PHILIP'S

STRE[...]S Glasgow and West Central Scotland

C000292331

www.philips-maps.co.uk
First published in 1995 by Philip's,
a division of Octopus Publishing Group Ltd
www.octopusbooks.co.uk
2–4 Heron Quays, London E14 4JP
An Hachette UK Company
www.hachette.co.uk

Fourth colour edition 2009
First impression 2009
GLWDA

978-1-84907-017-1 (pocket)

Speed camera data provided by **PocketGPSWorld.com Ltd**

Printed by Toppan, China

Contents

II Mobile safety cameras
III **Key to map symbols**
IV **Key to map pages**
VI **Route planning**
X Major administrative and Postcode boundaries

1 **Street maps** at 2⅔ inches to 1 mile
240 **Street map of Glasgow city centre** at 5⅓ inches to 1 mile

242 **Index** of towns, villages, streets, hospitals, industrial estates, railway stations, schools, shopping centres, universities and places of interest

Digital Data

The exceptionally high-quality mapping found in this atlas is available as digital data in TIFF format, which is easily convertible to other bitmapped (raster) image formats.

The index is also available in digital form as a standard database table. It contains all the details found in the printed index together with the National Grid reference for the map square in which each entry is named.

For further information and to discuss your requirements, please contact victoria.dawbarn@philips-maps.co.uk

Mobile safety cameras

For locations of mobile safety camera sites, please check the safety camera partnership websites for the latest 'located' mobile sites on your route prior to every journey.

Some safety camera partnerships post a weekly list of the locations in which they will be operating mobile speed cameras. Others have a general list of those places where mobile cameras will be used.

Please note, however, that local authorities can now place mobile cameras at different locations which may not be listed on the partnership website. Always drive within the speed limit.

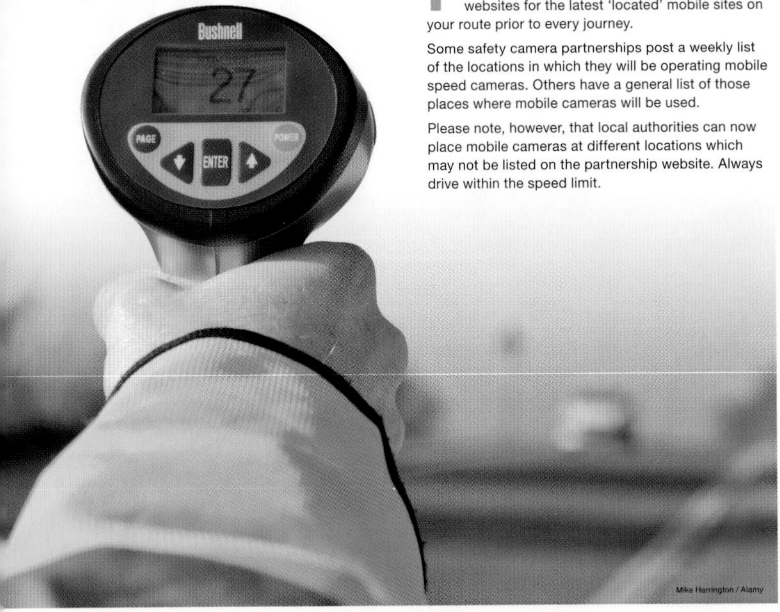

Mike Harrington / Alamy

Useful websites

Strathclyde Safety Camera Partnership
http://strathclydecameras.com/

Central Scotland Safety Camera Partnership
www.centralsafetycameras.co.uk

Further information
www.dvla.gov.uk
www.thinkroadsafety.gov.uk
www.dft.gov.uk
www.road-safe.org

Key to map symbols

Motorway with junction number
Primary route – dual/single carriageway
A road – dual/single carriageway
B road – dual/single carriageway
Minor road – dual/single carriageway
Other minor road – dual/single carriageway
Road under construction
Tunnel, covered road
Speed cameras – single, multiple
Rural track, private road or narrow road in urban area
Gate or obstruction to traffic – restrictions may not apply at all times or to all vehicles
Path, bridleway, byway open to all traffic, restricted byway
Pedestrianised area

Postcode boundaries
County or unitary authority boundaries

Railway with station
Tunnel
Railway under construction
Metro station
Private railway station
Miniature railway
Tramway, tramway under construction
Tram stop, tram stop under construction
Bus, coach station

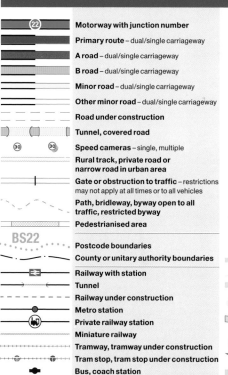

Ambulance station
Coastguard station
Fire station
Police station

Accident and Emergency entrance to hospital
Hospital

Place of worship
Information centre – open all year
Shopping centre, parking
Park and Ride, Post Office
Camping site, caravan site
Golf course, picnic site
Church ROMAN FORT **Non-Roman antiquity, Roman antiquity**

Important buildings, schools, colleges, universities and hospitals
Woods, built-up area

Water name
River, weir
Stream
Canal, lock, tunnel
Water
Tidal water

Adjoining page indicators and overlap bands – the colour of the arrow and band indicates the scale of the adjoining or overlapping page (see scales below)

The dark grey border on the inside edge of some pages indicates that the mapping does not continue onto the adjacent page

The small numbers around the edges of the maps identify the 1-kilometre National Grid lines

Abbreviations

Acad	**Academy**	Meml	**Memorial**
Allot Gdns	**Allotments**	Mon	**Monument**
Cemy	**Cemetery**	Mus	**Museum**
C Ctr	**Civic centre**	Obsy	**Observatory**
CH	**Club house**	Pal	**Royal palace**
Coll	**College**	PH	**Public house**
Crem	**Crematorium**	Recn Gd	**Recreation ground**
Ent	**Enterprise**	Resr	**Reservoir**
Ex H	**Exhibition hall**	Ret Pk	**Retail park**
Ind Est	**Industrial Estate**	Sch	**School**
IRB Sta	**Inshore rescue boat station**	Sh Ctr	**Shopping centre**
Inst	**Institute**	TH	**Town hall / house**
Ct	**Law court**	Trad Est	**Trading estate**
L Ctr	**Leisure centre**	Univ	**University**
LC	**Level crossing**	W Twr	**Water tower**
Liby	**Library**	Wks	**Works**
Mkt	**Market**	YH	**Youth hostel**

Enlarged maps only

Railway or bus station building
Place of interest
Parkland

The map scale on the pages numbered in blue is 2⅔ inches to 1 mile
4.2 cm to 1 km • 1:23810

0 ¼ mile ½ mile ¾ mile **1 mile**
0 250m 500m 750m **1km**

The map scale on the pages numbered in red is 5⅓ inches to 1 mile
8.4 cm to 1 km • 1:11900

0 220yds 440yds 660yds **½ mile**
0 125m 250m 375m **500m**

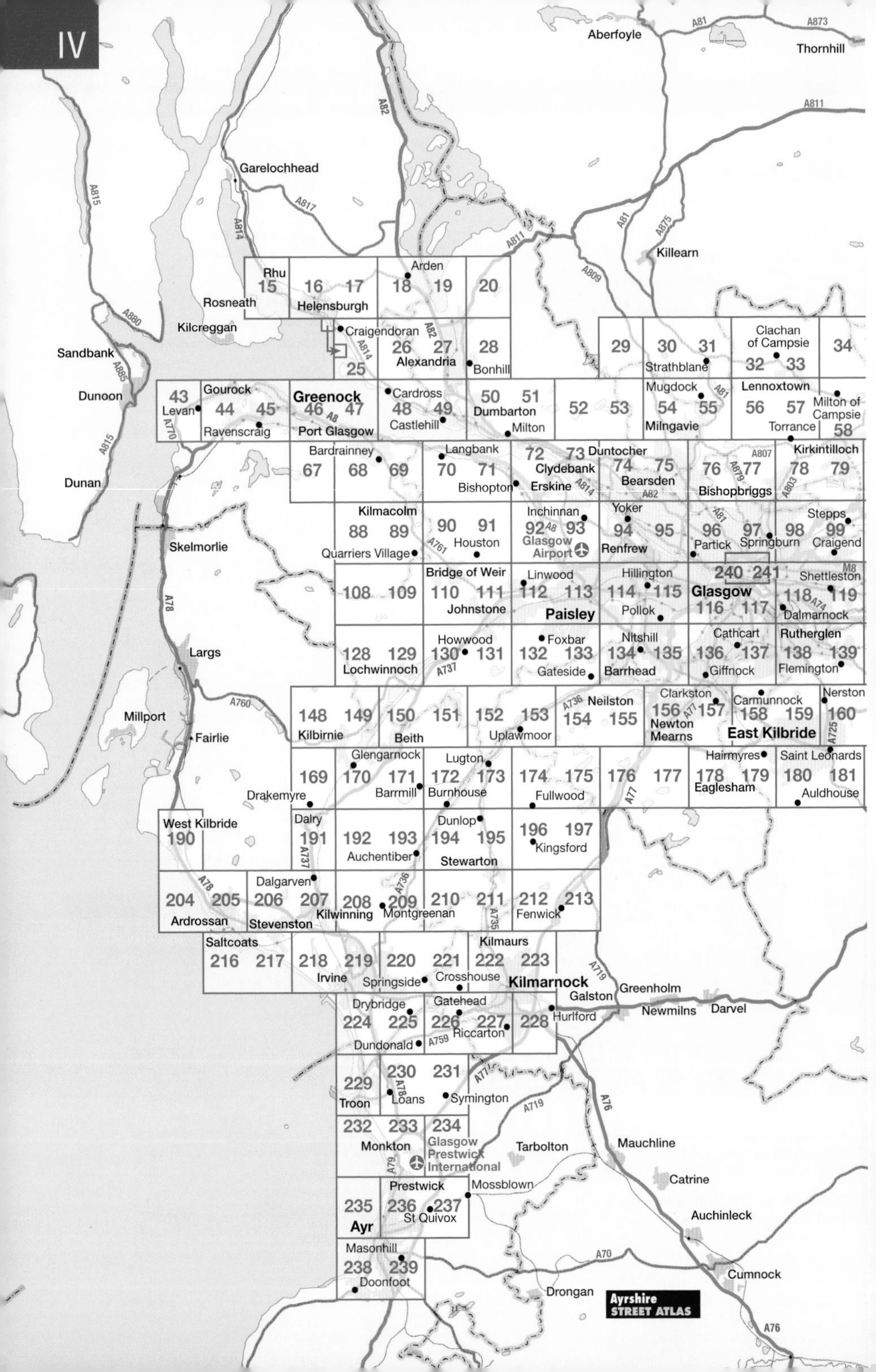
Aberfoyle
A81
A873
Thornhill
A811
A82
Garelochhead
A815
A817
A814
A81
A875
A811
Killearn
A809
Rhu
15
16
17
Arden
18
19
20
Rosneath
Helensburgh
A880
Kilcreggan
Craigendoran
A82
A814
26
27
Alexandria
28
Bonhill
25
29
30
31
Strathblane
Clachan of Campsie
32
33
34
Sandbank
A885
Dunoon
43
Levan
A770
Gourock
44
45
Ravenscraig
Greenock
46
A8
47
Port Glasgow
Cardross
48
49
Castlehill
50
51
Dumbarton
Milton
52
53
Mugdock
54
55
Milngavie
A81
Lennoxtown
56
57
Torrance
Milton of Campsie
58
A815
Dunan
Bardrainney
67
68
69
Langbank
70
71
Bishopton
72
73
Duntocher
Clydebank
Erskine
A814
74
75
Bearsden
A82
A807
A879
76
77
Bishopbriggs
A803
Kirkintilloch
78
79
Skelmorlie
Kilmacolm
88
89
Quarriers Village
A761
90
91
Houston
Inchinnan
92
A8
93
Glasgow Airport
Yoker
94
95
Renfrew
96
A81
97
Partick
Springburn
98
99
Stepps
Craigend
A78
108
109
Bridge of Weir
110
111
Johnstone
Linwood
112
113
Paisley
Hillington
114
115
Pollok
240
241
Glasgow
116
117
M8
Shettleston
118
119
A74
Dalmarnock
Largs
128
129
Lochwinnoch
Howwood
130
131
A737
132
133
Foxbar
Gateside
Nitshill
134
135
Barrhead
Cathcart
136
137
Giffnock
Rutherglen
138
139
Flemington
A760
Millport
Fairlie
148
149
Kilbirnie
150
151
Beith
152
153
Uplawmoor
A736
Neilston
154
155
Clarkston
156
A77
157
Newton Mearns
Carmunnock
158
159
East Kilbride
Nerston
160
A725
169
Drakemyre
Glengarnock
170
171
Barrmill
Lugton
172
173
Burnhouse
174
175
Fullwood
176
177
A77
Hairmyres
178
179
Eaglesham
Saint Leonards
180
181
Auldhouse
West Kilbride
190
Dalry
191
A737
192
193
Auchentiber
Dunlop
194
195
Stewarton
196
197
Kingsford
A78
204
205
Ardrossan
Dalgarven
206
207
Stevenston
208
Kilwinning
A736
209
Montgreenan
210
211
A735
212
213
Fenwick
Saltcoats
216
217
218
219
Irvine
220
221
Springside
Crosshouse
Kilmaurs
222
223
Kilmarnock
A719
Galston
Greenholm
Newmilns
Darvel
Drybridge
224
225
Dundonald
Gatehead
226
227
Riccarton
A759
228
Hurlford
229
Troon
230
A78
231
Loans
Symington
A77
A719
A76
232
233
Monkton
234
Glasgow Prestwick International
A79
Tarbolton
Mauchline
Catrine
Prestwick
235
Ayr
236
237
St Quivox
Mossblown
Auchinleck
Masonhill
238
239
Doonfoot
A70
Cumnock
Drongan
Ayrshire STREET ATLAS
A76

Key to map pages

123	Map pages at 2⅔ inches to 1 mile
241	Map pages at 5⅓ inches to 1 mile

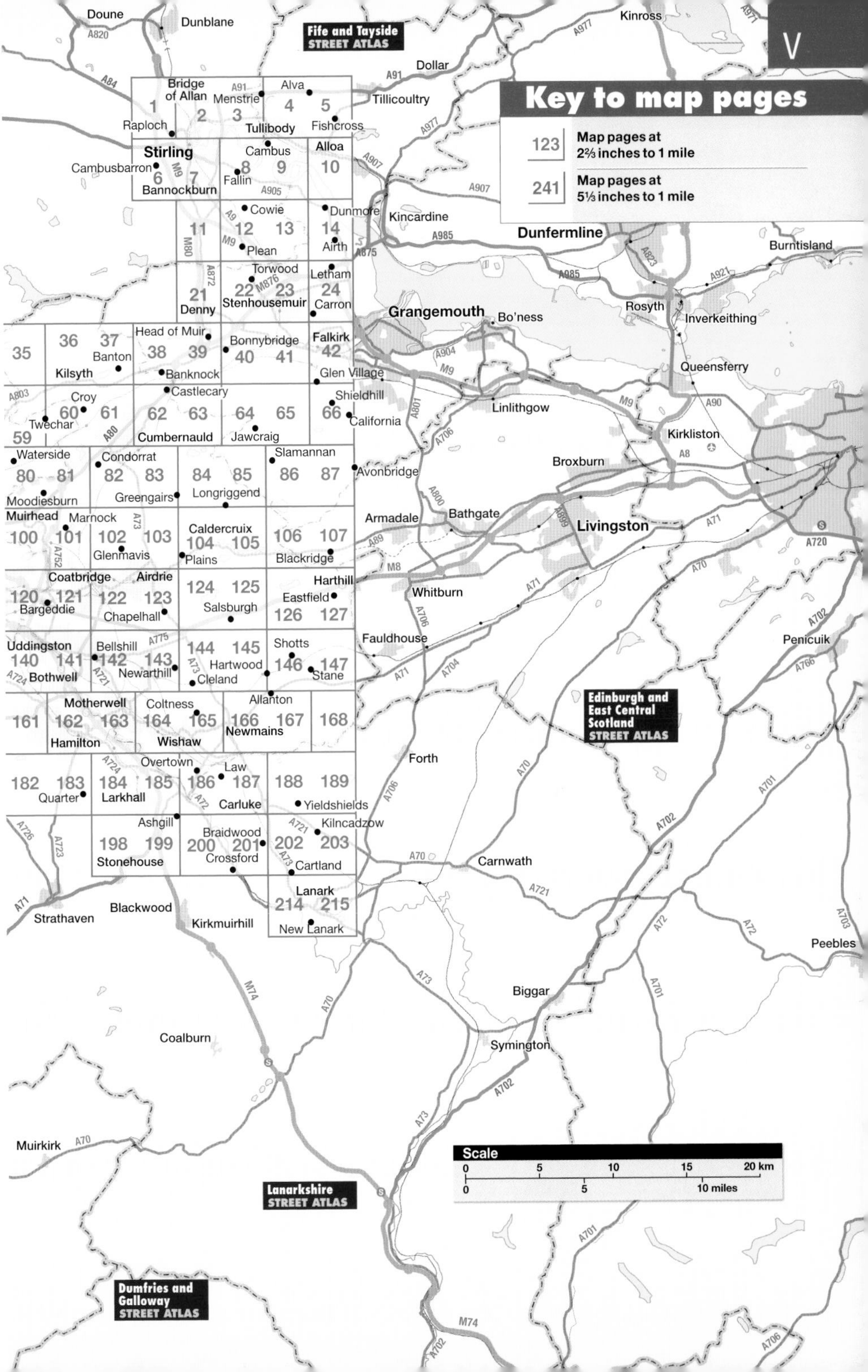

Route planning

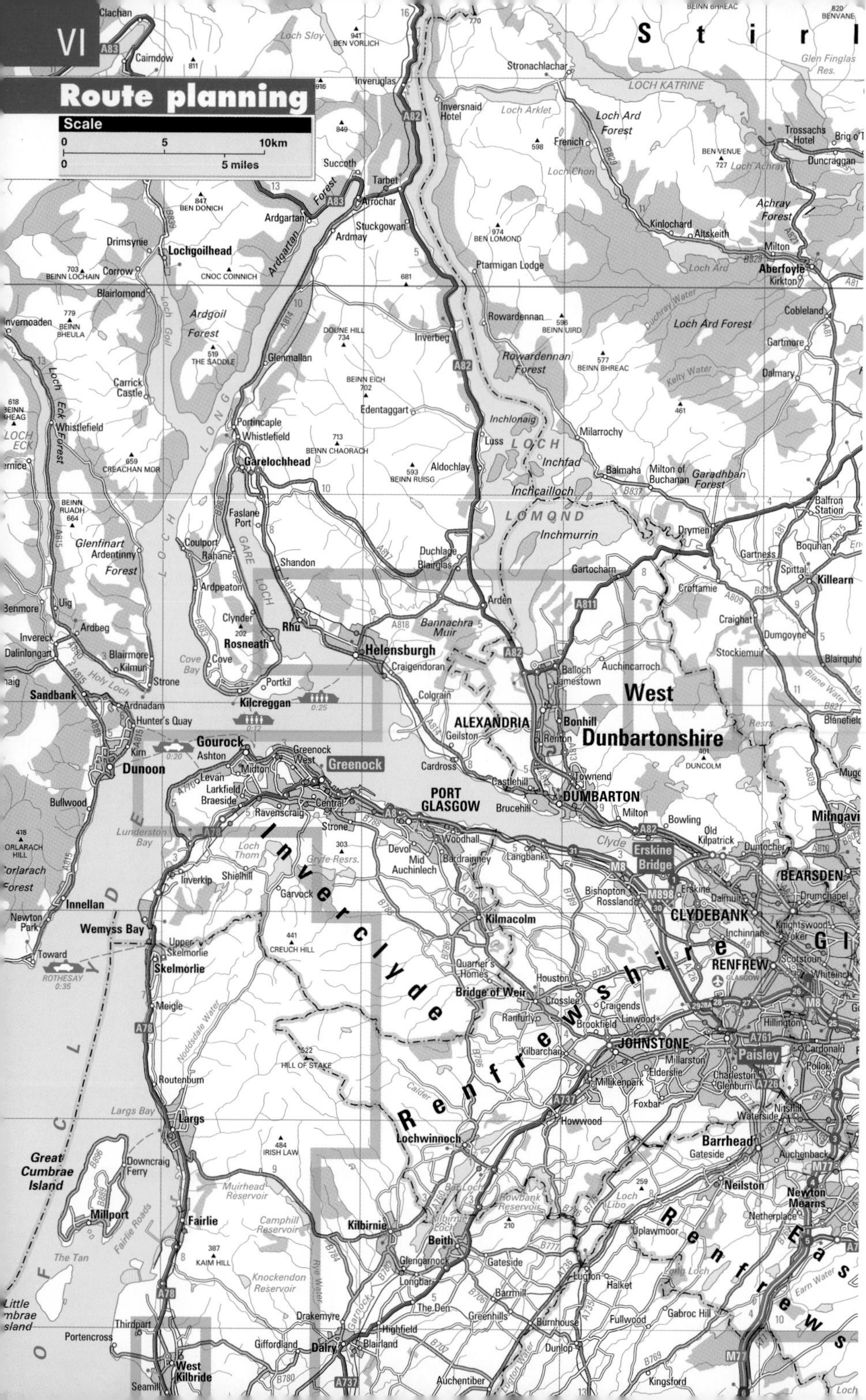

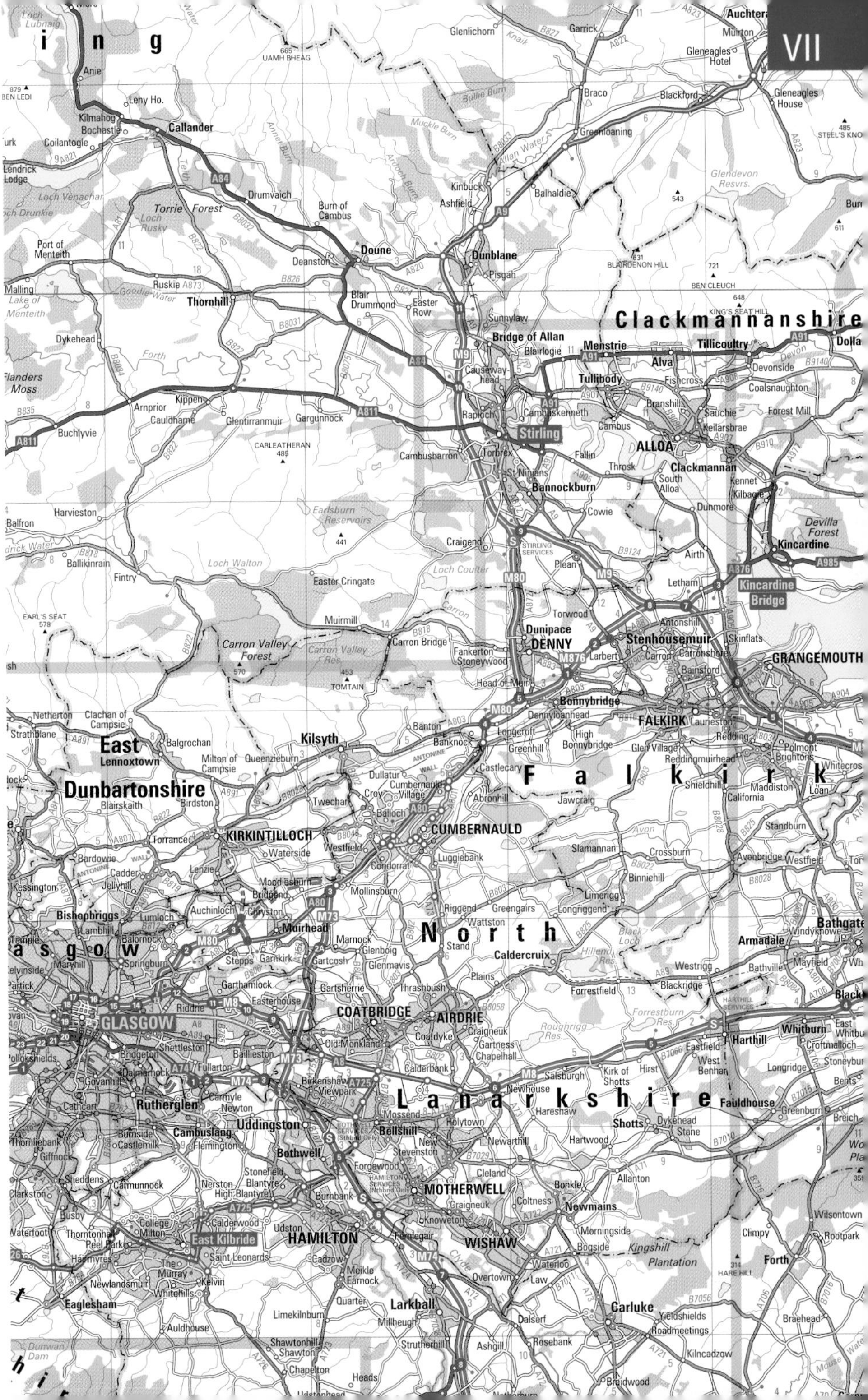
Clackmannanshire
East Dunbartonshire
Falkirk
North Lanarkshire
Stirling
Callander
Doune
Dunblane
Bridge of Allan
Menstrie
Tillicoultry
Alva
Tullibody
ALLOA
Clackmannan
Kincardine
Kincardine Bridge
Bannockburn
Cowie
Plean
Airth
Stenhousemuir
Larbert
DENNY
Dunipace
Bonnybridge
FALKIRK
GRANGEMOUTH
Polmont
Kilsyth
KIRKINTILLOCH
CUMBERNAULD
Lennoxtown
Bishopbriggs
GLASGOW
Rutherglen
Cambuslang
Uddingston
Bothwell
Bellshill
COATBRIDGE
AIRDRIE
Caldercruix
MOTHERWELL
HAMILTON
WISHAW
East Kilbride
Larkhall
Carluke
Shotts
Harthill
Whitburn
Fauldhouse
Armadale
Bathgate
Eaglesham
Kippen
Gargunnock
Buchlyvie
Thornhill
Port of Menteith
Fintry
Balfron
Strathblane
Torrie Forest
Carron Valley Forest
Devilla Forest
Kingshill Plantation
Earlsburn Reservoirs
Loch Coulter
Carron Valley Res.
Glendevon Resvrs.
Gleneagles Hotel
Braco
Blackford
Greenloaning
Muirhead
Stepps
Newmains
Kirk of Shotts
Salsburgh
Forth
Allanton
Cleland
Uamh Bheag
Ben Ledi
Ben Cleuch
Blairdenon Hill
King's Seat Hill
Earl's Seat
Tomtain
Carleatheran
Hare Hill
Steel's Knowe

GLASGOW
Braeside
Ravenscraig
Central
Brucehill
Milton
Bowling
Old Kilpatrick
Milngavie
Duntocher
BEARSDEN
Lunderston Bay
Corlarach Forest
Innellan
Newton Park
Toward
ROTHESAY 0:35
Wemyss Bay
Upper Skelmorlie
Skelmorlie
Meigle
Inverkip
Shielhill
Loch Thom
Gryfe Resrs.
Strone
Devol
Mid Auchinlech
Woodhall
Bardrainney
Langbank
Clyde
Erskine Bridge
Bishopton
Rossland
Erskine
Dalmuir
Drumchapel
CLYDEBANK
Knightswood
Yoker
Scotstoun
Whiteinch
Inchinnan
RENFREW
GLASGOW
Garvock
Kilmacolm
CREUCH HILL
Inverclyde
Quarrier's Homes
Houston
Bridge of Weir
Crosslee
Craigends
Linwood
Ranfurly
Brookfield
Hillington
Cardonald
Pollok
Kilbarchan
JOHNSTONE
Millarston
Paisley
Elderslie
Charleston
Glenburn
Milliken Park
Foxbar
Nitshill
Waterside
Routenburn
HILL OF STAKE
Noddsdale Water
Largs Bay
Largs
Renfrewshire
Howwood
Lochwinnoch
Barrhead
Gateside
Auchenback
Great Cumbrae Island
Downcraig Ferry
Millport
Fairlie Roads
Fairlie
IRISH LAW
Muirhead Reservoir
Camphill Reservoir
Barr Loch
Kilbirnie Loch
Rowbank Reservoir
Loch Libo
Neilston
Newton Mearns
Netherplace
Uplawmoor
Kilbirnie
Beith
KAIM HILL
The Tan
Knockendon Reservoir
Rye Water
Glengarnock
Gateside
Lugton
Halket
Long Loch
East Renfrewshire
Earn Water
Longbar
Barrmill
The Den
Drakemyre
Greenhills
Burnhouse
Fullwood
Gabroc Hill
Little Cumbrae Island
North Ayrshire
Thirdpart
Portencross
Highfield
Blairland
Giffordland
Dalry
Dunlop
West Kilbride
Seamill
Kingsford
Auchentiber
Stewarton
Loch
Flow Moss
Laighmuir
Dalgarven
Torranyard
Annick Water
Waterside
Fenwick
Laigh Fenwick
Chapelhill
Kilwinning
Benslie
Cunninghamhead
Dykesmains
Ardrossan
Stevenston
Saltcoats
Kilmaurs
CRINS
Wallace Muir
Moscow
Girdle Toll
Perceton
Onthank
Springside
Knockentiber
Knockinlaw
Irvine
Crosshouse
Kilmarnock
Dreghorn
Fullarton
Grange
Irvine Bay
Crookedholm
Hurlford
KILMARNOCK SERVICES
Galston
Green
Newmiln
Drybridge
Gatehead
Riccarton
Earlston
Dundonald
Shortlees
Crossroads
Sornhill
Barassie
North Bay
Muirhead
Craigie
Bogend
Loans
Symington
Troon
South Bay
Hansel Village
Millburn
Auchmillan
Cessnock Water
Mossgiel
LARNE 1:50 (March-Oct)
Monkton
GLASGOW PRESTWICK INTERNATIONAL
Tarbolton
Mauchline
Catrine
Prestwick
Failford
Haugh
St Quivox
Mossblown
Woodfield
Crosshill
Stair
Newton on Ayr
Wallacetown
Annbank
Whitletts
Lugar Water
Ayr
Trabboch
Ochiltree
Seafield
Belston
Masonhill
Coylton
Coalhall
Belmont
Joppa
Hillhead
Drongan
Doonfoot
Laigh Glengall
Alloway
Martnaham Loch
Barbieston
Skares
Fisherton
Sinclairston
Dunure
Hayhill
Littlemill
Hollybush
Rankinston
Culroy
Minishant
Dalrymple
Water of Coyle
Culzean Bay
Polnessan
KILMEIN HILL
Patna
Burnfoot
Whitefaulds
Maybole
Kirkmichael
Waterside
Maidenhead Bay
BENBEOCH
FIRTH OF CLYDE

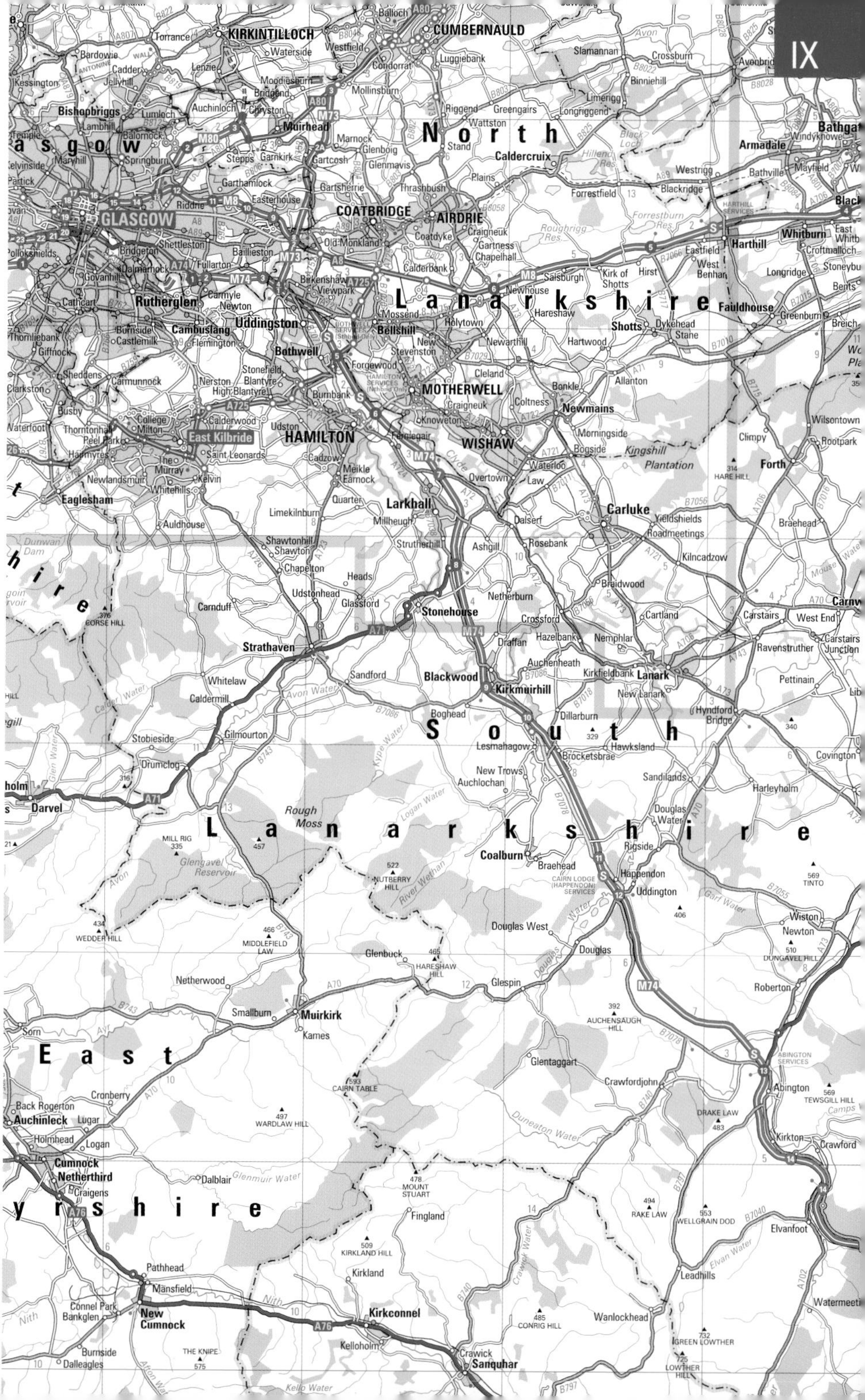
KIRKINTILLOCH
CUMBERNAULD
Balloch
Torrance
Bardowie
Lenzie
Waterside
Westfield
Luggiebank
Condorrat
Slamannan
Crossburn
Avonbridge
Binniehill
Cadder
Jellyhill
Kessington
Moodiesburn
Bridgend
Mollinsburn
Limerigg
Longriggend
Riggend
Greengairs
Bishopbriggs
Lumloch
Auchinloch
Chryston
Lambhill
Balornock
Muirhead
Wattston
North
Bathgate
Windyknowe
Armadale
Glasgow
Maryhill
Springburn
Stepps
Garnkirk
Marnock
Glenboig
Gartcosh
Stand
Caldercruix
Glenmavis
Hillend Res.
Black Loch
Westrigg
Bathville
Mayfield
Kelvinside
Partick
Garthamlock
Gartsherrie
Thrashbush
Plains
Forrestfield
Blackridge
Easterhouse
Riddrie
GLASGOW
COATBRIDGE
AIRDRIE
Forrestburn Res.
HARTHILL SERVICES
Roughrigg Res.
Shettleston
Old Monkland
Coatdyke
Craigneuk
Gartness
Chapelhall
Eastfield
Harthill
Whitburn
East Whitburn
Pollokshields
Bridgeton
Baillieston
Dalmarnock
Calderbank
Croftmalloch
Stoneybu
Govanhill
Fullarton
Birkenshaw
Viewpark
Salsburgh
Kirk of Shotts
Hirst
West Benhar
Longridge
Newhouse
Bents
Cathcart
Rutherglen
Carmyle
Newton
Lanarkshire
Fauldhouse
Uddingston
Mossend
Holytown
Hareshaw
Dykehead
Greenburn
Breich
Thornliebank
Burnside
Castlemilk
Cambuslang
BOTHWELL SERVICES
Bellshill
Shotts
Stane
Giffnock
Flemington
Bothwell
New Stevenston
Newarthill
Hartwood
Sheddens
Carmunnock
Forgewood
Cleland
Clarkston
Nerston
Stonefield
Blantyre
High Blantyre
HAMILTON SERVICES
MOTHERWELL
Allanton
Bonkle
Busby
Burnbank
Craigneuk
Coltness
Newmains
Waterfoot
Thorntonhall
Peel Park
College Milton
Calderwood
East Kilbride
Udston
HAMILTON
Ferniegair
Knowetop
WISHAW
Morningside
Wilsontown
Climpy
Rootpark
Hairmyres
Saint Leonards
Bogside
Kingshill Plantation
The Murray
Newlandsmuir
Kelvin
Whitehills
Cadzow
Meikle Earnock
Clyde
Overtown
Waterloo
Law
314 HARE HILL
Forth
Eaglesham
Quarter
Larkhall
Dalserf
Carluke
Yieldshields
Roadmeetings
Limekilnburn
Millheugh
Auldhouse
Braehead
Dunwan Dam
Shawtonhill
Shawton
Struthérhill
Ashgill
Rosebank
Kilncadzow
Chapelton
Heads
Braidwood
Mouse Water
Udstonhead
Glassford
Netherburn
Carnduff
Stonehouse
376 CORSE HILL
Crossford
Cartland
Carstairs
West End
Carnwath
Strathaven
Draffan
Hazelbank
Nemphlar
Ravenstruther
Carstairs Junction
Whitelaw
Sandford
Blackwood
Auchenheath
Kirkfieldbank
Lanark
Pettinain
Caldermill
Calder Water
Avon Water
Kirkmuirhill
New Lanark
Boghead
Dillarburn
Hyndford Bridge
340
Stobieside
Gilmourton
South
Lesmahagow
329
Hawksland
Brocketsbrae
Covington
Drumclog
316
New Trows
Auchlochan
Sandilands
Harleyholm
Darvel
Rough Moss
Logan Water
Douglas Water
Lanarkshire
MILL RIG 335
457
Glengavel Reservoir
Coalburn
Braehead
Rigside
522 NUTBERRY HILL
CAIRN LODGE (HAPPENDON) SERVICES
Happendon
Uddington
569 TINTO
River Wethan
Garf Water
434 WEDDER HILL
466 MIDDLEFIELD LAW
Douglas West
406
Wiston
Newton
510 DUNGAVEL HILL
Glenbuck
465 HARESHAW HILL
Douglas
Netherwood
Glespin
Roberton
Smallburn
Muirkirk
Kames
392 AUCHENSAUGH HILL
Sorn
East
Glentaggart
ABINGTON SERVICES
593 CAIRN TABLE
Crawfordjohn
Abington
569 TEWSGILL HILL
Cronberry
Back Rogerton
Auchinleck
Lugar
497 WARDLAW HILL
DRAKE LAW 483
Camps
Holmhead
Logan
Duneaton Water
Kirkton
Crawford
Cumnock
Netherthird
Craigens
Dalblair
Glenmuir Water
478 MOUNT STUART
Ayrshire
494 RAKE LAW
553 WELLGRAIN DOD
Elvanfoot
Fingland
509 KIRKLAND HILL
Crawick Water
Elvan Water
Pathhead
Kirkland
Leadhills
Mansfield
Connel Park
Bankglen
New Cumnock
Nith
Kirkconnel
485 CONRIG HILL
Wanlockhead
Watermeeting
732 GREEN LOWTHER
Burnside
Dalleagles
THE KNIPE 575
Kelloholm
Crawick
Sanquhar
725 LOWTHER HILL
Afton Water
Kello Water

Major administrative and Postcode boundaries

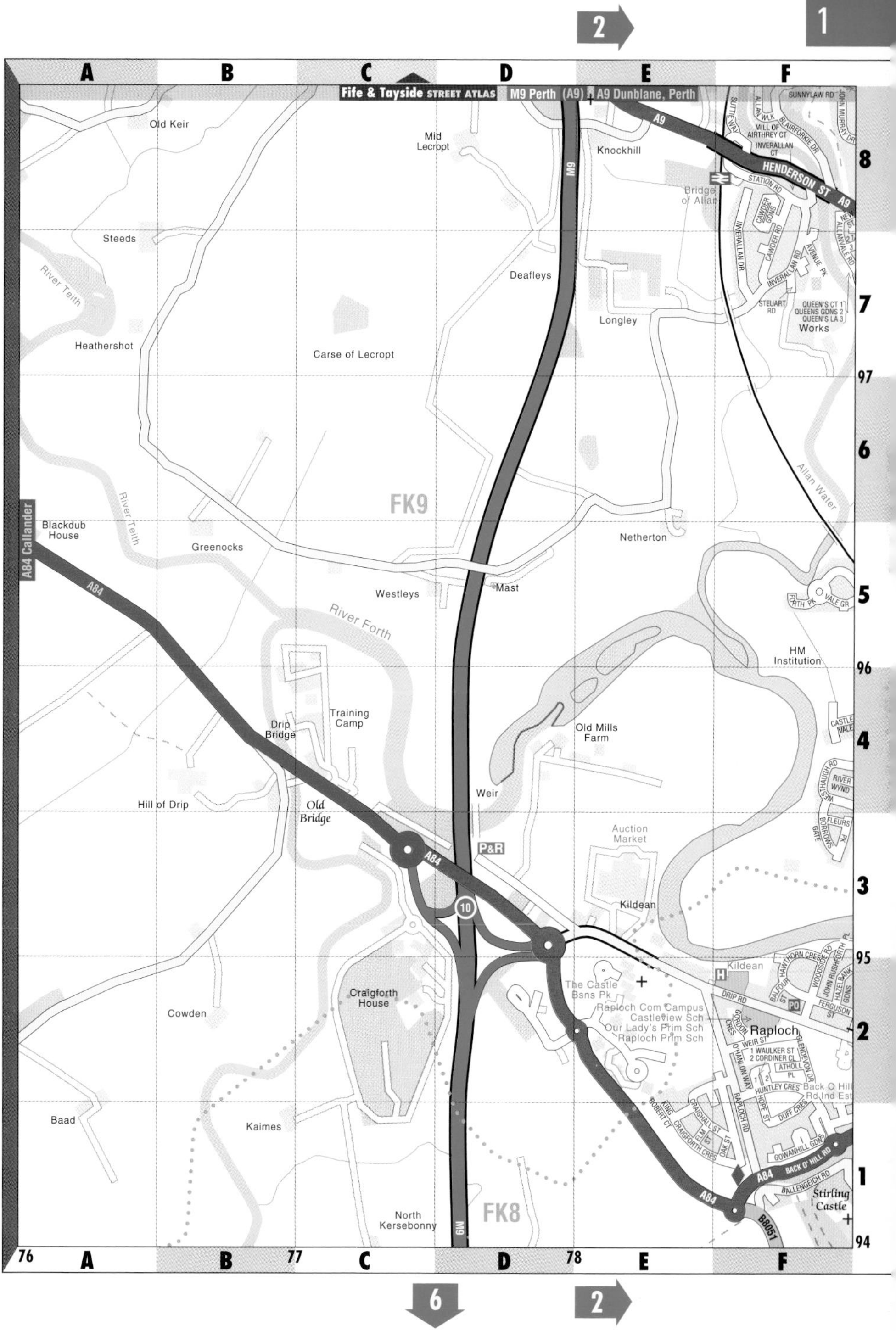
2
A
B
C
D
E
F
Fife & Tayside STREET ATLAS
M9 Perth (A9)
A9 Dunblane, Perth
Old Keir
Mid Lecropt
Knockhill
Bridge of Allan
HENDERSON ST
STATION RD
Steeds
River Teith
Deafleys
Longley
Works
Heathershot
Carse of Lecropt
FK9
Allan Water
A84 Callander
Blackdub House
River Teith
Greenocks
Netherton
Westleys
Mast
River Forth
HM Institution
Training Camp
Drip Bridge
Old Mills Farm
Hill of Drip
Old Bridge
Weir
P&R
Auction Market
Kildean
Kildean
The Castle Bsns Pk
Raploch Com Campus
Castleview Sch
Our Lady's Prim Sch
Raploch Prim Sch
Raploch
Craigforth House
Cowden
Back O Hill Rd Ind Est
Baad
Kaimes
Stirling Castle
North Kersebonny
FK8
M9
A84
B8051
8
7
97
6
5
96
4
3
95
2
1
94
76
77
78
6
2

1

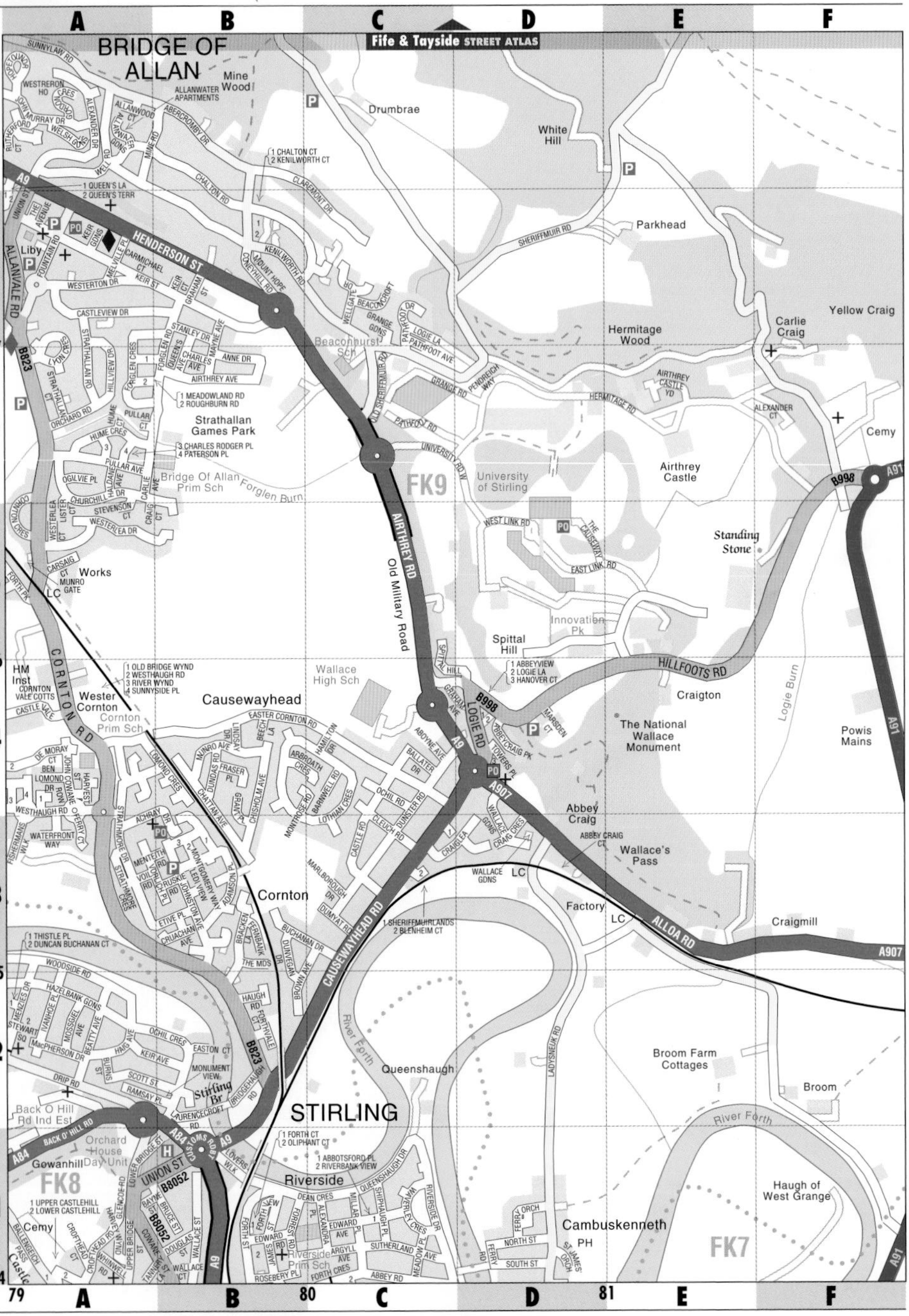

B3
1 WESTWOOD CRES
2 SMILLIE TERR
3 PORTER AVE

1
7

4

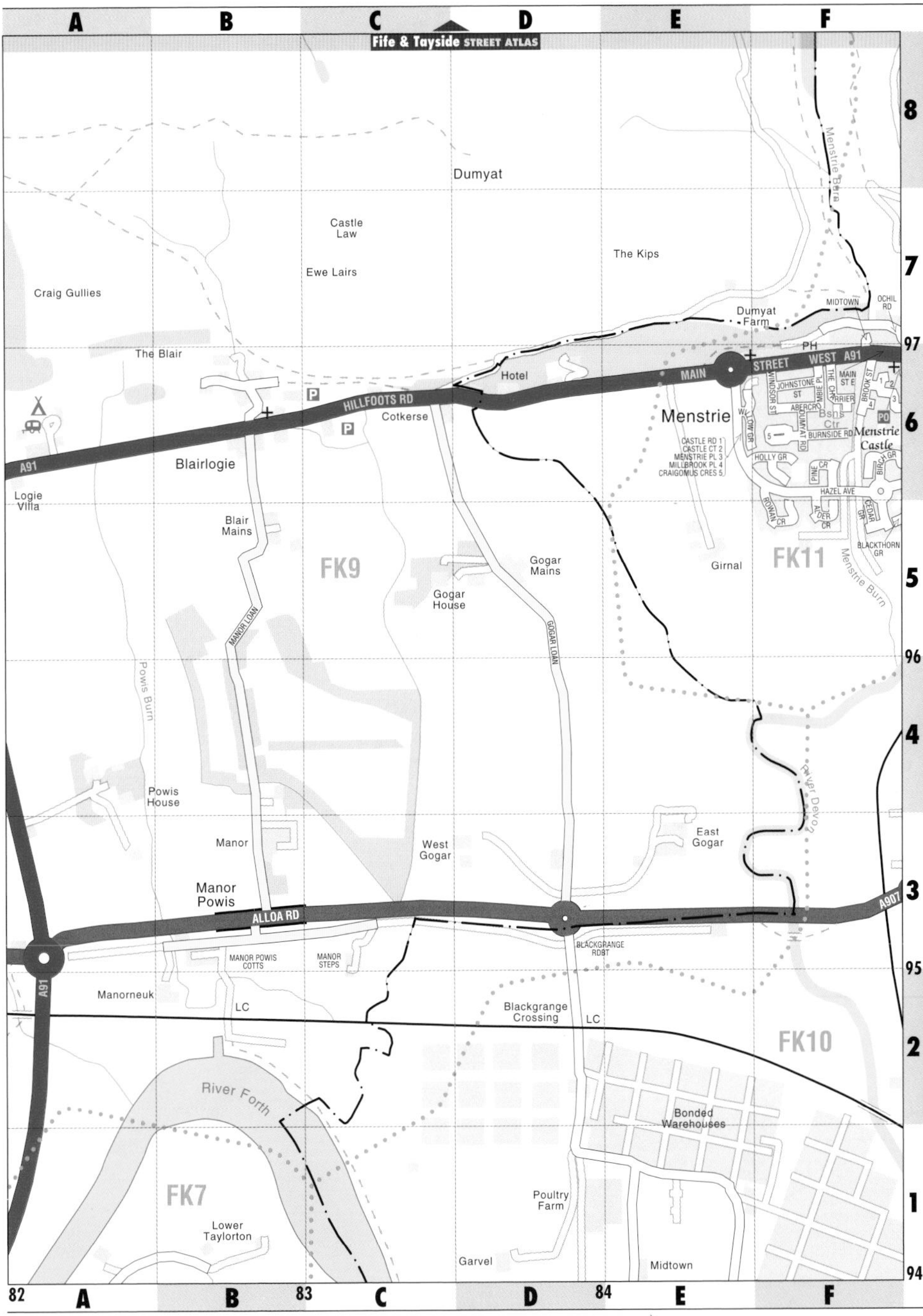
A
B
C
D
E
F
Fife & Tayside STREET ATLAS
8
7
97
6
5
96
4
3
95
2
1
94
82
83
84
Dumyat
Castle Law
Ewe Lairs
The Kips
Craig Gullies
Menstrie Burn
Dumyat Farm
MIDTOWN
OCHIL RD
PH
The Blair
Hotel
MAIN STREET WEST A91
HILLFOOTS RD
Cotkerse
Menstrie
JOHNSTONE ST
WINDSOR ST
ABERCROMBIE PL
THE CAIRNRIGG
BROOK ST
MAIN ST E
DUMYAT RD
WILLOW GR
Bsns Ctr
BURNSIDE RD
PO
Menstrie Castle
CASTLE RD 1
CASTLE CT 2
MENSTRIE PL 3
MILLBROOK PL 4
CRAIGOMUS CRES 5
HOLLY GR
PINE CR
BIRCH GR
HAZEL AVE
ROWAN CR
ALDER CR
CEDAR GR
BLACKTHORN GR
A91
Blairlogie
Logie Villa
Blair Mains
FK9
Gogar Mains
Gogar House
Girnal
FK11
MANOR LOAN
GOGAR LOAN
Powis Burn
River Devon
Powis House
Manor
West Gogar
East Gogar
Manor Powis
ALLOA RD
A907
BLACKGRANGE RDBT
MANOR POWIS COTTS
MANOR STEPS
Manorneuk
LC
Blackgrange Crossing
FK10
River Forth
Bonded Warehouses
FK7
Poultry Farm
Lower Taylorton
Garvel
Midtown

8
4

3

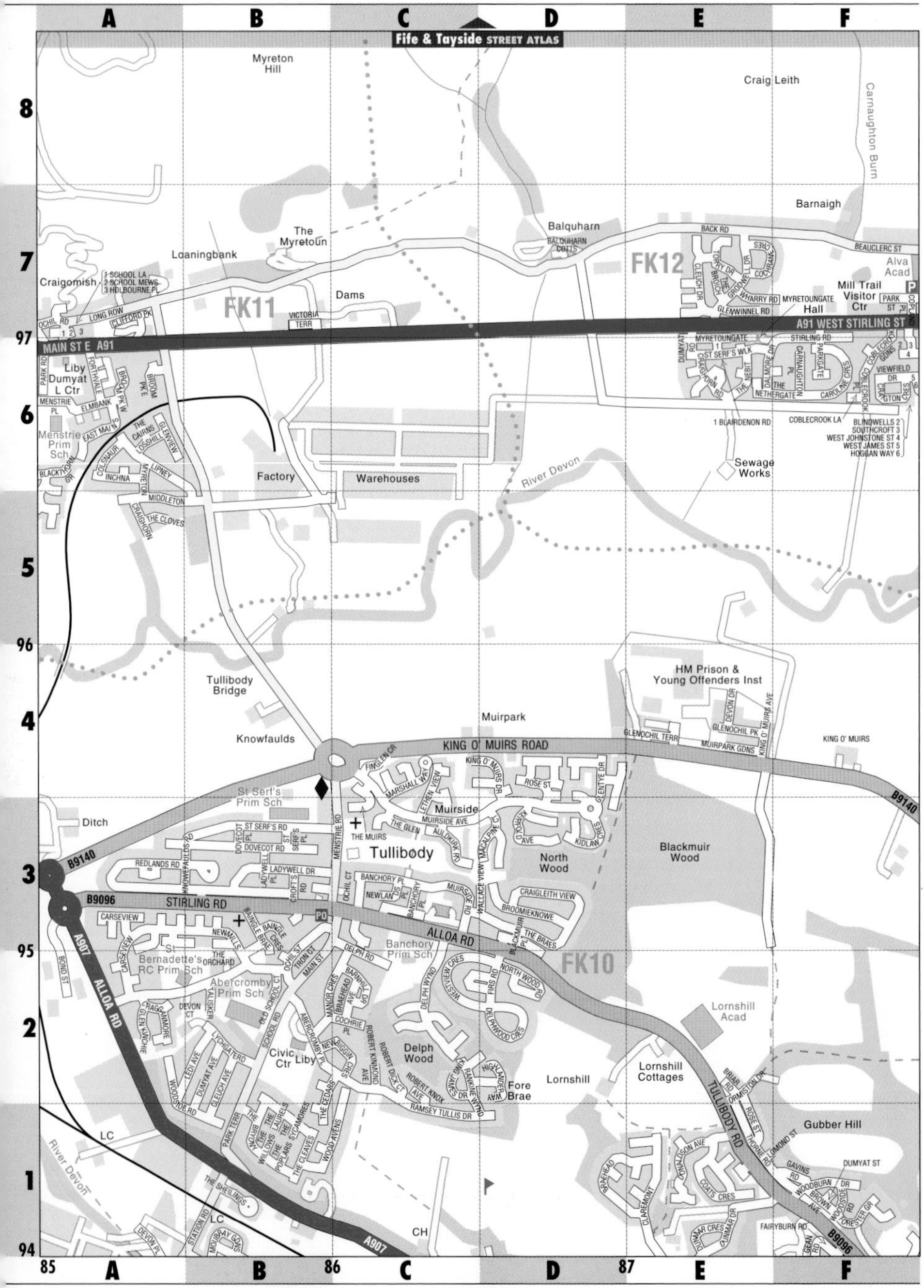
A
B
C
D
E
F
Fife & Tayside STREET ATLAS
8
7
97
6
5
96
4
3
95
2
1
94
85
86
87
Myreton Hill
Craig Leith
Carnaughton Burn
Barnaigh
The Myretoun
Balquharn
BALQUHARN COTTS
Loaningbank
Craigomish
1 SCHOOL LA
2 SCHOOL MEWS
3 HOLBOURNE PL
Dams
FK11
FK12
VICTORIA TERR
OCHIL RD
LONG ROW
CLIFFORD PK
MAIN ST E A91
A91 WEST STIRLING ST
BACK RD
BEAUCLERC ST
Alva Acad
Mill Trail Visitor Ctr
Hall
PARK ST
COPLAND PL
MYRETOUNGATE
GLENWINNIEL RD
WHARRY RD
CLEUCH DR
TORRY DR
GRODWELL DR
COCHRANE CRES
STIRLING RD
ST SERF'S WLK
DUMYAT RD
CRAIGHORN RD
THE NEBIT
DALMORE DR
CARNAUGHTON PL
PARKGATE
CAROLINE CRES
THE NETHERGATE
COBLECROOK GDNS
COBLECROOK PL
VIEWFIELD DR
CRAIGTON CRES
COBLECROOK LA
1 BLAIRDENON RD
BLINDWELLS 2
SOUTHCROFT 3
WEST JOHNSTONE ST 4
WEST JAMES ST 5
HOGGAN WAY 6
Sewage Works
River Devon
PARK RD
FORTHVALE
Liby
Dumyat L Ctr
BROOM PK W
BROOM PK E
MENSTRIE PL
ELMBANK
EAST MAINS
Menstrie Prim Sch
THE CAIRNS
GLENVIEW
MOSSHILL
COLSNAUR
LIPNEY
INCHNA
MYRETON
BLACKTHORN GR
MIDDLETON
CRAIGHORN
THE CLOVES
Factory
Warehouses
Tullibody Bridge
Knowfaulds
Muirpark
HM Prison & Young Offenders Inst
DEVON DR
GLENOCHIL PK
KING O' MUIRS AVE
GLENOCHIL TERR
MUIRPARK GDNS
KING O' MUIRS ROAD
KING O' MUIRS
B9140
FINGLEN CR
MARSHALL WAY
LETHEN VIEW
KING O' MUIRS DR
ROSE ST
GLENTYE DR
St Serf's Prim Sch
Ditch
Muirside
MUIRSIDE AVE
THE GLEN
AULDKIRK RD
HAROLD AVE
MACALPINE CT
KIDLAW CRES
THE MUIRS
Tullibody
North Wood
Blackmuir Wood
ST SERF'S RD
DOVECOT PL
DOVECOT RD
ST SERF'S PL
KNOWEFAULDS RD
REDLANDS RD
LADYWELL PL
LADYWELL DR
CROFT'S RD
MENSTRIE RD
OCHIL CT
BANCHORY PL
NEWLANDS
BANCHORY PL
MUIRSIDE RD
WALLACE VIEW
CRAIGLEITH VIEW
BROOMIEKNOWE
BLACKMUIR PL
THE BRAES
B9096
STIRLING RD
PO
ALLOA RD
CARSEVIEW
BAINGLE BRAE
BAINGLE CRES
NEWMILLS
St Bernadette's RC Prim Sch
THE ORCHARD
OCHIL ST
TRON CT
MAIN ST
DELPH RD
Banchory Prim Sch
FK10
BOND ST
A907
ALLOA RD
Abercromby Prim Sch
DEVON CT
TALISKER
OLD SCHOOL CT
SCHOOL RD
CRAIGANMORE
GLEN KINCHIE
LYCHGATE RD
LEDI AVE
DUMYAT AVE
CLEUCH AVE
WOODSIDE RD
Civic Ctr
Liby
MANOR CRES
BRAEHEAD
BARNHILL AVE
BARNHILL DR
COCHRIE PL
ABERCROMBY PL
NEWBIGGIN CRES
ROBERT KINMOND AVE
ROBERT DICK CT
DELPH WYND
WESTVIEW CRES
FIRS RD
NORTH WOOD RD
DELPHWOOD CRES
Delph Wood
ROBERT KNOX AVE
KING JAMES DR
RANKINE WYND
HIGHLANDER WAY
Fore Brae
RAMSEY TULLIS DR
Lornshill
Lornshill Acad
Lornshill Cottages
TULLIBODY RD
BRIAR RD
ORMISTON DR
ROSE ST
THORNE RD
LOMOND ST
Gubber Hill
GAVINS RD
DUMYAT ST
WOODBURN DR
BROWN AVE
WOODSIDE RD
FORESTER GR
FAIRYBURN RD
GEAN RD
B9096
PARK TERR
THE BRYONY
THE WILLOWS
THE LAURELS
THE POPLARS
THE SYCAMORES
THE CLEAVES
THE CEDARS
WOOD AVENS
THE SHEILINGS
STATION RD
MOUBRAY GDNS
DEVON PL
LC
River Devon
CH
DONALDSON AVE
BRAEHEAD
COATS CRES
CLAREMONT
DUNMAR CRES
DUNMAR DR

3

9

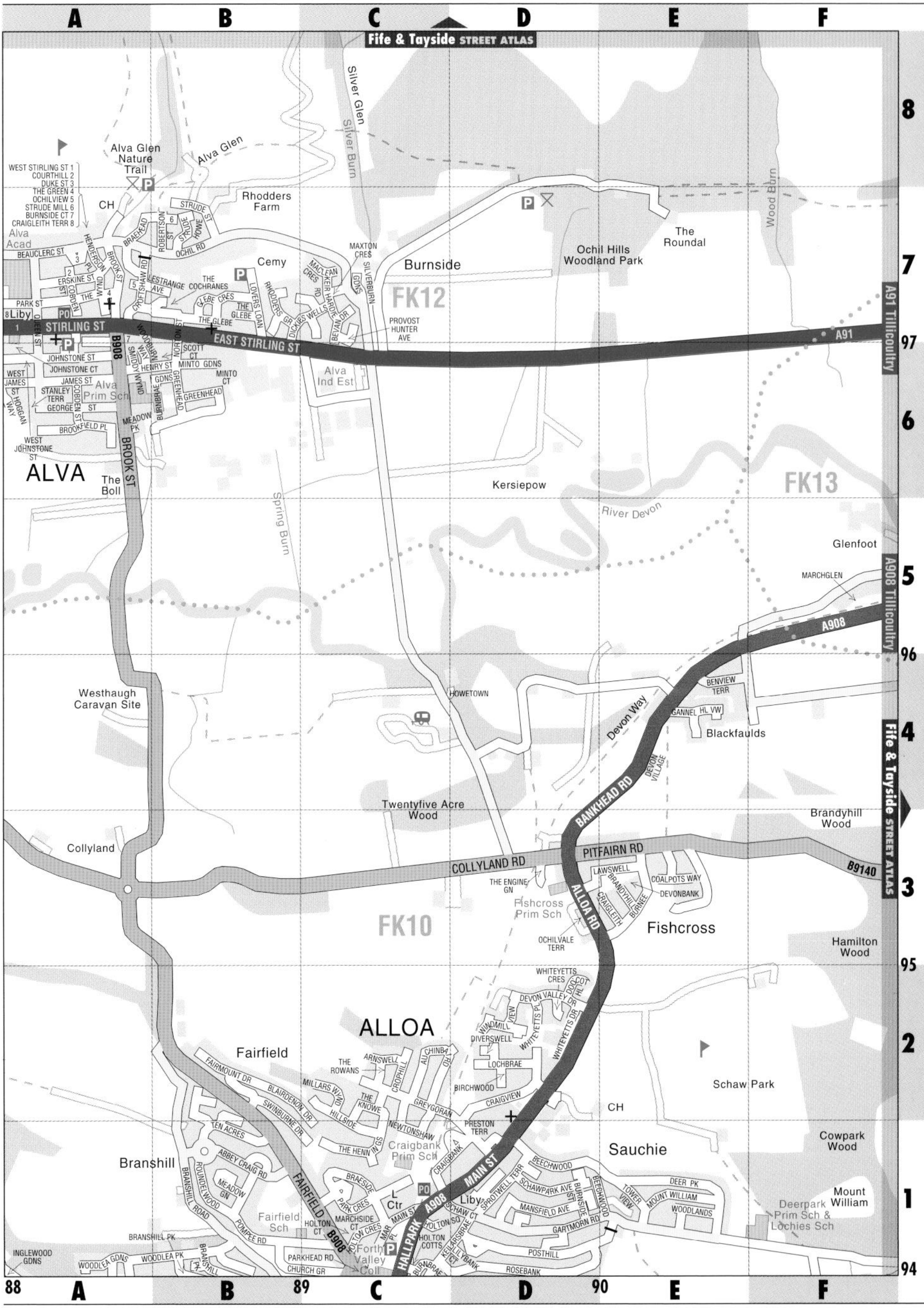
Fife & Tayside STREET ATLAS
A91 Tillicoultry
A908 Tillicoultry
ALVA
ALLOA
Fishcross
Sauchie
FK12
FK13
FK10
Alva Glen Nature Trail
Alva Glen
Silver Glen
Silver Burn
Wood Burn
Rhodders Farm
Burnside
Ochil Hills Woodland Park
The Roundal
WEST STIRLING ST 1
COURTHILL 2
DUKE ST 3
THE GREEN 4
OCHILVIEW 5
STRUDE MILL 6
BURNSIDE CT 7
CRAIGLEITH TERR 8
CH
Alva Acad
Cemy
STIRLING ST
EAST STIRLING ST
BROOK ST
B908
A91
Alva Ind Est
Alva Prim Sch
PROVOST HUNTER AVE
The Boll
Kersiepow
River Devon
Spring Burn
Glenfoot
MARCHGLEN
A908
HOWETOWN
Westhaugh Caravan Site
Devon Way
BENVIEW TERR
GANNEL HL VW
Blackfaulds
DEVON VILLAGE
BANKHEAD RD
Twentyfive Acre Wood
Brandyhill Wood
Collyland
COLLYLAND RD
PITFAIRN RD
B9140
THE ENGINE GN
Fishcross Prim Sch
ALLOA RD
LAWSWELL
COALPOTS WAY
DEVONBANK
OCHILVALE TERR
Hamilton Wood
WHITEYETTS CRES
Fairfield
Schaw Park
Branshill
Craigbank Prim Sch
MAIN ST
HALLPARK
FAIRFIELD
L Ctr
Liby
Fairfield Sch
Forth Valley Coll
CH
Cowpark Wood
Mount William
Deerpark Prim Sch & Lochies Sch
INGLEWOOD GDNS
BRANSHILL PK
WOODLEA PK
PARKHEAD RD
CHURCH GR
POSTHILL
ROSEBANK
GARTMORN RD
MOUNT WILLIAM
WOODLANDS
DEER PK
TOWER VIEW
BEECHWOOD
88
89
90
94
95
96
97
A B C D E F
1 2 3 4 5 6 7 8

10

1

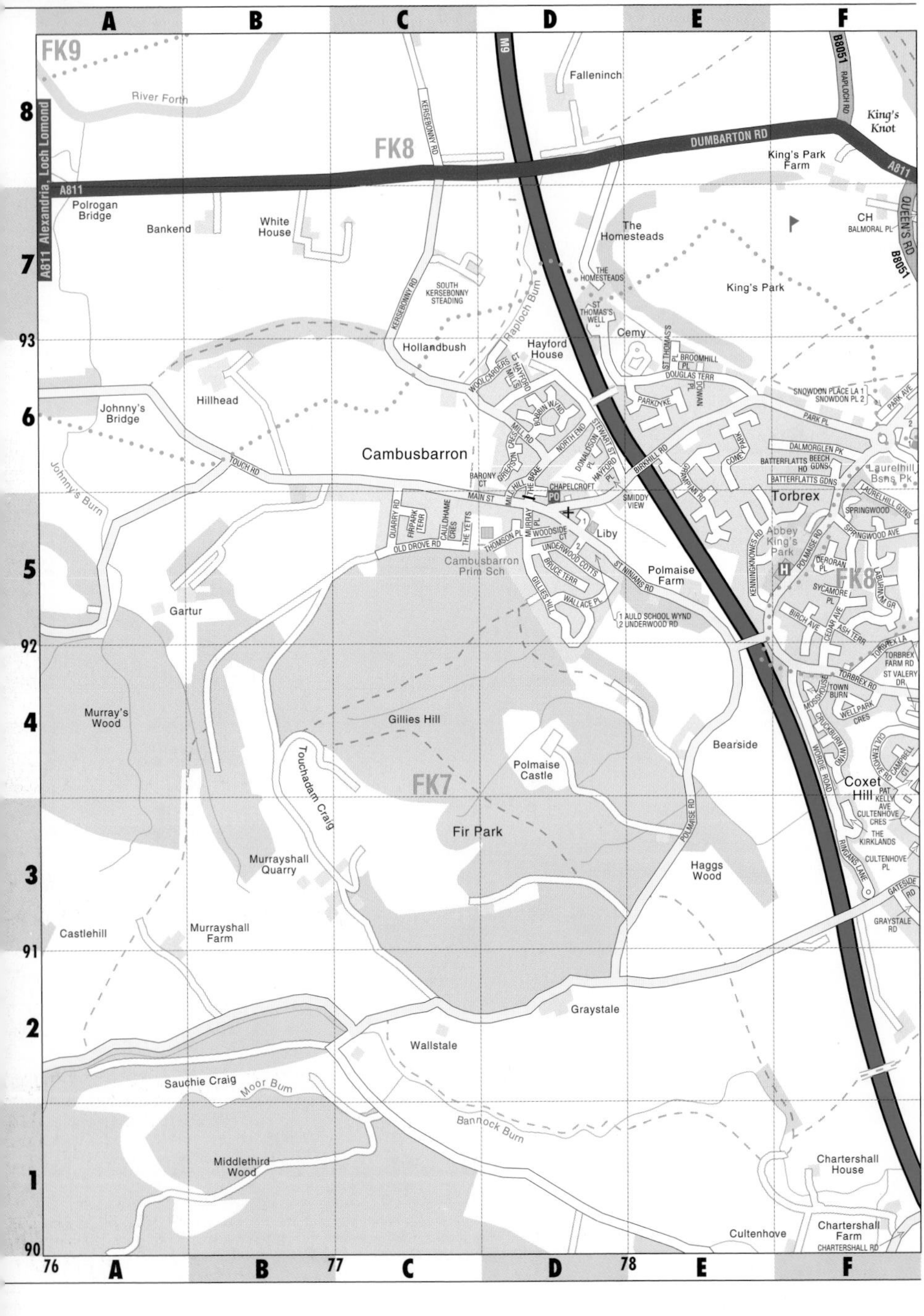
A
B
C
D
E
F
FK9
River Forth
FK8
Falleninch
M9
B8051
RAPLOCH RD
King's Knot
DUMBARTON RD
King's Park Farm
A811
QUEEN'S RD
A811 Alexandria, Loch Lomond
Polrogan Bridge
Bankend
White House
The Homesteads
CH
BALMORAL PL
KERSEBONNY RD
SOUTH KERSEBONNY STEADING
THE HOMESTEADS
ST THOMAS'S WELL
King's Park
Raploch Burn
Hollandbush
Hayford House
Cemy
ST THOMAS'S PL
BROOMHILL PL
DOUGLAS TERR
DOWAN PL
PARKDYKE
SNOWDON PLACE LA 1
SNOWDON PL 2
PARK AVE
PARK PL
Hillhead
Johnny's Bridge
WOOLCARDERS CT
HAYFORD MILLS
BOBBIN WYND
MILL RD
NORTH END
STEWART ST
DONALDSON PL
HAYFORD PL
BIRKHILL RD
GRAMPIAN RD
CONEY PARK
DALMORGLEN PK
BATTERFLATTS HO
BEECH GDNS
BATTERFLATTS GDNS
Laurelhill Bsns Pk
LAURELHILL GDNS
Torbrex
SPRINGWOOD
SPRINGWOOD AVE
Johnny's Burn
TOUCH RD
Cambusbarron
BARONY CT
GRIERSON CRES
MILL HILL
THE BRAE
CHAPELCROFT
PO
MAIN ST
SMIDDY VIEW
QUARRY RD
FIRPARK TERR
CAULDHAME CRES
THE YETTS
THOMSON PL
MURRAY PL
WOODSIDE CT
Liby
OLD DROVE RD
UNDERWOOD COTTS
ST NINIANS RD
Abbey King's Park
KENNINGKNOWES RD
POLMAISE RD
DERORAN PL
LABURNUM GR
Cambusbarron Prim Sch
BRUCE TERR
Polmaise Farm
H
FK8
SYCAMORE PL
GILLIES HILL
WALLACE PL
1 AULD SCHOOL WYND
2 UNDERWOOD RD
BIRCH AVE
CEDAR AVE
ASH TERR
Gartur
TORBREX LA
TORBREX FARM RD
ST VALERY DR
TORBREX RD
TOWN BURN
MOSSHOUSE
WELLPARK CRES
Murray's Wood
Gillies Hill
CRUCKBURN WYND
CULTENHOVE RD
CAMPBELL CT
Bearside
Touchadam Craig
Polmaise Castle
WORDIE ROAD
Coxet Hill
PAT KELLY AVE
CULTENHOVE CRES
FK7
Fir Park
POLMAISE RD
THE KIRKLANDS
Murrayshall Quarry
Haggs Wood
CULTENHOVE PL
RINGANS LANE
GATESIDE RD
GRAYSTALE RD
Castlehill
Murrayshall Farm
Graystale
Wallstale
Sauchie Craig
Moor Burn
Bannock Burn
Chartershall House
Middlethird Wood
Cultenhove
Chartershall Farm
CHARTERSHALL RD
8
7
93
6
5
92
4
3
91
2
1
90
76
77
78

A8
1 ESPLANADE
2 UPPER CASTLEHILL
3 KINGSTABLES LA
4 CASTLE WYND
5 ST MARY'S WYND
6 BANK ST

B7
1 CORN EXCHANGE RD
2 BACK WLK
3 THE CRAWFORD SH ARC
4 THISTLE CHAMBERS
5 ORCHARDCROFT
6 CASTLEGAIT
7 BASTION WYND
8 THE MARCHES
9 CAMERONIAN ST
10 ALLAN PARK HO

B8
1 WALLACE ST
2 COWANE ST
3 VIEWFIELD PL
4 VIEWFIELD ST
5 SEAFORTH PL
6 MAXWELL PL
7 STATION RD

2
8

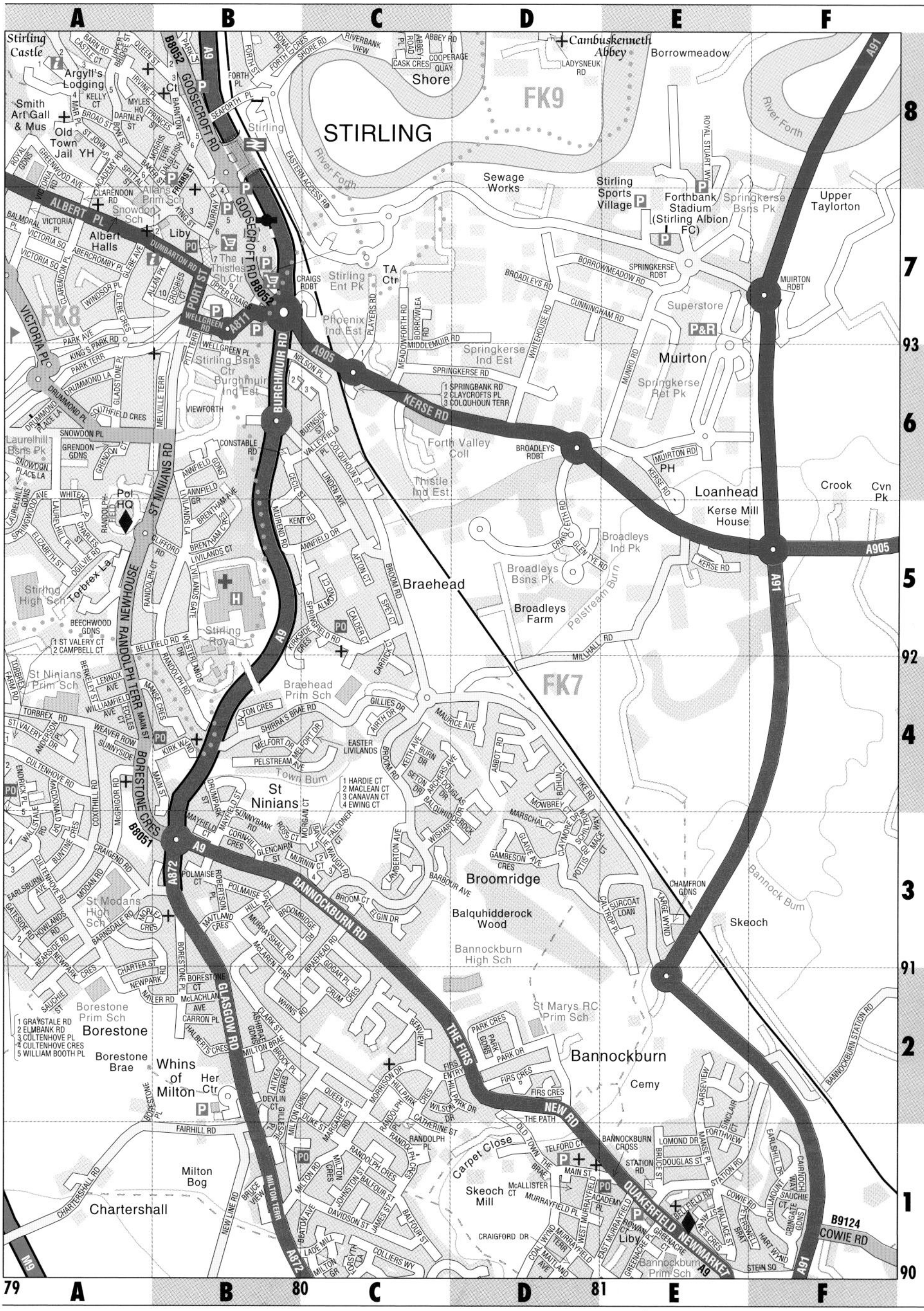

11
8

7
3

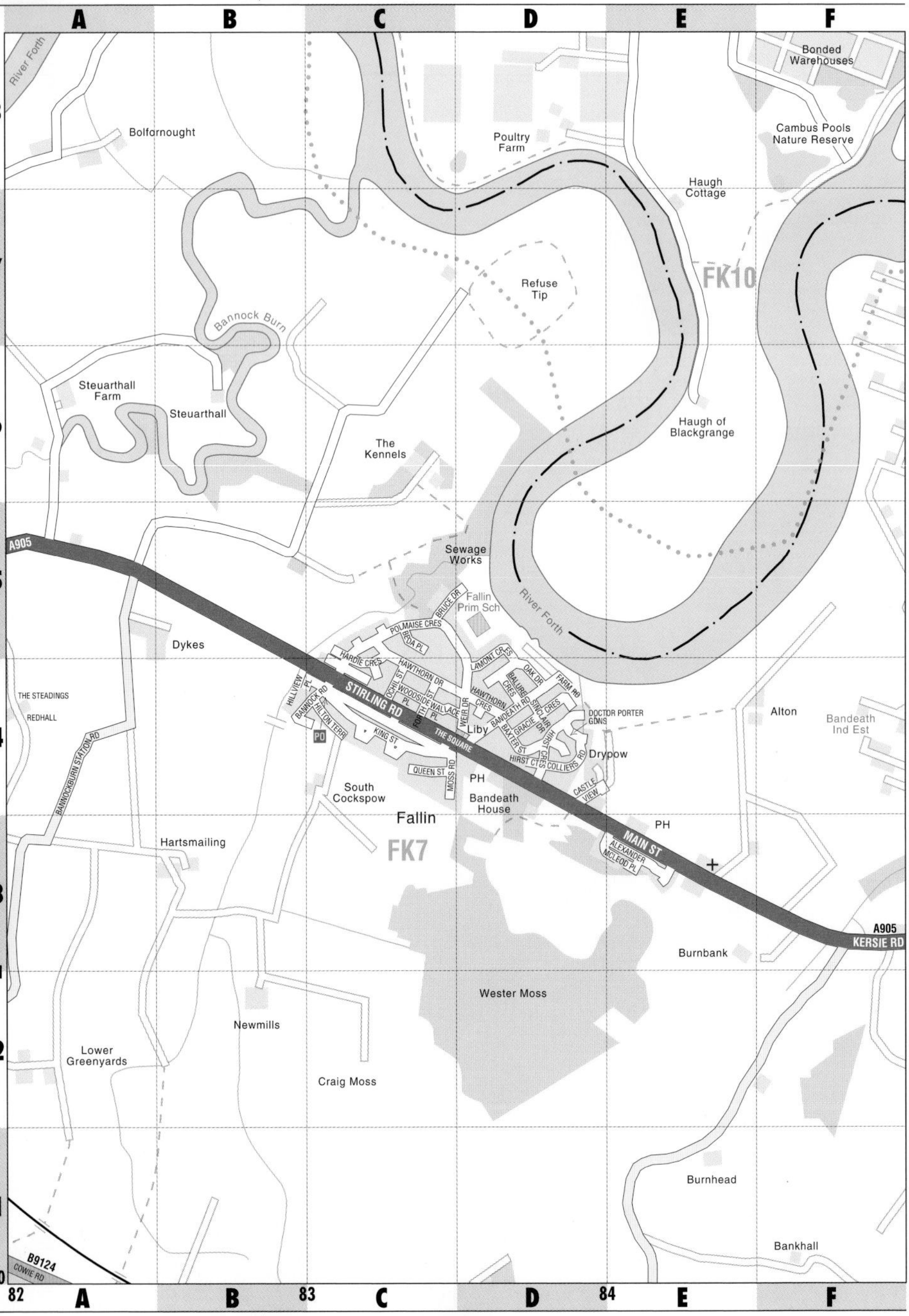
River Forth
Bolfornought
Poultry Farm
Bonded Warehouses
Cambus Pools Nature Reserve
Haugh Cottage
Refuse Tip
FK10
Bannock Burn
Steuarthall Farm
Steuarthall
The Kennels
Haugh of Blackgrange
A905
Sewage Works
Fallin Prim Sch
River Forth
Dykes
POLMAISE CRES
BRUCE DR
BEDA PL
HARDIE CRES
HAWTHORN DR
LAMONT CRES
OAK DR
FARM RD
BALURE CRES
HILLVIEW PL
BANNOCK RD
STIRLING RD
OCHIL ST
WOODSIDE PL
WALLACE PL
WEIR DR
HAWTHORN CRES
BANDEATH RD
SINCLAIR DR
DOCTOR PORTER GDNS
THE STEADINGS
REDHALL
HILTON TERR
KING ST
FORTH PL
THE SQUARE
Liby
GRACIE DR
BAXTER ST
HIRST CRES
COLLIERS RD
Drypow
Alton
Bandeath Ind Est
BANNOCKBURN STATION RD
PO
QUEEN ST
MOSS RD
HIRST CT
CASTLE VIEW
South Cockspow
PH
Bandeath House
Fallin
PH
MAIN ST
ALEXANDER MCLEOD PL
FK7
Hartsmailing
A905
KERSIE RD
Burnbank
Wester Moss
Newmills
Lower Greenyards
Craig Moss
Burnhead
Bankhall
B9124
COWIE RD
A B C D E F
8 7 93 6 5 92 4 3 91 2 1 90
82 83 84

7
12

4
10

A
B
C
D
E
F
MOUBRAY GDNS
Cambus Farm
STATION RD
MAIN ST
SOUTH ST
PO
PH
FORTH ST
DEVON PL
Cambus
A907
Arnsbrae
DUNMAR DR
Gean House
ARNS GR
Alloa Acad
CLAREMONT
Claremont Prim Sch
KENT RD
FAIRYBURN RD
CROWN GDNS
WINDSOR GDNS
GEAN RD
LORNSHILL CRES
EDEN RD
INGLEWOOD RD
CHURCHILL ST
CHARLES ST
ANNE ST
B9096
TULLIBODY RD
WEST LODGE GDNS
TITANIA
OBERON
DAWSON AVE
PAVILION VIEW
ACADEMY ST
CARSE TERR
NORWOOD GR
NORWOOD AVE
REDWELL PL
NORWOOD CRES
ALEXANDRA DR
STIRLING RD
8
7
93
6
5
92
4
3
91
2
1
90
FK10
Pavilions Bsns Pk
THE PAVILIONS
ALLOA
THE PLEASURES
Smart Village Bsns Campus
LC
A907
Orchard Farm
Orchard House
Pier
SMITHFIELD LOAN
MITCHELL CRES
DIRLETON GDNS
DIRLETON LA
St John's Prim Sch
THE HARLAWS
OLD MDWS
GRANGE RD
MEDWYN PL
Works
New Struan Sch
BELLEVUE RD
BELLEVUE PK
FORBES ST
STANTON AVE
SHIRE WAY
CARPENTERS WYND
GRANT ST
CALEDONIAN RD
KELLIEBANK
DOWNS CRES
KEVERKAE
MUNRO PL
Longcarse
Works
KELLIEBANK
CRAIGWARD
Bandeath Ind Est
Tullibody Inch
Longcarse Reach
Rhind
Inch
Bandeath Ind Est
Throsk House
Works
FERRY RD
Pier
THE HAVEN
South Alloa
Bandeath Ind Est
River Forth
KERSIE RD
Throsk
KERSIE RD
Kersie Mains
KERSIE TERR
Mains of Throsk
Poppletrees
Kersie Bridge
FK7
South Kersie
Willowbank
Meadowfield
SOUTH MAINS
FK2
A905
85
86
87
13
10

B6
1 BURGH MEWS
2 MERCAT WYND
3 STRIPEHEAD
4 UNION ST
5 BREWHOUSE CT
6 WEST VENNEL
7 CANDLERIGGS CT
8 THE CROSS
9 TOWNHEAD APARTMENTS
10 MAPLE CT
11 OLD BRIDGE ST
12 JUNCTION PL
13 BRIDGE TERR

B7
1 Sunnyside Prim Sch

9
5

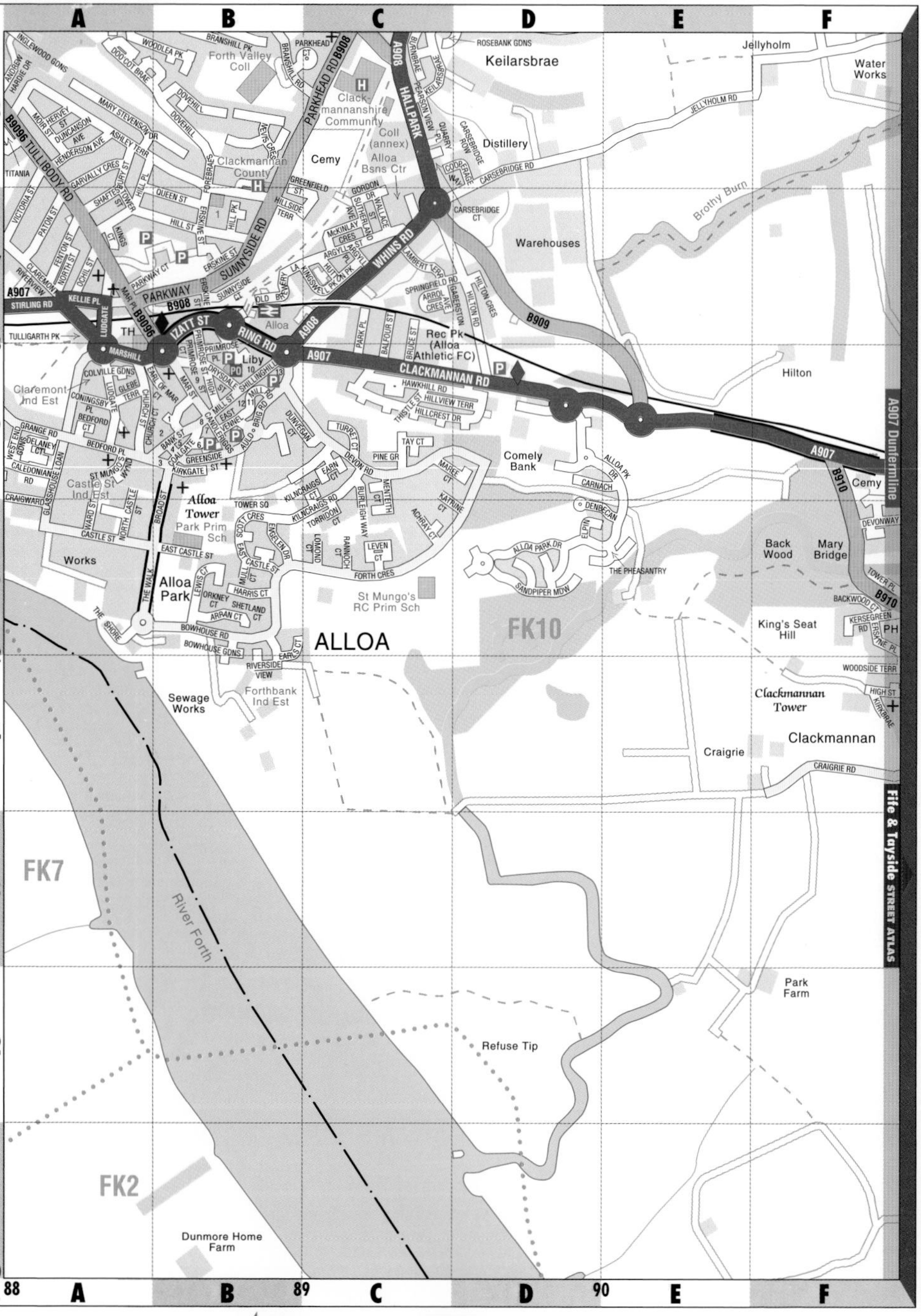

9
14

7
12

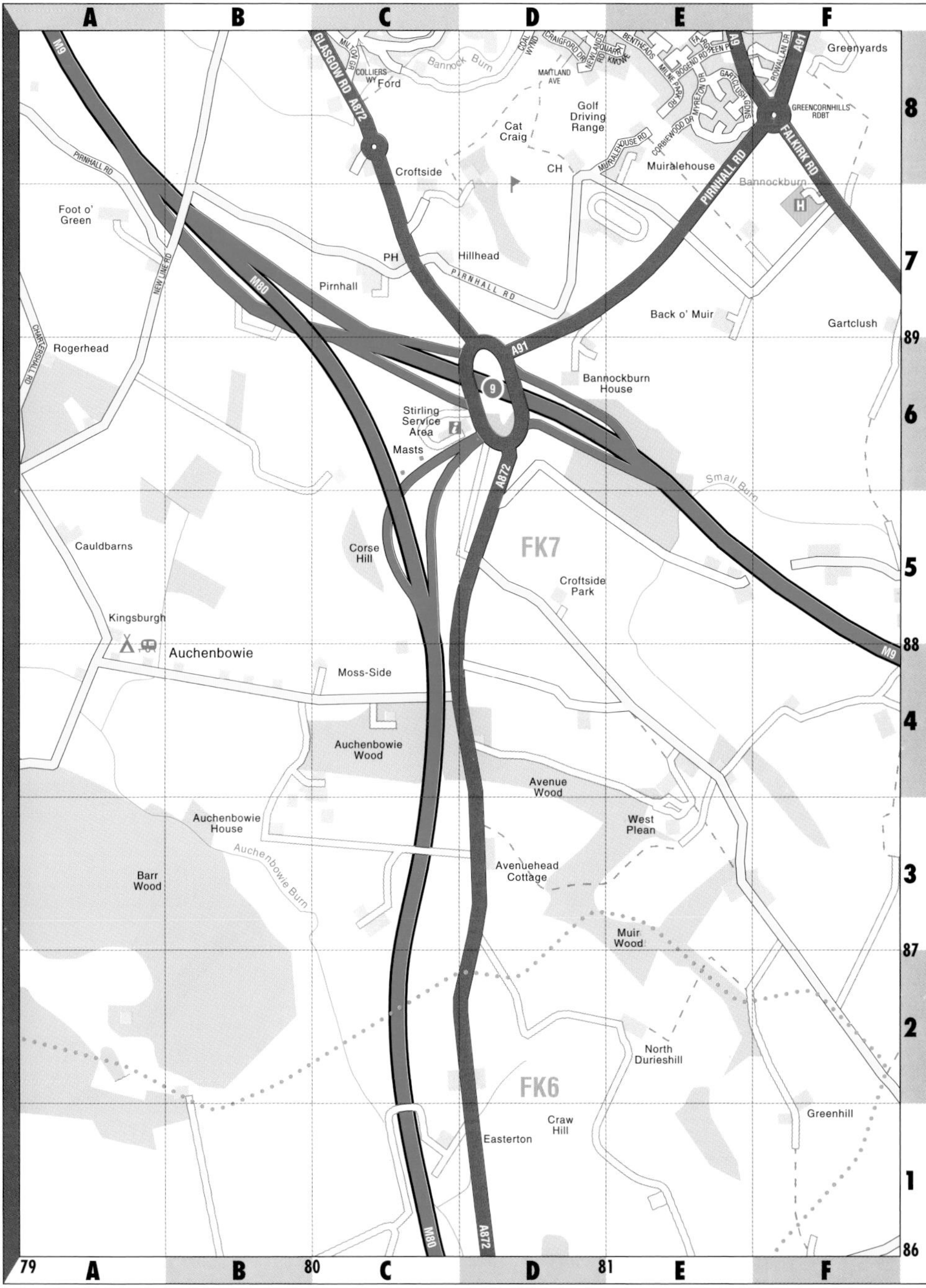
A
B
C
D
E
F
8
7
89
6
5
88
4
3
87
2
1
86
79
80
81
M9
M80
A872
A91
A9
GLASGOW RD
FALKIRK RD
PIRNHALL RD
NEW LINE RD
CHARTERSHALL RD
MURALEHOUSE RD
COAL WYND
CRAIGFORD DR
NEWLANDS RD
MILNE PARK RD
MYRETON DR
CORBIEWOOD DR
GARTCLUSH GDNS
ROWALLAN DR
BENTHEADS
COLLIERS WY
MAITLAND AVE
GREENCORNHILLS RDBT
Ford
Bannock Burn
Greenyards
Golf Driving Range
Cat Craig
Croftside
CH
Muiralehouse
Bannockburn
Foot o' Green
PH
Hillhead
Pirnhall
Back o' Muir
Gartclush
Rogerhead
Bannockburn House
9
Stirling Service Area
Masts
Small Burn
FK7
Cauldbarns
Corse Hill
Croftside Park
Kingsburgh
Auchenbowie
Moss-Side
Auchenbowie Wood
Avenue Wood
Auchenbowie House
West Plean
Auchenbowie Burn
Barr Wood
Avenuehead Cottage
Muir Wood
North Durieshill
FK6
Greenhill
Craw Hill
Easterton

21
12

11
8

COWIE RD
B9124
Westerton
of Cowie
Easter
Greenyards
Sewage
Works
Hilton
Farm
1 MURRAY ROW
2 ROXBURGH ROW
3 MOUBREY ROW
RICHARD QUINN ST
FINCASTLE PL
ARDGOWAN PL
TIBBIES LOAN
WESTERTON
FARM RD
FLINT CRES
OCHRE CRES
CARNOCK ST
PARK ST
HILTON
COWIEHALL RD
BANNOCKBURN RD
SCOTSTOUN RD
Cowie
Prim Sch
St Margarets
RC Prim Sch
PO
Berry
Hills
Cowie
Cowiehall
BERRYHILL
MOUNT OLIPHANT
EASTERTON DR
EASTERTON GR
ALLOWAY DR
BURNS TERR
KYLE AVE
OCHILVIEW
MAIN ST
Gartclush
A9
89
Liby
Sink
MAIN ST
STATION RD
Works
Plean
Junction
Plean
Farm
FK7
Gallamuir
Wood
SAUCHENFORD
SMALLHOLDINGS
B9124
GALLAMUIR RD
FALKIRK RD
88
M9
Gallamuir
Pleanbank
Wood
Pleanbank
Farm
MCCANN CT
CAREY CT
HENDERSON PL
Sauchinford Burn
BURNSIDE CRES
LOANFOOT GDNS
Liby
PO
WALLACE CRES
PARKSIDE CT
PRESIDENT KENNEDY DR
KIRKSIDE TERR
TOUCHHILL CRES
OAK CRES
BRUCE CRES
BRUCE ST
CARBROOK DR
BEECH AVE
GALLAMUIR DR
BALFOUR CT
BALFOUR CRES
CUSHENQUARTER DR
PLEANBANK COTTS
FK2
Plean
STIRLING PL
WILLOW BRAE
THORNYCROFT TERR
MCAULAY BRAE
TORBURN AVE
MAIN ST
Works
Sewage
Works
Gartwhinnie
Farm
87
East Plean
Prim Sch
CADGERS LOAN
CHURCH LA
Cushenquarter
Plean
Country Park
Plean
House
NEWLANDS CT
GILLESPIE TERR
Plean Burn
CARDROWAN RD
M9
GLEN RD
Plean
Ind Est
FK5
Muirmailing
Carbrook Mains
A9
86
82
83
84
A
B
C
D
E
F
8
7
6
5
4
3
2
1

11
22

9
14

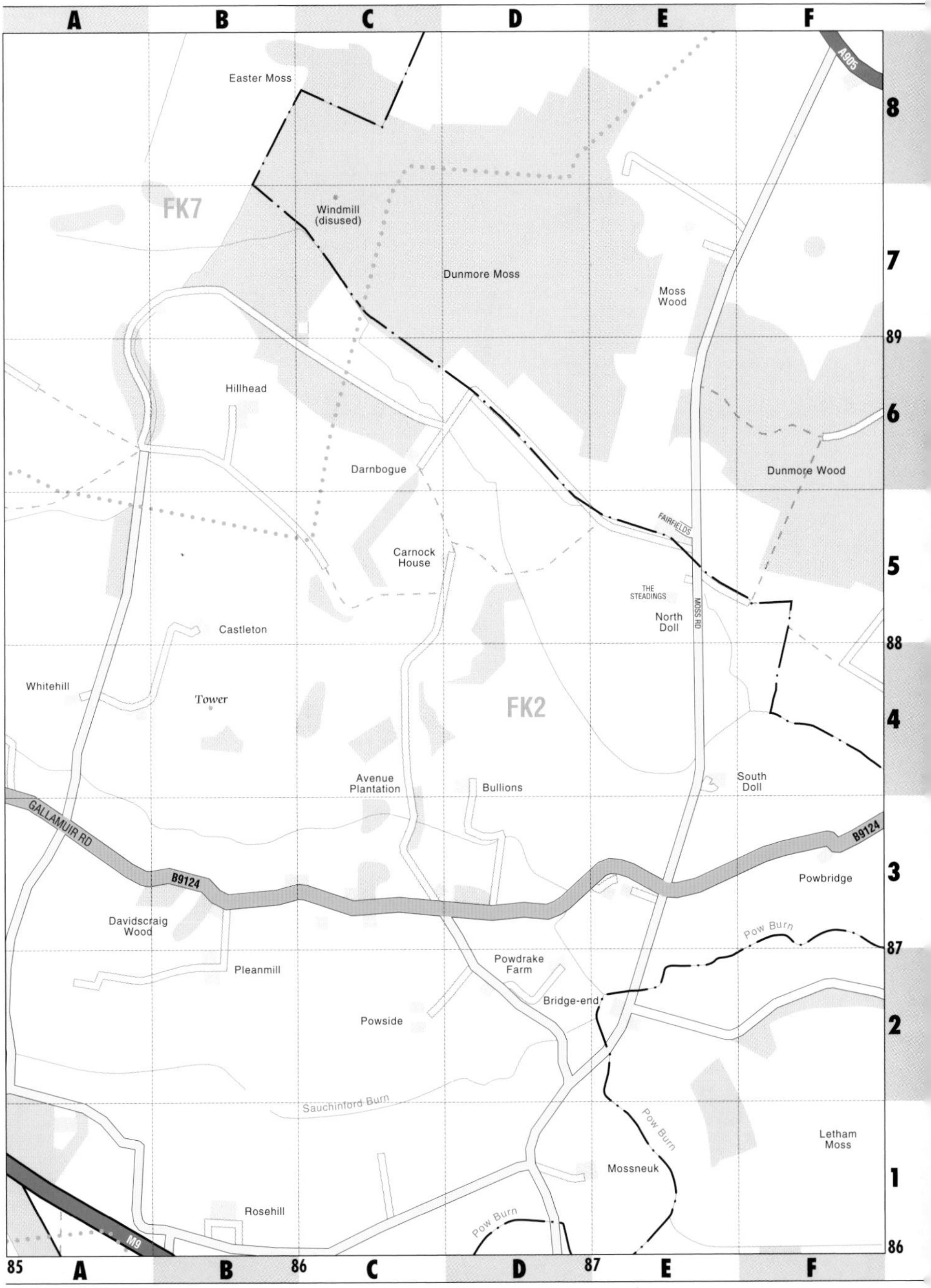
A
B
C
D
E
F
8
7
89
6
5
88
4
3
87
2
1
86
85
86
87
Easter Moss
FK7
Windmill
(disused)
Dunmore Moss
Moss
Wood
A905
Hillhead
Darnbogue
Dunmore Wood
FAIRFIELDS
Carnock
House
THE
STEADINGS
North
Doll
MOSS RD
Castleton
Whitehill
Tower
FK2
Avenue
Plantation
Bullions
South
Doll
GALLAMUIR RD
B9124
B9124
Powbridge
Davidscraig
Wood
Pow Burn
Pleanmill
Powdrake
Farm
Bridge-end
Powside
Sauchinford Burn
Pow Burn
Letham
Moss
Mossneuk
Rosehill
Pow Burn
M9

23
14

13
10
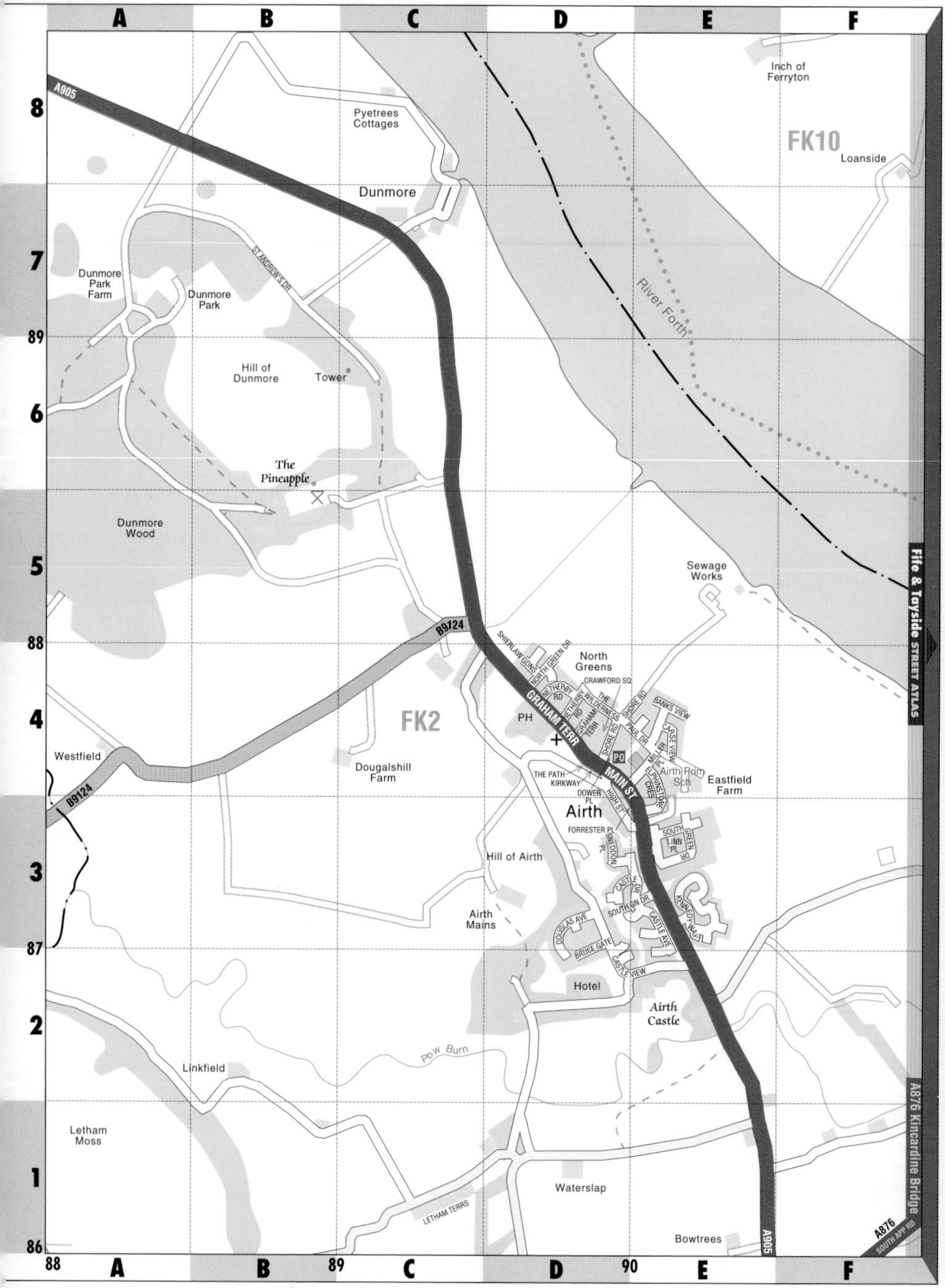
A905
Inch of Ferryton
Pyetrees Cottages
FK10
Loanside
Dunmore
ST ANDREW'S DR
Dunmore Park Farm
Dunmore Park
River Forth
Hill of Dunmore
Tower
The Pineapple
Dunmore Wood
Sewage Works
B9124
SHIERLAW GDNS
NORTH GREEN DR
North Greens
NETHERBY RD
CRAWFORD SQ
THE WILDERNESS
GRAHAM TERR
SHORE RD
BANKS VIEW
PAUL DR
CARSE VIEW
PH
FK2
MILLER PL
PO
Westfield
Dougalshill Farm
THE PATH
KIRKWAY
MAIN ST
ELPHINSTONE CRES
Airth Prim Sch
Eastfield Farm
DOWER PL
HIGH ST
Airth
FORRESTER PL
SOUTH GREEN DR
LINN PL
SNEDDON PL
Hill of Airth
CASTLE DR
SOUTH GN DR
KENNEDY WAY
Airth Mains
DOUGLAS AVE
CASTLE AVE
BRIDGE GATE
CASTLE VIEW
Hotel
Airth Castle
Pow Burn
Linkfield
Letham Moss
Waterslap
LETHAM TERRS
Bowtrees
A876
SOUTH APP RD
Fife & Tayside STREET ATLAS
A876 Kincardine Bridge
13
24

16

A B C D E F
A814 Garelochhead
A814
ARDGARE
QUEENS POINT
Croy
BROOMFIELD GDNS
Blairvadach
Aldownick Glen
Resrs
Letrualt Farm
G84
ALEXANDER PL
JUPITER PL
BEECH GR
AROS RD
ARDEN HILL
ARDENCONNEL MEWS
EDEN GR
ARDENCONNEL HQ
Rhu
EMPRESS RD
ARDENCONNEL WAY
QUARRY KNOWE
LINESIDE WLK
STATION RD
Torr
CUMBERLAND RD
UPPER HALL RD
HALL RD
CUMBERLAND TERR
SCHOOL RD
INCHGOWER GR
MANSE BRAE
GLEBEFIELD RD
LAGGARY RD
TORR CRES
1 BRAEHEAD PL
2 CALDWELL PL
BARGE CT
MANSE PL
Pier
Yacht Club
Rhu Prim Sch
Liby
ARDWELL PL
PO
GUTHRIE PL
LAGGARY PK
SPY'S LA
GLENARN RD
UPPER TORWOODHILL RD
GLENORAN RD
CHURCH PL 1
BRAEHOUSE 2
RHU-ELLEN CT 3
WATERSEDGE CT 4
Gare Loch
ROWMORE QUAYS
PIER RD
Rhu Bay
WOODSTONE CT
ARTARMAN RD
ARMADALE RD
TORWOODHILL RD
TORWOODHILL PL
TORWOODHILL
Tor Wood
GARELOCH RD
B833
Stroul Bay
Jetty
Works
Limekiln Point
Rosneath Prim Sch
COURT HILL
Clachan Burn
HOWIE CRES
CLACHAN RD
MAIN RD
ST MODAN'S WAY
FERRY RD
GARE RD
1 NAVY WAY
2 PRINCESS WAY
Rosneath
THE CLACHAN
PO
ARGYLL RD
CEDAR VIEW
CAMSAIL RD
THE LOCHANS
ROSNEATH RD
Marina
IRB Sta
RHU RD HIGHER
A814
RHU RD LOWER
DALMORE CRES 1
CUMBERLAND AVE 2
KIDSTON DR 3
Cairndhu Point
P
Broom Plantation
Clachan Glen
Clachan Burn
G84
Pier
Clachan Farm
Rosneath Bay
Castle Point
Hill of Camsail Plantation
Camsail Wood
Creag na Goibhre
Crane Rock
Castle Bay
Camsail Bay
Rosneath Castle Caravan Pk
Dark Wood
B833
8 7 85 6 5 84 4 3 83 2 1 82
25 26 27

16

15

A
B
C
D
E
F
8
7
85
6
5
84
4
3
83
2
1
82
28
29
30
Green Burn
Drumford Wood
Highlandman's Wood
Millig Burn
Reservoir
Highlandman's Road
G84
Ardencaple Wood
Ardencaple Farm
Blackhill Plantation
Reservoirs
Glennan Burn
Duchess Wood
Hill House
LUSS RD
A818
Helensburgh Upper
Castle Wood
Lomond Sch
Parklands Sch
Hermitage Prim Sch
St Josephs Prim Sch
CH
SINCLAIR ST
WEST CLYDE ST
EAST CLYDE ST
RHU RD LOWER
RHU RD HIGHER
A814
HELENSBURGH
Liby
Helensburgh Central
Swimming Pool
Victoria
Cemy
STRATHCLYDE PL 1
MACAULAY PL 2
COVE PL 3
ROSNEATH DR 4
BONAR LAW AVE 5
CAMSAIL AVE 6
SUTHERLAND PL 7
WESTBORNE GDNS 8
COLERIDGE GDNS 9
PRINCESS CT 1
SCOTT CT 2
COLQUHOUN SQ 3
HANOVER ST 1
ROSEDALE GDNS 2
MILLERSLEA GDNS 3
STUCKLECKIE RD 1
ATHOLE ST 2
WILLIAMSON DR 3
UPPER SUTHERLAND ST 1
LOWER SUTHERLAND CRES 2

15

18

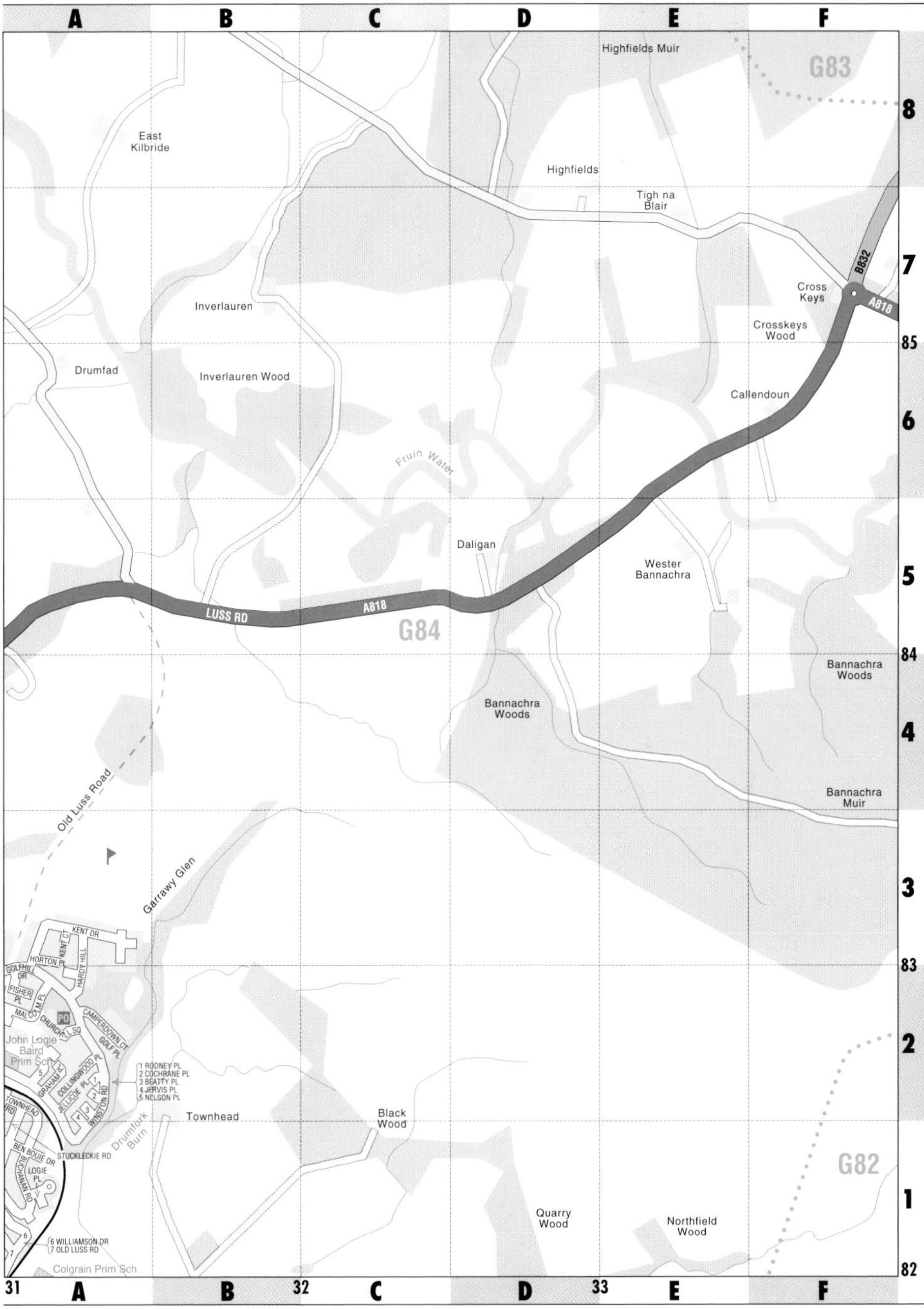
A
B
C
D
E
F
Highfields Muir
G83
8
East Kilbride
Highfields
Tigh na Blair
7
B832
Cross Keys
A818
Inverlauren
Crosskeys Wood
85
Drumfad
Inverlauren Wood
Callendoun
6
Fruin Water
Daligan
Wester Bannachra
5
LUSS RD
A818
G84
84
Bannachra Woods
Bannachra Woods
4
Old Luss Road
Bannachra Muir
Garrawy Glen
3
KENT DR
KENT CT
HORTON PL
HARDY HILL
GOLFHILL DR
FISHER PL
MALCOLM PL
83
PO
CHURCHILL SQ
CAMPERDOWN CT
GOLF PL
John Logie Baird Prim Sch
2
1 RODNEY PL
2 COCHRANE PL
3 BEATTY PL
4 JERVIS PL
5 NELSON PL
GRAHAM PL
COLLINGWOOD PL
JELLICOE PL
WINSTON RD
TOWNHEAD RD
Townhead
Black Wood
Drumfork Burn
BEN BOUIE DR
STUCKLECKIE RD
BUCHANAN RD
LOGIE PL
G82
1
Quarry Wood
Northfield Wood
6 WILLIAMSON DR
7 OLD LUSS RD
Colgrain Prim Sch
82
31
32
33

25
18

17

A
B
C
D
E
F
A82 Tarbet, Crianlarich
Midross
Auchentullich Namoin
Mungo's Hill
8
B832
A82
Blairkatie Wood
7
Meikle Dumfin
Hole Wood
A818
Nether Ross
85
Little Dumfin
Fruin Water
Dumfin Mill House
Rossbank
Burnfoot
Saw Mill
6
Arden
A818
ARDEN HO
Wester Auchendennan
Pier
5
Bannachra
G84
LOMOND CASTLE
84
Redburn Plantation
Strone Wood
Auchendennan Cottages
Auchendennan
G83
A82
4
Red Burn
Loch Lomond YH
Goukhill Farm
Holy Wood
3
Goukhill Plantation
Garden Wood
Auchendennan Glen
Goukhill Muir
Ben Bowie
83
2
Tank Wood
Gouk Hill
Auchendennan Muir
G82
1
Cameron Wood
Darleith Muir
82
34
35
36

20

A
B
C
D
E
F
Knockour Wood
Lorn
8
Knockour Hill
Knockour
7
Black Roundel
85
6
Boturich Castle
Meikle Boturich
Loch Lomond
Whinny Hill
5
Loch Lomond & The Trossachs National Park
84
Ledrishmore Wood
G83
Burn of Balloch
4
Over Balloch
Duck Bay
Horsehouse Wood
Stable Wood
Cameron Bay
3
Hotel
83
Balloch Castle
Cameron House Farm
Balloch Castle Country Park
2
Ledrishbeg
Balloch Pier
INCHFAD RD
INCHCONNACHAN AVE
TORRINCH DR
LEDRISH AVE
MOLLANBOWIE RD
CREINCH DR
INCHMURRIN CRES
INCHLONAIG DR
LORN DR
1 MCLEAN CRES
2 HARAN RD
3 SHANDON CRES
4 SHANDON BRAE
5 DUMBAIN RD
6 HALDANE TERR
OLD LUSS RD
Moss o' Balloch Plantations
Sea Life Loch Lomond
Loch Lomond Shores
River Leven
Balloch
ENDRICK DR
MOSSBURN AVE
A811
BOTURICH DR
PARK AVE
CASTLE AVE
LAWRENCE DR
1
BEN LOMOND WAY
PIER RD
DRYMEN RD
GALLACHER CRES
McKENZIE DR
LOMOND RD
MAIN ST
A82
INCHCRUIN
CLAIRINSH
BALLOCH RD
82
37
38
39

27

20

19
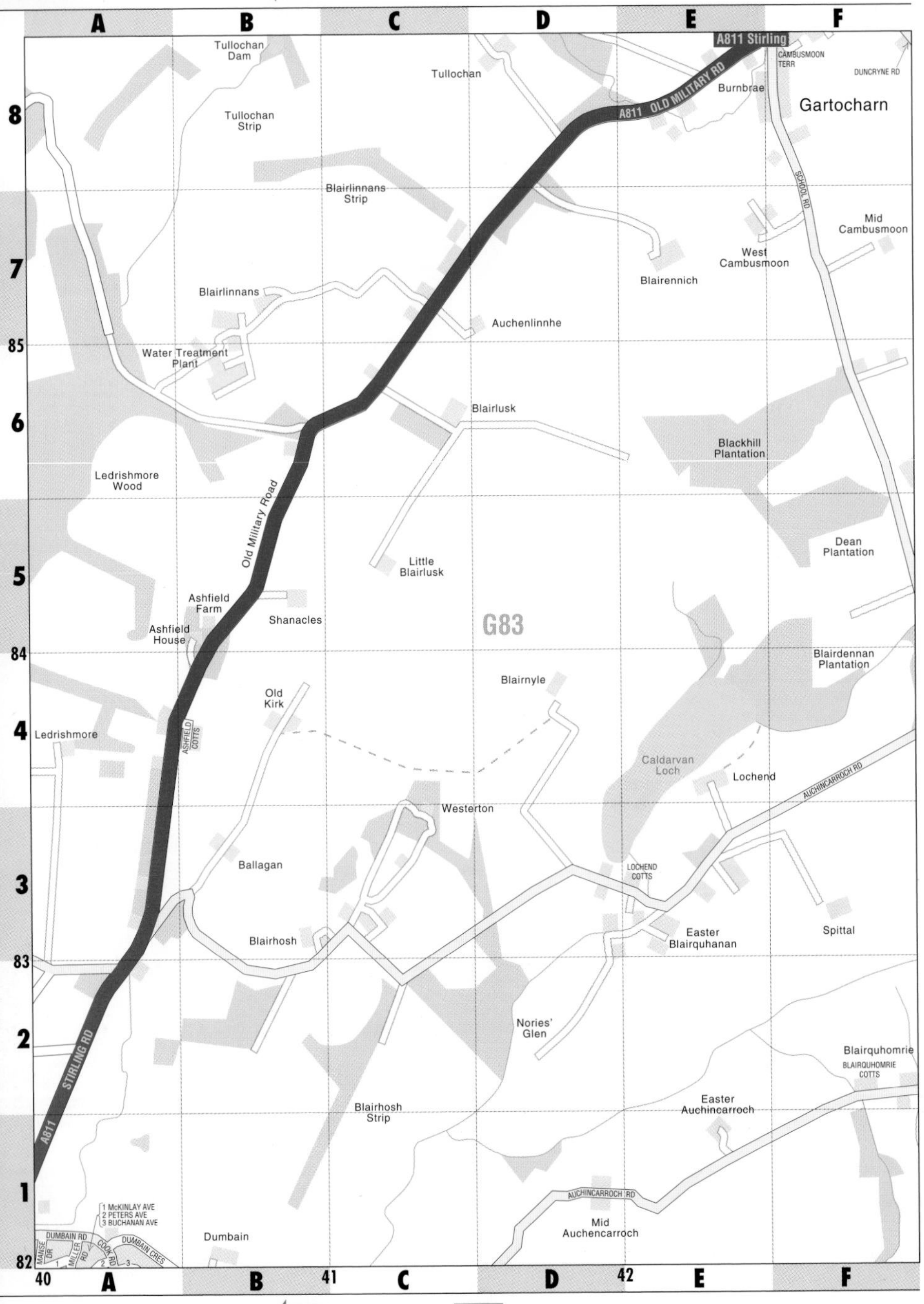
A
B
C
D
E
F
8
7
85
6
5
84
4
3
83
2
1
82
40
41
42
A811 Stirling
A811 OLD MILITARY RD
Tullochan Dam
Tullochan
Tullochan Strip
Burnbrae
CAMBUSMOON TERR
DUNCRYNE RD
Gartocharn
SCHOOL RD
Blairlinnans Strip
Mid Cambusmoon
West Cambusmoon
Blairennich
Blairlinnans
Auchenlinnhe
Water Treatment Plant
Blairlusk
Blackhill Plantation
Ledrishmore Wood
Old Military Road
Dean Plantation
Little Blairlusk
Ashfield Farm
Shanacles
G83
Ashfield House
Blairdennan Plantation
Old Kirk
Blairnyle
Ledrishmore
ASHFIELD COTTS
Caldarvan Loch
Lochend
AUCHINCARROCH RD
Westerton
Ballagan
LOCHEND COTTS
Easter Blairquhanan
Spittal
Blairhosh
Nories' Glen
STIRLING RD
Blairquhomrie
BLAIRQUHOMRIE COTTS
Blairhosh Strip
Easter Auchincarroch
A811
AUCHINCARROCH RD
1 McKINLAY AVE
2 PETERS AVE
3 BUCHANAN AVE
DUMBAIN RD
MANSE DR
MILLER RD
COOK RD
DUMBAIN CRES
Dumbain
Mid Auchencarroch
19
28

11 22

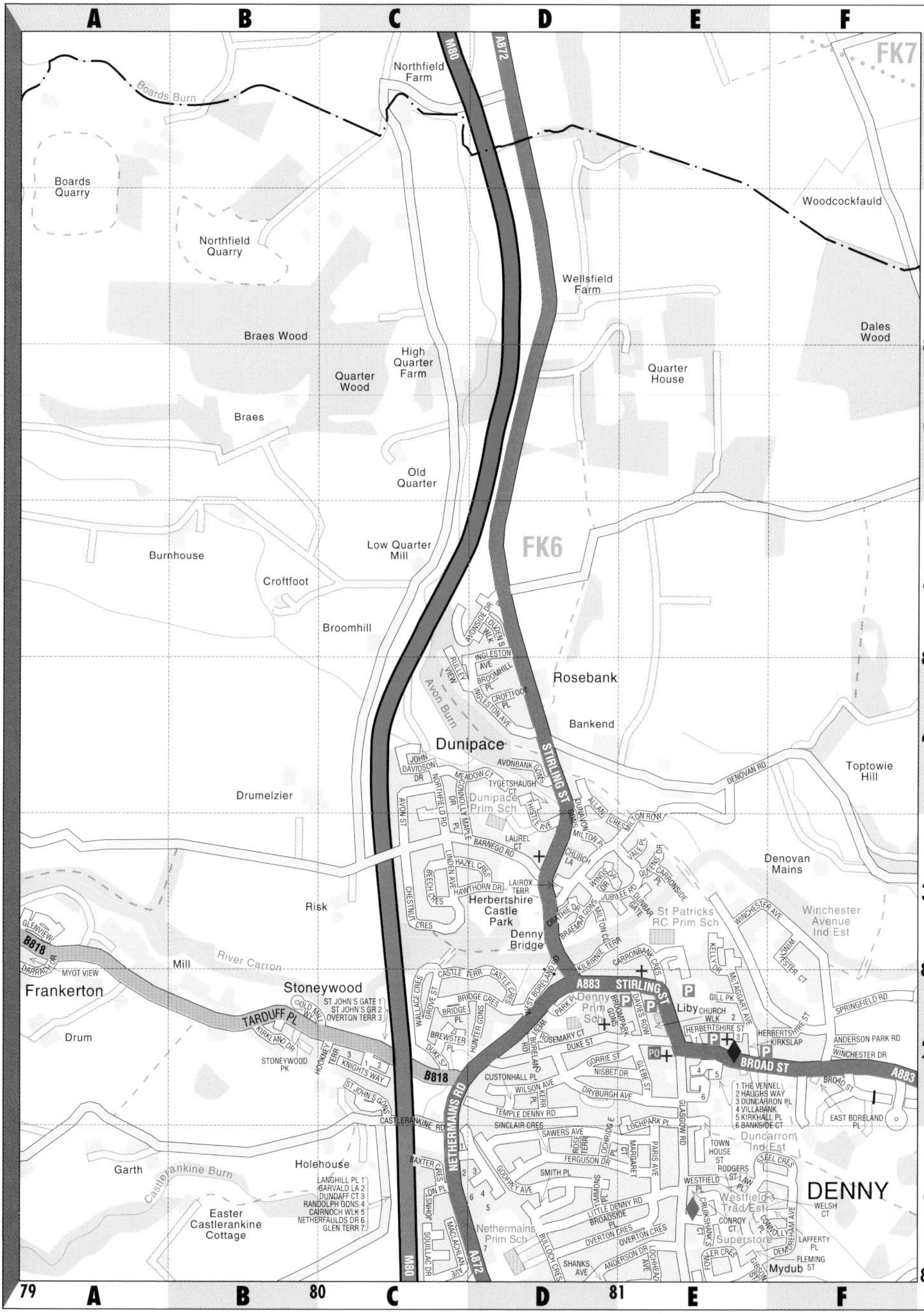
Northfield Farm
Boards Burn
Boards Quarry
Northfield Quarry
Wellsfield Farm
Woodcockfauld
Dales Wood
Braes Wood
High Quarter Farm
Quarter Wood
Quarter House
Braes
Old Quarter
FK6
FK7
Burnhouse
Low Quarter Mill
Croftfoot
Broomhill
Rosebank
Bankend
Dunipace
Toptowie Hill
Drumelzier
Denovan Mains
Risk
Herbertshire Castle Park
Denny Bridge
St Patricks RC Prim Sch
Winchester Avenue Ind Est
Frankerton
Mill
River Carron
Stoneywood
Drum
Liby
Garth
Holehouse
Easter Castlerankine Cottage
Castlerankine Burn
Duncarron Ind Est
Westfield Trad Est
Superstore
DENNY
Nethermains Prim Sch
Dunipace Prim Sch
Denny Prim Sch
Mydub
STIRLING ST
BROAD ST
NETHERMAINS RD
M80
A872
A883
B818
1 THE VENNEL
2 HAUGHS WAY
3 DUNCARRON PL
4 VILLABANK
5 KIRKHALL PL
6 BANKSIDE CT
ST JOHN'S GATE 1
ST JOHN'S GR 2
OVERTON TERR 3
LANGHILL PL 1
GARVALD LA 2
DUNDAFF CT 3
RANDOLPH GDNS 4
CAIRNOCH WLK 5
NETHERFAULDS DR 6
GLEN TERR 7
A B C D E F
8 7 85 6 5 84 4 3 83 2 1 82
79 80 81

39 22

21
12

A
B
C
D
E
F
8
7
85
6
5
84
4
3
83
2
1
82
82
83
84
FK7
Glenside
GLEN RD
Tor Burn
A9
Hollings
BOGEND RD
Langlands
GLEN RD
CASTLE CRES
NEWINGTON LA
FORRESTER GAIT
The Rocks
Tappoch
Torwood
Whinnie Muir
Torwood Sch
Tor Wood
Torwood Castle
Torwoodhead
FK5
STIRLING RD
CH
Doghillock
Tod Hill
Pamphellgoat Wood
M876
A9
STIRLING RD
2
M876
Denovan
Baxter Wood
FK6
DENOVAN RD
OLD DENNY RD
Oakbank Wood
Forth Valley
Under construction – due to open 2010
Big Wood
H
Sewage Works
Kirkland
River Carron
P
A883
Evergreen Trailer Court
Larbert House
PH
Works
Househill Farm
Cemy
Headswood House
DENNY RD
A883
M876
B905

21
40

13 24

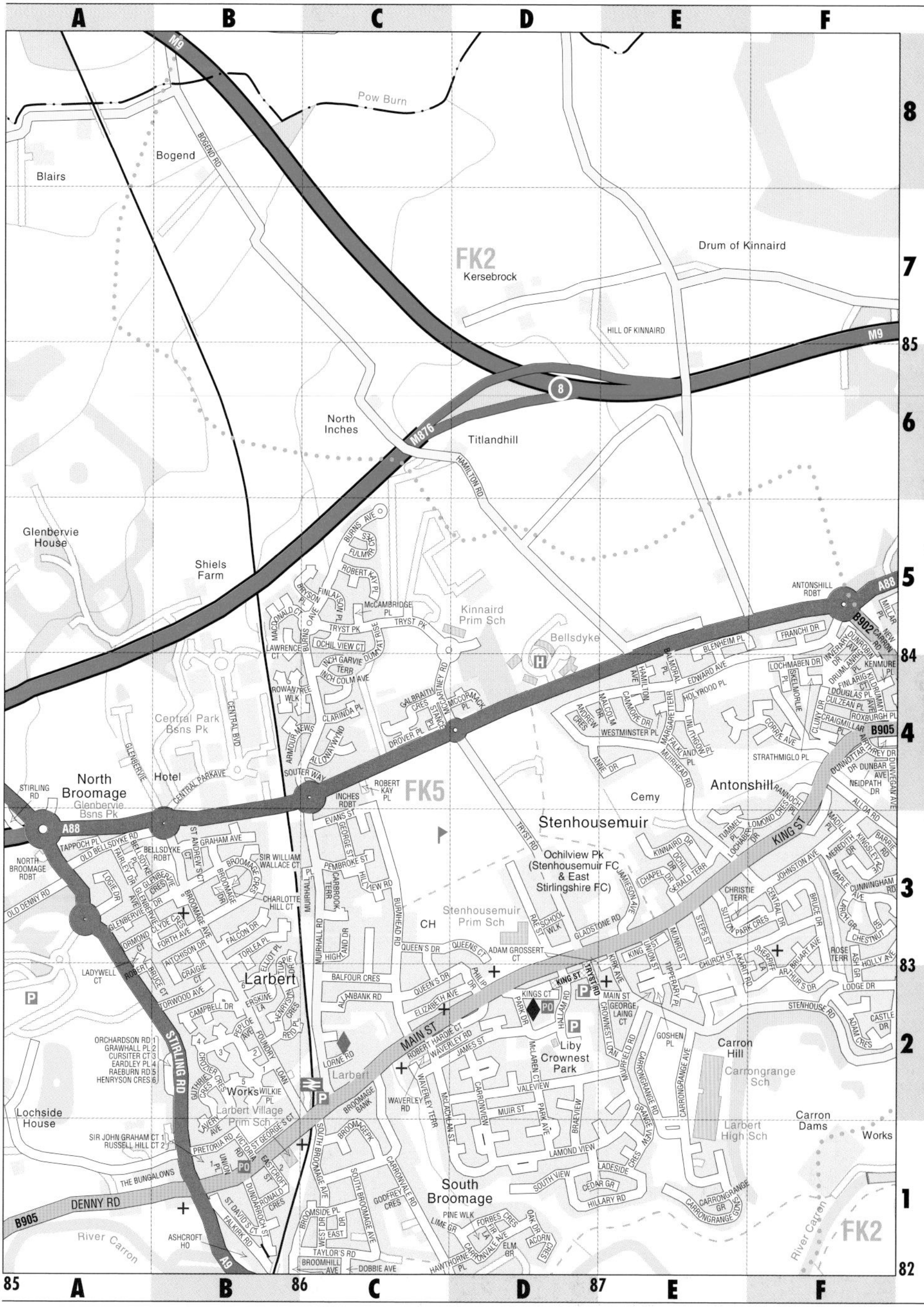
A B C D E F
8 7 6 5 4 3 2 1
85 84 83 82
85 86 87
M9
Pow Burn
Bogend
BOGEND RD
Blairs
FK2
Kersebrock
Drum of Kinnaird
HILL OF KINNAIRD
8
M876
North Inches
Titlandhill
HAMILTON RD
Glenbervie House
Shiels Farm
Kinnaird Prim Sch
Bellsdyke
ANTONSHILL RDBT
A88
B902
B905
Central Park Bsns Pk
CENTRAL BVD
North Broomage
Glenbervie Bsns Pk
Hotel
STIRLING RD
INCHES RDBT
FK5
Stenhousemuir
Antonshill
Cemy
Ochilview Pk
(Stenhousemuir FC & East Stirlingshire FC)
Stenhousemuir Prim Sch
CH
KING ST
MAIN ST
Larbert
Works
Larbert Village Prim Sch
ORCHARDSON RD 1
GRAWHALL PL 2
CURSITER CT 3
EARDLEY PL 4
RAEBURN RD 5
HENRYSON CRES 6
SIR JOHN GRAHAM CT 1
RUSSELL HILL CT 2
Lochside House
LADYWELL CT
STIRLING RD
DENNY RD
THE BUNGALOWS
River Carron
ASHCROFT HO
A9
South Broomage
Liby
Crownest Park
Carron Hill
Carrongrange Sch
Larbert High Sch
Carron Dams
Works
FK2
River Carron

23
14
A B C D E F
8 7 85 6 5 84 4 3 83 2 1 82
88 89 90
Letham
Lochs of Airth
LETHAM COTTS
Letham Farm
North Langdyke
M876
SOUTH APPROACH RD
A905
Southfield
North Bellsdyke
M9
7
Kinnaird House
South Bellsdyke
BRACKENLEES RD
A88
BELLSDYKE RD
Muirdyke Burn
Bensfield
FK2
Kirkton
Howkerse
Carronshore Prim Sch
Roughlands
Carronshore
Westertown
Bothkennar Prim Sch
Dutch Inn (PH)
Skinflats
BOTHKENNAR RD
Backrow Farm
Carron House
CORONATION PL
NEWTON AVE
EDWARD PL
BINNIE PL
WESTERTON TERR
NORTH MAIN ST
THE AVENUE
MAIN ST
FRIENDSHIP GDNS
CASTLE AVE
MURDYKE AVE
Carron Prim Sch
Carrongrove Bsns Pk
NEW CARRON RD
B902
B905
CARRON RDBT
STENHOUSE RD
Carron
River Carron
MONTGOMERY WELL
MONTGOMERY CRES
MONTGOMERY PL
FALKIRK
Langlees
Yonderhaugh
Sewage Works
FK3
A905 Grangemouth (A904)
Edinburgh STREET ATLAS
DAVID'S LOAN
ABBOTS RD
1 BUCHAN AVE
2 STEVENSON CT
3 CROCKETT PL
CHURCH ST 1
WADDELL ST 2
1 BARRA PL
2 ROXBURGH PL
3 NEIDPATH DR
4 CRATHES AVE
ADAMS LOAN
SINCLAIR PL
CANNONS WAY
PARK RD
CARRON RD
LANGLEES ST
SEAFORTH RD
TORRIDON AVE
DUNVEGAN DR
MORAR DR
STRIVEN DR
COBBLEBRAE CRES
ABBOTSFORD GDNS
CROSS ST
HAUGH ST
HAUGH GDNS
MILLFLATS ST
RIVER ST
FARM ST
CARRONSIDE ST
ABBOTSFORD ST
BEAUMONT DR
CARRONSHORE RD
LORIMAR PL
WATERS END
THE MEADOWS
MONTGOMERY DR
BURNSIDE PL
BURNSIDE

23
42

17
26

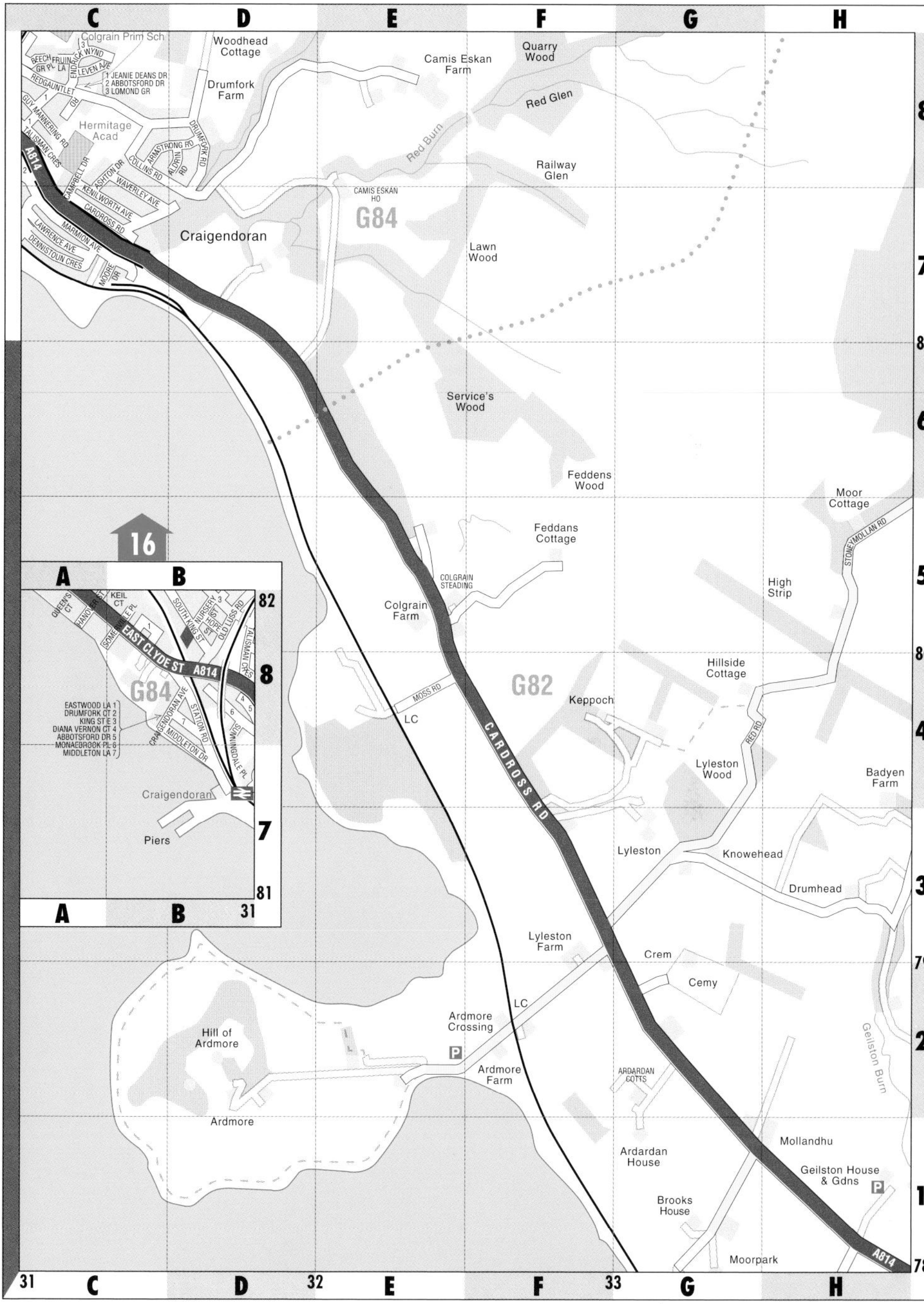
C
D
E
F
G
H
Colgrain Prim Sch
Woodhead Cottage
Camis Eskan Farm
Quarry Wood
Drumfork Farm
Red Glen
Hermitage Acad
Red Burn
Railway Glen
CAMIS ESKAN HO
G84
Craigendoran
Lawn Wood
A814
1 JEANIE DEANS DR
2 ABBOTSFORD DR
3 LOMOND GR
REDGAUNTLET RD
GUY MANNERING RD
TALISMAN CRES
CAMPBELL DR
ASHTON DR
COLLINS RD
ARMSTRONG RD
ALDRIN RD
DRUMFORK RD
WAVERLEY AVE
KENILWORTH AVE
CARDROSS RD
MARMION AVE
LAWRENCE AVE
DENNISTOUN CRES
MOORE DR
LEVEN AVE
BEECH GR
FRUIN PL
ENDRICK WYND
LA
8
7
81
6
Service's Wood
Feddens Wood
Moor Cottage
Feddans Cottage
STONEYMOLLAN RD
5
COLGRAIN STEADING
High Strip
Colgrain Farm
80
Hillside Cottage
MOSS RD
G82
Keppoch
LC
4
CARDROSS RD
RED RD
Lyleston Wood
Badyen Farm
Lyleston
Knowehead
3
Drumhead
Lyleston Farm
Crem
79
Cemy
LC
Ardmore Crossing
2
Geilston Burn
Hill of Ardmore
P
Ardmore Farm
ARDARDAN COTTS
Ardmore
Mollandhu
Ardardan House
Geilston House & Gdns
P
1
Brooks House
Moorpark
A814
78
31
32
33
16
A
B
QUEEN'S CT
HANOVER ST
KEIL CT
SOMERVILLE PL
EAST CLYDE ST
A814
SOUTH KING ST
NURSERY ST
HOPE ST
OLD LUSS RD
TALISMAN CRES
82
8
G84
EASTWOOD LA 1
DRUMFORK CT 2
KING ST E 3
DIANA VERNON CT 4
ABBOTSFORD DR 5
MONAEBROOK PL 6
MIDDLETON LA 7
CRAIGENDORAN AVE
STATION RD
MIDDLETON DR
SUNNINGDALE PL
Craigendoran
Piers
7
81
A
B
31

47
26

25
18

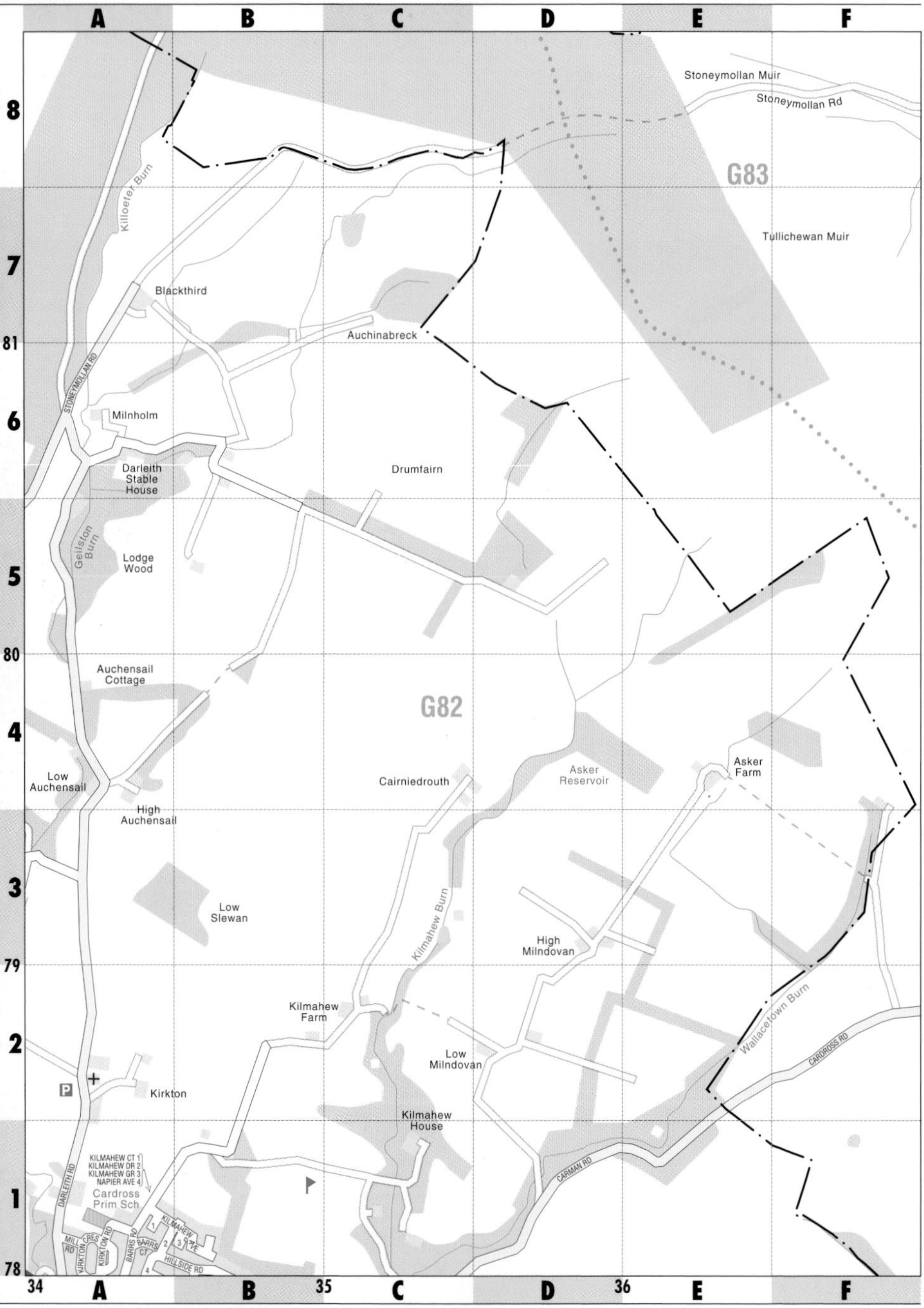
A
B
C
D
E
F
8
7
81
6
5
80
4
3
79
2
1
78
34
35
36
Stoneymollan Muir
Stoneymollan Rd
G83
Tullichewan Muir
Killoeter Burn
Blackthird
Auchinabreck
STONEYMOLLAN RD
Milnholm
Darleith
Stable
House
Drumfairn
Geilston
Burn
Lodge
Wood
Auchensail
Cottage
G82
Low
Auchensail
High
Auchensail
Cairniedrouth
Asker
Reservoir
Asker
Farm
Low
Slewan
Kilmahew Burn
High
Milndovan
Kilmahew
Farm
Low
Milndovan
Wallacetown Burn
CARDROSS RD
P
Kirkton
Kilmahew
House
KILMAHEW CT 1
KILMAHEW DR 2
KILMAHEW GR 3
NAPIER AVE 4
Cardross
Prim Sch
DARLEITH RD
CARMAN RD
MILL CRES
KIRKTON RD
BARRS RD
BARRS CT
HILLSIDE RD

25
48

19

E5
1 ALEXANDER ST
2 SUSANNAH ST
3 JAMES ST
4 MUNRO ST

28

E8
1 BALLOCH RD
2 DALVAIT GDNS
3 LYNN WLK
4 OLD MILL WLK
5 MACDONALD WLK
6 MCINTYRE TERR
7 LENNOXBANK HO
8 RIVERSIDE GDNS

F8
1 St Kessog's Prim Sch

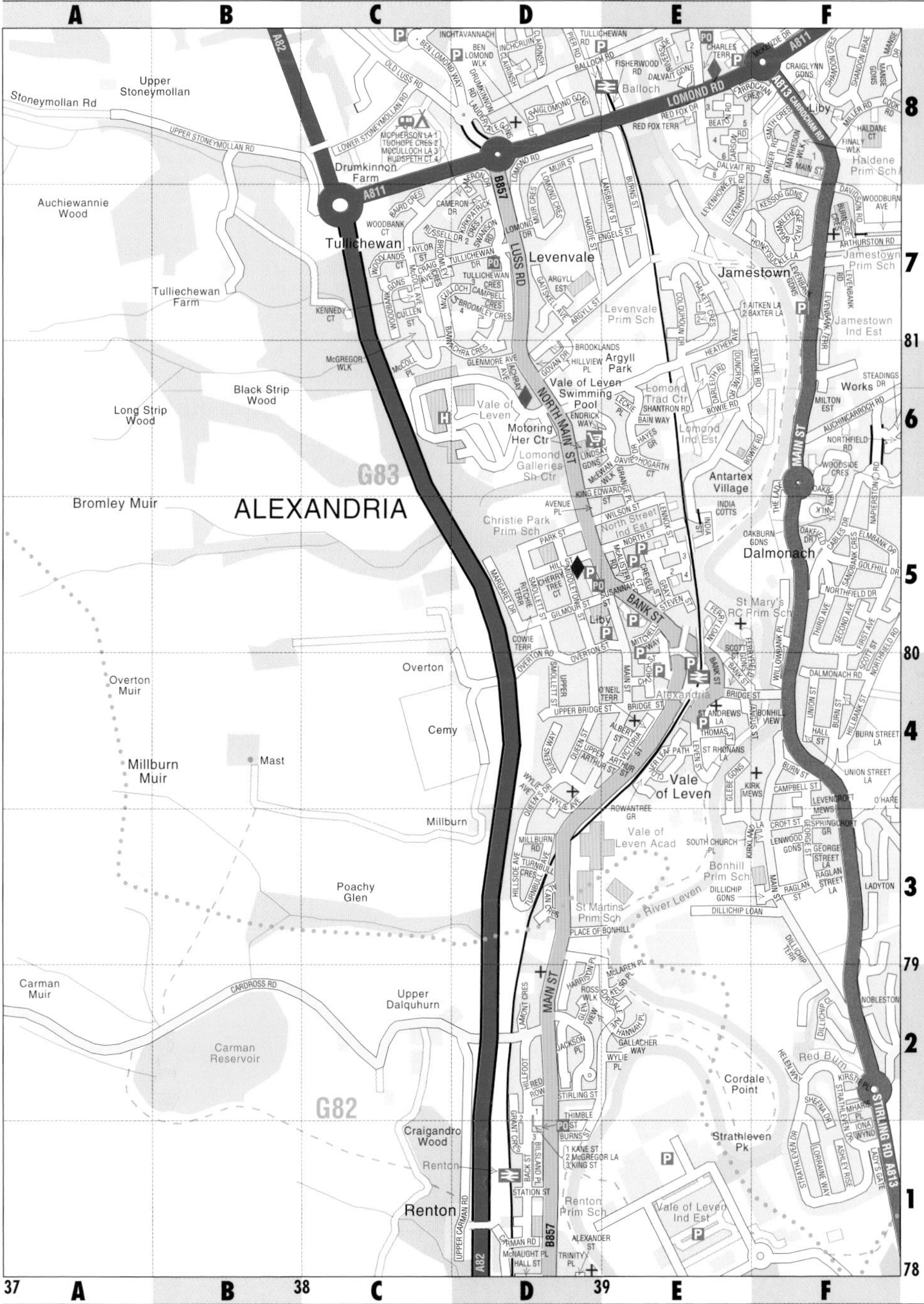

49

28

27
20

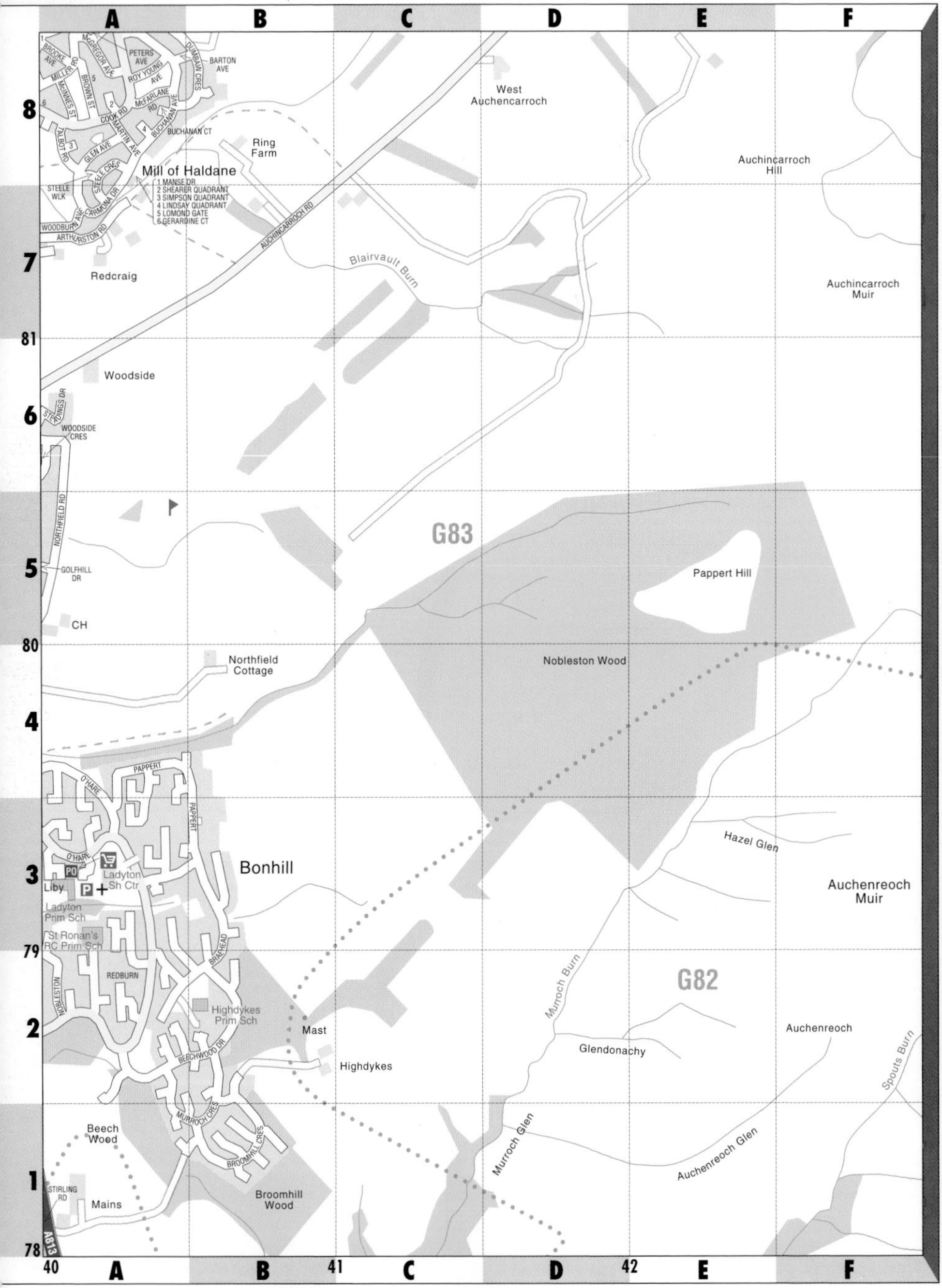
A
B
C
D
E
F
8
7
81
6
5
80
4
3
79
2
1
78
40
41
42
PETERS AVE
BARTON AVE
West Auchencarroch
Ring Farm
Mill of Haldane
1 MANSE DR
2 SHEARER QUADRANT
3 SIMPSON QUADRANT
4 LINDSAY QUADRANT
5 LOMOND GATE
6 GERARDINE CT
BUCHANAN CT
AUCHINCARROCH RD
Auchincarroch Hill
Blairvault Burn
Redcraig
Auchincarroch Muir
Woodside
WOODSIDE CRES
NORTHFIELD RD
G83
GOLFHILL DR
Pappert Hill
CH
Northfield Cottage
Nobleston Wood
PAPPERT
O'HARE
Bonhill
Hazel Glen
Ladyton Sh Ctr
Liby
Ladyton Prim Sch
St Ronan's RC Prim Sch
Auchenreoch Muir
REDBURN
BRAEHEAD
NOBLESTON
Highdykes Prim Sch
G82
Murroch Burn
Mast
Auchenreoch
Glendonachy
BEECHWOOD DR
Highdykes
Spouts Burn
MURROCH CRES
BROOMHILL CRES
Beech Wood
Murroch Glen
Auchenreoch Glen
STIRLING RD
Mains
Broomhill Wood
A813

27
50

30

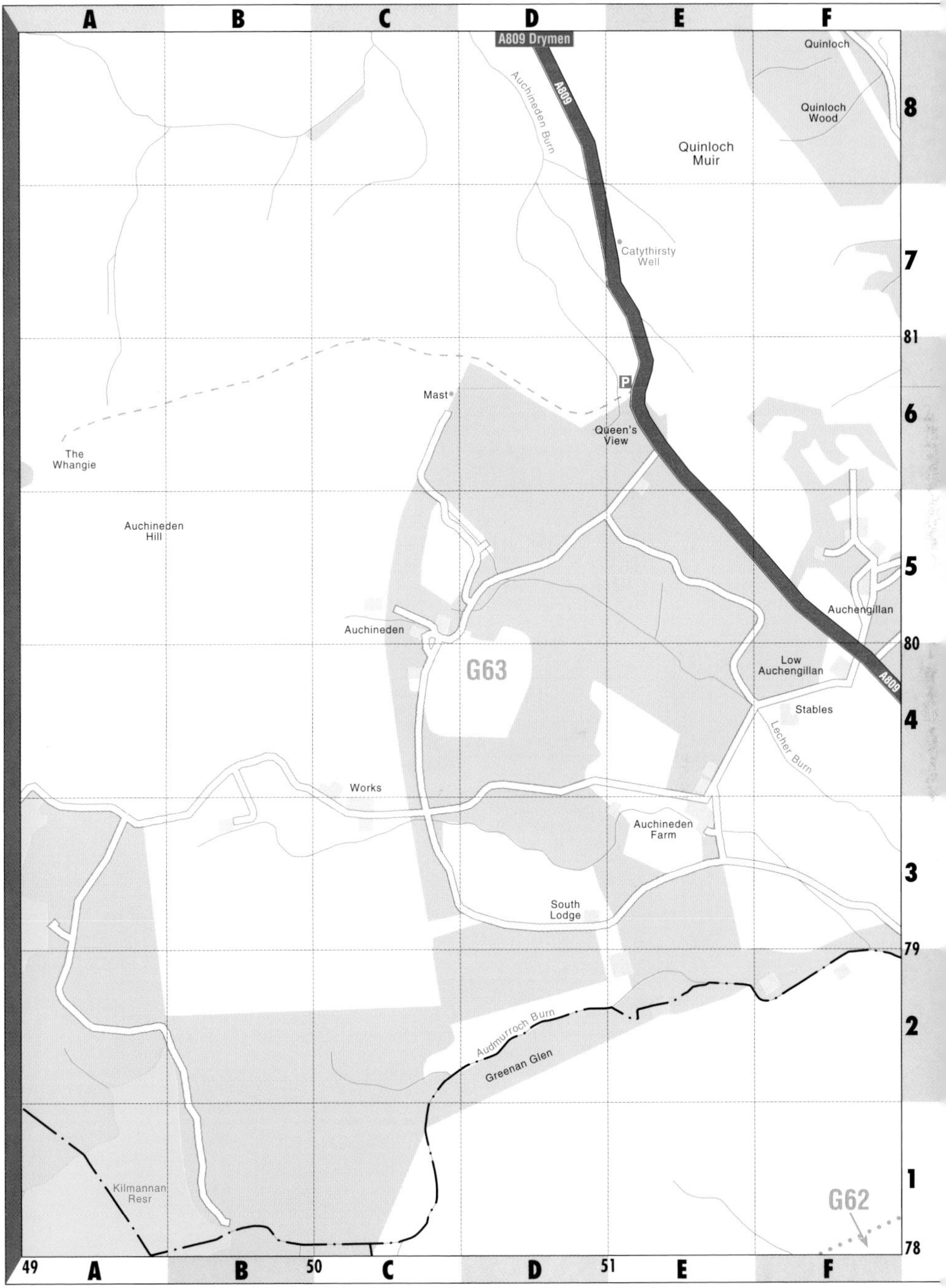
A
B
C
D
E
F
A809 Drymen
A809
Auchineden Burn
Quinloch
Quinloch Wood
Quinloch Muir
8
Catythirsty Well
7
81
Mast
P
Queen's View
6
The Whangie
Auchineden Hill
5
Auchengillan
Auchineden
G63
80
Low Auchengillan
A809
Stables
4
Lecher Burn
Works
Auchineden Farm
3
South Lodge
79
2
Audmurroch Burn
Greenan Glen
1
Kilmannan Resr
G62
78
49
50
51

53

30

29

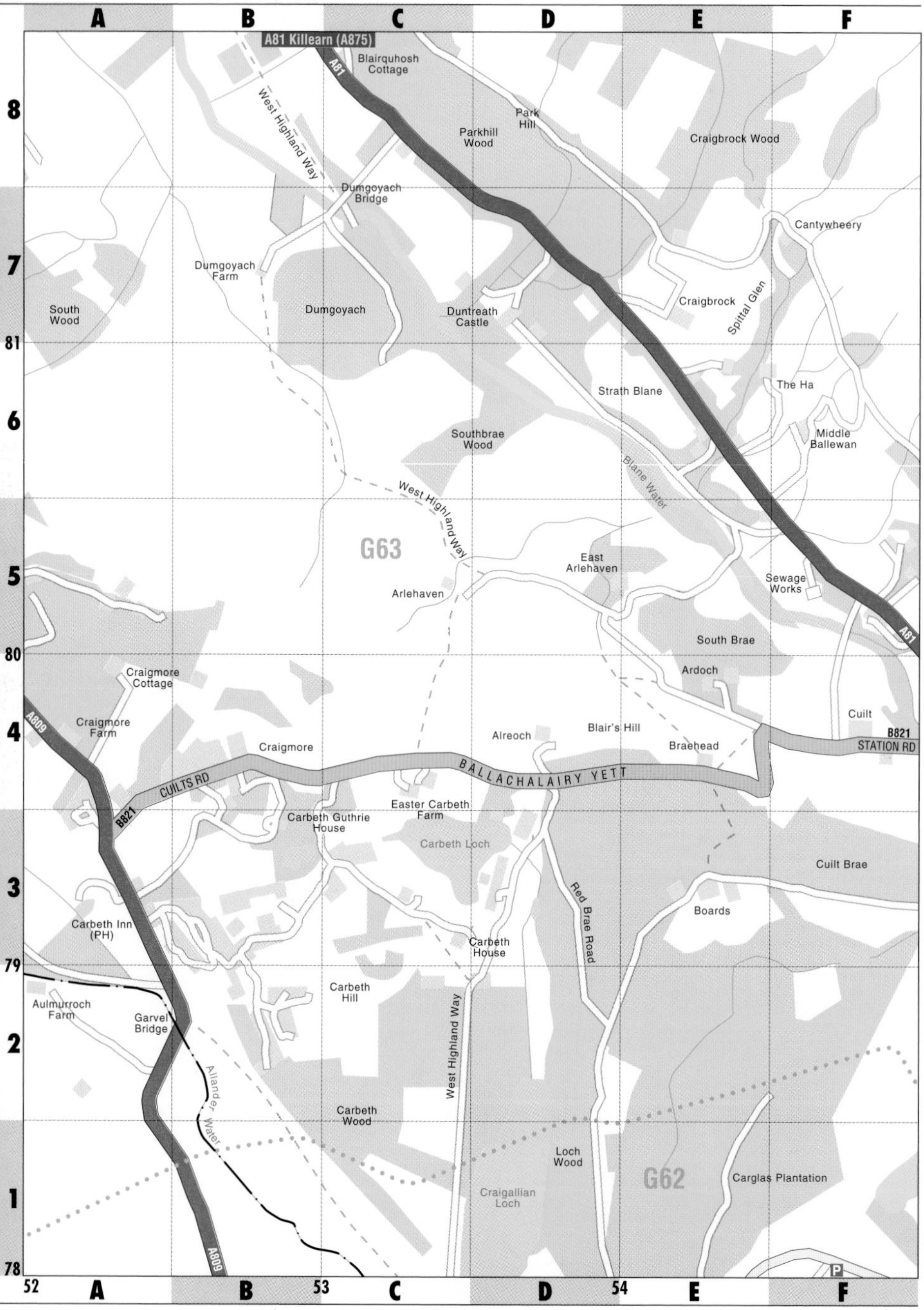
A
B
C
D
E
F
A81 Killearn (A875)
A81
Blairquhosh Cottage
West Highland Way
Park Hill
Parkhill Wood
Craigbrock Wood
Dumgoyach Bridge
Cantywheery
Dumgoyach Farm
South Wood
Dumgoyach
Duntreath Castle
Craigbrock
Spittal Glen
Strath Blane
The Ha
Southbrae Wood
Middle Ballewan
Blane Water
West Highland Way
G63
East Arlehaven
Sewage Works
Arlehaven
A81
South Brae
Ardoch
Craigmore Cottage
Craigmore Farm
A809
Alreoch
Blair's Hill
Cuilt
B821
STATION RD
Braehead
Craigmore
CUILTS RD
B821
BALLACHALAIRY YETT
Easter Carbeth Farm
Carbeth Guthrie House
Carbeth Loch
Cuilt Brae
Red Brae Road
Boards
Carbeth Inn (PH)
Carbeth House
Aulmurroch Farm
Garvel Bridge
Carbeth Hill
West Highland Way
Allander Water
Carbeth Wood
Loch Wood
G62
Carglas Plantation
Craigallian Loch
A809
P
8
7
81
6
5
80
4
3
79
2
1
78
52
53
54

29

54

32

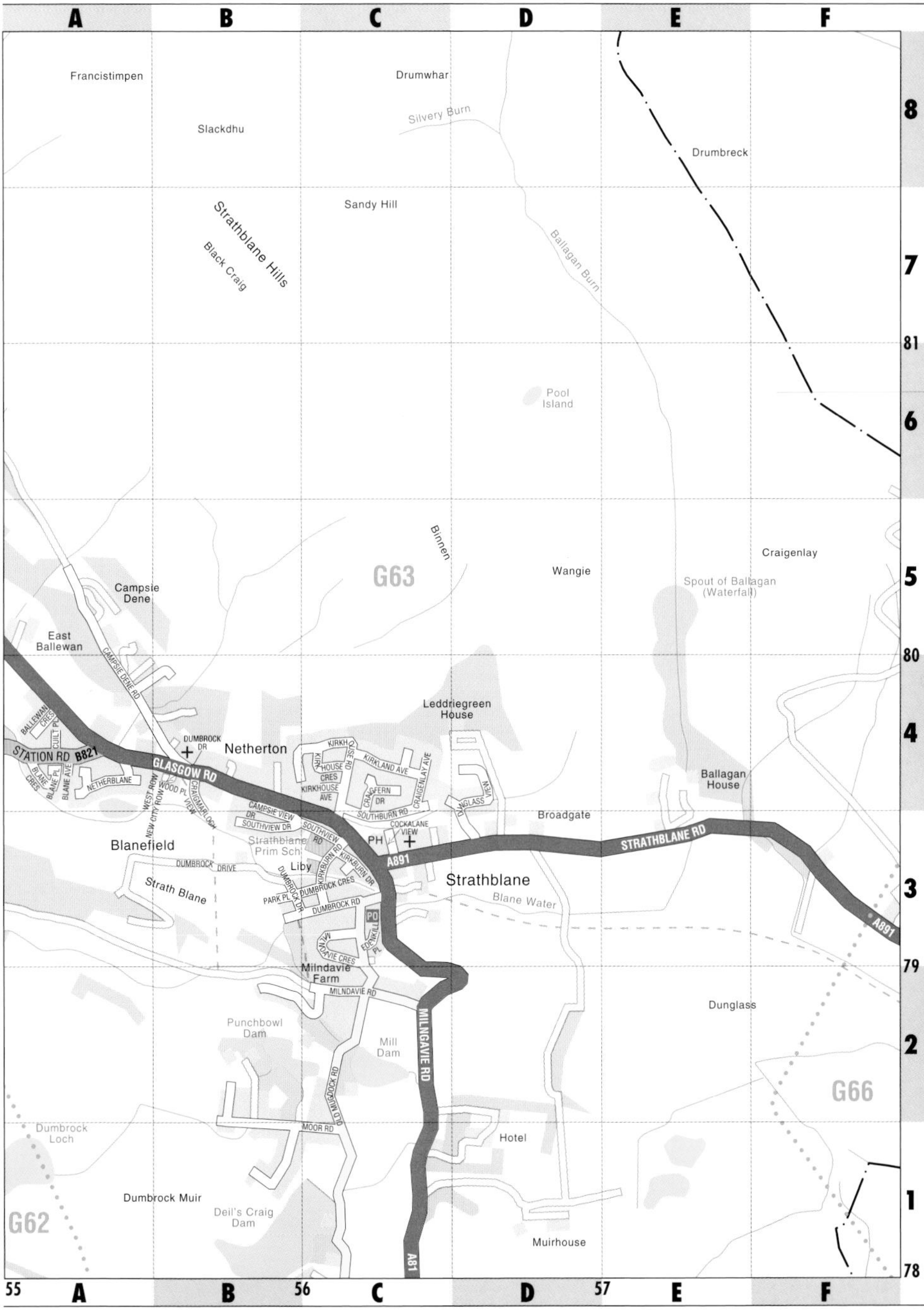
A
B
C
D
E
F
8
7
81
6
5
80
4
3
79
2
1
78
55
56
57
Francistimpen
Drumwhar
Silvery Burn
Slackdhu
Drumbreck
Sandy Hill
Strathblane Hills
Black Craig
Ballagan Burn
Pool Island
Binnen
G63
Wangie
Craigenlay
Spout of Ballagan (Waterfall)
Campsie Dene
East Ballewan
CAMPSIE DENE RD
Leddriegreen House
BALLEWAN CRES
CUILT PL
DUMBROCK DR
Netherton
STATION RD
B821
GLASGOW RD
KIRKHOUSE CRES
KIRKLAND AVE
CRAIGENLAY AVE
KIRKHOUSE AVE
CRAIGFERN DR
SOUTHBURN RD
DUNGLASS VIEW
Ballagan House
BLANE CRES
BLANE PL
BLANE AVE
NETHERBLANE
WEST ROW
NEW CITY ROW
WOOD PL
CRAIGMARLOCH VIEW
CAMPSIE VIEW DR
SOUTHVIEW DR
SOUTHVIEW RD
COCKALANE VIEW
Broadgate
STRATHBLANE RD
Blanefield
Strathblane Prim Sch
PH
A891
DUMBROCK DRIVE
Liby
KIRKBURN RD
KIRKBURN DR
Strathblane
Strath Blane
DUMBROCK CRES
PARK PL
DUMBROCK DR
DUMBROCK RD
Blane Water
PO
MILNDAVIE CRES
EDENKILL PL
Milndavie Farm
MILNDAVIE RD
Dunglass
Punchbowl Dam
Mill Dam
MILNGAVIE RD
OLD MUGDOCK RD
G66
Dumbrock Loch
MOOR RD
Hotel
Dumbrock Muir
Deil's Craig Dam
G62
Muirhouse
A81

55
32

31

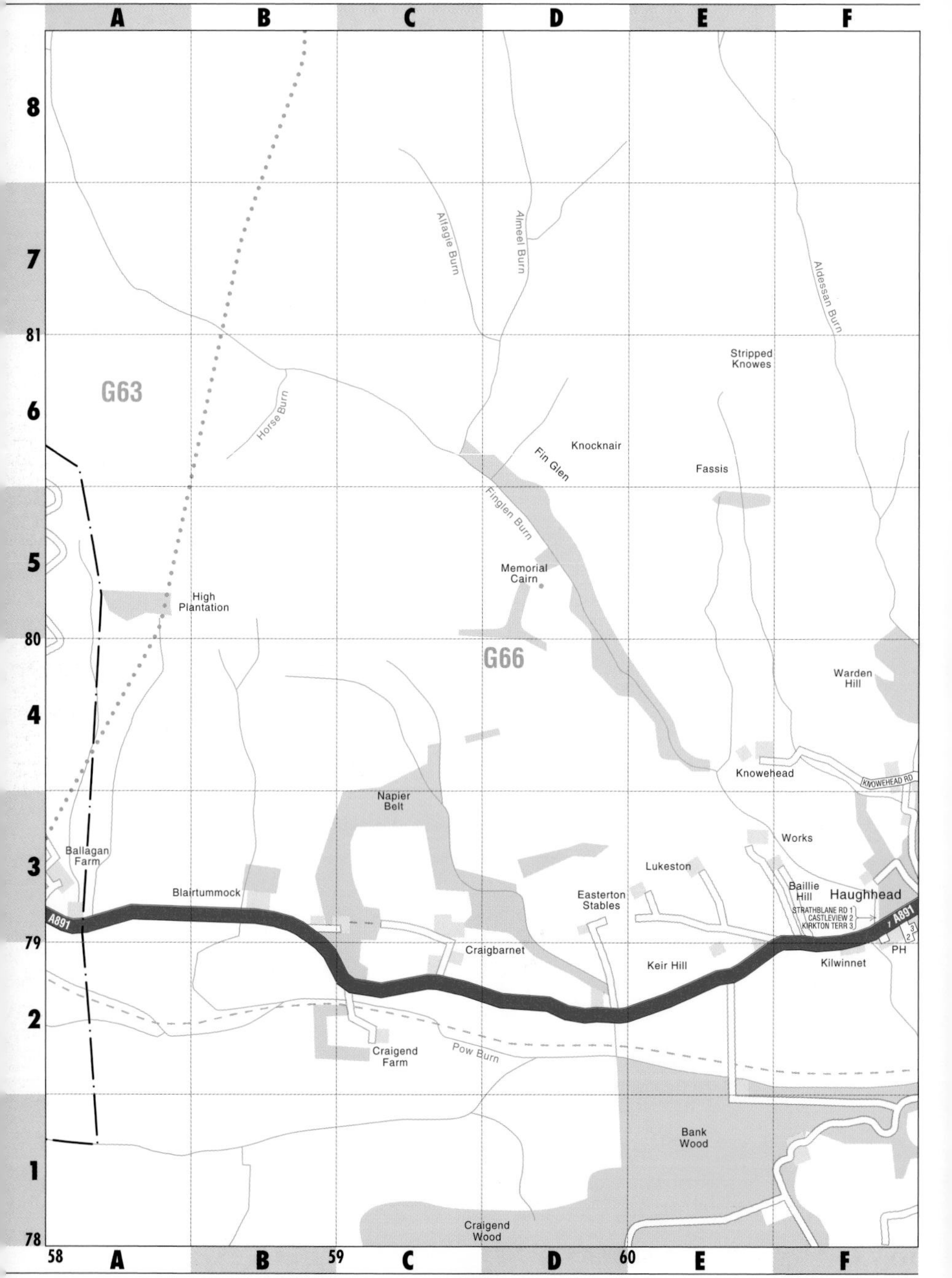
A
B
C
D
E
F
8
7
81
6
5
80
4
3
79
2
1
78
58
59
60
G63
G66
Alfagie Burn
Almeel Burn
Aldessan Burn
Stripped Knowes
Horse Burn
Knocknair
Fin Glen
Fassis
Finglen Burn
Memorial Cairn
High Plantation
Warden Hill
Knowehead
KNOWEHEAD RD
Napier Belt
Works
Ballagan Farm
Lukeston
Baillie Hill
Haughhead
Blairtummock
Easterton Stables
STRATHBLANE RD 1
CASTLEVIEW 2
KIRKTON TERR 3
A891
Craigbarnet
Keir Hill
Kilwinnet
PH
Craigend Farm
Pow Burn
Bank Wood
Craigend Wood

31
56

34

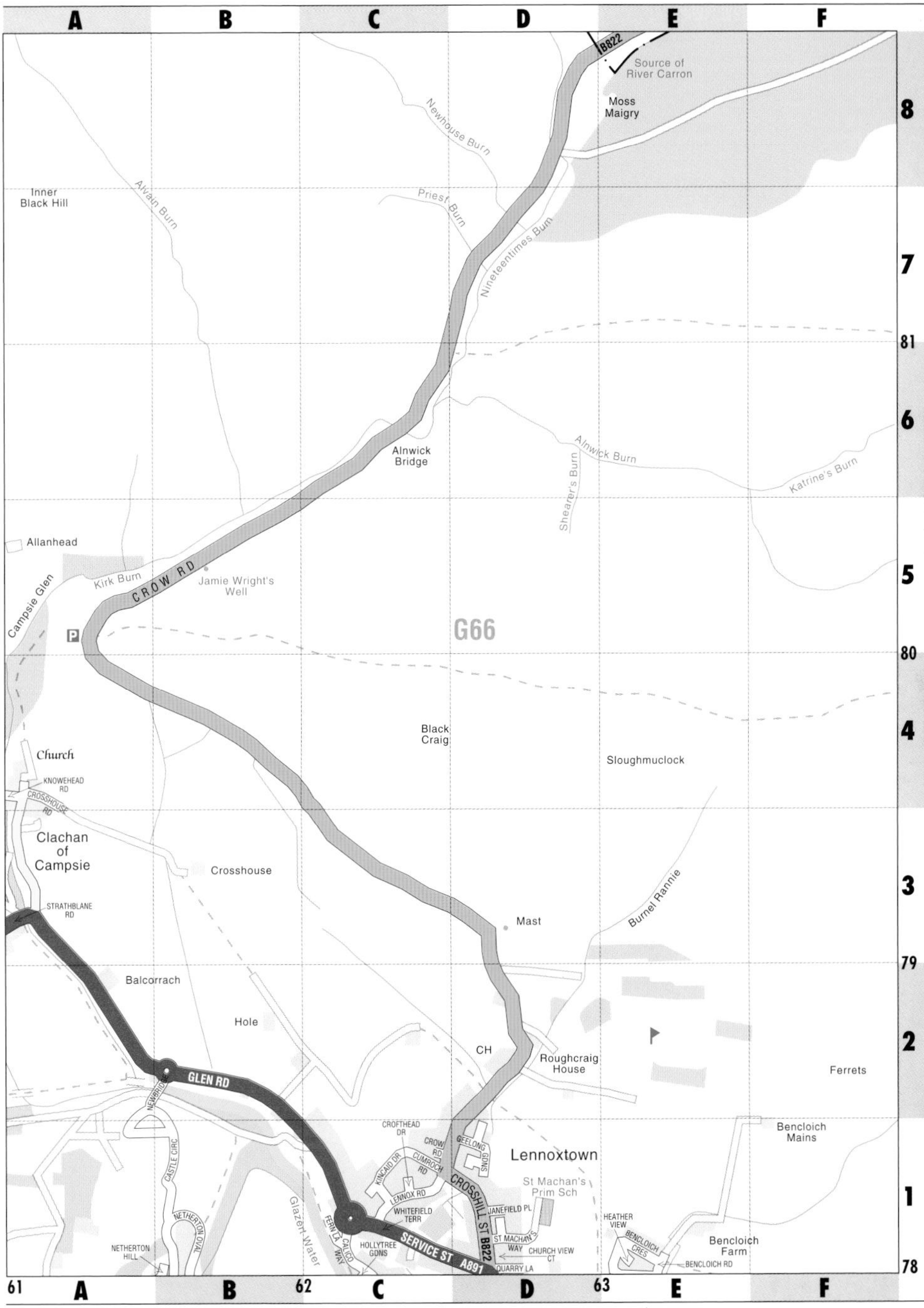

A
B
C
D
E
F
8
7
81
6
5
80
4
3
79
2
1
78
61
62
63
B822
Source of River Carron
Moss Maigry
Newhouse Burn
Inner Black Hill
Alvain Burn
Priest Burn
Nineteentimes Burn
Alnwick Bridge
Alnwick Burn
Shearer's Burn
Katrine's Burn
Allanhead
Campsie Glen
Kirk Burn
CROW RD
Jamie Wright's Well
P
G66
Black Craig
Sloughmuclock
Church
KNOWEHEAD RD
CROSSHOUSE RD
Clachan of Campsie
Crosshouse
STRATHBLANE RD
Burnel Rannie
Mast
Balcorrach
Hole
CH
Roughcraig House
Ferrets
GLEN RD
NEWBRIDGE
CASTLE CIRC
NETHERTON OVAL
NETHERTON HILL
Glazert Water
FERN LA
CALICO WAY
HOLLYTREE GDNS
SERVICE ST
A891
CROFTHEAD DR
KINCAID DR
CROW RD
CUMROCH RD
LENNOX RD
WHITEFIELD TERR
GEELONG GDNS
CROSSHILL ST
B822
Lennoxtown
St Machan's Prim Sch
JANEFIELD PL
ST MACHAN'S WAY
CHURCH VIEW CT
QUARRY LA
HEATHER VIEW
BENCLOICH CRES
BENCLOICH RD
Bencloich Mains
Bencloich Farm

57

34

33

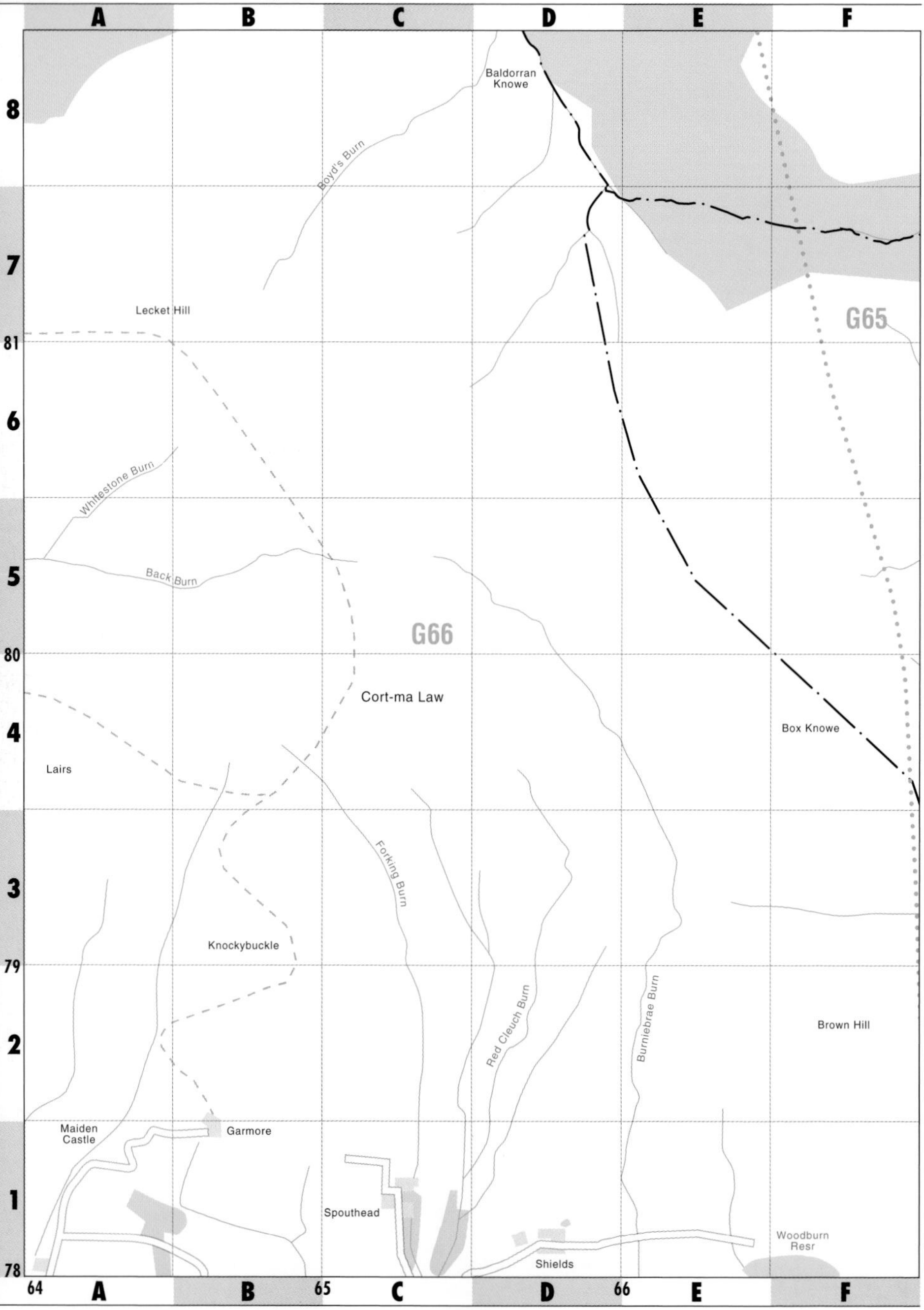
A
B
C
D
E
F
8
7
81
6
5
80
4
3
79
2
1
78
64
65
66
Baldorran Knowe
Boyd's Burn
Lecket Hill
G65
Whitestone Burn
Back Burn
G66
Cort-ma Law
Box Knowe
Lairs
Forking Burn
Knockybuckle
Red Cleuch Burn
Burniebrae Burn
Brown Hill
Maiden Castle
Garmore
Spouthead
Shields
Woodburn Resr

33

58

36

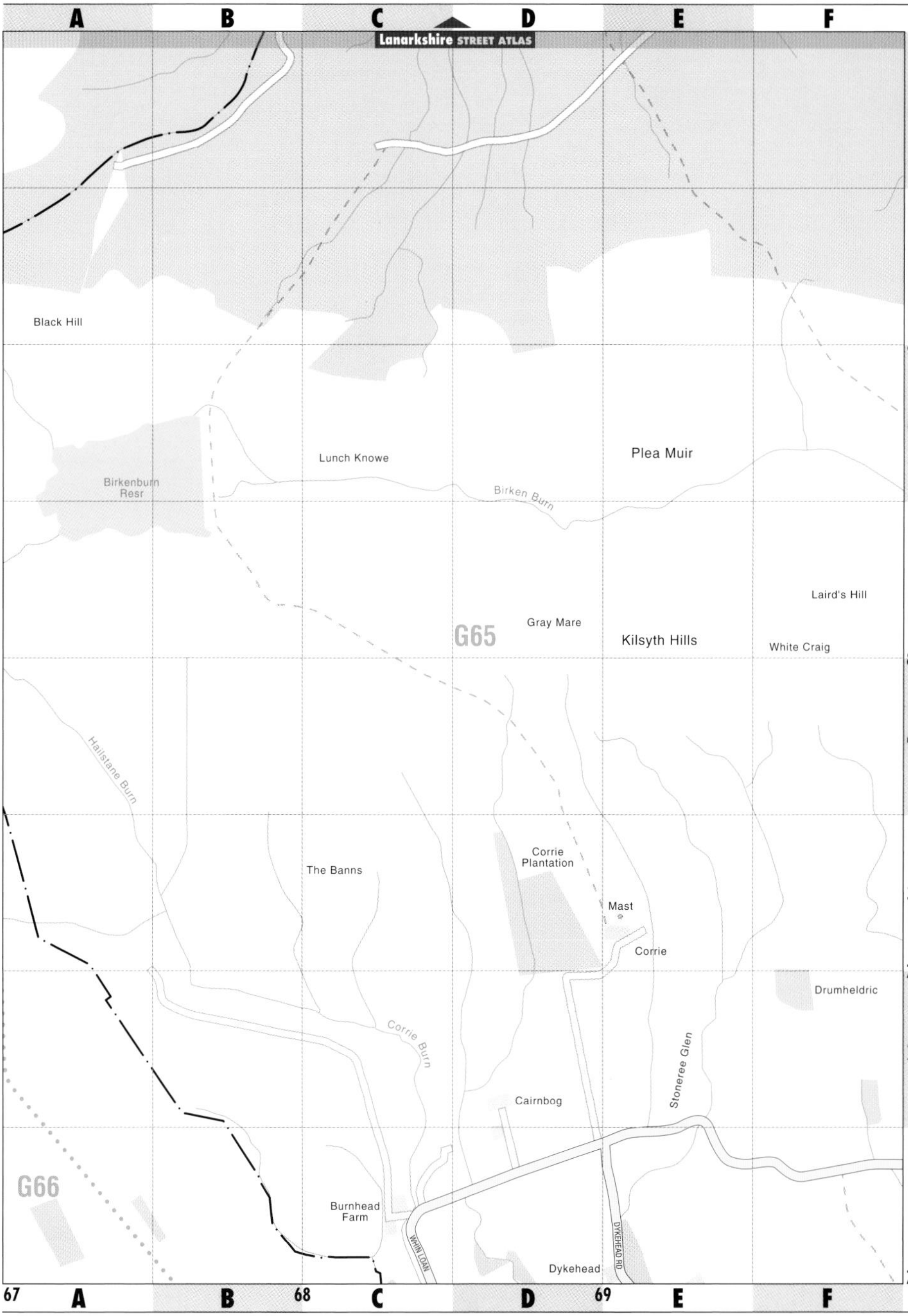

Lanarkshire STREET ATLAS
A
B
C
D
E
F
8
7
81
6
5
80
4
3
79
2
1
78
67
68
69
Black Hill
Birkenburn Resr
Lunch Knowe
Plea Muir
Birken Burn
G65
Gray Mare
Kilsyth Hills
Laird's Hill
White Craig
Hailstane Burn
Corrie Plantation
The Banns
Mast
Corrie
Drumheldric
Corrie Burn
Stoneree Glen
Cairnbog
G66
Burnhead Farm
WHIN LOAN
DYKEHEAD RD
Dykehead

59
36

35

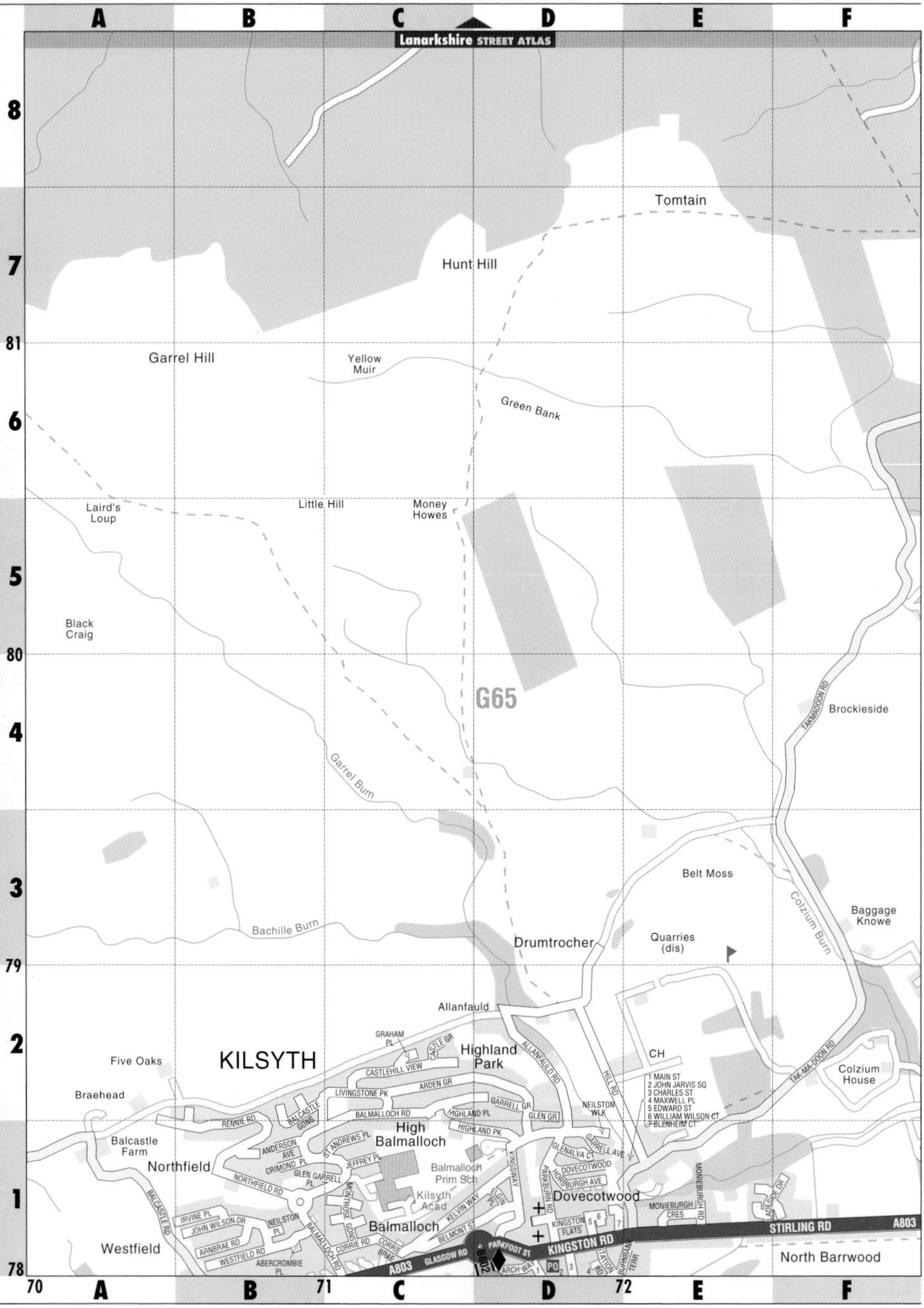
Lanarkshire STREET ATLAS
A B C D E F
8 7 81 6 5 80 4 3 79 2 1 78
70 71 72
Tomtain
Hunt Hill
Garrel Hill
Yellow Muir
Green Bank
Laird's Loup
Little Hill
Money Howes
Black Craig
G65
Brockieside
Garrel Burn
TAKMADOON RD
Belt Moss
Colzium Burn
Baggage Knowe
Bachille Burn
Drumtrocher
Quarries (dis)
Allanfauld
GRAHAM PL
CASTLE GR
Highland Park
KILSYTH
Five Oaks
Braehead
CASTLEHILL VIEW
ARDEN GR
LIVINGSTONE PK
ALLANFAULD RD
HILL RD
CH
1 MAIN ST
2 JOHN JARVIS SQ
3 CHARLES ST
4 MAXWELL PL
5 EDWARD ST
6 WILLIAM WILSON CT
7 BLENHEIM CT
TAK-MA-DOON RD
Colzium House
GARRELL GR
GLEN GR
NEILSTON WLK
BALMALLOCH RD
HIGHLAND PL
HIGHLAND PK
RENNIE RD
BALCASTLE GDNS
High Balmalloch
Balcastle Farm
Northfield
ANDERSON AVE
CRIMOND PL
ST ANDREWS PL
JEFFREY PL
GLEN GARRELL PL
NORTHFIELD RD
Balmalloch Prim Sch
Kilsyth Acad
KINGSWAY
GLENALVA CT
GARRELL AVE
DOVECOTWOOD
HORSBURGH AVE
PARKBURN RD
Dovecotwood
MONIEBURGH CRES
MONIEBURGH RD
LADESIDE DR
BALCASTLE RD
IRVINE PL
JOHN WILSON DR
NEILSTON PL
ARNBRAE RD
WESTFIELD RD
ABERCROMBIE PL
BALMALLOCH RD
MONTROSE GDNS
CORRIE RD
CORRIE BRAE
Balmalloch
KELVIN WAY
ELGIN PL
BELMONT ST
Westfield
A803
GLASGOW RD
B802
PARKFOOT ST
KINGSTON FLATS
KINGSTON RD
ARCH WAY
STATION RD
BURNBANK TERR
STIRLING RD
A803
North Barrwood

35

60

Lanarkshire STREET ATLAS
A
B
C
D
E
F
8
7
81
6
5
80
4
3
79
2
1
78
73
74
75
FK6
Doups
Mast
TAKMADOON RD
Craigdouffie Burn
Boiling Glen
Drumnessie
Berryhill
Mast
Banton Burn
Glenhead
Banton Mains
High Banton
Binniemyre
HIGH BANTON RD
Easter Auchinrivock
G65
Wester Auchinrivock
THE MAILINGS
Meadowside
Slaughter Howe
Drum Burn
PH
MAILINGS CT
MAILINGS RD
Banton Prim Sch
HILLVIEW
MILL RD
MAIN ST
KELVINSIDE CRES
LAMMERKNOWES RD
VALLEYBANK
Banton
PO
FK4
Auchinvalley
Riskend
Riskend Strip
Craigs
KELVINHEAD RD
Kelvinhead Farm
A803
KELVINHEAD
Dam Wood
Banton Loch
BANTON RD
Ruchill
Speirs Island
Gateside
Craigstone Wood
Castle Hill
Townhead
Girnal Hill
River Kelvin
Forth & Clyde Canal
Kelvinhead Jetty
Back Drain
STIRLING RD
A803
Bullet Knowes
A803

37

A
B
C
D
E
F
8
7
81
6
5
80
4
3
79
2
1
78
76
77
78
Tappetknowe
Leysbent
Leys
Castlerankine
Linns
Rashiehill
Castlerankine Burn
FK6
Glenhead
Drumbowie
Resr
Bottomhead
Bowridge
Bottomhead
Resr
Whitehill
Easter
Wairds
Craigs
Plantation
G65
Braeface
KELT RD
Tomfyne
Cowden
Hill
Wester
Thomaston
Cloybank
Doups Burn
BRAEFACE RD
Banknock
HOLLANDBUSH AVE
KILSYTH RD
FK4
M80
4
A80
A803
KILSYTH RD
CONEYPARK CRES
CONEYPARK CRES
CONEYPARK PL
VIEWFIELD RD
JOHN BASSY DR
Bankier
Prim
Sch
BANKIER TERR
HOLLANDBUSH CRES
BANKIER RD
BOG RD
BALLINKIER AVE
Bog
HILLHEAD AVE
GLENVIEW AVE
PO
GARNGREW RD
CASTLEVIEW TERR
AUCHINCLOCH DR
LINDEN DR
WELLPARK RD
ROWAN DR
LABURNUM RD
MAPLE PL
ASH PL
KELVINVIEW AVE
CASTLEHILL CRES
HOLLY GR
LAUREL SQ
WILLOW DR
HAWTHORN DR
CEDAR RD
LARCH DR
ALMOND DR
CHERRY LA
HAZEL RD
CUMBERNAULD RD
Orchard
Farm
West
Auchincloch
P
Bonny Water
Auchincloch
Wyndford
Lock
Forth & Clyde Canal
A803
Netherwood
WYNDFORD RD
B816
Red Burn
Works
Hirst
House
G65
G68
BRIDGEND CT
CASTLECARY RD
Hotel
GARNHALL
DITCH
B816
A80
Hirst

37

62

21
40

A
B
C
D
E
F
8
7
81
6
5
80
4
3
79
2
1
78
80
81
Blaefaulds
Little Denny Reservoir
FK6
Whitehill
East Kelt
KELT ROAD
Easter Banknock
Banknock
Wester Banknock
Wester Bankhead
Dennyloanhead
Longcroft
Longcroft Farm
No 1 Holding
Parkfoot
FK4
Bonny Water
Haggs
Underwood Farm
Underwood House
Forth & Clyde Canal
Castlecary Mill Farm
Allandale
Woodend
Skipperton
Dalnair
South Woodend
Clayfolds
Forresterquarter
Greenhill Upper Junction
Castlecary Low Wood
Lochdrum
Head of Muir
Bankhead
Bonded Warehouses
SEABEGS WOOD ANTONINE WALL
Denny High Sch
Head of Muir Prim Sch
M80
A872
M876
A803
A80
B816
NETHERMAINS RD
GLASGOW RD
DENNY RD
KILSYTH RD
BONNYBRIDGE RD
BONNYFIELD RD
SEABEGS RD
STATION RD
CUMBERNAULD RD
MYOTHILL RD
HAYPARK RD
REEDLANDS DR
GLASGOW RD
DEMOREHAM AVE
SOUILLAC DR
SCLANDERSBURN RD
LITHGOW PL
FLEMING CT
OCHIL VIEW
BRAES VIEW
WOODLAND WAY
BLAEFAULDS CRES
BULLOCH CRES
SHANKS AVE
LONEY CRES
LOCHHEAD AVE
ANDERSON DR
ARGYLL PATH
SUTHERLAND DR
KARRIES CT
GIBBDUN PL
HEATHERDALE GDNS
AFTON DR
GLENBO DR
HILLHOUSE RD
CHACEFIELD WOOD
GLOWRORUM DR
LEITH PL
GARVALD RD
SOLWAY DR
HILLCREST PL
LAXDALE DR
HAYFIELD TERR
ENDRICK DR
EARN PL
DROVE LOAN CRES
DROVE LOAN
HOME FARM COTTS
SPENCE ST 1
CLAREMONT ST 2
HOPEPARK TERR 3
ANNET RD
LOMOND WAY
BANKHEAD CRES
LOANHEAD AVE
PARK AVE
BANKVIEW TERR
KATRINE PL
CRERAN DR
ELMBANK CRES
BALFOUR ST
ASHLEY ST
DUNCAIRN AVE
MORRISON AVE
GLENMORE DR
ALLOWAY CRES
DUNVEGAN PL
DUNCAN ST
LARBERT RD
DICKBURN CRES
SINGERS PL
MOCHRAY CT
BONNYMUIR CRES
BONNYVIEW
WOODLEA GDNS
EMMAS WAY
CROWN CRES
PEARSON AVE
PEARSON PL
GLEN VIEW
RUSSELL PL
MONTROSE WAY
RANKIN CRES
BELMONT AVE
WALKER DR
BY-PASS RD
CALEDONIA TERR 1
JUBILEE WAY 2
VALE OF BONNY VIEW 3
STEWART ST 4
BOWLING GREEN PL 5
BROOMBRIDGE PL
LIND PL
WATSON PL
LYONCROSS
McVEAN PL
SEABEGS CRES
MANNFIELD AVE
SEABEGS PL
GREENHILL RD
WOODBURN CRES
GRAHAMSDYKE RD 1
ANTONINE GR 2
GRAHAMSDYKE CRES 3
LEAPARK DR
LAUREL PL
LAUREL GR
ANDERSON TERR
MAYFIELD DR
CROFT EST
JOHN ST
JAMES ST
CASTLEVIEW TERR
MARGARET AVE
LONGCROFT HOLDINGS
GARNGREW RD
THORNDALE GDNS
ALLANDALE COTTS
DUNDAS COTTS
ANTONINE GATE
OCHIL GDNS
GLENYARDS RD
P
PO
5

63
40

39
22

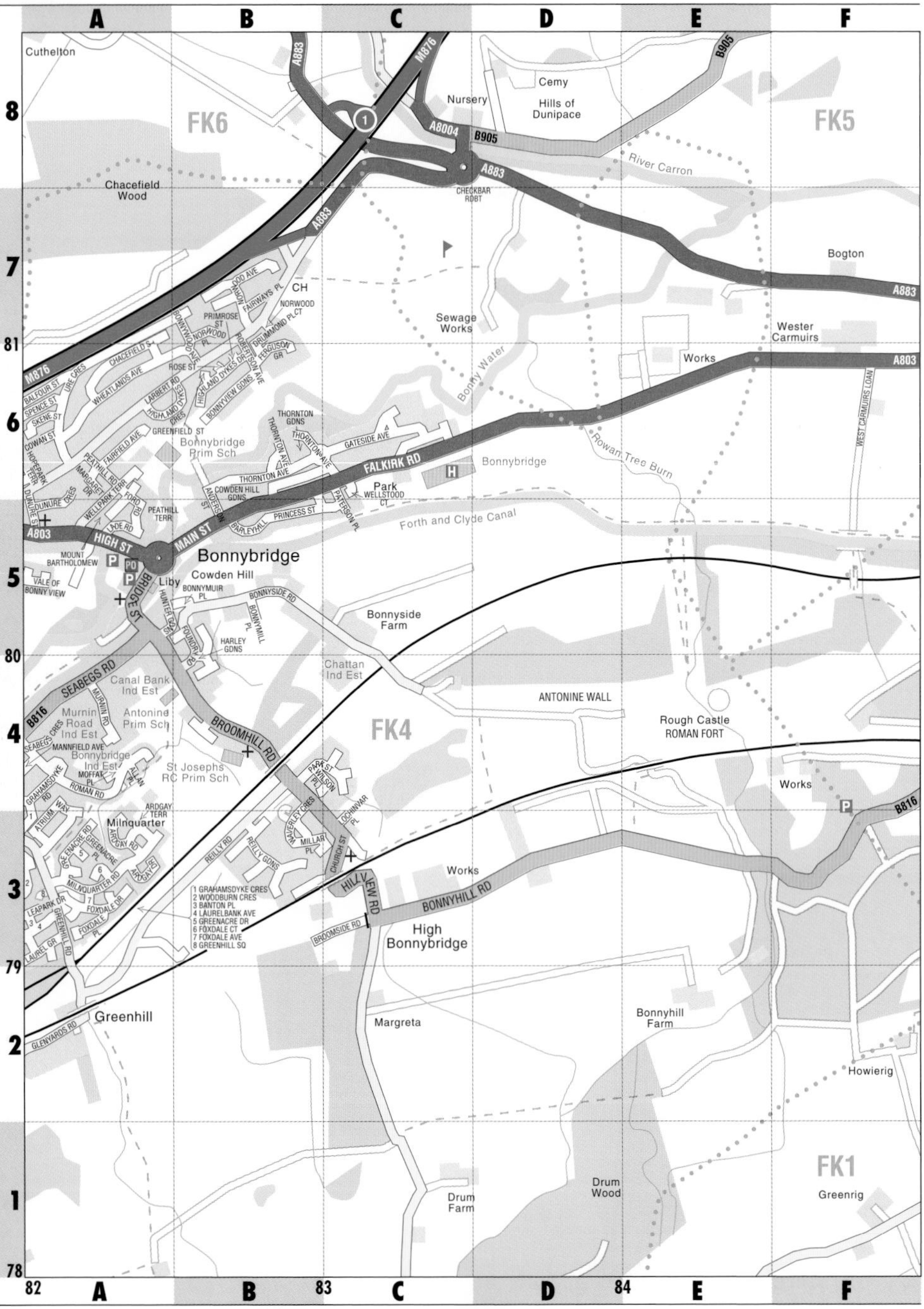
A
B
C
D
E
F
8
7
81
6
5
80
4
3
79
2
1
78
82
83
84
Cuthelton
FK6
FK5
FK4
FK1
A883
M876
B905
A8004
A803
B816
Cemy
Nursery
Hills of
Dunipace
River Carron
CHECKBAR
RDBT
Chacefield
Wood
Bogton
Sewage
Works
Wester
Carmuirs
Works
Bonny Water
CH
NORWOOD
CT
PRIMROSE
ST
FAIRWAYS PL
DRUMMOND PL
ROBERTSON AVE
FERGUSON
GR
CHACEFIELD ST
WHEATLANDS AVE
BALFOUR ST
SPENCE ST
SKENE ST
COWAN ST
HOPEPARK
TERR
ROSE ST
LARBERT RD
HIGHLAND DYKES
BONNYVIEW GDNS
GREENFIELD ST
Bonnybridge
Prim Sch
THORNTON
GDNS
THORNTON AVE
GATESIDE AVE
FALKIRK RD
Bonnybridge
WEST CARMUIRS LOAN
Rowan Tree Burn
FAIRFIELD AVE
PEATHILL RD
MARGARET
DR
WELLPARK TERR
FORD
RD
PEATHILL
TERR
DUNURE CRES
DUNURE ST
COWDEN HILL
GDNS
ANDERSON
ST
Park
WELLSTOOD
CT
PATERSON PL
PRINCESS ST
BARLEYHILL
Forth and Clyde Canal
HIGH ST
MAIN ST
MOUNT
BARTHOLOMEW
PO
Bonnybridge
Cowden Hill
VALE OF
BONNY VIEW
Liby
BONNYMUIR
PL
BONNYSIDE RD
BONNYMILL
PL
HUNTER
BRIDGE ST
FOUNDRY
RD
HARLEY
GDNS
Bonnyside
Farm
Chattan
Ind Est
SEABEGS RD
Canal Bank
Ind Est
Murnin
Road
Ind Est
MURNIN RD
Antonine
Prim Sch
SEABEGS CRES
MANNFIELD AVE
Bonnybridge
Ind Est
MOFFAT
PL
ALLAN
ROMAN RD
St Josephs
RC Prim Sch
BROOMHILL RD
ANTONINE WALL
Rough Castle
ROMAN FORT
Works
GRAHAMSDYKE
RD
ATRIUM
WAY
ARDGAY
TERR
Milnquarter
GREENACRE
ARDGAY RD
ARDGAY ST
MILNQUARTER RD
LEAPARK DR
FOXDALE DR
FOXDALE
PL
GREENHILL RD
LAUREL GR
PARK ST
WILSON
PL
LOCHINVAR
PL
WAVERLEY CRES
MILLAR
PL
CHURCH ST
REILLY RD
REILLY GDNS
1 GRAHAMSDYKE CRES
2 WOODBURN CRES
3 BANTON PL
4 LAURELBANK AVE
5 GREENACRE DR
6 FOXDALE CT
7 FOXDALE AVE
8 GREENHILL SQ
HILLVIEW RD
BONNYHILL RD
Works
BROOMSIDE RD
High
Bonnybridge
Greenhill
GLENYARDS RD
Margreta
Bonnyhill
Farm
Howierig
Drum
Farm
Drum
Wood
Greenrig

39
64

23

42

F8
1 CAULDHAME FARM RD
2 CAULDHAME ST
3 WESTPARK CRES
4 MUNGAL MILL CT
5 GOOSEDUBS PL
6 STEPHENS CFT
7 COTLAND DR
8 WESTPARK CT

65

42

A8
1 MULLOCH AVE
2 ANDERSON AVE
3 NEWCARRON CT
4 WILLIAMSON AVE
5 DUNDEE CT
6 JARVIE PL
7 JOHNSTON CT
8 GASCOIGNE CT
9 STEPHENS CFT

41
24

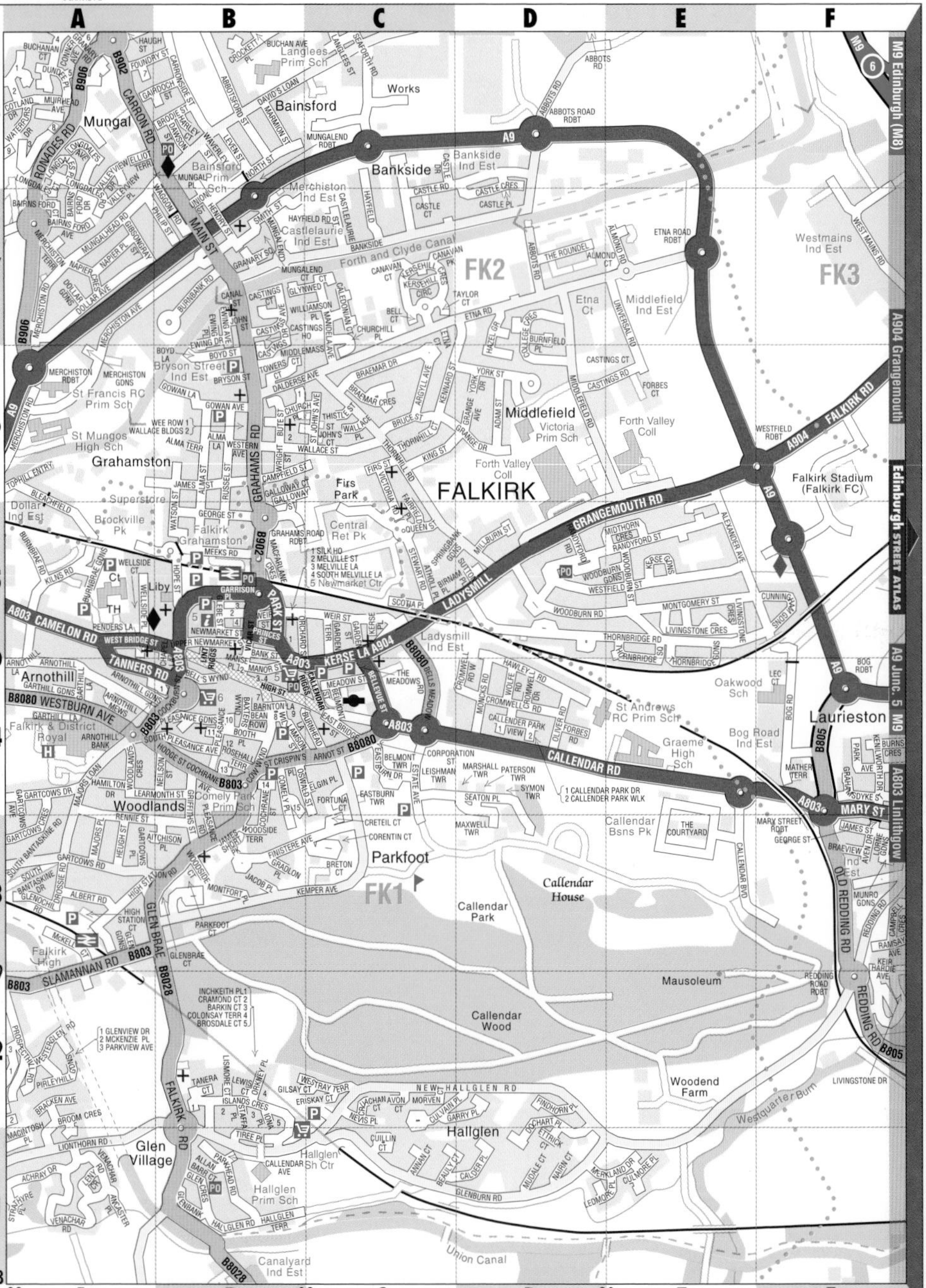

B4
1 BURNFOOT LA
2 KIRK WYND
3 TOLBOOTH ST
4 WODER ST
5 Callendar Square Sh Ctr
6 Howgate Sh Ctr
7 KINGS CT
8 MISSION LA
9 MELROSE PL
10 ST ANDREWS PL
11 PLEASANCE SQ
12 PLEASANCE CT
13 ST MODANS CT
14 COMELY PARK TERR
15 COMELY PK GDNS

41
66

44

A
B
C
D
E
F
8
7
77
6
5
76
4
3
75
2
1
74
McInroy's Point
Ferry Terminal
A770
CAMERON CT
LEVAN POINT
CASTLE LEVAN MANOR
LEVANNE LEVANNE PL
GDNS
DUNROBIN DR
CLOCH RD
BALMORAL PL
DUNVEGAN AVE
STIRLING DR
AVE
Hotel
EDINBURGH DR
CULZEAN DR
BLAIR GDNS
TANTALLON
BLAIRBEG PL
Levan
BRODICK DR
BALLOCHYLE PL
ARDYNE PL
URQUHART DR
TAYMOUTH DR
FAULDS PARK RD
BLAIRMORE PL
FINBRAKEN DR
Cloch Point
Works
KNOCKDHU PL
Levan Burn
KILLELLAN PL
Faulds Park
Cloch Lighthouse
HILLSIDE
Caravan Pk
Cloch Plantation
Tannel Hill
Underheugh Cottage
PA19
Burneven Hill
Underheugh Quarry (dis)
Underheugh
Mast
Clyde Muirshiel Regional Park
North Knowe
Lunderston Bay
PA16
Curling Pond
A770
A770 Wemyss Bay, Largs (A78)
Ayrshire STREET ATLAS
19
20
21

44

A
B
C
D
E
F
8
7
77
6
5
76
4
3
75
2
1
74
22
23
24
Kempock Point
Gourock
KEMPOCK ST
SHORE ST
Liby
1 CASTLE GDNS
2 ADELAIDE ST
3 HOPETON ST
Ferry Terminal
ST JOHN'S RD
ROYAL ST
Gourock Prim Sch
West Bay
Gourock Bay
SHARP ST 1
MARGARET ST 2
ADAM ST 3
JOHN CAMPBELL ST 4
JOHN CAMPBELL CT 5
RIVERSIDE GDNS 6
MURIEL BLUE CT 7
CALEDONIA GDNS 8
Pier
COVE RD
A771
TARBET ST
CHAPEL ST
CARDWELL RD
A770
CALEDONIA CRES
ALBERT RD
CRAGBURN GATE
ASHGROVE AVE 1
ASHTON TERR 2
ESPLANADE
ASHTON RD
Ashton
Tower
Tower Hill
Barr Hill
GOUROCK
DRUMSHANTIE TERR
Gourock High Sch
BROOMBERRY DR
DAVIDSON DR
VICTORIA RD
MOORFIELD RD
MOORFIELD LA
GOLF RD
PRESTON PL
JACOBS DR
FINNIE TERR
DRUMSHANTIE RD
MANOR CRES
BAY VIEW RD
GLYDE RD
ARGYLE RD
CLOCH RD
A770
CLOCH BRAE
TURNBERRY AVE
COWAL CRES
DIVERT RD
CUMBRAE PL
TOWER DR
IONA CRES
BUTE ST
DIVERT WLK 1
IONA WLK 2
Midton
ROSE CRES
FIR TERR
ELM TERR
STAFFA ST
RESERVOIR RD
OXFORD AVE
GRENVILLE RD
GARVIE AVE
COLLINGWOOD TERR
ST ANDREWS LA
ST ANDREWS DR
BELLEISLE PL
GLENBERVIE PL
COWAL VIEW
CH
HAWTHORNE PL
MOORFOOT DR
POPLAR PL
MACMILLAN DR
KIRN DR
St Ninian's Prim Sch
GEORGE RD
MATHIE CRES
HILLTOP CRES
GLENEAGLES DR
CARNOUSTIE AVE
ROSEMOUNT PL
DOUNE GDNS
PA19
Moorfoot Prim Sch
Coves Reservoirs
Trumpethill
EARNHILL PL
Larkfield Ind Est
Mast
EARNHILL RD
BARMOUTH AVE
1 AVONMOUTH PL
2 LYNMOUTH PL
Cemy
YORK RD
PLYMOUTH AVE
FALMOUTH DR
BOURNEMOUTH RD
DURHAM RD
76
Garvel Specl Sch
Earnhill Prim Sch
Inverclyde Royal
Larkfield
14 OBAN TERR
15 MALLAIG TERR
16 PORTREE TERR
17 BROADFORD TERR
18 CUMBERLAND WLK
Sacred Heart Prim Sch
FANCY FARM PL 1
NEIL ST 2
GLENINVER RD 3
FANCY FARM RD
STAFFORD RD
BERWICK RD
LOTHIAN RD
WESTMORLAND RD
CUMBERLAND RD
AUCHMEAD RD
WARWICK RD
Ravenscraig Stad & Rec Ctr
Inverclyde Acad
A78
PA16
MINERVA LA 1
BRAESIDE LA 2
ATHOLE LA 3
JUNO LA 4
JUPITER LA 5
MERCURY LA 6
Braeside
Ravenscraig Prim Sch
KIRKWALL RD
BRANCHTON RD
ROTHESAY RD
Banks
Earn Hill
Gallow Hill
St Gabriels Prim Sch
KYLEMORE TERR
Branchton
WELLYARD LA
WELLYARD WAY
WELLYARD WYND
DRUMILLAN HILL
CRISSWELL CRES
FLATTERTON LA
CRISSWELL CL
Glenburn Sch
7 KYLEMORE LA
8 BENMORE LA
9 KINLOCH LA
10 MAUCHLINE LA
11 AYR LA
12 CARRICK LA
13 JEAN ARMOUR LA
INVERKIP RD
Leitchland Farm
Flatterton Farm
Drumillan Hill
FLATTERTON RD
Spango Burn
Spango Valley
Spango
Howford Glen
IBM
Greenock Cut
Factory
Hole of Spango
Chrisswell
A78 Largs
Ayrshire STREET ATLAS

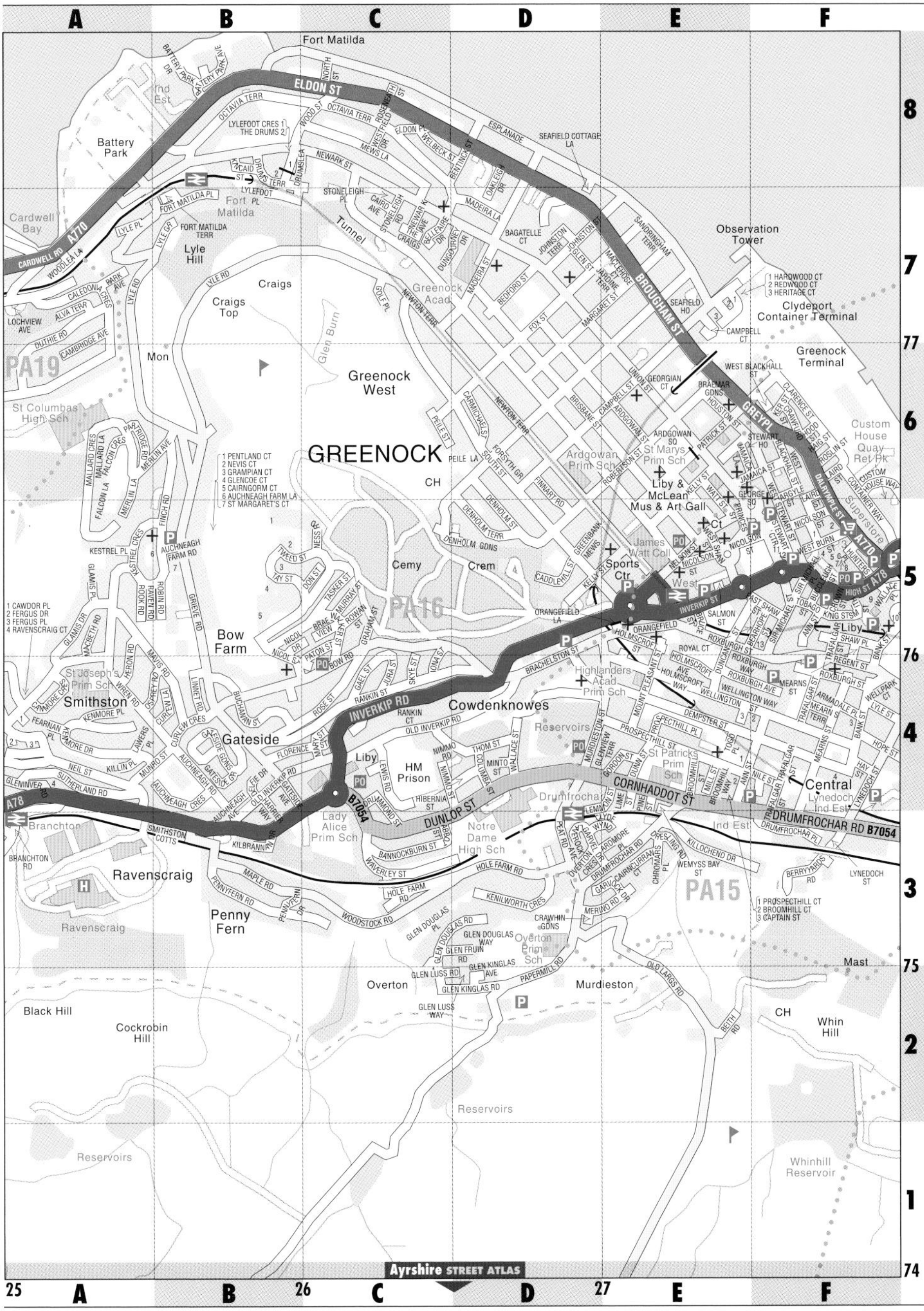

A B C D E F
8 7 77 6 5 76 4 3 75 2 1 74
25 26 27
Fort Matilda
ELDON ST
Battery Park
Ind Est
Cardwell Bay
CARDWELL RD A770
Lyle Hill
Craigs
Craigs Top
Tunnel
Greenock Acad
Glen Burn
Greenock West
GREENOCK
PA19
PA16
PA15
Mon
St Columbas High Sch
CH
Cemy
Crem
Observation Tower
Clydeport Container Terminal
Greenock Terminal
Custom House Quay Ret Pk
BROUGHAM ST
GREY PL
Ardgowan Prim Sch
St Marys Prim Sch
Liby & McLean Mus & Art Gall
James Watt Coll
Sports Ctr
West
INVERKIP ST
INVERKIP RD
A78
A770
Superstore
Bow Farm
St Joseph's Prim Sch
Smithston
Gateside
Cowdenknowes
HM Prison
Highlanders Acad Prim Sch
Reservoirs
St Patricks Prim Sch
Central
Lynedoch Ind Est
CORNHADDOT ST
DRUMFROCHAR RD B7054
Ind Est
Drumfrochar
Lady Alice Prim Sch
B7054
DUNLOP ST
Notre Dame High Sch
Branchton
Ravenscraig
Penny Fern
Overton Prim Sch
Overton
Murdieston
Mast
Black Hill
Cockrobin Hill
Whin Hill
Reservoirs
Whinhill Reservoir
1 PROSPECTHILL CT
2 BROOMHILL CT
3 CAPTAIN ST
1 PENTLAND CT
2 NEVIS CT
3 GRAMPIAN CT
4 GLENCOE CT
5 CAIRNGORM CT
6 AUCHNEAGH FARM LA
7 ST MARGARET'S CT
1 CAWDOR PL
2 FERGUS DR
3 FERGUS PL
4 RAVENSCRAIG CT
1 HARDWOOD CT
2 REDWOOD CT
3 HERITAGE CT
Ayrshire STREET ATLAS

45

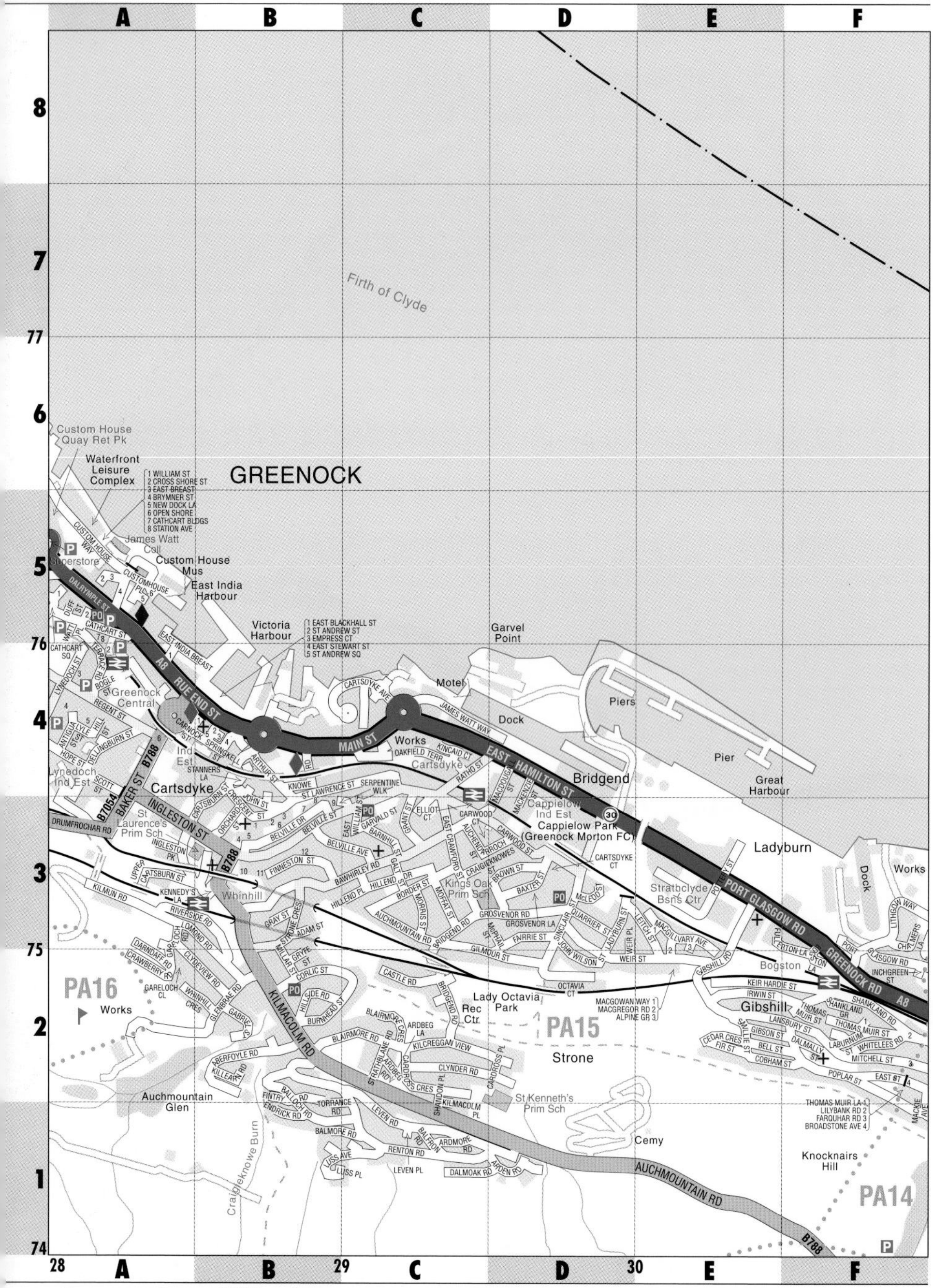

A4
1 VIRGINIA ST
2 STATION AVE
3 WELLPARK BLDGS
4 LYNEDOCH CT
5 ANTIGUA CT
6 DELLINGBURN ST

B3
1 TREVIOT PL
2 DUNS PL
3 ETTRICK PL
4 JEDBURGH CT
5 KELSO CT
6 LANGHOLM CT
7 MELROSE CT
8 PEEBLES CT
9 SELKIRK CT
10 HAWICK CT
11 FINNESTON LA
12 FINNESTON WAY

45

67

25
48

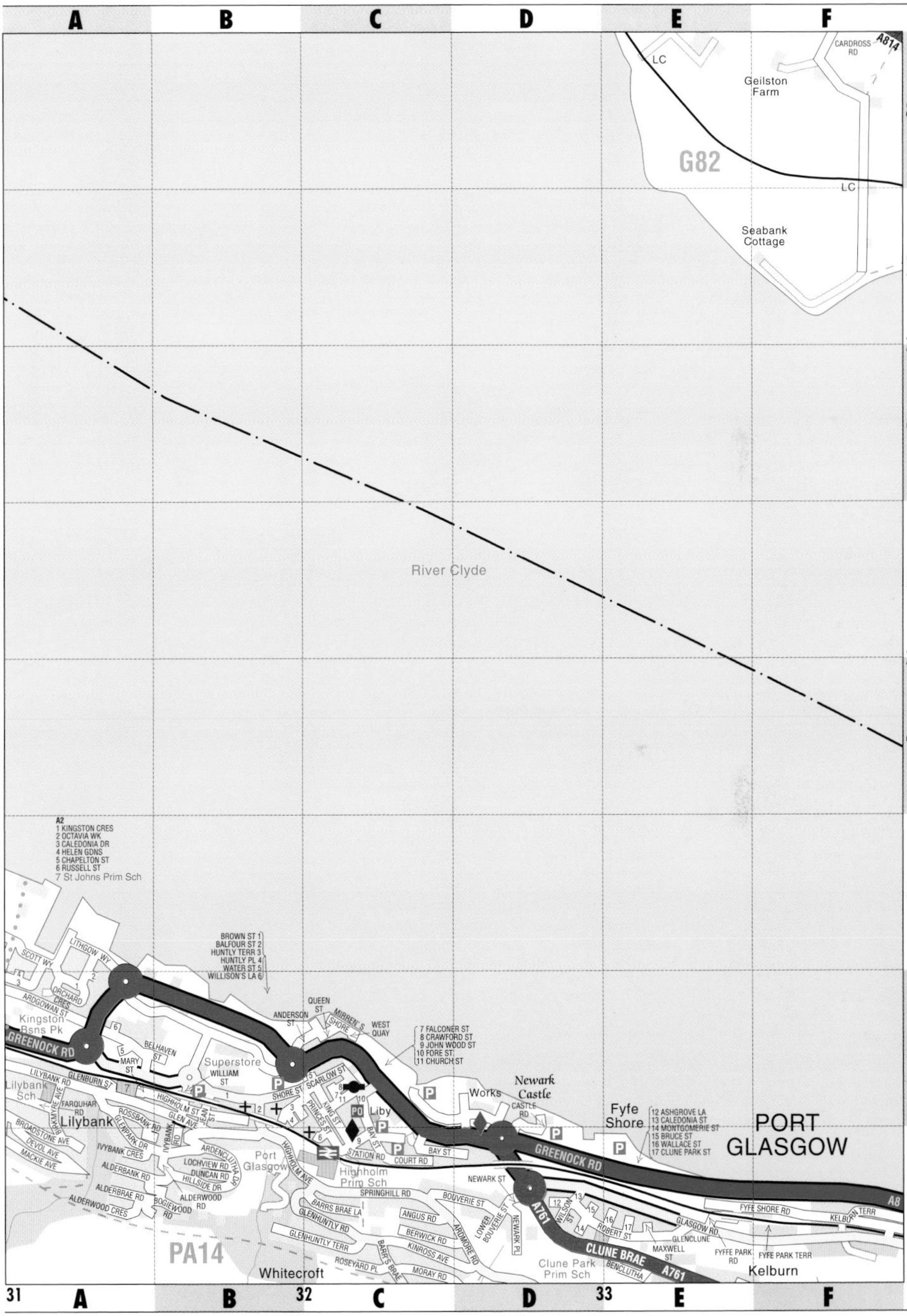
A
B
C
D
E
F
8
7
77
6
5
76
4
3
75
2
1
74
31
32
33
CARDROSS RD
A814
LC
Geilston Farm
G82
LC
Seabank Cottage
River Clyde
A2
1 KINGSTON CRES
2 OCTAVIA WK
3 CALEDONIA DR
4 HELEN GDNS
5 CHAPELTON ST
6 RUSSELL ST
7 St Johns Prim Sch
BROWN ST 1
BALFOUR ST 2
HUNTLY TERR 3
HUNTLY PL 4
WATER ST 5
WILLISON'S LA 6
SCOTT WY
LITHGOW WY
ORCHARD CRES
ARDGOWAN ST
Kingston Bsns Pk
GREENOCK RD
BELHAVEN ST
MARY ST
Superstore
WILLIAM ST
ANDERSON ST
QUEEN ST
MIRREN'S SHORE
WEST QUAY
7 FALCONER ST
8 CRAWFORD ST
9 JOHN WOOD ST
10 FORE ST
11 CHURCH ST
LILYBANK RD
GLENBURN ST
Lilybank Sch
FARQUHAR RD
BIRKMYRE AVE
Lilybank
ROSSBANK RD
GLENPARK DR
BROADSTONE AVE
DEVOL AVE
MACKIE AVE
IVYBANK CRES
IVYBANK RD
HIGHHOLM ST
GLEN AVE
JEAN ST
SHORE ST
SCARLOW ST
KING ST
PRINCES ST
Liby
BAY ST
STATION RD
COURT RD
ARDENCLUTHA DR
LOCHVIEW RD
DUNCAN RD
HILLSIDE DR
ALDERBANK RD
ALDERBRAE RD
ALDERWOOD CRES
BOGIEWOOD RD
ALDERWOOD RD
Port Glasgow
HIGHHOLM AVE
Highholm Prim Sch
SPRINGHILL RD
BARRS BRAE LA
GLENHUNTLY RD
GLENHUNTLY TERR
ROSEYARD PL
BARR'S BRAE
ANGUS RD
BERWICK RD
KINROSS AVE
MORAY RD
PA14
Whitecroft
Works
Newark Castle
CASTLE RD
NEWARK ST
BOUVERIE ST
LOWER BOUVERIE ST
NEWARK PL
ARDMORE RD
A761
WILSON ST
CLUNE BRAE
A761
Clune Park Prim Sch
BENCLUTHA
ROBERT ST
MAXWELL ST
GLENCLUNE
GLASGOW RD
Fyfe Shore
12 ASHGROVE LA
13 CALEDONIA ST
14 MONTGOMERIE ST
15 BRUCE ST
16 WALLACE ST
17 CLUNE PARK ST
PORT GLASGOW
A8
FYFE SHORE RD
KELBURN TERR
FYFFE PARK RD
FYFE PARK TERR
Kelburn

68
48

47
26

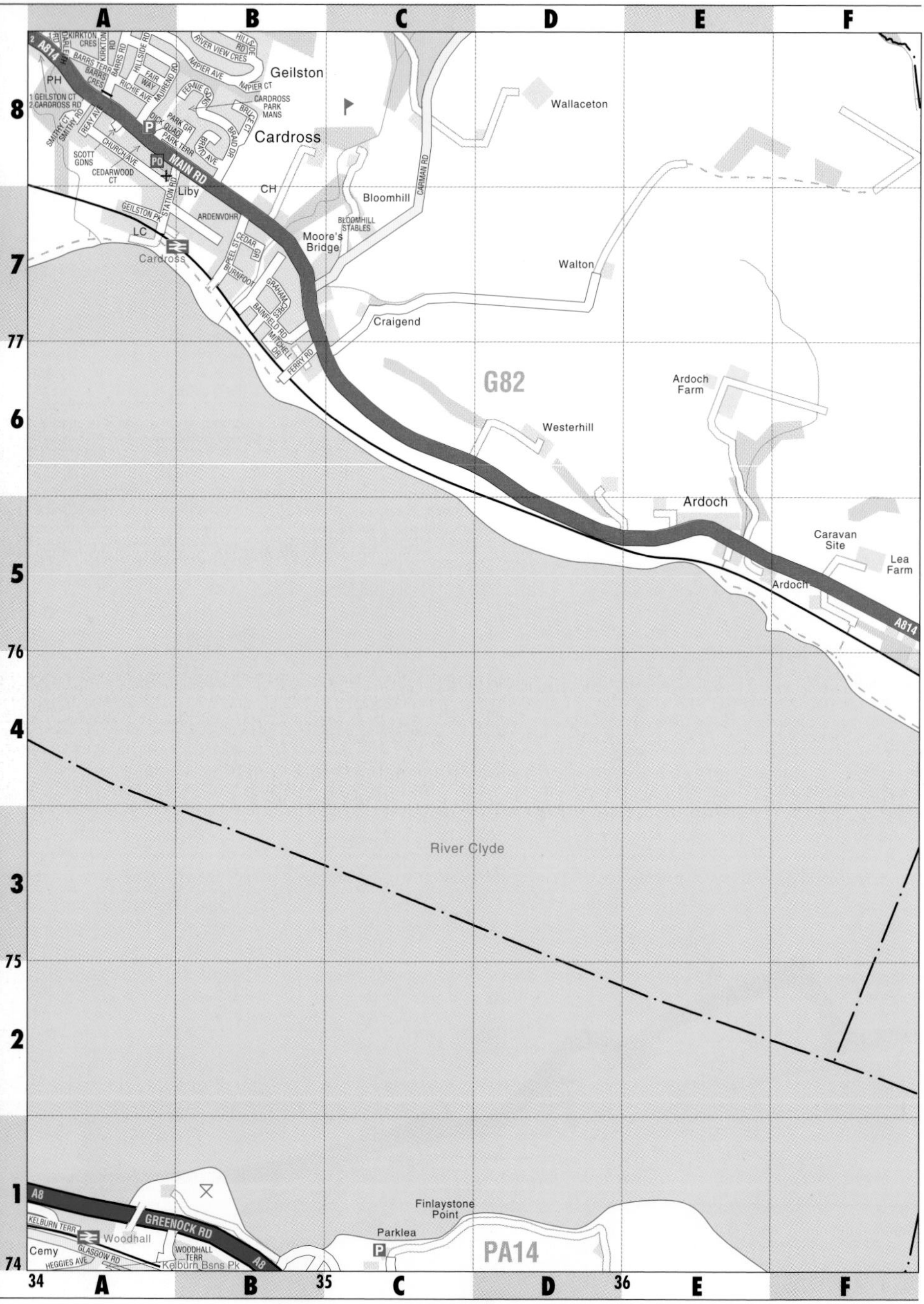
A
B
C
D
E
F
8
7
77
6
5
76
4
3
75
2
1
74
34
35
36
A814
KIRKTON CRES
BARRS TERR
BARRS CRES
HILLSIDE RD
RIVER VIEW CRES
NAPIER AVE
NAPIER CT
Geilston
PH
1 GEILSTON CT
2 CARDROSS RD
FAIR WAY
RICHIE AVE
MUIREND RD
CARDROSS PARK MANS
BRUCE CT
SMITHY CT
REAY AVE
DICK QUAD
PARK GR
PARK TERR
BRAID DR
BRAID AVE
Cardross
SCOTT GDNS
CHURCH AVE
CEDARWOOD CT
PO
MAIN RD
STATION RD
Liby
CH
GEILSTON PK
ARDENVOHR
LC
Cardross
PEEL ST
CEDAR GR
BURNFOOT
GRAHAM CRES
BAINFIELD RD
MITCHELL DR
FERRY RD
Moore's Bridge
BLOOMHILL STABLES
Bloomhill
CARMAN RD
Craigend
Wallaceton
Walton
G82
Westerhill
Ardoch Farm
Ardoch
Caravan Site
Lea Farm
Ardoch
A814
River Clyde
A8
GREENOCK RD
KELBURN TERR
Woodhall
Cemy
HEGGIES AVE
GLASGOW RD
WOODHALL TERR
Kelburn Bsns Pk
A8
Finlaystone Point
Parklea
P
PA14

47
69

27
50

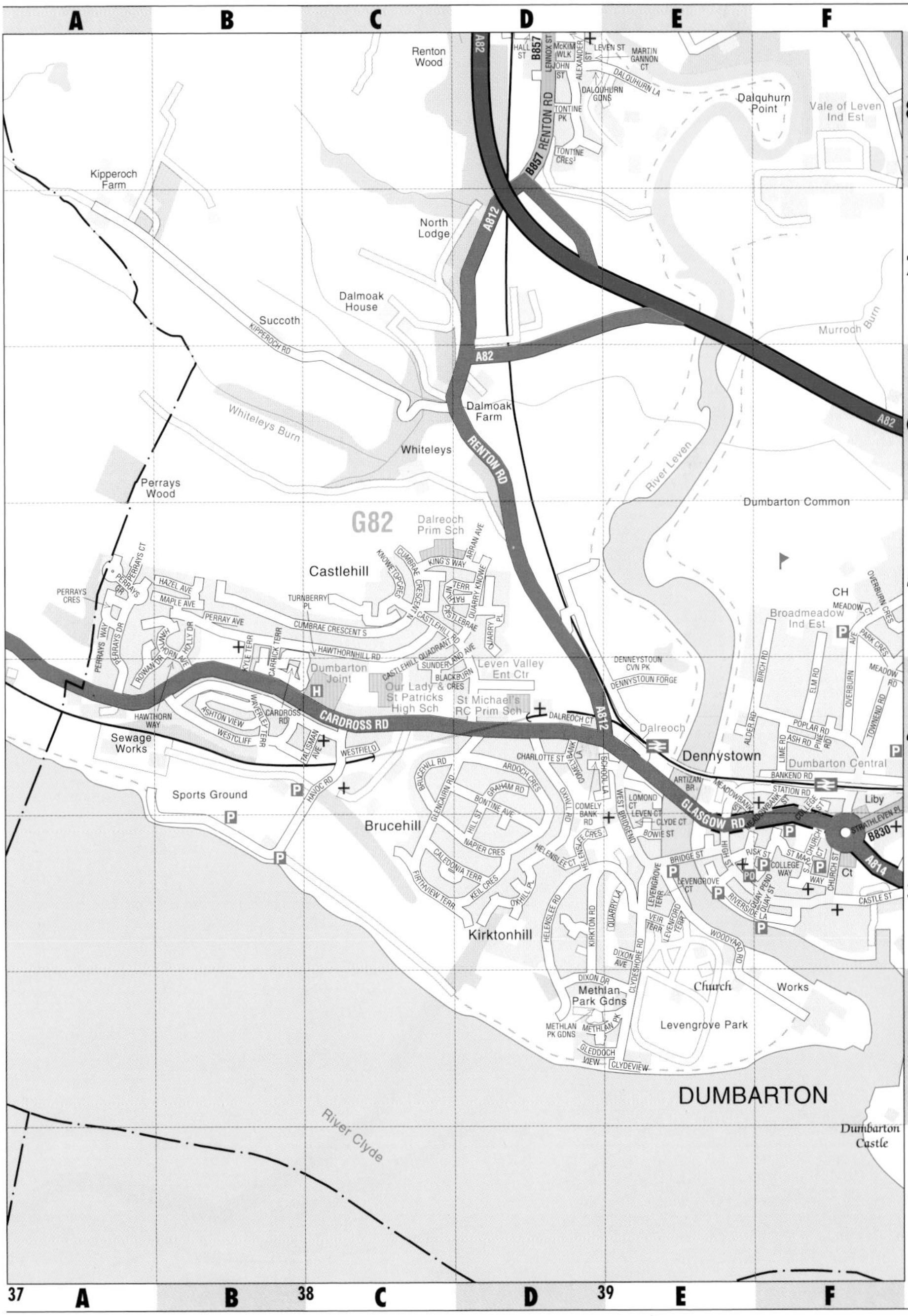
A
B
C
D
E
F
8
7
77
6
5
76
4
3
75
2
1
74
37
38
39
Renton Wood
A82
HALL ST
B857
LENNOX ST
McKIM WLK
JOHN ST
ALEXANDER ST
LEVEN ST
MARTIN GANNON CT
DALQUHURN LA
DALQUHURN GDNS
Dalquhurn Point
Vale of Leven Ind Est
B857 RENTON RD
TONTINE PK
TONTINE CRES
Kipperoch Farm
North Lodge
A812
Dalmoak House
Succoth
KIPPEROCH RD
Murroch Burn
A82
Dalmoak Farm
Whiteleys Burn
Whiteleys
RENTON RD
Perrays Wood
River Leven
Dumbarton Common
G82
Dalreoch Prim Sch
Castlehill
KING'S WAY
ARRAN AVE
CUMBRAE CRESCENT N
KNOWETOP CRES
PERRAYS CT
PERRAYS GR
PERRAYS CRES
HAZEL AVE
MAPLE AVE
PERRAY AVE
TURNBERRY PL
CUMBRAE CRESCENT S
CASTLEHILL RD
CASTLEBRAE
QUARRY KNOWE
QUARRY PL
CH
MEADOW CT
OVERBURN CRES
Broadmeadow Ind Est
PARK CRES
PERRAYS WAY
PERRAYS DR
ROWAN DR
HOLLY DR
KYLE TERR
CARRICK TERR
HAWTHORNHILL RD
CASTLEHILL QUADRANT
SUNDERLAND AVE
Dumbarton Joint
BLACKBURN CRES
Leven Valley Ent Ctr
Our Lady & St Patricks High Sch
St Michael's RC Prim Sch
DENNEYSTOUN CVN PK
DENNYSTOUN FORGE
BIRCH RD
ELM RD
OVERBURN AVE
MEADOW RD
TOWNEND RD
HAWTHORN WAY
ASHTON VIEW
WAVERLEY TERR
CARDROSS RD
CARDROSS RD
WESTCLIFF
DALREOCH CT
A812
Dalreoch
ALDER RD
POPLAR RD
ASH RD
PINE RD
LIME RD
Sewage Works
TALISMAN AVE
WESTFIELD
CHARLOTTE ST
COMELYBANK LA
SCHOOL LA
Dennystown
Dumbarton Central
BANKEND RD
Sports Ground
HAVOC RD
BRUCEHILL RD
GLENCAIRN RD
ARDOCH CRES
GRAHAM RD
BONTINE AVE
OXHILL RD
ARTIZAN BR
MEADOWBANK ST
STATION RD
COLLEGE ST
Liby
STRATHLEVEN PL
B830
Brucehill
HILL ST
COMELY BANK RD
LOMOND CT
LEVEN CT
WEST BRIDGEND
CLYDE CT
BOWIE ST
GLASGOW RD
HIGH ST
A814
NAPIER CRES
HELENSLEE CT
HELENSLEE CRES
CALEDONIA TERR
KEIL CRES
FIRTHVIEW TERR
OXHILL PL
BRIDGE ST
LEVENGROVE CT
LEVENGROVE TERR
RISK ST
QUAY PEND
QUAY ST
RIVERSIDE LA
COLLEGE WAY
ST MARY'S WAY
CHURCH CT
CHURCH ST
Ct
CASTLE ST
PO
Kirktonhill
HELENSLEE RD
KIRKTON RD
QUARRY LA
CLYDESHORE RD
VEIR TERR
LEVENFORD TERR
WOODYARD RD
DIXON AVE
DIXON DR
Methlan Park Gdns
Church
Works
METHLAN PK GDNS
METHLAN PK
Levengrove Park
GLEDDOCH VIEW
CLYDEVIEW
DUMBARTON
Dumbarton Castle
River Clyde

70
50

49
28

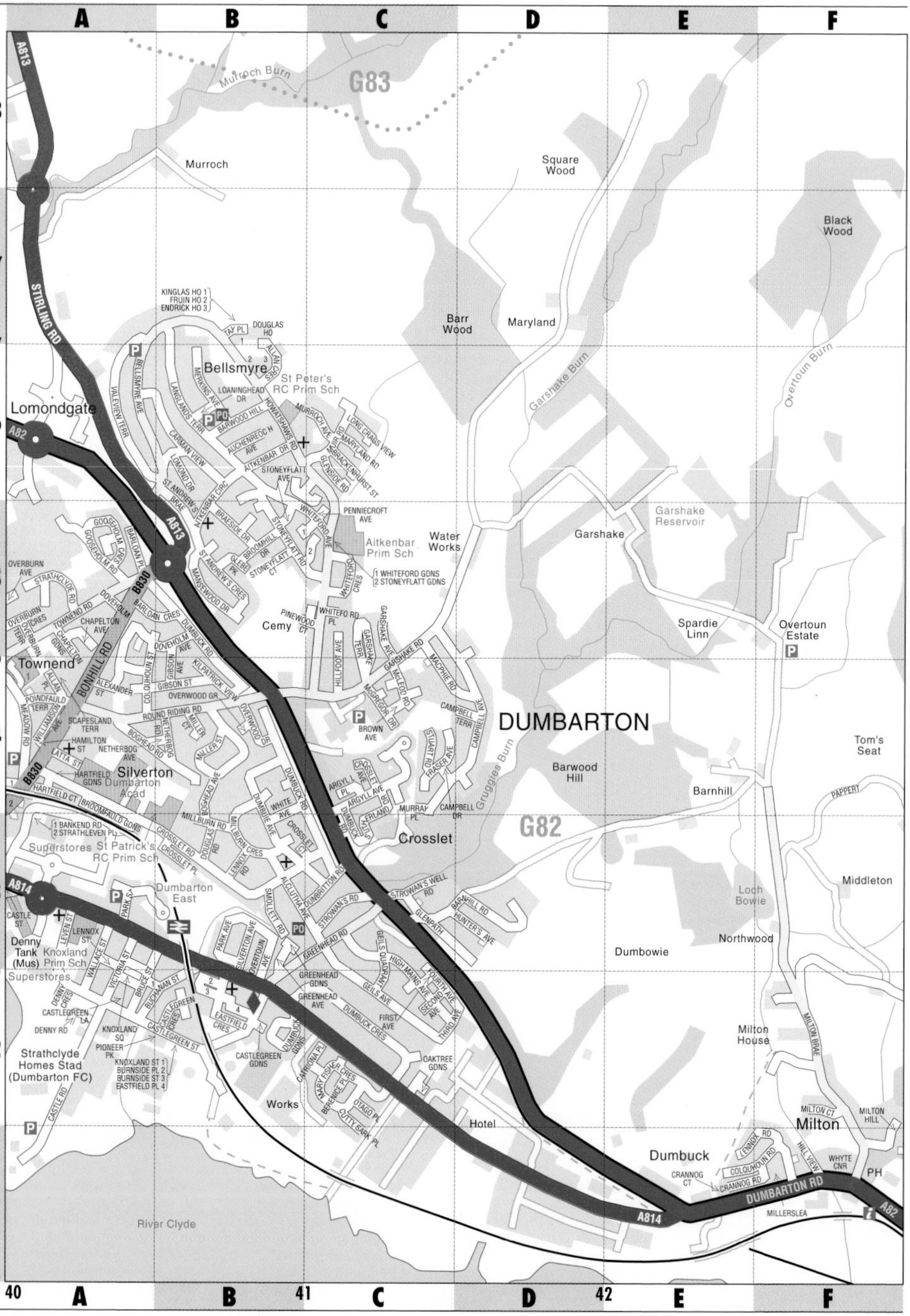
A
B
C
D
E
F
8
7
77
6
5
76
4
3
75
2
1
74
40
41
42
A813
STIRLING RD
A82
A814
B830
BONHILL RD
DUMBARTON RD
G83
G82
Murroch Burn
Murroch
Square Wood
Black Wood
Barr Wood
Maryland
Bellsmyre
St Peter's RC Prim Sch
Lomondgate
Garshake Burn
Overtoun Burn
Aitkenbar Prim Sch
Water Works
Garshake
Garshake Reservoir
Spardie Linn
Overtoun Estate
Cemy
Townend
DUMBARTON
Tom's Seat
Barwood Hill
Barnhill
Silverton
Dumbarton Acad
Gruggies Burn
Crosslet
Superstores
St Patrick's RC Prim Sch
Dumbarton East
Middleton
Loch Bowie
Northwood
Dumbowie
Denny Tank (Mus)
Knoxland Prim Sch
Strathclyde Homes Stad (Dumbarton FC)
Milton House
MILTON BRAE
Works
Hotel
Milton
Dumbuck
PH
River Clyde
MILLERSLEA
KINGLAS HO 1
FRUIN HO 2
ENDRICK HO 3
TAY PL
DOUGLAS HO
1 WHITEFORD GDNS
2 STONEYFLATT GDNS
1 BANKEND RD
2 STRATHLEVEN PL
KNOXLAND ST 1
BURNSIDE PL 2
BURNSIDE ST 3
EASTFIELD PL 4

52

A
B
C
D
E
F
8
7
77
6
5
76
4
3
75
2
1
74
43
44
45
Roughting Burn
Overtoun Burn
Doughnot Hill
Meikle Soughen Brae
G82
Fyn
Loch
Black Linn
Reservoir
Cairn
of Fyn Loch
Lang Craigs
Darnycaip
Brown
Hill
Greenland Reservoir
No 1
Greenland Reservoir
No 2
Loch Humphrey
(Reservoir)
Greenland Reservoir
No 3
Craigarestie
Milton Burn
Middleton
Wood
Rigangower
Greenland
Auchentorlie Burn
Auchentorlie Glen
Reservoir
G60
Craigunnock
Glenarbuck
MILTON
HILL
Auchentorlie
Wood
Haw Craig
Sheep
Hill
Hill of Dun
DUMBARTON RD A82
Auchentorlie
House
High
Auchentorlie

72
52

51

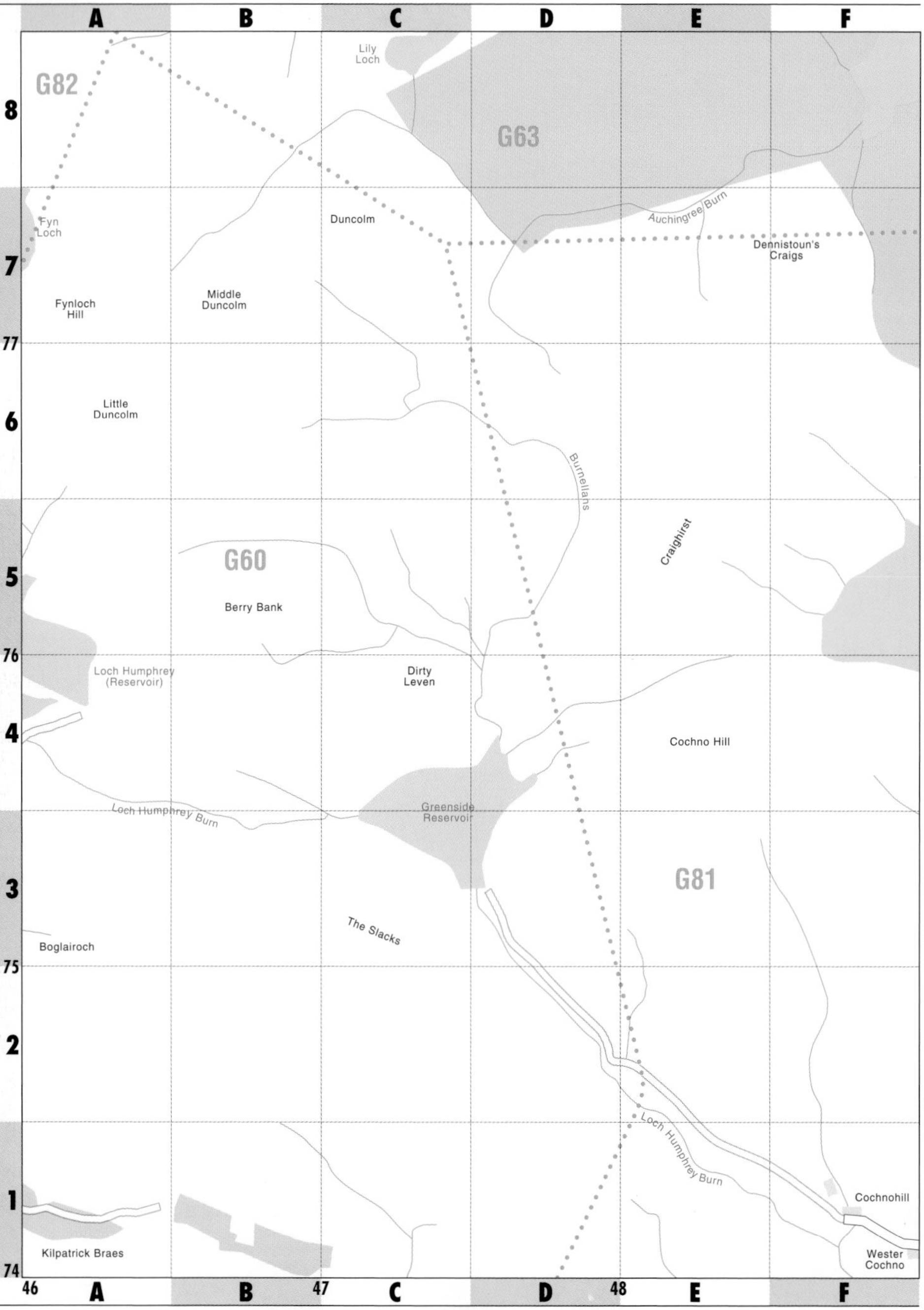

A
B
C
D
E
F
8
7
77
6
5
76
4
3
75
2
1
74
46
47
48
G82
Lily Loch
G63
Fyn Loch
Duncolm
Auchingree Burn
Dennistoun's Craigs
Fynloch Hill
Middle Duncolm
Little Duncolm
Burnellans
Craighirst
G60
Berry Bank
Loch Humphrey (Reservoir)
Dirty Leven
Cochno Hill
Loch Humphrey Burn
Greenside Reservoir
G81
The Slacks
Boglairoch
Loch Humphrey Burn
Cochnohill
Kilpatrick Braes
Wester Cochno

51

73

29
54

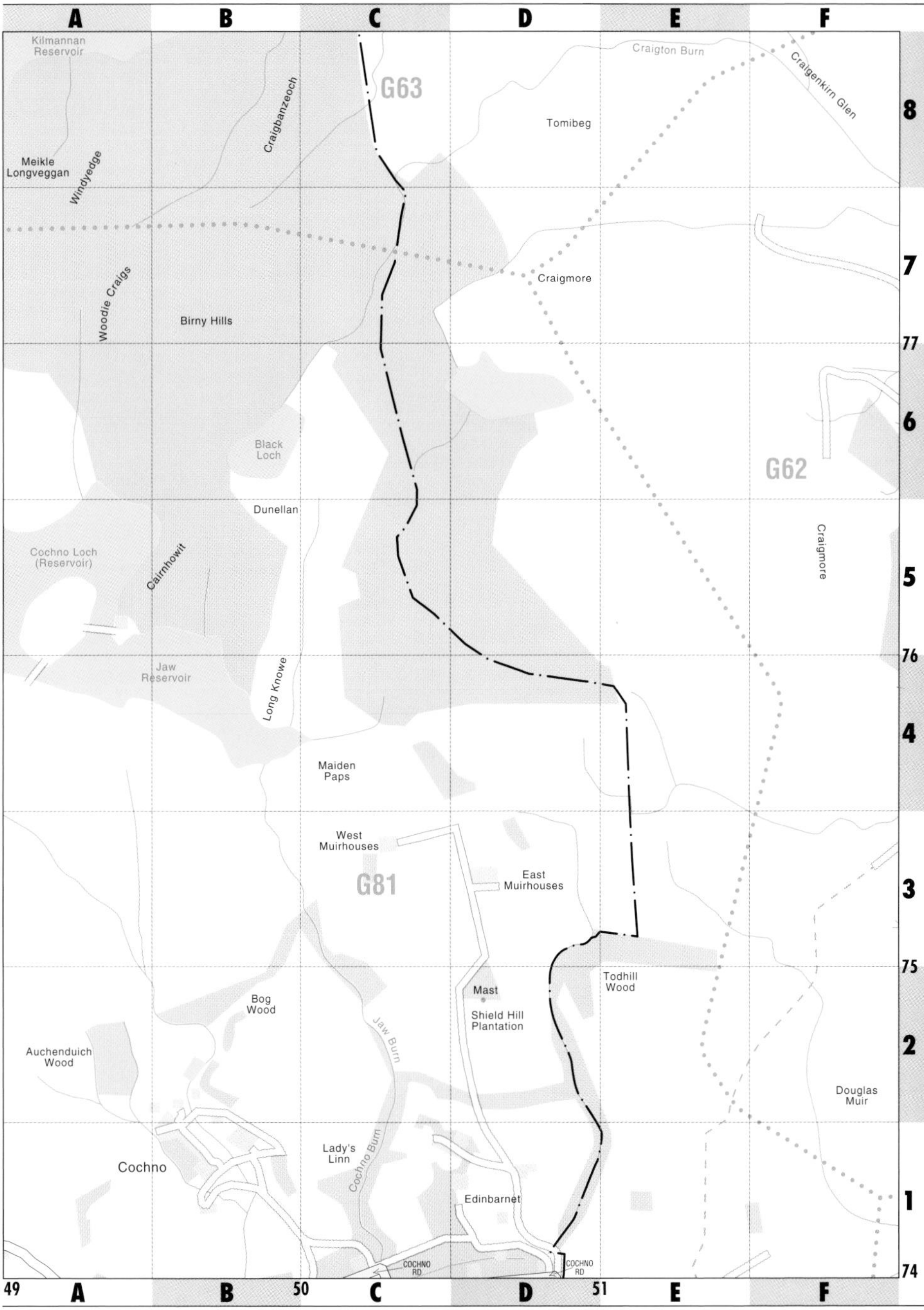
A
B
C
D
E
F
Kilmannan Reservoir
G63
Craigton Burn
Craigenkirn Glen
Craigbanzeoch
Tomibeg
8
Meikle Longveggan
Windyedge
7
Craigmore
Woodie Craigs
Birny Hills
77
6
Black Loch
G62
Dunellan
Craigmore
Cochno Loch (Reservoir)
Cairnhowit
5
76
Jaw Reservoir
Long Knowe
4
Maiden Paps
West Muirhouses
East Muirhouses
G81
3
75
Todhill Wood
Mast
Bog Wood
Shield Hill Plantation
Jaw Burn
Auchenduich Wood
2
Douglas Muir
Lady's Linn
Cochno
Cochno Burn
Edinbarnet
1
COCHNO RD
COCHNO RD
74
49
50
51

74
54

53
30

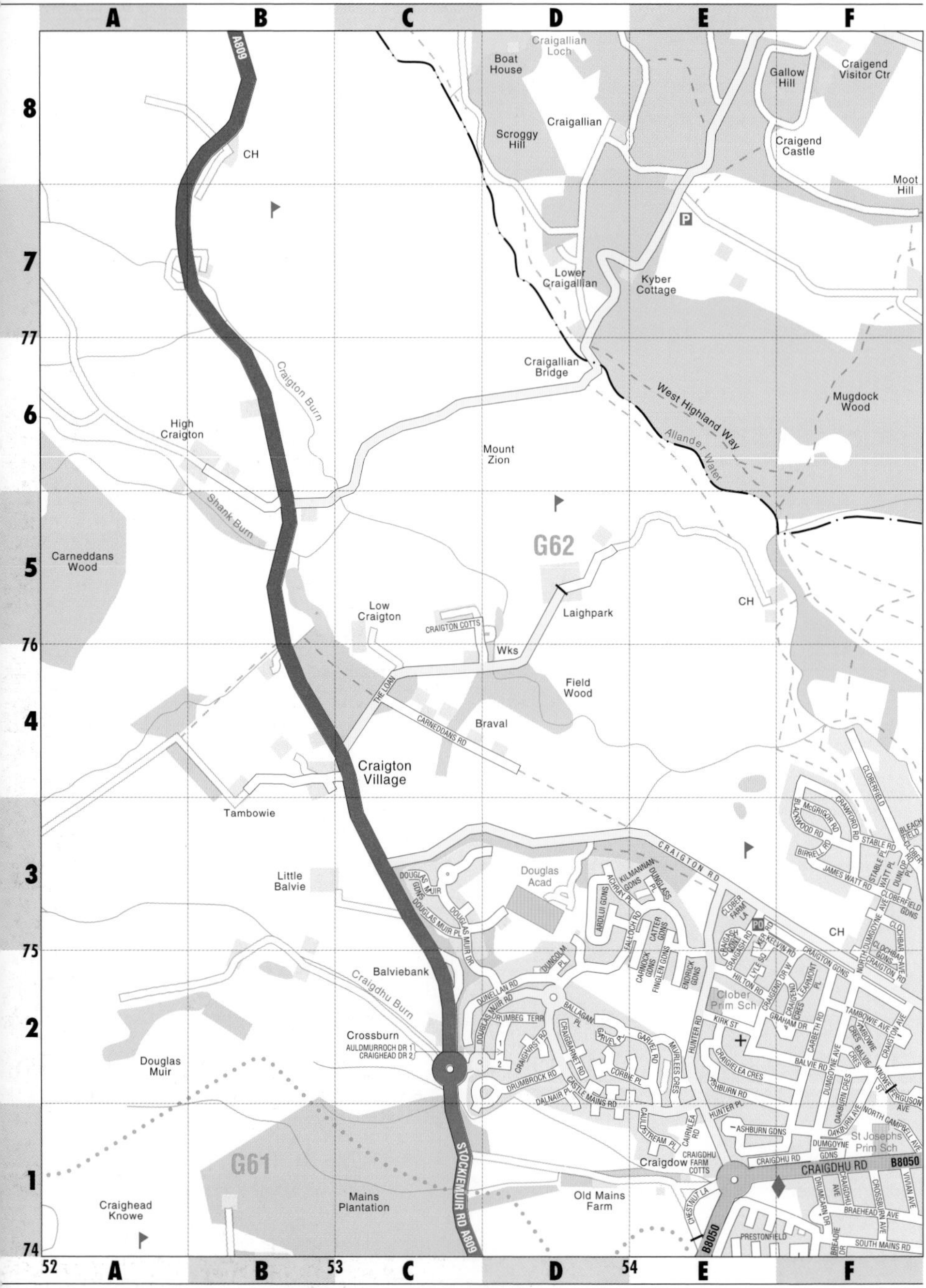
A
B
C
D
E
F
8
7
77
6
5
76
4
3
75
2
1
74
52
53
54
A809
Craigallian Loch
Boat House
Gallow Hill
Craigend Visitor Ctr
Scroggy Hill
Craigallian
CH
Craigend Castle
Moot Hill
Lower Craigallian
Kyber Cottage
Craigallian Bridge
Craigton Burn
West Highland Way
Allander Water
Mugdock Wood
High Craigton
Mount Zion
Shank Burn
G62
Carneddans Wood
Low Craigton
Laighpark
CH
CRAIGTON COTTS
Wks
Field Wood
THE LOAN
CARNEDDANS RD
Braval
Craigton Village
Tambowie
CLOBERFIELD
McGRIGOR RD
CRAWFORD RD
BLACKWOOD RD
BIRRELL RD
STABLE RD
BLEACHFIELD
CLOBER RD
STABLE PL
WATT PL
DUNLOP PL
JAMES WATT RD
CLOBERFIELD GDNS
CRAIGTON RD
Little Balvie
Douglas Acad
DOUGLAS MUIR GDNS
DOUGLAS MUIR PL
DOUGLAS MUIR DR
KILMANNAN GDNS
DUNGLASS PL
ARDLUI GDNS
ACHRAY PL
CLOBER FARM LA
PO
CH
CATTER GDNS
FALLOCH RD
CARNOCK GDNS
FINGLEN GDNS
ENDRICK GDNS
KELVIN RD
LYLE SQ
HILTON RD
CRAIGTON GDNS
LEARMONT PL
CLOCHBAR AVE
CRAIGTON RD
NORTH DUMGOYNE AVE
DUNCOLM PL
Balviebank
Craigdhu Burn
DUNELLAN RD
DOUGLAS MUIR RD
DRUMBEG TERR
BALLAGAN PL
Clober Prim Sch
KIRK ST
GRAHAM DR
CRAIGEND DR W
CRAIGEND CRES
CARBETH RD
TAMBOWIE AVE
CRAIGTON AVE
BALVIE CRES
Crossburn
AULDMURROCH DR 1
CRAIGHEAD DR 2
CRAIGHIRST RD
CRAIGBARNET RD
GARVEL PL
GARVEL RD
CORBIE PL
MUIRLEES CRES
HUNTER RD
CRAIGIELEA CRES
BALVIE RD
DUMGOYNE AVE
KNOWE ST
FERGUSON AVE
Douglas Muir
DRUMBROCK RD
CASTLE MAINS RD
DALNAIR PL
ASHBURN RD
HUNTER PL
ASHBURN GDNS
OAKBURN AVE
DUMGOYNE GDNS
NORTH CAMPBELL AVE
St Josephs Prim Sch
CAULDSTREAM PL
CAIRNLEA RD
G61
STOCKIEMUIR RD A809
Craigdow
CRAIGDHU FARM COTTS
CRAIGDHU RD
B8050
Craighead Knowe
Mains Plantation
Old Mains Farm
CHESTNUT LA
DRUMCAIRN DR
CRAIGDHU AVE
CROSSBURN AVE
VIVIAN AVE
BRAEHEAD AVE
PRESTONFIELD
BREADIE DR
SOUTH MAINS RD

53
75

31
56

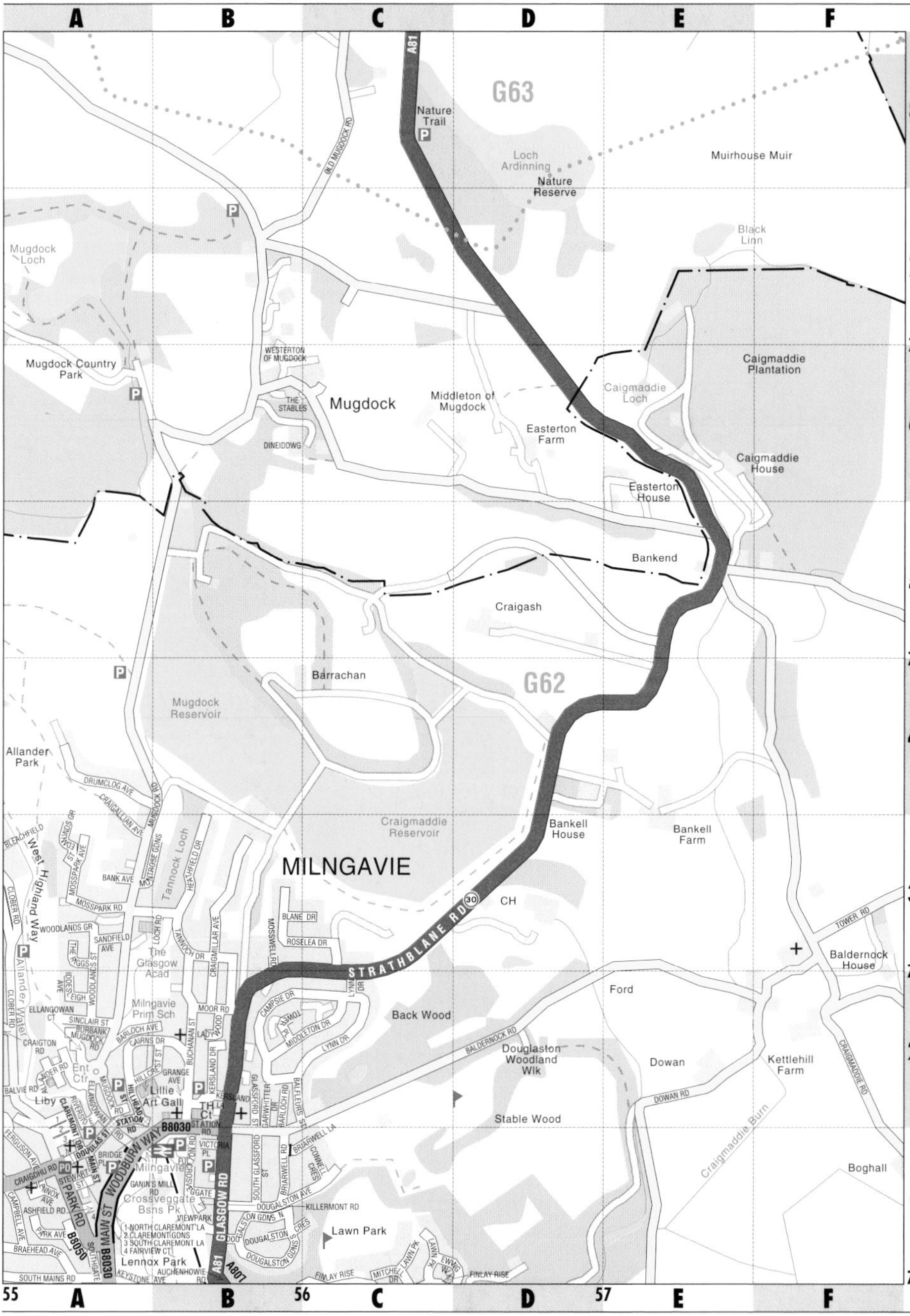
A
B
C
D
E
F
8
7
77
6
5
76
4
3
75
2
1
74
55
56
57
A81
G63
Nature Trail
Loch Ardinning
Nature Reserve
Muirhouse Muir
OLD MUGDOCK RD
Black Linn
Mugdock Loch
Mugdock Country Park
WESTERTON OF MUGDOCK
THE STABLES
Mugdock
DINEIDDWG
Middleton of Mugdock
Caigmaddie Loch
Caigmaddie Plantation
Easterton Farm
Caigmaddie House
Easterton House
Bankend
Craigash
Barrachan
G62
Mugdock Reservoir
Allander Park
DRUMCLOG AVE
CRAIGALLIAN AVE
MUGDOCK RD
Craigmaddie Reservoir
Bankell House
Bankell Farm
MILNGAVIE
West Highland Way
Tannock Loch
CH
TOWER RD
Baldernock House
STRATHBLANE RD
BLANE DR
ROSELEA DR
MOSSWELL RD
Ford
Back Wood
The Glasgow Acad
Milngavie Prim Sch
CAMPSIE DR
MIDDLETON DR
LYNN DR
BALDERNOCK RD
Douglaston Woodland Wlk
Dowan
Kettlehill Farm
CRAIGMADDIE RD
DOWAN RD
Stable Wood
Craigmaddie Burn
Boghall
Ent Ctr
Lillie Art Gall
Liby
TH Ct
STATION RD
B8030
WOODBURN WAY
Milngavie
Crossveggate Bsns Pk
GLASGOW RD
KILLERMONT RD
Lawn Park
DOUGALSTON AVE
MAIN ST
PARK RD
B8050
Lennox Park
A807
SOUTH MAINS RD
FINLAY RISE
1 NORTH CLAREMONT LA
2 CLAREMONT GDNS
3 SOUTH CLAREMONT LA
4 FAIRVIEW CT

76
56

55
32

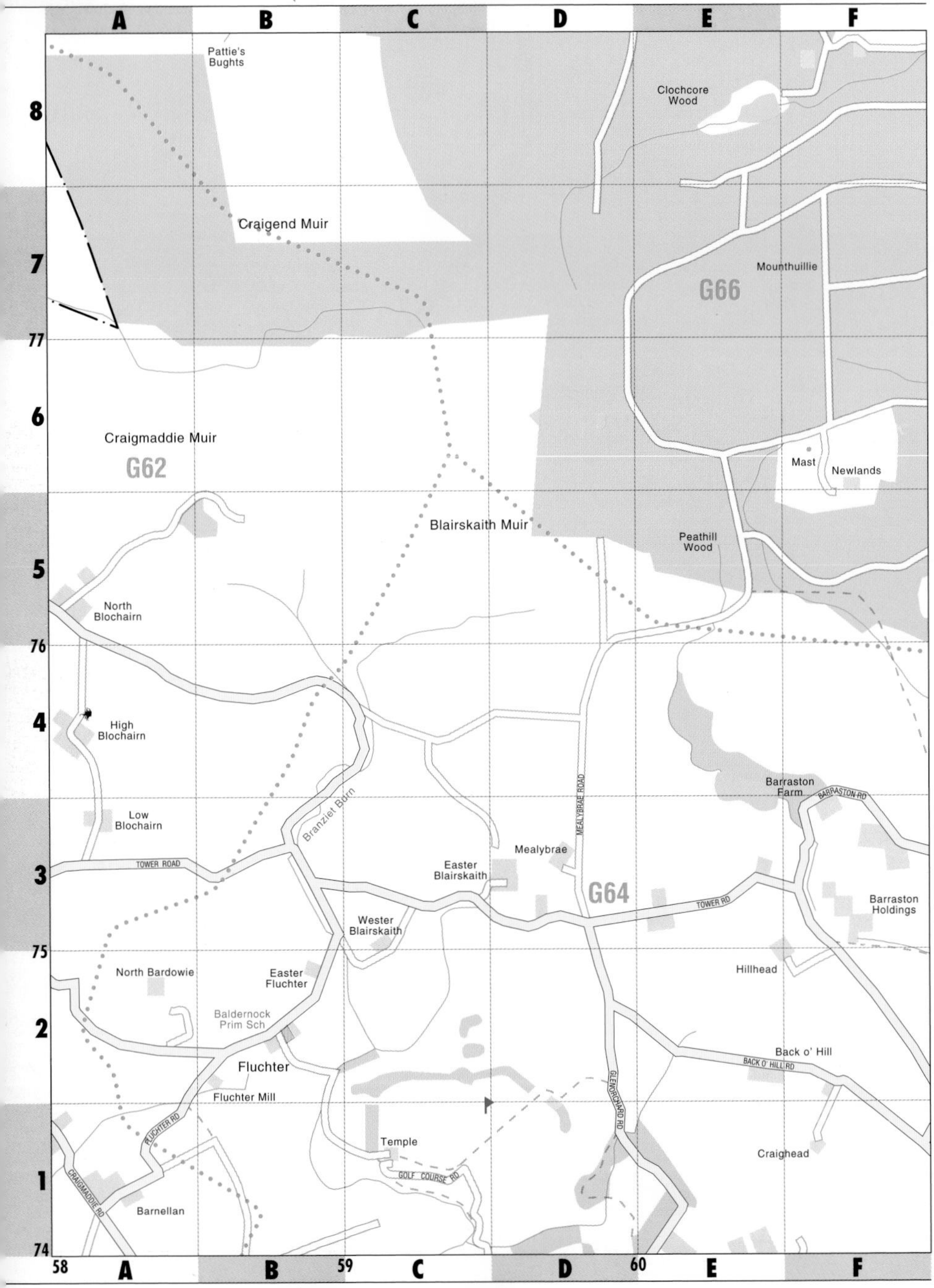
A
B
C
D
E
F
8
7
77
6
5
76
4
3
75
2
1
74
58
59
60
Pattie's Bughts
Clochcore Wood
Craigend Muir
Mounthuillie
G66
Craigmaddie Muir
G62
Mast
Newlands
Blairskaith Muir
Peathill Wood
North Blochairn
High Blochairn
Low Blochairn
Branziet Burn
MEALYBRAE ROAD
Barraston Farm
BARRASTON RD
Mealybrae
TOWER ROAD
Easter Blairskaith
G64
TOWER RD
Barraston Holdings
Wester Blairskaith
North Bardowie
Easter Fluchter
Hillhead
Baldernock Prim Sch
Back o' Hill
Fluchter
BACK O' HILL RD
Fluchter Mill
GLENORCHARD RD
FLUCHTER RD
Temple
Craighead
GOLF COURSE RD
CRAIGMADDIE RD
Barnellan

55
77

33
58

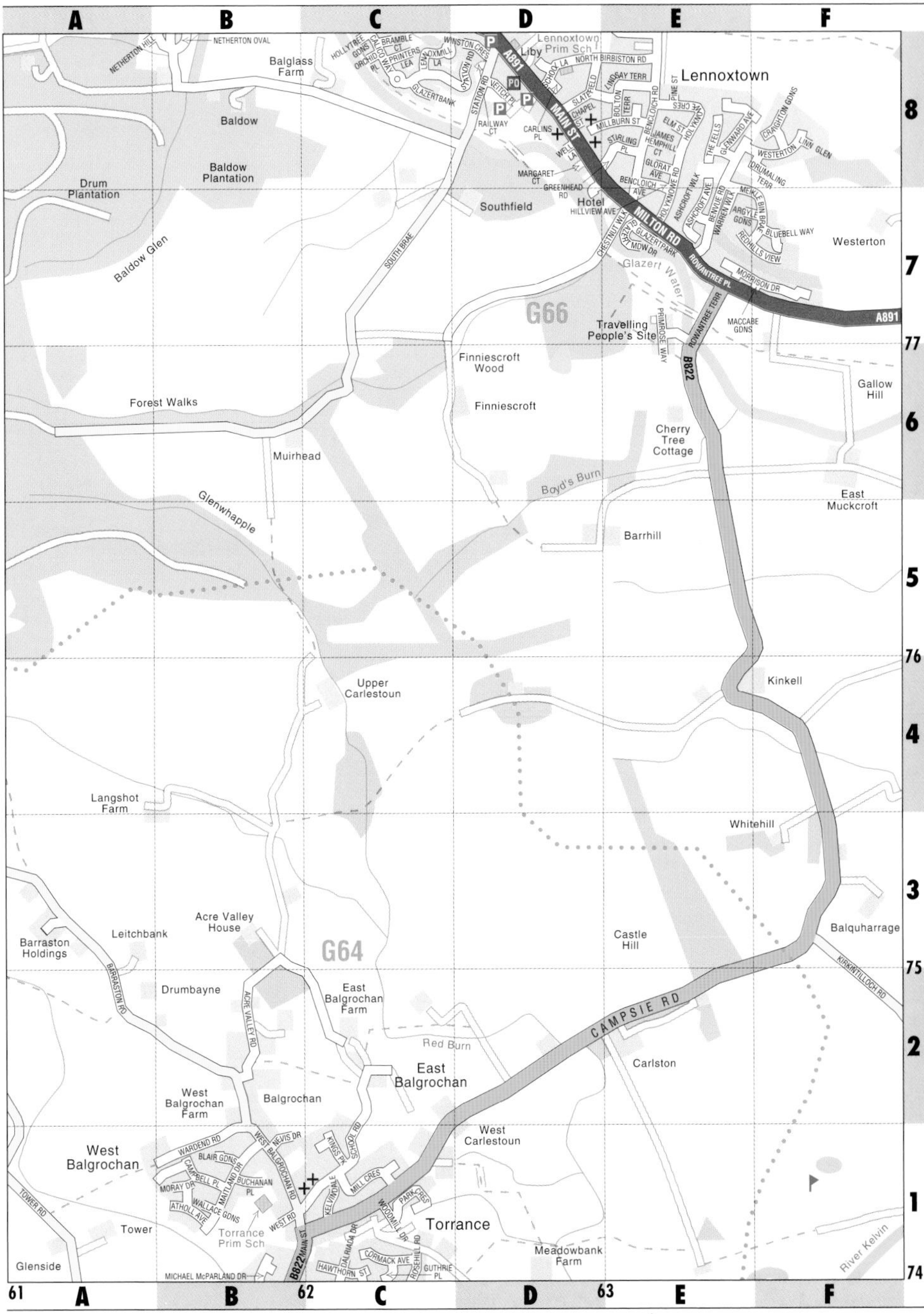
A B C D E F
8 7 77 6 5 76 4 3 75 2 1 74
61 62 63
Lennoxtown
Lennoxtown Prim Sch
Liby
NETHERTON HILL
NETHERTON OVAL
Balglass Farm
Baldow
Baldow Plantation
Drum Plantation
Baldow Glen
HOLLYTREE GDNS
BRAMBLE CT
ORCHID PL
PRINTERS LEA
OXMILL LA
WINSTON CRES
STATION RD
GLAZERTBANK
VEITCH PL
RAILWAY CT
SCHOOL LA
NORTH BIRBISTON RD
SLATEFIELD
LINDSAY TERR
BOLTON TERR
BENCLOICH RD
PINE ST
MAIN ST
A891
CARLINS PL
CHAPEL ST
MILLBURN ST
STIRLING PL
JAMES HEMPHILL CT
ELM ST
GLORAT AVE
MARGARET CT
GREENHEAD RD
BENCLOICH AVE
HOLYKNOWE RD
Hotel
HILLVIEW AVE
Southfield
MILTON RD
CHESTNUT WLK
GLAZERT MDW DR
GLAZERTPARK
ASHCROFT WLK
ASHCROFT AVE
BENVUE RD
WARREN WLK
THE FELLS
GLENWARD AVE
CRAIGHTON GDNS
WESTERTON
LINN GLEN
DRUMALING TERR
MEIKLE BIN BRAE
ARGYLE GDNS
BLUEBELL WAY
REDHILLS VIEW
Westerton
MORRISON DR
ROWANTREE PL
ROWANTREE TERR
MACCABE GDNS
Glazert Water
G66
Travelling People's Site
PRIMROSE WAY
SOUTH BRAE
B822
Finniescroft Wood
Finniescroft
Gallow Hill
Forest Walks
Muirhead
Cherry Tree Cottage
Boyd's Burn
East Muckcroft
Glenwhapple
Barrhill
Upper Carlestoun
Kinkell
Langshot Farm
Whitehill
Acre Valley House
Leitchbank
Barraston Holdings
G64
Castle Hill
Balquharrage
BARRASTON RD
Drumbayne
ACRE VALLEY RD
East Balgrochan Farm
KIRKINTILLOCH RD
CAMPSIE RD
Red Burn
Carlston
East Balgrochan
West Balgrochan Farm
Balgrochan
West Carlestoun
West Balgrochan
WARDEND RD
NEVIS DR
BLAIR GDNS
WEST BALGROCHAN RD
KINGS PL
SCHOOL RD
CAMPBELL PL
MAITLAND DR
BUCHANAN PL
MORAY DR
WALLACE GDNS
ATHOLL AVE
MILL CRES
KELVINDALE
PARK CRES
WOODMILL DR
TOWER RD
Tower
Torrance Prim Sch
WEST RD
Torrance
Meadowbank Farm
River Kelvin
Glenside
MICHAEL McPARLAND DR
MAIN ST
DALRIADA DR
CORMACK AVE
ROSEHILL RD
HAWTHORN ST
GUTHRIE PL

78
58

57
34

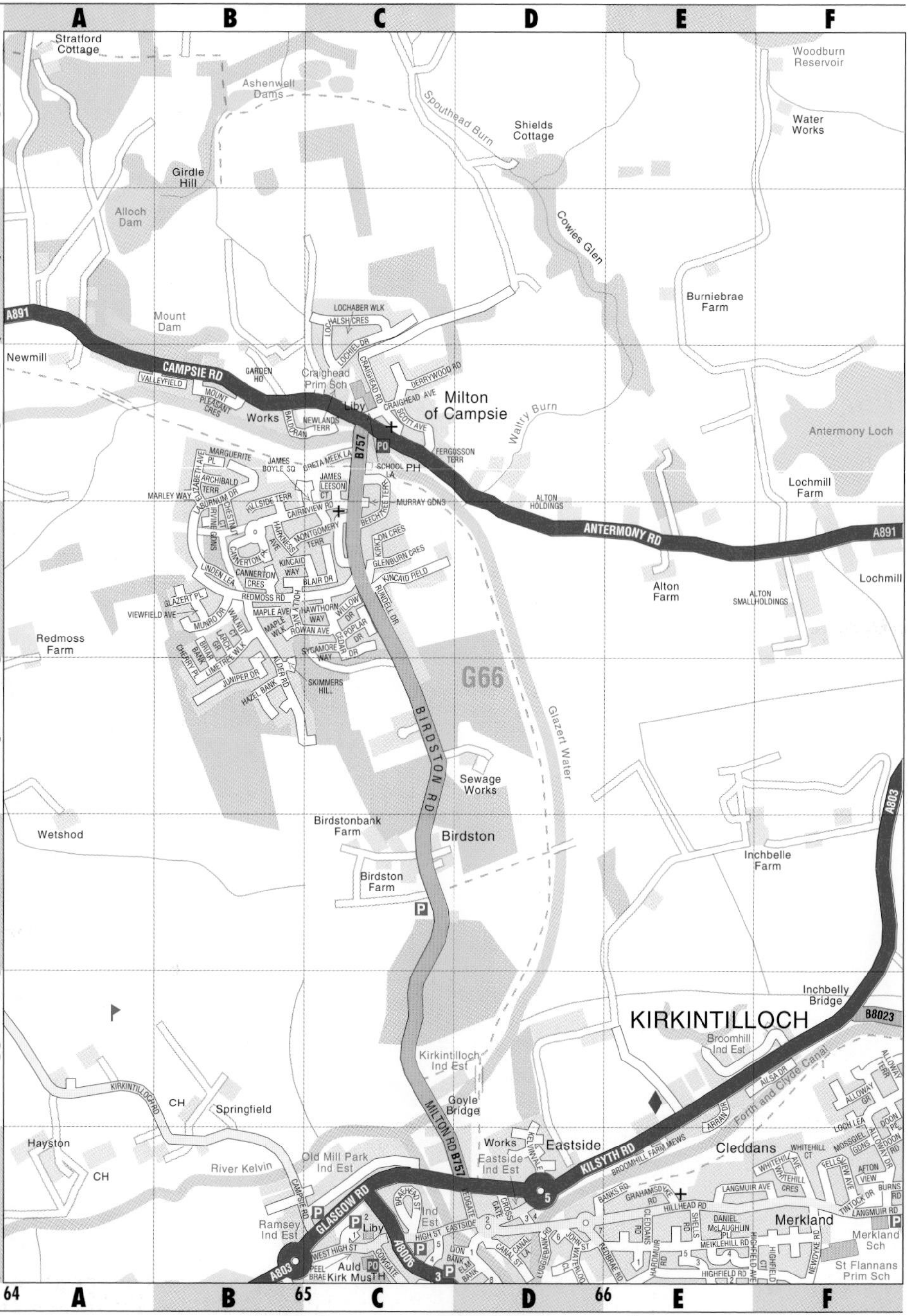

57
79

C1
1 KELVIN CT
2 SALFORD PL
3 ROCHDALE PL
4 BROADCROFT
5 BROADCROFT RD

D1
1 PETER D.STIRLING RD
2 HILLHEAD RDBT
3 HOPKIN'S BRAE
4 BROOMHILL CT
5 EASTSIDE RDBT
6 WATERLOO GDNS
7 REDBRAE PL
8 GLENVIEW

E1
1 HARDMUIR GDNS
2 HIGHFIELD GR
3 HIGHFIELD CRES
4 MEIKLEHILL AVE
5 FERNLEA RD

35
60

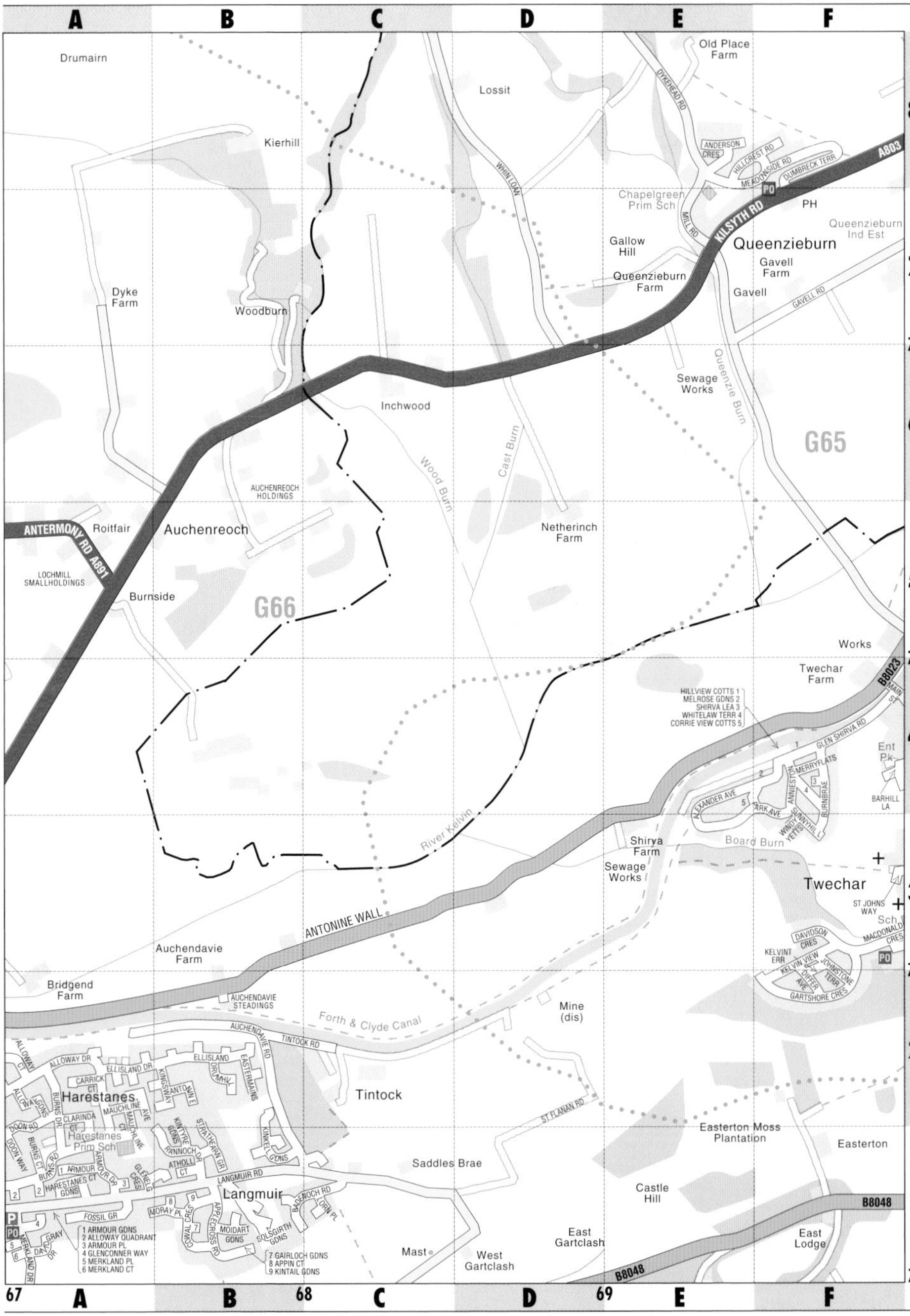
A
B
C
D
E
F
8
7
77
6
5
76
4
3
75
2
1
74
67
68
69
Drumairn
Lossit
Old Place Farm
DYKEHEAD RD
ANDERSON CRES
HILLCREST RD
MEADOWSIDE RD
DUMBRECK TERR
A803
Kierhill
WHIN LOAN
Chapelgreen Prim Sch
PO
PH
KILSYTH RD
MILL RD
Queenzieburn Ind Est
Gallow Hill
Queenzieburn
Gavell Farm
Queenzieburn Farm
Gavell
GAVELL RD
Dyke Farm
Woodburn
Sewage Works
Queenzie Burn
Inchwood
G65
Wood Burn
Cast Burn
AUCHENREOCH HOLDINGS
Netherinch Farm
ANTERMONY RD A891
Roitfair
Auchenreoch
LOCHMILL SMALLHOLDINGS
Burnside
G66
Works
Twechar Farm
B8023
MAIN ST
HILLVIEW COTTS 1
MELROSE GDNS 2
SHIRVA LEA 3
WHITELAW TERR 4
CORRIE VIEW COTTS 5
GLEN SHIRVA RD
MERRYFLATS
Ent Pk
ANNIESTON
BURNBRAE
ALEXANDER AVE
PARK AVE
SUNNYHILL
WINDY YETTS
BARHILL LA
River Kelvin
Shirva Farm
Board Burn
Sewage Works
Twechar
ST JOHNS WAY
Sch
ANTONINE WALL
DAVIDSON CRES
MACDONALD CRES
KELVINT ERR
KELVIN VIEW
JOHNSTONE TERR
DIFFER AVE
GARTSHORE CRES
Auchendavie Farm
Bridgend Farm
AUCHENDAVIE STEADINGS
Forth & Clyde Canal
Mine (dis)
AUCHENDAVIE RD
TINTOCK RD
ALLOWAY DR
ELLISLAND DR
ELLISLAND
CARRICK CT
KINGSWAY
ANTONINE
DRUMHILL
EASTERMAINS
Harestanes
BURNS DR
MAUCHLINE AVE
CLARINDA CT
DOON RD
DOON WAY
BURNS CT
Harestanes Prim Sch
KINTYRE GDNS
STRATHEARN GR
RANNOCH DR
ATHOLL CT
KINKELL GDNS
ARMOUR DR
GLENELG CRES
HARESTANES CT
HARESTANES GDNS
LANGMUIR RD
Tintock
ST FLANAN RD
Easterton Moss Plantation
Easterton
Saddles Brae
Langmuir
BADENOCH RD
LORN PL
Castle Hill
B8048
FOSSIL GR
MORAY PL
APPLECROSS RD
COWAL CRES
MOIDART GDNS
SOLSGIRTH GDNS
P
PO
GRAY DR
DAVID DR
MERKLAND DR
1 ARMOUR GDNS
2 ALLOWAY QUADRANT
3 ARMOUR PL
4 GLENCONNER WAY
5 MERKLAND PL
6 MERKLAND CT
7 GAIRLOCH GDNS
8 APPIN CT
9 KINTAIL GDNS
Mast
West Gartclash
East Gartclash
East Lodge

80
60

59
36

D8
1 CHARLES ST
2 EAST BURNSIDE ST
3 KING ST LA
4 KING ST
5 MARKET PL
6 MARKET SQ
7 MARKET CL
8 CHURCH LA
9 FINDLAY ST
10 WESTPORT ST
11 WILLIAM ST
12 PARKER PL
13 KEIR HARDIE DR
14 ARRAN VIEW
15 MARKET CT
16 LENNOX CT
17 BACKBRAE ST

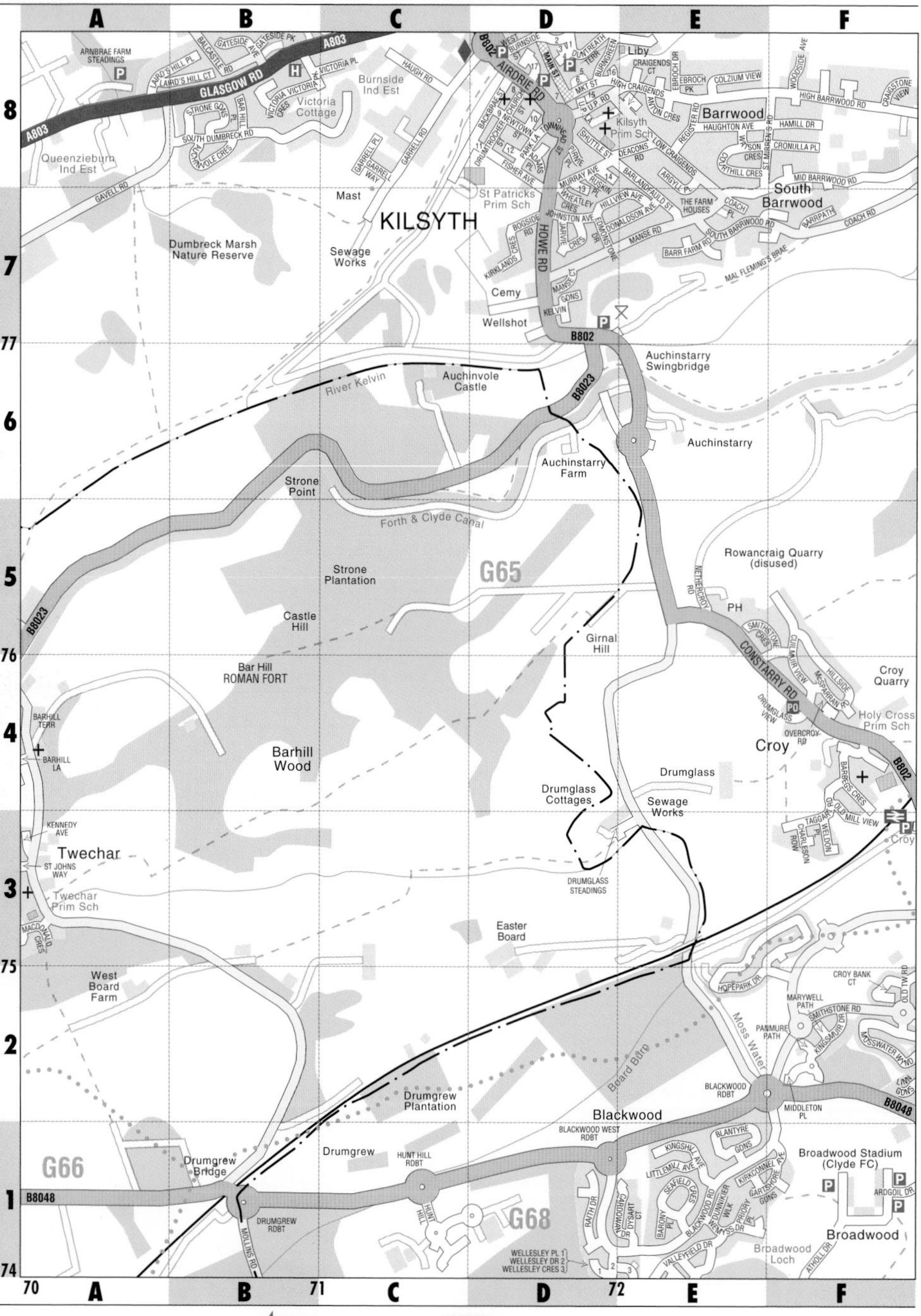

59
81

37
62

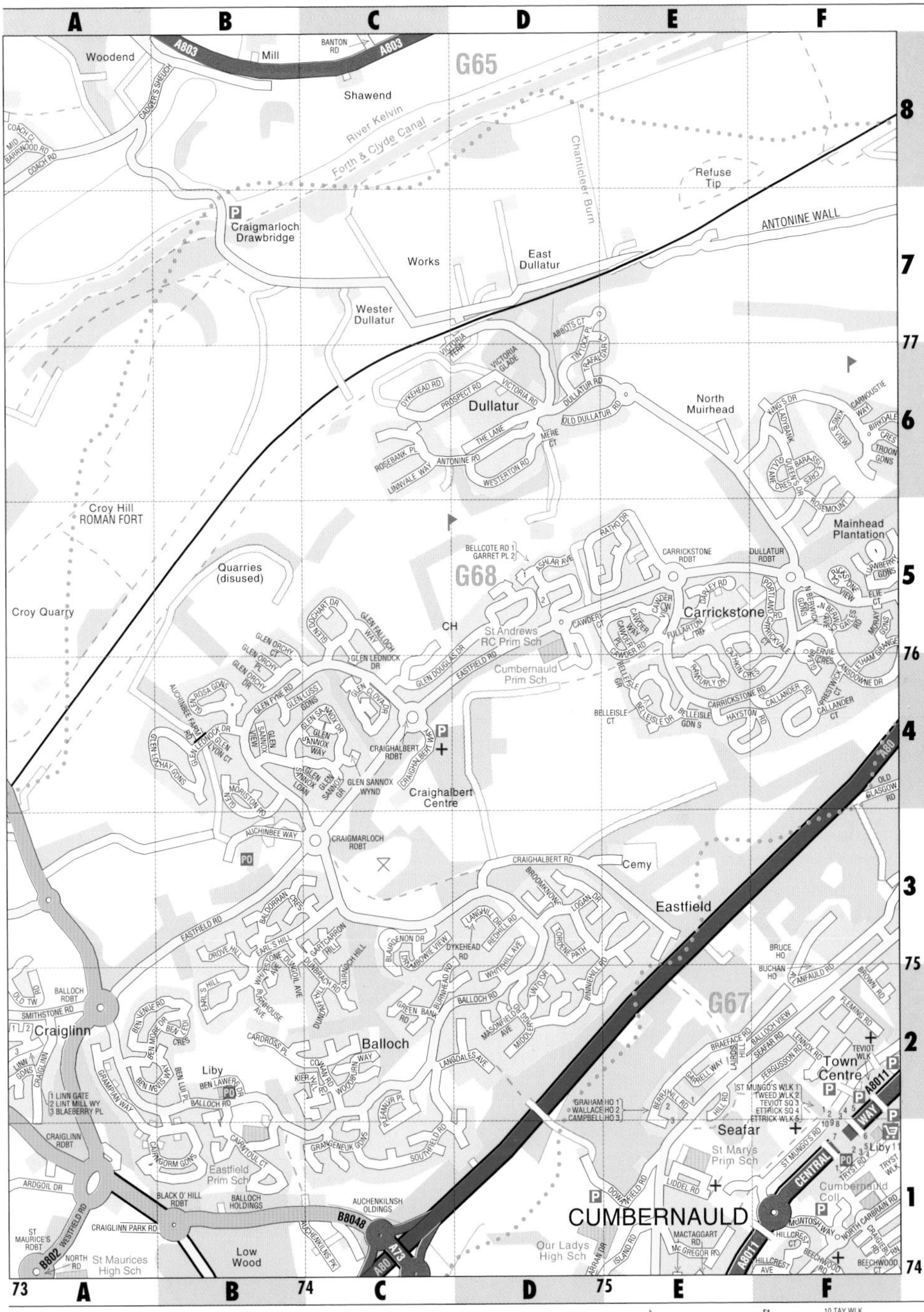

82
62

F1
1 CLYDE WLK
2 CLYDE SQ
3 CLYDE WAY
4 AVON WLK
5 FORTH WLK
6 LEVEN WAY
7 ANNAN WAY
8 SPEY WLK
9 ETTRICK WAY
10 TAY WLK
11 Antonine Sh Ctr

61
38

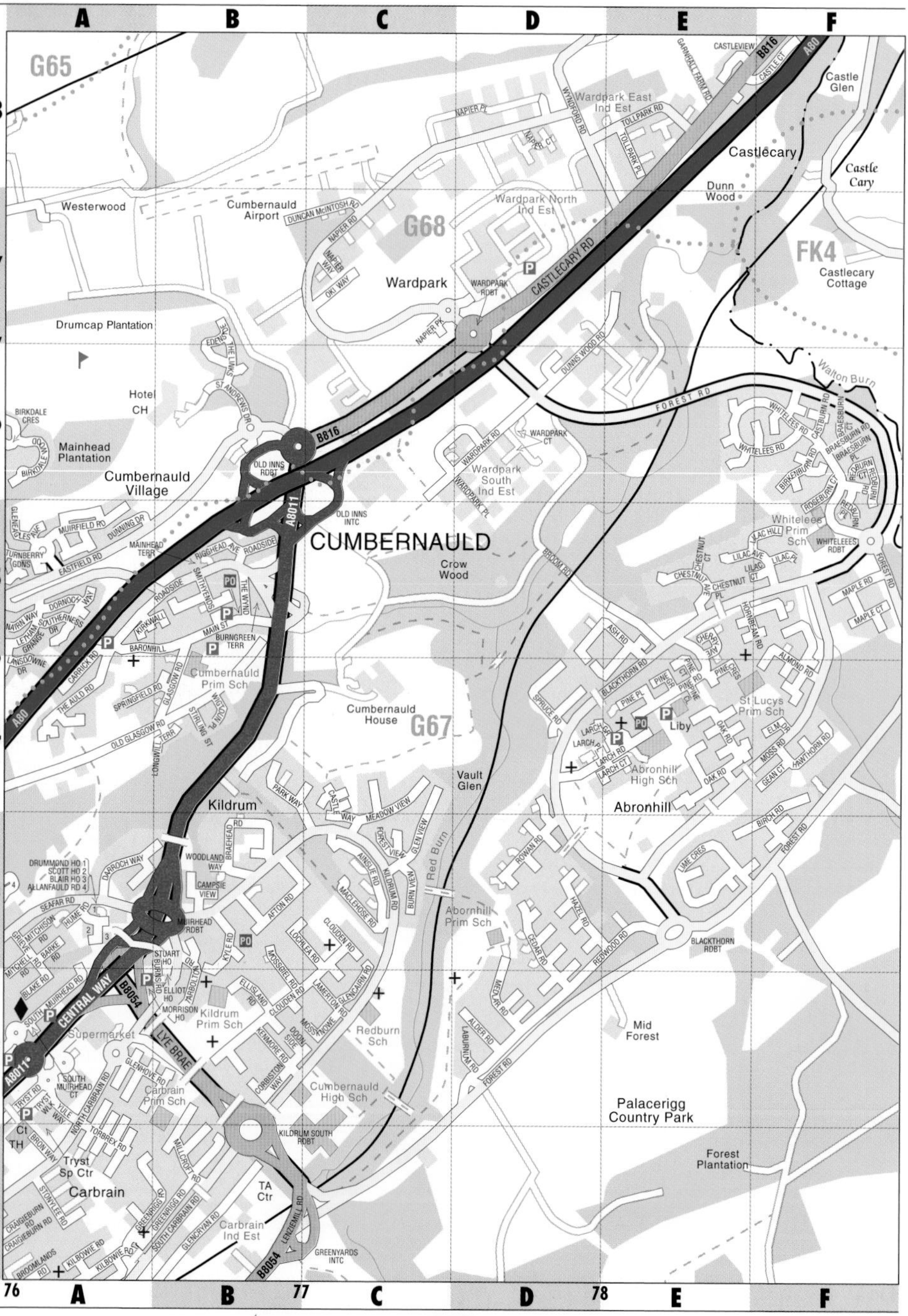
A
B
C
D
E
F
8
7
77
6
5
76
4
3
75
2
1
74
76
77
78
G65
G68
G67
FK4
CUMBERNAULD
Westerwood
Cumbernauld Airport
DUNCAN McINTOSH RD
NAPIER RD
NAPIER WAY
OKI WAY
NAPIER PL
NAPIER CT
NAPIER PK
Wardpark
Wardpark East Ind Est
Wardpark North Ind Est
WARDPARK RDBT
CASTLECARY RD
WYNDFORD RD
TOLLPARK RD
GARNHALL FARM RD
CASTLEVIEW
CASTLE CT
B816
A80
Castle Glen
Castlecary
Castle Cary
Dunn Wood
Castlecary Cottage
Walton Burn
Drumcap Plantation
EDEN
THE LINKS
ST ANDREWS DR
Hotel
CH
BIRKDALE CRES
BIRKDALE WOOD
BIRKDALE
Mainhead Plantation
Cumbernauld Village
OLD INNS RDBT
OLD INNS INTC
A8011
DUNNS WOOD RD
FOREST RD
WARDPARK RD
WARDPARK CT
WARDPARK PL
Wardpark South Ind Est
WHITELEES RD
CASTBURN RD
BRAESBURN RD
BRAESBURN CT
BRAESBURN PL
BIRKENBURN RD
ROSEBURN CT
REDBURN CT
REDBURN RD
REDBURN PL
Whitelees Prim Sch
WHITELEES RDBT
LILAC HILL
LILAC AVE
LILAC PL
LILAC CT
CHESTNUT CT
CHESTNUT PL
CHESTNUT AVE
MAPLE RD
MAPLE CT
GLENEAGLES AVE
MUIRFIELD RD
DUNNING DR
TURNBERRY GDNS
EASTFIELD RD
MAINHEAD TERR
RIGGHEAD AVE
ROADSIDE
SMITHYENDS
THE WYND
Crow Wood
BROOM RD
NAIRN WAY
DORNOCH WAY
LETHAM GRANGE
SOUTHERNESS DR
KIRKWALL
MAIN ST
BURNGREEN TERR
BARONHILL
LANSDOWNE DR
CARRICK RD
THE AULD RD
SPRINGFIELD RD
GLASGOW RD
WIGTON PL
STIRLING ST
Cumbernauld Prim Sch
OLD GLASGOW RD
LONGWILL TERR
Cumbernauld House
ASH RD
BLACKTHORN RD
PINE PL
PINE CT
PINE GR
PINE CRES
CHERRY AVE
HORNBEAM RD
ALMOND RD
SPRUCE RD
LARCH GR
LARCH PL
LARCH RD
LARCH CT
Liby
St Lucys Prim Sch
OAK RD
ELM DR
MOSS RD
HAWTHORN RD
GEAN CT
Abronhill High Sch
Abronhill
Vault Glen
BIRCH RD
FOREST RD
LIME CRES
Kildrum
PARK WAY
CASTLE WAY
MEADOW VIEW
FOREST VIEW
GLEN VIEW
BRAEHEAD RD
WOODLAND WAY
CAMPSIE VIEW
DARROCH WAY
AINSLIE RD
KILDRUM RD
BURN VIEW
Red Burn
ROWAN RD
HAZEL RD
CEDAR RD
DRUMMOND HO 1
SCOTT HO 2
BLAIR HO 3
ALLANFAULD RD 4
SEAFAR RD
HUME RD
MITCHISON RD
GRIEVE RD
BARKE RD
MITCHELL RD
BLAKE RD
MUIRHEAD RD
MUIRHEAD RDBT
AFTON RD
MACLEHOSE RD
CLOUDEN RD
LOCHLEA RD
KYLE RD
MOSSGIEL RD
LAMERTON RD
GLENCAIRN RD
Abornhill Prim Sch
REDWOOD RD
BLACKTHORN RDBT
STUART HO
BURNS RD
ELLIOT HO
MORRISON HO
ARBOLTON RD
ELLISLAND RD
CLOUDEN RD
MOSSGIEL
DOON SIDE
KENMORE RD
Kildrum Prim Sch
Redburn Sch
MEDLAR RD
ALDER RD
LABURNUM RD
Mid Forest
CENTRAL WAY
B8054
SOUTH MUIRHEAD RD
Supermarket
LYE BRAE
GLENHOVE RD
CORBISTON WAY
Cumbernauld High Sch
Carbrain Prim Sch
SOUTH MUIRHEAD CT
TRYST RD
TRYST WLK
YULE WAY
NORTH CARBRAIN RD
TORBREX RD
Palacerigg Country Park
Forest Plantation
KILDRUM SOUTH RDBT
Ct
TH
BRON WAY
Tryst Sp Ctr
Carbrain
MILLCROFT RD
TA Ctr
LENZIEMILL RD
CRAIGIEBURN RD
STONYLEE RD
GREENRIGG RD
SOUTH CARBRAIN RD
GLENCRYAN RD
Carbrain Ind Est
KILBOWIE RD
KILBOWIE RD
BROOMLANDS RD
GREENYARDS INTC
B8054

61
83

39
64

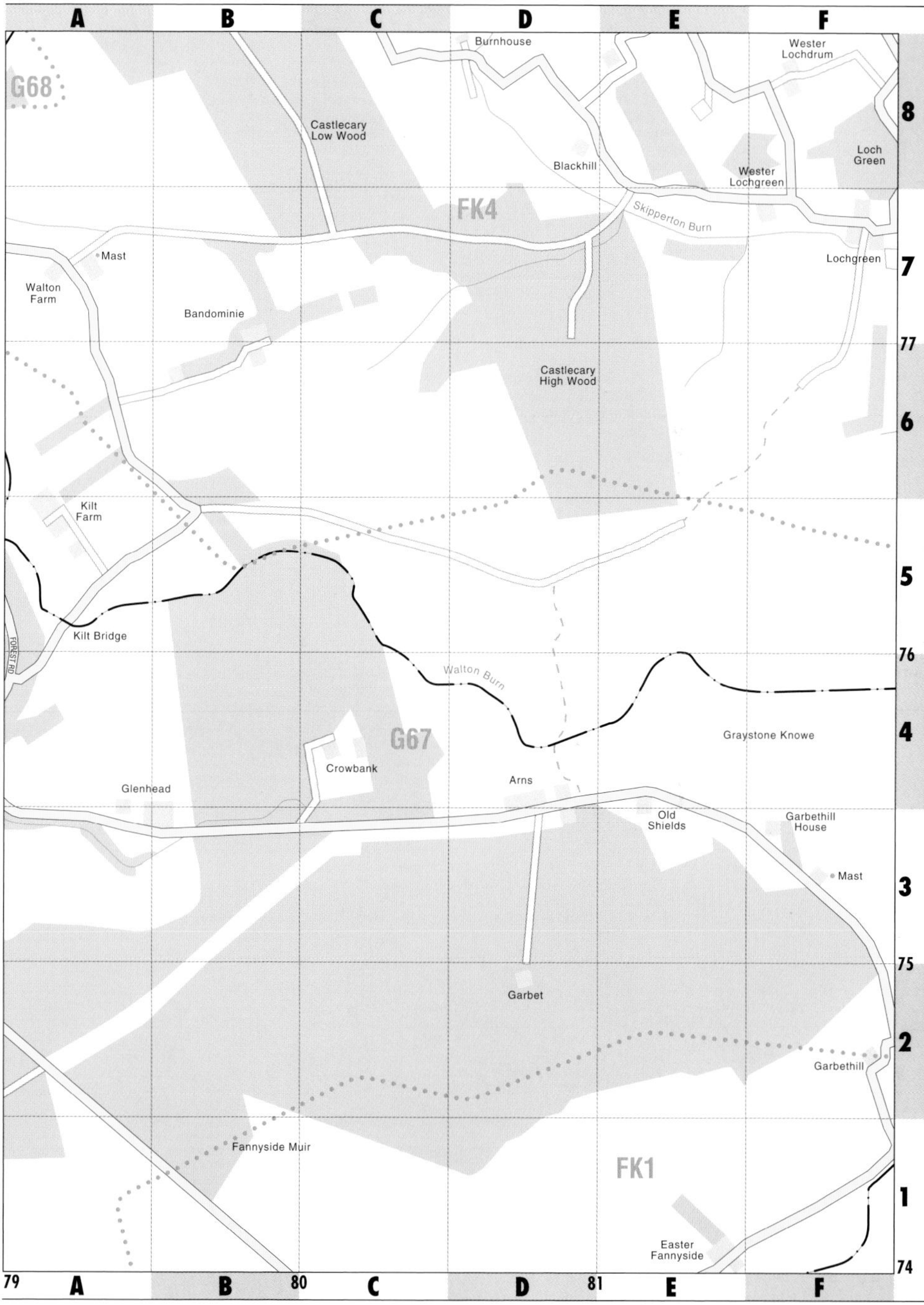
A
B
C
D
E
F
G68
Burnhouse
Wester
Lochdrum
Castlecary
Low Wood
Blackhill
Loch
Green
Wester
Lochgreen
FK4
Skipperton Burn
8
Mast
Lochgreen
7
Walton
Farm
Bandominie
77
Castlecary
High Wood
6
Kilt
Farm
5
Kilt Bridge
FOREST RD
Walton Burn
76
G67
Graystone Knowe
4
Crowbank
Glenhead
Arns
Old
Shields
Garbethill
House
Mast
3
75
Garbet
2
Garbethill
Fannyside Muir
FK1
1
Easter
Fannyside
74
79
80
81

84
64

63
40

A
B
C
D
E
F
8
7
77
6
5
76
4
3
75
2
1
74
82
83
84
Drum Wood
South Drum
Cadgersloan
FK4
Tippetcraig
Loanfoot
Beam
G67
FK1
Newcraig
Cottage
B803
Garbethill Muir
Easter
Jawcraig
Wester
Jawcraig
Jawcraig
Farm
Jawcraig
Threaprig
Easter
Greenrig
Oakersdykes
Wester Jaw
Cottage

63
85

41
66

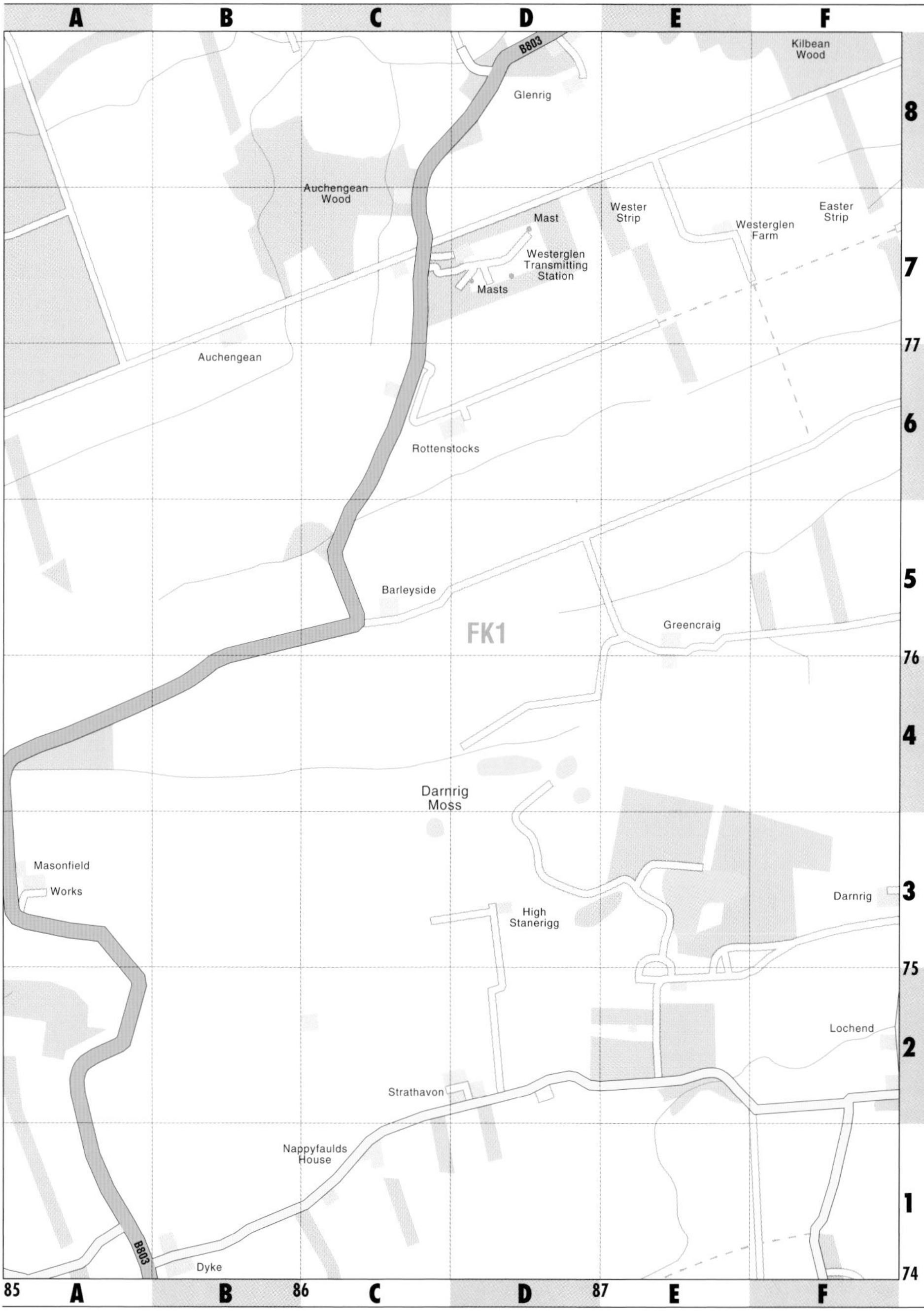
A
B
C
D
E
F
B803
Kilbean Wood
Glenrig
8
Auchengean Wood
Mast
Wester Strip
Westerglen Farm
Easter Strip
Westerglen Transmitting Station
Masts
7
77
Auchengean
6
Rottenstocks
5
Barleyside
FK1
Greencraig
76
4
Darnrig Moss
Masonfield
Works
3
Darnrig
High Stanerigg
75
Lochend
2
Strathavon
Nappyfaulds House
1
B803
Dyke
74
85
86
87

86
66

65
42

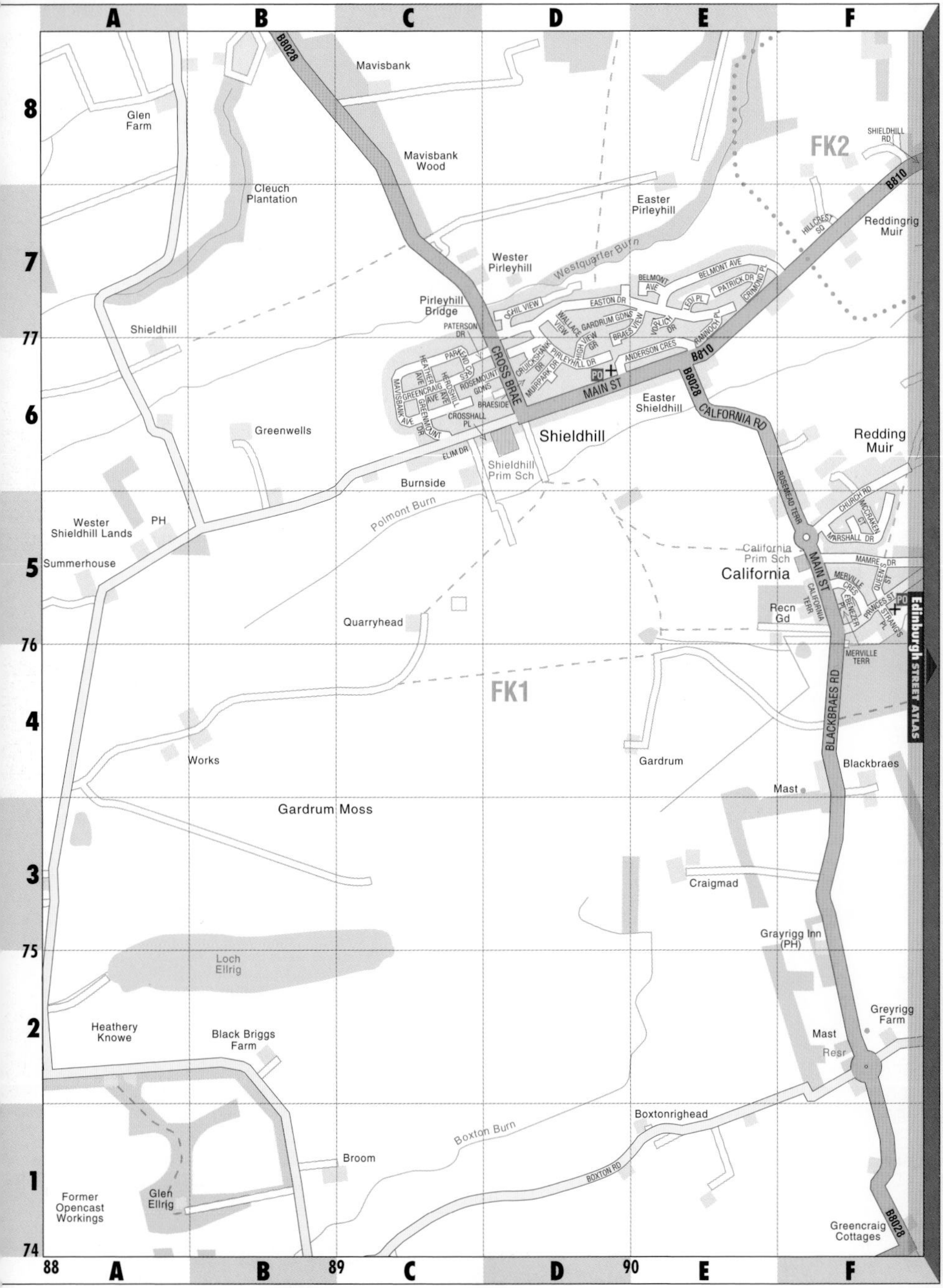
A
B
C
D
E
F
8
7
77
6
5
76
4
3
75
2
1
74
88
89
90
B8028
Mavisbank
Glen Farm
Mavisbank Wood
Cleuch Plantation
Easter Pirleyhill
FK2
SHIELDHILL RD
B810
HILLCREST SQ
Reddingrig Muir
Westquarter Burn
Wester Pirleyhill
BELMONT AVE
BELMONT AVE
PATRICK DR
CRIMOND PL
LEDI PL
Pirleyhill Bridge
SHIELDHILL VIEW
EASTON DR
GARDRUM GDNS
WALLACE VIEW
BRAES VIEW
VORLICH DR
RANNOCH PL
Shieldhill
PATERSON DR
HIGH VIEW GR
ANDERSON CRES
PARKEND CRES
HEATHER AVE
HEROHILL AVE
CRUICKSHANK DR
PIRLEYHILL DR
CROSS BRAE
GREENCRAIG AVE
ROSEMOUNT GDNS
MUIRPARK DR
PO
MAIN ST
MAVISBANK AVE
GREENMOUNT DR
BRAESIDE
CROSSHALL PL
Easter Shieldhill
CALIFORNIA RD
Greenwells
Shieldhill
Redding Muir
ELIM DR
Shieldhill Prim Sch
Burnside
ROSEHEAD TERR
CHURCH RD
MCCRAKEN CT
Polmont Burn
Wester Shieldhill Lands
PH
MARSHALL DR
California Prim Sch
Summerhouse
MAMRE DR
QUEEN'S ST
California
MAIN ST
MERVILLE CRES
EBENEZER PL
PRINCES ST
STRANG'S PL
Recn Gd
CALIFORNIA TERR
Quarryhead
MERVILLE TERR
FK1
BLACKBRAES RD
Edinburgh STREET ATLAS
Works
Gardrum
Blackbraes
Mast
Gardrum Moss
Craigmad
Grayrigg Inn (PH)
Loch Ellrig
Greyrigg Farm
Heathery Knowe
Black Briggs Farm
Mast
Resr
Boxtonrighead
Boxton Burn
Broom
BOXTON RD
Former Opencast Workings
Glen Ellrig
Greencraig Cottages

65
87

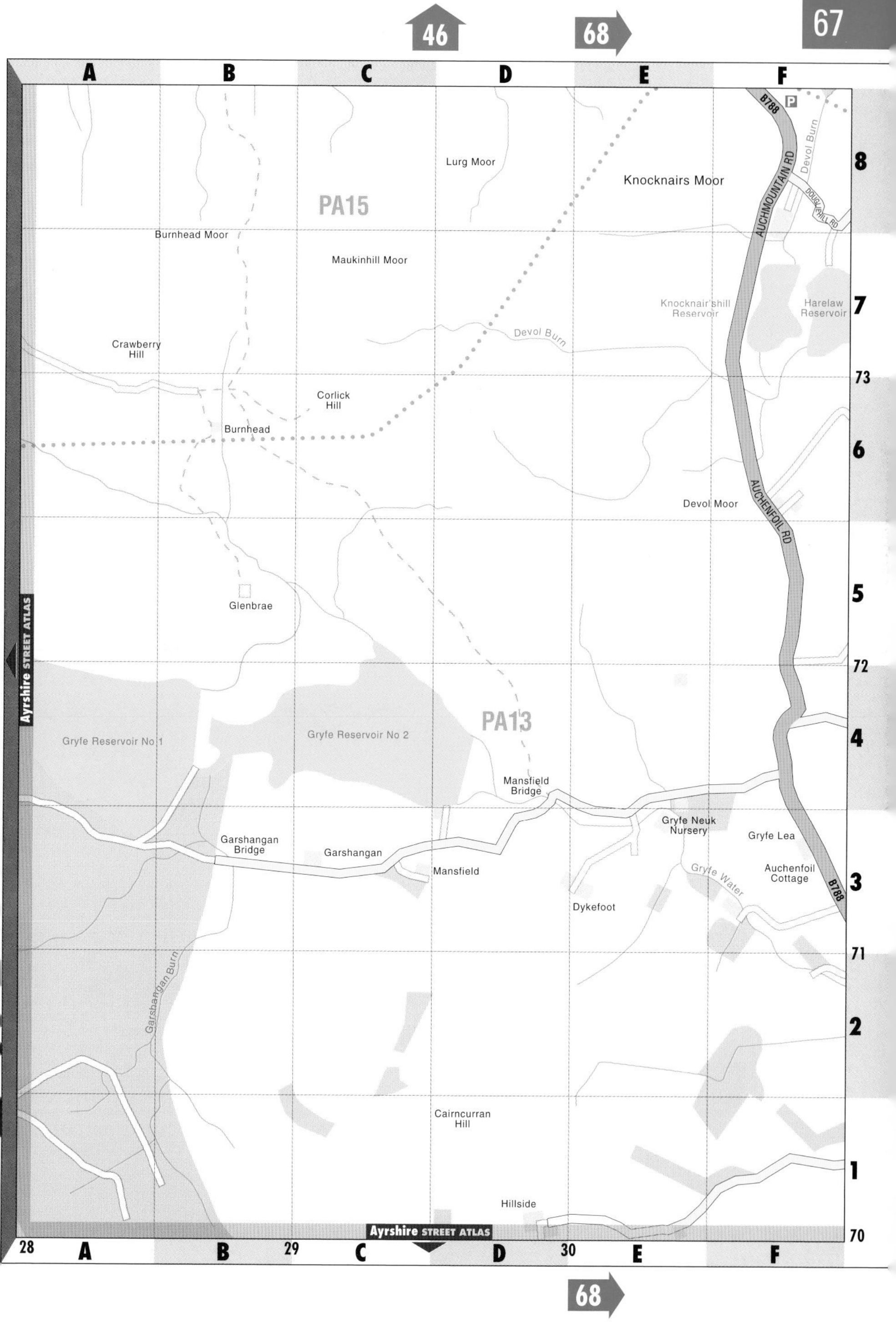
46
68
A
B
C
D
E
F
8
7
73
6
5
72
4
3
71
2
1
70
28
29
30
Lurg Moor
Knocknairs Moor
PA15
Burnhead Moor
Maukinhill Moor
B788
AUCHMOUNTAIN RD
Devol Burn
DOUGLIEHILL RD
Knocknair'shill Reservoir
Harelaw Reservoir
Crawberry Hill
Devol Burn
Corlick Hill
Burnhead
Devol Moor
AUCHENFOIL RD
Glenbrae
Ayrshire STREET ATLAS
Gryfe Reservoir No 1
Gryfe Reservoir No 2
PA13
Mansfield Bridge
Garshangan Bridge
Garshangan
Mansfield
Gryfe Neuk Nursery
Gryfe Lea
Gryfe Water
Auchenfoil Cottage
Dykefoot
Garshangan Burn
Cairncurran Hill
Hillside
Ayrshire STREET ATLAS
68

67
47

F8
1 St Michaels Prim Sch
2 Newark Prim Sch

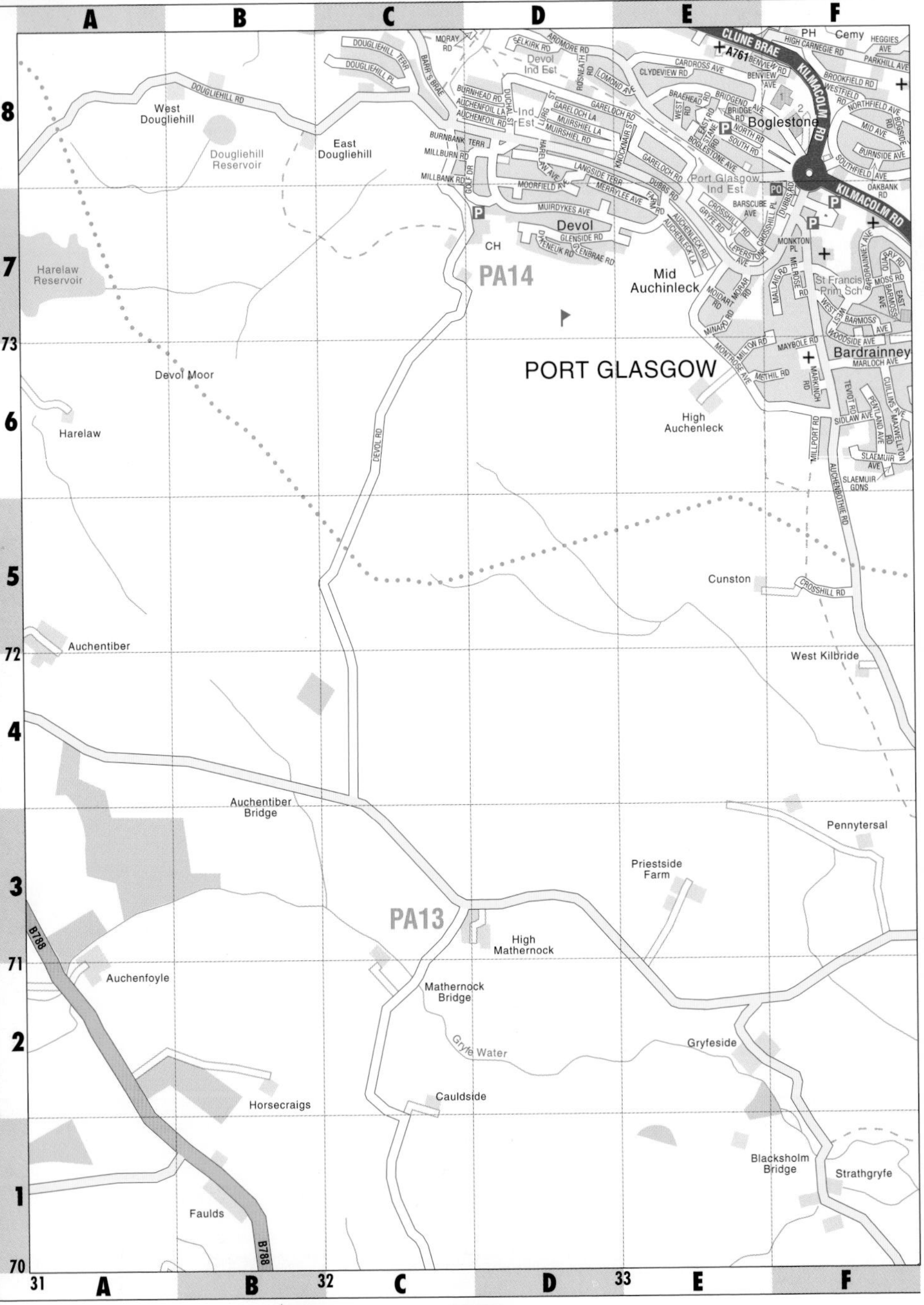

67
88

48
70

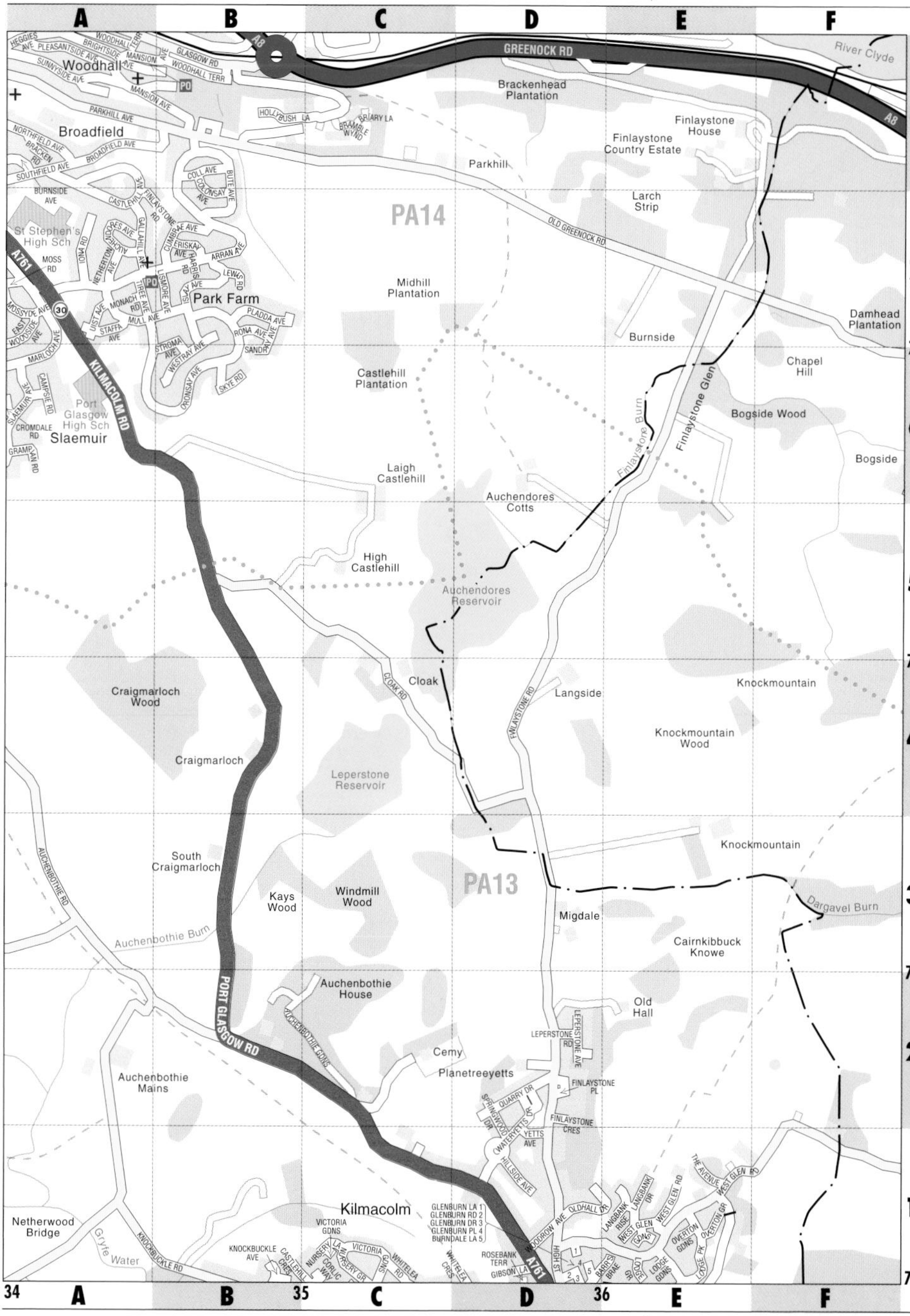
A
B
C
D
E
F
Woodhall
Broadfield
HEGGIES AVE
PLEASANTSIDE AVE
BRIGHTSIDE AVE
WOODHALL TERR
MANSION AVE
GLASGOW RD
WOODHALL TERR
SUNNYSIDE AVE
PO
MANSION AVE
PARKHILL AVE
NORTHFIELD AVE
BRACKEN RD
BROADFIELD AVE
SOUTHFIELD AVE
BURNSIDE AVE
HOLLYBUSH LA
BRIARY LA
BRAMBLE WYND
COLL AVE
COLONSAY AVE
BUTE AVE
CASTLEHILL AVE
FINLAYSTONE RD
St Stephen's High Sch
MOSS RD
IONA RD
NETHERTON AVE
GALLAHILL AVE
CUMBRAE AVE
ERISKAY AVE
HARRIS RD
ARRAN AVE
LEWIS RD
ISLAY AVE
Park Farm
PO
MONACH RD
TIREE AVE
LISMORE AVE
MULL AVE
UIST AVE
STAFFA AVE
PLADDA AVE
RONA AVE
SANDRAY AVE
STROMA AVE
WESTRAY AVE
ORONSAY AVE
SKYE RD
MOSSVIEW AVE
EAST WOODSIDE AVE
MARLOCH AVE
CAMPSIE RD
SLAEMUIR AVE
CROMDALE RD
GRAMPIAN RD
Port Glasgow High Sch
Slaemuir
A761
30
KILMACOLM RD
A8
GREENOCK RD
Brackenhead Plantation
Parkhill
PA14
Midhill Plantation
Castlehill Plantation
Laigh Castlehill
High Castlehill
Auchendores Cotts
Auchendores Reservoir
OLD GREENOCK RD
River Clyde
A8
Finlaystone House
Finlaystone Country Estate
Larch Strip
Burnside
Damhead Plantation
Chapel Hill
Bogside Wood
Bogside
Finlaystone Burn
Finlaystone Glen
8
7
73
6
5
72
4
3
71
2
1
70
Craigmarloch Wood
Craigmarloch
Cloak
CLOAK RD
Langside
FINLAYSTONE RD
Knockmountain
Knockmountain Wood
Leperstone Reservoir
Knockmountain
South Craigmarloch
Kays Wood
Windmill Wood
PA13
Migdale
Dargavel Burn
Cairnkibbuck Knowe
AUCHENBOTHIE RD
Auchenbothie Burn
Auchenbothie House
AUCHENBOTHIE GDNS
PORT GLASGOW RD
Old Hall
LEPERSTONE RD
LEPERSTONE AVE
Cemy
Planetreeyetts
FINLAYSTONE PL
QUARRY DR
SPRINGWOOD DR
YETTS DR
WATERYETTS DR
YETTS AVE
FINLAYSTONE CRES
HILLSIDE AVE
Auchenbothie Mains
Netherwood Bridge
Gryfe Water
Kilmacolm
KNOCKBUCKLE RD
KNOCKBUCKLE AVE
CASTLEHILL CRES
VICTORIA GDNS
NURSERY LA
CORLIC WAY
NURSERY GR
VICTORIA GDNS
WHITELEA RD
WHITELEA CRES
GLENBURN LA 1
GLENBURN RD 2
GLENBURN DR 3
GLENBURN PL 4
BURNDALE LA 5
ROSEBANK TERR
GIBSON LA
A761
WOODROW AVE
HIGH ST
OLDHALL DR
LANGBANK RISE
LANGBANK DR
WEST GLEN GDNS
WEST GLEN RD
BARRS BRAE
LODGE GR
LODGE GDNS
LODGE PK
OVERTON GDNS
OVERTON GR
THE AVENUE
WEST GLEN RD
34
A
B
35
C
D
36
E
F

89
70

69
49

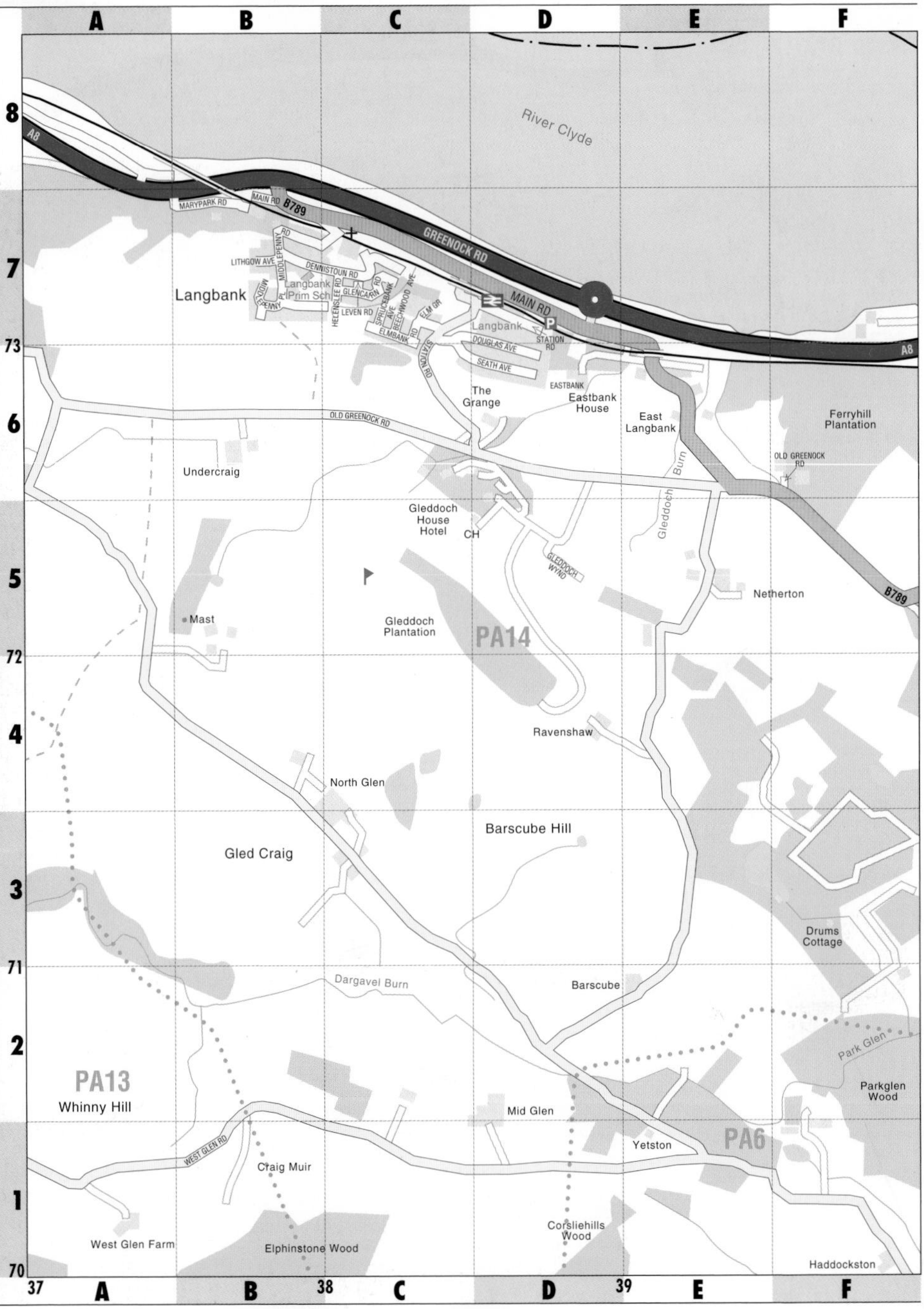
River Clyde
A8
GREENOCK RD
B789
MARYPARK RD
MAIN RD
LITHGOW AVE
MIDDLEPENNY RD
DENNISTOUN RD
Langbank
Langbank Prim Sch
GLENCAIRN RD
HELENSLEE RD
SPRUCEBANK AVE
BEECHWOOD AVE
LEVEN RD
ELM GR
ELMBANK RD
STATION RD
DOUGLAS AVE
SEATH AVE
EASTBANK
Eastbank House
The Grange
East Langbank
Ferryhill Plantation
OLD GREENOCK RD
Undercraig
Gleddoch Burn
Gleddoch House Hotel
CH
GLEDDOCH WYND
Netherton
Mast
Gleddoch Plantation
PA14
Ravenshaw
North Glen
Barscube Hill
Gled Craig
Drums Cottage
Dargavel Burn
Barscube
Park Glen
Parkglen Wood
PA13
Whinny Hill
Mid Glen
Yetston
PA6
WEST GLEN RD
Craig Muir
Corsliehills Wood
West Glen Farm
Elphinstone Wood
Haddockston
A
B
C
D
E
F
8
7
73
6
5
72
4
3
71
2
1
70
37
38
39

69
90

50
72

A
B
C
D
E
F
G82
Milton Island
River Clyde
Inner Clyde
Nature Reserve
Longhaugh
Point
M8
31
Fornet Cottage
A8
Ferryhill
Plantation
Convent
High
Hatton
Laigh
Hatton
Lodge
Cora
Campus
GREENOCK RD
OLD GREENOCK RD
B789
Lodge
PA14
Slateford
CHESTNUT AVE
Whitemoss Dam
Bishopton Tunnels
KINGSWOOD RD
LYLE CRES
PA7
Ingliston
House
Mast
Drums
Castlehill
Cottage
Whitemoss
NEWTON RD 1
CROSSGATES 2
WEST PORTON PL 3
WRAISLAND CRES 4
Cemy
HAMILTON CRES
INGLISTON DR
Ingliston
Easter Newton
Barbeg Hill
Formakin
Barmore Hill
Paddockcraig
Gatehead
Formakin
Estate
P
Parkglen Wood
Nether Mill
West
Glenshinnoch
Meiklefield
BAROCHAN RD
Dargavel Burn
B789
REILLY RD
PA6
8
7
73
6
5
72
4
3
71
2
1
70
40
41
42

91
72

71
51
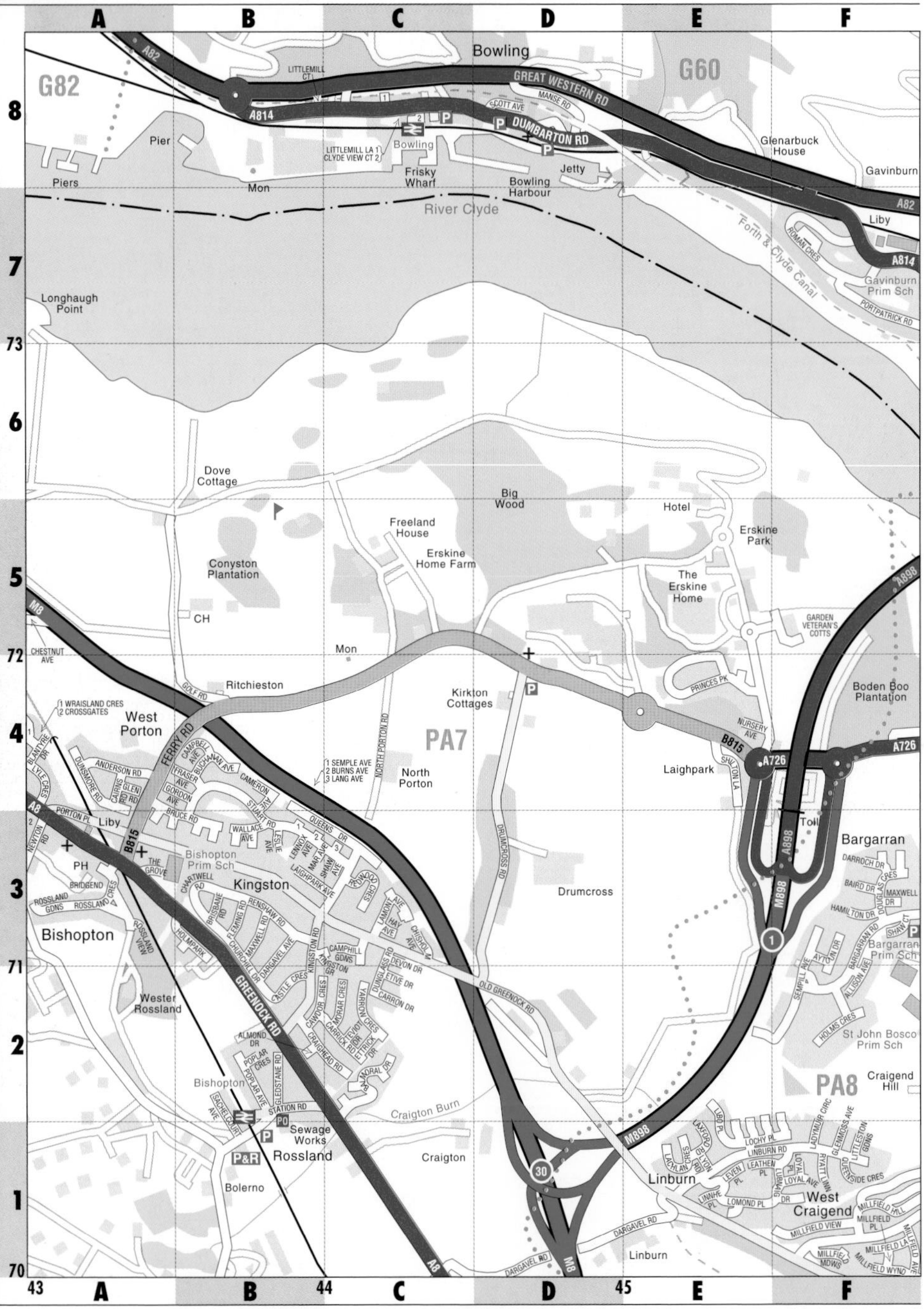
A
B
C
D
E
F
8
7
73
6
5
72
4
3
71
2
1
70
43
44
45
Bowling
G82
G60
A82
GREAT WESTERN RD
A814
DUMBARTON RD
LITTLEMILL CT
MANSE RD
SCOTT AVE
LITTLEMILL LA 1
CLYDE VIEW CT 2
Pier
Piers
Mon
Frisky Wharf
Bowling Harbour
Jetty
Glenarbuck House
Gavinburn
River Clyde
Liby
ROMAN CRES
Forth & Clyde Canal
Gavinburn Prim Sch
PORTPATRICK RD
Longhaugh Point
Dove Cottage
Big Wood
Hotel
Erskine Park
Freeland House
Erskine Home Farm
Conyston Plantation
The Erskine Home
GARDEN VETERAN'S COTTS
A898
M8
CH
CHESTNUT AVE
Mon
Ritchieston
Kirkton Cottages
PRINCES PK
NURSERY AVE
Boden Boo Plantation
1 WRAISLAND CRES
2 CROSSGATES
West Porton
GOLF RD
FERRY RD
PA7
B815
A726
Laighpark
SHILTON LA
1 SEMPLE AVE
2 BURNS AVE
3 LANG AVE
NORTH PORTON RD
North Porton
BLANTYRE DR
LYLE CRES
DUNSMORE RD
ANDERSON RD
CAIRNS RD
GLEN RD
CAMPBELL AVE
BUCHANAN AVE
FRASER AVE
GORDON AVE
CAMERON
STUART RD
A8
PORTON PL
Liby
BRUCE RD
WALLACE AVE
LESLIE AVE
LENNOX AVE
MAR AVE
SHAW AVE
QUEENS DR
LAIGHPARK AVE
REDWOOD CRES
Toll
Bargarran
NEWTON RD
PH
THE GROVE
Bishopton Prim Sch
CHARTWELL RD
Kingston
Drumcross
DRUMCROSS RD
DARROCH DR
BAIRD DR
DOUGLAS CRES
MAXWELL DR
HAMILTON DR
M898
BRIDGEND
ROSSLAND GDNS
ROSSLAND CRES
Bishopton
ROSSLAND VIEW
BRISBANE RD
FLEMING RD
RENSHAW RD
LAMONT AVE
HAY AVE
CHISHOLM
HOLMPARK
CHURCHILL DR
MAXWELL DR
DARGAVEL AVE
KINGSTON RD
CAMPHILL GDNS
KINGSTON GR
DUNGLASS RD
DEVON DR
ETIVE DR
CARRON DR
OLD GREENOCK RD
SEMPILL AVE
AYTOUN DR
BARGARRAN RD
ALLISON AVE
SHAW CT
Bargarran Prim Sch
Wester Rossland
CASTLE CRES
CAWDOR CRES
MOIDART CRES
YARROW CRES
HOLMS CRES
St John Bosco Prim Sch
GREENOCK RD
ALMOND DR
CARRICK RD
TEVIOT DR
ETTRICK DR
CRAIGHEAD RD
POPLAR CRES
POPLAR AVE
GLEDSTANE RD
BALMORAL DR
PA8
Craigend Hill
Bishopton
SACHELCOURT AVE
STATION RD
PO
Sewage Works
Craigton Burn
Rossland
Craigton
P&R
30
LOCHY PL
LINBURN RD
LAXFORD RD
LYON RD
LACHLAN CRES
LEVEN PL
LEATHEN PL
LUBNAIG
LOYAL AVE
RYATT LINN
LADYMUIR CIRC
GLENMOSS AVE
LITTLESTON GDNS
QUEENSIDE CRES
Linburn
LINNHE PL
LOMOND PL
West Craigend
MILLFIELD HILL
MILLFIELD PL
MILLFIELD VIEW
Bolerno
DARGAVEL RD
Linburn
MILLFIELD LA
MILLFIELD MDWS
MILLFIELD WYND
MILLFIELD AVE
1
71
92

52
74

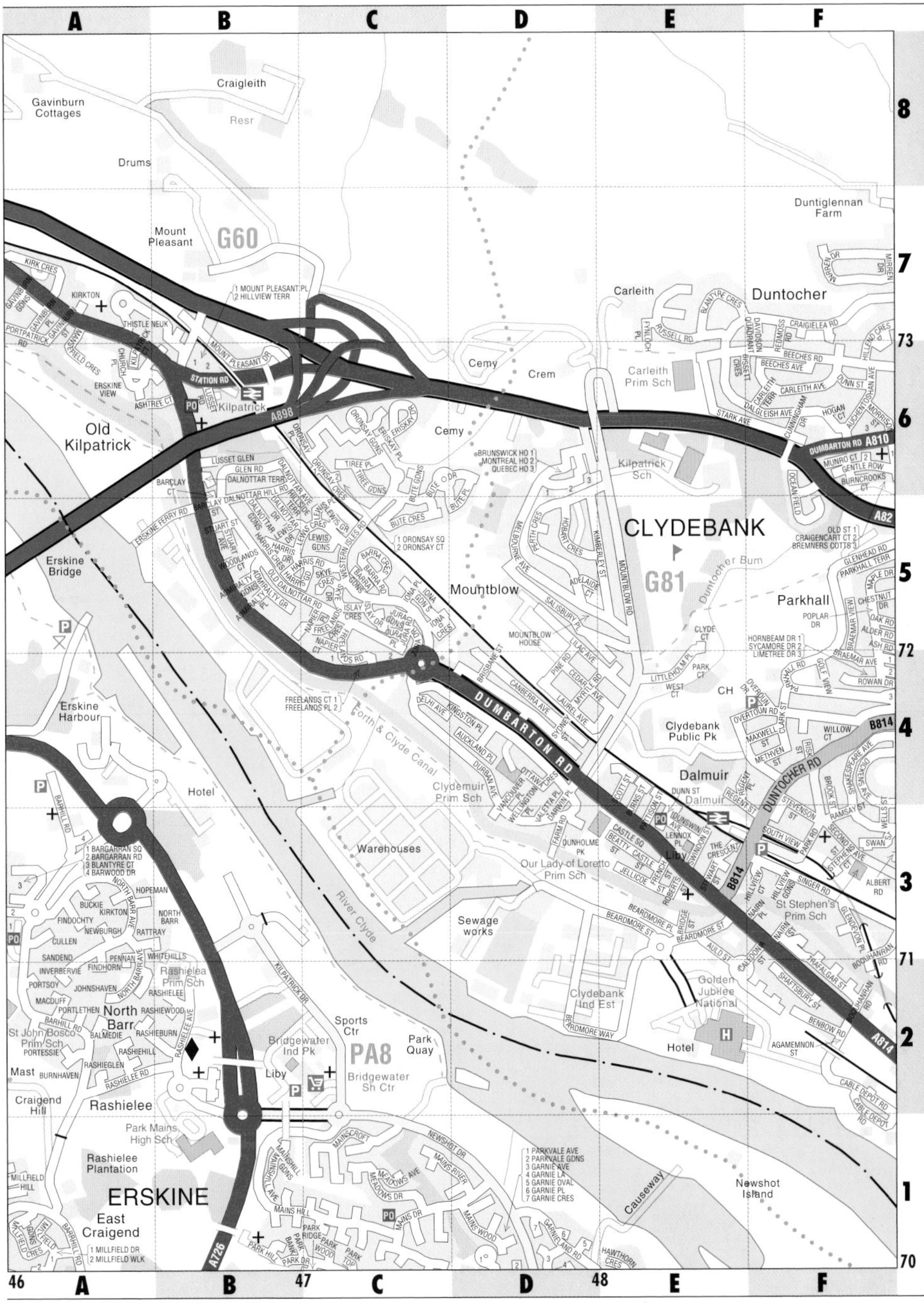
A
B
C
D
E
F
8
7
73
6
5
72
4
3
71
2
1
70
46
47
48
Craigleith
Resr
Gavinburn
Cottages
Drums
Mount
Pleasant
G60
Duntiglennan
Farm
Carleith
Duntocher
Kirkton
Old
Kilpatrick
Kilpatrick
STATION RD
A898
Cemy
Crem
Carleith
Prim Sch
Kilpatrick
Sch
CLYDEBANK
G81
Duntocher Burn
Parkhall
Mountblow
MOUNTBLOW HOUSE
DUMBARTON RD
A810
A82
B814
DUNTOCHER RD
Erskine
Bridge
Erskine
Harbour
Hotel
Forth & Clyde Canal
Clydemuir
Prim Sch
Warehouses
Clydebank
Public Pk
Dalmuir
Our Lady of Loretto
Prim Sch
St Stephen's
Prim Sch
Sewage
works
River Clyde
Clydebank
Ind Est
Golden
Jubilee
National
Hotel
A814
North
Barr
Rashielea
Prim Sch
St John Bosco
Prim Sch
Mast
Craigend
Hill
Rashielee
Park Mains
High Sch
Rashielee
Plantation
ERSKINE
East
Craigend
Bridgewater
Ind Pk
PA8
Sports
Ctr
Park
Quay
Liby
Bridgewater
Sh Ctr
Causeway
Newshot
Island
A726
1 MOUNT PLEASANT PL
2 HILLVIEW TERR
1 ORONSAY SQ
2 ORONSAY CT
BRUNSWICK HO 1
MONTREAL HO 2
QUEBEC HO 3
FREELANDS CT 1
FREELANDS PL 2
1 BARGARRAN SQ
2 BARGARRAN RD
3 BLANTYRE CT
4 BARWOOD DR
1 PARKVALE AVE
2 PARKVALE GDNS
3 GARNIE AVE
4 GARNIE LA
5 GARNIE OVAL
6 GARNIE PL
7 GARNIE CRES
1 MILLFIELD DR
2 MILLFIELD WLK
OLD ST 1
CRAIGENCART CT 2
BREMNERS COTTS 3
HORNBEAM DR 1
SYCAMORE DR 2
LIMETREE DR 3

93
74

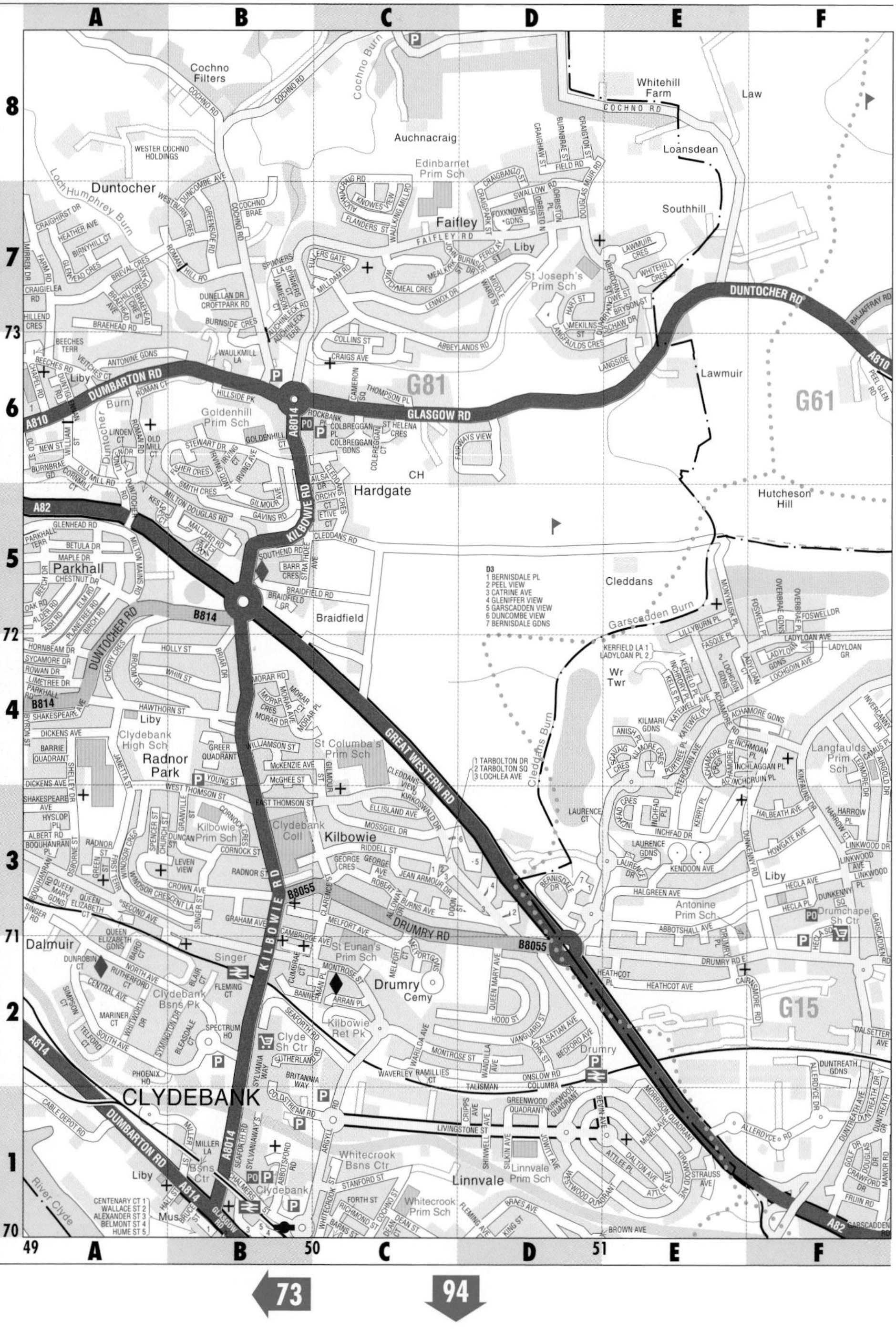
A B C D E F
8 7 6 5 4 3 2 1
73 72 71 70
49 50 51
Cochno Filters
WESTER COCHNO HOLDINGS
Duntocher
Auchnacraig
Edinbarnet Prim Sch
Faifley
Whitehill Farm
Law
Loansdean
Southhill
COCHNO RD
DUNTOCHER RD
St Joseph's Prim Sch
Liby
G81
G61
Lawmuir
DUMBARTON RD
GLASGOW RD
A810
A8014
Goldenhill Prim Sch
Hardgate
CH
Hutcheson Hill
A82
KILBOWIE RD
Parkhall
Cleddans
Braidfield
B814
D3
1 BERNISDALE PL
2 PEEL VIEW
3 CATRINE AVE
4 GLENIFFER VIEW
5 GARSCADDEN VIEW
6 DUNCOMBE VIEW
7 BERNISDALE GDNS
Garscadden Burn
KERFIELD LA 1
LADYLOAN PL 2
Wr Twr
GREAT WESTERN RD
Clydebank High Sch
Radnor Park
St Columba's Prim Sch
Langfaulds Prim Sch
1 TARBOLTON DR
2 TARBOLTON SQ
3 LOCHLEA AVE
Cleddans Burn
Kilbowie Prim Sch
Clydebank Coll
Kilbowie
Antonine Prim Sch
Drumchapel Sh Ctr
B8055
DRUMRY RD
Dalmuir
Singer
St Eunan's Prim Sch
Drumry Cemy
Clydebank Bsns Pk
Kilbowie Ret Pk
G15
Clyde Sh Ctr
Drumry
A814
CLYDEBANK
Whitecrook Bsns Ctr
Linnvale
Linnvale Prim Sch
Whitecrook Prim Sch
Bsns Ctr
Clydebank
Mus
River Clyde
CENTENARY CT 1
WALLACE ST 2
ALEXANDER ST 3
BELMONT ST 4
HUME ST 5
A82

54
76

E5
1 DOUGLAS PL
2 KIRK LA
3 JEDWORTH CT
4 THE LOANING

B3
1 KINCLAVEN PL
2 KINCLAVEN GDNS
3 MERRYTON GDNS
4 LINKWOOD GR
5 SOUTHDEEN GR

95
76

F3
1 PINEWOOD
2 CANNIESBURN TOLL
3 KILLERMONT RD
4 SECOND AVE 5
5 MACFARLANE RD
6 CARRICKARDEN RD
7 BEECHWOOD LA
8 DRYMEN RD

75
55

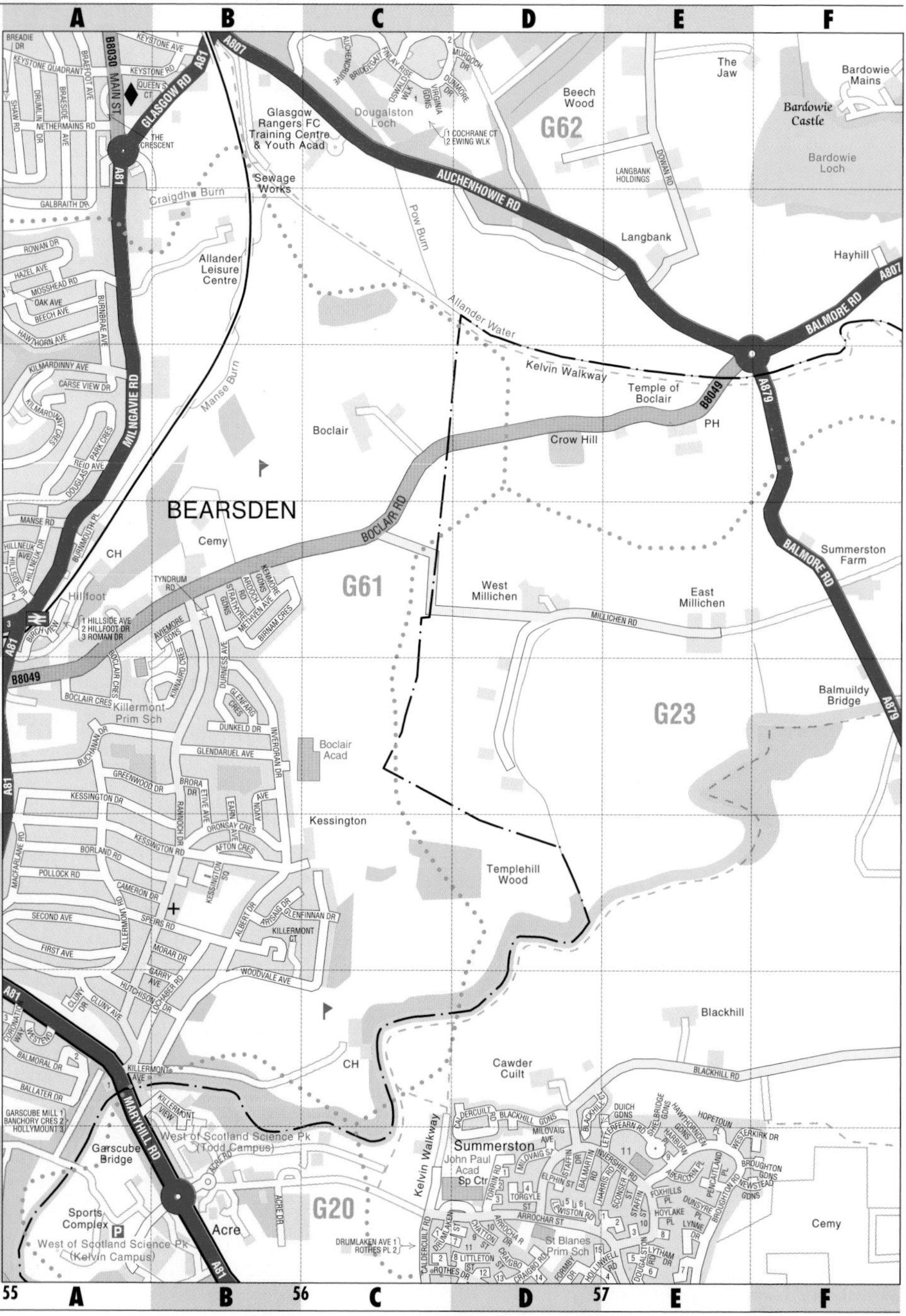

75
96

D1
1 CARNOCH ST
2 ARDESSIE ST
3 GEARY ST
4 CARBOST ST
5 LEWISTON DR
6 LEWISTON PL
7 DRUMLAKEN CT
8 LITTLETON DR
9 DRUMLAKEN PL
10 ARROCHAR PATH
11 DRUMLAKEN PATH
12 MULLARDOCH ST
13 CRAIGBO DR
14 CRAIGBO AVE
15 GLENBERVIE PL

E1
1 FORRES ST
2 TOLSTA ST
3 GALLAN AVE
4 LINDRICK DR
5 WENTWORTH DR
6 MUIRFIELD CRES
7 CROSSFORD DR
8 CROSSPOINT DR
9 NEWCASTLETON DR
10 STAFFIN PATH
11 Caldercuilt Prim Sch

56
78

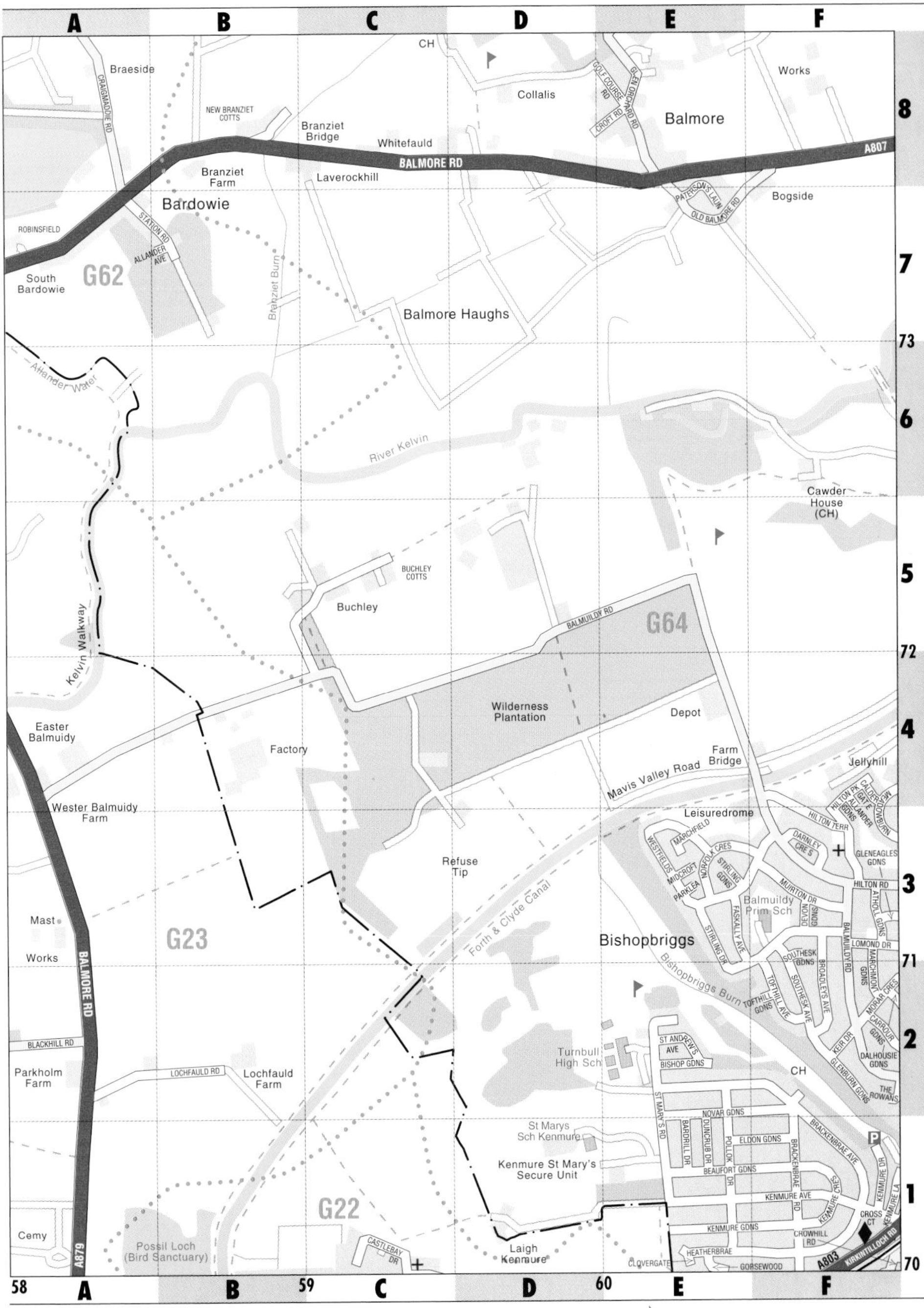
A
B
C
D
E
F
CH
Braeside
CRAIGMADDIE RD
NEW BRANZIET COTTS
Branziet Bridge
Whitefauld
Collalis
GOLF COURSE RD
GLEN ORCHARD RD
CROFT RD
Balmore
Works
BALMORE RD
A807
Branziet Farm
Laverockhill
Bardowie
ROBINSFIELD
STATION RD
ALLANDER AVE
G62
South Bardowie
Branziet Burn
PATERSON'S LAW
OLD BALMORE RD
Bogside
Balmore Haughs
Allander Water
River Kelvin
Cawder House (CH)
BUCHLEY COTTS
Buchley
BALMUILDY RD
G64
Kelvin Walkway
Wilderness Plantation
Depot
Easter Balmuidy
Factory
Farm Bridge
Mavis Valley Road
Jellyhill
Wester Balmuidy Farm
Leisuredrome
HILTON TERR
DARNLEY CRES
MARCHFIELD
WESTFIELDS
MIDCROFT
PARKLEA
NORFOLK CRES
STIRLING GDNS
Refuse Tip
GLENEAGLES GDNS
HILTON RD
MUIRTON DR
ATHOLL GDNS
Balmuildy Prim Sch
FASKALLY AVE
STIRLING DR
Mast
G23
Forth & Clyde Canal
Bishopbriggs
LOMOND DR
Works
BALMORE RD
SOUTHESK GDNS
BROADLEYS AVE
Bishopbriggs Burn
TOFTHILL GDNS
TOFTHILL AVE
SOUTHESK AVE
BALMUILDY RD
MARCHMONT GDNS
MORAR CRES
CARROUR GDNS
KEIR DR
BLACKHILL RD
ST ANDREWS AVE
BISHOP GDNS
Turnbull High Sch
DALHOUSIE GDNS
Parkholm Farm
LOCHFAULD RD
Lochfauld Farm
CH
GLENBURN GDNS
THE ROWANS
ST MARY'S RD
NOVAR GDNS
BARDRILL DR
DUNCRUB DR
POLLOK DR
ELDON GDNS
BRACKENBRAE AVE
St Marys Sch Kenmure
BEAUFORT GDNS
BRACKENBRAE RD
Kenmure St Mary's Secure Unit
KENMURE AVE
KENMURE CRES
KENMURE DR
G22
CROSS CT
KENMURE GDNS
CROWHILL RD
Cemy
A879
Possil Loch (Bird Sanctuary)
CASTLEBAY DR
Laigh Kenmure
CLOVERGATE
HEATHERBRAE
GORSEWOOD
A803
KIRKINTILLOCH RD
8
7
73
6
5
72
4
3
71
2
1
70
58
59
60

97
78

77
57

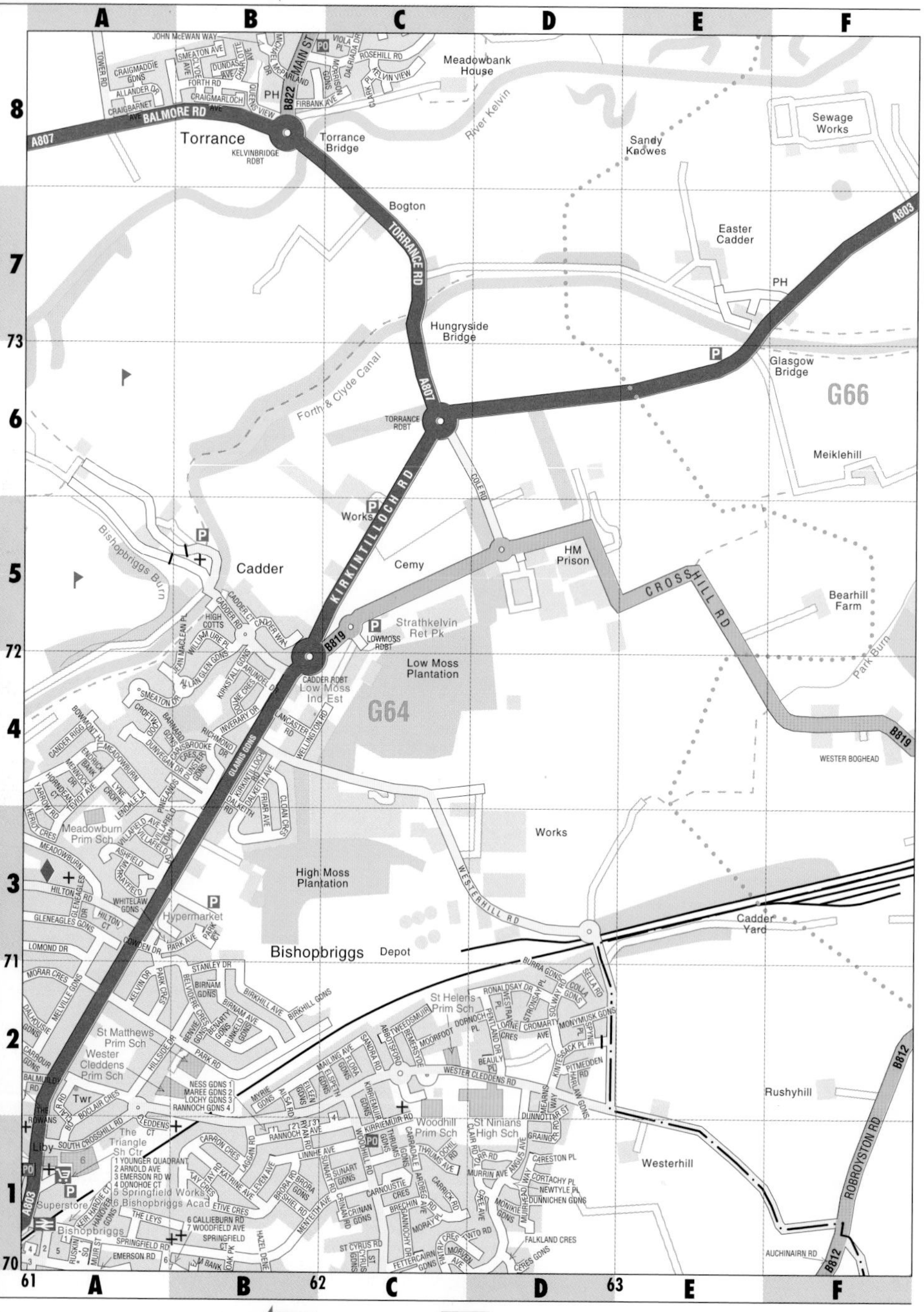
A
B
C
D
E
F
8
7
73
6
5
72
4
3
71
2
1
70
61
62
63
JOHN McEWAN WAY
TOWER RD
CRAIGMADDIE GDNS
ALLANDER DR
CRAIGBARNET AVE
SMEATON AVE
CLYDE AVE
DUNDAS AVE
CHARLOTTE AVE
FORTH RD
CRAIGMARLOCH AVE
QUEENS VIEW
MICHAEL McPARLAND DR
B822
MAIN ST
PO
VIOLA PL
DALRIADA DR
MORRISON GDNS
ROSEHILL RD
KELVIN VIEW
CLARK PL
FIRBANK AVE
PH
BALMORE RD
A807
Torrance
KELVINBRIDGE RDBT
Torrance Bridge
Meadowbank House
River Kelvin
Sandy Knowes
Sewage Works
Bogton
TORRANCE RD
Easter Cadder
A803
PH
Hungryside Bridge
P
Glasgow Bridge
G66
Forth & Clyde Canal
TORRANCE RDBT
Meiklehill
KIRKINTILLOCH RD
COLE RD
P
Works
Bishopbriggs Burn
P
Cadder
Cemy
HM Prison
CROSSHILL RD
Bearhill Farm
Strathkelvin Ret Pk
LOWMOSS RDBT
B819
HIGH COTTS
CADDER RD
CADDER CT
CADDER WAY
WILLIAM URE PL
JEAN MACLEAN PL
ALLAN GLEN GDNS
KIRKSTALL GDNS
ARUNDEL DR
SMEATON DR
CADDER RDBT
Low Moss Ind Est
Low Moss Plantation
Park Burn
G64
B819
WESTER BOGHEAD
CROFTWOOD
BARNARD GDNS
CARISBROOKE CRES
DUNVEGAN DR
DUNVEGAN QUAD
RICHMOND GDNS
INVERARY DR
DOUNE CRES
LANCASTER RD
WELLINGTON RD
GLAMIS GDNS
KIRKINTILLOCH RD
DALKEITH AVE
DALKEITH RD
FRIAR AVE
CLOAN CRES
BOWMONT HILL
CANDER RIGG
ENDRICK BANK
MEADOWBURN
MENNOCK DR
HORNDEAN CT
YARROW RD
TEVIOT AVE
LYNE CROFT
LENDALE LA
PINELANDS
HILLFOOT DR
VILLAFIELD AVE
VILLAFIELD LOAN
HERIOT CRES
Meadowburn Prim Sch
ASHFIELD
MAYFIELD
RAYFIELD
MEADOWBURN
Works
WESTERHILL RD
High Moss Plantation
HILTON RD
GLENEAGLES LA
WHITELAW GDNS
HILTON CT
GLENEAGLES GDNS
P
Hypermarket
PARK AVE
PARK CT
COWDEN DR
LOMOND DR
Bishopbriggs
Depot
Cadder Yard
MORAR CRES
MELVILLE GDNS
KELVIN DR
PARK CRES
STANLEY DR
BIRNAM GDNS
BIRNAM AVE
BIRKHILL AVE
BIRKHILL GDNS
BURRA GDNS
COLLA GDNS
SELLA RD
RONALDSAY DR
STRONSAY PL
SOLWAY RD
St Helens Prim Sch
DALHOUSIE GDNS
BELVIDERE CRES
BENVIE GDNS
BENARTY GDNS
DUNKELD GDNS
TWEEDSMUIR
ABBOTSFORD
BEMERSYDE
MOORFOOT
DORNOCH PL
WESTRAY CIRC
LORNE CRES
CROMARTY AVE
MONYMUSK GDNS
SPYNIE PL
KINTESSACK PL
PENTLAND DR
BEAULY PL
St Matthews Prim Sch
Wester Cleddens Prim Sch
CARROUR GDNS
HILLSIDE DR
PARK RD
MAILING AVE
SANDRA RD
FLORA GDNS
ELSPETH GDNS
EILEEN GDNS
MYRIE GDNS
AILSA RD
WESTER CLEDDENS RD
PITMEDDEN RD
HARLAW GDNS
MEARNS WAY
B812
Rushyhill
BALMUILDY RD
Twr
BOCLAIR CRES
THE ROWANS
SOUTH CROSSHILL RD
CLEDDENS CT
NESS GDNS 1
MAREE GDNS 2
LOCHY GDNS 3
RANNOCH GDNS 4
RANNOCH AVE
RYAN RD
KIRRIEMUIR GDNS
KIRRIEMUIR RD
KIRRIEMUIR AVE
WOODHILL RD
Woodhill Prim Sch
St Ninians High Sch
DUNNOTTAR ST
GRAINGER RD
The Triangle Sh Ctr
1 YOUNGER QUADRANT
2 ARNOLD AVE
3 EMERSON RD W
4 DONOHOE CT
5 Springfield Works
6 Bishopbriggs Acad
CARRON CRES
LAGGAN RD
LINNHE AVE
SUNART RD
SUNART GDNS
THRUMS GDNS
CARRADALE GDNS
THRUMS AVE
OCHIL RD
CLAIR RD
TOBAR RD
MURRIN AVE
ANGUS AVE
CARESTON PL
CORTACHY PL
NEWTYLE PL
DUNNICHEN GDNS
Westerhill
Liby
PO
P
Superstore
A803
KATRINE AVE
TAY CRES
LEVEN AVE
BRORA RD
BRORA GDNS
SHIEL RD
ETIVE CRES
MENTEITH AVE
CRINAN RD
CRINAN GDNS
CARNOUSTIE CRES
ARDBEG AVE
CARRICK RD
BRECHIN RD
BANNOCHY DR
MORAY PL
MONIKIE GDNS
MUIRHEAD WAY
ROBROYSTON RD
KEIR HARDIE CT
HANOVER GDNS
Bishopbriggs
THE LEYS
6 CALLIEBURN RD
7 WOODFIELD AVE
SPRINGFIELD CT
SPRINGFIELD RD
RUSKIN SQ
MUIR ST
EMERSON RD
HAZEL DENE
OAK PK
ELM BANK
ST CYRUS RD
ST CYRUS GDNS
FETTERCAIRN GDNS
FINTRY CRES
MORVEN AVE
ANTO RD
FALKLAND CRES
CERES GDNS
AUCHINAIRN RD
B812

77
98

C8
1 YORK PL
2 Regent Sh Ctr
3 BROADCROFT
4 ROCHDALE PL
5 Lairdsland Prim Sch

58

D8
1 GLENVIEW
2 PETER D.STIRLING RD
3 GLENBURN CT
4 STRATHALLAN GDNS
5 BROOMFIELD WLK
6 BELMONT CT

80

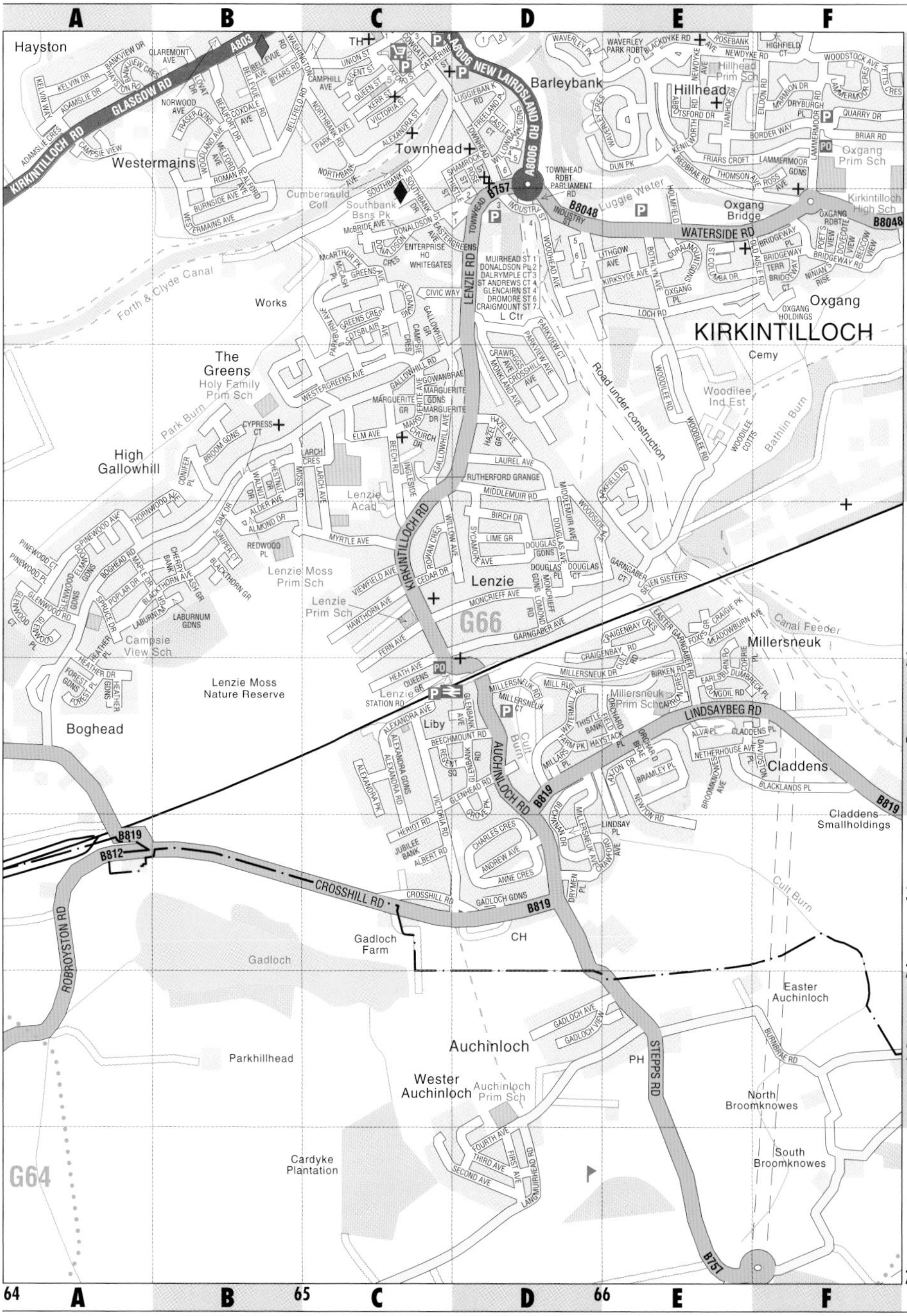

99
80

79
59

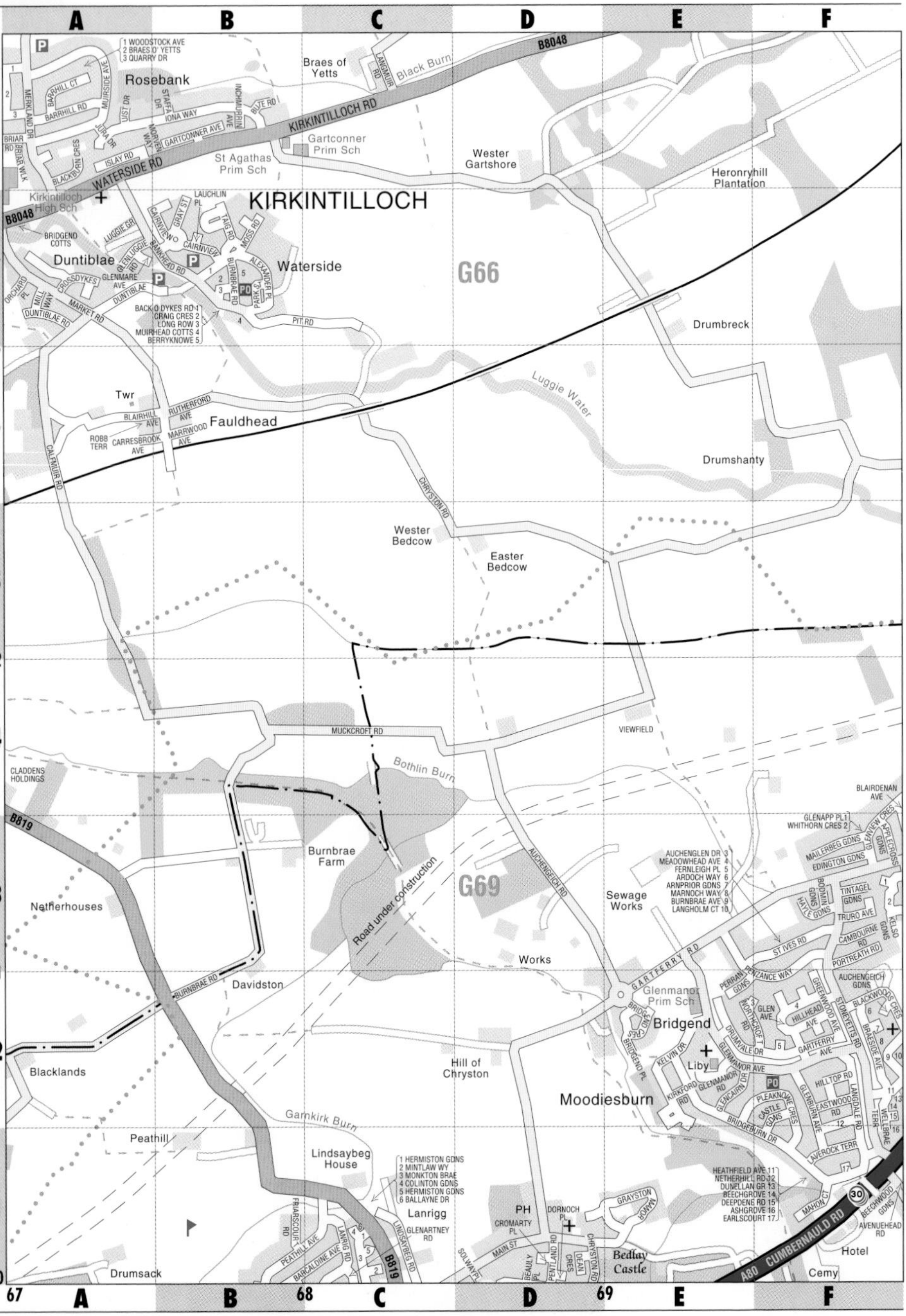
A
B
C
D
E
F
8
7
73
6
5
72
4
3
71
2
1
70
67
68
69
Rosebank
1 WOODSTOCK AVE
2 BRAES O' YETTS
3 QUARRY DR
Braes of Yetts
Black Burn
B8048
KIRKINTILLOCH RD
WATERSIDE RD
Gartconner Prim Sch
St Agathas Prim Sch
Wester Gartshore
Heronryhill Plantation
KIRKINTILLOCH
Kirkintilloch High Sch
BRIDGEND COTTS
Duntiblae
Waterside
G66
BACK O DYKES RD 1
CRAIG CRES 2
LONG ROW 3
MUIRHEAD COTTS 4
BERRYKNOWE 5
PIT RD
Drumbreck
Luggie Water
Twr
Fauldhead
Drumshanty
CHRYSTON RD
Wester Bedcow
Easter Bedcow
MUCKCROFT RD
VIEWFIELD
CLADDENS HOLDINGS
Bothlin Burn
B819
Burnbrae Farm
Road under construction
G69
AUCHENGEICH RD
Sewage Works
Netherhouses
Works
BURNBRAE RD
Davidston
GARTFERRY RD
Glenmanor Prim Sch
Bridgend
Blacklands
Hill of Chryston
Liby
Moodiesburn
Garnkirk Burn
Peathill
Lindsaybeg House
1 HERMISTON GDNS
2 MINTLAW WY
3 MONKTON BRAE
4 COLINTON GDNS
5 HERMISTON GDNS
6 BALLAYNE DR
Lanrigg
PH
AUCHENGLEN DR 3
MEADOWHEAD AVE 4
FERNLEIGH PL 5
ARDOCH WAY 6
ARNPRIOR GDNS 7
MARNOCH WAY 8
BURNBRAE AVE 9
LANGHOLM CT 10
GLENAPP PL 1
WHITHORN CRES 2
HEATHFIELD AVE 11
NETHERHILL RD 12
DUNELLAN GR 13
BEECHGROVE 14
DEEPDENE RD 15
ASHGROVE 16
EARLSCOURT 17
Bedlay Castle
A80 CUMBERNAULD RD
30
Hotel
Cemy
Drumsack

79
100

60
82
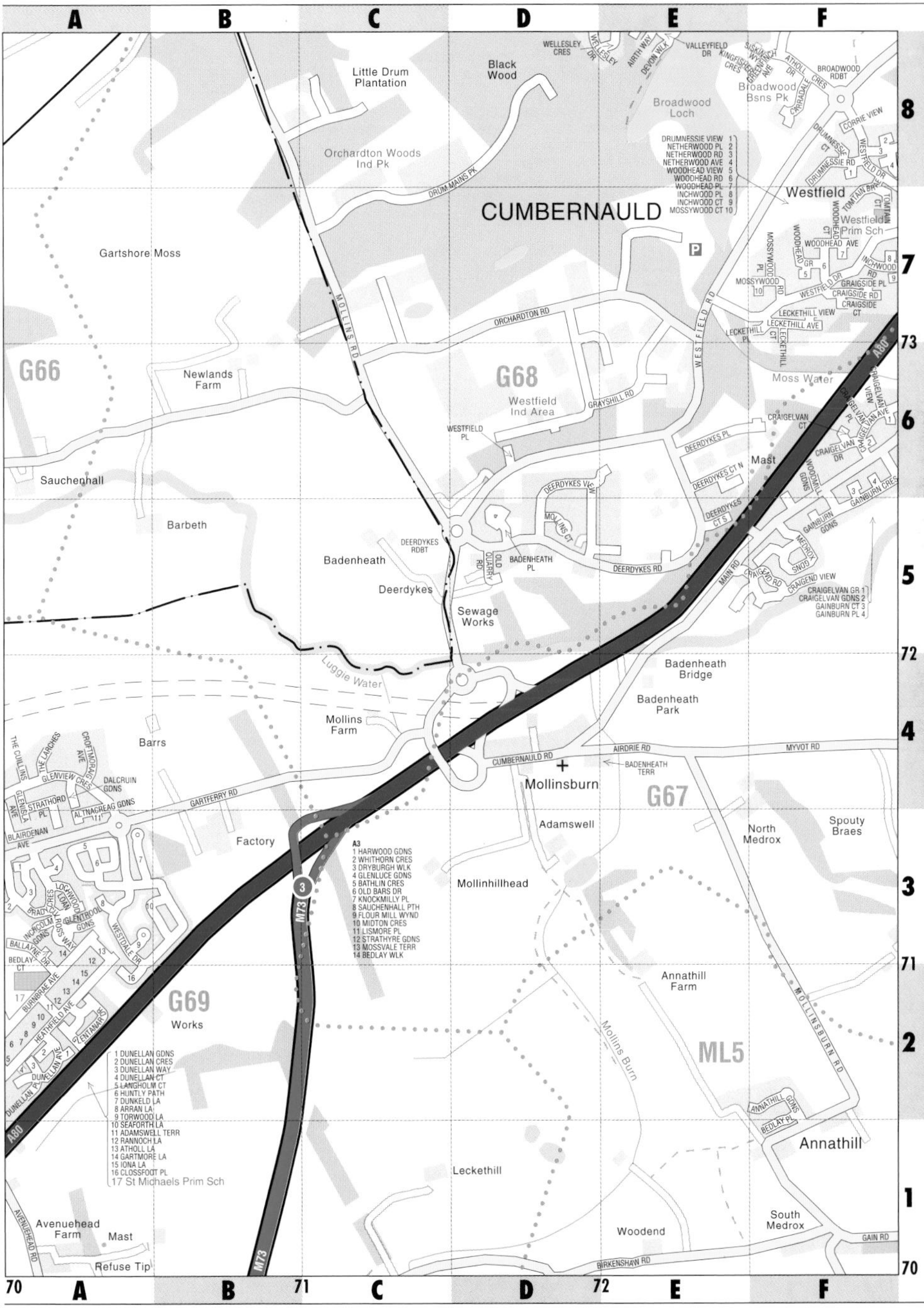
A B C D E F
8 7 6 5 4 3 2 1
73 72 71 70
70 71 72
CUMBERNAULD
G66
G68
G67
G69
ML5
Little Drum Plantation
Black Wood
Orchardton Woods Ind Pk
DRUM MAINS PK
Broadwood Loch
Broadwood Bsns Pk
WELLESLEY CRES
WELLESLEY DR
AIRTH WAY
DEVON WLK
VALLEYFIELD DR
KINGFISHER CRES
SISKIN
GREENFINCH AVE
ATHOLL CRES
BROADWOOD RDBT
CORRIE VIEW
CRRADALE
DRUMNESSIE VIEW 1
NETHERWOOD PL 2
NETHERWOOD RD 3
NETHERWOOD AVE 4
WOODHEAD VIEW 5
WOODHEAD RD 6
WOODHEAD PL 7
INCHWOOD PL 8
INCHWOOD CT 9
MOSSYWOOD CT 10
Westfield
Westfield Prim Sch
TOMTAIN BRAE
WESTFIELD DR
DRUMNESSIE RD
DRUMNESSIE CT
WOODHEAD AVE
WOODHEAD CT
WOODHEAD GR
MOSSYWOOD PL
MOSSYWOOD RD
INCHWOOD RD
WESTFIELD DR
GRAIGSIDE PL
CRAIGSIDE RD
CRAIGSIDE CT
LECKETHILL VIEW
LECKETHILL AVE
LECKETHILL PL
LECKETHILL CT
Gartshore Moss
MOLLINS RD
ORCHARDTON RD
WESTFIELD RD
Newlands Farm
Westfield Ind Area
GRAYSHILL RD
WESTFIELD PL
Moss Water
A80
CRAIGELVAN VIEW
CRAIGELVAN PL
CRAIGELVAN AVE
CRAIGELVAN CT
CRAIGELVAN DR
DEERDYKES PL
DEERDYKES CT N
DEERDYKES CT S
Mast
Sauchenhall
Barbeth
DEERDYKES VIEW
MOLLINS CT
DEERDYKES RDBT
OLD QUARRY RD
BADENHEATH PL
DEERDYKES RD
Badenheath
Deerdykes
Sewage Works
WOODMILL GDNS
GAINBURN CRES
GAINBURN GDNS
METHROX
MAIN RD
CRAIGEND RD
CRAIGEND VIEW
CRAIGELVAN GR 1
CRAIGELVAN GDNS 2
GAINBURN CT 3
GAINBURN PL 4
Luggie Water
Badenheath Bridge
Badenheath Park
Mollins Farm
Barrs
AIRDRIE RD
MYVOT RD
CUMBERNAULD RD
BADENHEATH TERR
Mollinsburn
THE CUILLINS
THE LARCHES
CROFTMORAIG AVE
GLENVIEW CRES
DALCRUIN GDNS
STRATHORD PL
GLENISLA AVE
ALTNACREAG GDNS
GARTFERRY RD
BLAIRDENAN AVE
Factory
Adamswell
North Medrox
Spouty Braes
A3
1 HARWOOD GDNS
2 WHITHORN CRES
3 DRYBURGH WLK
4 GLENLUCE GDNS
5 BATHLIN CRES
6 OLD BARS DR
7 KNOCKMILLY PL
8 SAUCHENHALL PTH
9 FLOUR MILL WYND
10 MIDTON CRES
11 LISMORE PL
12 STRATHYRE GDNS
13 MOSSVALE TERR
14 BEDLAY WLK
Mollinhillhead
M73
LOCHWOOD LOAN
GLENTROOL GDNS
INCHCOLM GDNS
ROSS WAY
WESTDALE DR
BALLAYNE DR
BEDLAY CT
BURNBRAE AVE
HEATHFIELD AVE
LENTANAR
Annathill Farm
Mollins Burn
MOLLINSBURN RD
Works
1 DUNELLAN GDNS
2 DUNELLAN CRES
3 DUNELLAN WAY
4 DUNELLAN CT
5 LANGHOLM CT
6 HUNTLY PATH
7 DUNKELD LA
8 ARRAN LA
9 TORWOOD LA
10 SEAFORTH LA
11 ADAMSWELL TERR
12 RANNOCH LA
13 ATHOLL LA
14 GARTMORE LA
15 IONA LA
16 CLOSSFOOT PL
17 St Michaels Prim Sch
DUNELLAN PL
ANNATHILL GDNS
BEDLAY PL
Annathill
Leckethill
AVENUEHEAD RD
Avenuehead Farm
Mast
Refuse Tip
Woodend
South Medrox
GAIN RD
BIRKENSHAW RD
101
82

81
61

F8
1 St Margaret of Scotland Prim Sch

81
102

A
B
C
D
E
F
8
7
73
6
5
72
4
3
71
2
1
70
76
77
78
GLENCRYAN RD
B8054
Cumbernauld
GREENFAULDS RD
St Margaret of Scotland
Prim Sch
Ind
Est
LENZIEMILL RD
Lenziemill
JANE'S BRAE
Greenside
Glencryan
Plantation
Glencryan Burn
Palacerigg
Country Park
Visitor
Ctr
Palacerigg
Cottage
CH
West
Waterhead
East
Waterhead
G67
Sandyknowes
Tannoch
BROOMLEE
RD
Blairlinn
Ind Est
STIRLING RD
Luggiebank
Luggie Water
Acrecroft
Farm
Easter Blairlinn
Cottages
Glenhove
Craigelvan
Fedderland
Wester
Glentore
Greens
Coathill
MILLCROFT RD
HULKS RD
SPAIRDRUM
RD
SPAIRDRUM RD
Muirhead
Muirhead
Glen
Boglea
Loanhead
Auldshields
Bridge
STIRLING RD
BRACKENKNOWE RD
Staylee
Glen
Staylee
ML6
BLACKBOG RD
Blacktongue
Farm
Cameron Burn
Whinrigg
Farm
B8039
CAMERON RD
Cameron
Cameron
Glen
Greengairs
Prim Sch
B803
RANKIN CRES
HILLVIEW
ANNANDALE
COALBURN ST
LAUREL GR
Greengairs
GREENGAIRS RD
Cullochrig
Plantation
OLD BIGGAR RD
DRUMGRAY GDNS
Drumgray
Farm
MILL RD
BRACKENHIRST RD
Berryhill
Cottage
Riggend
DRUMGRAY LA
MEIKLE DRUMGRAY RD
HILLRIGG
A73

83
63

A
B
C
D
E
F
8
7
73
6
5
72
4
3
71
2
1
70
79
80
81
Palacerigg Country Park
G67
Herd's Hill
Fannyside Lochs
Fannyside Lodge
Fannyside Mill
Garbethill Burn
Jawhills
River Avon
Thieves Hill
Scar Hill
West Fannyside
FK1
Toddle Knowe
Bog Bridge
Luggie Water
Avon Water
Black Hill
Blackhill
Torbrex
HULKS RD
Bogside
Netherton of Glentore
B803
P
Easter Glentore Farm
Shielhill Burn
Langdales
ML6
DERVAIG GDNS
LUCKENHILL DR
AVON AVE
SCAMADALE RD
Easter Glentore
Upperton Farm
GREENGAIRS RD
THE CRESCENT
Meadowfield
B803
PH
Greendykeside
Avalon
BRIDGE ST

83
104

64
86

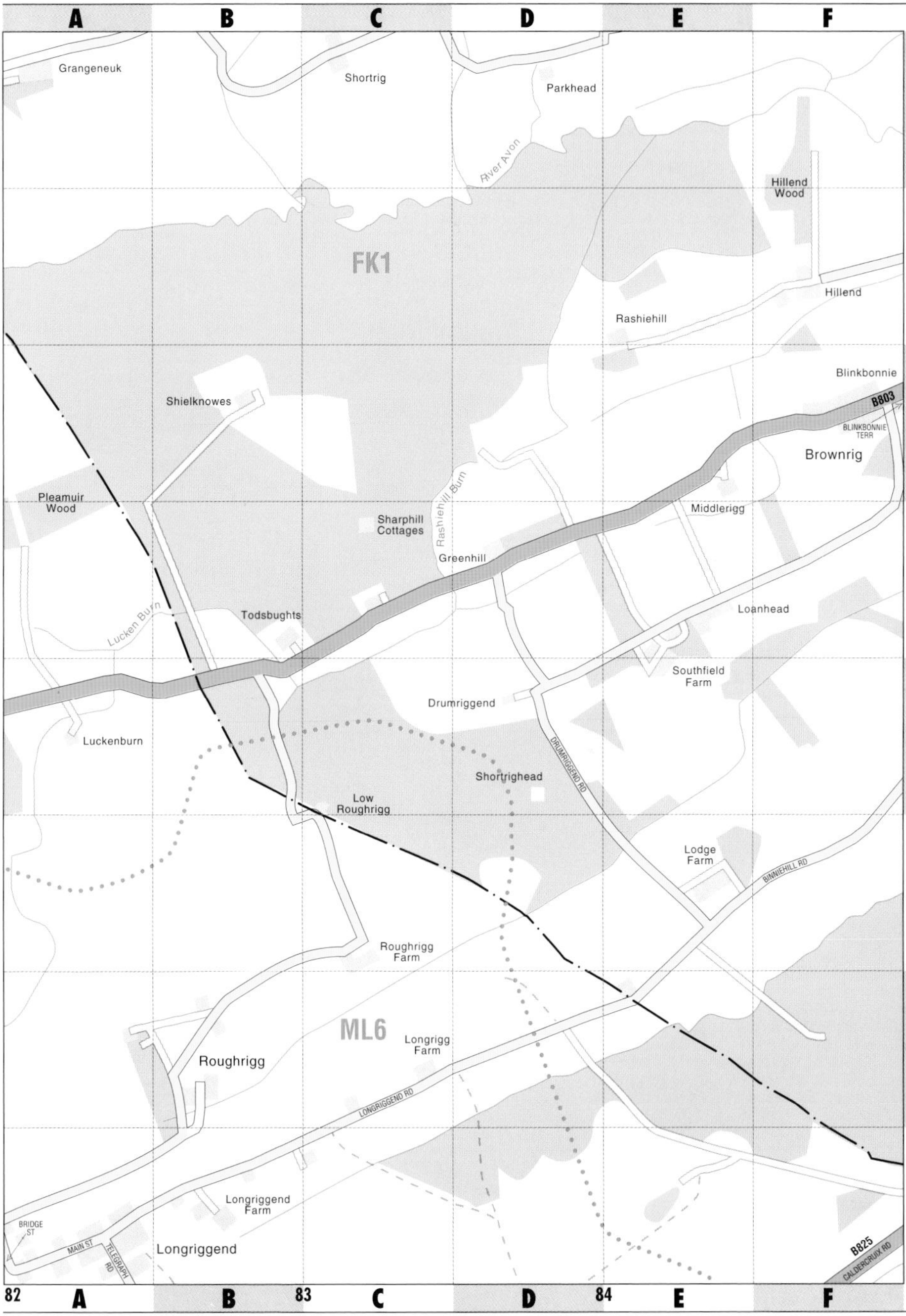
A
B
C
D
E
F
Grangeneuk
Shortrig
Parkhead
River Avon
Hillend Wood
FK1
Hillend
Rashiehill
73
Blinkbonnie
B803
BLINKBONNIE TERR
Brownrig
Shielknowes
Pleamuir Wood
Rashiehill Burn
Sharphill Cottages
Greenhill
Middlerigg
Lucken Burn
Todsbughts
Loanhead
72
Southfield Farm
Drumriggend
Luckenburn
DRUMRIGGEND RD
Shortrighead
Low Roughrigg
Lodge Farm
BINNIEHILL RD
Roughrigg Farm
71
ML6
Longrigg Farm
Roughrigg
LONGRIGGEND RD
Longriggend Farm
BRIDGE ST
MAIN ST
TELEGRAPH RD
Longriggend
B825
CALDERCRUIX RD
70
8
7
6
5
4
3
2
1
82
83
84

105
86

85
65

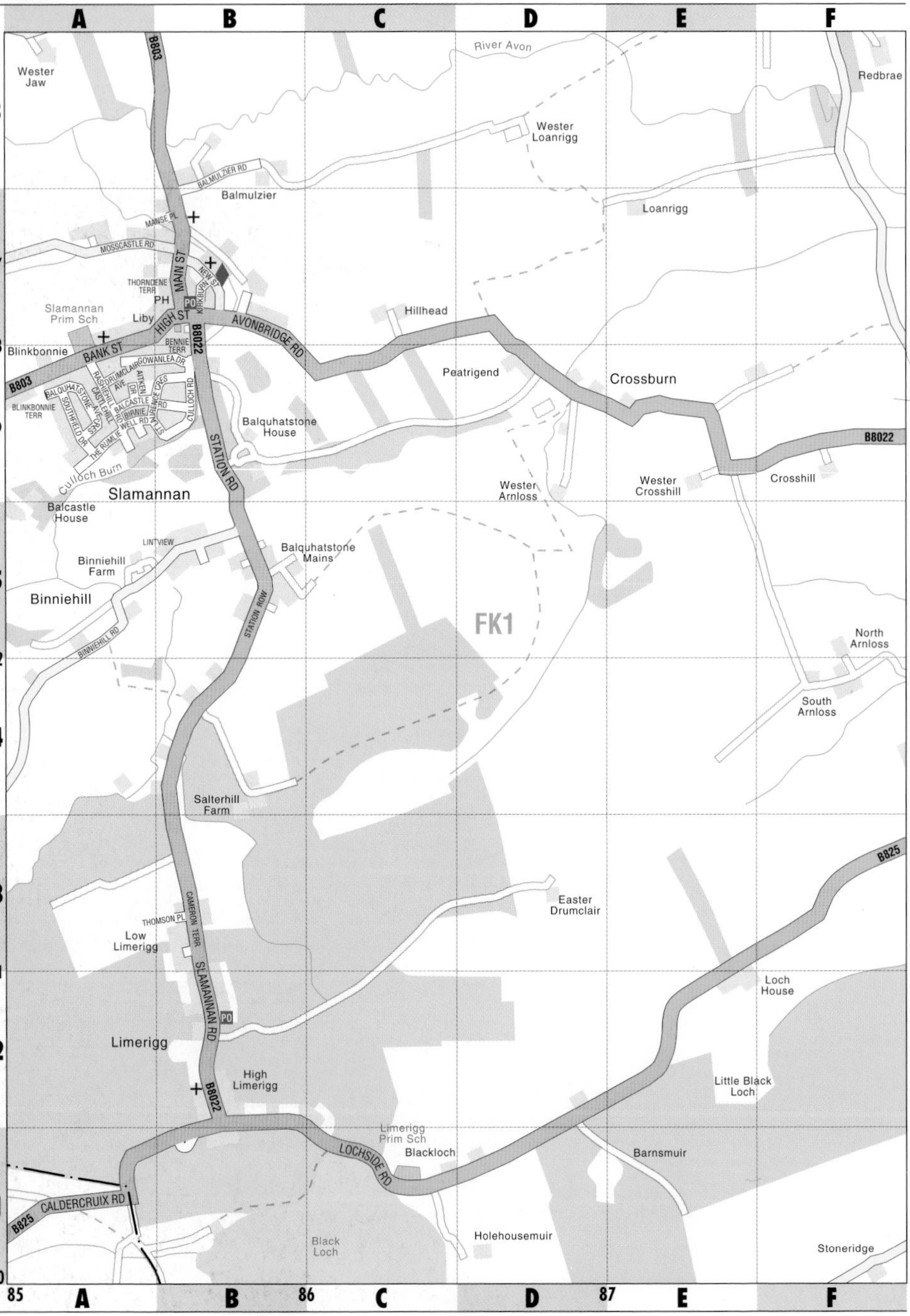
A
B
C
D
E
F
8
7
73
6
5
72
4
3
71
2
1
70
85
86
87
River Avon
Wester Jaw
Redbrae
Wester Loanrigg
B803
BALMULZIER RD
Balmulzier
Loanrigg
MANSE PL
MOSSCASTLE RD
MAIN ST
NEW ST
KIRKBURN
THORNDENE TERR
PH
PO
Slamannan Prim Sch
Liby
HIGH ST
AVONBRIDGE RD
Hillhead
B8022
BENNIE TERR
Blinkbonnie
BANK ST
GOWANLEA DR
Peatrigend
Crossburn
DRUMCLAIR AVE
BALQUHATSTONE CRES
CULLOCH RD
BLINKBONNIE TERR
SOUTHFIELD DR
BALCASTLE RD
BIRNIE
WELL RD
THE RUMLIE
Balquhatstone House
B8022
STATION RD
Crosshill
Culloch Burn
Slamannan
Wester Arnloss
Wester Crosshill
Balcastle House
LINTVIEW
Balquhatstone Mains
Binniehill Farm
Binniehill
STATION ROW
FK1
BINNIEHILL RD
North Arnloss
South Arnloss
Salterhill Farm
B825
Easter Drumclair
CAMERON TERR
THOMSON PL
Low Limerigg
SLAMANNAN RD
Loch House
PO
Limerigg
High Limerigg
B8022
Little Black Loch
Limerigg Prim Sch
Blackloch
LOCHSIDE RD
Barnsmuir
CALDERCRUIX RD
B825
Black Loch
Holehousemuir
Stoneridge

85
106

66

A
B
C
D
E
F
BOXTON RD
Lower Boxton
Boagstown
B8028
Hareburn
8
North Bankhead
Balmitchell
Windy-yett
Avonview
7
Manse
Whinny Knowes
B8028
South Bankhead
73
River Avon
Bogo
The Neucks
Avonvale
Avonbridge
6
AVONPARK
Summerhouse
SLAMANNAN RD
B825
Avonbridge Prim Sch
B8022
Babbithill
5
Crossroads
Craigend
Bulliondale House
72
FK1
Dykehead
Edinburgh STREET ATLAS
4
Wester Holehouse
North East Holehouse
Holehouse
Redhall
Lin Mill Burn
Elrigside Wood
South Holehouse
Easter Greenhill
Linhouse Farm
3
East Plantation
Wester Greenhill
71
Drumtassie Burn
Barns
2
North Rhodens Plantation
1
70
88
A
B
89
C
D
90
E
F

107

68

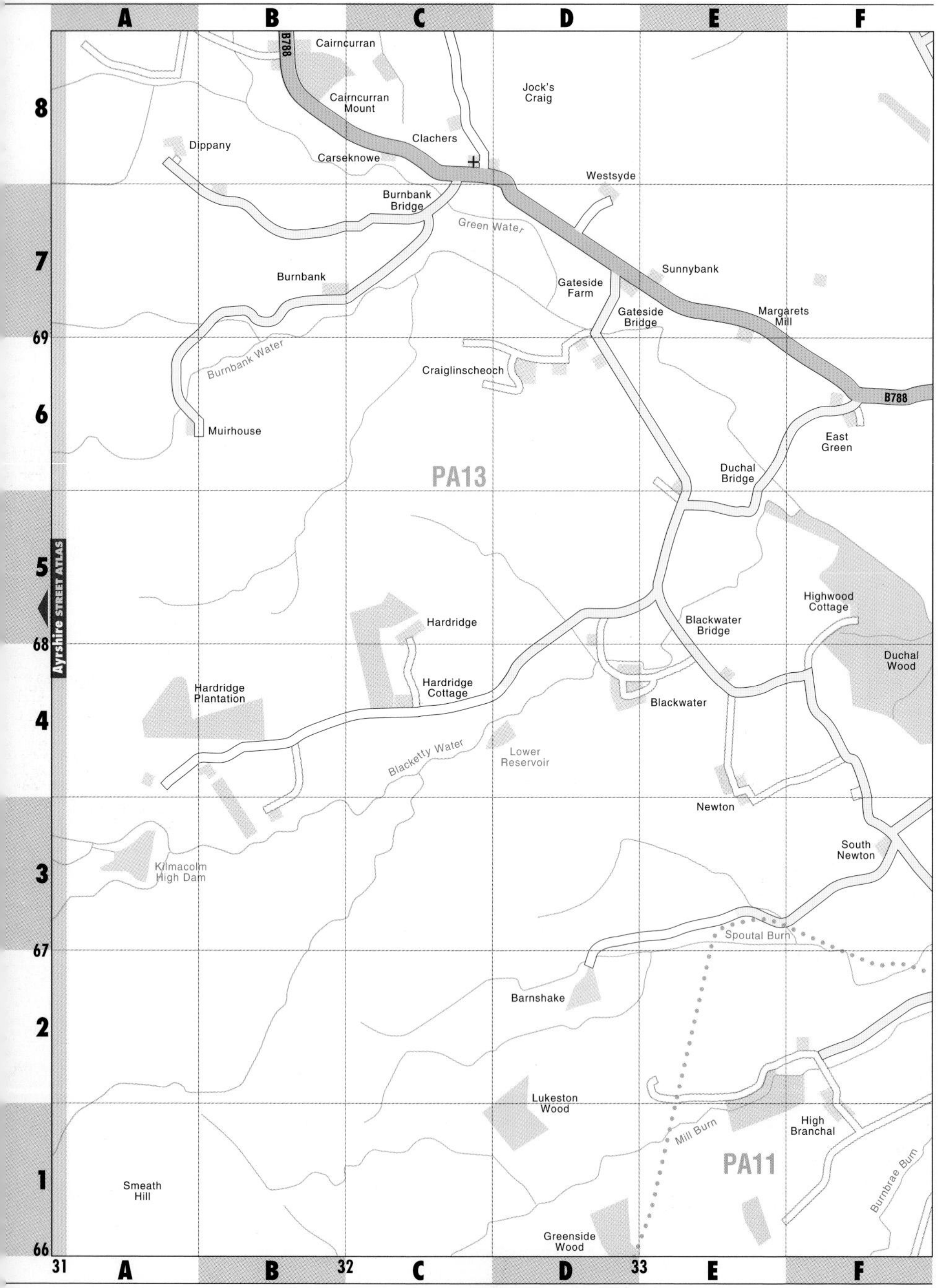
A
B
C
D
E
F
8
7
69
6
5
68
4
3
67
2
1
66
31
32
33
B788
Cairncurran
Cairncurran
Mount
Jock's
Craig
Dippany
Clachers
Carseknowe
Westsyde
Burnbank
Bridge
Green Water
Burnbank
Sunnybank
Gateside
Farm
Gateside
Bridge
Margarets
Mill
Craiglinscheoch
Burnbank Water
B788
Muirhouse
East
Green
PA13
Duchal
Bridge
Highwood
Cottage
Hardridge
Blackwater
Bridge
Duchal
Wood
Hardridge
Plantation
Hardridge
Cottage
Blackwater
Blacketty Water
Lower
Reservoir
Newton
South
Newton
Kilmacolm
High Dam
Spoutal Burn
Barnshake
Lukeston
Wood
High
Branchal
Mill Burn
PA11
Burnbrae Burn
Smeath
Hill
Greenside
Wood
Ayrshire STREET ATLAS

108

69 90

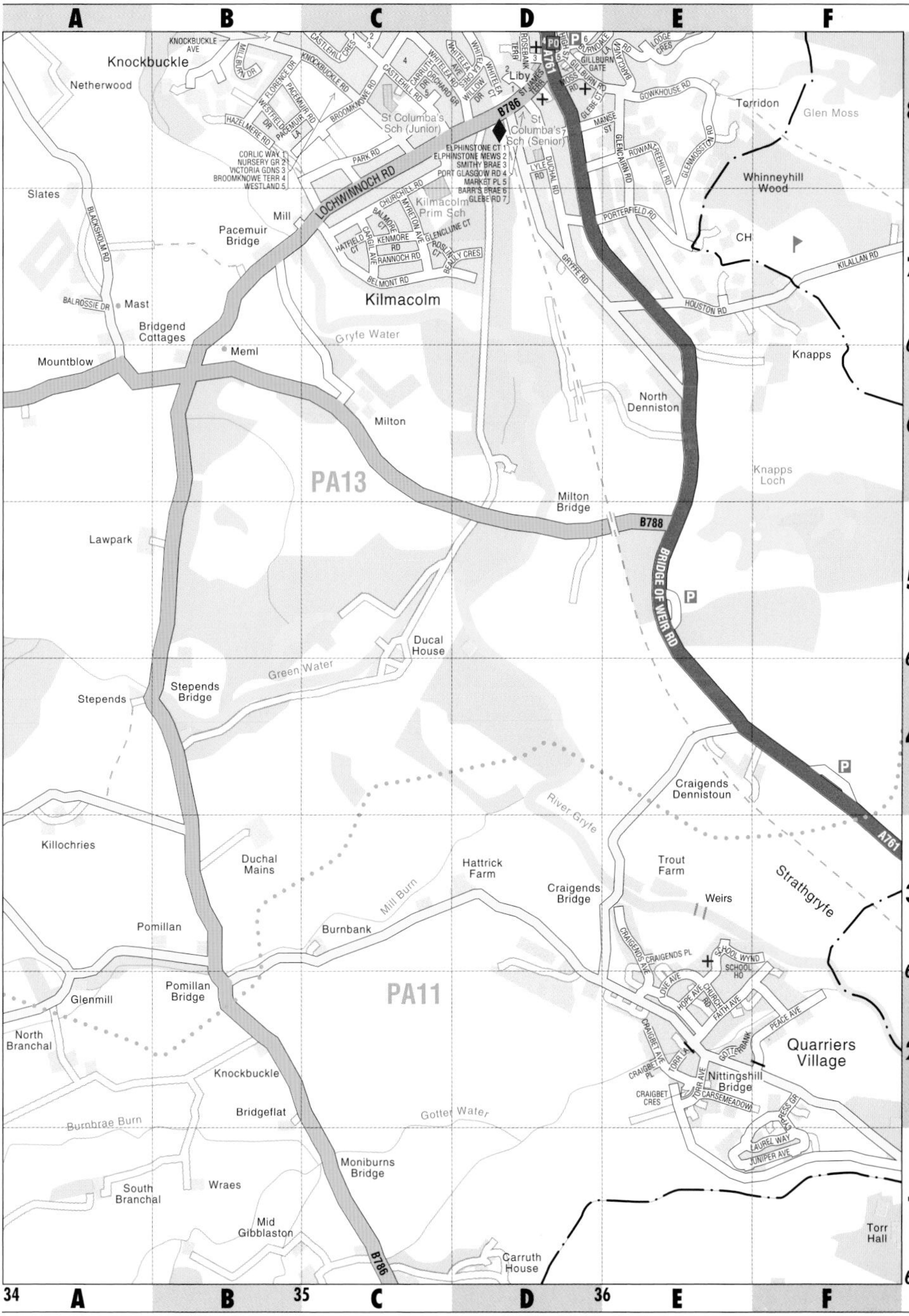
A B C D E F
Knockbuckle
Netherwood
Slates
Mill
Pacemuir Bridge
Mast
Bridgend Cottages
Meml
Mountblow
Kilmacolm
Gryfe Water
Milton
PA13
St Columba's Sch (Junior)
St Columba's Sch (Senior)
Kilmacolm Prim Sch
Liby
LOCHWINNOCH RD
B786
A761
B788
PARK RD
CHURCHILL RD
BELMONT RD
RANNOCH RD
KENMORE RD
GLENCLUNE CT
HATFIELD CT
BALMORE CT
ROSLIN CT
BEAULY CRES
MYRETON AVE
CARGILL AVE
HAZELMERE RD
WESTFIELD DR
PACEMUIR RD
FLORENCE DR
KNOCKBUCKLE AVE
MILLBURN DR
KNOCKBUCKLE RD
CASTLEHILL CRES
CASTLEHILL RD
BROOMKNOWE RD
WHITELEA RD
ORCHARD GR
WILLOW DR
WHITELEA CT
ROSEBANK TERR
ST JAMES TERR
CORLIC WAY 1
NURSERY GR 2
VICTORIA GDNS 3
BROOMKNOWE TERR 4
WESTLAND 5
ELPHINSTONE CT 1
ELPHINSTONE MEWS 2
SMITHY BRAE 3
PORT GLASGOW RD 4
MARKET PL 5
BARR'S BRAE 6
GLEBE RD 7
MOSS RD
HIGH ST
BURNDALE
GILLBURN GATE
GILLBURN RD
BARCLAY
LODGE CRES
GOWKHOUSE RD
GLEBE CT
MANSE ST
LYLE RD
DUCHAL RD
GLENCAIRN RD
ROWAN
REEHILL RD
GLENMOSSTON RD
PORTERFIELD RD
GRYFFE RD
HOUSTON RD
KILALLAN RD
Torridon
Glen Moss
Whinneyhill Wood
CH
Knapps
North Denniston
Knapps Loch
Milton Bridge
BRIDGE OF WEIR RD
Lawpark
Ducal House
Green Water
Stepends
Stepends Bridge
Craigends Dennistoun
River Gryfe
Killochries
Duchal Mains
Hattrick Farm
Trout Farm
Craigends Bridge
Weirs
Strathgryfe
Pomillan
Burnbank
Mill Burn
PA11
Glenmill
Pomillan Bridge
North Branchal
CRAIGENDS AVE
CRAIGENDS PL
SCHOOL WYND
SCHOOL HO
LOVE AVE
HOPE AVE
CHURCH RD
FAITH AVE
PEACE AVE
CRAIGBET AVE
CRAIGBET PL
CRAIGBET CRES
TORR LA
TORR AVE
GOTTERBANK
CARSEMEADOW
Quarriers Village
Nittingshill Bridge
CYPRESS GR
LAUREL WAY
JUNIPER AVE
Knockbuckle
Bridgeflat
Burnbrae Burn
Gotter Water
Moniburns Bridge
South Branchal
Wraes
Mid Gibblaston
Carruth House
Torr Hall
8 7 69 6 5 68 4 3 67 2 1 66
34 35 36

109 90

89
70

A
B
C
D
E
F
8
7
69
6
5
68
4
3
67
2
1
66
37
38
39
PA14
PA13
PA6
PA11
Elphinstone Wood
Corsliehills Wood
Lawfield Dam
Corsliehills Cottage
CORSLIEHILL RD
Kirkton Wood
High Lawfield
Shovelboard
Hogs Burn
Kilallan
Wraes
Kirkton Farm
Wraes Wood
North Barlogan Wood
KILALLAN RD
Houston Burn
Mashington Wood
Wellees Farm
Peter's Burn
Ennelly Wood
Barfillan Cottage
Barfillan
Ennelly
Barlogan Wood
Barlogan Farm
Waterlea
BRIDGE OF WEIR RD
A761
WARLOCK RD
Botherickfield Wood
Scart Wood
Botherickfield
Scart
Houstonfield Dam
West Yonderton
East Yonderton
KILMACOLM RD
Law Hill
Girthill
River Gryfe
Gryffe Wraes
B790
GRYFFE CASTLE
Bridge of Weir Prim Sch
CASTLE RD
Fodston
HOUSTON RD
PARK RD
BEECH AVE
FREELAND DR
SOUTHVIEW
CRES
Threeply
WARLOCK DR
ELM RD
LOCH RD
THISTLEBANK 1
GLENGOWAN RD 2
STRATHGRYFFE CRES
GRYFFE AVE
KILALLAN AVE
WOODSIDE AVE
Houstonhead Dam

89
110

71
92

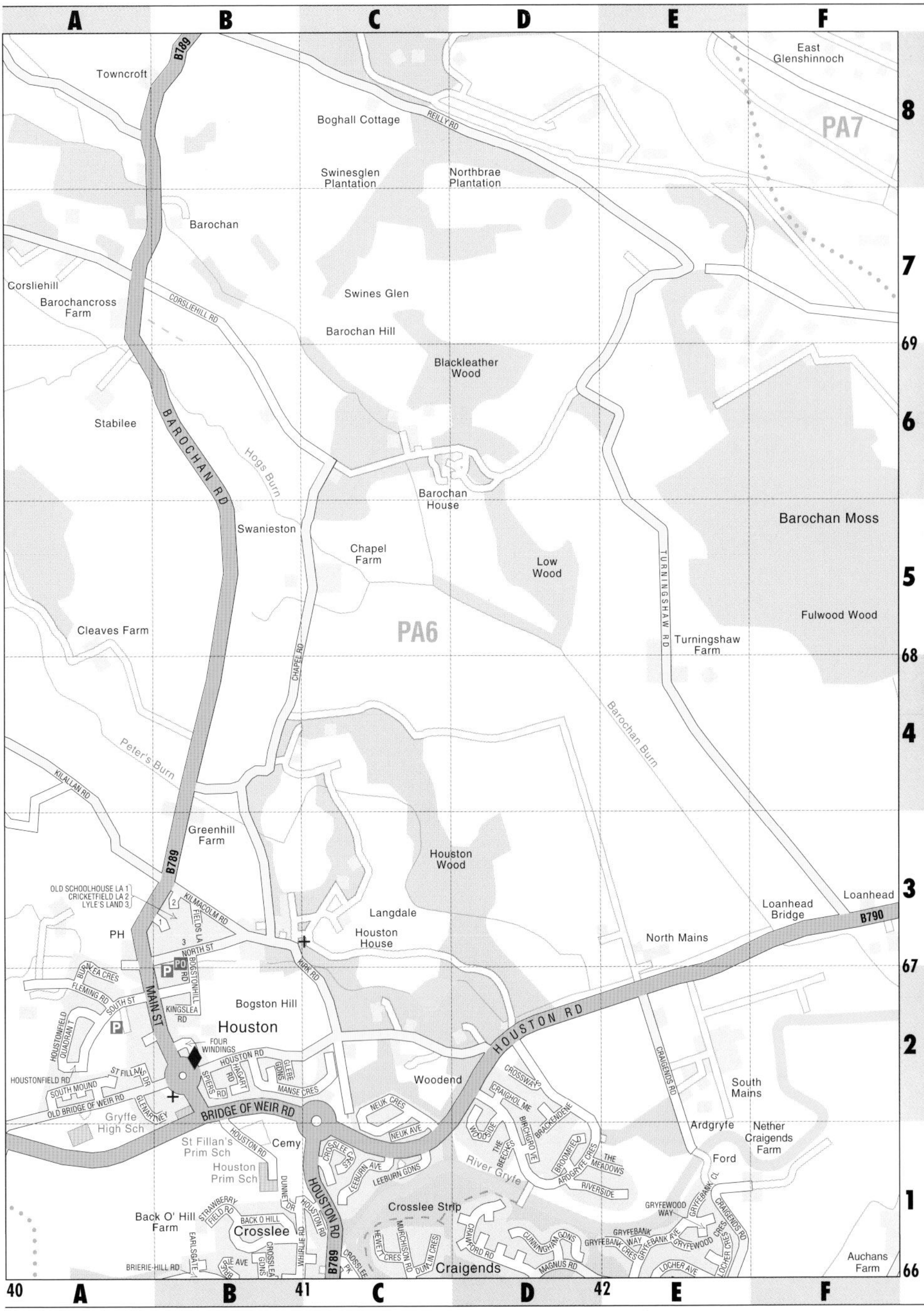
A
B
C
D
E
F
8
7
69
6
5
68
4
3
67
2
1
66
40
41
42
Towncroft
B789
Boghall Cottage
REILLY RD
East Glenshinnoch
PA7
Swinesglen Plantation
Northbrae Plantation
Barochan
Corsliehill
Barochancross Farm
CORSLIEHILL RD
Swines Glen
Barochan Hill
Blackleather Wood
Stabilee
BAROCHAN RD
Hogs Burn
Barochan House
Swanieston
Chapel Farm
Low Wood
Barochan Moss
TURNINGSHAW RD
Fulwood Wood
Cleaves Farm
PA6
Turningshaw Farm
CHAPEL RD
Barochan Burn
Peter's Burn
KILALLAN RD
Greenhill Farm
Houston Wood
OLD SCHOOLHOUSE LA 1
CRICKETFIELD LA 2
LYLE'S LAND 3
KILMACOLM RD
FIELDS LA
Langdale
Loanhead Bridge
Loanhead
B790
PH
NORTH ST
Houston House
North Mains
BURNLEA CRES
FLEMING RD
BOGSTONHILL RD
KIRK RD
SOUTH ST
KINGSLEA RD
Bogston Hill
MAIN ST
HOUSTONFIELD QUADRANT
Houston
HOUSTON RD
FOUR WINDINGS
HOUSTON RD
GLEBE
GDNS
HAGART RD
SPIERS RD
MANSE CRES
Woodend
CROSSWAY
CRAIGENDS RD
South Mains
HOUSTONFIELD RD
ST FILLANS DR
SOUTH MOUND
OLD BRIDGE OF WEIR RD
GLENARTNEY
BRIDGE OF WEIR RD
NEUK CRES
NEUK AVE
CRAIGHOLME
WOODSIDE
BIRCHGROVE
BRACKENDENE
Gryffe High Sch
St Fillan's Prim Sch
Cemy
CROSSLEE CRES
THE BEECHES
BROOMFIELD
ARDGRYFE CRES
THE MEADOWS
Ardgryfe
Nether Craigends Farm
Houston Prim Sch
LEEBURN AVE
LEEBURN GDNS
River Gryfe
RIVERSIDE
Ford
DUNNET DR
HOUSTON RD
Crosslee Strip
GRYFEWOOD WAY
GRYFEBANK CL
Back O' Hill Farm
STRAWBERRY FIELD RD
BACK O HILL
Crosslee
WHIRLIE RD
CRAWFORD RD
CUNNINGHAM GDNS
GRYFEBANK WAY
GRYFEBANK CRES
GRYFEBANK AVE
GRYFEWOOD CRES
CRAIGENDS RD
HEWETT CRES
MURCHISON RD
DUNLIN CRES
MAGNUS RD
LOCHER AVE
LOCHER CRES
EARLSGATE
BRIERIE-HILL RD
BRIERIE AVE
CROSSLEE GDNS
B789
CROSSLEE PK
Craigends
Auchans Farm

111
92

91
72

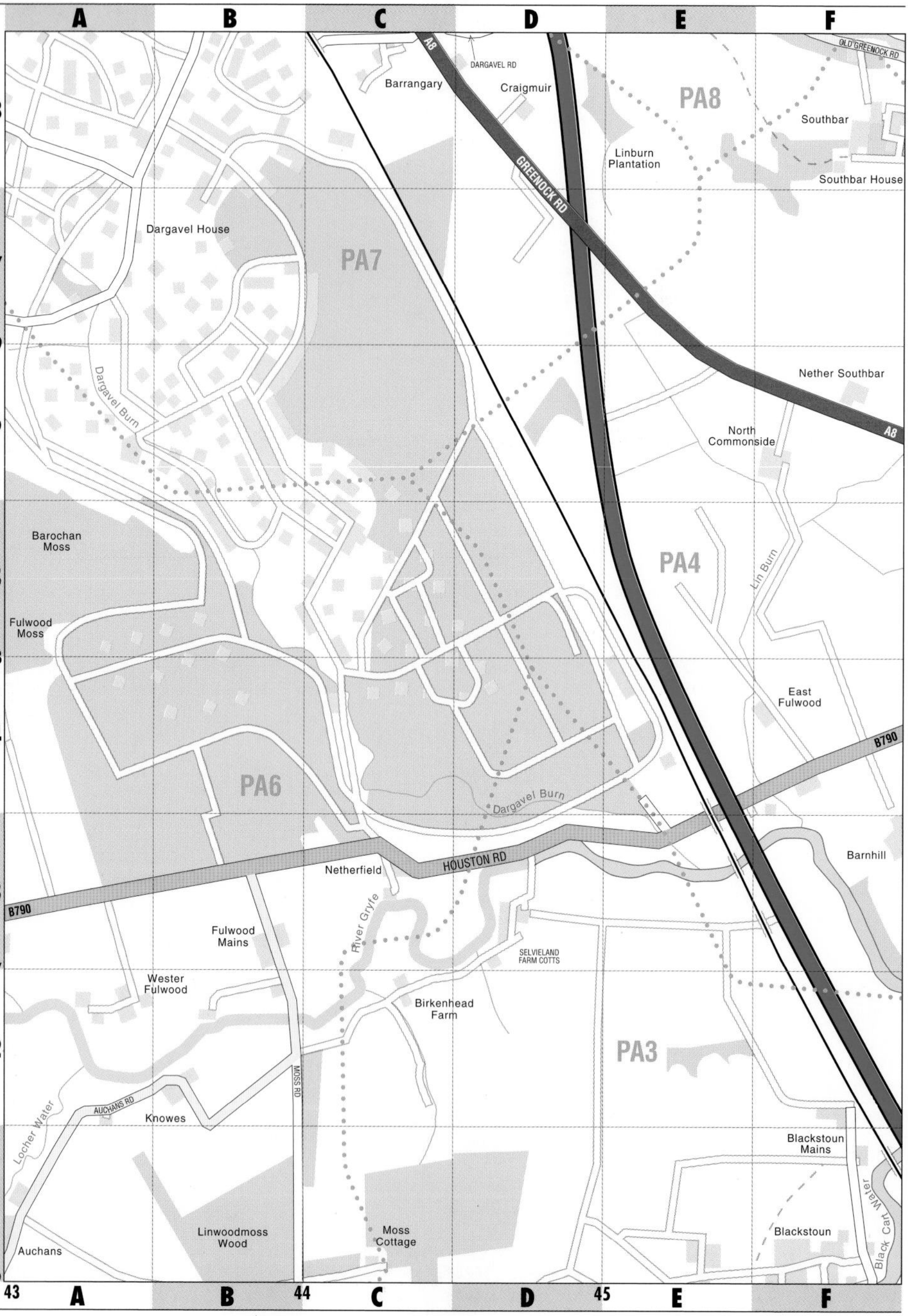
A
B
C
D
E
F
8
7
69
6
5
68
4
3
67
2
1
66
43
44
45
DARGAVEL RD
OLD GREENOCK RD
Barrangary
Craigmuir
PA8
Southbar
Linburn
Plantation
Southbar House
GREENOCK RD
A8
Dargavel House
PA7
Dargavel Burn
Nether Southbar
North
Commonside
A8
Barochan
Moss
PA4
Lin Burn
Fulwood
Moss
East
Fulwood
B790
PA6
Dargavel Burn
Barnhill
HOUSTON RD
Netherfield
B790
River Gryfe
Fulwood
Mains
SELVIELAND
FARM COTTS
Wester
Fulwood
Birkenhead
Farm
PA3
MOSS RD
AUCHANS RD
Knowes
Locher Water
Blackstoun
Mains
Black Cart Water
Linwoodmoss
Wood
Moss
Cottage
Blackstoun
Auchans

91
112

73
94

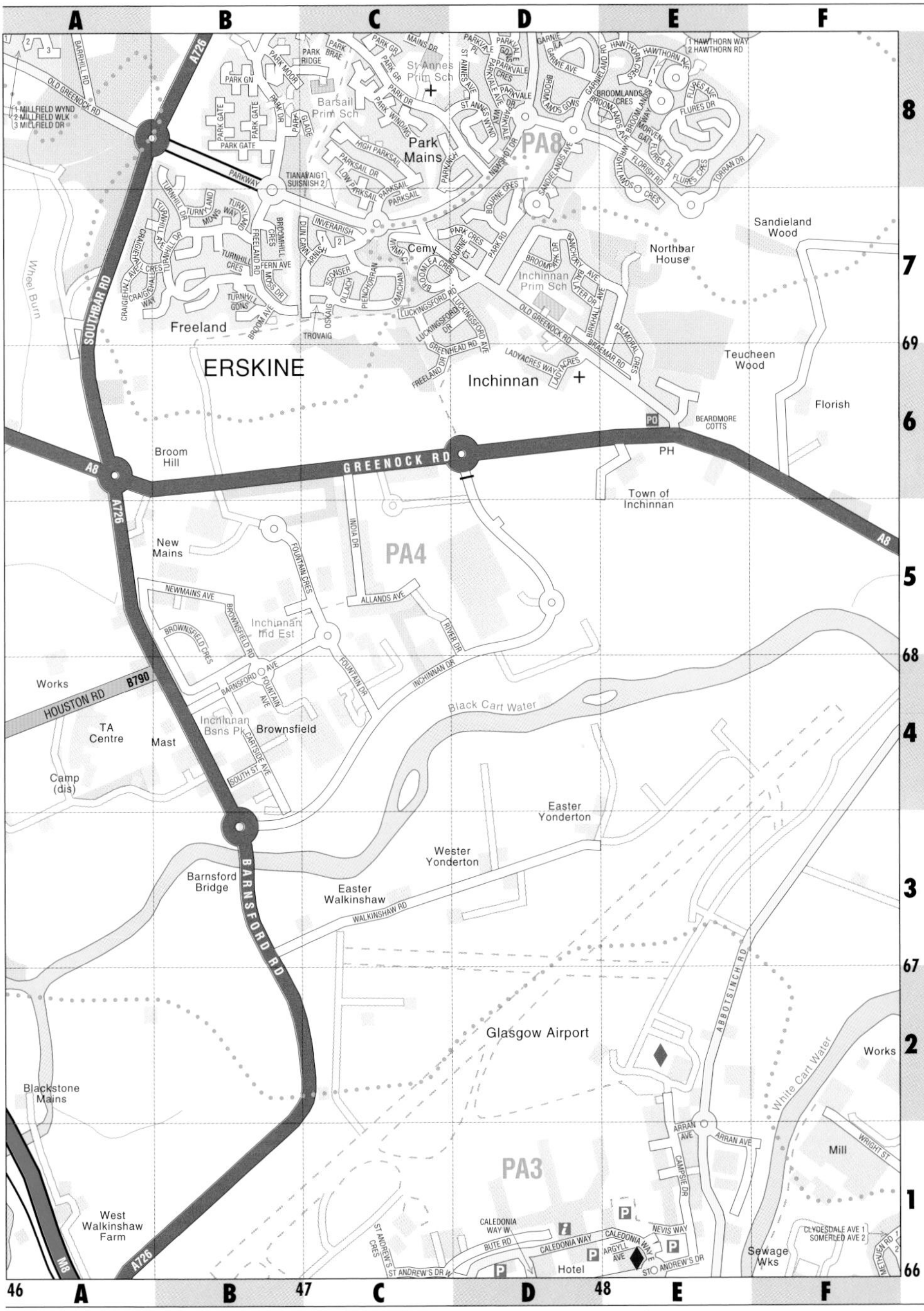
A
B
C
D
E
F
8
7
69
6
5
68
4
3
67
2
1
66
46
47
48
ERSKINE
Freeland
Park Mains
PA8
St Annes Prim Sch
Barsail Prim Sch
Cemy
Inchinnan Prim Sch
Inchinnan
Northbar House
Sandieland Wood
Teucheen Wood
Florish
BEARDMORE COTTS
PH
PO
Town of Inchinnan
Broom Hill
GREENOCK RD
A8
A726
SOUTHBAR RD
OLD GREENOCK RD
PARKWAY
Wheel Burn
New Mains
PA4
INDIA DR
FOUNTAIN CRES
ALLANDS AVE
RIVER DR
INCHINNAN DR
NEWMAINS AVE
BROWNSFIELD CRES
BROWNSFIELD RD
Inchinnan Ind Est
BARNSFORD AVE
FOUNTAIN AVE
FOUNTAIN DR
Inchinnan Bsns Pk
Brownsfield
CARTSIDE AVE
SOUTH ST
Works
HOUSTON RD
B790
TA Centre
Mast
Camp (dis)
Black Cart Water
Easter Yonderton
Wester Yonderton
Barnsford Bridge
BARNSFORD RD
Easter Walkinshaw
WALKINSHAW RD
ABBOTSINCH RD
Glasgow Airport
White Cart Water
Works
Blackstone Mains
West Walkinshaw Farm
M8
PA3
ARRAN AVE
CAMPSIE DR
Mill
WRIGHT ST
CALEDONIA WAY W
BUTE RD
CALEDONIA WAY
CALEDONIA WAY E
ARGYLL AVE
NEVIS WAY
ST ANDREW'S DR
ST ANDREW'S CRES
Hotel
Sewage Wks
1 CLYDESDALE AVE
2 SOMERLED AVE
METHVEN RD
1 MILLFIELD WYND
2 MILLFIELD WLK
3 MILLFIELD DR
BARRHILL RD
1 HAWTHORN WAY
2 HAWTHORN RD
FLURES AVE
FLURES DR
FLURES CRES
TORRAN DR
LADYACRES WAY
LADYACRES
BALMORAL CRES
BRAEMAR RD
BIRKHALL AVE
LUCKINGSFORD AVE
LUCKINGSFORD DR
GREENHEAD RD
FREELAND DR
TROVAIG
TURNHILL DR
TURNHILL CRES
TURNHILL GDNS
CRAIGIEHALL AVE
CRAIGIEHALL WAY
BROOM AVE
FERN AVE
FREELAND RD
INVERARISH
PARKSAIL DR
LOW PARKSAIL
HIGH PARKSAIL
PARK DR
PARK GATE
PARK GN
PARK RIDGE
PARK BRAE
PARK RD
PARK CRES
BOURNE CRES
NEWSHOT DR
SANDIELANDS AVE
BROOMLANDS CRES
BROOMLANDS AVE
FLORISH RD

113
94

93
74

A B C D E F

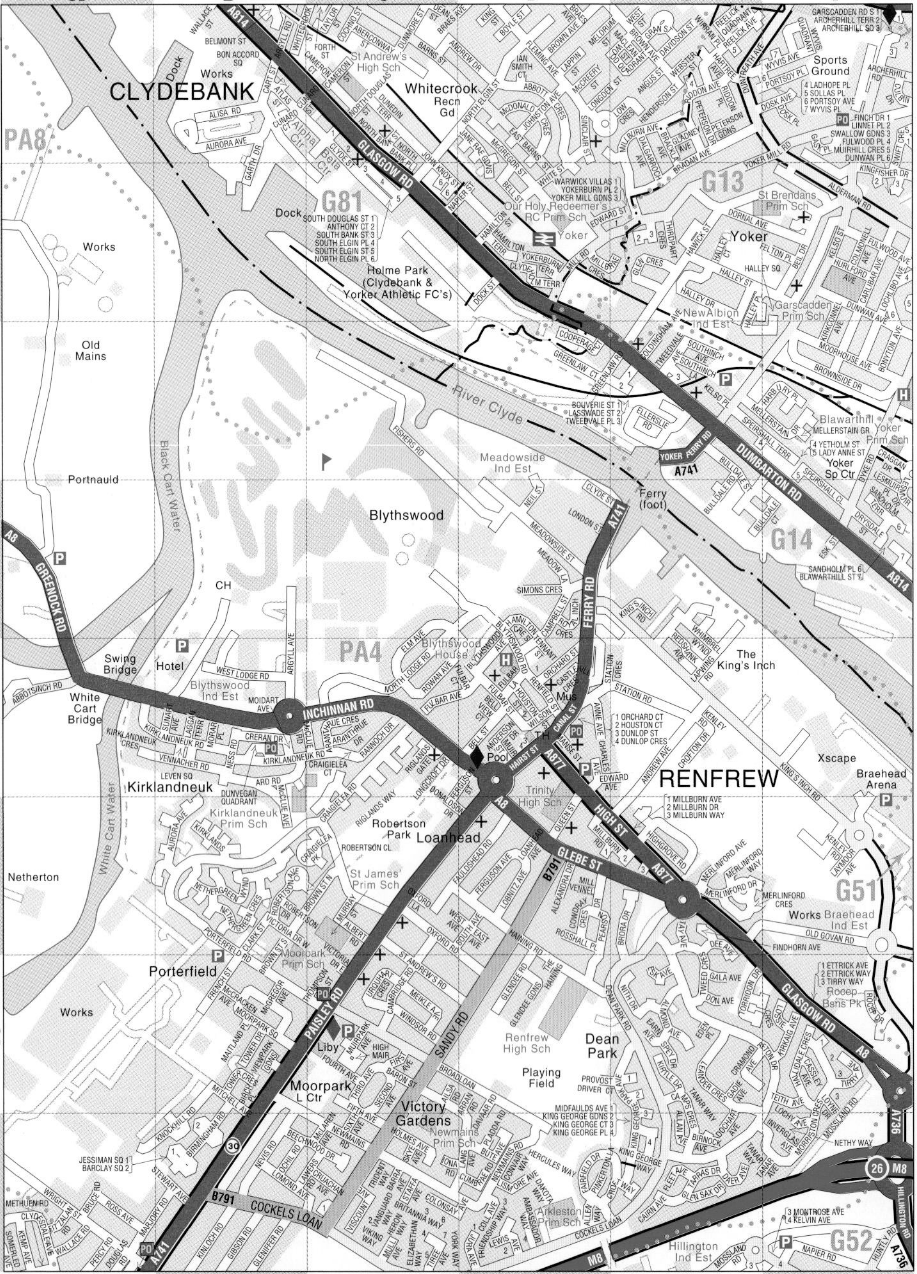

49 A B 50 C D 51 E F

93
114

C1
1 CLAIRINSH GDNS
2 HERALD WAY
3 ARGOSY WAY
4 LANCASTER WAY
5 WELLINGTON WAY
6 ANSON WAY
7 HALIFAX WAY

D1
1 STIRLING WAY
2 LYSANDER WAY
3 CARAVELLE WAY
4 HAMPDEN WAY

D6
1 DUTHIE PARK PL
2 DUTHIE PARK GDNS
3 PRIORWOOD GDNS
4 BRANKLYN CL
5 BRANKLYN PL
6 BRANKLYN CT
7 PRIORWOOD CT

D8
1 ROTHERWOOD PL

E5
1 SELBORNE PL
2 WOODEND LA
3 SOUTHBRAE LA
4 BORDEN RD

75

F5
1 FERN COTTS
2 ALBANY COTTS
3 AIGAS COTTS
4 Anniesland Coll

96

F7
1 TEMPLE LOCKS CT
2 TEMPLE LOCKS PL
3 WALDO ST
4 STRATHCONA DR

F8
1 NETHERTON FARM LA
2 OLD FARM RD

52 A B 53 C D 54 E F

C4
1 DANES AVE
2 UPLAND LA
3 DANES LA N
4 VERONA GDNS
5 DUNGLASS LA N
6 ORMISTON LA N
7 DUNCAN LA N
8 DUNGLASS LA
9 EARLBANK LA N
10 ORMISTON LA
11 DUNGLASS LA S
12 ORMISTON LA S
13 DUNCAN LA S
14 NORSE LA S
15 VANCOUVER LA

115

D3
1 PRIMROSE CT
2 BOWLING GREEN LA
3 BOWLING GREEN RD
4 LIME LA
5 ELM LA W
6 ELM LA E
7 VICTORIA PARK ST
8 WESTLAND DRIVE LA
9 HALDANE LA

96

F1
1 GLASGOW HARBOUR TERR
2 CASTLEBANK PL

F3
1 MARLBOROUGH LA N
2 BALSHAGRAY PL

F4
1 MITRE GATE
2 MITRE CT

A3
1 MONKSCROFT AVE
2 KIRKMICHAEL GDNS
3 KIRKMICHAEL AVE
4 THORNWOOD DR
5 BLAIRATHOLL GDNS
6 TIBBERMORE RD

B3
1 KINGSBOROUGH GATE
2 TURNBERRY AVE
3 HILLSIDE GARDENS LA
4 QUEENSBOROUGH GDNS
5 PRINCES GARDENS LA
6 NORTH GARDNER ST

95

B4
1 DEVONSHIRE GDNS
2 DEVONSHIRE GDNS LA
3 WESTBOURNE TERR LA S

C5
1 THORNBRIDGE AVE
2 BELLSHAUGH PL

76

D5
1 GARRIOCH CRES
2 GARRIOCH QUADRANT
3 WYNDFORD PL
4 DUNBEITH PL
5 LATHERTON DR
6 INVERSHIN DR
7 KIRKHILL PL
8 GARRIOCH GATE

For full street detail of the highlighted area see page 240.

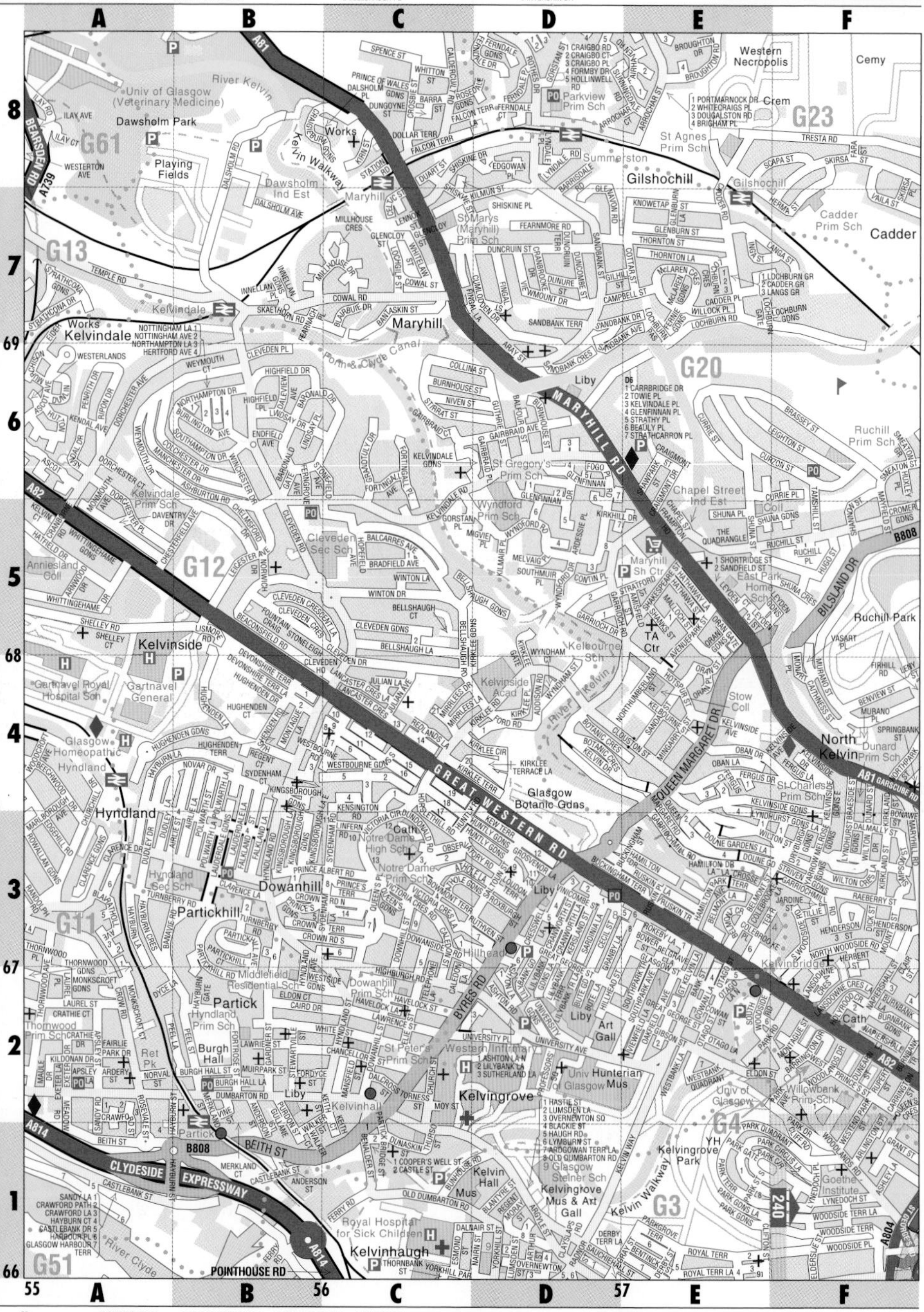

C3
1 DOWANSIDE LA
2 MARCHMONT TERR
3 BOWMONT GDNS
4 VICTORIA CRES PL
5 BEAUMONT GATE
6 FOREMOUNT TERR LA
7 CROWN CIR
8 PRINCE'S PL
9 QUEENS GATE LA
10 EAMONT LODGE
11 HYNDLAND CT
12 ROSSLYN CT
13 ROSEBERRY HO
14 CROWN GDNS

C4
1 KENSINGTON GATE
2 KENSINGTON GATE LA
3 LORRAINE RD
4 LORRAINE GDNS
5 WESTBOURNE GDNS LA
6 WESTBOURNE GDNS N
7 WESTBOURNE GDNS W
8 WESTBOURNE TERR LA N
9 LANCASTER TERR LA
10 LANCASTER TERR
11 GREAT WESTERN TERR LA
12 GREAT WESTERN TERR
13 REDLANDS TERR
14 LOWTHER TERR
15 BELHAVEN TERR W
16 BELHAVEN TERR W LA
17 ROSSLYN TERR
18 BELHAVEN TERR LA
19 BELHAVEN TERR
20 KIRKLEE TERR RD
21 REDLANDS RD

D3
1 KERSLAND LA
2 SANDRINGHAM LA
3 VINICOMBE LA
4 BURGH LA
5 CRESSWELL ST
6 GREAT GEORGE LA
7 RUTHVEN LA
8 Hillhead Prim Sch
9 GROSVENOR CRES
10 OBSERVATORY LA
11 GROSVENOR CRES
12 GROSVENOR TERR

116

D4
1 KIRKLEE QUADRANT

E1
1 PARK TERR LA
2 LA BELLE PL
3 LA BELLE ALLEE
4 N CLAREMONT ST
5 KELVINGROVE ST
6 PARKGROVE TERR LA
7 CRAIGMADDIE TERR LA
8 WOODLANDS CT
9 CLIFTON HO

E2
1 Hillhead High Sch
2 OAKFIELD LA
3 ETON LA
4 BOTHWELL LA
5 CALEDONIAN CRES
6 WEST PRINCE'S ST
7 WESTBANK CT

E3
1 LOTHIAN GDNS
2 KELVINSIDE TERR W
3 KELVINSIDE TERR S
4 DOUNE QUADRANT
5 ALFRED LA
6 ALFRED TERR
7 OAKFIELD AVE
8 GRANBY HO
9 COLEBROOKE ST

E4
1 CLOUSTON CT
2 OBAN CT
3 QUEEN MARGARET CT
4 KELVINSIDE GDNS LA

F2
1 WILLOWBANK CRES
2 HOLYROOD QUADRANT
3 NAPIERSHALL PL
4 SEAMORE ST

F3
1 JEDBURGH GDNS
2 YARROW GDNS LA
3 GARRIOCHMILL WAY
4 The Glasgow Acad

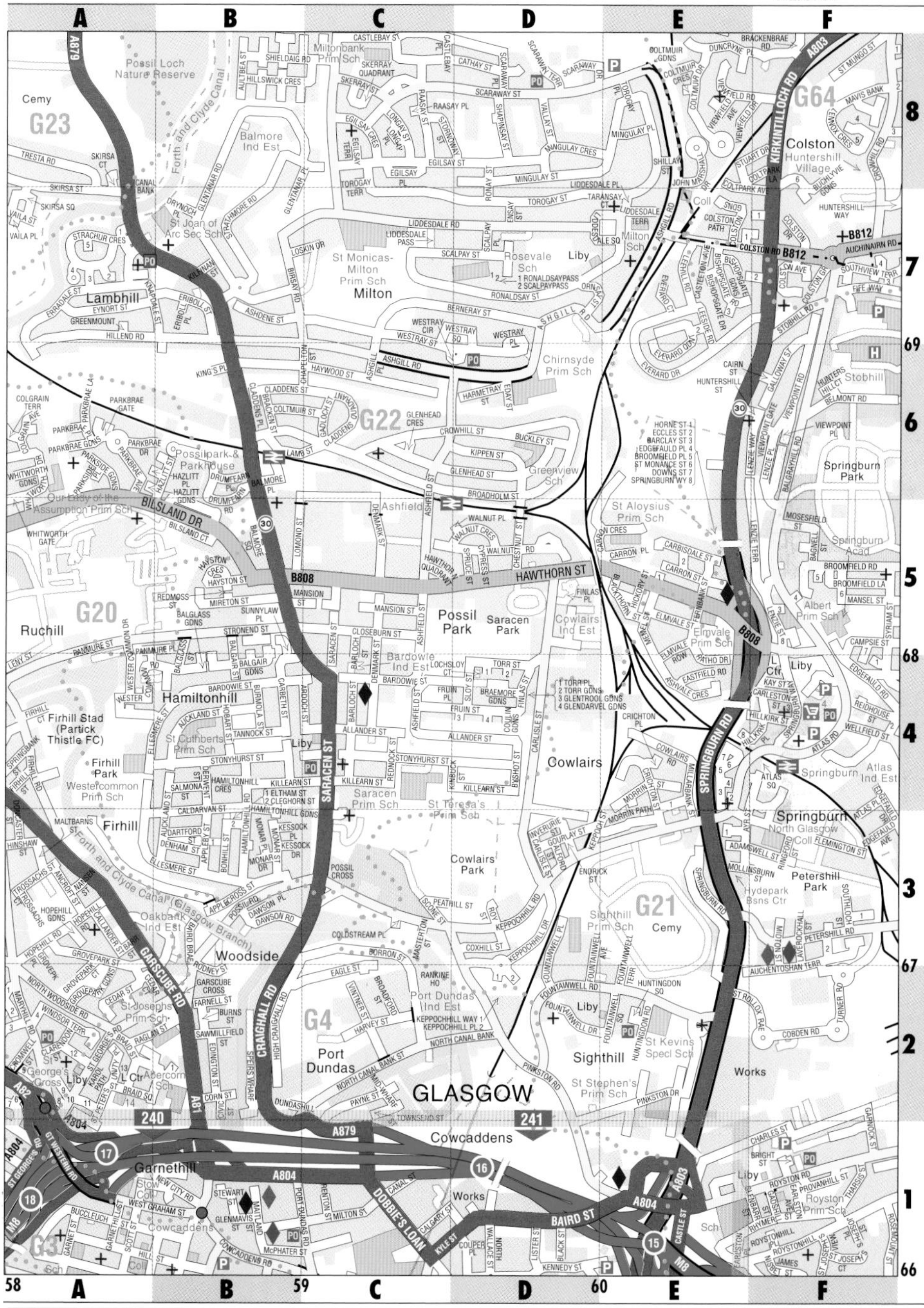
A
B
C
D
E
F
8
7
69
6
5
68
4
3
67
2
1
66
58
59
60
Possil Loch Nature Reserve
Forth and Clyde Canal
Cemy
G23
Balmore Ind Est
Miltonbank Prim Sch
St Joan of Arc Sec Sch
Lambhill
St Monicas-Milton Prim Sch
Milton
Rosevale Sch
Liby
Milton Sch
Coll
G64
Colston
Huntershill Village
Chirnsyde Prim Sch
G22
Possilpark & Parkhouse
Our Lady of the Assumption Prim Sch
BILSLAND DR
Ashfield
Greenview Sch
St Aloysius Prim Sch
Stobhill
Springburn Park
Springburn Acad
B808
HAWTHORN ST
G20
Ruchill
Possil Park
Saracen Park
Cowlairs Ind Est
Elmvale Prim Sch
Albert Prim Sch
Hamiltonhill
Bardowie Ind Est
Firhill Stad (Partick Thistle FC)
Firhill Park
Westercommon Prim Sch
St Cuthberts Prim Sch
Cowlairs
Saracen Prim Sch
St Teresa's Prim Sch
Springburn
Atlas Ind Est
Firhill
North Glasgow Coll
Cowlairs Park
Petershill Park
Hydepark Bsns Ctr
Oakbank Ind Est
Forth and Clyde Canal (Glasgow Branch)
G21
Sighthill Prim Sch
Woodside
GARSCUBE RD
CRAIGHALL RD
SARACEN ST
SPRINGBURN RD
KIRKINTILLOCH RD
Port Dundas Ind Est
G4
Port Dundas
Sighthill
St Kevins Specl Sch
St Stephen's Prim Sch
Works
St Josephs Prim Sch
St George's Cross
Liby
L Ctr
Abercorn Sch
GLASGOW
240
241
Cowcaddens
Garnethill
Stow Coll
Works
A804
A879
A803
M8
BAIRD ST
DOBBIE'S LOAN
Cowcaddens
Royston Prim Sch
G3
B812
A879
A803

97
78

D8
1 WALLACE PL
2 WALLACE GATE
3 WALLACE DR
4 GREENACRES RDBT
5 MILLAR PL

A B C D E F

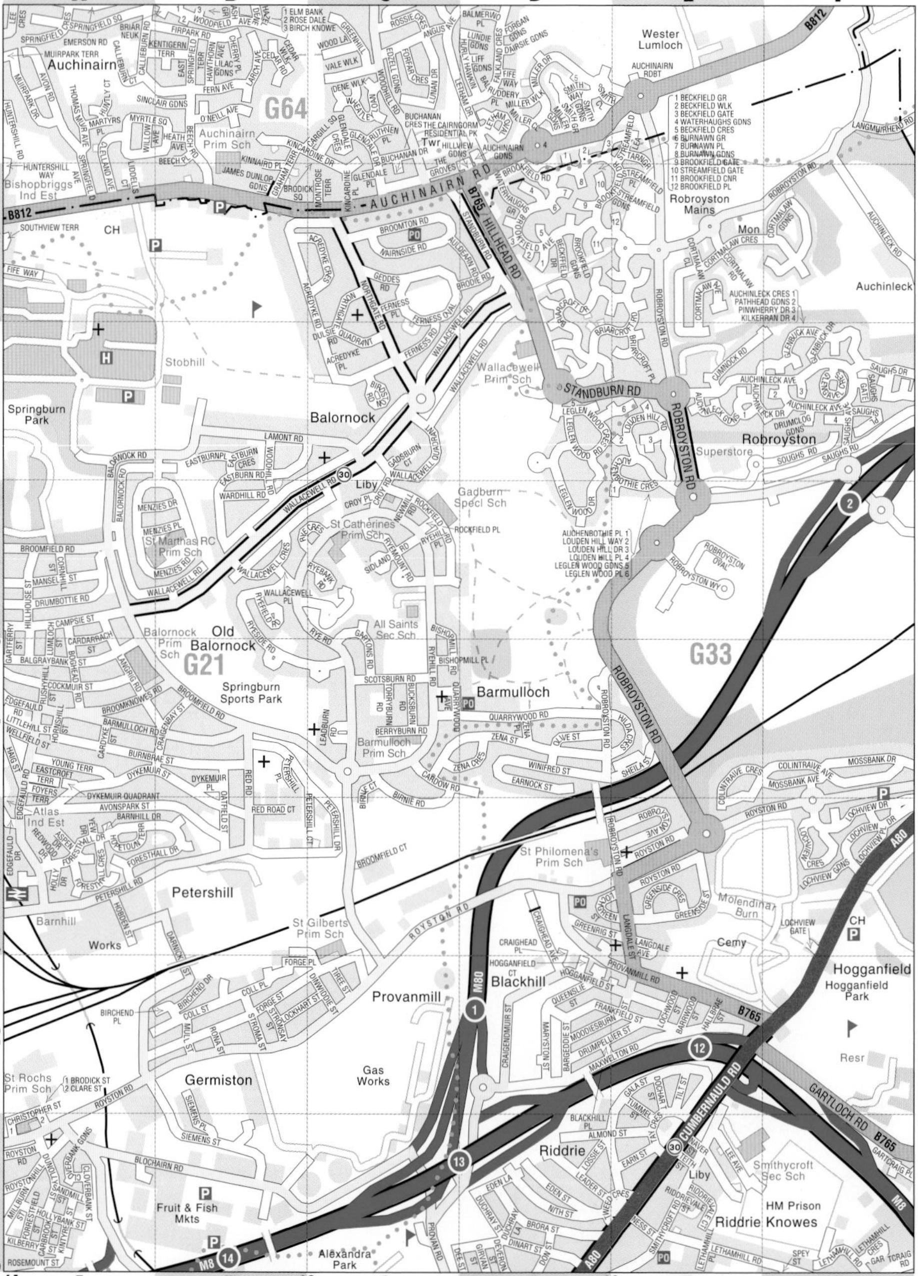

A B C D E F

97
118

79
100

B2
1 Avenue End Prim Sch
2 Croftcroighn Sch

119
100

99
C8
1 FLEMINGTON WY
2 MONKTON BRAE
3 CLIFFVALE RD
80

99
120

81
102

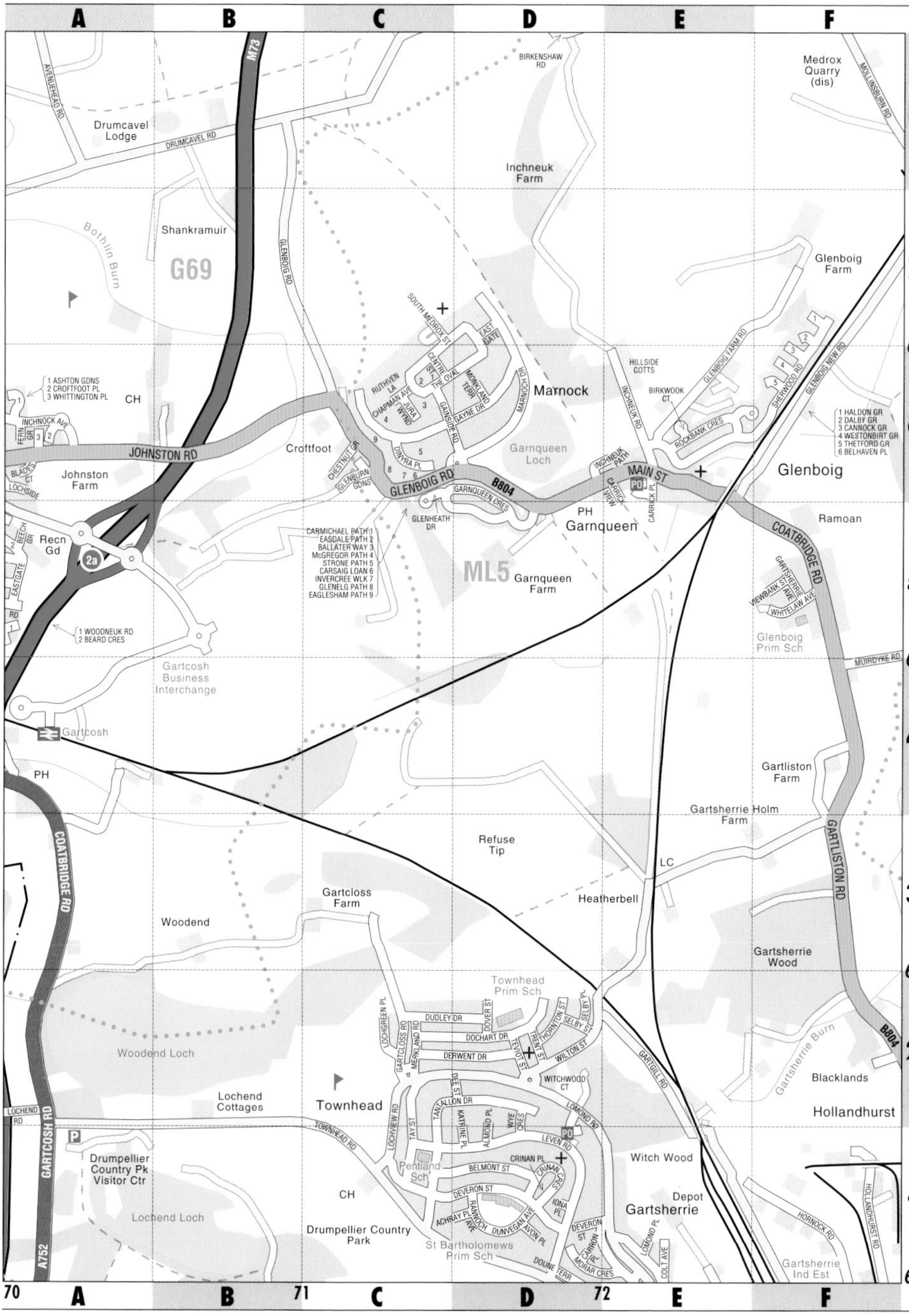

121
102

101
82

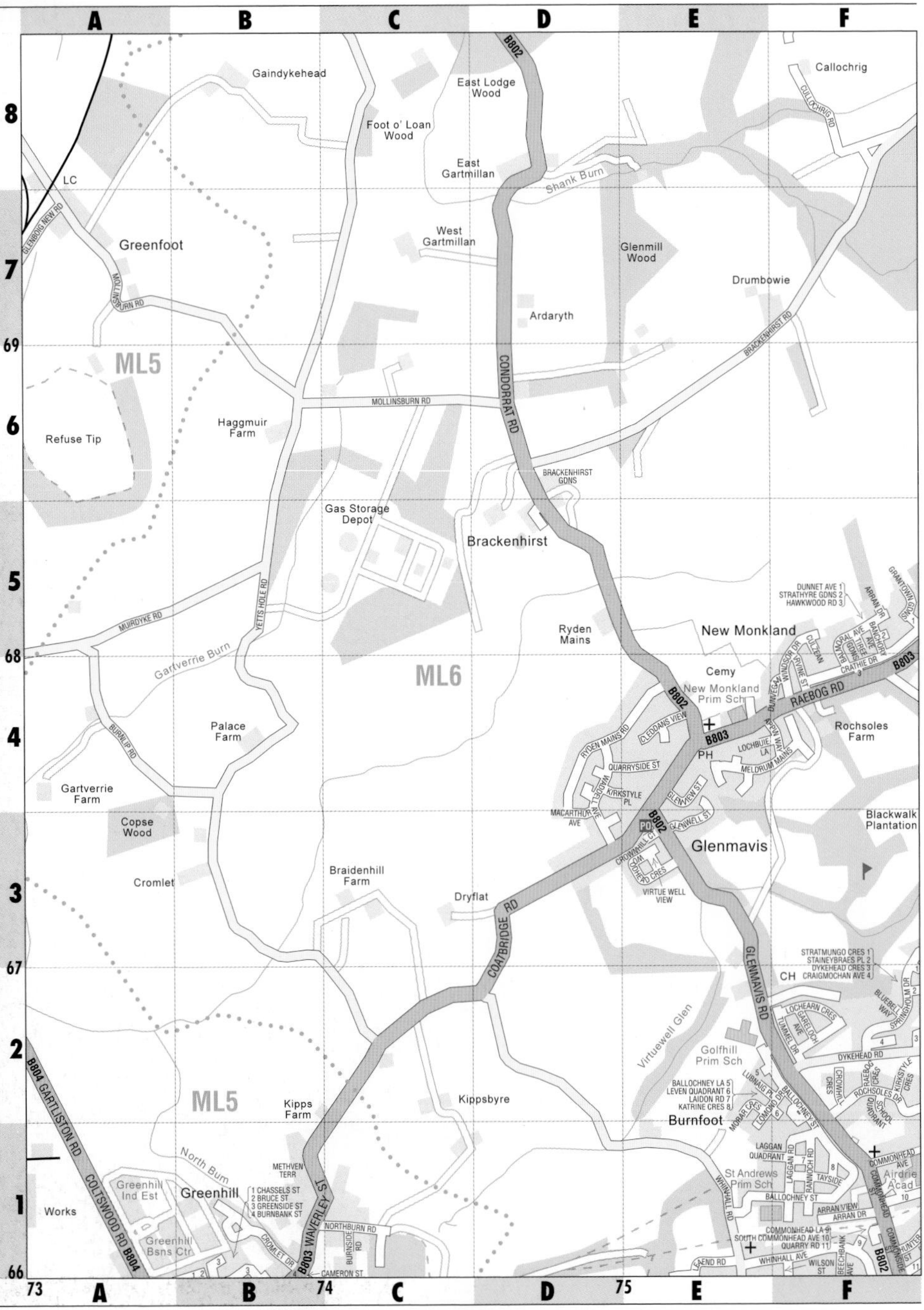

A
B
C
D
E
F
8
7
69
6
5
68
4
3
67
2
1
66
73
74
75
B802
Gaindykehead
East Lodge Wood
Foot o' Loan Wood
East Gartmillan
Callochrig
CULLOCHRIG RD
LC
GLENBOIG NEW RD
Greenfoot
Shank Burn
West Gartmillan
Glenmill Wood
Drumbowie
MOLLINSBURN RD
Ardaryth
BRACKENHIRST RD
ML5
CONDORRAT RD
MOLLINSBURN RD
Haggmuir Farm
Refuse Tip
BRACKENHIRST GDNS
Gas Storage Depot
Brackenhirst
MUIRDYKE RD
YETTS HOLE RD
Ryden Mains
New Monkland
DUNNET AVE 1
STRATHYRE GDNS 2
HAWKWOOD RD 3
Gartverrie Burn
ML6
Cemy
New Monkland Prim Sch
RAEBOG RD
B803
CRATHIE DR
Rochsoles Farm
Palace Farm
BURNLIP RD
RYDEN MAINS RD
CLEDDANS VIEW
QUARRYSIDE ST
PH
LOCHBUIE LA
MELDRUM MAINS
KIRKSTYLE PL
Gartverrie Farm
MACARTHUR AVE
GLENVIEW ST
GLENWELL ST
PO
Glenmavis
Blackwalk Plantation
Copse Wood
CROWHILL CT
VIRTUE WELL VIEW
Cromlet
Braidenhill Farm
Dryflat
COATBRIDGE RD
GLENMAVIS RD
STRATMUNGO CRES 1
STAINEYBRAES PL 2
DYKEHEAD CRES 3
CRAIGMOCHAN AVE 4
CH
Virtuewell Glen
Golfhill Prim Sch
DYKEHEAD RD
B804 GARTLISTON RD
ML5
Kipps Farm
Kippsbyre
BALLOCHNEY LA 5
LEVEN QUADRANT 6
LAIDON RD 7
KATRINE CRES 8
Burnfoot
North Burn
METHVEN TERR
Greenhill Ind Est
Greenhill
1 CHASSELS ST
2 BRUCE ST
3 GREENSIDE ST
4 BURNBANK ST
Works
COLTSWOOD RD B804
Greenhill Bsns Ctr
NORTHBURN RD
BURNSIDE RD
CROMLET DR
B803 WAVERLEY ST
CAMERON ST
WHINHALL RD
St Andrews Prim Sch
LAGGAN QUADRANT
LAGGAN RD
RANNOCH RD
TAYSIDE
BALLOCHNEY ST
Airdrie Acad
COMMONHEAD AVE
ARRAN VIEW
ARRAN DR
COMMONHEAD LA 9
SOUTH COMMONHEAD AVE 10
QUARRY RD 11
WHINHALL AVE
WILSON ST
BEECHBANK AVE
B802

83
104

123
104

A1
1 COTTONMILL CT

A2
1 STRATHMORE CRES
2 STRATHMUNGO CRES
3 STAINEYBRAES PL
4 DYKEHEAD CRES
5 STRATHPEFFER CRES

A3
1 STRATHSPEY CRES
2 STRATHBLANE CRES
3 STRATHTUMMEL CRES
4 SPRINGHOLM DR
5 ARDBEG CRES
6 LOCHSIDE CRES
7 TOBERMORY GDNS
8 SPEYBURN PL
9 ARDMORE CRES

B1
1 BRAMBLE GDNS
2 THORNLEA GDNS

103
84

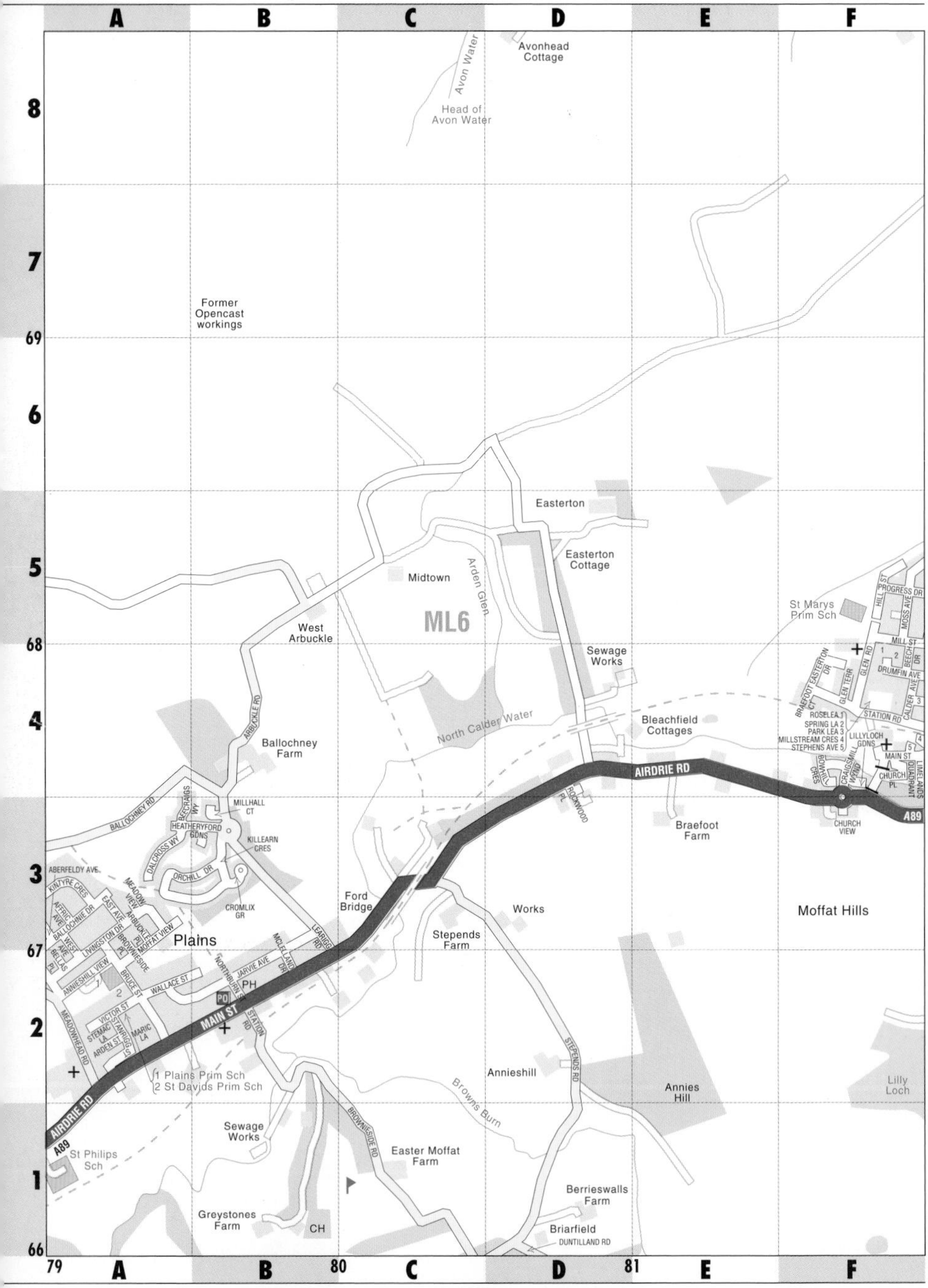

103
124

85
106

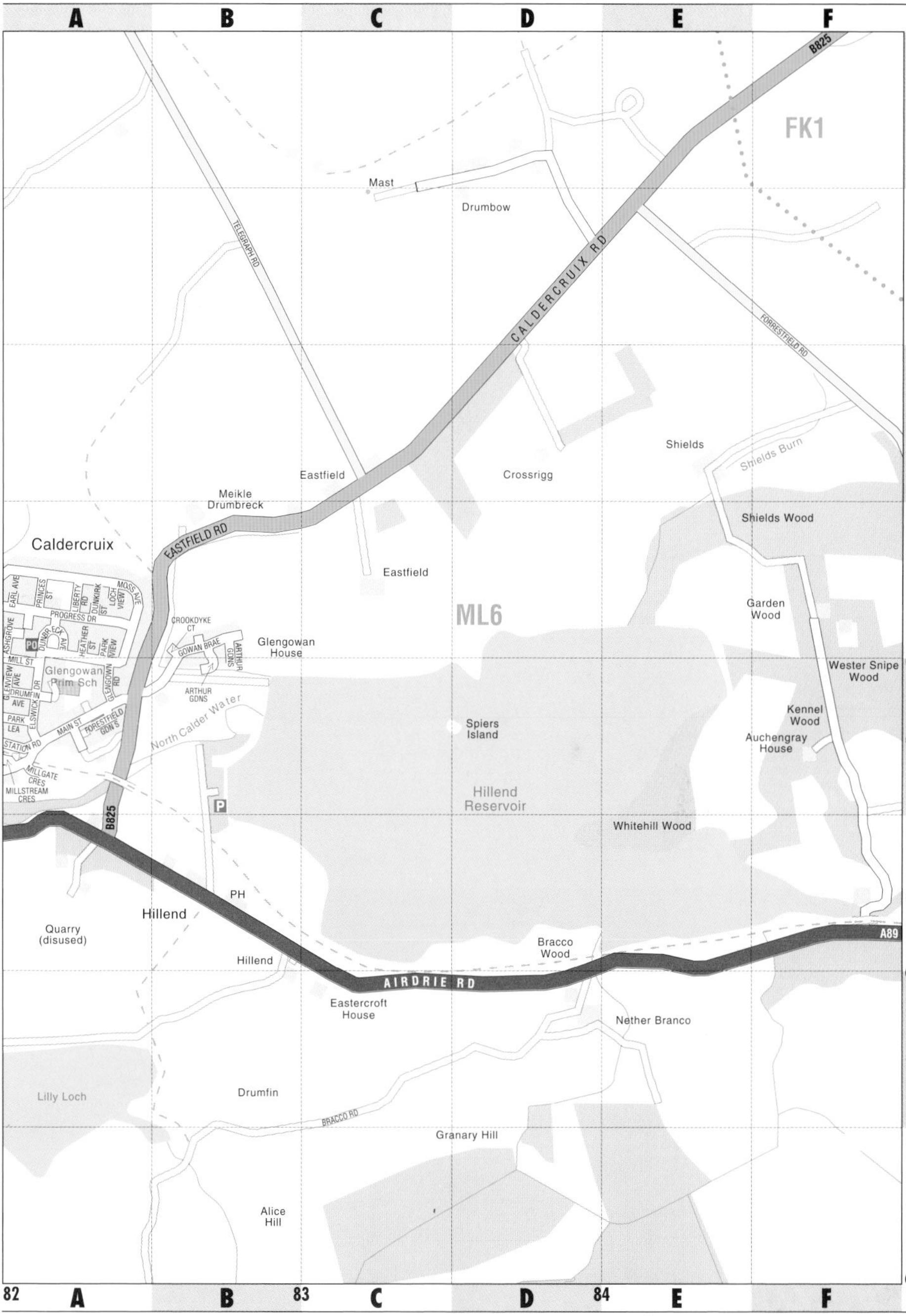

125
106

105 86

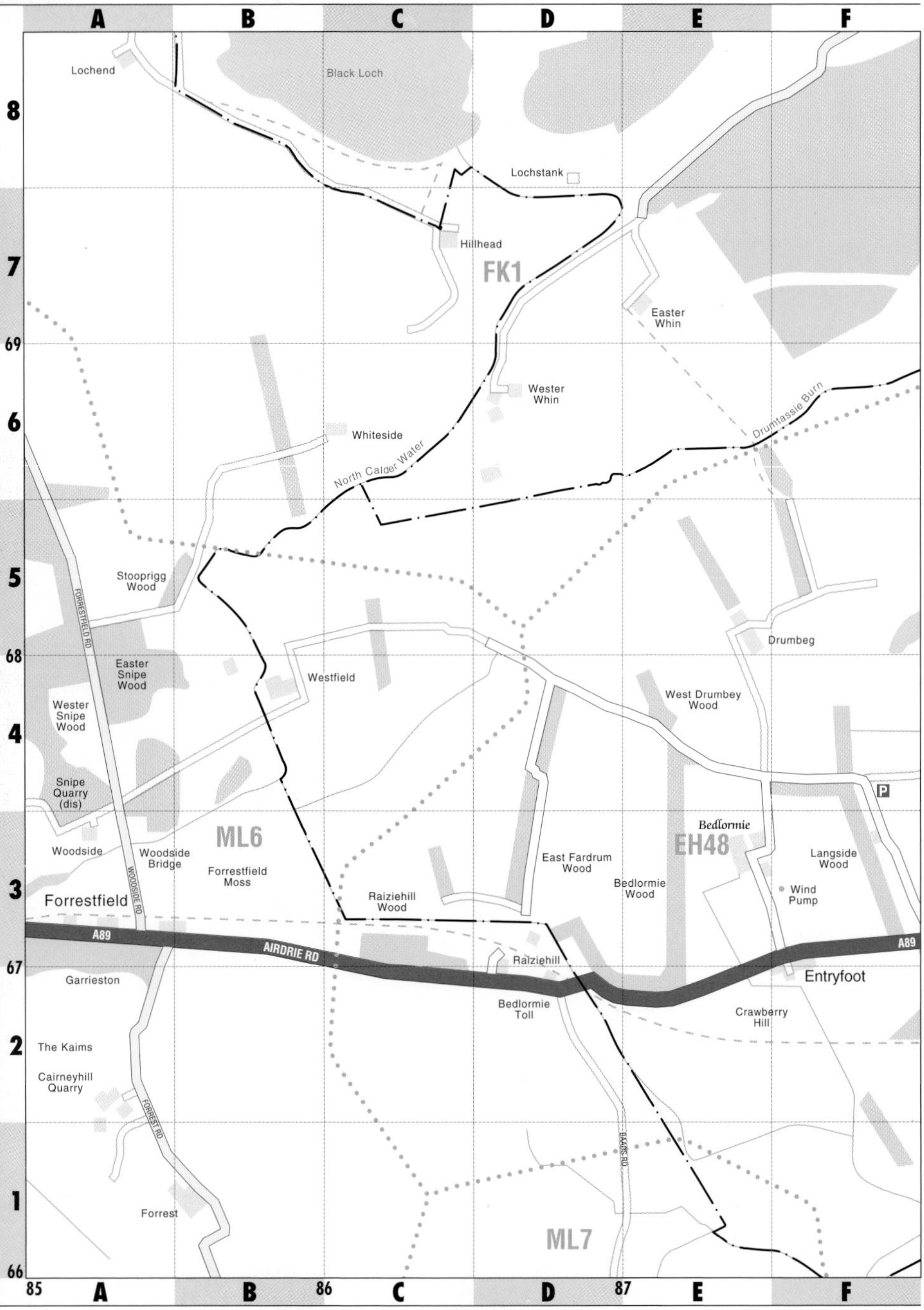

105 126

87

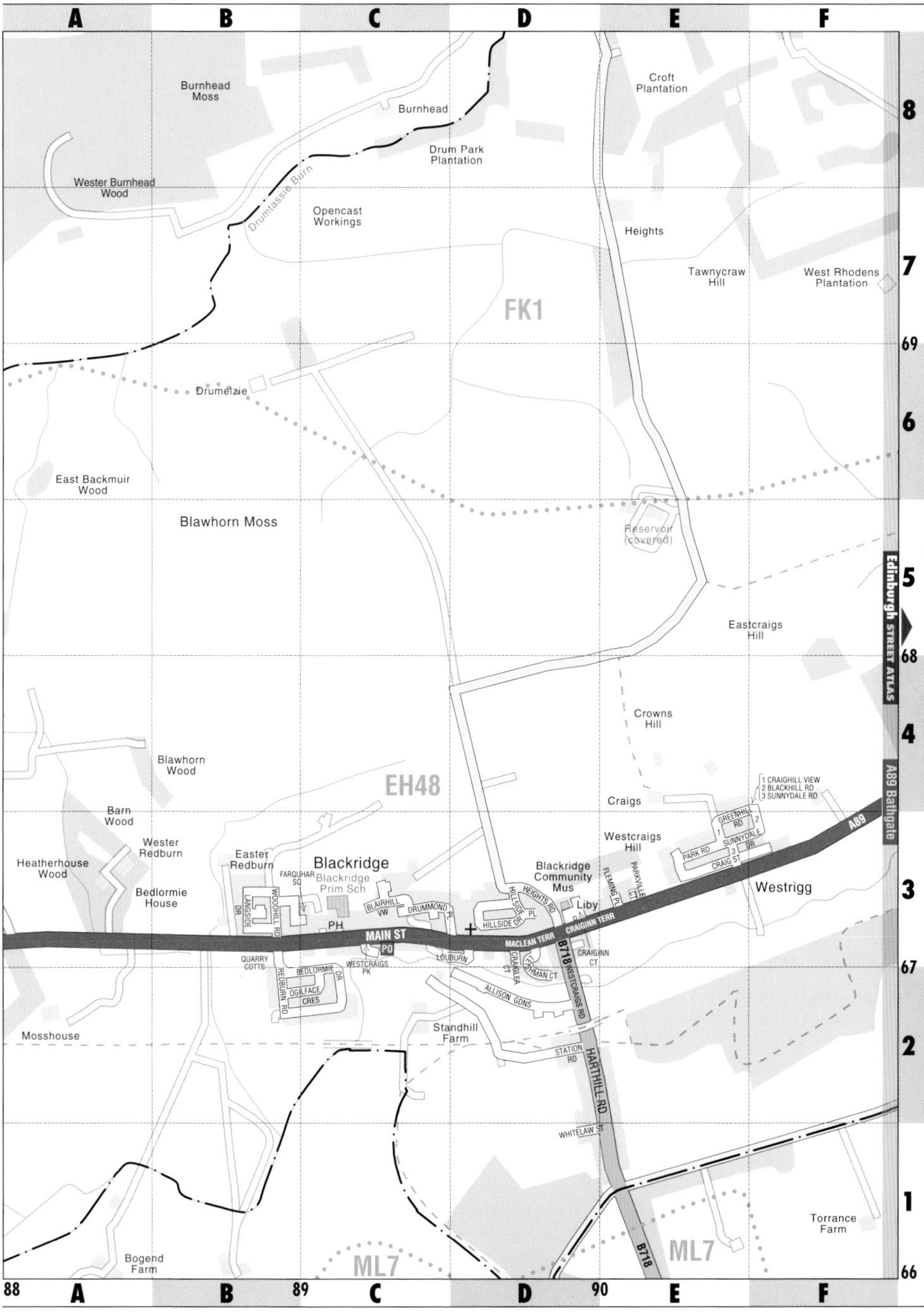
A
B
C
D
E
F
8
7
69
6
5
68
4
3
67
2
1
66
88
89
90
Burnhead Moss
Burnhead
Drum Park Plantation
Croft Plantation
Wester Burnhead Wood
Drumtassie Burn
Opencast Workings
Heights
Tawnycraw Hill
West Rhodens Plantation
FK1
Drumelzie
East Backmuir Wood
Blawhorn Moss
Reservoir (covered)
Eastcraigs Hill
Edinburgh STREET ATLAS
Crowns Hill
Blawhorn Wood
EH48
Craigs
1 CRAIGHILL VIEW
2 BLACKHILL RD
3 SUNNYDALE RD
A89 Bathgate
A89
Barn Wood
Wester Redburn
Heatherhouse Wood
Easter Redburn
Blackridge
Blackridge Prim Sch
Westcraigs Hill
Blackridge Community Mus
Westrigg
Bedlormie House
FARQUHAR SQ
LANGSIDE DR
WOODHILL RD
PH
BLAIRHILL VW
DRUMMOND PL
HILLSIDE PL
HEIGHTS RD
HILLSIDE DR
Liby
FLEMING PL
PARKVILLE CT
GREENHILL RD
SUNNYDALE DR
PARK RD
CRAIG ST
MAIN ST
PO
MACLEAN TERR
CRAIGINN TERR
B718
CRAIGINN CT
QUARRY COTTS
BEDLORMIE DR
REDBURN RD
OGILFACE CRES
WESTCRAIGS PK
LOUBURN
CRAIGLEA CT
LOCHMAN CT
WESTCRAIGS RD
ALLISON GDNS
Mosshouse
Standhill Farm
STATION RD
HARTHILL RD
WHITELAW ST
Torrance Farm
ML7
Bogend Farm

88

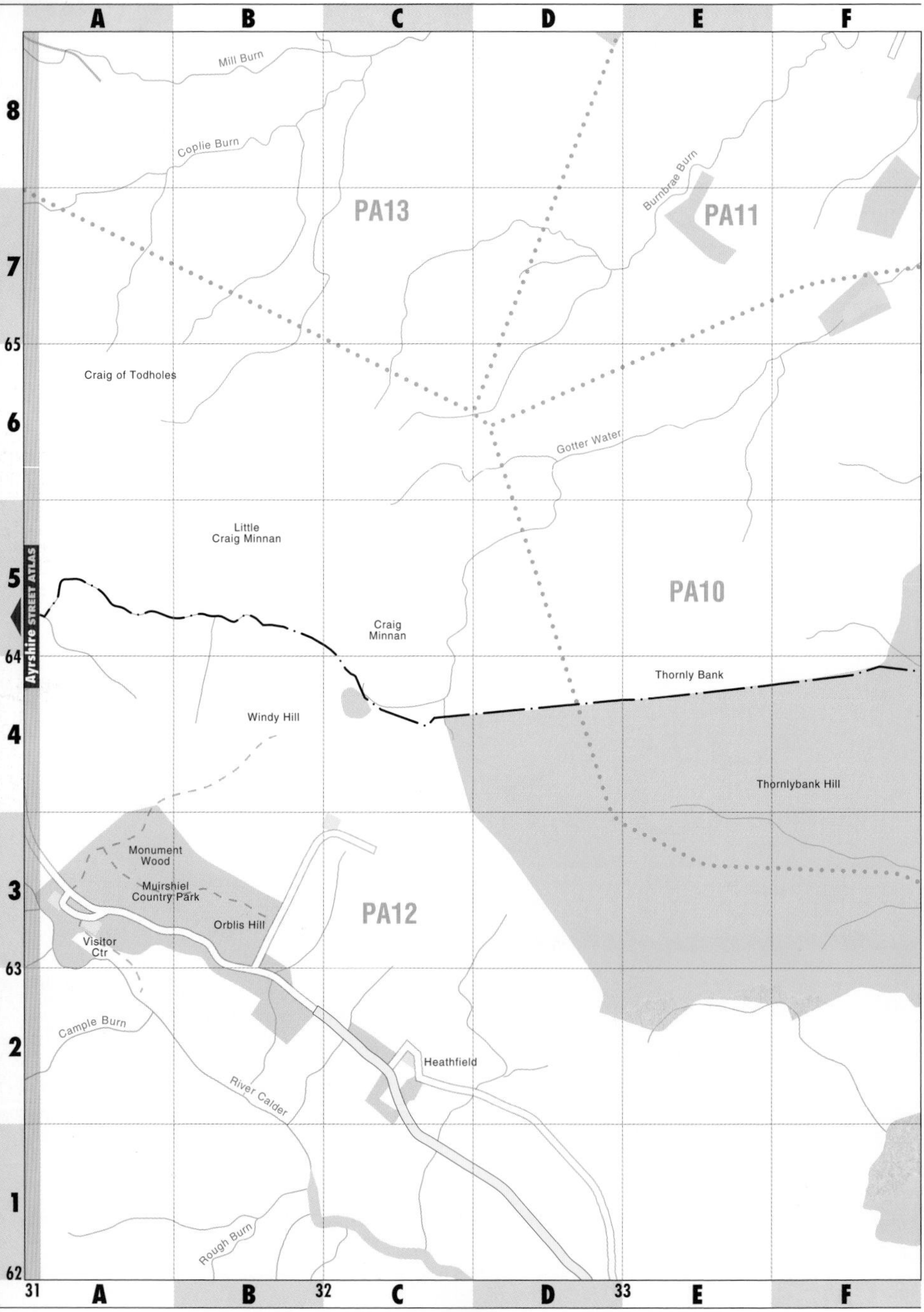
A
B
C
D
E
F
8
7
65
6
5
64
4
3
63
2
1
62
31
32
33
Mill Burn
Coplie Burn
PA13
Burnbrae Burn
PA11
Craig of Todholes
Gotter Water
Little
Craig Minnan
PA10
Craig
Minnan
Thornly Bank
Windy Hill
Thornlybank Hill
Monument
Wood
Muirshiel
Country Park
Orblis Hill
PA12
Visitor
Ctr
Campl e Burn
Heathfield
River Calder
Rough Burn
Ayrshire STREET ATLAS

128

89
110

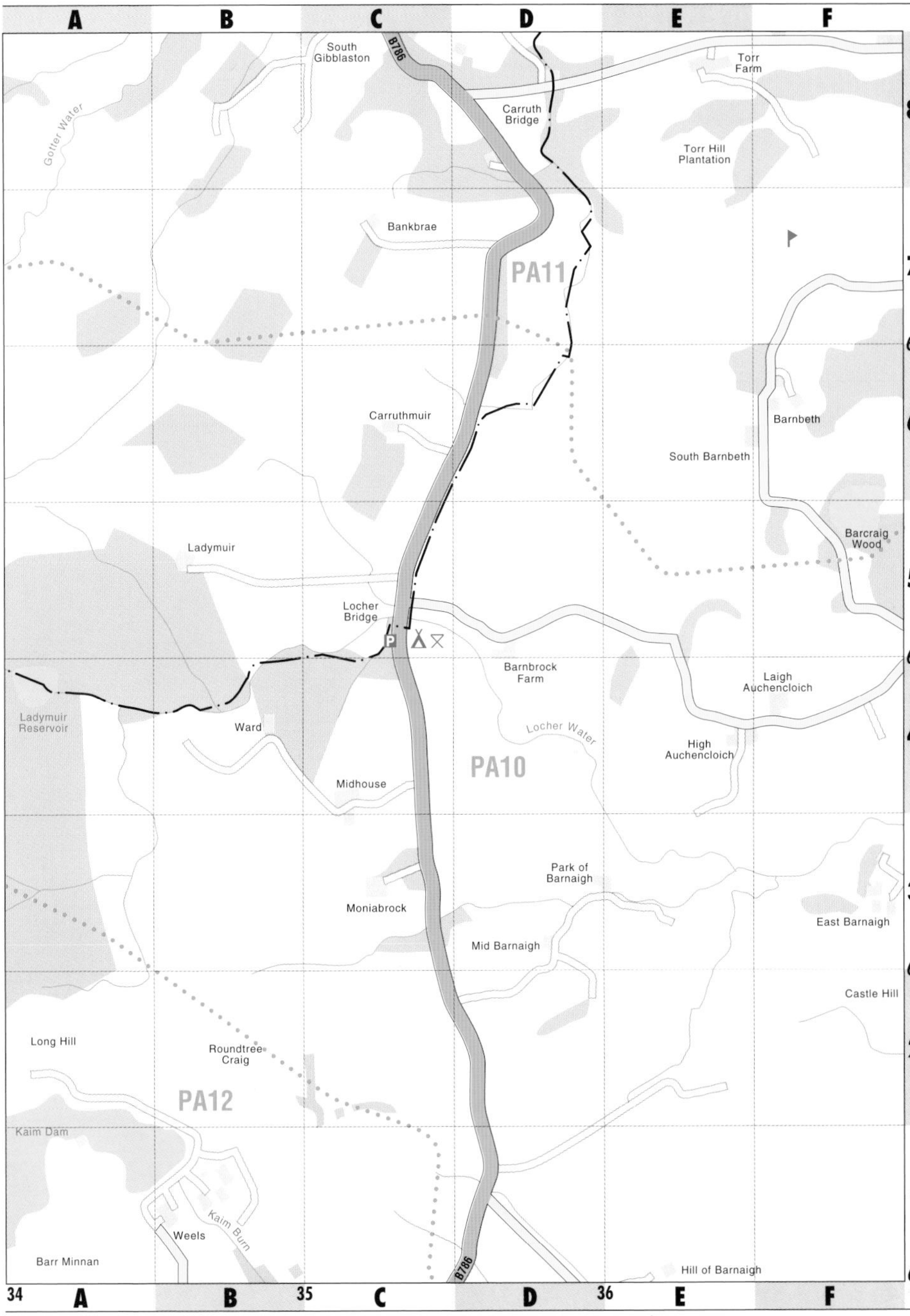

129
110

109
90

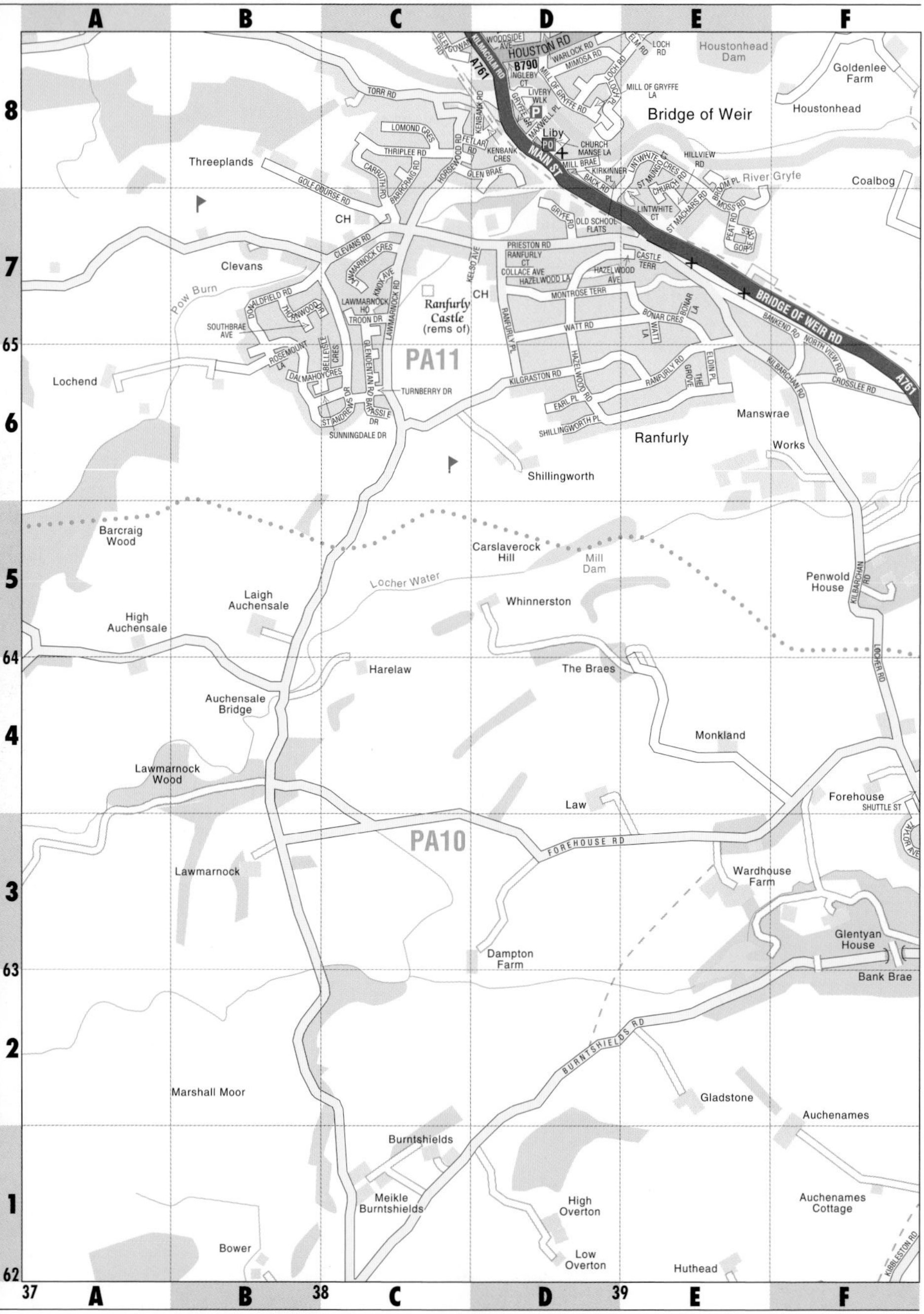

109
130

91
112

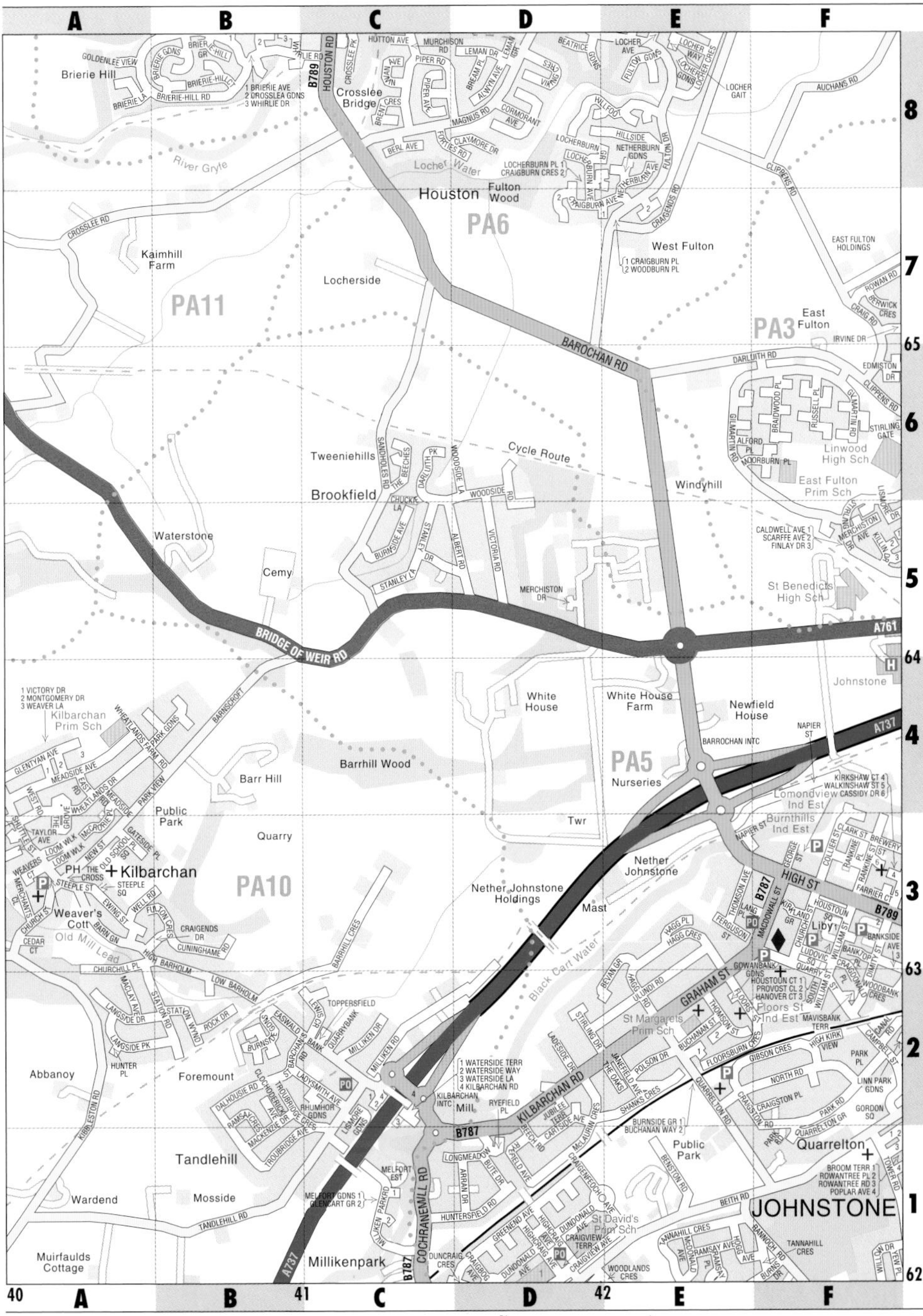

D1
1 Cochrane Castle Prim Sch

131
112

111
92

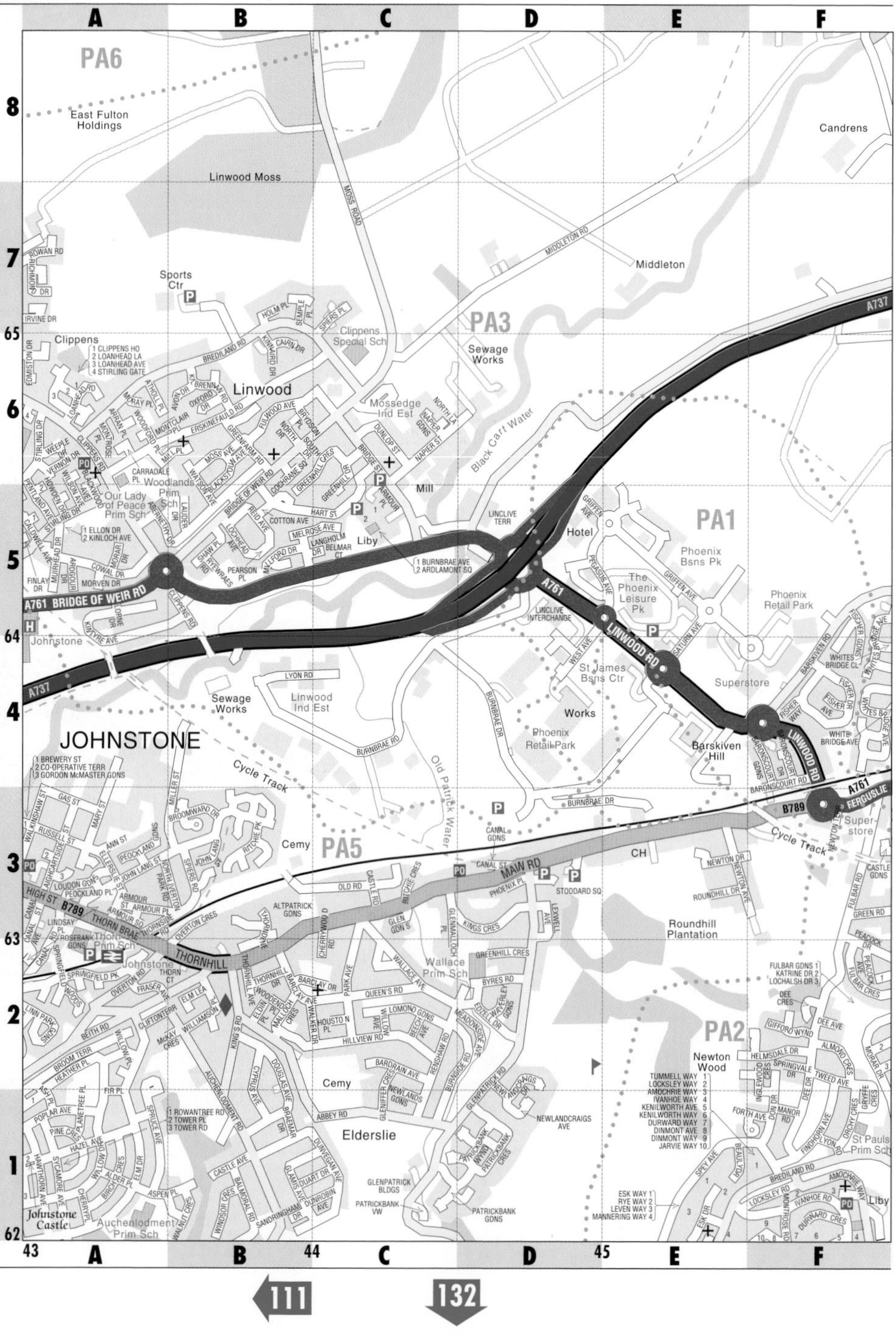

111
132

E5
1 MONCRIEFF ST
2 STONEY BRAE
3 BACK SNEDDON ST
4 MAXWELL ST
5 MEETINGHOUSE LA
6 COUNTY SQ
7 COUNTY PL
8 CENTRAL WAY

93

D8
1 ABBOTSBURN WAY
2 BROOMDYKE WAY
3 CONVAL WAY
4 MALVERN WAY
5 WENDUR WAY

114

F5
1 BRICK LA
2 WALLNEUK
3 EAST BUCHANAN MEWS

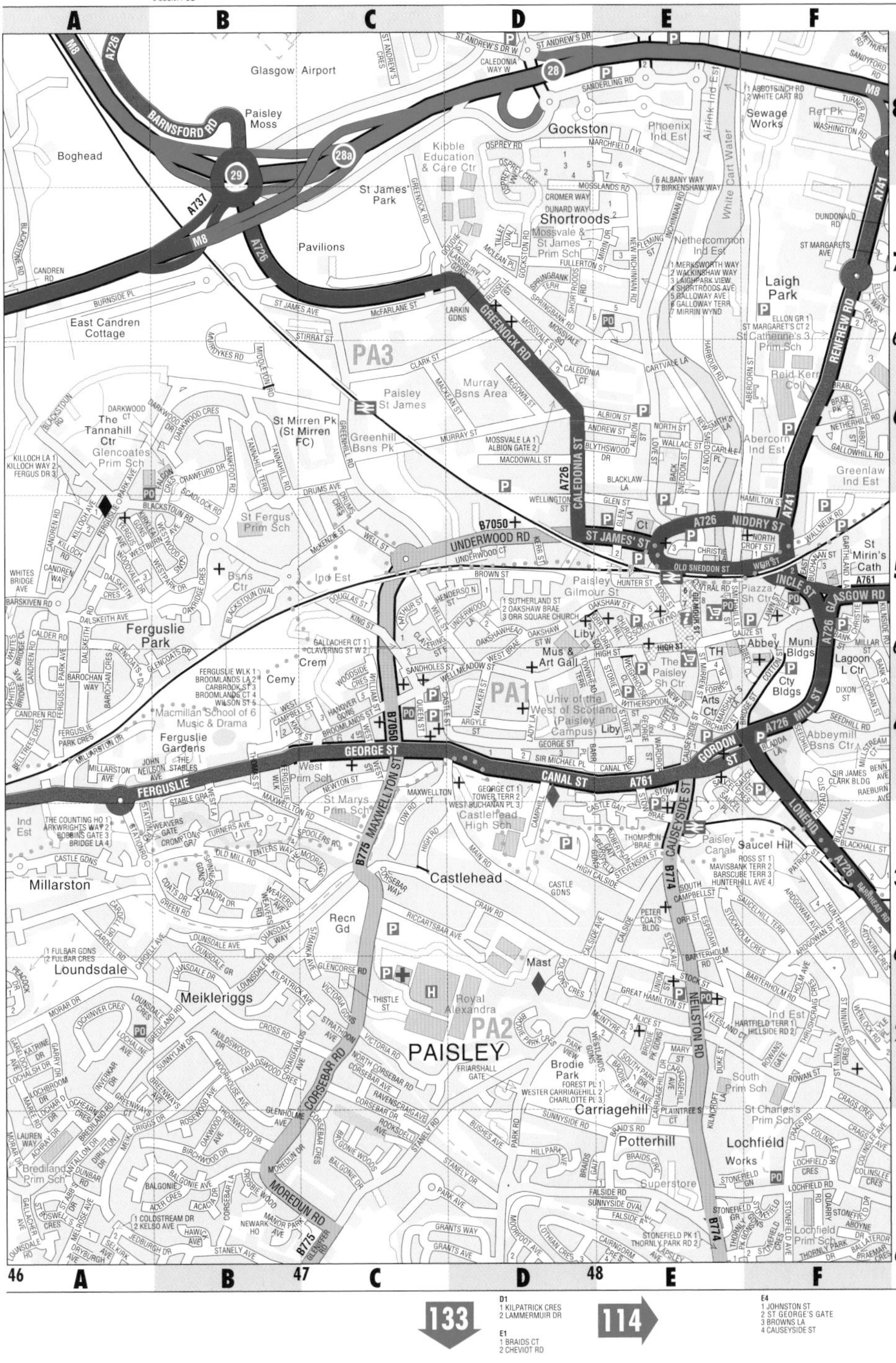

D1
1 KILPATRICK CRES
2 LAMMERMUIR DR

E1
1 BRAIDS CT
2 CHEVIOT RD

133

114

E4
1 JOHNSTON ST
2 ST GEORGE'S GATE
3 BROWNS LA
4 CAUSEYSIDE ST

113
94

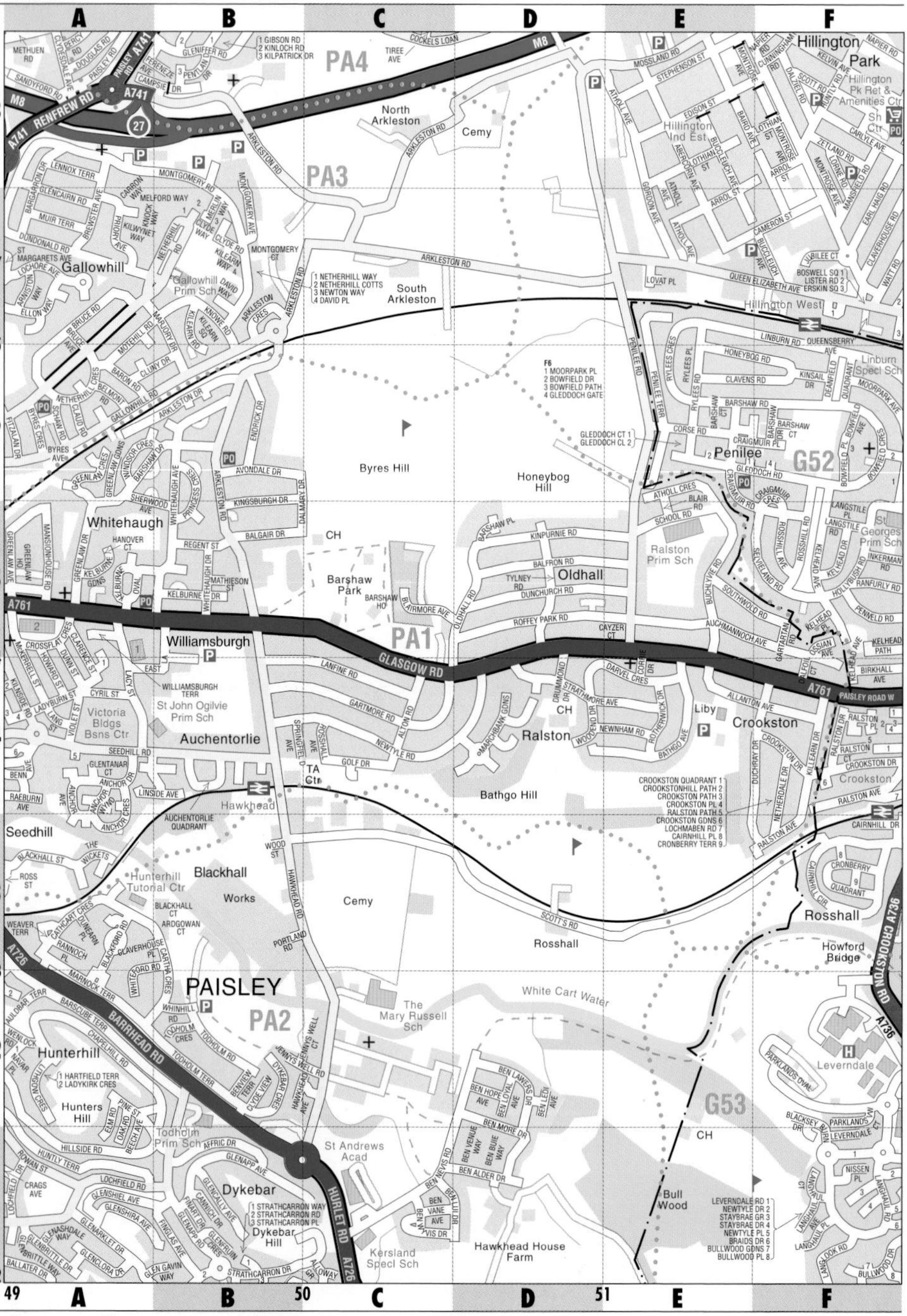

A4
1 CLARENCE DR
2 DIXON ST
3 BANK ST
4 UNSTED PL
5 RALSTON ST
6 MILLSTREAM CT

A5
1 Williamsburgh Prim Sch
2 Paisley Grammar Sch

113
134

D6
1 TORMORE ST
2 DAVIOT ST
3 MONTGARRIE ST
4 HILLBRAE ST

95

D7
1 MARCHGLEN PL
2 MELNESS PL
3 MELVICK PL
4 SILVER BIRCH DR
5 SILVER BIRCH GDNS
6 ELDER GROVE PL

116

7 ELDER GROVE CT
8 MOUNTGARRIE PATH
9 MOUNTGARRIE RD
10 MOREFIELD RD
E8
1 LINTHOUSE BLDGS
2 HOLMFAULD RD

3 HOLMFAULDHEAD PL
4 CLACHAN DR
F7
1 ELDERPARK GR
2 CROSSLOAN TERR

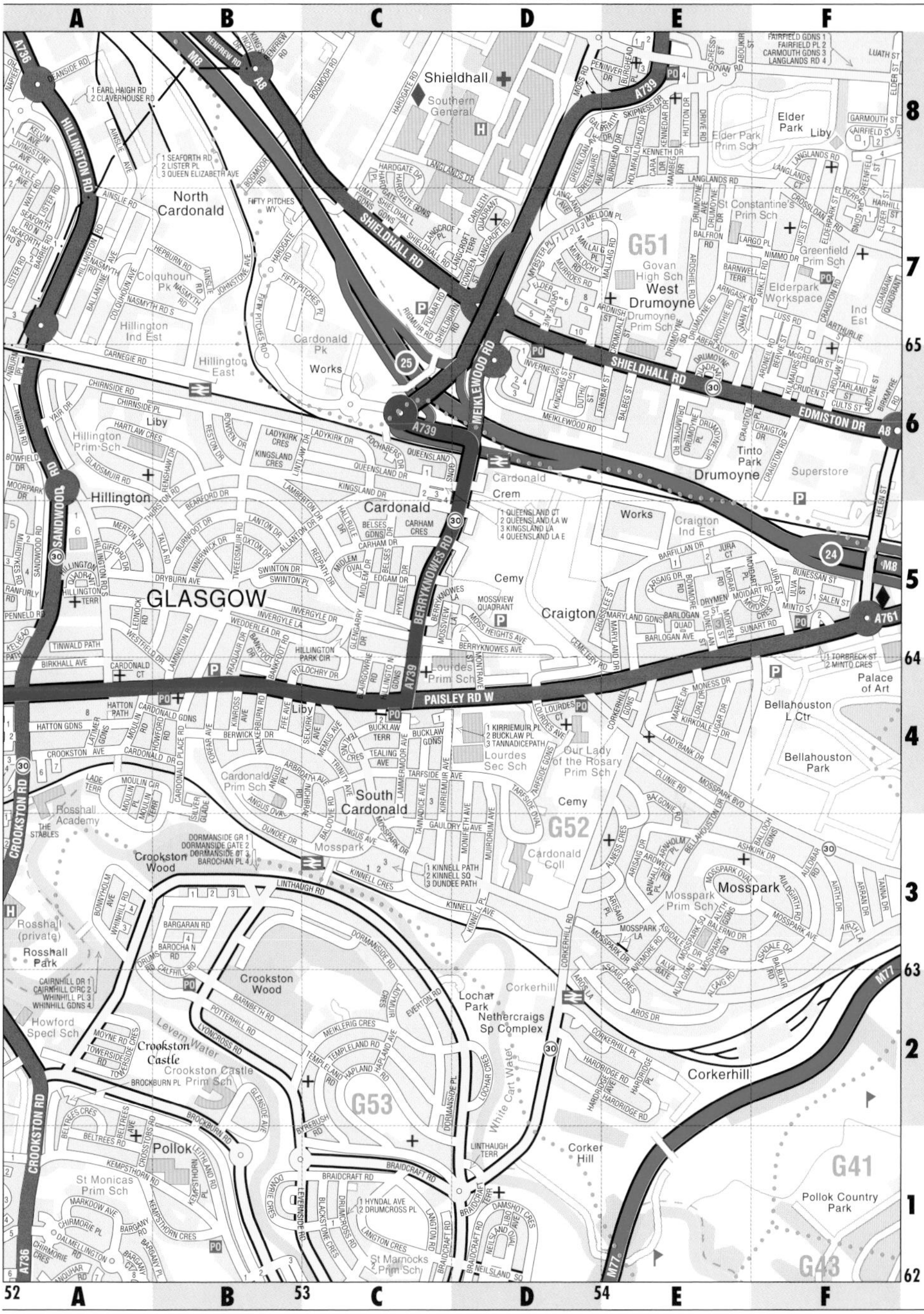

A1
1 LEVERNDALE RD
2 NEWTYLE DR
3 NEWTYLE PL
4 BRAIDS DR
5 BULLWOOD DR
6 BULLWOOD CT
7 BALLOCHMYLE DR
8 BARGANY PL

A4
1 CROOKSTON QUADRANT2
CROOKSTON TERR
3 CROOKSTON DR
4 RALSTON AVE
5 LOCHMABEN RD
6 CROOKSTON GR
7 CROOKSTON CT
8 LATIMER PATH

A5
1 SANDWOOD PATH
2 MUIRDYKES AVE
3 INKERMAN RD
4 SANDWOOD CRES
5 St Georges Prim Sch
6 Sandwood Prim Sch

B1
1 DEVOL CRES
2 LEITHLAND AVE
3 LEVERNSIDE CRES

135

116

E5
1 LUING RD
2 COLONSAY RD
3 Craigton Prim Sch

A8
1 HARMONY ROW
2 WARDROP ST
3 GARMOUTH CT
4 GARMOUTH GDNS
D5
1 CLIFFORD PL

2 LANGSHOT ST
3 PLANTATION PARK GDNS
E5
1 MILNPARK GDNS
2 LAMBHILL QUADRANT
3 SEAWARD ST

115

E6
1 EAGLESHAM CT
2 EAGLESHAM PL
3 MIDDLESEX GDNS

96

E8
1 CLIFTON PL
2 FITZROY PL
3 WESTMINSTER TERR
4 DERBY TERRACE LA
5 CORUNNA ST
6 Stobcross Bsns Pk

7 HOULDSWORTH LA
8 Clydeway Ind Est
9 FINNIESTON SQ
10 MINERVA CT
11 SANFORD PL

For full street detail of the highlighted area see page 240.

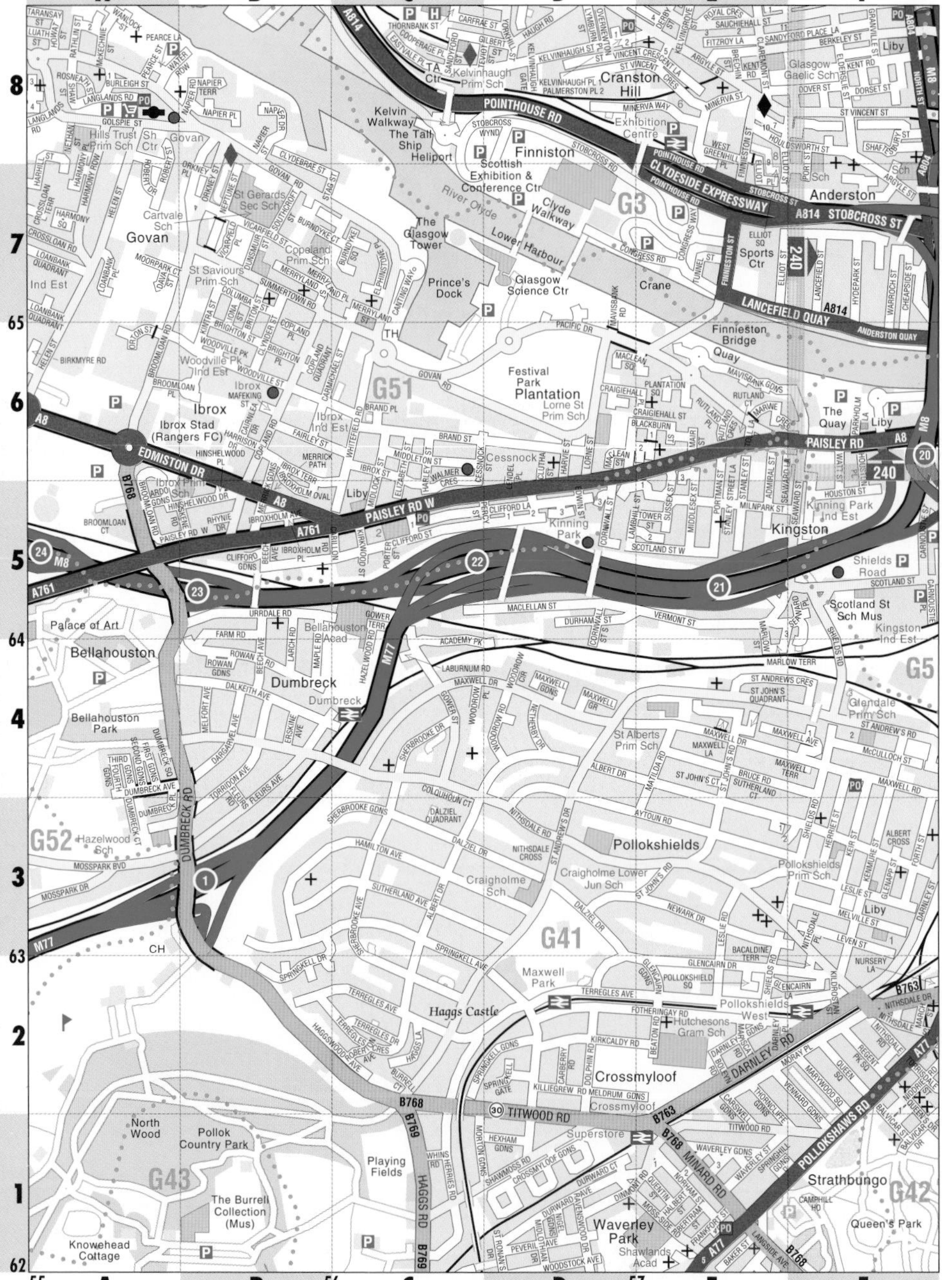

A
B
C
D
E
F

115

C5
1 NORTH GOWER ST
2 Bellahouston Prim Sch

136

E1
1 DINMONT PL
2 LOCHSIDE ST
3 WESTCLYFFE ST
4 ABBOT ST
5 SHAWLANDS CROSS
E3
1 KNOWEHEAD TERR
2 KNOWEHEAD GDNS

F2
1 NIDDRIE SQ
2 BARBRECK RD
F4
1 MAXWELL OVAL
2 LINCLUDEN PATH
3 ST ANDREWS CL

F3
1 Pollokshields Prim Sch Annexe

For full street detail of the highlighted area see pages 240 and 241.

B5
1 LANGBANK ST
2 KILBARCHAN ST
3 COBURG ST
4 HERBERTSON ST
5 S PORTLAND ST
6 BEDFORD LA
7 STIRLINGFAULD PL

97

F5
1FORBESDR
2 REDAN ST
3 OLYMPIA ST
4 Bridgeton Bsns Ctr
F6
1 ABERCROMBY SQ

118

2 MILLROAD GDNS
E5
1 ABERCROMBY ST
2 GRAIGNESTOCK PL
3 MONTEITH PL
F7
1 McINTOSH CT

2 CARDROSS CT
3 SETON TERR
4 OAKLEY TERR
5 CLAYTON TERR
6 BROOMPARK ST
7 WESTERCRAIGS CT
8 BROOMPARK CIR

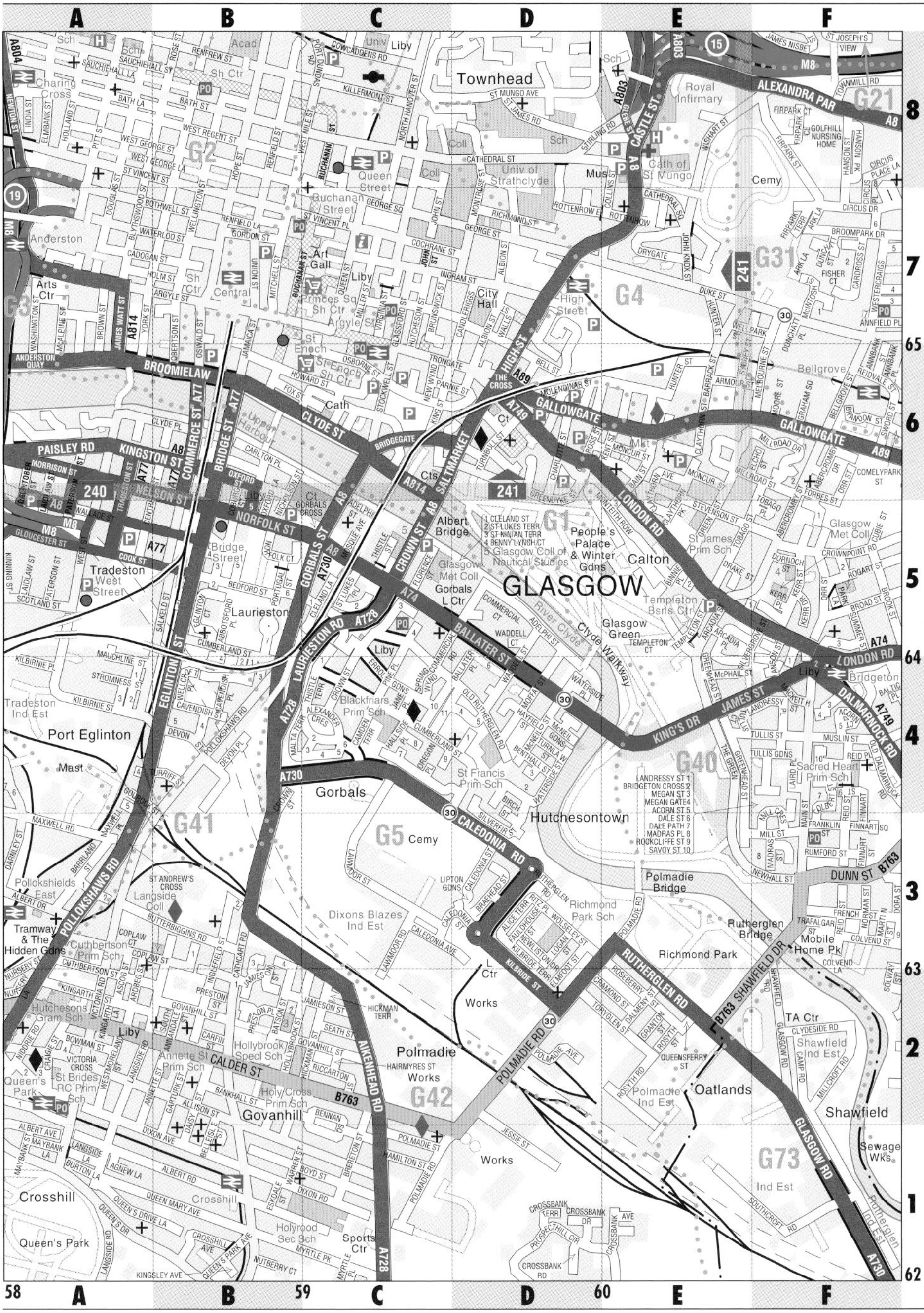

A2
1 TORRISDALE ST
2 PRINCE EDWARD ST
3 ALLISON PL
4 CHAPMAN ST
A3
1 MUIRHOUSE ST
2 BUTTERFIELD PL
A4
1 FALFIELD ST
2 FRANCIS ST
3 RITCHIE ST
4 LAUDER ST
5 CARDWELL ST
6 ST ANDREW'S RD
7 McCULLOCH ST
B2
1 JAMIESON CT
2 HOLLYBROOK PL
3 Victoria Prim Sch
B3
1 ANNANDALE ST
2 LARKFIELD ST
3 ROBSON GR
4 MORGAN MEWS
B4
1 SURREY LA
2 SALISBURY ST
3 SURREY ST
4 ABBOTSFORD PL
5 CAVENDISH CT
C4
1 SANDIEFIELD RD
2 SOUTHSIDE CRES
3 HANDEL PL
4 KIDSTON TERR
5 KIDSTON PL
6 NABURN GATE
7 GILMOUR PL
8 HUTCHINSON TOWN CT
9 CUMBERLAND PL
10 QUEEN ELIZABETH GDNS
11 QUEEN ELIZABETH SQ

137

D4
1 SANDYFAULDS ST
2 SNOWDON PL
3 SNOWDON ST
4 ST FRANCIS RIGG
5 ST VALENTINE TERR
6 MATHIESON TERR

118

A8
1 ALEXANDRA GATE
2 Alexandra Parade Prim Sch

117
98

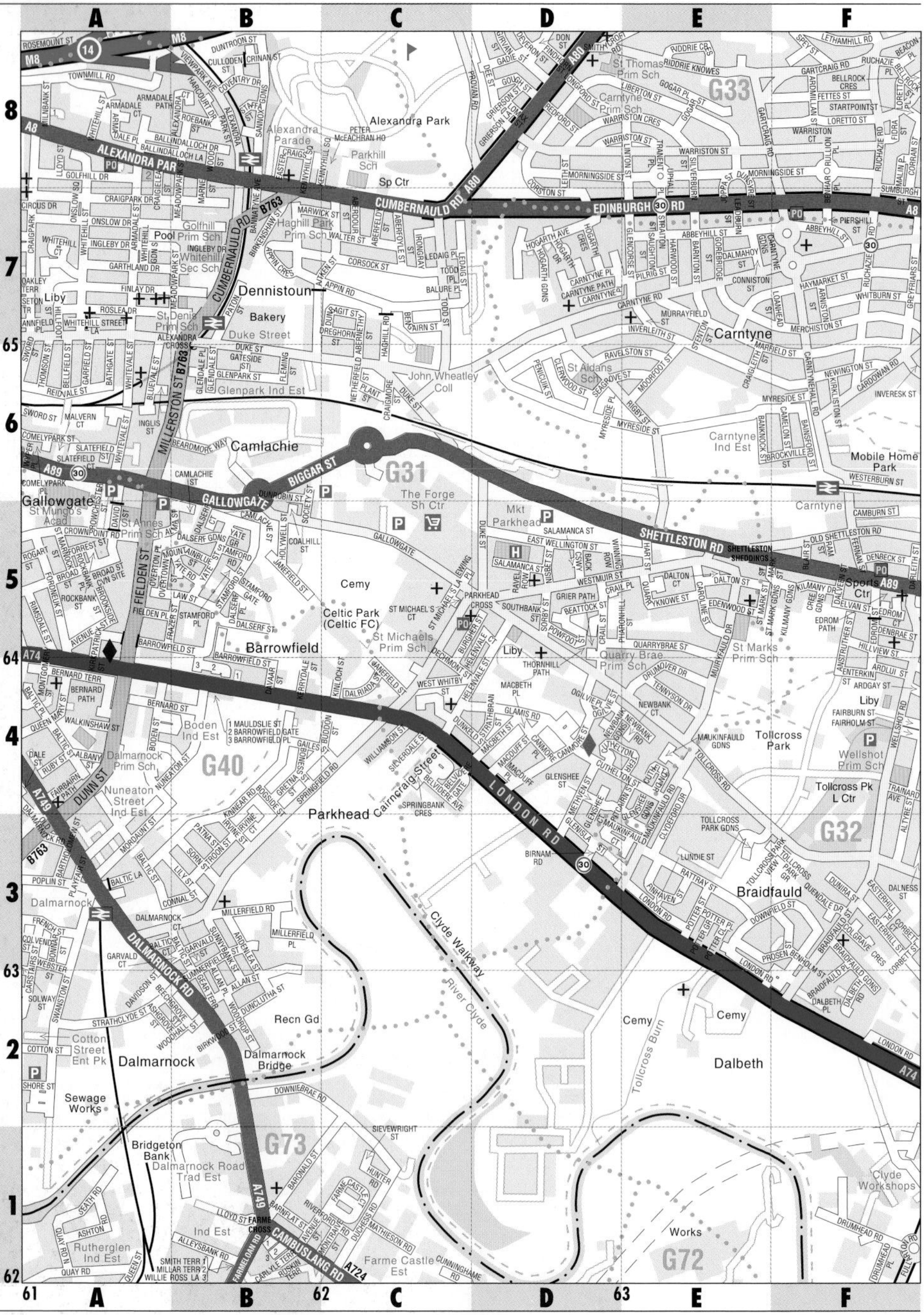

117
138

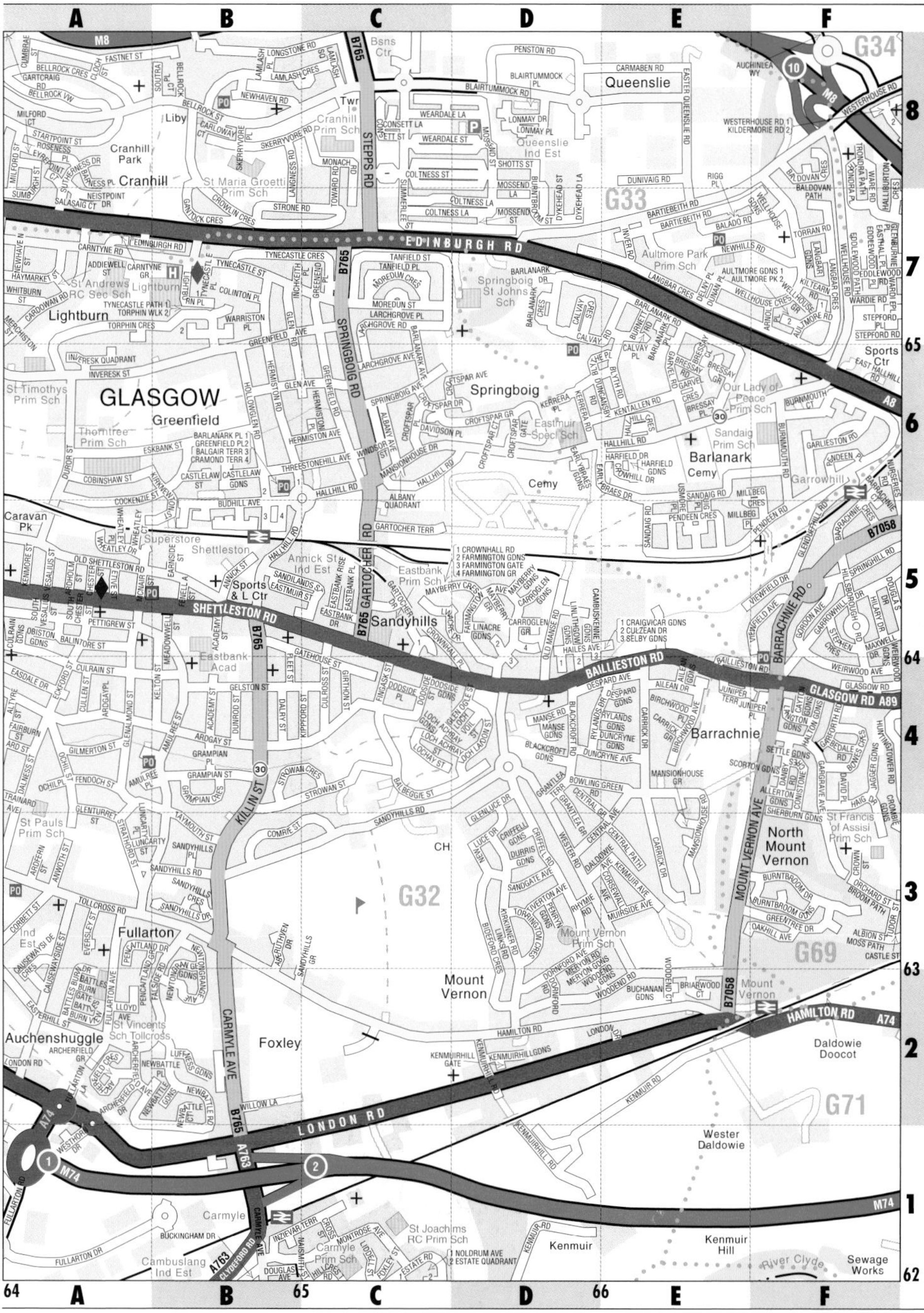
A
B
C
D
E
F
8
7
6
5
4
3
2
1
65
64
63
62
66
M8
Queenslie
Queenslie Ind Est
G34
G33
Liby
Cranhill Park
Cranhill
St Maria Goretti Prim Sch
Cranhill Prim Sch
STEPPS RD
EDINBURGH RD
Lightburn
St Andrews RC Sec Sch
GLASGOW
Greenfield
St Timothys Prim Sch
Thorntree Prim Sch
Springboig
Springboig St Johns Sch
SPRINGBOIG RD
Eastmuir Specl Sch
Barlanark
Aultmore Park Prim Sch
Our Lady of Peace Prim Sch
Sandaig Prim Sch
Cemy
Garrowhill
A8
Sports Ctr
Caravan Pk
Superstore
Shettleston
Annick St Ind Est
Eastbank Prim Sch
Sports & L Ctr
SHETTLESTON RD
Sandyhills
BAILLIESTON RD
GLASGOW RD A89
Eastbank Acad
Barrachnie
B7058
BARRACHNIE RD
MOUNT VERNON AVE
North Mount Vernon
St Francis of Assisi Prim Sch
St Pauls Prim Sch
KILLIN ST
G32
CH
Fullarton
Mount Vernon Prim Sch
Mount Vernon
G69
Auchenshuggle
St Vincents Sch Tollcross
Foxley
CARMYLE AVE
HAMILTON RD
A74
Daldowie Doocot
LONDON RD
G71
Wester Daldowie
M74
Carmyle
Carmyle Prim Sch
St Joachims RC Prim Sch
Kenmuir
Kenmuir Hill
River Clyde
Sewage Works
Cambuslang Ind Est
A763

119

C8
1 MILLENNIUM GR
2 HONEYWELL CT

100

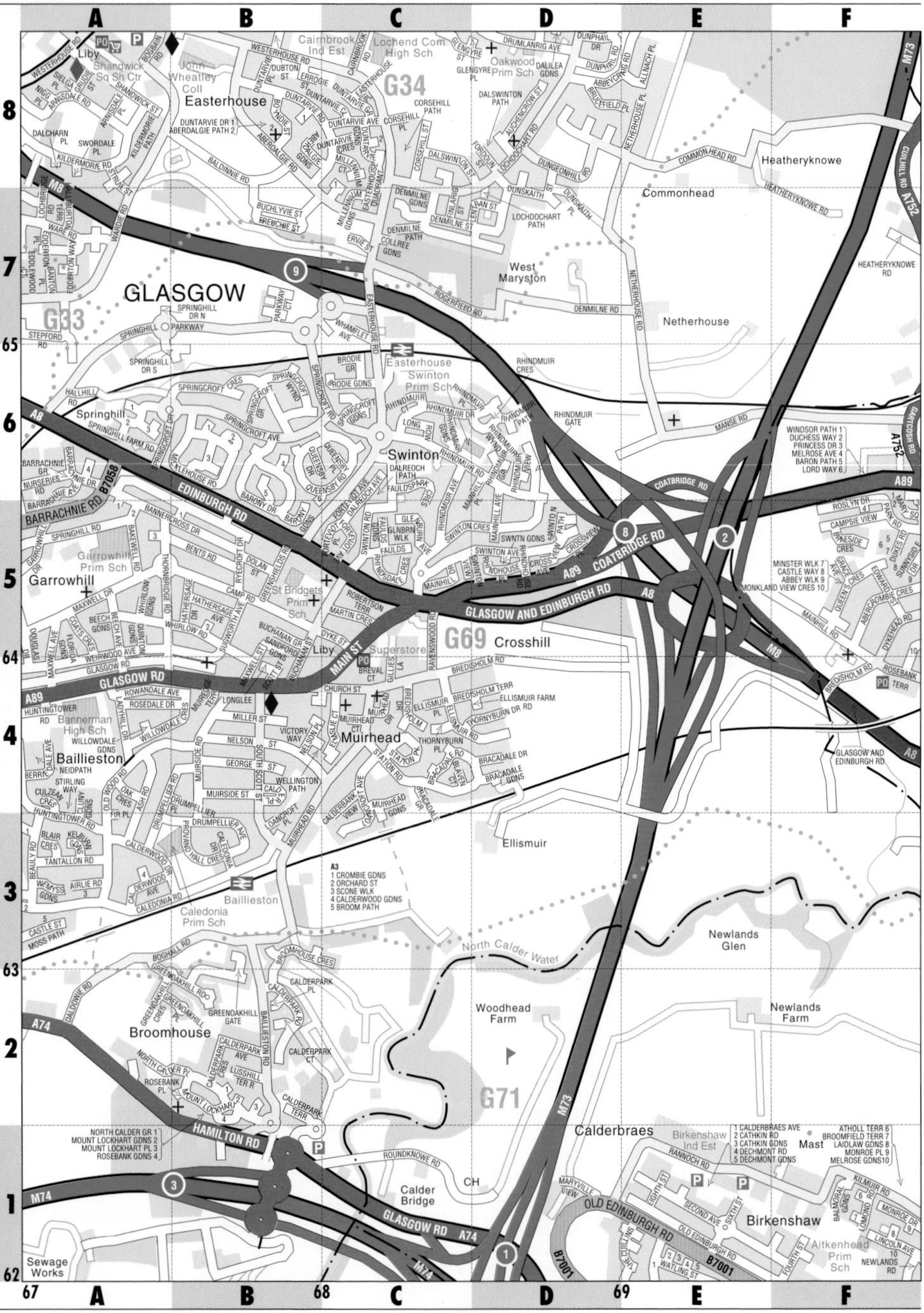

A6
1 SPRINGHILL FARM PL
2 SPRINGHILL FARM WAY
3 SPRINGHILL FARM GR
4 BARRACHNIE PL

A5
1 BANNERCROSS GDNS
2 BANNERCROSS AVE
3 THORNBRIDGE GDNS

B6
1 MICKLEHOUSE PL
2 MICKLEHOUSE OVAL
3 MICKLEHOUSE WYND
4 BARONY CT
5 BARONY WYND
6 QUEENSBY AVE

B5
1 THORNBRIDGE AVE
2 HATHERSAGE GDNS

119

140

101 122

A B C D E F

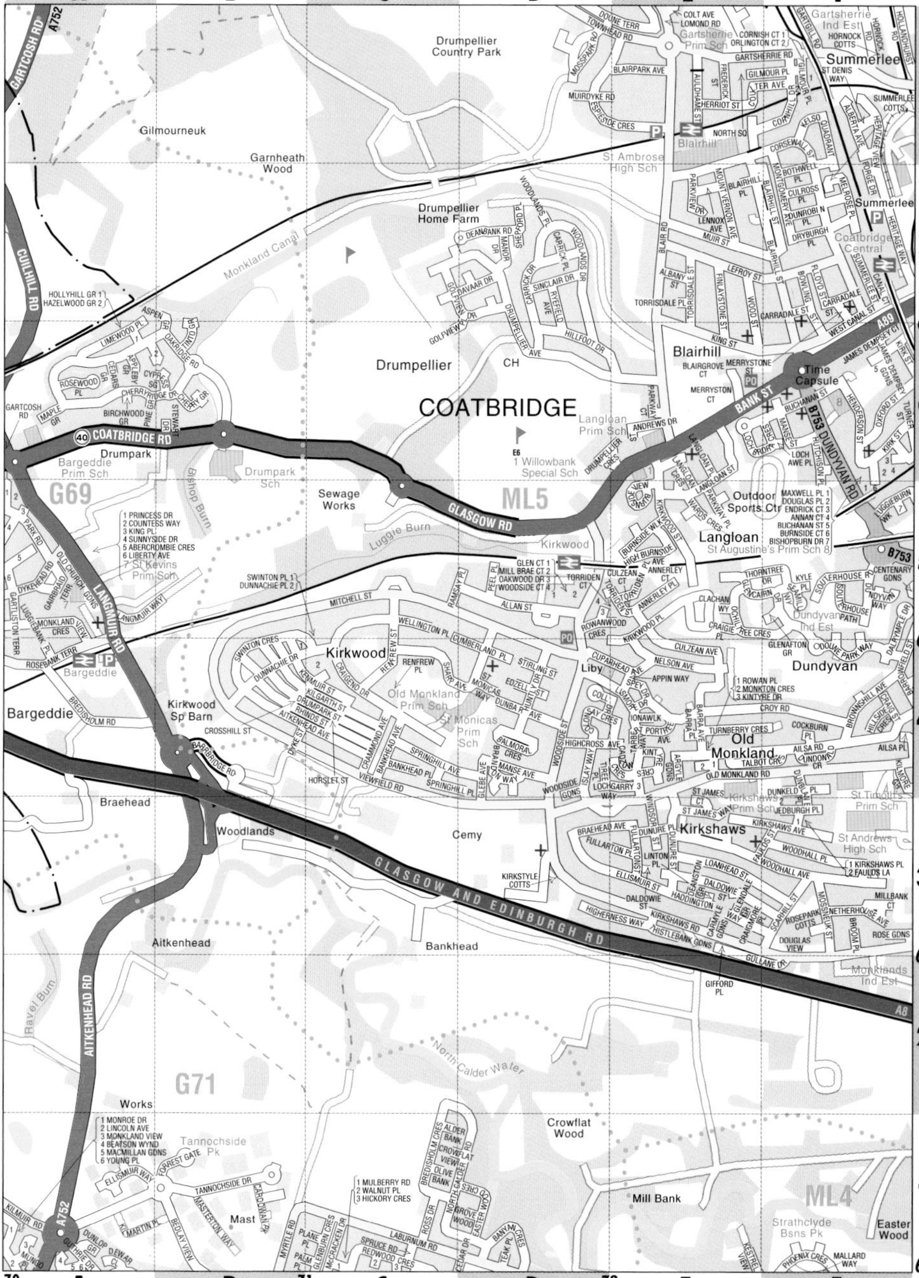

8 7 6 5 4 3 2 1

70 A B 71 C D 72 E F

141 122

A8
1 COLTSWOOD CT
2 RONALD ST
3 RED BRIDGE CT
4 LINCOLN CT
5 CALEDONIAN GATE

121
102

F8
1 NORTH BRIDGE ST
2 WELLWYND GDNS
3 WILLOWPARK CT
4 AITCHISON CT

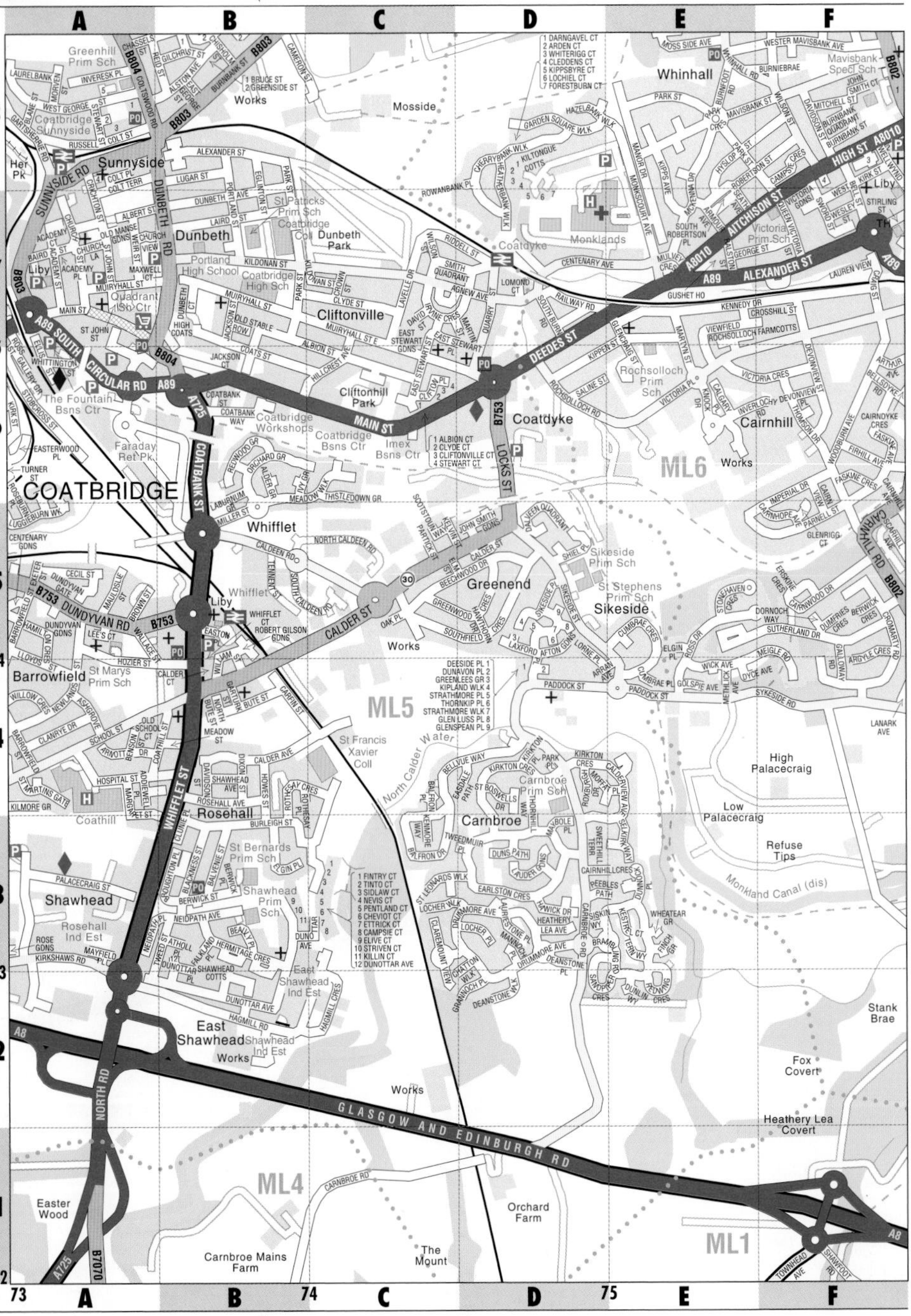

121
142

A8
1 ANDERSON LA
2 AULD'S BRAE
3 PARKHEAD LA
4 OLD CROSS
5 ANDERSON ST

B7
1 GARTLEA GDNS
2 SOUTH NIMMO ST
3 ALBERT CRES

C7
1 KINGSTON AVE
2 COLSTON PL
3 COLSTON ROW
4 COLSTON TERR

E7
1 FINLAYSON QUADRANT
2 WESTER MOFFAT CRES
3 MOORPARK AVE
4 CRAIGNURE CRES

103
124

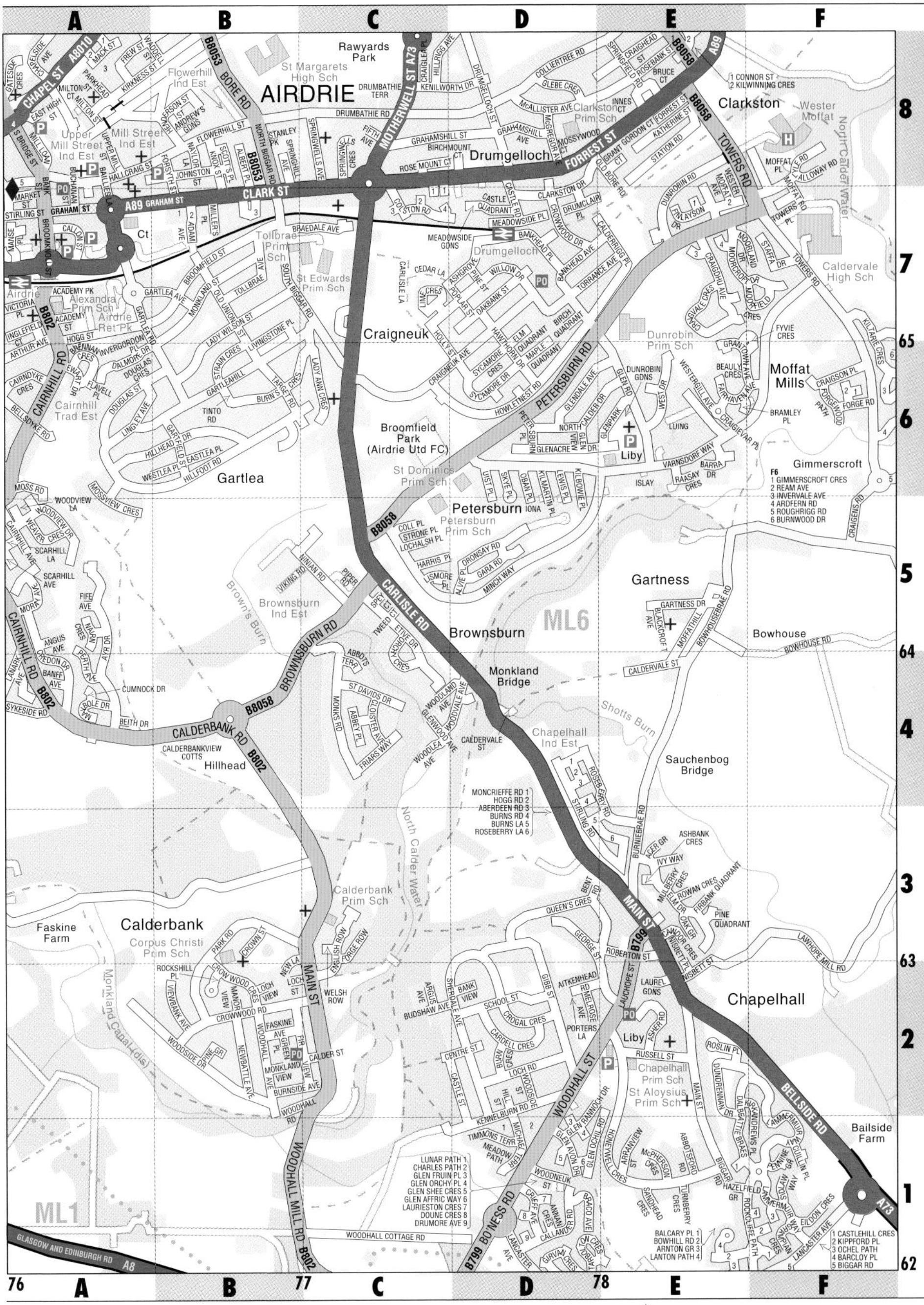

143
124

123
104

123
144

105
126

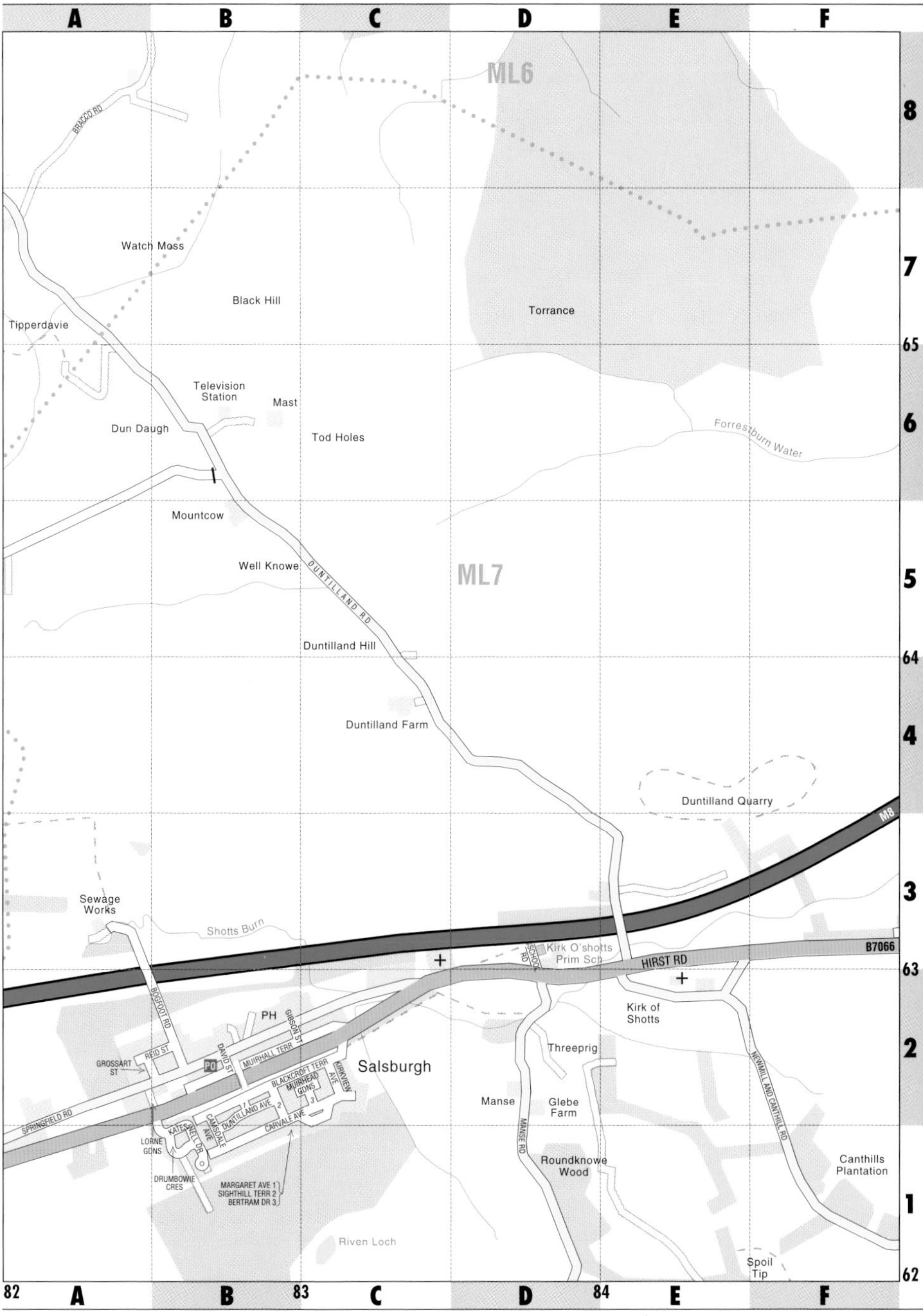

145
126

125
106

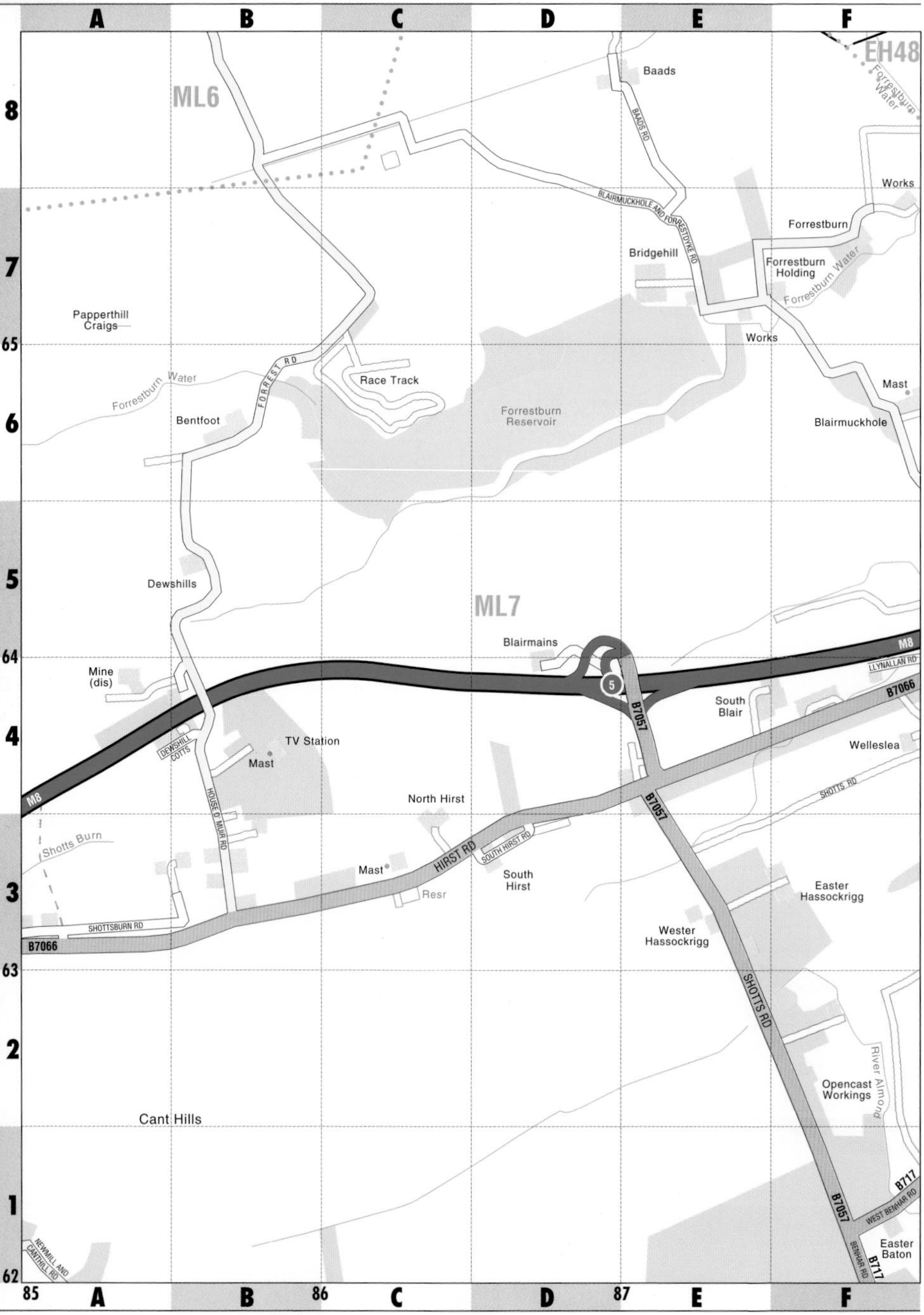

125
146

A
B
C
D
E
F
Blairhill Quarry
EH48
Loan Farm
B718
EH48
8
Forrestburn Water
Hill Farm
Netherton Farm
Blairmuckhill Farm
7
M8 Edinburgh (A71)
M8
Knowehead
Mast
65
Harthill Service Area
Sewage Works
WESTCRAIGS RD
Greenrigg Prim Sch
6
Treesbank Farm
Service Area
MILLER ST
HOWBURN RD
HOWBURN CRES
HAWTHORN DR
LOAN PL
PAXSTONE DR
PAXSTONE CRES
FORREST PL
DUNN TERR
DEER PATH
Harthill Ind Est
GIBBSHILL PL
MOSSBURN AVE
BANK RD
PRIG WAY
EAST MAIN ST B7066
WEST MAIN ST
POLKEMMET LA
GREENRIGG COTTS
How Burn
Mossburn Ind Est
BLAIRMUCKHOLE AND FORRESTDYKE RD
ALMOND TERR
OLD EASTFIELD ST
B717 CHURCH ST
B717
5
Edinburgh STREET ATLAS
BERTRAM ST
BROOMHILL ST
VICTORIA RD
ALBERT RD
BALBAKIE RD
Alexander Peden Prim Sch
Harthill
PEDEN ST
BRESLIN TERR
BAIRD TERR
MINTHILL PL
HEATHERBELL CT
LYNALLAN RD
HIRST RD
64
Tam's Loup Quarry
Eastfield
Paxtane
LIVINGSTONE QUADRANT
COVENANTER RD
CUNNINGHAM DR
MUIRHEAD PL
SPOUTS RD
4
ML7
West Benhar
WEST BENHAR RD
River Almond
Works
3
63
Active Workings
Spoil Heap
2
Mon
Brownhill Farm
1
62
88
89
90

108

A
B
C
D
E
F
8
7
61
6
5
60
4
3
59
2
1
58
31
32
33
Ayrshire STREET ATLAS
Rough Burn
Glenward Hill
Clovenstone
Calder Bank
River Calder
Tandlemuir
Turnave Hill
PA12
Lairdside Hill
Garpel Burn
Muirfauldhouse
High Linthills
Maws Law
North Plantation
Maich Water
The Ward
Dunconnel Hill
Kilbanes Burn
Kilbanes Law
Barnbeth Hill
Gillsyard
Fairhills
Startle Hill
KA25
Castle Hill
Glenlora
Cockston
Lorabank
Glenlora Bridge
Easthills
Lamb Hill
Lady Burn
Lora Burn
Mast
Hills Bridge
Gavelmoss
Midhills
Weshills

149

109
130

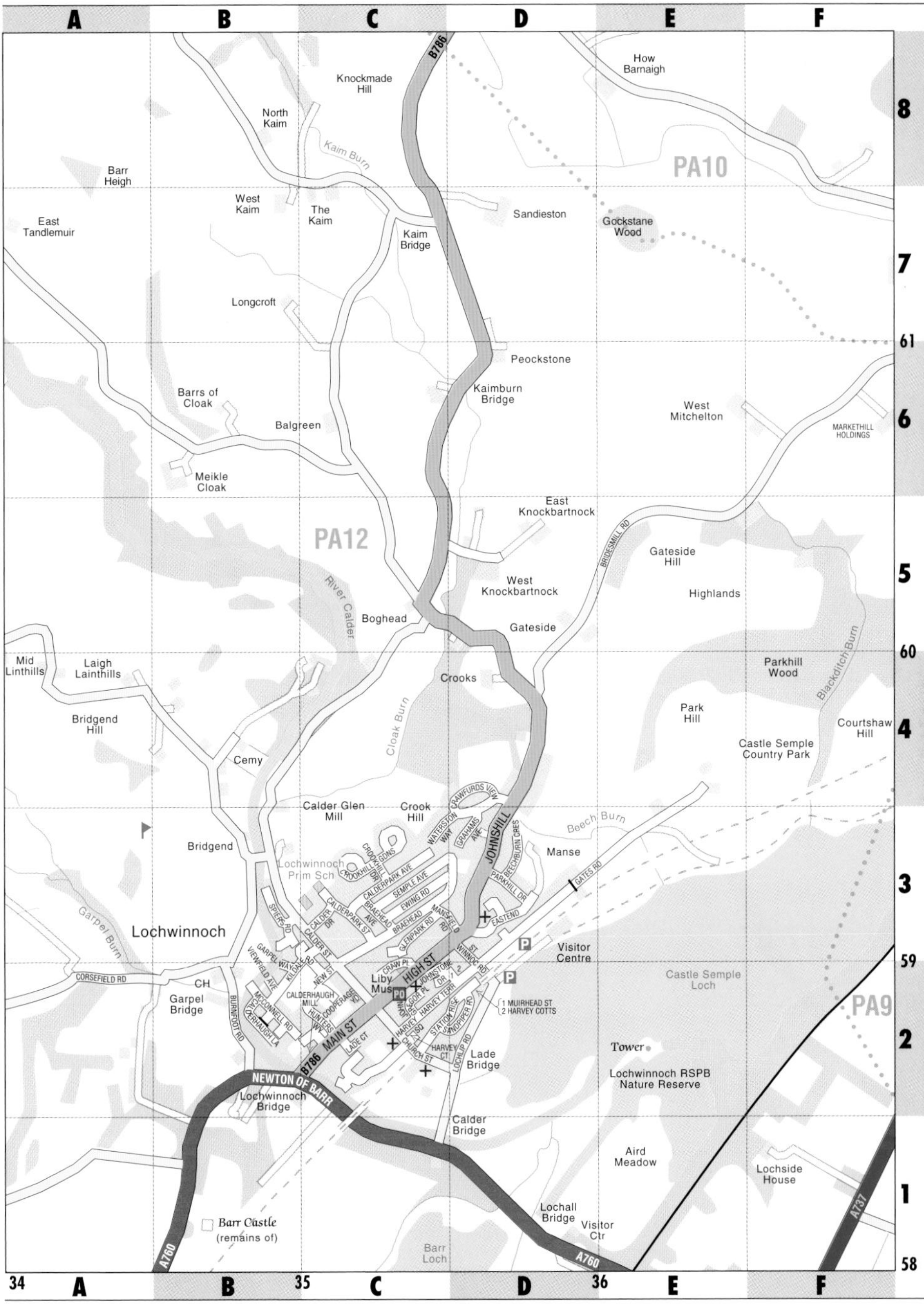

150
130

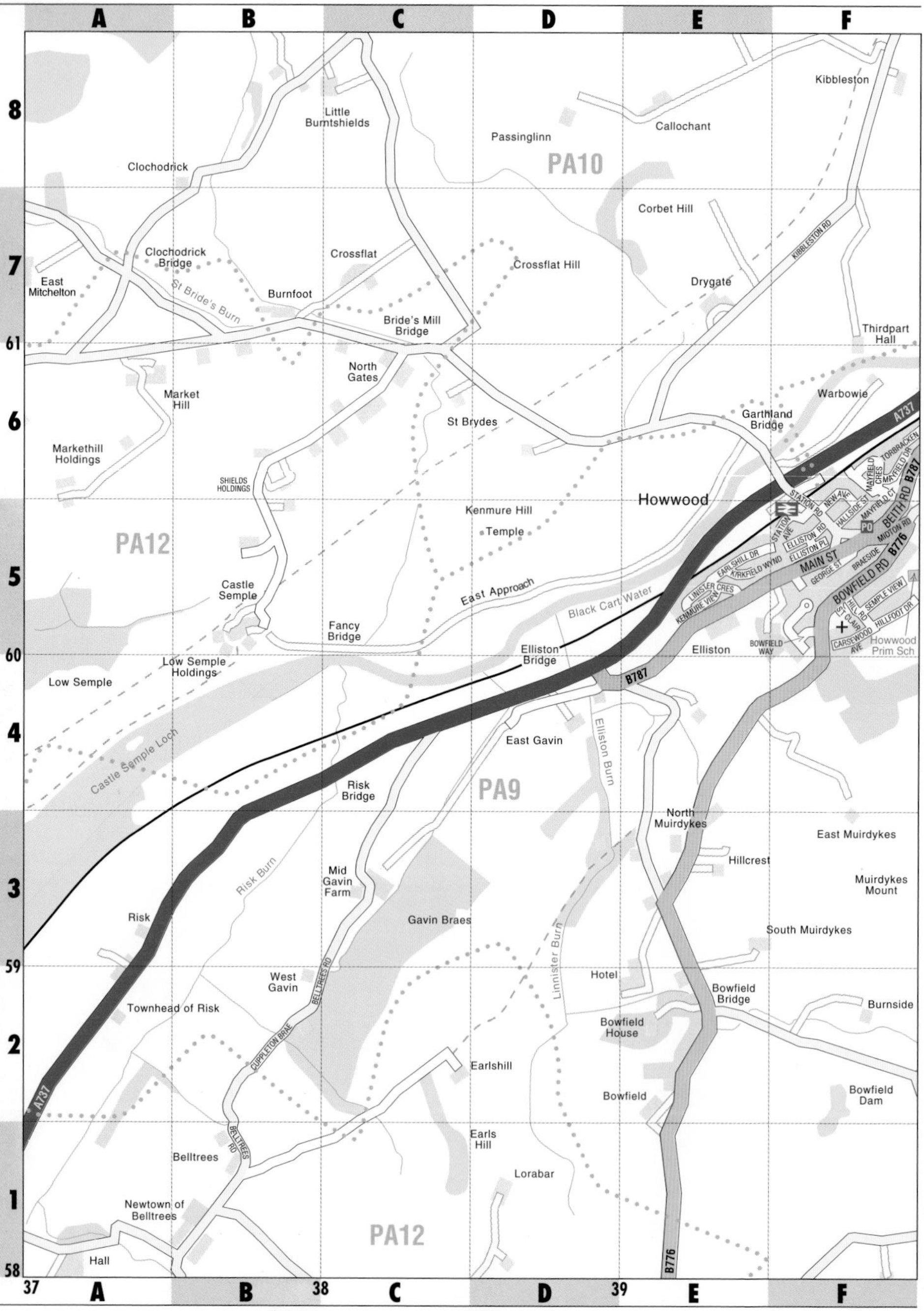
A
B
C
D
E
F
8
7
61
6
5
60
4
3
59
2
1
58
37
38
39
Little Burntshields
Passinglinn
Callochant
Kibbleston
PA10
Clochodrick
Corbet Hill
Clochodrick Bridge
Crossflat
Crossflat Hill
Drygate
KIBBLESTON RD
East Mitchelton
St Bride's Burn
Burnfoot
Bride's Mill Bridge
Thirdpart Hall
North Gates
Market Hill
Warbowie
St Brydes
Garthland Bridge
A737
Markethill Holdings
SHIELDS HOLDINGS
Howwood
Kenmure Hill
Temple
PA12
Castle Semple
East Approach
Black Cart Water
STATION RD
STATION AVE
NEW AVE
HALLSIDE ST
MAYFIELD CRES
MAYFIELD CT
MAYFIELD DR
TORBRACKEN
BEITH RD
B787
PO
MIDTON RD
B776
ELLISTON RD
ELLISTON PL
EARLSHILL DR
KIRKFIELD WYND
MAIN ST
GEORGE ST
BRAESIDE
BOWFIELD RD
LINNISTER CRES
KENMURE VIEW
SEMPLE VIEW
HILLFOOT DR
HILL RD
ST CLAIR
CARSEWOOD AVE
BOWFIELD WAY
Howwood Prim Sch
Fancy Bridge
Elliston Bridge
Elliston
Low Semple
Low Semple Holdings
B787
East Gavin
Elliston Burn
Castle Semple Loch
Risk Bridge
PA9
North Muirdykes
East Muirdykes
Hillcrest
Risk Burn
Mid Gavin Farm
Muirdykes Mount
Risk
Gavin Braes
South Muirdykes
Linnister Burn
West Gavin
Hotel
Bowfield Bridge
Burnside
BELLTREES RD
Townhead of Risk
Bowfield House
CUPPLETON BRAE
Earlshill
A737
Bowfield
Bowfield Dam
BELLTREES RD
Earls Hill
Belltrees
Lorabar
Newtown of Belltrees
PA12
Hall
B776

111
132

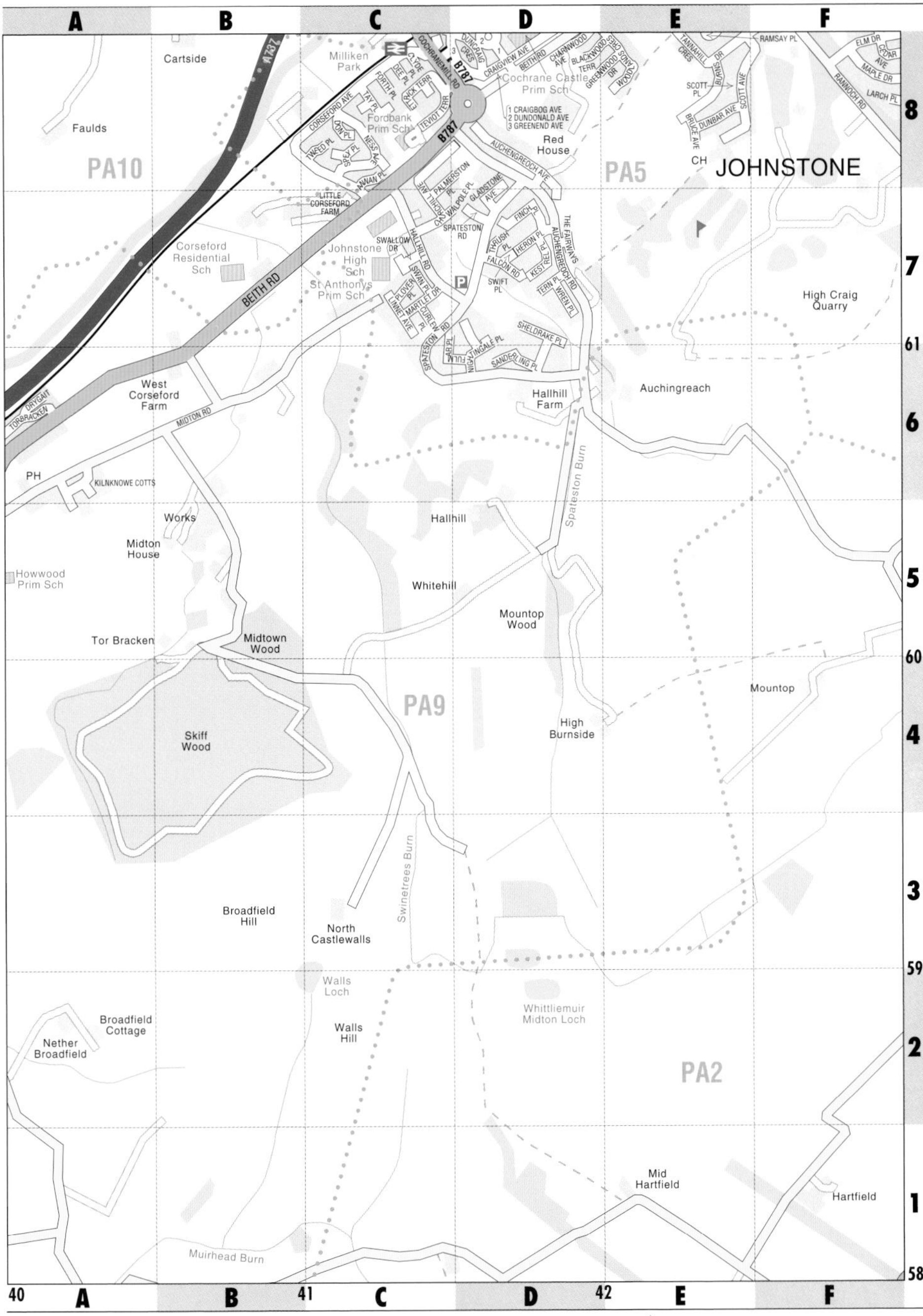

152
132

131
112

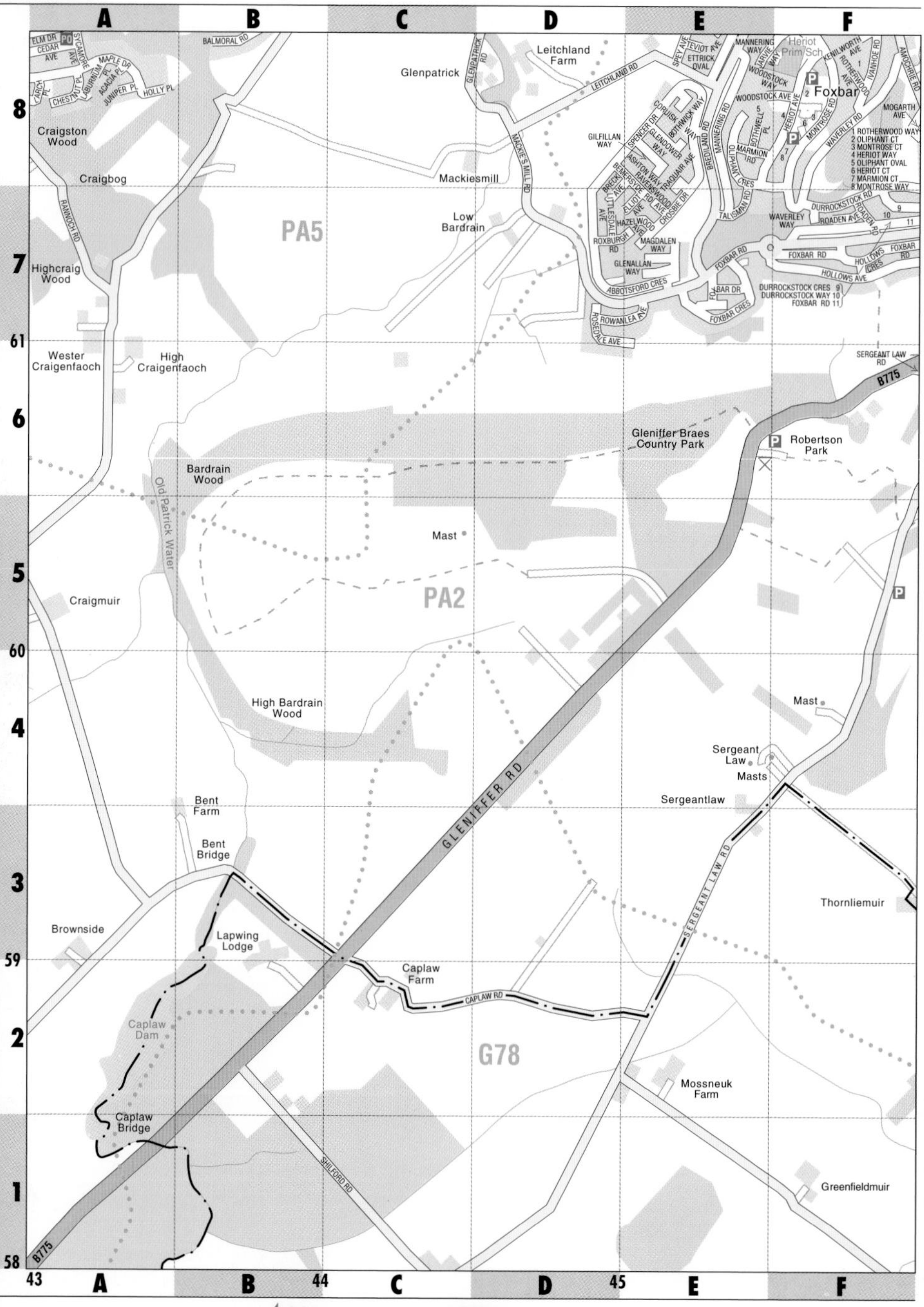

131
153

113
134

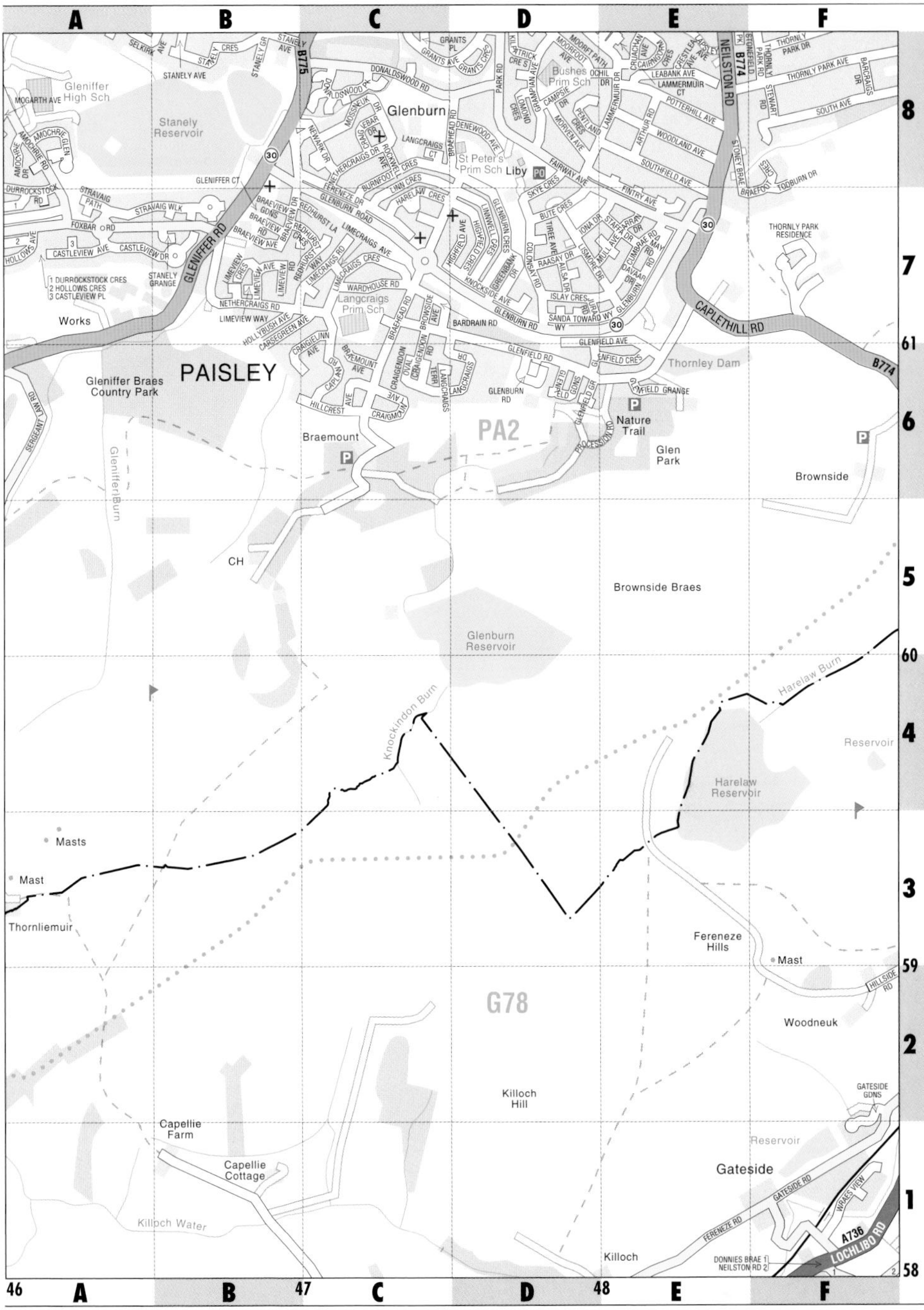

154
134

133
114

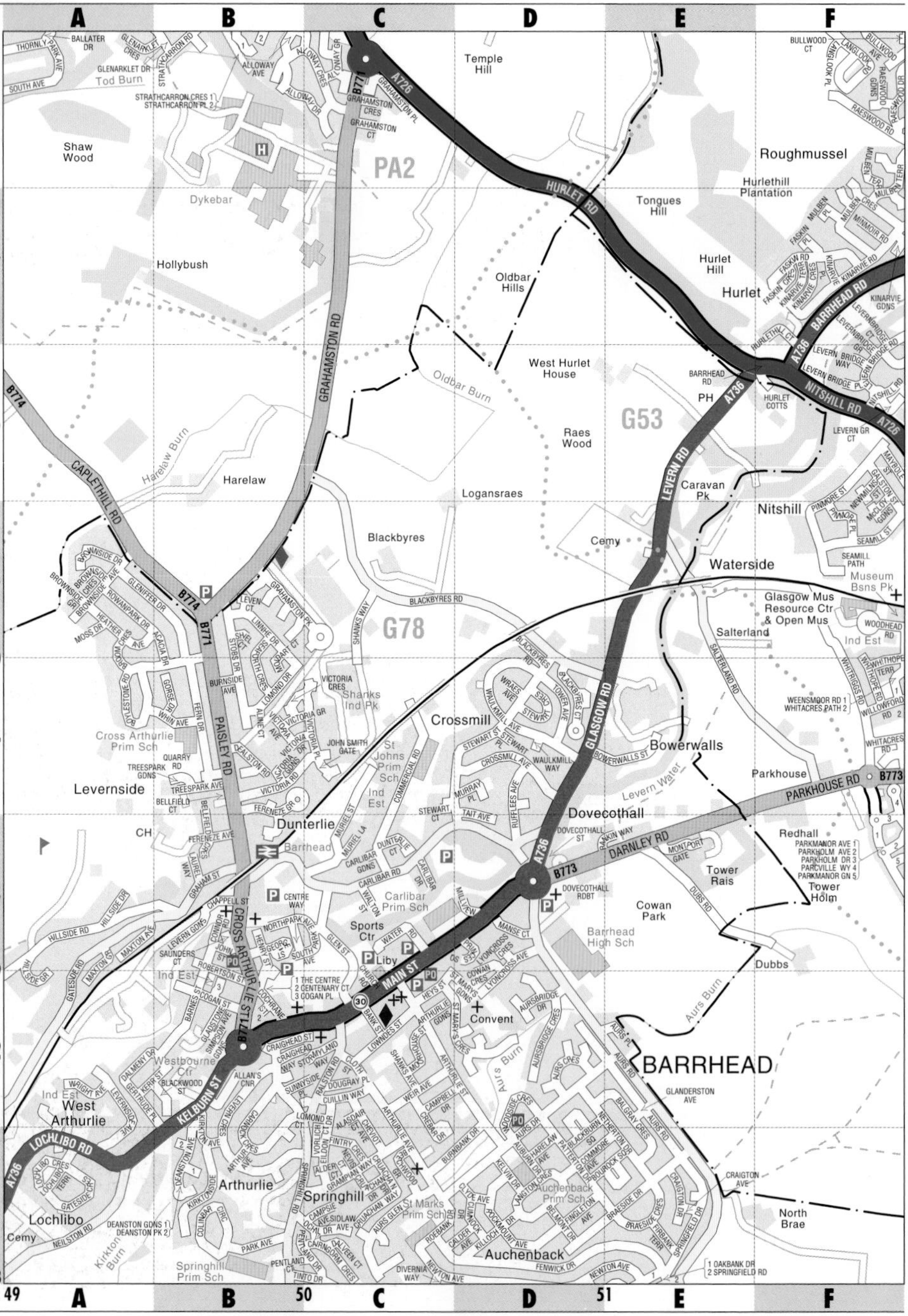

133
155

A8
1 SANQUHAR GDNS
2 SANQUHAR PL
3 RAESWOOD PL
4 POLQUHAP CT
5 POLQUHAP PL
6 POLQUHAP GDNS
7 CATRINE GDNS
8 CATRINE CT
9 DALMELLINGTON DR
10 LITTLEMILL GDNS
11 BALLOCHMYLE CRES
12 BALLOCHMYLE PL
13 MARLACH PL
14 BALLOCHMYLE DR
15 BARGANY PL

115
136

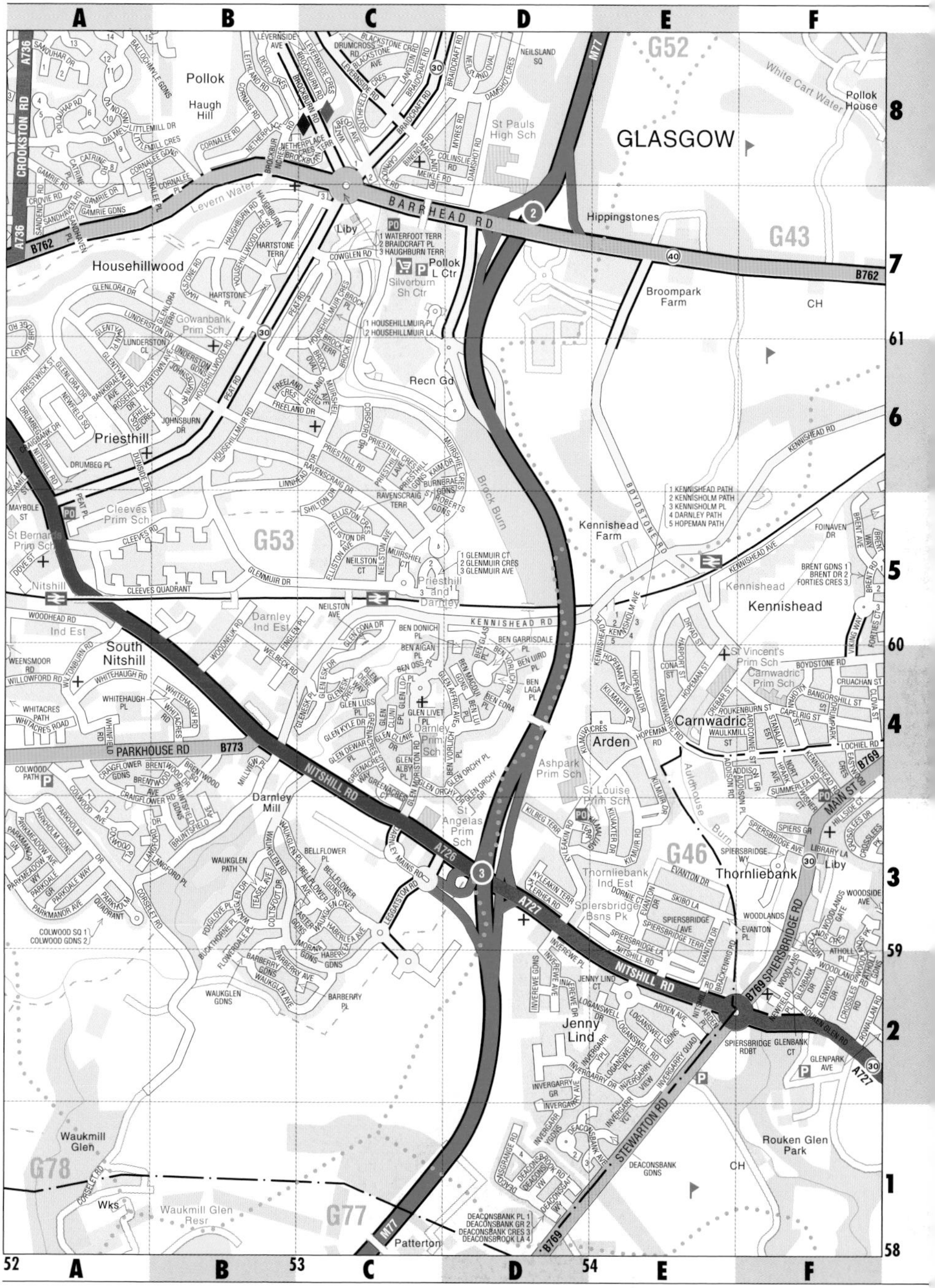

C7
1 JOHNSHAVEN ST
2 BENGAL PL

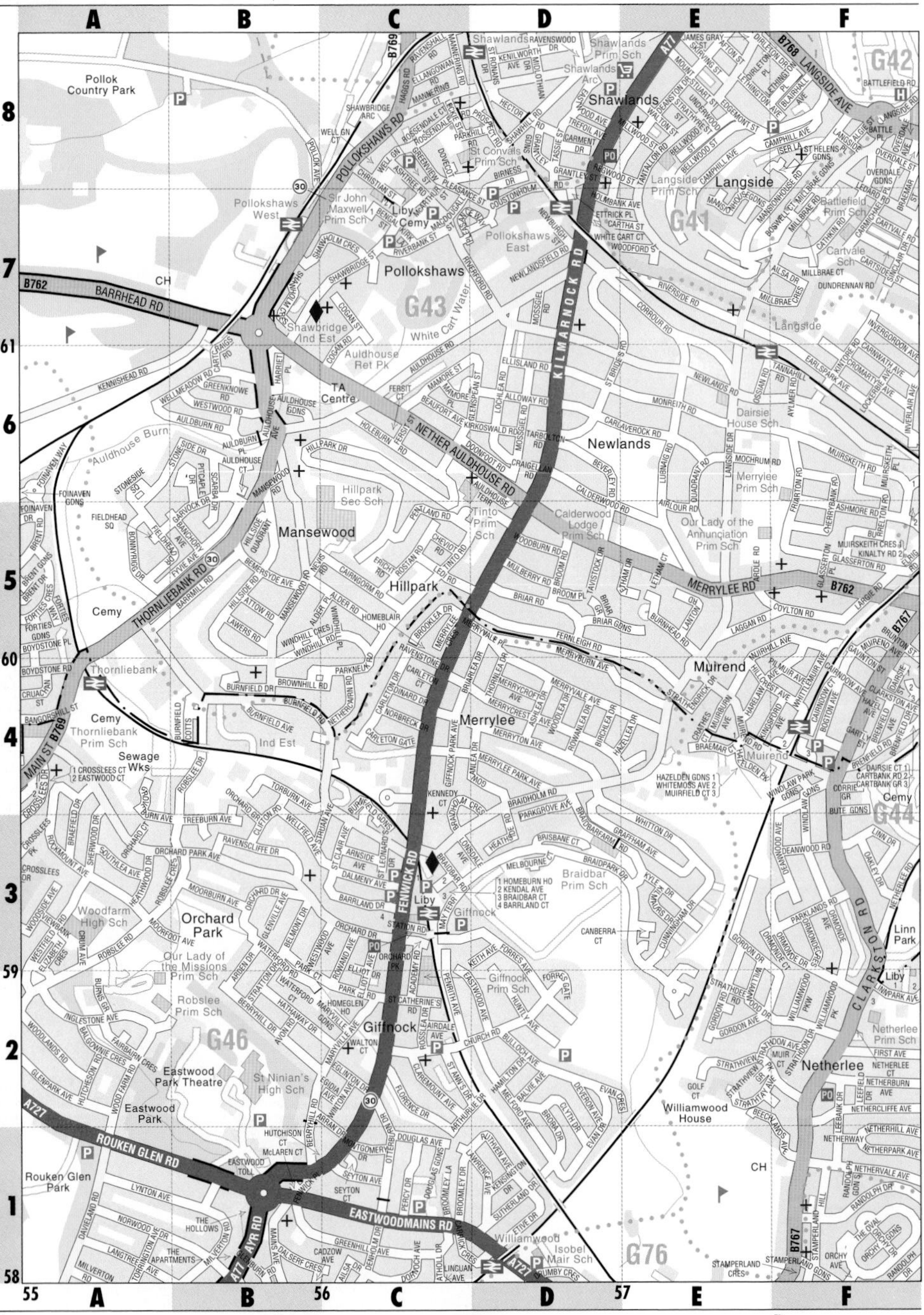

F2
1 RIVERSIDE CT
2 LINNPARK CT
3 MACLAREN PL

117
138

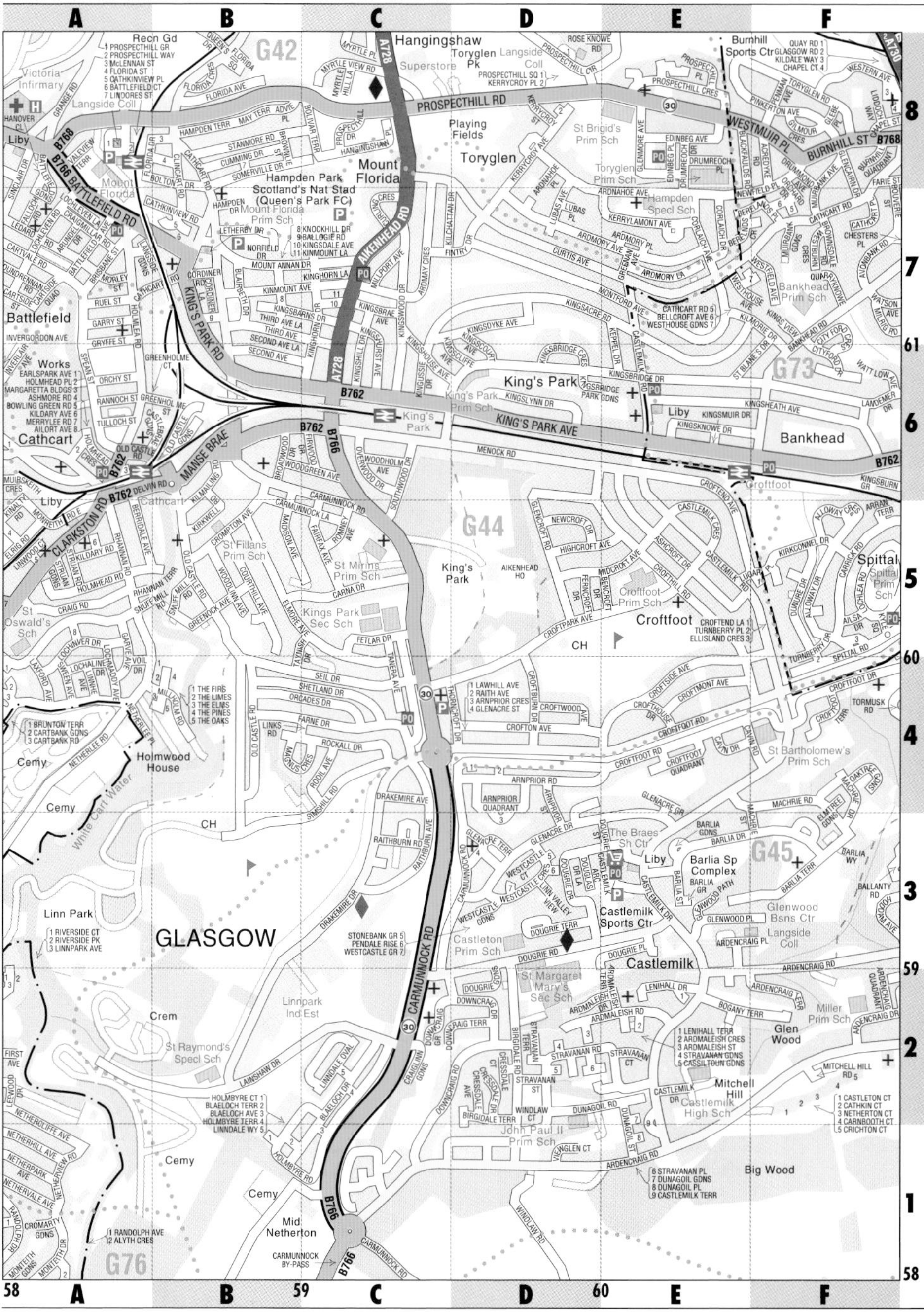

158
138

A7
1 MACDONALD ST
2 BALVAIRD CRES
3 CHESTERS PL

A8
1 WESTERN AVE
2 CHAPEL ST
3 GREENBANK ST
4 VICTORIA PL
5 KING STREET LA

137

B7
1 St Columbkilles Prim Sch
2 Stonelaw High Sch

118

E6
1 SILVERBANKS RD
2 SILVERBANKS GAIT
3 SILVERBANKS CT

F6
1 BRIDGE ST
2 LIBRARY GDNS
3 ARDOCH GDNS
4 CENTRAL GR
5 SIR THOMAS LIPTON WY

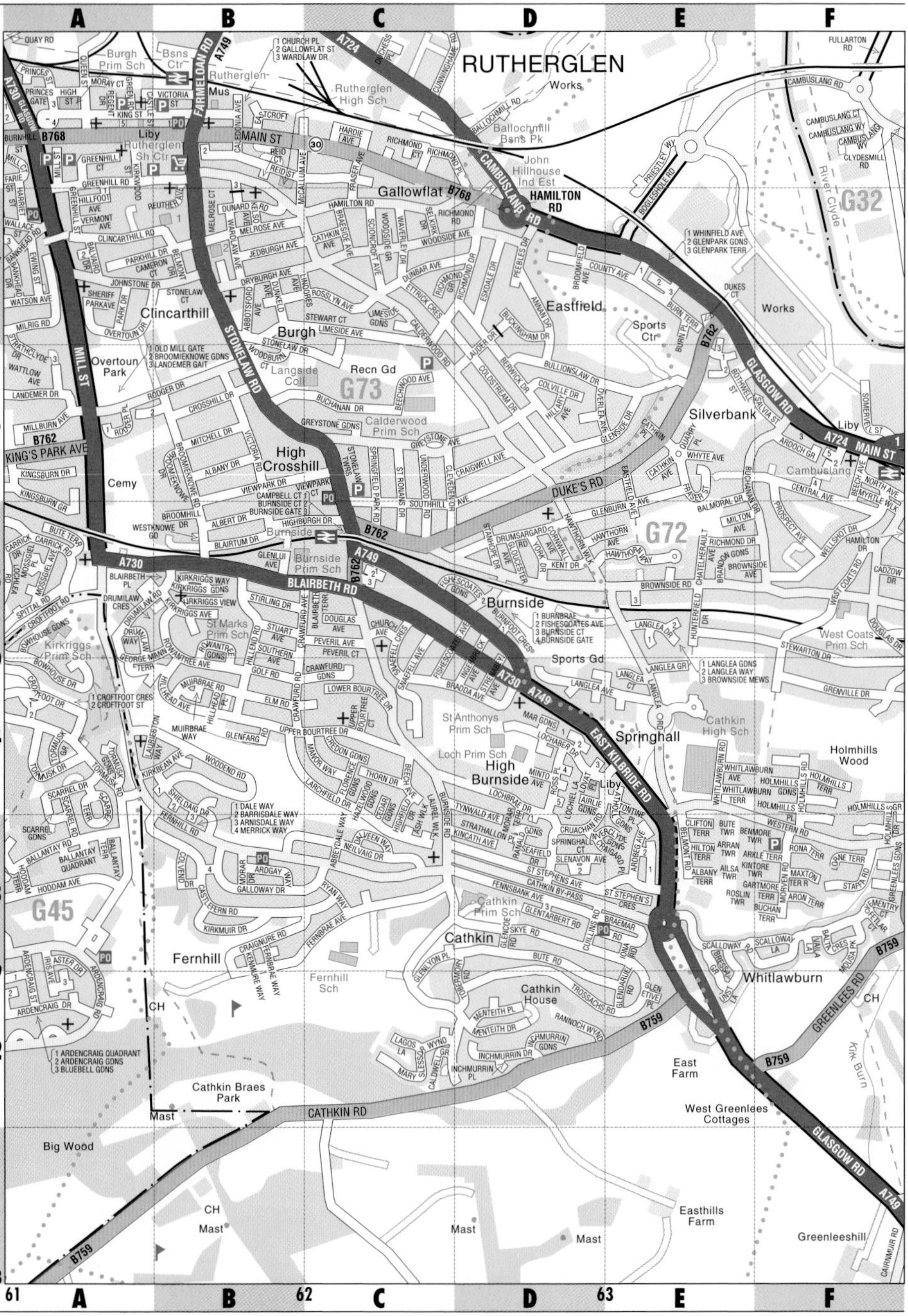

137

159

D3
1 TULLOCHARD PL
2 LYBSTER CRES
3 GLENALMOND RD

D4
1 WARRISTON WAY
2 STRATHMORE GDNS
3 APPIN TERR
4 BREADALBANE GDNS
5 STRATHCONA PL

E3
1 ISLAY AVE
2 BOWMORE GDNS

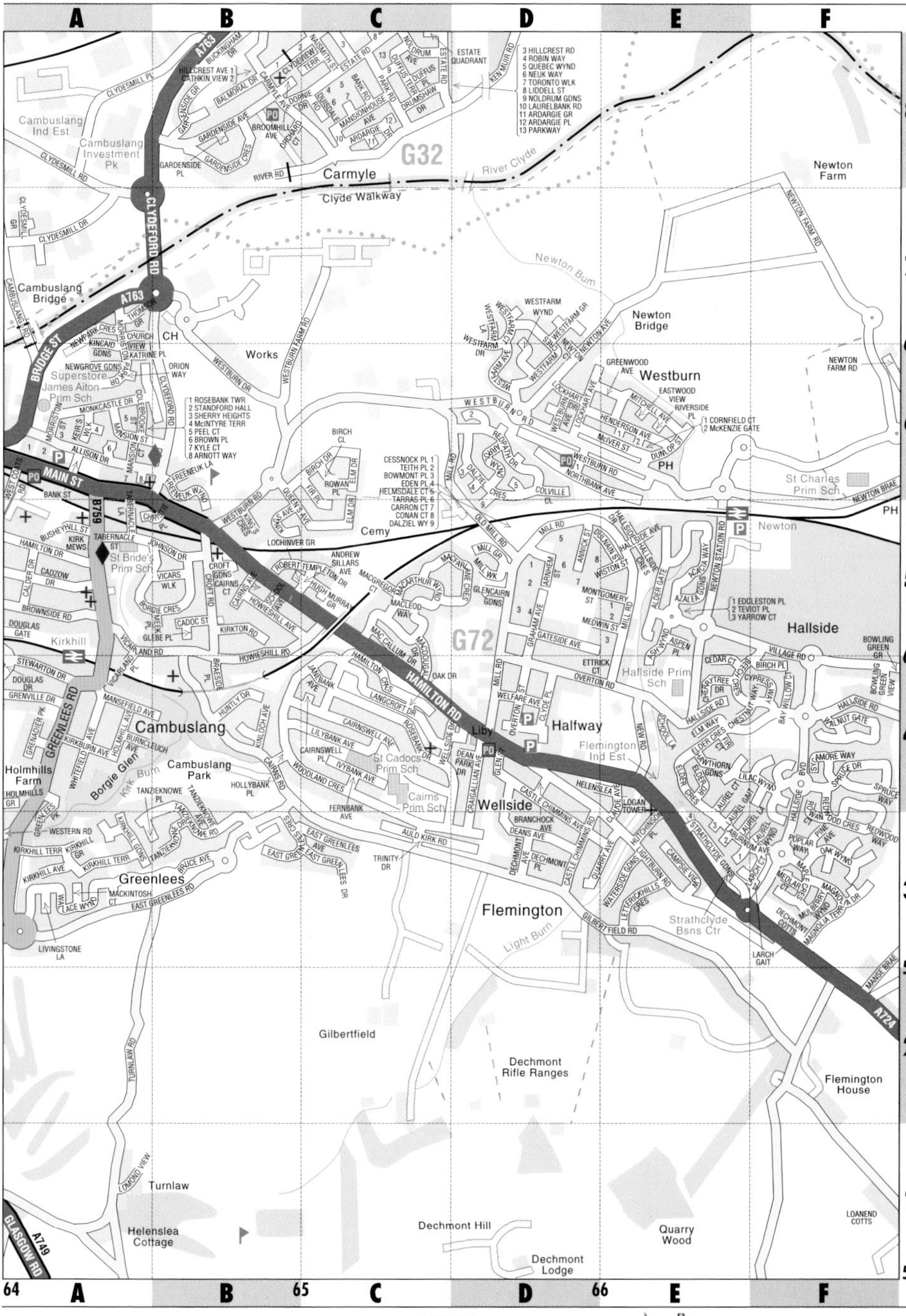
A
B
C
D
E
F
8
7
61
6
5
60
4
3
59
2
1
58
64
65
66
A763
CLYDEFORD RD
BRIDGE ST
MAIN ST
B759
HAMILTON RD
A724
GLASGOW RD
A749
G32
G72
Cambuslang Ind Est
Cambuslang Investment Pk
CLYDESMILL PL
CLYDESMILL RD
CLYDESMILL DR
CLYDESMILL GR
Cambuslang Bridge
CAMBUSLANG RD
BUCKINGHAM DR
HILLCREST AVE 1
CATHKIN VIEW 2
BALMORAL DR
GARDENSIDE GR
GARDENSIDE AVE
GARDENSIDE CRES
GARDENSIDE PL
BROOMHILL AVE
ORCHARD CT
CARMYLE AVE
DORNIE DR
CLYDEVIEW TERR
NAISMITH ST
ESTATE RD
DUISDALE RD
BAIRK RD
MANSIONHOUSE AVE
PARK RD
DUFFUS TERR
DUFFUS PL
NOLDRUM AVE
DRUMSHAW DR
ARDARGIE PL
ESTATE QUADRANT
KEN MUIR RD
3 HILLCREST RD
4 ROBIN WAY
5 QUEBEC WYND
6 NEUK WAY
7 TORONTO WLK
8 LIDDELL ST
9 NOLDRUM GDNS
10 LAURELBANK RD
11 ARDARGIE GR
12 ARDARGIE PL
13 PARKWAY
RIVER RD
Carmyle
Clyde Walkway
River Clyde
Newton Farm
NEWTON FARM RD
Newton Burn
Newton Bridge
NEWTON AVE
WESTFARM WYND
WESTFARM GR
WESTFARM CT
WESTFARM LA
WESTFARM DR
WESTFARM AVE
WESTFARM CRES
NEWTON FARM RD
Westburn
GREENWOOD AVE
EASTWOOD VIEW
RIVERSIDE PL
1 CORNFIELD CT
2 McKENZIE GATE
MITCHELL AVE
HENDERSON AVE
McIVER ST
DUNLOP ST
LOCKHART AVE
LOCKHART DR
WESTBURN AVE
WESTBURN RD
WESTBURN DR
NORTHBANK AVE
COLVILLE CL
PH
St Charles Prim Sch
NEWTON BRAE
THOMSON DR
NEWPARK CRES
MORRISTON PARK DR
KINCAID GDNS
CHURCH VIEW
KATRINE PL
CH
Works
WESTBURN FARM RD
ORION WAY
NEWGROVE GDNS
Superstore
James Aiton Prim Sch
MONKCASTLE DR
COLEBROOKE ST
MORRISTON ST
KEIR'S WLK
MANSION ST
MANSION CT
1 ROSEBANK TWR
2 STANDFORD HALL
3 SHERRY HEIGHTS
4 McINTYRE TERR
5 PEEL CT
6 BROWN PL
7 KYLE CT
8 ARNOTT WAY
ALLISON DR
FREENEUK LA
FREENEUK WYND
BIRCH CL
BIRCH DR
ROWAN PL
FIR PL
ELM DR
CESSNOCK PL 1
TEITH PL 2
BOWMONT PL 3
EDEN PL 4
HELMSDALE CT 5
TARRAS PL 6
CARRON CT 7
CONAN CT 8
DALZIEL WY 9
MILL RD
REDPATH DR
DALZIEL CRES
OLD MILL RD
WEST COATS RD
BANK ST
TABERNACLE LA
CHRISTIE PL
WESTBURN RD
KING'S CRES
QUEEN'S AVE
KING'S AVE
LOCHINVER GR
Cemy
ANDREW SILLARS AVE
MACGREGOR CT
BUSHEYHILL ST
KIRK MEWS
TABERNACLE ST
St Bride's Prim Sch
JOHNSON DR
HAMILTON DR
CALDER DR
CADZOW DR
BROWNSIDE RD
DOUGLAS GATE
Kirkhill
VICARS WLK
BORGIE CRES
GLEBE PL
MEEK PL
CADOC ST
CROFT GDNS
CAIRNS CT
CROFT RD
CAIRNS AVE
SCHOOL AVE
ROBERT TEMPLETON DR
HUGH MURRAY GR
HOWIESHILL AVE
KIRKTON RD
HOWIESHILL RD
VICARLAND RD
VICARLAND PL
MACARTHUR WYND
MACLAREN CRES
MILL GR
MILL WK
GLENCAIRN GDNS
MACLEOD WAY
MACCALLUM DR
MACDOUGAL DR
OAK DR
MILL RD
ARNHEM ST
ANNICK ST
DUNAIN ST
WISTON ST
HALLSIDE DR
HALLSIDE AVE
HALLSIDE CRES
MONTGOMERY ST
MEDWIN ST
GRAHAM AVE
GATESIDE AVE
ALDER GATE
ACACIA WAY
AZALEA GDNS
NEWTON STATION RD
Newton
1 EDDLESTON PL
2 TEVIOT PL
3 YARROW CT
Hallside
ASH WYND
ASPEN PL
VILLAGE RD
BOWLING GREEN GR
BOWLING GREEN VIEW
CEDAR CT
BEECH CRES
BIRCH PL
CHERRYTREE DR
CYPRESS WAY
CHESTNUT WAY
BAY WILLOW CT
HALLSIDE RD
WALNUT GATE
ETTRICK CT
OVERTON RD
Hallside Prim Sch
STEWARTON DR
DOUGLAS DR
GRENVILLE DR
GRENADIER PK
GREENLEES RD
BRAESIDE PL
HUNTLY DR
JANEBANK AVE
HAMILTON CRES
LANGCROFT DR
MANSEFIELD AVE
HOLMHILL AVE
BURNCLEUCH AVE
KIRKBURN AVE
WHITEFIELD AVE
Cambuslang
KINLOCH AVE
CAIRNSWELL AVE
LILYBANK AVE
ROSEBANK DR
WELLSIDE DR
Liby
WELFARE AVE
OVERTON ST
CLYDE PL
Halfway
Flemington Ind Est
NEW RD
SCHOOL LA
ELM WAY
ELDER CRES
FIR CT
HAWTHORN GDNS
ELDER GR
LILAC WYND
SYCAMORE WAY
SPRUCE DR
SPRUCE WAY
HALLSIDE BLVD
ROWAN CT
REDWOOD CRES
REDWOOD WAY
Holmhills Farm
HOLMHILLS GR
Borgie Glen
Kirk Burn
Cambuslang Park
CAIRNSWELL PL
IVYBANK AVE
WOODLAND CRES
St Cadocs Prim Sch
CAIRNS RD
HOLLYBANK PL
DEAN PARK DR
CRAIGALLIAN AVE
GLEN ST
Cairns Prim Sch
FERNBANK AVE
Wellside
CASTLE CHIMMINS AVE
CASTLE CHIMMINS RD
HELENSLEA
LOGAN TOWER
BRANCHOCK AVE
DEANS AVE
DECHMONT AVE
DECHMONT PL
QUARRY AVE
CLYDE AVE
HUTCHINSON PL
LAUREL CT
LAUREL GAIT
LAUREL LA
LAUREL WYND
LABURNUM AVE
STRATHCLYDE GDNS
POPLAR WAY
PINE AVE
OAK WYND
MAPLE CRES
MEDLAR CT
MULBERRY WYND
MAGNOLIA DR
MAGNOLIA TERR
DECHMONT COTTS
LARCH CT
TANZIEKNOWE PL
TANZIEKNOWE AVE
TANZIEKNOWE RD
TANZIEKNOWE DR
KIRKHILL GDNS
WESTERN RD
GREENLEES PK
KIRKHILL TERR
KIRKHILL GR
KIRKHILL AVE
BRUCE AVE
Greenlees
WALLACE WYND
MACKINTOSH CT
EAST GREENLEES RD
EAST GREENLEES AVE
EAST GREENLEES DR
EAST GREENLEES CRES
AULD KIRK RD
TRINITY DR
LIVINGSTONE LA
Flemington
GILBERTFIELD RD
WATERSIDE GDNS
LETTERICKHILLS CRES
LIGHTBURN RD
CAMPSIE VIEW
Strathclyde Bsns Ctr
LARCH GAIT
MANSE BRAE
Light Burn
Gilbertfield
TURNLAW RD
Dechmont Rifle Ranges
Flemington House
LOMOND VIEW
Turnlaw
Helenslea Cottage
Dechmont Hill
Dechmont Lodge
Quarry Wood
LOANEND COTTS

139
120

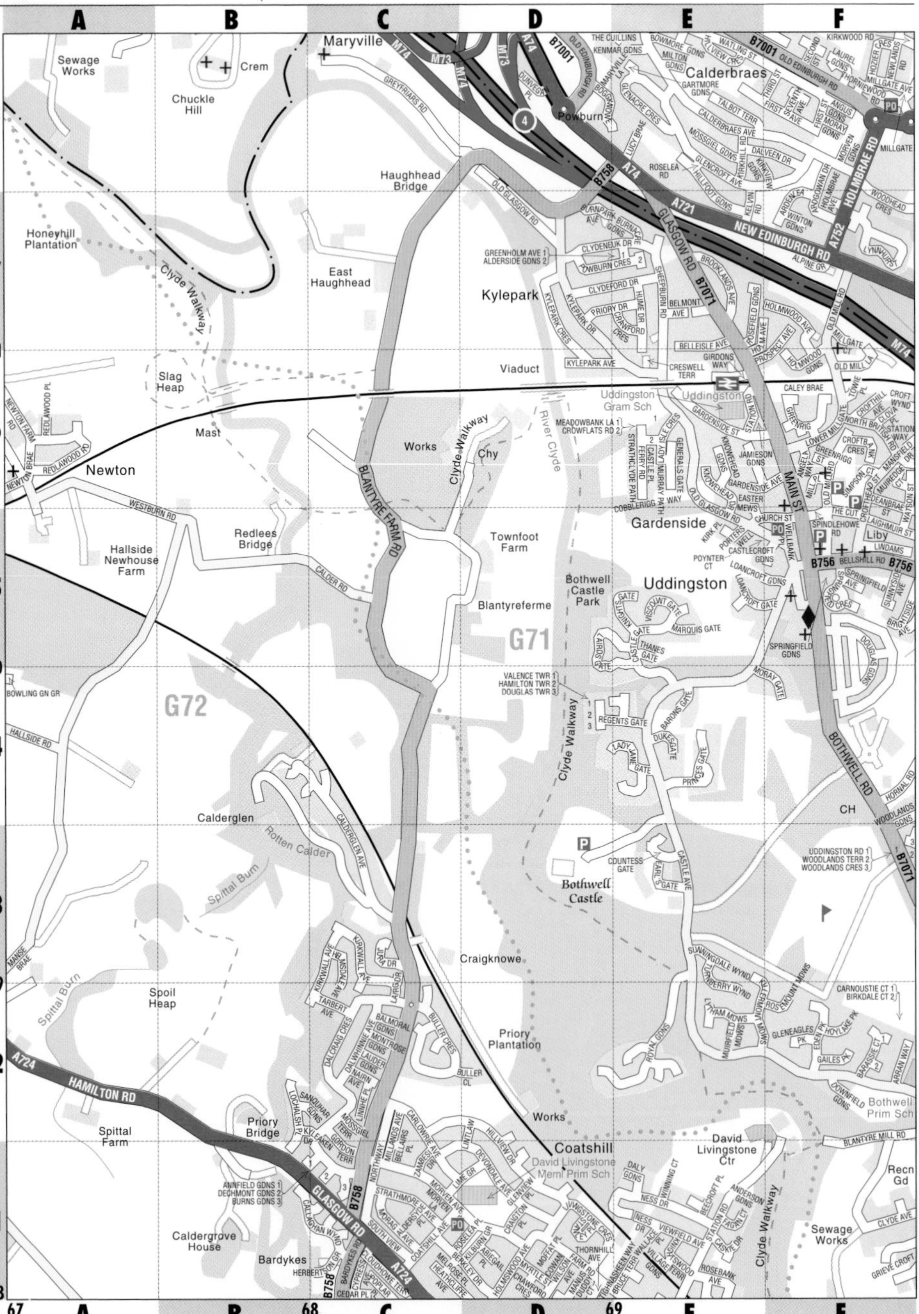

139
161

A8
1 YOUNG PL
2 WALKER PATH
3 CHRIGHTON GN
4 MUIRHEAD GATE
5 PRENTICE LA
6 HADDOW GR
7 CAMPSIE VIEW
8 OCHIL VIEW
9 KILPATRICK WAY
10 RUSSELL GDNS
11 BAILLE WYND
12 KIRKWOOD RD

121
142

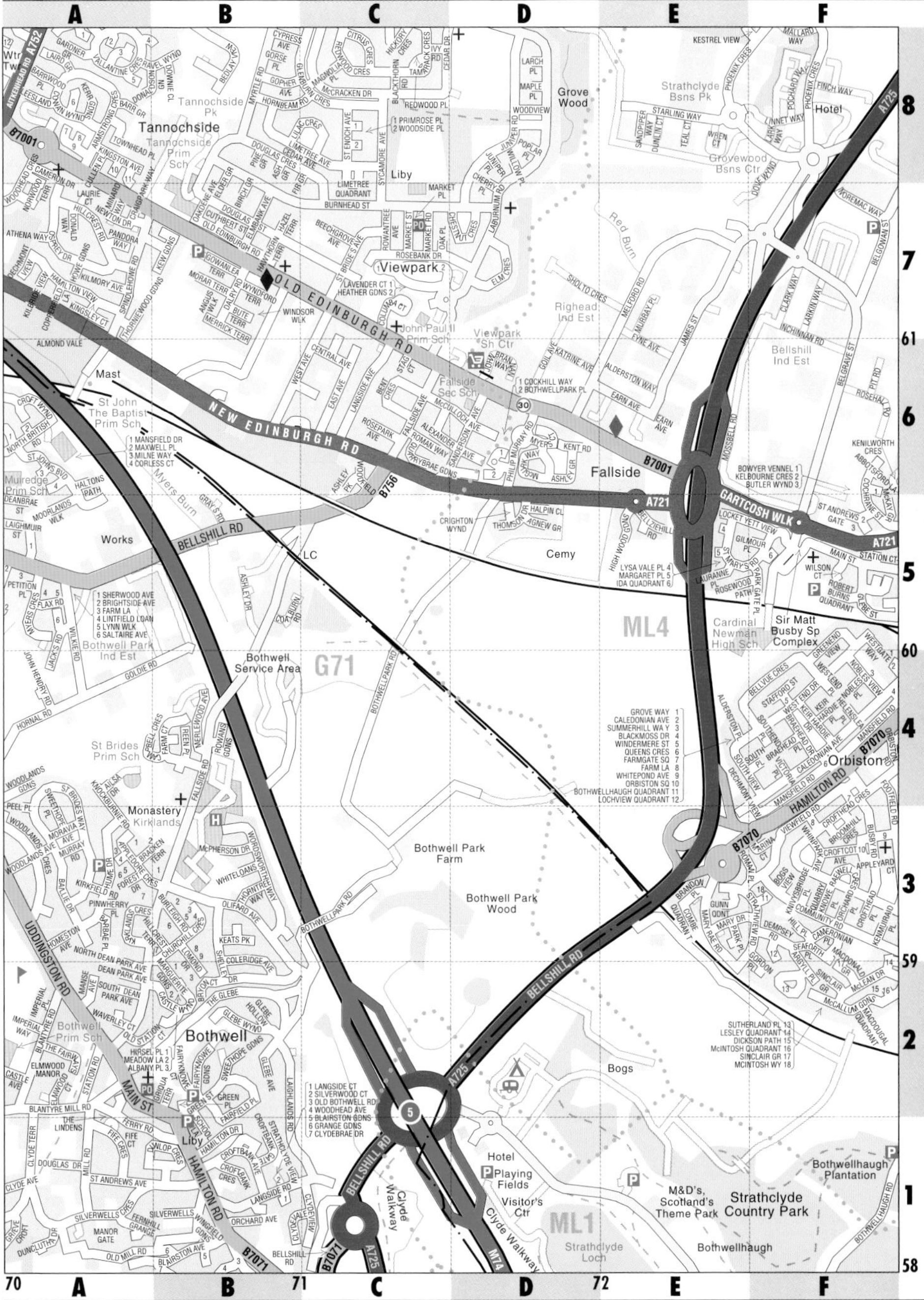

A3
1 KELVIN WAY
2 APPIN WAY
3 LIVINGSTONE LA
4 BELSTANE PL
5 KATRINE WAY
6 RANNOCH WAY
7 CARRICK WAY

B3
1 MORVEN WAY
2 TANTALLON RD
3 ROSEBANK LA
4 THORNHILL LA
5 ALDERSIDE PL
6 BARNSWOOD PL
7 MALLARD LA
8 NEWFIELD LA
9 HOZIER PL

162
142

141
122

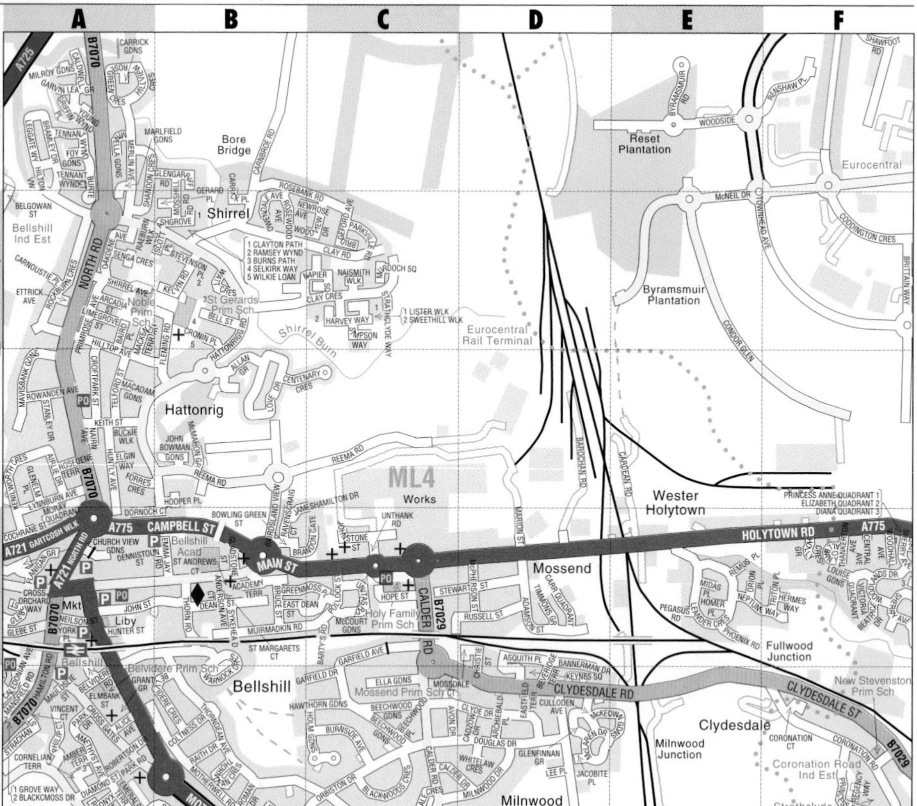

141
163

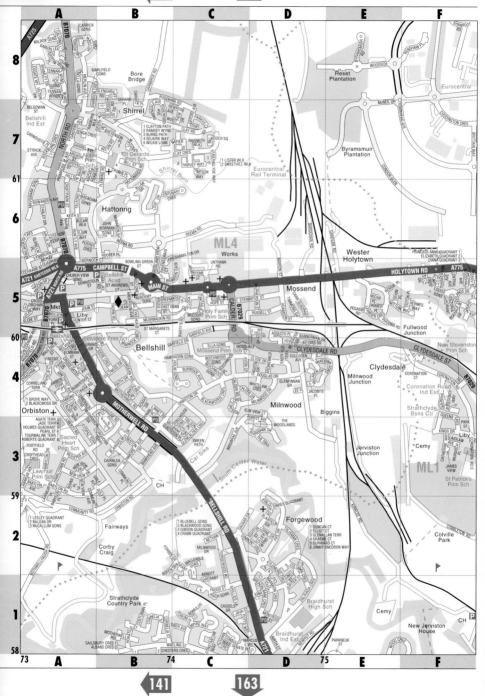

123
144

A2
1 DALMORE CRES
2 INCHGOWER PL
3 GLENGOYNE DR

B1
1 DERBY WYND
2 BYRESKNOWE LA

B2
1 LONGMORN PL
2 LOCHRANZA CT
3 STRATHISLA WAY
4 BLAIRATHOL WYND
5 ST MUNGOS CRES
6 THE LAURELS
7 MONTROSE CT

164
144

143
124

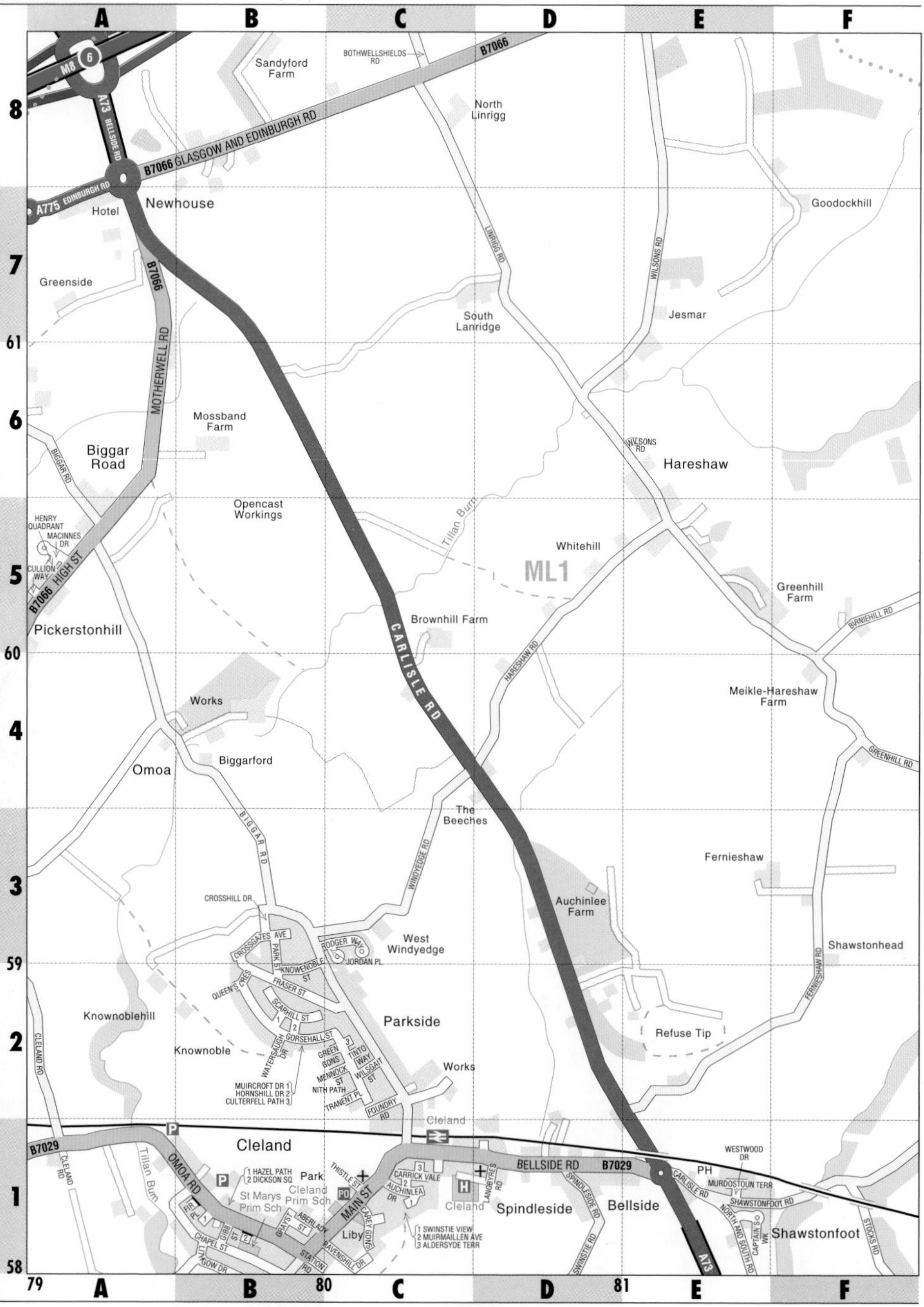

143
165

125
146

166
146

145
126

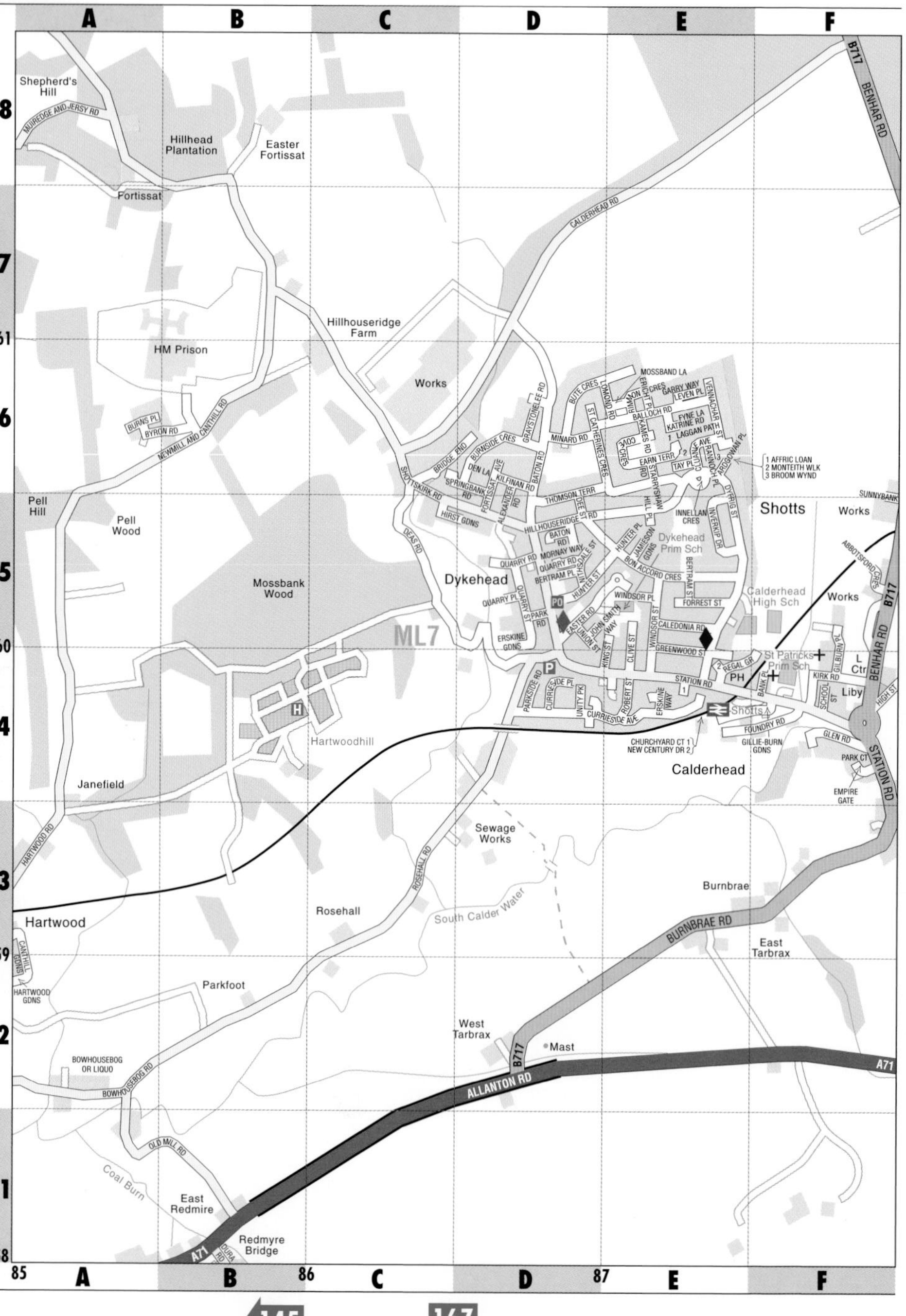

145
167

127

A
B
C
D
E
F
8
7
61
6
5
60
4
3
59
2
1
58
88
89
90
B717
BENHAR RD
CH
Starryshaw Farm
South Calder Water
Stanebent
Spoil Heap
Cairneyhead
ML7
Stane
GRAY ST
HIGH ST
STABLE RD
CEDAR WYND
ROWAN CRES
HAZEL GR
CHARLES ST
TORBOTHIE RD
CLYDE DR
KELVIN DR
CALDER DR
HAWTHORN DR
SOUTHFIELD AVE
SOUTHFIELD RD
SOUTHFIELD CRES
Torbothie
Stane Prim Sch
STANE GR
MANSE RD
CEMETERY RD
CHARLOTTE ST
NEVIS PL
ELGOL PATH
Cemy
GARTEN DR
MAIN ST
PO
SANDYHILL AVE
REDHAWS RD
SANDVALE PL
Stane
BLINNY CT 1
TARBRAX PATH 2
LOCHABER CRES
SHIEL GDNS
NAVAR CT
APPIN TERR
MELFORD AVE
WYVIS PL
TULLOCH RD
ONICH PL
LANSDOWNE CRES
LAGGAN AVE
BRIDGE PL
KNOLL CROFT RD
HUNTLY TERR
1 ETIVE WLK
2 UIG WAY
3 GAIR WYND
4 BOWMORE WLK
5 TORRIN LOAN
6 SPRINGHILL VIEW
7 DORNIE WYND
8 MORAR WAY
9 COIRE LOAN
10 SUNA PATH
11 SALEN LOAN
B7010
SPRINGHILL RD
Springhill
BLACKHALL ST
BELMONT DR
BROWN ST
BEECHMOUNT PL
BERRYHILL PL
MULDRON TERR
ELMWOOD RD
LARCHFIELD PATH
NORTHFIELD AVE
STANE RD
Works
Springhill
SPRINGHILL AND LEADLOCH RD
EH47
B7010
B715
HEADLESSCROSS RD
Knowton Farm
Works
Lingore Linn
A71
Edinburgh STREET ATLAS
A71 Livingston, Edinburgh

168

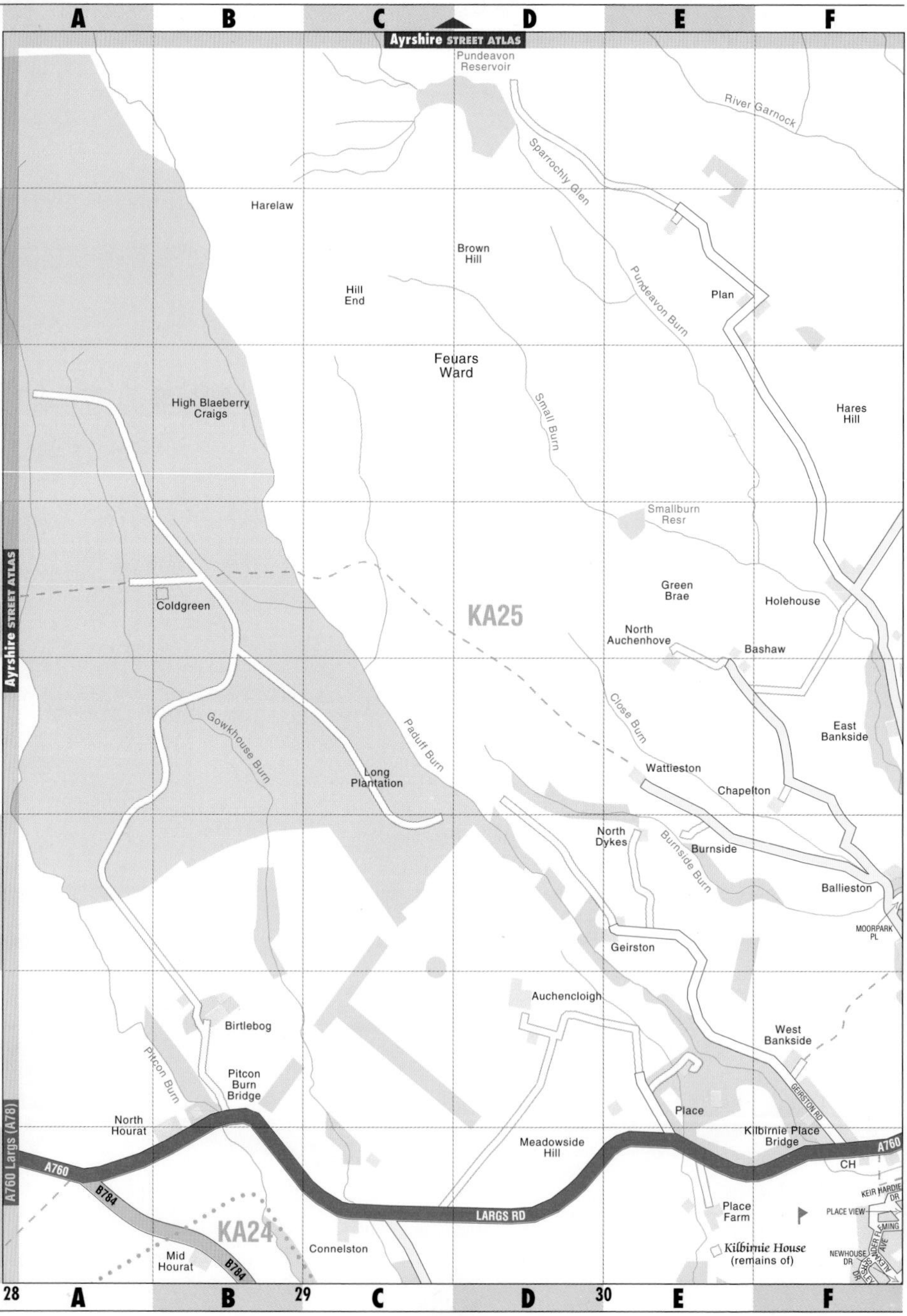
Ayrshire STREET ATLAS
Pundeavon Reservoir
River Garnock
Sparrochly Glen
Harelaw
Brown Hill
Hill End
Pundeavon Burn
Plan
Feuars Ward
High Blaeberry Craigs
Small Burn
Hares Hill
Smallburn Resr
Green Brae
Holehouse
Coldgreen
KA25
North Auchenhove
Bashaw
Gowkhouse Burn
Paduff Burn
Close Burn
East Bankside
Long Plantation
Wattieston
Chapelton
North Dykes
Burnside Burn
Burnside
Ballieston
MOORPARK PL
Geirston
Auchencloigh
Birtlebog
West Bankside
Pitcon Burn
Pitcon Burn Bridge
GEIRSTON RD
Place
North Hourat
Kilbirnie Place Bridge
Meadowside Hill
A760
CH
A760 Largs (A78)
B784
LARGS RD
Place Farm
KEIR HARDIE DR
PLACE VIEW
FLEMING AVE
KA24
Mid Hourat
Connelston
Kilbirnie House (remains of)
NEWHOUSE DR
A B C D E F
8 7 57 6 5 56 4 3 55 2 1 54
28 29 30

169

128
150

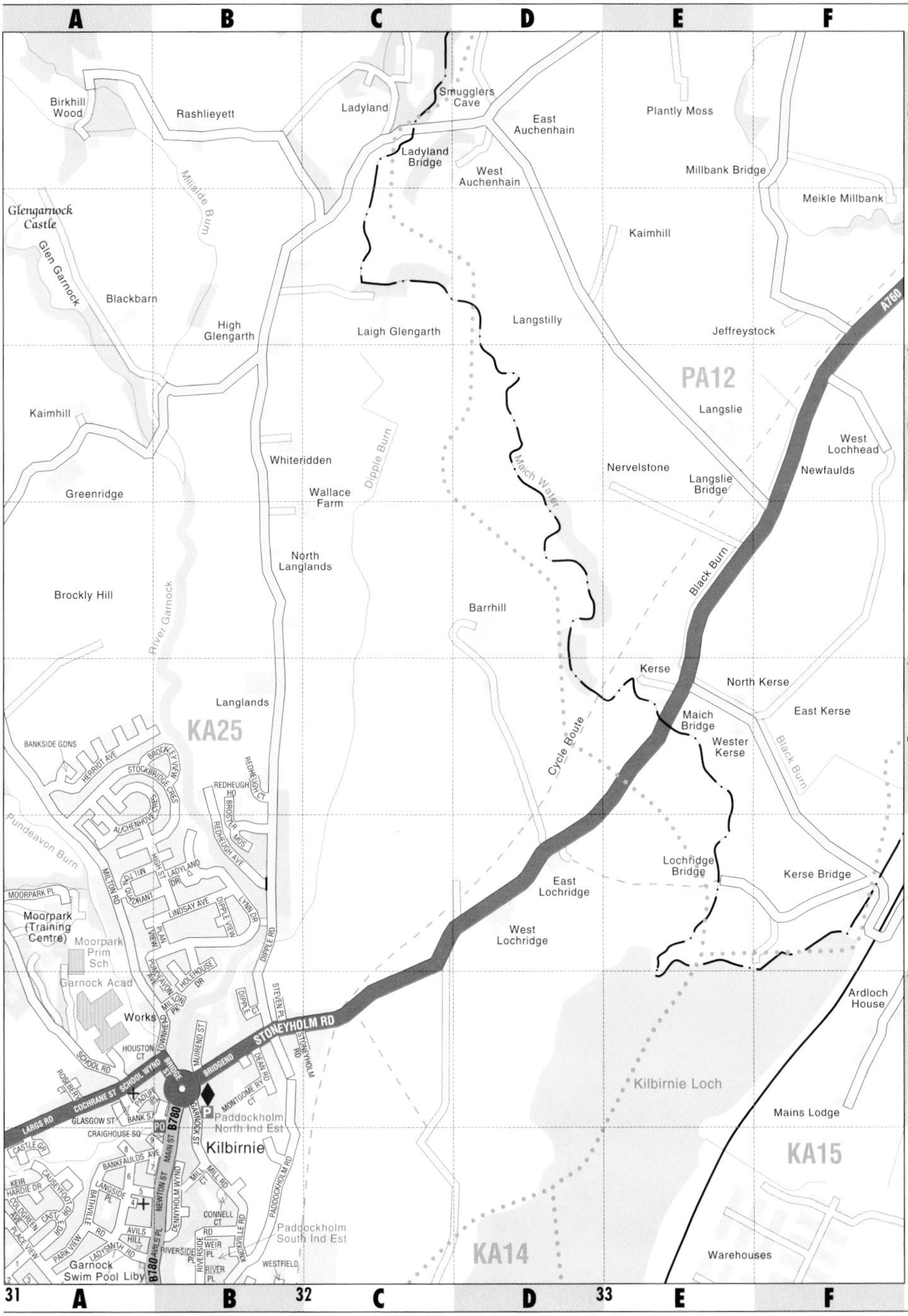

170
150

A1
1 NEWHOUSE DR
2 BROWNHILL DR
3 LADESIDE CT
4 GARNOCK CT
5 WALKER ST
6 PARKHOUSE DR
7 BANKFAULDS CT
8 MONTGOMERIESTON PL
9 MONTGOMERIESTON ST

149
129

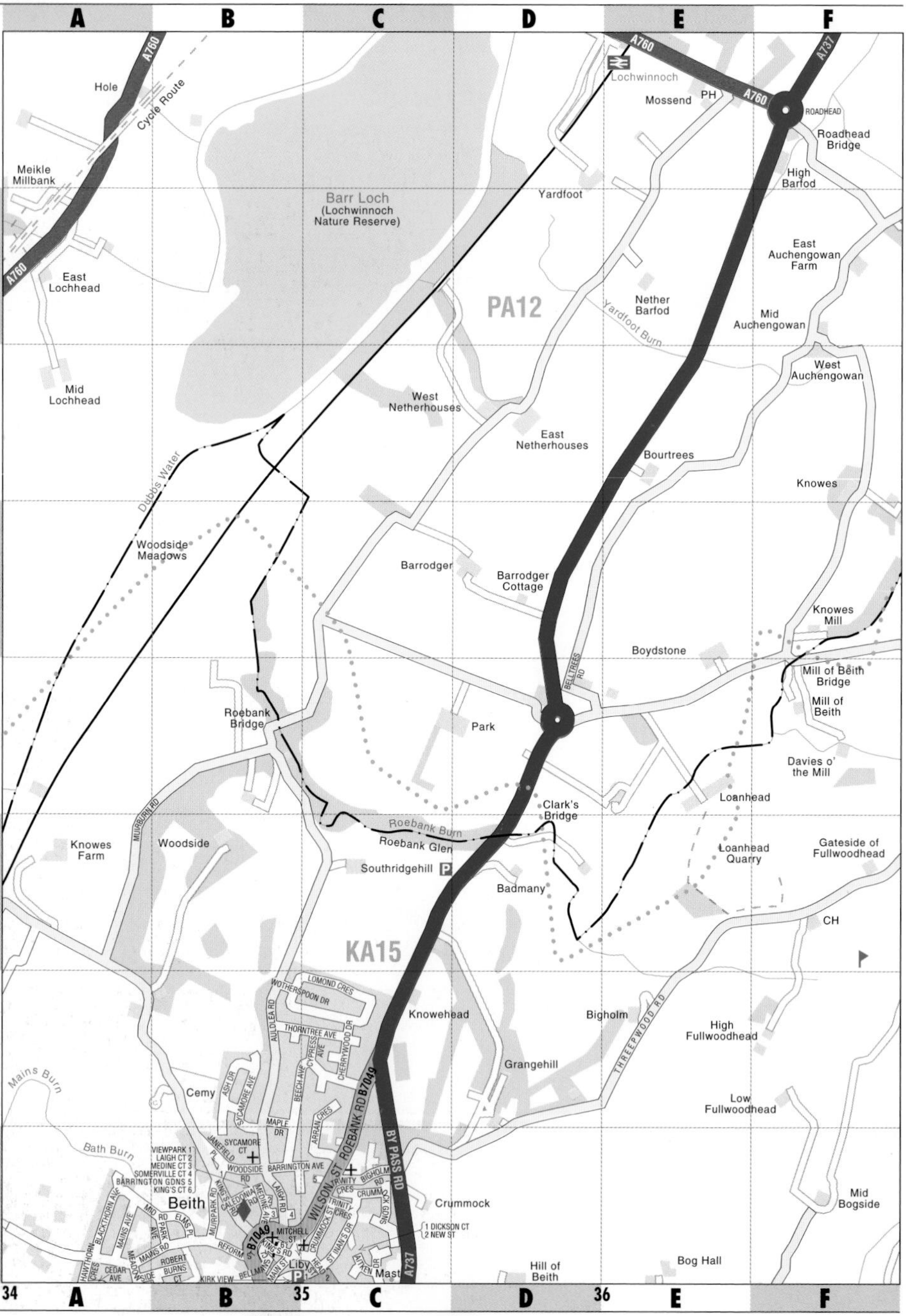

149
171

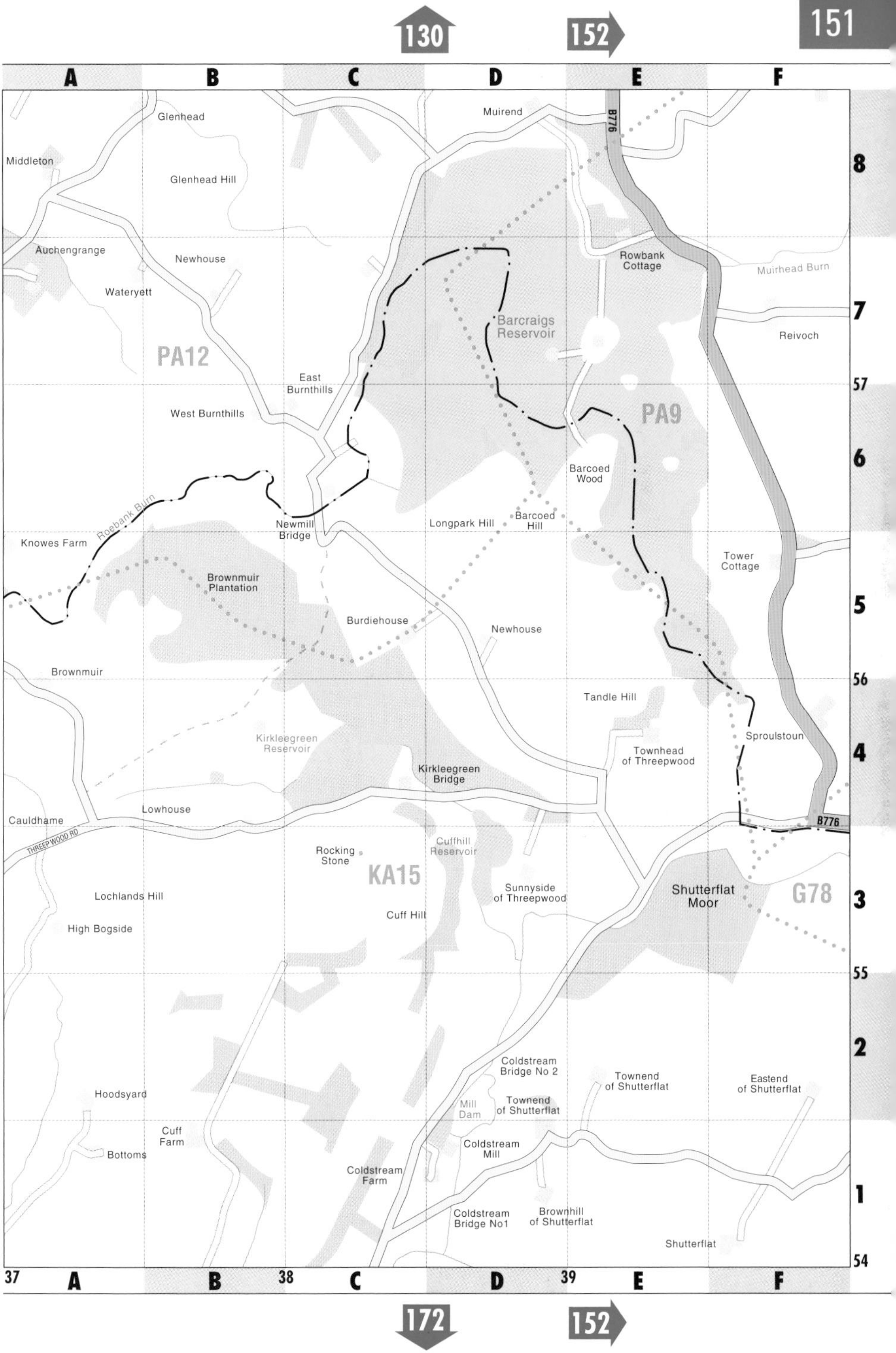
130
152
A
B
C
D
E
F
Glenhead
Muirend
B776
Middleton
Glenhead Hill
8
Auchengrange
Newhouse
Rowbank Cottage
Muirhead Burn
Wateryett
Barcraigs Reservoir
7
Reivoch
PA12
East Burnthills
57
West Burnthills
PA9
6
Barcoed Wood
Roebank Burn
Newmill Bridge
Longpark Hill
Barcoed Hill
Knowes Farm
Tower Cottage
Brownmuir Plantation
5
Burdiehouse
Newhouse
Brownmuir
56
Tandle Hill
Sproulstoun
Kirkleegreen Reservoir
Townhead of Threepwood
4
Kirkleegreen Bridge
Lowhouse
Cauldhame
B776
THREEP WOOD RD
Rocking Stone
Cuffhill Reservoir
KA15
Shutterflat Moor
G78
Sunnyside of Threepwood
3
Lochlands Hill
Cuff Hill
High Bogside
55
2
Coldstream Bridge No 2
Townend of Shutterflat
Eastend of Shutterflat
Hoodsyard
Mill Dam
Townend of Shutterflat
Cuff Farm
Coldstream Mill
Bottoms
Coldstream Farm
1
Coldstream Bridge No1
Brownhill of Shutterflat
Shutterflat
54
37
38
39
172
152

151
131

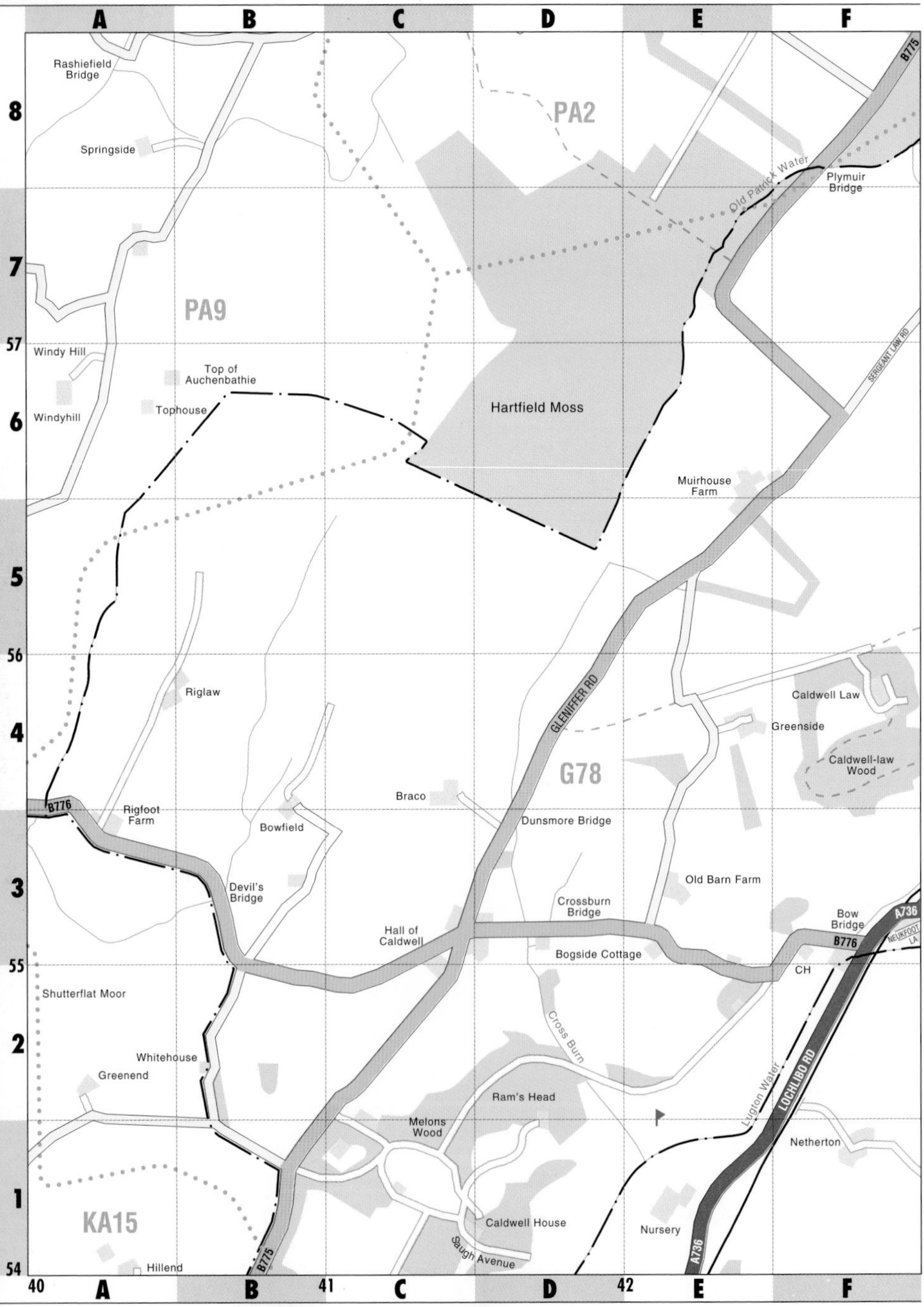

151
173

132
154

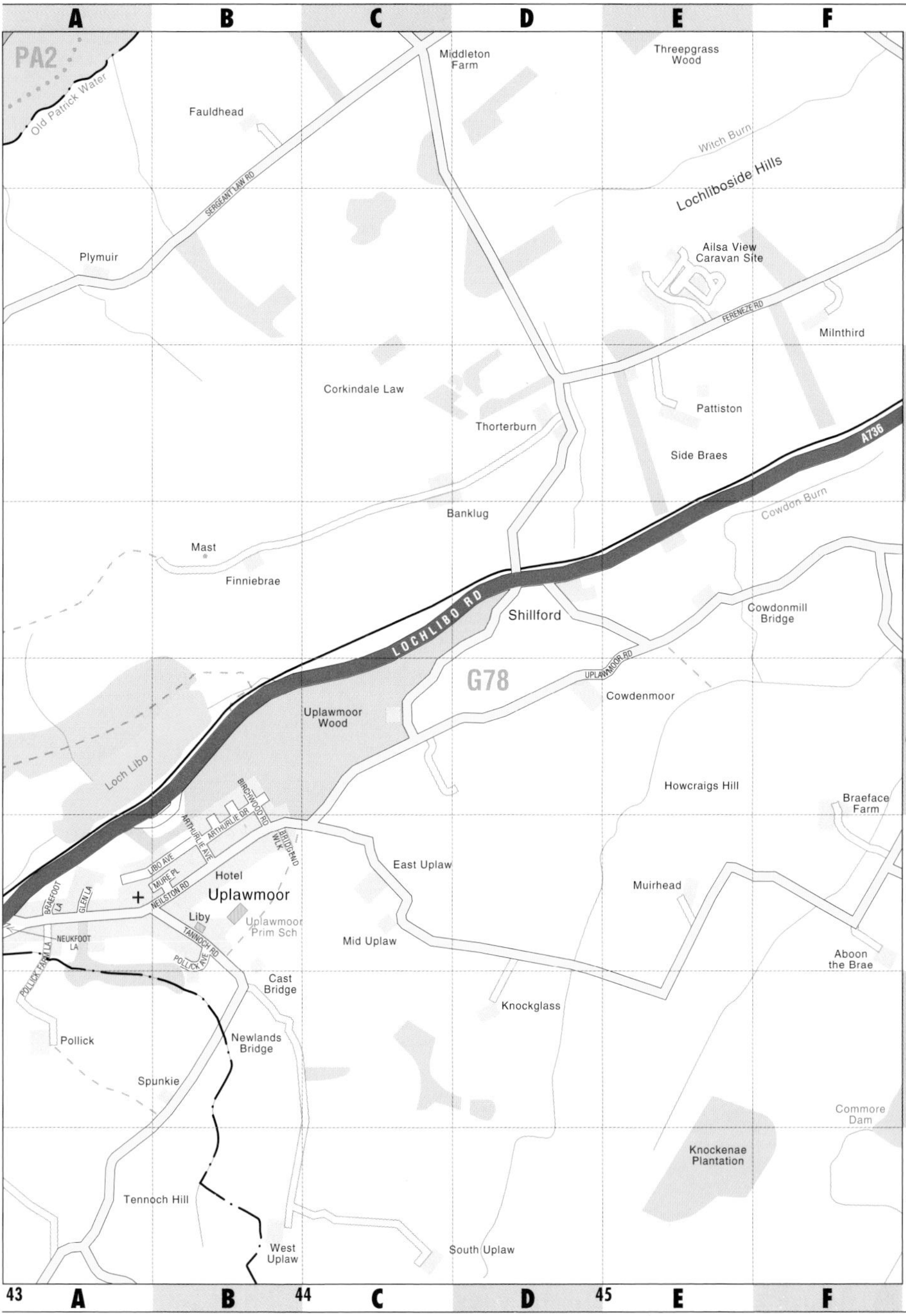

174
154

153 133

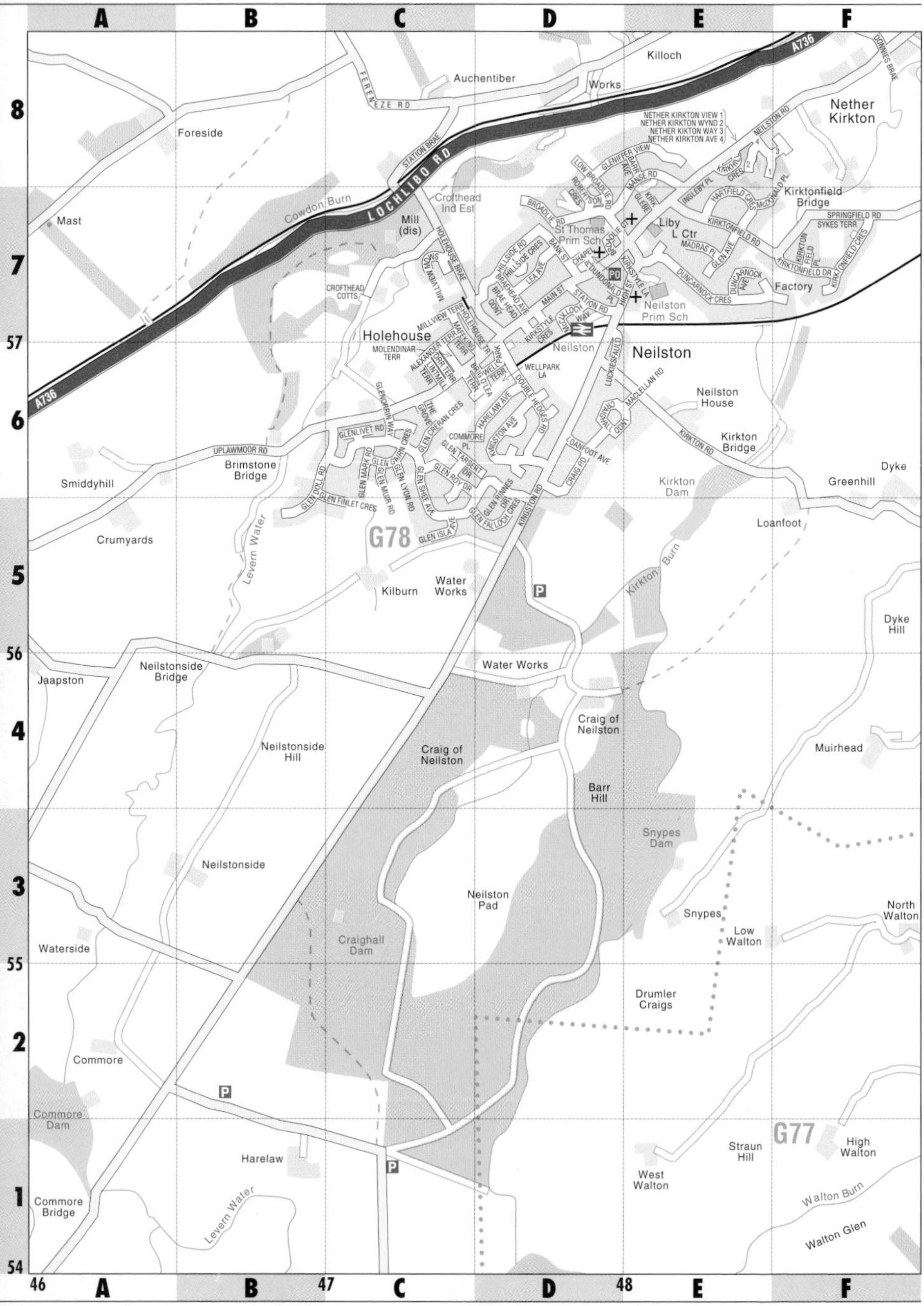

153 175

134
156

176
156

155
135

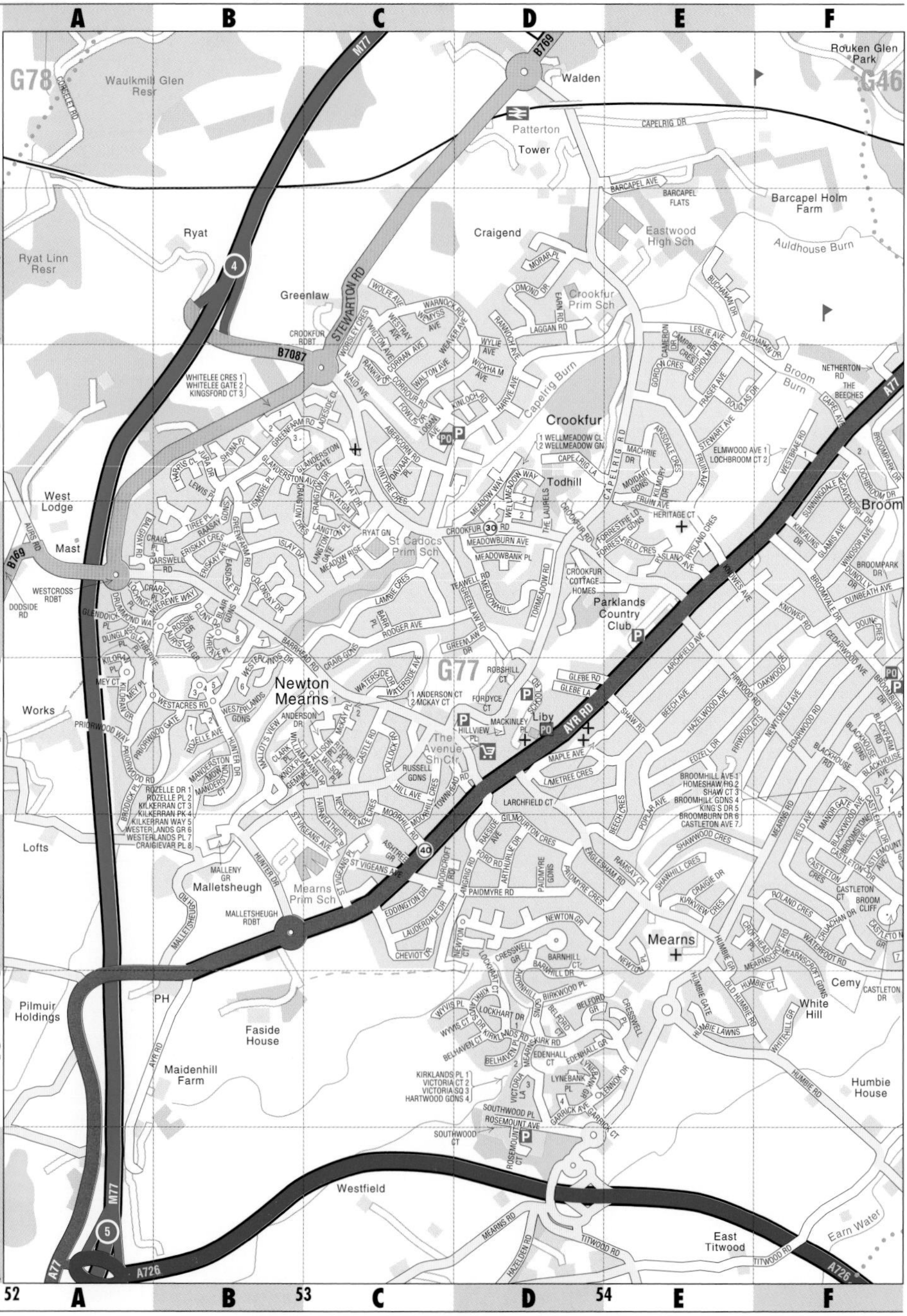

155
177

136
158

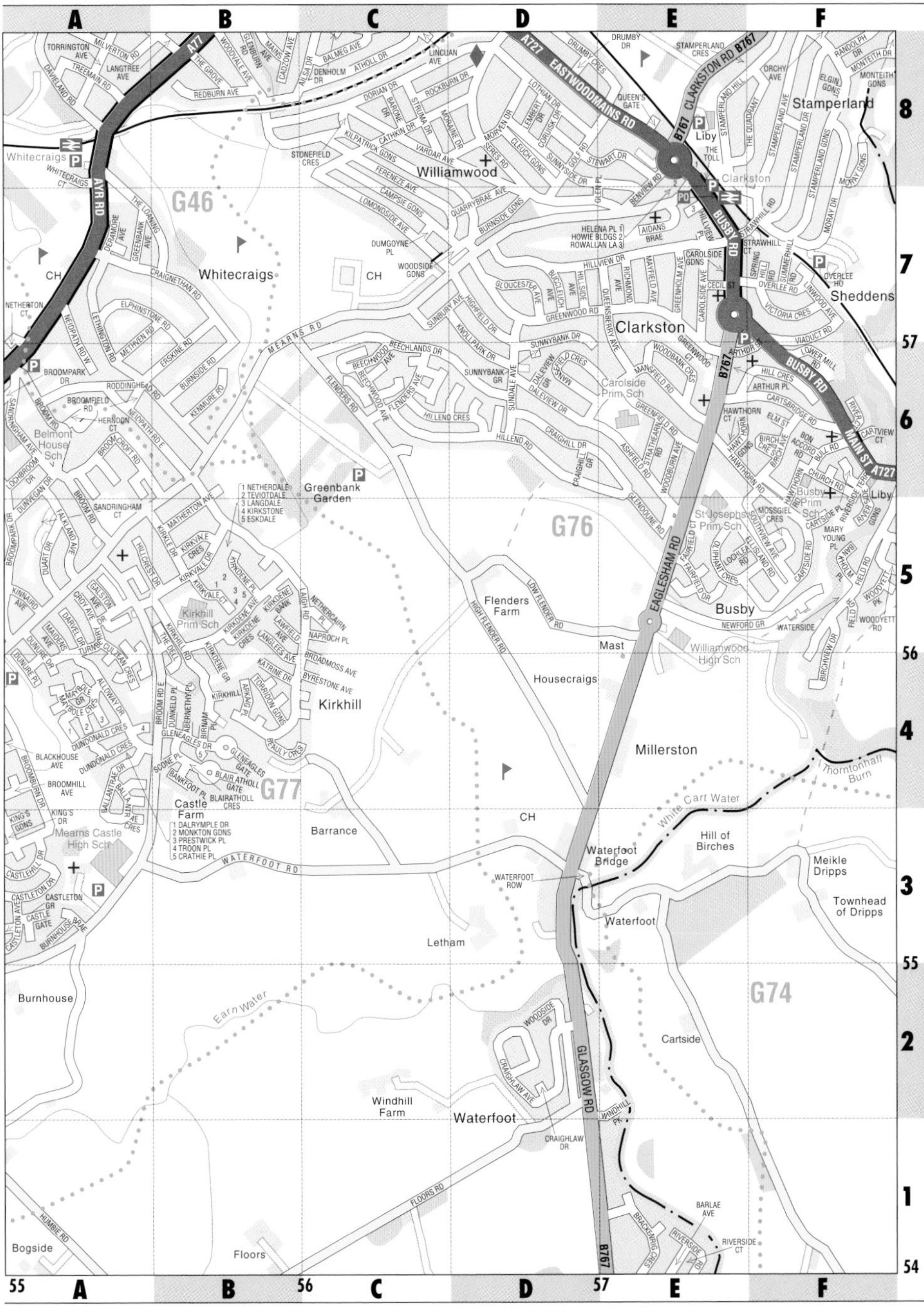

178
158

157
137

157
179

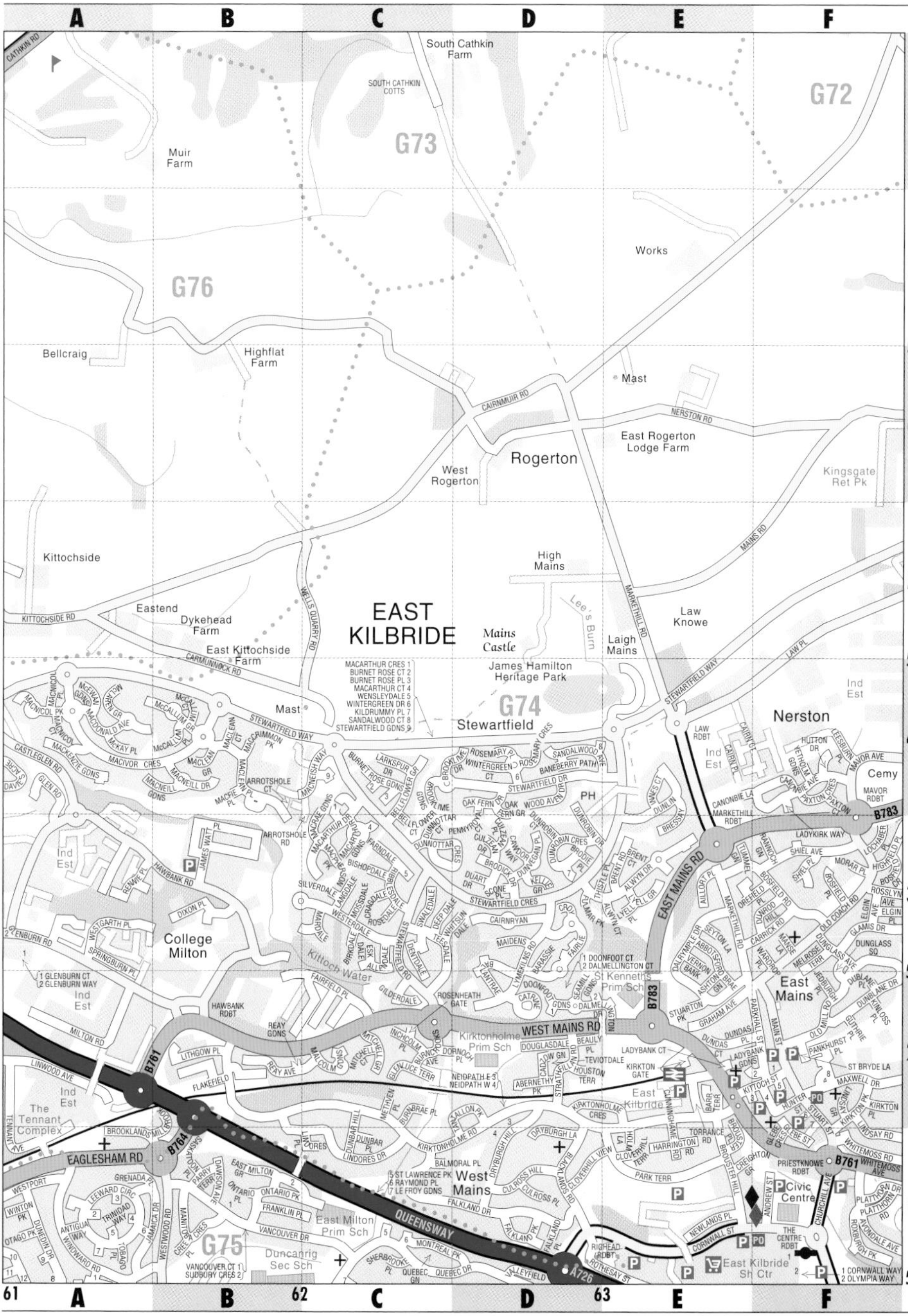

A1
1 NASSAU PL
2 MONTEGO GN
3 TRINIDAD GN
4 DOMINICA GN
5 BARBADOS GN
6 BAHAMAS WAY
7 WATLING PL
8 AUCKLAND PK
9 HAVELOCK PK
10 STRATHALLAN WYND
11 STRATHALLAN GATE
12 STRATHALLAN AVE

F2
1 WEAVERS CT
2 LADYBANK PL
3 MONTGOMERY PL
4 MONTGOMERY ST
5 KITTOCH PL
6 ELIZABETH CT
7 WELLBECK HO
8 ST BRYDE ST

159
139

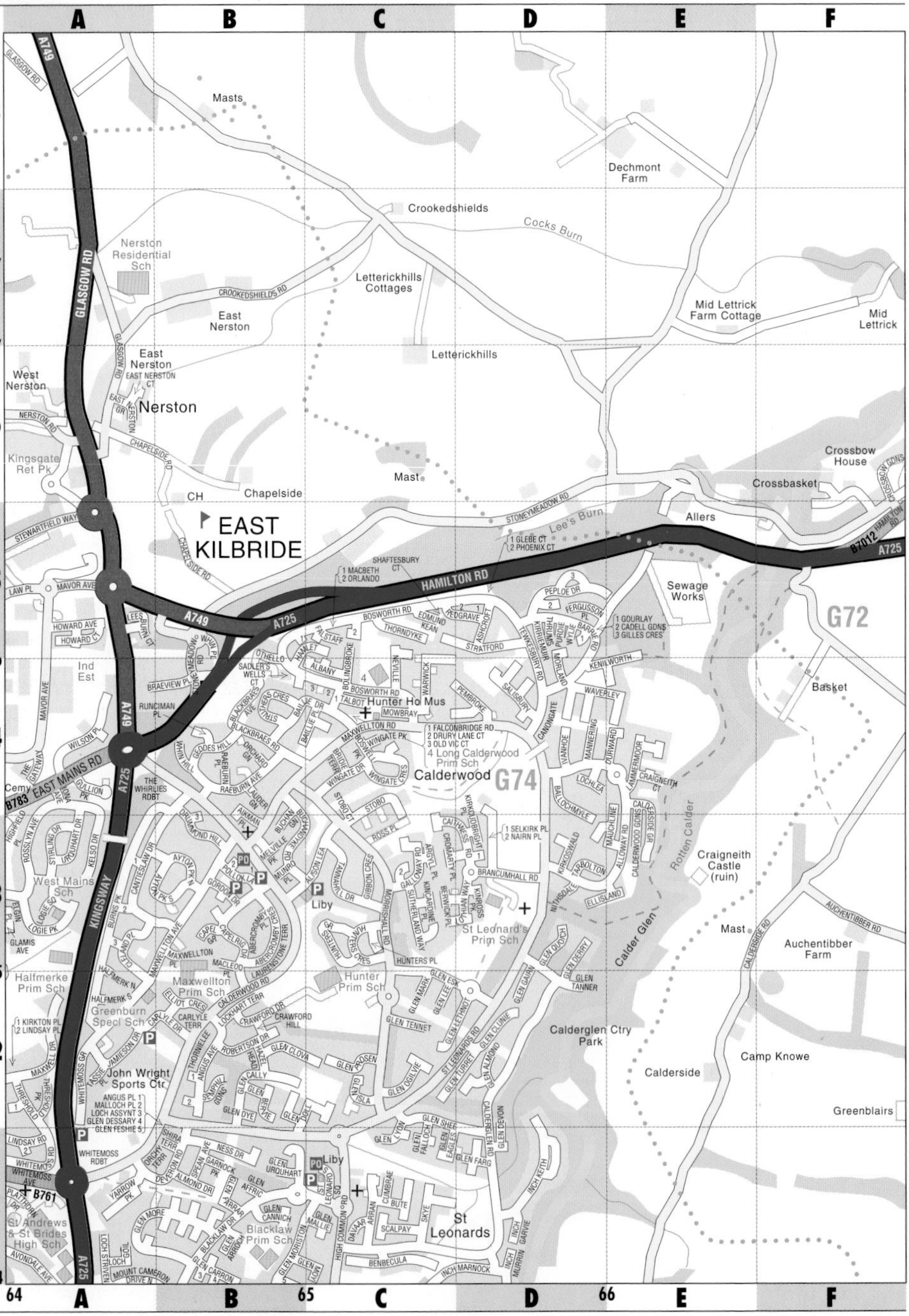

A3
1 SCOTT HILL
2 ETTRICK HILL
3 RAMSAY HILL

B3
1 CALDERWOOD SQ
2 POLLOK PL
3 DRUMMOND PL

159
181

C6
1 CAERLAVEROCK PL
2 SANDALE PATH
3 MALVAIG LA

D7
1 DRYBURGH WAY
2 ALLENDALE PATH
3 BARNETT PATH
4 CAUSEYSTANES
5 ROXBURGH PL
6 GREENBANK
7 LIBERTY PATH
8 LOCHABER PATH
9 MADISON PATH
10 TOURNAI PATH

140

162

E7
1 ELM CT
2 HERBERTSON ST
3 NORDIC GDNS
4 ALPINE WLK
5 ALPINE PATH
6 NORDIC GR
7 ANFORD LA

A B C D E F

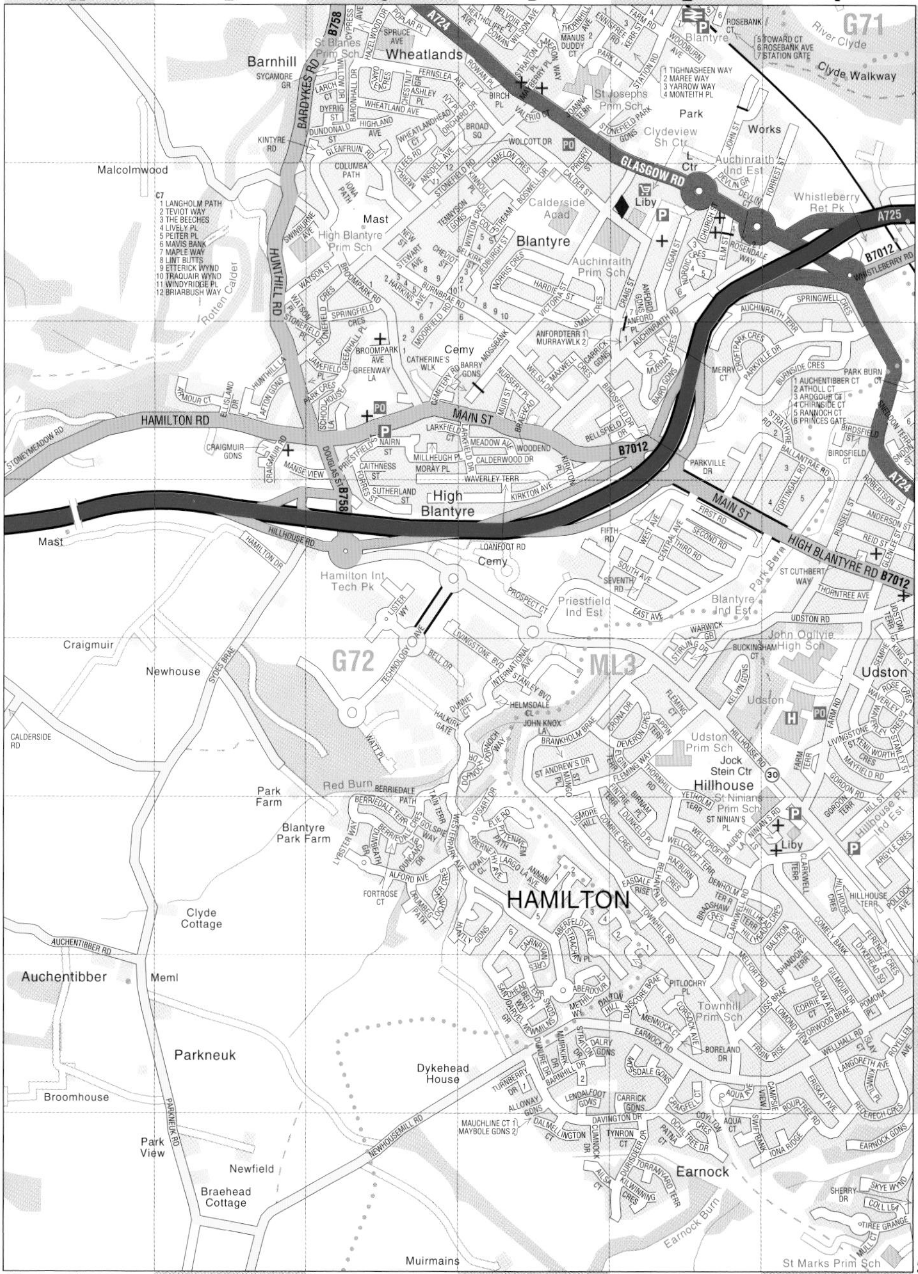

A B C D E F

67 68 69

182

D3
1 DALBEATTIE DR
2 THORN AVE
3 GLAMIS CRES
4 GLAMIS LA
5 BLACKCRAIG BRAE
6 KIRKMAIDEN WY

162

E3
1 TOWNHILL TERR
2 GLAMIS GAIT

A5
1 GLADSTONE CT
2 LIMETREE CT
3 GEORGE STEWART GDNS
4 WILSON CT
5 GEORGE CT
6 BURNBANK GDNS
7 GEORGES CL
8 Glenlee Prim Sch
9 Hamilton Sch for the Deaf
10 St Cuthberts Prim Sch

161

A6
1 PARKWOOD LEA
2 PARKWOOD TERR
3 JAMES MURDIE GDNS
4 ALBERT LA

141

B5
1 COPPERWOOD CT
2 COPPERWOOD WYND
3 COPPERWOOD CRES

A B C D E F

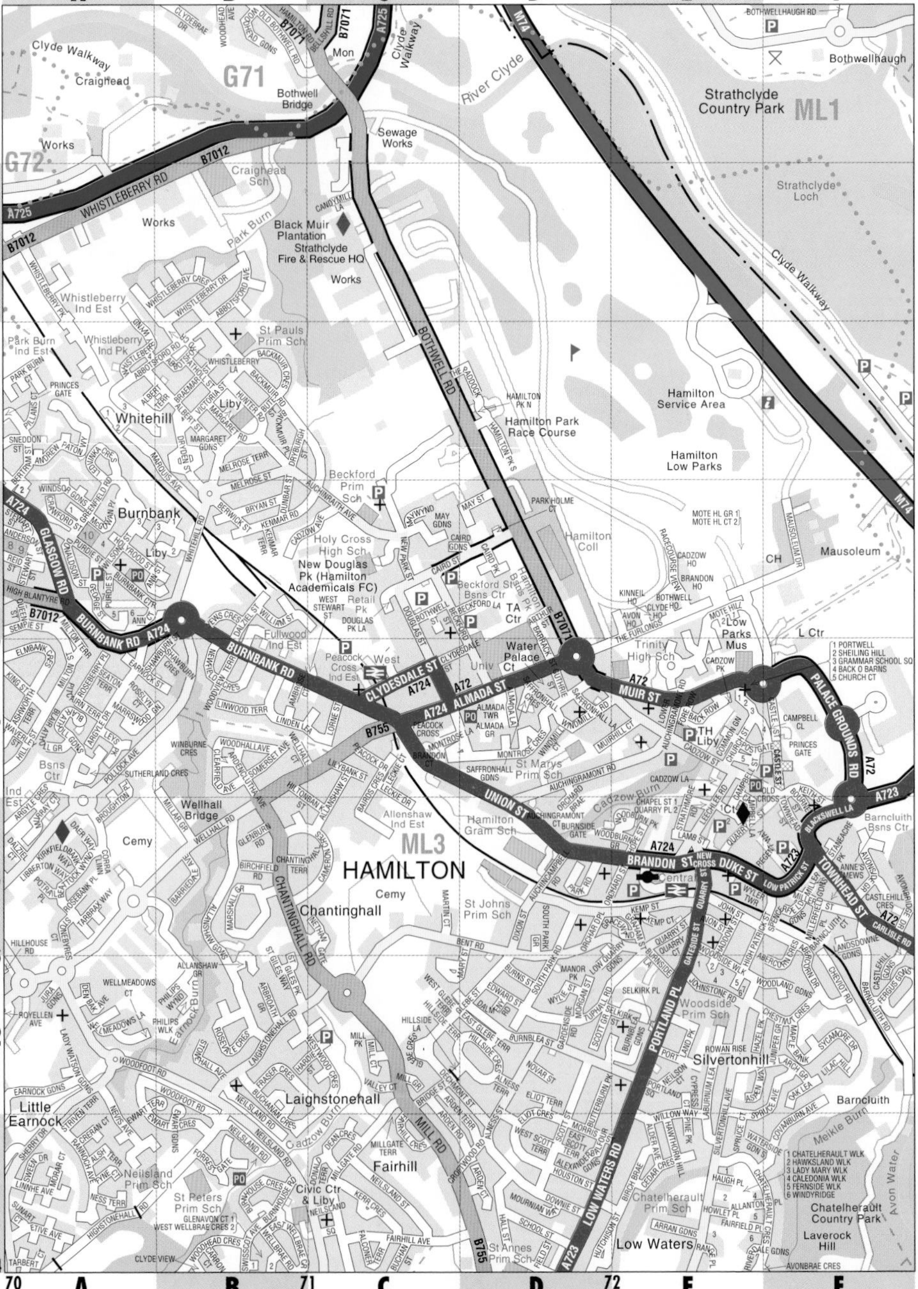

70 A B 71 C D 72 E F

161

183

E2
1 BROWN ST
2 CENTENARY GDNS
3 WEAVERS CT
4 WOODSIDE CT
5 WOODSIDE AVE
6 CARLTON CT
7 HILTON CT

C8
1 MARIUS CRES
2 SENATE PL
3 MARCUS WY
4 TARQUIN PL

142

D8
1 LANTANA GR
2 Braidhurst Ind Est
3 FINDLAY CT
4 CERES PL
5 Muir St Prim Sch

164

E5
1 OAKFIELD TWR
2 ALBION TWR
3 McCLURG CT
4 ELVAN TWR
5 KERR GRIEVE CT
6 CALDER TWR
7 AVON TWR
8 CLYDE TWR
E6
1 BRANDON ARC
2 OAKFIELD DR
3 WATSONVILLE PK
4 WATSON ST
F5
1 GLENCAIRN TWR
2 CAIRN CT
3 MACDONALD ST
4 CIVIC SQ
5 BLAIR PATH
6 ELLIS WAY

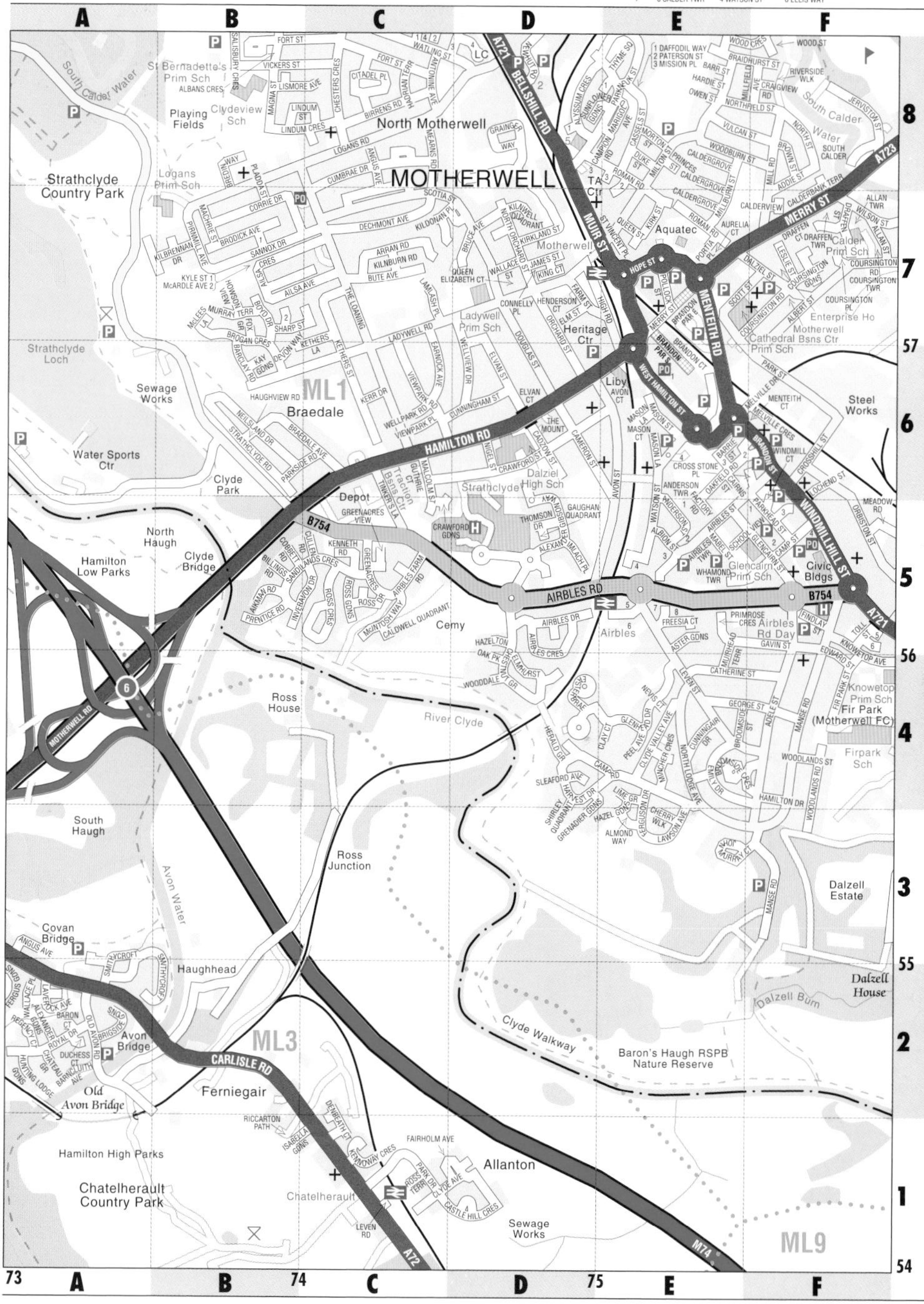

184

164

163
143

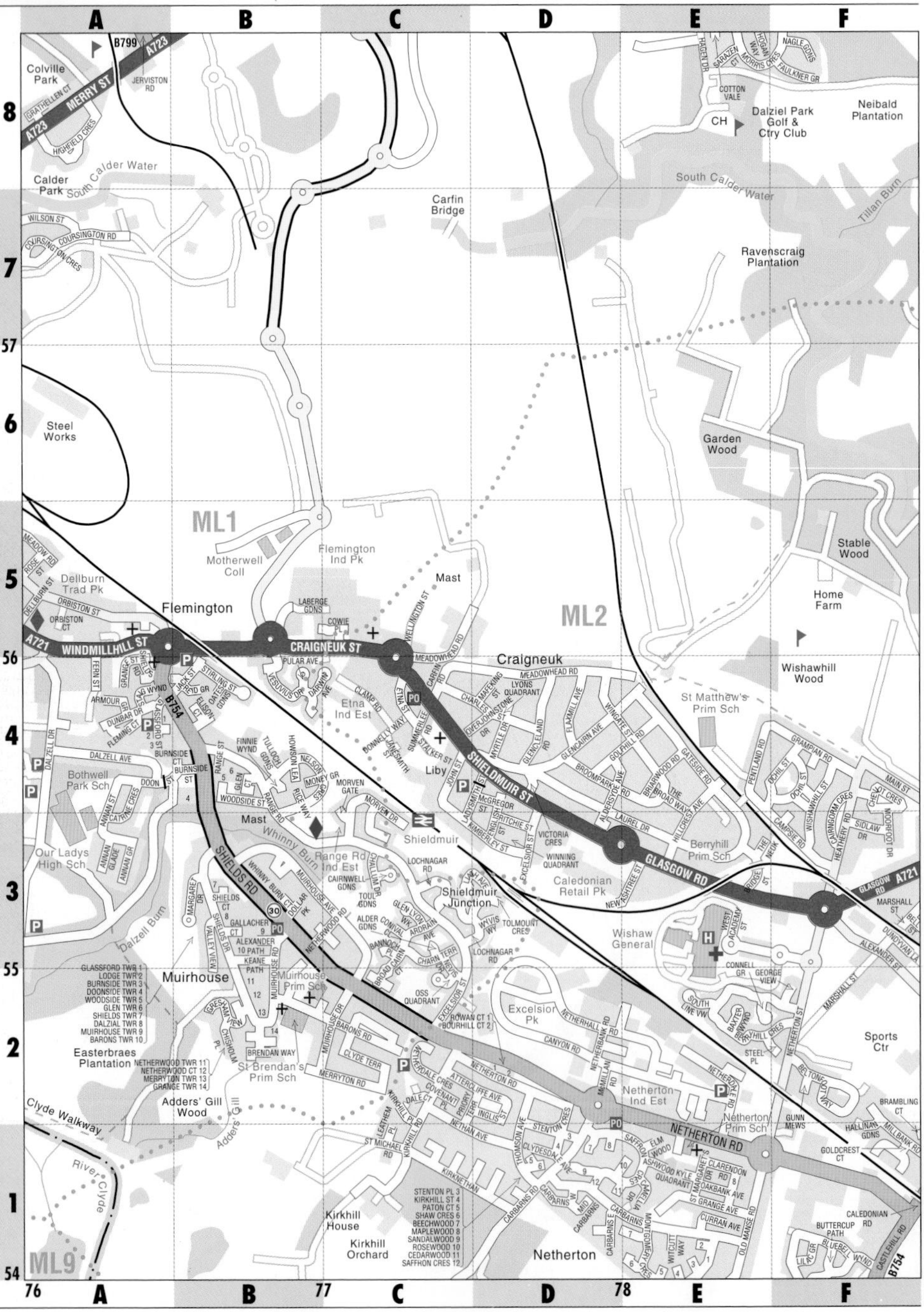

163
185

E1
1 MONTGOMERY CRES
2 ISLAY QUADRANT
3 JURA QUADRANT
4 GIGHA QUADRANT
5 SCARBA QUADRANT
6 PARK QUADRANT
7 STUART QUADRANT
8 ROSEHALL TERR

144 166

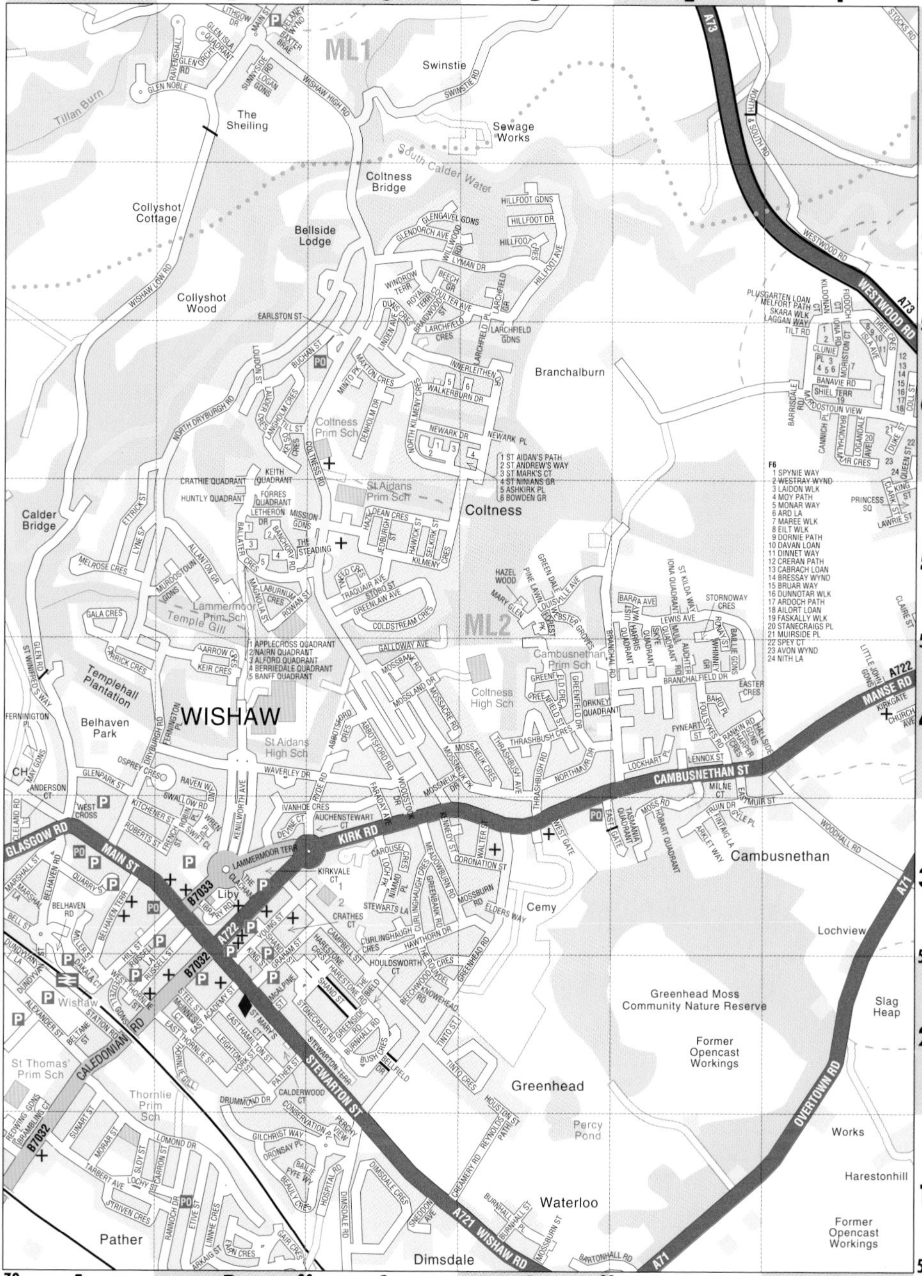

B2
1 Wishaw Bsns Ctr

C3
1 St Ignatius' RC Prim Sch
2 Wishaw Acad Prim Sch

186 166

165
145

165
187

146
168

188
168

167
147

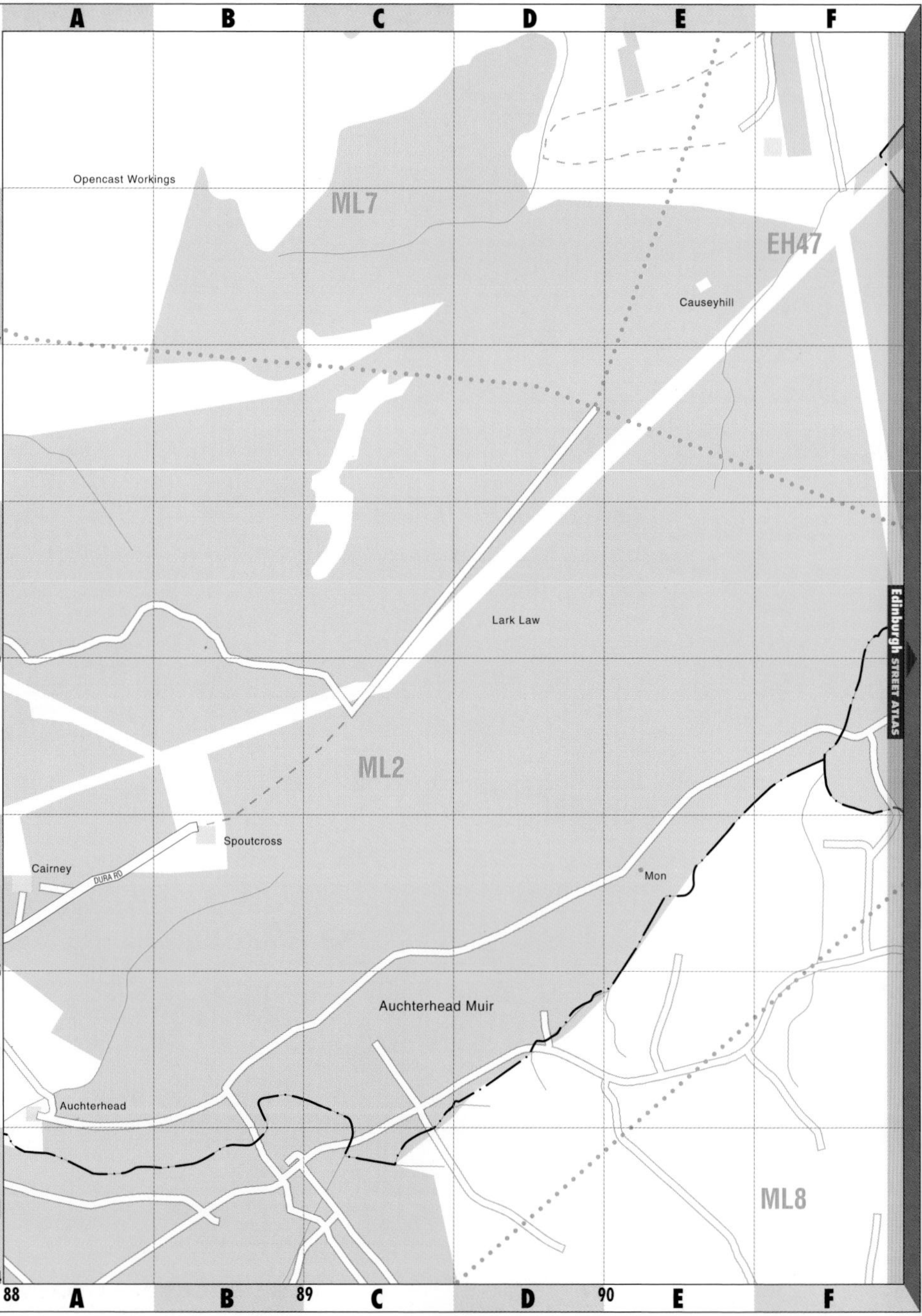

167
189

148
170

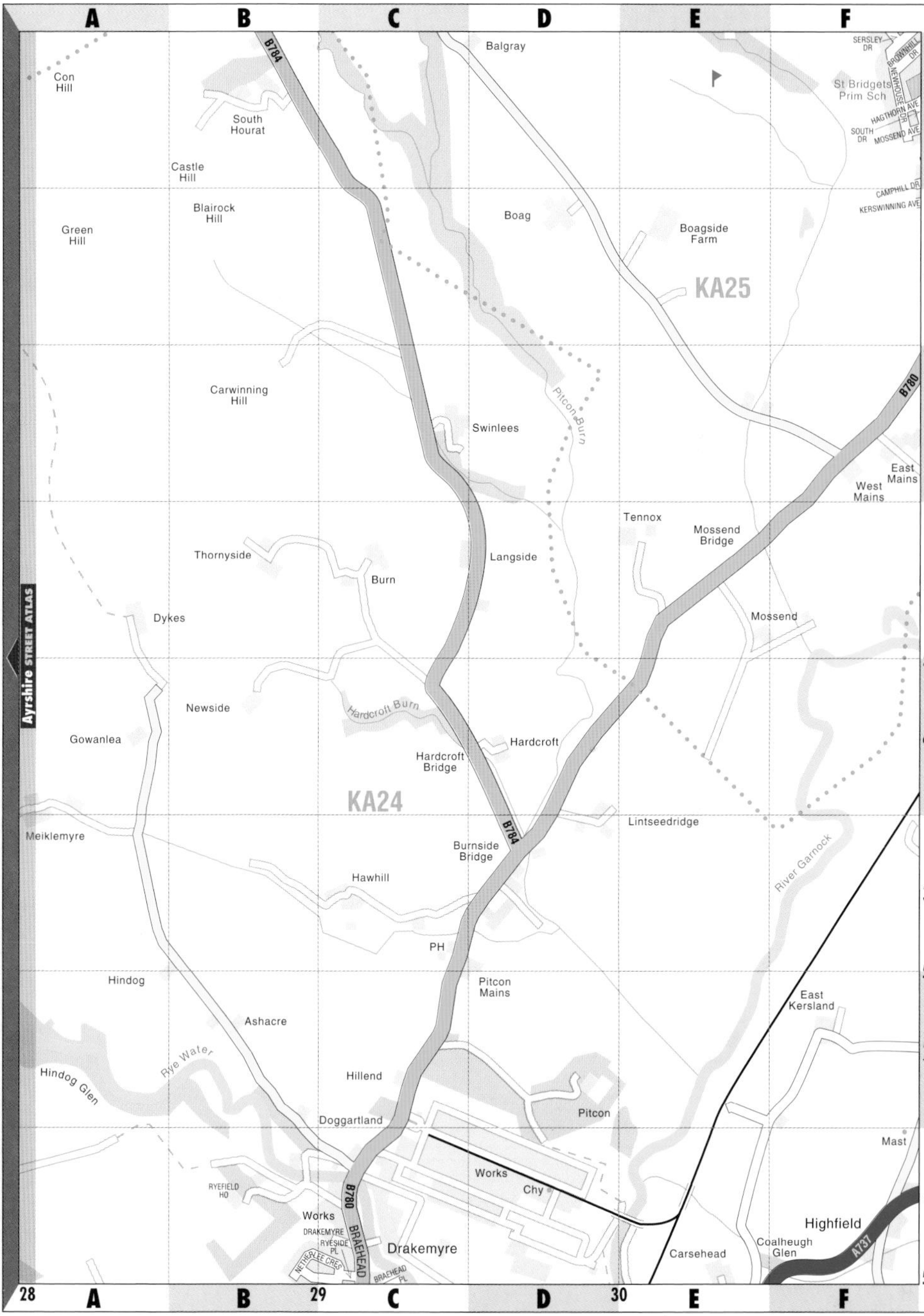

191
170

169
149

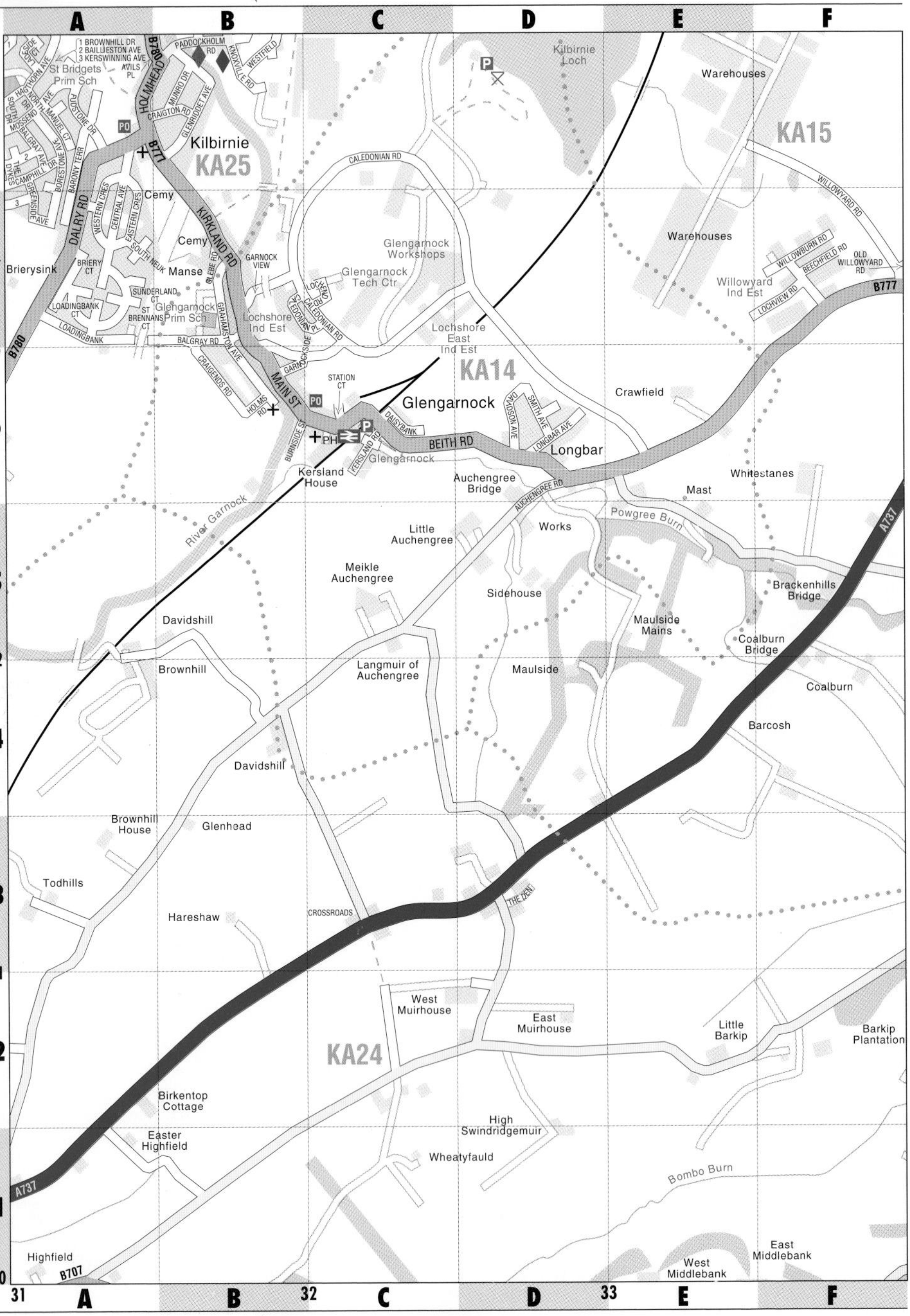
Kilbirnie
KA25
St Bridgets Prim Sch
Cemy
Manse
Glengarnock Prim Sch
Brierysink
Lochshore Ind Est
Glengarnock Workshops
Glengarnock Tech Ctr
Lochshore East Ind Est
KA14
Glengarnock
Longbar
Kilbirnie Loch
Warehouses
KA15
Willowyard Ind Est
Crawfield
Whitestanes
Mast
Kersland House
Auchengree Bridge
Little Auchengree
Meikle Auchengree
Works
Sidehouse
Powgree Burn
River Garnock
Brackenhills Bridge
Maulside Mains
Coalburn Bridge
Maulside
Coalburn
Davidshill
Brownhill
Langmuir of Auchengree
Barcosh
Brownhill House
Glenhead
Todhills
Hareshaw
CROSSROADS
THE DEN
West Muirhouse
East Muirhouse
KA24
Little Barkip
Barkip Plantation
Birkentop Cottage
Easter Highfield
High Swindridgemuir
Wheatyfauld
Bombo Burn
Highfield
West Middlebank
East Middlebank
A737
B777
B780
B707
DALRY RD
KIRKLAND RD
MAIN ST
BEITH RD
CALEDONIAN RD
AUCHENGREE RD
1 BROWNHILL DR
2 BAILLIESTON AVE
3 KERSWINNING AVE
A B C D E F
8 7 6 5 4 3 2 1
53 52 51 50
31 32 33

150
172

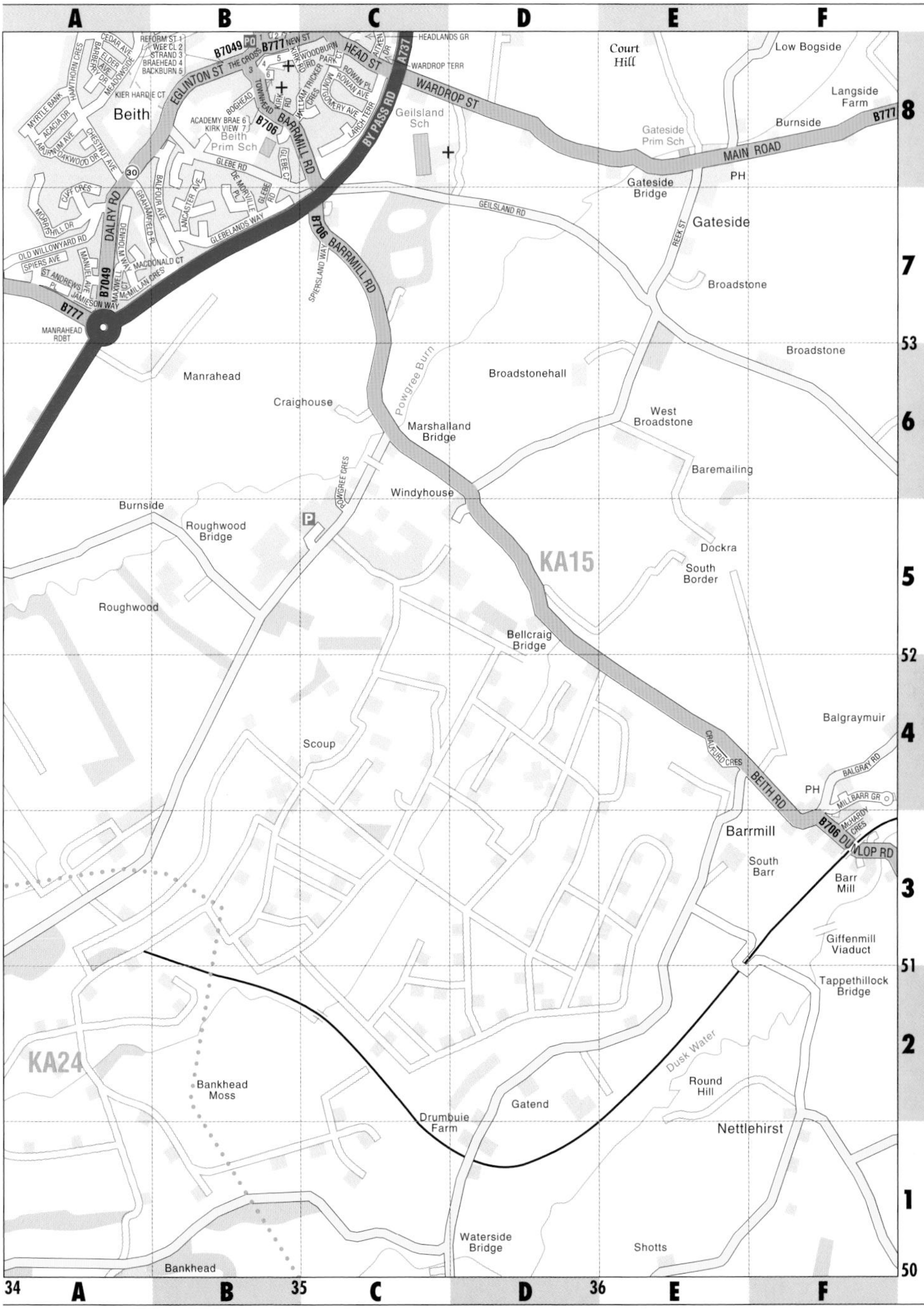

193
172

171
151

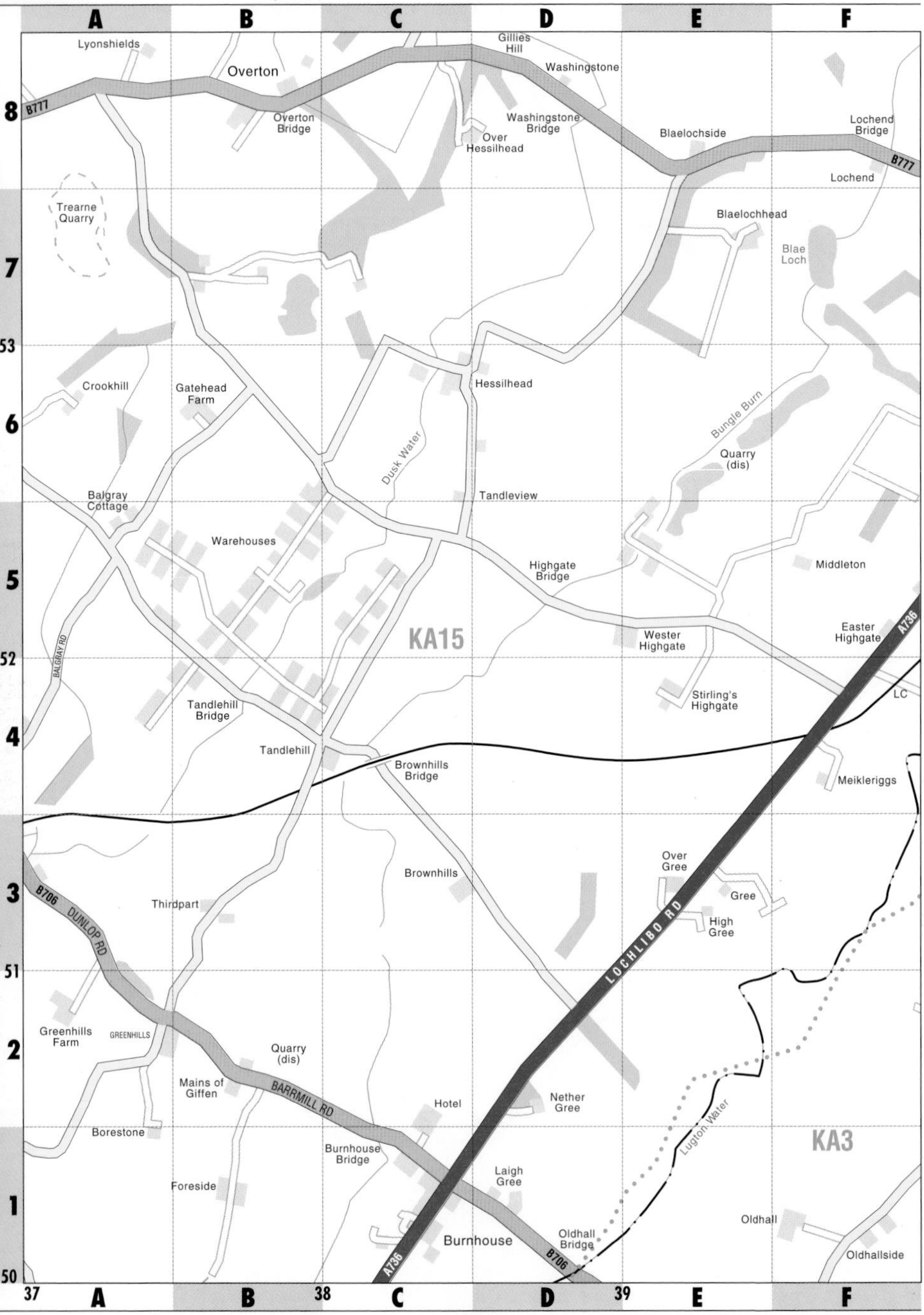
A
B
C
D
E
F
8
7
53
6
5
52
4
3
51
2
1
50
37
38
39
Lyonshields
Overton
Gillies Hill
Washingstone
B777
Overton Bridge
Washingstone Bridge
Over Hessilhead
Blaelochside
Lochend Bridge
Lochend
Trearne Quarry
Blaelochhead
Blae Loch
Crookhill
Gatehead Farm
Hessilhead
Bungle Burn
Dusk Water
Quarry (dis)
Balgray Cottage
Tandleview
Warehouses
Highgate Bridge
Middleton
BALGRAY RD
KA15
Wester Highgate
Easter Highgate
A736
LC
Tandlehill Bridge
Stirling's Highgate
Tandlehill
Brownhills Bridge
Meikleriggs
Brownhills
Over Gree
Gree
B706
DUNLOP RD
Thirdpart
LOCHLIBO RD
High Gree
Greenhills Farm
GREENHILLS
Quarry (dis)
Mains of Giffen
BARRMILL RD
Hotel
Nether Gree
Lugton Water
Borestone
Burnhouse Bridge
KA3
Laigh Gree
Foreside
Oldhall
Burnhouse
Oldhall Bridge
Oldhallside

171
194

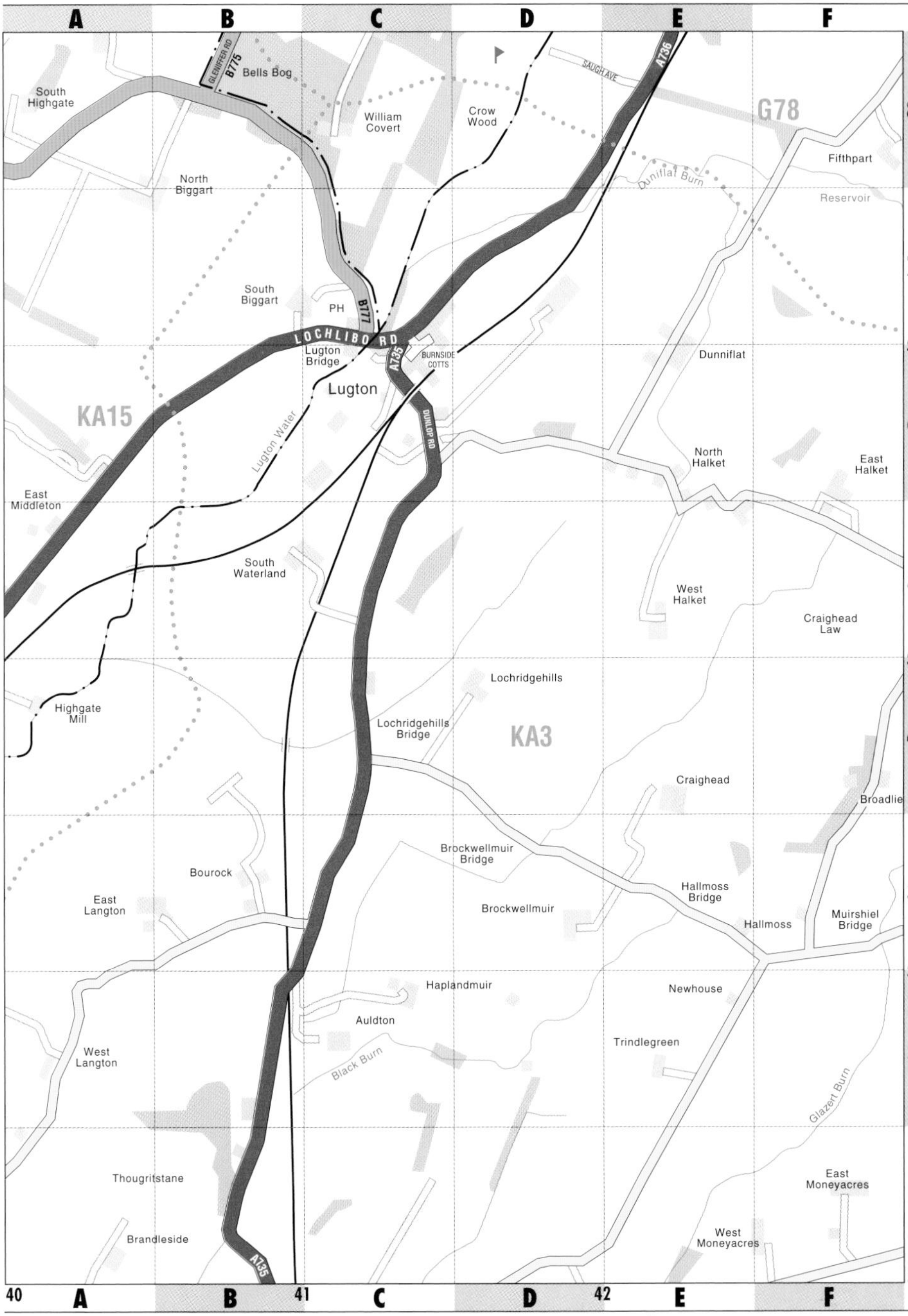
A
B
C
D
E
F
GLENIFFER RD
B775
Bells Bog
South Highgate
William Covert
Crow Wood
SAUGH AVE
A736
G78
8
Fifthpart
North Biggart
Dunniflat Burn
Reservoir
7
South Biggart
PH
B777
LOCHLIBO RD
Lugton Bridge
A735
BURNSIDE COTTS
Lugton
53
Dunniflat
KA15
Lugton Water
DUNLOP RD
6
North Halket
East Halket
East Middleton
South Waterland
5
West Halket
Craighead Law
52
Lochridgehills
Highgate Mill
Lochridgehills Bridge
KA3
4
Craighead
Broadlie
Brockwellmuir Bridge
Bourock
Hallmoss Bridge
3
East Langton
Brockwellmuir
Hallmoss
Muirshiel Bridge
51
Haplandmuir
Newhouse
Auldton
West Langton
Trindlegreen
2
Black Burn
Glazert Burn
Thougritstane
East Moneyacres
1
Brandleside
West Moneyacres
A735
50
40
41
42

173
153

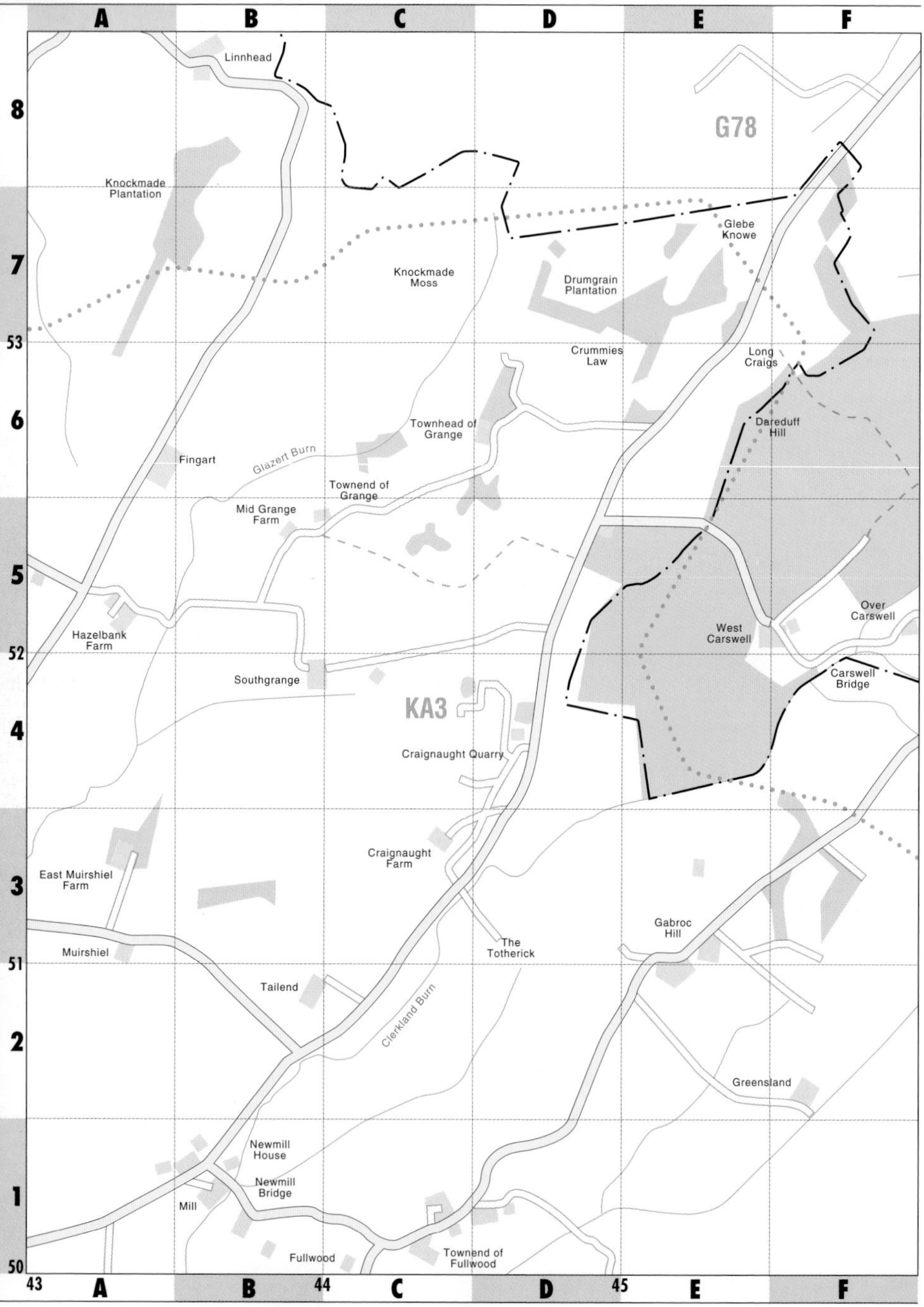

173
196

154
176

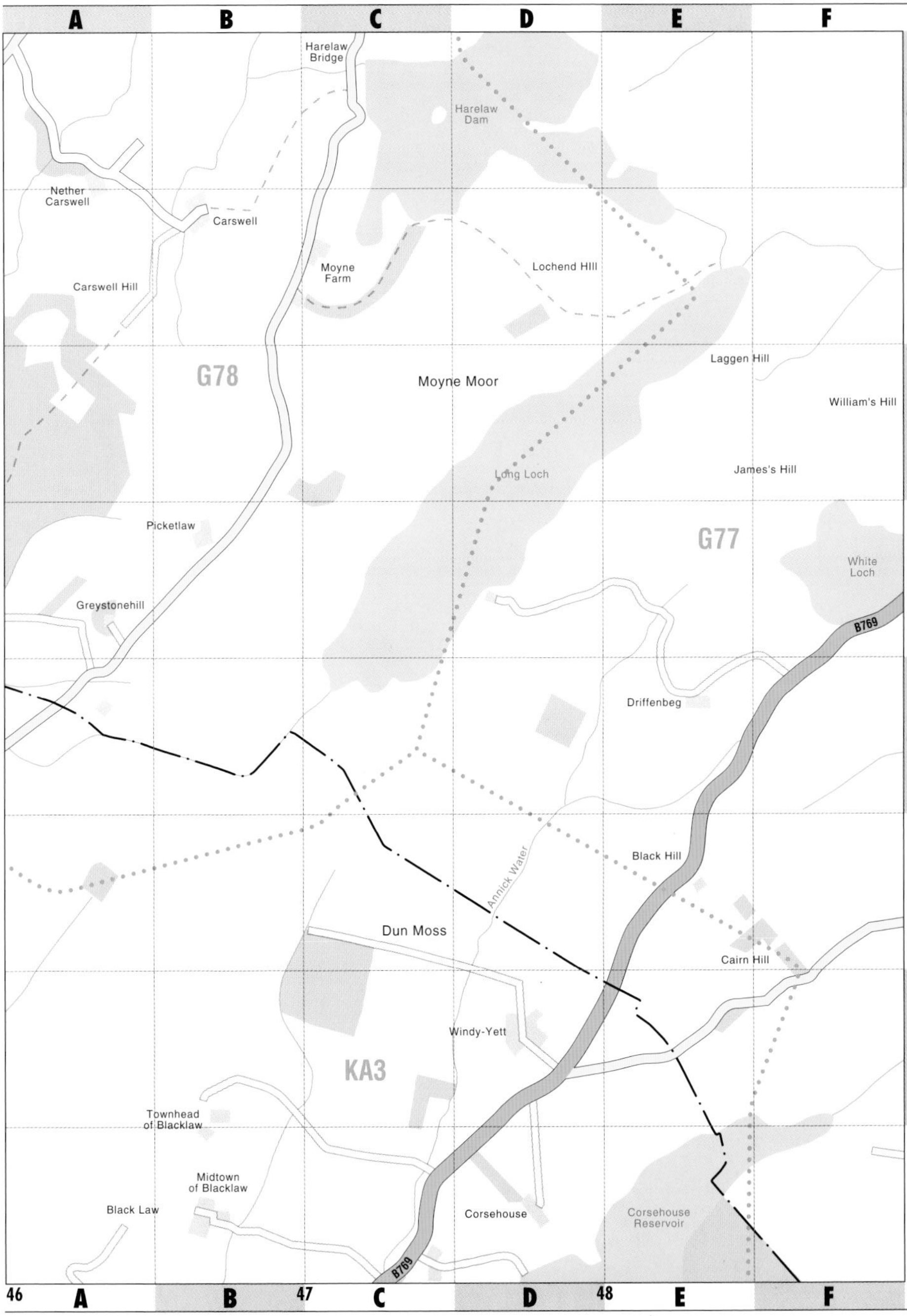

197
176

175
155

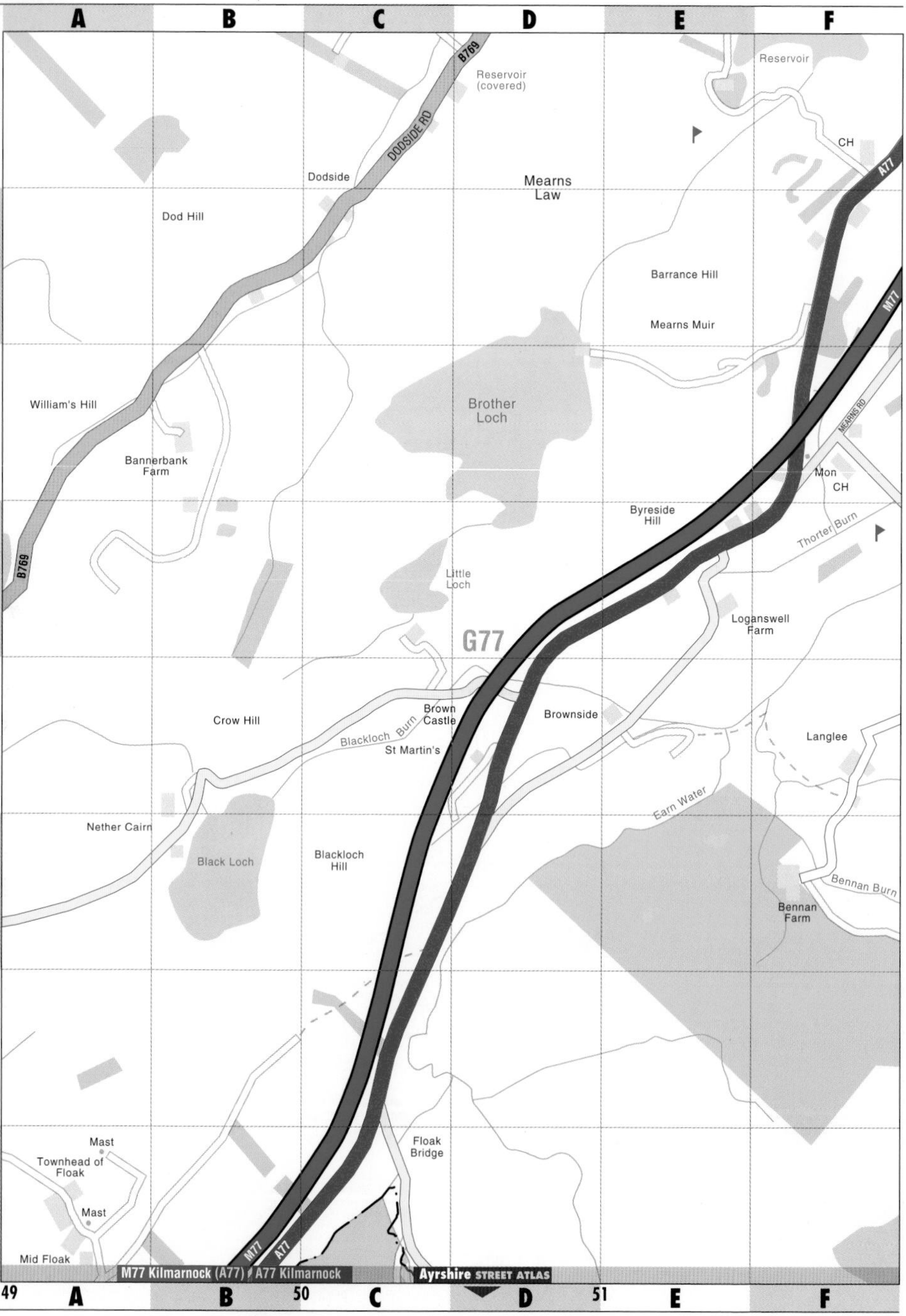
A
B
C
D
E
F
8
7
53
6
5
52
4
3
51
2
1
50
49
50
51
B769
DODSIDE RD
Reservoir (covered)
Reservoir
CH
A77
M77
Dodside
Mearns Law
Dod Hill
Barrance Hill
Mearns Muir
William's Hill
Brother Loch
MEARNS RD
Bannerbank Farm
Mon
CH
Byreside Hill
Thorter Burn
Little Loch
Loganswell Farm
G77
Brown Castle
Brownside
Crow Hill
Blackloch Burn
St Martin's
Langlee
Earn Water
Nether Cairn
Black Loch
Blackloch Hill
Bennan Burn
Bennan Farm
Mast
Townhead of Floak
Floak Bridge
Mast
Mid Floak
M77 Kilmarnock (A77)
A77 Kilmarnock
Ayrshire STREET ATLAS

175

156
178

A
B
C
D
E
F
A77
M77
A726
Nursery
Crook
HAZELDEN RD
Hazeldean House
TITWOOD RD
West Titwood
MEARNS RD
Harelea Hill
Mast
Star and Garter
Hazeldenhill
Hazelden Mains
G77
Broadlees
Earn Water
Fauldside Hill
Blackhouse Farm
Bonnyton Moor
Thorter Burn
Long Wood
BONNYTON MOOR RD
North Moorhouse
Muirshield Bridge
KIRKTON MOOR RD
East Moorhouse
Boshee Hill
G76
Water Works
South Moorhouse
Lochcraig Reservoir
Bennan Burn
Rieve Hill
Melowther
Bennan Loch
Ballageich Hill
8
7
53
6
5
52
4
3
51
2
1
50
52
53
54

178

177
157

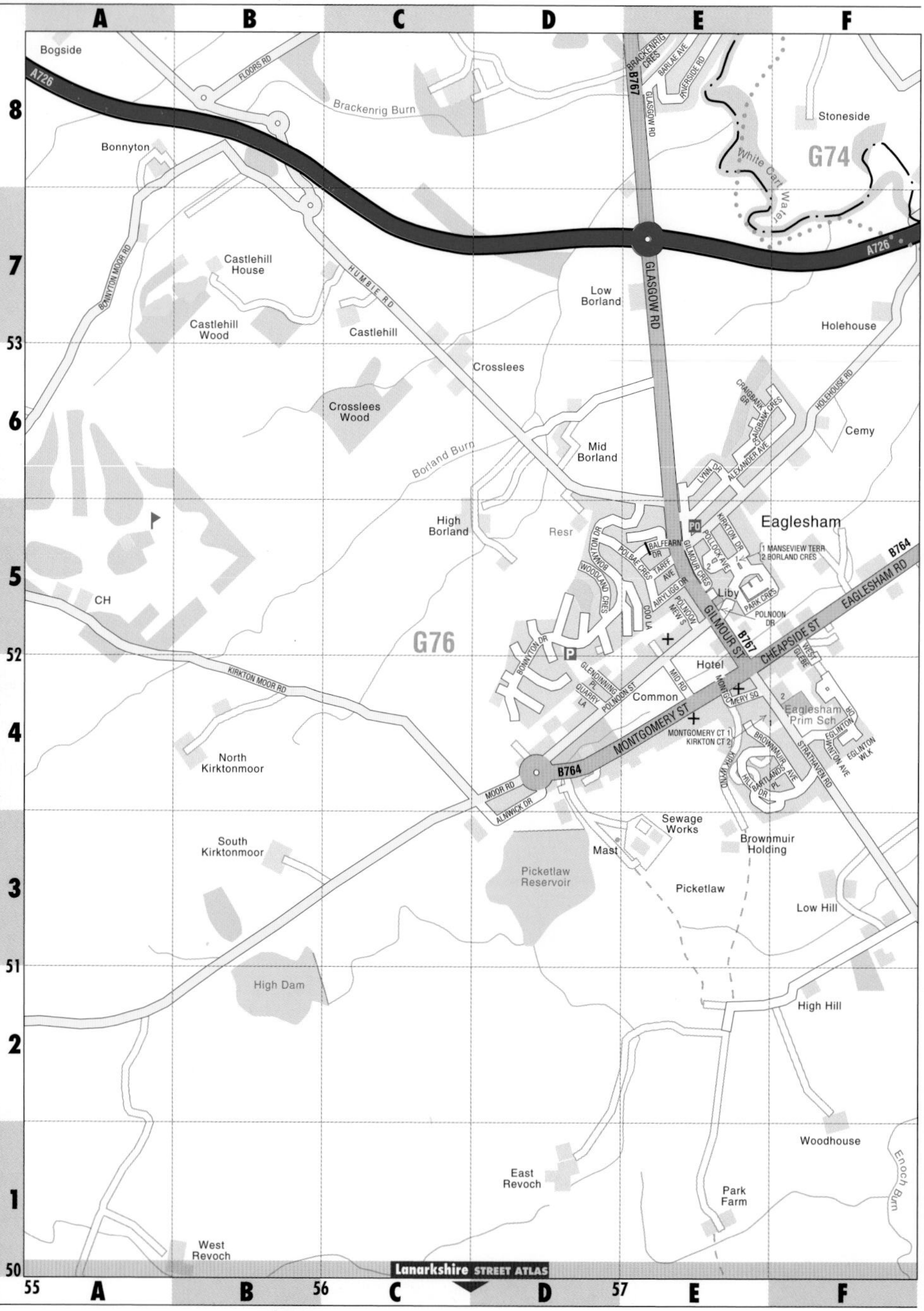
A
B
C
D
E
F
8
7
53
6
5
52
4
3
51
2
1
50
55
56
57
Bogside
A726
FLOORS RD
Brackenrig Burn
BRACKENRIG CRES
BARLAE AVE
RIVERSIDE RD
B767
GLASGOW RD
Stoneside
White Cart Water
G74
Bonnyton
A726
Castlehill House
HUMBIE RD
BONNYTON MOOR RD
GLASGOW RD
Low Borland
Castlehill Wood
Castlehill
Holehouse
Crosslees
Crosslees Wood
CRAIGBANK GR
CRAIGBANK CRES
HOLEHOUSE RD
Cemy
Borland Burn
Mid Borland
LYNN DR
ALEXANDER AVE
High Borland
Resr
Eaglesham
KIRKTON DR
BALFEARN DR
POLBAE CRES
TARFF AVE
GILMOUR CRES
POLLOCK AVE
1 MANSEVIEW TERR
2 BORLAND CRES
B764
BONNYTON DR
WOODLAND CRES
AIRYLIGG DR
Liby
PARK CRES
EAGLESHAM RD
CH
COO LA
POLNOON MEWS
POLNOON DR
G76
BONNYTON DR
GILMOUR ST
B767
CHEAPSIDE ST
WEST GLEBE
Hotel
GLENDINNING PL
QUARRY LA
POLNOON ST
MID RD
Common
MONTGOMERY SQ
KIRKTON MOOR RD
Eaglesham Prim Sch
EGLINTON DR
MONTGOMERY ST
MONTGOMERY CT 1
KIRKTON CT 2
EGLINTON WLK
WINTON AVE
North Kirktonmoor
BROWNMUIR AVE
STRATHAVEN RD
B764
KIRK WYND
BARTLANDS PL
HILL DR
MOOR RD
ALNWICK DR
Sewage Works
South Kirktonmoor
Mast
Brownmuir Holding
Picketlaw Reservoir
Picketlaw
Low Hill
High Dam
High Hill
Woodhouse
East Revoch
Park Farm
Enoch Burn
West Revoch

177

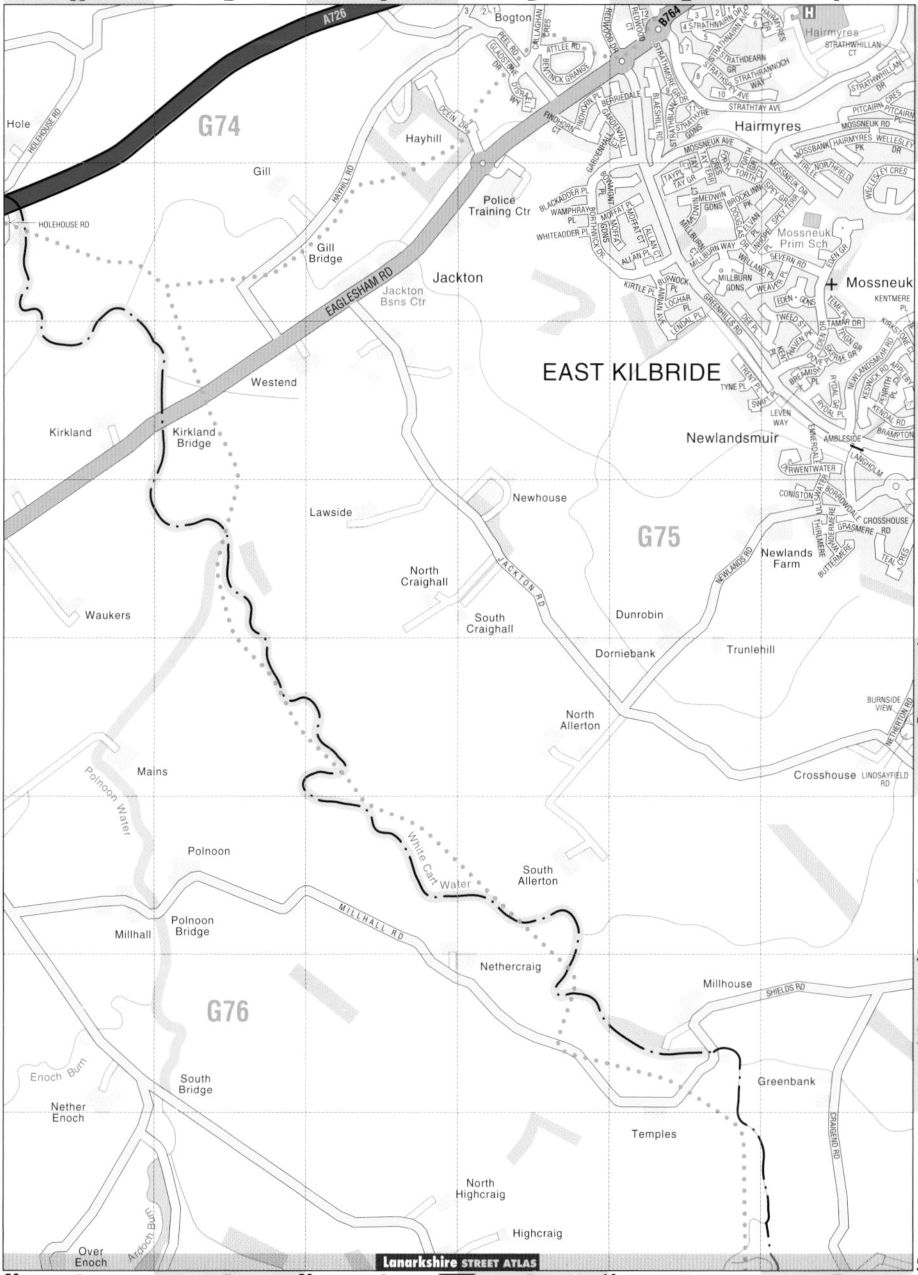
A
B
C
D
E
F
8
7
53
6
5
52
4
3
51
2
1
50
58
59
60
A726
B764
G74
G75
G76
EAST KILBRIDE
Bogton
Hairmyres
Hole
HOLEHOUSE RD
Gill
Hayhill
HAYHILL RD
Police
Training Ctr
Gill
Bridge
Jackton
Jackton
Bsns Ctr
EAGLESHAM RD
Westend
Kirkland
Kirkland
Bridge
Lawside
Newhouse
North
Craighall
South
Craighall
JACKTON RD
Waukers
Dunrobin
Dorniebank
Trunlehill
North
Allerton
Mains
Polnoon Water
Polnoon
South
Allerton
White Cart Water
Millhall
Polnoon
Bridge
MILLHALL RD
Nethercraig
Millhouse
SHIELDS RD
Greenbank
Enoch Burn
Nether
Enoch
South
Bridge
Temples
North
Highcraig
Highcraig
Over
Enoch
Ardoch Burn
Mossneuk
Mossneuk
Prim Sch
Newlandsmuir
NEWLANDS RD
Newlands
Farm
Crosshouse
LINDSAYFIELD
RD
BURNSIDE
VIEW
NETHERTON RD
CRAIGEND RD
STRATHWHILLAN
CT
STRATHTAY AVE
MOSSNEUK AVE
MOSSNEUK DR
PITCAIRN CRES
WELLESLEY CRES
BLACKADDER PL
WAMPHRAY
PL
WHITEADDER PL
MILLBURN WAY
MILLBURN
GDNS
GREENHILLS RD
KIRTLE PL
LENDAL PL
SEVERN RD
WELLAND PL
TWEED ST
TRENT PL
TYNE PL
SWIFT PL
LEVEN
WAY
AMBLESIDE
LANGHOLM
DERWENTWATER
CONISTON
BORROWDALE
CROSSHOUSE
RD
GRASMERE
THIRLMERE
BUTTERMERE
TEAL CRES
KENTMERE
PL
KIRKSTONE PL
NEWLANDSMUIR RD
KENDAL RD
BRAMPTON
RYDAL PL
FINDHORN
CT
BERRIEDALE
BLAESHILL RD
GARDENHALL
ATTLEE RD
BENTINCK GRANGE
PEEL RD
GLADSTONE
DR
DISRAELI
WAY
OCEIN DR
REDWOOD DR
REDWOOD
CT

C7
1 COOLGARDIE PL
2 COOLGARDIE GN

179

C8
1 ALBERTA CRES
2 BARKLY TERR
3 BUNBURY TERR
4 LETHBRIDGE PL
5 MELBOURNE GN
6 SYDNEY PL

D8
1 CALGARY PL
2 ALBERTA PL
3 STEPHENSON PL
4 STEPHENSON SQ

159

E7
1 CULLEN LA
2 THE MURRAY SQ
3 HEATHER GR
4 STRATHCONA LA

F7
1 SOMERVILLE TERR
2 SOMERVILLE LA
3 SHEILDHILL

F8
1 East Kilbride Shop Ctr
2 DENHOLM GN
3 SINCLAIR PK
4 MUIRHOUSE LA
5 HENRY BELL GN
6 FREELAND LA
7 TELFORD TERR
8 SYMINGTON SQ
9 TODHILLS

A B C D E F

8
7
53
6
5
52
4
3
51
2
1
50

61 A B 62 C D 63 E F

179

A8
1 AVONDALE AVE
2 LOCH STRIVEN
3 MOUNT CAMERON DR N

160
182

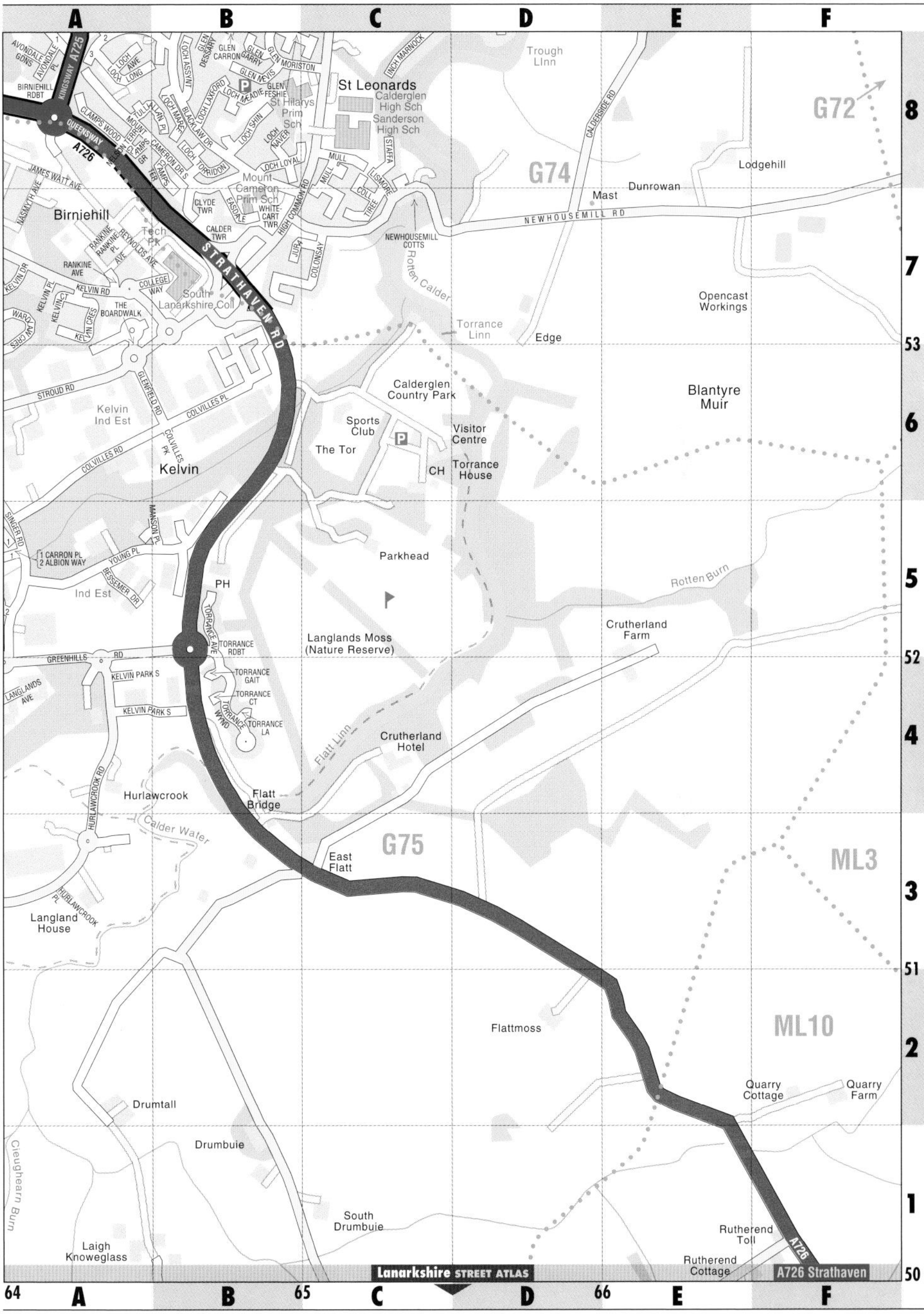

182

181
161

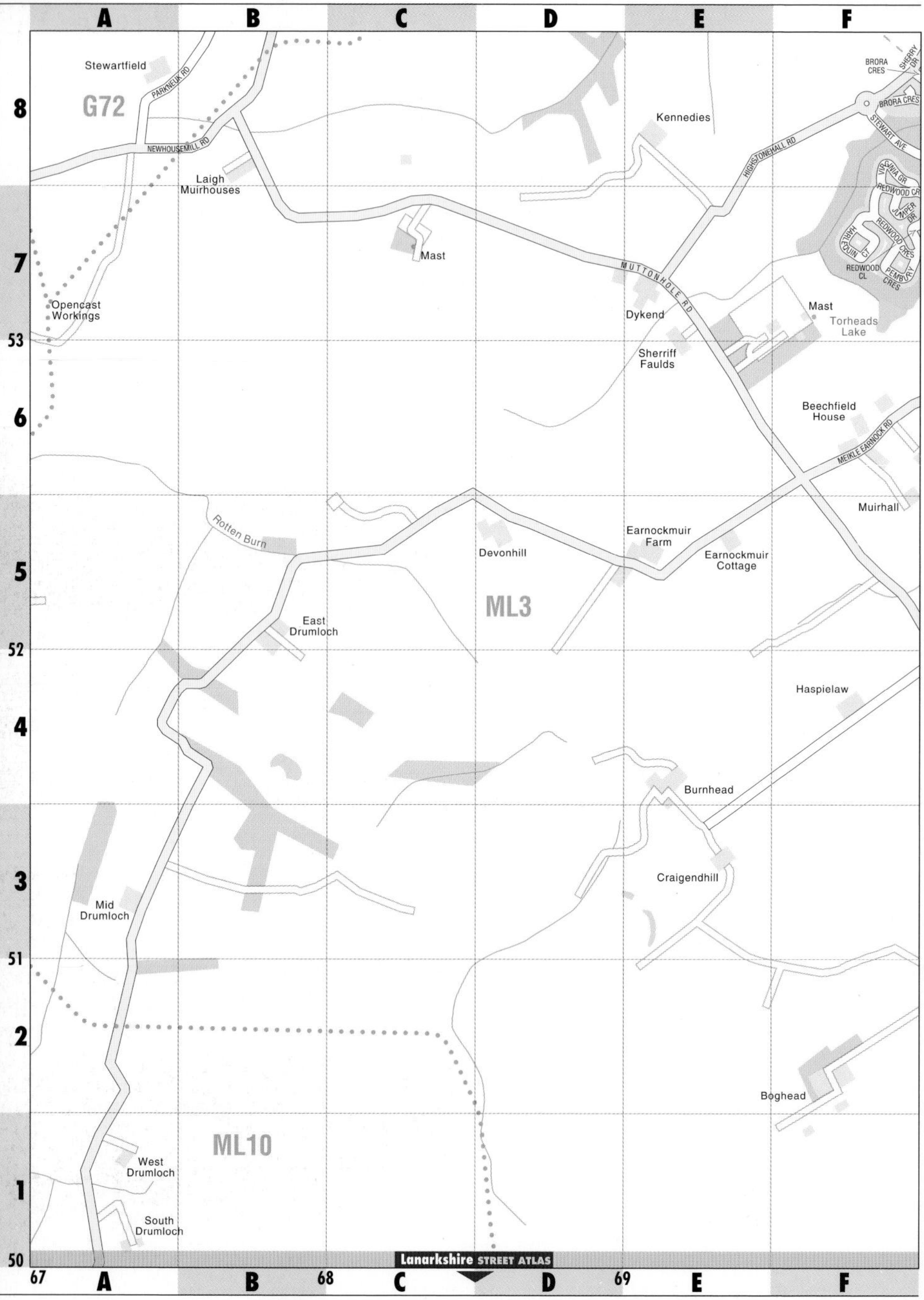
A
B
C
D
E
F
8
7
6
5
4
3
2
1
53
52
51
50
67
68
69
G72
ML3
ML10
Stewartfield
PARKNEUK RD
NEWHOUSEMILL RD
Laigh
Muirhouses
Opencast
Workings
Mast
Kennedies
HIGHSTONEHALL RD
BRORA
CRES
SHERRY
DR
BRORA CRES
STEWART AVE
VIRGINIA GR
REDWOOD CR
JUNIPER
DR
REDWOOD
CRES
HARLEQUIN CT
REDWOOD
CL
PEMBURY
CRES
MUTTONHOLE RD
Dykend
Mast
Torheads
Lake
Sherriff
Faulds
Beechfield
House
MEIKLE EARNOCK RD
Muirhall
Rotten Burn
Devonhill
Earnockmuir
Farm
Earnockmuir
Cottage
East
Drumloch
Haspielaw
Burnhead
Craigendhill
Mid
Drumloch
Boghead
West
Drumloch
South
Drumloch

181

162
184

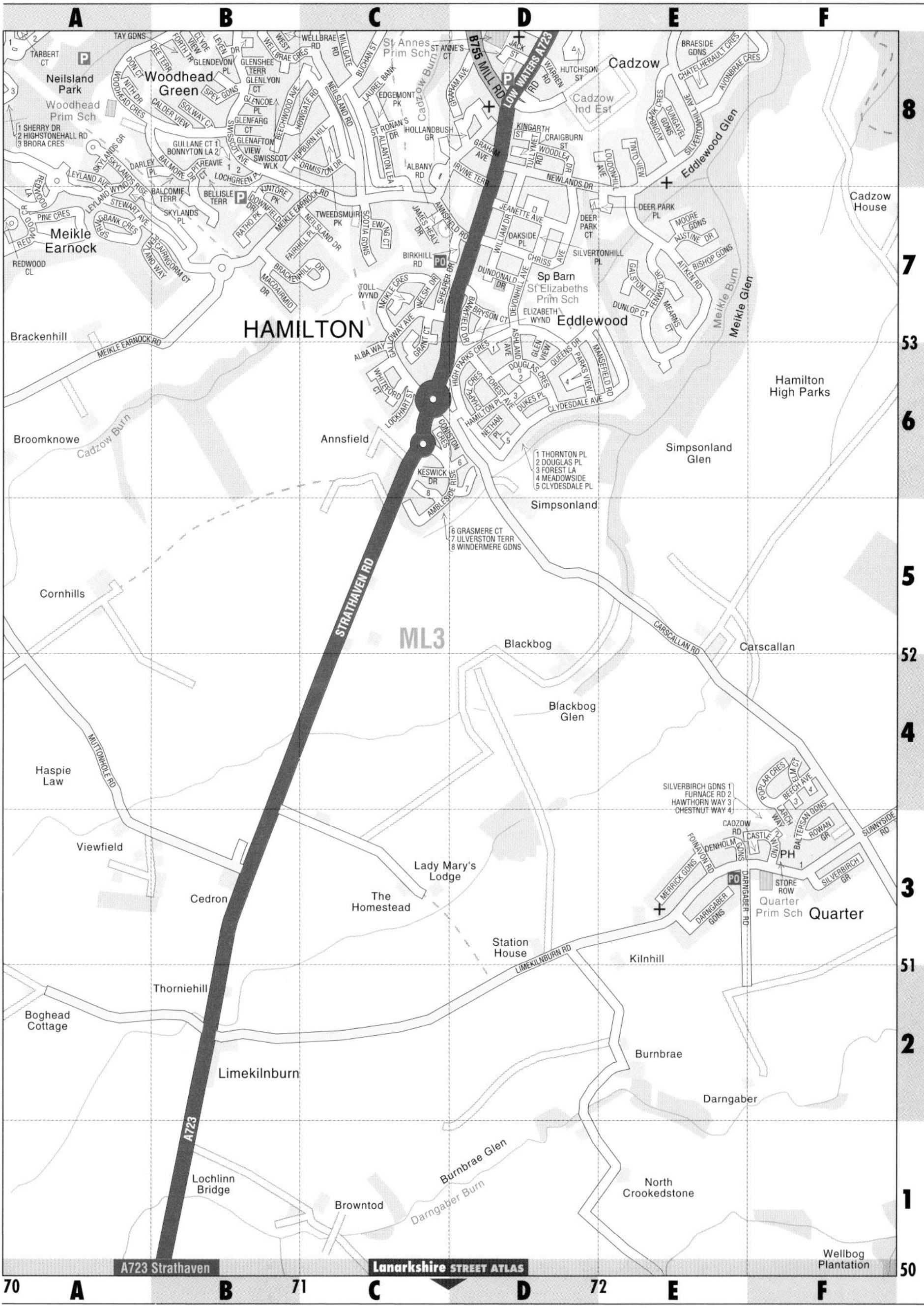
A
B
C
D
E
F
8
7
53
6
5
52
4
3
51
2
1
50
70
71
72
Neilsland Park
Woodhead Prim Sch
Woodhead Green
Meikle Earnock
HAMILTON
St Annes Prim Sch
Cadzow
Cadzow Ind Est
Eddlewood Glen
Cadzow House
Sp Barn
St Elizabeths Prim Sch
Eddlewood
Meikle Glen
Meikle Burn
Brackenhill
Hamilton High Parks
Broomknowe
Cadzow Burn
Annsfield
Simpsonland Glen
Simpsonland
Cornhills
ML3
Blackbog
Carscallan
Blackbog Glen
Haspie Law
Viewfield
Lady Mary's Lodge
Cedron
The Homestead
Quarter
Quarter Prim Sch
Station House
Kilnhill
Thorniehill
Boghead Cottage
Burnbrae
Limekilnburn
Darngaber
Burnbrae Glen
Darngaber Burn
Lochlinn Bridge
Browntod
North Crookedstone
Wellbog Plantation
STRATHAVEN RD
A723
B755 MILL RD
LOW WATERS A723
CARSCALLAN RD
LIMEKILNBURN RD
MUTTONHOLE RD
MEIKLE EARNOCK RD
1 SHERRY DR
2 HIGHSTONEHALL RD
3 BRORA CRES
1 THORNTON PL
2 DOUGLAS PL
3 FOREST LA
4 MEADOWSIDE
5 CLYDESDALE PL
6 GRASMERE CT
7 ULVERSTON TERR
8 WINDERMERE GDNS
SILVERBIRCH GDNS 1
FURNACE RD 2
HAWTHORN WAY 3
CHESTNUT WAY 4
A723 Strathaven

184

183
163

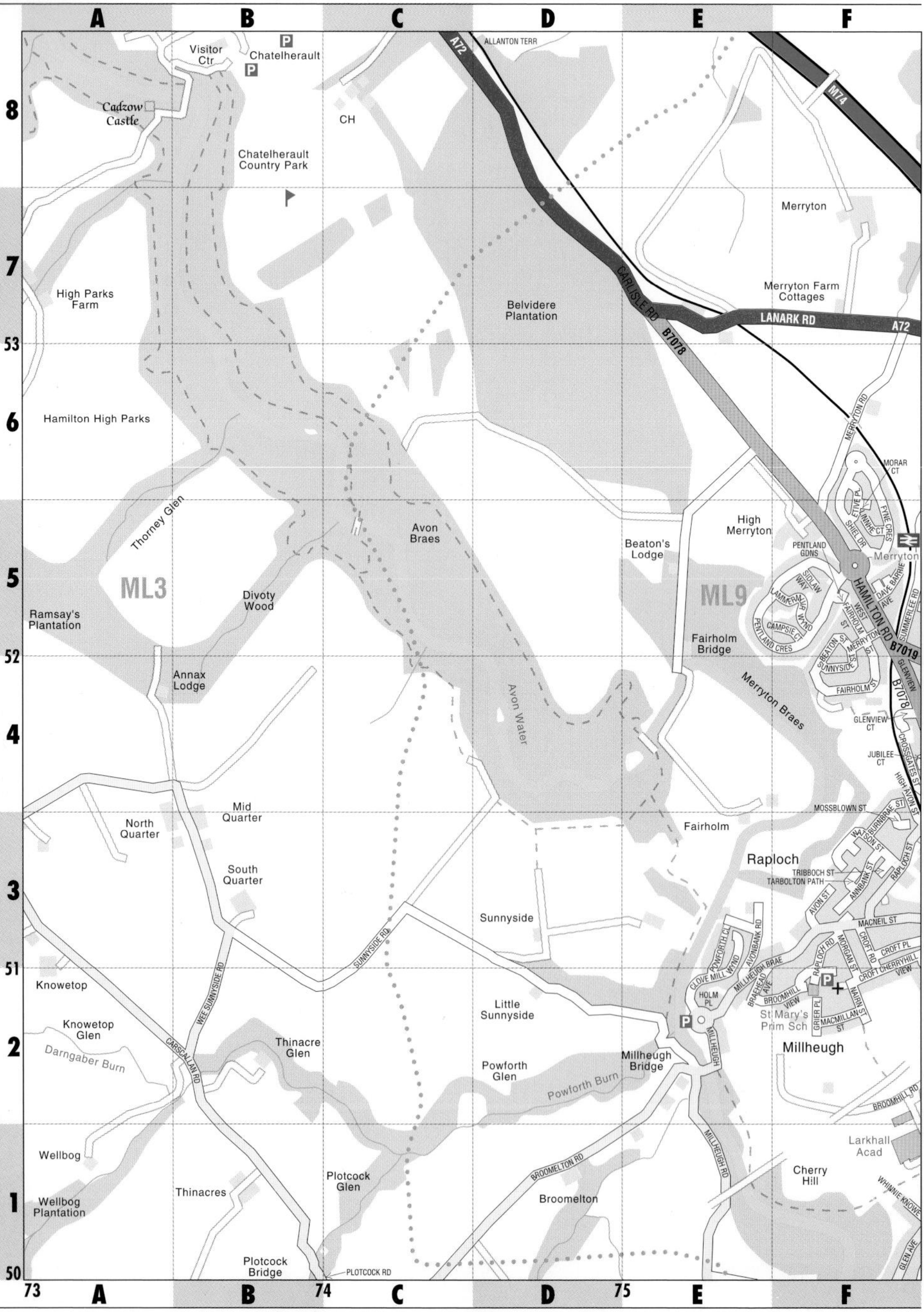

183
198

164
186

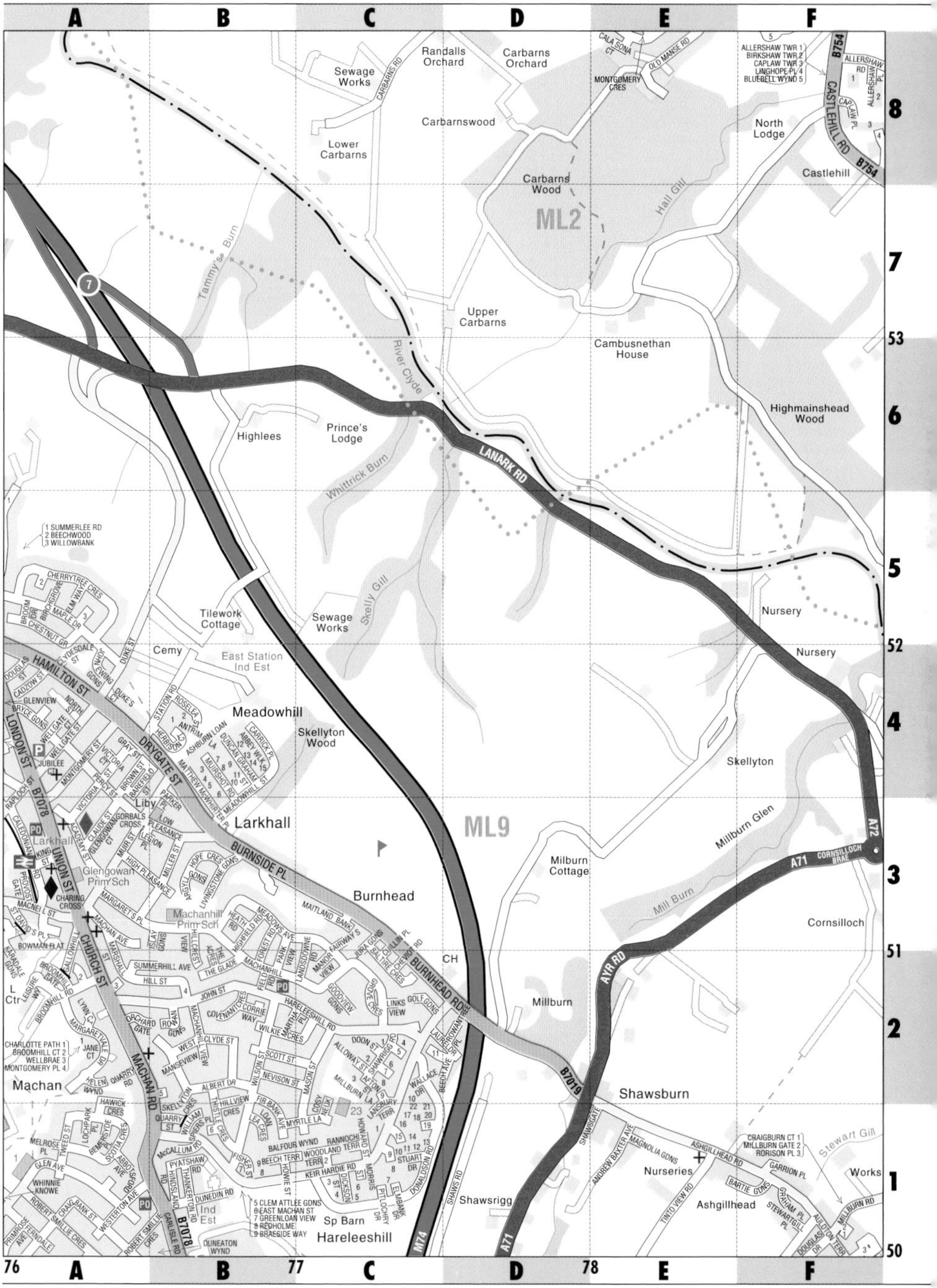

A1
1 Robert Smillie Meml Prim Sch

B4
1 GLENORAN LA
2 EASTWOOD WAY
3 GLENBURN WYND
4 PORTLAND WYND
5 SIGHTHILL LOAN
6 PARKNOOK WAY
7 LOMOND WLK
8 HOZIER LOAN
9 CRAIGIE LA
10 GEORGE WAY
11 ALBANY WYND
12 CRAIGMORE WYND
13 BURNS LOAN
14 BANK WAY
15 BRAESIDE LA

C2
1 LOANING
2 LOVAT PATH
3 BALMORAL PATH
4 LOCHLEA LOAN
5 CATRINE ST
6 GILLBANK LA
7 CARRICK ST
8 WINDSOR PATH
9 WOODBURN TERR
10 MAXWELL PATH
11 HAWTHORN GDNS

C1
1 MOSSGIEL LA
2 BERTRAM ST
3 HAZELDENE LA
4 ROSEMOUNT LA
5 LAUREL LA
6 BRACKEN WAY
7 LAMMER WYND
8 CAMERONIAN WAY
9 GLEN FRUIN DR
10 ST ANDREWS PATH
11 LAWRIE WAY
12 KATRIONA PATH
13 CAMERON PATH
14 TRINITY WAY
15 BLAIR ATHOLL DR
16 ALBA WAY
17 ARRAN PATH
18 DALSERF PATH
19 BANNOCKBURN DR
20 LOCHNAGAR WAY
21 FLEMING WAY
22 BRUCE'S LOAN
23 Hareleeshill Prim Sch

199
186

185
165

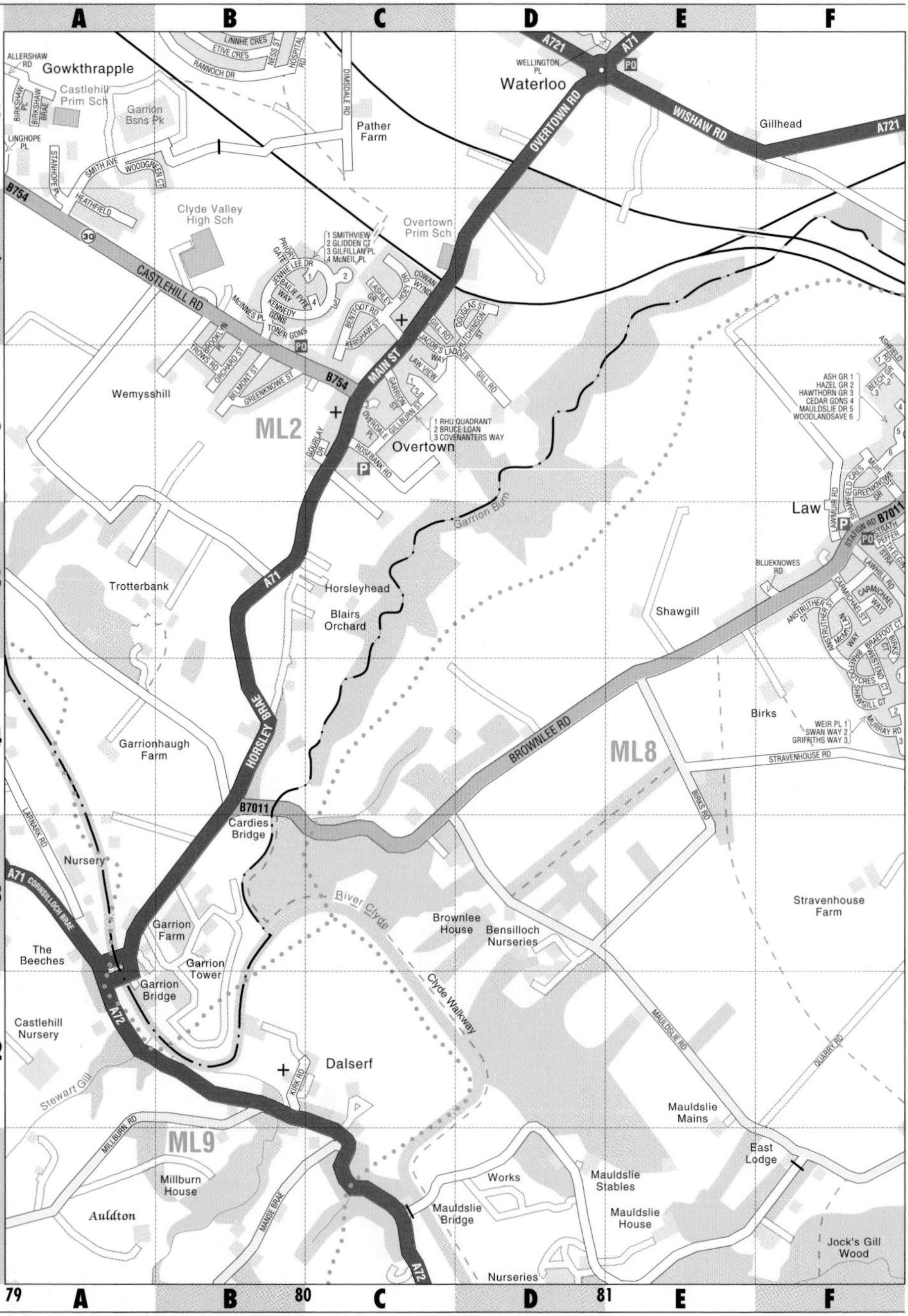

185
200

166
188

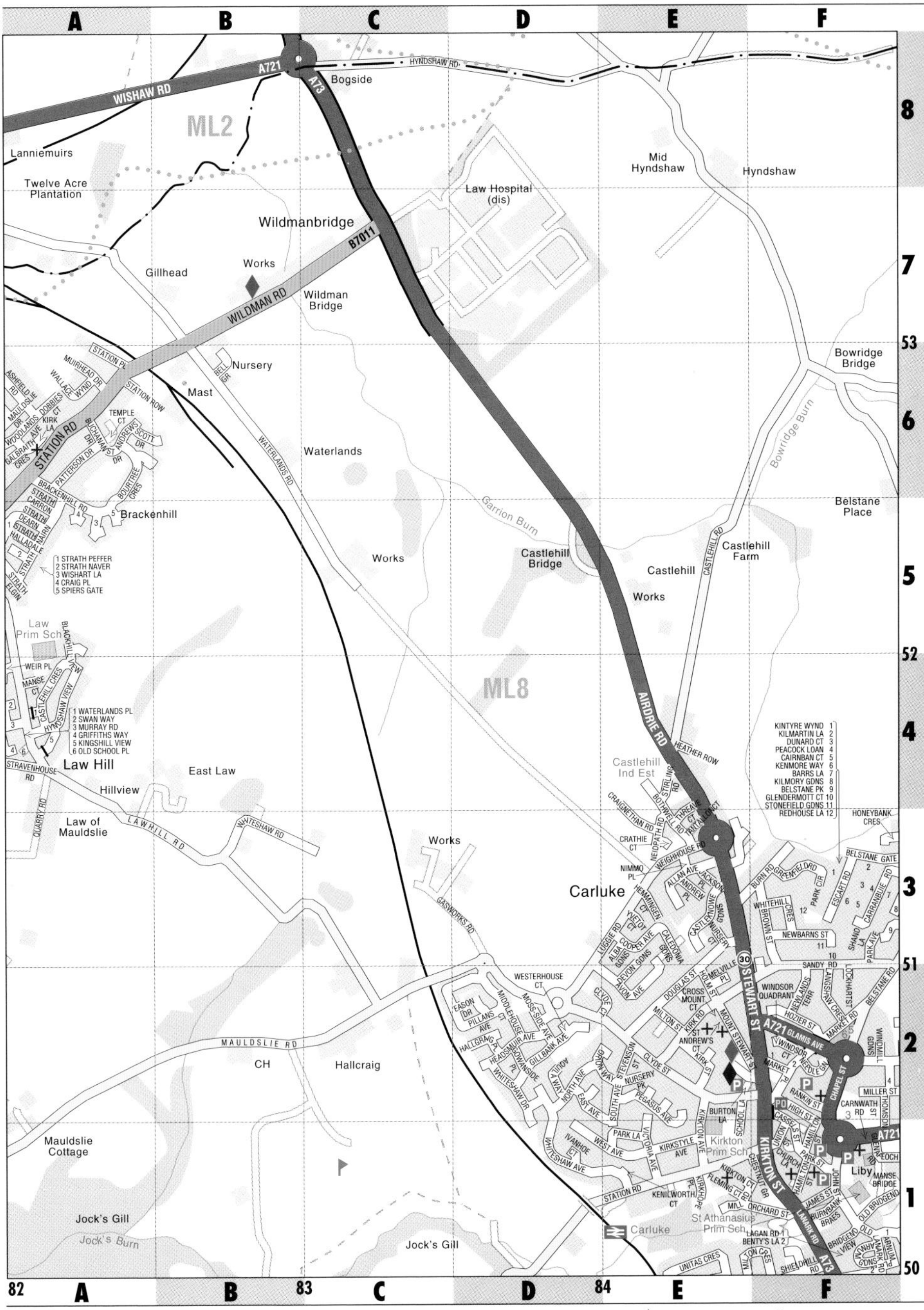

201
188

F2
1 STEWART PL
2 MARKET RD
3 Rankin Gate Ctr
4 GREENBANK TERR
5 High Mill Prim Sch
6 Victoria Park Sch

187 167

187 202

168

A B C D E F
Black Law
Wind Farm
ML2
Black Law
8
7
53
Birniehall
6
Netherton Burn
Thornmuir
5
Springfield
Reservoir
ML8
52
Hill of
Westerhouse
Middlehope
Farm
Easterseat
4
Springfield
Knowehead
Middlehouse
YIELDSHIELDS RD
B7056
3
Westerhouse
Damhead
Netherton Burn
51
East
Highcross
2
Coldstream Burn
Candymill Burn
1
Mid
Coldstream
Craigend
50
88 A B 89 C D 90 E F
Lanarkshire STREET ATLAS

203

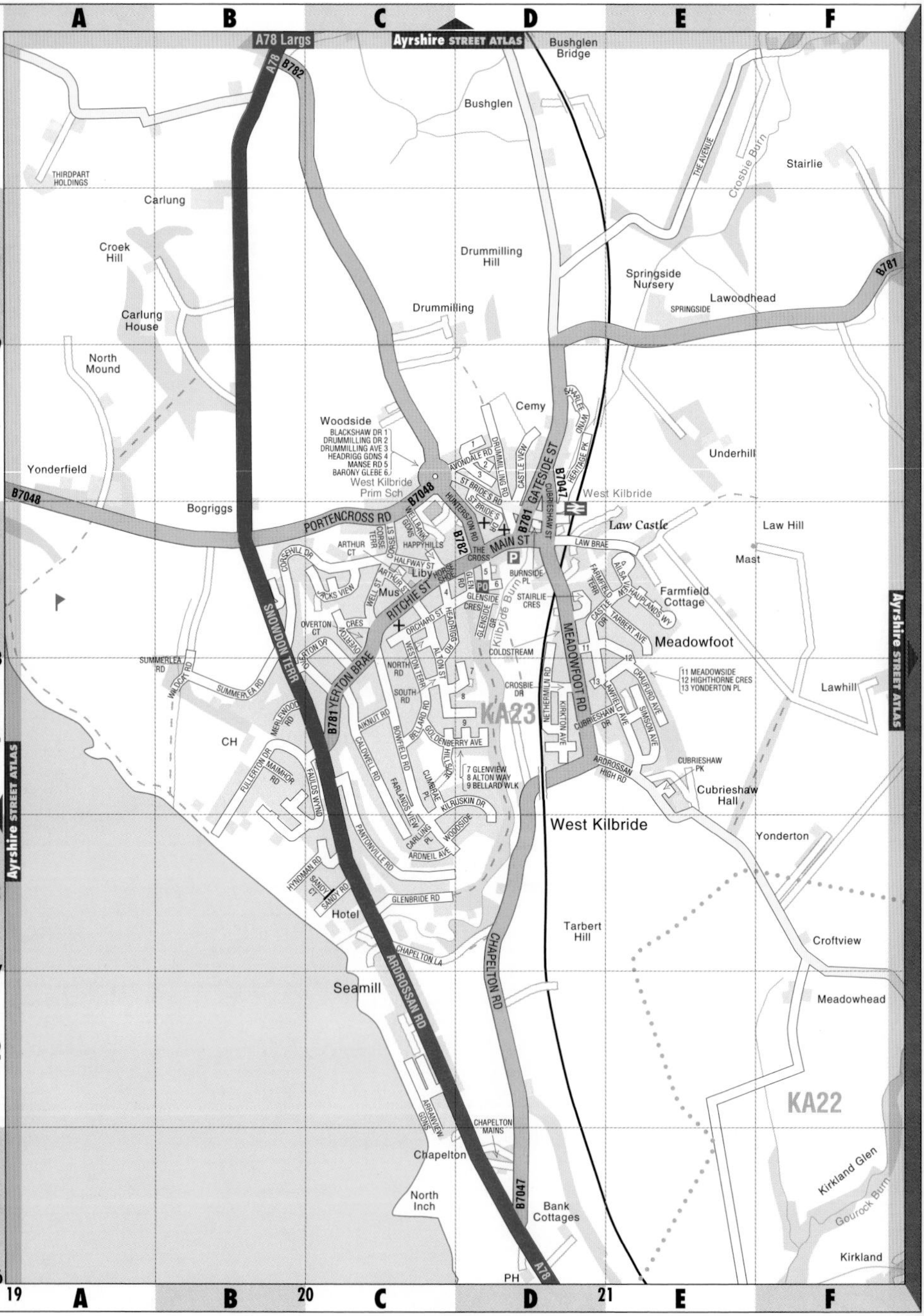
A
B
C
D
E
F
A78 Largs
Ayrshire STREET ATLAS
Bushglen Bridge
Bushglen
THIRDPART HOLDINGS
Carlung
Croek Hill
Carlung House
North Mound
Drummilling Hill
Drummilling
Springside Nursery
SPRINGSIDE
Lawoodhead
Stairlie
Crosbie Burn
THE AVENUE
B781
B782
A78
Woodside
BLACKSHAW DR 1
DRUMMILLING DR 2
DRUMMILLING AVE 3
HEADRIGG GDNS 4
MANSE RD 5
BARONY GLEBE 6
West Kilbride Prim Sch
Cemy
Underhill
Yonderfield
B7048
Bogriggs
PORTENCROSS RD
West Kilbride
Law Castle
Law Hill
Mast
GATESIDE ST
B7047
CUBRIESHAW ST
HERITAGE PK
CHARLES WYND
AVONDALE RD
DRUMMILLING RD
CASTLE VIEW
ST BRIDE'S RD
HUNTERSTON RD
MAIN ST
LAW BRAE
THE CROSS
HAPPYHILLS
ARTHUR CT
CORSE TERR
HALFWAY ST
Liby
Mus
PO
BURNSIDE PL
STAIRLIE CRES
Farmfield Cottage
Meadowfoot
FARMFIELD TERR
CASTLE DR
TARBERT AVE
HAUPLANDS WY
CORSEHILL DR
JACKS VIEW
WELL ST
RITCHIE ST
HORSE SHOE
GLENSIDE CRES
GLENSIDE GR
Kilbride Burn
OVERTON CT
OVERTON CRES
OVERTON DR
ORCHARD ST
HEADRIGG RD
COLDSTREAM
MEADOWFOOT RD
11 MEADOWSIDE
12 HIGHTHORNE CRES
13 YONDERTON PL
CRAUFURD AVE
SUMMERLEA RD
WILDCAT RD
SUMMERLEA RD
SNOWDON TERR
B781 YERTON BRAE
NORTH RD
SOUTH RD
WESTON TERR
ALTON ST
CROSBIE DR
KA23
NETHERMILN RD
KIRKTON AVE
CUBRIESHAW DR
LAWFIELD AVE
SIMSON AVE
Lawhill
MERLEWOOD RD
AIKNUT RD
BOWFIELD RD
BELLARD RD
GOLDENBERRY AVE
HILLSIDE
CH
FULLERTON DR
MAIMHOR RD
FAULDS WYND
CALDWELL RD
7 GLENVIEW
8 ALTON WAY
9 BELLARD WLK
ARDROSSAN HIGH RD
CUBRIESHAW PK
Cubrieshaw Hall
FARLANDS VIEW
CUMBRAE PL
KILRUSKIN DR
West Kilbride
Yonderton
PANTONVILLE RD
CARLUNG PL
WOODSIDE
ARDNEIL AVE
HYNDMAN RD
SANDY CT
SANDY RD
Hotel
GLENBRIDE RD
Tarbert Hill
Croftview
CHAPELTON LA
Seamill
ARDROSSAN RD
CHAPELTON RD
Meadowhead
KA22
ARRANVIEW GDNS
CHAPELTON MAINS
Chapelton
Kirkland Glen
North Inch
B7047
Bank Cottages
Gourock Burn
Kirkland
PH
8
7
49
6
5
48
4
3
47
2
1
46
19
20
21

169
192

B7
1 CARSWELL CT
2 ARCHIBALD DR

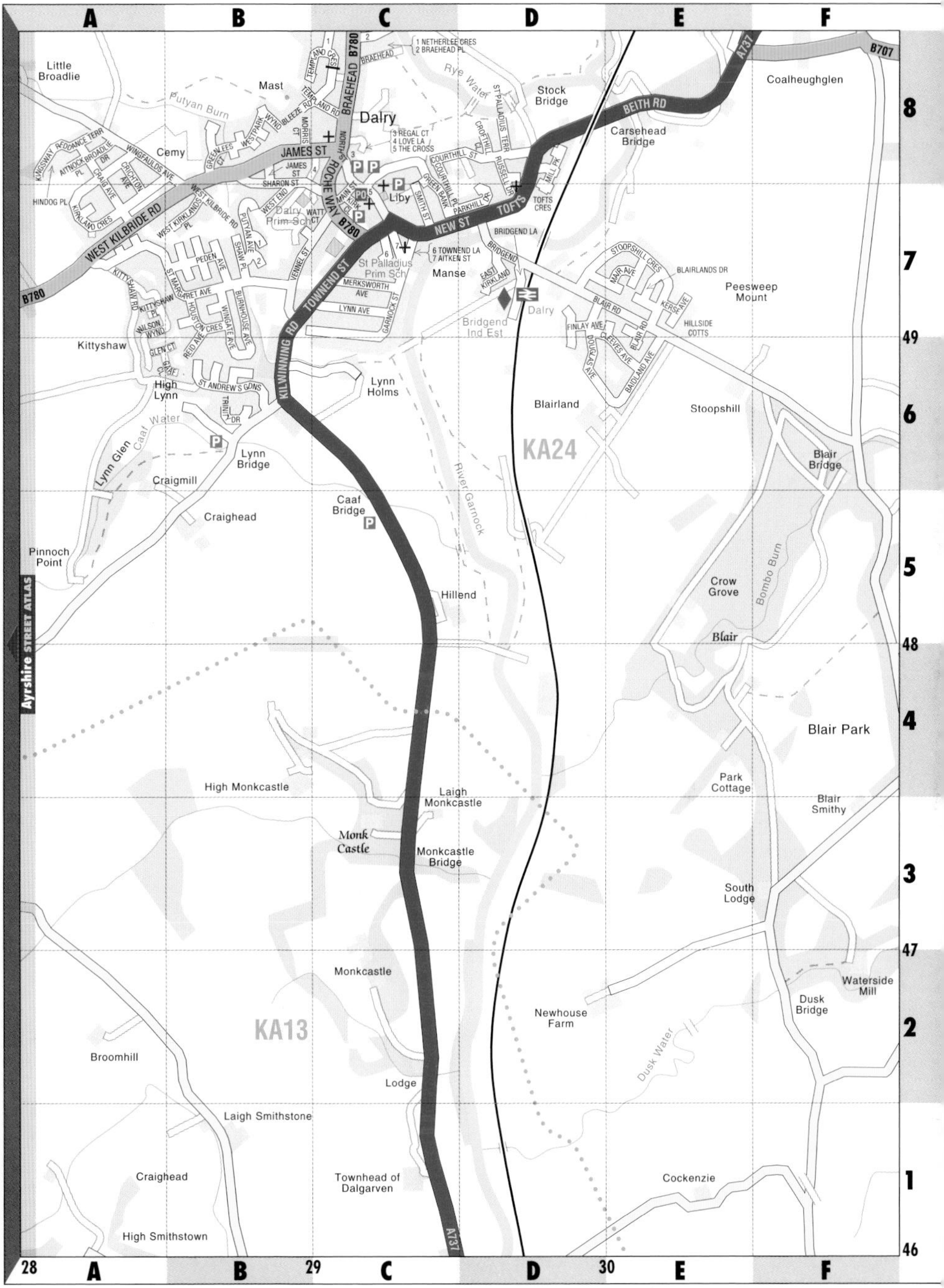

207
192

191
170

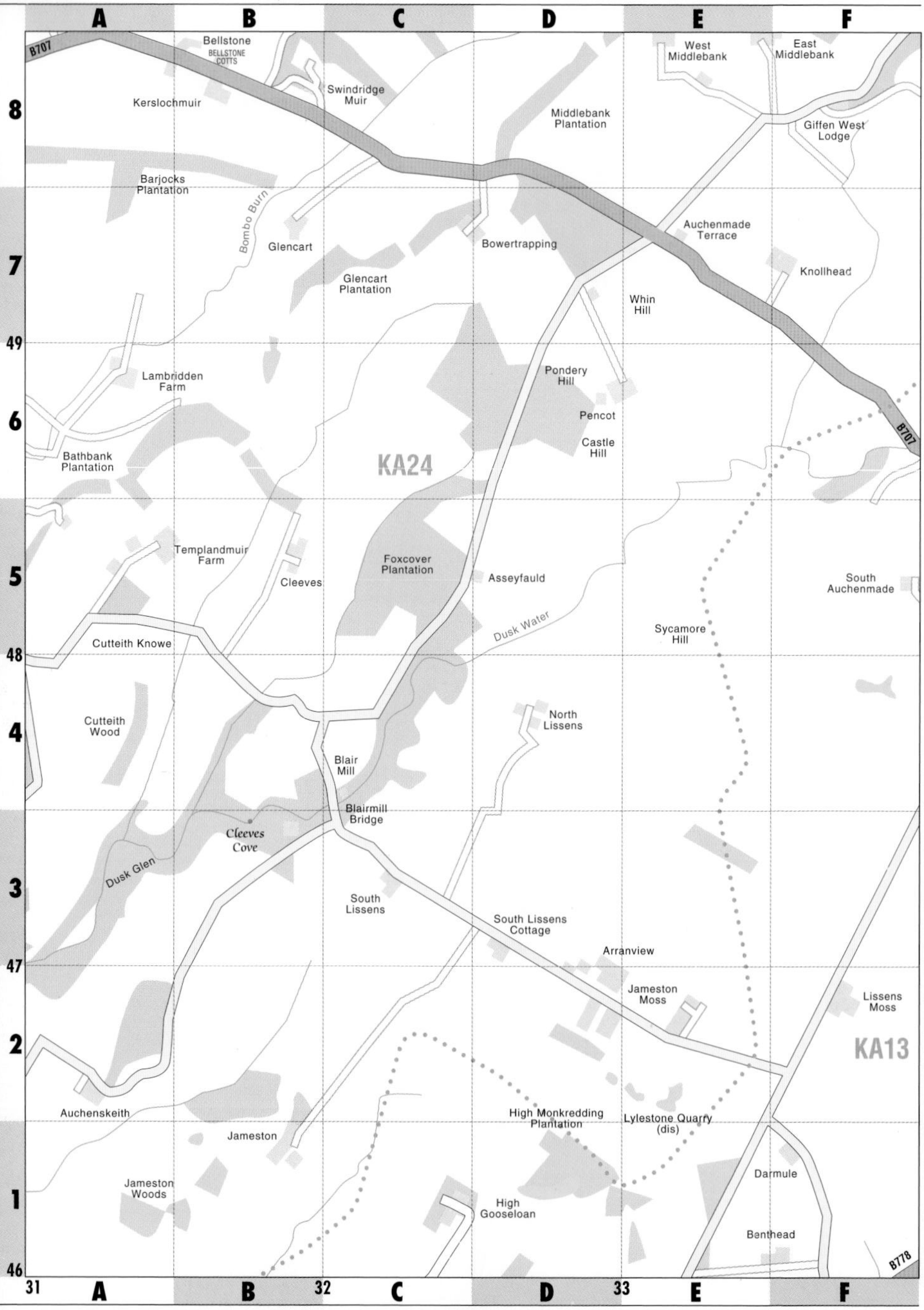

191
208

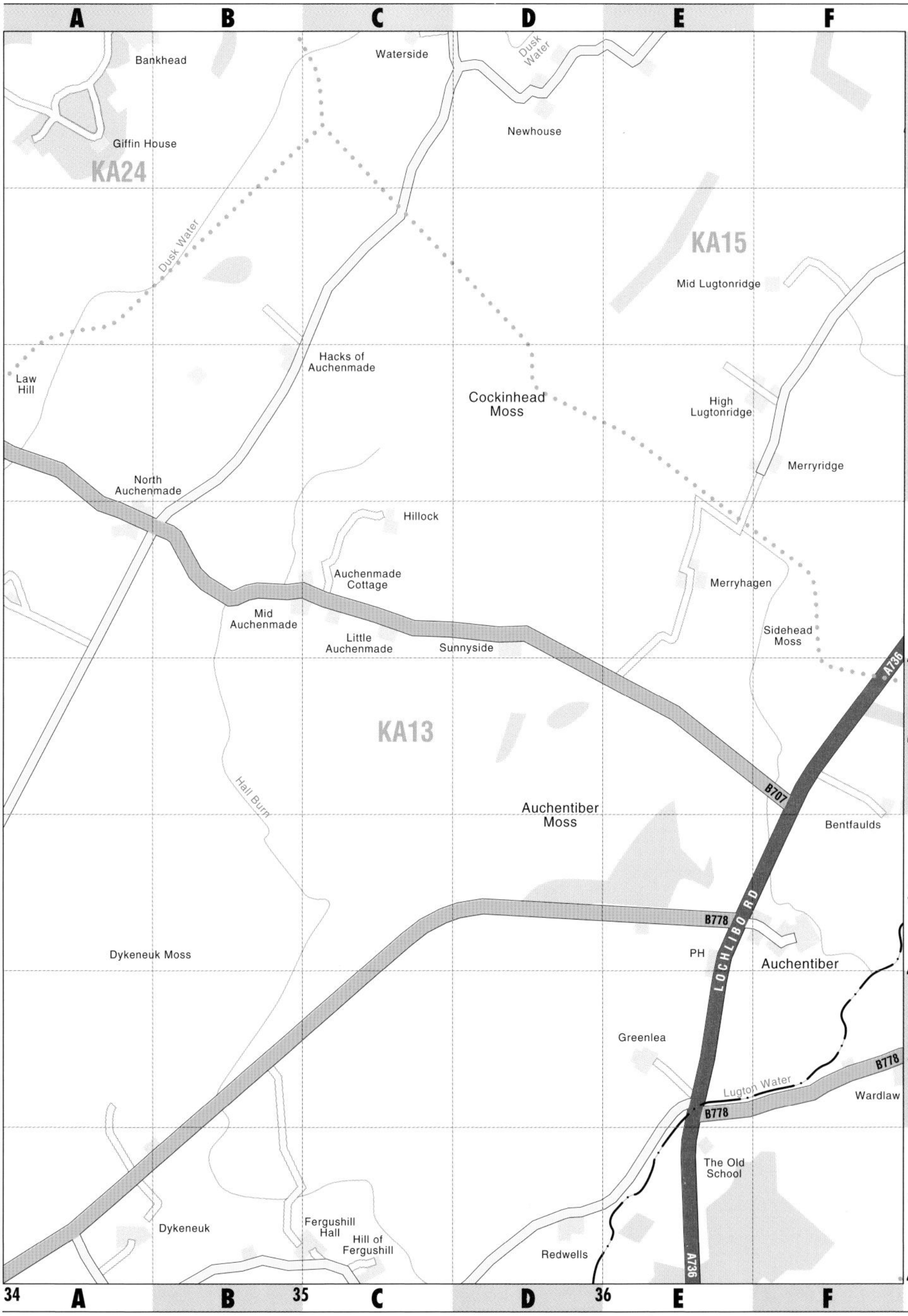
A
B
C
D
E
F
Bankhead
Waterside
Dusk Water
Newhouse
Giffin House
KA24
8
KA15
Dusk Water
7
Mid Lugtonridge
49
Law Hill
Hacks of Auchenmade
Cockinhead Moss
High Lugtonridge
6
Merryridge
North Auchenmade
Hillock
Auchenmade Cottage
Merryhagen
5
Mid Auchenmade
Little Auchenmade
Sunnyside
Sidehead Moss
A736
48
KA13
4
Hall Burn
B707
Auchentiber Moss
Bentfaulds
3
LOCHLIBO RD
B778
Dykeneuk Moss
PH
Auchentiber
47
Greenlea
2
B778
Lugton Water
Wardlaw
B778
The Old School
1
Dykeneuk
Fergushill Hall
Hill of Fergushill
Redwells
A736
46
34
35
36

193
172

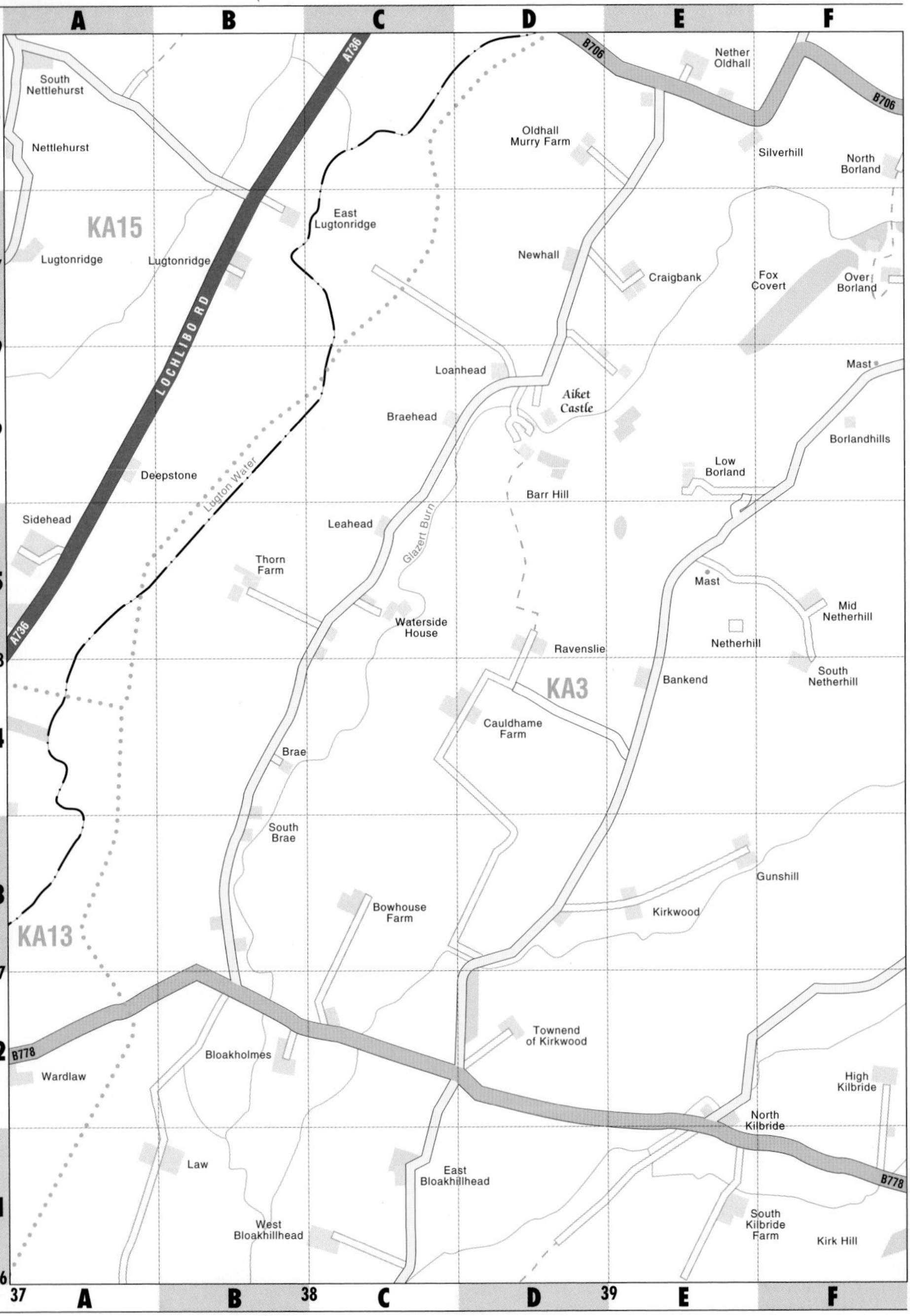

193
210

173
196

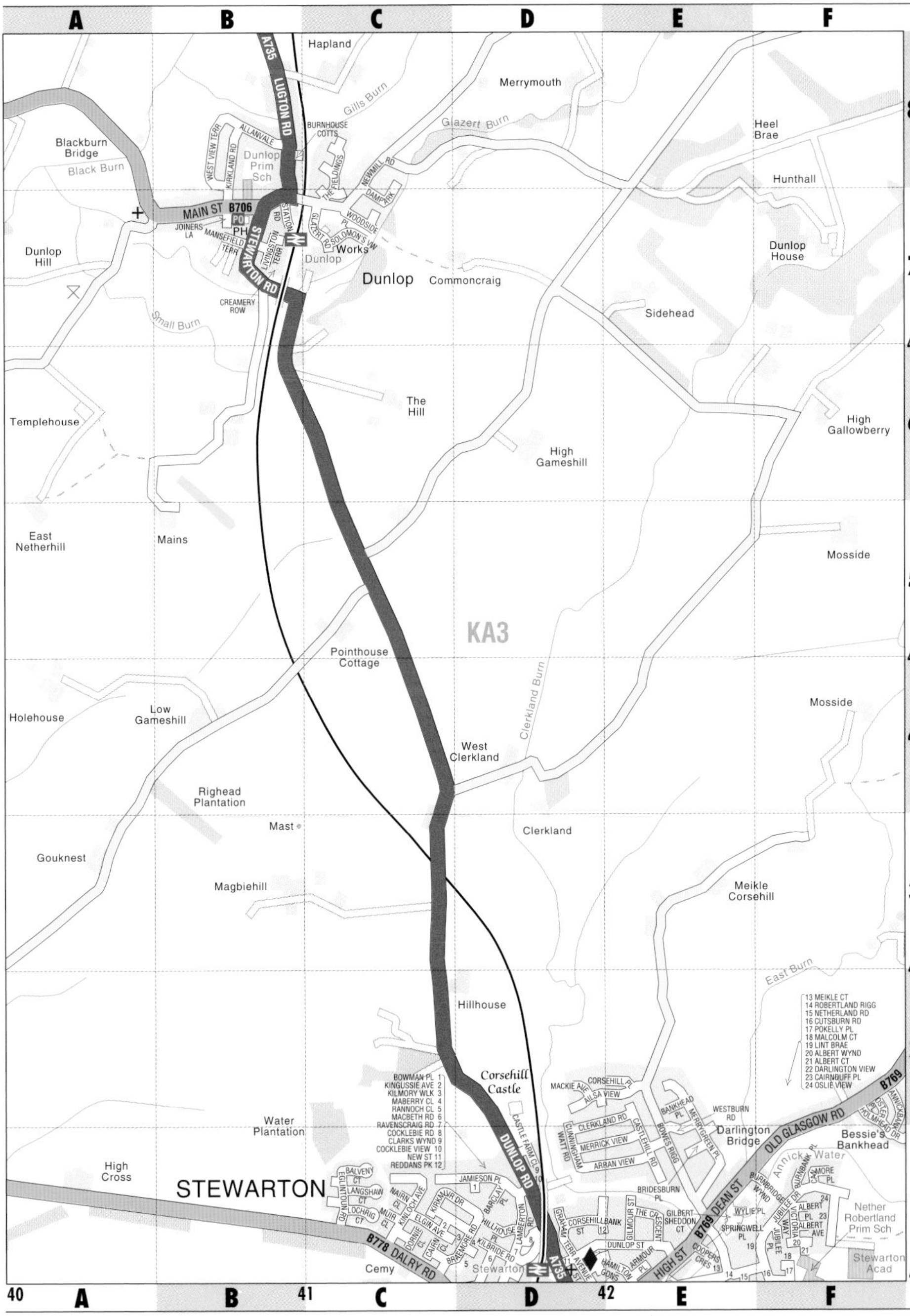

211
196

195
174

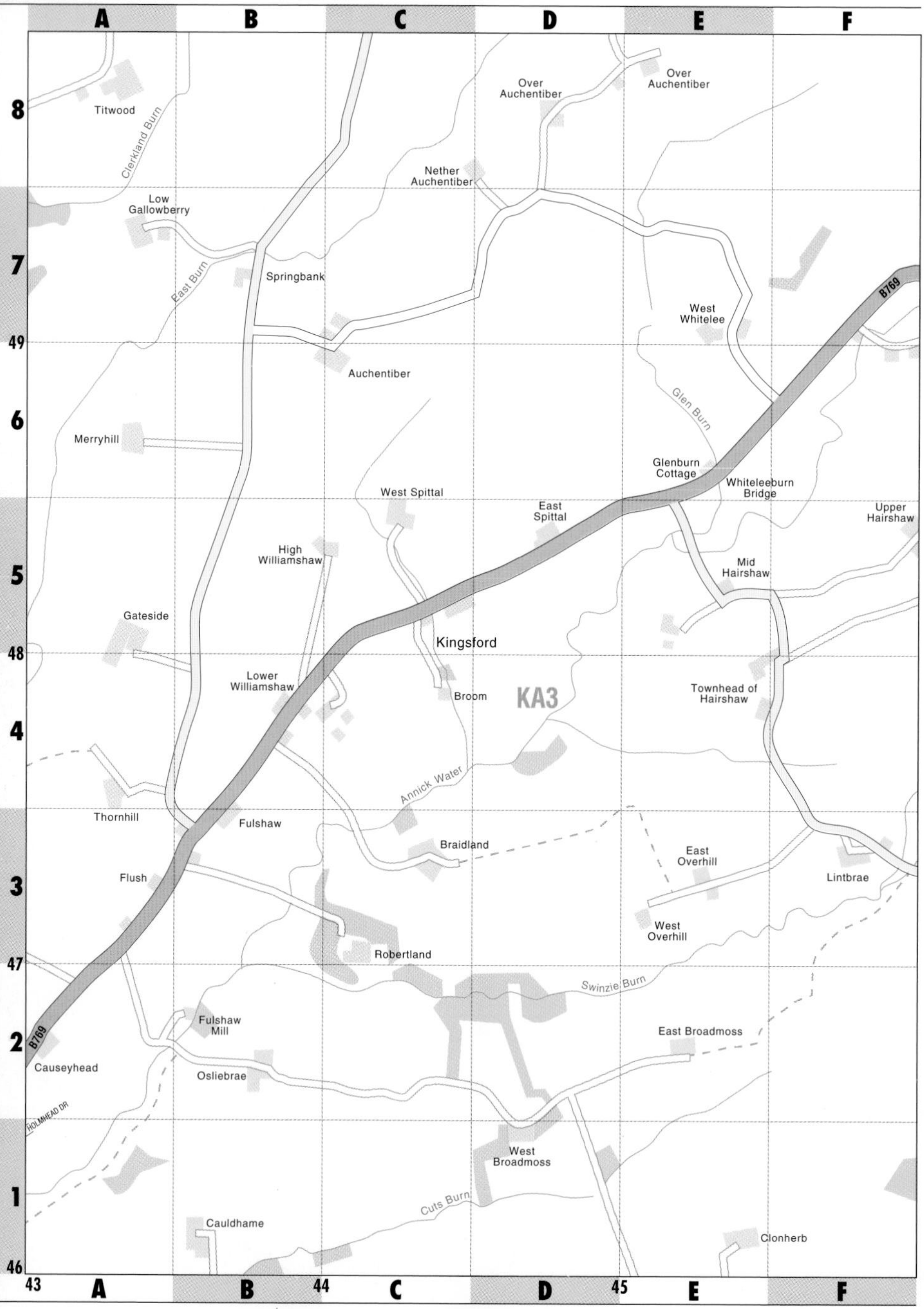

195
212

175

A
B
C
D
E
F
8
7
49
6
5
48
4
3
47
2
1
46
47
48
Blacklawhill
Low Blacklaw
B769
Corsehouse Resr
Annick Water
Blacklaw Cottage
Blacklaw Bridge
Glenouther Rig
G77
East Whitelee
Glenouther Moor
Swinzie Burn
Glenouther
Ayrshire STREET ATLAS
KA3
Low Clunch
Clunch Hill
High Clunch
Gree Law
Blair
Harelaw
A77 Glasgow (M77)
M77 Glasgow (M8)
Gree Cottage
Townhead of Gree
Crofthead
Townend of Gree
Raithill
A77
Kingswell Burn
M77
Tam's Hill
Dunton Water
Fenwick Water
Damhead Wood
Ladeside
Raithburn
Mast
Benthouse Bridge

213

184

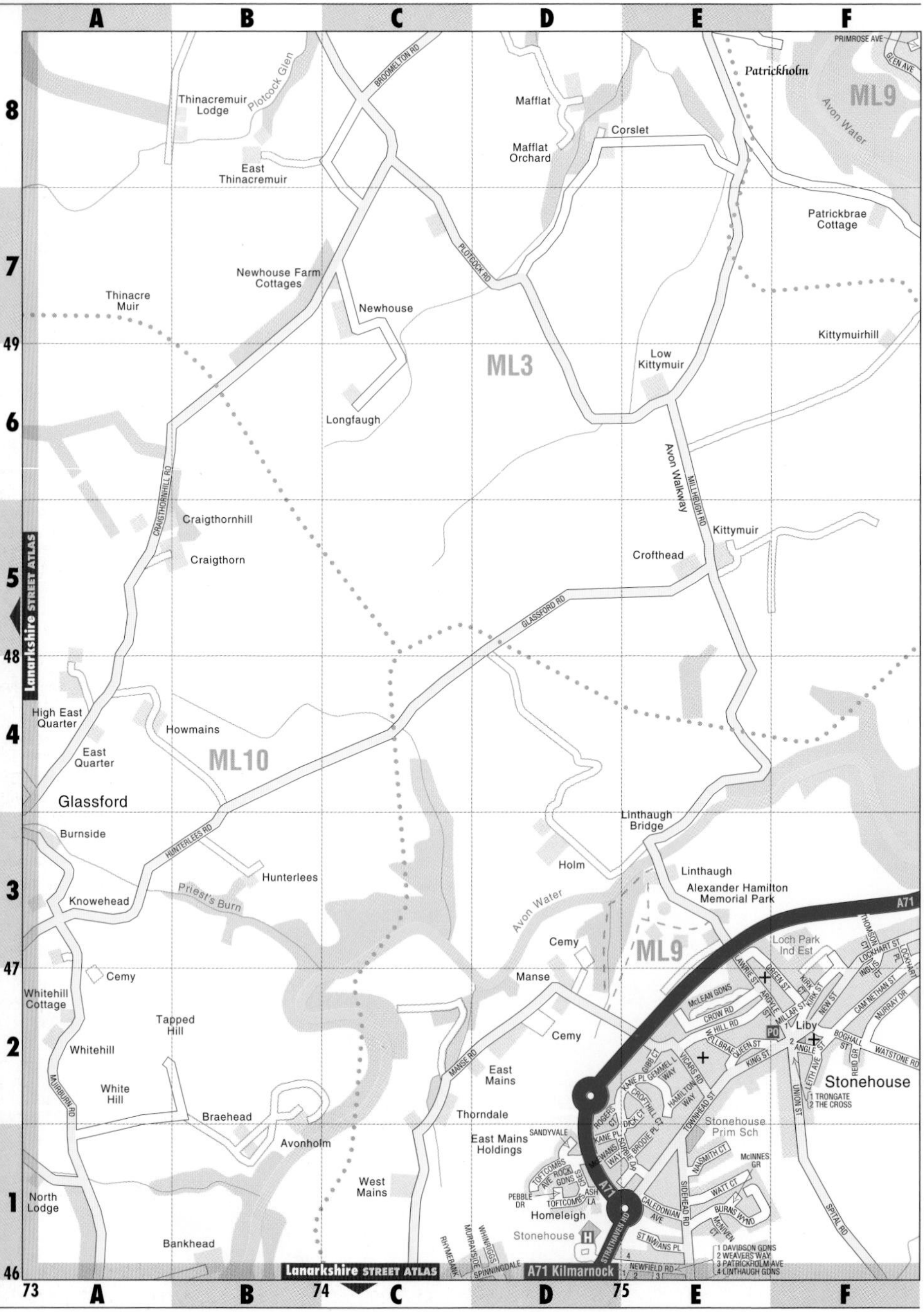
A
B
C
D
E
F
8
7
49
6
5
48
4
3
47
2
1
46
73
74
75
PRIMROSE AVE
GLEN AVE
Patrickholm
ML9
Avon Water
Thinacremuir Lodge
Plotcock Glen
BROOMELTON RD
Mafflat
Corslet
Mafflat Orchard
East Thinacremuir
Patrickbrae Cottage
PLOTCOCK RD
Newhouse Farm Cottages
Thinacre Muir
Newhouse
Kittymuirhill
ML3
Low Kittymuir
Longfaugh
Avon Walkway
MILLHAUGH RD
CRAIGTHORNHILL RD
Craigthornhill
Kittymuir
Craigthorn
Crofthead
GLASSFORD RD
Lanarkshire STREET ATLAS
High East Quarter
Howmains
East Quarter
ML10
Glassford
Linthaugh Bridge
Burnside
HUNTERLEES RD
Holm
Hunterlees
Linthaugh
Alexander Hamilton Memorial Park
Priest's Burn
Knowehead
Avon Water
A71
Cemy
ML9
Loch Park Ind Est
Cemy
Manse
Whitehill Cottage
Tapped Hill
Cemy
Whitehill
MANSE RD
East Mains
MUIRBURN RD
White Hill
Thorndale
Braehead
East Mains Holdings
SANDYVALE
Avonholm
Stonehouse Prim Sch
West Mains
North Lodge
PEBBLE DR
Homeleigh
Stonehouse
Bankhead
RHYMEBANK
MURRAYSIDE
WHINRIGGS
SPINNINGDALE
A71 Kilmarnock
STRATHAVEN RD
NEWFIELD RD
ST NINIANS PL
CALEDONIAN AVE
SIDEHEAD RD
TOWNHEAD ST
UNION ST
SPITAL RD
LEITH AVE
Liby
Stonehouse
1 TRONGATE
2 THE CROSS
1 DAVIDSON GDNS
2 WEAVERS WAY
3 PATRICKHOLM AVE
4 LINTHAUGH GDNS
McLEAN GDNS
CROW RD
HILL RD
WELLBRAE
QUEEN ST
KING ST
VICARS RD
HAMILTON WAY
LAWRIE ST
GREEN ST
ARGYLE ST
MILLAR ST
KIRK ST
NEW ST
THOMSON CT
LOCKHART ST
INGLIS CT
CAMNETHAN ST
MURRAY DR
BOGHALL ST
REID GR
WATSTONE RD
ANGLE ST
NASMITH CT
McINNES GR
WATT CT
BURNS WYND
McNIVEN CT
ROGERS CT
KANE PL
McEWANS WAY
GIBB CT
GEMMELL WAY
CROFTHILL CT
DICK CT
SORBIE DR
BRODIE PL
TOFTCOMBS AVE
ROCK GDNS
TOFTCOMBS CRES
ASH LA
PO
Lanarkshire STREET ATLAS

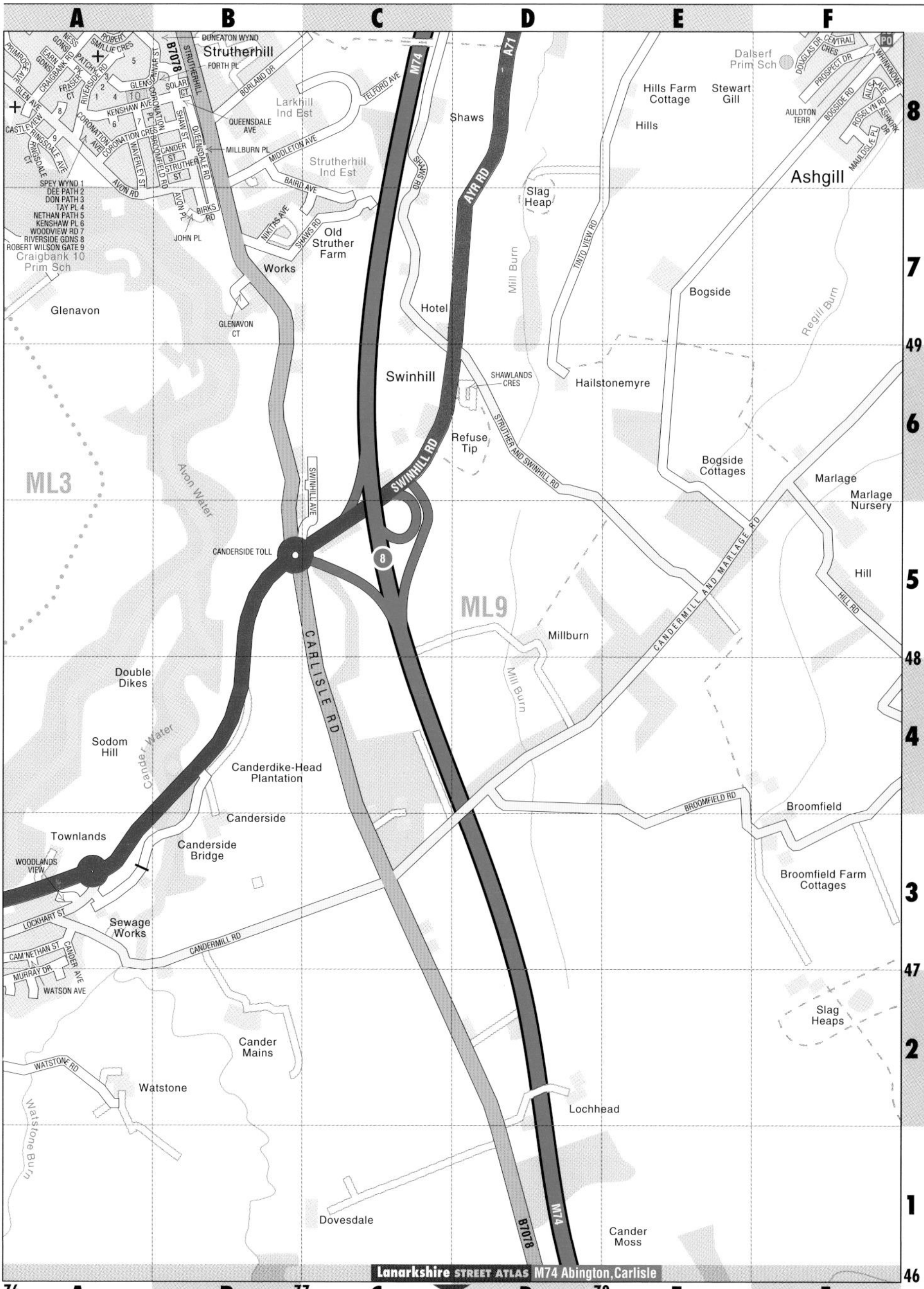
Strutherhill
Larkhill Ind Est
Strutherhill Ind Est
Shaws
Hills Farm Cottage
Stewart Gill
Hills
Dalserf Prim Sch
Ashgill
Slag Heap
Old Struther Farm
Works
Craigbank 10 Prim Sch
Glenavon
Hotel
Bogside
Swinhill
Hailstonemyre
Refuse Tip
ML3
Bogside Cottages
Marlage
Marlage Nursery
Hill
ML9
Millburn
Double Dikes
Sodom Hill
Canderdike-Head Plantation
Canderside
Broomfield
Townlands
Canderside Bridge
Broomfield Farm Cottages
Sewage Works
Slag Heaps
Cander Mains
Watstone
Lochhead
Dovesdale
Cander Moss
M74
A71
AYR RD
SWINHILL RD
CARLISLE RD
B7078
CANDERSIDE TOLL
CANDERMILL AND MARLAGE RD
CANDERMILL RD
BROOMFIELD RD
STRUTHER AND SWINHILL RD
TINTO VIEW RD
HILL RD
Avon Water
Cander Water
Mill Burn
Regill Burn
Watstone Burn
SPEY WYND 1
DEE PATH 2
DON PATH 3
TAY PL 4
NETHAN PATH 5
KENSHAW PL 6
WOODVIEW RD 7
RIVERSIDE GDNS 8
ROBERT WILSON GATE 9
LOCKHART ST
WATSON AVE
WATSTONE RD
A B C D E F
76 77 78
46 47 48 49

199
186

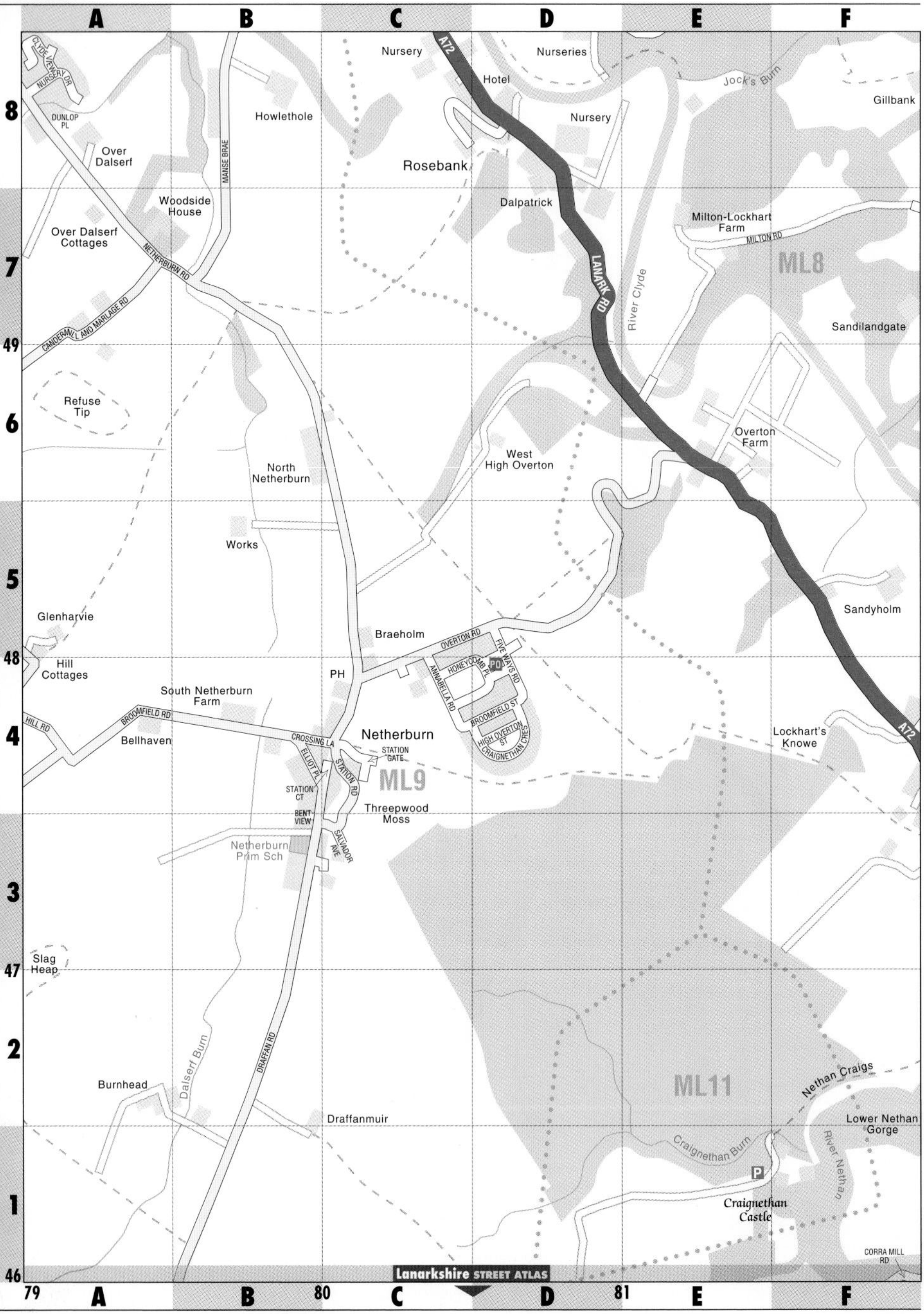
A
B
C
D
E
F
8
7
49
6
5
48
4
3
47
2
1
46
79
80
81
CLYDE VIEW
NURSERY DR
DUNLOP PL
Over Dalserf
Howlethole
MANSE BRAE
Nursery
A72
Hotel
Nurseries
Jock's Burn
Gillbank
Nursery
Rosebank
Woodside House
Dalpatrick
Milton-Lockhart Farm
MILTON RD
Over Dalserf Cottages
NETHERBURN RD
LANARK RD
River Clyde
ML8
CANDERMILL AND MARLAGE RD
Sandilandgate
Refuse Tip
Overton Farm
North Netherburn
West High Overton
Works
Glenharvie
Sandyholm
Braeholm
OVERTON RD
FIVE WAYS RD
HONEYCOMB PL
PO
ANNABELLA RD
Hill Cottages
PH
South Netherburn Farm
BROOMFIELD RD
BROOMFIELD ST
HIGH OVERTON ST
CRAIGNETHAN CRES
HILL RD
Bellhaven
Netherburn
CROSSING LA
ELLIOT PL
STATION RD
STATION GATE
Lockhart's Knowe
A72
ML9
STATION CT
BENT VIEW
Threepwood Moss
Netherburn Prim Sch
SALVADOR AVE
Slag Heap
Dalserf Burn
DRAFFAN RD
Burnhead
Draffanmuir
ML11
Nethan Craigs
Lower Nethan Gorge
Craignethan Burn
River Nethan
P
Craignethan Castle
CORRA MILL RD

199

187
202

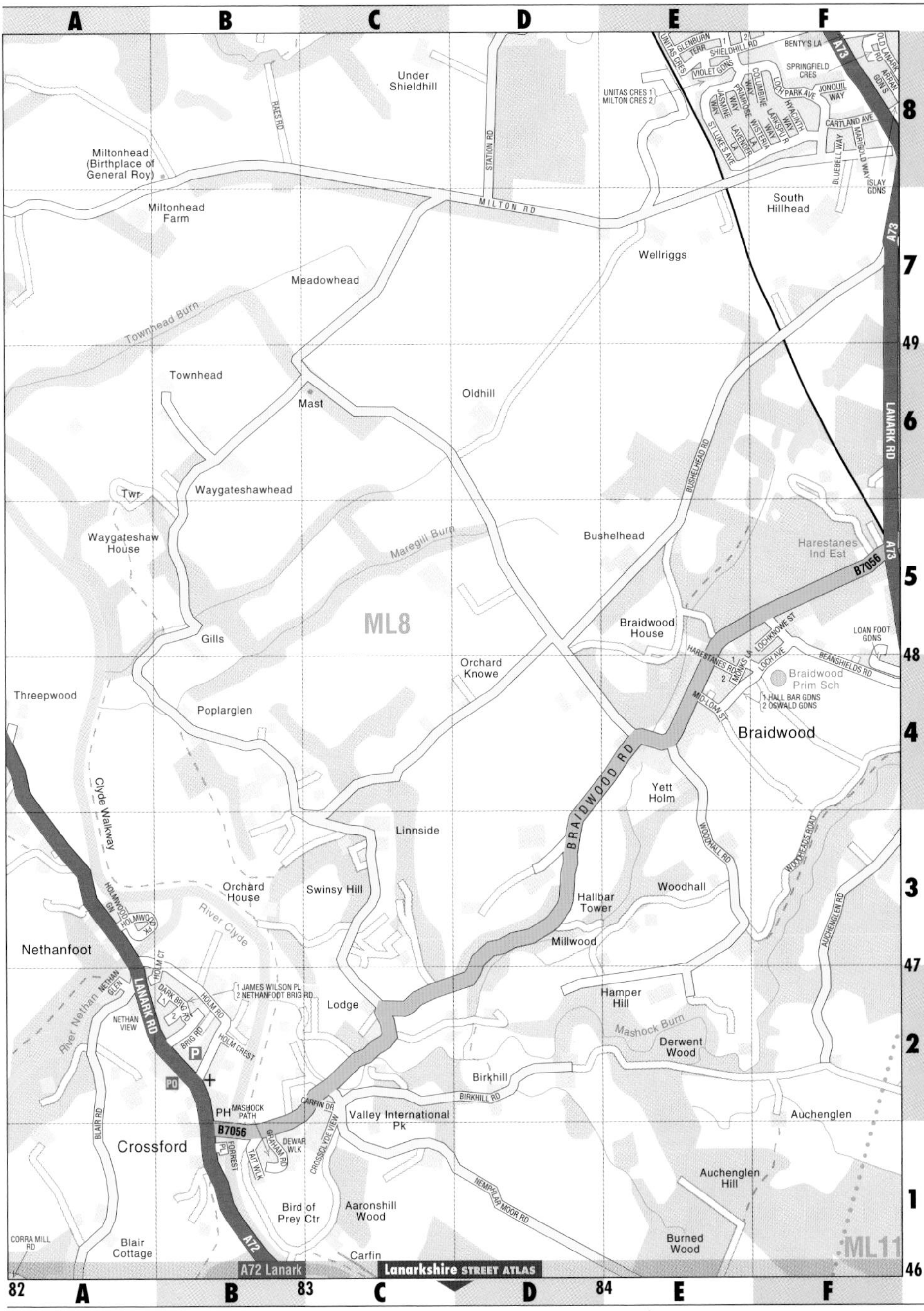
A
B
C
D
E
F
8
7
49
6
5
48
4
3
47
2
1
46
82
83
84
Under Shieldhill
RAES RD
STATION RD
Miltonhead (Birthplace of General Roy)
Miltonhead Farm
MILTON RD
UNITAS CRES 1
MILTON CRES 2
GLENBURN TERR
SHIELDHILL RD
BENTY'S LA
SPRINGFIELD CRES
OLD LANARK RD
ARRAN GDNS
VIOLET GDNS
COLUMBINE WAY
LOCH PARK AVE
JONQUIL WAY
HYACINTH WAY
LARKSPUR WAY
WISTERIA LA
PRIMROSE WAY
JASMINE WAY
LAVENDER LA
ST LUKE'S AVE
CARTLAND AVE
MARIGOLD WAY
BLUEBELL WAY
ISLAY GDNS
South Hillhead
A73
Wellriggs
Meadowhead
Townhead Burn
Townhead
Mast
Oldhill
LANARK RD
BUSHELHEAD RD
Twr
Waygateshawhead
Waygateshaw House
Maregill Burn
Bushelhead
Harestanes Ind Est
B7056
ML8
Gills
Braidwood House
LOCHKNOWE ST
LOAN FOOT GDNS
HARESTANES RD
MONKS LA
LOCH AVE
BEANSHIELDS RD
Orchard Knowe
Braidwood Prim Sch
1 HALL BAR GDNS
2 OSWALD GDNS
MID LOAN ST
Threepwood
Poplarglen
Braidwood
BRAIDWOOD RD
Yett Holm
Clyde Walkway
Linnside
WOODNALL RD
WOODHEADS ROAD
Orchard House
Swinsy Hill
Hallbar Tower
Woodhall
AUCHENGLEN RD
HOLMWOOD GN
HOLMWOOD PK
River Clyde
Millwood
Nethanfoot
HOLM CT
NETHAN GLEN
1 JAMES WILSON PL
2 NETHANFOOT BRIG RD
DARK BRIG RD
HOLM RD
Lodge
Hamper Hill
River Nethan
NETHAN VIEW
BRIG RD
HOLM CREST
Mashock Burn
Derwent Wood
PO
Birkhill
BIRKHILL RD
PH
MASHOCK PATH
CARFIN DR
Valley International Pk
Auchenglen
BLAIR RD
B7056
FORREST PL
GRAHAM RD
DEWAR WLK
TAIT WLK
CROSSCLYDE VIEW
Crossford
NEMPHLAR MOOR RD
Auchenglen Hill
Bird of Prey Ctr
Aaronshill Wood
A72
Burned Wood
CORRA MILL RD
Blair Cottage
Carfin
ML11
A72 Lanark

202

B8
1 CAMERON RD
2 BRAEHEAD LOAN
3 CHARLES CRES
4 GLEN MS

201
188

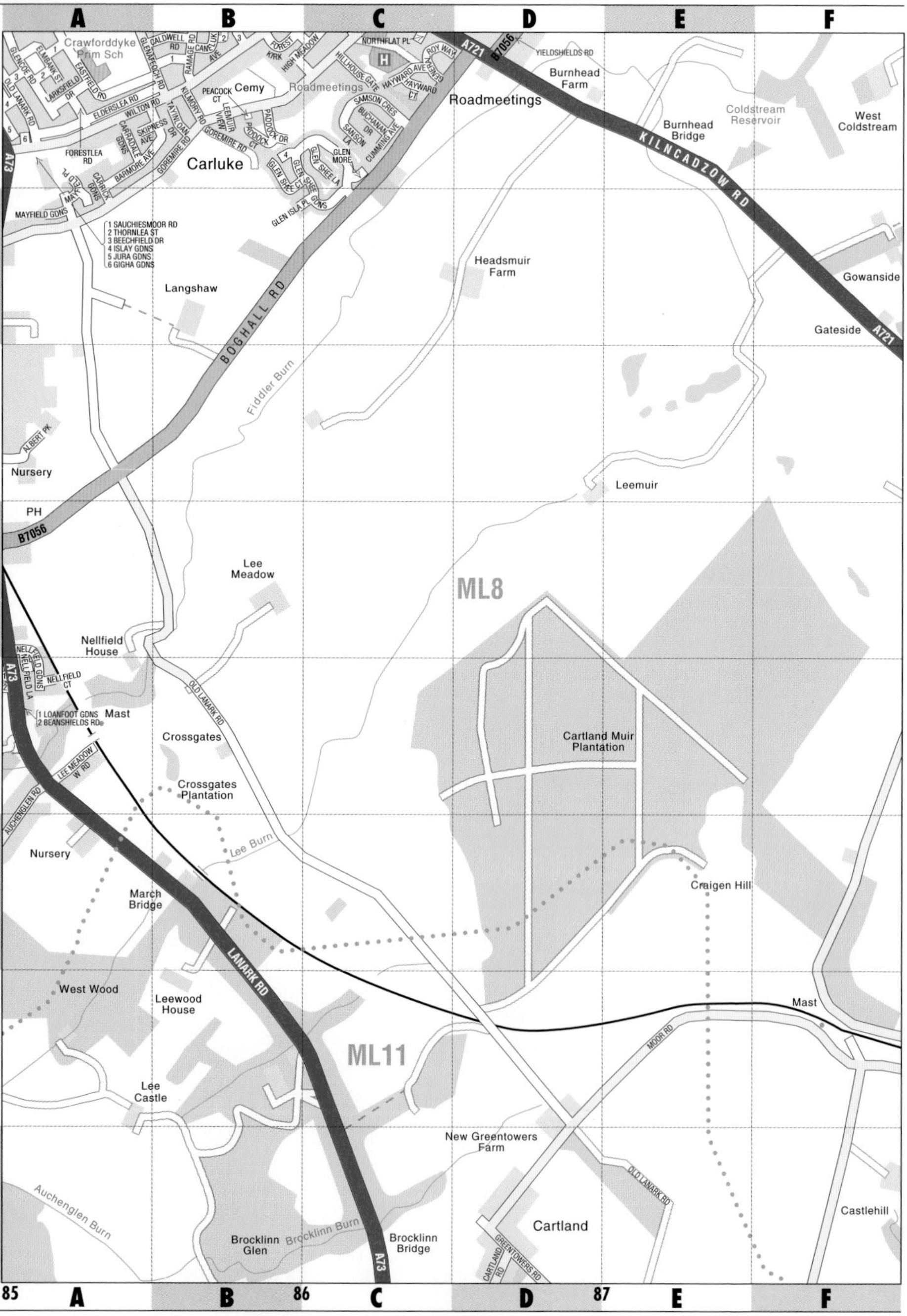

201
214

189

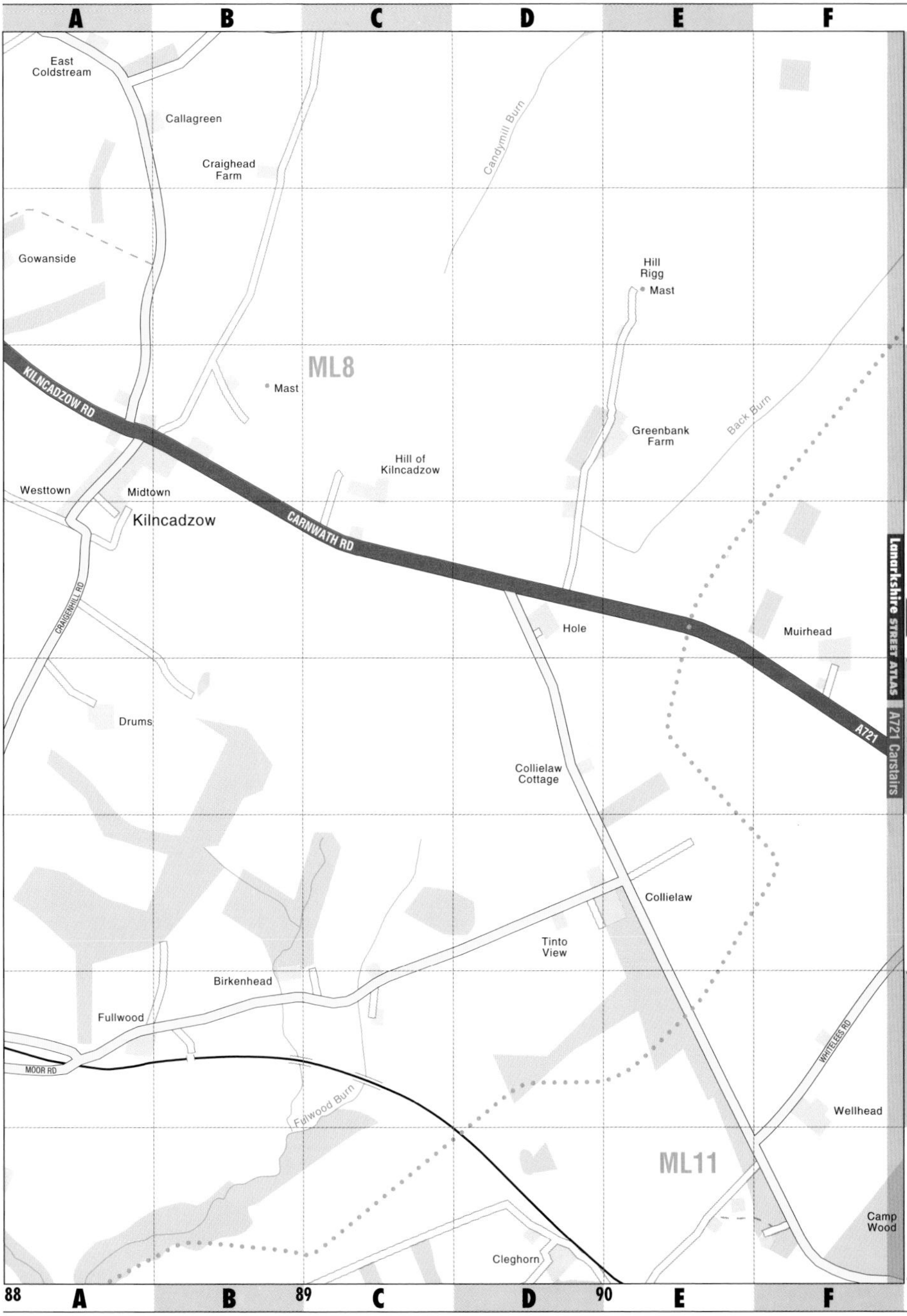
A
B
C
D
E
F
East Coldstream
Callagreen
Craighead Farm
Candymill Burn
Gowanside
Hill Rigg
Mast
ML8
Mast
KILNCADZOW RD
Greenbank Farm
Back Burn
Hill of Kilncadzow
Westtown
Midtown
Kilncadzow
CARNWATH RD
CRAIGENHILL RD
Hole
Muirhead
Drums
A721
Collielaw Cottage
Collielaw
Tinto View
Birkenhead
Fullwood
MOOR RD
WHITELEES RD
Wellhead
Fulwood Burn
ML11
Camp Wood
Cleghorn
8
7
49
6
5
48
4
3
47
2
1
46
88
89
90
Lanarkshire STREET ATLAS
A721 Carstairs

215

190

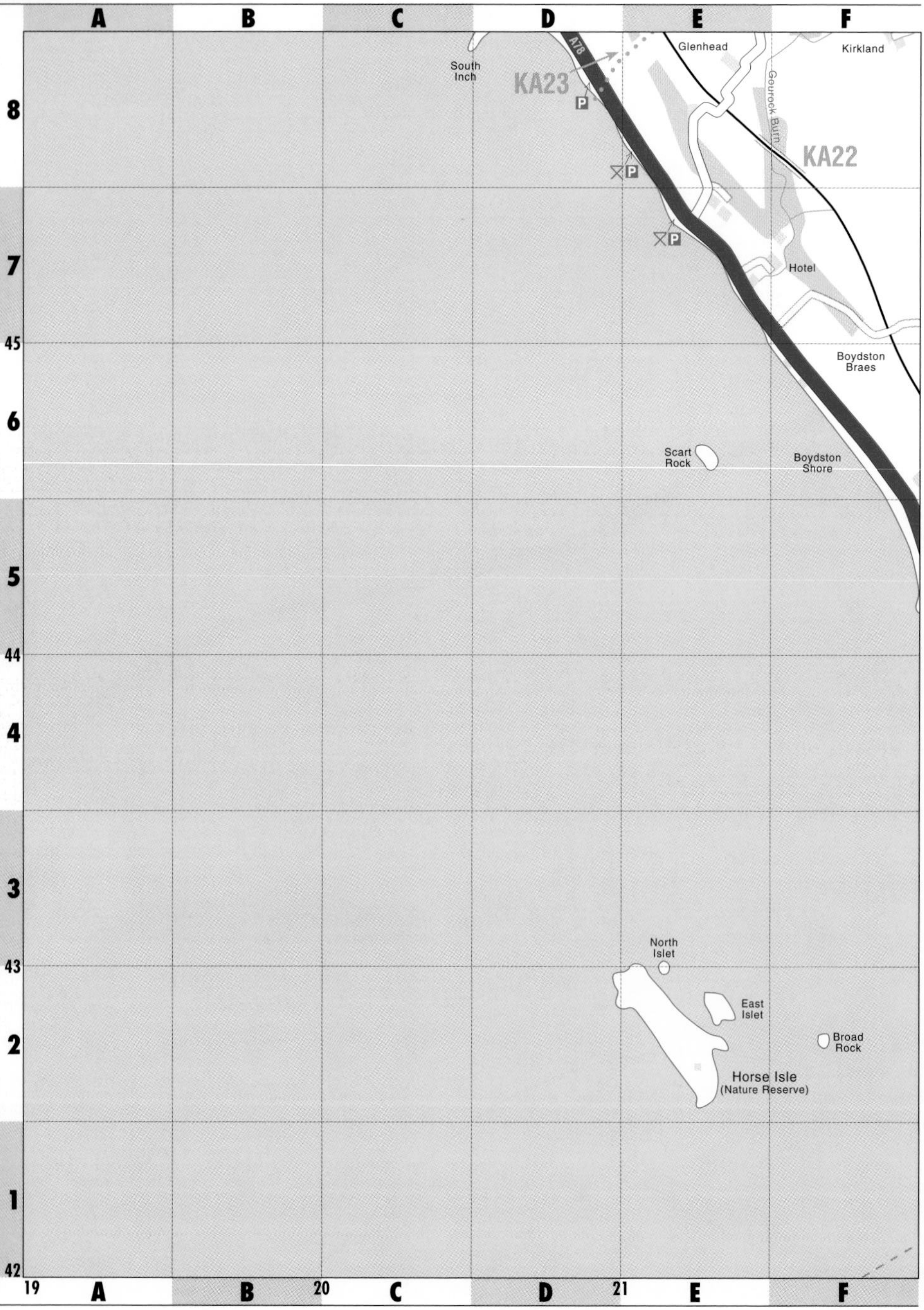
A
B
C
D
E
F
8
7
45
6
5
44
4
3
43
2
1
42
19
20
21
South Inch
A78
KA23
Glenhead
Kirkland
Gourock Burn
KA22
Hotel
Boydston Braes
Scart Rock
Boydston Shore
North Islet
East Islet
Broad Rock
Horse Isle
(Nature Reserve)

206

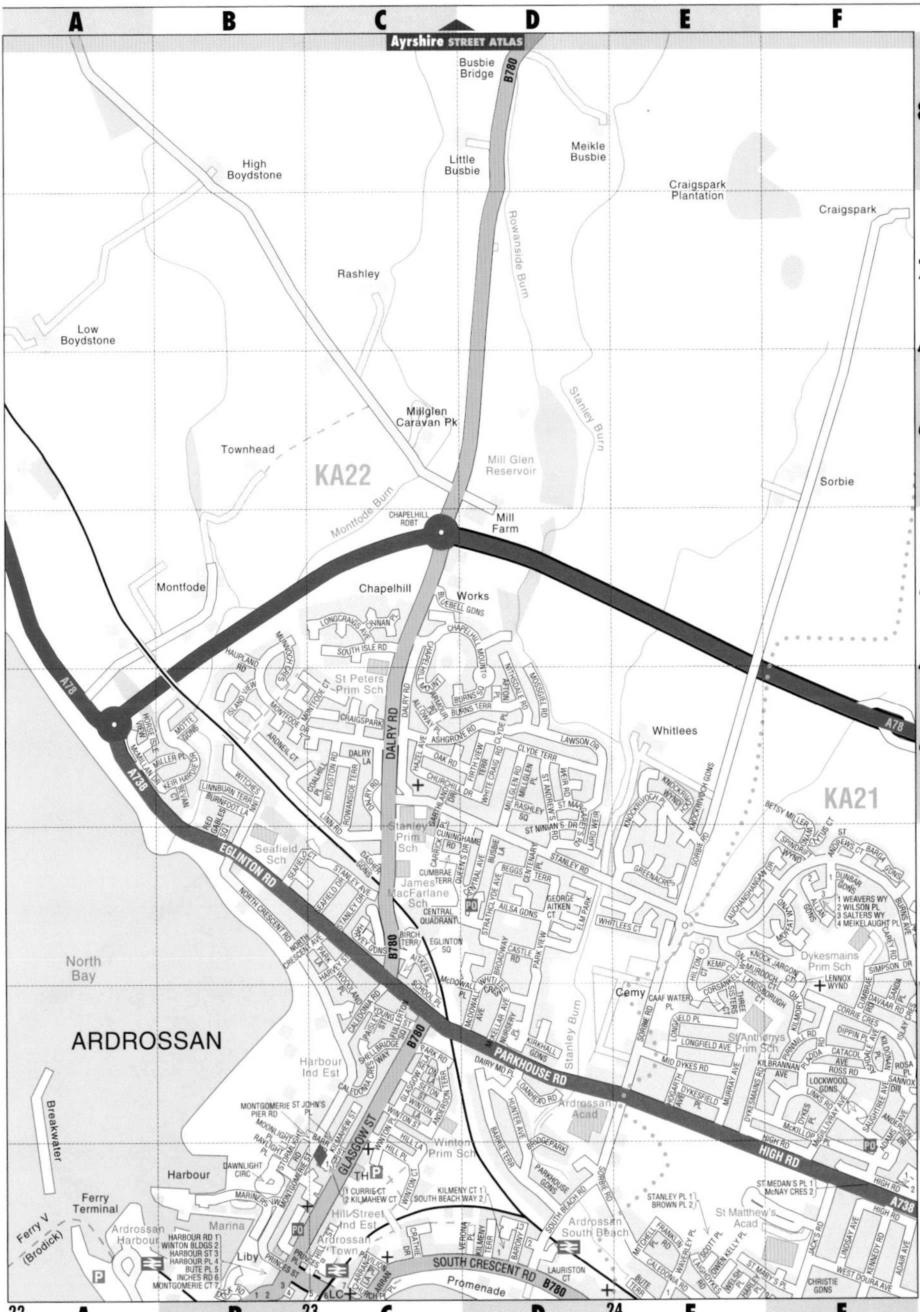

A
B
C
D
E
F
Ayrshire STREET ATLAS
8
7
45
6
5
44
4
3
43
2
1
42
22
23
24
Busbie Bridge
B780
High Boydstone
Little Busbie
Meikle Busbie
Craigspark Plantation
Craigspark
Rowanside Burn
Rashley
Low Boydstone
Millglen Caravan Pk
Stanley Burn
Townhead
KA22
Mill Glen Reservoir
Sorbie
Montfode Burn
CHAPELHILL RDBT
Mill Farm
Montfode
Chapelhill
Works
A78
Whitlees
KA21
DALRY RD
St Peters Prim Sch
Stanley Prim Sch
Seafield Sch
James MacFarlane Sch
EGLINTON RD
A738
North Bay
Dykesmains Prim Sch
Cemy
ARDROSSAN
PARKHOUSE RD
St Anthonys Prim Sch
Harbour Ind Est
Ardrossan Acad
Breakwater
GLASGOW ST
Winton Prim Sch
HIGH RD
Harbour
TH
Ferry Terminal
Ferry V (Brodick)
Marina
Ardrossan Harbour
Hill Street Ind Est
Ardrossan Town
Ardrossan South Beach
St Matthew's Acad
Liby
SOUTH CRESCENT RD
Promenade
LAURISTON CT
HARBOUR RD 1
WINTON BLDGS 2
HARBOUR ST 3
HARBOUR PL 4
BUTE PL 5
INCHES RD 6
MONTGOMERIE CT 7
1 WEAVERS WY
2 WILSON PL
3 SALTERS WY
4 MEIKELAUGHT PL
KILMENY CT 1
SOUTH BEACH WAY 2
1 CURRIE CT
2 KILMAHEW CT
ST MEDAN'S PL 1
McNAY CRES 2
STANLEY PL 1
BROWN PL 2

216

206

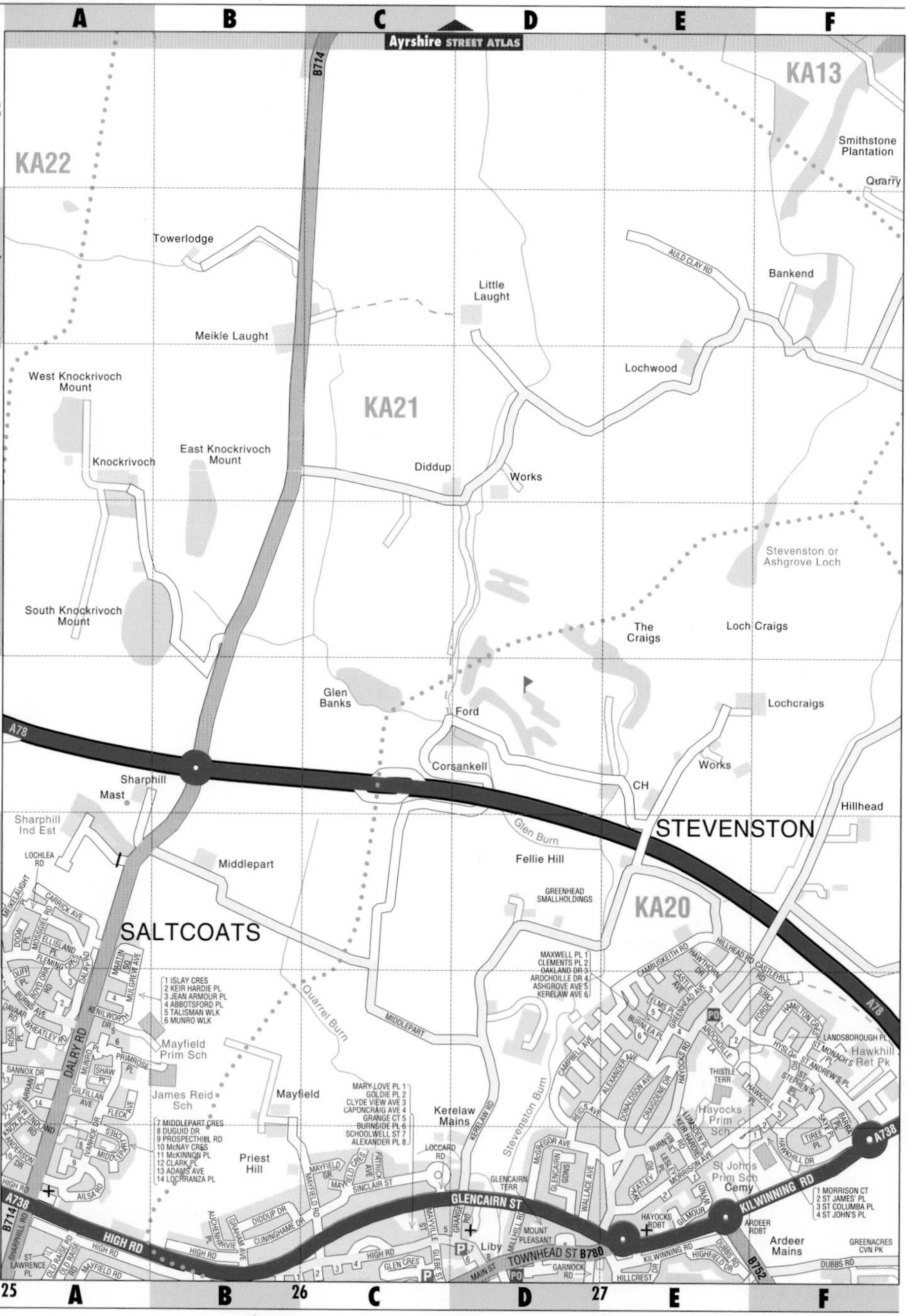
Ayrshire STREET ATLAS
KA22
KA21
KA13
KA20
Towerlodge
Meikle Laught
Little Laught
West Knockrivoch Mount
East Knockrivoch Mount
Knockrivoch
South Knockrivoch Mount
Diddup
Works
Lochwood
Bankend
Smithstone Plantation
Quarry
AULD CLAY RD
Stevenston or Ashgrove Loch
The Craigs
Loch Craigs
Lochcraigs
Glen Banks
Ford
Corsankell
Works
CH
Hillhead
STEVENSTON
Glen Burn
Fellie Hill
GREENHEAD SMALLHOLDINGS
Sharphill
Mast
Sharphill Ind Est
Middlepart
SALTCOATS
Mayfield Prim Sch
James Reid Sch
Mayfield
Priest Hill
Kerelaw Mains
Quarrel Burn
Stevenston Burn
MIDDLEPART
KERELAW RD
Hayocks Prim Sch
St Johns Prim Sch
Cemy
Hawkhill Ret Pk
Ardeer Mains
Liby
MOUNT PLEASANT
GLENCAIRN ST
TOWNHEAD ST B780
KILWINNING RD
HIGH RD
A738
A78
B714
B752
DALRY RD
1 ISLAY CRES
2 KEIR HARDIE PL
3 JEAN ARMOUR PL
4 ABBOTSFORD PL
5 TALISMAN WLK
6 MUNRO WLK
7 MIDDLEPART CRES
8 DUGUID DR
9 PROSPECTHILL RD
10 McNAY CRES
11 McKINNON PL
12 CLARK PL
13 ADAMS AVE
14 LOCHRANZA PL
MARY LOVE PL 1
GOLDIE PL 2
CLYDE VIEW AVE 3
CAPONCRAIG AVE 4
GRANGE CT 5
BURNSIDE PL 6
SCHOOLWELL ST 7
ALEXANDER PL 8
MAXWELL PL 1
CLEMENTS PL 2
OAKLAND DR 3
ARDCHOILLE DR 4
ASHGROVE AVE 5
KERELAW AVE 6
1 MORRISON CT
2 ST JAMES' PL
3 ST COLUMBA PL
4 ST JOHN'S PL
LANDSBOROUGH PL
GREENACRES CVN PK
DUBBS RD
HAYOCKS RDBT
ARDEER RDBT
E1
1 MOSSGIEL PL
2 LOCHLIE PL

191
208

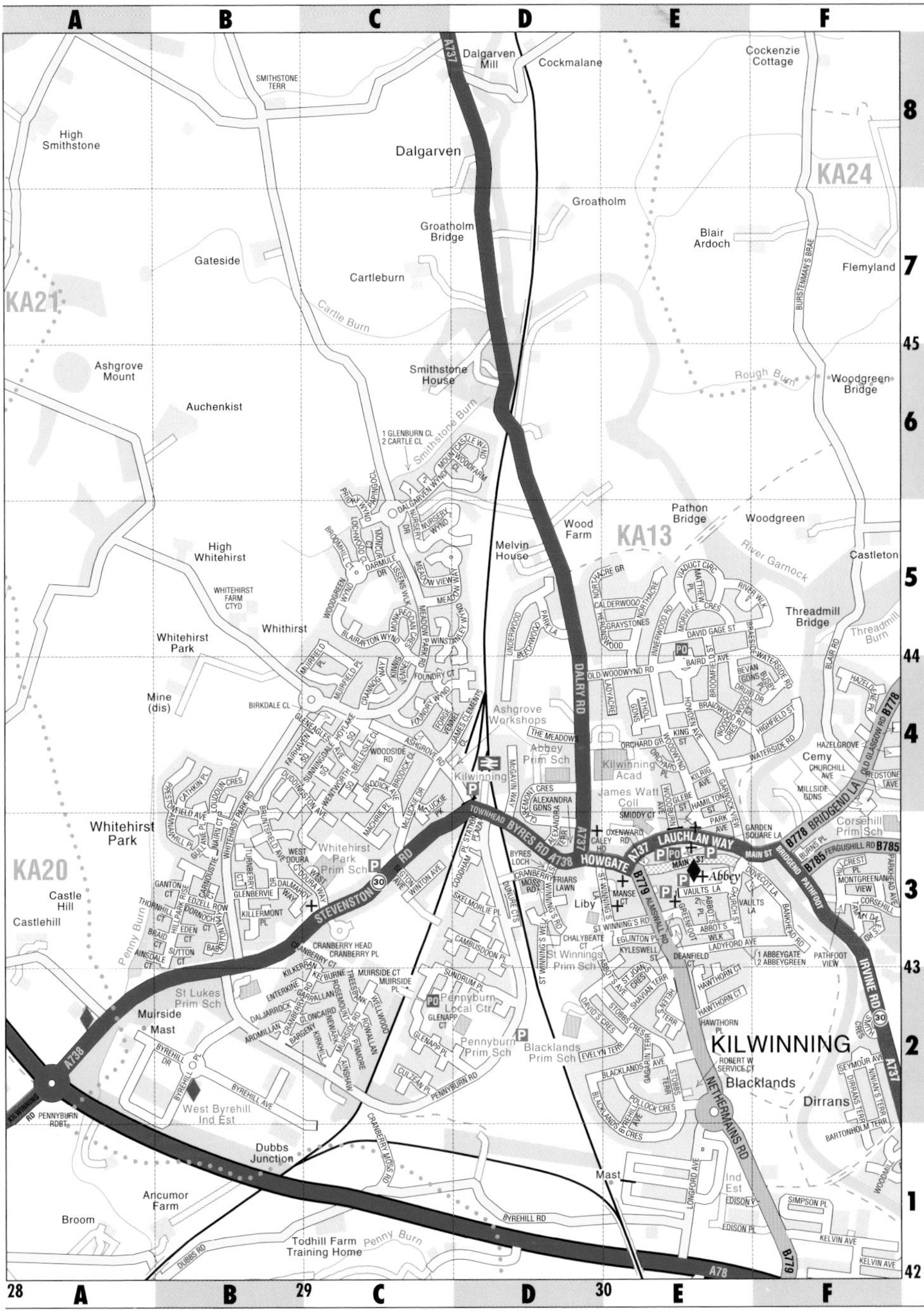

218
208

207
192

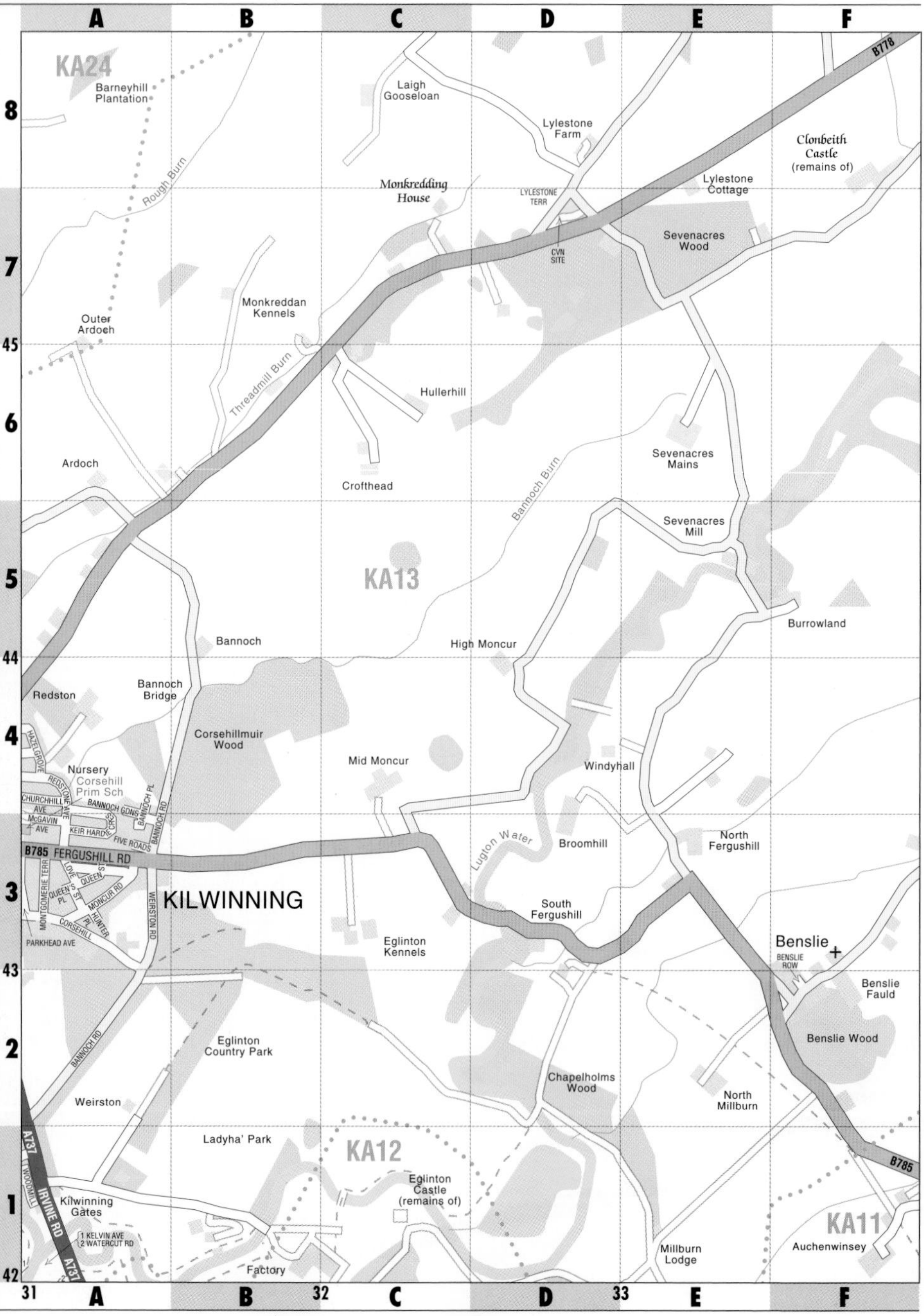

207
219

193
210
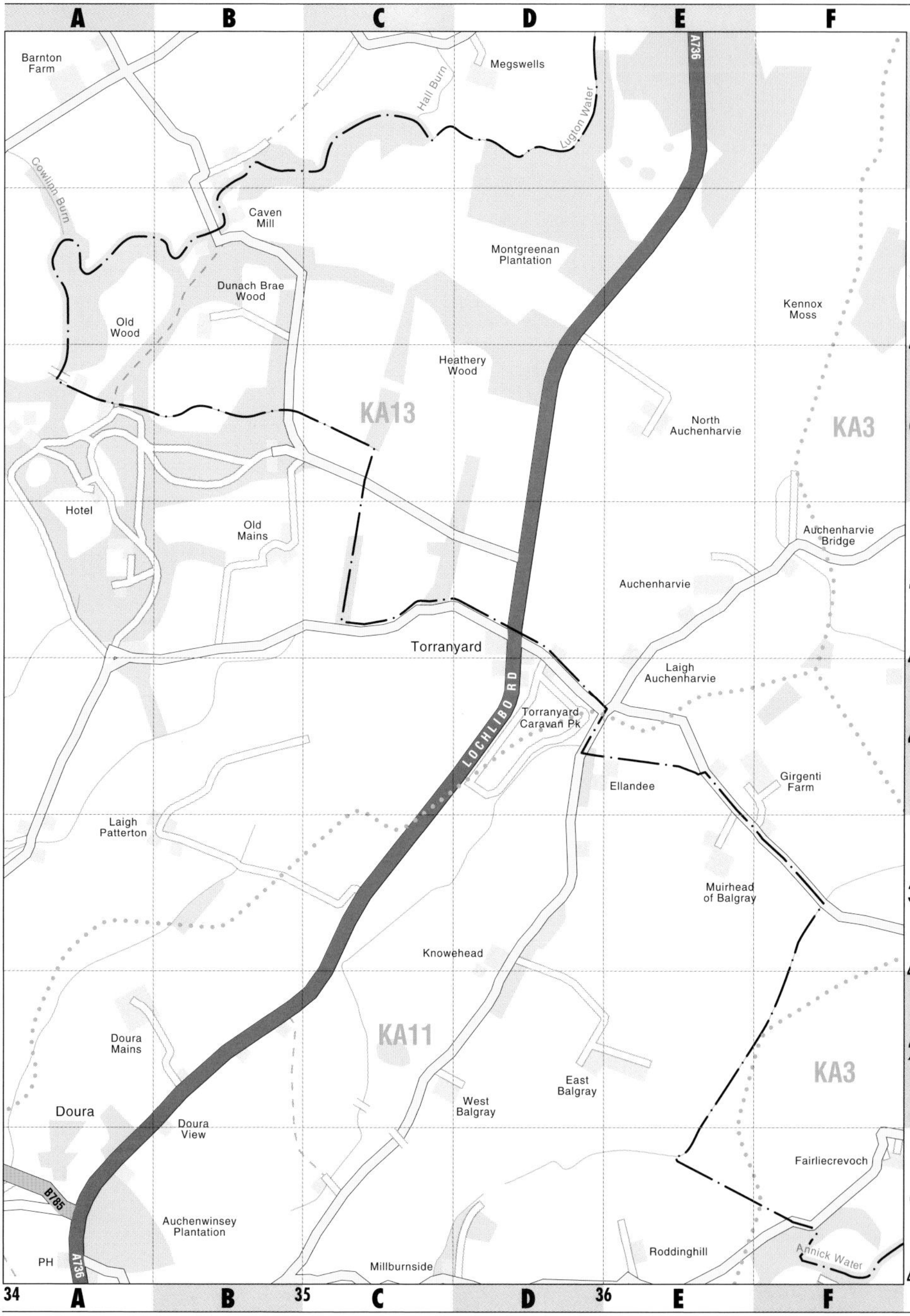

220
210

209
194

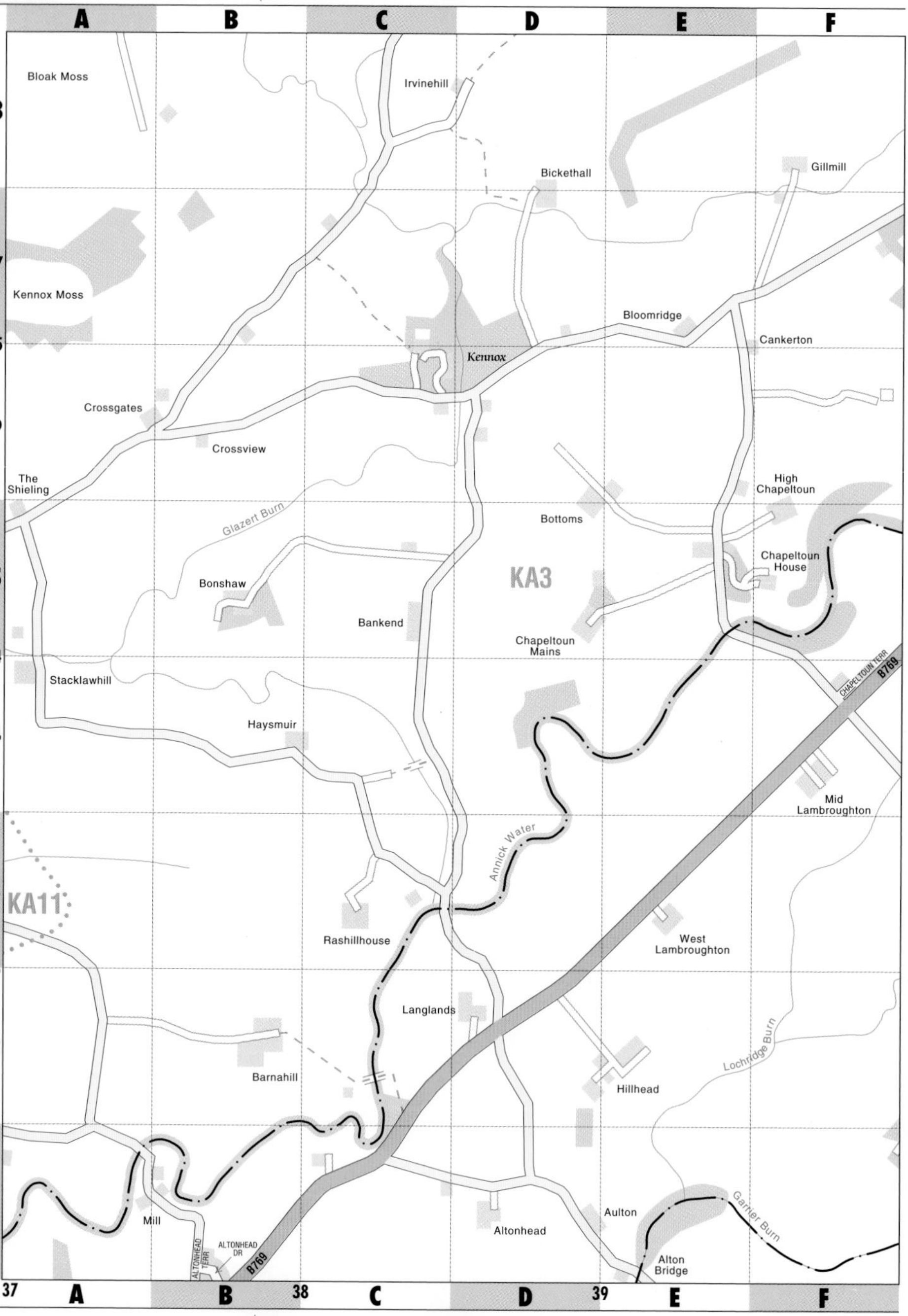

209
221

195
212

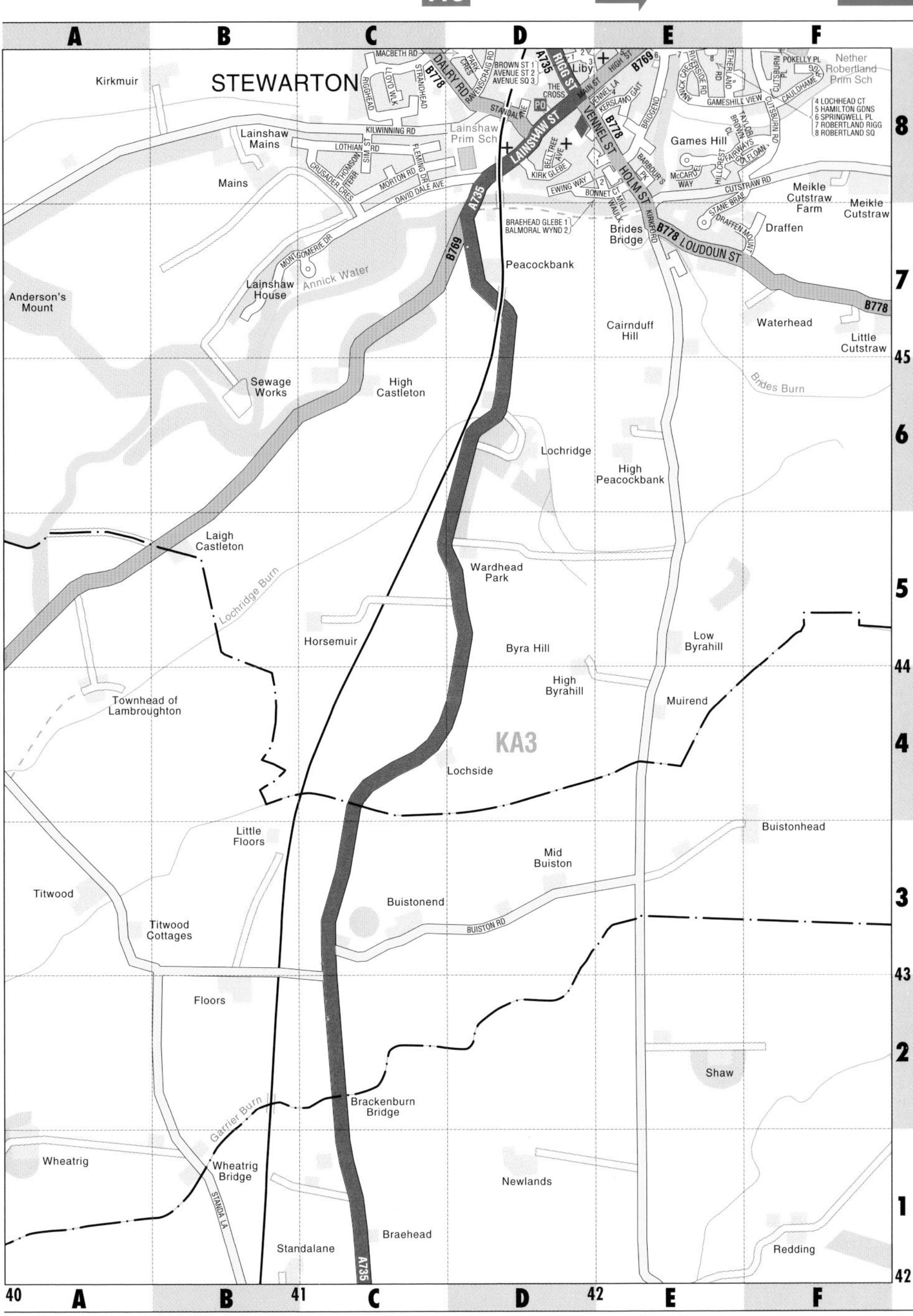

222
212

211
196

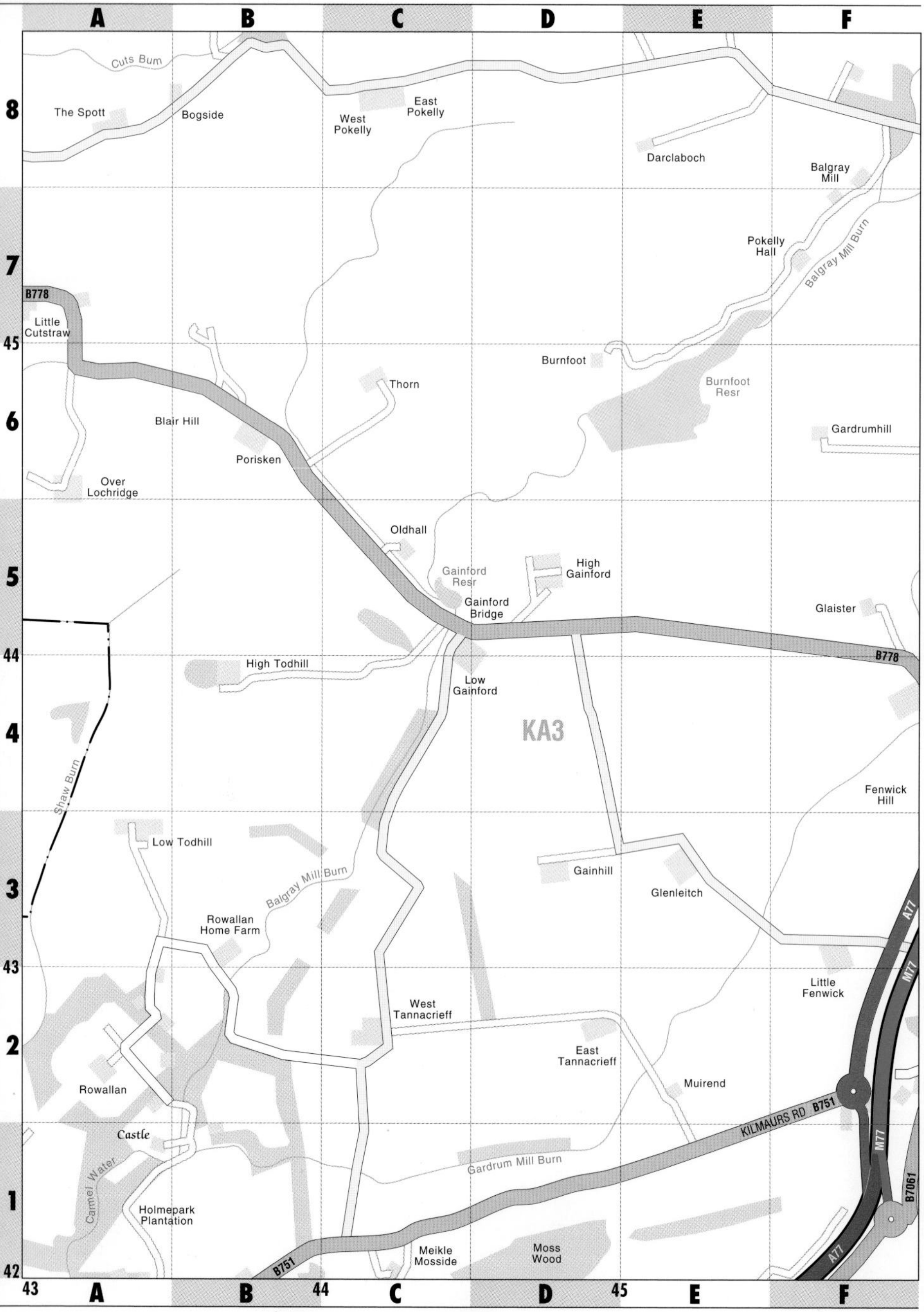

211
223

197

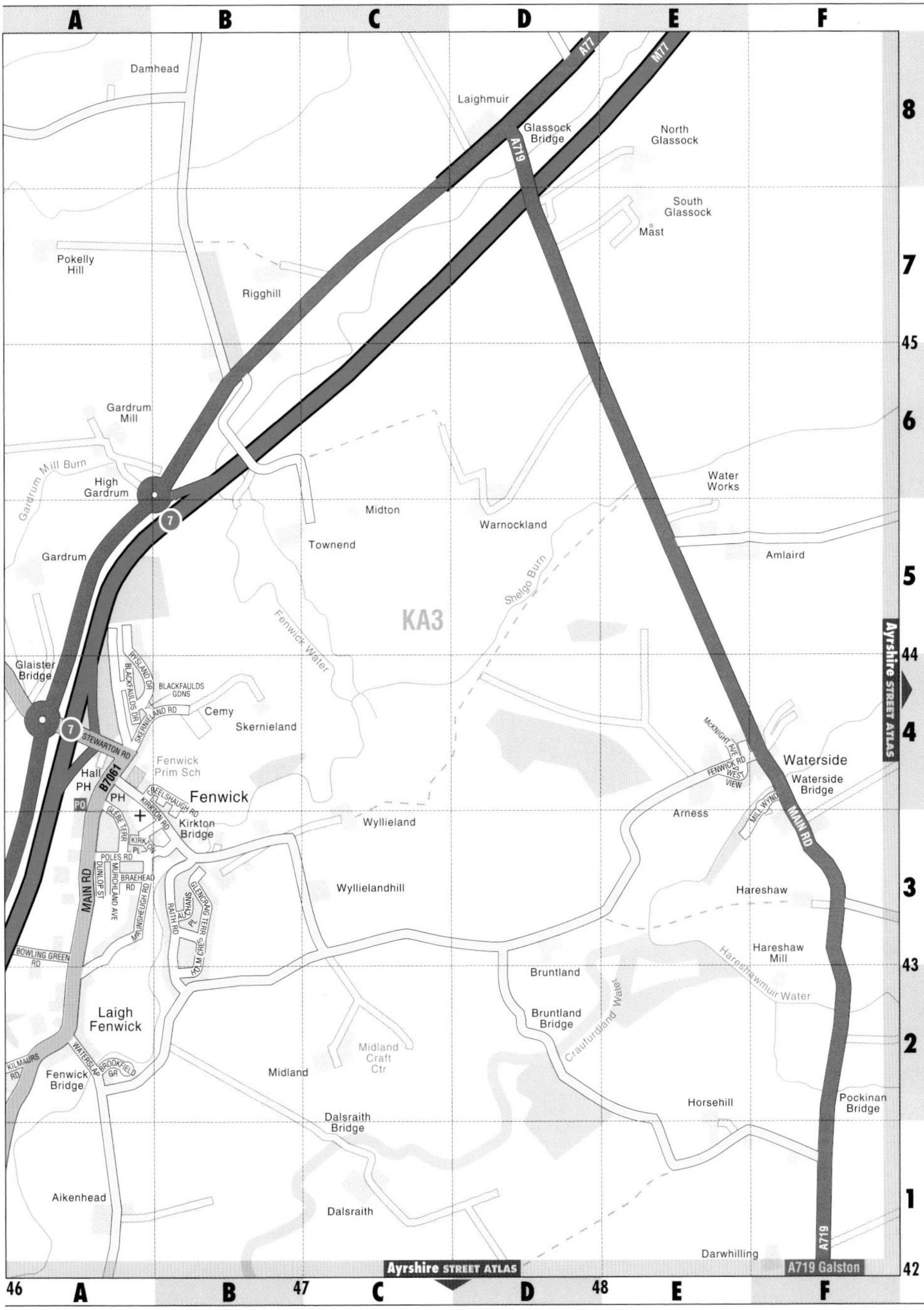
A
B
C
D
E
F
8
7
45
6
5
44
4
3
43
2
1
42
46
47
48
Damhead
Laighmuir
A77
M77
Glassock Bridge
A719
North Glassock
South Glassock
Mast
Pokelly Hill
Rigghill
Gardrum Mill
Gardrum Mill Burn
High Gardrum
7
Midton
Warnockland
Water Works
Townend
Gardrum
Amlaird
Shelgo Burn
KA3
Fenwick Water
Glaister Bridge
RYSLAND DR
BLACKFAULDS DR
BLACKFAULDS GDNS
SKERNIELAND RD
Cemy
Skernieland
STEWARTON RD
Fenwick Prim Sch
Hall
PH
B7061
PO
Fenwick
KIRKTON RD
Kirkton Bridge
GLEBE TERR
KIRKTON PL
POLES RD
DUNLOP ST
MURCHLAND AVE
BRAEHEAD RD
MAUNSHEIGH RD
RAITH RD
AUCHANS PL
GLENCRAIG TERR
HOLM CRES
MAIN RD
Wyllieland
Wyllielandhill
McKNIGHT AVE
FENWICK RD
WEST VIEW
Waterside
Waterside Bridge
MILL WYND
Arness
MAIN RD
Hareshaw
Hareshaw Mill
Hareshawmuir Water
BOWLING GREEN RD
Bruntland
Bruntland Bridge
Craufurdland Water
Laigh Fenwick
KILMAURS RD
WATERSLAP
BROOKFIELD GR
Fenwick Bridge
Midland
Midland Craft Ctr
Horsehill
Pockinan Bridge
Dalsraith Bridge
Aikenhead
Dalsraith
Darwhilling
A719
Ayrshire STREET ATLAS
A719 Galston

202

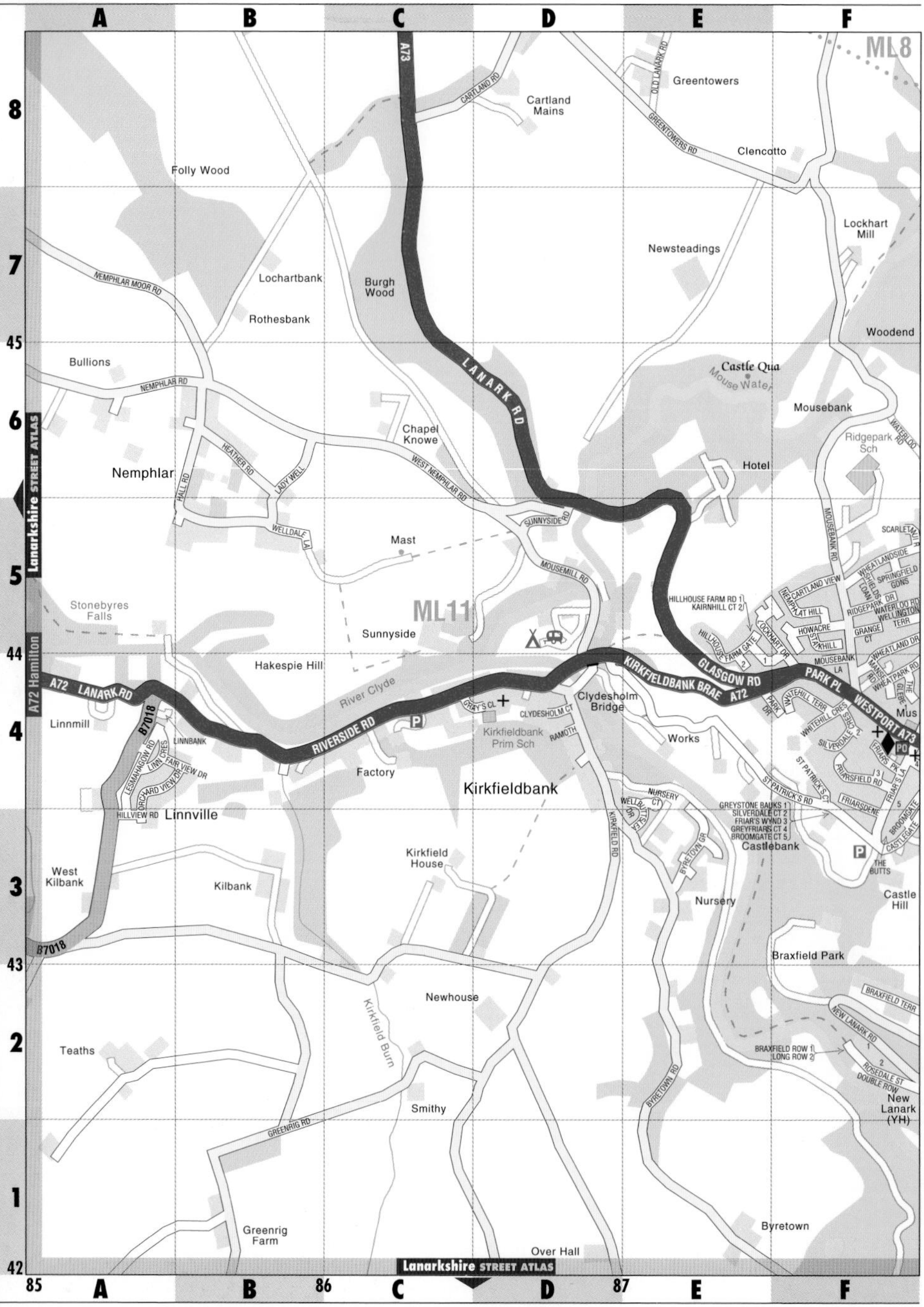
A
B
C
D
E
F
8
7
6
5
4
3
2
1
45
44
43
42
85
86
87
ML8
ML11
A73
CARTLAND RD
Cartland Mains
OLD LANARK RD
Greentowers
GREENTOWERS RD
Clencotto
Folly Wood
Lockhart Mill
Newsteadings
NEMPHLAR MOOR RD
Lochartbank
Burgh Wood
Rothesbank
Woodend
Bullions
LANARK RD
Castle Qua
Mouse Water
NEMPHLAR RD
Mousebank
Chapel Knowe
WATERLOO
Ridgepark Sch
HEATHER RD
Nemphlar
HALL RD
LADY WELL
WEST NEMPHLAR RD
Hotel
MOUSEBANK RD
SUNNYSIDE RD
WELLDALE LA
Mast
SCARLETMUIR
MOUSEMILL RD
WHEATLANDSIDE
CARTLAND VIEW
SPRINGFIELD GDNS
Stonebyres Falls
HILLHOUSE FARM RD 1
KAIRNHILL CT 2
NEMPHLAT HILL
RIDGEPARK DR
WATERLOO RD
WELLINGTON TERR
HOWACRE
GRANGE CT
Sunnyside
STAKHILL
WHEATLAND DR
MOUSEBANK LA
WHEATPARK RD
HILLHOUSE FARM GATE
LOCKHART DR
Hakespie Hill
A72 Hamilton
A72 LANARK RD
KIRKFIELDBANK BRAE A72
GLASGOW RD
PARK PL
WESTPORT A73
River Clyde
Clydesholm Bridge
GRAY'S CL
CLYDESHOLM CT
Mus
Linnmill
B7018
RIVERSIDE RD
PARK DR
WHITEHILL TERR
WHITEHILL CRES
LINNBANK
Kirkfieldbank Prim Sch
RAMOTH
Works
SILVERDALE
PO
LESMAHAGOW RD
LINN CRES
FAIR VIEW DR
Factory
FRIARS PK
ST PATRICK'S CT
FRIARSFIELD RD
ORCHARD VIEW DR
Kirkfieldbank
NURSERY CT
ST PATRICK'S RD
FRIAR'S LA
WELLBUTTS LEA DR
FRIARSDENE
HILLVIEW RD
Linnville
GREYSTONE BAUKS 1
SILVERDALE CT 2
FRIAR'S WYND 3
GREYFRIARS CT 4
BROOMGATE CT 5
BROOMGATE
KIRKFIELD RD
BYRETOWN GR
Castlebank
CASTLEGATE
West Kilbank
Kirkfield House
THE BUTTS
Kilbank
Nursery
Castle Hill
B7018
Braxfield Park
Newhouse
BRAXFIELD TERR
Kirkfield Burn
NEW LANARK RD
Teaths
BRAXFIELD ROW 1
LONG ROW 2
ROSEDALE ST
DOUBLE ROW
BYRETOWN RD
Smithy
New Lanark (YH)
GREENRIG RD
Greenrig Farm
Byretown
Over Hall
Lanarkshire STREET ATLAS

203

A4
1 GLEBE DR
2 WALLACE CT
3 BONNET RD
4 WHEATPARK RD
5 GREYSTONE BAULKS
6 GREENSIDE CL
7 GREENSIDE LA
8 AITKEN PL
9 BLOOMGATE
10 SHIRLEY'S CL
11 DUNCAN'S CL
12 CROSS KEY'S CL
13 RITCHIE'S CL
14 HUNTER'S CL
15 BULL'S CL
16 McKENZIES CL
17 MARKET END
18 MARKET CT
19 HYNDFORD PL
20 BERNARD'S WYND
21 BERNARD'S CT
22 THOMSON'S CL
23 GLEBE CT

205

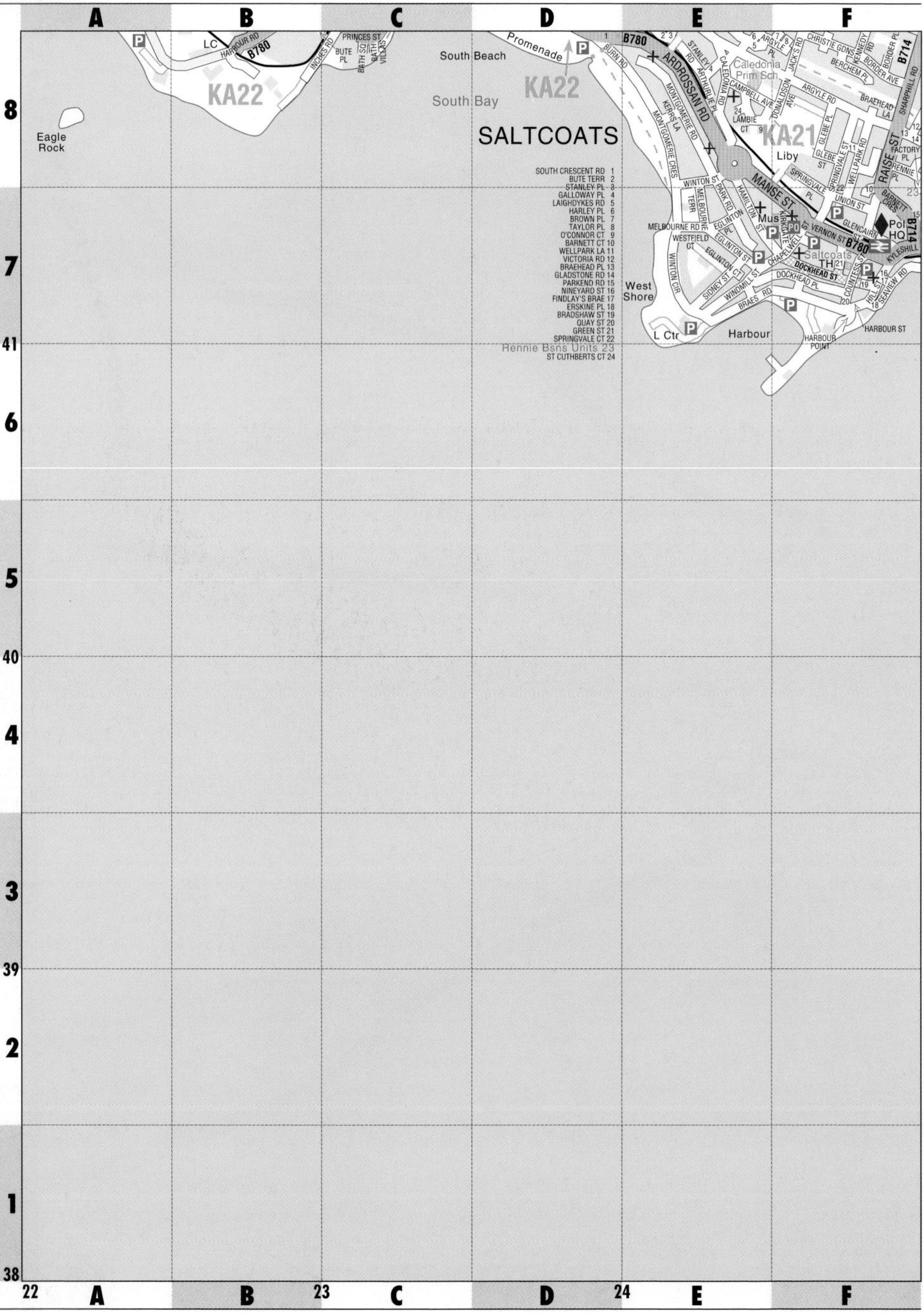

A
B
C
D
E
F
8
7
41
6
5
40
4
3
39
2
1
38
22
23
24
Eagle Rock
LC
HARBOUR RD
B780
KA22
INCHES RD
PRINCES ST
BUTE PL
BATH SQ
BATH VILLAS
South Beach
Promenade
KA22
South Bay
SALTCOATS
BURN RD
B780
ARDROSSAN RD
STANLEY RD
ARTHURLIE PL
CALEDONIA RD
Caledonia Prim Sch
CAMPBELL AVE
LAMBIE CT
DONALDSON AVE
JACK'S RD
ARGYLE PL
CHRISTIE GDNS
KENNEDY RD
BORDER PL
BORDER AVE
BERCHEM PL
B714
SHARPHILL RD
ARGYLE RD
BRAEHEAD LA
KA21
Liby
GLEBE PL
GLEBE ST
SPRINGVALE ST
WELLPARK RD
RAISE ST
FACTORY PL
RENNIE PL
BARNETT CRES
MONTGOMERIE RD
KERRS LA
MONTGOMERIE CRES
WINTON ST
MELBOURNE TERR
PARK RD
HAMILTON ST
MANSE ST
SPRINGVALE PL
UNION ST
GLENCAIRN ST
Pol HQ
B714
Mus
KIRKGATE
PO
VERNON ST
B780
KYLESHILL
MELBOURNE RD
EGLINTON PL
WESTFIELD CT
EGLINTON ST
EGLINTON CT
CHAPELWELL ST
Saltcoats TH
DOCKHEAD ST
DOCKHEAD PL
COUNTESS ST
HILL ST
SEAVIEW RD
WINTON CIR
SIDNEY ST
WINDMILL ST
BRAES RD
West Shore
L Ctr
Harbour
HARBOUR POINT
HARBOUR ST
SOUTH CRESCENT RD 1
BUTE TERR 2
STANLEY PL 3
GALLOWAY PL 4
LAIGHDYKES RD 5
HARLEY PL 6
BROWN PL 7
TAYLOR PL 8
O'CONNOR CT 9
BARNETT CT 10
WELLPARK LA 11
VICTORIA RD 12
BRAEHEAD PL 13
GLADSTONE RD 14
PARKEND RD 15
NINEYARD ST 16
FINDLAY'S BRAE 17
ERSKINE PL 18
BRADSHAW ST 19
QUAY ST 20
GREEN ST 21
SPRINGVALE CT 22
Rennie Bsns Units 23
ST CUTHBERTS CT 24

206
218
A
B
C
D
E
F
8
7
6
5
4
3
2
1
41
40
39
38
25
26
27
STEVENSTON
Auchenharvie
Auchenharvie Acad
L Ctr
KA21
KA20
SALTCOATS RD
CANAL ST
BOGLEMART ST
B780
B714
B752
CALEDONIAN RD
Saltcoats Campbell
CH
Cemy
Liby
Glencairn Prim Sch
Ardeer Stad
Ardeer Park
Portland Place Ind Est
Moorpark Ind Est
Mast
Stevenston
Ardeer Prim Sch
East Shore
Beach Park
Sewage Works
Stevenston Ind Est
Stevenston Burn
SANDYLANDS PROM
1 THOMAS CAMPBELL ST
2 McISAAC RD
3 PARKEND GDNS
4 CANAL CT
5 PARKEND AVE
6 PARKEND TERR
MOORPARK RD W
MOORPARK RD E
PORTLAND PL
WARNER ST
LIMEKILN RD
GEORGE ST
SHORE RD
ARDOCH TERR
THISTLE MEWS
MORRIS MOODIE AVE
DEER PARK AVE
SOMMERVILLE DR
MISK KNOWES
ARDOCH CRES
ARDOCH CT
TRELAWNEY TERR
LUNDHOLM RD
ARDEER LA
GOLF AVE
FIRST AVE
CLARK CRES
CARMYLE PL
ROBERTSON CRES
ARTHUR ST
JAMES MILLER CRES
BLAKELY RD
SEABANK ST
REID TERR
GUTHRIE RD
PARKEND RD
GLADSTONE RD
VICTORIA RD
KERR AVE
CUNNINGHAME CR
CUNNINGHAME RD
JOHN BROGAN PL
MARY LOVE PL
RIGGS COTTS
GLEBE ST
HILLSIDE ST
HILLSIDE CT
FULLARTON PL
AFTON CT
AFTON RD
NEW ST
DARG RD
GARNOCK RD
OLD QUARRY RD
MOORE PL
WESTPARK CT
BURNBANK
STATION RD
CALEY CT
CANAL CRES
MILLAR RD
MAYFIELD RD
NELSON RD
TOWNHEAD RD
KINNIER RD
HALKETT PL

217
207

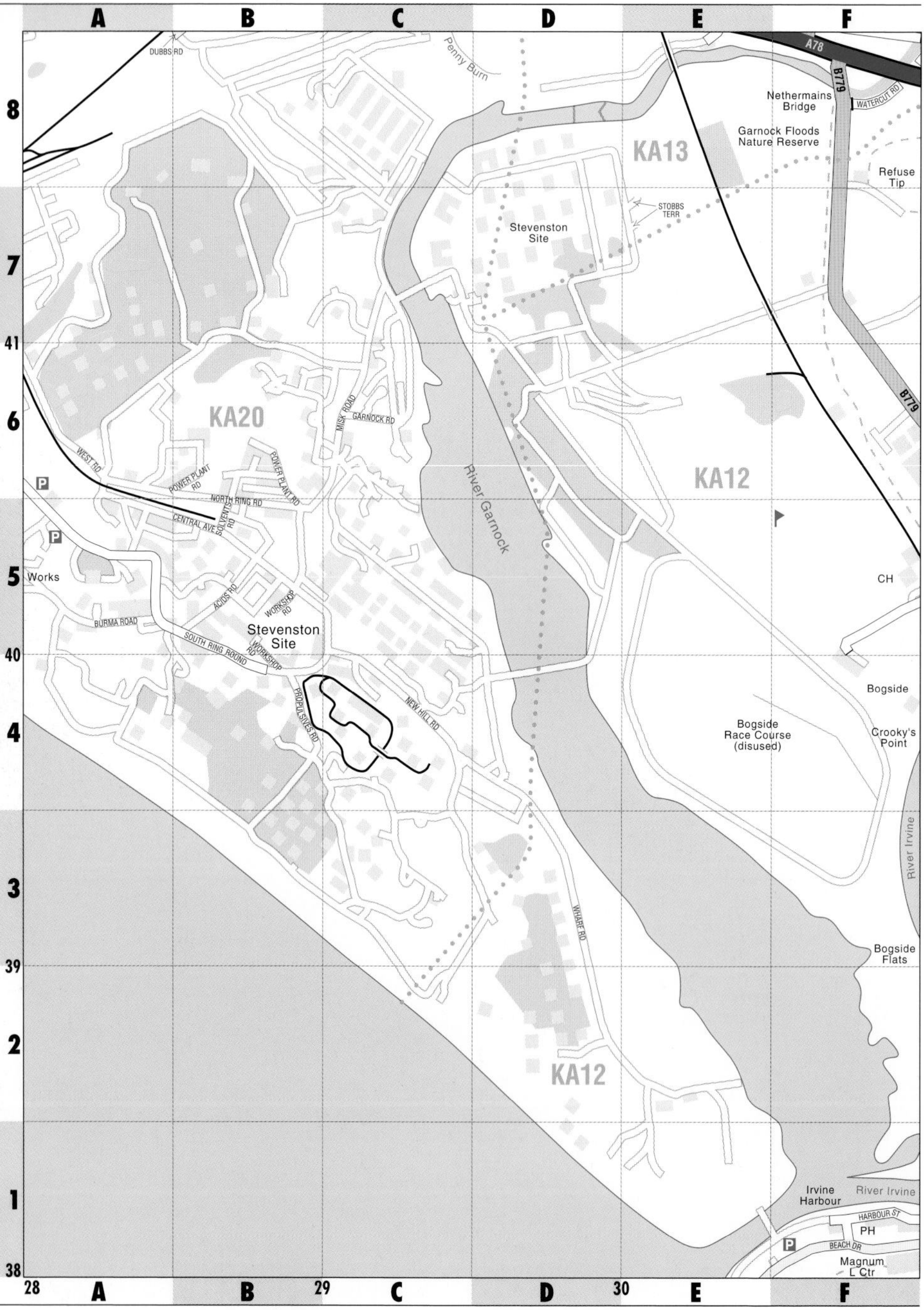
A
B
C
D
E
F
8
7
41
6
5
40
4
3
39
2
1
38
28
29
30
DUBBS RD
Penny Burn
A78
B779
Nethermains
Bridge
WATERCUT RD
Garnock Floods
Nature Reserve
KA13
Refuse
Tip
STOBBS
TERR
Stevenston
Site
KA20
MISK ROAD
GARNOCK RD
WEST RD
POWER PLANT
RD
POWER PLANT RD
NORTH RING RD
CENTRAL AVE
SOLVENTS
RD
River Garnock
KA12
P
Works
CH
ACIDS RD
WORKSHOP
RD
BURMA ROAD
Stevenston
Site
SOUTH RING ROUND
WORKSHOP
RD
PROPULSIVES RD
NEW HILL RD
Bogside
Bogside
Race Course
(disused)
Crooky's
Point
River Irvine
WHARF RD
Bogside
Flats
KA12
Irvine
Harbour
River Irvine
HARBOUR ST
PH
BEACH DR
Magnum
L Ctr

217

208
220

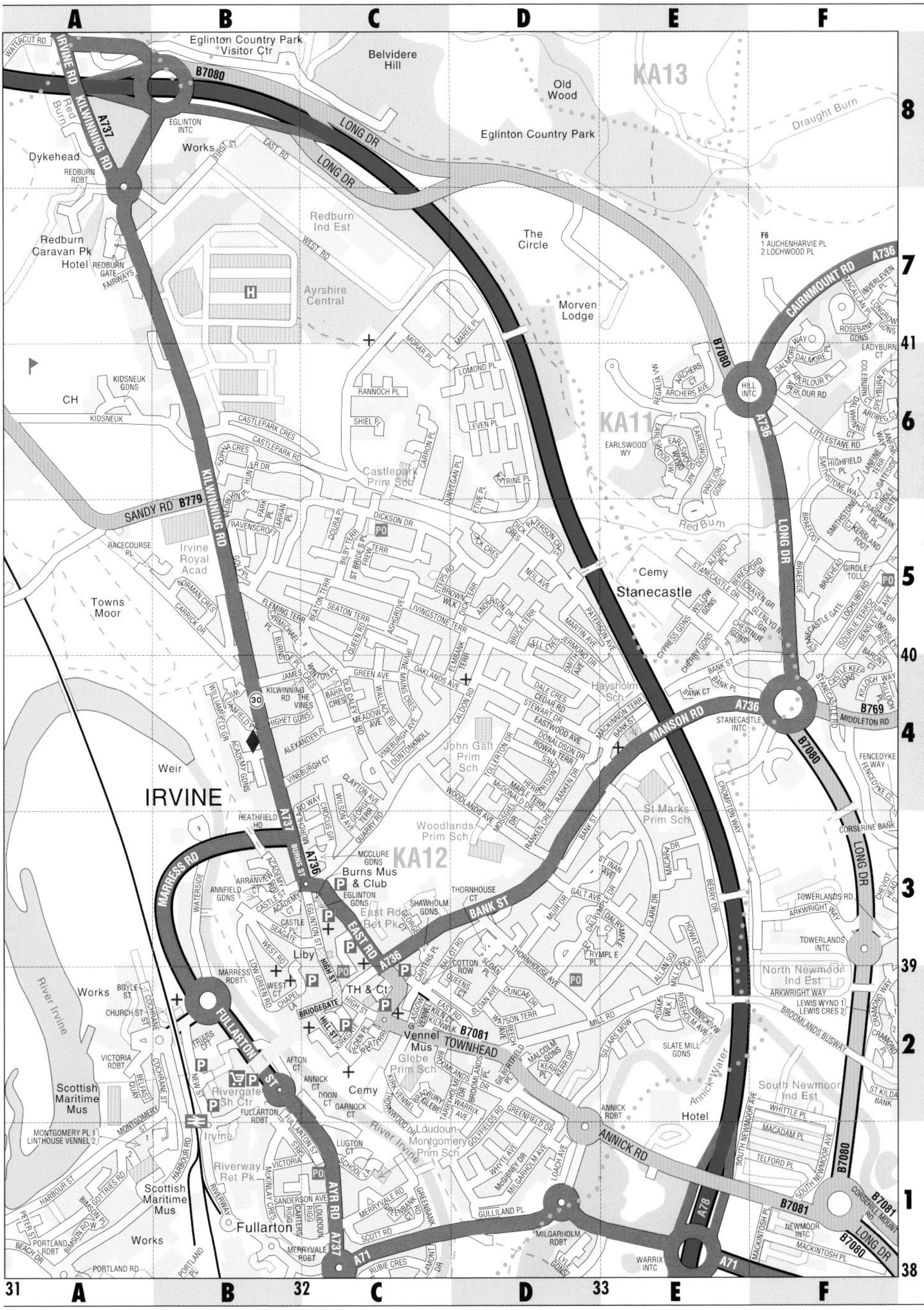

224
220

219
209

219
225

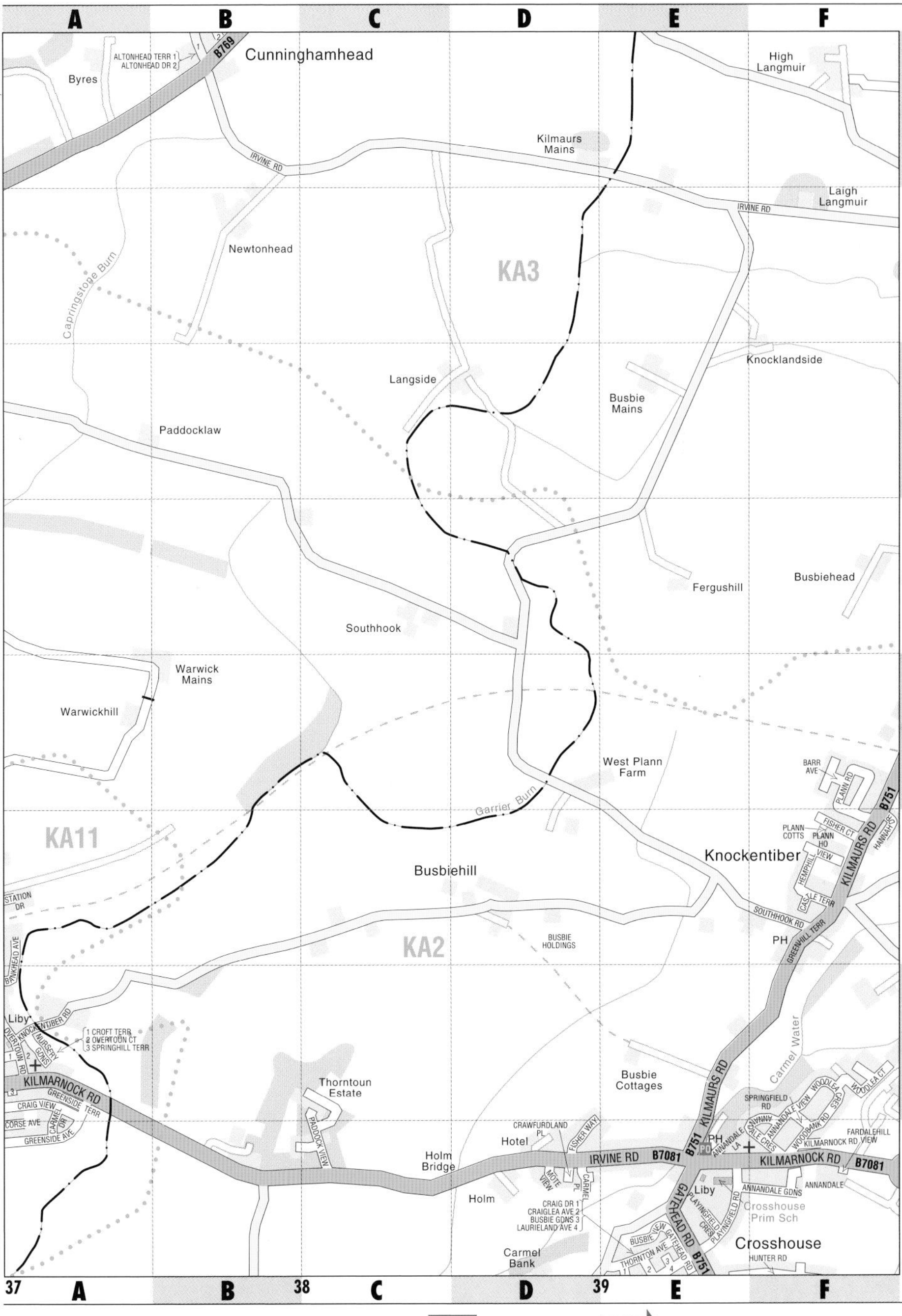
A
B
C
D
E
F
Cunninghamhead
Byres
ALTONHEAD TERR 1
ALTONHEAD DR 2
B769
High Langmuir
8
Kilmaurs Mains
IRVINE RD
Laigh Langmuir
IRVINE RD
Newtonhead
KA3
7
Capringstone Burn
41
Knocklandside
Langside
Busbie Mains
6
Paddocklaw
Fergushill
Busbiehead
5
Southhook
40
Warwick Mains
Warwickhill
4
West Plann Farm
BARR AVE
PLANN RD
B751
Garrier Burn
KA11
FISHER CT
PLANN COTTS
PLANN HO
HANNAH DR
KILMAURS RD
VIEW
Knockentiber
HEMPHILL
Busbiehill
3
STATION DR
CASTLE TERR
SOUTHHOOK RD
KA2
BUSBIE HOLDINGS
PH
GREENVILL TERR
BANKHEAD AVE
39
Liby
KNOCKENTIBER RD
OVERTOUN RD
NURSERY GDNS
1 CROFT TERR
2 OVERTOUN CT
3 SPRINGHILL TERR
2
Carmel Water
KILMARNOCK RD
Thorntoun Estate
Busbie Cottages
KILMAURS RD
WOODLEA CT
CRAIG VIEW
GREENSIDE TERR
CARMEL DR
CORSE AVE
GREENSIDE AVE
SPRINGFIELD RD
WOODLEA CRES
ANNANDALE VIEW
WOODBANK RD
FARDALEHILL VIEW
KILMARNOCK RD
CRAWFURDLAND PL
FISHER WAY
PADDOCK VIEW
Hotel
Holm Bridge
IRVINE RD
B7081
B751
PH
PO
ANNANDALE LA
KILMARNOCK RD
B7081
MOTE VIEW
PL
CARMEL
Liby
ANNANDALE GDNS
ANNANDALE
1
Holm
CRAIG DR 1
CRAIGLEA AVE 2
BUSBIE GDNS 3
LAURIELAND AVE 4
GATEHEAD RD
PLAYINGFIELD CRES
PLAYINGFIELD RD
Crosshouse Prim Sch
BUSBIE VIEW
Crosshouse
Carmel Bank
THORNTON AVE
GATEHEAD RD
B751
HUNTER RD
38
37
38
39

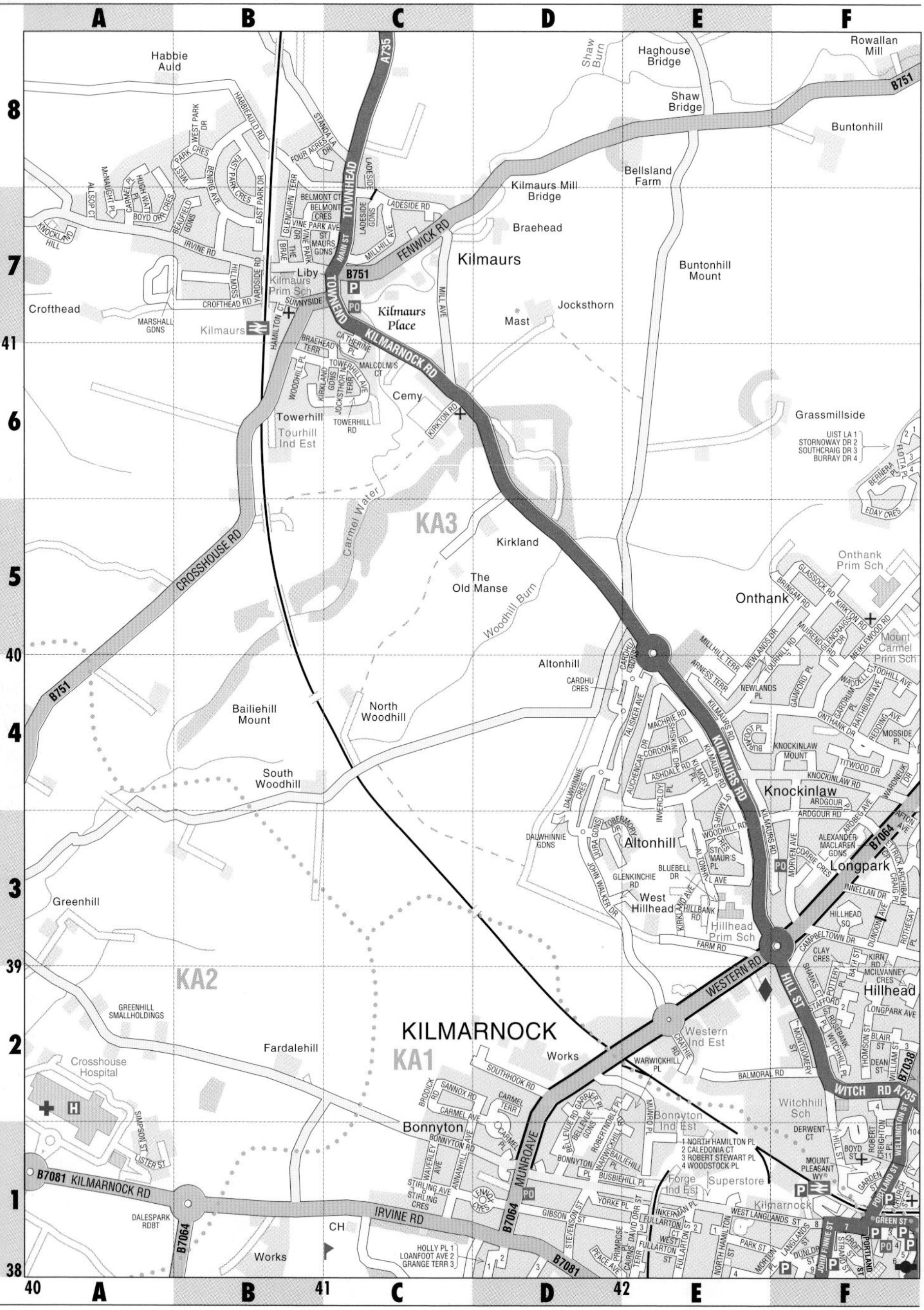

F1
1 UNION ST
2 HIGH CHURCH LA
3 SQUARE OF ALES
4 THE FOREGATE
5 JAMES SHAW LA
6 FOREGATE SQ
7 WEST GEORGE ST
8 LANGLANDS BRAE
9 JOHN DICKIE ST
10 FULTON'S LA
11 DEAN CT

F2
1 MONTGOMERY PL
2 HILLPARK DR
3 ORCHARD ST
4 WELLINGTON PL

212

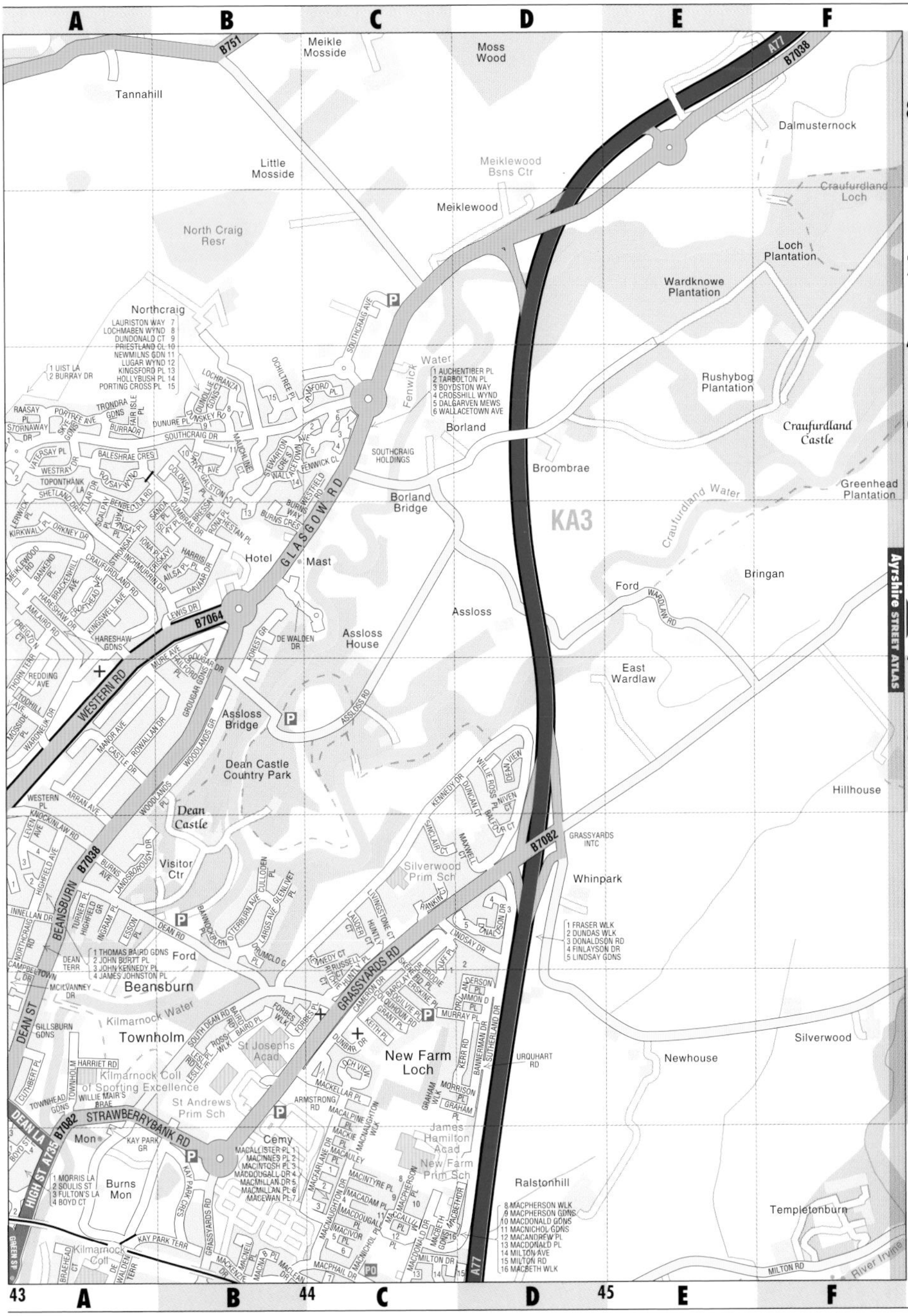
A
B
C
D
E
F
Meikle Mosside
Moss Wood
Tannahill
Dalmusternock
Little Mosside
Meiklewood Bsns Ctr
Craufurdland Loch
Meiklewood
North Craig Resr
Loch Plantation
Wardknowe Plantation
Northcraig
LAURISTON WAY 7
LOCHMABEN WYND 8
DUNDONALD CT 9
PRIESTLAND CL 10
NEWMILNS GDN 11
LUGAR WYND 12
KINGSFORD PL 13
HOLLYBUSH PL 14
PORTING CROSS PL 15
1 UIST LA
2 BURRAY DR
Fenwick Water
1 AUCHENTIBER PL
2 TARBOLTON PL
3 BOYDSTON WAY
4 CROSSHILL WYND
5 DALGARVEN MEWS
6 WALLACETOWN AVE
Rushybog Plantation
Borland
Craufurdland Castle
SOUTHCRAIG HOLDINGS
Broombrae
Greenhead Plantation
Craufurdland Water
Borland Bridge
KA3
GLASGOW RD
Hotel
Mast
Bringan
Ford
Assloss
Assloss House
East Wardlaw
Assloss Bridge
Dean Castle Country Park
Hillhouse
Dean Castle
GRASSYARDS INTC
Visitor Ctr
Silverwood Prim Sch
Whinpark
1 FRASER WLK
2 DUNDAS WLK
3 DONALDSON RD
4 FINLAYSON DR
5 LINDSAY GDNS
1 THOMAS BAIRD GDNS
2 JOHN BURTT PL
3 JOHN KENNEDY PL
4 JAMES JOHNSTON PL
Ford
Beansburn
Kilmarnock Water
Townholm
St Josephs Acad
New Farm Loch
Silverwood
Newhouse
URQUHART RD
Kilmarnock Coll of Sporting Excellence
St Andrews Prim Sch
WILLIE MAIR'S BRAE
STRAWBERRYBANK RD
Mon
Cemy
James Hamilton Acad
New Farm Prim Sch
Ralstonhill
1 MORRIS LA
2 SOULIS ST
3 FULTON'S LA
4 BOYD CT
Burns Mon
MACALLISTER PL 1
MACINNES PL 2
MACINTOSH PL 3
MACDOUGALL DR 4
MACMILLAN DR 5
MACMILLAN PL 6
MACEWAN PL 7
8 MACPHERSON WLK
9 MACPHERSON GDNS
10 MACDONALD GDNS
11 MACNICHOL GDNS
12 MACANDREW PL
13 MACDONALD PL
14 MILTON AVE
15 MILTON RD
16 MACBETH WLK
Templetonburn
Kilmarnock Coll
MILTON RD
River Irvine
A77
B7038
B751
B7064
B7082
A735
Ayrshire STREET ATLAS
8
7
41
6
5
40
4
3
39
2
1
38
43
44
45

219

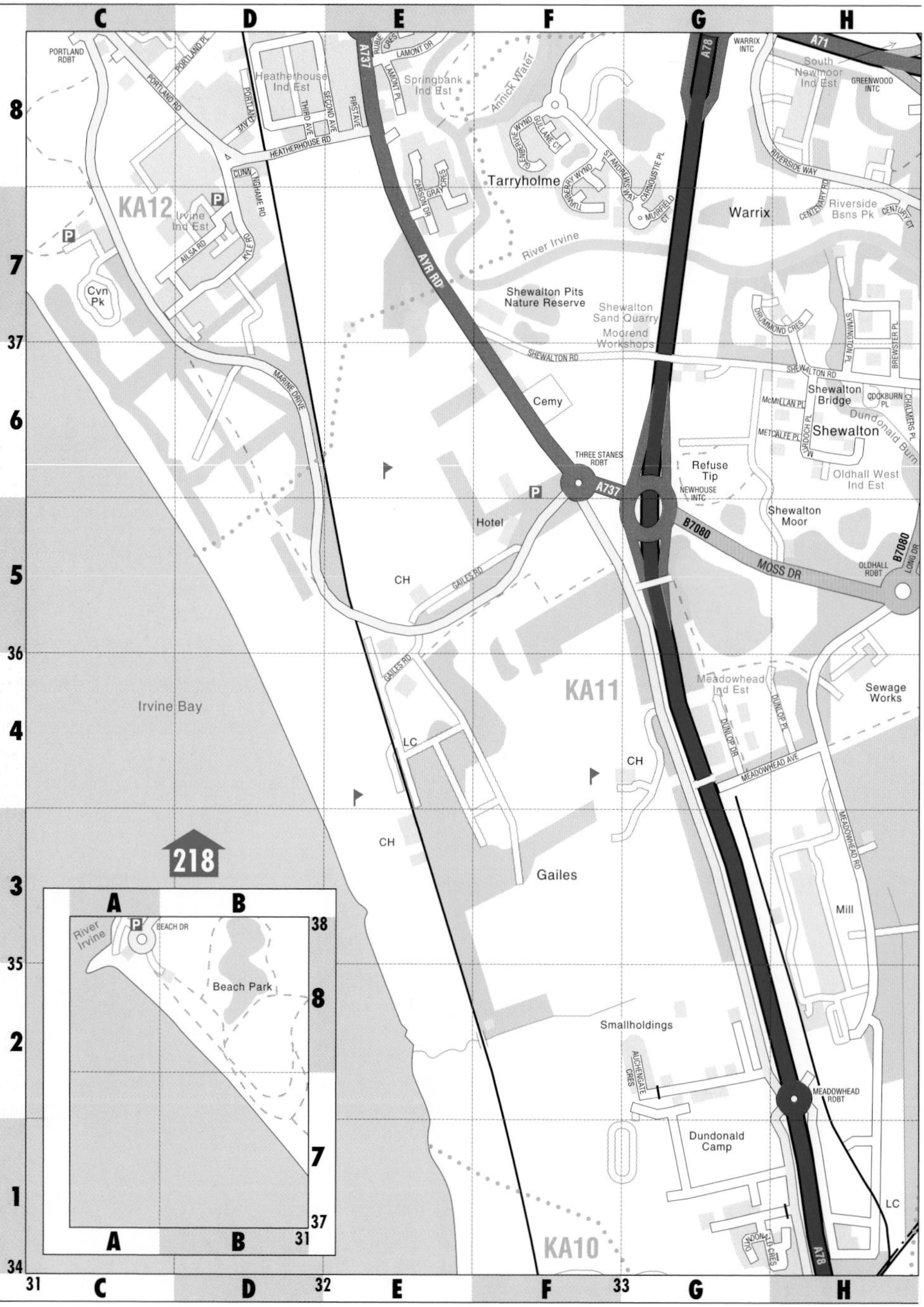
C
D
E
F
G
H
8
7
37
6
5
36
4
3
35
2
1
34
31
32
33
PORTLAND RDBT
PORTLAND PL
PORTLAND RD
PORTLAND AVE
Heatherhouse Ind Est
THIRD AVE
SECOND AVE
FIRST AVE
HEATHERHOUSE RD
A737
RUBIE CRES
LAMONT DR
LAMONT PL
Springbank Ind Est
Annick Water
GLENBERVIE WYND
GULLANE CT
TURNBERRY WYND
ST ANDREWS WAY
CARNOUSTIE PL
MUIRFIELD CT
A78
WARRIX INTC
A71
South Newmoor Ind Est
GREENWOOD INTC
RIVERSIDE WAY
CENTENARY RD
Riverside Bsns Pk
CENTURY CT
Warrix
Tarryholme
CARSON DR
GRAY CRES
CUNNINGHAME RD
KA12
Irvine Ind Est
AILSA RD
KYLE RD
Cvn Pk
AYR RD
River Irvine
Shewalton Pits Nature Reserve
Shewalton Sand Quarry
Moorend Workshops
DRUMMOND CRES
SYMINGTON PL
BREWSTER PL
SHEWALTON RD
MARINE DRIVE
Cemy
Shewalton Bridge
COCKBURN PL
McMILLAN PL
METCALFE PL
MURDOCH PL
Shewalton
CHALMERS PL
Dundonald Burn
THREE STANES RDBT
A737
Refuse Tip
Oldhall West Ind Est
NEWHOUSE INTC
Hotel
Shewalton Moor
B7080
MOSS DR
B7080
OLDHALL RDBT
LONG DR
CH
GAILES RD
GAILES RD
Meadowhead Ind Est
KA11
Sewage Works
Irvine Bay
DUNLOP DR
DUNLOP PL
LC
CH
MEADOWHEAD AVE
MEADOWHEAD RD
CH
Gailes
218
A
B
River Irvine
BEACH DR
38
Beach Park
8
7
37
31
Mill
Smallholdings
AUCHENGATE CRES
MEADOWHEAD RDBT
Dundonald Camp
LC
DUNDONALD CRES
KA10
A78

229

220
226

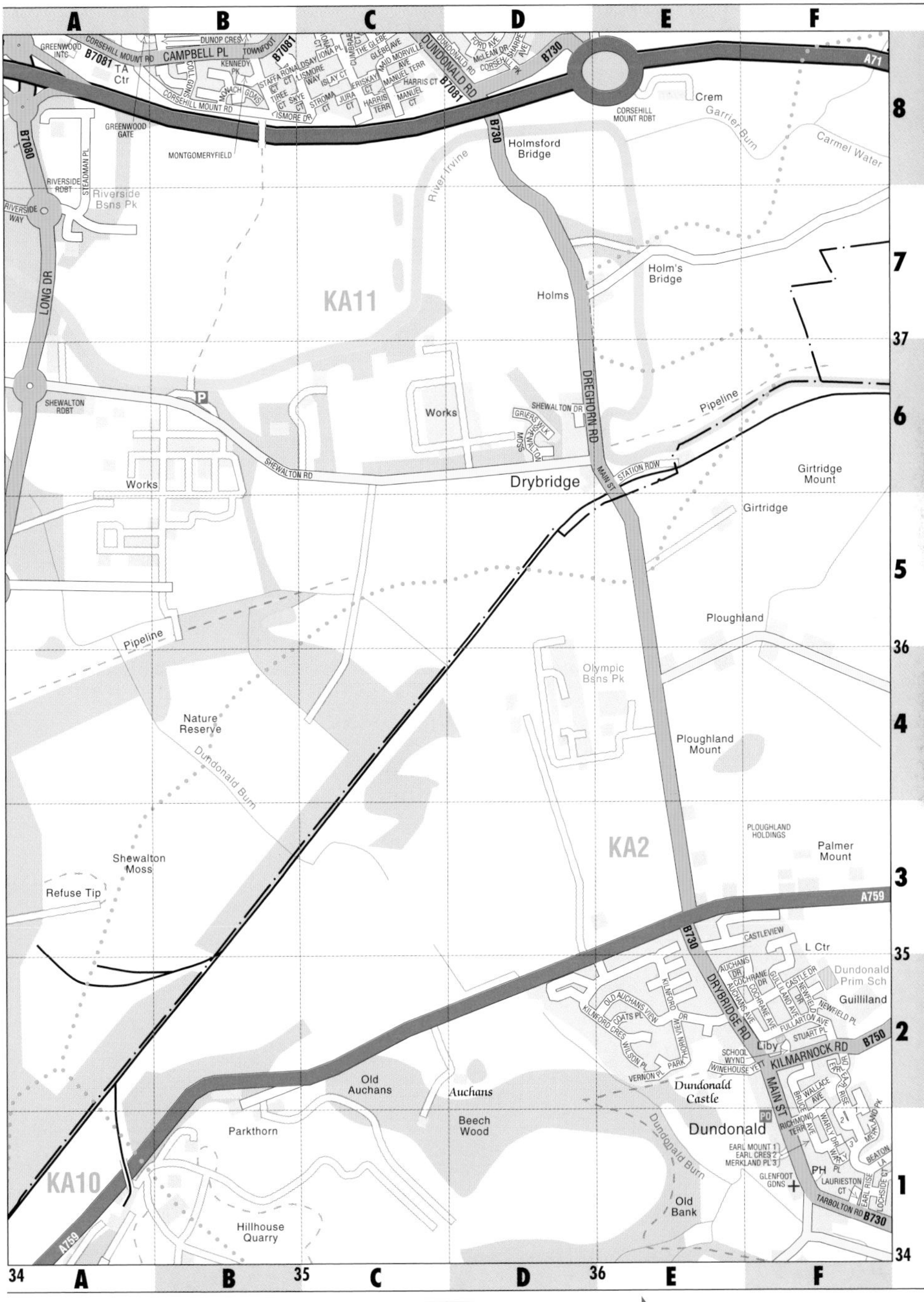

230
226

225
221

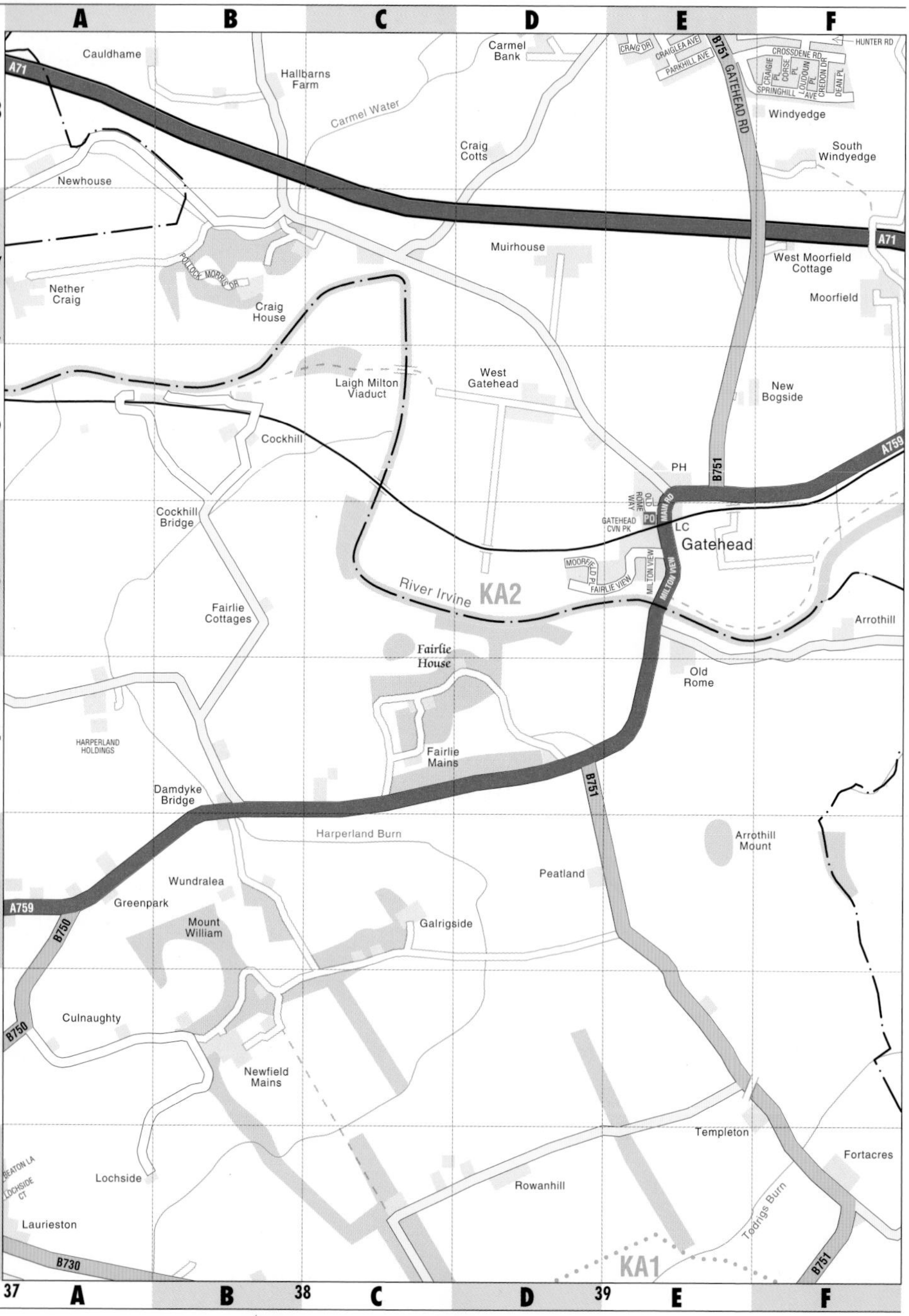

225
231

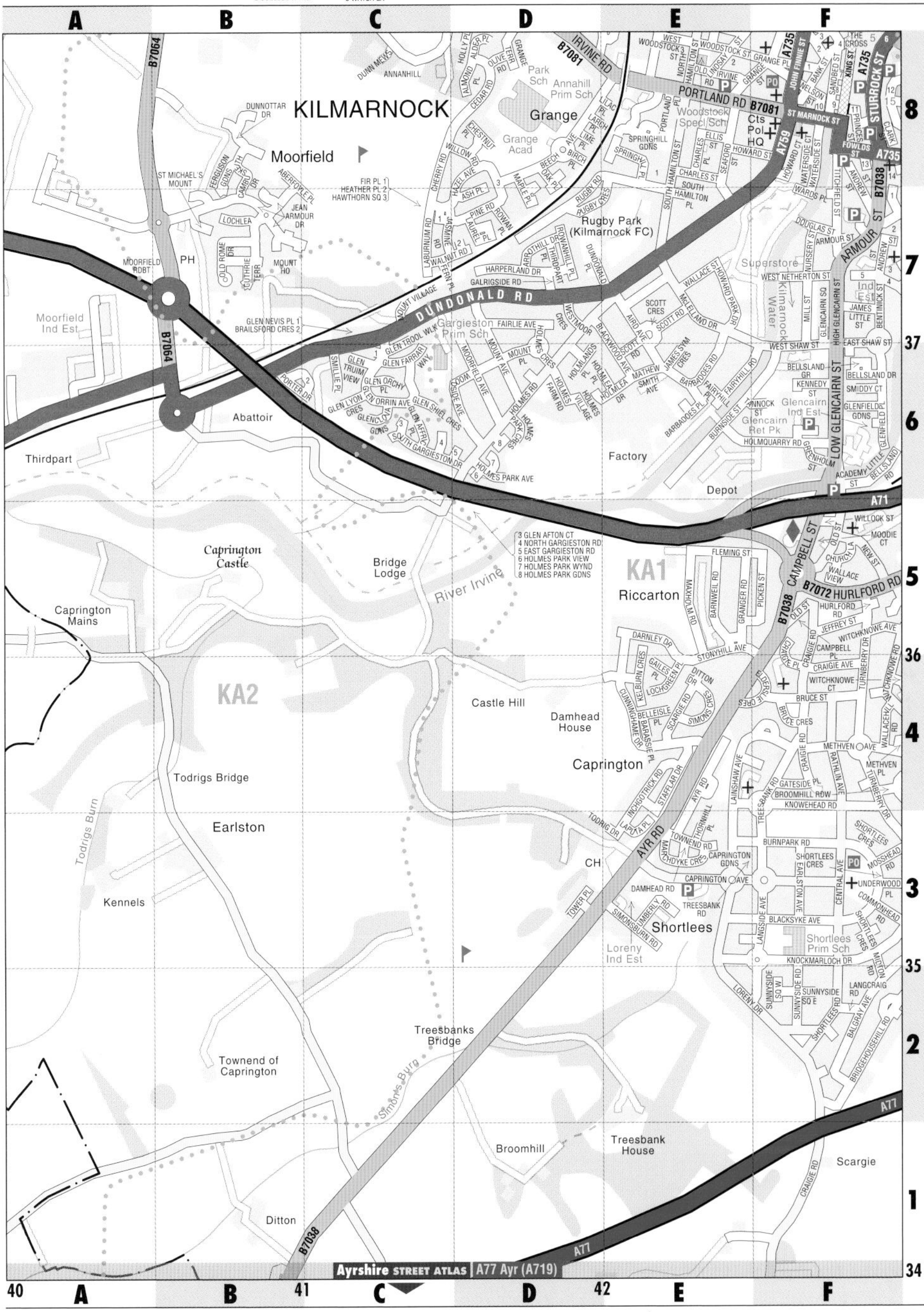
A
B
C
D
E
F
KILMARNOCK
Moorfield
Grange
Park Sch
Annahill Prim Sch
Grange Acad
Rugby Park (Kilmarnock FC)
PORTLAND RD
DUNDONALD RD
Moorfield Ind Est
MOORFIELD RDBT
PH
Abattoir
Thirdpart
Gargieston Prim Sch
Factory
Depot
Superstore
Kilmarnock Water
Glencairn Ind Est
Glencairn Ret Pk
LOW GLENCAIRN ST
HIGH GLENCAIRN ST
Woodstock Spec Sch
Cts
Pol HQ
A71
Caprington Castle
Bridge Lodge
River Irvine
KA1
Riccarton
CAMPBELL ST
B7072 HURLFORD RD
Caprington Mains
KA2
Castle Hill
Damhead House
Caprington
Todrigs Bridge
Earlston
Todrigs Burn
Kennels
AYR RD
CH
Shortlees
Loreny Ind Est
Shortlees Prim Sch
Treesbanks Bridge
Townend of Caprington
Simons Burn
Broomhill
Treesbank House
Scargie
Ditton
A77
B7038
B7064
B7081
8
7
37
6
5
36
4
3
35
2
1
34
40
41
42

A8
1 ACADAEMY APARTMENTS
2 GLEBE CT
3 MITCHELL CT
4 Loanhead Prim Sch

227
223

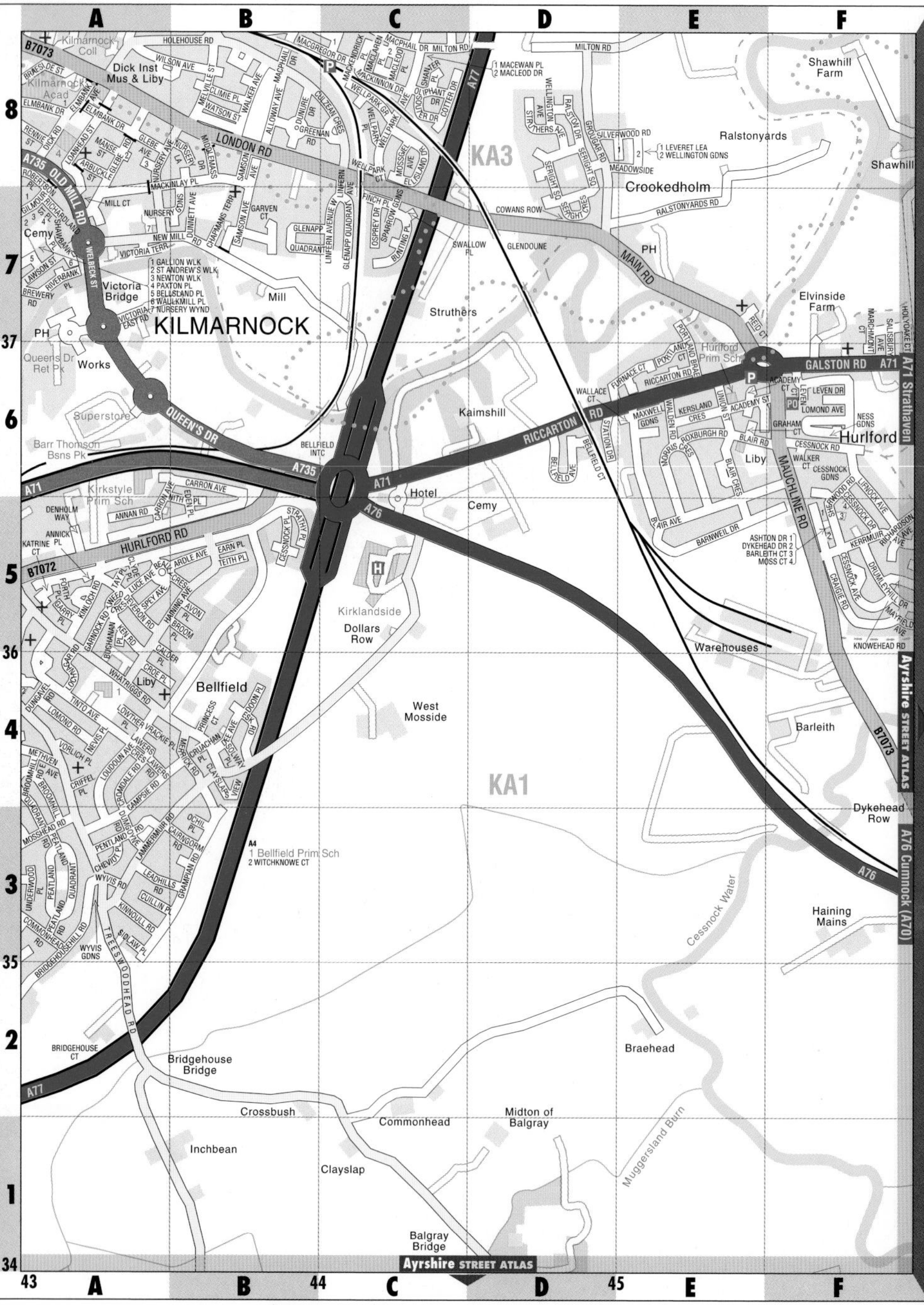

227

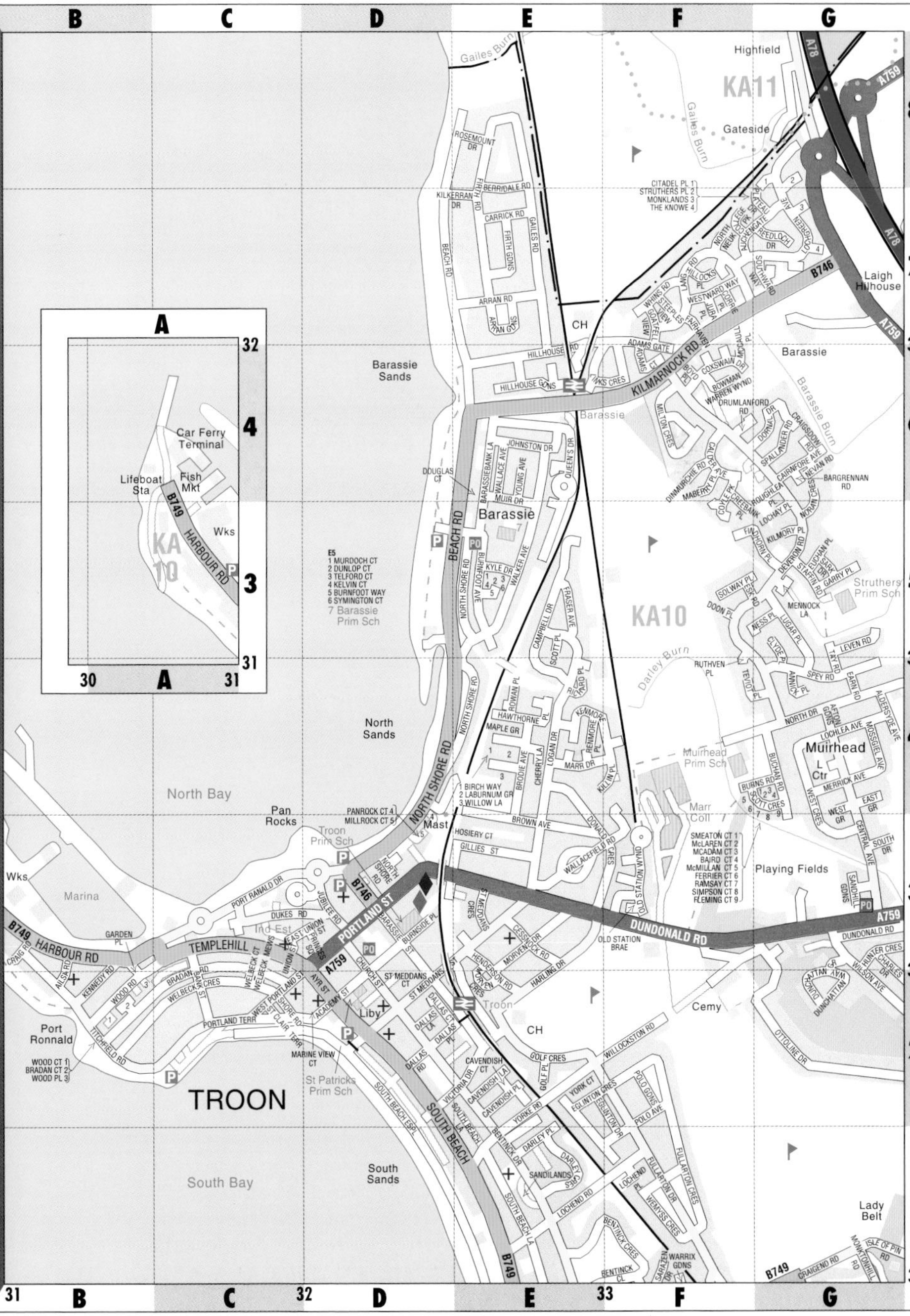
B
C
D
E
F
G
8
7
6
5
4
3
2
1
33
32
31
30
Highfield
KA11
Gateside
Gailes Burn
A78
A759
ROSEMOUNT DR
BERRIDALE RD
KILKERRAN DR
FIRTH RD
CARRICK RD
FIRTH GDNS
GAILES RD
BEACH RD
ARRAN RD
ARRAN GDNS
CITADEL PL 1
STRUTHERS PL 2
MONKLANDS 3
THE KNOWE 4
Laigh Hilhouse
B746
CH
HILLHOUSE RD
HILLHOUSE GDNS
KILMARNOCK RD
Barassie
Barassie Sands
Barassie Burn
JOHNSTON DR
QUEEN'S DR
DOUGLAS CT
BARASSIEBANK LA
WALLACE AVE
YOUNG AVE
MUIR DR
BARGRENNAN RD
E5
1 MURDOCH CT
2 DUNLOP CT
3 TELFORD CT
4 KELVIN CT
5 BURNFOOT WAY
6 SYMINGTON CT
7 Barassie Prim Sch
KYLE DR
WALKER AVE
NORTH SHORE RD
Struthers Prim Sch
KA10
MENNOCK LA
Darley Burn
LEVEN RD
RUTHVEN PL
SPEY RD
North Sands
North Bay
HAWTHORNE PL
MAPLE GR
ROWAN PL
FRASER AVE
CAMPBELL DR
SCOTT PL
Muirhead
Muirhead Prim Sch
L Ctr
1 BIRCH WAY
2 LABURNUM GR
3 WILLOW LA
Pan Rocks
PANROCK CT 4
MILLROCK CT 5
Troon Prim Sch
Mast
BROWN AVE
HOSIERY CT
GILLIES ST
Marr Coll
SMEATON CT 1
McLAREN CT 2
MCADAM CT 3
BAIRD CT 4
McMILLAN CT 5
FERRIER CT 6
RAMSAY CT 7
SIMPSON CT 8
FLEMING CT 9
Playing Fields
Wks
Marina
PORT RANALD DR
DUKES RD
Ind Est
PORTLAND ST
B746
A759
DUNDONALD RD
OLD STATION BRAE
B749
HARBOUR RD
TEMPLEHILL
GARDEN PL
PO
Troon
Cemy
CH
Liby
Port Ronnald
WOOD CT 1
BRADAN CT 2
WOOD PL 3
PORTLAND TERR
MARINE VIEW CT
St Patricks Prim Sch
TROON
SOUTH BEACH ESPL
SOUTH BEACH
GOLF CRES
WILLOCKSTON RD
OTTOLINE DR
South Bay
South Sands
SANDILANDS
LOCHEND RD
FULLARTON CRES
Lady Belt
CRAIGEND RD
MONKTONHILL RD
ISLE OF PIN RD
BENTINCK CL
WARRIX GDNS
A
32
4
Car Ferry Terminal
Lifeboat Sta
Fish Mkt
Wks
KA 10
HARBOUR RD
3
30
31

229
225

229
233

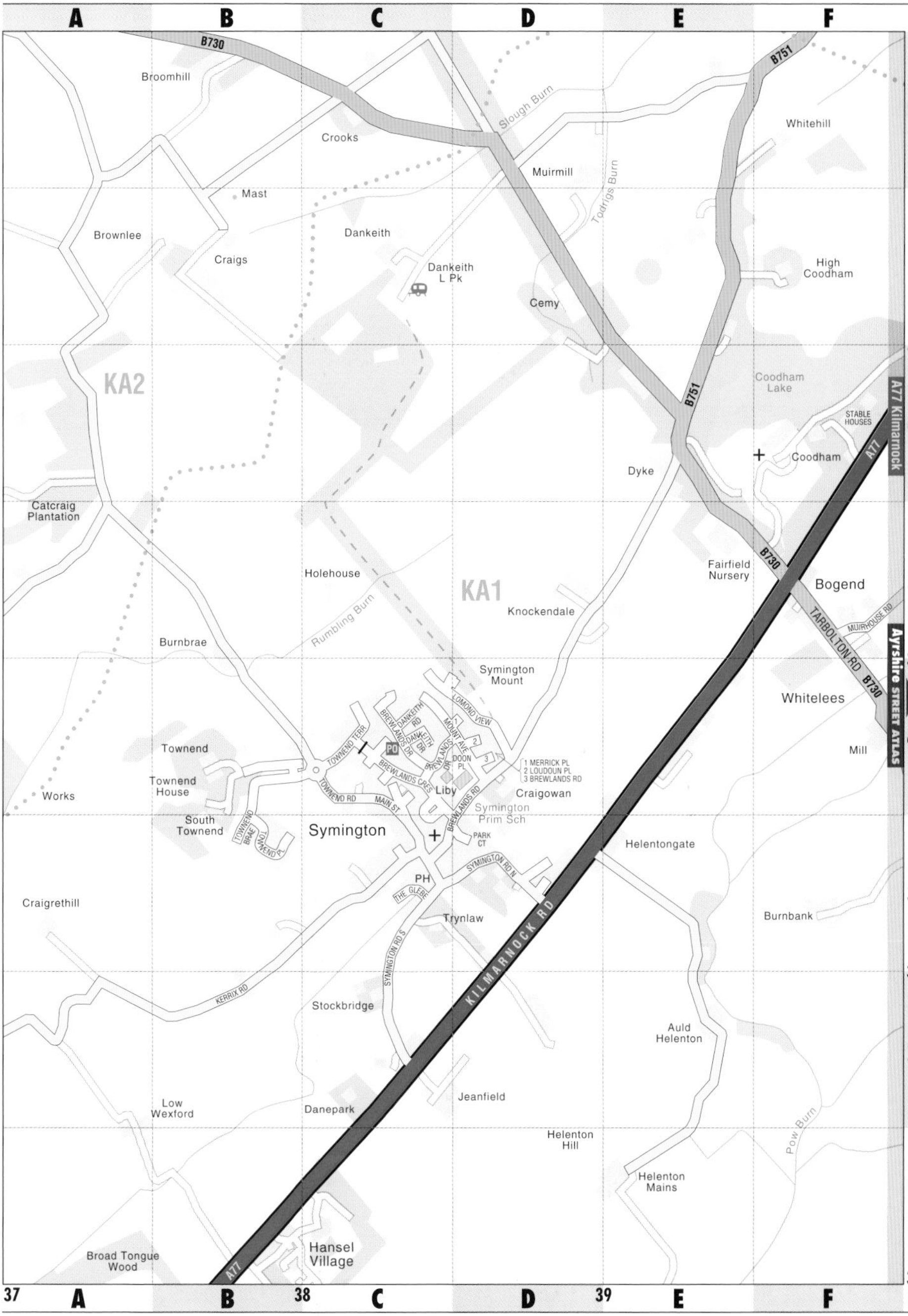
A
B
C
D
E
F
8
7
6
5
4
3
2
1
33
32
31
30
37
38
39
B730
B751
Broomhill
Crooks
Slough Burn
Whitehill
Muirmill
Todrigs Burn
Mast
Brownlee
Dankeith
Craigs
Dankeith
L Pk
High
Coodham
Cemy
KA2
Coodham
Lake
A77 Kilmarnock
STABLE
HOUSES
Coodham
A77
Dyke
Catcraig
Plantation
Fairfield
Nursery
Bogend
Holehouse
KA1
Knockendale
Rumbling Burn
TARBOLTON RD
MUIRHOUSE RD
Burnbrae
Symington
Mount
Ayrshire STREET ATLAS
Whitelees
LOMOND VIEW
Townend
TOWNEND TERR
BREWLANDS DR
DANKEITH RD
DANKEITH DR
MOUNT AVE
DOON PL
BREWLANDS CRES
BREWLANDS DR
PO
Mill
1 MERRICK PL
2 LOUDOUN PL
3 BREWLANDS RD
Townend
House
Works
TOWNEND RD
MAIN ST
Liby
BREWLANDS RD
Craigowan
Symington
Prim Sch
South
Townend
TOWNEND BRAE
TOWNEND PL
Symington
PARK CT
Helentongate
PH
SYMINGTON RD N
THE GLEBE
Craigrethill
Trynlaw
Burnbank
KILMARNOCK RD
SYMINGTON RD S
KERRIX RD
Stockbridge
Auld
Helenton
Low
Wexford
Jeanfield
Danepark
Helenton
Hill
Pow Burn
Helenton
Mains
Broad Tongue
Wood
Hansel
Village

229

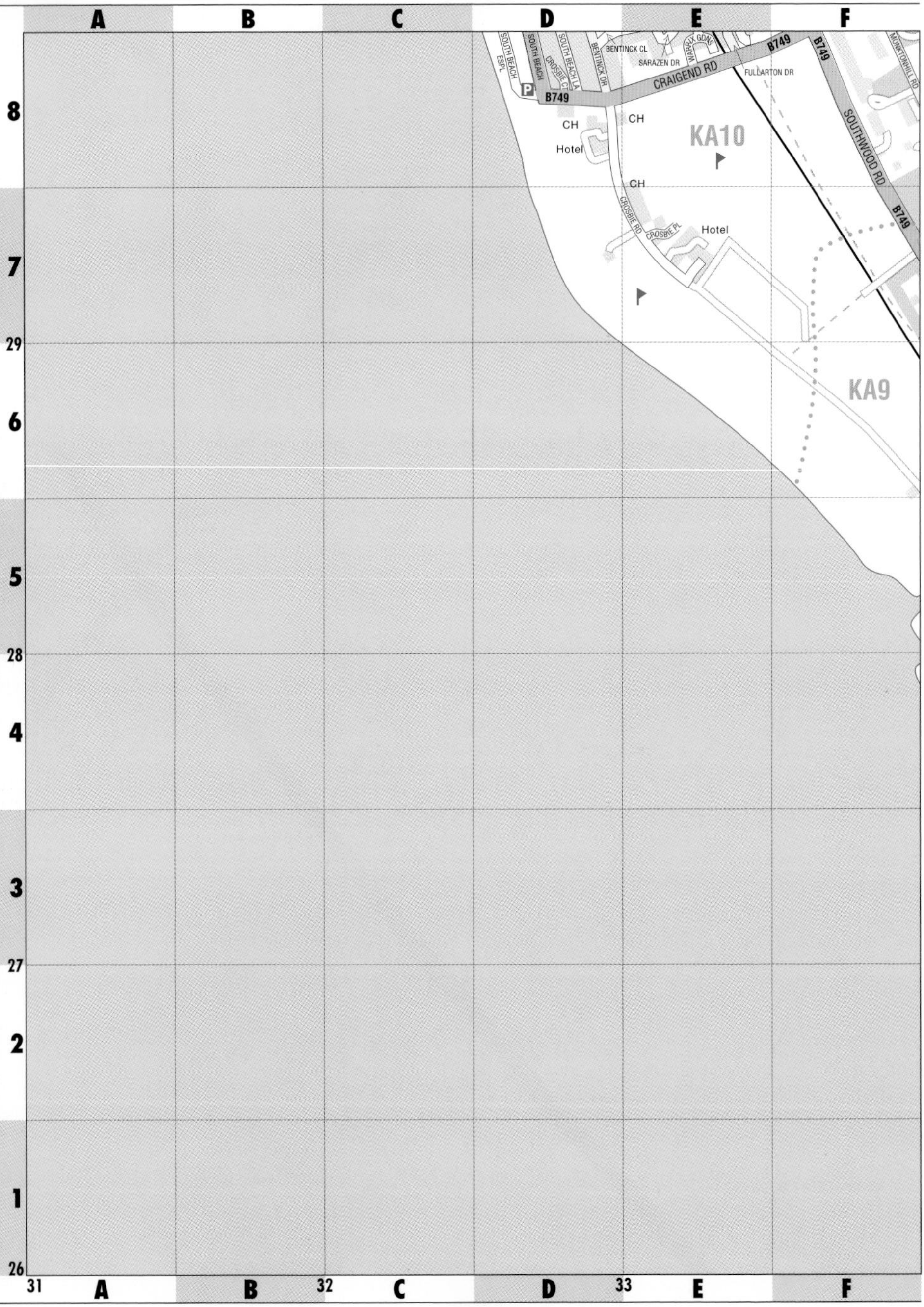

A
B
C
D
E
F
8
7
29
6
5
28
4
3
27
2
1
26
31
32
33
SOUTH BEACH ESPL
SOUTH BEACH
CROSBIE CT
SOUTH BEACH LA
BENTINCK DR
BENTINCK CL
SARAZEN DR
WARRIX GDNS
CRAIGEND RD
B749
FULLARTON DR
MONKTONHILL RD
SOUTHWOOD RD
P
CH
Hotel
KA10
CROSBIE RD
CROSBIE PL
KA9

235

230
234

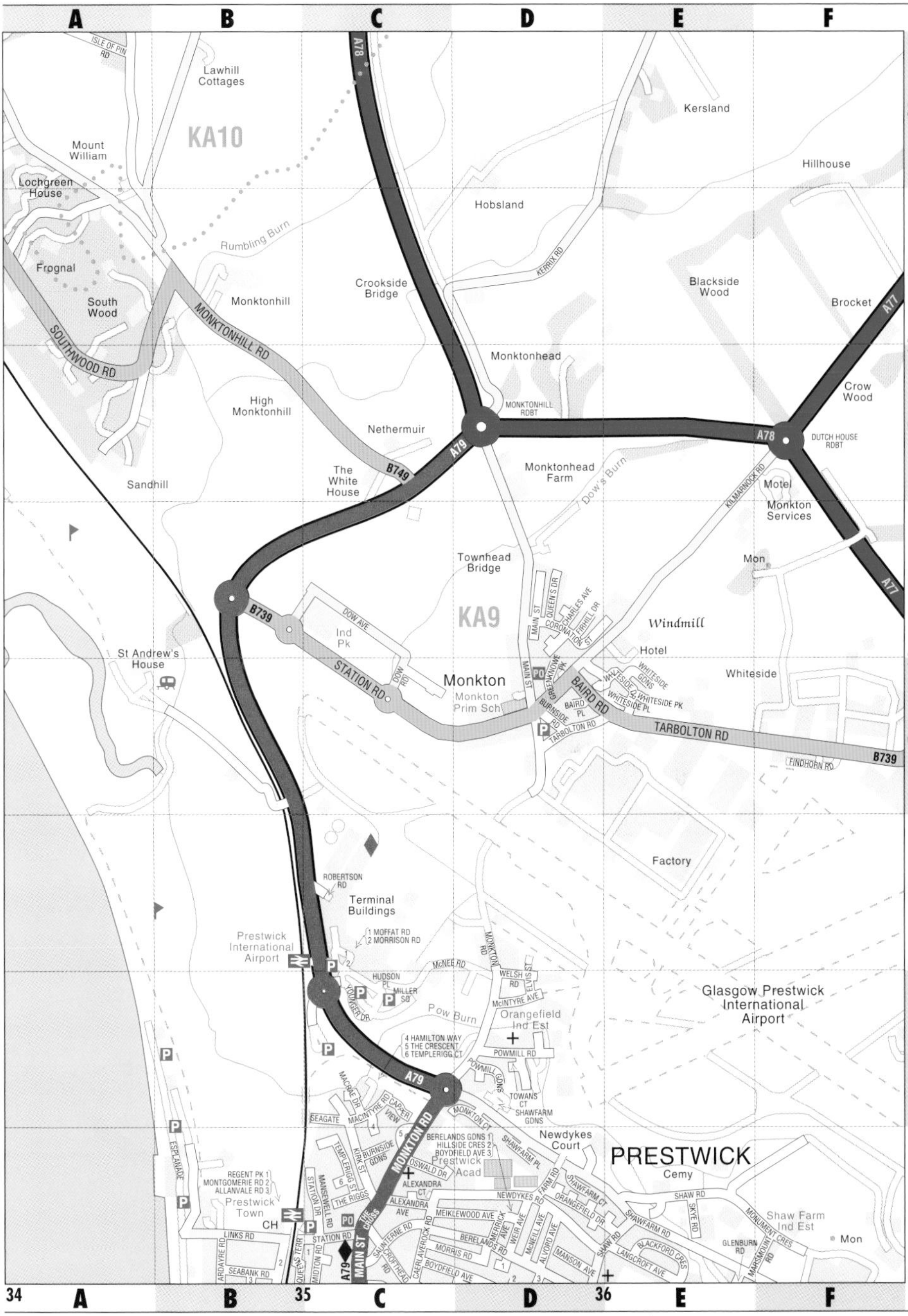

236
234

233
231

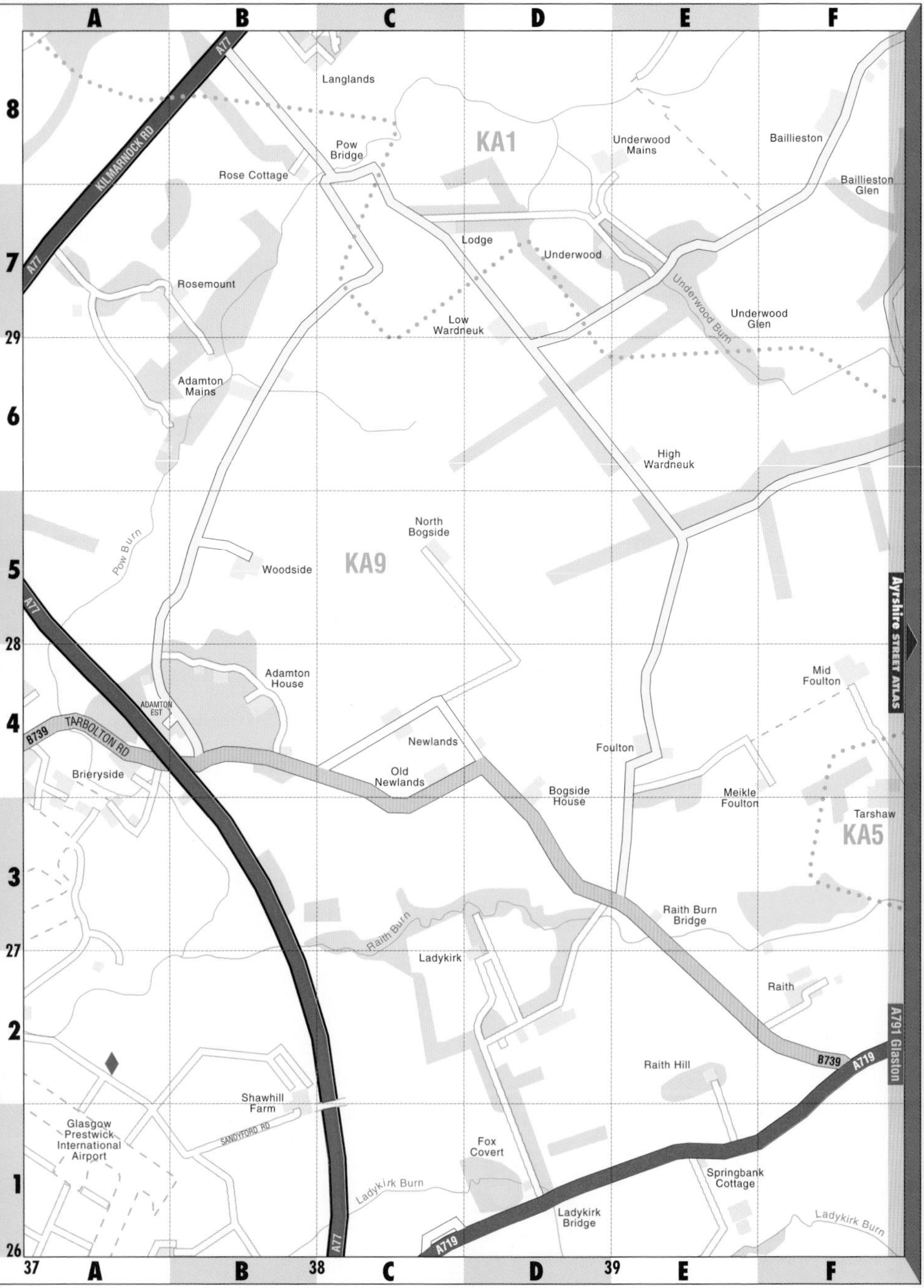

233
237

232
236

238
236

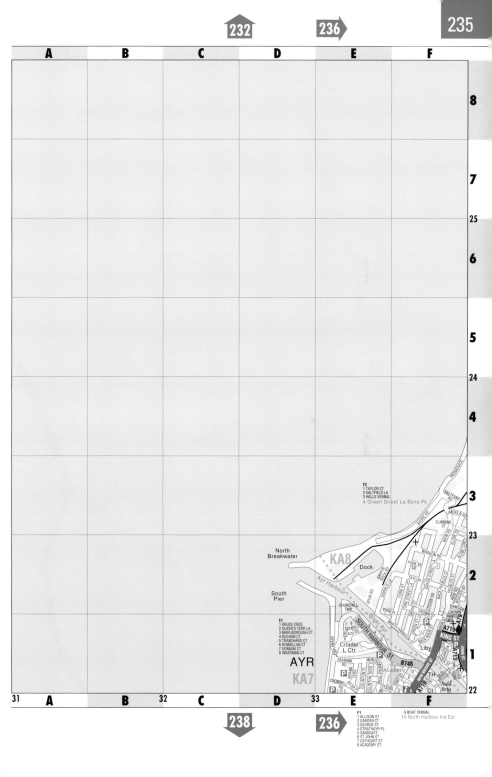

F1
1 ALLISON ST
2 GARDEN CT
3 GEORGE ST
4 STRATHAYR PL
5 SANDGATE
6 ST JOHN ST
7 CATHCART ST
8 ACADEMY ST
9 BOAT VENNAL
10 North Harbour Ind Est

235
233

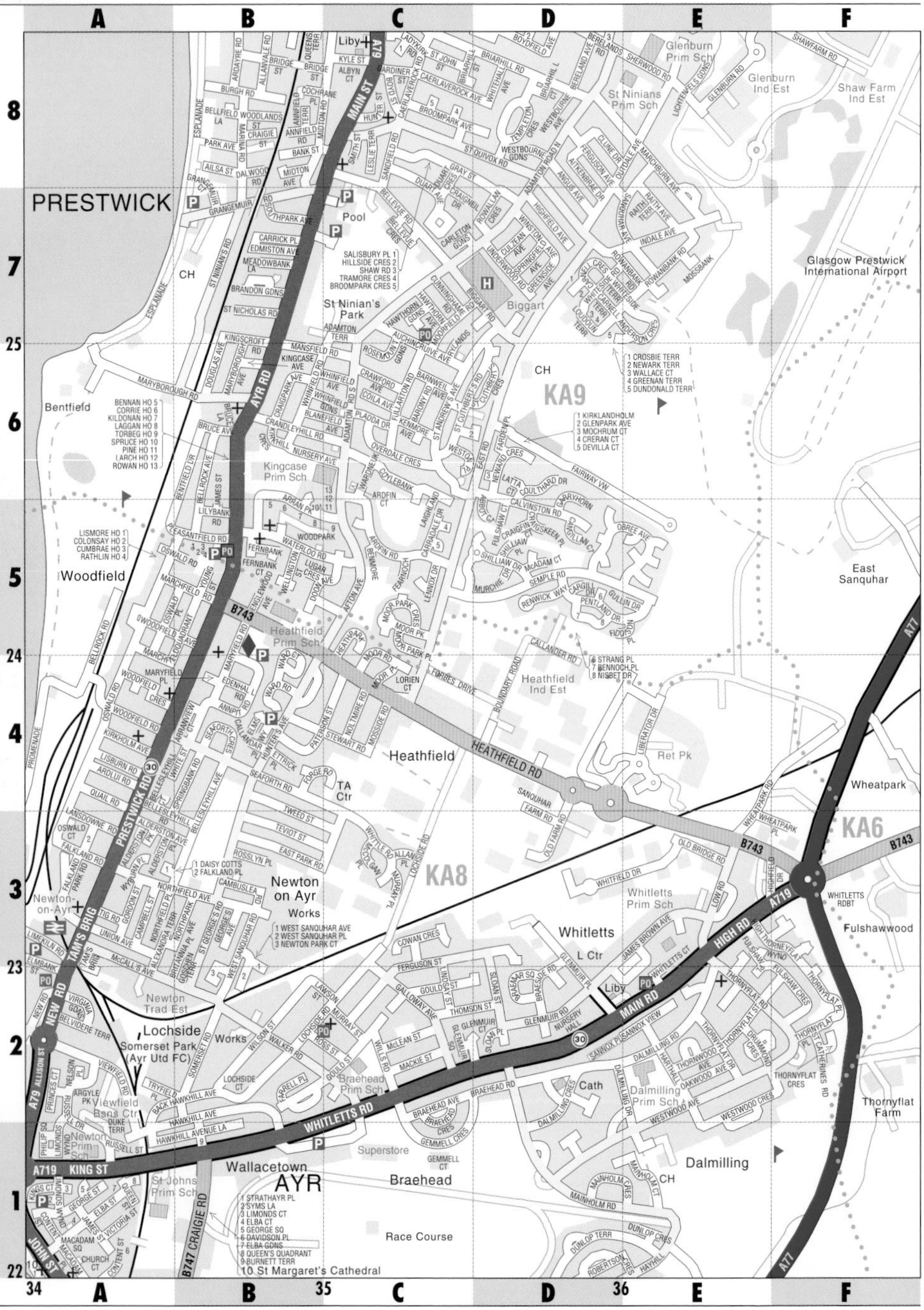

235
239

Ayrshire STREET ATLAS
Ayrshire STREET ATLAS

235
A
B
C
D
E
F
8
7
21
6
5
20
4
3
19
2
1
18
31
32
33
Ayrshire STREET ATLAS
A719 Turnberry, Girvan (A77)
QUEEN'S TERRACE LA 1
CROMWELL RD 2
AILSA PL 3
BRUCE CRES 4
DOUGLAS LA 5
DOUGLAS ST 6
HOPE ST 7
LORNE ARC 8
BLACKFRIARS WLK 9
HOMEBRIAR HO 10
ARRAN MALL 11
KILLOCH PL 13
BURNS STATUE SQ 14
SMITH ST 15
PARKHOUSE ST 16
BURNS STATUE ARC 17
AYR
Low Green
ESPLANADE
CHARLOTTE ST
QUEEN'S TERR
BATH PL
PAVILION RD
WELLINGTON SQ
WELLINGTON LA
PARK TERR
ALLOWAY PL
SANDGATE
A719
NEWMARKET ST
RIVER VIEW
BARNS ST
BARNS PK
DALBLAIR RD
Kyle Ctr
MILLER RD
A70
FAIRFIELD RD
FAIRFIELD PK
BERESFORD CT
BERESFORD TERR
A79
PARK CIR
BELLEVUE ST
BELLEVUE CRES
BELLEVUE LA
SHIELING PK
SAVOY PK
SAVOY CT
WELLSBOURNE HO
WHEATFIELD RD
Wellington Sch
CRAIGWEIL RD
CRAIGWEIL PL
BLACKBURN DR
BLACKBURN RD
BLACKBURN PL
RACECOURSE RD
MARCHMONT RD
DORNOCH PK
Grammar Prim Sch
SOUTH LODGE CT
SPRINGVALE RD
SPRINGVALE PK
RONALDSHAW PK
CARRICK RD
CARRICK PK
CARRICK AVE
BOWMAN RD
BALLANTINE DR
WESTFIELD RD
CLARKE AVE
SEA TOWER CT
BENTFIELD AVE
SOUTHPARK RD
BROOMFIELD RD
CHALMERS RD
AIRLIE CT
VICTORIA PK
VICTORIA MANS
SEAFIELD RD
SEAFIELD CRES
RACECOURSE VIEW
ST LEONARD'S WYND
ST LEONARD'S RD
HAZELWOOD RD
B7024
HARTFIELD RD
Seafield
Playing Fields
ARROL PK
ARROL DR
SEAFIELD DR
CORSEHILL RD
CORSEHILL PK
CHAPELPARK RD
BELLEVALE AVE
EWENFIELD RD
EWENFIELD GDNS
CARWINSHOCH VIEW
AUCHENTRAE CRES
AUCHENDOON CRES
DOONFOOT RD
Cunning Park
KA7
Slaphouse Burn
Slaphouse
MONUMENT RD
LONGBANK RD
LONGBANK DR
LONGLANDS PK
KNOLL PK
Belleisle Bridge
Slaphouse Bridge
Belleisle
Hotel
CH
Belleisle Park
Longhill Point
GEARHOLM RD
GOUKSCROFT CT
CASTLE WLK
GREENAN RD
GREENAN PL
SCAUR O DOON RD
Doonfoot Prim Sch
LOCHPARK
ABBOTS WAY
Greenan
Rozelle Park
BELLEISLE COTTS
KNOWEHOLM
Rozelle House MacLaurin Galleries
ST VINCENT CRES
EARLS WAY
DOONVIEW GDNS
GREENFIELD AVE
ABBOTS CRES
CRAIG DR
DALTON PK
AILSA VW GDNS
AILSA VIEW WYND
GEORGE PL
AILSA VW PL
STRATHDOON PL
MOUNT CHARLES CRES
Mill
MOUNTCHARLES
Burns Cottage & Mus
Burton Smithy
DUNURE RD
Doonfoot
River Doon
SHALLOCH PK
Doonbank Farm
CAMBUSDOON DR
WRIGHTFIELD PL
ALLOWAY
High Greenan
CROSSBURN
NEWARK CRES
BROWNCARRICK DR
CORSERINE RD
CAIRNSMORE DR
GLENALLA CRES
Alloway
Alloway Prim Sch
Burns Mon
SHANTER WYND
SHANTER PL
SHANTER WAY
Liby
UPPER CROFTS
DOONHOLM RD
WOODEND RD
LAIGH MOUNT
A719
LONGHILL AVE
LAMFORD DR
PORTMARK AVE
CRAIGSTEWART CRES
BALMINNOCH PK
MURDOCH'S LONE
B7024
AULD NICKS VIEW
Tam O'Shanter Experience

236

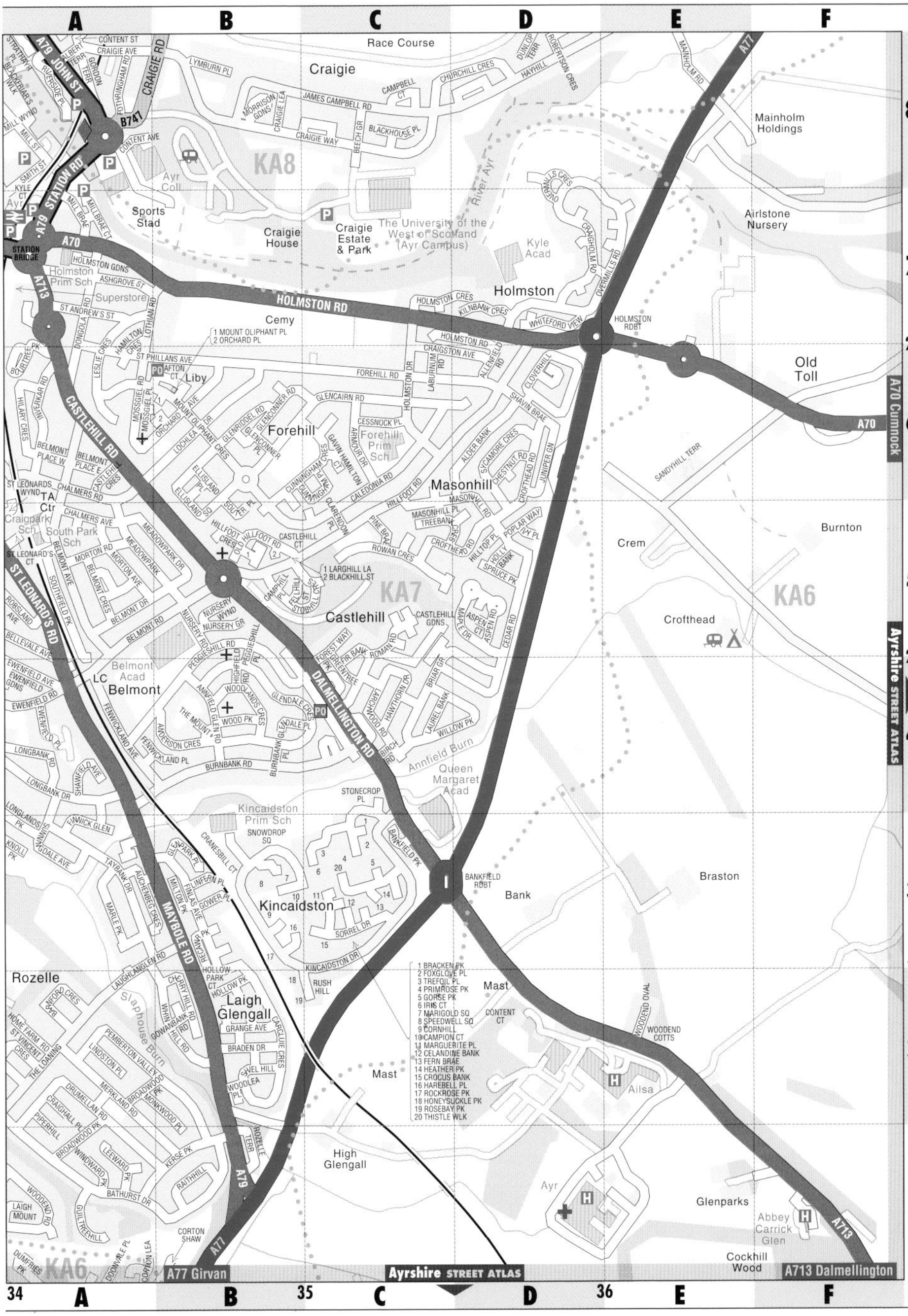
A
B
C
D
E
F
8
7
21
6
5
20
4
3
19
2
1
18
34
35
36
Race Course
Craigie
KA8
LYMBURN PL
JAMES CAMPBELL RD
CRAIGIE WAY
CAMPBELL CT
CHURCHILL CRES
BLACKHOUSE PL
BEECH GR
MORRISON GDNS
CRAIGIE LEA
DUNLOP TERR
ROBERTSON CRES
HAYHILL
MAINHOLM RD
Mainholm Holdings
A77
River Ayr
Ayr Coll
Sports Stad
Craigie House
Craigie Estate & Park
The University of the West of Scotland (Ayr Campus)
Kyle Acad
Airlstone Nursery
CRAIGHOLM RD
OVERMILLS RD
OVERMILLS CRES
CONTENT ST
CRAIGIE AVE
CRAIGIE RD
A79 JOHN ST
ALBERT TERR
GORDON
ROTHINGHAM RD
RIVERSIDE PL
MILL WYND
MILL ST
SMITH ST
KYLE CT
STATION RD
MILL BRAE
MILLBRAE CT
CONTENT AVE
B747
A79
A70
STATION BRIDGE
A713
HOLMSTON GDNS
ASHGROVE ST
Holmston Prim Sch
Superstore
ST ANDREW'S ST
HOLMSTON RD
Cemy
Holmston
HOLMSTON CRES
KILNBANK CRES
WHITEFORD VIEW
HOLMSTON RDBT
HOLMSTON RD
CRAIGSTON AVE
Old Toll
A70
A70 Cumnock
1 MOUNT OLIPHANT PL
2 ORCHARD PL
ST PHILLANS AVE
AFTON CT
Liby
FOREHILL RD
GLENCAIRN RD
HOLMSTON DR
LABURNUM RD
ALLENFIELD RD
CLOVERHILL
SHAVIN BRAE
CASTLEHILL RD
Forehill
Forehill Prim Sch
CESSNOCK PL
GAVIN HAMILTON CT
ARMOUR DR
CALEDONIA RD
HILLFOOT RD
Masonhill
MASONHILL RD
ALDER BANK
SYCAMORE CRES
CHESTNUT RD
CROFTHEAD RD
JUNIPER GN
SANDYHILL TERR
LESLIE CRES
HAMILTON CRES
DONGOLA RD
LOTHIAN RD
MOSSGIEL RD
MOSSGIEL PL
ORCHARD AVE
MOUNT OLIPHANT CRES
LOCHLEA AVE
GLENRIDDELL RD
GLENCONNER RD
GLENCONNER PL
CUNNINGHAM CRES
CLARENDON PL
ELLISLAND PL
ELLISLAND SQ
SOUTAR PL
HILLFOOT CRES
OLD HILLFOOT RD
CASTLEHILL CT
PINE BRAE
ROWAN CRES
MASONHILL PL
TREEBANK CRES
CROFTHEAD RD
HILLTOP PL
HOLLY BANK
SPRUCE PK
POPLAR WAY
IVY PL
BOURTREE PK
INVERKAR RD
HILARY CRES
BELMONT PLACE W
BELMONT PLACE E
CASTLEHILL CRES
ST LEONARDS WYND
CHALMERS RD
TA Ctr
Craigpark Sch
South Park Sch
CHALMERS AVE
MEADOWPARK
MEADOWPARK DR
MORTON RD
MORTON AVE
BELMONT CRES
BELMONT DR
BELMONT RD
BELMONT AVE
SOUTHFIELD PK
ST LEONARD'S CT
ST LEONARD'S RD
ROBSLAND AVE
BELLEVALE AVE
Burnton
Crem
KA6
1 LARGHILL LA
2 BLACKHILL ST
KA7
Castlehill
CAMPHILL PL
FELLHILL ST
STOBHILL GDS
CASTLEHILL GDNS
ASPEN CT
ASPEN RD
MAPLE DR
CEDAR RD
Crofthead
NURSERY WYND
NURSERY GR
PEGGIESHILL RD
PEGGIESHILL PL
HIGHFIELD RD
FOREST WAY
FIR BANK
ROMAN RD
GREENTREE PK
BRIAR GR
HAWTHORN DR
LARCHWOOD RD
LAUREL BANK
WILLOW PK
BIRCH RD
DALMELLINGTON RD
Belmont Acad
LC
Belmont
EWENFIELD AVE
EWENFIELD GDNS
EWENFIELD RD
EWENFIELD PL
FENWICKLAND AVE
FENWICKLAND PL
ANNFIELD GLEN RD
THE MOUNT
WOODLANDS CRES
WOOD PK
GLENDALE CRES
DALE PL
ANDERSON CRES
BURNBANK RD
BURNBANK GLEN
Annfield Burn
Queen Margaret Acad
LONGBANK RD
LONGBANK DR
SHAWFIELD AVE
LONGLANDS PK
FINWICK GLEN
KNOLL PK
GLENDALE AVE
Kincaidston Prim Sch
SNOWDROP SQ
STONECROP PL
CRANESBILL CT
BANKFIELD PK
BANKFIELD RDBT
Bank
Braston
TAYBANK DR
AUCHENBEG CRES
MARLE PK
MILTON PK
FINLAS AVE
GLEN PARK PL
LINFERN PL
GOWER PL
MAYBOLE RD
Kincaidston
SORREL DR
KINCAIDSTON DR
RUSH HILL
1 BRACKEN PK
2 FOXGLOVE PL
3 TREFOIL PL
4 PRIMROSE PK
5 GORSE PK
6 IRIS CT
7 MARIGOLD SQ
8 SPEEDWELL SQ
9 CORNHILL
10 CAMPION CT
11 MARGUERITE PL
12 CELANDINE BANK
13 FERN BRAE
14 HEATHER PK
15 CROCUS BANK
16 HAREBELL PL
17 ROCKROSE PK
18 HONEYSUCKLE PK
19 ROSEBAY PK
20 THISTLE WLK
Mast
CONTENT CT
WOODEND OVAL
WOODEND COTTS
Rozelle
LAUGHLANGLEN RD
CHERRY HILL RD
HOLLOW PARK CT
HOLLOW PK
Laigh Glengall
GRANGE AVE
BRADEN DR
CARCLUIE CRES
SHIEL HILL
WOODLEA PL
Slaphouse Burn
GOWANBANK RD
WHINHILL RD
HOME FARM RD
ST VINCENT CRES
THE LOANING
PEMBERTON VALLEY
LINDSTON PL
BROADWOOD PK
MONKWOOD PL
MERKLAND RD
DRUMELLAN RD
CRAIGHALL PL
PIPERHILL
BROADWOOD PK
WINDWARD PK
LEEWARD PK
KERSE PK
RAITHHILL
BATHURST DR
ROZELLE TERR
Mast
Ailsa
High Glengall
Ayr
Glenparks
Abbey Carrick Glen
Cockhill Wood
A713
LAIGH MOUNT
WOODEND RD
GULTREE HILL
DUMFRIES PK
DOONVALE PL
COTTON LEA
CORTON SHAW
KA6
A77 Girvan
A713 Dalmellington
Ayrshire STREET ATLAS

96 96 97

Scale: 5⅓ inches to 1 mile
0 110 yards 220 yards
0 125 m 250 m

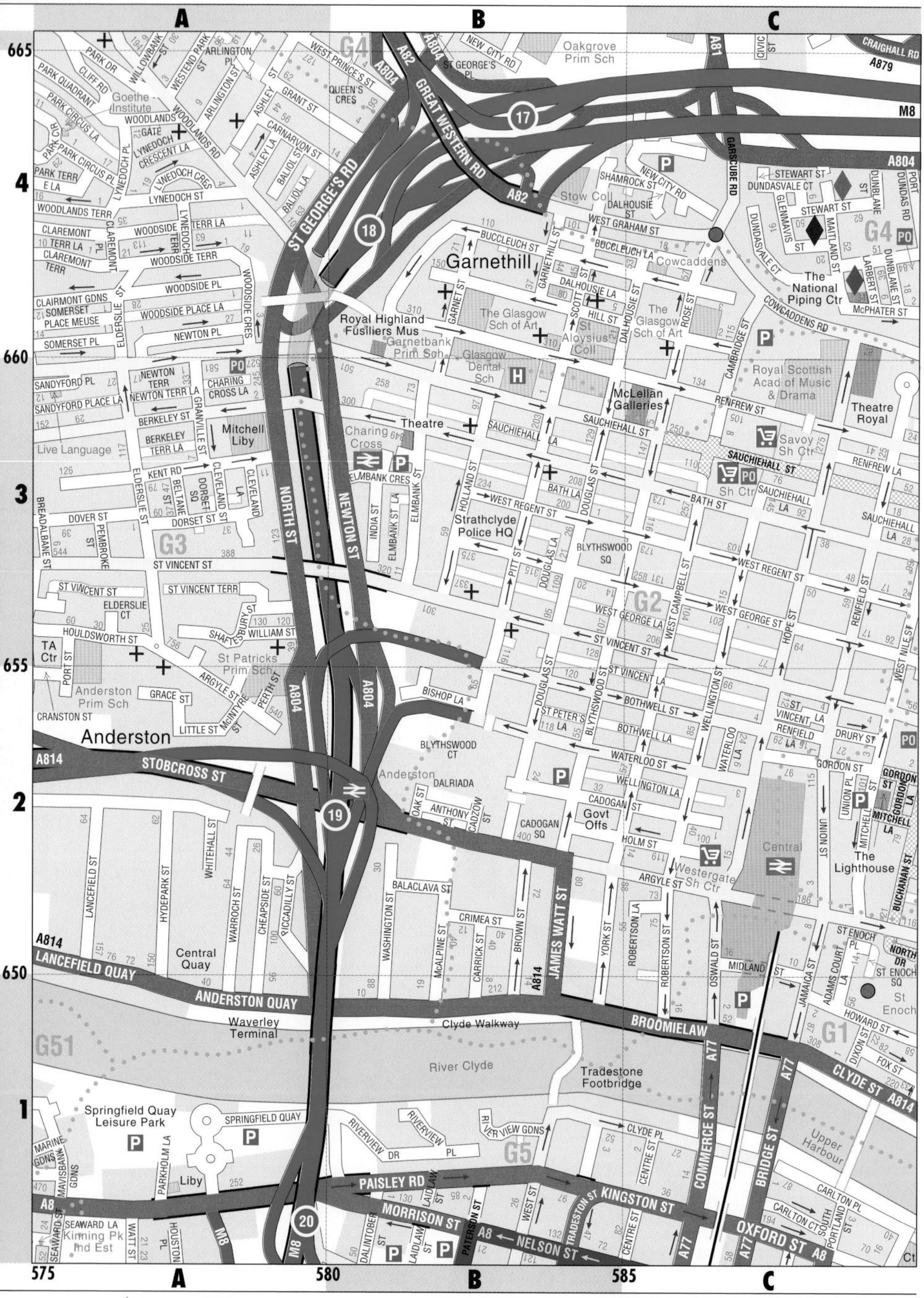

116 116 117

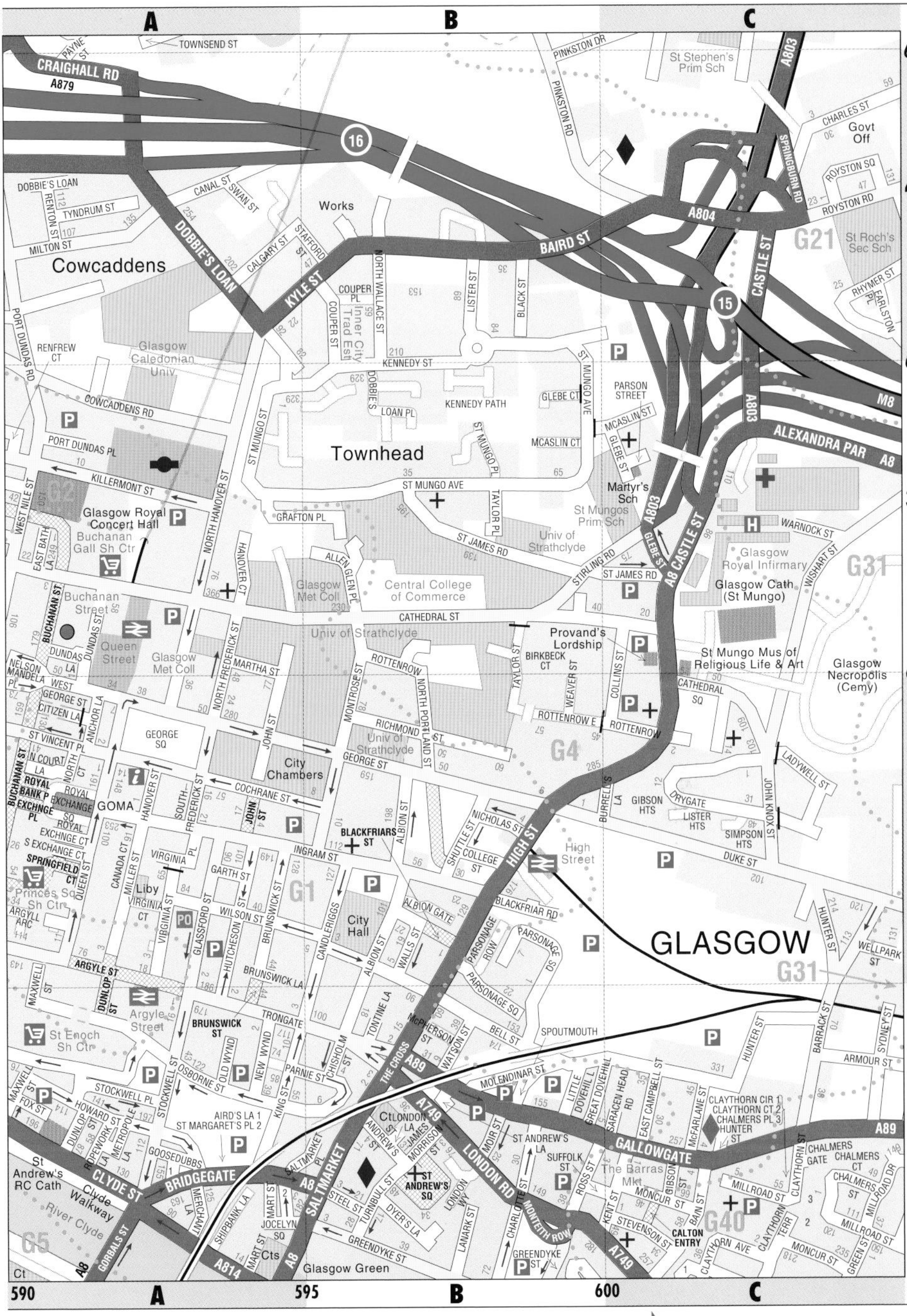
A
B
C
665
660
655
650
4
3
2
1
590
595
600
TOWNSEND ST
PAYNE ST
CRAIGHALL RD
A879
PINKSTON DR
PINKSTON RD
St Stephen's Prim Sch
A803
CHARLES ST
Govt Off
ROYSTON SQ
ROYSTON RD
SPRINGBURN RD
16
15
DOBBIE'S LOAN
RENTON ST
TYNDRUM ST
MILTON ST
CANAL ST
SWAN ST
Works
A804
BAIRD ST
G21
St Roch's Sec Sch
CASTLE ST
RHYMER ST
EARLSTON PL
Cowcaddens
CALGARY ST
STAFFORD ST
KYLE ST
COUPER PL
COUPER ST
NORTH WALLACE ST
Inner City Trad Est
LISTER ST
BLACK ST
PORT DUNDAS RD
RENFREW CT
Glasgow Caledonian Univ
KENNEDY ST
DOBBIE'S LOAN
KENNEDY PATH
ST MUNGO AVE
GLEBE CT
PARSON STREET
MCASLIN ST
M8
ALEXANDRA PAR
A8
COWCADDENS RD
PORT DUNDAS PL
ST MUNGO ST
LOAN PL
ST MUNGO PL
MCASLIN CT
GLEBE ST
Townhead
KILLERMONT ST
NORTH HANOVER ST
ST MUNGO AVE
TAYLOR PL
Martyr's Sch
St Mungos Prim Sch
A803
WARNOCK ST
GRAFTON PL
ST JAMES RD
Univ of Strathclyde
WEST NILE ST
Glasgow Royal Concert Hall
Buchanan Gall Sh Ctr
EAST BATH LA
HANOVER CT
ALLEN GLEN PL
STIRLING RD
ST JAMES RD
A8 CASTLE ST
GLEBE ST
Glasgow Royal Infirmary
WISHART ST
G31
Glasgow Met Coll
Central College of Commerce
Glasgow Cath (St Mungo)
BUCHANAN ST
Buchanan Street
DUNDAS ST
Queen Street
CATHEDRAL ST
Provand's Lordship
Univ of Strathclyde
BIRKBECK CT
TAYLOR ST
WEAVER ST
COLLINS ST
St Mungo Mus of Religious Life & Art
Glasgow Necropolis (Cemy)
NELSON MANDELA PL
DUNDAS LA
Glasgow Met Coll
MARTHA ST
NORTH FREDERICK ST
ROTTENROW
NORTH PORTLAND ST
CATHEDRAL SQ
WEST GEORGE ST
CITIZEN LA
ANCHOR LA
GEORGE SQ
JOHN ST
MONTROSE ST
RICHMOND ST
Univ of Strathclyde
ROTTENROW E
ROTTENROW
G4
ST VINCENT PL
N COURT LA
NORTH CT
GEORGE ST
City Chambers
LADYWELL ST
ROYAL BANK PL
ROYAL EXCHANGE SQ
EXCHNGE PL
GOMA
HANOVER ST
SOUTH FREDERICK ST
COCHRANE ST
JOHN ST
BURRELL'S LA
GIBSON HTS
DRYGATE
LISTER HTS
SIMPSON HTS
JOHN KNOX ST
BUCHANAN ST
ROYAL EXCHNGE CT
S EXCHANGE CT
CANADA CT
MILLER ST
VIRGINIA PL
BLACKFRIARS ST
ALBION ST
NICHOLAS ST
SHUTTLE ST
COLLEGE ST
HIGH ST
High Street
DUKE ST
SPRINGFIELD CT
QUEEN ST
Liby
GARTH ST
INGRAM ST
G1
Princes Sq Sh Ctr
VIRGINIA CT
VIRGINIA ST
GLASSFORD ST
WILSON ST
BRUNSWICK ST
CANDLERIGGS
City Hall
ALBION GATE
BLACKFRIAR RD
ARGYLL ARC
HUTCHESON ST
WALLS ST
PARSONAGE ROW
PARSONAGE SQ
GLASGOW
HUNTER ST
WELLPARK ST
MAXWELL ST
ARGYLE ST
DUNLOP ST
BRUNSWICK LA
G31
Argyle Street
BRUNSWICK ST
TRONGATE
NEW WYND
OLD WYND
TONTINE LA
McPHERSON ST
WATSON ST
BELL ST
SPOUTMOUTH
BARRACK ST
SYDNEY ST
St Enoch Sh Ctr
CHISHOLM ST
HUNTER ST
ARMOUR ST
MAXWELL ST
FOX ST
STOCKWELL PL
HOWARD ST
STOCKWELL ST
OSBORNE ST
PARNIE ST
KING ST
THE CROSS
A89
MOLENDINAR ST
LITTLE DOVEHILL
GREAT DOVEHILL
SARACEN HEAD RD
EAST CAMPBELL ST
MCFARLANE ST
CLAYTHORN CIR 1
CLAYTHORN CT 2
CHALMERS PL 3
HUNTER ST
A89
DUNLOP ST
ROPEWORK LA
METROPOLE LA
AIRD'S LA 1
ST MARGARET'S PL 2
London LA
JAMES MORRISON ST
A749
GALLOWGATE
CLAYTHORN ST
CHALMERS GATE
CHALMERS CT
CHALMERS ST
MILLROAD DR
St Andrew's RC Cath
CLYDE ST
GOOSEDUBBS
ST ANDREW'S LA
SUFFOLK ST
The Barras Mkt
GIBSON ST
MILLROAD ST
Clyde Walkway
River Clyde
BRIDGEGATE
SALTMARKET PL
SALTMARKET
ANDREW'S S
ST ANDREW'S SQ
LONDON RD
LONDON WY
MOIR ST
ROSS ST
MONCUR ST
BAIN ST
G40
MILLROAD ST
MERCHANT LA
MART ST
A8
STEEL ST
TURNBULL ST
DYER'S LA
CHARLOTTE ST
MONTEITH ROW
KENT ST
STEVENSON ST
CALTON ENTRY
CLAYTHORN TERR
CLAYTHORN AVE
MONCUR ST
GREEN ST
G5
GORBALS ST
SHIPBANK LA
JOCELYN SQ
GREENDYKE ST
LANARK ST
GREENDYKE ST
A749
Ct
A8
A814
Cts
A8
Glasgow Green

Index

Church Rd **6** Beckenham BR2..........**53** C6

Place name May be abbreviated on the map

Location number Present when a number indicates the place's position in a crowded area of mapping

Locality, town or village Shown when more than one place has the same name

Postcode district District for the indexed place

Page and grid square Page number and grid reference for the standard mapping

Cities, towns and villages are listed in CAPITAL LETTERS **Public and commercial buildings** are highlighted in magenta

Places of interest are highlighted in blue with a star★

Abbreviations used in the index

Acad	**Academy**	Comm	**Common**	Gd	**Ground**	L	**Leisure**	Prom	**Promenade**
App	**Approach**	Cott	**Cottage**	Gdn	**Garden**	La	**Lane**	Rd	**Road**
Arc	**Arcade**	Cres	**Crescent**	Gn	**Green**	Liby	**Library**	Recn	**Recreation**
Ave	**Avenue**	Cswy	**Causeway**	Gr	**Grove**	Mdw	**Meadow**	Ret	**Retail**
Bglw	**Bungalow**	Ct	**Court**	H	**Hall**	Meml	**Memorial**	Sh	**Shopping**
Bldg	**Building**	Ctr	**Centre**	Ho	**House**	Mkt	**Market**	Sq	**Square**
Bsns, Bus	**Business**	Ctry	**Country**	Hospl	**Hospital**	Mus	**Museum**	St	**Street**
Bvd	**Boulevard**	Cty	**County**	HQ	**Headquarters**	Orch	**Orchard**	Sta	**Station**
Cath	**Cathedral**	Dr	**Drive**	Hts	**Heights**	Pal	**Palace**	Terr	**Terrace**
Cir	**Circus**	Dro	**Drove**	Ind	**Industrial**	Par	**Parade**	TH	**Town Hall**
Cl	**Close**	Ed	**Education**	Inst	**Institute**	Pas	**Passage**	Univ	**University**
Cnr	**Corner**	Emb	**Embankment**	Int	**International**	Pk	**Park**	Wk, Wlk	**Walk**
Coll	**College**	Est	**Estate**	Intc	**Interchange**	Pl	**Place**	Wr	**Water**
Com	**Community**	Ex	**Exhibition**	Junc	**Junction**	Prec	**Precinct**	Yd	**Yard**

Index of towns, villages, streets, hospitals, industrial estates, railway stations, schools, shopping centres, universities and places of interest

Abb–Ade

A

Abbey Carrick Glen Hospl KA6 ....239 F1
Abbey Cl PA1 ....113 F4
Abbey Craig Ct FK9 ....2 D3
Abbeycraig Pk FK9 ....2 D4
Abbeycraig Rd G34 ....100 E1
Abbey Craig Rd FK10 ....5 B1
Abbeydale Way G73 ....138 C3
Abbey Dr G14 ....95 E4
Abbeygate KA13 ....207 E3
Abbeygreen KA13 ....207 E3
Abbeygreen St G34 ....100 E1
Abbeyhill St G32 ....118 E7
Abbey King's Park Hospl FK7 ....6 F5
Abbeylands Rd G81 ....74 D6
Abbey Mill FK8 ....7 C8
Abbeymill Bsns Ctr PA1 ....113 F4
Abbey Pl ML6 ....123 C4
Abbey Prim Sch KA13 ....207 D4
Abbey Rd
Elderslie PA5 ....112 C1
Stirling FK8 ....2 C1
Abbey Road Pl FK8 ....7 C8
Abbeyview FK9 ....2 D4
Abbey Wlk
Coatbridge G69 ....120 F5
Larkhall ML9 ....185 B4
Abbot Ct KA9 ....236 D5
Abbot Rd FK7 ....7 D4
Abbot's Ave KA13 ....207 E2
Abbotsburn Way 1 PA3 ....113 D8
Abbots Cres KA7 ....238 B2
Abbots Ct G68 ....61 D7
Abbotsford G64 ....78 C2
Abbotsford Ave
Hamilton ML3 ....162 B7
Larkhall ML9 ....185 A1
Rutherglen G73 ....138 B7
Abbotsford Brae G74 ....159 E3
Abbotsford Cres
Hamilton ML3 ....162 B6
Paisley PA2 ....132 E7
Shotts ML7 ....146 F5
Wishaw ML2 ....165 C4
Abbotsford Ct G67 ....82 F7
Abbotsford Dr
Helensburgh G84 ....25 B8
Kirkintilloch G66 ....79 E8
Abbotsford Gdns FK2 ....24 B1
Abbotsford La ML4 ....141 F6
Abbotsford Pl
Cumbernauld G67 ....82 F7
4 Glasgow G5 ....117 B4
Glasgow, Laurieston G5 ....117 B5
Motherwell ML1 ....143 B5
Saltcoats KA21 ....206 A2
Stirling FK8 ....2 C1
Abbotsford Rd
Bearsden G61 ....75 C6
Chapelhall ML6 ....123 E1
Clydebank G81 ....74 B1
Cumbernauld G67 ....82 F7
Hamilton ML3 ....162 B6
Wishaw ML2 ....165 C4
Abbotsford St FK2 ....42 B8
Abbotsford Terr ML11 ....215 C4
Abbotshall Ave G15 ....74 E3
Abbotsinch Rd
Paisley PA3 ....113 E8
Renfrew PA3 ....93 E2
Abbots Moss Dr FK1 ....41 F1
Abbot's Pl KA13 ....207 E3
Abbots Rd FK2 ....42 D7
Abbots Road Rdbt FK2 ....42 D8
Abbot St
4 Glasgow G41 ....116 E1
Greenock PA16 ....45 C3
Paisley PA3 ....113 F6
Abbots Terr ML6 ....123 C4
Abbots Way KA7 ....238 C3
Abbot's Wlk KA13 ....207 E3
Abbott Cres G81 ....94 D8
Aberconway St G81 ....94 C8
Abercorn Ave G52 ....114 E8
Abercorn Cres ML3 ....162 F2
Abercorn Dr ML3 ....162 F2
Abercorn Ind Est PA3 ....113 F6
Abercorn Pl G23 ....76 E1
Abercorn Rd G77 ....156 C6
Abercorn Sch G4 ....97 B2
Abercorn St
Clydebank G81 ....74 E7
Paisley PA3 ....113 F6
Abercrombie Cres G69 ....120 F5
Abercrombie Dr G61 ....75 B8
Abercrombie Pl
Kilsyth G65 ....36 B1
Menstrie FK11 ....3 F6
Abercrombie St FK1 ....41 E6
Abercromby Cres
East Kilbride G74 ....160 B3
Helensburgh G84 ....16 F3
Abercromby Dr
Ayr KA7 ....238 D4
Bridge of Allan FK9 ....2 B8
Glasgow G40 ....117 F6
Abercromby Pl
East Kilbride G74 ....160 B3
Stirling FK8 ....7 A7
Tullibody FK10 ....4 B2
Abercromby Place W G84 ....16 D3
Abercromby Prim Sch FK10 ....4 B2
Abercromby Sq 1 G40 ....117 F6
Abercromby St 1 G40 ....117 E5
Abercromby Street E G84 ....16 E2
Aberdalgie Gdns G34 ....120 B8
Aberdalgie Path G34 ....120 B8
Aberdalgie Rd G34 ....120 B8
Aberdeen Rd ML6 ....123 D4
Aberdour Ct G72 ....161 D2
Aberdour St G31 ....118 C7
Aberfeldy Ave
Hamilton G72 ....161 D3
Plains ML6 ....103 F3
Aberfeldy St G31 ....118 C7
Aberfeldy Terr KA11 ....220 A6
Aberfoyle Pl KA1 ....227 B8
Aberfoyle Rd PA15 ....46 B2
Aberfoyle St G31 ....118 C7
Aberlady Rd G51 ....115 E6
Aberlady St ML1 ....144 B1
Aberlour Pl
Irvine KA11 ....219 F6
Motherwell ML1 ....143 A2
Aberlour Rd KA11 ....219 F6
Abernethy Ave G72 ....161 D3
Abernethy Dr PA3 ....112 A5
Abernethyn Rd ML2 ....166 B6
Abernethy Pk G74 ....159 D2
Abernethy Pl G77 ....157 B4
Abernethy St G31 ....118 C7
Aberuthven Dr G32 ....119 B3
Abiegail Pl G72 ....140 D1
Aboukir St G51 ....115 E8
Aboyne Ave FK9 ....2 C4
Aboyne Dr PA2 ....113 F1
Aboyne St G51 ....115 F6
ABRONHILL 62 E4
Abronhill High Sch G67 ....62 E4
Abronhill Prim Sch G67 ....62 D3
Acacia Dr
Barrhead G78 ....134 B5
Beith KA15 ....171 A8
Paisley PA2 ....113 B1
Acacia Pl PA5 ....132 A8
Acacia Way G72 ....139 E5
Academy Apartments 1 KA1 ....228 A8
Academy Brae KA15 ....171 B8
Academy Ct
Coatbridge ML5 ....122 A7
Hurlford KA1 ....228 E6
Irvine KA12 ....219 B3
Academy Gdns KA12 ....219 B4
Academy Pk
Airdrie ML6 ....123 A7
Glasgow G51 ....116 C4
Academy Pl
Bannockburn FK7 ....7 E1
Coatbridge ML5 ....122 A7
Academy Rd
Glasgow G46 ....136 C2
Irvine KA12 ....219 B3
Stirling FK8 ....7 A8
Academy St
Airdrie ML6 ....123 A7
Alloa FK10 ....9 F8
8 Ayr KA7 ....235 F1
Coatbridge ML5 ....122 A7
Glasgow G32 ....119 B4
Hurlford KA1 ....228 E6
Kilmarnock KA1 ....227 F6
Larkhall ML9 ....185 A3
Troon KA10 ....229 D2
Academy Terr ML4 ....142 B5
Acer Cres PA2 ....113 B1
Acer Gr ML6 ....123 E3
Achamore Cres G15 ....74 E4
Achamore Dr G15 ....74 E4
Achamore Gdns G15 ....74 E4
Achamore Rd G15 ....74 E4
Achnasheen Rd ML6 ....124 A6
Achray Ave G83 ....27 D6
Achray Ct FK10 ....10 C5
Achray Dr
Falkirk FK1 ....42 A1
Paisley PA2 ....113 A1
Stirling FK9 ....2 A4
Achray Pl
Coatbridge ML5 ....101 D1
Milngavie G62 ....54 D3
Achray Rd G67 ....82 C6
Acids Rd KA20 ....218 B5
Acorn Cres FK5 ....23 D1
Acorn Ct G40 ....117 F4
Acorn Rd ML11 ....215 E1
Acorn St G40 ....117 F4
ACRE 76 B1
Acre Dr G20 ....76 B1
Acredyke Cres G21 ....98 C7
Acredyke Pl G21 ....98 C6
Acredyke Rd
Glasgow G21 ....98 C7
Rutherglen G73 ....137 F8
Acre Rd G20 ....76 B1
Acres The ML9 ....185 B2
Acre Valley Rd G64 ....57 B2
Adair Ave KA21 ....205 F1
Adam Ave ML6 ....123 B7
Adam Cres FK5 ....23 F2
Adam Grossert Ct FK5 ....23 D3
Adams Ave KA21 ....205 F2
Adams Court La G1 ....240 C1
Adams Ct KA10 ....229 F6
Adams Gate KA10 ....229 F6
Adamslie Cres G66 ....79 A8
Adamslie Dr G66 ....79 A8
Adams Loan FK2 ....24 A1
Adamson Pl FK9 ....2 B3
Adamson St ML4 ....142 D5
Adams Pl G65 ....60 D8
Adam St
Falkirk FK2 ....42 D6
Gourock PA19 ....44 F7
Greenock PA15 ....46 B3
Adamswell St G21 ....97 F3
Adamswell Terr G69 ....81 A2
Adams Wlk KA12 ....219 E2
Adamton Est KA9 ....234 A4
Adamton Road N KA9 ....236 D8
Adamton Road S KA9 ....236 C6
Adamton Terr KA9 ....236 C7
Addie St ML1 ....163 F8
Addiewell Pl ML5 ....122 A4
Addiewell St G32 ....119 A7
Addison Gr G46 ....135 F4
Addison Pl G46 ....135 F4
Addison Rd
Glasgow, Carnwadric G46 ....135 E4
Glasgow, Dowanhill G12 ....96 D4
Adelaide Ct G81 ....73 D5
Adelaide Rd G75 ....180 C7
Adelaide St
Gourock PA19 ....44 E8
Helensburgh G84 ....16 E1

Adele St ML1 163 F4
Adelphi St
Glasgow G5 117 C5
Glasgow G5 117 D5
Admiral St G41 116 E5
Admiralty Gdns G60 73 B5
Admiralty Gr G60 73 B5
Admiralty Pl G60 73 B5
Advie Pl G42 137 B8
Affric Ave ML6 104 A3
Affric Dr
Falkirk FK2 24 C1
Paisley PA2 114 B1
Affric Loan ML7 146 E6
Afton Ave
Kilmarnock KA3 222 F3
Prestwick KA9 236 C5
Afton Cres G61 76 B3
Afton Ct
Ayr KA7 239 B6
Irvine KA12 219 B2
Stevenston KA20 217 D8
Stirling FK7 7 C5
Afton Dr
Denny FK6 39 D7
Renfrew PA4 94 F2
Afton Gdns
Coatbridge ML5 122 D5
Hamilton G72 161 B6
Troon KA10 229 G4
Afton Pl KA22 205 D4
Afton Rd
Cumbernauld G67 62 B3
Stevenston KA20 217 D8
Afton St
Glasgow G41 136 E8
Larkhall ML9 185 C2
Afton View G66 58 F1
Agamemnon St G81 73 F2
Agate Terr ML4 142 A4
Agnew Ave ML5 122 D7
Agnew Gr ML4 141 D5
Agnew La G42 117 A1
Aidans Brae G76 157 E7
Aidrie L Ctr ML6 103 C1
Aigas Cotts 3 G13 95 F5
Aikenhead House G44 137 D5
Aikenhead Rd
Glasgow, Mount Florida G44 137 C7
Glasgow, Polmadie G42 117 C2
Aikman Pl G74 160 B4
Aikman Rd ML1 163 B5
Aiknut Rd KA23 190 C4
Ailean Dr G32 119 E4
Ailean Gdns G32 119 E4
Aileymill Gdns PA16 44 E2
Ailort Pl G74 159 E3
Ailort Ave G44 137 A5
Ailort Loan 18 ML2 165 F6
Ailsa Ave
Ashgill ML9 199 F8
Motherwell ML1 163 B7
Ailsa Cres ML1 163 B7
Ailsa Ct ML3 161 D1
Ailsa Dr
Bothwell G71 141 A4
Clydebank G81 74 C6
Giffnock G46 136 C1
Glasgow G42 136 F7
Kirkintilloch G66 58 F2
Paisley PA2 133 D7
Rutherglen, Croftfoot G73 137 F5
Rutherglen G46 157 C8
Stevenston KA20 217 C8
Ailsa Gdns KA22 205 D3
Ailsa Hospl KA6 239 E2
Ailsa Pl
Ayr KA7 235 E1
Coatbridge ML5 121 F4
Kilmarnock KA3 223 B5
Ailsa Rd
Bishopbriggs G64 78 B2
Coatbridge ML5 121 F4
Gourock PA19 44 C6
Irvine KA12 224 D7
Renfrew PA4 94 C2
Saltcoats KA21 206 A1
Troon KA10 229 B3
Ailsa St KA9 236 B8
Ailsa Twr G72 138 E3
Ailsa View
Doonfoot KA7 238 B2
Stewarton KA3 195 E2
West Kilbride KA23 190 E5
Ailsa View Cvn Site G78 153 E7
Ailsa View Gdns KA7 238 B2
Ailsa View Pl KA7 238 C2
Ailsa View Wynd KA7 238 C2
Ainsdale Ct KA13 207 B3
Ainslie Ave G52 115 A8
Ainslie Rd
Cumbernauld G67 62 C3
Glasgow G52 115 A7
Glasgow G52 115 B7
Airbles Cres ML1 163 D5
Airbles Dr ML1 163 D5
Airbles Farm Rd ML1 163 C5
Airbles Rd ML1 163 D5
Airbles Road Day Hospl ML1 163 F5
Airbles St ML1 163 E5
Airbles Sta ML1 163 E5
Airbles Twr ML1 163 E5
Airdale Ave G46 136 C2
Aird Ave KA1 227 E7
AIRDRIE 123 B8
Airdrie Acad ML6 103 A1
Airdriehill Rd ML6 103 D3
Airdriehill St ML6 103 C2
Airdrie Rd
Caldercruix ML6 105 C2
Carluke ML8 187 E4
Cumbernauld G67 82 A7
Cumbernauld G67 82 B6
Cumbernauld, Mollinsburn G67 81 E4
Kilsyth G65 60 D8
Plains ML6 103 F1
Airdrie Ret Pk ML6 123 A7
Airdrie Sta ML6 123 A7
Aird's La G1 241 A1
Airgold Dr G15 74 F4
Airlie Ave G61 75 E7
Airlie Ct KA7 238 E6
Airlie Dr ML4 142 A6
Airlie Gdns G73 138 D4
Airlie La G12 96 B3
Airlie Rd G69 120 A3
Airlie St G12 96 B3
Airlink Ind Est PA3 113 E8
Airlour Rd G44 136 E5
AIRTH 14 D3
Airth Ct ML1 142 D1
Airth Dr
Glasgow G52 115 F3
Stirling FK7 7 C4
Airth La G52 115 F3
Airth Prim Sch FK2 14 E4
Airthrey Ave
Bridge of Allan FK9 2 B6
Glasgow G14 95 E4
Airthrey Castle Yd FK9 2 E6
Airthrey Dr FK5 23 F4
Airthrey La G14 95 E4
Airthrey Rd FK9 2 C5
Airth Way G68 81 E8
Airyligg Dr G76 178 E5
Aitchison Ct 4 ML6 122 F8
Aitchison Dr FK5 23 B3
Aitchison Pl FK1 42 B3
Aitchison St ML6 122 E7
Aitkenbar Circ G82 50 B6
Aitkenbar Dr G82 50 B6
Aitkenbar Prim Sch G82 50 C5
Aitkenbrae Dr KA9 236 D8
Aitken Cl ML2 166 A7
Aitken Cres FK7 7 B2
Aitken Dr
Beith KA15 150 C1
Slamannan FK1 86 A6
Aitken Gdns FK1 41 E6
Aitkenhead Ave ML5 121 B4
Aitkenhead Prim Sch G71 120 F1
Aitkenhead Rd
Chapelhall ML6 123 D2
Uddingston G71 121 A2
Aitken La G83 27 E7
Aitken Pl
Ardrossan KA22 205 C3
8 Lanark ML11 215 A4
Aitken Rd
Falkirk FK1 41 D6
Hamilton ML3 183 E7
Aitken St
Airdrie ML6 103 B1
Dalry KA24 191 C7
Glasgow G31 118 C7
Aitken Terr FK1 41 D6
Aitnock Pl KA24 191 A8
Akarit Rd FK5 23 E2
Alasdair Ct G78 134 C2
Alba Gdns ML8 187 E3
Albans Cres ML1 163 B8
Albany G74 160 C4
Albany Ave G32 119 C6
Albany Cotts 2 G13 95 F5
Albany Dr
Lanark ML11 215 B3
Rutherglen G73 138 B6
Albany Pl G71 141 B2
Albany Quadrant G32 119 C6
Albany Rd ML3 183 C7
Albany St
Coatbridge ML5 121 E7
Glasgow G40 118 A4
Albany Terr G72 138 E3
Albany Way PA3 113 E8
Albany Wynd 11 ML9 185 B4
Alba Way
Hamilton ML3 183 C6
16 Larkhall ML9 185 C1
Alberta Ave
Coatbridge ML5 121 F8
East Kilbride G75 180 C8
Alberta Cres 1 G75 180 C8
Alberta Pk G75 180 D8
Alberta Pl 2 G75 180 D8
Albert Ave
Glasgow G42 117 A1
Stewarton KA3 195 F1
Albert Cres 3 ML6 123 B7
Albert Cross G41 116 F3
Albert Ct KA3 195 F1
Albert Dr
Bearsden G61 76 B3
Glasgow G41 116 D4
Helensburgh G84 16 F2
Larkhall ML9 185 B2
Rutherglen G73 138 B5
Albert Halls* FK8 7 A7
Albert La 4 ML3 162 A6
Albert Pk ML8 202 A6
Albert Pl
Airdrie ML6 123 B8
Albert Pl continued
Stewarton KA3 195 F1
Stirling FK8 7 A7
Albert Prim Sch G21 97 F5
Albert Quadrant ML1 143 A5
Albert Rd
Brookfield PA5 111 D5
Clydebank G81 74 A3
Falkirk FK1 42 A3
Glasgow G42 117 B1
Gourock PA19 44 D8
Harthill ML7 127 E5
Kirkintilloch G66 79 C3
Renfrew PA4 94 C3
Albert St
Alexandria G83 27 E4
Coatbridge ML5 122 A7
Hamilton ML3 162 B6
Helensburgh G84 16 E2
Motherwell ML1 163 F7
Albert Terr
Ayr KA8 239 A8
Hamilton ML3 162 A6
Albert Wynd KA3 195 F1
Albion Ct ML5 122 C6
Albion Gate
Glasgow G1 241 B2
Paisley PA3 113 D6
Albion St
Coatbridge ML5 122 C6
Glasgow G1 241 B2
Glasgow, North Mount Vernon G69 119 F3
Motherwell ML1 163 E5
Paisley PA3 113 E6
Albion Twr 2 ML1 163 E5
Albion Way G75 180 F5
Albyn Ct KA9 236 C8
Alcaig Rd G52 115 E2
Alcath Rd ML2 166 B6
Alclutha Ave G82 50 B3
Alder Ave
Hamilton ML3 162 E1
Kirkintilloch G66 79 B5
Alder Bank
Ayr KA7 239 D6
Motherwell G71 121 C1
Alderbank Rd PA14 47 A1
Alderbrae Rd PA14 47 A1
Alder Cres
East Kilbride G75 180 C5
Menstrie FK11 3 F5
Alder Ct
Barrhead G78 134 C1
East Kilbride G75 180 C5
Alder Gate G72 139 E5
Alder Gdns ML1 164 C3
Alder Gn KA11 220 A4
Alder Gr ML5 122 B6
Alder La
Motherwell, Clydesdale ML1 143 A3
Motherwell, Holytown ML1 143 C5
Alderman Pl G13 95 C6
Alderman Rd G13 95 B6
Alder Pl
East Kilbride G75 180 C5
Glasgow G43 136 C5
Johnstone PA5 112 A1
Kilmarnock KA1 227 D8
Alder Rd
Clydebank G81 74 A5
Cumbernauld G67 62 D2
Dumbarton G82 49 E4
Glasgow G43 136 C5
Milton of Campsie G66 58 B4
Alderside Gdns G71 140 E7
Alderside Pl 5 G71 141 B8
Alderstocks G75 180 E5
Alderston Ave KA8 236 A3
Alderston Pk KA8 236 A3
Alderston Pl
Ayr KA8 236 A3
Bellshill ML4 141 E4
Alderston Way ML4 141 E6
Aldersyde Ave
Troon KA10 229 G4
Wishaw ML2 164 D4
Aldersyde Pl G72 140 C1
Aldersyde Terr ML1 144 C1
Alderwood Cres PA14 47 A1
Alderwood Rd PA14 47 B1
Aldrin Rd G84 25 D8
Alexander Ave
Eaglesham G76 178 E6
Falkirk FK2 42 E5
Stevenston KA20 206 E2
Twechar G65 59 E4
Uddingston G71 141 C6
Alexander Balfour Gdns ML3 162 D1
Alexander Cres G5 117 C4
Alexander Ct FK9 2 F6
Alexander Dr FK9 2 A8
Alexander Fleming Ave KA25 148 F1
Alexander Gdns ML3 163 A2
Alexander Gibson Way ML1 163 D5
Alexander MacLaren Gdns KA3 222 F3
Alexander McLeod Pl FK7 8 E3
Alexander Path ML1 164 B3
Alexander Peden Prim Sch ML7 127 E5
Alexander Pl
Irvine KA12 219 C4
Kirkintilloch G66 80 B7
Alexander Pl continued
Rhu G84 15 D6
Stevenston KA20 206 D1
Alexander Rd ML7 146 D6
Alexander St
Airdrie ML6 122 F7
1 Alexandria G83 27 E5
Clydebank G81 74 B1
Coatbridge ML5 122 B8
Dumbarton G81 50 A4
Renton G82 49 D8
Wishaw ML2 165 A2
Alexander Stephen Ho G51 95 E1
Alexander Terr G78 154 C6
Alexandra Ave
Kirkintilloch G66 79 C4
Prestwick KA9 233 C1
Stepps G33 99 D6
Alexandra Cross G31 118 B7
Alexandra Ct
Glasgow G31 118 B8
Prestwick KA9 233 C1
Alexandra Dr
Alloa FK10 9 F7
Paisley PA2 113 B3
Renfrew PA4 94 D3
Alexandra Gate 1 G31 118 A8
Alexandra Gdns
Kilwinning KA13 207 D3
Kirkintilloch G66 79 C4
Alexandra Par G31 118 A8
Alexandra Parade Prim Sch
2 G31 118 A8
Alexandra Parade Sta G31 118 B8
Alexandra Park St G31 118 B8
Alexandra Pk G66 79 C4
Alexandra Pl FK8 2 C1
Alexandra Prim Sch ML6 123 A7
Alexandra Rd G66 79 C4
Alexandra St G66 79 C8
Alexandra Terr
Ayr KA8 236 A3
Kilwinning KA13 207 D3
ALEXANDRIA 27 B5
Alexandria Quadrant ML1 143 A5
Alexandria Sta G83 27 E4
Alexandria Terr KA8 236 A3
Alford Ave
Hamilton G72 161 C3
Kirkintilloch G66 79 B8
Alford Pl
Irvine KA11 219 E5
Linwood PA3 111 E6
Alford Quadrant ML2 165 B5
Alford St G21 97 D3
Alfred La 5 G12 96 E3
Alfred Terr 6 G12 96 E3
Algie St G41 136 F8
Algoma Pl G75 180 B8
Alice Ave ML4 142 A4
Alice St PA2 113 E2
Alice Terr G5 117 D3
Aline Ct G78 134 B4
Alisa Rd G81 94 B8
Alison Lea G74 160 C3
Allan Ave
Carluke ML8 187 E3
Renfrew PA4 94 E1
Allanbank Rd FK5 23 C2
Allanbank St ML7 166 F8
Allan Barr Ct FK1 42 B1
Allan Cres
Alexandria G83 27 D3
Denny FK6 21 D3
Dumbarton G82 50 B6
Allan Ct G75 179 E7
ALLANDALE 39 C2
Allandale Ave ML1 143 F5
Allandale Cotts FK4 39 C2
Allander Ave G62 77 B7
Allander Dr G64 78 A8
Allander Gdns G64 77 F4
Allander L Ctr G61 76 B7
Allander Rd
Bearsden G61 75 D2
Milngavie G62 55 A2
Allander St
Glasgow G22 97 C4
Glasgow G22 97 D4
Allands Ave PA4 93 C5
Allanfauld Rd
Cumbernauld G67 61 F2
Kilsyth G65 36 D2
Allan Gdns KA21 205 F3
Allan Glen Gdns G64 78 B4
Allan Gr ML4 142 B6
Allan Park Ho 10 FK8 7 B7
Allan Pk FK8 7 A7
Allan Pl
Ayr KA8 236 C3
Dumbarton G82 50 A4
East Kilbride G75 179 E7
Glasgow G40 118 B2
Allan's Cnr G78 134 B2
Allanshaw Gdns ML3 162 B3
Allanshaw Gr ML3 162 B3
Allanshaw St ML3 162 C3
Allans Prim Sch FK8 7 A7
Allan Sq KA12 219 E2
Allan St
Coatbridge ML5 121 D5
Glasgow G40 118 B2
Motherwell ML1 163 F7
ALLANTON
Hamilton 163 D1
Wishaw 167 A8
Allanton Ave PA1 114 E4
Allanton Dr G52 115 C5
Allanton Gr ML2 165 B5
Allanton Lea ML3 183 C8
Allanton Pl ML3 162 E1
Allanton Prim Sch ML7 167 B8
Allanton Rd
Crosshill ML2, ML7 166 E7
Shotts ML7 146 D2
Allanton Terr ML3 184 D8
Allan Twr ML1 163 F7
Allanvale KA3 195 B8
Allanvale Rd
Bridge of Allan FK9 1 F7
Prestwick KA9 236 B8
Allanwater Apartments FK9 2 A8
Allanwater Gdns FK9 2 A8
Allan Wlk FK9 1 F8
Allanwood Ct FK9 2 A8
Allbany Cres ML1 142 F5
Allendale G74 159 C3
Allendale Path 2 G72 161 D7
Allenfield Rd KA7 239 D6
Allen Glen Pl G1 241 B3
Allenshaw Ind Est ML3 162 C3
Allen Way PA4 94 D1
Allerdyce Dr G15 74 F1
Allerdyce Rd G15 74 F1
Allershaw Pl ML2 185 F8
Allershaw Rd ML2 185 F8
Allershaw Tower ML2 185 F8
Allerton Gdns G69 119 F4
Alleysbank Rd G73 118 B1
Allison Ave PA8 72 F2
Allison Dr G72 139 A6
Allison Gdns EH48 107 D2
Allison Hall PA1 114 B5
Allison Pl
Gartcosh G69 100 E4
3 Glasgow G42 117 A2
Newton Mearns G77 156 C4
Allison St
Ayr KA8 236 A2
Glasgow G42 117 B2
Allnach Pl G34 120 E8
ALLOA 10 C5
Alloa Acad FK10 9 E8
ALLOA PARK 10 B5
Alloa Park Dr FK10 10 E6
Alloa Rd
Fishcross FK10 5 D3
Menstrie FK9 3 B3
Stenhousemuir FK5 23 F4
Stirling FK9 2 E3
Tullibody FK10 4 A2
Tullibody FK10 4 C3
Alloa Sta FK10 10 B7
Alloa Tower* FK10 10 B5
Alloa Trad Ctr FK10 10 C7
ALLOWAY 238 E1
Alloway KA7 238 E1
Alloway Ave
Kilmarnock KA3 228 B8
Paisley PA2 134 B8
Alloway Cres
Bonnybridge FK4 39 F6
Paisley PA2 134 C8
Rutherglen G73 137 F5
Alloway Ct G66 59 A2
Alloway Dr
Clydebank G81 74 C3
Cowie FK7 12 D7
Kirkintilloch G66 59 A2
Newton Mearns G77 157 A4
Paisley PA2 134 B8
Rutherglen G73 137 F5
Alloway Gdns
Hamilton ML3 161 D2
Kirkintilloch G66 59 A2
Alloway Gr
Kirkintilloch G66 58 F2
Paisley PA2 114 C1
Alloway Pk KA7 238 E8
Alloway Pl
Ardrossan KA22 205 C4
Ayr KA7 238 E8
Alloway Place La KA7 238 E8
Alloway Prim Sch KA7 238 F1
Alloway Quadrant G66 59 A1
Alloway Rd
Airdrie ML6 123 F8
East Kilbride G74 160 E3
Glasgow G43 136 D6
Alloway St
Ayr KA7 238 F8
Larkhall ML9 185 C2
Alloway Terr G66 58 F2
Alloway Wynd
Motherwell ML1 143 E4
Stenhousemuir FK5 23 C4
All Saints Sec Sch G21 98 C5
Allsop Ct KA3 222 A7
Almada Gr ML3 162 D4
Almada La ML3 162 D4
Almada St ML3 162 D4
Almada Twr ML3 162 D4
Alma La FK2 42 B6
Alma St
Falkirk FK2 42 B6
Glasgow G31 118 B5
Alma Terr FK2 42 B6

Almond Ave PA4 .... 94 E2
Almondbank ML6 .... 103 F3
Almond Bank G61 .... 75 C2
Almond Cres PA2 .... 112 F2
Almond Ct
Falkirk FK2 .... 42 E7
Stirling FK7 .... 7 C5
Almond Dr
Banknock FK4 .... 38 E2
Bishopton PA7 .... 72 B2
East Kilbride G74 .... 160 B1
Kirkintilloch G66 .... 79 B5
Almond Pl
Coatbridge ML5 .... 101 D1
Kilmarnock KA1 .... 227 D8
Motherwell ML1 .... 143 B5
Almond Rd
Bearsden G61 .... 75 D2
Cumbernauld G67 .... 62 F4
Falkirk FK2 .... 42 E7
Stepps G33 .... 99 C5
Almond St G33 .... 98 D1
Almond Terr ML7 .... 127 C5
Almond Vale G71 .... 141 A7
Almond Way ML1 .... 163 E3
Almswall Rd KA13 .... 207 E3
Alness Cres G52 .... 115 E3
Alness St ML3 .... 162 D1
Alness Terr ML3 .... 162 D2
Alnwick Dr G76 .... 178 D4
Alpha Ctr G81 .... 94 C8
Alpine Gr
Greenock PA15 .... 46 E3
Uddingston G71 .... 140 F7
Alpine Path 5 G72 ...... 161 E7
Alpine Wlk 4 G72 .... 161 E7
Alsatian Ave G81 .... 74 D2
Alsh Terr ML3 .... 162 A1
Alston Ave ML5 .... 122 B8
Alston Gdns G61 .... 75 B8
Altnacreag Gdns G69 ..... 81 A3
Altonhead Dr KA3 .... 210 B1
Altonhead Terr KA3 ...... 210 B1
ALTONHILL 222 E3
Altonhill Ave KA3 .... 222 E3
Alton Holdings
Auchenreoch G66 .... 58 F5
Milton of Campsie G66 .... 58 D5
Alton Rd PA1 .... 114 C4
Alton St KA23 .... 190 C5
Alton Way KA23 .... 190 D4
Altpatrick Gdns PA5 ..... 112 B3
Altry Pl KA7 .... 238 B1
Altyre St G32 .... 118 F4
ALVA 5 A6
Alva Acad FK12 .... 5 A7
Alva Gate G52 .... 115 E3
Alva Gdns
Bearsden G61 .... 75 D8
Glasgow G52 .... 115 E2
Alva Glen Nature Trail*
FK12 .... 5 A8
Alva Ind Est FK12 .... 5 C6
Alva Pl G66 .... 79 E4
Alva Prim Sch FK12 .... 5 A6
Alva Terr PA19 .... 45 A7
Alvie Pl ML6 .... 123 D5
Alvord Ave KA9 .... 233 D1
Alwyn Ave PA6 .... 111 D8
Alwyn Ct G74 .... 159 E3
Alwyn Dr G74 .... 159 E3
Alyssum Cres ML1 ...... 163 D8
Alyth Cres G76 .... 158 A8
Alyth Gdns
Clarkston G76 .... 158 A8
Glasgow G52 .... 115 E3
Ambassador Way PA4 ..... 94 D1
Amber Terr ML4 .... 142 A4
Ambleside G75 .... 180 A6
Ambleside Rise ML3 .... 183 D6
Ambrose Ct ML3 .... 162 B4
Amethyst Ave ML4 ...... 142 A4
Amisfield St G20 .... 96 E5
Amlaird Rd KA3 .... 223 A5
Amochrie Dr PA2 .... 133 A8
Amochrie Glen PA2 ..... 133 A8
Amochrie Rd PA2 .... 133 A8
Amochrie Way PA2 ...... 112 F1
Amulree Pl G32 .... 119 A4
Amulree St G32 .... 119 B4
Ancaster Dr G13 .... 95 F6
Ancaster La G13 .... 95 F6
Ancaster Pl FK1 .... 42 A1
Anchor Ave PA1 .... 114 A4
Anchor Cres PA1 .... 114 A3
Anchor Dr PA1 .... 114 A4
Anchor La G1 .... 241 A2
Anchor Wynd PA1 .... 114 A4
Ancroft St G20 .... 97 A3
Andersen Ct G75 .... 180 E6
Anderside G75 .... 180 E5
Anderson Ave
2 Falkirk FK2 .... 42 A8
Kilsyth G65 .... 36 B1
Anderson Cres
Ayr KA7 .... 239 B4
Prestwick KA9 .... 236 E7
Queenzieburn G65 .... 59 E8
Shieldhill FK1 .... 66 E6
Anderson Ct
Bellshill ML4 .... 142 B5
Newton Mearns G77 ...... 156 C4
Wishaw ML2 .... 165 A3
Anderson Dr
Denny FK6 .... 21 E1
Anderson Dr *continued*
Falkirk FK2 .... 24 B2
Irvine KA12 .... 219 D5
Newton Mearns G77 ...... 156 C4
Renfrew PA4 .... 94 D4
Saltcoats KA21 .... 206 A1
Anderson Gdns G72 ..... 140 E1
Anderson La 1 ML6 .... 123 A8
Anderson Park Rd FK6 ... 21 F2
Anderson Pl
Kilmarnock KA3 .... 223 D2
Stirling FK7 .... 7 A4
Anderson Rd PA7 .... 72 A4
Anderson St
5 Airdrie ML6 .... 123 A8
Bonnybridge FK4 .... 40 B5
Glasgow G11 .... 96 B1
Hamilton ML3 .... 161 F5
Motherwell ML1 .... 163 E5
Port Glasgow PA14 .... 47 C2
Anderson Terr
Ardrossan KA22 .... 205 C2
Longcroft FK4 .... 39 B3
Anderson Twr ML1 ...... 163 E6
ANDERSTON 240 A2
Anderston Prim Sch G3 . 240 A2
Anderston Quay G3 ..... 240 A1
Anderston Sta G3 .... 240 B2
Andrew Ave
Kirkintilloch G66 .... 79 D3
Renfrew PA4 .... 94 E3
Andrew Baxter Ave ML9 . 185 E1
Andrew Cres FK5 .... 23 D4
Andrew Dr G81 .... 94 D8
Andrew Hardie Dr FK10 ... 10 A8
Andrew Paton Way ML3 . 162 A6
Andrew Pl ML8 .... 187 E3
Andrew Sillars Ave G72 . 139 C5
Andrew St
East Kilbride G74 .... 159 F1
Paisley PA3 .... 113 E6
Anford Gdns G72 .... 161 E7
Anford La 7 G72 .... 161 E7
Anford Pl G72 .... 161 E7
Anford Terr G72 .... 161 E6
Angela Way G71 .... 140 F6
Angle Gate G14 .... 95 D4
Angle St ML9 .... 198 F2
Angus Ave
Airdrie ML6 .... 123 A5
Bishopbriggs G64 .... 78 D1
East Kilbride G74 .... 160 B2
Glasgow G52 .... 115 C3
Hamilton ML3 .... 163 A3
Motherwell ML1 .... 163 C8
Prestwick KA9 .... 236 D8
Angus Gdns G71 .... 140 F8
Angus Oval G52 .... 115 B4
Angus Pl
East Kilbride G74 .... 160 B2
Glasgow G52 .... 115 B4
Angus Rd
Carluke ML8 .... 188 B1
Greenock PA16 .... 44 D4
Port Glasgow PA14 .... 47 C1
Angus St
Alexandria G83 .... 27 F4
Clydebank G81 .... 94 E8
6 Glasgow G21 .... 97 E4
Angus Wlk G71 .... 141 B7
Anish Pl G15 .... 74 E4
Annabella Rd ML9 ...... 200 C4
Annan Ave
East Kilbride G75 .... 179 E7
Hamilton G72 .... 161 D3
Annan Cres ML6 .... 123 D1
Annan Ct
Coatbridge ML5 .... 121 F6
Falkirk FK1 .... 42 C1
Annandale
Crosshouse KA2 .... 221 F1
Greengairs ML6 .... 83 F2
Annandale Cres KA2 .... 221 F1
Annandale Gdns KA2 .... 221 F1
Annandale La KA2 ...... 221 E1
Annandale St 1 G42 .... 117 B3
Annandale View KA2 .... 221 F2
Annandale Way KA11 ... 220 A5
Annan Dr
Bearsden G61 .... 75 D3
Rutherglen G73 .... 138 D7
Annan Glade ML1 .... 164 A3
Annan Gr ML1 .... 164 A3
Annanhill KA1 .... 227 C8
Annanhill Ave KA1 ...... 222 C1
Annanhill Pl KA13 .... 207 B3
Annanhill Prim Sch KA1 . 227 D8
Annan Pl PA5 .... 131 C8
Annan Rd KA1 .... 228 A5
Annan St ML1 .... 164 A3
Annan Way 7 G67 .... 61 F1
ANNATHILL 81 F1
Annathill Gdns ML5 .... 81 F2
Annbank Pl G31 .... 117 F6
Annbank St
Glasgow G31 .... 117 F6
Larkhall ML9 .... 184 F3
Ann Ct ML3 .... 162 A5
Anne Ave PA4 .... 94 D4
Anne Cres G66 .... 79 D3
Anne Dr
Bridge of Allan FK9 .... 2 B6
Stenhousemuir FK5 .... 23 E4
Annerley Ct ML5 .... 121 E5
Annerley Pl ML5 .... 121 E5
Anne's Mews ML3 .... 162 F3
Anne St FK10 .... 9 F8
Annet Rd FK6 .... 39 D6
Annette St G42 .... 117 A2
Annette Street Prim Sch
G42 .... 117 B2
Annfield Dr FK7 .... 7 C5
Annfield Gdns
Blantyre G72 .... 140 C1
Irvine KA12 .... 219 B3
Stirling FK8 .... 7 B6
Annfield Glen Rd KA7 ... 239 B4
Annfield Gr FK8 .... 7 B6
Annfield Pl G31 .... 117 F7
Annfield Rd KA9 .... 236 B8
Annfield Terr KA9 ...... 236 B8
Annickbank KA3 .... 195 F2
Annick Cres KA3 .... 211 E8
Annick Ct KA12 .... 219 C2
Annick Dr
Bearsden G61 .... 75 C2
Irvine KA11 .... 220 B1
Annick Pl
Kilmarnock KA1 .... 228 A5
Troon KA10 .... 229 G4
Annick Prim Sch 1
KA11 .... 220 A5
Annick Rd
Irvine, Dreghorn KA11 ..... 220 B1
Irvine KA11, KA12 .... 219 E1
Annick Rdbt KA12 .... 219 E2
Annick St
Cambuslang G72 .... 139 D5
Glasgow G32 .... 119 B5
Annick Street Ind Est
G32 .... 119 C5
Annick View KA12 ...... 219 E2
ANNICK WATER 220 B3
Anniesdale Ave G33 ...... 99 D6
Annieshill View ML6 .... 104 A2
ANNIESLAND 95 E6
Anniesland Coll (Balshagray
Campus) G11 .... 95 F2
Anniesland Coll (Hatfield
Campus) G12 .... 96 A5
Anniesland Coll (Milton
Resource Ctr) G22 .... 97 E7
Anniesland Coll (Ruchill Com
Learning Ctr) G20 .... 96 E5
Anniesland Cres G14 ..... 95 A5
Anniesland Ind Est G13 ... 95 E8
Anniesland Rd
Glasgow, Anniesland G14 ... 95 C5
Glasgow, Scotstounhill G14 .. 95 A5
Anniesland Sta G13 .... 95 F6
Annieston G65 .... 59 F4
Anniversary Ave G75 .... 180 C7
Annpit Rd KA8 .... 236 B4
Annsfield Rd ML3 .... 183 D7
Ann St
Greenock, Central PA15 ..... 45 E4
Greenock PA15 .... 45 F5
Hamilton ML3 .... 162 A5
Johnstone PA5 .... 112 A3
Ansdell Ave G72 .... 161 C8
Anson Ave FK1 .... 41 E4
Anson St G40 .... 117 F4
Anson Way 6 PA4 .... 94 C1
Anstruther Ct ML8 ...... 186 F5
Anstruther St
Glasgow G32 .... 118 F5
Law ML8 .... 186 F5
Antermony Rd G66 .... 58 E5
Anthony Ct G81 .... 94 C8
Anthony St G2 .... 240 B2
Antigua Ct 5 PA15 .... 46 A4
Antigua St PA15 .... 46 A4
Antigua Way G75 .... 159 A1
Anton Cres G65 .... 60 E8
Antonine G66 .... 59 B2
Antonine Ave ML1 ...... 163 C8
Antonine Gate FK4 .... 39 A1
Antonine Gdns
Clydebank G81 .... 74 A6
Falkirk FK1 .... 41 C5
Antonine Gr FK4 .... 39 F3
Antonine Prim Sch
Bonnybridge FK4 .... 40 A4
Clydebank G15 .... 74 E3
Antonine Rd
Bearsden G61 .... 75 B6
Dullatur G68 .... 61 D6
Antonine Sh Ctr 11 G67 ... 61 F1
Antonine St FK1 .... 41 C5
Antonine Wall*
Bonnybridge FK4 .... 40 D4
Kirkintilloch G66 .... 59 C3
ANTONSHILL 23 E4
Antonshill Rdbt FK5 ...... 23 F5
Antrim La ML9 .... 185 B4
Anwoth St G32 .... 119 A3
Apartments The G46 .... 136 B1
Apollo Path ML1 .... 143 B5
Appin Cres G31 .... 118 B7
Appin Ct G66 .... 59 B1
Appin Rd G31 .... 118 C7
Appin Terr
Hamilton ML3 .... 161 E4
3 Rutherglen G73 .... 138 D4
Shotts ML7 .... 147 B3
Appin Way
2 Bothwell G71 .... 141 A3
Coatbridge ML5 .... 121 E4
Glenmavis ML6 .... 102 F4
Appleby Cl G75 .... 179 F6
Appleby Gr G69 .... 121 A6
Appleby St G22 .... 97 B3
Applecross Gdns G69 ..... 80 F3
Applecross Quadrant
ML2 .... 165 B5
Applecross Rd G66 .... 59 B1
Applecross St G4, G22 ..... 97 B3
Appledore Cres G71 .... 141 A3
Apple Way G75 .... 180 F6
Appleyard Ct ML4 ...... 141 F3
Apsley La G11 .... 96 A2
Apsley St G11 .... 96 A2
Aqua Ave ML3 .... 161 E2
Aqua Ct ML3 .... 161 E2
Aquatech ML1 .... 163 E7
Aquila Way ML8 .... 187 D2
Araburn Dr G75 .... 180 E5
Aranthrue Cres PA4 ...... 94 C4
Aranthrue Dr PA4 .... 94 C4
Aray St G20 .... 96 D6
Arbroath Ave G52 ...... 115 B4
Arbroath Cres FK9 .... 2 B4
Arbroath Gr ML3 .... 162 B2
Arbuckle Pl ML6 .... 104 A3
Arbuckle Rd ML6 ...... 104 B4
Arbuckle St KA1 .... 228 A8
Arbuthnot St FK1 .... 41 E6
Arcadia Bsns Ctr G81 ..... 74 B1
Arcadia Pl G40 .... 117 E5
Arcadia St
Bellshill ML4 .... 142 A7
Glasgow G40 .... 117 E5
Arcan Cres G15 .... 75 B2
Archerfield Ave G32 .... 119 A2
Archerfield Cres G32 ... 119 A2
Archerfield Dr G32 ..... 119 A2
Archerfield Gr G32 ..... 119 A2
Archerhill Ave G13 .... 95 A8
Archerhill Cotts G13 ..... 95 A8
Archerhill Cres G13 ...... 95 B8
Archerhill Gdns G13 ..... 95 A8
Archerhill Rd G13 .... 95 B7
Archerhill Sq G13 .... 94 F8
Archerhill Terr G13 ...... 95 A8
Archers Ave
Irvine KA11 .... 219 E6
Stirling FK7 .... 7 C4
Archers Ct KA11 .... 219 E6
Archibald Craig Pl KA3 .. 222 F3
Archibald Dr 2 KA24 .... 191 B7
Archibald Kelly Ct G75 .. 180 E7
Archibald Terr G66 .... 58 B6
Archiebald Pl ML4 ...... 142 D4
Arch Way G65 .... 36 D1
Arcon Ave KA6 .... 237 F6
Ardardan Cotts G82 .... 25 G2
Ardargie Dr G32 .... 139 C8
Ardargie Gr G32 .... 139 C8
Ardargie Pl G32 .... 139 C8
Ardayre Rd KA9 .... 236 B8
Ardbeg Ave
Bishopbriggs G64 .... 78 C1
Kilmarnock KA3 .... 222 F3
Rutherglen G73 .... 138 E3
Ardbeg Cres 5 ML6 .... 103 A3
Ardbeg Ct KA11 .... 219 F6
Ardbeg La
Glasgow G42 .... 117 A2
Greenock PA15 .... 46 C2
Thorntonhall G74 .... 158 C3
Ardbeg Rd
Greenock PA15 .... 46 C2
Motherwell ML1 .... 143 B2
Ardbeg St G42 .... 117 A2
Ardchoille Dr KA20 ..... 206 E2
Ardchoille La KA20 ..... 206 E2
Ardconnel St G46 ...... 135 F4
Ardeer La KA20 .... 217 F6
Ardeer Prim Sch KA20 .. 217 D7
Ardeer Rdbt KA20 ...... 206 E1
ARDEN
Glasgow 135 E4
Helensburgh 18 D6
Arden Ave G46 .... 135 E2
Ardencaple Dr G84 ...... 16 A2
Ardencaple Quadrant G84 16 B2
Ardenclutha Ave ML3 ... 162 B4
Ardenclutha Dr PA14 .... 47 B1
Ardenconnel Ho G84 ..... 15 D5
Ardenconnel Mews G84 .. 15 D6
Ardenconnel Way G84 .... 15 D5
Ardencraig Cres G45 ... 137 C1
Ardencraig Dr G45 ..... 138 A2
Ardencraig Gdns G45 .. 138 A2
Ardencraig Pl G45 ...... 137 E3
Ardencraig Quadrant
G45 .... 137 F2
Ardencraig Rd
Glasgow G45 .... 137 E1
Glasgow G45 .... 137 F3
Ardencraig St G45 ..... 138 A2
Ardencraig Terr G45 ... 137 F2
Arden Ct
Airdrie ML6 .... 122 D8
Hamilton ML3 .... 162 D1
Arden Dr G46 .... 136 B3
Arden Gr G65 .... 36 C2
Arden Hill G84 .... 15 D6
Arden Ho G83 .... 18 E6
Ardenlea G71 .... 140 F7
Ardenlea St G40 .... 118 B3
Arden Pl G46 .... 135 E2
Arden Rd
Greenock PA15 .... 46 D1
Hamilton ML3 .... 162 C1
Arden St ML6 .... 104 A2
Arden Terr ML3 .... 162 C2
Ardenvohr G82 .... 48 B7
Ardery St G11 .... 96 A2
Ardessie Pl G20 .... 96 D5
Ardessie St 2 G23 .... 76 D1
Ardfern Rd ML6 .... 124 A6
Ardfern St G32 .... 119 A3
Ardfin Ct KA9 .... 236 C6
Ardfin Rd KA9 .... 236 C5
Ardgare G84 .... 15 A7
Ardgay Dr FK4 .... 40 A3
Ardgay Pl G32 .... 119 A4
Ardgay Rd FK4 .... 40 A3
Ardgay St G32 .... 119 B4
Ardgay Terr FK4 .... 40 A4
Ardgay Way G73 .... 138 B3
Ardgoil Dr G68 .... 61 A1
Ardgour Ct G72 .... 161 F6
Ardgour Dr PA3 .... 112 A5
Ardgour Par ML1 .... 143 C1
Ardgour Pl KA3 .... 222 F4
Ardgour Rd KA3 .... 222 F3
Ardgowan Ave PA2 ..... 113 F3
Ardgowan Ct PA2 ...... 114 B3
Ardgowan Dr G71 ...... 140 F7
Ardgowan Pl
Cowie FK7 .... 12 D8
Shotts ML7 .... 146 E6
Ardgowan Prim Sch PA16 . 45 D6
Ardgowan Sq PA16 .... 45 E6
Ardgowan St
Greenock PA16 .... 45 E6
Paisley PA2 .... 113 F3
Port Glasgow PA14 .... 47 A2
Ardgowan Terrace La G3 .. 96 D1
Ardgryfe Cres PA6 .... 91 D1
Ardholm St G32 .... 119 A5
Ardhu Pl G15 .... 75 A4
Ard La 6 ML2 .... 165 F6
Ardlamont Sq PA3 ..... 112 C5
Ardlaw St G51 .... 115 F6
Ardle Ave KA1 .... 228 B5
Ardle Rd G43 .... 136 E5
Ard Loan ML1 .... 143 A5
Ardlui Gdns G62 .... 54 D3
Ardlui Rd KA8 .... 236 A4
Ardlui St G32 .... 118 F4
Ardmaleish Cres G45 ... 137 E2
Ardmaleish Dr G45 .... 137 D2
Ardmaleish Rd G45 .... 137 E2
Ardmaleish St G45 ..... 137 D2
Ardmaleish Terr G45 ... 137 E2
Ardmay Cres G44 ...... 137 C7
Ardmillan KA13 .... 207 B2
Ardmillan St G33 ...... 118 F8
Ardmore Cresent 9
ML6 .... 103 A3
Ardmore Ct KA11 ...... 220 A6
Ardmore Pl PA15 .... 45 E3
Ardmore Rd
Greenock PA15 .... 46 C1
Port Glasgow PA14 .... 68 D8
Ardmory Ave G42 ...... 137 D7
Ardmory La G42 .... 137 E7
Ardmory Pl G42 .... 137 E7
Ardnahoe Ave G42 ..... 137 E7
Ardnahoe Pl G42 ...... 137 D8
Ardneil Ave KA23 ...... 190 C3
Ardneil Ct KA22 .... 205 B4
Ardneil Rd G51 .... 115 F6
Ardnish St G51 .... 115 E7
ARDOCH 48 E5
Ardoch Cres
Dumbarton G82 .... 49 D4
Stevenston KA20 .... 217 E6
Ardoch Ct KA20 .... 217 E6
Ardoch Gdns 3 G72 .... 138 F6
Ardoch Gr G72 .... 138 F6
Ardoch Path 17 ML2 ... 165 F6
Ardoch Rd G61 .... 76 B5
Ardochrig G75 .... 180 F5
Ardoch St G22 .... 97 C4
Ardoch Terr KA20 ...... 217 E7
Ardoch Way G69 .... 80 F2
Ardo Gdns G51 .... 116 A5
Ardrain Ave ML1 ...... 164 C3
Ard Rd PA4 .... 94 B4
ARDROSSAN 205 A2
Ardrossan Acad KA22 ... 205 D2
Ardrossan Harbour Sta
KA22 .... 205 A1
Ardrossan High Rd KA23 . 190 E4
Ardrossan Rd
Saltcoats KA21 .... 216 E8
West Kilbride KA23 ...... 190 C2
Ardrossan South Beach Sta
KA22 .... 205 D1
Ardrossan Town Sta
KA22 .... 205 C1
Ardshiel Rd G51 .... 115 E7
Ardsloy La G14 .... 95 A4
Ardsloy Pl G14 .... 95 A4
Ard St G32 .... 119 A4
Ardtoe Cres G33 .... 99 E5
Ardtoe Pl G33 .... 99 E5
Arduthie Rd G51 .... 115 E7
Ardvreck Pl FK2 .... 24 A3
Ardwell Pl G84 .... 15 D4
Ardwell Rd G52 .... 115 E3
Ardyne Pl PA19 .... 43 F5
Argosy Way 3 PA4 .... 94 C1
Argus Ave ML6 .... 123 C2
Argyle Cres
Airdrie ML6 .... 122 F5
Hamilton ML3 .... 162 A3
Argyle Dr ML3 .... 162 A4
Argyle Gdns
Coatbridge ML5 .... 121 E4
Lennoxtown G66 .... 57 E7
Argyle Pk KA8 .... 236 A2
Argyle Pl KA21 .... 216 F8
Argyle Rd
Gourock PA19 .... 44 F6
Saltcoats KA21 .... 216 F8
Argyle St
Glasgow, Anderston G3 ... 240 A2

Argyle St *continued*
Glasgow, Cranston Hill G3 . 116 E8
Glasgow G2 . 240 C2
Glasgow, Kelvingrove G3 . 96 D1
Greenock PA15 . 45 F6
Paisley PA1 . 113 D4
Stonehouse ML9 . 198 F2
Argyle Street E G84 . 16 E1
Argyle Street Sta G1 . 241 A1
Argyll Arc G2 . 241 A2
Argyll Ave
Dumbarton G82 . 50 C4
Falkirk FK2 . 42 C6
Renfrew, Kirklandneuk PA4 . 94 B4
Renfrew PA3 . 93 E1
Stirling FK8 . 2 C1
Argyll Ct ML7 . 127 F5
Argyll Est G83 . 27 D7
Argyll Gdns ML9 . 185 B3
Argyll Path FK6 . 39 D8
Argyll Pl
Alloa FK10 . 10 C7
Bellshill ML4 . 141 F2
Dumbarton G82 . 50 C4
East Kilbride G74 . 160 C3
Kilsyth G65 . 60 E8
Argyll Rd
Bearsden G61 . 75 E7
Clydebank G81 . 74 C1
Rosneath G84 . 15 B3
Argyll's Lodging* FK8 . 7 A8
Argyll St
Alexandria G83 . 27 D7
Alloa FK10 . 10 C7
Argyll Street W G84 . 16 C2
Argyll View G84 . 16 A2
Argyll Wynd ML1 . 143 B2
Arisaig Dr
Bearsden G61 . 76 B3
Glasgow G52 . 115 E3
Arisaig Pl G52 . 115 E3
Arisdale Cres G77 . 156 E6
Arkaig Ave ML6 . 103 F3
Arkaig Pl G77 . 157 B4
Arkaig St ML2 . 165 B1
Ark La G31 . 117 F7
Arkleston Cres PA3 . 114 B7
Arkleston Dr PA1 . 114 B6
Arkleston Prim Sch PA4 . 94 D1
Arkleston Rd PA4, PA3 . 114 C8
Arkle Terr G72 . 138 F3
Arklet Rd G51 . 115 F7
Arklet Way ML2 . 165 E3
Arkwrights Way PA1 . 113 B3
Arkwright Way
Irvine KA11 . 219 F2
Irvine KA11 . 219 F3
Arlington Pl G3 . 240 A4
Arlington St G3 . 240 A4
Armadale Ct
Glasgow G31 . 118 A8
3 Greenock PA15 . 45 F4
Armadale Path G31 . 118 A8
Armadale Pl
Glasgow G31 . 118 A8
Greenock PA15 . 45 F4
Armadale Rd
Lanark ML11 . 215 C4
Rhu G84 . 15 F4
Armadale St G31 . 118 A7
Armine Path ML1 . 143 C4
Armour Ave
Airdrie ML6 . 122 E7
Cowie FK7 . 12 D7
Armour Ct
Hamilton G72 . 161 B6
Kirkintilloch G66 . 59 A1
Armour Dr
Ayr KA7 . 239 C6
Kirkintilloch G66 . 59 A1
Armour Gdns G66 . 59 A1
Armour Gr ML1 . 164 A4
Armour Mews FK5 . 23 B4
Armour Pl
Ardrossan KA22 . 205 C4
Johnstone PA5 . 112 A3
Kirkintilloch G66 . 59 A1
Linwood PA3 . 112 C5
Motherwell ML1 . 143 C4
Stewarton KA3 . 195 E1
Armour Sq PA5 . 112 A3
Armour St
Glasgow G4 . 241 C1
Johnstone PA5 . 112 A3
Kilmarnock KA1 . 227 F7
Armstrong Cres G71 . 141 A8
Armstrong Gr G75 . 180 D7
Armstrong Rd
Helensburgh G84 . 25 D8
Kilmarnock KA3 . 223 C2
Arnbrae Farm Steadings
G65 . 60 A8
Arnbrae Rd G65 . 36 B1
Arness Terr KA3 . 222 E4
Arngask Rd G51 . 115 E7
Arnhall Pl G52 . 115 E3
Arnhem St G72 . 139 D5
Arnholm Pl G52 . 115 E3
Arnisdale Pl G34 . 120 A8
Arnisdale Rd G34 . 120 A8
Arnisdale Way G73 . 138 B3
Arnish PA4 . 93 C7
Arniston St G32 . 118 F7
Arniston Way PA3 . 114 A7
Arnold Ave G64 . 78 A1
Arnol Pl G33 . 119 F7
ARNOTHILL . 42 A4
Arnothill FK1 . 42 A4
Arnothill Bank FK1 . 42 A4
Arnothill Ct FK1 . 41 F5
Arnothill Gdns FK1 . 42 A4
Arnothill La FK1 . 41 F4
Arnothill Mews FK1 . 42 A4
Arnot St FK1 . 42 C4
Arnott Dr ML5 . 122 A4
Arnott Quadrant ML1 . 142 C1
Arnott Way G72 . 139 A6
Arnprior Cres G45 . 137 D3
Arnprior Gdns G69 . 80 F2
Arnprior Pl KA7 . 238 F2
Arnprior Quadrant G45 . 137 D4
Arnprior Rd G45 . 137 D4
Arnprior St G45 . 137 D4
Arns Gr FK10 . 9 E8
Arnside Ave G46 . 136 C3
Arnswell FK10 . 5 C2
Arnton Gr ML6 . 123 E1
Arnum Gdns ML8 . 187 F1
Arnum Pl ML8 . 187 F1
Arnwood Dr G12 . 96 A5
Arondale Rd ML6 . 103 F3
Aron Terr G72 . 138 F3
Aros Dr G52 . 115 E2
Aros La G52 . 115 D2
Aros Rd G84 . 15 D6
Arran G74 . 160 C1
Arran Ave
Coatbridge ML5 . 122 D4
Dumbarton G82 . 49 D5
Kilmarnock KA3 . 223 A4
Port Glasgow PA14 . 69 B7
Renfrew PA3 . 93 E1
Arran Cres KA15 . 150 C1
Arran Ct
Alloa FK10 . 10 B5
Stevenston KA20 . 217 C8
Arran Dr
Airdrie ML6 . 102 F1
Cumbernauld G67 . 82 D8
Glasgow G52 . 115 F3
Glasgow, Giffnock G46 . 136 C2
Glenmavis ML6 . 102 F5
Johnstone PA5 . 111 D1
Kirkintilloch G66 . 58 E2
Paisley PA2 . 133 E7
Arran Gdns
Carluke ML8 . 201 F8
Hamilton ML3 . 162 E1
Troon KA10 . 229 E7
Arran La
Ardrossan KA22 . 205 C1
Moodiesburn G69 . 81 A2
Arran Mall KA7 . 238 F8
Arran Path 17 ML9 . 185 C1
Arran Pk KA9 . 236 B6
Arran Pl
Ardrossan KA22 . 205 C1
Clydebank G81 . 74 C2
Coatbridge ML5 . 122 D4
Irvine KA12 . 219 B5
Linwood PA3 . 112 A6
Saltcoats KA21 . 206 A2
Arran Rd
Gourock PA19 . 44 D6
Motherwell ML1 . 163 C7
Renfrew PA4 . 94 D2
Troon KA10 . 229 E7
Arran Terr
Ayr KA7 . 235 E1
Falkirk FK1 . 41 C4
Rutherglen G73 . 137 F5
Arran Twr G72 . 138 E3
Arran View
Airdrie ML6 . 102 F1
14 Kilsyth G65 . 60 D8
Stewarton KA3 . 195 E1
Troon KA10 . 229 D3
Arranview Ct
Ayr KA8 . 236 B4
Irvine KA12 . 219 B3
Arranview Gdns KA23 . 190 C2
Arranview St ML6 . 123 E1
Arran Way G71 . 140 F2
Arrochar Ct G23 . 96 E8
Arrochar Dr G23 . 76 D1
Arrochar Path 10 G23 . 76 D1
Arrochar St G23 . 76 D1
Arrol Cres FK10 . 10 C7
Arrol Dr KA7 . 238 D5
Arrol Pk KA7 . 238 E5
Arrol Pl G40 . 118 B4
Arrol St
Glasgow G52 . 114 E7
Glasgow G52 . 114 F8
Arrol Wynd G72 . 139 D6
Arrothill Dr KA1 . 227 D7
Arrotshole Ct G74 . 159 B4
Arrotshole Rd G74 . 159 B3
Arrowsmith Ave G13 . 95 D8
Artarman Rd G84 . 15 E4
Artartex Village* G83 . 27 E6
Arthur Ave
Airdrie ML6 . 123 A6
Barrhead G78 . 134 B1
Arthur Ct KA23 . 190 C5
Arthur Gdns ML6 . 105 B4
ARTHURLIE . 134 B1
Arthurlie Ave
Barrhead G78 . 134 C1
Uplawmoor G78 . 153 B3
Arthurlie Dr
Glasgow G46 . 136 C2
Newton Mearns G77 . 156 D3
Uplawmoor G78 . 153 B3
Arthurlie Gdns G78 . 134 C2
Arthurlie Pl KA21 . 216 E8
Arthurlie St
Barrhead G78 . 134 C2
Glasgow G51 . 115 F6
Arthur Pl G76 . 157 E6
Arthur Rd PA2 . 133 E8
Arthur's Dr FK5 . 23 F2
Arthur St
Alexandria G83 . 27 E4
Ayr KA7 . 238 F8
Clarkston G76 . 157 E6
Glasgow G3 . 96 D1
Greenock PA15 . 46 B4
Hamilton ML3 . 162 D5
Paisley PA1 . 113 C5
Saltcoats KA21 . 217 A7
Stevenston KA20 . 217 D8
West Kilbride KA23 . 190 C5
Arthurston Rd
Alexandria G83 . 27 F7
Balloch G83 . 28 A7
Artizan Br G82 . 49 E3
Arundel Dr
Bishopbriggs G64 . 78 B4
Glasgow G42 . 137 A7
Ascaig Cres G52 . 115 E2
Ascog Rd G61 . 75 F2
Ascog St G42 . 117 A2
Ascot G12 . 96 A6
Ascot Ave G12 . 95 F6
Ascot Gate G12 . 95 F6
Ash Ave G75 . 180 C6
Ashbank Cres ML6 . 123 E3
Ashbrae Gdns FK7 . 7 B2
Ashburn Gate PA19 . 44 C7
Ashburn Gdns
Gourock PA19 . 44 C7
Milngavie G62 . 54 E1
Ashburn Loan ML9 . 185 B4
Ashburn Rd G62 . 54 E2
Ashburton Pk G75 . 180 A7
Ashburton Rd G12 . 96 B6
Ashby Cres G13 . 75 E1
Ashcraig Sch G33 . 99 B3
Ashcroft G74 . 160 D5
Ashcroft Ave G66 . 57 E7
Ashcroft Dr G44 . 137 E5
Ashcroft Ho FK5 . 23 B1
Ashcroft Wlk G66 . 57 E7
Ash Ct G75 . 180 C6
Ashdale Ave KA21 . 205 F2
Ashdale Dr G52 . 115 E3
Ashdale Rd KA3 . 222 E4
Ashdene St G22 . 97 B7
Ash Dr KA15 . 150 B2
Asher Rd ML6 . 123 E2
Ashfield G64 . 78 A3
Ashfield Rd
Clarkston G76 . 157 E6
Milngavie G62 . 55 A1
Ashfield St
Glasgow G22 . 97 C4
Glasgow G22 . 97 C5
Ashfield Sta G22 . 97 C5
ASHGILL . 199 F8
Ashgillhead Rd ML9 . 185 E1
Ashgill Pl G22 . 97 C6
Ashgill Rd G22 . 97 D7
Ash Gr
Bishopbriggs G64 . 98 B8
Kirkintilloch G66 . 79 B5
Law ML8 . 186 F6
Stenhousemuir FK5 . 23 F2
Uddingston G71 . 141 B8
Ashgrove
Airdrie ML6 . 123 D7
Caldercruix ML6 . 105 A5
Coatbridge ML5 . 122 A4
Hartwood ML7 . 145 F3
Irvine KA12 . 219 C5
Moodiesburn G69 . 80 F1
Ashgrove Ave
Gourock PA19 . 44 C7
Stevenston KA20 . 206 E2
Ashgrove La PA14 . 47 D1
Ashgrove Rd
Ardrossan KA22 . 205 C4
Bellshill ML4 . 142 B7
Kilwinning KA13 . 207 C4
Ashgrove St
Ayr KA7 . 239 A7
Glasgow G40 . 118 A2
Ashgrove Workshops
KA13 . 207 D4
Ashiestiel Ct G67 . 82 E7
Ashiestiel Pl G67 . 82 E7
Ashiestiel Rd G67 . 82 E7
Ashkirk Dr
Ashgill ML9 . 199 F8
Glasgow G52 . 115 F3
Ashkirk Pl ML2 . 165 C6
Ash La ML9 . 198 D1
Ashland Ave ML3 . 183 D6
Ashlar Ave G68 . 61 D5
Ashlea Dr G46 . 136 D4
Ashlea Gdns ML6 . 103 F3
Ashley Dr G71 . 141 B5
Ashley Gr ML4 . 141 D6
Ashley La G3 . 240 A4
Ashley Pk G71 . 141 C6
Ashley Pl G72 . 161 C8
Ashley Rise G83 . 27 F1
Ashley St
Bonnybridge FK4 . 39 F6
Glasgow G3 . 240 A4
Ashley Terr FK10 . 10 A8
Ashmore Rd G44 . 136 F5
Ashpark Prim Sch G46 . 135 D4
Ash Pl
Banknock FK4 . 38 E2
East Kilbride G75 . 180 C6
Johnstone PA5 . 112 A1
Kilmarnock KA1 . 227 D7
Ash Rd
Clydebank G81 . 74 A5
Cumbernauld G67 . 62 E5
Dumbarton G82 . 49 F4
Glasgow G69 . 120 A4
Ash Terr FK8 . 6 F5
Ashton Dr
Helensburgh G84 . 25 C8
Hurlford KA1 . 228 F5
Ashton Gdns G69 . 101 A6
Ashton Gn G74 . 159 E2
Ashton La G12 . 96 D2
Ashton Lane N G12 . 96 D2
Ashton Pl PA19 . 44 C7
Ashton Rd
Glasgow, Dalmarnock
G73 . 118 A1
Glasgow, Kelvingrove G12 . 96 D2
Gourock PA19 . 44 C7
Ashton St ML1 . 142 D2
Ashton Terr PA19 . 44 C7
Ashton View G82 . 49 B4
Ashton Way PA2 . 132 E8
Ashtree Ct G60 . 73 B6
Ashtree Gr G77 . 156 C3
Ashtree Rd G43 . 136 C8
Ashvale Cres G21 . 97 E4
Ash Wlk
Motherwell ML1 . 143 B5
Rutherglen G73 . 138 C3
Ashwood ML2 . 164 E1
Ashwood Gdns G13 . 95 F5
Ashworth Terr ML3 . 162 A4
Ash Wynd G72 . 139 E5
Aspen Ct KA7 . 239 D5
Aspen Dr G21 . 98 A3
Aspen Gdns ML1 . 143 D2
Aspen Gr G69 . 121 B6
Aspen Pl
Cambuslang G72 . 139 E5
Johnstone PA5 . 112 A1
Aspen Rd KA7 . 239 D5
Aspen Way ML3 . 162 E2
Asquith Pl ML4 . 142 D5
Assloss Rd KA3 . 223 C4
Aster Dr G45 . 138 A3
Aster Gdns
Glasgow G53 . 135 C3
Motherwell ML1 . 163 E5
Athelstane Dr G67 . 82 D7
Athelstane Rd G13 . 95 C7
Athena Way G71 . 141 A7
Athole Gdns G12 . 96 C3
Athole La
Glasgow G12 . 96 D3
Greenock PA16 . 44 D3
Athole St G84 . 16 F1
Athole Terr PA16 . 44 D3
Atholl Ave
Glasgow G52 . 114 E7
Torrance G64 . 57 B1
Atholl Cres PA1 . 114 E6
Atholl Ct
Hamilton G72 . 161 F6
Kirkintilloch G66 . 59 B1
Atholl Dr
Cumbernauld G68 . 81 F8
Giffnock G46 . 136 C1
Rutherglen G46 . 157 C8
Atholl Gdns
Bearsden G61 . 75 E7
Bishopbriggs G64 . 77 F3
Glasgow G46 . 135 F2
Kilwinning KA13 . 207 E4
Rutherglen G73 . 138 E4
Atholl La G69 . 81 A2
Atholl Pl
Coatbridge ML5 . 122 B3
Falkirk FK2 . 42 C5
Glasgow G46 . 135 F2
Linwood PA3 . 112 A6
Stirling FK8 . 1 F2
Atholl St ML3 . 162 B6
Atholl Terr G71 . 120 F1
Atlas Ind Est G21 . 97 E4
Atlas Pl G21 . 97 F4
Atlas Rd G21 . 97 F4
Atlas Sq G21 . 97 F4
Atlas St G81 . 94 B8
Atlin Dr ML1 . 143 B3
Atrium Way FK4 . 40 A3
Attercliffe Ave ML2 . 164 D2
Attlee Ave G81 . 74 E1
Attlee Pl G81 . 74 E1
Attlee Rd G75 . 179 D8
Attow Rd G43 . 136 B5
Auburn Dr G78 . 134 D1
Auchans Ave KA2 . 225 E2
Auchans Dr KA2 . 225 E2
Auchanshangan Dr KA21 . 205 E3
Auchans Pl KA3 . 213 B3
Auchans Rd PA6 . 92 A2
AUCHENBACK . 134 D1
Auchenback Prim Sch
G78 . 134 D1
Auchenbeg Cres KA7 . 239 A3
Auchenbothie Cres G33 . 98 E5
Auchenbothie Gdns PA13 . 69 C2
Auchenbothie Pl G33 . 98 E5
Auchenbothie Rd PA14 . 68 F6
AUCHENBOWIE . 11 B4
Auchencar Dr KA3 . 222 E4
Auchencrow St G34 . 120 D8
Auchencruive G62 . 76 C8
Auchendarroch St PA15 . 46 C3
Auchendavie Rd G66 . 59 B2
Auchendavie Steadings
G66 . 59 B2
Auchendoon Cres KA7 . 238 D4
Auchendores Ave PA14 . 69 A7
Auchenfoil La PA14 . 68 D8
Auchenfoil Rd
Knocknairs Moor PA13 . 67 F6
Port Glasgow PA14 . 68 D8
Auchengate KA10 . 229 G7
Auchengate Cres KA11 . 224 G2
Auchengeich Gdns G69 . 80 F2
Auchengeich Rd G69 . 80 D3
Auchengilloch G75 . 180 E5
Auchenglen Dr G69 . 80 E2
Auchenglen Rd ML8 . 201 F3
Auchengree Rd KA14 . 170 D6
Auchengreoch Ave PA5 . 131 D8
Auchengreoch Rd PA5 . 131 D7
AUCHENHARVIE . 217 B8
Auchenharvie Acad
KA21 . 217 B8
Auchenharvie L Ctr
KA21 . 217 B8
Auchenharvie Pl
Irvine KA11 . 219 F6
Stevenston KA20 . 206 B1
Auchenharvie Rd KA21 . 217 A8
Auchenhove Cres KA25 . 149 A3
Auchenhowie Rd G62 . 76 D7
Auchenkilns Holdings
Cumbernauld, Balloch G68 . 61 C1
Cumbernauld, Condorrat
G67 . 82 D6
Auchenkilns Pk G68 . 61 C1
Auchenkilns Rd G67 . 82 D6
Auchenleck La PA14 . 68 E7
Auchenleck Rd PA14 . 68 E7
Auchenlodment Prim Sch
PA5 . 112 A1
Auchenlodment Rd PA5 . 112 B1
AUCHENREOCH . 59 B5
Auchenreoch Ave G82 . 50 B6
Auchenreoch Holdings
G66 . 59 B6
AUCHENSHUGGLE . 119 A2
Auchenstewart Ct ML2 . 165 C3
AUCHENTIBBER . 161 A2
Auchentibber Ct G72 . 161 F6
Auchentibber Rd G72 . 161 A3
AUCHENTIBER . 193 F3
Auchentiber Pl KA3 . 223 C6
AUCHENTORLIE . 114 B4
Auchentorlie Quadrant
PA1 . 114 B4
Auchentorlie St G11 . 95 F2
Auchentoshan Ave G81 . 73 F6
Auchentoshan Terr G21 . 97 F2
Auchentrae Cres KA7 . 238 D5
Auchentyre Pl FK2 . 24 C3
AUCHINAIRN . 98 A8
Auchinairn Gdns G64 . 98 D8
Auchinairn Prim Sch G64 . 98 B8
Auchinairn Rd G64 . 98 C7
Auchinairn Rdbt G64 . 98 E8
Auchinbaird FK10 . 5 C2
Auchinbee Farm Rd G68 . 61 B4
Auchinbee Way G68 . 61 B3
Auchincampbell Rd ML3 . 162 D3
Auchincarroch Rd
Alexandria G83 . 27 F6
Bonhill G83 . 28 B7
Gartocharn G83 . 20 F4
Auchincloch Dr FK4 . 38 F3
Auchincruive Ave KA9 . 236 C6
Auchineden Ct G61 . 75 C7
Auchingill Pl G34 . 100 D1
Auchingill Rd
Glasgow G34 . 100 C1
Glasgow G34 . 100 D1
Auchingramont Ct ML3 . 162 D3
Auchingramont Rd ML3 . 162 D4
Auchinlea Dr ML1 . 144 C1
Auchinlea Rd G34 . 99 F1
Auchinleck Ave G33 . 98 F6
Auchinleck Cres G33 . 98 E6
Auchinleck Dr G33 . 98 E6
Auchinleck Gdns G33 . 98 E6
Auchinleck Rd
Clydebank G81 . 74 B7
Glasgow G33 . 98 F7
Auchinleck Terr G81 . 74 B7
AUCHINLOCH . 79 D2
Auchinloch Prim Sch G66 . 79 D2
Auchinloch Rd G66 . 79 D4
Auchinloch St 2 G21 . 97 F3
Auchinraith Ave ML3 . 162 C5
Auchinraith Ind Est G72 . 161 E7
Auchinraith Prim Sch
G72 . 161 D7
Auchinraith Rd G72 . 161 E6
Auchinraith Terr G72 . 161 F7
Auchinvole Cres G65 . 60 B8
Auchmannoch Ave PA1 . 114 E5
Auchmead Rd PA16 . 44 E4
Auchmountain Rd
Greenock, Bridgend PA15 . 46 C3
Greenock PA15, PA13 . 46 E1
Auchnacraig Rd G81 . 74 C7
Auchneagh Ave PA16 . 45 B4
Auchneagh Cres PA16 . 45 B4
Auchneagh Farm La PA16 . 45 A5
Auchneagh Farm Rd PA16 . 45 B5

Auchneagh Rd PA16 45 B4
Auchter Ave ML2 166 C5
Auchterburn Rd ML7 166 F8
Auchter Rd ML2 165 E4
Auckland Pk 8 G75 159 A1
Auckland Pl G81 73 D4
Auckland St
Glasgow G22 97 B3
Glasgow G22 97 B4
Auctioneers Way 3
ML11 215 C3
Auldbar Rd G52 115 F3
Auldbar Terr PA2 114 A2
Auld Brig Rd FK10 10 B6
Auldburn Pl G43 136 B6
Auldburn Rd G43 136 B6
Auld Clay Rd KA21 206 E7
Auldearn Rd G21 98 D7
Auldgirth Rd G52 115 F3
Auldhame St ML5 121 E8
AULDHOUSE 180 D1
Auldhouse Ave G43 136 B6
Auldhouse Ct G43 136 B6
Auldhouse Gdns G43 136 B6
Auldhouse Prim Sch
G75 180 C1
Auldhouse Rd
East Kilbride G75 180 C2
Glasgow G43 136 C6
Auldhouse Ret Pk G43 136 C6
Auldhouse Terr G43 136 D6
Auld Kirk Mus* G66 58 C1
Auldkirk Rd FK10 4 C3
Auld Kirk Rd G72 139 C3
Auld Kirk The G76 158 A5
Auldlea Rd KA15 150 B2
Auldmurroch Dr G62 54 D2
Auld Nicks View KA7 238 E1
Auld Rd The G67 62 A4
Auld's Brae 2 ML6 123 A8
Auld School Wynd FK7 6 D5
Auld St G81 73 E3
Auldton Terr ML9 185 F1
Aultbea St G22 97 B8
Aultmore Dr ML1 143 B2
Aultmore Gdns G33 119 F7
Aultmore Park Prim Sch
G33 119 E7
Aultmore Pk G33 119 F7
Aultmore Rd G33 119 F7
Aurelia Ct ML1 163 E7
Aurora Ave
Clydebank G81 94 B8
Renfrew PA4 94 B3
Aursbridge Cres G78 134 D2
Aursbridge Dr G78 134 D2
Aurs Cres G78 134 D2
Aurs Dr G78 134 D2
Aurs Glen G78 134 C1
Aurs Pl G78 134 E2
Aurs Rd
Barrhead G78 134 E2
Newton Mearns G77 155 F7
Austen Rd G13 95 E5
Austine Dr ML3 183 E7
Aven Dr FK2 42 F3
Avenel Rd G13 75 E1
Avenue End Gate G33 99 B2
Avenue End Prim Sch 1
G33 99 B2
Avenue End Rd G33 99 B3
Avenuehead Rd
Moodiesburn G69 81 A1
Muirhead G69 101 A8
Avenuepark St G20 96 E5
Avenue Pk FK9 1 F7
Avenue Pl G83 27 D5
Avenue Sh Ctr The G77 156 D4
Avenue Sq KA3 211 D8
Avenue St
Glasgow G40 118 A5
Rutherglen G73 118 B1
Stewarton KA3 195 D1
Avenue The
Bridge of Allan FK9 2 A7
Falkirk FK2 24 D2
Kilmacolm PA13 69 E1
West Kilbride KA23 190 E8
Aviemore Gdns G61 76 B5
Aviemore Rd G52 115 E3
Avils Hill KA25 149 A1
Avils Pl KA25 149 B1
Avoch St G34 100 B1
Avon Ave
Bearsden G61 76 B4
Carluke ML8 187 E2
Longriggend ML6 84 D3
Avonbank Cres ML3 183 E8
Avonbank Gdns FK6 21 D4
Avonbank Rd
Larkhall ML9 184 E3
Rutherglen G73 137 F7
Avonbrae Cres ML3 183 E8
AVONBRIDGE 87 F6
Avonbridge Dr ML3 162 F3
Avonbridge Prim Sch FK1 87 F5
Avonbridge Rd FK1 86 B7
Avon Ct
Falkirk FK1 42 C2
Irvine KA11 220 A4
Motherwell ML1 163 E6
Avondale Ave G74 159 F1
Avondale Dr PA1 114 B6
Avondale Gdns G74 181 A8
Avondale Pl G74 181 A8
Avondale Rd KA23 190 D6
Avondale St G33 99 A1
Avon Dr
Bellshill ML4 142 C4
Linwood PA3 112 B6
Avonhead G75 180 E5
Avonhead Ave G67 82 C7
Avonhead Gdns G67 82 C7
Avonhead Pl G67 82 C7
Avonhead Rd G67 82 C7
Avon Ho ML3 162 E5
Avonmouth Pl PA19 44 F5
Avonpark FK1 87 F6
Avon Pl
Coatbridge ML5 101 D1
Kilmarnock KA1 228 B5
Larkhall ML9 199 B7
Avon Rd
Bishopbriggs G64 98 A8
Glasgow G46 136 B2
Larkhall ML9 199 A7
Avonside Dr FK6 21 D5
Avonside Gr ML3 162 F3
Avonspark St G21 98 A3
Avon St
Denny FK6 21 C4
Hamilton ML3 162 E3
Larkhall ML9 184 F3
Motherwell ML1 163 E6
Avon Twr 7 ML1 163 E5
Avon Wlk 4 G67 61 F1
Avon Wynd 23 ML2 165 F6
Aylmer Rd G43 136 F6
AYR 238 D7
Ayr Acad KA7 235 E1
Ayr Coll (Dam Park Campus)
KA8 239 B8
Ayr Dr ML6 123 A5
Ayr Hospl KA6 239 D1
Ayr La PA16 44 E3
Ayr Rd
Ashgill ML9 185 E2
Giffnock G46 136 B1
Irvine KA11, KA12 224 E7
Kilmarnock KA1 227 E3
Newton Mearns G77 156 B2
Newton Mearns G77 156 D4
Prestwick KA9 236 B6
Rutherglen G77 157 A7
Ayrshire Central Hospl
KA12 219 B7
Ayr St
Glasgow G21 97 E3
Troon KA10 229 D2
Ayr Sta KA7 239 A7
Ayr Terr PA16 44 E3
Ayton Park N G74 160 B3
Ayton Park S G74 160 A3
Aytoun Dr PA8 72 F3
Aytoun Rd G41 116 E3
Azalea Gdns G72 139 E5

B

Baads Rd ML7 126 E8
Baberton Way KA13 207 B3
Babylon Ave ML4 142 A3
Babylon Dr ML4 142 A3
Babylon Pl ML4 142 A3
Babylon Rd ML4 142 A3
Backbrae St 17 G65 60 D8
Backburn KA15 171 B8
Back Cswy G31 118 D5
Back Hawkhill Ave KA8 236 B2
Back Main St KA8 235 F1
Backmuir Cres ML3 162 B6
Backmuir Pl ML3 162 B6
Backmuir Rd
Clydebank G15 75 B4
Hamilton ML3 162 B6
Back O Barns ML3 162 E4
Back O Dykes Rd G66 80 B7
Back O Hill PA6 91 B1
Back O' Hill Ind Est FK8 2 A2
Back O' Hill Rd
Fluchter G64 56 E2
Stirling FK8 1 F1
Back Peebles St KA8 235 F2
Back Rd
Alva FK12 4 E7
Bridge of Weir PA11 110 D8
Back Row ML3 162 E4
Back Sneddon St PA3 113 E6
Back St G82 27 D1
Back Wlk 2 FK8 7 B7
Backwood Ct FK10 10 F5
Badenheath Pl G68 81 D5
Badenheath Terr G67 81 E4
Badenoch Rd G66 59 C1
Bagatelle Ct PA16 45 D7
Bagnell St G21 97 F5
Bahamas Way 6 G75 159 A1
Baidland Ave KA24 191 E6
Bailie Dr G61 75 D7
Bailie Fyfe Way
Overtown ML2 186 B7
Wishaw ML2 165 C1
Bailiehill Pl KA1 222 D1
Baillie Ave ML7 127 F5
Baillie Dr
Bothwell G71 141 A3
East Kilbride G74 160 C4
Baillie Gdns ML2 165 E4
Baillie Pl G74 160 C4
Baillies La ML6 123 A8
Bailliesmuir Pl ML2 166 A6
BAILLIESTON 120 A4
Baillieston Ave KA25 170 A8
Baillieston Rd
Glasgow, Barrachnie
G32 119 E4
Glasgow, Broomhouse
G71 120 B2
Baillieston Sta G69 120 B3
Baillie Waugh Rd FK7 7 C3
Baillie Wynd 11 G71 141 A8
Bain Cres G84 16 E3
Bainfield Rd G82 48 B7
Baingle Brae FK10 4 B3
Baingle Cres FK10 4 B3
BAINSFORD 42 B8
Bainsford Prim Sch FK2 42 B8
Bainsford St G32 118 F6
Bain St G40 241 C1
Bain Way G83 27 E6
Baird Ave
Airdrie ML6 103 B2
Glasgow G52 114 E8
Helensburgh G84 16 B2
Kilwinning KA13 207 E4
Larkhall ML9 199 C8
Baird Brae G4 97 B3
Baird Cres
Alexandria G83 27 C7
Cumbernauld G67 82 B7
Baird Ct
Clydebank G81 74 A2
Troon KA10 229 G4
Baird Dr
Bearsden G61 75 D5
Erskine PA8 72 F3
Baird Gdns G72 161 E6
Baird Hill G75 180 E8
Baird Memorial Prim Sch
G67 82 C7
Baird Pl
Bellshill ML4 142 A7
Kilmarnock KA3 223 B2
Monkton KA9 233 D4
Wishaw ML2 165 E4
Baird Rd
Alloway KA7 238 E2
Kilmarnock KA3 223 B2
Monkton KA9 233 D4
Bairds Cres ML3 162 C3
Bairdsland View ML4 142 B6
Baird St
Coatbridge ML5 122 A7
Falkirk FK1 41 D5
Glasgow G4 241 B4
Baird Terr ML7 127 C5
Bairns Ford Ave FK2 42 A7
Bairns Ford Ct FK2 42 A7
Bairns Ford Dr FK2 42 A7
Baker St
Glasgow G41 116 E1
Greenock PA15 46 A3
Stirling FK8 7 A8
Bakewell Rd G69 120 A5
Balaclava St G2, G3 240 B2
Balado Rd G33 119 E7
Balbakie Rd ML7 127 E5
Balbeggie St G32 119 C4
Balbeg St G51 115 E6
Balblair Rd
Airdrie ML6 103 A3
Glasgow G52 115 F2
Balcarres Ave G12 96 C5
Balcary Pl ML6 123 E1
Balcastle Gdns G65 36 B2
Balcastle Rd
Kilsyth G65 36 A1
Slamannan FK1 86 A6
Balcomie Cres KA10 230 A2
Balcomie St G33 99 A1
Balcomie Terr ML3 183 B8
Balcurvie Rd G34 100 A2
Baldernock Prim Sch G64 56 B2
Baldernock Rd G62 55 D2
Baldinnie Rd G34 120 B8
Baldoran Dr G66 58 B6
Baldorran Cres G68 61 B3
Baldovan Cres G33 119 F8
Baldovan Path G33 119 F7
Baldovie Rd G52 115 C3
Baldragon Rd G34 100 C1
Baldric Rd G13 95 C6
Baldwin Ave G13 95 D8
Balerno Dr G52 115 E3
Baleshrae Cres KA3 223 A6
Balfearn Dr G76 178 E5
Balfleurs St G62 55 B2
Balfluig St G34 99 F1
Balfour Ave KA15 171 B7
Balfour Cres
Plean FK7 12 D3
Stenhousemuir FK5 23 C2
Balfour Ct
Kilmarnock KA3 223 D3
Plean FK7 12 D3
Balfour St
Alloa FK10 10 C7
Bannockburn FK7 7 C1
Bonnybridge FK4 39 F6
Glasgow G20 96 D6
Port Glasgow PA14 47 B2
Stirling FK8 1 F2
Balfour Terr G75 180 F7
Balfour Wynd ML9 185 B1
Balfron Cres ML3 161 F3
Balfron Dr ML5 122 C3
Balfron Pl ML5 122 C4
Balfron Rd
Glasgow G51 115 E7
Greenock PA15 46 C1
Balfron Rd *continued*
Paisley PA1 114 D5
Balgair Dr PA1 114 B5
Balgair Pl G22 97 B5
Balgair St G22 97 B4
Balgair Terr G32 119 B5
Balglass Gdns G22 97 B4
Balglass St G22 97 B4
Balgonie PA2 113 B1
Balgonie Ave PA2 113 B1
Balgonie Dr PA2 113 C1
Balgonie Rd G52 115 E4
Balgonie Woods PA2 113 C1
Balgownie Cres G46 136 A2
Balgray Ave
Kilbirnie KA25 170 A8
Kilmarnock KA1 227 F2
Balgraybank St G21 98 A4
Balgray Cres G78 134 E2
Balgrayhill Rd G21 97 F6
Balgray Rd
Barrmill KA15 172 A5
Glengarnock KA14 170 B7
Newton Mearns G77 156 A5
Balgraystone Rd G78 155 D7
Balgray Way KA11 220 A6
Balintore St G32 119 A5
Baliol La G3 240 A4
Baliol St G3 240 A4
Baljaffray Prim Sch G61 75 C8
Baljaffray Rd G61 75 B8
Baljaffrey Sh Ctr G61 75 C8
Ballachalairy Yett G63 30 D4
Ballagan Pl G62 54 D2
Ballaig Ave G61 75 D5
Ballaig Cres G33 99 C5
Ballantay Quadrant G45 138 A3
Ballantay Rd G45 138 A3
Ballantay Terr G45 138 A3
Ballantine Ave G52 115 A7
Ballantine Dr KA7 238 F6
Ballantrae G74 159 D2
Ballantrae Cres G77 157 A4
Ballantrae Dr G77 157 A4
Ballantrae Rd G72 161 F6
Ballantrae Wynd ML1 143 B5
Ballantyne Drive La KA7 238 F6
Ballater Cres ML2 165 B5
Ballater Dr
Bearsden G61 76 A2
Inchinnan PA4 93 D7
Paisley PA2 114 A1
Stirling FK9 2 C4
Ballater Pl G5 117 D4
Ballater St G5 117 D5
Ballater Way ML5 101 C6
Ballayne Dr
Chryston G69 80 C1
Moodiesburn G69 81 A3
Ballengeich Pass FK8 2 A1
Ballengeich Rd FK8 1 F1
Ballerup Terr G75 180 E6
Ballewan Cres G63 31 A4
Ballindalloch Dr G31 118 B8
Ballindalloch La G31 118 A8
Ballinkier Ave FK4 38 E3
BALLOCH
Alexandria 19 E1
Cumbernauld 61 C2
Balloch Castle* G83 19 D2
Balloch Castle Ctry Pk*
G83 19 D2
Balloch Gdns G52 115 F3
Balloch Holdings G68 61 B1
Ballochmill Bsns Pk G73 138 D8
Ballochmill Rd G73 138 D8
Ballochmyle G74 160 D4
Ballochmyle Cres 11
G53 135 A8
Ballochmyle Dr 14 G53 135 A8
Ballochmyle Gdns G53 135 A8
Ballochmyle Pl 12 G53 135 A8
Ballochney La ML6 102 E2
Ballochney Rd
Plains ML6 103 E3
Plains ML6 104 A3
Ballochney St
Airdrie ML6 102 F1
Airdrie ML6 102 F2
Ballochnie Dr ML6 104 A3
Ballochnie View ML6 103 F2
Balloch Rd
Airdrie ML6 124 A6
Balloch G83 27 D8
Cumbernauld G68 61 D2
Greenock PA15 46 B1
Shotts ML7 146 E6
Balloch Rdbt G68 61 A2
Balloch Sta G83 27 E8
Balloch View G67 61 F2
Ballochyle Pl PA19 43 F5
Ballogie Rd G44 137 B7
Ballot Rd KA12 219 C3
BALMALLOCH 36 C1
Balmalloch Prim Sch G65 36 C1
Balmalloch Rd G65 36 B1
Balmartin Rd G23 76 D1
Balmedie PA8 73 A2
Balmeg Ave G46 157 C8
Balmerino Pl G64 98 D8
Balminnoch Pk KA7 238 D1
Balmoral Ave ML6 102 F5
Balmoral Cres
Coatbridge ML5 121 D4
Inchinnan PA4 93 E6
Balmoral Dr
Bearsden G61 76 A2
Bishopton PA7 72 C2
Balmoral Dr *continued*
Cambuslang G72 138 E6
Falkirk FK1 41 E3
Glasgow G32 139 B8
Balmoral Gdns
Blantyre G72 140 C2
Uddingston G71 120 F1
Balmoral Path 3 ML9 185 C2
Balmoral Pl
East Kilbride G74 159 C1
Gourock PA19 43 E5
Stenhousemuir FK5 23 E4
Stirling FK8 7 A7
Balmoral Rd
Elderslie PA5 112 B1
Kilmarnock KA3 222 E2
Balmoral St
Falkirk FK1 41 E3
Glasgow G14 95 B3
Balmoral Wynd KA3 211 E8
BALMORE 77 E8
Balmore Ct PA13 89 C7
Balmore Dr ML3 183 B8
Balmore Ind Est G22 97 B8
Balmore Pl G22 97 B6
Balmore Rd
Balmore G62, G64 77 C8
Bardowie G62, G64 77 C8
1 Glasgow G22 97 A7
Glasgow G22, G23 77 A2
Greenock PA15 46 C1
Balmore Sq G22 97 B5
Balmuildy Prim Sch G64 77 F3
Balmuildy Rd G64 77 D5
Balmulzier Rd FK1 86 B8
BALORNOCK 98 C6
Balornock Prim Sch G21 98 A4
Balornock Rd G64 98 A6
Balquharn Cotts FK12 4 D7
Balquhatstone Cres FK1 86 A6
Balquhiderock FK7 7 C4
Balrossie Dr PA13 89 A7
Balruddery Pl G64 98 D8
Balshagray Ave G11 95 F3
Balshagray Cres G14 95 E2
Balshagray Dr G11 95 F3
Balshagray La G11 95 F3
Balshagray Pl 2 G11 95 F3
Balta Cres G72 138 F3
Baltersan Gdns ML3 183 F3
Baltic Ct G40 118 A3
Baltic La G40 118 A3
Baltic Pl G40 118 A4
Baltic St
Glasgow G40 118 A3
Glasgow G40 118 A4
Glasgow G40 118 B3
Balure Cres FK7 8 D4
Balure Pl G31 118 C7
Balvaird Cres 2 G73 138 A7
Balvaird Dr G73 138 A7
Balvenie Dr ML1 143 B1
Balvenie St ML5 122 B3
Balveny Ave 3 G33 99 D2
Balveny Ct KA3 195 C1
Balveny Dr 2 G33 99 D2
Balveny Pl 1 G33 99 D2
Balveny St G33 99 D2
Balvicar Dr G42 116 F1
Balvicar St G42 116 F1
Balvie Ave
Clydebank G15 75 A1
Glasgow, Giffnock G46 136 D2
Balvie Cres G62 54 F2
Balvie Rd G62 54 F2
Banavie La G11 96 A3
Banavie Rd ML2 165 F6
Banchory Ave
Glasgow G43 136 B5
Glenmavis ML6 102 F5
Inchinnan PA4 93 D7
Banchory Cres G61 76 A2
Banchory Pl FK10 4 C3
Banchory Prim Sch FK10 4 C3
Banchory Rd ML2 165 B5
Bandeath Ind Est FK7 9 A5
Bandeath Rd FK7 8 D4
Baneberry Path G74 159 D4
Banff Ave ML6 123 A4
Banff Pl
East Kilbride G75 180 C8
Greenock PA16 44 D5
Banff Quadrant ML2 165 B5
Banff Rd PA16 44 D5
Banff St G33 99 B2
Bangorshill St
Glasgow G46 135 F4
Thornliebank G46 136 A4
Bank Ave G62 55 A3
Bankbrae Ave G53 135 A6
Bank Ct KA12 219 E4
Bankend Pl KA3 223 A5
Bankend Rd
Bridge of Weir PA11 110 E7
Dumbarton G82 49 F4
Bankend St G33 99 A1
Bankfaulds Ave KA25 149 A1
Bankfaulds Ct 7 KA25 149 A1
Bankfield Dr ML3 183 D7
Bankfield Pk KA7 239 C3
Bankfield Rdbt KA7 239 D3
Bankfoot Dr G52 115 B4
Bankfoot Pl G77 157 B4
Bankfoot Rd
Glasgow G52 115 B4
Paisley PA3 113 B6
Bankglen Rd G15 75 B4
Bankhall St G42 117 B2

BANKHEAD
Denny 39 E6
Rutherglen 137 F6
Bankhead Ave
Airdrie ML6 123 D7
Bellshill ML4 142 B3
Coatbridge ML5 121 C4
Glasgow G13 95 A6
Springside KA11 221 A2
Bankhead Cres FK4 39 D6
Bankhead Dr G73 138 A7
Bankhead Pl
Airdrie ML6 123 D7
Coatbridge ML5 121 C4
Stewarton KA3 195 E2
Bankhead Prim Sch
Glasgow G13 95 A6
Rutherglen G73 137 F7
Bankhead Rd
Carmunnock G76 158 D7
Fishcross FK10 5 D3
Kilwinning KA13 207 F3
Kirkintilloch G66 80 B7
Rutherglen G73 137 F7
Bankhead Terr ML11 215 B2
Bankholm Pl G76 157 F5
Bankier Prim Sch FK4 38 E3
Bankier Rd FK4 38 E3
Bankier Terr FK4 38 E3
BANKNOCK 38 E3
Banknock St G32 118 E6
Bank Pk G75 180 D8
Bank Pl
Irvine KA12 219 E4
1 Kilmarnock KA1 227 F8
Shotts ML7 146 F4
Bank Rd
Glasgow G32 139 C8
Harthill ML7 127 E5
BANKSIDE 42 C8
Bankside FK2 42 C7
Bankside Ave PA5 111 F3
Bankside Ct FK6 21 E2
Bankside Gdns KA25 149 A4
Bankside Ind Est FK2 42 D8
Banks Rd G66 58 E1
Bank St
Airdrie ML6 123 A8
Alexandria G83 27 E5
Alloa FK10 10 B6
Barrhead G78 134 C2
Cambuslang G72 139 A6
Coatbridge ML5 121 E6
Falkirk FK1 42 B5
Glasgow G12 96 E2
Greenock PA15 45 F4
Greenock PA15 45 F5
Irvine KA12 219 D3
Irvine, Stanecastle KA12 219 E4
Kilbirnie KA25 149 A2
Kilmarnock KA1 227 F8
Neilston G78 154 D7
Paisley PA1 113 F5
Prestwick KA9 236 B8
Slamannan FK1 86 A6
6 Stirling FK8 7 A8
Troon KA10 229 C2
Banks View FK2 14 E4
Banktop Pl PA5 111 F3
Bank View ML6 123 D2
Bankview Cres G66 79 A8
Bankview Dr G66 79 A8
Bankview Terr FK4 39 E6
Bank Way 14 ML9 185 B4
Bannachra Cres G83 27 D6
Bannachra Dr G84 16 B2
Bannatyne Ave G31 118 B7
Bannatyne St ML11 215 B4
Bannercross Ave 2 G69 120 A5
Bannercross Dr G69 120 A5
Bannercross Gdns 1
G69 120 A5
Banner Dr G13 75 C1
Bannerman Dr
Bellshill ML4 142 D5
Kilmarnock KA3 223 D2
Bannerman High Sch
G69 120 A4
Bannerman Pl G81 74 B2
Banner Rd G13 75 D1
Bannoch Gdns KA13 208 A4
Bannoch Pl
Kilwinning KA13 208 A3
Motherwell ML1 164 C3
Bannoch Rd
Kilwinning KA13 208 A2
Kilwinning KA13 208 A3
BANNOCKBURN 7 E2
Bannockburn Cross FK7 7 E1
Bannockburn Dr 10 ML9 185 C1
Bannockburn Heritage Ctr*
FK7 7 B2
Bannockburn High Sch
FK7 7 D2
Bannockburn Hospl FK7 11 F7
Bannockburn Pl
Kilmarnock KA3 223 B3
Motherwell ML1 143 A2
Bannockburn Prim Sch
FK7 7 E1
Bannockburn Rd
Cowie FK7 12 C8
Stirling FK7 7 C3
Bannockburn St PA16 45 C3
Bannockburn Station Rd
Bannockburn FK7 7 F2
Fallin FK7 8 A4
Bannock Rd FK7 8 C4
BANTASKIN 41 F4
Bantaskine Dr FK1 41 F4
Bantaskine Gdns FK1 41 E3
Bantaskine Rd FK1 41 F4
Bantaskine St FK1 41 E3
Bantaskin Prim Sch FK1 41 E4
Bantaskin St G20 96 C7
BANTON 37 E3
Banton Pl
Bonnybridge FK4 40 A3
Glasgow G33 120 A7
Banton Prim Sch G65 37 E3
Banton Rd G65 37 D2
Banyan Cres G71 121 D1
BARASSIE 229 E5
Barassie G74 159 D3
Barassiebank La KA10 229 E6
Barassie Cres G68 61 F6
Barassie Ct G71 140 F2
Barassie Dr PA11 110 C6
Barassie Pl KA1 227 E4
Barassie Prim Sch 7
KA10 229 E5
Barassie St KA10 229 D3
Barassie Sta KA10 229 E6
Barbadoes Pl KA1 227 E6
Barbadoes Rd KA1 227 E6
Barbados Gn 5 G75 159 A1
Barbae Pl G71 141 A3
Barbana Rd G74 158 E2
Barbegs Cres G65 60 F4
Barberry Ave G53 135 B2
Barberry Cres G67 82 D6
Barberry Dr KA15 171 A8
Barberry Gdns G53 135 B2
Barberry Pl G53 135 C2
Barbeth Gdns G67 82 B6
Barbeth Pl
Cumbernauld G67 82 B6
Irvine KA11 220 A5
Barbeth Rd G67 82 B6
Barbeth Way G67 82 A6
Barbour Ave FK7 7 C3
Barbour's Pk KA3 211 E8
Barbreck Rd 2 G42 116 F2
Barcaldine Ave G69 80 B1
Barcaldine Terr G41 116 F2
Barcapel Ave G77 156 E8
Barcapel Flats G77 156 E7
Barclaven Rd PA13 89 E8
Barclay Ave PA5 112 B2
Barclay Ct G60 73 B6
Barclay Dr
Helensburgh G84 16 C3
Johnstone PA5 112 B2
Kilmarnock KA3 223 C2
Barclay Gdns KA11 220 D6
Barclay Pl KA3 195 D1
Barclay Rd ML1 163 B6
Barclay Sq PA4 94 B1
Barclay St
Glasgow G21 97 F5
Old Kilpatrick G60 73 B5
Barcloy Pl ML6 123 F1
Barcraigs Dr PA2 133 F8
Bard Ave G13 95 B8
BARDOWIE 77 B7
Bardowie Ind Est G22 97 C4
Bardowie St
Glasgow G22 97 B4
Glasgow G22 97 C4
Bardrain Ave PA5 112 C2
BARDRAINNEY 68 F6
Bardrainney Ave PA14 68 F7
Bardrain Rd PA2 133 C7
Bardrill Dr G64 77 E1
Bardykes Rd
Blantyre G72 140 C1
Hamilton G72 161 B8
Barefield St ML9 185 A4
Barfillan Dr G52 115 E5
Barga Gdns KA21 205 F3
Bargany Ct G53 115 A1
Bargany Pl
8 Glasgow G53 115 A1
Glasgow G53 115 B1
Bargany Rd G53 115 A1
Bargaran Rd G53 115 B3
BARGARRAN 72 F3
Bargarran Prim Sch PA8 72 F2
Bargarran Rd PA8 72 F3
Bargarran Sq PA8 73 A3
Bargarron Dr PA3 114 A8
Barge Ct G84 15 D5
BARGEDDIE 121 A4
Bargeddie Prim Sch
G69 121 A6
Bargeddie St G33 98 D2
Bargeddie Sta G69 121 A4
Bargeny KA13 207 B2
Bargrennan Rd KA10 229 G6
Barhill La G65 59 F4
Bar Hill Pl G65 60 B8
Barhill Rd PA8 73 A2
Bar Hill Roman Fort*
G65 60 B4
Barhill Terr G65 60 A4
Barholm Sq G33 99 D1
Barholm St G33 99 D1
Barke Rd G67 62 A3
Barkin Ct FK1 42 B2
Barkly Terr 2 G75 180 C8
Barlae Ave G76 178 E8
BARLANARK 119 E6
Barlanark Ave G32 119 C6
Barlanark Cres G33 119 D7
Barlanark Dr G33 119 D7
Barlanark Pl
Glasgow G33 119 E7
Glasgow, Greenfield G32 119 B6
Barlanark Rd G33 119 E7
Barlandfauld St G65 60 E7
Barleith Ct KA1 228 F5
BARLEYBANK 79 D8
Barleyhill FK4 40 B5
Barlia Dr G45 137 E3
Barlia Gdns G45 137 E3
Barlia Gr G45 137 E3
Barlia Sports Complex
G45 137 E3
Barlia St G45 137 E3
Barlia Terr G45 137 F3
Barlia Way G45 137 F3
Barloan Cres G82 50 A5
Barloan Pl G82 50 A5
Barloch Ave G62 55 A2
Barloch Rd G62 55 B2
Barloch St G22 97 C4
Barlogan Ave G52 115 E5
Barlogan Quadrant G52 115 E5
Barmore Ave ML8 202 A8
Barmouth Ave PA19 44 F5
BARMULLOCH 98 D4
Barmulloch Prim Sch
G21 98 C4
Barmulloch Rd G21 98 B4
Barnard Gdns G64 78 B4
Barnbeth Rd G53 115 B2
Barncluith Ave ML3 163 A2
Barncluith Bsns Ctr ML3 162 F3
Barncluith Ct ML3 162 F3
Barncluith Rd ML3 162 F2
Barnego Rd FK6 21 D3
Barness Pl G33 119 A8
Barnes St G78 134 B2
Barnett Cres KA21 216 F7
Barnett Ct KA21 216 F7
Barnett Path 3 G72 161 D7
Barnflat St G73 118 B1
Barnford Cres KA7 239 A2
Barn Gn PA10 111 A3
BARNHILL 161 B8
Barnhill Ct G77 156 D3
Barnhill Dr
Glasgow G21 98 A3
Hamilton ML3 161 D2
Newton Mearns G77 156 D2
Tullibody FK10 4 C2
Barnhill Rd G82 50 D3
Barnhill St PA15 46 C3
Barnhill Sta G21 98 A3
Barnkirk Ave G15 75 A3
Barn Rd FK8 7 A8
Barns Cres KA7 238 F8
Barnscroft PA5, PA10 111 B4
Barnsdale Rd FK7 7 A3
Barnsford Ave PA4 93 B4
Barnsford Rd
Inchinnan PA4 93 B3
Paisley PA3 113 B8
Barns Pk KA7 238 F8
Barns St
Ayr KA7 238 F8
Clydebank G81 94 C8
Barns Street La KA7 238 F8
Barns Terr KA7 238 F8
Barnswood Pl 6 G71 141 B3
Barnton La FK1 42 B4
Barnton St
Glasgow G32 118 E7
Stirling FK8 7 B8
Barnweil Ave KA9 236 C6
Barnweil Dr KA1 228 E5
Barnweil Rd KA1 227 E5
Barnwell Rd FK9 2 C4
Barnwell Terr G51 115 E7
Barochan Cres PA3 113 A4
Barochan Pl G53 115 B3
Barochan Rd
Bellshill ML4 142 D6
Brookfield PA3, PA6, PA10,
PA11 111 D6
Glasgow G53 115 B3
Houston PA6 91 B6
Barochan Way PA3 113 A4
Baronald Dr G12 96 B6
Baronald Gate G12 96 B6
Baronald St G73 118 B1
Baron Ct ML3 163 A2
Barone Dr G76 157 C8
Baronhall Dr G72 161 C8
Baronhill G67 62 B5
Baron Path G69 120 F5
Baron Rd PA3 114 A6
Baronscourt Dr PA1 112 F4
Baronscourt Gdns PA1 112 F4
Baronscourt Rd PA1 112 F4
Barons Gate G71 140 E4
Baron's Haugh RSPB Nature
Reserve* ML1 163 E2
Barons Rd ML1 164 C2
Baron St PA4 94 C2
Barons Twr ML1 164 B3
Barony Ct
Ardrossan KA22 205 D1
Cambusbarron FK7 6 D6
4 Glasgow G69 120 B6
Irvine KA11 219 F5
Barony Dr G69 120 B5
Barony Gdns G69 120 B5
Barony Glebe KA23 190 D5
Barony Gr 4 G72 139 E3
Barony Pl G68 60 E1
Barony Rd KA9 236 C6
Barony Terr KA25 170 A8
Barony Wynd 5 G69 120 B6
Barra Ave
Coatbridge ML5 121 E4
Renfrew PA4 94 C1
Wishaw ML2 165 E5
BARRACHNIE 119 E4
Barrachnie Ave G69 120 A6
Barrachnie Cres G69 119 F5
Barrachnie Ct G69 119 F6
Barrachnie Dr G69 120 A5
Barrachnie Gr G69 120 A6
Barrachnie Pl 4 G69 120 A6
Barrachnie Rd G69 119 F5
Barrack St
Glasgow G4 241 C1
Hamilton ML3 162 D4
Barra Cres
Irvine KA11 220 C2
Old Kilpatrick G60 73 C5
Barra Dr ML6 123 E6
Barra Gdns G60 73 C5
Barra La KA11 220 C2
Barra Pl
Coatbridge ML5 121 E4
Irvine KA11 220 C2
Stenhousemuir FK5 24 A4
Stevenston KA20 206 F2
Barra Rd G60 73 C5
Barras Mkt The G4 241 C1
Barra St G20 96 C8
Barraston Holdings G64 57 A3
Barraston Rd
Fluchter G64 56 F4
Torrance G64 57 A2
Barr Ave
Crosshouse KA2 221 F4
Neilston G78 154 E8
Barra Wynd KA11 220 C2
Barrbridge Rd ML5 121 B4
Barrcraig Rd PA11 110 C8
Barr Cres
Clydebank G81 74 B5
Irvine KA12 219 C4
Barr Farm Rd G65 60 E7
Barr Gr G71 141 A8
BARRHEAD 134 E2
Barrhead High Sch G78 134 D3
Barrhead Rd
Glasgow G43, G53 135 C7
Newton Mearns G77 156 B5
Paisley PA2 114 A2
Barrhead Sp Ctr G78 134 C3
Barrhead Sta G78 134 B3
Barrhill Cres PA10 111 C3
Barrhill Ct G66 80 A8
Barrhill Rd
Erskine PA8 73 A2
Gourock PA19 44 D8
Kirkintilloch G66 80 A8
Barriedale Ave ML3 162 B3
Barrie Quadrant G81 74 A4
Barrie Rd
East Kilbride G74 160 D5
Glasgow G52 115 A7
Stenhousemuir FK5 23 F3
Barrie St ML1 163 E6
Barrie Terr KA22 205 D1
Barrington Ave KA15 150 B1
Barrington Dr G4 96 F2
Barrington Gdns KA15 150 C1
Barrisdale Rd
Glasgow G20 96 D8
Wishaw ML2 165 F6
Barrisdale Way G73 138 B4
Barrland Ct G46 136 C3
Barrland Dr G46 136 C3
Barrland St G41 117 A3
BARRMILL 171 F3
Barrmill Rd
Beith KA15 171 C8
Burnhouse KA15 172 B2
Glasgow G43 136 B5
Barrochan Intc PA5 111 E4
BARROWFIELD
Coatbridge 122 A4
Glasgow 118 B5
Barrowfield Gate G40 118 B4
Barrowfield Pl G40 118 B4
Barrowfield St
Coatbridge ML5 121 F4
Glasgow G40 118 A5
Barrpath G65 60 F7
Barr Pl
Newton Mearns G77 156 C5
Paisley PA1 113 D4
Barr's Brae
Kilmacolm PA13 69 D1
Port Glasgow PA14 68 C8
Barrs Brae La PA14 47 C1
Barrs Cres G82 48 A8
Barrs Ct G82 26 A1
Barrs La ML8 187 F3
Barrs Rd G82 48 A8
Barr St
Ardrossan KA22 205 C1
Glasgow G20 97 A3
Motherwell ML1 163 E8
Barrs Terr G82 48 A8
Barr Terr G74 159 E2
Barr Thomson Bsns Pk
KA1 228 A6
BARRWOOD 60 E8
Barrwood Pl G71 141 A8
Barrwood St G33 98 E2
Barry Gdns G72 161 D6
Barsail Prim Sch PA8 93 C8
Barscube Ave PA14 68 E7
Barscube Terr PA2 114 A2
Barshaw Ct G52 114 E6
Barshaw Dr PA1 114 A6
Barshaw Ho PA1 114 C5
Barshaw Pl PA1 114 D5
Barshaw Rd G52 114 F6
Barskiven Rd PA1 112 F4
Barterholm Rd PA2 113 F2
Bartholomew St G40 118 A3
Bartiebeith Rd G33 119 E7
Bartie Gdns ML9 185 F1
Bartlands Pl G76 178 F4
Barton Ave G83 28 A8
Bartonhall Rd ML2 165 D1
Bartonholm Terr KA13 207 F1
Barty's Rd ML4 142 C5
Barwheys Dr KA6 237 F6
Barwood Dr PA8 73 A3
Barwood Hill G82 50 B6
Bassett Ave G13 95 B8
Bassett Cres G13 95 B8
Bastion Wynd 7 FK8 7 B7
Bathgate St G31 118 A6
Bathgo Ave PA1 114 E4
Bath La G2 240 B3
Bathlin Cres 5 G69 81 A3
Bath Pl KA7 238 E8
Bath Sq KA22 216 C8
Bath St
Glasgow G2 240 C3
Gourock PA19 44 E8
Kilmarnock KA3 222 F3
Bathurst Dr KA7 239 A1
Bath Villas KA22 216 C8
Bathville Rd KA25 149 A1
Baton Rd ML7 146 D6
Batson St G42 117 B2
Batterflatts Gdns FK7 6 F6
Batterflatts Ho FK7 6 F6
Battery Park Ave PA16 45 B8
Battery Park Dr PA16 45 B8
Battismains ML11 215 C4
BATTLEFIELD 137 A7
Battlefield Ave G42 137 A7
Battlefield Ct G42 137 B7
Battlefield Gdns G42 137 A8
Battlefield Prim Sch
G42 136 F7
Battlefield Rd G42 137 A7
Battle Pl G42 136 F8
Battles Burn Dr G32 119 A2
Battles Burn Gate G32 119 A2
Battles Burn View G32 119 A2
Bavelaw St G33 99 D2
Bawhirley Rd PA15 46 C3
Baxter Brae ML1 165 B8
Baxter Cres FK6 21 C1
Baxter La
Alexandria G83 27 E7
Lanark ML11 215 A4
Baxter St
Fallin FK7 8 D4
Greenock PA15 46 D3
Baxters Wynd FK1 42 B4
Baxter Wynd ML2 164 E2
Bayfield Ave G15 75 A3
Bayfield Terr G15 75 A3
Bayne St FK8 2 A1
Bay St PA14 47 C1
Bay View Rd PA19 44 F7
Bay Willow Ct G72 139 F4
Beach Dr KA12 218 F1
Beach Rd
Troon KA10 229 D7
Troon KA10 229 E5
Beaconcroft FK9 2 C7
Beaconhurst Sch FK9 2 C6
Beacon Pl G33 118 F8
Beaconsfield Rd G12 96 B5
Beagle Cres KA7 238 C3
Bean Row FK1 42 B4
BEANSBURN 223 A2
Beansburn KA3 223 A3
Beanshields Rd ML8 201 F4
Beard Cres G69 101 A5
Beardmore Cotts PA4 93 E6
Beardmore Pl G81 73 E3
Beardmore St G81 73 E3
Beardmore Way
Clydebank G81 73 D2
Glasgow G31 118 B6
Bearford Dr G52 115 B6
Bearhope St PA15 45 F5
BEARSDEN 75 E6
Bearsden Acad G61 75 D7
Bearsden Bath House*
G61 75 F5
Bearsden Prim Sch G61 75 E5
Bearsden Rd
Bearsden G61 95 F7
Bearsden G61 95 F8
Bearsden Sta G61 75 E4
Bearside Rd FK7 7 A3
Beaton Ave FK7 7 C1
Beaton La KA2 225 F1
Beaton Rd
Balloch G83 27 E8
Glasgow G41 116 E2
Beaton St ML9 184 F5
Beaton Terr KA12 219 C5
Beatrice Dr ML1 142 F5
Beatrice Gdns PA6 111 D8
Beatson Wynd G71 121 A1
Beattie Ct KA20 217 D7
Beattock St G31 118 D5

Beattock Wynd ML3 . . . . . 162 A3
Beatty Ave FK8 . . . . . 2 A2
Beatty Pl G84 . . . . . 17 A2
Beatty St G81 . . . . . 73 E3
Beauclerc St FK12 . . . . . 5 A7
Beaufield Gdns KA3 . . . . . 222 B7
Beaufort Ave G43 . . . . . 136 C6
Beaufort Dr
Falkirk FK2 . . . . . 24 A3
Kirkintilloch G66 . . . . . 79 B8
Beaufort Gdns G64 . . . . . 77 E1
Beauly Cres
Airdrie ML6 . . . . . 123 E6
Kilmacolm PA13 . . . . . 89 D7
Kilmarnock KA1 . . . . . 228 A5
Newton Mearns G77 . . . . . 157 B4
Wishaw ML2 . . . . . 165 B1
Beauly Ct FK1 . . . . . 42 C1
Beauly Dr PA2 . . . . . 112 E1
Beauly Pl
Bishopbriggs G64 . . . . . 78 D2
Chryston G69 . . . . . 80 D1
Coatbridge ML5 . . . . . 122 B3
East Kilbride G74 . . . . . 159 D2
6 Glasgow G20 . . . . . 96 D6
Motherwell ML1 . . . . . 143 A5
Beauly Rd G69 . . . . . 120 A3
Beaumont Dr FK2 . . . . . 24 B2
Beaumont Gate 5 G12 . . . 96 C3
Beckfield Cres G33 . . . . . 98 D7
Beckfield Dr G33 . . . . . 98 D7
Beckfield Gate G33 . . . . . 98 D7
Beckfield Gr G33 . . . . . 98 D7
Beckfield Wlk G33 . . . . . 98 D7
Beckford La ML3 . . . . . 162 D5
Beckford Prim Sch ML3 . 162 C5
Beckford St Bsns Ctr
ML3 . . . . . 162 D5
Beckford St ML3 . . . . . 162 D5
Bedale Rd G69 . . . . . 119 F4
Beda Pl FK7 . . . . . 8 C5
Bedcow View G66 . . . . . 79 F7
Bedford Ave G81 . . . . . 74 D2
Bedford Ct FK10 . . . . . 10 A6
Bedford La 6 G5 . . . . . 117 B5
Bedford Pl FK10 . . . . . 10 A6
Bedford St
Glasgow G5 . . . . . 117 B5
Greenock PA16 . . . . . 45 D7
Bedlay Ct G69 . . . . . 81 A3
Bedlay Pl ML5 . . . . . 81 F1
Bedlay View G71 . . . . . 141 B8
Bedlay Wlk 14 G69 . . . . . 81 A3
Bedlormie Dr EH48 . . . . . 107 C2
Beech Ave
Bearsden G61 . . . . . 76 A7
Beith KA15 . . . . . 150 B2
Bridge of Weir PA11 . . . . . 90 D1
Cambuslang G72 . . . . . 138 F6
Elderslie PA5 . . . . . 112 C2
Glasgow, Dumbreck G41 . . . 116 B4
Glasgow, Garrowhill G69 . . 120 A5
Glasgow, Ibrox G41 . . . . . 116 B5
Irvine KA12 . . . . . 219 D2
Kilmarnock KA1 . . . . . 227 D8
Larkhall ML9 . . . . . 185 D2
Motherwell ML1 . . . . . 143 B3
Newton Mearns G77 . . . . . 156 E4
Paisley PA2 . . . . . 114 A1
Plean FK7 . . . . . 12 C3
Quarter ML3 . . . . . 183 F4
Rutherglen G73 . . . . . 138 C4
Beechbank Ave ML6 . . . . . 102 F1
Beechburn Cres PA12 . . . 129 D3
Beech Cres
Cambuslang G72 . . . . . 139 E4
Denny FK6 . . . . . 21 C3
Larbert FK5 . . . . . 41 C8
Motherwell ML1 . . . . . 143 D7
Newton Mearns G77 . . . . . 156 E4
Beech Dr
Caldercruix ML6 . . . . . 104 F4
Clydebank G81 . . . . . 74 A5
Beeches Ave G81 . . . . . 73 F6
Beeches Rd G81 . . . . . 73 F6
Beeches Terr G81 . . . . . 74 A6
Beeches The
Brookfield PA5 . . . . . 111 C6
3 Hamilton G72 . . . . . 161 C7
Houston PA6 . . . . . 91 D1
Lanark ML11 . . . . . 215 B2
Newton Mearns G77 . . . . . 156 F6
Beechfield Dr ML8 . . . . . 202 A8
Beechfield Rd KA15 . . . . . 170 F7
Beech Gdns
Glasgow G69 . . . . . 120 A5
Stirling FK7 . . . . . 6 F6
Beech Gr
Ayr KA8 . . . . . 239 C8
East Kilbride G75 . . . . . 180 B6
Gartcosh G69 . . . . . 101 A5
Law ML8 . . . . . 186 F6
Rhu G84 . . . . . 15 D6
Wishaw ML2 . . . . . 165 C7
Beechgrove G69 . . . . . 80 F2
Beechgrove Ave G71 . . . . . 141 C7
Beechgrove Pl G84 . . . . . 25 C8
Beechgrove Quadrant
ML1 . . . . . 143 A5
Beechgrove St G40 . . . . . 118 B2
Beech La FK9 . . . . . 2 B4
Beechlands Ave G44 . . . . . 136 F1
Beechlands Dr G76 . . . . . 157 C6
Beechmount Ct ML7 . . . . . 147 B2
Beechmount Rd G66 . . . . . 79 D4
Beech Pl
Bishopbriggs G64 . . . . . 98 B8
Gourock PA19 . . . . . 44 C6
Beech Rd
Bishopbriggs G64 . . . . . 98 B8
Johnstone PA5 . . . . . 111 D1
Kirkintilloch G66 . . . . . 79 C6
Beech Terr ML9 . . . . . 185 B1
Beechtree Terr G66 . . . . . 58 C6
Beechwood
Alloa FK10 . . . . . 5 E1
Kilwinning KA13 . . . . . 207 D5
Larkhall ML9 . . . . . 185 A5
Sauchie FK10 . . . . . 5 D1
Wishaw ML2 . . . . . 164 D1
Beechwood Ave
Clarkston G76 . . . . . 157 C6
Hamilton ML3 . . . . . 183 B8
Langbank PA14 . . . . . 70 C7
Rutherglen G73 . . . . . 138 C6
Beechwood Cres ML2 . . . 165 C2
Beechwood Ct
Bearsden G61 . . . . . 75 F3
Cumbernauld G67 . . . . . 82 F8
1 Lanark ML11 . . . . . 215 C3
Beechwood Dr
Bonhill G83 . . . . . 28 B2
Coatbridge ML5 . . . . . 122 D5
Glasgow G11 . . . . . 95 F4
Renfrew PA4 . . . . . 94 C1
Beechwood Gate 2
ML11 . . . . . 215 C3
Beechwood Gdns
Bellshill ML4 . . . . . 142 C4
Moodiesburn G69 . . . . . 80 F1
Stirling FK8 . . . . . 7 A5
Beechwood Gr G78 . . . . . 134 C1
Beechwood La 7 G61 . . . . . 75 F3
Beechwood Paddock
KA10 . . . . . 230 B4
Beechwood Pl
Bellshill ML4 . . . . . 142 C4
Glasgow G11 . . . . . 95 F4
Beechwood Rd G67 . . . . . 82 F8
Beechworth Dr ML1 . . . . . 143 D2
Beecraigs Way ML6 . . . . . 104 A3
Beecroft Pl G72 . . . . . 140 E1
Begg Ave FK1 . . . . . 41 E4
Beggs Terr KA22 . . . . . 205 D3
Beil Dr G13 . . . . . 94 F7
BEITH 150 B1
Beith Dr ML6 . . . . . 123 A4
Beith Prim Sch KA15 . . . . . 171 B8
Beith Rd
Barrmill KA15 . . . . . 171 F4
Dalry KA24 . . . . . 191 E8
Glengarnock KA14 . . . . . 170 C6
Greenock PA16 . . . . . 45 E2
Johnstone PA9, PA10, PA5 . . 131 B7
Johnstone, Quarrelton
PA5 . . . . . 111 E1
Beith St G11 . . . . . 96 B1
Beith Way G72 . . . . . 161 D2
Belfast Quay KA12 . . . . . 219 A2
Belford Ct G77 . . . . . 156 D2
Belford Gr G77 . . . . . 156 D2
Belgowan St ML4 . . . . . 141 F7
Belgrave La G12 . . . . . 96 E3
Belgrave St ML4 . . . . . 141 F6
Belhaven Ct G77 . . . . . 156 D2
Belhaven Pk G69 . . . . . 100 C7
Belhaven Pl
Glenboig ML5 . . . . . 101 F6
Newton Mearns G77 . . . . . 156 D2
Belhaven Rd
Hamilton ML3 . . . . . 161 E3
Wishaw ML2 . . . . . 165 A3
Belhaven St PA14 . . . . . 47 B2
Belhaven Terr
20 Glasgow G12 . . . . . 96 C4
Wishaw ML2 . . . . . 165 A3
Belhaven Terrace La 19
G12 . . . . . 96 C4
Belhaven Terrace West La 17
G12 . . . . . 96 C4
Belhaven Terr W 18 G12 . . . 96 C4
BELLAHOUSTON 116 A4
Bellahouston Acad G41 . 116 C5
Bellahouston Dr G52 . . . . . 115 E3
Bellahouston L Ctr G52 . . 115 F4
Bellahouston Pk* G41 . . . 115 F4
Bellahouston Prim Sch 2
G51 . . . . . 116 C5
Bellairs Pl G72 . . . . . 140 C1
Bellard Rd KA23 . . . . . 190 C4
Bellard Wlk KA23 . . . . . 190 D4
Bellas Pl ML6 . . . . . 104 A2
Bellaville Gr G69 . . . . . 100 D8
Bellcote Rd G68 . . . . . 61 D5
Bellcraig Ct G76 . . . . . 158 A5
Bell Cres KA12 . . . . . 219 D5
Bell Ct FK2 . . . . . 42 C7
Bell Dr G72 . . . . . 161 C4
Belleaire Dr PA16 . . . . . 45 C7
Bellefield Cres ML11 . . . . . 215 A6
Bellefield Rd ML11 . . . . . 215 A5
Bellefield Way ML11 . . . . . 215 A6
BELLEISLE 238 E3
Belleisle Ave G71 . . . . . 140 E7
Belleisle Cl KA13 . . . . . 207 C4
Belleisle Cotts KA7 . . . . . 238 D3
Belleisle Cres PA11 . . . . . 110 C6
Belleisle Ct G68 . . . . . 61 E4
Belleisle Dr G68 . . . . . 61 E4
Belleisle Gdns G68 . . . . . 61 E4
Belleisle Gr G68 . . . . . 61 E4
Belleisle Pk* KA7 . . . . . 238 E3
Belleisle Pl
Gourock PA19 . . . . . 44 A6
Kilmarnock KA1 . . . . . 227 E4
Belleisle St G42 . . . . . 117 B1
Bellesleyhill Ave KA8 . . . . . 236 B3
Bellesleyhill Ct KA8 . . . . . 236 A4
Bellesleyhill Rd KA8 . . . . . 236 A3
Bellevale Ave KA7 . . . . . 239 A5
Bellevale Quadrant KA7 . . 238 F5
Bellevue Ave G66 . . . . . 79 B8
Bellevue Cotts KA7 . . . . . 238 F7
Bellevue Cres
Ayr KA7 . . . . . 238 F7
Prestwick KA9 . . . . . 236 C7
Bellevue Gdns KA1 . . . . . 222 D1
Bellevue La KA7 . . . . . 238 F7
Bellevue Pk FK10 . . . . . 9 E6
Bellevue Rd
Alloa FK10 . . . . . 9 F6
Ayr KA7 . . . . . 238 F7
Kilmarnock KA1 . . . . . 222 D1
Kirkintilloch G66 . . . . . 79 B8
Prestwick KA9 . . . . . 236 C7
Bellevue St
Ayr KA7 . . . . . 238 F7
Falkirk FK1 . . . . . 42 C4
BELLFIELD 228 B4
Bellfield Ave KA1 . . . . . 228 D6
Bellfield Cres G78 . . . . . 134 B3
Bellfield Ct
Barrhead G78 . . . . . 134 B4
Hurlford KA1 . . . . . 228 D6
Bellfield Dr ML2 . . . . . 165 C1
Bellfield Intc KA1 . . . . . 228 C6
Bellfield La KA9 . . . . . 236 B8
Bellfield Prim Sch 1
KA1 . . . . . 228 A4
Bellfield Rd
Bannockburn FK7 . . . . . 7 E1
Kirkintilloch G66 . . . . . 79 B8
Stirling FK8 . . . . . 7 B5
Bellfield St G31 . . . . . 118 A6
Bellflower Ave G53 . . . . . 135 C3
Bellflower Ct G74 . . . . . 159 C3
Bellflower Gdns G53 . . . . . 135 C3
Bellflower Gr G74 . . . . . 159 C4
Bellflower Pl G53 . . . . . 135 C3
Bell Gr ML8 . . . . . 187 B6
Bell Green E G75 . . . . . 180 F8
Bell Green W G75 . . . . . 180 E8
Bellgrove St G31 . . . . . 117 F6
Bellgrove Sta G31 . . . . . 117 F6
Bellisle Terr ML3 . . . . . 183 B8
Bellmans Cl KA15 . . . . . 150 B1
Bellrock Ave KA9 . . . . . 236 B6
Bellrock Cres G33 . . . . . 119 A8
Bellrock Ct G33 . . . . . 119 B8
Bellrock Rd KA8 . . . . . 236 A4
Bellrock St G33 . . . . . 119 B8
Bellrock View G33 . . . . . 119 A8
Bellscroft Ave G73 . . . . . 137 F7
Bellsdyke Hospl FK5 . . . . . 23 D5
Bellsdyke Pl FK5 . . . . . 23 A3
Bellsdyke Rd
Airdrie ML6 . . . . . 123 A6
Falkirk FK2 . . . . . 24 C6
Stenhousemuir FK5 . . . . . 23 D4
Bellsdyke Rdbt FK5 . . . . . 23 B3
Bellsfield Dr G72 . . . . . 161 E6
Bellshaugh Ct G12 . . . . . 96 C5
Bellshaugh Gdns G12 . . . . . 96 C5
Bellshaugh La G12 . . . . . 96 C5
Bellshaugh Pl 2 G12 . . . . . 96 C5
Bellshaugh Rd G12 . . . . . 96 C4
BELLSHILL 142 B4
Bellshill Acad ML4 . . . . . 142 B5
Bellshill Ind Est ML4 . . . . . 141 F6
Bellshill Rd
Bellshill G71, ML1, ML4 . . . 141 D2
Bothwell G71 . . . . . 141 B5
Motherwell ML1 . . . . . 142 C2
Bellshill Sta ML4 . . . . . 142 A5
BELLSIDE 144 E1
Bellside Rd
Chapelhall ML6 . . . . . 123 F2
Cleland ML1 . . . . . 144 D1
Motherwell ML1 . . . . . 144 A8
Bellsland Dr KA1 . . . . . 227 F6
Bellsland Gr KA1 . . . . . 227 F6
Bellsland Pl KA1 . . . . . 228 A7
Bellsmeadow Rd FK1 . . . . . 42 C4
BELLSMYRE 50 B6
Bellsmyre Ave G82 . . . . . 50 A6
Bell St
Airdrie ML6 . . . . . 122 F7
Bellshill ML4 . . . . . 142 B7
Clydebank G81 . . . . . 94 D7
Glasgow G1 . . . . . 241 B1
Greenock PA15 . . . . . 46 E2
Renfrew PA4 . . . . . 94 D4
Wishaw ML2 . . . . . 165 A3
Bellstone Cotts KA24 . . . . . 192 B8
Bells Wynd ML11 . . . . . 215 C5
Bell's Wynd
Falkirk FK1 . . . . . 42 B4
Lanark ML11 . . . . . 215 C5
Belltree Ave KA3 . . . . . 211 D8
Belltrees Cres PA3 . . . . . 113 A4
Belltrees Rd
Howwood PA9 . . . . . 130 C2
Lochwinnoch PA12 . . . . . 150 D4
Bell View ML2 . . . . . 166 A6
Bell View Ct PA4 . . . . . 94 D4
Bellvue Cres ML4 . . . . . 141 F4
Bellvue Way ML5 . . . . . 122 D4
Bellwood St G41 . . . . . 136 E8
Bellziehill Rd ML4 . . . . . 141 E5
Belmar Ct PA3 . . . . . 112 C5
BELMONT 239 A4
Belmont Acad KA7 . . . . . 239 B5
Belmont Ave
Ayr KA7 . . . . . 239 A5
Bonnybridge FK4 . . . . . 39 D5
Shieldhill FK1 . . . . . 66 E7
Uddingston G71 . . . . . 140 E7
Belmont Cres
Ayr KA7 . . . . . 239 A5
Glasgow G12 . . . . . 96 E3
Kilmaurs KA3 . . . . . 222 B7
Belmont Ct
Kilmaurs KA3 . . . . . 222 C7
6 Kirkintilloch G66 . . . . . 79 D8
Belmont Dr
Ayr KA7 . . . . . 239 A5
Barrhead G78 . . . . . 134 D1
East Kilbride G75 . . . . . 180 B8
Glasgow G46 . . . . . 136 B3
Rutherglen G73 . . . . . 138 B7
Shotts ML7 . . . . . 147 B2
Belmont House Sch G77 157 A6
Belmont La G12 . . . . . 96 E3
Belmont Place E KA7 . . . 239 A6
Belmont Place W KA7 . . . 239 A6
Belmont Rd
Ayr KA7 . . . . . 239 A5
Cambuslang G72 . . . . . 138 E3
Glasgow G21 . . . . . 97 F6
Kilmacolm PA13 . . . . . 89 C7
Paisley PA3 . . . . . 114 A6
Belmont St
Clydebank G81 . . . . . 94 B8
Coatbridge ML5 . . . . . 101 D1
Falkirk FK1 . . . . . 42 C4
Glasgow G12 . . . . . 96 E3
Kilsyth G65 . . . . . 36 C1
Overtown ML2 . . . . . 186 B6
Belmont Twr FK1 . . . . . 42 C4
Belses Dr G52 . . . . . 115 C5
Belses Gdns G52 . . . . . 115 C5
Belstane Gate ML8 . . . . . 188 A3
Belstane Mews ML8 . . . . . 188 A3
Belstane Pk ML8 . . . . . 187 F3
Belstane Pl 4 G71 . . . . . 141 A3
Belstane Rd
Carluke ML8 . . . . . 188 A3
Cumbernauld G67 . . . . . 82 F5
Belsyde Ave G15 . . . . . 75 B2
Beltane St
Glasgow G3 . . . . . 240 A3
Wishaw ML2 . . . . . 165 A2
Beltonfoot Way ML2 . . . . . 164 F2
Beltrees Ave G53 . . . . . 115 A2
Beltrees Cres G53 . . . . . 115 A2
Beltrees Rd G53 . . . . . 115 A1
Belvidere Ave G31 . . . . . 118 C4
Belvidere Cres
Bellshill ML4 . . . . . 142 B4
Bishopbriggs G64 . . . . . 78 B2
Belvidere Gate G31 . . . . . 118 C4
Belvidere Prim Sch ML4 . 142 A4
Belvidere Rd ML4 . . . . . 142 A4
Belvidere Terr KA8 . . . . . 236 A2
Belville Ave PA15 . . . . . 46 C3
Belville Dr PA15 . . . . . 46 B3
Belville St PA15 . . . . . 46 B3
Belvoir Pl G72 . . . . . 161 D8
Bemersyde G64 . . . . . 78 C2
Bemersyde Ave G43 . . . . . 136 B5
Bemersyde Pl ML9 . . . . . 185 A1
Bemersyde Rd PA2 . . . . . 132 E8
Ben Aigan Pl G53 . . . . . 135 C4
Ben Alder Dr PA2 . . . . . 114 D1
Benalder St G11 . . . . . 96 C1
Benarty Gdns G64 . . . . . 78 B2
Benbain Pl KA11 . . . . . 220 B6
Benbecula G74 . . . . . 160 C1
Benbecula Rd KA3 . . . . . 223 A5
Ben Bouie Dr G84 . . . . . 16 F1
Benbow Rd G81 . . . . . 73 F2
Ben Buie Way PA2 . . . . . 114 D1
Bencleuch Pl KA11 . . . . . 220 B3
Bencloich Ave G66 . . . . . 57 E8
Bencloich Cres G66 . . . . . 33 E1
Bencloich Rd G66 . . . . . 57 E8
Benclutha PA14 . . . . . 47 E1
Bencroft Dr G44 . . . . . 137 E5
Bendigo Pl ML11 . . . . . 215 A4
Ben Donich Pl G53 . . . . . 135 D4
Ben Edra Pl G53 . . . . . 135 D4
Benford Ave ML1 . . . . . 143 D4
Benford Knowe ML1 . . . . . 143 E4
Bengairn St G31 . . . . . 118 C7
Bengal Pl 2 G43 . . . . . 136 C7
Bengal St G43 . . . . . 136 C7
Ben Garrisdale Pl G53 . . 135 D4
Ben Glas Pl G53 . . . . . 135 D4
Benhar Pl G33 . . . . . 118 F8
Benhar Rd ML7 . . . . . 147 A6
Benholm St G32 . . . . . 118 F3
Ben Hope Ave PA2 . . . . . 114 D2
Ben Laga Pl G53 . . . . . 135 D4
Ben Lawers Dr
Cumbernauld G68 . . . . . 61 B2
Paisley PA2 . . . . . 114 D2
Ben Ledi Ave PA2 . . . . . 114 D2
Ben Ledi Cres G68 . . . . . 61 B2
Ben Lomond Dr FK9 . . . . . 2 A4
Ben Lomond Way G83 . . . . . 19 D1
Ben Lomond Wlk G83 . . . . . 27 D8
Ben Loyal Ave PA2 . . . . . 114 D2
Ben Lui Dr PA2 . . . . . 114 D1
Ben Lui Pl
Cumbernauld G68 . . . . . 61 B2
Glasgow G53 . . . . . 135 D4
Ben MacDui Gdns G53 . . 135 D4
Benmore KA9 . . . . . 236 C5
Ben More Dr
Cumbernauld G68 . . . . . 61 A2
Paisley PA2 . . . . . 114 D1
Benmore La PA16 . . . . . 44 E3
Benmore Twr G72 . . . . . 138 E3
Bennan Ho KA9 . . . . . 236 B5
Bennan Pl G75 . . . . . 180 C4
Bennan Sq G42 . . . . . 117 C2
Benn Ave PA1 . . . . . 114 A4
Ben Nevis Rd PA2 . . . . . 114 C1
Ben Nevis Way G68 . . . . . 61 B2
Bennie Terr FK1 . . . . . 86 B7
Bennoch Pl KA9 . . . . . 236 D5
Benny Lynch Ct G5 . . . . . 117 C5
Ben Oss Pl G53 . . . . . 135 C4
Benrig Ave KA3 . . . . . 222 B8
Bensley Ave KA11 . . . . . 219 F5
Bensley Rise KA11 . . . . . 219 F5
BENSLIE 208 F3
Benslie Row KA13 . . . . . 208 F2
Benson St ML5 . . . . . 122 A4
Benston Rd PA5 . . . . . 111 E1
Bent Cres G71 . . . . . 141 C6
Bentfield Ave KA7 . . . . . 238 E6
Bentfield Dr KA9 . . . . . 236 B6
Bentfoot Rd ML2 . . . . . 186 C7
Benthall St G5 . . . . . 117 D4
Bentheads FK7 . . . . . 11 E8
Bentinck Cres KA10 . . . . . 229 F1
Bentinck Dr KA10 . . . . . 229 E1
Bentinck Grange G75 . . . 179 D8
Bentinck St
Glasgow G3 . . . . . 96 E1
Greenock PA16 . . . . . 45 D8
Kilmarnock KA1 . . . . . 227 F7
Bent Rd
Chapelhall ML6 . . . . . 123 D3
Hamilton ML3 . . . . . 162 D3
Bents Rd G69 . . . . . 120 B5
Bent View ML9 . . . . . 200 B3
Benty's La ML8 . . . . . 201 F8
Ben Uird Pl G53 . . . . . 135 D4
Ben Vane Ave PA2 . . . . . 114 C1
Ben Venue Rd G68 . . . . . 61 A2
Ben Venue Way PA2 . . . . . 114 D1
Benvie Gdns G64 . . . . . 78 B2
Benview FK7 . . . . . 7 C2
Benview Ave PA14 . . . . . 68 F8
Benview Rd
Clarkston G76 . . . . . 157 E7
Port Glasgow PA14 . . . . . 68 F8
Benview St G20 . . . . . 96 F4
Benview Terr
Fishcross FK10 . . . . . 5 E4
Paisley PA2 . . . . . 114 B2
Ben Vorlich Dr G53 . . . . . 135 D4
Ben Vorlich Pl G53 . . . . . 135 D4
Benvue Rd G66 . . . . . 57 E7
Ben Wyvis Dr PA2 . . . . . 114 C1
Berchem Pl KA21 . . . . . 216 F8
Bereland Ave KA9 . . . . . 236 D8
Berelands Cres G73 . . . . . 137 E7
Berelands Gdns KA9 . . . . . 233 D1
Berelands Pl G73 . . . . . 137 F7
Berelands Rd KA9 . . . . . 233 D1
Berenice Pl G82 . . . . . 50 C2
Beresford Ave G14 . . . . . 95 E4
Beresford Ct KA7 . . . . . 238 F7
Beresford Gr KA11 . . . . . 219 E5
Beresford La KA7 . . . . . 238 F7
Beresford Terr KA7 . . . . . 238 F7
Berkeley St
Glasgow G3 . . . . . 240 A3
Stirling FK7 . . . . . 7 A4
Berkeley Terrace La G3 . 240 A3
Berkley Dr G72 . . . . . 140 D1
Berl Ave PA6 . . . . . 111 C8
Bernadette Cres ML1 . . . 143 D2
Bernadette St ML1 . . . . . 143 D3
Bernard Path G40 . . . . . 118 A4
Bernard's Ct 21 ML11 . . . 215 A4
Bernard St G40 . . . . . 118 A4
Bernard's Wynd 20 ML11 215 A4
Bernard Terr G40 . . . . . 118 A4
Bernera Pl KA3 . . . . . 222 F6
Berneray St G22 . . . . . 97 C7
Bernisdale Dr G15 . . . . . 74 D3
Bernisdale Gdns 7 G15 . . 74 D3
Bernisdale Pl 1 G15 . . . . . 74 D3
Berridale Ave G44 . . . . . 137 A5
Berridale Rd KA10 . . . . . 229 E7
Berriedale G75 . . . . . 179 E8
Berriedale Ave G69 . . . . . 120 A4
Berriedale Cres G72 . . . . . 161 C3
Berriedale Path G72 . . . . . 161 C3
Berriedale Quadrant
ML2 . . . . . 165 B5
Berriedale Terr G72 . . . . . 161 C3
Berryburn Rd G21 . . . . . 98 C4
Berry Dr KA12 . . . . . 219 E3
Berryhill FK7 . . . . . 12 E7
Berryhill Ave KA11 . . . . . 220 B6
Berryhill Cres ML2 . . . . . 164 F2
Berryhill Dr G46 . . . . . 136 B2
Berryhill Pl ML7 . . . . . 147 B2
Berryhill Prim Sch ML2 . . 164 E3
Berryhill Rd
Cumbernauld G67 . . . . . 61 E2
Glasgow G46 . . . . . 136 B2
Berryknowe G66 . . . . . 80 B7
Berryknowe Ave G69 . . . . . 100 C7
Berryknowes Ave G52 . . . 115 D5
Berryknowes La G52 . . . . . 115 C5
Berryknowes Rd G52 . . . . . 115 C5
Berryyards Rd PA15 . . . . . 45 F3
Bertram Dr ML7 . . . . . 125 C2
Bertram Pl ML7 . . . . . 146 D5

Bertram St
Glasgow G41 116 E1
Hamilton ML3 162 A6
Harthill ML7 127 C5
2 Larkhall ML9 185 C1
Shotts ML7 146 E5
Bervie St G51 115 F6
Berwick Cres
Airdrie ML6 122 F5
Linwood PA3 111 F7
Berwick Dr
Glasgow G52 115 B4
Rutherglen G73 138 D6
Berwick Pl
Coatbridge ML5 122 B3
East Kilbride G74 160 C3
Greenock PA16 44 D4
Berwick Rd
Greenock PA16 44 D4
Port Glasgow PA14 47 C1
Berwick St
Coatbridge ML5 122 B3
Hamilton ML3 162 B5
Bessemer Dr G75 181 A5
Beta Ctr G81 94 C8
Bethal La G75 180 A4
Betsy Miller Wynd KA21 205 F4
Betula Dr G81 74 A5
Bevan Ct KA22 205 B4
Bevan Dr FK12 5 C7
Bevan Gdns KA13 207 E4
Bevan Gr PA5 111 E2
Beveridge Terr ML4 142 D4
Beverley Rd G43 136 D6
Bevin Ave G81 74 D1
Bidders Gait ML11 215 B3
Bideford Cres G32 119 D3
Bield The ML2 165 C2
Biggar Rd
Biggar Road ML1 144 A6
Chapelhall ML6 123 E1
Newhouse ML1, ML6 143 F7
Parkside ML1 144 B3
BIGGAR ROAD 143 F5
Biggar St G31 118 B6
Biggart Hospl KA9 236 D7
Biggart Rd KA9 236 D7
Bigholm Rd KA15 150 C1
Bigton St G33 99 B2
Bilby Terr KA12 219 C5
Billings Rd ML1 163 B5
Bilsland Ct G20 97 B5
Bilsland Dr G20 97 A5
Bilsland Pl G82 27 D1
Bimson Pl KA12 219 A1
Bimson Row KA12 219 A1
Binend Rd G53 135 C8
BINNIEHILL 86 A5
Binniehill Rd
Cumbernauld G68 61 D2
Slamannan FK1 85 F3
Binnie La PA19 44 E7
Binnie Pl
Glasgow G40 117 E5
Skinflats FK2 24 F2
Binnie St PA19 44 E8
Binns Rd G33 99 C2
Birch Ave
Clarkston G76 157 F6
Stirling FK8 6 F5
Birch Brae ML3 162 E1
Birch Cl G72 139 C6
Birch Cotts G84 16 D2
Birch Cres
Clarkston G76 157 F6
Johnstone PA5 112 A1
Birch Dr
Cambuslang G72 139 C6
Kirkintilloch G66 79 D5
Birchend Dr G21 98 B2
Birchend Pl G21 98 B2
Birchfield Dr G14 95 B4
Birchfield Rd ML3 162 B3
Birch Gr
Menstrie FK11 3 F6
Uddingston G71 141 B7
Birchgrove
Houston PA6 91 D1
Larkhall ML9 185 A5
Birch Knowe G64 98 B8
Birchlea Dr G46 136 D4
Birchmount Ct ML6 123 D8
Birch Pl
Cambuslang G72 139 F4
Hamilton G72 161 D8
Kilmarnock KA1 227 D8
Renfrew PA4 94 B2
Birch Quadrant ML6 123 D7
Birch Rd
Ayr KA7 239 C4
Clydebank G81 74 A5
Cumbernauld G67 62 F3
Dumbarton G82 49 F4
Birch St
Glasgow G5 117 D3
Motherwell ML1 143 B5
Birch Terr KA22 205 C3
Birch View G61 76 A5
Birchview Dr G76 157 F4
Birch Way KA10 229 E4
Birchwood FK10 5 D2
Birchwood Ave G32 119 E4
Birchwood Dr PA2 113 B1
Birchwood Gr G69 121 A6
Birchwood Pl G32 119 E4
Birchwood Rd G78 153 B4
Bird of Prey Ctr* ML8 201 B1
Birdsfield Ct G72 161 F6
Birdsfield Dr G72 161 E6
Birdsfield St ML3 161 F6
BIRDSTON 58 D3
Birdston Rd
Glasgow G21 98 C6
Milton of Campsie G66 58 C4
Birgidale Rd G45 137 D2
Birgidale Terr G45 137 D2
Birkbeck Ct G4 241 B3
Birkdale G74 159 C3
Birkdale Cl KA13 207 C4
Birkdale Cres G68 61 F6
Birkdale Ct G71 140 F2
Birkdale Wood G68 62 A6
Birkenburn Rd G67 62 F6
Birken Rd G66 79 E4
BIRKENSHAW 120 F1
Birkenshaw Ind Est G71 120 E1
Birkenshaw Rd ML5 81 E1
Birkenshaw St G31 118 B7
Birkenshaw Way PA3 113 E8
Birkfield Loan ML8 188 C1
Birkfield Pl ML8 188 C1
Birkhall Ave
Glasgow G52 115 A4
Inchinnan PA4 93 D7
Birkhall Dr G61 75 F2
Birkhill Ave G64 78 B2
Birkhill Gdns G64 78 B2
Birkhill Rd
Crossford ML8 201 D2
Hamilton ML3 183 D7
Stirling FK7 6 E6
Birkmyre Ave PA14 47 A2
Birkscairn Pl KA11 220 C2
Birkscairn Way KA11 220 C2
Birks Ct ML8 186 F5
Birkshaw Brae ML2 186 A8
Birkshaw Pl ML2 186 A8
Birkshaw Tower ML2 185 F8
Birks Hill KA11 220 A4
Birks Pl ML11 215 A5
Birks Rd
Larkhall ML9 199 B7
Law ML8 186 E3
Birkwood Pl G77 156 D2
Birkwood St G40 118 B2
Birkwook Ct ML5 101 E6
Birmingham Rd PA4 94 B1
Birnam Ave G64 78 B2
Birnam Cres G61 76 B5
Birnam Gdns G64 78 B2
Birnam Pl
Falkirk FK2 42 C5
Hamilton ML3 161 E3
Newton Mearns G77 157 B4
Birnam Rd G31 118 D3
Birness Dr G43 136 D7
Birnie Ct G21 98 C4
BIRNIEHILL 181 A7
Birniehill Rd ML1 145 A5
Birniehill Rdbt G74 181 A8
Birnie Rd G21 98 C3
Birnie Well Rd FK1 86 A6
Birnock Ave PA4 94 E1
Birnyhill Ct G81 74 A7
Birrell Rd G62 54 F3
Birrens Rd ML1 163 C8
Birsay Rd G22 97 B7
BISHOPBRIGGS 78 B3
Bishopbriggs Acad G64 78 A1
Bishopbriggs Ind Est G21 98 A7
Bishopbriggs Sta G64 78 A1
Bishopburn Dr ML5 121 F5
Bishopdale G74 159 C3
Bishop Gdns
Bishopbriggs G64 77 E2
Hamilton ML3 183 E7
Bishop La G3 240 B2
Bishopmill Pl G21 98 C4
Bishopmill Rd G21 98 C4
Bishops Gate G74 158 C3
Bishopsgate Dr G21 97 E7
Bishopsgate Gdns G21 97 E7
Bishopsgate Pl 3 G21 97 E7
Bishopsgate Rd G21 97 E7
Bishops Pk G74 158 B3
BISHOPTON 72 A3
Bishopton Prim Sch PA7 72 A3
Bishopton Sta PA7 72 B2
Bissett Cres G81 73 E6
Blacader Dr G69 100 C3
Blackadder Pl G75 179 D7
Blackbog Rd ML6 82 F2
Blackbraes Rd
California FK1 66 F4
East Kilbride G75 160 B4
Blackburn Cres
Dumbarton G82 49 D4
Kirkintilloch G66 80 A8
Blackburn Dr KA7 238 E6
Blackburn Pl KA7 238 E6
Blackburn Rd KA7 238 E6
Blackburn Sq G78 134 D1
Blackburn St G51 116 E6
Blackbyres Ct G78 134 D4
Blackbyres Rd G78 134 C5
Blackcraig Ave G15 75 A3
Blackcraig Brae 5 G72 161 D3
Blackcroft Ave ML6 123 E5
Blackcroft Gdns G32 119 D4
Blackcroft Rd G32 119 D4
Blackcroft Terr ML7 125 B2
Blackdyke Rd G66 79 E8
Blackfarm Rd G77 156 F4
Blackfaulds Dr KA3 213 A4
Blackfaulds Gdns KA3 213 A4
Blackfaulds Rd G73 137 E8
Blackford Cres KA9 233 E1
Blackford Rd PA2 114 A3
Blackfriar Rd G1 241 B2
Blackfriars Ct KA7 238 F8
Blackfriars Prim Sch G5 117 C4
Blackfriars St G1 241 B2
Blackfriars Wlk KA7 238 F8
Blackgrange Rdbt FK9 3 D3
BLACKHALL 114 B3
Blackhall Ct PA2 114 B3
Blackhall La PA1 113 F3
Blackhall St
Paisley PA1 114 A3
Shotts ML7 147 B3
BLACKHILL 98 D2
Blackhill Ct G23 76 D2
Blackhill Dr G84 16 D4
Blackhill Gdns G23 76 D2
Blackhill Pl G33 98 D2
Blackhill Rd
Blackridge EH48 107 F3
Glasgow G23 76 E2
Blackhill St KA7 239 B5
Blackhill View ML8 187 A4
Blackhouse Ave G77 156 F4
Blackhouse Gdns G77 156 F4
Blackhouse Pl KA8 239 C8
Blackhouse Rd G77 156 F4
Blackie St G3 96 D1
BLACKLANDS 207 E2
Blacklands Ave KA13 207 E2
Blacklands Cres KA13 207 E1
Blacklands Pl G66 79 F4
Blacklands Prim Sch
KA13 207 D2
Blacklands Rd G74 159 D1
Blacklaw Dr G74 181 B8
Blacklaw La PA3 113 E6
Blacklaw Prim Sch G74 160 B1
Blackmill Cres FK2 24 B3
Blackmoor Pl ML1 143 A3
Blackmoss Dr ML4 141 F4
Blackmuir Pl FK10 4 D3
Blackness St ML5 122 B3
Black O' Hill Rdbt G68 61 B1
BLACKRIDGE 107 C3
Blackridge Community Mus*
EH48 107 C3
Blackridge Prim Sch
EH48 107 C3
Blacksey Burn Dr G53 114 F2
Blackshaw Dr KA23 190 D6
Blacksholm Rd PA13 89 A7
Black St
Airdrie ML6 103 B1
Glasgow G4 241 B4
Blackstone Ave G53 135 C8
Blackstone Cres G53 115 C1
Blackstone Rd PA3 113 A7
Blackstoun Ave PA3 112 B6
Blackstoun Oval PA3 113 B5
Blackstoun Rd PA3 113 B5
Blackswell La ML3 162 F3
Blacksyke Ave KA1 227 F3
Blackthorn Ave
Beith KA15 150 A1
Kirkintilloch G66 79 B5
Blackthorn Gr
Kirkintilloch G66 79 B5
Menstrie FK11 3 F5
Blackthorn Rd
Cumbernauld G67 62 E4
Uddingston G71 141 C8
Blackthorn Rdbt G67 62 E3
Blackthorn St G22 97 E5
Blacktongue Farm Rd
ML6 83 E2
BLACKWOOD 60 E2
Blackwood G75 180 D5
Blackwood Ave
Kilmarnock KA1 227 E6
Linwood PA3 112 A5
Newton Mearns G77 156 F3
Blackwood Gdns ML1 142 C2
Blackwood Rd
Cumbernauld G68 60 E1
Milngavie G62 54 F3
Blackwood Rdbt G68 60 F2
Blackwoods Cres
Bellshill ML4 142 C4
Moodiesburn G69 80 F2
Blackwood St
Barrhead G78 134 B2
Glasgow G13 95 E7
Blackwood Terr PA5 131 D8
Blackwood West Rdbt
G68 60 D1
Bladda La PA1 113 F4
Blades Ct G69 101 A6
Bladnoch Dr G15 75 C2
Blaeberry Pl G68 61 A2
Blaefaulds Cres FK6 39 D8
Blaeloch Ave G45 137 C1
Blaeloch Dr G45 137 C2
Blaeloch Terr G45 137 B1
Blaeshill Rd G75 179 E8
Blairafton Wynd KA13 207 C5
Blairatholl Ave G11 96 A3
Blairatholl Cres G77 157 B4
Blair Atholl Dr 15 ML9 185 C1
Blair Atholl Gate G77 157 B4
Blairatholl Gdns 5 G11 96 A3
Blair Atholl Gdns ML3 162 A4
Blair Atholl Gr ML3 162 A4
Blairathol Wynd 4 ML1 143 B2
Blair Ave KA1 228 E5
Blairbeg Pl PA19 43 E5
Blairbeth Dr G44 137 B7
Blairbeth Pl G73 138 A5
Blairbeth Rd G73 138 C5
Blairbeth Terr G73 138 C5
Blairbuie Dr G20 96 C7
Blair Cres
Glasgow G69 120 A3
Hurlford KA1 228 E6
Blair Ct G81 74 B2
BLAIRDARDIE 75 B1
Blairdardie Prim Sch G15 75 B1
Blairdardie Rd
Clydebank G15 75 B1
Glasgow G13 75 C1
Blairdenan Ave G69 81 A3
Blairdenon Cres FK1 41 F3
Blairdenon Dr
Alloa FK10 5 B2
Cumbernauld G68 61 C3
Blairdenon Rd FK12 4 E6
Blairdenon Way KA11 220 B2
Blair Dr G66 58 C5
Blairforkie Dr FK9 1 F8
Blair Gdns
Gourock PA19 43 F5
Newton Mearns G77 156 B5
Torrance G64 57 B1
Blairgowrie Rd G52 115 C4
Blairgrove Ct ML5 121 E6
Blairhall Ave G41 136 F8
BLAIRHILL 121 E6
Blairhill Ave G66 80 A6
Blairhill Pl ML5 121 E7
Blairhill St ML5 121 F7
Blairhill Sta ML5 121 E8
Blairhill View EH48 107 C3
Blair Ho G67 62 A3
Blairholm Dr ML4 142 B3
Blairlands Dr KA24 191 E7
Blairlinn Ind Est G67 82 F6
Blairlinn Rd G67 82 F6
Blairlinn View G67 83 A6
BLAIRLOGIE 3 B6
Blairlogie St G33 99 B2
Blairmore Ave PA1 114 C5
Blairmore Cres PA15 46 C2
Blairmore Pl PA19 43 F5
Blairmore Rd PA15 46 C2
Blairmuckhole & Forrestdyke
Rd ML7 126 E7
Blairpark Ave ML5 121 E8
Blair Path 5 ML1 163 F5
Blair Pl 2 FK2 41 F7
Blairquhomrie Cotts G83 20 F2
Blair Rd
Coatbridge ML5 121 E7
Crossford ML8 201 A1
Dalry KA24 191 E7
Hurlford KA1 228 E6
Kilwinning KA13 207 F5
Paisley PA1 114 E5
Blair St
Glasgow G32 118 F5
Kilmarnock KA3 222 F2
Blairston Ave G71 141 B1
Blairston Gdns G71 141 B1
Blair Terr FK5 24 A4
Blairtum Dr G73 138 B5
Blairtummock Pl G33 119 D8
Blairtummock Rd G33 119 D8
Blakely Rd KA21 217 B7
Blake Rd G67 62 A2
Blane Ave G63 31 A4
Blane Cres G63 31 A4
Blane Dr G62 55 B3
BLANEFIELD 31 A3
Blanefield Ave KA9 236 B6
Blanefield Gdns G13 95 F8
Blane Pl G63 31 A4
Blane St ML5 122 A8
Blaneview G33 99 D4
BLANTYRE 161 D7
Blantyre Cres G81 73 E7
Blantyre Ct PA8 73 A3
Blantyre Dr PA7 72 A4
Blantyre Farm Rd G71,
G72 140 C5
Blantyre Gdns G68 60 E1
Blantyre Ind Est G72 161 E5
Blantyre L Ctr G72 161 E8
Blantyre Mill Rd G71 141 A2
Blantyre Rd G71 141 A2
Blantyre St G3 96 D1
Blantyre Sta G72 161 E8
Blaven Ct G69 120 C4
Blaven Head KA11 220 A4
Blawarthill Hospl G14 95 A6
Blawarthill St G14 94 F5
Bleachfield
Falkirk FK2 42 A5
Milngavie G62 55 A3
Bleasdale Ct G81 74 B2
Bleeze Rd KA24 191 B8
Blendon Ho KA7 238 F7
Blenheim Ave
East Kilbride G75 180 C7
Stepps G33 99 E6
Blenheim Ct
Carluke ML8 188 B1
Kilsyth G65 36 D1
Stepps G33 99 C5
Stirling FK9 2 C3
Blenheim Pl FK5 23 E5
Blindwells FK12 4 F6
Blinkbonnie Terr FK1 86 A6
Blinkbonny Rd FK1 41 E4
Blinny Ct ML7 147 A3
Blochairn Rd G21 98 B1
Bloomgate 9 ML11 215 A4
Bloomhill Stables G82 48 C7
Bluebell Dr KA3 222 E3
Bluebell Gdns
Ardrossan KA22 205 C5
Glasgow G45 138 A2
Motherwell ML1 142 C2
Bluebell Way
Airdrie ML6 102 F2
Carluke ML8 201 F8
Lennoxtown G66 57 F7
Bluebell Wlk ML1 143 A3
Bluebell Wynd ML2 164 F1
Blueknowes Rd ML8 186 F5
Bluevale St G31 118 A6
Blythe Pl G33 119 D6
Blyth Rd G33 119 E6
BLYTHSWOOD 94 C5
Blythswood Ave PA4 94 D4
Blythswood Ct G2 240 B2
Blythswood Dr PA3 113 E6
Blythswood House Hospl
PA4 94 D4
Blythswood Ind Est PA4 94 B4
Blythswood Rd PA4 94 D4
Blythswood Sq G2 240 B3
Blythswood St G2 240 B2
Boardwalk The G75 181 A7
Boat Vennal 9 KA7 235 F1
Bobbins Gate PA1 113 B3
Bobbin Wynd FK7 6 D6
Boclair Acad G61 76 C4
Boclair Ave G61 75 F4
Boclair Cres
Bearsden G61 76 A4
Bishopbriggs G64 78 A2
Boclair Rd
Bearsden G62 76 C5
Bishopbriggs G64 78 A2
Boclair St G13 95 E8
Bodden Sq ML1 143 E7
Boden Ind Est G40 118 B4
Boden Quadrant ML1 142 C2
Boden St G40 118 A4
Bodesbeck Ct KA11 220 A3
Bodmin Gdns G69 80 F3
Bogany Terr G45 137 E2
Bogbain Rd G34 120 A8
BOGEND 231 F5
Bogend Rd
Bannockburn FK7 11 E8
Larbert FK2 23 B8
Torwood FK5 22 F8
Bogfoot Rd ML7 125 B2
Boggknowe G71 140 D8
Boghall Rd
Carluke ML8 202 B7
Glasgow G69 120 B3
Boghall St
Glasgow G33 99 B1
Stonehouse ML9 198 F2
BOGHEAD 79 A4
Boghead KA15 171 B8
Boghead Ave G82 50 B4
Boghead Rd
Dumbarton G82 50 B4
Glasgow G21 98 A4
Kirkintilloch G66 79 A5
Bogiewood Rd PA14 47 B1
Boglemart St KA20 217 C8
Bogleshole Rd G72 138 E7
Bogle St PA15 46 A4
BOGLESTONE 68 F8
Boglestone Ave PA14 68 E8
Bogmoor Pl G51 95 C1
Bogmoor Rd G51 115 C8
Bog Rd
Banknock FK4 38 E3
Laurieston FK2 42 F4
Bog Rdbt FK2 42 F4
Bog Road Ind Est FK2 42 F4
Bogside Rd
Ashgill ML9 199 F8
Kilsyth G65 60 D7
Millerston G33 99 A5
Port Glasgow PA14 68 F8
Bogside St G40 118 B4
Bogstonhill Rd PA6 91 B2
Bogston La PA15 46 F2
Bogston Sta PA15 46 F2
Bogs View ML4 141 F3
Bogton Ave G44 136 F4
Bohun Ct FK7 7 D4
Boleyn Ct ML2 166 B6
Boleyn Rd G41 116 E2
Bolingbroke G74 160 C4
Bolivar Terr G42 137 C8
Bolton Dr G42 137 B8
Bolton Terr G66 57 E8
Bon Accord Cres ML7 146 E5
Bon Accord Rd G76 157 F6
Bon Accord Sq G81 94 B8
Bonar Cres PA11 110 E7
Bonar La PA11 110 E7
Bonar Law Ave G84 16 B2
Bonawe St G20 96 F3
Bonds Dr ML2 166 B6
Bond St FK10 4 A3
Bo'ness Rd
Chapelhall ML6 123 D1
Motherwell ML1 143 C7
Boness St G40 118 B4
BONHILL 28 B3
Bonhill Prim Sch G83 27 F3
Bonhill Rd G82 50 A4
Bonhill St G22 97 B3

Bonhill View G83 27 F4
BONKLE 166 C6
Bonkle Gdns ML2 166 B5
Bonkle Rd ML2 166 B5
Bonnar St G40 118 A3
Bonnaughton Rd G61 75 B6
Bonnet Ct KA3 211 E8
Bonnet Rd 3 ML11 215 A4
Bonnie Lesley Ct KA20 217 C8
Bonnington Ave ML11 215 B3
BONNYBRIDGE 40 B5
Bonnybridge Hospl FK4 40 C6
Bonnybridge Ind Est FK4 40 A4
Bonnybridge Prim Sch FK4 40 B6
Bonnybridge Rd FK4 39 E5
Bonnyfield Rd FK4 39 F5
Bonnyhill Rd
Bonnybridge FK4 40 D3
Falkirk FK1 41 A4
Bonnyholm Ave G53 115 A3
Bonnymill Pl FK4 40 B5
Bonnymuir Cres FK4 39 F5
Bonnymuir Pl FK4 40 B5
Bonnyrigg Dr G43 136 A5
Bonnyside Rd FK4 40 B5
BONNYTON 222 C1
Bonnyton Dr G76 178 D5
Bonnyton Foot KA11 220 A5
Bonnyton Ind Est KA1 222 E1
Bonnyton La ML3 183 B8
Bonnyton Moor Rd G76 178 A7
Bonnyton Pl
Irvine KA11 220 A5
Kilmarnock KA1 222 D1
Bonnyton Rd KA1 222 C1
Bonnyton Row KA11 220 A5
Bonnyvale Pl FK4 39 F5
Bonnyview Gdns FK4 40 B6
Bonnywood Ave FK4 40 B7
Bontine Ave G82 49 D4
Bonyton Ave G13 94 F6
Boon Dr G15 75 B2
Booth Pl FK1 42 B4
Boquhanran Pl G81 74 A3
Boquhanran Rd G81 73 F2
Borden Rd 4 G13 95 E5
Border Ave KA21 216 F8
Border Pl KA21 216 F8
Border St PA15 46 C3
Border Way G66 79 F8
Boreland Dr
Glasgow G13 95 B6
Hamilton ML3 161 E2
Boreland Pl G13 95 B6
Bore Rd ML6 123 B8
BORESTONE 7 A2
Borestone Ave KA25 170 A8
Borestone Cres FK7 7 A4
Borestone Ct FK7 7 B2
Borestone Pl FK7 7 A2
Borestone Prim Sch FK7 7 A2
Borgie Cres G72 139 B5
Borland Cres G76 178 E5
Borland Dr ML9 199 B8
Borland Rd G61 76 A3
Borron St G4 97 C3
Borrowdale G75 179 F5
Borrowlea Rd FK7 7 C7
Borrowmeadow Rd FK7 7 E7
Borrows Gate FK9 1 F3
Borthwick Dr G75 179 D7
Borthwick Pl G69 100 F4
Borthwick St G33 99 B1
Bosfield Cnr G74 159 F3
Bosfield Pl G74 159 F3
Bosfield Rd G74 159 F3
Boston Dr G84 16 F3
Boswell Ct G42 136 F7
Boswell Dr G72 161 D7
Boswell Pk
Ayr KA7 238 F8
East Kilbride G74 160 C4
Boswell Sq G52 114 F7
Bosworth Rd G74 160 C5
Botanic Cres G20 96 D4
Botanic Crescent La G20 96 D4
Bothkennar Prim Sch FK2 24 F3
Bothkennar Rd FK2 24 E3
Bothlin Dr G33 99 D6
Bothlyn Ave G66 79 E7
Bothlyn Cres G69 100 F7
Bothlyn Rd G69 100 D8
BOTHWELL 141 B2
Bothwell Castle* G72 140 D3
Bothwellhaugh Quadrant ML4 141 F3
Bothwellhaugh Rd ML4 142 A2
Bothwell Ho ML3 162 E5
Bothwell La
Glasgow G2 240 C2
4 Glasgow, Kelvingrove G12 96 E2
Bothwell Park Ind Est G71 141 A5
Bothwellpark Pl ML4 141 D6
Bothwellpark Rd
Bothwell G71 141 C3
Fallside G71, ML4 141 C4
Bothwell Park Sch ML1 164 A4
Bothwell Pl
Coatbridge ML5 121 F7
Paisley PA2 132 E8
Bothwell Prim Sch G71 141 A2
Bothwell Rd
Bothwell G71 140 F4
Carluke ML8 187 E3
Hamilton ML3 162 C6
Bothwellshields Rd ML1 124 C2
Bothwell St
Cambuslang G72 138 E6
Glasgow G2 240 C2
Hamilton ML3 162 C5
Bothwick Way PA2 132 E8
Boturich Dr G83 19 E1
Boundary Rd KA8 236 D4
Bourhill Ct ML2 164 D2
Bourne Cres PA4 93 D7
Bourne Ct PA4 93 D7
Bournemouth Rd PA19 44 E5
Bourne St ML3 162 F3
Bourock Sq G78 134 E1
Bourtree Cres ML8 187 A6
BOURTREEHILL 220 C2
Bourtree Pk KA7 239 A6
Bourtree Rd ML3 161 F2
Bouverie St
Glasgow G14 94 E6
Port Glasgow PA14 47 D1
Rutherglen G73 137 F7
Bowden Dr G52 115 B6
Bowden Gr ML2 165 D6
Bowden Pk G75 180 C8
Bower St G12 96 E3
BOWERWALLS 134 E4
Bowerwalls St G78 134 E4
Bowes Cres G69 119 F4
Bowes Rigg KA3 195 E1
BOW FARM 45 B5
Bowfield Ave G52 114 F6
Bowfield Cres G52 114 F6
Bowfield Dr G52 115 A6
Bowfield Path G52 114 F6
Bowfield Pl 3 G52 114 F6
Bowfield Rd
Howwood PA9 130 F5
West Kilbride KA23 190 C4
Bowfield Way PA9 130 F5
Bowhill Cres ML6 104 F4
Bowhill Rd ML6 123 E1
Bowhousebog or Liquo ML7 146 A2
Bowhousebog Rd ML7 146 A2
Bowhousebrae Rd ML6 123 E5
Bowhouse Dr G45 138 A4
Bowhouse Gdns
Alloa FK10 10 B5
Glasgow G45 138 A5
Bowhouse Head KA11 220 B5
Bowhouse Rd
Airdrie ML6 123 F5
Alloa FK10 10 B5
Bowhouse Rise KA11 220 B5
Bowie Rd G83 27 E6
Bowie St G82 49 E3
BOWLING 72 D8
Bowling Green Gr G72 139 F4
Bowling Green La 2 G14 95 D3
Bowling Green Pl FK4 39 F5
Bowling Green Rd
Chryston G69 100 D8
Fenwick KA3 213 A3
Glasgow, Barrachnie G32 119 D4
Glasgow G44 137 A5
3 Glasgow, Whiteinch G14 95 D3
Bowling Green St ML4 142 B5
Bowling Green View G72 139 F4
Bowling St ML5 121 F7
Bowling Sta G60 72 C8
Bowmanflat ML9 185 A3
Bowman Flat ML9 185 A3
Bowman Pl KA3 195 D1
Bowman Rd KA7 238 F6
Bowman St G42 117 A2
Bowman Warren Wynd KA10 229 F6
Bowmont Gdns 3 G12 96 C3
Bowmont Hill G64 78 A4
Bowmont Pl
Cambuslang G72 139 D5
East Kilbride G75 179 D7
Bowmont Terr G12 96 C3
Bowmore Cres G74 158 C3
Bowmore Ct KA11 220 A6
Bowmore Gdns
Rutherglen G73 138 E3
Uddingston G71 140 E8
Bowmore Rd G52 115 E5
Bowmore Wlk ML7 147 A3
Bow Rd PA16 45 C4
Bow St FK8 7 A8
Bowyer Vennel ML4 141 F6
Boxton Rd FK1 66 D1
Boyd Ct KA3 223 A1
Boyd Dr ML1 163 B7
Boydfield Ave KA9 236 D8
Boyd La FK2 42 B6
Boyd Orr Cres KA3 222 A7
Boyd Orr Rd KA21 206 A2
Boyd Pl KA10 229 F6
Boyd St
Falkirk FK2 42 B6
Glasgow G42 117 C1
Kilmarnock KA3 223 A1
Prestwick KA9 236 C8
Boydstone Pl G46 136 A5
Boydstone Rd
Glasgow G53, G46, G43 135 E5
Thornliebank G46 136 A4
Boydston Rd KA22 205 C4
Boydston Way KA3 223 C6
Boyle St
Clydebank G81 94 D8
Irvine KA12 219 A2
Boylestone Rd G78 134 A4
Boyndie St G34 120 B8
Brabloch Cres PA3 113 F6
Brabloch Pk PA3 113 F6
Bracadale Dr G69 120 D4
Bracadale Gdns G69 120 D4
Bracadale Gr G69 120 C4
Bracadale Rd G69 120 C4
Bracco Rd ML6 105 C2
Brachelston St PA16 45 D4
Bracken Ave FK1 42 A2
Brackenbrae Ave G64 77 F1
Brackenbrae Rd G64 77 F1
Brackendene PA6 91 D2
Brackenhill Ave KA3 223 A5
Brackenhill Dr ML3 183 C7
Brackenhill Rd ML8 187 A6
BRACKENHIRST 102 D5
Brackenhirst Gdns ML6 102 D6
Brackenhirst Rd ML6 102 E7
Brackenhurst St G82 50 C6
Brackenknowe Rd ML6 83 D3
Bracken La FK9 2 B3
Brackenlees Rd FK2 24 F4
Bracken Pk KA7 239 C3
Bracken Rd PA14 69 A8
Brackenrig Cres G76 157 E1
Brackenrig Rd G46 135 E2
Bracken St
Glasgow G22 97 B6
Motherwell ML1 143 A3
Bracken Terr G71 141 A3
Bracken Way 6 ML9 185 C1
Brackla Ave G13, G81 94 E8
Bracklinn Pl FK1 41 F1
Braco Ave ML6 123 D1
Bradan Ave G13 94 E7
Bradan Ct KA10 229 B2
Bradan Rd KA10 229 C2
Bradbury Glebe KA12 219 C2
Bradbury St FK2 24 B2
Bradda Ave G73 138 D4
Braden Dr KA7 239 B2
Bradfield Ave G12 96 C5
Bradley Ct G33 99 F5
Bradshaw Cres ML3 161 E3
Bradshaw St KA21 216 F7
Brady Cres G69 81 A3
BRAEDALE 163 C6
Braedale Ave
Airdrie ML6 123 C7
Motherwell ML1 163 C6
Braedale Cres ML2 166 B5
Braedale Pl ML2 166 C5
Braedale Rd ML11 215 A5
Braeface Rd
Banknock FK4 38 E3
Cumbernauld G67 61 E2
Braefield Dr G46 136 A3
Braefoot KA11 219 F5
Braefoot Ave G62 76 A8
Braefoot Cres
Law ML8 186 F4
Paisley PA2 133 F8
Braefoot Ct
Caldercruix ML6 104 F4
Law ML8 186 F5
Braefoot La G78 153 A3
BRAEHEAD
Ayr 236 C1
Sterling 7 C5
Thorntonhall 158 D3
Braehead
Alexandria G83 28 B3
Alloa FK10 4 D1
Alva FK10 5 A7
Beith KA15 171 B8
Dalry KA24 191 C8
Hamilton G72 161 D6
Irvine KA11 219 F5
Lochwinnoch PA12 129 C3
Braehead Arena* PA4 94 F4
Braehead Ave
Ayr KA8 236 C2
Clydebank G81 74 A7
Coatbridge ML5 121 D3
Larkhall ML9 184 E2
Lochwinnoch PA12 129 C3
Milngavie G62 54 F1
Neilston G78 154 D7
Tullibody FK10 4 C2
Braehead Cres
Ayr KA8 236 C2
Clydebank G81 74 A7
Braehead Ct KA3 223 A1
Braehead Dr ML4 141 F4
Braehead Glebe KA3 211 E8
Braehead Ind Est PA4 94 F3
Braehead La KA21 216 F8
Braehead Loan 2 ML8 202 B8
Braehead Pl
Bellshill ML4 141 F4
Dalry KA24 191 C8
Rhu G84 15 E5
Saltcoats KA21 216 F8
Braehead Prim Sch
Ayr KA8 236 C2
7 Carluke ML8 187 F2
1 Dumbarton G82 50 A4
Stirling FK7 7 C4
Braehead Quadrant ML1 143 D4
Brae Head Quadrant G78 154 D7
Braehead Rd
Ayr KA8 236 D2
Braehead Rd *continued*
Clydebank G81 74 A7
Cumbernauld G67 62 B3
Fenwick KA3 213 A3
Paisley PA2 133 C7
Paisley PA2 133 D8
Port Glasgow PA14 68 E8
Stirling FK7 7 C3
Thorntonhall G74 158 C3
Braehead (Sh Ctr) G51 95 A3
Braehead St
Glasgow G5 117 D3
Kirkintilloch G66 58 C1
Braehead Terr KA3 222 C6
Braehouse G84 15 D4
Braemar Ave G81 73 F4
Braemar Cres
Bearsden G61 75 F2
Carluke ML8 188 A3
Falkirk FK2 42 C6
Paisley PA2 113 F1
Braemar Ct G44 136 E4
Braemar Dr
Elderslie PA5 112 B1
Falkirk FK2 42 C6
Braemar Gdns
Denny FK6 21 D3
Greenock PA16 45 E6
Braemar Pl FK5 24 A4
Braemar Rd
Inchinnan PA4 93 E6
Rutherglen G73 138 E3
Braemar Sq KA8 236 D2
Braemar St
Glasgow G42 136 F7
Hamilton ML3 162 B6
Braemar View G81 73 F5
Braemore Gdns G22 97 D4
Braemore Rd KA3 195 D1
Braemount Ave PA2 133 C6
Braes Ave G81 74 D1
Braesburn Ct G67 62 F6
Braesburn Pl G67 62 F6
Braesburn Rd G67 62 F6
BRAESIDE 44 D3
Braeside
Alloa FK10 5 C1
Howwood PA9 130 F5
Irvine KA11 219 F5
Kilwinning KA13 207 E5
Shieldhill FK1 66 D6
Braeside Ave
Milngavie G62 76 A8
Moodiesburn G69 80 F2
Rutherglen G73 138 C7
Braeside Cres
Barrhead G78 134 E1
Coatbridge G69 120 F5
Braeside Dr
Barrhead G78 134 E1
Dumbarton G82 50 B5
Braeside Gdns ML3 183 E8
Braeside La
Greenock PA16 44 D3
15 Larkhall ML9 185 B4
Braeside Pl G72 139 B4
Braeside Rd
Ayr KA8 236 D2
Greenock PA16 44 D3
Motherwell ML1 143 D4
Braeside St
Glasgow G20 96 F4
Kilmarnock KA1 228 A8
Braeside Way ML9 185 B1
Braes O' Yetts G66 80 A8
Braes Rd KA21 216 E7
Braes Sh Ctr The G45 137 E3
Braes The FK10 4 D3
Braes View
Denny FK6 39 D8
Shieldhill FK1 66 E7
Brae The
Bannockburn FK7 7 D1
Cambusbarron FK7 6 D6
Kilmaurs KA3 222 B7
Braeval Way G33 99 E5
Braeview
Laurieston FK2 42 F3
Stenhousemuir FK5 23 D2
Brae View PA16 45 C5
Braeview Ave PA2 133 B7
Braeview Dr PA2 133 B7
Braeview Gdns PA2 133 B7
Braeview Pl G74 160 B4
Braeview Rd PA2 133 B7
Braid Ave
Cardross G82 48 B8
Motherwell ML1 143 F1
Braidbar Ct G46 136 C3
Braidbar Farm Rd G46 136 D3
Braidbar Prim Sch G46 136 D3
Braidbar Rd G46 136 C3
Braidcraft Pl G53 135 C8
Braidcraft Rd
Glasgow G53 115 C1
Glasgow G53 115 D1
Braidcraft Terr G53 115 D1
Braid Ct KA13 207 B3
Braid Dr G82 48 B8
BRAIDFAULD 118 E3
Braidfauld Gdns G32 118 F3
Braidfauld Pl G32 118 F2
Braidfauld St G32 118 F3
Braidfield Gr G81 74 B5
Braidfield Rd G81 74 B5
Braidfute ML11 215 C5
Braidholm Cres G46 136 C4
Braidholm Rd G46 136 D4
Braidhurst High Sch ML1 142 D1
Braidhurst Ind Est ML1 142 D1
Braidhurst St ML1 163 E8
Braidley Cres G75 180 E5
Braidpark Dr G46 136 D3
Braids Circ PA2 113 E1
Braids Ct 1 PA2 113 E1
Braids Dr G53 114 F1
Braids Gait PA2 113 D1
Braid Sq G4 97 A2
Braid's Rd PA2 113 E1
Braid St G4 97 A2
BRAIDWOOD 201 F4
Braidwood Pl PA3 111 F6
Braidwood Prim Sch ML8 201 F4
Braidwood Rd
Braidwood ML8 201 D4
Kilwinning KA13 207 E4
Braidwood St ML2 165 C7
Brailsford Cres KA2 227 C6
Bramah Ave G75 180 F8
Bramble Ct G66 57 C8
Bramble Gdns 1 ML6 103 B1
Bramblehedge Path G83 27 F7
Bramble Wynd PA14 69 C8
Brambling Ct ML2 165 A1
Brambling Rd ML5 122 D3
Bramley Dr ML4 142 A8
Bramley Pl
Airdrie ML6 123 E6
Kirkintilloch G66 79 E4
Brampton G75 179 F6
Branchalfield Dr ML2 165 E4
Branchalmuir Cres ML2 165 F6
Branchal Rd ML2 165 E4
Branchline Ind Est KA10 229 C3
Branchock Ave G72 139 D4
BRANCHTON 44 F3
Branchton Rd PA16 44 F3
Branchton Sta PA16 45 A3
Brancumhall Rd G74 160 D3
Brandon Arc 1 ML1 163 E6
Brandon Ct
Hamilton ML3 162 C4
Motherwell ML1 163 E6
Brandon Dr G61 75 E7
Brandon Gate ML4 142 B5
Brandon Gdns
Cambuslang G72 138 E5
Prestwick KA9 236 B7
Brandon Ho ML3 162 E5
Brandon Parade E ML1 163 E7
Brandon Parade S ML1 163 E6
Brandon Pl ML4 141 E3
Brandon St
Glasgow G31 117 F6
Hamilton ML3 162 E3
Motherwell ML1 163 F6
Brandon Way ML5 121 D4
Brand Pl G51 116 C6
Brand St G51 116 C6
Brandyhill FK10 5 E3
Brankholm Brae ML3 161 D4
Branklyn Cl 4 G13 95 D6
Branklyn Cres G13 95 D6
Branklyn Ct 6 G13 95 D6
Branklyn Gr G13 95 D6
Branklyn Pl 5 G13 95 D6
Brannock Ave ML1 143 D4
Brannock High Sch ML1 143 C3
Brannock Pl ML1 143 D4
Brannock Rd ML1 143 D4
BRANSHILL 5 A1
Branshill Pk
Alloa FK10 10 B8
Sauchie FK10 5 B1
Branshill Rd FK10 10 B8
Brassey St G20 96 F6
Braxfield Rd ML11 215 A2
Braxfield Row ML11 214 F2
Braxfield Terr ML11 214 F2
Breadalbane Cres ML1 142 D1
Breadalbane Gdns 4 G73 138 D4
Breadalbane St G3 240 A3
Breadie Dr G62 75 F8
Breamish Pl G75 179 F6
Bream Pl PA6 111 D8
Brechin Rd G64 78 C1
Brechin St G3 116 E8
Breck Ave PA2 132 D7
Brediland Prim Sch PA2 113 A1
Brediland Rd
Linwood PA3 112 B6
Paisley PA2 112 F1
Bredin Way ML1 163 B8
Bredisholm Cres G71 121 C1
Bredisholm Dr G69 120 C4
Bredisholm Rd
Coatbridge G69 120 F4
Glasgow G69 120 D4
Bredisholm Terr G69 120 D4
Bremners Cotts G81 73 F6
Brendan Way ML1 164 B2
Brendon Ave G75 180 A4
Brenfield Ave G44 136 F4
Brenfield Dr G44 136 F4
Brenfield Rd G44 136 F4
Brennan Cres ML6 123 A6
Brent Ave G46 135 F5
Brent Cres PA6 111 C8
Brent Ct G74 159 E3
Brent Dr
Glasgow G46 135 F5
Thornliebank G46 136 A5

Brent Gdns
Glasgow G46 135 F5
Thornliebank G46 136 A5
Brentham Ave FK8 7 B5
Brentham Cres FK8 7 B5
Brent Rd
East Kilbride G74 159 E3
Glasgow G46 135 F5
Thornliebank G46 136 A5
Brent Way G46 135 F5
Brentwood Ave G53 135 B4
Brentwood Dr G53 135 B4
Brentwood Sq G53 135 B4
Brereton St G42 117 C1
Breslin Terr ML7 127 C5
Bressay G74 159 E4
Bressay Cl G33 119 E6
Bressay Gr
Cambuslang G72 138 E3
Glasgow G33 119 E6
Bressay Pl
Glasgow G33 119 E6
Kilmarnock KA3 223 B5
Bressay Rd G33 119 E6
Bressay Wynd 14 ML2 165 F6
Breton Ct FK1 42 C3
Breval Cres G81 74 A7
Breval Ct G69 120 C4
Brewery Rd 4 KA1 227 F7
Brewery St PA5 111 F3
Brewhouse Ct 5 FK10 10 B6
Brewlands Cres KA1 231 C4
Brewlands Dr KA1 231 C4
Brewlands Rd KA1 231 D4
Brewster Ave PA3 114 A7
Brewster Pl
Denny FK6 21 C2
Irvine KA11 224 H6
Briar Bank G66 58 B5
Briarbush Way 12 G72 161 C7
Briarcroft Dr G33 98 D7
Briarcroft Pl G33 98 E6
Briarcroft Rd G33 98 D6
Briar Dr G81 74 B4
Briar Gdns G43 136 D5
Briar Gr
Ayr KA7 239 C4
Glasgow G43 136 D5
Briarhill Ct KA9 236 D8
Briarhill Rd KA9 236 D8
Briarhill St KA9 236 C8
Briarlea Dr G46 136 C4
Briar Neuk G64 98 B8
Briar Pl PA19 44 D6
Briar Rd
Alloa FK10 4 E2
Glasgow G43 136 D5
Kirkintilloch G66 79 F8
Briarwell La G62 55 B1
Briarwell Rd G62 55 B1
Briar Wlk G66 80 A8
Briarwood Ct G32 119 E2
Briarwood Rd ML2 164 E4
Briary La PA14 69 C8
Brick La 1 PA3 113 F5
Bridesburn Pl KA3 195 E1
Bridesmill Rd PA12 129 E5
Bridgeburn Dr G69 80 F1
Bridge Cres FK6 21 D2
Bridge End ML7 146 C6
Bridgeford Ave ML4 142 C7
Bridgegait G62 76 C8
Bridgegate
Glasgow G1 241 A1
Irvine KA12 219 C2
Bridgehaugh Rd FK9 2 B2
Bridgehouse Ct KA1 228 A2
Bridgehousehill Rd KA1 228 A3
Bridge La
9 Kilmarnock KA1 227 F8
Paisley PA2 113 B3
BRIDGEND
Greenock 46 D4
Moodiesburn 80 E2
Bridgend
Bishopton PA7 72 A3
Dalry KA24 191 D7
Kilbirnie KA25 149 B2
Kilwinning KA13 207 F3
Stewarton KA3 211 E8
Bridgend Ave PA14 68 E8
Bridgend Cotts G66 80 A7
Bridgend Cres G69 80 E2
Bridgend Ct G68 38 F1
Bridgend Ind Est KA24 191 D7
Bridgend La
Dalry KA24 191 D7
Kilwinning KA13 207 F4
Bridgend Pl G69 80 E2
Bridgend Rd PA15 46 C2
Bridgend View ML8 187 F1
Bridgend Wlk G78 153 B3
BRIDGE OF ALLAN 2 A8
Bridge of Allan Prim Sch
FK9 2 B6
Bridge of Allan Sta FK9 1 E8
BRIDGE OF WEIR 110 E8
Bridge of Weir Prim Sch
PA11 90 D1
Bridge of Weir Rd
Bridge of Weir PA11 110 F7
Brookfield PA5, PA11 111 C5
Houston PA6 91 B2
Kilmacolm PA13 89 E6
Linwood PA3 112 B5
Bridgepark KA22 205 D2
Bridge Pl
Denny FK6 21 C2

Bridge Pl *continued*
Milngavie G62 55 A1
Shotts ML7 147 A3
Bridge Rd PA14 68 E8
Bridge St
Alexandria G83 27 E4
Bonnybridge FK4 40 A5
Cambuslang G72 139 A6
Clydebank G81 73 E3
Dumbarton G82 49 E3
Glasgow G5 240 C1
Hamilton ML3 162 C2
Kilbirnie KA25 149 B2
Linwood PA3 112 C6
Longriggend ML6 84 F1
Paisley PA1 113 F4
Prestwick KA9 236 B8
Wishaw ML2 164 E3
Bridge Street Underground
Sta G5 117 B5
Bridge Terr 13 FK10 10 B6
Bridgeton Bsns Ctr 4
G40 117 F5
Bridgeton Cross G40 117 F4
Bridgeton Sta G40 117 F4
Bridgewater Ind Pk PA8 73 C2
Bridgewater Sh Ctr PA8 73 C2
Bridgeway Ct G66 79 F7
Bridgeway Pl G66 79 F7
Bridgeway Rd G66 79 F7
Bridgeway Terr G66 79 F7
Bridie Terr G74 160 C4
Brierie Ave PA6 91 B1
Brierie Gdns PA6 111 B8
Brierie Hill Ct PA6 111 B8
Brierie-Hill Gr PA6 111 B8
Brierie-Hill Rd PA6 111 B8
Brierie La PA6 111 A8
Brierybank Ave ML11 215 A3
Briery Ct KA25 170 A7
Brigbrae Ave ML4 142 C3
Brigham Pl G23 96 E8
Brighton Pl G51 116 B6
Brighton St G51 116 B6
Brightside Ave
Port Glasgow PA14 69 A8
Uddingston G71 140 F5
Bright St G21 97 F1
Brig-O-Doon Gr FK7 12 E7
Brig O'lea Terr G78 154 D6
Brigside Gdns ML3 163 A2
Bringan Rd KA3 222 F5
Brisbane Ct G46 136 D3
Brisbane Rd PA7 72 B3
Brisbane St
Clydebank G81 73 D4
Glasgow G42 137 A7
Greenock PA16 45 D6
Brisbane Terr G75 180 C7
Britannia Pl KA8 236 B2
Britannia Way
Clydebank G81 74 B2
Renfrew PA4 94 C1
Briton St G51 116 B7
Brittain Way ML1 142 F7
Broad Cairn Ct ML1 164 C2
Broadcroft 4 G66 58 C1
Broadcroft Rd 5 G66 58 C1
BROADFIELD 69 A8
Broadfield Ave PA14 69 A8
Broadford St G4 97 C2
Broadford Terr PA16 44 E4
Broadholm St G22 97 C6
Broadleys Ave G64 77 F2
Broadleys Bsns Pk FK7 7 D5
Broadleys Ind Pk FK7 7 E5
Broadleys Rd FK7 7 D7
Broadleys Rdbt FK7 7 D6
Broadlie Ct G78 154 D7
Broadlie Dr
Dalry KA24 191 A8
Glasgow G13 95 A6
Broadlie Rd G78 154 D7
Broadloan PA4 94 C2
Broadmeadow Ind Est
G82 49 F5
Broadmoss Ave G77 157 C4
Broad St Cvn Site G40 118 A5
Broadside Pl FK6 21 D1
Broad Sq G72 161 D8
Broad St
Alloa FK10 10 B5
Denny FK6 21 F2
Glasgow G40 118 A5
Stirling FK8 7 A8
Broadstone Ave
Greenock PA14 46 F2
Port Glasgow PA14 47 A1
Broadway KA22 205 D3
Broad Way The ML2 164 E4
BROADWOOD 60 F1
Broadwood Bsns Pk G68 81 F8
Broadwood Dr G44 137 B6
Broadwood Pk KA7 239 A1
Broadwood Rdbt G68 81 F8
Broadwood Stadium (Clyde
FC) G68 60 F1
Brockburn Cres G53 135 B8
Brockburn Pl G53 115 A2
Brockburn Rd G53 115 B1
Brockburn Terr G53 135 C8
Brockley View KA25 149 B4
Brocklinn Pk G75 179 E7
Brock Oval G53 135 C6
Brock Pl
Glasgow G53 135 C7
Stirling FK7 7 B2
Brock Rd G53 135 C6

Brock Terr G53 135 C6
Brockville St G32 118 F6
Brodick Ave
Kilwinning KA13 207 C4
Motherwell ML1 163 B7
Brodick Cl KA13 207 C4
Brodick Dr
East Kilbride G74 159 D3
Gourock PA19 43 F5
Helensburgh G84 16 F3
Brodick Pl
Falkirk FK1 41 C4
Newton Mearns G77 156 A4
Brodick Rd KA1 222 C2
Brodick Sq G64 98 C7
Brodick St G21 98 A1
Brodie Ave KA10 229 E4
Brodie Gdns G69 120 C6
Brodie Gr G69 120 C6
Brodie Park Ave PA2 113 E2
Brodie Park Cres PA2 113 D2
Brodie Park Gdns PA2 113 E2
Brodie Pl
East Kilbride G74 159 D3
Kilmarnock KA3 223 C2
Stonehouse ML9 198 E1
Brodie Rd G21 98 D7
Brodie St FK2 42 B8
Brogan Cres ML1 163 B7
Broich The FK12 4 E7
Bronte Pl FK5 24 A3
Bron Way G67 62 A1
Brookbank Terr ML8 188 A1
Brooke Ave G83 28 A8
BROOKFIELD 111 C6
Brookfield Ave G33 98 D7
Brookfield Cnr G33 98 D7
Brookfield Dr G33 98 D7
Brookfield Gate G33 98 D8
Brookfield Gdns G33 98 D7
Brookfield Gr KA3 213 A2
Brookfield Pl
Alva FK12 5 A6
Glasgow G33 98 E7
Brookfield Rd
Glasgow G33 98 D7
Port Glasgow PA14 68 F8
Brooklands
Alexandria G83 27 D6
East Kilbride G74 159 A1
Brooklands Ave G71 140 E7
Brooklea Dr G46 136 C5
Brooklime Dr G74 159 D4
Brooklime Gdns G74 159 C4
Brooklyn Pl ML2 186 B7
Brookside St G40 118 A5
Brook St
Alva FK12 5 A7
Clydebank G81 73 F4
Glasgow G40 117 F5
Menstrie FK11 3 F6
BROOM 156 F5
Broomage Ave FK5 23 B3
Broomage Bank FK5 23 C2
Broomage Cres FK5 23 B3
Broomage Dr FK5 23 B3
Broomage Pk FK5 23 C1
Broom Ave PA8 93 B7
Broomberry Dr PA19 44 E7
Broomburn Dr G77 157 A4
Broom Cliff G77 156 F3
Broom Cres
Barrhead G78 134 A5
East Kilbride G75 180 D5
Falkirk FK1 42 A2
Broomcroft Rd G46 157 A6
Broom Ct FK7 7 C3
Broom Dr
Clydebank G81 74 A4
Larkhall ML9 185 A5
Broomdyke Way 2 PA3 113 D8
Broomelton Rd ML3, ML9 184 D1
Broomfauld Gdns G82 50 A3
Broomfield PA6 91 D1
Broomfield Ave
Cambuslang G72 138 D7
Newton Mearns G77 156 F3
Broomfield Ct G21 98 C3
Broomfield Gdn KA7 238 F6
Broomfield Gdns G84 15 C7
Broomfield La G21 97 F5
Broomfield Pl G21 97 F5
Broomfield Rd
Ayr KA7 238 F6
Glasgow G21 98 B4
Larkhall ML9 199 B8
Netherburn ML9 199 E4
Rutherglen G46 157 A6
Broomfield St
Airdrie ML6 123 B7
Kilwinning KA13 207 E4
Netherburn ML9 200 D4
Broomfield Terr G71 120 F1
Broomfield Wlk 5 G66 79 D8
Broomgate ML11 215 A4
Broomgate Ct ML11 214 F4
Broom Gdns G66 79 B6
Broomhill Ave
Glasgow G32 139 B8
Glasgow, Whiteinch G11 95 F2
Larbert FK5 41 C8
Newton Mearns G77 156 F4
Broomhill Cres
Bellshill ML4 141 F3
Bonhill G83 28 B1
Erskine PA8 93 B7
Broomhill Ct
Greenock PA15 45 E4

Broomhill Ct *continued*
Kilwinning KA13 207 C5
4 Kirkintilloch G66 58 D1
Larkhall ML9 185 A2
Broomhill Dr
Dumbarton G82 50 B5
Glasgow G11 95 F3
Rutherglen G73 138 B5
Broomhill Farm Mews
G66 58 E1
Broomhill Gate ML9 185 A2
Broomhill Gdns
Glasgow G11 95 F3
Newton Mearns G77 156 F4
Broomhill Ind Est G66 58 E2
Broomhill La G11 95 F3
Broomhill Path G11 95 F2
Broomhill Pl
Denny FK6 21 D4
Glasgow G11 95 F2
Stirling FK7 6 E6
Broomhill Prim Sch G11 95 F4
Broomhill Quadrant KA1 228 A4
Broomhill Rd
Bonnybridge FK4 40 B4
Larkhall ML9 185 A2
Broomhill Road E KA1 228 A4
Broomhill Road W KA1 227 F4
Broomhill St
Greenock PA15 45 E4
Harthill ML7 127 C5
Broomhill Terr G11 95 F2
Broomhill View ML9 184 F2
Broomhill Way PA15 45 E4
BROOMHOUSE 120 B2
Broomhouse Cres G71 120 B3
Broomieknowe FK10 4 D3
Broomieknowe Dr G73 138 B6
Broomieknowe Gdns
G73 138 B6
Broomieknowe Rd G73 138 B6
Broomielaw G1, G2 240 C1
Broomknoll St ML6 123 A7
Broomknowe G68 61 D3
Broomknowe Rd PA13 89 C8
Broomknowes Ave G66 79 E4
Broomknowes Rd G21 98 A4
Broomknowe Terr PA13 89 C8
BROOMLANDS 220 A1
Broomlands Ave PA8 93 E8
Broomlands Busway
KA11 220 A2
Broomlands Cres PA8 93 E8
Broomlands Ct
Irvine KA11 220 A2
Paisley PA1 113 C4
Broomlands Dr KA12 219 D2
Broomlands Gdns PA8 93 D8
Broomlands La PA1 113 B4
Broomlands Pl KA12 219 D2
Broomlands Prim Sch
KA11 220 A2
Broomlands Rd
Cumbernauld G67 83 A8
Irvine KA11 220 B1
Broomlands St PA1 113 C4
Broomlands Way PA8 93 E8
Broomlea Cres PA4 93 D7
Broomlee Rd G67 82 F6
Broomley Cres G83 27 D7
Broomley Dr G46 136 C1
Broomley La G46 136 C1
Broomloan Ct G51 116 A5
Broomloan Pl G51 116 B6
Broomloan Rd
Glasgow G51 116 A5
Glasgow G51 116 A6
Broompark Ave
Hamilton G72 161 C6
Prestwick KA9 236 C8
Broompark Cir 8 G31 117 F7
Broompark Cres
Airdrie ML6 103 A3
Prestwick KA9 236 C8
Broompark Dr
Glasgow G31 117 F7
Inchinnan PA4 93 D7
Newton Mearns G77 157 A5
Broompark E FK11 4 A6
Broompark Gdns FK6 21 E2
Broompark Rd
Hamilton G72 161 C7
Wishaw ML2 164 D4
Broompark St 6 G31 117 F7
Broompark W FK11 4 A6
Broom Path G69 119 F3
Broom Pl
Bridge of Weir PA11 110 E7
Coatbridge ML5 121 F3
Glasgow G43 136 D5
Kilmarnock KA1 228 B5
Motherwell ML1 143 C4
Broom Rd
Cumbernauld G67 62 D5
Glasgow G43 136 D5
Newton Mearns G77 157 A6
Rosneath G84 15 B3
Stirling FK7 7 C4
BROOMRIDGE 7 D3
Broomridge Pl FK4 39 D4
Broomridge Rd FK7 7 B3
Broom Road E G77 157 B4
Broomside Cres ML1 163 E4
Broomside Pl FK5 23 C1
Broomside Rd FK4 40 B3
Broomside St ML1 163 E4
Broomstone Ave G77 156 F3
Broom Terr PA5 112 A2

Broomton Rd G21 98 C7
Broomvale Dr G77 156 F5
Broomward Dr PA5 112 B3
Broom Wynd ML7 146 E6
Brora Cres ML3 182 F8
Brora Dr
Bearsden G61 76 B4
Glasgow G46 136 D2
Renfrew PA4 94 E3
Brora Gdns G64 78 B1
Brora Rd G64 78 B1
Brora St G33 98 D1
Brosdale Ct FK1 42 B2
Broster Mdws KA25 149 B3
Brougham St PA16 45 E7
Broughton G75 180 E5
Broughton Dr G23 96 E8
Broughton Gdns G23 76 F1
Broughton Gn KA11 220 B6
Broughton Pl
Coatbridge ML5 122 B3
Hamilton ML3 162 A3
Broughton Rd G23 76 E1
Broun Dr KA7 238 E1
Brouster Hill G74 159 E1
Brouster Pl G74 159 E1
Brown Ave
Alloa FK10 4 F1
Clydebank G81 94 E8
Dumbarton G82 50 C4
Stirling FK9 2 B2
Troon KA10 229 E3
Browncarrick Dr KA7 238 B1
Brown Ct G33 99 E5
Brownhill Dr KA25 169 F8
Brownhill Rd G43 136 B4
Brownhill View ML2 166 D6
Brownieknowe Pl FK2 41 F8
Brownieside Pl ML6 104 A3
Brownieside Rd ML6 104 C1
Brownlee Rd ML8 186 D4
Brownlie St G42 137 B8
Brownmuir Ave G76 178 F4
Brown Pl
Cambuslang G72 139 A6
Saltcoats KA21 205 F1
Brown Rd G67 61 F2
BROWNRIG 85 F6
BROWNSBURN 123 D5
Brownsburn Ind Est ML6 123 B5
Brownsburn Rd ML6 123 C5
Brownsdale Rd G73 137 F7
Brownsfield Cres PA4 93 B5
Brownsfield Rd PA4 93 B5
Brownshill Ave ML5 121 F4
Brownside Ave
Barrhead G78 134 A5
Cambuslang G72 138 E5
Brownside Cres G78 134 A5
Brownside Dr
Barrhead G78 134 A5
Glasgow G13 94 F6
Brownside Gr G78 134 A5
Brownside Mews G72 138 E5
Brownside Rd G72, G73 138 E5
Browns La 3 PA1 113 E4
Brownsland Ct G69 100 F6
Brown St
Balloch G83 28 A8
Carluke ML8 187 F3
Coatbridge ML5 122 A5
Falkirk FK1 41 D5
Glasgow G2 240 B2
Greenock PA15 46 D3
1 Hamilton ML3 162 E2
Larkhall ML9 185 A4
Motherwell ML1 163 F8
Paisley PA1 113 D5
Port Glasgow PA14 47 B2
Shotts ML7 147 B3
Stewarton KA3 211 D8
Wishaw ML2 166 A4
Brown Street N PA4 94 C3
Brown Street S PA4 94 B3
Brown Wlk
Irvine KA12 219 D5
Wishaw ML2 166 B5
Browside Ave PA2 133 C7
Bruart Ave FK5 23 F3
Bruar Way 15 ML2 165 F6
Bruce Ave
Cambuslang G72 139 B3
Dundonald KA2 225 F1
Johnstone PA5 131 E8
Motherwell ML1 163 D7
Paisley PA3 114 A7
Prestwick KA9 236 B6
Bruce Cres
1 Ayr KA7 235 E1
Falkirk FK2 24 B3
Kilmarnock KA1 227 F4
Plean FK7 12 D3
Bruce Ct
Airdrie ML6 123 E8
Cardross G82 48 B8
Bruce Dr
Fallin FK7 8 C5
Stenhousemuir FK5 23 F3
Brucefield Pl G34 120 D8
Bruce Gate FK2 14 D2
BRUCEHILL 49 C3
Brucehill Rd G82 49 C4
Bruce Ho G67 61 F3
Bruce La KA9 236 B6
Bruce Loan ML2 186 C6

Bruce Pl G75 180 F7
Bruce Rd
Bishopton PA7 72 B3
Glasgow G41 116 E4
Motherwell ML1 143 B2
Paisley PA3 114 A7
Renfrew PA4 94 A1
Bruce's Loan 22 ML9 185 C1
Bruce St
Alloa FK10 10 C7
Bannockburn FK7 7 E1
Bellshill ML4 142 B5
Clydebank G81 74 B1
Coatbridge ML5 122 B8
Dumbarton G82 50 A2
Falkirk FK2 42 C6
Greenock PA15 45 E5
Kilmarnock KA1 227 F4
Plains ML6 104 A2
Plean FK7 12 D3
Port Glasgow PA14 47 D1
Stirling FK8 2 B1
Bruce Terr
Blantyre G72 140 E1
Cambusbarron FK7 6 D5
East Kilbride G75 180 F7
Irvine KA12 219 D5
Bruce View FK7 7 B1
Brunel Way G75 180 F8
Brunstane Rd G34 100 A1
Brunswick Ho G81 73 D6
Brunswick La G1 241 A2
Brunswick St G1 241 A2
Brunton St G44 137 A5
Brunton Terr G44 137 A4
Bruntsfield Ave
Glasgow G53 135 B3
Kilwinning KA13 207 B3
Bruntsfield Gdns G53 135 B3
Bryan St ML3 162 B5
Bryce Ave FK2 24 B2
Bryce Gdns ML9 185 A4
Bryce Knox Ct KA11 220 A6
Bryce Pl G75 180 D6
Brydson Pl PA3 112 B6
Brymner St PA15 46 A5
Bryon Ct G71 141 B2
Bryony The FK10 4 B1
Bryson Ct ML3 183 D7
Bryson Pl FK5 23 C5
Bryson St
Clydebank G81 74 E7
Falkirk FK2 42 B6
Bryson Street Ind Est FK2 42 B6
Buccleuch Ave
Clarkston G76 157 D7
Glasgow G52 114 E8
Glasgow G52 114 F7
Buccleuch Ct G61 75 E7
Buccleuch Dr G61 75 E7
Buccleuch La G3 240 B4
Buccleuch St G3 240 B4
Buccleugh St PA15 45 F5
Buchanan Ave
Balloch G83 28 A8
Bishopton PA7 72 B4
Buchanan Bsns Pk G33 99 E6
Buchanan Cres
Bishopbriggs G64 98 C7
Hamilton ML3 162 B2
Buchanan Ct
Balloch G83 28 A8
Falkirk FK2 42 A8
Stepps G33 99 F6
Buchanan Dr
Bearsden G61 76 A4
Bishopbriggs G64 98 C8
Cambuslang G72 138 E6
Carluke ML8 202 C8
Kirkintilloch G66 79 D3
Law ML8 187 A6
Newton Mearns G77 156 E7
Rutherglen G73 138 C6
Stirling FK9 2 B3
Buchanan Galleries Sh Ctr
G1 241 A3
Buchanan Gate G33 99 F6
Buchanan Gdns G32 119 E2
Buchanan Gr G69 120 B5
Buchanan Pl
Kilmarnock KA1 228 A5
Torrance G64 57 B1
Buchanan Rd G84 17 A1
Buchanan St
Airdrie ML6 123 A7
Coatbridge ML5 121 F6
Dumbarton G82 50 B2
Glasgow G1 240 C2
Glasgow G1 241 A3
Glasgow, Muirhead G69 120 B4
Greenock PA16 45 B4
Johnstone PA5 111 E2
Milngavie G62 55 B2
Buchanan Street
Underground Sta G1 241 A3
Buchanan Way PA5 111 E2
Buchan Ave FK2 24 B1
Buchan Ct 4 KA7 235 E1
Buchandyke Rd G74 160 B3
Buchan Gn G74 160 B3
Buchan Ho G67 61 F2
Buchan Rd
Motherwell ML1 143 B2
Troon KA10 229 G4
Buchan St
Hamilton ML3 183 C8
Wishaw ML2 165 B6
Buchan Terr G72 138 F3
Buchley Cotts G64 77 C5
Buchlyvie Gdns G64 97 F8
Buchlyvie Rd PA1 114 E5
Buchlyvie St G34 120 B7
Buckie PA8 73 A3
Buckie Wlk ML4 142 A6
Buckingham Ct ML3 161 E4
Buckingham Dr
Glasgow G32 139 B8
Rutherglen G73 138 D7
Buckingham St G12 96 D3
Buckingham Terr G12 96 D3
Bucklaw Gdns G52 115 C4
Bucklaw Pl G52 115 C4
Bucklaw Terr G52 115 C4
Buckley St G22 97 D6
Bucksburn Rd G21 98 C4
Buckthorne Pl G53 135 B3
Buddon St G31 118 C4
Budhill Ave G32 119 B5
Budshaw Ave ML6 123 C2
Buiston Rd KA3 211 D3
Bulldale Ct G14 94 F5
Bulldale Rd G14 94 E5
Bulldale St G14 94 E6
Buller Cl G72 140 D2
Buller Cres G72 140 C2
Bullionslaw Dr G73 138 D6
Bulloch Ave G46 136 D2
Bulloch Cres FK6 21 D1
Bull Rd G76 157 F6
Bull's Cl 15 ML11 215 A4
Bullwood Ave G53 134 F8
Bullwood Ct 6 G53 115 A1
Bullwood Dr G53 114 F1
Bullwood Gdns G53 114 F1
Bullwood Pl G53 114 F1
Bunbury Terr 3 G75 180 C8
Bunessan St G52 115 F5
Bungalows The FK5 23 B1
Bunhouse Rd G3 96 C1
Buntine Cres FK7 7 A3
Bunting Pl KA1 228 C7
Burbank G62 55 A2
Burder Pk FK2 24 A2
BURGH 138 B7
Burghead Dr G51 115 E8
Burghead Pl G51 115 E8
Burgher St G31 118 C5
Burgh Hall La G11 96 B2
Burgh Hall St G11 96 B2
Burgh La 4 G12 96 D3
Burgh Mews 1 FK10 10 B6
Burghmuir Ind Est FK8 7 B6
Burghmuir Rd FK7 7 B6
Burgh Prim Sch G73 138 A8
Burgh Rd KA9 236 B8
Burgh Wlk PA19 44 E8
Burleigh Rd G71 141 B3
Burleigh St
Coatbridge ML5 122 B3
Glasgow G51 116 A8
Burleigh Way FK10 10 C6
Burley Pl G74 158 F2
Burlington Ave G12 96 B6
Burma Rd KA20 218 A5
Burmola St G22 97 B4
Burnacre Gdns G71 140 E7
Burnawn Gdns G33 98 D7
Burnawn Gr G33 98 D7
Burnawn Pl G33 98 D7
BURNBANK 162 A5
Burnbank Braes ML8 187 F1
Burnbank Ctr ML3 162 A5
Burnbank Dr G78 134 D1
Burnbank Gdns
Glasgow G20 96 F2
6 Hamilton ML3 162 A5
Burnbank La G20 96 F2
Burnbank Pl
Ayr KA7 239 B4
2 Glasgow G20 97 A2
Stewarton KA3 195 F1
Burnbank Quadrant ML6 122 F8
Burnbank Rd
Ayr KA7 239 B4
Falkirk FK2 42 B7
Hamilton ML3 162 B4
Burnbank St
Airdrie ML6 122 F8
Coatbridge ML5 122 B8
Stevenston KA20 217 D8
Burnbank Terr
Glasgow G20 96 F2
Kilsyth G65 36 D1
Port Glasgow PA14 68 D8
Burnblea Gdns ML3 162 E2
Burnblea St ML3 162 D2
Burnbrae
Alloa FK10 10 C8
Clydebank G81 74 A6
Sauchie FK10 5 C1
Twechar G65 59 F4
Burnbrae Ave
Bearsden G61 76 A7
Linwood PA3 112 C5
Moodiesburn G69 81 A2
Burnbrae Cres KA11 220 C5
Burnbrae Dr
Linwood PA3 112 D4
Perceton KA11 220 C5
Rutherglen G73 138 D5
Burnbrae Gdns
Alva FK12 5 B6
Burnbrae Gdns *continued*
Falkirk FK1 42 A5
Glasgow G53 135 D6
Burnbrae Pl G74 159 C2
Burnbrae Rd
Falkirk FK1 42 A5
Hamilton G72 161 C7
Harthill ML7 127 F6
Kirkintilloch, Auchinloch G66 79 F2
Kirkintilloch G66 80 B2
Kirkintilloch, Waterside G66 80 B7
Linwood PA3 112 C4
Shotts ML7 146 E3
Burnbrae St
Clydebank G81 74 D8
Glasgow G21 98 A4
Larkhall ML9 184 F3
Burnbridge Wynd KA3 195 F1
Burncleuch Ave G72 139 A4
Burn Cres
Chapelhall ML6 123 D2
Motherwell ML1 143 B4
Burncrooks Ave
Bearsden G61 75 D7
East Kilbride G74 159 C2
Burncrooks Ct G81 73 F6
Burndale La PA13 89 D8
Burn Dr FK7 7 C4
Burndyke Ct G51 116 C7
Burndyke Sq G51 116 C7
Burnee FK10 5 E3
Burness Ave KA7 238 F2
Burnet Rose Ct G74 159 C4
Burnet Rose Gdns G74 159 C4
Burnet Rose Pl G74 159 C4
Burnett Ct G69 100 C8
Burnett Rd G33 119 E7
Burnett Terr KA8 236 B1
Burnfield Ave G46 136 B4
Burnfield Cotts G46 136 B4
Burnfield Dr G43 136 B4
Burnfield Gdns G46 136 C4
Burnfield Pl FK2 42 D7
Burnfield Rd G46 136 B4
BURNFOOT 102 E1
Burnfoot G82 48 B7
Burnfoot Ave KA10 229 E5
Burnfoot Cres
Paisley PA2 133 C8
Rutherglen G73 138 D5
Burnfoot Dr G52 115 B5
Burnfoot La
Ardrossan KA22 205 B4
1 Falkirk FK1 42 B4
Burnfoot Pl KA3 222 E4
Burnfoot Rd
Airdrie ML6 122 E8
Lochwinnoch PA12 129 B2
Burnfoot Way 5 KA10 229 E5
Burngreen G65 60 D8
Burngreen Terr G67 62 B5
Burnhall Pl ML2 165 D1
Burnhall Rd ML2 165 C2
Burnhall St ML2 165 D1
Burnham Rd G14 95 A4
Burnhaven PA8 73 A2
BURNHEAD 185 C3
Burnhead La FK1 42 C4
Burnhead Rd
Airdrie ML6 103 D1
Cumbernauld G68 61 C2
Glasgow G43 136 E5
Larkhall ML9 185 C2
Port Glasgow PA14 68 D8
Stenhousemuir FK5 23 C3
Burnhead St
Greenock PA15 46 B2
Uddingston G71 141 C7
Burnhill Quadrant G73 137 F8
Burnhill Sp Ctr G73 137 F8
Burnhill St G73 137 F8
BURNHOUSE 172 C1
Burnhouse Ave
Cumbernauld G68 61 B2
Dalry KA24 191 B7
Burnhouse Brae G77 157 A3
Burnhouse Cotts KA3 195 B8
Burnhouse Cres ML3 162 B1
Burnhouse Rd
East Kilbride G75 180 A1
Hamilton ML3 162 B1
Burnhouse St
Glasgow G20 96 C6
Glasgow G20 96 D6
Burniebrae ML6 122 F8
Burniebrae Rd ML6 123 E3
Burn La ML1 143 A4
Burnlea Cres PA6 91 A3
Burnlea Pl KA20 206 E2
Burnlip Rd ML6 102 A4
Burnmouth Ct G33 119 F6
Burnmouth Pl G61 76 A5
Burnmouth Rd G33 119 F6
Burnock Pl G75 179 E7
Burnpark Ave G71 140 D7
Burnpark Rd KA1 227 F3
Burn Pl G72 138 E7
Burn Rd
Carluke ML8 187 F3
Saltcoats KA21 216 D8
Burns Ave
Bishopton PA7 72 B3
Kilmarnock KA3 223 A3
Saltcoats KA21 205 F3
Stenhousemuir FK5 23 C5
Burns Cottage & Mus★
KA7 238 E2
Burns Cres
Harthill ML7 127 F6
Irvine KA11 220 A5
Kilmarnock KA3 223 B5
Laurieston FK2 42 F4
Burn's Cres ML6 123 B6
Burns Ct G66 59 A1
Burns Dr
Johnstone PA5 131 E8
Kirkintilloch G66 59 A2
Burns Gdns G72 140 C1
Burns Gr G46 136 A2
BURNSIDE
Alva 5 C7
Rutherglen 138 D5
Burnside G61 75 C7
Burnside Ave
Barrhead G78 134 B4
Bellshill ML4 142 C4
Brookfield PA5 111 C5
Calderbank ML6 123 B2
Kirkintilloch G66 79 B7
Port Glasgow PA14 68 F8
Burnside Cotts KA3 173 C6
Burnside Cres
Balloch G83 27 F7
Clydebank G81 74 B7
Hamilton G72 161 F6
Plean FK7 12 C4
Shotts ML7 146 D6
Burnside Ct
Alva FK12 5 A7
Bearsden G61 75 C7
Coatbridge ML5 121 F5
Falkirk, Camelon FK1 41 E5
Motherwell ML1 164 B4
Rutherglen G73 138 C5
Burnside Gate
Hamilton ML3 162 D3
Rutherglen G73 138 C5
Burnside Gdns
Clarkston G76 157 D7
Johnstone PA10 111 B2
Prestwick KA9 233 C1
Burnside Gr PA5 111 E2
Burnside Ind Est G65 60 C8
Burnside La ML3 162 E2
Burnside Pl
Dumbarton G82 50 B2
Falkirk FK2 24 B3
Irvine KA12 219 B4
Larkhall ML9 185 B3
Paisley PA3 113 A7
Stevenston KA20 206 D1
Troon KA10 229 D3
West Kilbride KA23 190 D5
Burnside Prim Sch G73 138 B5
Burnside Quadrant ML1 143 A5
Burnside Rd
Elderslie PA5 112 D2
Glenmavis ML5 102 C1
Gourock PA19 44 F6
Menstrie FK11 3 F6
Monkton KA9 233 D4
Motherwell ML1 143 D4
Rutherglen G46 157 B6
Rutherglen, High Burnside
G73 138 C4
Burnside St
Alloa FK10 5 D1
Dumbarton G82 50 B2
Glengarnock KA14 170 B6
Kilmarnock KA1 227 E6
Motherwell ML1 164 B4
Stirling FK7 7 C6
Burnside Sta G73 138 C5
Burnside Terr FK1 41 E5
Burnside Twr ML1 164 B3
Burnside View
Coatbridge ML5 121 E5
East Kilbride G75 180 A4
Burnside Wlk
Bearsden G61 75 C7
Coatbridge ML5 121 E5
Burns La ML6 123 D3
Burns Loan 13 ML9 185 B4
Burns Mon★
Ayr KA7 238 E1
Kilmarnock KA3 223 A1
Burns Path ML4 142 B7
Burns Pk G74 160 A3
Burns Pl
Kilwinning KA13 207 F3
Shotts ML7 146 A6
Burn's Pl KA20 206 E1
Burns Prec 5 KA1 227 F8
Burns Rd
Chapelhall ML6 123 D4
Cumbernauld G67 62 B2
Greenock PA16 44 D4
Kirkintilloch G66 59 A1
Troon KA10 229 G4
Burns Sq
Ardrossan KA22 205 D4
Greenock PA16 44 D4
Burns St
Alexandria G83 27 E7
Clydebank G81 73 E4
Glasgow G4 97 B2
Hamilton ML3 162 D2
Irvine KA12 219 B3
Renton G82 27 D1
Stirling FK8 2 A2
Burns Statue Arc KA7 238 F7
Burns Statue Sq KA7 238 F7
Burn St G83 27 F4
Burns Terr
Ardrossan KA22 205 D4
Burns Terr *continued*
Cowie FK7 12 D7
Burn Street La G83 27 F4
Burns Way
Kilmarnock KA3 223 B5
Motherwell ML1 143 C4
Burns' Wicket KA7 238 E1
Burns Wynd ML9 198 E1
Burntbroom Dr G69 119 F3
Burntbroom Gdns G69 119 F3
Burntbroom Rd G69 119 F2
Burntbroom St G33 119 D7
Burn Terr G72 138 E7
Burnthills Ind Est PA5 111 F3
Burntshields Rd PA10 110 D2
Burn View G67 62 C3
Burnwood Dr ML6 124 A6
Burra Gdns G64 78 D2
Burray Dr KA3 223 A6
Burrell Collection The
(Mus)★ G43 116 B1
Burrell Ct G41 116 C2
Burrell's La G4 241 C2
Burrelton Rd G43 136 F5
Burstenman's Brae KA13,
KA24 207 F7
Burte Ct ML4 142 A7
Burton La
Carluke ML8 187 E2
Glasgow G42 117 A1
Busbie Gdns KA2 221 E1
Busbiehead KA11 220 B5
Busbiehill Pl KA1 222 D1
Busbie Holdings KA2 221 D3
Busbie La KA22 205 D3
Busbie View KA2 221 E1
BUSBY 158 B5
Busby Pl KA13 207 F4
Busby Prim Sch G76 157 F6
Busby Rd
Bellshill ML4 141 F3
Carmunnock G76 158 C7
Clarkston G76 157 E7
Busby Sta G76 158 A5
Bush Cres ML2 165 C2
Bushelhead Rd ML8 201 E6
Bushes Ave PA2 113 D1
Bushes Prim Sch PA2 133 D8
Busheyhill St G72 139 A5
Bute G74 160 C1
Bute Ave
Motherwell ML1 163 C7
Port Glasgow PA14 69 B8
Renfrew PA4 94 D1
Bute Cres
Bearsden G61 75 F2
Old Kilpatrick G60 73 C5
Paisley PA2 133 D7
Shotts ML7 146 D6
Bute Ct
Irvine KA11 220 C1
Stevenston KA20 217 C8
Bute Dr
Johnstone PA5 111 D1
Old Kilpatrick G60 73 C6
Bute Gdns
Glasgow G44 136 F4
Glasgow, Kelvingrove G12 96 D2
Old Kilpatrick G60 73 C6
Bute La G12 96 D2
Bute Pl
Ardrossan KA22 205 C1
Old Kilpatrick G60 73 D5
Bute Rd
Kirkintilloch G66 80 B8
Renfrew PA3 93 D1
Rutherglen G73 138 D3
Bute St
Coatbridge ML5 122 B4
Falkirk FK2 42 B6
Gourock PA19 44 D6
Hamilton ML3 162 B6
Bute Terr
Rutherglen G73 138 A5
Saltcoats KA21 205 E1
Uddingston G71 141 B7
Bute Twr G72 138 E3
Butler Wynd ML4 141 F5
Butt Ave G84 16 E3
Butterbiggins Rd G42 117 B3
Butterburnpark St ML3 162 D2
Buttercup Path ML2 164 F1
Butterfield Pl 2 G41 117 A3
Buttermere G75 179 F5
Buttsley Ct ML11 214 E4
Butts The ML11 214 F3
Byars Rd G66 79 B8
By Pass Rd KA15 150 C1
By-Pass Rd FK4 39 E5
Byramsmuir Rd ML1 142 E8
Byrebush Rd G53 115 C1
Byrehill Ave KA13 207 B2
Byrehill Dr KA13 207 B2
Byrehill Pl KA13 207 B2
Byrehill Rd KA13, KA20 207 D1
Byres Ave PA3 114 A6
Byres Cres PA3 114 A6
Byresknowe La 2 ML1 143 B1
Byres Loch KA13 207 D3
Byres Rd
Elderslie PA5 112 D2
Glasgow G12 96 C2
Kilwinning KA13 207 D3
Motherwell ML1 143 E4
Byrestone Ave G77 157 C4
Byretown Gr ML11 214 E3
Byretown Rd ML11 214 E2
Byron Rd ML7 146 B6

Byron St
Clydebank G81 . . . 74 A4
Glasgow G11 . . . 95 F2
Byshot St G22 . . . 97 D4

C

Caafwater Pl KA21 . . . 205 E2
Cable Depot Rd G81 . . . 73 F2
Cables Dr G83 . . . 27 F5
Cabrach Loan 13 ML2 . . . 165 F6
CADDER
Bishopbriggs . . . 78 B5
Glasgow . . . 96 F7
Cadder Cl G69 . . . 100 F5
Cadder Ct G64 . . . 78 B5
Cadder Gr G20 . . . 96 E7
Cadder Pl G20 . . . 96 E7
Cadder Prim Sch G23 . . . 96 F7
Cadder Rd
Bishopbriggs G64 . . . 78 B5
Glasgow G23 . . . 96 E7
Cadder Rdbt G64 . . . 78 B4
Cadder Way G64 . . . 78 B5
Caddlehill St PA16 . . . 45 D5
Cadell Dr FK2 . . . 24 A5
Cadell Gdns G74 . . . 160 D5
Cadgers Loan FK7 . . . 12 B2
Cadger's Sheuch G68 . . . 61 B8
Cadoc St G72 . . . 139 B5
Cadogan Sq G2 . . . 240 B2
Cadogan St G2 . . . 240 B2
CADZOW . . . 183 E8
Cadzow Ave
Hamilton ML3 . . . 162 C5
Rutherglen G46 . . . 157 B8
Cadzow Cres ML5 . . . 121 E4
Cadzow Dr
Bellshill ML4 . . . 142 D4
Cambuslang G72 . . . 139 A5
Cadzow Gn G74 . . . 159 D2
Cadzow Ho ML3 . . . 162 E5
Cadzow Ind Est ML3 . . . 183 D8
Cadzow La ML3 . . . 162 E4
Cadzow Pk ML3 . . . 162 E4
Cadzow Rd ML3 . . . 183 F3
Cadzow St
Glasgow G2 . . . 240 B2
Hamilton ML3 . . . 162 E4
Larkhall ML9 . . . 185 A4
Motherwell ML1 . . . 163 D6
Caerlaverock Ave KA9 . . . 236 C8
Caerlaverock Pl 1 G72 . . . 161 C6
Caerlaverock Rd KA9 . . . 236 C8
Caird Ave PA16 . . . 45 C7
Caird Dr G11 . . . 96 B2
Caird Gdns ML3 . . . 162 D5
Caird Pk ML3 . . . 162 D5
Caird St ML3 . . . 162 C5
Caird Terr G61 . . . 75 D7
Cairn Ave PA4 . . . 94 E1
Cairnban Ct ML8 . . . 187 F3
Cairnbrook Ind Est G34 . . . 120 C8
Cairnbrook Rd G34 . . . 120 C8
Cairn Cl KA3 . . . 195 C1
Cairn Cres KA7 . . . 238 D2
Cairn Ct
East Kilbride G74 . . . 159 E4
2 Motherwell ML1 . . . 163 F5
Cairncurran Ct PA15 . . . 45 E3
Cairndhu Ave G84 . . . 16 A2
Cairndhu Gdns G84 . . . 16 A2
Cairndow Ave G44 . . . 136 F4
Cairndow Ct G44 . . . 136 F4
Cairn Dr PA3 . . . 112 B6
Cairnduff Pl KA3 . . . 195 F1
Cairndyke Cres ML6 . . . 123 A6
Cairneymount Rd ML8 . . . 188 A2
Cairney Pl ML2 . . . 166 D6
Cairnfore Ave KA10 . . . 229 G6
Cairngorm Cres
Barrhead G78 . . . 134 C1
Bearsden G61 . . . 75 B6
Paisley PA2 . . . 113 E1
Wishaw ML2 . . . 164 F3
Cairngorm Ct
Greenock PA16 . . . 45 B5
Hamilton ML3 . . . 183 B7
Irvine KA11 . . . 220 B5
Cairngorm Gdns G68 . . . 61 B1
Cairngorm Pl G75 . . . 180 B4
Cairngorm Rd
Glasgow G43 . . . 136 C5
Kilmarnock KA1 . . . 228 B3
Cairngorm Residential Pk
The G64 . . . 98 C8
CAIRNHILL . . . 122 F6
Cairnhill Ave ML6 . . . 123 A5
Cairnhill Cir G53 . . . 114 F3
Cairnhill Cres ML5 . . . 122 D3
Cairnhill Ct ML8 . . . 188 A2
Cairnhill Dr G53 . . . 114 F3
Cairnhill Pl G53 . . . 114 F3
Cairnhill Rd
Airdrie ML6 . . . 123 A6
Bearsden G61 . . . 75 F1
Cairnhill Trad Est ML6 . . . 123 A6
Cairnhill View G61 . . . 75 E2
Cairnhope Ave ML6 . . . 122 F5
Cairnlea Dr G51 . . . 116 B6
Cairnlea Gdns ML4 . . . 142 B3
Cairnlea Rd G62 . . . 54 E1
Cairnmount Rd KA11 . . . 219 F7
Cairnmuir Rd G74 . . . 159 D6
Cairnoch Hill G68 . . . 61 C2
Cairnoch Way FK7 . . . 7 F1
Cairnoch Wlk FK6 . . . 21 D1
Cairn Pl G74 . . . 159 E4
Cairnryan G74 . . . 159 D3
Cairnryan Cres G72 . . . 161 D3
Cairns Ave G72 . . . 139 B5
Cairns Ct G72 . . . 139 B5
Cairns Dr G62 . . . 55 A2
Cairnsgarroch Way
KA11 . . . 220 B2
Cairnsmore Dr
Bearsden G61 . . . 75 B7
Doonfoot KA7 . . . 238 C1
Cairnsmore Rd G15 . . . 74 F2
Cairnsmore Way KA11 . . . 220 B2
Cairns Prim Sch G72 . . . 139 C4
Cairns Rd
Bishopton PA7 . . . 72 A4
Cambuslang G72 . . . 139 B4
Cairns St ML1 . . . 163 E6
Cairn St G21 . . . 97 F6
Cairns Terr KA1 . . . 222 E1
Cairns The FK11 . . . 4 A6
Cairnswell Ave G72 . . . 139 C4
Cairnswell Pl G72 . . . 139 C4
Cairntoul Ct G68 . . . 61 B1
Cairntoul Dr G14 . . . 95 A5
Cairntoul Pl G14 . . . 95 A5
Cairnview G66 . . . 80 B7
Cairn View ML6 . . . 122 F6
Cairnview Rd G66 . . . 58 C5
Cairnwell Gdns ML1 . . . 164 C3
Cairnwood Dr ML6 . . . 122 F5
Caithness Rd
East Kilbride G74 . . . 160 D3
Greenock PA16 . . . 44 D4
Caithness Row ML11 . . . 215 A2
Caithness St
Glasgow G20 . . . 96 F4
Hamilton G72 . . . 161 C6
Cala Sona Ct ML2 . . . 185 E8
Calcots Path G34 . . . 100 C1
Calcots Pl G34 . . . 100 D1
Caldarvan St G22 . . . 97 B3
Caldeen Rd ML5 . . . 122 B5
Calder Ave
Barrhead G78 . . . 134 D1
Caldercruix ML6 . . . 104 F4
Coatbridge ML5 . . . 122 B4
Troon KA10 . . . 229 F6
Wishaw ML2 . . . 166 A6
CALDERBANK . . . 123 B3
Calderbank Prim Sch
ML6 . . . 123 C3
Calderbank Rd ML6 . . . 123 B4
Calderbank Terr ML1 . . . 163 F7
Calderbank View G69 . . . 120 C4
Calderbankview Cotts
ML6 . . . 123 B4
CALDERBRAES . . . 140 E8
Calderbraes Ave G71 . . . 140 E8
CALDERBREAS . . . 120 E1
CALDERCRUIX . . . 105 A5
Caldercruix Rd ML6 . . . 105 D7
Calder Ct
Coatbridge ML5 . . . 122 B4
Stirling FK7 . . . 7 C5
Caldercuilt Prim Sch 11
G23 . . . 76 E1
Caldercuilt Rd
Glasgow G20 . . . 96 C8
Glasgow G23 . . . 76 D2
Calder Dr
Bellshill ML4 . . . 142 C4
Cambuslang G72 . . . 139 A5
Lochwinnoch PA12 . . . 129 C3
Shotts ML7 . . . 147 B4
Calder Gate G64 . . . 77 F4
Calderglen Ave G72 . . . 140 C3
Calderglen Ctry Pk*
G75 . . . 181 C6
Calderglen High Sch
G74 . . . 181 C8
Calderglen Rd G74 . . . 160 D1
Caldergrove ML1 . . . 163 E8
Calderhaugh La PA12 . . . 129 B2
Calderhaugh Mill PA12 . . . 129 C2
CALDERHEAD . . . 146 E4
Calderhead High Sch
ML7 . . . 146 F5
Calderhead Rd ML7 . . . 146 D7
Calderpark Ave
Glasgow G71 . . . 120 B2
Lochwinnoch PA12 . . . 129 C3
Calderpark Cres G71 . . . 120 B2
Calderpark Ct G71 . . . 120 B2
Calderpark Pl G71 . . . 120 B2
Calderpark Rd G71 . . . 120 B2
Calderpark St PA12 . . . 129 C3
Calderpark Terr G71 . . . 120 B2
Calder Pl
Falkirk FK1 . . . 42 D1
Glasgow G69 . . . 120 B4
Kilmarnock KA1 . . . 228 A5
Calder Prim Sch ML1 . . . 163 F7
Calder Rd
Bellshill ML4 . . . 142 C4
Paisley PA3 . . . 113 A5
Shotts ML7 . . . 166 F8
Uddingston G71, G72 . . . 140 C5
Calderrigg Pl ML6 . . . 123 E7
Calderside Acad G72 . . . 161 D7
Calderside Gr G74 . . . 160 E3
Calderside Rd G72, G74 . . . 160 E3
Calder St
Calderbank ML6 . . . 123 C2
Coatbridge ML5 . . . 122 C5
Glasgow G42 . . . 117 B2
Hamilton G72 . . . 161 D7
Lochwinnoch PA12 . . . 129 C3
Calder Twr
East Kilbride G74 . . . 181 B7
6 Motherwell ML1 . . . 163 E5
Caldervale High Sch
ML6 . . . 123 F7
Caldervale St ML6 . . . 123 E4
Calderview ML1 . . . 163 F7
Calder View ML3 . . . 183 B8
Calderview Ave ML5 . . . 122 E4
CALDERWOOD . . . 160 C4
Calderwood KA13 . . . 207 E5
Calderwood Ave 4 G69 . . . 120 A3
Calderwood Ct ML2 . . . 165 B2
Calderwood Dr
Glasgow G69 . . . 120 A3
Hamilton G72 . . . 161 D6
Calderwood Gdns
East Kilbride G74 . . . 160 E3
Glasgow G69 . . . 120 A3
Calderwood Lodge Prim Sch
G43 . . . 136 E5
Calderwood Prim Sch
G73 . . . 138 C6
Calderwood Rd
East Kilbride G74 . . . 160 B2
Glasgow G43 . . . 136 D6
Rutherglen G73 . . . 138 C7
Calderwood Sq 1 G74 . . . 160 B3
Caldon Rd KA12 . . . 219 D4
Caldwell Ave
Glasgow G13 . . . 95 A6
Linwood PA3 . . . 112 A5
Caldwell Gr
Bellshill ML4 . . . 142 A8
Rutherglen G73 . . . 138 C2
Caldwell Pl G84 . . . 15 E5
Caldwell Quadrant ML1 . . . 163 C5
Caldwell Rd
Carluke ML8 . . . 202 B8
West Kilbride KA23 . . . 190 C4
Caldwellside Ind Est
ML11 . . . 215 E5
Caledonia Ave
Glasgow G5 . . . 117 C3
Rutherglen G73 . . . 138 B8
Caledonia Cres
Ardrossan KA22 . . . 205 C2
Gourock PA19 . . . 44 F7
Caledonia Ct
Kilmarnock KA1 . . . 222 E1
Paisley PA3 . . . 113 D6
Caledonia Dr
Glasgow G69 . . . 120 B3
Motherwell ML1 . . . 143 E4
3 Port Glasgow PA14 . . . 47 A2
Caledonia Gdns
Carluke ML8 . . . 187 E3
Gourock PA19 . . . 44 F7
Caledonian Ave
Bellshill ML4 . . . 141 F4
Stonehouse ML9 . . . 198 E1
Caledonian Cres 5 G12 . . . 96 E2
Caledonian Ct
East Kilbride G75 . . . 180 E8
Falkirk FK2 . . . 42 C7
Caledonian Gate 5 ML5 . . . 122 A8
Caledonian Pl KA14 . . . 170 B7
Caledonian Rd
Alloa FK10 . . . 9 F6
Glengarnock KA14 . . . 170 C7
Larkhall ML9 . . . 185 A3
Stevenston KA20 . . . 217 E7
Wishaw ML2 . . . 165 A2
Caledonian Ret Pk ML2 . . . 164 D3
Caledonia Prim Sch
Glasgow G69 . . . 120 A3
Saltcoats KA21 . . . 216 E8
Caledonia Rd
Ardrossan KA22 . . . 205 C2
Ayr KA7 . . . 239 C6
Beith KA15 . . . 150 B1
Glasgow G69 . . . 120 A3
Glasgow, Gorbals G5 . . . 117 C4
Saltcoats KA21 . . . 205 E1
Shotts ML7 . . . 146 E5
Caledonia St
Clydebank G81 . . . 73 F3
Glasgow G5 . . . 117 D3
Paisley PA3 . . . 113 D6
Port Glasgow PA14 . . . 47 D1
Caledonia Terr
Bonnybridge FK4 . . . 39 F5
Dumbarton G82 . . . 49 D3
Caledonia Way PA3 . . . 93 D1
Caledonia Way E PA3 . . . 93 E1
Caledonia Way W PA3 . . . 93 D1
Caledonia Wlk ML3 . . . 162 E1
Caledon La G12 . . . 96 C2
Caledon St G12 . . . 96 C3
Caley Brae G71 . . . 140 F6
Caley Ct KA20 . . . 217 D7
Caley Ho KA13 . . . 207 D3
Calfhill Rd G53 . . . 115 B2
Calfmuir Rd G66 . . . 80 A6
Calgary Pk G75 . . . 180 D8
Calgary Pl
Airdrie ML6 . . . 122 E6
1 East Kilbride G75 . . . 180 D8
Calgary St G4 . . . 241 A4
Calico Way G66 . . . 33 C1
CALIFORNIA . . . 66 E5
California Prim Sch FK1 . . . 66 F5
California Rd FK1 . . . 66 E6
California Terr FK1 . . . 66 F5
Callaghan Cres G74 . . . 179 D8
Callaghan Wynd G72 . . . 140 C1
Callandar Pl KA8 . . . 236 B4
Callander Ct G68 . . . 61 F4
Callander Dr FK5 . . . 41 C8
Callander Rd
Ayr KA8 . . . 236 D5
Chapelhall ML6 . . . 123 D1
Cumbernauld G68 . . . 61 F4
Callander St G20 . . . 97 A3
Callendar Ave FK1 . . . 42 B1
Callendar Bsns Pk FK1 . . . 42 E3
Callendar Bvd FK1 . . . 42 E3
Callendar House* FK1 . . . 42 D3
Callendar Park Dr FK1 . . . 42 D4
Callendar Rd FK1 . . . 42 D4
Callendar Riggs FK1 . . . 42 C4
Callendar Square Sh Ctr 5
FK1 . . . 42 B4
Callender Park View FK1 . . . 42 D4
Callender Park Wlk FK1 . . . 42 D4
Callieburn Ct G64 . . . 98 A8
Callieburn Rd G64 . . . 98 A8
Callon St ML6 . . . 123 A7
Cally Ave G15 . . . 75 A3
Calside PA2 . . . 113 E3
Calside Ave PA2 . . . 113 E3
CALTON . . . 117 E5
Calton Cres FK7 . . . 7 B4
Calton Entry G40 . . . 241 C1
Caltrop Pl FK7 . . . 7 E3
Calvay Cres G33 . . . 119 D7
Calvay Pl G33 . . . 119 E7
Calvay Rd G33 . . . 119 E7
Calvinston Rd KA9 . . . 236 D5
Cambourne Rd G69 . . . 80 F3
Cambridge Ave
Clydebank G81 . . . 74 B3
Gourock PA19 . . . 45 A7
Cambridge Rd
Greenock PA16 . . . 44 D4
Renfrew PA4 . . . 94 C2
Cambridge St G3 . . . 240 C3
Camburn St G32 . . . 118 F5
CAMBUS . . . 9 B8
CAMBUSBARRON . . . 6 C6
Cambusbarron Prim Sch
FK7 . . . 6 D5
Cambusdoon Dr KA7 . . . 238 E2
Cambusdoon Pl KA13 . . . 207 D3
Cambusdoon Rd G33 . . . 99 C2
Cambuskeith Dr KA1 . . . 227 B8
Cambuskeith Rd KA20 . . . 206 E3
Cambuskenneth Abbey*
FK9 . . . 7 D8
Cambuskenneth Gdns
G32 . . . 119 D5
Cambuskenneth Pl G33 . . . 99 C2
CAMBUSLANG . . . 139 B4
Cambuslang Ct G32 . . . 138 F8
Cambuslang Ind Est G32 . . . 139 A8
Cambuslang Investment Pk
G32 . . . 139 A8
Cambuslang Rd
Cambuslang G32, G72 . . . 138 F8
Rutherglen G72, G73 . . . 138 D8
Cambuslang Sta G72 . . . 138 F6
Cambuslang Way G32 . . . 138 F8
Cambuslea Rd KA8 . . . 236 B3
CAMBUSLENNETH . . . 2 D1
Cambusmoon Terr G83 . . . 20 F8
CAMBUSNETHAN . . . 165 E3
Cambusnethan Prim Sch
ML2 . . . 165 D4
Cambusnethan St ML2 . . . 165 E4
Cambus Pl G33 . . . 99 C2
Cambus Pools Nature
Reserve* FK10 . . . 8 F8
Camden Terr G5 . . . 117 C4
Camellia Dr ML2 . . . 164 E1
CAMELON . . . 41 C5
Camelon Cres G72 . . . 161 D8
Camelon Ed Ctr FK1 . . . 41 E6
Camelon Rd FK1 . . . 41 F5
Camelon Rdbt FK1 . . . 41 D6
Camelon St G32 . . . 118 F6
Camelon Sta FK1 . . . 41 D6
Cameron Ave PA7 . . . 72 B4
Cameron Cres
Carmunnock G76 . . . 158 E8
Hamilton ML3 . . . 162 C3
Cameron Ct
Clydebank G81 . . . 94 C8
Gourock PA19 . . . 43 F6
Rutherglen G73 . . . 138 A7
Cameron Dr
Alexandria G83 . . . 27 D7
Bearsden G61 . . . 76 A3
Kilmarnock KA3 . . . 223 C2
Newton Mearns G77 . . . 156 E7
Uddingston G71 . . . 141 A8
Cameronian Ct ML11 . . . 215 C5
Cameronian Dr ML8 . . . 188 B1
Cameronian Pl ML4 . . . 141 F3
Cameronian St 9 FK8 . . . 7 B7
Cameronian Way 8
ML9 . . . 185 C1
Cameron Path 13 ML9 . . . 185 C1
Cameron Pl FK2 . . . 24 B2
Cameron Rd
1 Carluke ML8 . . . 202 B8
Wattston ML6 . . . 83 C2
Cameron Sq G81 . . . 74 C6
Cameron St
Clydebank G81 . . . 94 C8
Coatbridge ML5 . . . 122 B8
Glasgow G52 . . . 114 F7
Motherwell ML1 . . . 163 D6
Cameron Terr FK1 . . . 86 B3
Cameron Way G72 . . . 161 D8
Camis Eskan Ho G84 . . . 25 E7
CAMLACHIE . . . 118 B6
Camlachie St G31 . . . 118 B5
Cam'nethan St ML9 . . . 198 F2
Campbell Ave
Bishopton PA7 . . . 72 B4
Dumbarton G82 . . . 50 D4
Milngavie G62 . . . 55 A1
Saltcoats KA21 . . . 216 E8
Stevenston KA20 . . . 206 D2
Campbell Cl ML3 . . . 162 F4
Campbell Cres
Alexandria G83 . . . 27 D7
Bothwell G71 . . . 141 A4
Laurieston FK2 . . . 42 F3
Newton Mearns G77 . . . 156 E6
Campbell Ct
Ayr KA8 . . . 239 C8
Greenock PA16 . . . 45 E7
Rutherglen G73 . . . 138 C5
Stirling FK7 . . . 6 F4
Campbell Dr
Barrhead G78 . . . 134 C2
Bearsden G61 . . . 75 D5
Dumbarton G82 . . . 50 C4
Helensburgh G84 . . . 25 C7
Larbert FK5 . . . 23 B2
Troon KA10 . . . 229 E5
Campbell Ho G67 . . . 61 E2
Campbell La ML3 . . . 162 E3
Campbell Pl
East Kilbride G75 . . . 180 E7
3 Falkirk FK2 . . . 41 F7
Irvine KA11 . . . 225 B8
Kilmarnock KA1 . . . 227 F5
Torrance G64 . . . 57 B1
Campbell St
Alexandria G83 . . . 27 F4
Ayr KA8 . . . 236 A3
Bellshill ML4 . . . 142 B5
Glasgow G20 . . . 96 E7
Greenock PA16 . . . 45 E6
Hamilton ML3 . . . 162 E4
Helensburgh G84 . . . 16 C2
Johnstone PA5 . . . 111 F2
Kilmarnock KA1 . . . 227 F5
Renfrew PA4 . . . 94 D5
Wishaw ML2 . . . 165 C2
Campbell Terr G82 . . . 50 D4
Campbeltown Dr KA3 . . . 222 F3
Camperdown Ct G84 . . . 17 A2
Campfield St FK2 . . . 42 B6
Camphill PA1 . . . 113 D3
Camphill Ave
Glasgow G41 . . . 136 E8
Kirkintilloch G66 . . . 79 C8
Camphill Dr KA25 . . . 170 A8
Camphill Gdns PA7 . . . 72 C3
Camphill Ho G41 . . . 116 F1
Camphill Pl KA7 . . . 239 B5
Campie Terr FK2 . . . 24 F2
Campion Ct KA7 . . . 239 B3
Campion Rd ML1 . . . 163 E8
Camp Rd
Glasgow G69 . . . 120 B5
Motherwell ML1 . . . 163 E4
Rutherglen G73 . . . 117 F2
Camps Cres PA4 . . . 94 E1
Campsie Ave
Barrhead G78 . . . 134 C1
Irvine KA11 . . . 220 B3
Campsie Cres
Airdrie ML6 . . . 122 F8
Kirkintilloch G66 . . . 79 C6
Campsie Ct
Coatbridge ML5 . . . 122 C3
Larkhall ML9 . . . 184 F5
Campsie Dene Rd G63 . . . 31 A5
Campsie Dr
Bearsden G61 . . . 75 E7
Milngavie G62 . . . 55 B2
Paisley, Glenburn PA2 . . . 133 D8
Paisley PA4 . . . 114 B8
Renfrew PA3 . . . 93 E1
Campsie Gdns G76 . . . 157 C7
Campsie Pl G69 . . . 100 C8
Campsie Rd
East Kilbride G75 . . . 180 A3
Kilmarnock KA1 . . . 228 A4
Kirkintilloch G66 . . . 58 B1
Milton of Campsie G66 . . . 58 B6
Port Glasgow PA14 . . . 69 A6
Torrance G64 . . . 57 E2
Wishaw ML2 . . . 164 F3
Campsie St G21 . . . 98 A5
Campsie View
Cambuslang G72 . . . 139 E3
Chryston G69 . . . 100 C8
Coatbridge G69 . . . 120 F5
Cumbernauld G67 . . . 62 B3
Hamilton ML3 . . . 161 F2
Kirkintilloch G66 . . . 79 A8
Stepps G33 . . . 99 D4
7 Uddingston G71 . . . 141 A8
Campsie View Dr G63 . . . 31 B4
Campsie View Sch G66 . . . 79 A5
Campsie Way KA11 . . . 220 A3
Campsie Wlk KA11 . . . 220 B3
Camp St ML1 . . . 163 F5
Campston Pl G33 . . . 99 B1
Camsail Ave G84 . . . 16 B2
Camsail Rd G84 . . . 15 B3
Camsbusmore Pl G33 . . . 99 C2
Camsdale Ave ML7 . . . 125 B2
Camstradden Drive E G61 . . . 75 D4
Camstradden Drive W
G61 . . . 75 C4

Camstradden Prim Sch G15 75 B4
Camus Pl G15 74 F4
Canada Ct G1 241 A2
Canal Ave PA5 112 A3
Canal Bank G22 97 A7
Canal Bank Ind Est FK4 40 A4
Canal Cres KA20 217 D7
Canal Ct
Coatbridge ML5 121 F7
Saltcoats KA21 217 A7
Canal Gdns PA5 112 D3
Canal La G66 58 D1
Canal Pl KA21 217 A7
Canal Rd PA5 112 A2
Canal St
Elderslie PA5 112 D3
Falkirk, Camelon FK1 41 D5
Falkirk FK2 42 B7
Glasgow G4 241 A4
Johnstone PA5 112 A3
Kirkintilloch G66 58 D1
Paisley PA1 113 D4
Renfrew PA4 94 D4
Saltcoats KA21 217 A7
Canal Terr PA1 113 E4
Canalyard Ind Est FK1 42 B1
Canavan Ct
Falkirk FK2 42 C7
Stirling FK7 7 C3
Canavan Pk FK2 42 C7
Canberra Ave G81 73 D4
Canberra Ct G46 136 E3
Canberra Dr G75 180 D8
Canberra Prim Sch G75 180 B8
Cander Ave ML9 199 A3
Candermill & Marlage Rd
Ashgill ML9 199 E5
Ashgill ML9 200 A7
Candermill Rd ML9 199 B3
Cander Rigg G64 78 A4
Canderside Toll ML9 199 B5
Cander St ML9 199 B8
Candimilne Ct ML8 188 B1
Candleriggs
Alloa FK10 10 B6
Glasgow G1 241 B2
Candleriggs Ct 7 FK10 10 B6
Candren Rd
Linwood PA3 112 E6
Paisley PA3 113 A4
Candren Way PA3 113 A5
Candymill La ML3 162 C7
Caneluk Ave ML8 188 B1
Cangillan Ct KA9 236 D5
Canmore Cres PA16 45 A4
Canmore Dr FK5 23 E4
Canmore Pl
Glasgow G31 118 D4
Stewarton KA3 195 F1
Canmore St G31 118 D4
Cannerton Cres G66 58 B5
Cannerton Pk G66 58 B5
Cannich Dr PA2 114 B1
Cannich Pl ML2 165 F6
Canniesburn Dr G61 75 F2
Canniesburn Quadrant G61 75 E2
Canniesburn Rd G61 75 D3
Canniesburn Sq G61 75 F2
Canniesburn Toll 2 G61 75 F3
Cannock Gr ML5 101 F6
Cannons Way FK2 24 A1
Canonbie Ave G74 159 F4
Canonbie La G74 159 E4
Canonbie St G34 100 D1
Canon Ct ML1 143 D2
Canongate G74 160 D4
Canterbury G75 180 C7
Canthill Gdns ML7 146 A3
Cantieslaw Dr G74 160 A3
Canting Way G51 116 C7
Canyon Rd ML2 164 D2
Caol Ct G74 158 C3
Capel Ave G77 156 F6
Capel Gr G74 160 B3
Capel Pl KA11 220 B2
Capelrig Cotts G77 155 F4
Capelrig Dr
East Kilbride G74 160 B3
Newton Mearns G77 156 E8
Capelrig La G77 156 D6
Capelrig Rd G77 156 E6
Capelrig St G46 135 F4
Caplaw Pl ML2 185 F8
Caplaw Rd
Johnstone G78 132 D2
Paisley PA2 133 C6
Caplaw Tower ML2 185 E7
Caplethill Rd
Barrhead G78 134 A6
Paisley PA2 133 E7
Caponcraig Ave KA20 206 C1
Capper View KA9 233 C2
Cappielow Ind Est PA15 46 D3
Cappielow Pk (Greenock Morton FC) PA15 46 D3
Capringstone Foot KA11 220 B5
CAPRINGTON 227 E4
Caprington Ave KA1 227 E3
Caprington Gdns KA1 227 E3
Caprington Pl G33 99 A1
Caprington St G33 99 A1
Captain St PA15 45 E4
Captain's Wlk
Cleland ML1 144 E1
Shawstonfoot ML1 144 E1
Cara Dr G51 115 E8
Caravelle Way 3 PA4 94 D1
Carbarns ML2 164 E1
Carbarns E ML2 164 D1
Carbarns Rd ML2 164 D1
Carbarns W ML2 164 D1
Carberry Rd G41 116 D2
Carbeth Rd G62 54 F2
Carbeth St G22 97 B4
Carbisdale St G22 97 E5
Carbost St 4 G23 76 D1
CARBRAIN 62 A1
Carbrain Ind Est G67 62 B1
Carbrain Prim Sch G67 62 B2
Carbrook Dr FK7 12 C3
Carbrook St
Glasgow G21 98 A1
Paisley PA1 113 C4
Carbrook Terr FK5 23 C3
Carcluie Cres KA7 239 B2
Cardarrach St G21 98 A4
Cardean Rd ML4 142 E6
Cardell Ave PA2 113 A3
Cardell Cres ML6 123 D2
Cardell Dr PA2 113 A3
Cardell Rd PA2 113 A3
Cardhu Cres KA3 222 D4
Cardhu Gdns KA3 222 D4
Cardinal Newman High Sch ML4 141 F5
CARDONALD 115 C5
Cardonald Coll G52 115 D3
Cardonald Ct G52 115 A4
Cardonald Dr G52 115 A4
Cardonald Gdns G52 115 B4
Cardonald Pk G51 115 C7
Cardonald Place Rd G52 115 B4
Cardonald Prim Sch G52 115 B4
Cardonald Sta G52 115 D6
Cardon Pl KA11 220 B2
Cardowan Dr
Cumbernauld G68 60 E1
Stepps G33 99 E5
Cardowan Pk G71 121 B1
Cardowan Rd
Glasgow G32 119 A7
Stepps G33 99 E5
Cardow Cres KA11 220 A6
Cardow Rd G21 98 C4
Cardrona St G33 99 B3
CARDROSS 48 B8
Cardross Ave PA14 68 E8
Cardross Cres PA15 46 C2
Cardross Ct 2 G31 117 F7
Cardross Park Mans G82 48 B8
Cardross Pl
Cumbernauld G68 61 B2
Greenock PA15 46 D2
Cardross Prim Sch G82 26 A1
Cardross Rd
Cardross G82 48 A8
Dumbarton G82 49 B4
Helensburgh G82, G84 25 F4
Renton G82 27 B2
Cardross St G31 117 F7
Cardross Sta G82 48 A7
Cardrowan Rd FK7 12 D1
Cardwell Rd PA19 44 F7
Cardwell St 5 G5 117 A4
Cardyke St G21 98 A4
Careston Pl G64 78 D1
Carey Ct FK7 12 C4
Carey Gdns ML1 144 C1
Carey Rd KA21 205 F3
CARFIN 143 D2
Carfin Dr ML8 201 C2
Carfin Ind Est ML1 143 A2
Carfin Lourdes Grotto* ML1 143 D2
Carfin Rd
Motherwell ML1 143 D3
Wishaw ML2 164 C4
Carfin St
Coatbridge ML5 122 B4
Glasgow G42 117 B2
Motherwell ML1 143 A3
Motherwell ML1 143 A3
Carfin Sta ML1 143 C2
Carfrae St G3 116 C8
Cargil Ave PA13 89 C7
Cargill Dr KA9 236 D5
Cargill Pl ML6 103 E1
Cargill Sq G64 98 C8
Carham Cres G52 115 C5
Carham Dr G52 115 C5
Caribou Gn G75 180 B8
Carillon Rd G51 116 C5
Carisbrooke Cres G64 78 B4
Carlaverock Rd G43 136 E6
Carleith Ave G81 73 F6
Carleith Prim Sch G81 73 E6
Carleith Quadrant G51 115 D7
Carleith Terr G81 73 F6
Carleston St G21 97 F4
Carleton Ct G46 136 C4
Carleton Dr G46 136 C4
Carleton Gate G46 136 C4
Carleton Gdns KA9 236 C7
Carlibar Ave G13 94 F7
Carlibar Dr G78 134 C3
Carlibar Gdns G78 134 C3
Carlibar Prim Sch G78 134 C3
Carlibar Rd G78 134 C3
Carlie Ave FK9 2 A6
Carlile Pl PA3 113 E6
Carlin La ML8 188 B1
Carlins Pl G66 57 D8
Carlisle La ML6 123 C7
Carlisle Rd
Airdrie ML6 123 C5
Cleland, Omoa ML1 144 C4
Cleland, Shawstonfoot ML1 144 E1
Hamilton ML3 163 B2
Larkhall ML3, ML9 184 E7
Stonehouse ML9 199 C4
Carlisle St G21, G22 97 D4
Carlouk La ML8 188 B1
Carloway Ct G33 119 B8
Carlowrie Ave G72 140 C2
Carlton Ct
Glasgow G5 240 C1
6 Hamilton ML3 162 E2
Carlton Pl G5 240 C1
CARLUKE 187 D3
Carluke High Sch ML8 188 A2
Carluke L Ctr ML8 188 B2
Carluke Prim Sch ML8 188 A3
Carluke Sta ML8 187 E1
Carlung Ho KA23 190 B7
Carlung Pl KA23 190 C3
Carlyle Ave
Glasgow G52 114 F8
Hillington Industrial Estate G52 115 A8
Carlyle Dr G74 160 B2
Carlyle Terr
East Kilbride G74 160 B2
Rutherglen G73 118 B1
Carmaben Rd G33 119 E8
Carman Rd
Cardross G82 48 C8
Renton G82 27 D1
Carman View G82 50 B6
Carmel Ave KA1 222 C2
Carmel Dr KA11 221 A1
Carmel Pl
Crosshouse KA2 221 D1
Kilmarnock KA1 222 D1
Kilmaurs KA3 222 A7
Carmel Terr KA1 222 D2
Carment Dr
Glasgow G41 136 D8
Stevenston KA20 217 E7
Carmichael Ct
Bridge of Allan FK9 2 A7
Lanark ML11 215 C4
Carmichael Path ML5 101 C6
Carmichael Pl
Glasgow G42 136 F7
Irvine KA12 219 B5
Carmichael St
Glasgow G51 116 C6
Greenock PA16 45 D6
Law ML8 186 F5
Carmichael Way ML8 186 F5
Carmona Dr G83 28 A7
CARMUIRS 41 B5
Carmuirs Ave FK1 41 C5
Carmuirs Dr FK1 41 B6
Carmuirs Prim Sch FK1 41 D5
Carmuirs St FK1 41 D5
CARMUNNOCK 158 E7
Carmunnock By-Pass
Carmunnock G45, G76 158 C7
Glasgow G45 137 C1
Carmunnock La G44 137 C5
Carmunnock Prim Sch G76 158 D7
Carmunnock Rd
Clarkston G76 158 B6
East Kilbride G76, G74 159 B4
Glasgow G45 137 C2
Glasgow G45 137 D3
CARMYLE 139 C8
Carmyle Ave
Glasgow, Carmyle G32 139 B8
Glasgow, Foxley G32 119 B2
Carmyle Gdns ML5 121 E3
Carmyle Pl KA20 217 D7
Carmyle Prim Sch G32 119 C1
Carmyle Station G32 119 B1
Carnach FK10 10 A6
Carna Dr G44 137 C5
Carnarvon St G3 240 A4
Carnaughton Pl FK12 4 F6
Carnbooth Ct G45 137 F2
CARNBROE 122 D3
Carnbroe Prim Sch ML5 122 D4
Carnbroe Rd
Bellshill ML4 142 B8
Coatbridge ML5 122 D3
Carneddans Rd G62 54 C4
Carnegie Dr FK1 41 D6
Carnegie Hill G75 180 D8
Carnegie Pl G75 180 D8
Carnegie Rd G52 115 A6
Carnell Cres KA9 236 D7
Carnell Terr KA9 236 D7
Carnoch St 1 G23 76 D1
Carnock Cres G78 134 B1
Carnock Gdns G62 54 E2
Carnock Rd G53 135 C8
Carnock St
Cowie FK7 12 E8
Greenock PA15 46 A4
Carnoustie Ave PA19 44 A6
Carnoustie Cres
Bishopbriggs G64 78 C1
East Kilbride G75 180 A6
Carnoustie Ct
Bothwell G71 140 F2
Kilwinning KA13 207 B3
Carnoustie Pl
Bellshill ML4 142 A7
Glasgow G5 116 F5
Irvine KA11 224 G7
Carnoustie St G5 116 F5
Carnoustie Way G68 61 F6
CARNTYNE 118 E7
Carntyne Gdns G33 118 E7
Carntyne Gr G32 119 A7
Carntynehall Rd G32 118 F6
Carntyne Ind Est G32 118 E6
Carntyne Path G32 118 D7
Carntyne Pl G32 118 D7
Carntyne Prim Sch G33 118 D8
Carntyne Rd
Glasgow, Cartyne G32 118 E7
Glasgow, Lightburn G32 119 A7
Carntyne Sta G32 118 F6
CARNWADRIC 135 E4
Carnwadric Prim Sch G46 135 F4
Carnwadric Rd G46 135 E4
Carnwath Ave G43 136 F6
Carnwath Rd
Carluke ML8 188 A1
Kilncadzow ML8 203 C5
Caroline Cres FK12 4 F6
Caroline St G31 118 E5
Carolside Ave G76 157 E7
Carolside Dr G15 75 B3
Carolside Gdns G76 157 E7
Carolside Prim Sch G76 157 E6
Carousel Cres ML2 165 C3
Carpenters Wynd FK10 9 F6
Carradale Ave FK1 41 C4
Carradale Cres G68 81 F8
Carradale Dr KA9 236 C5
Carradale Gdns
Bishopbriggs G64 78 C1
Carluke ML8 202 A8
Carradale Pl PA3 112 A6
Carradale St ML5 121 F7
Carranbuie Rd ML8 187 F3
Carrbridge Dr 1 G20 96 D6
Carresbrook Ave G66 80 A6
CARRIAGEHILL 113 E1
Carriagehill Ave PA2 113 E2
Carriagehill Dr PA2 113 E2
Carrickarden Rd 6 G61 75 F3
Carrick Ave
Ayr KA7 238 F6
Saltcoats KA21 206 A3
Carrick Cres
Glasgow G46 136 C1
Wishaw ML2 165 A4
Carrick Ct
Kirkintilloch G66 59 A2
Stirling FK7 7 C5
Carrick Dr
Coatbridge ML5 121 D7
Glasgow G32 119 E4
Irvine KA12 219 B5
Rutherglen G73 138 A5
Carrick Gdns
Ayr KA7 238 F6
Bellshill ML4 142 A8
Carluke ML8 202 A7
Hamilton, Blantyre G72 161 D6
Hamilton, Earnock ML3 161 E2
Carrick Gr G32 119 E4
Carrick La PA16 44 E3
Carrick Pk KA7 238 F6
Carrick Pl
Ardrossan KA22 205 C3
Bellshill ML4 142 B7
Coatbridge ML5 121 D7
Falkirk FK2 24 A3
Falkirk, Tamfourhill FK1 41 C4
Glenboig ML5 101 E6
Larkhall ML9 185 B4
Prestwick KA9 236 B7
Carrick Rd
Ayr KA7 238 F6
Bishopbriggs G64 78 C1
Bishopton PA7 72 C2
Cumbernauld G67 62 A4
East Kilbride G74 159 F3
Rutherglen G73 137 F5
Rutherglen G73 138 A5
Troon KA10 229 E7
Carrick St
Ayr KA7 238 F8
Glasgow G2 240 B2
7 Larkhall ML9 185 C2
CARRICKSTONE 61 E5
Carrickstone Rd G68 61 E4
Carrickstone Rdbt G68 61 E5
Carrickstone View G68 61 F5
Carrick Terr
Dumbarton G82 49 B4
Greenock PA16 44 E3
Carrick Vale ML1 144 C1
Carrickvale Ct G68 61 F5
Carrick View ML5 101 E6
Carrick Way 7 G71 141 A3
Carrington St G4 96 F2
Carrochan Cres G83 27 F8
Carrochan Rd G83 27 F8
Carroglen Gdns G32 119 D5
Carroglen Gr G32 119 D5
Carroll Cres ML1 143 D2
CARRON 24 A2
Carronade Pl FK2 41 E8
Carron Ave KA1 228 B6
Carronbank Ave FK2 24 B2
Carronbank Cres FK6 21 E3
Carronbank Ct FK2 24 B2
Carron Cres
Bearsden G61 75 C3
Bishopbriggs G64 78 B1
Glasgow G22 97 D5
Kirkintilloch G66 79 E4
Carron Ct
Cambuslang G72 139 D5
Hamilton ML3 162 B1
Carron Dr PA7 72 C2
Carrongrange Ave FK5 23 E2
Carrongrange Gdns FK5 23 E1
Carrongrange Gr FK5 23 E1
Carrongrange Rd FK5 23 E2
Carrongrange Sch FK5 23 E2
Carrongrove Ave FK2 24 A2
Carrongrove Bsns Pk FK2 24 A2
Carrongrove Rd FK2 24 A2
Carronhall Ave FK2 24 C4
Carronlea Dr FK2 24 A2
Carron Pl
Coatbridge ML5 101 D1
East Kilbride G75 180 F5
Glasgow G22 97 E5
Irvine KA12 219 C6
Stirling FK7 7 B2
Carron Prim Sch FK2 24 A2
Carron Rd
Falkirk FK2 24 A1
Falkirk FK2 42 A8
Carron Rdbt FK2 24 A2
CARRONSHORE 24 C3
Carronshore Prim Sch FK2 24 C4
Carronshore Rd FK2 24 B2
Carronside Pl FK6 21 E3
Carronside St FK2 42 B8
Carron St
Glasgow G22 97 E5
Wishaw ML2 165 B1
Carronvale Ave FK5 23 D1
Carronvale Rd
Larbert FK5 41 D8
Stenhousemuir FK5 23 C1
Carronview FK5 23 D2
Carron Way
Motherwell ML1 143 C4
Paisley PA3 114 A7
Carrour Gdns G64 77 F2
Carr Quadrant ML4 142 D5
Carruth Dr PA13 89 C8
Carruth Rd PA11 110 C8
Carsaig Ct FK9 2 A5
Carsaig Dr G52 115 E5
Carsaig Loan ML5 101 C6
Carscallan Rd ML3 183 E5
Carsebridge Ct FK10 10 C8
Carsebridge Rd FK10 10 D8
Carsebridge Row FK10 10 D8
Carsegreen Ave PA2 133 B7
Carseloch Rd KA7 238 F1
Carsemeadow PA11 89 E2
Carse Terr FK10 9 F8
Carseview
Bannockburn FK7 7 E2
Tullibody FK10 4 A3
Carse View FK2 14 E4
Carse View Dr G61 76 A6
Carsewood Ave PA9 130 F5
Carson Dr KA12 224 E7
Carson Rd G83 27 E8
Carstairs St G40 118 A2
Carswell Ct 1 KA24 191 B7
Carswell Gdns G41 116 E2
Carswell Rd G77 156 B5
Cartbank Gdns G44 137 A4
Cartbank Gr G44 136 F4
Cartbank Rd G44 137 A4
Cartcraigs Rd G43 136 B6
Carters Pl KA12 219 C2
Carters Rigg KA12 219 B1
Cartha Cres PA2 114 B3
Cartha St G41 136 E7
CARTLAND 202 D1
Cartland Ave ML8 201 F8
Cartland Rd ML11 214 D8
Cartland View ML11 214 F5
Cartle Cl KA13 207 C6
Cartsbridge Rd G76 157 F6
Cartsburn St PA15 46 B3
CARTSDYKE 46 A4
Cartsdyke Ave PA15 46 C4
Cartsdyke Ct PA15 46 D3
Cartsdyke Sta PA15 46 C4
Cartside Ave
Inchinnan PA4 93 B4
Johnstone PA5 111 D1
Cartside Dr G76 158 A6
Cartside Pl G76 157 F5
Cartside Quadrant G42 137 A7
Cartside Rd G76 157 F5
Cartside St G42 136 F7
Cart St G81 94 B8
Cartvale La PA3 113 E6
Cartvale Rd G42 136 F7
Cartvale Sch
Glasgow, Govan G51 116 B7
Glasgow, Langside G42 136 F7
Cartview Ct G76 157 F6
Carvale Ave ML7 125 B2
Carwinshoch View KA7 238 D5
Carwood Ct PA15 46 C3
Carwood St PA15 46 D3
Cask Cres FK8 7 C8
Caskie Dr G72 140 E1
Cassels Gr ML1 142 C1
Cassels St
Carluke ML8 187 F1
Motherwell ML1 163 E8

Cassidy Dr PA5 111 F3
Cassillis St KA7 238 E8
Cassiltoun Gdns G45 137 D2
Cassley Ave PA4 94 F2
Castburn Rd G67 62 F6
Castelmilk Sp Ctr G45 137 E3
Castings Ave FK2 42 B7
Castings Ct
Falkirk FK2 42 B7
Falkirk, Middlefield FK2 42 E6
Castings Dr FK2 42 B6
Castings Ho FK2 42 B7
Castings Rd FK2 42 E6
Castle Ave
Airth FK2 14 E3
Balloch G83 19 F1
Bothwell G71 140 E3
Elderslie PA5 112 B1
Falkirk FK2 24 C3
Helensburgh G84 16 A2
Motherwell ML1 143 B6
Stevenston KA20 206 E2
Castlebank Ct G13 95 E6
Castlebank Dr G11 96 A1
Castlebank Gdns G13 95 E6
Castlebank St
Glasgow G11 96 A1
Glasgow G11 96 B1
Castlebank Villas G13 95 E6
Castlebay Dr G22 77 C1
Castlebay Pl G22 97 C8
Castlebay St G22 97 C8
Castlebrae G82 49 D5
Castlebrae Gdns G44 137 B6
Castle Bsns Pk The FK9 1 E2
CASTLECARY 62 F8
Castlecary Rd G67, G68 62 D7
Castle Chimmins Ave
G72 139 D4
Castle Chimmins Rd
G72 139 D3
Castle Circ G66 33 B1
Castle Cres
Bishopton PA7 72 B2
Denny FK6 21 D2
Falkirk FK2 42 D7
Torwood FK5 22 E7
Castlecroft Gdns G71 140 F5
Castle Ct
Cumbernauld G68 62 F8
Falkirk FK2 42 C7
Kirkintilloch G66 79 D8
Menstrie FK11 3 F6
Stirling FK8 7 A8
Castle Dr
Airth FK2 14 E3
Dundonald KA2 225 F2
Falkirk FK2 42 C8
Kilbirnie KA25 149 A1
Kilmarnock KA3 223 A4
Motherwell ML1 143 B6
Stenhousemuir FK5 23 F2
West Kilbride KA23 190 D5
Castle Farm Cl KA3 195 D1
Castlefern Rd G73 138 B3
Castlefield Ct G33 99 B4
Castlefield Gdns G75 180 B5
Castlefield Prim Sch
G75 180 B6
Castlegait 6 FK8 7 B7
Castle Gait PA1 113 E3
Castlegate ML11 215 A4
Castle Gate
Newton Mearns G77 157 A3
Uddingston G71 140 E5
Castle Gdns
Gourock PA19 44 E8
Moodiesburn G69 80 F2
Paisley, Castlehead PA2 113 D3
Paisley PA2 113 A3
Castleglen Rd G74 159 A4
Castle Gr
Kilbirnie KA25 149 A1
Kilsyth G65 36 C2
Castlegreen Cres G82 50 B2
Castlegreen Gdns G82 50 B2
Castlegreen La G82 50 A2
Castlegreen St G82 50 B2
CASTLEHEAD 113 D3
Castlehead High Sch
PA1 113 D3
CASTLEHILL
Ayr 239 C5
Dumbarton 49 C5
Castlehill Ave
Port Glasgow PA14 69 A7
Slamannan FK1 86 A6
Castlehill Cres
Ayr KA7 239 A6
Banknock FK4 38 E2
Chapelhall ML6 123 F1
Hamilton, Allanton ML3 163 D1
Hamilton ML3 162 F3
Kilmacolm PA13 89 C8
Law ML8 187 A4
Renfrew PA4 94 D4
Castlehill Ct KA7 239 B5
Castlehill Dr G77 156 F3
Castlehill Gdns
Ayr KA7 239 C5
Hamilton ML3 162 F2
Castlehill Gn G74 158 F4
Castlehill Ind Est ML8 187 E4
Castlehill Prim Sch
Bearsden G61 75 C6
Wishaw ML2 186 A8
Castlehill Quadrant G82 49 C5
Castlehill Rd
Ayr KA7 239 A6
Bearsden G61 75 C6
Carluke ML8 187 E5
Dumbarton G82 49 C5
Kilmacolm PA13 89 C8
Overtown ML2 186 B7
Stevenston KA20 206 F2
Stewarton KA3 195 E1
Castlehill View G65 36 C2
Castle Keep Gdns KA11 219 F4
Castleknowe Gdns ML8 187 E3
Castlelaurie Ind Est FK2 42 C7
Castlelaurie St FK2 42 C7
Castlelaw Gdns G32 119 B6
Castlelaw St G32 119 B6
Castle Levan Manor PA19 43 F5
Castle Mains Rd G62 54 D2
CASTLEMILK 137 E3
Castlemilk Arc G45 137 D3
Castlemilk Cres G44 137 E5
Castlemilk Dr G45 137 E3
Castlemilk High Sch
G45 137 E2
Castlemilk Rd
Glasgow, Croftfoot G44 137 E5
Glasgow, King's Park G44 137 E6
Castlemilk Terr G45 137 E1
Castlemount Ave G77 156 F3
Castlepark Cres KA12 219 B6
Castlepark Prim Sch
KA12 219 C6
Castlepark Rd KA12 219 B6
Castle Pl
Falkirk FK2 42 D7
Irvine KA12 219 B3
Uddingston G71 140 E6
Castle Quadrant ML6 123 D7
Castlerankine Rd FK6 21 C2
Castle Rd
Airdrie ML6 123 D7
Ardrossan KA22 205 D3
Bridge of Weir PA11 90 D1
Dumbarton G82 50 A2
Elderslie PA5 112 C3
Falkirk FK2 42 C8
Greenock PA15 46 C2
Menstrie FK11 3 F6
Newton Mearns G77 156 C4
Port Glasgow PA14 47 D1
Stirling FK9 2 C3
Castle St Ind Est FK10 10 A6
Castle Semple Ctry Pk*
PA12 129 E3
Castle Sq
Clydebank G81 73 E3
Doonfoot KA7 238 B3
Castle St
Alloa FK10 10 A5
Chapelhall ML6 123 D2
Clydebank G81 73 E3
Dumbarton G82 49 F3
Glasgow, Baillieston G69 120 A3
Glasgow G4 241 C3
Glasgow, Kelvinhaugh G11 96 C1
Hamilton ML3 162 F4
Irvine KA12 219 B3
Paisley PA1 113 C4
Rutherglen G73 138 A8
Castle Terr
Bridge of Weir PA11 110 E7
Denny FK6 21 C2
Knockentiber KA2 221 F3
Castleton Ave
Bishopbriggs G64 97 E7
Newton Mearns G77 157 A3
Castleton Cres G77 156 F3
Castleton Ct
Glasgow G45 137 F2
Newton Mearns G77 156 F3
Castleton Dr G77 156 F3
Castleton Gr G77 156 F3
Castleton Prim Sch G45 137 D3
Castle Vale FK9 2 A4
Castleview
Clachan of Campsie G66 32 F3
Cumbernauld G68 62 E8
Dundonald KA2 225 F3
Larkhall ML9 199 A8
Castle View
Airth FK2 14 D2
Doonfoot KA7 238 B3
Fallin FK7 8 D4
West Kilbride KA23 190 D6
Wishaw ML2 166 A6
Castleview Ave PA2 133 A7
Castleview Dr
Bridge of Allan FK9 2 A7
Paisley PA2 133 A7
Castleview Pl PA2 133 A7
Castleview Sch FK8 1 E2
Castleview Terr FK4 39 A3
Castle Way
Coatbridge G69 120 F5
Cumbernauld G67 62 C4
Castle Wlk KA7 238 C3
Castle Wynd
Bothwell G71 141 B2
Quarter ML3 183 F3
4 Stirling FK8 7 A8
Catacol Ave KA21 205 F2
Cathay St G22 97 C8
Cathburn Holdings ML2 166 D5
Cathburn Rd ML2 166 C5
CATHCART 137 A6
Cathcart Bldgs PA15 46 A5
Cathcart Cres PA2 114 A3
Cathcart Pl G73 137 F7
Cathcart Rd
Glasgow, Govanhill G42 117 B2
Glasgow, Mount Florida
G42 137 B8
Cathcart Sq PA15 46 A5
Cathcart St
7 Ayr KA7 235 F1
Greenock PA15 46 A5
Cathcart Sta G44 137 A6
Cathedral Prim Sch ML1 163 E7
Cathedral Sq G4 241 C2
Cathedral St G1, G4 241 B3
Catherine Pl KA3 222 C6
Catherine St
Bannockburn FK7 7 C1
Kirkintilloch G66 79 C8
Motherwell ML1 163 E4
Catherine's Wlk G72 161 D6
Catherine Way ML1 142 F3
CATHKIN 138 D3
Cathkin Ave
Cambuslang G72 138 E6
Rutherglen G73 138 C7
Cathkin By-Pass G73 138 D3
Cathkin Cres G68 61 E4
Cathkin Ct G45 137 F2
Cathkin Dr G76 157 C8
Cathkin Gdns G71 120 E1
Cathkin High Sch G72 138 E4
Cathkin Pl
Cambuslang G72 138 E6
Kilwinning KA13 207 B4
Cathkin Prim Sch G73 138 D3
Cathkin Rd
Carmunnock G76 158 F8
Glasgow G42 136 F7
Rutherglen G73 138 C2
Uddingston G71 120 E1
Cathkin View G32 139 B8
Cathkinview Pl G42 137 B7
Cathkinview Rd G42 137 B7
Catrine G74 159 D2
Catrine Ave 3 G81 74 A3
Catrine Cres ML1 164 A4
Catrine Ct 8 G53 135 A8
Catrine Gdns 7 G53 135 A8
Catrine Pl G53 135 A8
Catrine Rd G53 135 A8
Catrine St 5 ML9 185 C2
Catriona Pl G82 50 C2
Catriona Way ML1 143 B4
Catter Gdns G62 54 E3
Cauldhame Cres FK7 6 C5
Cauldhame Farm Rd 1
FK2 41 F8
Cauldhame Rigg KA3 211 F8
Cauldhame St 2 FK2 41 F8
Cauldstream Pl G62 54 E1
CAUSEWAYHEAD 2 B4
Causewayhead Rd FK9 2 C3
Causewayside Cres G32 119 A2
Causewayside St G32 119 A2
Causeway The FK9 2 D5
Causeyfoot Dr KA25 149 A1
Causeyside St 4 PA1 113 E4
Causeystanes 4 G72 161 D7
Cavendish Ct
5 Glasgow G5 117 B4
Troon KA10 229 E2
Cavendish Dr G77 156 F5
Cavendish La KA10 229 E2
Cavendish Pl
Glasgow G5 117 B4
Troon KA10 229 E2
Cavendish St G5 117 B4
Cavin Dr G45 137 E4
Cavin Rd G45 137 F4
Cawder Ct G68 61 D5
Cawder Gdns FK9 1 F8
Cawder Pl G68 61 E5
Cawder Rd
Bridge of Allan FK9 1 F7
Cumbernauld G68 61 E5
Cawder View G68 61 E5
Cawder Way G68 61 E5
Cawdor Cres
Bishopton PA7 72 B2
Chapelhall ML6 123 E3
Greenock PA16 45 A4
Cawdor Pl PA16 45 A4
Cawdor Way G74 159 D3
Cayton Gdns G69 119 F4
Cayzer Ct PA1 114 E5
Cecil St
Clarkston G76 157 E7
Coatbridge ML5 122 A5
Glasgow G12 96 D3
Stirling FK7 7 B6
Cedar Ave
Beith KA15 171 A8
Clydebank G81 73 D4
Johnstone PA5 132 A8
Stirling FK8 6 F5
Uddingston G71 141 B8
Cedar Cres
Greenock PA15 46 E2
Hamilton ML3 162 E1
Cedar Ct
Cambuslang G72 139 E4
East Kilbride G75 180 C5
Glasgow G20 97 A2
Kilbarchan PA10 111 A3
Cedar Dr
East Kilbride G75 180 C5
Kirkintilloch G66 79 C5
Milton of Campsie G66 58 C5
Uddingston G71 141 C8
Cedar Gdns
Law ML8 186 F6
Motherwell ML1 143 C4
Rutherglen G73 138 C4
Cedar Gr
Cardross G82 48 B7
Menstrie FK11 3 F5
Stenhousemuir FK5 23 D1
Cedar La
Airdrie ML6 123 C7
Motherwell ML1 143 B4
Cedar Pl
Barrhead G78 155 D8
Blantyre G72 140 C1
East Kilbride G75 180 C5
Gourock PA19 44 D6
Cedar Rd
Ayr KA7 239 D5
Banknock FK4 38 E2
Bishopbriggs G64 98 B8
Cumbernauld G67 62 D3
Irvine KA12 219 D4
Kilmarnock KA1 227 D8
Cedars Gr G69 121 A6
Cedars Sch of Excellance
PA16 45 E6
Cedar St G20 97 A2
Cedars The FK10 4 B2
Cedar View G84 15 A3
Cedar Wlk
Bishopbriggs G64 98 B8
Motherwell ML1 143 D2
Cedarwood ML2 164 D1
Cedarwood Ave G77 156 F5
Cedarwood Ct G82 48 A8
Cedarwood Rd G77 156 F4
Cedar Wynd ML7 147 B4
Cedric Pl G13 95 D7
Cedric Rd G13 95 D7
Celandine Bank KA7 239 C3
Celtic Pk (Celtic FC)*
G40 118 C5
Celtic St G20 96 C7
Cemetery Rd
Glasgow G52 115 E4
Hamilton G72 161 C6
Shotts ML7 147 B4
Centenary Ave ML6 122 D7
Centenary Cres ML4 142 B6
Centenary Ct
Barrhead G78 134 B2
Clydebank G81 74 B1
Centenary Gdns
Coatbridge ML5 122 A5
2 Hamilton ML3 162 E2
Centenary Pl KA22 205 D3
Centenary Quadrant
ML1 143 A5
Centenary Rd KA11 224 H7
CENTRAL 45 F4
Central Ave
Ardrossan KA22 205 D3
Cambuslang G72 138 F6
Clydebank G81 74 A2
Glasgow G11 95 F2
Glasgow, North Mount Vernon
G32 119 E3
Hamilton G72 161 E5
Kilbirnie KA25 170 A7
Kilmarnock KA1 227 F3
Motherwell, Holytown ML1 142 F5
Stevenston KA20 218 B5
Troon KA10 229 G3
Uddingston G71 141 C6
Central Bvd FK5 23 B4
Central College of
Commerce G1, G4 241 B3
Central Cres ML9 199 F8
Central Dr FK5 23 F3
Central Gr
4 Cambuslang G72 138 F6
Glasgow G32 119 D4
Central Park Ave FK5 23 B4
Central Park Bsns Pk FK5 23 B4
Central Path G32 119 E3
Central Quadrant KA22 205 C3
Central Rd PA1 113 E5
Central Ret Pk FK1 42 C5
Central Way
Cumbernauld G67 61 F1
8 Paisley PA1 113 E5
Centre Rdbt The G74 159 F1
Centre St
Chapelhall ML6 123 D2
Glasgow G5 240 C1
Glenboig ML5 101 C6
Centre Way G78 134 B3
Centurion Pl ML1 142 B1
Centurion Way FK2 41 D6
Century Ct KA11 224 H7
Ceres Gdns G64 78 D1
Ceres Pl 4 ML1 163 D8
Cessnock Ave KA1 228 F5
Cessnock Dr KA1 228 F5
Cessnock Gdns KA1 228 F6
Cessnock Pl
Ayr KA7 239 C6
Cambuslang G72 139 D5
Kilmarnock KA1 228 B5
Cessnock Rd
Hurlford KA1 228 F6
Millerston G33 99 B4
Troon KA10 229 E3
Cessnock St G51 116 C6
Cessnock Underground Sta
G51 116 C6
Chacefield St FK4 40 A6
Chacefield Wood FK6 39 E7
Challum Dr ML1 164 C3
Chalmers Ave KA7 239 A5
Chalmers Cres G75 180 F7
Chalmers Ct
Glasgow G40 241 C1
Uddingston G71 140 F6
Chalmers Dr G75 180 F7
Chalmers Gate G40 241 C1
Chalmers La PA15 46 F3
Chalmers Pl
Glasgow G40 241 C1
Irvine KA11 224 H6
Chalmers Rd KA7 239 A6
Chalmers St
Clydebank G81 74 B1
Glasgow G40 241 C1
Gourock PA19 44 F7
Chalmerston Rd FK9 1 B3
Chalton Ct FK9 2 B7
Chalton Rd FK9 2 B7
Chalybeate Ct KA13 207 D3
Chamberlain Rd
Glasgow, Anniesland G13 95 E6
Glasgow, Jordanhill G13 95 E5
Chambers Dr FK2 24 B2
Chamfron Gdns FK7 7 E3
Chancellor St G11 96 C2
CHANTINGHALL 162 C3
Chantinghall Rd ML3 162 B3
Chantinghall Terr ML3 162 B3
CHAPEL 166 C2
Chapelacre Gr G84 16 E2
Chapel Cres
Falkirk FK2 24 B3
Hamilton ML3 183 D6
Chapelcroft FK7 6 D6
Chapelcross Ave ML6 103 A1
Chapel Ct G73 137 F8
Chapel Dr FK5 23 E3
Chapelgill Pl KA11 220 A4
Chapelgreen Prim Sch
G65 59 E7
CHAPELHALL 123 F2
Chapelhall Ind Est ML6 123 D4
Chapelhall Prim Sch
ML6 123 E2
Chapelhill Mount KA22 205 D5
Chapelhill Rd PA2 114 A2
Chapelhill Rdbt KA22 205 C5
Chapelknowe Rd ML1 143 E1
Chapel La
Falkirk FK1 42 B5
Irvine KA12 219 C2
Chapelpark Rd KA7 238 F4
Chapel Pl G78 154 D7
Chapel Rd
Clydebank G81 74 A6
Houston PA6 91 B4
Wishaw ML2 166 C2
Chapelside Ave ML6 123 A8
Chapelside Prim Sch
ML6 103 A1
Chapelside Rd
East Kilbride G74 160 B5
Nerston G74 160 A6
Chapel St
Airdrie ML6 123 A8
Carluke ML8 187 F2
Cleland ML1 144 B1
Glasgow G20 96 E5
Gourock PA19 44 F7
Hamilton ML3 162 E3
Lennoxtown G66 57 D8
Rutherglen G73 137 F8
Chapel Street Ind Est G20 96 E5
Chapelton Ave
Bearsden G61 75 F4
Dumbarton G82 50 A5
Chapelton Gdns
Bearsden G61 75 F4
Dumbarton G82 50 A5
Chapelton La KA23 190 C3
Chapelton Mains KA23 190 D1
Chapelton Rd
Cumbernauld G67 82 D6
West Kilbride KA23 190 D2
Chapelton St 5 PA14 47 A2
Chapeltoun Terr KA3 210 F4
Chapelwell St KA21 216 F7
Chapland Rd ML11 215 A5
Chaplet Ave G13 95 C8
Chapman Ave ML5 101 C6
Chapman St 4 G42 117 A2
Chapmans Terr KA1 228 B7
Chappell St G78 134 B3
Charing Cross ML9 185 A3
Charing Cross La G3 240 A3
Charing Cross Sta G2 240 B3
Charles Ave
Bridge of Allan FK9 2 B6
Monkton KA9 233 D5
Renfrew PA4 94 D4
Charles Cres
Carluke ML8 188 B1
Kirkintilloch G66 79 D3
Charles Dr
Larbert FK5 41 C8
Troon KA10 230 A2
Charleson Row G65 60 F3
Charles Path ML6 123 D1
Charles Pl
4 Greenock PA15 45 F5
Kilmarnock KA1 227 E8
Charles Quadrant ML1 143 A5
Charles Rodger Pl FK9 2 A6

Charles St
Alloa FK10 ... 9 F8
Glasgow G21 ... 97 F1
Kilmarnock KA1 ... 227 E8
Kilsyth G65 ... 36 D1
Shotts ML7 ... 147 B4
Stirling FK8 ... 7 A5
Wishaw ML2 ... 164 D4
Charles Terr G83 ... 27 E8
Charlotte Ave G64 ... 78 B8
Charlotte Hill Ct FK5 ... 23 B3
Charlotte Path ML9 ... 185 A2
Charlotte Pl PA2 ... 113 E2
Charlotte St
Ayr KA7 ... 238 E8
Dumbarton G82 ... 49 D4
Glasgow G1 ... 241 B1
Helensburgh G84 ... 16 E2
Shotts ML7 ... 147 A3
Charnwood Ave PA5 ... 131 D8
Charrier The FK11 ... 3 F6
CHARTERSHALL ... 7 A1
Chartershall Rd
Bannockburn FK7 ... 11 A6
Stirling FK7 ... 7 A1
Charter St FK7 ... 7 A3
Chartwell Rd PA7 ... 72 B3
Chassels St ML5 ... 122 A8
Chateau Gr ML3 ... 163 A2
Chatelherault Ave G72 ... 138 E5
Chatelherault Country Pk* ML3 ... 184 B8
Chatelherault Cres ML3 ... 162 F1
Chatelherault Prim Sch ML3 ... 162 E1
Chatelherault Sta ML3 ... 163 C1
Chatelherault Wlk ML3 ... 162 E1
Chatham G75 ... 180 C7
Chattan Ave FK9 ... 2 B4
Chattan Ind Est FK4 ... 40 C4
Chatton St G23 ... 76 D1
Chatton Wlk ML5 ... 122 D3
Cheapside St
Eaglesham G76 ... 178 F5
Glasgow G3 ... 240 A2
4 Kilmarnock KA1 ... 227 F8
Checkbar Rdbt FK5 ... 40 C7
Chelmsford Dr G12 ... 96 B5
Cherry Ave G67 ... 62 E5
Cherry Bank G66 ... 79 B5
Cherrybank Rd G43 ... 136 F5
Cherrybank Wlk ML6 ... 122 D8
Cherry Cres G81 ... 74 A4
Cherry Gdns KA11 ... 219 E5
Cherry Gr G69 ... 121 B6
Cherry Hill Rd KA7 ... 239 B2
Cherryhill View ML9 ... 184 F3
Cherry La
Banknock FK4 ... 38 E2
Troon KA10 ... 229 E4
Cherry Pl
Bishopbriggs G64 ... 98 B8
Johnstone PA5 ... 112 A1
Milton of Campsie G66 ... 58 B4
Motherwell ML1 ... 143 B5
Uddingston G71 ... 141 D7
Cherry Rd KA1 ... 227 C8
Cherryridge Dr G69 ... 121 A6
Cherrytree Cres ML9 ... 185 A5
Cherry Tree Ct G83 ... 27 D5
Cherrytree Dr G72 ... 139 E4
Cherrytree Wynd G75 ... 180 F6
Cherry Wlk ML1 ... 163 E3
Cherrywood Dr KA15 ... 150 C2
Cherrywood Rd PA5 ... 112 C2
Chesterfield Ave G12 ... 96 B5
Chester Rd PA16 ... 44 E4
Chesters Cres ML1 ... 163 C8
Chesters Pl 3 G73 ... 138 A7
Chesters Rd G61 ... 75 D4
Chester St G32 ... 119 A5
Chestnut Ave
Beith KA15 ... 171 A8
Bishopton PA7 ... 71 F5
Cumbernauld G67 ... 62 E5
Chestnut Cres
Denny FK6 ... 21 C3
East Kilbride G75 ... 180 C6
Hamilton ML3 ... 162 F2
Uddingston G71 ... 141 D7
Chestnut Ct
Cumbernauld G67 ... 62 E5
Milton of Campsie G66 ... 58 B5
Chestnut Dr
Clydebank G81 ... 74 A5
Kirkintilloch G66 ... 79 B6
Chestnut Gdns KA11 ... 219 E5
Chestnut Gr
Carluke ML8 ... 187 F1
Glenboig G69 ... 101 C6
Hamilton G72 ... 161 C8
Larkhall ML9 ... 185 A5
Motherwell ML1 ... 163 D4
Stenhousemuir FK5 ... 23 F3
Chestnut La G62 ... 54 E1
Chestnut Pl
Cumbernauld G67 ... 62 E5
Johnstone PA5 ... 132 A8
Kilmarnock KA1 ... 227 D8
Chestnut Rd KA7 ... 239 D6
Chestnut St G22 ... 97 D5
Chestnut Way
Cambuslang G72 ... 139 E4
Quarter ML3 ... 183 F4
Chestnut Wlk G66 ... 57 E7
Cheviot Ave G78 ... 134 C1
Cheviot Cres
East Kilbride G75 ... 180 B4
Wishaw ML2 ... 164 F4
Cheviot Ct
Airdrie ML6 ... 103 B2
Coatbridge ML5 ... 122 C3
Irvine KA11 ... 220 A3
Cheviot Dr G77 ... 156 C3
Cheviot Gdns G61 ... 75 D7
Cheviot Head
Irvine, Bourtreehill KA11 ... 220 A3
Irvine KA11 ... 219 F3
Cheviot Pl KA1 ... 228 A3
Cheviot Rd
Glasgow G43 ... 136 C5
Hamilton ML3 ... 162 F2
Larkhall ML9 ... 185 C2
2 Paisley PA2 ... 113 E1
Cheviot St G72 ... 161 C7
Cheviot Way KA11 ... 220 A3
Chirmorie Cres G53 ... 115 A1
Chirmorie Pl G53 ... 115 A1
Chirnside Ct G72 ... 161 F5
Chirnside Pl G52 ... 115 B6
Chirnside Rd G52 ... 115 A6
Chirnsyde Prim Sch G22 ... 97 D6
Chisholm Ave
Bishopton PA7 ... 72 C3
Stirling FK9 ... 2 B4
Chisholm Dr G77 ... 156 E6
Chisholm Pl ML1 ... 164 B2
Chisholm St
Coatbridge ML5 ... 122 B8
Glasgow G1 ... 241 B1
Chrighton Gn 3 G71 ... 141 A8
Chriss Ave ML3 ... 183 D7
Christchurch Pl G75 ... 180 B7
Christian St G43 ... 136 C8
Christie Gdns KA21 ... 216 F8
Christie La PA3 ... 113 E5
Christie Park Prim Sch G83 ... 27 D5
Christie Pl G72 ... 139 B5
Christie St
Bellshill ML4 ... 142 D5
Paisley PA1 ... 113 F5
Christie Terr FK5 ... 23 E3
Christopher St G21 ... 98 A1
Christ the King Prim Sch ML1 ... 143 B6
Chromars Pl PA15 ... 45 E3
CHRYSTON ... 100 D8
Chryston Bsns Ctr G69 ... 100 C8
Chryston High Sch G69 ... 100 C8
Chryston Prim Sch G69 ... 100 D8
Chryston Rd
Chryston G69 ... 100 D8
Kirkintilloch G69, G66 ... 80 C5
Chuckie La PA5 ... 111 C6
Church Ave
Cardross G82 ... 48 A8
Rutherglen G73 ... 138 C5
Stepps G33 ... 99 D6
Wishaw ML2 ... 166 A4
Church Cres ML6 ... 103 E1
Church Ct
Alloa FK10 ... 10 A6
Ayr KA8 ... 236 A1
Dumbarton G82 ... 49 F3
Hamilton ML3 ... 162 E4
Church Dr G66 ... 79 C6
Church Gr FK10 ... 5 C1
Church Hill PA1 ... 113 E5
Churchhill Ave KA13 ... 208 A4
Churchill Ave
East Kilbride G74 ... 159 F1
Johnstone PA5 ... 131 C7
Churchill Cres
Ayr KA8 ... 239 D8
Bothwell G71 ... 141 B3
Churchill Dr
Ardrossan KA22 ... 205 D4
Bishopton PA7 ... 72 B3
Bridge of Allan FK9 ... 2 A6
Glasgow G11 ... 96 A4
Churchill Pl
Falkirk FK2 ... 42 C7
Kilbarchan PA10 ... 111 A3
Churchill Rd PA13 ... 89 C7
Churchill Sq G84 ... 17 A2
Churchill St FK10 ... 9 F8
Churchill Twr KA7 ... 235 E2
Church La
Carluke ML8 ... 187 F1
Coatbridge ML5 ... 122 A7
Denny FK6 ... 21 D3
Kilmarnock KA1 ... 227 F5
8 Kilsyth G65 ... 60 D8
Plean FK7 ... 12 D2
Church Manse La PA11 ... 110 D8
Church Pl
Ardrossan KA22 ... 205 C1
Caldercruix ML6 ... 104 F4
Falkirk FK2 ... 42 B6
Old Kilpatrick G60 ... 73 A6
Rhu G84 ... 15 D4
Rutherglen G73 ... 138 B8
Church Rd
Barrhead G78 ... 134 C2
Bridge of Weir PA11 ... 110 E8
California FK1 ... 66 F5
Clarkston G76 ... 157 F6
Glasgow G46 ... 136 D2
Muirhead G69 ... 100 C7
Quarriers Village PA11 ... 89 E2
Rhu G84 ... 15 D5
Church Rd *continued*
Wishaw ML2 ... 166 D6
Church St
Alexandria G83 ... 27 E4
Alloa FK10 ... 10 A6
Bonnybridge FK4 ... 40 C3
Clydebank G81 ... 74 A3
Coatbridge ML5 ... 122 A7
Dumbarton G82 ... 49 F3
Falkirk FK2 ... 24 C2
Glasgow, Kelvingrove G11 ... 96 C2
Glasgow, Muirhead G69 ... 120 C4
Gourock PA19 ... 44 E8
Hamilton, Blantyre G72 ... 161 E7
Hamilton ML3 ... 162 E4
Harthill ML7 ... 127 C5
Irvine KA12 ... 219 B2
Johnstone PA5 ... 111 F3
Kilbarchan PA10 ... 111 A3
Kilmarnock KA3 ... 222 F1
Kilsyth G65 ... 60 D8
Kilwinning KA13 ... 207 E3
Larkhall ML9 ... 185 A2
Lochwinnoch PA12 ... 129 C2
Motherwell ML1 ... 143 F4
Port Glasgow PA14 ... 47 C2
Stenhousemuir FK5 ... 23 E3
Troon KA10 ... 229 D2
Uddingston G71 ... 140 F5
Church View
Caldercruix ML6 ... 104 F3
Cambuslang G72 ... 139 A7
Coatbridge ML5 ... 122 A7
Church View Ct G66 ... 33 D1
Church View Gdns ML4 ... 142 A5
Church Wlk FK6 ... 21 E2
Churchyard Ct ML7 ... 146 E4
Circus Dr G31 ... 117 F7
Circus Pl G31 ... 117 F8
Circus Place La G31 ... 117 F8
Citadel L Ctr KA7 ... 235 E1
Citadel Pl
Ayr KA7 ... 235 E1
Motherwell ML1 ... 163 C8
Citadel Way KA10 ... 229 G8
Citizen La G1 ... 241 A2
Citrus Cres G71 ... 141 C8
Cityford Cres G73 ... 137 F7
Cityford Dr G73 ... 137 F6
Civic Sq 4 ML1 ... 163 F5
Civic St G4 ... 97 B2
Civic Way G66 ... 79 C7
Clachaig Pl PA19 ... 43 F5
Clachan Dr 4 G51 ... 115 E8
CLACHAN OF CAMPSIE ... 33 A3
Clachan Rd G84 ... 15 A3
Clachan The
Rosneath G84 ... 15 A3
Wishaw ML2 ... 165 B3
Clachan Way ML5 ... 121 E5
CLACKMANNAN ... 10 F4
Clackmannan County Hospl FK10 ... 10 B8
Clackmannan Rd FK10 ... 10 D6
Clackmannanshire Com Hospl FK10 ... 10 C8
Clackmannan Tower* FK10 ... 10 F4
CLADDENS ... 79 F4
Claddens Holdings G66 ... 80 A4
Claddens Pl
Glasgow G22 ... 97 B6
Kirkintilloch G66 ... 79 E4
Claddens Quadrant G22 ... 97 C6
Claddens St G22 ... 97 B6
Cladence Gr G75 ... 180 F5
Claire St ML2 ... 166 A5
Clairinsh G83 ... 27 D8
Clairinsh Gdns 1 PA4 ... 94 C1
Clairmont Gdns G3 ... 240 A4
Clair Rd G64 ... 78 D1
Clamp Rd ML2 ... 164 C4
Clamps Gr G74 ... 181 A8
Clamps Terr G74 ... 181 B8
Clamps Wood G74 ... 181 A8
Clanranald Pl FK1 ... 41 F1
Clanrye Dr ML5 ... 122 A4
Clapperhow Rd ML1 ... 143 B1
Claremont FK10 ... 9 F8
Claremont Ave G66 ... 79 B8
Claremont Cres KA13 ... 207 D4
Claremont Dr
Bridge of Allan FK9 ... 2 C7
Milngavie G62 ... 55 A2
Claremont Gdns G62 ... 55 A1
Claremont Ind Est FK10 ... 10 A6
Claremont Passage G3 ... 240 A4
Claremont Pl G3 ... 240 A4
Claremont Prim Sch FK10 ... 9 E8
Claremont St
Bonnybridge FK4 ... 39 F6
Glasgow G3 ... 116 E8
Claremont Terr G3 ... 240 A4
Claremont Terrace La G3 ... 240 A4
Claremount Ave G46 ... 136 C2
Claremount View ML5 ... 122 C3
Clarence Dr
Glasgow G12 ... 96 A3
1 Paisley PA1 ... 114 A4
Clarence Gdns G11 ... 96 A3
Clarence La G12 ... 96 B3
Clarence St
Clydebank G81 ... 74 C3
Greenock PA15 ... 45 F6
Paisley PA1 ... 114 A5
Clarendon Pl
Ayr KA7 ... 239 C5
Clarendon Pl *continued*
9 Glasgow G20 ... 97 A2
Stepps G33 ... 99 D5
Stirling FK8 ... 7 A7
Clarendon Rd
Stirling FK8 ... 7 A7
Wishaw ML2 ... 164 E1
Clarendon St G20 ... 97 A2
Clare St G21 ... 98 A2
Clarinda Ave FK1 ... 41 B5
Clarinda Ct G66 ... 59 A2
Clarinda Pl
Motherwell ML1 ... 143 C3
Stenhousemuir FK5 ... 23 C4
Clarion Cres G13 ... 95 A8
Clarion Rd G13 ... 95 B7
Clark Cres KA20 ... 217 D7
Clark Dr KA12 ... 219 E3
Clarke Ave KA7 ... 238 E6
Clarkin Ave G75 ... 180 A4
Clark Pl
Newton Mearns G77 ... 156 B4
Saltcoats KA21 ... 206 A2
Torrance G64 ... 78 C8
Clark St
Airdrie ML6 ... 123 B7
Clydebank G81 ... 73 F4
Johnstone PA5 ... 111 F3
Kilmarnock KA1 ... 227 F8
Paisley PA3 ... 113 C6
Renfrew PA4 ... 94 B3
Stirling FK7 ... 7 B2
Wishaw ML2 ... 165 F5
CLARKSTON
Airdrie ... 123 E8
Newton Mearns ... 157 E7
Clarkston Ave G44 ... 136 F4
Clarkston Dr ML6 ... 123 D7
Clarkston Prim Sch ML6 ... 123 D8
Clarkston Rd
Clarkston G76 ... 157 E8
Glasgow G44, G76 ... 136 F3
Clarkston Sta G76 ... 157 E7
Clark Way ML4 ... 141 F7
Clarkwell Rd ML3 ... 161 E3
Clarkwell Terr ML3 ... 161 F3
Clathic Ave G61 ... 76 A4
Claude Ave G72 ... 139 E4
Claude St ML9 ... 185 A3
Claud Rd PA3 ... 114 A6
Clavens Rd G52 ... 114 E6
Claverhouse Pl PA2 ... 114 B3
Claverhouse Rd G52 ... 114 F7
Clavering Street E PA1 ... 113 C5
Clavering Street W PA1 ... 113 C4
Clay Cres
Bellshill ML4 ... 142 C7
Kilmarnock KA3 ... 222 F2
Claycrofts Pl FK7 ... 7 B6
Clay Ct ML1 ... 163 E4
Clayhouse Rd G33 ... 99 E5
Claymore Dr
Houston PA6 ... 111 D8
Stirling FK7 ... 7 D3
Claypotts Pl G33 ... 99 A1
Claypotts Rd G33 ... 99 A1
Clay Rd ML4 ... 142 C7
Clayslaps Rd G3 ... 96 D1
Clayslaps View KA1 ... 228 B4
Claythorn Ave G40 ... 241 C1
Claythorn Cir G40 ... 241 C1
Claythorn Ct G40 ... 241 C1
Claythorn Pk G40 ... 117 E5
Claythorn St G40 ... 241 C1
Claythorn Terr G40 ... 241 C1
Clayton Ave KA12 ... 219 C4
Clayton Path ML4 ... 142 B7
Clayton Terr 5 G31 ... 117 F7
Clearfield Ave ML3 ... 162 B4
Cleaves The FK10 ... 4 B1
CLEDDANS ... 58 E1
Cleddans Cres G81 ... 74 C5
Cleddans Rd
Clydebank G81 ... 74 C5
Kirkintilloch G66 ... 58 E1
Cleddans View
Clydebank G81 ... 74 C4
Glenmavis ML6 ... 102 E4
Cleddens Ct
Airdrie ML6 ... 122 D8
Bishopbriggs G64 ... 78 A1
CLEEKHIMIN ... 143 B1
Cleeves Ave KA24 ... 191 E6
Cleeves Prim Sch G53 ... 135 A5
Cleeves Quadrant G53 ... 135 B5
Cleeves Rd G53 ... 135 A5
CLEGHORN ... 215 F7
Cleghorn Ave ML11 ... 215 B5
Cleghorn Dr ML11 ... 215 A5
Cleghorn Rd ML11 ... 215 A5
Cleghorn St G22 ... 97 B3
Cleish Ave G61 ... 75 C8
CLELAND ... 144 B1
Cleland Hospl ML1 ... 144 C1
Cleland La G5 ... 117 C5
Cleland Pl G74 ... 160 A3
Cleland Prim Sch ML1 ... 144 C1
Cleland Rd
Cleland ML1 ... 144 A2
Wishaw ML2 ... 165 A3
Cleland St G5 ... 117 C5
Cleland Sta ML1 ... 144 C1
Clelland Ave G64 ... 98 A8
Clem Attlee Gdns ML9 ... 185 B2
Clement Dr ML6 ... 103 D1
Clements Pl KA20 ... 206 E2
Clerkland Rd KA3 ... 195 D2
Clerwood St G32 ... 118 D6
Cleuch Ave FK10 ... 4 B2
Cleuch Dr FK12 ... 4 E7
Cleuch Gdns G76 ... 157 D8
Cleuch Rd FK9 ... 2 C3
Cleughearn Rd G75 ... 180 D1
Clevans Rd PA11 ... 110 C7
Cleveden Cres G12 ... 96 B5
Cleveden Crescent La G12 ... 96 B5
Cleveden Dr
Glasgow G12 ... 96 C4
Rutherglen G73 ... 138 C6
Cleveden Gdns G12 ... 96 C5
Cleveden Pl G12 ... 96 C4
Cleveden Pl G12 ... 96 B6
Cleveden Rd G12 ... 96 B5
Cleveden Sec Sch G12 ... 96 C5
Cleveland La G3 ... 240 A3
Cleveland St G3 ... 240 A3
Clifford Gdns G51 ... 116 B5
Clifford La G51 ... 116 D5
Clifford Pk FK11 ... 4 A7
Clifford Pl 1 G51 ... 116 D5
Clifford Rd FK8 ... 7 B5
Clifford St G51 ... 116 C5
Cliff Rd G3 ... 240 A4
Cliffvale Rd 3 G69 ... 100 C8
Clifton Ho 9 G3 ... 96 E1
Clifton Pl
Coatbridge ML5 ... 122 C6
1 Glasgow G3 ... 116 E8
Clifton Rd G46 ... 136 B3
Clifton St G3 ... 96 E1
Clifton Terr
Cambuslang G72 ... 138 E3
Johnstone PA5 ... 112 A2
CLIFTONVILLE ... 122 C7
Cliftonville Ct ML5 ... 122 C6
Climie Pl KA3 ... 228 B8
CLINCARTHILL ... 138 B7
Clincarthill Rd G73 ... 138 A7
Clincart Rd G42 ... 137 B8
Clippens Ho PA3 ... 112 A6
Clippens Rd
Houston PA3, PA6 ... 111 F8
Linwood PA3 ... 112 A6
Clippens Sch PA3 ... 112 C6
Clive St ML7 ... 146 E5
Cloak Rd PA13 ... 69 C4
Cloan Ave G15 ... 75 B2
Cloan Cres G64 ... 78 B3
Clober Farm La G62 ... 54 E3
Cloberfield G62 ... 54 F4
Cloberfield Gdns G62 ... 54 F3
Cloberhill Rd G13 ... 75 D1
Clober Prim Sch G62 ... 54 E2
Clober Rd G62 ... 55 A2
Clochbar Ave G62 ... 54 F3
Clochbar Gdns G62 ... 54 F2
Cloch Brae PA19 ... 44 A6
Clochoderick Ave PA10 ... 111 B2
Clochranhill Rd KA7 ... 238 F2
Cloch Rd PA19 ... 43 E5
Cloch St G33 ... 119 A8
Clockenhill Pl ML1 ... 143 E4
Cloister Ave ML6 ... 123 C4
Cloncaird KA13 ... 207 C2
Closeburn St G22 ... 97 C5
Clossfoot Pl G69 ... 81 A2
Cloth St G78 ... 134 C2
Clouden Rd G67 ... 62 B2
Cloudhowe Terr G72 ... 140 C1
Clouston Ct 1 G20 ... 96 E4
Clouston St G20 ... 96 E4
Clova Pl G71 ... 140 F6
Clova St G46 ... 135 F4
Clove Mill Wynd ML9 ... 184 E2
Cloverbank Gdns G21 ... 98 A1
Cloverbank St G21 ... 98 A1
Clovergate G64 ... 77 E1
Cloverhill KA7 ... 239 D6
Cloverhill Pl G69 ... 100 C8
Cloverhill Terr G74 ... 159 E1
Cloverhill View G74 ... 159 D1
Clover Leaf Path G83 ... 27 E4
Cloves The FK11 ... 4 A5
Cluanie Ave ML7 ... 146 E6
Clune Brae PA14 ... 47 E1
Clune Dr KA9 ... 236 D8
Clune Park Prim Sch PA14 ... 47 E1
Clune Park St PA14 ... 47 E1
Clunie Pl
Coatbridge ML5 ... 122 B3
Wishaw ML2 ... 165 F6
Clunie Rd G52 ... 115 E4
Cluny Ave G61 ... 76 A2
Cluny Dr
Bearsden G61 ... 76 A2
Newton Mearns G77 ... 156 B5
Paisley PA3 ... 114 A6
Stenhousemuir FK5 ... 23 F4
Cluny Gdns
Glasgow, Baillieston G69 ... 120 A4
Glasgow, Jordanhill G14 ... 95 E4
Cluny Villas G14 ... 95 E4
Clutha Pl G75 ... 180 A7
Clutha St G51 ... 116 D6
Clyde Ave
Barrhead G78 ... 134 D1
Bothwell G71 ... 140 F1
Hamilton ML3 ... 163 C1
Torrance G64 ... 78 B8
CLYDEBANK ... 74 B1
Clydebank Bsns Pk G81 ... 74 B2
Clydebank Coll G81 ... 74 B3
Clydebank High Sch G81 ... 74 A4

Clydebank Ind Est G81 73 D2
Clydebank Mus* G81 74 B1
Clydebank Sta G81 74 B1
Clydebrae Dr G71 162 B8
Clydebrae St G51 116 B8
Clydebuilt (Mus)* G51 95 A3
Clyde Cres
 Lanark ML11 215 B5
 Larbert FK5 23 B3
Clyde Ct
 Carluke ML8 187 E2
 Clydebank G81 73 E5
 Coatbridge ML5 122 C6
 Dumbarton G82 49 E3
Clyde Dr
 Bellshill ML4 142 D4
 Shotts ML7 147 B4
Clydeford Dr
 Glasgow G32 118 E3
 Uddingston G71 140 E7
Clydeford Rd G32, G72 139 A7
Clyde Ho ML3 162 E5
Clydeholm Rd G14 95 D2
Clydeholm Terr G81 94 D7
Clyde La ML1 143 A4
Clydemuir Prim Sch G81 73 D4
Clyde Muirshiel Regional Pk* PA19 43 D2
Clydeneuk Dr G71 140 D7
Clyde Pl
 Ardrossan KA22 205 D4
 Cambuslang G72 139 D4
 Glasgow G5 240 C1
 Johnstone PA5 131 C8
 Kilmarnock KA1 228 A5
 Motherwell ML1 143 A4
 Troon KA10 229 G5
Clyde Rd
 Gourock PA19 44 F6
 Paisley PA3 114 B7
CLYDESDALE 142 E4
Clydesdale Ave
 Hamilton ML3 183 D6
 Paisley PA3 94 A1
 Wishaw ML2 164 D1
Clydesdale Pl ML3 183 D6
Clydesdale Rd ML4 142 D4
Clydesdale St
 Hamilton ML3 162 C4
 Larkhall ML9 185 A4
 Motherwell ML1 142 F4
Clyde Sh Ctr G81 74 B2
Clydesholm Ct ML11 214 D4
Clydeshore Rd G82 49 E3
Clydeside Expressway G3 116 E7
Clydeside Ind Est G14 95 E1
Clydeside Rd G73 117 F2
Clydesmill Dr G32 139 A7
Clydesmill Gr G32 139 A7
Clydesmill Pl G32 139 A8
Clydesmill Rd G32 139 A8
Clyde Sq
 2 Cumbernauld G67 61 F1
 9 Greenock PA15 45 F5
Clyde St
 Carluke ML8 187 E2
 Clydebank G81 94 C8
 Coatbridge ML5 122 C7
 Falkirk FK1 41 E5
 Glasgow G1 241 A1
 Renfrew PA4 94 D5
Clyde Terr
 Ardrossan KA22 205 D4
 Bothwell G71 141 A1
 Motherwell ML1 164 C2
Clyde Twr
 East Kilbride G74 181 B7
 8 Motherwell ML1 163 E5
Clydevale G71 141 B1
Clyde Valley Ave ML1 163 E4
Clyde Valley High Sch ML2 186 B7
Clydeview
 Bothwell G71 141 C1
 Dumbarton G82 49 E2
Clyde View
 Ashgill ML9 200 A8
 Hamilton ML3 162 B1
 Paisley PA2 114 B2
Clyde View Ave KA20 206 C1
Clyde View Ct G60 72 C8
Clydeview Rd
 Greenock PA15 46 B2
 Port Glasgow PA14 68 E8
Clydeview Sch ML1 163 B8
Clydeview Sh Ctr G72 161 E7
Clydeview Terr G32 139 C8
Clyde Way
 3 Cumbernauld G67 61 F1
 Paisley PA3 114 B7
Clydeway Ind Est 8 G3 116 E8
Clyde Wlk
 1 Cumbernauld G67 61 F1
 Wishaw ML2 166 A6
Clyde Workshops G32 118 F1
Clyde Wynd PA15 45 E3
Clynder Rd PA15 46 C2
Clynder St G51 116 B6
Clyth Dr G46 136 D2
Clytus Ct KA21 205 F3
Coach Brae View KA11 220 E2
Coach Cl G65 61 A8
Coach Pl G65 60 E7
Coach Rd G65 60 F7
Coalburn Rd G71 141 B5
Coalburn St ML6 83 F2
Coalgate FK10 10 B6
Coalhall Ave ML1 143 A1
Coalhill Pl KA22 205 C4
Coalhill St G31 118 B5
Coalpots Way FK10 5 E3
Coal Wynd FK7 7 D1
Coatbank St ML5 122 B6
Coatbank Way ML5 122 B6
COATBRIDGE 122 A6
Coatbridge Bsns Ctr ML5 122 C6
Coatbridge Central Sta ML5 121 F7
Coatbridge Coll ML5 122 B7
Coatbridge High Sch ML5 122 B7
Coatbridge Outdoor Sp Ctr ML5 121 E5
Coatbridge Rd
 Coatbridge G69 121 A6
 Gartcosh G69 101 A3
 Glasgow G69 120 E5
 Glenboig ML5 101 F5
 Glenmavis ML6 102 D3
Coatbridge Sunnyside Sta ML5 122 A8
Coatbridge Workshops ML5 122 B6
COATDYKE 122 D6
Coatdyke Sta ML5 122 D7
Coathill Hospl ML5 122 A4
Coathill St ML5 122 B4
Coats Cres
 Glasgow G69 120 A5
 Tullibody FK10 4 E1
Coats Dr PA2 113 B3
COATSHILL 140 D1
Coatshill Ave G72 140 C1
Coats Pl KA2 225 E2
Coats St ML5 122 B6
Cobbett Rd ML1 163 B5
Cobblebrae Cres FK2 24 B1
Cobblerigg Way G71 140 E6
Cobbleton Rd ML1 142 F2
Cobden St
 Alva FK12 5 A6
 Alva FK12 5 A7
Cobham St PA15 46 E2
Cobington Pl G33 99 B1
Cobinshaw St G32 119 A6
Coblecrook Gdns FK12 4 F6
Coblecrook La FK12 4 F6
Coblecrook Pl FK12 4 F6
Coburg St 3 G5 117 B5
COCHNO 53 B1
Cochno Brae G81 74 B7
Cochno Rd
 Clydebank, Duntocher G81 74 B8
 Clydebank, Faifley G81 74 E8
Cochno St G81 74 C1
Cochrane Ave
 Dundonald KA2 225 F2
 Falkirk FK1 42 B4
Cochrane Castle Prim Sch 1 PA5 111 D1
Cochrane Cres FK12 4 E7
Cochrane Ct G62 76 C8
Cochrane Dr KA2 225 E2
Cochranemill Rd PA5 111 C1
Cochrane Pl
 Helensburgh G84 17 A2
 Prestwick KA9 236 B8
Cochrane Sq PA3 112 B6
Cochrane St
 Barrhead G78 134 B2
 Bellshill ML4 141 F5
 Falkirk FK1 42 B4
 Glasgow G1 241 A2
 Irvine KA12 219 B2
 Kilbirnie KA25 149 A2
Cochranes The FK12 5 A7
Cochran St PA1 113 F4
Cochrie Pl FK10 4 C2
Cockalane View G63 31 C3
Cockburn Pl
 Coatbridge ML5 121 F4
 Irvine KA11 224 H6
Cockburn St FK1 42 B4
Cockels Loan PA4 94 D1
Cockenzie St G32 119 A6
Cockhill Way ML4 141 D6
Cocklebie Rd KA3 195 D1
Cocklebie View KA3 195 D1
Cockmuir St G21 98 A4
Coddington Cres ML1 142 F7
Cogan Pl G78 134 B2
Cogan Rd G43 136 C6
Cogan St
 Barrhead G78 134 B2
 Glasgow G43 136 C7
Coila Ave KA9 236 C6
Coire Loan ML7 147 B3
Colbert St G40 117 F4
Colbreggan Ct G81 74 C6
Colbreggan Gdns G81 74 C6
Colbreggan Pl G81 74 C6
Colchester Dr G12 96 B6
Coldgreen Ave KA25 149 A1
Coldingham Ave G14 94 E6
Coldstream KA23 190 D5
Coldstream Cres ML2 165 C5
Coldstream Dr
 Paisley PA2 113 A1
 Rutherglen G73 138 D6
Coldstream Pl G21 97 C3
Coldstream Rd G81 74 B1
Coldstream St G72 161 D7
Colebrooke Pl G12 96 E3
Colebrooke St
 Cambuslang G72 139 A6
 9 Glasgow G12 96 E3
Colebrooke Terr G12 96 E3
Coleburn Ct KA11 219 F6
Cole Rd G64 78 D6
Coleridge G75 180 A7
Coleridge Ave G71 141 B3
Coleridge Gdns G84 16 C2
Colfin St G34 100 C1
Colgrain Ave G20 97 A6
Colgrain Prim Sch G84 25 C8
Colgrain Steading G82 25 E5
Colgrain Terr G20 97 A6
Colgrave Cres G32 118 F3
Colinbar Circ G78 134 B1
Colinslee Ave PA2 113 F1
Colinslee Cres PA2 113 F1
Colinslee Dr PA2 113 F1
Colinslie Rd G53 135 D8
Colinton Gdns G69 80 C1
Colinton Pl G32 119 B7
Colintraive Ave G33 98 F4
Colintraive Cres G33 98 E4
Coll G74 181 C7
Collace Ave PA11 110 D7
Colla Gdns G64 78 D2
Coll Ave
 Port Glasgow PA14 69 B8
 Renfrew PA4 94 D1
Coll Dr ML5 121 E4
College Cres FK2 42 D7
College Gate G61 75 C6
College La G1 241 B2
COLLEGE MILTON 159 B3
College Pk KA10 229 F7
College St
 Dumbarton G82 49 F4
 Glasgow G1 241 B2
College Way
 Dumbarton G82 49 F3
 East Kilbride G75 181 A7
College Wynd 2 KA1 227 F8
COLLENAN 230 A6
Collenan Ave KA10 230 A4
Collenan Smallholdings KA10 230 B6
Collessie Dr G33 99 C2
Coll Gdns KA11 225 B8
Colliers Rd FK7 8 D4
Collier St PA5 111 F3
Colliers Way FK7 7 C1
Colliertree Rd ML6 123 D8
Collina St G20 96 C6
Collingwood Ct FK1 41 E5
Collingwood Pl G84 17 A2
Collingwood Terr PA19 44 F6
Collins Dr KA10 230 A4
Collins Rd G84 25 C8
Collins St
 Clydebank G81 74 C6
 Glasgow G4 241 C2
Coll Lea ML3 161 F1
Coll Pl
 Airdrie ML6 123 C5
 Glasgow G21 98 B2
Collree Gdns G34 120 C7
Coll St
 Glasgow G21 98 B2
 Wishaw ML2 165 F6
Collyland Rd FK10 5 D3
Collylinn Rd G61 75 E4
Colmonell Ave G13 94 F7
Colonsay G74 181 C7
Colonsay Ave
 Port Glasgow PA14 69 B7
 Renfrew PA4 94 C1
Colonsay Cres ML5 121 D4
Colonsay Dr G77 156 B5
Colonsay Ho KA9 236 B5
Colonsay Pl KA3 223 B6
Colonsay Rd
 2 Glasgow G52 115 E5
 Paisley PA2 133 D7
Colonsay Terr FK1 42 B2
Colquhoun G82 50 A4
Colquhoun Ave G52 115 A7
Colquhoun Ct G41 116 C3
Colquhoun Dr
 Alexandria G83 27 E7
 Bearsden G61 75 E5
Colquhoun Park Prim Sch G61 75 D3
Colquhoun Pk G52 115 B7
Colquhoun Rd
 Kilmarnock KA3 223 C2
 Milton G82 50 F1
Colquhoun Sq G84 16 C1
Colquhoun St
 Dumbarton G82 50 A4
 Helensburgh G84 16 D2
 Stirling FK7 7 C6
Colquhoun Terr FK7 7 C6
Colsnaur FK11 4 A6
Colson Pl ML4 142 C3
COLSTON 97 F8
Colston Ave G64 97 F7
Colston Dr G64 97 F7
Colston Gdns G64 97 E7
Colston Gr G64 97 F7
Colston Path G64 97 E7
Colston Pl
 2 Airdrie ML6 123 C7
 1 Bishopbriggs G64 97 E7
Colston Rd
 Airdrie ML6 123 C7
 Bishopbriggs G64 97 F7
Colston Row 3 ML6 123 C7
Colston Terr 4 ML6 123 C7
Colt Ave ML5 101 E1
Coltmuir Cres G64 97 E8
Coltmuir Dr G64 97 E8
Coltmuir Gdns G64 97 E8
Coltmuir St G22 97 B6
COLTNESS 165 D5
Coltness Ave ML7 166 F8
Coltness Dr ML4 142 B4
Coltness High Sch ML2 165 D4
Coltness La G33 119 D7
Coltness Prim Sch ML2 165 C6
Coltness Rd ML2 165 C6
Coltness St G33 119 C8
Coltpark Ave G64 97 E7
Coltpark La G64 97 F8
Colt Pl ML5 122 A8
Coltsfoot Dr G53 135 B3
Coltswood Ct 1 ML5 122 A8
Coltswood Rd ML5 122 A8
Colt Terr ML5 122 A8
Columba G81 74 D2
Columba Cres ML1 142 D2
Columba Ct G71 141 C7
Columba Path G72 161 C8
Columba St
 Glasgow G51 116 B7
 Greenock PA16 45 D4
 Helensburgh G84 16 D2
Columbia Pl G75 180 B8
Columbia Way G75 180 B8
Columbine Way ML8 201 F8
Colvend Dr G73 138 B3
Colvend La G40 117 F3
Colvend St G40 117 F3
Colville Cl G72 139 D6
Colville Ct ML1 143 C1
Colville Dr G73 138 D6
Colville Gdns FK10 10 A6
Colvilles Pk G75 181 B6
Colvilles Pl G75 181 B6
Colvilles Rd G75 181 A6
Colwood Ave G53 135 A3
Colwood Gdns G53 135 A3
Colwood Path G53 135 A4
Colwood Pl G53 135 A3
Colwood Sq G53 135 A3
Colwyn Ct ML6 103 A1
Colzium Ho* G65 36 F2
Colzium View G65 60 E8
Combe Quadrant ML4 141 E3
Comedie Rd G33 99 E4
Comely Bank ML3 161 F3
Comelybank La G82 49 D4
Comelybank Rd G82 49 D4
Comely Park Gdns
 15 Falkirk FK1 41 B4
 15 Falkirk FK1 42 B4
Comelypark Pl G31 118 A6
Comely Park Prim Sch FK1 42 B4
Comelypark St G31 118 A6
Comely Park Terr 14 FK1 42 B4
Comely Pl FK1 42 B4
Commerce St G5 240 C1
Commercial Ct G5 117 D5
Commercial Rd
 Barrhead G78 134 C4
 Glasgow G5 117 D5
Common Gn ML3 162 E4
Commonhead Ave ML6 102 F1
Commonhead La ML6 102 F1
Commonhead Rd
 Glasgow G34, G69 120 E8
 Kilmarnock KA1 228 A3
Commonhead St ML6 102 F1
Commonside St ML6 102 F1
Commore Ave G78 134 D1
Commore Dr G13 95 A7
Commore Pl G78 154 C6
Community Ave ML4 142 A2
Community Pl ML4 142 B3
Community Rd ML4 142 A2
Comrie Cres ML3 161 E3
Comrie Rd G33 99 C5
Comrie St G32 119 B3
Conan Ct G72 139 D5
Cona St G46 135 E4
Condor Glen ML1 142 E7
CONDORRAT 82 B7
Condorrat Intc G67 82 C8
Condorrat Prim Sch G67 82 B7
Condorrat Rd
 Cumbernauld G67, ML6 82 B3
 Glenmavis ML6 102 D6
Condorrat Ring Rd
 Cumbernauld, Condorrat G67 82 A6
 Cumbernauld, Dalshannon G67 82 C7
Coneyhill Rd FK9 2 B7
Coneypark FK7 6 E6
Coneypark Cres FK4 38 C3
Coneypark Pl FK4 38 C3
Congress Rd G3 116 D7
Congress Way G3 116 E7
Conifer Pl G66 79 B6
Coningsby Pl FK10 10 A6
Conisborough Cl G34 100 A1
Conisborough Path G34 99 F1
Conisborough Rd G34 100 A1
Coniston G75 179 F5
Coniston Cres ML3 183 C6
Coniston Dr ML4 142 B3
Conistone Cres G69 119 F4
Conival Cl ML1 164 C3
Connal St G40 118 B3
Connell Cres G62 55 C1
Connell Ct KA25 149 B1
Connell Gr ML2 164 E2
Connelly Pl ML1 163 D7
Conner Ave FK2 42 A8
Conniston St G32 118 E7
Connolly Dr FK6 21 C4
Connolly Pl FK6 21 F1
Connor Rd G78 134 B3
Connor St ML6 103 E1
Conon Ave G61 75 D3
Conroy Ct FK6 21 E1
Conservation Pl ML2 165 C1
Consett La G33 119 C8
Consett St G33 119 C8
Constable Rd FK7 7 B6
Constantine Way ML1 142 C1
Constarry Rd G65 60 F4
Consul Way ML1 142 C1
Container Way PA15 45 F5
Content Ave KA8 239 A8
Content Ct KA6 239 D2
Content St KA8 239 A8
Contin Pl G20 96 D5
Convair Way PA4 94 D1
Conval Way 3 PA3 113 D8
Conway Ct FK1 41 F4
Coodham Pl KA13 207 D3
Cook Rd G83 28 A8
Cook St G5 117 A5
Coo La G76 178 E5
Coolgardie Gn 2 G75 180 C7
Coolgardie Pl 1 G75 180 C7
Cooperage Ct G14 94 D6
Cooperage Pl G3 116 C8
Cooperage Quay FK8 7 C8
Cooperage Way FK10 10 D8
Cooperage Yd PA12 129 C2
Co-Operative Terr PA5 112 A3
Cooper Ave ML8 187 E3
Coopers Cres KA3 195 E1
Cooper's Well St G11 96 C1
Copeland Prim Sch G51 116 B7
Copenhagen Ave G75 180 E6
Copland Pl
 Alva FK12 4 F7
 Glasgow G51 116 B6
Copland Quadrant G51 116 B6
Copland Rd G51 116 B6
Coplaw Ct G42 117 A3
Coplaw St G42 117 A3
Copperfield La G71 141 A7
Copperwood Cres 3 ML3 162 B5
Copperwood Ct 1 ML3 162 B5
Copperwood Wynd 2 ML3 162 B5
Coralmount Gdns G66 79 E7
Coranbae Pl KA7 238 B1
Corbett Ct G32 118 F3
Corbett St G32 119 A3
Corbie Pl G62 54 D2
Corbiewood Dr FK7 11 E8
Corbiston Way G67 62 B2
Cordale Ave G82 27 E2
Cordiner Cl FK8 1 F2
Cordiner La G44 137 D2
Cordiner St G44 137 B7
Cordon Rd KA3 222 E4
Corentin Ct FK1 42 C3
CORKERHILL 115 E2
Corkerhill Gdns G52 115 E4
Corkerhill Pl G52 115 E2
Corkerhill Rd G52 115 D3
Corkerhill Sta G52 115 D2
Corlaich Ave G42 137 E7
Corlaich Dr G42 137 E7
Corless Ct G71 141 A6
Corlic St PA15 46 B2
Corlic Way PA13 69 C1
Cormack Ave G64 57 C1
Cormorant Ave PA6 111 D8
Cornaig Rd G53 135 B8
Cornalee Gdns G53 135 B8
Cornalee Pl G53 135 B8
Cornalee Rd G53 135 B8
Cornelian Terr ML4 142 A4
Cornelia St ML1 142 B1
Corn Exchange Rd 1 FK8 7 B7
Cornfield Ct G72 139 E6
Cornhaddock St PA15 45 E4
Cornhill KA7 239 B3
Cornhill Cres FK7 7 B3
Cornhill Dr ML5 121 F8
Cornhill St G21 98 A5
Cornish Ct ML5 121 F8
Cornmill Ct G81 74 A6
Cornock Cres G81 74 B3
Cornock St G81 74 B3
Cornsilloch Brae ML9 186 A3
Corn St G4 97 B2
CORNTON 2 B3
Cornton Bsns Pk FK9 2 B3
Cornton Cres FK9 2 A5
Cornton Prim Sch FK9 2 A4
Cornton Rd FK9 2 A4
Cornton Vale Cotts FK9 2 A4
Cornwall Ave G73 138 D5
Cornwall St
 East Kilbride G74 159 E1
 Glasgow G41 116 D5
Cornwall Street S G41 116 D5
Cornwall Way G74 159 F1
Corona Cres FK4 39 F5
Coronation Ave ML9 199 A8
Coronation Cres ML9 199 A8

Coronation Ct ML1 142 F4
Coronation Pl
Larkhall ML9 199 B8
Mount Ellen G69 100 E7
Skinflats FK2 24 F3
Coronation Rd ML1 142 F4
Coronation Road E ML1 142 F3
Coronation Road Ind Est ML1 142 F4
Coronation St
Monkton KA9 233 D5
Wishaw ML2 165 D3
Coronation Way G61 76 A2
Corpach Pl G34 100 D1
Corporation St FK1 42 C4
Corpus Christi Prim Sch
Airdrie ML6 123 B3
Glasgow G13 95 C6
Corra Linn ML3 162 A3
Corran Ave G77 156 C6
Corran St G33 118 F8
Correen Gdns G61 75 B7
Corrie Ave FK5 23 F4
Corrie Brae G65 36 C1
Corrie Cres
Kilmarnock KA3 222 F3
Saltcoats KA21 205 F2
Corrie Ct ML3 161 F2
Corrie Dr
Motherwell ML1 163 B7
Paisley PA1 114 E4
Corrie Gdns G75 180 B4
Corrie Gr G44 136 F4
Corrie Ho KA9 236 B5
Corrie Pl
Falkirk FK1 41 C4
Helensburgh G84 16 F3
Kirkintilloch G66 79 E4
Troon KA10 229 F7
Corrie Rd G65 36 C1
Corrie View G68 81 F8
Corrie View Cotts G65 59 E4
Corrie Way ML9 185 B2
Corrour Rd
Glasgow G43 136 E7
Newton Mearns G77 156 C6
Corsankell Wynd KA21 205 E3
Corse Ave KA11 221 A1
Corsebar Ave PA2 113 C2
Corsebar Cres PA2 113 C1
Corsebar Dr PA2 113 C2
Corsebar La PA2 113 B1
Corsebar Rd PA2 113 C2
Corsebar Way PA2 113 C3
Corsefield Rd PA12 128 E2
Corseford Ave PA5 131 C8
Corseford Residential Sch PA10 131 B7
Corsehill KA13 208 A3
Corsehillbank St KA3 195 D1
Corsehill Dr KA23 190 B5
Corsehill Mount Rd KA11 220 A1
Corsehill Mount Rdbt KA11 225 E8
Corsehill Path G34 120 C8
Corsehill Pk
Ayr KA7 238 F5
Irvine KA11 225 D8
Corsehill Pl
Ayr KA7 238 F5
Glasgow G34 120 C8
Stewarton KA3 195 E2
Corsehill Prim Sch KA13 207 F3
Corsehill Rd KA7 238 F5
Corsehill St G34 120 C8
Corsehill Terr KA11 220 F2
Corselet Rd
Glasgow G53 135 A3
Glasgow G78, G53 135 A1
Corse Pl KA2 226 F8
Corse Rd G52 114 E6
Corserine Bank KA11 219 F3
Corserine Rd KA7 238 B1
Corse St KA23 190 C5
Corse Terr KA23 190 C5
Corsewall Ave G32 119 E3
Corsewall St ML5 121 F8
Corsford Dr G53 135 C6
Corsliehill Rd PA6 90 D7
Corsock Ave ML3 161 E2
Corsock St G31 118 C7
Corston St G33 118 D7
Cortachy Ave FK2 24 A3
Cortachy Pl G64 78 D1
Cortmalaw Ave G33 98 E7
Cortmalaw Cl G33 98 E7
Cortmalaw Cres G33 98 E7
Cortmalaw Gdns G33 98 F7
Cortmalaw Rd G33 98 E7
Corton Lea KA7 239 A1
Corton Shaw KA7 239 B1
Coruisk Dr G76 157 D8
Coruisk Way PA2 132 E8
Corunna Ct ML8 188 B1
Corunna St 5 G3 116 E8
Coshneuk Rd G33 99 B4
Cosy Neuk ML9 185 C1
Cotland Dr FK2 41 F8
Cottage Cres FK1 41 E5
Cottar St G20 96 E7
Cotter Dr KA3 228 C8
Cotton Ave PA3 112 B5
Cottonmill Ct 1 ML6 103 A1
Cotton Row KA12 219 C2
Cotton St
Glasgow G40 118 A2
Paisley PA1 113 F4
Cotton Street Ent Pk G40 118 A2
Cotton Vale ML1 143 E1
Coulin Gdns G22 97 D4
Coulport Pl G84 16 B2
Coulter Ave
Coatbridge ML5 121 E8
Wishaw ML2 165 C7
Coulthard Dr KA9 236 D6
Countess Gate G71 140 E3
Countess St KA21 216 F7
Countess Way G69 121 A5
Counting Ho The PA1 113 B3
County Ave G72 138 E7
County Dr ML11 215 C3
County Pl 7 PA1 113 E5
County Sq 6 PA1 113 E5
Couper Pl G4 241 B4
Couper St G4 241 B4
Coursington Cres ML1 164 A7
Coursington Gdns ML1 163 F7
Coursington Pl ML1 163 F7
Coursington Rd ML1 164 A7
Coursington Twr ML1 163 F7
Courthill
Alva FK12 5 A7
Bearsden G61 75 D6
Court Hill G84 15 A3
Courthill Ave G44 137 B5
Courthill Cres G65 60 E8
Courthill Pl KA24 191 C8
Courthill St KA24 191 C8
Courtrai Ave G84 16 B2
Court Rd PA14 47 C1
Courtyard The FK1 42 E3
Coustonholm Rd G43 136 D8
Couther Quadrant ML6 103 A2
Covanburn Ave ML3 162 F1
Cove Cres ML7 146 E6
Covenant Cres ML9 185 B2
Covenanter Rd ML7 127 D4
Covenanters Way ML2 186 C6
Covenant Pl ML2 164 C2
Coventry Dr G31 118 B8
Cove Pl G84 16 B2
Cove Rd PA19 44 F7
Cowal Cres
Gourock PA19 44 B6
Kirkintilloch G66 59 B1
Cowal Dr PA3 112 A5
Cowal Rd G20 96 C7
Cowal St G20 96 C7
Cowal View PA19 44 B6
Cowan Cres
Ayr KA8 236 C3
Barrhead G78 134 D3
Cowane St 2 FK8 7 B8
Cowan La G12 96 E2
Cowan Rd G68 61 C2
Cowans Row KA3 228 D7
Cowan St
Bonnybridge FK4 40 A6
Glasgow G12 96 E2
Cowan Wilson Ave
Blantyre G72 140 D1
Hamilton G72 161 D8
Cowan Wynd
Overtown ML2 186 C7
Uddingston G71 141 A8
COWCADDENS 241 A4
Cowcaddens Rd G2, G3, G4 240 C4
Cowcaddens Underground Sta G4 240 C4
Cowden Dr G64 78 A3
Cowdenhill Circ G13 95 D8
Cowden Hill Gdns FK4 40 B6
Cowdenhill Pl G13 95 D8
Cowdenhill Rd G13 95 D8
COWDENKNOWES 45 D4
Cowden St G51 115 D7
Cowdray Cres PA4 94 D3
Cowgate G66 79 C8
Cowglen Rd G53 135 C7
COWIE 12 C7
Cowiehall Rd FK7 12 D8
Cowie Pl ML1 164 C5
Cowie Prim Sch FK7 12 D7
Cowie Rd
Bannockburn FK7 7 E1
Cowie FK7 12 A8
Cowie Terr G83 27 D5
COWLAIRS 97 D4
Cowlairs Ind Est G22 97 D5
Cowlairs Rd 5 G21 97 E4
Cow Wynd FK1 42 B4
Coxdale Ave G66 79 B8
COXET HILL 6 F4
Coxhill St G21 97 D3
Coxithill Rd FK7 7 A3
Coxswain Dr KA10 229 F6
Coxton Pl G33 99 D1
Coylebank KA9 236 C6
Coyle Pk KA10 229 F6
Coylton Cres ML3 161 E1
Coylton Rd G43 136 F5
Crabb Quadrant ML1 142 C1
Cragburn Gate PA19 44 D7
Cragdale G74 159 C3
Craggan Dr G14 95 A5
Cragganmore FK10 4 A2
Crags Ave PA2 113 F1
Crags Cres PA2 113 F2
Crags Rd PA2 113 F1
Cragwell Pk G76 158 E7
Craigallian Ave
Cambuslang G72 139 D4
Milngavie G62 55 A3
Craigard Pl G73 138 D3
Craigash Quadrant G62 54 E3
Craigash Rd G62 54 E3
Craig Ave
Alexandria G83 27 C7
Dalry KA24 191 A8
Craigbank FK10 5 C1
Craigbank Cres G76 178 E6
Craigbank Dr G53 135 A6
Craigbank Gr G76 178 E6
Craigbank Prim Sch
Alloa FK10 5 C1
Larkhall ML9 199 A8
Craigbank Rd ML9 199 A8
Craigbank St ML9 185 A1
Craigbanzo St G81 74 D8
Craigbarnet Ave G66 78 A8
Craigbarnet Cres G33 99 B4
Craigbarnet Rd G62 54 D2
Craigbet Ave PA11 89 E2
Craigbet Cres PA11 89 E2
Craigbet Pl PA11 89 E2
Craigbo Ave 14 G23 76 D1
Craigbo Ct G23 96 D8
Craigbo Dr 13 G23 76 D1
Craigbog Ave PA5 131 D8
Craigbo Pl G23 96 D8
Craigbo Rd G23 76 D1
Craigbo St G23 76 D1
Craigburn Ave PA6 111 D7
Craigburn Cres PA6 111 D7
Craigburn Ct
Ashgill ML9 185 F1
Falkirk FK1 41 F2
Craigburn Pl PA6 111 E7
Craigburn St ML3 183 D8
Craig Cotts KA2 226 D8
Craig Cres
Kirkintilloch G66 80 B7
Stirling FK9 2 D3
Craig Ct FK9 2 A5
Craigdene Dr KA20 206 E2
Craigdhu Ave
Airdrie ML6 123 E7
Milngavie G62 54 F1
Craigdhu Farm Cotts G62 54 E1
Craigdhu Prim Sch G62 75 F8
Craigdhu Rd
Bearsden G61 75 E8
Milngavie G62 54 F1
Craigdonald Pl PA5 111 F3
Craig Dr
Crosshouse KA2 226 E8
Doonfoot KA7 238 B2
Craigellan Rd G43 136 D6
Craigelvan Ave G67 81 F6
Craigelvan Ct G67 81 F6
Craigelvan Dr G67 81 F6
Craigelvan Gdns G67 81 F6
Craigelvan Gr G67 81 F6
Craigelvan Pl G67 81 F6
Craigelvan View G67 81 F6
Craigenbay Cres G66 79 E5
Craigenbay Rd G66 79 E5
Craigenbay St G21 98 B4
Craigencart Ct G81 73 F6
CRAIGEND 99 D2
Craigend Cir G13 95 E6
Craigend Cres G62 54 F2
Craigend Ct G13 95 E6
Craigend Dr ML5 121 C4
Craigend Drive W G62 54 F2
CRAIGENDMUIR 99 E4
Craigendmuir Pk G33 99 E4
Craigendmuir Rd G33 99 E4
Craigendmuir St G33 98 D2
Craigendon Oval PA2 133 C6
Craigendon Rd PA2 133 C6
CRAIGENDORAN 25 D7
Craigendoran Ave G84 25 B8
Craigendoran Sta G84 25 B7
Craigend Pl G13 95 E6
Craigend Rd
Cumbernauld G67 81 F5
East Kilbride G75 179 F1
Stirling FK7 7 A3
Troon KA10 232 E8
CRAIGENDS 91 D1
Craigends Ave PA11 89 E3
Craigends Ct G65 60 E8
Craigends Dr PA10 111 B3
Craigends Pl PA11 89 E3
Craigends Rd
Glengarnock KA14 170 B6
Houston PA6 91 E2
Craigend St G13 95 E6
Craigend View G67 81 F5
Craigend Visitor Ctr★ G62 54 F8
Craigenfeoch Ave PA5 111 D1
Craigenhill Rd ML8 203 A5
Craigenlay Ave G63 31 C4
Craigens Rd ML1, ML6 124 C3
Craigfaulds Ave PA2 113 B2
Craigfell Ct ML3 161 E2
Craigfern Dr G63 31 C4
Craigfin Ct KA9 236 D5
Craigflower Gdns G53 135 A4
Craigflower Rd G53 135 B3
Craigford Dr FK7 7 D1
Craigforth Cres FK8 1 F1
Craig Gdns G77 156 C5
Craighalbert Rd G68 61 D3
Craighalbert Rdbt G68 61 C4
Craighalbert Way G68 61 C4
Craighall Pl KA7 239 A2
Craighall Quadrant G78 154 D6
Craighall Rd G4 97 B2
Craighall St FK8 1 E1
Craighaw St G81 74 D8
Craighead Ave
Glasgow G33 98 D3
Milton of Campsie G66 58 C6
Craighead Dr G62 54 D2
Craighead Pl G33 98 D3
Craighead Prim Sch G66 58 C6
Craighead Rd
Bishopton PA7 72 B2
Milton of Campsie G66 58 C6
Craighead Sch ML3 162 B7
Craighead St
Airdrie ML6 123 E8
Barrhead G78 134 B2
Craighead Way G78 134 B2
Craig Hill G75 180 C7
Craighill Dr G76 157 D6
Craighill Gr G76 157 D6
Craighill View EH48 107 E3
Craighirst Dr G81 74 A7
Craighirst Rd G62 54 D2
Craighlaw Ave G76 157 D2
Craighlaw Dr G76 157 D2
Craigholme PA6 91 D2
Craigholme Lower Jun Sch G41 116 D3
Craigholme Sch G41 116 D3
Craigholm Rd KA7 239 D7
Craighorn FK11 4 A5
Craighorn Dr FK1 41 E2
Craighorn Rd FK12 4 E6
Craighouse Sq KA25 149 B1
Craighouse St G33 99 A1
Craighton Gdns G66 57 F8
CRAIGIE 239 C8
Craigie Ave
Ayr KA8 239 A8
Kilmarnock KA1 227 F4
Craigiebar Dr PA2 133 C8
Craigieburn Gdns G20 96 B8
Craigieburn Rd G67 61 F1
Craigie Ct FK5 23 B2
Craigie Dr G77 156 E3
Craigie Est & Pk★ KA8 239 C7
Craigiehall Ave PA8 93 A7
Craigiehall Cres PA8 93 A7
Craigiehall Pl G51 116 D6
Craigiehall St G51 116 E6
Craigiehall Way PA8 93 A7
Craigieknowes St PA15 46 C3
Craigie La 9 ML9 185 B4
Craigie Lea KA8 239 B8
Craigielea Cres G62 54 E2
Craigielea Ct PA4 94 C4
Craigielea Pk PA4 94 C3
Craigielea Rd
Duntocher G81 73 F7
Renfrew PA4 94 C3
Craigielea St G31 118 A8
Craigielinn Ave PA2 133 C7
Craigie Pk G66 79 E5
Craigie Pl
Coatbridge ML5 121 E5
Crosshouse KA2 226 F8
Kilmarnock KA1 227 F4
Craigie Rd
Ayr KA8 236 B1
Hurlford KA1 228 F5
Kilmarnock KA1 227 F1
Craigie St
Glasgow G42 117 A2
Prestwick KA9 236 B8
Craigievar Ave
Falkirk FK2 24 A3
Glasgow G33 99 E2
Craigievar Pl
Airdrie ML6 123 E6
Newton Mearns G77 156 B5
Craigievar St G33 99 E2
Craigie Way KA8 239 C8
Craiginn Ct EH48 107 D3
Craiginn Terr EH48 107 D3
Craiglea FK9 2 C3
Craiglea Ave KA2 226 E8
Craiglea Ct EH48 107 D3
Craiglea Pl ML6 123 C8
Craiglea Terr ML6 103 F3
Craiglee G75 180 E5
Craigleith FK10 5 E3
Craigleith Ave FK1 41 E2
Craig Leith Rd FK7 7 D6
Craigleith St G32 118 E6
Craigleith Terr FK12 5 A7
Craigleith View FK10 4 D3
CRAIGLINN 61 A2
Craiglinn G68 61 A2
Craiglinn Gdns G45 137 C2
Craiglinn Park Rd G68 61 A1
Craiglinn Rdbt G68 61 A1
Craiglockhart Cres 5 G33 99 D2
Craiglockhart Dr 4 G33 99 D2
Craiglockhart Pl 6 G33 99 D2
Craiglockhart St G33 99 D1
Craiglomond Gdns G83 27 D8
Craiglynn Gdns G83 27 F8
Craigmaddie Gdns G64 78 A8
Craigmaddie Rd G62 56 A1
Craigmaddie Terrace La 7 G3 96 E1
Craigmark Pl KA11 219 F5
Craigmarloch Ave G64 78 B8
Craigmarloch Rdbt G68 61 C3
Craigmarloch View G63 31 B4
Craigmillar Ave G62 55 B3
Craigmillar Pl
Gartcosh G69 100 E4
Stenhousemuir FK5 23 F4
Craigmillar Rd G42 137 A7
Craigmochan Ave ML6 102 F2
Craigmont Dr G20 96 E6
Craigmont St G20 96 E6
Craigmore Pl ML5 121 E3
Craigmore Rd G61 75 B7
Craigmore St G31 118 C6
Craigmore Wynd 12 ML9 185 B4
Craigmount Ave PA2 133 C6
Craigmount St G66 79 D7
Craigmuir Cres G52 114 F6
Craigmuir Gdns G72 161 B6
Craigmuir Pl G52 114 E6
Craigmuir Rd
Glasgow G52 114 E6
Hamilton G72 161 B6
Craigmuschat Rd PA19 44 E7
Craignaw Pl KA11 220 B2
Craigneil Dr KA9 236 C7
Craigneil St G33 99 E2
Craigneith Ct G74 160 E4
Craignethan Castle★ ML11 200 F1
Craignethan Cres ML9 200 D4
Craignethan Rd
Carluke ML8 187 E3
Rutherglen G46 157 B7
CRAIGNEUK
Airdrie 123 C7
Wishaw 164 D4
Craigneuk Ave ML6 123 C6
Craigneuk St ML2 164 C5
Craignure Cres 4 ML6 123 E7
Craignure Rd G73 138 B3
Craigomus Cres FK11 3 F6
Craigpark G31 118 A7
Craigpark Ave KA9 236 B6
Craigpark Dr G31 118 A7
Craigpark Sch KA7 239 A5
Craigpark St G81 74 D7
Craigpark Way G71 141 A7
Craig Pl
Law ML8 187 A5
Newton Mearns G77 156 B5
Craig Rd
Glasgow G44 137 A5
Linwood PA3 111 F7
Neilston G78 154 D6
Troon KA10 229 B3
Craigrie Rd FK10 10 F4
Craigs Ave G81 74 C6
Craigsdow Rd KA10 229 G6
Craigsheen Ave G76 158 D7
Craigshiel Pl KA7 238 D4
Craigside Ct G68 81 F7
Craigside Rd G68 81 F7
Craigskeen Pl KA9 236 D5
Craigsmill Wynd ML6 104 F4
Craigson Pl ML6 123 F6
Craigspark KA22 205 C4
Craigs Pl KA21 217 B8
Craigs Rdbt FK7 7 B7
Craig St
Airdrie ML6 122 F7
Blackridge EH48 107 E3
Coatbridge ML5 121 F4
Hamilton G72 161 E7
Craigstewart Cres KA7 238 C1
Craigs The PA16 45 C7
Craigston Ave KA7 239 C6
Craigstone View G65 60 F8
Craigston Pl PA5 111 F2
Craigston Rd PA5 111 F2
Craigthornhill Rd ML3, ML10 198 A6
CRAIGTON 115 D5
Craigton Ave
Barrhead G78 134 E1
Milngavie G62 54 F2
Craigton Cotts G62 54 C5
Craigton Cres
Alva FK12 4 F6
Newton Mearns G77 156 B5
Craigton Dr
Barrhead G78 134 E1
Glasgow G51 115 F6
Newton Mearns G77 156 C6
Craigton Gdns G62 54 F2
Craigton Ind Est G52 115 E5
Craigton Pl
Blantyre G72 140 D1
Glasgow G51 115 E6
Craigton Prim Sch 3 G52 115 E5
Craigton Rd
Glasgow, Drumoyne G51 115 F6
Glasgow, West Drumoyne G51 115 F7
Kilbirnie KA25 170 B8
Milngavie G62 54 E3
Neilston G77 155 B3
Craigton St G81 74 D8
CRAIGTON VILLAGE 54 C4
Craigvale Cres ML6 123 E7
Craigvicar Gdns G32 119 D4
Craigview FK10 5 D2
Craig View KA11 221 A2
Craigview Ave PA5 111 E1
Craigview Rd ML1 163 F8
Craigview Terr PA5 111 D1
Craigward FK10 10 A6
Craigweil Pl KA7 238 E7
Craigweil Rd KA7 238 E7
Craigwell Ave G73 138 D6

Craiksland Pl KA10 230 A4
Craiksland Rd KA10 230 B4
Crail Cl G72 161 D3
Crail Pl G31 118 D5
Crail St G31 118 D5
Cramalt Ct KA11 220 A3
Crammond Ave ML5 121 C4
Cramond Ave PA4 94 E2
Cramond Ct FK1 42 B2
Cramond Pl KA11 219 F2
Cramond St G5 117 E2
Cramond Terr G32 119 B5
Cramond Way KA11 219 F2
Cranberry Ct KA13 207 C3
Cranberry Head KA13 207 C3
Cranberry Moss Rd
Kilwinning KA13 207 D3
Kilwinning KA13, KA20 207 C1
Cranberry Pl KA13 207 C2
Cranberry Rd KA13 207 B2
Cranborne Rd G12 96 A5
Cranbrooke Dr G20 96 D7
Crandleyhill Rd KA9 236 B6
Cranesbill Ct KA7 239 B3
CRANHILL 119 A8
Cranhill Prim Sch G33 119 C8
Crannog Ct G82 50 E1
Crannog Rd G82 50 F1
Crannog Way KA13 207 C4
Cranston Ave ML6 103 D1
CRANSTON HILL 116 D8
Cranston St G3 240 A2
Cranworth La G12 96 D3
Cranworth St G12 96 D3
Crarae Ave G61 75 E2
Crarae Pl G77 156 B5
Crathes Ave FK5 24 A4
Crathes Ct
Glasgow G44 136 E4
Wishaw ML2 165 B3
Crathie Ct
Carluke ML8 187 E3
Glasgow G11 96 A2
Crathie Dr
Ardrossan KA22 205 C1
Denny FK6 21 D3
Glasgow G11 96 A2
Glenmavis ML6 102 F4
Crathie Pl G77 157 B4
Crathie Quadrant ML2 165 B5
Crathie Rd KA3 222 E2
Craufurd Ave KA23 190 E4
Craufurd Cres KA15 171 E4
Craufurdland Rd KA3 223 A5
Craven Gr KA11 219 F5
Crawberry Rd PA15 46 A2
Crawford Ave
Kirkintilloch G66 79 E3
Prestwick KA9 236 C6
Crawford Cres
Blantyre G72 140 D1
Uddingston G71 140 E7
Crawford Dr
Clydebank G15 75 A1
East Kilbride G74 160 B2
Helensburgh G84 16 E4
Crawforddyke Prim Sch
ML8 202 A8
Crawford Gdns ML1 163 C5
Crawford Hill G74 160 B2
Crawford La G11 96 A2
Crawford Path G11 96 A2
Crawford Rd
Houston PA6 91 D1
Milngavie G62 54 F3
Crawford Sh Arc The 3
FK8 7 B7
Crawford Sq FK2 14 D4
Crawford St
Glasgow G11 96 A2
Hamilton ML3 162 A5
Motherwell ML1 163 D6
Port Glasgow PA14 47 C2
Crawfurd Ave G73 138 B5
Crawfurd Dr PA3 113 B6
Crawfurd Gdns G73 138 C4
Crawfurdland Pl KA2 221 D1
Crawfurd Rd G73 138 B4
Crawfurd St PA15 45 F6
Crawfurds View PA12 129 D4
Crawhin Gdns PA15 45 D3
Craw Pl PA12 129 C2
Craw Rd PA2 113 D3
Crawriggs Ave G66 79 D6
Creamery Rd ML2 165 D1
Creamery Row KA3 195 B7
Crebar Dr G78 134 C1
Crebar St G46 135 E4
Credon Dr
Airdrie ML6 123 A4
Crosshouse KA2 226 F8
Credon Gdns G73 138 C4
Cree Ave G64 78 D1
Creebank Pl KA10 229 F5
Cree Gdns G32 118 F5
Creelshaugh Rd KA3 213 B4
Cree Pl G75 159 B1
Creighton Gr G74 159 E1
Creigton Ct KA3 223 A5
Creinch Dr G83 19 F2
Creran Ct
Hamilton ML3 162 A1
Prestwick KA9 236 C5
Creran Dr
Denny FK6 39 D6
Renfrew PA4 94 B4
Creran Path 12 ML2 165 F6
Crescent Gr G13 95 B5
Crescent Rd G13 95 B5
Crescent St PA15 46 B3
Crescent The
Clarkston G76 158 A5
Clydebank G81 73 E3
Longriggend ML6 84 D2
Milngavie G62 76 A8
Prestwick KA9 233 C1
Stewarton KA3 195 E1
Cressdale Ave G45 137 C1
Cressdale Ct G45 137 D2
Cressdale Dr G45 137 D2
Cresswell Gr G77 156 D3
Cresswell La G12 96 D3
Cresswell Pl G77 156 E2
Cresswell St 5 G12 96 D3
Cressy St G51 115 E8
Crest Ave G13 95 B8
Crestlea Ave PA2 133 E8
Creswell Terr G71 140 E6
Creteil Ct FK1 42 C3
Creveul Ct G83 27 E5
Crichton Ave KA24 191 A8
Crichton Ct G45 137 F2
Crichton Pl G21 97 E4
Crichton St
Coatbridge ML5 122 A7
Glasgow G21 97 E4
Cricketfield La PA6 91 B3
Crieff Ave ML6 123 D1
Criffell Gdns G32 119 D3
Criffell Rd G32 119 D3
Criffel Pl
Kilmarnock KA1 228 A4
Motherwell ML1 143 C3
Crighton Wynd ML4 141 D5
Crimea St G2 240 B2
Crimond Pl
Kilsyth G65 36 B1
Shieldhill FK1 66 E7
Crinan Cres ML5 101 D1
Crinan Gdns G64 78 C1
Crinan Pl
Ardrossan KA22 205 C5
Bellshill ML4 142 B4
Coatbridge ML5 101 D1
Crinan Rd G64 78 C1
Crinan St G31 118 B8
CRINDLEDYKE 166 C6
Crindledyke Cres ML2 166 B5
Cringate Gdns FK7 7 F1
Cripps Ave G81 74 D1
Crisswell Cl PA16 44 C2
Crisswell Cres PA16 44 C2
Crockett Pl FK2 24 B1
Crocus Bank KA7 239 C3
Crocus Gr KA12 219 C3
Croe Pl KA1 228 A4
Croft ML9 184 F2
Croftbank Ave G71 141 B1
Croftbank Cres
Bothwell G71 141 B1
Uddingston G71 140 F6
Croftbank Gate G71 141 B1
Croftbank St 2 G21 97 F4
Croftburn Dr G44 137 D4
Croftcot Ave ML4 141 F3
Croftcroighn Rd G33 99 B1
Croftcroighn Sch 2 G33 99 B2
Croftend Ave G44 137 E6
Croftend La G44 137 F5
Croft Est FK4 39 B3
CROFTFOOT 137 E5
Croftfoot Cres G45 138 A4
Croftfoot Dr G45 137 F4
Croftfoot Pl
Denny FK6 21 D4
Gartcosh G69 101 A6
Croftfoot Prim Sch G44 137 E5
Croftfoot Quadrant G45 137 E4
Croftfoot Rd G45 137 E4
Croftfoot St G45 138 A4
Croftfoot Sta G44 137 E6
Croftfoot Terr G45 137 F4
Croft Gdns G72 139 B5
Crofthead KA11 220 A3
Crofthead Ave KA3 223 A5
Crofthead Cotts G78 154 C7
Crofthead Cres ML4 141 F3
Crofthead Ct
Irvine KA11 220 A3
Stirling FK8 2 A1
Crofthead Dr G66 33 C1
Crofthead Ind Est G78 154 C7
Crofthead Pl
Bellshill ML4 141 F3
Newton Mearns G77 156 F3
Crofthead Rd
Ayr KA7 239 D6
Kilmaurs KA3 222 B7
Prestwick KA9 233 C1
Stirling FK8 2 A1
Crofthead St
Falkirk FK2 41 F8
Uddingston G71 140 F6
Crofthill Ave G71 140 F6
Crofthill Cl KA24 191 D8
Crofthill Ct ML9 198 E2
Crofthill Rd G44 137 E5
Crofthouse Dr G44 137 E4
Croftmont Ave G44 137 E4
Croftmoraig Ave G69 81 A4
Crofton Ave G44 137 D4
Crofton Dr PA4 94 E4
Crofton Wynd ML6 103 D1
Croftpark Ave G44 137 D5
Croftpark Cres G72 161 E6
Croftpark Rd G81 74 B7
Croftpark St ML4 142 A6
Croft Pl ML9 184 F3
Croft Rd
Balmore G64 77 E8
Cambuslang G72 139 B5
East Kilbride G75 180 E7
Larkhall ML9 184 F3
Croftshaw Rd FK12 5 A7
Croftside Ave G44 137 E4
Croftspar Ave G32 119 C6
Croftspar Ct G32 119 D6
Croftspar Dr G32 119 C6
Croftspar Gate G32 119 D6
Croftspar Gr G32 119 D6
Croftspar Pl G32 119 C6
Croft's Rd FK10 4 B3
Croft St
Alexandria G83 27 F3
Kilmarnock KA1 222 F1
Croft Terr KA11 220 F2
Croft Way PA4 94 E1
Croftwood G64 78 A4
Croftwood Ave G44 137 D4
Croftwood Rd ML3 162 D1
Croft Wynd G71 141 A6
Crogal Cres ML6 123 D2
Cromalt Ave G75 180 B4
Cromalt Cres G61 75 D8
Cromarty Ave
Bishopbriggs G64 78 D2
Glasgow G43 136 F6
Cromarty Cres G61 75 F7
Cromarty Gdns G76 137 A1
Cromarty Pl
Chryston G69 80 D1
East Kilbride G74 160 C3
Cromarty Rd ML6 122 F5
Crombie Gdns 1 G69 120 A3
Cromdale Rd
Kilmarnock KA1 228 A4
Port Glasgow PA14 69 A6
Cromdale St G51 115 E7
Cromdale Way ML1 143 A2
Cromer Gdns G20 96 F5
Cromer Way PA3 113 D7
Cromlet Dr ML5 102 B1
Cromlix Gr ML6 104 B3
Crompton Ave G44 137 B5
Cromptons Gr PA1 113 B3
Crompton Way KA12 219 E4
Cromwell Dr FK1 42 D4
Cromwell La 5 G20 97 A2
Cromwell Rd
Ayr KA7 235 E1
Falkirk FK1 42 D4
Cromwell Road W FK1 42 D4
Cromwell St G20 97 A2
Crona Dr ML3 161 E4
Cronberry Quadrant G53 114 F3
Cronberry Terr G53 114 F3
Cronin Pl ML4 142 B7
Cronulla Pl G65 60 F8
Crook Castle Prim Sch
G53 115 B2
Crookdyke Ct ML6 105 B5
CROOKEDHOLM 228 E8
Crookedshields Rd G72,
G74 160 B7
CROOKFUR 156 D6
Crookfur Cottage Homes
G77 156 D5
Crookfur Prim Sch G77 156 D7
Crookfur Rd G77 156 D5
Crookfur Rdbt G77 156 C6
Crookhill Dr PA12 129 C3
Crookhill Gdns PA12 129 C3
CROOKSTON 114 F4
Crookston Ave G52 115 A4
Crookston Castle* G53 115 B2
Crookston Ct 7 G52 115 A4
Crookston Dr
3 Glasgow G52 115 A4
Paisley PA1, G52 114 F4
Crookston Gdns G52 114 F4
Crookston Gr 6 G52 115 A4
Crookstonhill Path G52 114 F4
Crookston Path G52 114 F4
Crookston Pl G52 114 F4
Crookston Quadrant 1
G52 115 A4
Crookston Rd
Glasgow, Crookston G52 115 A4
Glasgow, Pollok G53 115 A1
Crookston Sta G52 114 F4
Crookston Terr 2 G52 115 A4
Crophill FK10 5 C2
Crosbie Ct KA10 232 D8
Crosbie Dr
Paisley PA2 132 E7
West Kilbride KA23 190 D4
Crosbie La G20 96 C8
Crosbie Pl KA10 232 E7
Crosbie Rd KA10 232 E7
Crosbies Ct FK8 7 B7
Crosbie St G20 96 C8
Crosbie Terr KA9 236 D7
Crosbie Wood PA2 113 B1
Cross Arthurlie Sch G78 134 B4
Cross Arthurlie St G78 134 B3
Crossbank Ave G42 117 E1
Crossbank Dr G42 117 D1
Crossbank Rd G42 117 D1
Crossbank Terr G42 117 D1
Crossbow Gdns G72 160 F6
Cross Brae FK1 66 D6
CROSSBURN 86 E6
Crossburn KA7 238 B1
Crossburn Ave G62 54 F1
Crossburn Dr KA10 230 B4
Crossburn La KA10 230 B4
Crossburn Terr KA10 230 B4
Crossclyde View ML8 201 C2
Cross Ct G64 77 F1
Crossdene Rd KA2 226 F8
Crossdykes G66 80 A7
Crossen La ML8 188 B1
Crossflat Cres PA1 114 A5
CROSSFORD 201 B1
Crossford Dr 8 G23 76 E1
Crossgate G66 58 D1
Crossgates PA7 72 A3
Cross Gates ML4 142 A4
Crossgates St ML9 184 F4
Crosshall Pl FK1 66 D6
CROSSHILL
Allanton 166 F8
Baillieston 120 D5
Govanhill 117 A1
Crosshill Ave
Glasgow G42 117 B1
Kirkintilloch G66 79 D6
Crosshill Dr
Cleland ML1 144 B3
Rutherglen G73 138 B6
Crosshill Pl PA14 68 F7
Crosshill Rd
Bishopbriggs G64, G66 78 E5
Port Glasgow, Mid Auchinleck
PA14 68 E7
Port Glasgow PA14 68 F5
Crosshill St
Airdrie ML6 122 F7
Coatbridge ML5 121 B4
Lennoxtown G66 33 D1
Motherwell ML1 163 F6
Crosshill Sta G42 117 B1
Crosshill Wynd KA3 223 C6
CROSSHOUSE 221 F1
Crosshouse Hospl KA2 222 A2
Crosshouse Prim Sch
Crosshouse KA2 221 E1
East Kilbride G75 180 A5
Crosshouse Rd
East Kilbride G75 180 A5
Kilmaurs KA3 222 B5
Lennoxtown G66 33 A4
Crossing La ML9 200 B4
Cross Key's Ct 12 ML11 215 A4
Crosslaw Ave ML11 215 C3
Crosslaw Gdns ML11 215 C3
Crosslea Gdns PA6 111 B8
CROSSLEE 91 B1
Crosslee Cres PA6 91 C1
Crosslee Pk PA6 111 C8
Crosslee Rd
Bridge of Weir PA11 110 F6
Houston PA11 111 A7
Crosslees Ct G46 136 A4
Crosslees Dr
Glasgow G46 135 F3
Thornliebank G46 136 A4
Crosslees Pk G46 135 F3
Crosslees Rd G46 135 F2
Crosslee St G52 115 D5
CROSSLET 50 C3
Crosslet Ave G82 50 C4
Crosslet Ct G82 50 B3
Crosslet Pl G82 50 B3
Crosslet Rd G82 50 B3
Crossloan Rd G51 115 F7
Crossloan Terr G51 116 A7
CROSSMILL 134 C4
Crossmill Ave G78 134 D4
Crossmount Ct ML8 187 E1
CROSSMYLOOF 116 D2
Crossmyloof Gdns G41 116 D1
Crossmyloof Sta G41 116 E1
Cross Orchard Way ML4 142 A5
Crosspoint Dr 7 G23 76 E1
Cross Rd PA2 113 B2
Crossroads KA24 170 C3
Cross Shore St PA15 46 A5
Cross St
Falkirk FK2 24 B1
Glasgow G32 119 C1
Cross Stone Pl ML1 163 F6
Cross The
8 Alloa FK10 10 B6
Beith KA15 171 B8
Dalry KA24 191 C7
Glasgow G1 241 B1
Kilbarchan PA10 111 A3
Kilmarnock KA1 227 F8
Prestwick KA9 233 C1
Stewarton KA3 211 D8
Stonehouse ML9 198 F2
West Kilbride KA23 190 D5
Crosstobs Rd G53 115 A1
Crossveggate Bsns Pk
G62 55 B1
Crossview Ave G69 120 D5
Crossview Pl G69 120 D5
Crossways PA6 91 D2
Crosveggate G62 55 B1
Crovie Rd G53 135 A7
Crow Ave ML1 143 B5
Crowflats Rd G71 140 E6
Crowflat View G71 121 D1
Crowhill Cres ML6 102 F2
Crowhill Dr G33 119 E6
Crowhill Rd G64 97 F8
Crowhill St G22 97 D6
Crowlin Cres G33 119 B7
Crown Ave G81 74 B3
Crown Cir 7 G12 96 C3
Crownest Loan FK5 23 E2
Crown Gdns
Alloa FK10 9 F8
14 Glasgow G12 96 C3
Crownhall Pl G32 119 C5
Crownhall Rd G32 119 C5
Crownhill Ct ML6 102 E3
Crownpoint Rd G40 117 F5
Crown Road N G12 96 C3
Crown Road S G12 96 C3
Crown Sq KA8 235 F2
Crown St
Ayr KA8 235 F2
Calderbank ML6 123 B3
Coatbridge ML5 122 C7
Glasgow G5 117 B4
Glasgow G5 117 C4
Glasgow, Gorbals G5 117 C5
Glasgow, North Mount Vernon
G69 119 F3
Greenock PA15 45 F5
Crown Terr G12 96 C3
Crow Rd
Glasgow, Anniesland G13 95 F5
Glasgow, Hyndland G11 96 A2
Glasgow, Kelvindale G13 95 F7
Lennoxtown G66 33 A5
Stonehouse ML9 198 E2
Crow Wood Cres ML6 123 B2
Crowwood Dr ML6 123 D7
Crowwood Rd ML6 123 B2
Crow Wood Rd G69 100 B7
Crow Wood Terr G69 100 B7
CROY 60 F4
Croy G74 159 D3
Croy Ave G77 157 A5
Croy Bank Ct G68 60 F2
Croy Hill Roman Fort*
G68 61 A5
Croy Pl G21 98 C5
Croy Rd
Coatbridge ML5 121 F4
Glasgow G21 98 C5
Croy Sta G68 60 F3
Crozier Cres FK5 23 B2
Cruachan Ave
Paisley PA2 133 E8
Renfrew PA4 94 C1
Stirling FK9 2 B3
Cruachan Ct FK1 42 C2
Cruachan Dr
Barrhead G78 134 C1
Newton Mearns G77 156 F3
Cruachan Pl KA1 228 B4
Cruachan Rd
Bearsden G61 75 B7
Rutherglen G73 138 D3
Cruachan St
Glasgow G46 135 F4
Thornliebank G46 136 A4
Cruachan Way G78 134 C1
Cruckburn Wynd FK7 6 F4
Cruden St G51 115 F6
Cruickshank Dr FK1 66 D6
Cruikshank's Ct FK6 21 E1
Crum Ave G46 136 A3
Crum Cres FK7 7 C2
Crummieholm Gdns
KA10 230 A4
Crummock Gdns KA15 150 C1
Crummock St KA15 150 C1
Crusader Ave G13 75 D1
Crusader Cres KA3 211 C8
Cubie St G40 117 F5
Cubrieshaw Dr KA23 190 D4
Cubrieshaw Pk KA23 190 E4
Cubrieshaw St KA23 190 D5
Cuckoo Way ML1 143 B5
Cuff Cres KA15 171 A7
Cuilhill Rd G69 121 A7
Cuillin Ct FK1 42 C1
Cuillin Pl
Chapelhall ML6 123 F1
Irvine KA11 220 A4
Kilmarnock KA1 228 A3
Larkhall ML9 185 C2
Cuillins Ave PA14 68 F6
Cuillins Rd G73 138 D3
Cuillins The
Moodiesburn G69 81 A4
Uddingston G71 120 E1
Cuillin Way G78 134 C2
Cuilmuir Terr G65 60 F4
Cuilmuir View G65 60 F5
Cuilt Pl G63 31 A4
Cuilts Rd G63 30 B4
Culbin Dr G13 95 A8
Cullen PA8 73 A3
Cullen La 1 G75 180 E7
Cullen Pl G71 141 A8
Cullen Rd
East Kilbride G75 180 D7
Motherwell ML1 163 C5
Cullen St
Alexandria G83 27 C7
Glasgow G32 119 A4
Cullion Way ML1 144 A5
Culloch Rd
Bearsden G61 75 C8
Slamannan FK1 86 B6
Cullochrig Rd ML6 82 F1
Culloden Ave ML4 142 D4
Culloden Pl KA3 223 B3
Culloden St G31 118 B8
Culmore Pl FK1 42 E1
Culrain Gdns G32 119 A5

Culrain St G32 119 A4
Culross Hill G74 159 D1
Culross Pl
Coatbridge ML5 121 F7
East Kilbride G74 159 D1
Culross St G32 119 C4
Culross Way G69 81 A3
Cultenhove Cres FK7 7 A3
Cultenhove Pl FK7 7 A3
Cultenhove Rd
Stirling, Coxet Hill FK7 7 A3
Stirling FK7 7 A4
Culterfell Path ML1 144 C2
Cult Rd G66 79 E4
Cults St G51 115 F6
Culvain Ave G61 75 B7
Culvain Pl FK1 42 C2
Culzean ML6 102 F5
Culzean Ave
Coatbridge ML5 121 E4
Prestwick KA9 236 D7
Culzean Cres
Glasgow G69 120 A4
Kilmarnock KA3 228 C8
Newton Mearns G77 157 A4
Culzean Ct ML5 121 E5
Culzean Dr
East Kilbride G74 159 D3
Glasgow G32 119 D4
Gourock PA19 43 F5
Motherwell ML1 143 C3
Culzean Pl
East Kilbride G74 159 D3
Kilwinning KA13 207 C2
Stenhousemuir FK5 23 F4
Culzean Rd KA7 238 D3
Cumberland Ave G84 16 A3
Cumberland Ct PA16 44 E4
Cumberland Pl
Coatbridge ML5 121 D4
9 Glasgow G5 117 C4
Cumberland Rd
Greenock PA16 44 E4
Rhu G84 15 D5
Cumberland St
Glasgow G5 117 B5
Glasgow G5 117 C4
Cumberland Terr G84 15 D5
Cumberland Wlk PA16 44 E4
CUMBERNAULD 62 C5
Cumbernauld Airport G68 62 B7
Cumbernauld Coll (Cumbernauld Campus) G67 61 F1
Cumbernauld Coll (East Dunbartonshire Campus) G66 79 C8
Cumbernauld High Sch G67 62 C1
Cumbernauld Prim Sch
Cumbernauld, Carrickstone G68 61 D5
Cumbernauld, Kildrum G67 62 B4
Cumbernauld Rd
Chryston G69 100 C7
Cumbernauld G67 81 D4
Glasgow, Dennistoun G31 118 B7
Glasgow, Dennistoun G31, G33 118 C7
Glasgow, Riddrie G33 98 E1
Haggs FK4 39 A3
Moodiesburn G68, G69 81 B3
Muirhead G69 100 C7
Stepps G33 99 D5
Cumbernauld Sta G67 83 A8
CUMBERNAULD VILLAGE 62 A6
Cumbrae G74 160 C1
Cumbrae Ave PA14 69 B7
Cumbrae Cres ML5 122 E5
Cumbrae Crescent N G82 49 C5
Cumbrae Crescent S G82 49 C5
Cumbrae Ct
Clydebank G81 74 B2
Irvine KA11 225 C8
Cumbrae Dr
Falkirk FK1 41 C4
Kilmarnock KA3 223 B5
Motherwell ML1 163 C8
Cumbrae Ho KA9 236 B5
Cumbrae Pl
Coatbridge ML5 122 E4
Gourock PA19 44 D6
West Kilbride KA23 190 C4
Cumbrae Rd
Paisley PA2 133 E7
Renfrew PA4 94 D1
Saltcoats KA21 205 F2
Cumbrae St G33 119 A8
Cumbrae Terr KA22 205 C3
Cumlodden Dr G20 96 D7
Cumming Ave ML8 202 C8
Cumming Dr G42 137 B8
Cumnock Dr
Airdrie ML6 123 A4
Barrhead G78 134 D1
Hamilton ML3 161 D1
Cumnock Rd G33 98 E6
Cumroch Rd G66 33 C1
Cunard Ct G81 94 B8
Cunard St G81 94 B8
Cuninghame Dr KA20 206 B1
Cuninghame Rd
Ardrossan KA22 205 C3
Kilbarchan PA10 111 B3
Cunningair Dr ML1 163 E4
Cunningham Cres KA7 239 C6
Cunningham Dr
Duntocher G81 73 F6
Glasgow G46 136 E3
Harthill ML7 127 D5
Cunninghame Cres KA21 217 A8
Cunninghame Dr KA1 227 E4
Cunninghame Rd
East Kilbride G74 159 E1
Irvine KA12 224 D8
Prestwick KA9 236 C7
Rutherglen G73 138 C8
Saltcoats KA21 217 A8
Cunningham Gdns
Falkirk FK2 42 F5
Houston PA6 91 D1
CUNNINGHAMHEAD 221 B8
Cunninghamhead Est Cvn Pk KA3 220 F8
Cunningham Pl KA7 239 C6
Cunningham Rd
Glasgow G52 114 F8
Stenhousemuir FK5 24 A3
Stirling FK7 7 D7
Cunningham St ML1 163 D6
Cunningham Watt Rd KA3 195 D1
Cunning Park Dr KA7 238 D3
Cupar Dr PA16 44 F3
Cuparhead Ave ML5 121 E4
Cuppleton Brae PA9, PA12 130 B2
Curfew Rd G13 75 D1
Curle St
Glasgow G14 95 D2
Glasgow G14 95 E2
Curlew Cres PA16 45 B4
Curlew Dr G75 180 A5
Curlew La PA16 45 B4
Curlew Pl PA5 131 C7
Curling Cres G44 137 C7
Curlinghaugh Cres ML2 165 C3
Curlingmire G75 180 E7
Curran Ave ML2 164 E1
Currie Ct KA22 205 C1
Currie Pl G20 96 F6
Currieside Ave ML7 146 E4
Currieside Pl ML7 146 D4
Currie St G20 96 E6
Cursiter Ct FK5 23 B2
Curtecan Pl KA7 238 F6
Curtis Ave G44 137 D7
Curzon St G20 96 F6
Cushenquarter Dr FK7 12 D3
Custom House Mus* PA15 46 A5
Customhouse Pl PA15 46 A5
Custom House Quay Ret Pk PA15 46 A6
Custom House Way PA15 46 A5
Customs Rdbt FK8 2 B1
Custonhall Pl FK6 21 D2
Cuthbert Pl KA3 223 A2
Cuthbertson Prim Sch G42 117 A3
Cuthbertson St G42 117 A2
Cuthbert St G71 141 B7
Cuthelton Dr G31 118 E4
Cuthelton St G31 118 D4
Cuthelton Terr G31 118 D4
Cutsburn Pl KA3 211 F8
Cutsburn Rd KA3 211 F8
Cutstraw Rd KA3 211 F8
Cut The G71 140 F5
Cuttyfield Pl FK2 24 C3
Cutty Sark Pl G82 50 C2
Cypress Ave
Beith KA15 150 C2
Blantyre G72 140 C1
Uddingston G71 141 B8
Cypress Cres G75 180 C5
Cypress Ct
East Kilbride G75 180 C5
Hamilton ML3 162 E2
Kirkintilloch G66 79 B6
Cypress Gdns KA11 219 E5
Cypress Gr
Coatbridge G69 121 B6
Quarriers Village PA11 89 F2
Cypress Pl G75 180 C5
Cypress St G22 97 D5
Cypress Way G72 139 F4
Cyprus Ave PA5 112 B2
Cyril St PA1 114 A4

D

Daer Ave PA4 94 E1
Daer Way ML3 162 A3
Daffodil Way ML1 163 E8
Daintree Terr FK1 41 E5
Dairsie Ct G44 136 F4
Dairsie Gdns G64 98 D8
Dairsie House Sch G43 136 E6
Dairsie St G44 136 F4
Dairy Mead Pl KA22 205 D2
Daisybank KA14 170 C6
Daisy Cotts KA8 236 A3
Daisy St G42 117 B2
Dakala Ct ML2 165 A2
Dakota Way PA4 94 D1
Dalbeattie Braes ML6 123 E1
Dalbeattie Dr 1 G72 161 D3
DALBETH 118 E2
Dalbeth Pl G32 118 F2
Dalbeth Rd G32 118 F2
Dalblair Ct KA7 238 F8
Dalblair Rd KA7 238 F7
Dalby Gr ML5 101 F7
Dalcharn Pl G34 120 A8
Dalcraig Cres G72 140 C2
Dalcross St G11 96 C2
Dalcross Way ML6 104 A3
Dalcruin Gdns G69 81 A4
Dalderse Ave FK2 42 B6
Daldowie Ave G32 119 D3
Daldowie Doocot* G69 119 F2
Daldowie Rd G71 120 A2
Daldowie St ML5 121 E3
Dale Ave G75 180 D6
Dale Cres KA12 219 D4
Dale Ct ML2 164 C2
Dale Dr ML1 143 A4
Dale Path G40 117 F4
Dalespark Rdbt KA2 222 A1
Dale St
Glasgow G40 117 F4
Glasgow G40 118 A4
Daleview Ave G12 96 B6
Daleview Dr G76 157 D6
Daleview Gr G76 157 D6
Dale Way G73 138 B4
Dalfoil Ct PA1 114 F4
Dalgain Ct KA11 220 A5
Dalgarroch Ave G81 94 E8
DALGARVEN 207 D8
Dalgarven Mews KA3 223 C6
Dalgarven Mill-Ayrshire Mus of Country Life & Costume* KA13 207 D8
Dalgarven Wynd KA13 207 C6
Dalgleish Ave G81 73 F6
Dalgleish Ct FK8 7 B8
Dalgleish Pl ML2 166 B3
Dalhousie Gdns G64 78 A2
Dalhousie La G3 240 B4
Dalhousie Rd PA10 111 B2
Dalhousie St G3 240 C4
Dalilea Dr G34 100 D1
Dalilea Pl G34 100 D1
Dalintober St G5 240 B1
Daljarrock KA13 207 B2
Dalkeith Ave
Bishopbriggs G64 78 B4
Glasgow G41 116 B4
Dalkeith Rd G64 78 B4
Dallas Ct KA10 229 D2
Dallas La KA10 229 D2
Dallas Pl KA10 229 D2
Dallas Rd KA10 229 D2
Dalmacoulter Rd ML6 103 B3
Dalmahoy Cres PA11 110 C6
Dalmahoy St G32 118 E7
Dalmahoy Way KA13 207 B3
Dalmailing Ave KA11 220 B1
Dalmally St
Glasgow G20 96 F3
Greenock PA15 46 F2
DALMARNOCK 118 A2
Dalmarnock Ct G40 118 B3
Dalmarnock Prim Sch G40 118 A4
Dalmarnock Rd G40 118 A3
Dalmarnock Road Trad Est G73 118 B1
Dalmarnock Sta G40 118 A3
Dalmary Dr PA1 114 B5
Dalmellington Ct
East Kilbride G74 159 D2
Hamilton ML3 161 D1
Dalmellington Dr
East Kilbride G74 159 D2
9 Glasgow G53 135 A8
Dalmellington Rd
Ayr KA7 239 C4
Glasgow G53 115 A1
Dalmeny Ave G46 136 C3
Dalmeny Dr G78 134 A2
Dalmeny Rd ML3 162 D2
Dalmeny St G5 117 E2
DALMILLING 236 E1
Dalmilling Cres KA8 236 D2
Dalmilling Dr KA8 236 E2
Dalmilling Prim Sch KA8 236 E2
Dalmilling Rd KA8 236 E2
Dalmoak Rd PA15 46 C1
DALMONACH 27 F5
Dalmonach Rd G83 27 F4
Dalmore Cres
Helensburgh G84 16 A3
1 Motherwell ML1 143 A2
Dalmore Dr
Airdrie ML6 123 A6
Alva FK12 4 E6
Dalmore Ho G84 16 A3
Dalmore Pl KA11 219 F6
Dalmore Way KA11 219 F6
Dalmorglen Pk FK7 6 F6
DALMUIR 73 E4
Dalmuir Sta G81 73 E3
Dalnair Pl G62 54 D2
Dalnair St G3 96 D1
Dalness St G32 119 A4
Dalnottar Ave G60 73 B6
Dalnottar Dr G60 73 B5
Dalnottar Gdns G60 73 B5
Dalnottar Hill Rd G60 73 B6
Dalnottar Terr G60 73 B6
Dalquhurn Gdns G82 49 D8
Dalquhurn La
Dumbarton G82 49 E8
Renton G82 49 E8
Dalreoch Ave G69 120 C6
Dalreoch Ct G82 49 D4
Dalreoch Path G69 120 C5
Dalreoch Prim Sch G82 49 C5
Dalreoch Sta G82 49 E4
Dalriada G2 240 B2
Dalriada Cres ML1 142 D1
Dalriada Dr G64 78 C8
Dalriada Rd PA16 44 D3
Dalriada St G40 118 C4
DALRY 191 C8
Dalry Gdns ML3 161 D2
Dalry La KA22 205 C4
Dalrymple Ct
Irvine KA12 219 E3
Kirkintilloch G66 79 D7
Dalrymple Dr
Coatbridge ML5 121 F5
East Kilbride G74 159 E3
Irvine KA12 219 E3
Newton Mearns G77 157 A4
Dalrymple Pl KA12 219 D3
Dalrymple St PA15 45 F6
Dalry Pl ML6 143 D8
Dalry Prim Sch KA24 191 B7
Dalry Rd
Ardrossan KA22 205 C4
Beith KA15 171 A7
Kilbirnie KA25 170 A7
Kilwinning KA13 207 D4
Saltcoats KA21 206 A2
Stewarton KA3 211 C8
Uddingston G71 141 B7
Dalry St G32 119 B4
Dalry Sta KA24 191 D7
DALSERF 186 C2
Dalserf Cres G46 136 B1
Dalserf Ct G31 118 B5
Dalserf Gdns G31 118 B5
Dalserf Path 18 ML9 185 C1
Dalserf Pl G31 118 B5
Dalserf Prim Sch ML9 199 F8
Dalserf St G31 118 B5
Dalsetter Ave G15 75 A2
Dalsetter Bsns Ctr G15 75 A2
Dalsetter Pl G15 75 A2
DALSHANNON 82 A6
Dalshannon Pl G67 82 A7
Dalshannon Rd G67 82 B7
Dalshannon View G67 82 B7
Dalshannon Way G67 82 A7
Dalsholm Ave G20 96 B7
Dalsholm Rd G20 96 B8
Dalskeith Ave PA3 113 A5
Dalskeith Cres PA3 113 A5
Dalskeith Rd PA3 113 A5
Dalswinton Path G34 120 D8
Dalswinton St G34 120 C8
Dalton Ave G81 74 E1
Dalton Ct G31 118 E5
Dalton Hill ML3 161 E2
Dalton Pk KA7 238 B2
Dalton St G31 118 E5
Dalvait Ct G83 27 F8
Dalvait Gdns G83 27 E8
Dalvait Rd 2 G83 27 E8
Dalveen Ct G78 134 C1
Dalveen Dr G71 140 F8
Dalveen Quadrant ML5 122 D5
Dalveen St G32 118 F5
Dalveen Way G73 138 C3
Dalwhinnie Ave G72 140 C2
Dalwhinnie Cres KA3 222 D4
Dalwhinnie Ct KA11 219 F6
Dalwhinnie Gdns KA3 222 D3
Dalwood Rd KA9 236 B8
Daly Gdns G72 140 E1
Dalzell Ave ML1 164 A4
Dalzell Dr ML1 164 A4
Dalzell Estate* ML1 163 F3
Dalziel Cres G72 139 D6
Dalziel Ct ML3 162 A3
Dalziel Dr
Glasgow G41 116 C3
Glasgow G41 116 D3
Dalziel Gait 3 G72 139 D6
Dalziel Gr 5 G72 139 D6
Dalziel High Sch ML1 163 D6
Dalziel Path 4 G72 139 D6
Dalziel Quadrant G41 116 C3
Dalziel Rd G52 114 F8
Dalziel St
Hamilton ML3 162 B5
Motherwell ML1 163 F7
Dalziel Twr ML1 164 B3
Dalziel Way G72 139 D5
Damhead Rd KA1 227 E3
Dampark KA3 195 C7
Damshot Cres G53 115 D1
Damshot Rd G53 135 D8
Damside KA8 235 F2
Danby Rd G69 119 F4
Danes Ave 1 G14 95 C4
Danes Cres G14 95 B5
Danes Dr G14 95 C4
Danes Lane N 3 G14 95 C4
Danes Lane S G14 95 C4
Daniel McLaughlin Pl G66 58 E1
Dankeith Dr KA1 231 C4
Dankeith Rd KA1 231 C4
Dargarvel Ave G41 116 B4
Dargavel Ave PA7 72 B3
Dargavel Rd
Bishopton PA7 72 D1
Erskine PA8 72 E1
Darg Rd KA20 217 D8
Dark Brig Rd ML8 201 B2
Darkwood Cres PA3 113 B6
Darkwood Ct PA3 113 B6
Darkwood Dr PA3 113 B6
Darleith Rd
Alexandria G83 27 E6
Cardross G82 26 A1
Darleith St G32 118 F5
Darley Cres KA10 229 E1
Darley Pl
Hamilton ML3 183 B8
Troon KA10 229 E1
Darley Rd G68 61 E5
Darlington View KA3 195 F1
Darluith Pk PA5 111 C6
Darluith Rd PA3 111 F6
Darmeid Pl ML7 167 B8
Darmule Dr KA13 207 C5
Darnaway Ave G33 99 D2
Darnaway Dr G33 99 D2
Darnaway St G33 99 D2
Darndaff Rd PA15 46 A2
Darngaber Gdns ML3 183 E3
Darngaber Rd ML3 183 E3
Darngavel Ct ML6 122 D8
Darngavil Rd ML6 103 E6
Darnick St G21 98 B2
Darnley Cres G64 77 F3
Darnley Dr KA1 227 E5
Darnley Gdns G41 116 E2
Darnley Ind Est G53 135 B5
Darnley Mains Rd G53 135 C3
Darnley Path G46 135 E5
Darnley Pl G41 116 E2
Darnley Prim Sch G53 135 C4
Darnley Rd
Barrhead G78 134 E3
Glasgow G41 116 E2
Darnley St
Glasgow G41 116 F3
Stirling FK8 7 A8
Darnshaw Cl KA11 220 C5
Darrach Dr FK6 21 A2
Darragh Gn ML2 166 A6
Darroch Ave PA19 44 E7
Darroch Dr
Erskine PA8 72 F3
Gourock PA19 44 E7
Darroch Way G67 62 A3
Dartford St G22 97 B3
Dartmouth Ave PA19 44 E5
Darvel Ave KA3 223 B6
Darvel Cres PA1 114 E4
Darvel Dr G77 157 A5
Darvel Gr G72 161 D2
Darwin Ave ML2 164 B4
Darwin Pl G81 73 D4
Darwin Rd G75 180 C8
Davaar G74 160 C1
Davaar Dr
Coatbridge ML5 121 D7
Kilmarnock KA3 223 B5
Motherwell ML1 142 C2
Paisley PA2 133 E7
Davaar Pl
Falkirk FK1 41 C4
Newton Mearns G77 156 C6
Davaar Rd
Greenock PA16 44 D3
Renfrew PA4 94 D2
Saltcoats KA21 205 F2
Davaar St G40 118 B4
Davan Loan 10 ML2 165 F6
Dava St G51 116 A7
Dave Barrie Ave ML9 184 F5
Daventry Dr G12 96 A5
Davey St PA16 45 C5
David Dale Ave KA3 211 C8
David Gage St KA13 207 E5
David Gray Dr G66 59 A1
David Livingstone Ctr* G72 140 E2
David Livingstone Meml Prim Sch G72 140 D1
David Orr St KA1 222 E1
David Pl
Glasgow G69 119 F4
Paisley PA3 114 B7
David's Cres KA13 207 D2
David's Loan FK2 24 D1
Davidson Ave KA14 170 D6
Davidson Cres G65 59 F3
Davidson Dr PA19 44 E7
Davidson Gdns
Glasgow G14 95 E4
Stonehouse ML9 198 E1
Davidson La ML8 188 B1
Davidson Pl
Ayr KA8 236 A1
Glasgow G32 119 C6
Davidson Quadrant G81 73 F7
Davidson Rd G83 27 F7
Davidson St
Airdrie ML6 122 F8
Bannockburn FK7 7 C1
Clydebank G81 94 E8
Coatbridge ML5 122 B4
Glasgow G40 118 A2
David St
Coatbridge ML5 122 C7
Glasgow G40 118 A5
Salsburgh ML7 125 B2
Davidston Pl G66 79 F4
David Way PA3 114 B7
Davieland Rd G46 136 A1
Davie's Acre G74 158 F4
Davies Dr G83 27 E6
Davies Quadrant ML1 142 D2
Davies Row FK6 21 E2
Davington Dr ML3 161 D1
Daviot St 2 G51 115 D6

Dawnlight Circ KA22 205 B1
Dawsholm Ind Est G20 96 B7
Dawson Ave
Alloa FK10 9 F8
East Kilbride G75 159 B1
Dawson Pl G4 97 B3
Dawson Rd G4 97 B3
Dawson St FK2 42 B8
Deaconsbank Ave G46 135 E1
Deaconsbank Cres G46 135 D1
Deaconsbank Gdns G46 135 E1
Deaconsbank Gr G46 135 D1
Deaconsbank Pl G46 135 D1
Deaconsbrook La G46 135 D1
Deaconsbrook Rd G46 135 D1
Deaconsgait Way G46 135 D1
Deaconsgrange Rd G46 135 D1
Deacons Rd G65 60 E8
Deacons View G46 135 D1
Dealston Rd G78 134 B4
Deanbank Rd ML5 121 D7
Deanbrae St G71 140 F6
Dean Castle* KA3 223 B3
Dean Castle Ctry Pk* KA3 223 B4
Dean Cres
Chryston G69 80 D1
Hamilton ML3 162 C1
Stirling FK8 2 C1
Dean Ct
Clydebank G81 74 C1
11 Kilmarnock KA3 222 F1
Deanfield Ct KA13 207 E3
Deanfield Quadrant G52 114 F6
Dean La KA3 223 A1
DEAN PARK 94 D2
Dean Park Ave G71 141 A2
Dean Park Dr G72 139 D4
Dean Park Rd PA4 94 E2
Dean Pl KA2 226 F8
Dean Rd
Kilbirnie KA25 149 B2
Kilmarnock KA3 223 B3
Deans Ave G72 139 D3
Deanside Rd G52 115 A8
Dean St
Bellshill ML4 142 B5
Clydebank G81 74 C1
Kilmarnock KA3 223 A2
Stewarton KA3 195 E1
Deanston Ave G78 134 B1
Deanston Dr G41 136 E8
Deanstone Pl ML5 122 D3
Deanstone Wlk ML5 122 D2
Deanston Gdns G78 134 B1
Deanston Gr ML5 121 E3
Deanston Pk G78 134 B1
Dean Terr KA3 223 A3
Dean View KA3 223 D4
Deanwood Ave G44 136 F3
Deanwood Rd G44 136 F3
Deas Rd ML7 146 C5
Dechmont G75 180 D5
Dechmont Ave
Cambuslang G72 139 D3
Motherwell ML1 163 C7
Dechmont Cotts G72 139 F3
Dechmont Gdns
Blantyre G72 140 C1
Uddingston G71 120 E1
Dechmont Pl G72 139 D3
Dechmont Rd G71 120 E1
Dechmont St
Glasgow G31 118 C4
Hamilton ML3 162 C2
Dechmont View
Bellshill ML4 141 F3
Uddingston G71 141 A7
Dee Ave
Kilmarnock KA1 228 B4
Paisley PA2 112 F2
Renfrew PA4 94 E3
Dee Cres PA2 112 F2
Deedes St ML6 122 D6
Dee Dr PA2 112 F2
Dee Path
Larkhall ML9 199 A8
Motherwell ML1 143 B5
Deep Dale G74 159 C3
Deepdene Rd
Bearsden G61 75 D2
Moodiesburn G69 80 F2
Dee Pl
East Kilbride G75 179 E6
Johnstone PA5 131 C8
Deerdykes Court N G68 81 E6
Deerdykes Court S G68 81 E5
Deerdykes Pl G68 81 E6
Deerdykes Rd G67, G68 81 E5
Deerdykes Rdbt G68 81 C5
Deerdykes View G68 81 D6
Deer Park FK10 5 E1
Deer Park Ave KA20 217 E7
Deer Park Ct ML3 183 D7
Deer Park Pl ML3 183 E7
Deerpark Prim Sch FK10 5 F1
Deer Path ML7 127 E5
Deeside Dr ML8 188 A3
Deeside Pl ML5 122 D4
Dee St
Coatbridge ML5 101 D2
Glasgow G33 118 D8
Shotts ML7 146 D5
Dee Terr ML3 183 B8
Delaney Ct FK10 10 A6
Delaney Wynd ML1 165 B8
Delfie Dr PA16 45 B4
Delhi Ave G81 73 C4
Dellburn St ML1 164 A5
Dellburn Trad Pk ML1 164 A5
Dellingburn St 6 PA15 46 A4
Dell The
Bellshill ML4 142 D3
Newton Mearns G77 157 B5
Delny Pl G33 119 E7
Delph Rd FK10 4 C2
Delphwood Cres FK10 4 D2
Delph Wynd FK10 4 C2
Delves Ct ML11 215 A4
Delves Pk ML11 215 A4
Delves Rd ML11 215 A3
Delvin Rd G44 137 A6
De Moray Ct FK9 2 A4
Demoreham Ave FK6 21 F1
De Morville Pl KA15 171 B7
Dempsey Rd ML4 141 F3
Dempster Ct 4 PA15 45 F4
Dempster St PA15 45 E4
Den Bak Ave ML3 162 A2
Denbeath Ct ML3 163 C1
Denbecan FK10 10 D5
Denbeck St G32 118 F5
Denbrae St G32 118 F5
Dene Wlk G64 98 C8
Denewood Ave PA2 133 D8
Denham St G22 97 B3
Denholm Cres G75 180 E8
Denholm Dr
Glasgow G46 136 C1
Wishaw ML2 165 C6
Denholm Gdns
Greenock PA16 45 C5
Quarter ML3 183 E3
Denholm Gn 2 G75 180 F8
Denholm St PA16 45 D5
Denholm Terr
Greenock PA16 45 D5
Hamilton ML3 161 E3
Denholm Way
Beith KA15 171 A7
Kilmarnock KA1 228 A5
Den La ML7 146 D6
Denmark St
Glasgow G22 97 C4
Glasgow G22 97 C5
Denmilne Gdns G34 120 C7
Denmilne Path G34 120 C7
Denmilne Rd G34 120 D7
Denmilne St G34 120 C7
Denneystoun Cvn Pk G82 49 E4
Denniston Pl ML11 215 C5
DENNISTOUN 118 B7
Dennistoun Cres G84 25 C7
Dennistoun Rd PA14 70 C7
Dennistoun St ML4 142 B5
DENNY 21 F1
Denny Cres G82 50 A2
Denny High Sch FK6 39 E8
Dennyholm Wynd KA25 149 B1
DENNYLOANHEAD 39 D5
Denny Prim Sch FK6 21 D2
Denny Rd
Denny FK4 39 E6
Dumbarton G82 50 A2
Larbert FK5 23 A1
Dennystoun Forge G82 49 E4
DENNYSTOWN 49 E4
Denny Tank (Mus)* G82 50 A3
Denovan Rd FK6 21 E4
Dentdale G74 159 C3
Den The KA24 170 D3
Deramore Ave G46 157 A7
Derby St G3 96 E1
Derby Terrace La 4 G3 116 E8
Derby Wynd 1 ML1 143 B1
Deroran Pl FK8 6 F5
Derrywood Rd G66 58 C6
Dervaig Gdns ML6 84 D3
Derwent Ave FK1 41 F4
Derwent Ct KA3 222 F1
Derwent Dr ML5 101 D2
Derwent St G22 97 B4
Derwentwater G75 179 F6
Despard Ave G32 119 E4
Despard Gdns G32 119 E4
Deveron Ave G46 136 D2
Deveron Cres ML3 161 E4
Deveron Rd
Bearsden G61 75 D2
East Kilbride G74 160 B1
Kilmarnock KA1 228 A5
Motherwell ML1 143 B5
Troon KA10 229 G5
Deveron St
Coatbridge ML5 101 D1
Glasgow G33 98 D1
Devilla Ct KA9 236 C5
Devine Ct ML2 165 B3
Devine Gr ML2 166 A7
Devlin Ct
Hamilton G72 161 E7
Stirling FK7 7 B2
Devlin Gr G72 161 E7
DEVOL 68 D7
Devol Ave PA14 47 A1
Devol Cres G53 135 B8
Devol Ind Est PA14 68 D8
Devol Rd PA14 68 C6
Devonbank FK10 5 E3
Devon Ct FK10 4 B2
Devondale Ave G72 140 D1
Devon Dr
Bishopton PA7 72 C3
Tullibody FK10 4 E4
Devon Gdns
Bishopbriggs G64 77 F3
Devon Gdns *continued*
Carluke ML8 187 E2
Devonhill Ave ML3 183 D7
Devon Pl
Cambus FK10 4 A1
Glasgow G41 117 B4
Devonport Pk G75 180 A7
Devon Rd
Alloa FK10 10 C6
Greenock PA16 44 D4
Devonshire Gardens La 2 G12 96 B4
Devonshire Gdns 1 G12 96 B4
Devonshire Terr G12 96 B4
Devonshire Terrace La G12 96 B4
Devon St G5 117 B4
Devon Valley Dr FK10 5 D2
Devonview Pl ML6 122 F6
Devonview St ML6 122 F6
Devon Village FK10 5 E4
Devonway FK10 10 F5
Devon Way ML1 163 B6
Devon Wlk G68 81 E8
De Walden Dr KA3 223 B5
De Walden Terr KA3 223 A1
Dewar Cl G71 121 A1
Dewar Dr G15 75 A3
Dewar Gate G15 75 A3
Dewar Wlk ML8 201 B1
Dewshill Cotts ML7 126 B4
Dhuhill Drive E G84 16 E4
Diamond Cotts KA6 237 B4
Diamond St ML4 142 A4
Diana Ave G13 95 B8
Diana Quadrant ML1 143 A5
Diana Vernon Ct G84 25 B8
Dickburn Cres FK4 39 F5
Dick Cres KA12 219 D5
Dick Ct ML9 198 E2
Dickens Ave G81 74 A4
Dickens Gr ML1 143 D2
Dickies Wells FK12 5 C7
Dick Institute Mus* KA1 228 A8
Dick Quad G82 48 A8
Dick Rd KA1 228 A8
Dickson Ct KA15 150 C1
Dickson Dr KA12 219 C5
Dickson Path ML4 141 F2
Dickson Sq ML1 144 B1
Dickson St ML9 185 C1
Dicks Pk G75 180 D8
Dick St G20 96 F3
Dick Terr KA12 219 D5
Diddup Dr KA20 206 B1
Differ Ave G65 59 F2
Dillichip Cl G83 27 F2
Dillichip Gdns G83 27 F3
Dillichip Loan G83 27 E3
Dillichip Terr G83 27 F3
Dilwara Ave G14 95 E2
Dimity St PA5 111 F3
DIMSDALE 165 C1
Dimsdale Cres ML2 165 C1
Dimsdale Rd ML2 165 C1
Dinard Dr G46 136 C4
Dinart St G33 98 D1
Dinduff St G34 100 C1
Dineiddwg G62 55 B6
Dingwall Dr PA16 44 F3
Dinmont Ave PA2 112 F1
Dinmont Cres ML1 142 D2
Dinmont Pl 1 G41 116 E1
Dinmont Rd G41 116 D1
Dinmont Way PA2 112 F1
Dinmurchie Rd KA10 229 F6
Dinnet Way 11 ML2 165 F6
Dinwiddie St G21 98 C2
Dinyra Pl ML5 101 C6
Dippin Pl KA21 205 F2
Dipple Ct KA25 149 B2
Dipple Pl G15 75 B2
Dipple Rd KA25 149 B3
Dipple View KA25 149 B3
Dirleton Dr
Glasgow G41 136 F8
Paisley PA2 113 A1
Dirleton Gate G61 75 D2
Dirleton Gdns FK10 9 F7
Dirleton La FK10 9 F6
Dirleton Pl G41 136 E8
DIRRANS 207 F2
Dirrans Terr KA13 207 F2
Disraeli Way G75 179 D8
Ditton Dr KA1 227 E4
Divernia Way G78 155 D8
Diverswell FK10 5 D2
Divert Rd PA19 44 C6
Divert Wlk PA19 44 C6
Dixon Ave
Dumbarton G82 49 E3
Glasgow G42 117 B1
Dixon Dr G82 49 D2
Dixon Pl G74 159 B3
Dixon Rd
Glasgow G42 117 C1
Helensburgh G84 16 E3
Dixons Blazes Ind Est G42, G5 117 C3
Dixon St
Coatbridge ML5 122 B4
Glasgow G1 240 C1
Hamilton ML3 162 D3
Paisley PA1 113 F4
Dobbie Ave
Larbert FK5 41 C8
Stenhousemuir FK5 23 C1
Dobbies Ct ML8 187 A6
Dobbie's Loan G4 241 A4
Dobbie's Loan Pl G4 241 B3
Dochart Ave PA4 94 E1
Dochart Dr ML5 101 D2
Dochart Pl FK1 42 D2
Dochart St G33 98 E2
Dock Breast PA15 46 A5
Dockhead Pl KA21 216 F7
Dockhead St KA21 216 F7
Dock Rd KA22 205 B1
Dock St
Clydebank G81 94 D7
Falkirk FK2 24 C2
Dodhill Pl G13 95 B6
Dodside Gdns G32 119 C4
Dodside Pl G32 119 C4
Dodside Rd G77 155 E3
Dodside St G32 119 C4
Dolan St G69 120 B5
Dollar Ave FK2 42 A7
Dollar Gdns FK2 42 A7
Dollar Ind Est FK1, FK2 42 A5
Dollar Pk ML1 164 B3
Dollar Terr G20 96 C8
Dolphin Rd G41 116 D2
Dominica Gn 4 G75 159 A1
Donald Cres KA10 229 E3
Donal Dewar L Ctr G15 75 A3
Donaldfield Rd PA11 110 B7
Donaldson Ave
Alloa FK10 4 E1
Kilsyth G65 60 E7
Saltcoats KA21 216 F8
Stevenston KA20 206 E2
Donaldson Cres G66 79 C7
Donaldson Dr
Irvine KA12 219 D4
Kilmarnock KA3 223 D3
Renfrew PA4 94 D3
Donaldson Gn G71 141 B8
Donaldson Pl
Cambusbarron FK7 6 D6
Kirkintilloch G66 79 D7
Donaldson Rd
Kilmarnock KA3 223 D3
Larkhall ML9 185 C1
Donaldson St
Hamilton ML3 162 A5
Kirkintilloch G66 79 C7
Donaldswood Pk PA2 133 C8
Donaldswood Rd PA2 133 C8
Donald Terr ML3 162 C1
Donald Way G71 141 A7
Don Ave PA4 94 E2
Doncaster St G20 97 A3
Don Ct ML3 183 A8
Don Dr PA2 112 F1
Dongola Rd KA7 239 A7
Donnelly Way ML2 164 C4
Donnies Brae G78 154 F8
Donnini Ct 7 KA7 235 E1
Donohoe Ct G64 78 A1
Don Path ML9 199 A8
Don Pl PA5 131 C8
Don St
Glasgow G33 98 D1
Greenock PA16 45 C5
Doo'cot Brae FK10 10 A8
Doo'cot Hill FK10 5 D2
Doon Ave KA9 236 B5
Doon Cres G61 75 D3
Doon Ct KA12 219 C2
DOONFOOT 238 C2
Doonfoot Ct G74 159 D2
Doonfoot Gdns G74 159 D2
Doonfoot Prim Sch KA7 238 B3
Doonfoot Rd
Ayr KA7 238 E4
Glasgow G43 136 D6
Doonholm Pk KA6 238 F1
Doonholm Pl KA7 238 F1
Doonholm Rd KA7 238 F1
Doon Pl
Kilmarnock KA1 228 B4
Kirkintilloch G66 58 F2
Saltcoats KA21 206 A3
Symington KA1 231 D4
Troon KA10 229 F5
Doon Rd G66 59 A2
Doon Side G67 62 B2
Doonside Twr ML1 164 B3
Doon St
Clydebank G81 74 D3
Larkhall ML9 185 C2
Motherwell ML1 164 A4
Doonvale Pl KA7 239 A1
Doonview Gdns KA7 238 D2
Doonview Wynd KA7 238 C2
Doon Way G66 59 A1
Dorain Rd ML1 143 D3
Dora St G40 117 F3
Dorchester Ave G12 96 A6
Dorchester Ct G12 96 A6
Dorchester Pl G12 96 A5
Dorian Dr G76 157 C8
Dorlin Rd G33 99 F5
Dormanside Ct G53 115 B3
Dormanside Gate G53 115 B3
Dormanside Gr G53 115 B3
Dormanside Pl G53 115 C2
Dormanside Rd G53 115 C3
Dornal Ave G13 94 E7
Dornal Dr KA10 229 G6
Dornford Ave G32 119 D3
Dornford Rd G32 119 D2
Dornie Cl KA3 195 C1
Dornie Ct G46 135 E3
Dornie Dr G32 139 B8
Dornie Path 9 ML2 165 F6
Dornie Wynd ML7 147 B3
Dornoch Ave G46 136 C1
Dornoch Ct
Bellshill ML4 142 A5
Kilwinning KA13 207 B3
Dornoch Dr G72 161 D4
Dornoch Pk KA7 238 E6
Dornoch Pl
Bishopbriggs G64 78 D2
Chryston G69 80 D1
East Kilbride G74 159 C2
Dornoch Rd
Bearsden G61 75 D2
Motherwell ML1 143 B5
Dornoch St G40 117 F5
Dornoch Way
Airdrie ML6 122 F5
Cumbernauld G68 62 A5
Hamilton G72 161 D4
Dorrator Ct FK1 41 E5
Dorrator Rd FK1 41 E6
Dorset Rd PA16 44 E4
Dorset Sq G3 240 A3
Dorset St G3 240 A3
Dosk Ave G13 94 F8
Dosk Pl G13 94 F8
Double Hedges Rd G78 154 D6
Double Row ML11 214 F2
Dougalston Ave G62 55 B1
Dougalston Cres G62 55 B1
Dougalston Gardens N G62 55 B1
Dougalston Gardens S G62 55 B1
Dougalston Rd G23 76 E1
Dougan Dr ML2 166 B5
Douglas Acad G62 54 D3
Douglas Ave
Airth FK2 14 D3
Dalry KA24 191 D6
Elderslie PA5 112 B2
Glasgow, Carmyle G32 119 B1
Glasgow G46 136 C1
Kirkintilloch G66 79 D5
Langbank PA14 70 D7
Prestwick KA9 236 B6
Rutherglen G73 138 C5
Douglas Cres
Airdrie ML6 123 A6
Erskine PA8 72 F3
Hamilton ML3 183 D6
Uddingston G71 141 B8
Douglas Ct
Kirkintilloch G66 79 D5
Troon KA10 229 E6
Douglasdale G74 159 D2
Douglas Dr
Ashgill ML9 199 F8
Bellshill ML4 142 D4
Bothwell G71 141 A1
Cambuslang G72 138 F5
Clydebank G15 74 F1
East Kilbride G75 179 E7
Glasgow G69 119 F5
Helensburgh G84 16 D4
Newton Mearns G77 156 E6
Stirling FK7 7 C4
Douglas Drive E G84 16 E3
Douglas Drive La G45 137 D3
Douglas Gate G72 138 F5
Douglas Gdns
Bearsden G61 75 F4
Glasgow G46 136 C1
Kirkintilloch G66 79 D5
Uddingston G71 140 F5
Douglas Ho G82 50 B7
Douglas La
Ayr KA7 238 F8
Glasgow G2 240 B3
Douglas Muir Dr G62 54 C3
Douglas Muir Gdns G62 54 C3
Douglas Muir Pl G62 54 C3
Douglas Muir Rd
Clydebank G81 74 D7
Milngavie G62 54 D2
Douglas Park Cres G61 76 A6
Douglas Park La ML3 162 C5
Douglas Pl
1 Bearsden G61 75 E5
Coatbridge ML5 121 F6
Hamilton ML3 183 D6
Kirkintilloch G66 79 D5
Stenhousemuir FK5 23 F4
Douglas Rd
Dumbarton G82 50 B3
Paisley PA4 114 A8
Douglas St
Airdrie ML6 123 A6
Ayr KA7 238 F8
Bannockburn FK7 7 E1
Carluke ML8 187 E2
Glasgow G2 240 B3
Hamilton, High Blantyre G72 161 C6
Hamilton ML3 162 C5
Kilmarnock KA1 227 F7
Larkhall ML9 185 A4
Milngavie G62 55 A1
Motherwell ML1 163 D6
Overtown ML2 186 D7
Paisley PA1 113 C5
Stirling FK8 2 B1
Uddingston G71 141 B7

Douglas Terr FK7 6 E6
Douglaston Woodland Wlk* G62 55 D2
Douglas Twr G71 140 D4
Douglas View ML5 121 F3
Douglehill Pl PA14 68 C8
Dougliehill Rd
Knocknairs Moor PA13 67 F8
Port Glasgow PA14 68 B8
Dougliehill Terr PA14 68 C8
Dougray Pl G78 134 C2
Dougrie Dr G45 137 D3
Dougrie Gdns G45 137 D2
Dougrie Pl G45 137 E3
Dougrie Rd G45 137 D3
Dougrie St G45 137 E3
Dougrie Terr G45 137 D3
Doune Cres
Bishopbriggs G64 78 B4
Chapelhall ML6 123 D1
Newton Mearns G77 156 F5
Stenhousemuir FK5 24 A4
Doune Gardens La G20 96 E3
Doune Gdns
Glasgow G20 96 E3
Gourock PA19 44 A6
Doune Park Way ML5 121 F4
Doune Quadrant 4 G20 96 E3
Doune Terr ML5 121 E8
Doura Dr KA11 219 F5
Doura Pl KA12 219 C5
Dovecot G43 136 C8
Dovecote View G66 79 F7
DOVECOTHALL 134 D3
Dovecothall Rdbt G78 134 D3
Dovecothall St G78 134 D3
Dovecot La
Kilwinning KA13 207 F3
Lanark ML11 215 A4
Dovecot Pl FK10 4 B3
Dovecot Rd FK10 4 B3
DOVECOTWOOD 36 D1
Dovecotwood G65 36 D1
Dovehill FK10 10 B8
Doveholm G82 50 A5
Doveholm Ave G82 50 B5
Dove Pl G75 179 F6
Dover St
Coatbridge ML5 101 D2
Glasgow G3 240 A3
Dove St G53 135 A5
Dove Wynd ML4 141 F8
Dowanfield Rd G67 61 E1
DOWANHILL 96 C3
Dowanhill Prim Sch G11 96 C2
Dowanhill St G12 96 C2
Dowan Pl FK7 6 E6
Dowan Rd
Glasgow G62 76 E8
Milngavie G62 55 E2
Dowanside La 1 G12 96 C3
Dowanside Rd G12 96 C3
Dow Ave KA9 233 C5
Dower Pl FK2 14 D4
Downcraig Dr G45 137 D2
Downcraig Gr G45 137 C2
Downcraig Rd G45 137 C2
Downcraig Terr G45 137 D2
Downfield Dr ML3 183 B7
Downfield Gdns G71 140 F2
Downfield St G32 118 E3
Downhill St G12 96 C3
Downiebrae Rd G73 118 B2
Downie Cl G71 141 B8
Downie St ML3 162 D1
Downs Cres FK10 9 F6
Downs St G21 97 F5
Dow Rd KA9 233 C4
Dowrie Cres G53 115 B1
Draffan Rd ML9 200 B2
Draffen Ct ML1 163 F7
Draffen Mount KA3 211 F7
Draffen St ML1 163 F7
Draffen Twr ML1 163 F7
Drakemire Ave G45 137 C4
Drakemire Dr G45 137 C3
DRAKEMYRE 169 C1
Drakemyre KA24 169 C1
Drake St G40 117 E5
Dr Campbell Ave FK7 12 D8
DREGHORN 220 D1
Dreghorn Prim Sch KA11 220 D1
Dreghorn Rd KA11 225 D6
Dreghorn St G31 118 C7
Dresling Rd PA15 45 E3
Drimnin Rd G33 99 F5
Drip Rd FK9 1 F2
Drive Rd G51 115 E8
Drochil St G34 100 A1
Dromore St G66 79 D7
Drossie Rd FK1 42 A3
Drove Hill G68 61 B3
Drove Loan FK6 39 F6
Drove Loan Cres FK6 39 E7
Drover Pl FK5 23 C4
Dr Porter Gdns FK7 8 D4
Druid Dr KA13 207 E4
Drumadoon Dr G84 16 F2
Drumaling Terr G66 57 F8
Drumbathie Rd ML6 123 C8
Drumbathie Terr ML6 123 C8
Drumbeg Dr G53 135 A6
Drumbeg Path G72 161 C3
Drumbeg Pl G53 135 A6
Drumbeg Terr G62 54 D2
Drumbottie Rd G21 98 A5
Drumbowie Cres ML7 125 B1
Drumbowie View G68 61 C3
Drumbrock Rd G62 54 D2
Drumby Cres G76 157 D8
Drumby Dr G76 157 D8
Drumcarn Dr G62 54 F1
Drumcavel Rd
Mount Ellen G69 100 F7
Muirhead G69 100 D7
DRUMCHAPEL 75 A3
Drumchapel Gdns G15 75 A2
Drumchapel High Sch G15 75 A4
Drumchapel Hospl G15 75 B2
Drumchapel Pl G15 75 B2
Drumchapel Pool G15 74 F2
Drumchapel Rd G15 75 B2
Drumchapel Sh Ctr G15 74 F3
Drumchapel Sta G15 75 A1
Drumclair Ave FK1 86 A6
Drumclair Pl ML6 123 D7
Drumclog Ave G62 55 A4
Drumclog Gdns G33 98 F6
Drumclog Pl KA3 223 B3
Drumcross Pl G53 115 C1
Drumcross Rd
Erskine PA7 72 D3
Glasgow G53 115 C1
Drumduff G75 180 D5
Drumellan Rd KA7 239 A2
Drumelzier Ct KA11 220 A4
Drumfearn Pl G20 /G22 97 B6
Drumfearn Rd G20 /G22 97 B6
Drumfin Ave ML6 105 A4
Drumfork Ct G84 25 B8
Drumfork Rd G84 25 D8
Drumfrochar Rd
Greenock PA15 45 E3
Greenock PA15 45 F3
Drumfrochar Sta PA15 45 D4
Drumgarve Ct G84 16 C2
DRUMGELLOCH 123 D8
Drumgelloch St ML6 123 D8
Drumgelloch Sta ML6 123 D7
Drumglass Steadings G65 60 E3
Drumglass View G65 60 F4
Drumgray Gdns ML6 83 D1
Drumgray La ML6 83 D1
Drumgrew Rdbt G68 60 B1
Drumhead Pl G32 118 F1
Drumhead Rd G32 118 F1
Drumhill G66 59 B2
Drumilaw Cres G73 138 A5
Drumilaw Rd G73 138 A5
Drumilaw Way G73 138 A5
Drumillan Hill PA16 44 C2
Drumkinnon Rd G83 27 D8
Drumlaken Ave G23 76 C1
Drumlaken Ct 7 G23 76 D1
Drumlaken Path 11 G23 76 D1
Drumlaken Pl 9 G23 76 D1
Drumlaken St G23 76 C1
Drumlanford Rd KA10 229 F6
Drumlanrig Ave G34 120 D8
Drumlanrig Cres G69 100 E4
Drumlanrig Pl
Glasgow G34 100 D1
Stenhousemuir FK5 23 F4
Drumley Ave KA6 237 F6
Drumleyhill Dr KA1 228 F5
Drumlin Dr G62 75 F8
Drumloch Gdns G75 180 E5
Drumlochy Rd G33 99 B1
Drum Mains Pk G68 81 D8
Drummilling Ave KA23 190 D6
Drummilling Dr KA23 190 D6
Drummilling Rd KA23 190 D6
Drummond Ave G73 137 F8
Drummond Cres
Ayr KA8 236 E2
Irvine KA11 224 H7
Drummond Dr
Paisley PA1 114 D4
Wishaw ML2 165 B2
Drummond Hill G74 160 B3
Drummond Ho G67 62 A3
Drummond La FK8 7 A6
Drummond Pl
Blackridge EH48 107 C3
Bonnybridge FK4 40 A7
3 East Kilbride G74 160 B3
Falkirk FK1 41 F2
Kilmarnock KA3 223 D2
Stirling FK8 7 A6
Drummond Place La FK8 7 A6
Drummond St PA16 45 C4
Drummond Way G77 156 A5
Drummore Ave ML5 122 D3
Drummore Rd G15 75 B4
Drummore Sch G15 75 C4
Drummuir Foot KA11 220 B5
Drumnessie Ct G68 81 F8
Drumnessie Rd G68 81 F8
Drumnessie View G68 81 F8
Drumore Ave ML6 123 D1
Drumover Dr G31 118 E4
DRUMOYNE 115 E6
Drumoyne Ave G51 115 E7
Drumoyne Cir G51 115 E6
Drumoyne Dr G51 115 E7
Drumoyne Pl G51 115 E6
Drumoyne Prim Sch G51 115 E6
Drumoyne Quadrant G51 115 E6
Drumoyne Rd
Glasgow, Drumoyne G51 115 E6
Drumoyne Rd *continued*
Glasgow, West Drumoyne G51 115 E7
Drumoyne Sq G51 115 E7
Drumpark Sch G69 121 B6
Drumpark St
Coatbridge ML5 121 C4
Glasgow G46 135 F4
Stirling FK7 7 B3
DRUMPELLIER 121 C6
Drumpellier Ave
Coatbridge ML5 121 D6
Cumbernauld G67 82 C7
Glasgow G69 120 B3
Drumpellier Country Pk* ML5 101 C1
Drumpellier Cres ML5 121 D6
Drumpellier Ct G67 82 C7
Drumpellier Gdns G67 82 C7
Drumpellier Gr G67 82 C7
Drumpellier Pl
Cumbernauld G67 82 C7
Glasgow G69 120 B4
Drumpellier Rd G69 120 A4
Drumpellier St G33 98 D2
Drumreoch Dr G42 137 E8
Drumreoch Pl G42 137 E8
Drumriggend Rd FK1 85 D4
DRUMRY 74 C2
Drumry Pl G15 74 E2
Drumry Rd G81 74 C3
Drumry Road E G15 74 E2
Drumry Sta G81 74 D2
Drumsack Ave G69 100 C8
Drumsargard Rd G73 138 D5
Drums Ave PA3 113 C6
Drums Cres PA3 113 C5
Drumshangie Pl ML6 103 A2
Drumshangie St ML6 103 A2
Drumshantie Rd PA19 44 E6
Drumshantie Terr PA19 44 E7
Drumshaw Dr G32 139 C8
Drumslea PA16 45 C8
Drums Rd G53 115 A3
Drums Terr PA16 45 B8
Drums The PA16 45 B8
DRUMTROCHER 36 D3
Drumtrocher St G65 60 D8
Drumvale Dr G69 80 E2
Drury Lane Ct G74 160 C4
Drury St G2 240 C2
Dryad St G46 135 E5
DRYBRIDGE 225 D6
Drybridge Rd KA2 225 E2
Dryburgh Ave
Denny FK6 21 D2
Paisley PA2 113 A1
Rutherglen G73 138 B7
Dryburgh Gdns G20 96 F3
Dryburgh Hill G74 159 D1
Dryburgh La G74 159 D1
Dryburgh Pl
Coatbridge ML5 121 F7
Kirkintilloch G66 79 F8
Dryburgh Rd
Bearsden G61 75 C6
Wishaw ML2 165 B4
Dryburgh St ML3 162 B6
Dryburgh Way 1 G72 161 D7
Dryburgh Wlk 3 G69 81 A3
Dryburn Ave G52 115 B5
Dryden St ML3 162 B6
Drygait PA9 131 A6
Drygate G4 241 C2
Drygate St ML9 185 B4
Drygrange Rd G33 99 C2
Drymen Pl G66 79 D3
Drymen Rd
Balloch G83 19 F1
Bearsden G61 75 E5
8 Bearsden G61 75 F3
Drymen St G52 115 E5
Drymen Wynd G61 75 F3
Drynoch Pl G22 97 B7
Drysdale St
Alloa FK10 10 B6
Glasgow G14 94 F5
Duart Ave KA9 236 C8
Duart Cres KA9 236 C8
Duart Dr
East Kilbride G74 159 D3
Elderslie PA5 112 C1
Newton Mearns G77 157 A5
Duart St G20 96 C8
Duart Way G69 100 E4
Dubbs Rd
Kilwinning KA20 207 B1
Port Glasgow PA14 68 E7
Port Glasgow PA14 68 F7
Stevenston KA20 206 E1
Stevenston KA20 206 F1
Dubs Rd G78 134 E3
Dubton St G34 100 B1
Duchall Pl G14 95 B4
Duchal Rd PA13 89 D8
Duchal St PA14 68 D8
Duchess Ct ML3 163 A2
Duchess Dr G84 16 B3
Duchess Pk G84 16 B3
Duchess Pl G73 138 C8
Duchess Rd G73 118 C1
Duchess Way G69 120 F5
Duchray Dr PA1 114 F4
Duchray La G33 98 D1
Duchray St G33 98 D1
Duddingston Ave KA13 207 B4
Dudley Dr
Coatbridge ML5 101 C2
Dudley Dr *continued*
Glasgow G12 96 A3
Dudley La G12 96 A3
Duff Cres FK8 1 F1
Duff Pl
Kilmarnock KA3 223 C3
Saltcoats KA21 206 A2
Duff St PA15 46 A5
Duffus Pl G32 139 C8
Duffus St G34 100 A1
Duffus Terr G32 139 C8
Duguid Dr KA21 206 A1
Duich Gdns G23 76 E1
Duisdale Rd G32 139 C8
Dukes Ct G72 138 E7
Duke's Ct ML9 185 A4
Dukes Gate G71 140 E4
Dukes Pl ML3 183 D6
Dukes Rd
Coatbridge G69 120 F5
Troon KA10 229 C3
Duke's Rd G72, G73 138 D6
Duke St
Alva FK12 5 A7
Bannockburn FK7 7 C1
Denny FK6 21 C2
Glasgow, Barrowfield G31 118 D5
Glasgow, Dennistoun G31 118 B6
Glasgow G4 241 C2
Hamilton ML3 162 E3
Larkhall ML9 185 A4
Motherwell ML1 163 E8
Paisley PA2 113 E2
Wishaw ML2 165 F6
Duke Street Sta G31 118 B7
Duke Terr KA8 236 A1
DULLATUR 61 D6
Dullatur Rd G68 61 D6
Dullatur Rdbt G68 61 F5
Dulnain St G72 139 E5
Dulsie Rd G21 98 C6
Dumbain Cres G83 28 B8
Dumbain Rd G83 20 A1
DUMBARTON 49 E2
Dumbarton Acad G82 50 A4
Dumbarton Castle* G82 49 F2
Dumbarton Central Sta G82 49 F4
Dumbarton East Sta G82 50 B3
Dumbarton Joint Hospl G82 49 C4
Dumbarton Rd
Bowling G60 72 D8
Cambusbarron FK8 6 E8
Clydebank, Duntocher G81 74 A6
Clydebank G60, G81 73 D4
Glasgow G11 95 F2
Glasgow G14 94 E6
Glasgow, Partick G11 96 B2
Milton G82 50 F1
Stirling FK8 7 B7
DUMBRECK 116 B4
Dumbreck Ave G41 116 A4
Dumbreck Ct G41 116 A3
Dumbreck Marsh Nature Reserve* G65 60 B7
Dumbreck Pl
Glasgow G41 116 A3
Kirkintilloch G66 79 E4
Dumbreck Rd G41 116 B3
Dumbreck Sq G41 116 A4
Dumbreck Sta G41 116 C4
Dumbreck Terr G65 59 F8
Dumbrock Cres G63 31 C3
Dumbrock Dr G63 31 B3
Dumbrock Rd
Milngavie G62 54 D2
Strathblane G63 31 C3
DUMBUCK 50 E1
Dumbuck Cres G82 50 C2
Dumbuck Gdns G82 50 B2
Dumbuck Rd
Dumbarton G82 50 B4
Dumbarton G82 50 B5
Dumbuie Ave G82 50 B3
Dumfries Cres ML6 122 F5
Dumfries Pk KA6 239 A1
Dumgoyne Ave G62 54 F2
Dumgoyne Dr G61 75 D7
Dumgoyne Gdns G62 54 F1
Dumgoyne Pl G76 157 C7
Dumgoyne Rd KA1 228 A3
Dumyat Ave FK10 4 B2
Dumyat Dr FK1 41 E3
Dumyat Rd
Alva FK12 4 E6
Menstrie FK11 3 F6
Stirling FK9 2 C3
Dumyat Rise FK5 23 C5
Dumyat St FK10 4 F1
Dunagoil Gdns G45 137 E2
Dunagoil Pl G45 137 E1
Dunagoil Rd G45 137 D2
Dunagoil St G45 137 E1
Dunalastair Dr G33 99 B5
Dunan Pl G33 119 E7
Dunard Ct ML8 187 F3
Dunard Prim Sch G20 96 F4
Dunard Rd G73 138 B7
Dunard St G20 96 F4
Dunard Way PA3 113 D7
Dunaskin St G11 96 C1
Dunavon Gdns FK6 21 D4
Dunavon Pl ML5 122 D4
Dunbar Ave
Coatbridge ML5 121 D4
Johnstone PA5 131 E8
Rutherglen G73 138 C7
Dunbar Ave *continued*
Stenhousemuir FK5 23 F4
Dunbar Dr
Kilmarnock KA3 223 C2
Motherwell ML1 164 A4
Dunbar Gate FK6 21 E3
Dunbar Gdns KA21 205 F3
Dunbar Hill G74 159 C1
Dunbar La ML1 143 A2
Dunbar Pl G74 159 C1
Dunbar Rd PA2 113 A1
Dunbar St ML3 162 B5
Dunbeath Ave G77 156 F5
Dunbeath Gr G72 161 C3
Dunbeith Pl 4 G20 96 D5
DUNBETH 122 B7
Dunbeth Ave ML5 122 B7
Dunbeth Ct ML5 122 B7
Dunbeth Rd ML5 122 B7
Dunblane Dr G74 159 F2
Dunblane Pl
Coatbridge ML5 121 F4
East Kilbride G74 159 F2
Dunblane St G4 240 C4
Dunbrach Rd G68 61 C2
Dunbreck Ave ML6 105 A5
Dunbritton Rd G82 50 C3
Duncairn Ave FK4 39 F6
Duncan Ave
Falkirk FK2 24 B3
Glasgow G14 95 C4
Duncan Buchanan Ct FK8 2 A2
Duncan Ct
Kilmarnock KA3 223 D4
Motherwell ML1 142 D1
Duncan Dr KA12 219 D2
Duncan Graham St ML9 185 B4
Duncan La G14 95 C3
Duncan Lane N 7 G14 95 C4
Duncan Lane S 13 G14 95 C4
Duncan McIntosh Rd G68 62 C7
Dun Cann PA4 93 C7
Duncan Rd
Helensburgh G84 16 E3
Port Glasgow PA14 47 B1
Duncanrig Sec Sch G75 159 B1
Duncansby Dr G72 161 C3
Duncansby Rd G33 119 D6
Duncan's Cl 11 ML11 215 A4
Duncanson Ave FK10 10 A8
Duncan St
Bonnybridge FK4 39 F5
Clydebank G81 74 B3
Greenock PA15 45 E5
Duncarnock Ave G78 154 E7
Duncarnock Cres G78 154 E7
Duncarron Ind Est FK6 21 F1
Duncarron Pl FK6 21 E2
Dunchattan Gr KA10 229 G2
Dunchattan Pl G31 117 F7
Dunchattan St G31 117 F7
Dunchattan Way KA10 229 G2
Dunchurch Rd PA1 114 D5
Dunclutha Dr G71 141 A1
Dunclutha St G40 118 B2
Duncolm Pl G62 54 D2
Duncombe Ave G81 74 B7
Duncombe St G20 96 D7
Duncombe View 6 G81 74 D3
Duncraig Cres PA5 131 D8
Duncrub Dr G64 77 E1
Duncruin St G20 96 D7
Duncruin Terr G20 96 D7
Duncryne Ave G32 119 E4
Duncryne Gdns G32 119 E4
Duncryne Pl G64 97 E8
Duncryne Rd
Alexandria G83 27 E6
Gartocharn G83 20 F8
Dundaff Ct FK6 21 D1
Dundaff Hill G68 61 C2
Dundarroch St FK5 23 B1
Dundas Ave G64 78 B8
Dundas Cotts FK4 39 A2
Dundas Ct G74 159 E2
Dundashill G4 97 B2
Dundas La G1 241 A3
Dundas Pl G74 159 E2
Dundas Rd FK9 2 B4
Dundas St G1 241 A3
Dundasvale Ct
Glasgow G2 240 C4
Glasgow G4 240 C4
Dundas Wlk KA3 223 D3
Dundee Ct 5 FK2 42 A8
Dundee Dr G52 115 B3
Dundee Path G52 115 C3
Dundee Pl FK2 42 A8
DUNDONALD 225 E1
Dundonald Ave PA5 111 D1
Dundonald Castle* KA2 225 E2
Dundonald Cres
Coatbridge ML5 121 F4
Irvine KA11 224 H1
Newton Mearns G77 157 A4
Dundonald Ct KA3 223 B6
Dundonald Dr ML3 183 D7
Dundonald Pl
Kilmarnock KA1 227 D7
Neilston G78 154 D7
Dundonald Prim Sch KA2 225 F2
Dundonald Rd
Glasgow G12 96 C3
Irvine KA11 225 C8
Kilmarnock KA1, KA2 227 D7
Paisley PA3 114 A7
Troon KA10 229 F3

Dundonald St G72 161 C8
Dundonald Terr KA9 236 D7
Dundrennan Dr ML6 123 E2
Dundrennan Rd G42 136 F7
DUNDYVAN 121 F4
Dundyvan Gate ML5 122 A5
Dundyvan Gdns ML5 122 A5
Dundyvan Ind Est ML5 121 F5
Dundyvan La ML2 165 A2
Dundyvan Rd ML5 121 F5
Dundyvan St ML2 165 A2
Dundyvan Way ML5 121 F5
Dunearn Pl PA2 114 A3
Dunearn St G4 96 F2
Duneaton Wynd ML9 185 B1
Dunedin Ct G75 180 A8
Dunedin Dr G75 180 A8
Dunedin Rd ML9 185 B1
Dunedin Terr G81 94 C8
Dunellan Ave G69 81 A2
Dunellan Cres G69 81 A2
Dunellan Ct G69 81 A2
Dunellan Dr G81 74 B7
Dunellan Gdns G69 81 A2
Dunellan Gr G69 80 F2
Dunellan Pl G69 81 A2
Dunellan Rd G62 54 D2
Dunellan St G52 115 E5
Dunellan Way G69 81 A2
Dungavel Gdns ML3 183 E8
Dungavel La ML8 188 B1
Dungavel Rd KA1 228 A4
Dungeonhill Rd G34 120 D8
Dunglass Ave
East Kilbride G74 159 F3
Glasgow G14 95 C4
Dunglass La 8 G14 95 C4
Dunglass Lane N 5 G14 95 C4
Dunglass Lane S 11 G14 95 C4
Dunglass Pl
Milngavie G62 54 E3
Newton Mearns G77 156 A5
Dunglass Rd PA7 72 C2
Dunglass Sq G74 159 F3
Dunglass View G63 31 D4
Dungoil Ave G68 61 B3
Dungoil Rd G66 79 E4
Dungourney Dr PA16 45 D7
Dungoyne St G20 96 C8
Dunholme Pk G81 73 D3
DUNIPACE 21 D4
Dunipace Prim Sch FK6 21 D3
Dunira St G32 118 F3
Dunivaig Rd G33 119 E8
Dunkeld Ave G73 138 B7
Dunkeld Dr G61 76 B4
Dunkeld Gdns G64 78 B2
Dunkeld La G69 81 A2
Dunkeld Pl
Coatbridge ML5 121 F4
Falkirk FK2 24 C1
Hamilton ML3 161 E3
Newton Mearns G77 157 B4
Dunkeld St G31 118 C4
Dunkenny Rd G15 74 F3
Dunkenny Sq G15 74 F3
Dunkirk St ML6 105 A5
Dunlin
East Kilbride G74 159 E4
Glasgow G12 96 A6
Dunlin Cres PA6 91 C1
Dunlin Ct ML4 141 E8
Dunlin Way ML5 122 E2
DUNLOP 195 C7
Dunlop Cres
Ayr KA8 236 E1
Bothwell G71 141 B1
Irvine KA11 220 B1
Renfrew PA4 94 D4
Dunlop Ct
Hamilton ML3 183 E7
2 Troon KA10 229 E5
Dunlop Dr KA11 224 G4
Dunlop Gr G71 121 A1
Dunlop Pl
Ashgill ML9 200 A8
Irvine KA11 224 H4
Milngavie G62 54 F3
Dunlop Prim Sch KA3 195 B8
Dunlop Rd
Barrmill KA15 172 A3
Lugton KA3 173 C6
Stewarton KA3 195 D1
Dunlop St
Cambuslang G72 139 E6
Fenwick KA3 213 A3
Glasgow G2 241 A1
Greenock PA16 45 D3
Kilmarnock KA1 222 F1
Linwood PA3 112 C6
Renfrew PA4 94 D4
Stewarton KA3 195 E1
Dunlop Sta KA3 195 B7
Dunlop Terr KA8 236 D1
Dunlop Twr G75 180 E8
Dunmar Cres FK10 4 E1
Dunmar Dr FK10 4 E1
DUNMORE 14 C7
Dunmore Dr G62 76 D8
Dunmore St G81 94 C8
Dunnachie Dr ML5 121 B4
Dunnachie Pl ML5 121 C4
Dunnet Ave ML6 102 F5
Dunnet Ct G72 161 D4
Dunnet Dr PA6 91 B1
Dunnett Ave KA1 228 B7
Dunnichen Gdns G64 78 D1
Dunnikier Wlk G68 60 E1
Dunning Dr G68 62 A5
Dunning Pl FK2 24 C1
Dunn Mews KA1 227 C8
Dunnock Pl ML5 122 E3
Dunnotar Wlk 16 ML2 165 F6
Dunnottar Cres G74 159 D3
Dunnottar Ct G74 159 C3
Dunnottar Dr
Kilmarnock KA1 227 B8
Stenhousemuir FK5 23 F4
Dunnottar St
Bishopbriggs G64 78 D2
Glasgow G33 99 B2
Dunn St
Clydebank G81 73 E3
Duntocher G81 73 F6
Glasgow G40 118 A4
Greenock PA15 45 E4
Paisley PA1 114 A4
Dunns Wood Rd G67 62 D6
Dunn Terr ML7 127 F6
Dunollie Gdns KA3 223 B6
Dunollie Pl G69 100 E4
Dunolly Dr G77 156 F5
Dunolly St G21 98 A1
Dunoon Ave KA3 222 F3
Dunottar Ave ML5 122 B2
Dunottar Pl ML5 122 B3
Dunphail Dr G34 100 D1
Dunphail Rd G34 120 D8
Dun Pk G66 79 E8
Dunragit St G31 118 C7
Dunrobin Ave
Elderslie PA5 112 C1
Stenhousemuir FK5 23 F5
Dunrobin Cres G74 159 D3
Dunrobin Ct
Clydebank G81 74 A2
East Kilbride G74 159 D3
Dunrobin Dr
East Kilbride G74 159 D3
Gourock PA19 43 F6
Dunrobin Gdns ML6 123 E6
Dunrobin Pl ML5 121 F7
Dunrobin Prim Sch ML6 123 E7
Dunrobin Rd ML6 123 E7
Dunrobin St G31 118 B6
Dunrod Hill G74 159 F3
Dunrod St G32 119 B4
Dunscore Brae ML3 161 E2
Duns Cres ML2 165 C7
Dunside Dr G53 135 A6
Dunsiston Rd ML6 124 B4
Dunskaith Pl G34 120 D7
Dunskaith St G34 120 D7
Dunskey Rd KA3 223 B6
Dunsmore Rd PA7 72 A4
Dunsmuir St G51 116 B7
Duns Path ML5 122 D3
Duns Pl 2 PA15 46 B3
Dunster Gdns G64 78 B4
Dunster Rd FK9 2 C3
Dunswin Ave G81 73 E3
Dunsyre Pl G23 76 E1
Dunsyre St G33 118 E8
Duntarvie Ave G34 120 C8
Duntarvie Cl G34 120 C8
Duntarvie Cres G34 120 C8
Duntarvie Dr G34 120 B8
Duntarvie Gdns G34 120 C8
Duntarvie Gr G34 120 C8
Duntarvie Pl G34 120 B8
Duntarvie Rd G34 120 B8
DUNTERLIE 134 C3
Dunterlie Ave G13 95 B6
Dunterlie Ct G78 134 C3
DUNTIBLAE 80 A7
Duntiblae G66 80 A7
Duntiblae Rd G66 80 A7
Duntiglennan Rd G81 74 A6
Duntilland Ave ML7 125 B2
Duntilland Rd
Airdrie ML6 124 E8
Salsburgh ML7 125 C5
DUNTOCHER 74 A7
Duntocher Rd
Bearsden G61 75 B6
Clydebank G81 74 A4
Clydebank, Parkhall G81 74 A5
Duntonknoll KA12 219 C4
Duntreath Ave
Clydebank G15 74 F1
Glasgow G13 94 E8
Duntreath Dr G15 74 F1
Duntreath Gdns G15 74 F2
Duntreath Gr G15 74 F1
Duntreath Terr G65 60 D8
Duntroon Pl ML4 142 B3
Duntroon St G31 118 B8
Dunure Cres FK4 40 A5
Dunure Cts KA13 207 D3
Dunure Dr
Hamilton ML3 161 D2
Kilmarnock KA3 228 B8
Newton Mearns G77 157 A5
Rutherglen G73 137 F5
Dunure Pl
Coatbridge ML5 121 E3
Kilmarnock KA3 223 B6
Newton Mearns G77 157 A4
Dunure Rd KA7 238 B2
Dunure St
Bonnybridge FK4 40 A5
Coatbridge ML5 121 E3
Glasgow G20 96 D7
Dunvegan ML6 102 F4
Dunvegan Ave
Coatbridge ML5 101 D1
Dunvegan Ave *continued*
Elderslie PA5 112 C1
Gourock PA19 43 F5
Stenhousemuir FK5 23 F4
Dunvegan Ct FK10 10 B6
Dunvegan Dr
Bishopbriggs G64 78 A4
Falkirk FK2 24 C1
Newton Mearns G77 157 A5
Stirling FK9 2 B3
Dunvegan Pl
Bonnybridge FK4 39 F6
East Kilbride G74 159 D3
Irvine KA12 219 D6
Uddingston G71 140 D8
Dunvegan Quadrant PA4 94 B4
Dunwan Ave G13 94 F7
Dunwan Pl G13 94 F7
Dura Rd ML2, ML7 167 C5
Durban Ave
Clydebank G81 73 D4
East Kilbride G75 180 B4
Durham Rd PA16 44 E5
Durham St G41 116 D5
Durisdeer Dr ML3 161 E1
Durness Ave G61 76 B4
Duror St G32 119 A6
Durris Gdns G32 119 D3
Durrockstock Cres PA2 132 F7
Durrockstock Rd PA2 132 F7
Durrockstock Way PA2 132 F7
Durward G74 160 E4
Durward Ave G41 116 D1
Durward Cres PA2 112 F1
Durward Ct
Glasgow G41 116 D1
Motherwell ML1 142 D1
Durward Way PA2 112 F1
Dutch House Rdbt KA9 233 F6
Duthie Park Gdns 2 G13 95 D6
Duthie Park Pl 1 G13 95 D6
Duthie Rd PA19 45 A7
Duthil St G51 115 D6
Dyce Ave ML6 122 E4
Dyce La G11 96 A2
Dyer's La G1 241 B1
Dyfrig St
Hamilton G72 161 C8
Shotts ML7 146 E5
DYKEBAR 114 B1
Dykebar Ave G13 95 B6
Dykebar Cres PA2 114 B2
Dykebar Hospl PA2 134 B8
DYKEHEAD 146 D5
Dykehead Cres ML6 102 F2
Dykehead Dr KA1 228 F5
Dykehead La G33 119 D7
Dykehead Prim Sch ML7 146 E5
Dykehead Rd
Airdrie ML6 103 B3
Coatbridge G69 121 A5
Cumbernauld G68 61 D3
Dullatur G68 61 C6
Queenzieburn G65 59 E8
Dykehead Sq ML3 161 F2
Dykehead St G33 119 D7
Dykemuir Pl G21 98 B4
Dykemuir Quadrant G21 98 A4
Dykemuir St G21 98 A4
Dykeneuk Rd PA14 68 D7
Dyke Rd G13, G14 95 A7
Dykesfield Pl KA21 205 E2
Dykesmains Prim Sch
KA21 205 F3
Dykesmains Rd KA21 205 E2
Dykes Pl KA21 205 F2
Dyke St
Coatbridge ML5 121 B4
Glasgow G69 120 C5
Dykes The KA25 170 A8
Dysart Ct G68 60 E1
Dysart Dr G72 161 D3
Dysart Way ML6 124 A6

E

Eagle Cres G61 75 B5
EAGLESHAM 178 F5
Eaglesham Ct
East Kilbride G74, G75 158 F1
1 Glasgow G51 116 E6
Eaglesham Path ML5 101 C6
Eaglesham Pl 2 G51 116 E6
Eaglesham Prim Sch
G76 178 F4
Eaglesham Rd
Clarkston G76 157 E5
East Kilbride G75 179 C7
Newton Mearns G77 156 D3
Eagle St G4 97 C2
Eamont Lodge 10 G12 96 C3
Eardley Pl FK5 23 B2
Earl Ave ML6 105 A5
Earlbank Ave G14 95 C4
Earlbank Lane N 9 G14 95 C4
Earlbank Lane S G14 95 C4
Earl Cres KA2 225 F1
Earl Dr KA2 225 F2
Earl Haig Rd G52 114 F7
Earl Mount KA2 225 F2
Earl of Mar Ct FK10 10 B6
Earl Pl
Bridge of Weir PA11 110 D6
Glasgow G14 95 C4
Earl Rise KA2 225 F1
Earlsburn Ave FK7 7 A3
Earlsburn Rd G66 79 E4
Earlscourt G69 80 F1
Earls Ct FK10 10 B5
Earlsgate PA6 91 B1
Earl's Gate G71 140 E3
Earl's Hill G68 61 B3
Earlshill Dr
Bannockburn FK7 7 F1
Howwood PA9 130 E5
Earlspark Ave G43 136 F6
Earl St G14 95 B4
EARLSTON 227 B3
Earlston Ave KA1 227 F3
Earlston Cres ML5 122 D3
Earlston Pl G21 241 C4
Earlston St ML2 165 C6
Earls Way KA7 238 C2
Earlswood Ave KA11 219 E6
Earlswood View KA11 219 E6
Earlswood Way KA11 219 E6
Earlswood Wynd KA12 219 E6
Earl View ML1 143 A3
Earlybraes Dr G33 119 E6
Earlybraes Gdns G33 119 D6
Earn Ave
Bearsden G61 76 B3
Bellshill ML4 141 E6
Renfrew PA4 94 E2
Earncraig Gn KA11 220 A3
Earn Cres ML2 165 B1
Earn Ct FK10 10 C6
Earn Gdns ML9 199 A8
Earnhill La PA16 44 C5
Earnhill Pl PA16 44 D5
Earnhill Prim Sch PA16 44 E4
Earnhill Rd PA16 44 D5
Earn La ML1 143 A5
EARNOCK 161 E1
Earnock Ave ML1 163 C6
Earnock Gdns ML3 162 A2
Earnock Rd ML3 161 E2
Earnock St
Glasgow G33 98 D4
Hamilton ML3 162 A4
Earn Pl
Denny FK6 39 D6
Kilmarnock KA1 228 B5
Earn Rd
Newton Mearns G77 156 D7
Troon KA10 229 G4
Earnside St G32 119 B5
Earn St G33 98 E1
Earn Terr ML7 146 E6
Easdale G74 181 B7
Easdale Dr G32 119 A4
Easdale Path
Coatbridge ML5 122 D4
Glenboig ML5 101 C6
Easdale Pl G77 156 B5
Easdale Rise ML3 161 E3
Eason Dr ML8 187 D2
East Academy St ML2 165 B2
East Ave
Carluke ML8 187 D2
Hamilton G72 161 E5
Motherwell ML1 143 A2
Plains ML6 104 A3
Renfrew PA4 94 D3
Uddingston G71 141 C6
EAST BALGROCHAN 57 C2
Eastbank PA14 70 D6
Eastbank Acad G32 119 B4
Eastbank Dr G32 119 C5
Eastbank Pl G32 119 C5
Eastbank Prim Sch G32 119 C5
Eastbank Rise G32 119 C5
East Barmoss Ave PA14 68 F7
East Barns St G81 94 D7
East Bath La G1 241 A3
East Blackhall St PA15 46 B4
East Boreland Pl FK6 21 D3
East Bowhouse Head
KA11 220 B5
East Bowhouse Way
KA11 220 B5
East Breast PA15 46 A5
East Bridge St FK1 42 C4
East Broomlands KA11 220 B2
East Buchanan Mews 3
PA1 113 F5
East Buchanan St PA1 113 F5
Eastburn Cres G21 98 B6
Eastburn Dr FK1 42 C4
Eastburn Pl G21 98 B6
Eastburn Rd G21 98 B6
East Burnside St 2 G65 60 D8
Eastburn Twr FK1 42 C4
East Campbell St G1 241 C1
East Castle St FK10 10 B5
East Clyde St G84 16 E1
Eastcote Ave G14 95 E4
EAST CRAIGEND 73 A1
East Crawford St PA15 46 C3
Eastcroft G73 138 B8
Eastcroft St FK5 23 B1
Eastcroft Terr G21 98 A4
East Dean St ML4 142 B5
East Dr FK5 23 C1
Eastend PA12 129 D3
Eastend Ave ML1 143 B1
Easterbrae ML1 163 D4
Easter Carmuirs Prim Sch
FK1 41 B6
Easter Cornton Rd FK9 2 B4
Easter Craigs G31 118 B8
Easter Cres ML2 165 E4
Easter Garngaber Rd G66 79 E5
Eastergreens Ave G66 79 C7
Easterhill Pl G32 118 F3
Easterhill Rd G84 16 F3
Easterhill St G32 119 A2
EASTERHOUSE 120 B8
Easterhouse Pl G34 120 C8
Easterhouse Quadrant
G34 120 C7
Easterhouse Rd G69 120 C7
Easterhouse Sp Ctr G34 99 F1
Easterhouse Sta G69 120 C6
Easter Livilands FK7 7 C4
Eastermains G66 59 B2
Easter Mews G71 140 E5
Eastern Access Rd FK8 7 B8
Eastern Cres KA25 170 A7
Easter Queenslie Rd
G33 119 E8
Easter Rd
Clarkston G76 158 A6
Shotts ML7 146 D5
Easterton Ave G76 158 A5
Easterton Cres FK7 12 E7
Easterton Dr
Caldercruix ML6 104 F4
Cowie FK7 12 E7
Easterton Gr FK7 12 E7
Easterton Stables* G66 32 D3
Easter Wood Cres G71 121 D1
Easterwood Pl ML5 122 A6
East Faulds Rd ML11 215 E5
EASTFIELD
Cumbernauld 61 E3
Harthill 127 C4
Rutherglen 138 D7
Eastfield Ave G72 138 E6
Eastfield Cres G82 50 B2
Eastfield Pl G82 50 B2
Eastfield Prim Sch G68 61 B1
Eastfield Rd
Caldercruix ML6 105 B5
Carluke ML8 202 A8
Cumbernauld, Carrickstone
G68 61 D4
Cumbernauld, Cumbernauld
Village G68 62 A5
Glasgow G21 97 E4
Eastfield Terr ML4 142 D4
East Fulton Holdings
PA3 111 F7
East Fulton Prim Sch
PA3 111 F6
East Gargieston Ave
KA1 227 D6
Eastgate G69 101 A5
East Gate
Glenboig ML5 101 D7
Wishaw ML2 165 D3
East George St ML5 122 B8
East Glebe Terr ML3 162 D2
East Gr KA10 229 G4
East Greenlees Ave G72 139 C3
East Greenlees Cres G72 139 B3
East Greenlees Dr G72 139 C3
East Greenlees Gr G72 138 F3
East Greenlees Rd G72 139 B3
East Hallhill Rd
Baillieston G69 119 F6
Glasgow G33 119 F6
Easthall Pl G33 119 F7
East Hamilton St
Greenock PA15 46 D4
Wishaw ML2 165 B2
East High St ML6 123 A8
East Ho ML11 215 C4
East India Breast PA15 46 A4
EAST KILBRIDE 159 C5
East Kilbride Rd
Carmunnock G74, G76 158 D4
Clarkston G76 157 F6
Rutherglen G73 138 E4
East Kilbride Sh Ctr G74 159 E1
East Kilbride Sta G74 159 E2
East Kirkland KA24 191 D7
East La PA1 114 B4
Eastlea Pl ML6 123 B6
East Lennox Dr G84 16 F3
East Link Rd FK9 2 D5
East Machan St ML9 185 B1
EAST MAINS 159 F2
East Mains FK11 4 A6
East Mains Rd G74 159 E3
East Main St ML7 127 F5
East Milton Gr G75 159 B1
East Milton Prim Sch
G75 159 C1
East Montrose St G84 16 E2
Eastmuir Specl Sch G33 119 D6
Eastmuir St
Glasgow G32 119 B5
Wishaw ML2 165 E3
East Murrayfield FK7 7 E1
East Nerston Ct G74 160 A6
East Nerston Gr G74 160 A6
East Netherton St 5
KA1 227 F7
Easton Ct FK8 2 B2
Easton Dr FK1 66 D7
Easton Pl ML5 122 B5
East Park Cres KA3 222 B7
East Park Dr KA3 222 B7
East Park Rd KA8 236 B3
East Plean Prim Sch FK7 12 C3
East Princes St G84 16 D1
East Rd
Irvine KA12 219 B8
Irvine KA12 219 C2

East Rd *continued*
Irvine KA12 219 C3
Kilbarchan PA10 111 A4
Motherwell ML1 143 A4
Port Glasgow PA14 68 E8
Prestwick KA9 236 D6
East Road Ret Pk KA12 219 C3
East Rossdhu Dr G84 16 E3
East Scott Terr ML3 162 D1
EAST SHAWHEAD 122 B2
East Shawhead Ind Est ML5 122 B2
East Shaw St
Greenock PA15 45 F5
Kilmarnock KA1 227 F6
EASTSIDE 58 D1
Eastside G66 58 D1
Eastside Ind Est G66 58 D1
Eastside Rdbt 5 G66 58 D1
East Springfield Terr G64 98 B8
East St PA14, PA15 46 F2
East Station Ind Est ML9 185 B4
East Stewart Gdns ML5 122 C7
East Stewart Pl ML5 122 C7
East Stewart St
Coatbridge ML5 122 C6
Greenock PA15 46 B4
East Stirling St FK12 5 B7
East Thomson St G81 74 B3
East Thornlie St ML2 165 B2
East Union St KA10 229 C3
Eastvale Pl G3 116 C8
East Vennel FK10 10 B6
East Wellbrae Cres ML3 162 B1
East Wellington St G31 118 D5
East William St PA15 46 C3
Eastwood Ave
Giffnock G46 136 D2
Glasgow G41 136 D8
Irvine KA12 219 D4
Eastwood Cres G46 135 F4
Eastwood Ct G46 136 A4
Eastwood Dr ML2 166 A6
Eastwood High Sch G77 156 E7
Eastwood La G84 25 B8
Eastwoodmains Rd
Clarkston G46 157 D8
Glasgow G46 136 C1
Eastwood Park Theatre* G46 136 B2
Eastwood Rd G69 80 F2
East Woodside Ave PA14 69 A7
East Woodstock Ct 2 KA1 227 E8
Eastwood Toll G46 136 B1
Eastwood View G72 139 E6
Eastwood Way 2 ML9 185 B4
Easwald Bank PA10 111 C2
Ebenezer Pl FK1 66 F5
Ebroch Dr G65 60 E8
Ebroch Pk G65 60 E8
Eccles Ct FK7 7 A4
Eccles St G22 97 E5
Eckford St G32 119 A4
Eck Path ML1 143 A5
Eday Cres KA3 222 F5
Eday St G22 97 D6
Edderton Pl G34 120 A7
Edderton Way G34 120 A7
Eddington Dr G77 156 C3
Eddleston Pl G72 139 E5
EDDLEWOOD 183 D7
Eddlewood Ct G33 120 A7
Eddlewood Path G33 119 F7
Eddlewood Pl G33 119 F7
Eddlewood Rd G33 119 F7
Eddlewood Sp Barn ML3 183 D7
Eden Ct KA13 207 B3
Eden Dr G75 179 F6
Eden Gdns G75 179 F7
Eden Gr G75 179 F7
Edenhall Ct G77 156 D2
Edenhall Gr G77 156 D2
Edenhall Rd KA8 236 B4
Edenkill Pl G63 31 C3
Eden La G33 98 D1
Eden Pk G71 140 F2
Eden Pl
Cambuslang G72 139 D5
Kilmarnock KA1 228 B5
Renfrew PA4 94 E2
Eden Rd FK10 9 F8
Edenside G68 62 B7
Eden St G33 98 D1
Edenwood St G31 118 E5
Edgam Dr G52 115 C5
Edgefauld Ave G21 97 F3
Edgefauld Dr G21 97 F3
Edgefauld Pl G21 97 F5
Edgefauld Rd
Glasgow G21 97 F4
Glasgow G21 98 A3
Edgehill Rd
Bearsden G61 75 E6
Glasgow G11 95 F4
Glasgow G11 96 A4
Edgemont Pk ML3 183 C8
Edgemont St G41 136 E8
Edinbarnet Prim Sch G81 74 C7
Edinbeg Ave G42 137 E8
Edinbeg Pl G42 137 E8
Edinburgh Dr PA19 43 E5
Edinburgh Rd
Glasgow G33 119 D7
Harthill ML7 127 C5

Edinburgh Rd *continued*
Motherwell ML1 143 D7
Edington Gdns G69 80 F3
Edington St G4 97 B2
Edison Pl KA13 207 E1
Edison St G52 114 E8
Edmiston Ave KA9 236 B7
Edmiston Dr G51 116 A6
Edmonstone Dr G65 60 D7
Edmonton Terr G75 180 C8
Edmund Kean G74 160 C5
Edrom Ct G32 118 F5
Edrom Path G32 118 F5
Edrom St G32 118 F5
Edward Ave
Renfrew PA4 94 E4
Stenhousemuir FK5 23 E4
Stirling FK8 2 C1
Edward Dr G84 16 C3
Edward Pl
Skinflats FK2 24 F3
Stepps G33 99 D5
Edward Rd FK8 2 B1
Edward St
Clydebank G81 94 D7
Coatbridge G69 120 F5
Hamilton ML3 162 D2
Kilsyth G65 36 D1
Motherwell ML1 163 F4
Edwin St G51 116 D5
Edzell Ct G14 95 D2
Edzell Dr
Elderslie PA5 112 D2
Newton Mearns G77 156 E4
Edzell Gdns
Bishopbriggs G64 98 C8
Wishaw ML2 165 A2
Edzell Pl G14 95 D3
Edzell Row KA13 207 B3
Edzell St
Coatbridge ML5 121 D4
Glasgow G14 95 D2
Egidia Ave G46 136 C2
Egilsay Cres G22 97 C8
Egilsay Pl G22 97 C8
Egilsay St G22 97 C8
Egilsay Terr G22 97 C8
Eglinton Country Pk* KA13 208 B2
Eglinton Cres KA10 229 E1
Eglinton Ct
Glasgow G5 117 B5
Saltcoats KA21 216 E7
Eglinton Ctry Pk Visitor Ctr* KA12 219 B8
Eglinton Dr
Eaglesham G76 178 F4
Glasgow G46 136 C2
Troon KA10 229 F2
Eglinton Gdns KA12 219 C3
Eglinton Intc KA12 219 B8
Eglinton Pl
Ayr KA7 235 E1
Kilwinning KA13 207 E3
Saltcoats KA21 216 F7
Eglinton Rd KA22 205 B3
Eglinton Sq KA22 205 C3
Eglinton St
Beith KA15 171 B8
Coatbridge ML5 122 B7
Glasgow G5 117 B4
Irvine KA12 219 C3
Saltcoats KA21 216 E7
Eglinton Terr KA7 235 E1
Eglinton Wlk G76 178 F4
Eglintoun Rd KA3 195 C1
Egmont Pk G75 180 A7
Eider G12 96 A7
Eider Ave G75 180 A5
Eider Gr G75 180 A5
Eider Pl G75 180 A4
Eighth St G71 120 E1
Eildon Cres ML6 123 F1
Eildon Dr G78 134 C1
Eildon Rd G66 79 F8
Eileen Gdns G64 78 B2
Eilt Wlk 8 ML2 165 F6
Elba Ct KA8 236 A1
Elba Gdns KA8 236 A1
Elba St KA8 236 A1
Elcho St G40 117 F6
Elder Ave KA15 171 A8
Elderbank G61 75 E3
Elder Cres G72 139 E4
Elder Dr G72 139 E4
Elder Gr G71 141 B8
Elder Grove Ave G51 115 D7
Elder Grove Ct 7 G51 115 D7
Elder Grove Pl 6 G51 115 D7
Elderpark Gdns G51 115 F7
Elderpark Gr 1 G51 115 F7
Elder Park Prim Sch G51 115 E8
Elderpark St G51 115 F7
Elderpark Workspace G51 115 F7
Elderslea Rd ML8 202 A8
ELDERSLIE 112 C1
Elderslie Cres KA1 227 F4
Elderslie Ct G3 240 A3
Elderslie St G3 240 A3
Elder St
Glasgow G51 115 F7
Glasgow G51 115 F8
Elders Way ML2 165 D3
Elder Way ML1 143 D2
Eldin Pl
Bridge of Weir PA11 110 E6

Eldin Pl *continued*
Elderslie PA5 112 B2
Eldon Ct G11 96 B2
Eldon Gdns G64 77 F1
Eldon Pl PA16 45 C8
Eldon St
Glasgow G3 96 E2
Greenock PA16 45 C8
Elgin Ave
East Kilbride G74 159 F3
Stewarton KA3 195 C1
Elgin Dr FK7 7 C3
Elgin Gdns G76 157 F8
Elgin Pl
Airdrie ML6 122 E5
Coatbridge ML5 122 B3
East Kilbride G74 159 F3
Falkirk FK1 42 C4
Kilsyth G65 36 D1
Elgin Rd G61 75 F7
Elgin Terr ML3 161 E4
Elgin Way ML4 142 A6
Elgol Path ML7 147 B3
Elibank St G33 99 A1
Elie Ct G68 61 F5
Elie Rd G72 161 D3
Elie St G11 96 C2
Elim Dr FK1 66 C6
Eliot Cres ML3 162 D1
Eliot Terr ML3 162 D2
Elison Ct ML1 164 B4
Elive Ct ML5 122 B3
Elizabethan Way PA4 94 C1
Elizabeth Ave
Milton of Campsie G66 58 B6
Stenhousemuir FK5 23 C2
Elizabeth Cres
Falkirk FK1 41 B6
Glasgow G46 136 A3
Elizabeth Ct 6 G74 159 F2
Elizabeth Quadrant ML1 142 F5
Elizabeth St
Glasgow G51 116 C6
Stirling FK8 7 A5
Elizabeth Wynd ML3 183 D7
Ella Gdns ML4 142 C4
Ellangowan Ct G62 55 A2
Ellangowan Rd
Glasgow G41 136 C8
Milngavie G62 55 A2
Ellergreen Rd G61 75 E4
Ellerslie Rd G14 94 E6
Ellerslie St PA5 112 A3
Ellesmere St
Glasgow G22 97 B3
Glasgow G22 97 B4
Elliot Ave
Glasgow G46 136 C3
Paisley PA2 132 E7
Elliot Cres G74 160 B2
Elliot Ct
Greenock PA15 46 C3
Motherwell ML1 142 D1
Elliot Dr G46 136 C3
Elliot Ho G67 62 B2
Elliot Pl
Glasgow G3 116 E7
Larbert FK5 23 B2
Netherburn ML9 200 B4
Elliot Sq G3 116 E7
Elliot St G3 116 E8
Elliot Terr FK2 42 A8
Ellisland
East Kilbride G74 160 E3
Kirkintilloch G66 59 B2
Ellisland Ave G81 74 C3
Ellisland Cres G73 137 F5
Ellisland Dr
Hamilton G72 161 B6
Kilmarnock KA3 228 C8
Kirkintilloch G66 59 A2
Ellisland Pl
Ayr KA7 239 B6
Saltcoats KA21 206 A3
Ellisland Rd
Clarkston G76 157 F5
Cumbernauld G67 62 B2
Glasgow G43 136 D6
Ellisland Sq KA7 239 B6
Ellisland Wynd ML1 143 C3
Ellismuir Farm Rd G69 120 D4
Ellismuir Pl G69 120 C4
Ellismuir Rd G69 120 C4
Ellismuir St ML5 121 E3
Ellismuir Way G71 121 A1
Ellis St
Coatbridge ML5 122 A6
Kilmarnock KA1 227 E8
Elliston Ave G53 135 C5
Elliston Cres G53 135 C5
Elliston Dr G53 135 C5
Elliston Pl PA9 130 F5
Elliston Rd PA9 130 F5
Ellis Way 6 ML1 163 F5
Ellon Dr PA3 112 A5
Ellon Gr PA3 113 F7
Ellon Way PA3 114 A7
Ellrig G75 180 D5
Elm Ave
Kirkintilloch G66 79 C6
Renfrew PA4 94 C4
Elmbank FK11 4 A6
Elm Bank
Bishopbriggs G64 78 B1
Kirkintilloch G66 58 D1
Elmbank Ave
Kilmarnock KA1 228 A8
Uddingston G71 141 B7

Elmbank Cres
Denny FK4 39 D6
Glasgow G2 240 B3
Hamilton ML3 162 A4
Elmbank Dr
Alexandria G83 27 F5
Kilmarnock KA1 228 A8
Larkhall ML9 185 C1
Elmbank Rd
Langbank PA14 70 C7
Stirling FK7 7 A3
Elmbank St
Ayr KA8 236 A3
Bellshill ML4 142 A4
Carluke ML8 202 A8
Glasgow G2 240 B3
Elmbank Street La G2 240 B3
Elmbank Terr KA12 219 D4
Elm Cres G71 141 D7
Elm Ct
1 Hamilton G72 161 E7
Quarter ML3 183 F4
Elm Dr
Cambuslang G72 139 C6
Chapelhall ML6 123 E3
Cumbernauld G67 62 F4
Johnstone PA5 112 A1
Elmfoot St G5 117 D2
Elm Gdns
Bearsden G61 75 E6
Troon KA10 230 A2
Elm Gr
Langbank PA14 70 C7
Stenhousemuir FK5 23 D1
Elmhurst ML1 163 D4
Elmira Rd G69 100 D7
Elm Lane E 6 G14 95 D3
Elm Lane W 5 G14 95 D3
Elm Lea PA5 112 B2
Elmore Ave G44 137 B5
Elm Park Gr ML6 83 F2
Elm Pk KA22 205 D3
Elm Pl G75 180 C6
Elm Quadrant ML6 123 D7
Elm Rd
Bridge of Weir PA11 110 E8
Clydebank G81 74 A5
Dumbarton G82 49 F4
Motherwell, Carfin ML1 143 A2
Motherwell, Holytown ML1 143 B5
Paisley PA2 114 A2
Rutherglen G73 138 B4
Elmslie Ct G69 120 C4
Elms Pl
Beith KA15 150 B1
Stevenston KA20 206 E2
Elm St
Clarkston G76 157 F6
Coatbridge ML5 122 C5
Glasgow G14 95 D3
Hamilton G72 161 E7
Lennoxtown G66 57 E8
Motherwell ML1 163 D7
Stirling FK8 1 E1
Elms The G44 137 B4
Elms Way KA8 236 B4
Elm Terr PA19 44 E6
Elmtree Gdns G45 137 F4
Elmvale Prim Sch G22 97 E5
Elmvale Row G21 97 E5
Elmvale St G21 97 E5
Elm View Ct ML4 142 D4
Elm Way
Cambuslang G72 139 E4
Larkhall ML9 185 A5
Elm Wlk G61 75 E6
Elmwood ML2 164 E1
Elmwood Ave
Glasgow G11 95 F4
Newton Mearns G77 156 F6
Elmwood Ct G71 141 A2
Elmwood Gdns G66 79 A5
Elmwood La G11 95 F4
Elmwood Manor G71 141 A2
Elmwood Rd ML7 147 B2
Elphin St G23 76 D1
Elphinstone Cres
Airth FK2 14 E4
East Kilbride G75 180 F6
Elphinstone Ct PA13 89 D8
Elphinstone Mews PA13 89 D8
Elphinstone Pl G51 116 C7
Elphinstone Rd G46 157 A7
Elpin FK10 10 D5
Elrig Rd G44 137 A5
Elsinore Path G75 180 E6
Elspeth Gdns G64 78 C2
Elswick Dr ML6 105 A4
Eltham St G22 97 B3
Elvan Ct ML1 163 D6
Elvan Pl G75 179 E7
Elvan St
Glasgow G32 118 F5
Motherwell ML1 163 D6
Elvan Twr 4 ML1 163 E5
Elvis St KA9 233 D2
Embo Dr G13 95 B6
Emerald Terr ML4 142 A4
Emerson Rd G64 78 A1
Emerson Rd W G64 78 A1
Emily Dr ML1 163 E4
Emma Jay Rd ML4 142 B5
Emma's Way FK4 39 F5
Empire Gate ML7 146 F4
Empire Way ML1 142 C1
Empress Ct PA15 46 B4
Empress Dr G84 16 A3
Empress Rd G84 15 D5

Endfield Ave G12 96 B6
Endrick Bank G64 78 A4
Endrick Ct ML5 121 F6
Endrick Dr
Balloch G83 19 F1
Bearsden G61 75 F3
Denny FK6 39 E6
Paisley PA1 114 B6
Endrick Gdns G62 54 E2
Endrick Ho G82 50 B6
Endrick Pl FK7 7 A4
Endrick Rd PA15 46 B1
Endrick St G21 97 D3
Endrick Way G83 27 E6
Endrick Wynd G84 25 C8
Engelen Dr FK10 10 B5
Engels St G83 27 E7
Engine Gn The FK10 5 D3
Englewood Ave KA8 236 B5
English Row ML6 123 C3
English St ML2 164 D3
Ennerdale G75 179 F6
Ennisfree Rd G72 161 D8
Ensay St G22 97 D7
Enterkine KA13 207 B2
Enterkin St G32 118 F4
Enterprise Ho G66 79 C7
Enterprise Ho ML1 163 F7
ENTRYFOOT 106 F2
Eriboll Pl G22 97 B7
Eriboll St G22 97 B7
Eribol Wlk ML1 143 D3
Ericht Pl ML7 146 E6
Ericht Rd G43 136 C5
Eriska Ave G14 95 B5
Eriskay Ave
Hamilton ML3 161 F2
Newton Mearns G77 156 B5
Port Glasgow PA14 69 B7
Eriskay Cres G77 156 B5
Eriskay Ct
Falkirk FK1 42 C2
Irvine KA11 225 C8
Eriskay Dr G60 73 C6
Eriskay Pl
Kilmarnock KA3 223 B5
Old Kilpatrick G60 73 C6
Ermelo Gdns G75 180 B4
Erradale Pl 3 G22 97 A7
Erradale St G22 97 A7
Errogie St G34 120 B8
Errol Gdns G5 117 C4
ERSKINE 73 A1
Erskine Ave G41 116 B4
Erskine Cres ML6 122 F5
Erskinefauld Rd PA3 112 B6
Erskine Ferry Rd G60 73 B5
Erskine Gdns ML7 146 D5
Erskine La FK5 23 B2
Erskine Pl
Clackmannan FK10 10 F5
Kilmarnock KA3 223 C2
Saltcoats KA21 216 F7
Erskine Rd G46 157 B6
Erskine Sp Ctr PA8 73 C2
Erskine Sq G52 114 F7
Erskine St
Alloa FK10 10 B7
Alva FK12 5 A7
Erskine View G60 73 A6
Erskine Way ML7 146 E4
Ervie St G34 120 C7
Escart Rd ML8 187 F3
Esdaile Ct ML1 143 A3
Esk Ave PA4 94 E2
Eskbank St G32 119 B6
Eskdale G77 157 B5
Esk Dale G74 159 C3
Eskdale Dr G73 138 D7
Eskdale Rd G61 75 D2
Eskdale St G42 117 B1
Esk Dr PA2 112 E1
Esk Rd
Kilmarnock KA1 228 B4
Troon KA10 229 F5
Esk St G14 94 F5
Esk Way PA2 112 E1
Esmond St G3 96 C1
Espedair St PA2 113 E3
Espieside Cres ML5 121 D8
Esplanade
Ayr KA7 238 E8
Gourock PA19 44 C7
Greenock PA16 45 D8
Prestwick KA9 236 B8
1 Stirling FK8 7 A8
Essenside Ave G15 75 C2
Essex Dr G14 95 E4
Essex La G14 95 E3
Essex Rd PA16 44 E4
Esslemont Ave G14 95 C5
Esson Pl KA3 223 A3
Estate Ave FK1 42 C4
Estate Quadrant G32 139 C8
Estate Rd G32 139 C8
Etive Ave
Bearsden G61 76 B4
Hamilton ML3 162 A1
Etive Cres
Bishopbriggs G64 78 B1
Cumbernauld G67 82 B6
Etive Ct
Clydebank G81 74 C5
Cumbernauld G67 82 B6
Etive Dr
Airdrie ML6 123 C5
Bishopton PA7 72 C2
Cumbernauld G67 82 B6

Etive Dr *continued*
Glasgow G46 136 D1
Etive Pl
Cumbernauld G67 82 C6
Irvine KA12 219 D5
Larkhall ML9 184 F5
Stirling FK9 2 B3
Etive St
Glasgow G32 119 A5
Wishaw ML2 165 B1
Etive Wlk ML7 147 B3
Etna Ct FK2 42 D7
Etna Ind Est ML2 164 C4
Etna Rd FK2 42 D7
Etna Road Rdbt FK2 42 E7
Etna St ML2 164 C4
Eton La 3 G12 96 E2
Etterick Wynd 9 G72 161 C7
Ettrick Ave
Hattonrig ML4 142 A7
Renfrew PA4 94 F2
Ettrick Cres
Kilmarnock KA3 222 F3
Rutherglen G73 138 C7
Ettrick Ct
Cambuslang G72 139 D4
Coatbridge ML5 122 C3
Falkirk FK1 42 D1
Ettrick Dr
Bearsden G61 75 C7
Bishopton PA7 72 C2
Ettrick Hill 2 G74 160 A3
Ettrick Oval PA2 132 E8
Ettrick Pl
Ayr KA8 236 B4
Glasgow G43 136 D7
3 Greenock PA15 46 B3
Ettrick Sq G67 61 F2
Ettrick St ML2 165 A5
Ettrick Terr PA5 131 C8
Ettrick Way
9 Cumbernauld G67 61 F1
Renfrew PA4 94 F2
Ettrick Wlk G67 61 F2
Euchan Pl KA10 229 G5
Eurocentral ML4 142 F8
Eurocentral Rail Terminal ML1 142 D7
Evan Cres G46 136 D2
Evan Dr G46 136 D2
Evans St FK5 23 C3
Evanton Dr G46 135 E3
Evanton Pl G46 135 E3
Evelyn Terr KA13 207 E2
Everard Ct G21 97 E7
Everard Dr G21 97 E6
Everard Pl 2 G21 97 E7
Everard Quadrant G21 97 E7
Everglades The G69 100 B8
Evergreen Trailer Ct FK6 22 A2
Eversley St G32 119 A3
Everton Rd G53 115 C2
Ewart Cres ML3 162 B1
Ewart Dr ML6 123 A6
Ewart Gdns ML3 162 B1
Ewart Terr ML3 162 A2
Ewenfield Ave KA7 239 A4
Ewenfield Gdns KA7 239 A4
Ewenfield Pk KA7 238 F4
Ewenfield Pl KA7 239 A4
Ewenfield Rd KA7 239 A4
Ewing Ave FK2 42 B7
Ewing Ct
Hamilton ML3 183 C7
Stirling FK7 7 C3
Ewing Dr FK2 42 B7
Ewing Pl
Falkirk FK2 42 B7
Glasgow G31 118 C5
Ewing Rd PA12 129 C3
Ewing St
Kilbarchan PA10 111 A3
Rutherglen G73 138 A7
Ewing Way KA3 211 D8
Ewing Wlk G62 55 C1
Excelsior Pk ML2 164 D2
Excelsior St ML1 164 C2
Exchange Pl G1 241 A2
Exeter Dr G11 96 A2
Exeter La G11 96 A2
Exeter St ML5 122 A5
Exhibition Centre Sta G3 116 E8
Exmouth Pl PA19 44 E5
Eynort St G22 97 A7
Eyrepoint Ct G33 119 A8

F

Factory Pl KA21 216 F8
Factory Rd ML1 163 E5
Fagan Ct G72 140 E1
FAIFLEY 74 C7
Faifley Rd G81 74 C7
Failford Pl KA3 223 B4
Fairbairn Cres G46 136 A2
Fairbairn Path G40 118 A4
Fairburn St G32 118 F4
Fairfax Ave G44 137 C5
FAIRFIELD 5 B2
Fairfield FK10 5 C1
Fairfield Ave FK4 40 A6
Fairfield Ct G76 157 E5
Fairfield Dr
Clarkston G76 157 E5
Renfrew PA4 94 D1
Fairfield Gdns G51 115 F8
Fairfield Pk KA7 238 E7
Fairfield Pl
Bothwell G71 141 B2
East Kilbride G74 159 C2
Falkirk FK2 42 C5
Glasgow G51 115 F8
Hamilton ML3 162 E1
Fairfield Rd
Ayr KA7 238 E7
Sauchie FK10 5 C1
Fairfields FK2 13 E5
Fairfield Sch FK10 5 B1
Fairfield St G51 115 F8
Fairford Dr G67 82 D7
Fairgreen Pl FK7 11 E8
Fairhaven KA10 229 F7
Fairhaven Ave ML6 123 E6
Fairhaven Rd G23 96 E8
Fairhaven Sq KA13 207 B4
FAIRHILL 162 C1
Fairhill Ave ML3 162 C1
Fairhill Cres ML3 162 C1
Fairhill Pl ML3 183 C7
Fairhill Rd FK7 7 B1
Fairholm Ave ML3 163 D1
Fairholm St
Glasgow G32 118 F4
Larkhall ML9 184 F4
Fair Isle Pl KA3 223 A6
Fairley Dr FK5 23 A3
Fairley St G51 116 B6
Fairlie G74 159 D3
Fairlie Ave KA1 227 D7
Fairlie Dr
Falkirk FK1 41 D5
Irvine KA11 220 B6
Fairlie Gdns FK1 41 D5
Fairlie Park Dr G11 96 A2
Fairlie St FK1 41 C5
Fairlie View KA2 226 E5
Fairmount Dr FK10 5 B2
Fair Oaks G76 158 E8
Fairrie St PA15 46 D3
Fairview Ct G62 55 A1
Fair View Dr ML11 214 A4
Fairway G61 75 C5
Fair Way G82 48 A8
Fairway Ave PA2 133 D8
Fairways
Irvine KA12 219 A7
Larkhall ML9 185 C3
Stewarton KA3 211 E8
Fairways Pl FK4 40 B7
Fairways The
Bothwell G71 141 A2
Johnstone PA5 131 D7
Fairways View G81 74 D6
Fairway View KA9 236 D6
Fairweather Pl G77 156 C3
Fairyburn Rd FK10 9 F8
Fairyhill Pl KA1 227 E6
Fairyhill Rd KA1 227 E6
Fairyknowe Ct G71 141 B2
Fairyknowe Gdns G71 141 B2
Faith Ave PA11 89 E2
Falconbridge Rd G74 160 C4
Falcon Cres
Greenock PA16 45 A6
Paisley PA3 113 B6
Falcon Dr FK5 23 B3
Falconer Ct FK7 7 C3
Falconer St PA14 47 C2
Falconer Terr ML3 162 C1
Falcon La PA16 45 A5
Falcon Rd PA5 131 D7
Falcon Terr G20 96 C8
Falcon Terrace La G20 96 C8
Falfield St 1 G5 117 A4
FALKIRK 42 D6
Falkirk & District Royal Infmy FK1 42 A4
Falkirk Grahamston Sta FK1 42 B5
Falkirk High Sch FK1 41 E4
Falkirk High Sta FK1 42 A3
Falkirk Rd
Bannockburn FK7 11 F8
Bonnybridge FK4 40 C6
Cowie FK7 12 A6
Falkirk FK2, FK3 42 F6
Falkirk, Glen Village FK1 42 B1
Larbert FK5 23 B1
Falkirk Stadium (Falkirk FC) FK2 42 F6
Falkirk Wheel* FK1 41 A5
Falkland Ave G77 157 A5
Falkland Cres G64 98 D8
Falkland Dr G74 159 D1
Falkland La G12 96 B3
Falkland Park Rd KA8 236 A3
Falkland Pk G74 159 D1
Falkland Pl
Ayr KA8 236 A3
Coatbridge ML5 122 B3
East Kilbride G74 159 D1
Stenhousemuir FK5 23 E4
Falkland Rd KA8 236 A3
Falkland St G12 96 B3
FALLIN 8 C3
Fallin Prim Sch FK7 8 D5
Falloch Pl ML2 165 F6
Falloch Rd
Bearsden G61 75 C2
Glasgow G42 137 A7
Milngavie G62 54 E3
FALLSIDE 141 D6
Fallside Ave G71 141 C6
Fallside Rd G71 141 B4
Fallside Sec Sch G71 141 D6
Falmouth Dr PA19 44 F5
Falside Ave PA2 113 E1
Falside Rd
Glasgow G32 119 B2
Paisley PA2 113 E1
Falstaff G74 160 C5
Fancy Farm Pl PA16 44 F4
Fancy Farm Rd PA16 45 A4
Faraday Ave ML2 165 C3
Faraday Ret Pk ML5 122 A6
Faransay Pl KA3 223 A5
Fara St G23 96 F8
Fardalehill View KA2 221 F1
Farden Pl KA9 236 D6
Farie St G73 137 F8
Farlands View KA23 190 C4
Farm Cres ML1 143 F4
Farm Ct G71 141 B4
Farme Castle Ct G73 118 C1
Farme Castle Est G73 118 C1
Farme Cross G73 118 B1
Farmeloan Rd G73 138 B8
Farmfield Terr KA23 190 D5
Farmgate Sq ML4 141 F4
Farm Houses The G65 60 E7
Farmington Ave G32 119 D5
Farmington Gate G32 119 D4
Farmington Gdns G32 119 D5
Farmington Gr G32 119 D5
Farm La ML4 141 F3
Farm Pk G66 79 D4
Farm Rd
Blantyre G72 140 D1
Clydebank, Duntocher G81 74 A7
Clydebank G81 73 D3
Cowie FK7 12 D8
Fallin FK7 8 D4
Glasgow G41 116 B5
Hamilton ML3 161 F4
Kilmarnock KA3 222 E3
Port Glasgow PA14 68 E7
Prestwick KA9 233 D1
Farm St
Falkirk FK2 24 A1
Motherwell ML1 163 D7
Farm Terr ML3 161 F4
Farndale G74 159 C3
Farne Dr G44 137 C4
Farnell St G4 97 B2
Farquhar Rd
Greenock PA14 46 F2
Port Glasgow PA14 47 A2
Farquharson Way FK1 41 F1
Farquhar Sq EH48 107 C3
Farrell Pl KA8 236 B2
Farrier Ct PA5 111 F3
Faskally Ave G64 77 E3
Faskally Wlk 19 ML2 165 F6
Faskin Cres G53 134 F7
Faskine Ave
Airdrie ML6 122 F6
Calderbank ML6 123 B2
Faskine Cres ML6 122 F6
Faskin Pl G53 134 F7
Faskin Rd G53 134 F7
Fasque Pl G15 74 E4
Fastnet St G33 119 A8
FAULDHEAD 80 B6
Fauldhouse St G5 117 D3
Faulds G69 120 C5
Faulds Gdns G69 120 C5
Fauldshead Rd PA4 94 D3
Faulds La ML5 121 F3
Fauldspark Cres G69 120 C6
Faulds Park Rd PA19 43 E5
Faulds St ML5 121 F3
Fauldswood Cres PA2 113 B2
Fauldswood Dr PA2 113 B2
Faulds Wynd KA23 190 C4
Faulkner Gr ML1 164 F8
Fearnach Pl G20 96 B7
Fearnan Pl PA16 45 A4
Fearnmore Rd G20 96 D7
Fearnoch KA9 236 C5
Fellhill St KA7 239 B5
Fells The G66 57 E8
Fellsview Ave G66 58 F1
Felton Pl G13 94 F7
Fencedyke Cl KA11 219 F4
Fencedyke Prim Sch KA11 220 A3
Fencedyke Way KA11 220 A4
Fendoch St G32 119 A4
Fenella St G32 119 B5
Fennsbank Ave G73 138 D3
Fenton St FK10 10 A7
FENWICK 213 B4
Fenwick Cl KA3 223 C6
Fenwick Dr
Barrhead G78 134 D1
Hamilton ML3 183 E7
Fenwickland Ave KA7 239 A4
Fenwickland Pl KA7 239 B4
Fenwick Pl G46 136 B1
Fenwick Prim Sch KA3 213 A4
Fenwick Rd
Glasgow G46 136 C3
Kilmaurs KA3 222 C7
Waterside KA3 213 E4
Ferclay St G81 74 D7
Fereneze Ave
Barrhead G78 134 B3
Clarkston G76 157 C8
Paisley PA4 114 A8
Fereneze Cres
Glasgow G13 95 A7
Hamilton ML3 161 F3
Fereneze Dr PA2 133 C7
Fereneze Gr G78 134 B4
Fereneze Rd G78 154 C8
Fergus Ave PA3 113 A5
Fergus Ct G20 96 E4
Fergus Dr
Glasgow G20 96 E4
Greenock PA16 45 A4
Paisley PA3 113 A5
Fergus Gdns ML3 162 F2
Fergushill Rd KA13 208 A3
Fergus La G20 96 F4
Ferguslie PA1 113 B4
FERGUSLIE PARK 113 A5
Ferguslie Park Ave PA3 113 A5
Ferguslie Park Cres PA3 113 A4
Ferguslie Wlk PA1 113 B4
Ferguson Ave
Milngavie G62 55 A1
Prestwick KA9 236 D8
Renfrew PA4 94 D3
Ferguson Dr
Denny FK6 21 D1
Motherwell ML1 163 E3
Stenhousemuir FK2 24 A5
Ferguson Gdns KA1 227 B8
Ferguson Gr FK4 40 B6
Ferguson St
Ayr KA8 236 C3
Johnstone PA5 111 E3
Renfrew PA4 94 D3
Stirling FK8 1 F2
Ferguson Way ML6 103 B2
Fergus Pl PA16 45 A4
Fergus Rd PA16 45 A4
Fergusson Pl G74 160 D5
Fergusson Rd G67 61 F2
Fergusson Terr G66 58 C5
Ferguston Rd G61 75 F3
Fernan St G32 118 F5
Fern Ave
Bishopbriggs G64 98 B8
Erskine PA8 93 B7
Kirkintilloch G66 79 C5
Fernbank
Prestwick KA9 236 B5
Stirling FK9 2 B3
Fernbank Ave G72 139 C4
Fernbank Ct KA9 236 B5
Fernbank St G22 97 E5
Fern Brae KA7 239 C3
Fernbrae Ave G73 138 C3
Fernbrae Way G73 138 B3
Fern Cotts 1 G13 95 F5
Ferncroft Dr G44 137 D5
Ferndale ML9 185 A1
Ferndale Ct G23 96 D8
Ferndale Dr G23 96 D8
Ferndale Gdns G23 96 D8
Ferndale Pl G23 96 D8
Fern Dr G78 134 B4
Ferness Oval G21 98 C7
Ferness Pl G21 98 C7
Ferness Rd G21 98 C6
Fern Gr G69 101 A6
Ferngrove Ave G12 96 B6
FERNHILL 138 B3
Fernhill Grange G71 141 A1
Fernhill Rd G73 138 B3
Fernhill Sch G73 138 C3
FERNIEGAIR 163 B2
Ferniegair Ave G84 16 B2
Fernie Gdns
Cardross G82 48 B8
Glasgow G20 96 E7
Fernieshaw Rd ML1 144 F2
Fernington Pl ML2 165 B4
Ferninigton Pl ML2 165 A4
Fern La
Glasgow G13 95 F5
Lennoxtown G66 33 C1
Fernlea G61 75 E3
Fern Lea Gr FK2 24 C3
Fernlea Rd 5 G66 58 E1
Fernleigh Pl G69 80 F2
Fernleigh Rd G43 136 D5
Fern Pl KA1 227 C7
Fernside Wlk ML3 162 E1
Fernslea Ave G72 161 C8
Fern St ML1 164 A4
Ferrier Ct KA10 229 F4
Ferry Ct FK9 2 A3
Ferryden Ct G14 95 E2
Ferryden St G14 95 E2
Ferryfield Gdns G83 27 F4
Ferry Loan G83 27 E5
Ferry Orch FK9 2 D1
Ferry Rd
Bishopton PA7 72 B4
Bothwell G71 141 A1
Cardross G82 48 B6
Glasgow G3 96 B1
Glasgow G3 96 C1
Renfrew PA4 94 D5
Rosneath G84 15 B3
South Alloa FK7 9 F4
Stirling FK9 2 D1
Uddingston G71 140 E6
Fersit Ct G43 136 C6
Fersit St G43 136 C6
Fetlar Ct G72 138 F3
Fetlar Dr
Glasgow G44 137 C5
Kilmarnock KA3 223 A6
Fetlar Rd PA11 110 D8
Fettercairn Ave G15 74 E4
Fettercairn Gdns G64 78 C1
Fettercairn Pl ML6 103 B3
Fettes St G33 118 F8
Fiddison Pl KA9 236 E5
Fiddoch Ct ML2 165 F7
Fidra St G33 118 F8
Fielden Pl G40 118 A5
Fielden St G40 118 A5
Field Gr G76 157 F5
Fieldhead Dr G43 136 A5
Fieldhead Sq G43 136 A5
Fieldings The KA3 195 C8
Field Rd
Clarkston G76 157 F5
Clydebank G81 74 D8
Larkhall ML9 185 B2
Fields La PA6 91 B3
Field St ML3 162 D1
Fife Ave
Airdrie ML6 123 A5
Glasgow G52 115 B4
Fife Cres G71 141 A1
Fife Ct G71 141 A1
Fife Dr
Greenock PA16 44 D5
Motherwell ML1 142 D2
Fife Rd PA16 44 D5
Fife Way
Bishopbriggs G64 98 D8
Glasgow G64 97 F7
Fifth Ave
Airdrie ML6 123 C8
Glasgow G12 95 F5
Millerston G33 99 B5
Renfrew PA4 94 C1
Fifth Rd G72 161 E5
Fifty Pitches Pl G51 115 C7
Fifty Pitches Rd G52 115 B7
Fifty Pitches Way G51 115 B7
Finaly Wlk G83 27 F8
Finart Dr PA2 114 B1
Finaven Gdns G61 75 B8
Finbraken Dr PA19 43 E5
Fincastle Pl FK7 12 E8
Finch Dr G13 95 A8
Finch Gr ML5 122 E3
Finch Pl
Johnstone PA5 131 D7
Kilmarnock KA1 228 C7
Finch Rd PA16 45 B5
Finch Way ML4 141 F8
Findhorn PA8 73 A2
Findhorn Ave
Paisley PA2 112 F1
Renfrew PA4 94 E3
Findhorn Ct G75 179 D8
Findhorn Pl
East Kilbride G75 179 D8
Falkirk FK1 42 D2
Troon KA10 229 G5
Findhorn Rd KA9 233 F4
Findhorn St G33 118 D8
Findlay Ct 3 ML1 163 D8
Findlay's Brae KA21 216 F7
Findlay St
9 Kilsyth G65 60 D8
Motherwell ML1 163 F5
Findlay Terr 2 G72 139 D6
Findochty PA8 73 A3
Findochty Pl G33 99 E2
Findochty St G33 99 E2
Fingal La G20 96 C7
Fingal St G20 96 D7
Fingalton Rd G77 155 E5
Fingask St G32 119 C4
Finglas Ave PA2 114 B1
Finglen Cres FK10 4 C4
Finglen Gdns G62 54 E2
Finglen Pl G53 135 B5
Fingleton Ave G78 134 D1
Finhaven St G32 118 E3
Finistere Ave FK1 42 B3
Finlarig Ct FK5 23 F4
Finlarig St G34 120 C7
Finlas Ave KA7 239 B3
Finlas Pl G22 97 D5
Finlas St G22 97 D4
Finlay Ave KA24 191 D7
Finlay Dr
Glasgow G31 118 A7
Linwood PA3 111 F5
Finlay Rise G62 76 C8
Finlayson Dr
Airdrie ML6 123 E7
Kilmarnock KA3 223 D3
Finlayson Pl FK5 23 C5
Finlayson Quadrant 1 ML6 123 E7
Finlaystone Country Estate* PA14 69 E8
Finlaystone Cres PA13 69 D2
Finlaystone Pl PA13 69 D2
Finlaystone Rd
Kilmacolm PA13 69 D4
Port Glasgow PA14 69 A7
Finlaystone St ML5 121 E7
Finnart Cres PA19 44 C6
Finnart Rd PA16 45 D6
Finnart Sq G40 117 F3
Finnart St
Glasgow G40 117 F3
Glasgow G40 117 F4
Greenock PA16 45 D6
Finneston La 11 PA15 46 B3
Finneston St PA15 46 B3
Finneston Way 12 PA15 46 B3
Finnick Glen KA7 239 A3

Finnieston Sq [9] G3 116 E8
Finnieston St
Glasgow G3 116 E7
Glasgow G3 116 E8
Finnie Terr
Gourock PA19 44 D6
Springside KA11 220 F2
Finnie Wynd ML1 164 B4
FINNISTON 116 D8
Finsbay St G51 115 E6
Fintaig La ML2 165 E3
Fintrie Terr ML3 161 E4
Fintry Ave PA2 133 E7
Fintry Cres
Barrhead G78 134 C1
Bishopbriggs G64 78 C1
Fintry Ct ML5 122 C3
Fintry Dr G44 137 D7
Fintry Gdns G61 75 C8
Fintry Pl
East Kilbride G75 180 B4
Irvine KA11 220 B2
Fintry Rd PA15 46 B2
Fintry Terr KA11 220 B3
Fintry Wlk KA11 220 B2
Fir Bank KA7 239 C5
Firbank Ave G64 78 B8
Fir Bank Ave ML9 185 B1
Firbank Quadrant ML6 123 E3
Firbank Terr G78 134 E1
Fir Ct G72 139 E4
Firdon Cres G15 75 A1
Fir Dr G75 180 B5
Firethorn Dr G67 82 D6
Fir Gr
Motherwell ML1 143 A2
Uddingston G71 141 C8
FIRHILL 97 A3
Firhill Ave ML6 122 F6
Firhill Ct G20 97 A4
Firhill Dr KA9 233 D5
Firhill Rd G20 97 A4
Firhill St G20 97 A4
Firhill Stadium (Partick Thistle FC) G20 97 A4
Fir La FK5 23 D1
Firlee G75 179 F7
Firpark Cl G31 117 F8
Firpark Ct G31 117 F8
Firpark Rd G64 98 B8
Firpark Sch ML1 163 F4
Firpark St G31 117 F8
Fir Park St ML1 163 F4
Firpark Terr
Cambusbarron FK7 6 C5
Glasgow G31 117 F7
Fir Pk (Motherwell FC) ML1 163 F4
Fir Pl
Cambuslang G72 139 C6
Cleland ML1 144 B1
Glasgow G69 120 A3
Johnstone PA5 112 A1
Kilmarnock KA1 227 C7
Firs Cres FK7 7 D2
Firs Entry FK7 7 D2
Firs Pk FK2 42 C6
Firs Rd FK10 4 D2
Firs St FK2 42 C6
Fir St PA15 46 E2
First Ave
Alexandria G83 27 F5
Auchinloch G66 79 D1
Bearsden G61 76 A3
Dumbarton G82 50 C2
Glasgow G44 136 F2
Irvine KA12 224 E8
Millerston G33 99 B4
Renfrew PA4 94 C2
Stevenston KA20 217 F7
Uddingston G71 140 F8
First Gdns G41 116 A4
Firs The
Bannockburn FK7 7 D2
Glasgow G44 137 B4
First Rd G72 161 E5
First St
Irvine KA12 219 B8
Uddingston G71 140 F8
First Terr G81 74 A3
Fir Terr PA19 44 D6
Firth Cres PA19 44 C6
Firth Gdns KA10 229 E7
Firth Rd KA10 229 E7
Firthview Terr G82 49 C3
Firth View Terr KA22 205 D4
Firtree Pl ML2 166 B6
Firtree Rd ML2 166 B6
Fir View ML6 123 B2
Firwood Cts G77 156 E4
Firwood Dr G44 137 C6
Firwood Rd G77 156 E4
Fischer Gdns PA1 112 F5
FISHCROSS 5 E3
Fishcross Prim Sch FK10 5 D3
Fisher Ave
Kilsyth G65 60 D8
Paisley PA1 112 F4
Fisher Cres G81 74 B6
Fisher Ct
Glasgow G31 117 F7
Knockentiber KA2 221 F3
Fisher Dr PA1 112 F4
Fishermans Wlk FK9 2 A3
Fisher Pl G84 17 A2
Fishers Rd PA4 94 C6
Fisher St ML9 185 B1
Fisher Way
Crosshouse KA2 221 D1
Paisley PA1 112 F4
Fisherwood Rd G83 27 E8
Fishescoates Ave G73 138 C4
Fishescoates Gdns G73 138 D5
Fitzalan Dr PA3 114 A6
Fitzalan Rd PA4 94 A1
Fitzroy Gr [1] G74 179 D8
Fitzroy La G3 116 E8
Fitzroy Pl [2] G3 116 E8
Five Roads KA13 208 A3
Five Ways Rd ML9 200 D4
Flakefield G74 159 B2
Flanders St G81 74 C7
Flanigan Gr ML4 142 A5
Flatterton La PA16 44 D2
Flatterton Rd PA16 44 C2
Flavell Pl ML6 123 A6
Flaxfield Gr ML1 142 D2
Flaxmill Ave ML2 164 D4
Flax Mill Rd ML7 127 F5
Flax Rd G71 141 A5
Fleck Ave KA21 206 A2
Fleet Ave PA4 94 E1
Fleet St G32 119 B4
Fleming Ave
Chryston G69 100 C8
Clydebank G81 94 D8
Fleming Cres KA21 206 A3
Fleming Ct
Carluke ML8 187 E1
Clydebank G81 74 B2
Denny FK6 39 D8
Hamilton ML3 161 E4
Motherwell ML1 164 A4
Troon KA10 229 G4
Fleming Dr
Stenhousemuir FK5 24 A3
Stewarton KA3 211 C8
Fleming Gdns FK1 41 E6
Fleming Pl
Blackridge EH48 107 E3
East Kilbride G75 180 E8
Fleming Rd
Bellshill ML4 142 B7
Bishopton PA7 72 B3
Cumbernauld G67 61 F2
Houston PA6 91 A2
Fleming St
Denny FK6 21 F2
Glasgow G31 118 B6
Kilmarnock KA1 227 E5
Paisley PA3 113 E7
Fleming Terr KA12 219 B5
FLEMINGTON
Cambuslang 139 D3
Motherwell 164 B5
Flemington Ind Est G72 139 E4
Flemington Ind Pk ML1 164 C5
Flemington St G21 97 F3
Flemington Way [1] G69 100 C8
Fleming Way
Hamilton ML3 161 E4
[21] Larkhall ML9 185 C1
Flenders Ave G76 157 C6
Flenders Rd G76 157 C6
Fletcher Ave PA19 44 E7
Fleurs Ave G41 116 B4
Fleurs Pk FK9 1 F3
Fleurs Rd G41 116 B4
Flinders Pl G75 180 B8
Flint Cres FK7 12 D8
Flloyd St ML5 121 F7
Floorsburn Cres PA5 111 E2
Floors Rd G76 157 C1
Floors St PA5 111 F2
Floors Street Ind Est PA5 111 F2
Flora Gdns G64 78 C2
Florence Dr
Glasgow G46 136 C2
Kilmacolm PA13 89 B8
Florence Gdns G73 138 C4
Florence St
Glasgow G5 117 C5
Greenock PA16 45 B4
Florida Ave G42 137 B8
Florida Cres G42 137 B8
Florida Dr G42 137 A8
Florida Gdns G69 120 A5
Florida Sq G42 137 B8
Florida St G42 137 B8
Florish Rd PA8 93 E8
Flotta Pl KA3 222 F6
Flour Mill Wynd [9] G69 81 A3
Flowerdale Pl G53 135 B3
Flowerhill Ind Est ML6 123 B8
Flowerhill St ML6 123 B8
FLUCHTER 56 B2
Fluchter Rd G64 56 A1
Flures Ave PA8 93 E8
Flures Cres PA8 93 E8
Flures Dr PA8 93 E8
Flures Pl PA8 93 E8
Fochabers Dr G52 115 C6
Fogo Pl G20 96 D6
Foinaven Dr G46 136 A5
Foinaven Gdns G46 136 A6
Foinaven Way G46 136 A6
Foinavon Rd ML3 183 E3
Footfield Rd ML4 141 F3
Forbes Cres FK5 23 D1
Forbes Ct FK2 42 E6
Forbes Dr
Ayr KA8 236 C4
Forbes Dr *continued*
[1] Glasgow G40 117 F5
Motherwell ML1 142 C2
Forbes Pl
Kilmarnock KA3 223 B2
Paisley PA1 113 E4
Forbes Rd FK1 42 D4
Forbes St
Alloa FK10 9 F6
Glasgow G40 117 F6
Forbes Wlk KA3 223 B2
Ford Ave KA11 225 D8
Fordbank Prim Sch PA5 131 C8
Forde Cres KA20 206 F2
Fordneuk St G40 118 A5
Fordoun St G34 120 D8
Ford Rd
Bonnybridge FK4 40 A5
Glasgow G12 96 D4
Newton Mearns G77 156 D3
Fordyce Ct G77 156 D4
Fordyce Gdns FK1 41 E4
Fordyce St G11 96 C2
Forebraes FK10 10 B7
Foregate Sq [6] KA1 222 F1
Foregate The [4] KA1 222 F1
FOREHILL 239 B6
Forehill Prim Sch KA7 239 C6
Forehill Rd KA7 239 C6
Forehouse Rd PA10 110 D3
Foremount Terrace La [6] G12 96 C3
Fore Row ML3 162 E4
Fore St
Glasgow G14 95 C3
Port Glasgow PA14 47 C2
Forest Ave
Bellshill ML4 142 D3
Hamilton ML3 183 D6
Forestburn Ct ML6 122 D7
Forest Dr G71 141 A3
Forester Gr FK10 4 F2
Forestfield Gdns ML6 105 A4
Forest Gdns G66 79 A4
Forest Gr KA3 223 B5
Foresthall Cres G21 98 A3
Foresthall Dr G21 98 A3
Forest Kirk ML8 202 B8
Forest La ML3 183 D6
Forestlea Rd ML8 202 A8
Forest Pk ML2 165 D5
Forest Pl
Kirkintilloch G66 79 A4
Paisley PA2 113 E2
Forest Rd
Cumbernauld G67 62 D2
Cumbernauld G67 62 E6
Larkhall ML9 185 B3
Forest View G67 62 C3
Forest Way KA7 239 C5
Forfar Ave G52 115 B4
Forfar Cres G64 98 C8
Forfar Rd PA16 44 F3
Forgan Gdns G64 98 D8
Forge Dr ML5 121 F7
Forge Ind Est KA1 222 E1
Forge Pl G21 98 B2
Forge Rd
Airdrie ML6 123 F6
Ayr KA8 236 B4
Forge Row ML6 123 C3
Forge Sh Ctr The G31 118 C5
Forge St G21 98 B2
Forge Vennel KA13 207 C4
FORGEWOOD 142 D2
Forgewood Path ML6 123 F6
Forgewood Rd ML1 142 C2
Forglen Cres FK9 2 A6
Forglen Rd FK9 2 B6
Forglen St G34 100 B1
Formakin Estate* PA7 71 C2
Formby Dr G23 76 D1
Forres Ave G46 136 D3
Forres Cres ML4 142 A6
Forres Gate G46 136 D2
Forres Quadrant ML2 165 B5
Forres St
[1] Glasgow G23 76 E1
Hamilton G72 161 C5
Forrest Dr G61 75 B8
Forrester Ct [1] G64 97 F8
Forrester Gait FK5 22 E6
Forrester Pl FK2 14 D3
FORRESTFIELD 106 A3
Forrestfield Cres G77 156 E5
Forrestfield Gdns G77 156 E5
Forrestfield Rd ML6 105 F7
Forrestfield St G21 98 A1
Forrest Gate
Hamilton ML3 162 B1
Motherwell G71 121 B1
Forrest Pl
Crossford ML8 201 B1
Harthill ML7 127 E5
Forrest Rd
Forrestfield ML6 106 A1
Lanark ML11 215 B5
Salsburgh ML6, ML7 126 B6
Stirling FK8 2 B1
Forrest St
Airdrie, Clarkston ML6 123 E8
Airdrie ML6 123 D8
Glasgow G40 118 A5
Hamilton G72 161 F7
Shotts ML7 146 E5
Forsa Ct G75 180 C4
Forsyth Ct ML11 215 C4
Forsyth Gr PA16 45 D6
Forsyth La FK7 7 C1
Forsyth St
Airdrie ML6 123 B8
Greenock PA16 45 D6
Fortacre Pl KA11 220 B5
Forteviot Ave G69 120 C5
Forteviot Pl G69 120 C5
Forth Ave
Larbert FK5 23 B3
Paisley PA2 112 F1
Forthbank Ind Est FK10 10 B4
Forthbank Stadium (Stirling Albion FC) FK7 7 E7
Forth Cres
Alloa FK10 10 C5
East Kilbride G75 179 E7
Stirling FK8 7 B8
Forth Ct
East Kilbride G75 179 E7
Stirling FK8 2 B1
Forth Gr G75 179 E8
Forth Pk
Bridge of Allan FK9 2 A5
Stirling FK9 1 F5
Forth Pl
Johnstone PA5 131 C8
Kilmarnock KA1 228 A5
Larkhall ML9 199 B8
Stirling FK8 7 B8
Forth Rd
Bearsden G61 75 D2
Torrance G64 78 B8
Forth St
Cambus FK10 9 A8
Clydebank G81 94 C8
Fallin FK7 8 C4
Glasgow G41 116 F3
Stirling FK8 2 B1
Forth Terr ML3 183 B8
Forthvale FK11 4 A6
Forthvale Ct FK9 2 B2
Forth Valley Coll (Clackmannan Campus) FK10 10 B8
Forth Valley Coll (Clackmannan Campus annexe) FK10 10 C8
Forth Valley Coll (Falkirk Campus) FK2 42 E6
Forth Valley Coll (Stirling Campus) FK7 7 C6
Forth Valley Hospl (under construction) FK5 22 F3
Forthview FK7 7 E1
Forth View FK8 2 B1
Forthview Ct FK1 41 F2
Forth Wlk [5] G67 61 F1
Forties Cres G46 136 A5
Forties Ct G46 135 F5
Forties Gdns G46 136 A5
Forties Rd PA6 111 C8
Forties Way G46 136 A5
Fortieth Ave G75 180 F5
Fortingall Ave G12 96 C6
Fortingall Pl G12 96 C6
Fortingall Rd G72 161 F5
Fortissat Ave ML7 146 D6
Fort Matilda Pl PA16 45 B7
Fort Matilda Sta PA16 45 B8
Fort Matilda Terr PA16 45 B7
Fortrose Ct G72 161 C3
Fortrose St G11 96 B2
Fort St
Ayr KA7 235 F1
Motherwell ML1 163 B8
Fortuna Ct FK1 42 C4
Forum Pl ML1 142 C1
Fossil Gr* G14 95 E3
Fossil Gr G66 59 A1
Foswell Dr G15 74 F5
Foswell Pl G15 74 F5
Fotheringay Rd G41 116 E2
Fothringham Rd KA8 239 A8
Foulburn Rd ML7 145 D2
Foulis La G13 95 F6
Foulis St G13 95 F6
Foulsykes Rd ML2 165 E4
Foundry Ct KA13 207 C4
Foundry Loan FK5 23 B2
Foundry Rd
Bonnybridge FK4 40 B5
Cleland ML1 144 C2
Shotts ML7 146 F4
Foundry St FK2 42 A8
Foundry Wynd KA13 207 C4
Fountain Ave PA4 93 B4
Fountain Bsns Ctr The ML5 122 A6
Fountain Craig G12 96 B5
Fountain Cres PA4 93 C5
Fountain Dr PA4 93 C4
Fountain Rd FK9 2 A7
Fountainwell Ave G21 97 D3
Fountainwell Dr G21 97 D2
Fountainwell Pl G21 97 D3
Fountainwell Rd G21 97 D2
Fountainwell Sq G21 97 E2
Fountainwell Terr G21 97 E2
Four Acres Dr KA3 222 B8
Fourth Ave
Auchinloch G66 79 D1
Dumbarton G82 50 D2
Millerston G33 99 B5
Renfrew PA4 94 C2
Fourth Gdns G41 116 A4
Fourth St G71 120 F1
Four Windings PA6 91 B2
Fowlds St KA1 227 F8
Fowler Cres FK6 21 E1
Fowlis Dr G77 156 C6
FOXBAR 132 F8
Foxbar Cres PA2 132 E7
Foxbar Dr
Glasgow G13 95 B6
Paisley PA2 132 E7
Foxbar Rd PA2 132 E7
Foxdale Ave FK4 40 A3
Foxdale Ct FK4 40 A3
Foxdale Dr FK4 40 A3
Foxdale Pl FK4 40 A3
Foxes Gr G66 79 E5
Foxglove Pl
Ayr KA7 239 C3
Glasgow G53 135 B3
Fox Gr ML1 163 B7
Foxhills Pl G23 76 E1
Foxknowe Gdns G81 74 D7
FOXLEY 119 B2
Foxley St G32 119 C1
Fox St
Glasgow G1 240 C1
Greenock PA16 45 D7
Foyers Terr G21 98 A4
Foy Gdns ML4 142 A8
Frampton Ho G20 96 E5
Franchi Dr FK5 23 F5
Francis St [2] G5 117 A4
FRANKERTON 21 A2
Frankfield Rd G33 99 E5
Frankfield St G33 98 E2
Frankfort St G41 116 E1
Franklin Pl G75 159 B1
Franklin Rd KA21 205 E1
Franklin St G40 117 F3
Fraser Ave
Bishopton PA7 72 B4
Dumbarton G82 50 C4
Johnstone PA5 112 A2
Newton Mearns G77 156 E6
Rutherglen G73 138 C8
Troon KA10 229 E5
Fraser Cres ML3 162 B2
Fraser Ct ML9 199 A8
Fraser Gdns G66 79 B8
Fraser Pl FK9 2 B4
Fraser River Twr G75 180 D8
Fraser St
Cambuslang G72 138 E6
Cleland ML1 144 B2
Fraser Wlk KA3 223 C3
Frazer Ave G84 16 A3
Frazer St G40 118 B5
Frederick St ML5 121 E8
FREELAND 93 B7
Freeland Cres G53 135 B6
Freeland Ct G53 135 C6
Freeland Dr
Bridge of Weir PA11 90 D1
Glasgow G53 135 B6
Inchinnan PA4 93 C6
Freeland La [6] G75 180 F8
Freeland Pl G66 79 D8
Freeland Rd PA8 93 B7
Freelands Cres G60 73 C5
Freelands Ct G60 73 C4
Freelands Pl G60 73 C4
Freelands Rd G60 73 C4
Freeneuk La G72 139 B6
Freeneuk Wynd G72 139 B6
Freesia Ct ML1 163 E5
French St
Clydebank G81 73 E3
Glasgow G40 117 F3
Renfrew PA4 94 B2
Wishaw ML2 165 B3
Freuchie St G34 120 B7
Frew St ML6 123 A8
Frew Terr KA12 219 C5
Friar Ave G64 78 B3
Friarscourt Ave G13 95 D8
Friarscourt Rd G69 80 B1
Friars Croft
Irvine KA12 219 B2
Kirkintilloch G66 79 E8
Friarsdene ML11 214 F4
Friarsfield Rd ML11 214 F4
Friarshall Gate PA2 113 D2
Friar's La ML11 214 F4
Friars Lawn KA13 207 D3
Friars Pk ML11 214 F4
Friars Pl G13 95 D8
Friars St FK8 7 B8
Friars Way ML6 123 C4
Friar's Wynd ML11 214 F4
Friarton Rd G43 136 F6
Friendship Gdns FK2 24 C3
Friendship Way PA4 94 D1
Frobisher Ave FK1 41 F4
Frood St ML1 142 C1
Fruin Ave G77 156 E6
Fruin Dr ML2 165 E3
Fruin Ho G82 50 B6
Fruin La G84 25 C8
Fruin Pl G22 97 C4
Fruin Rd G15 74 F1
Fruin Rise ML3 161 F2
Fruin St G22 97 D4
Fudstone Dr KA25 170 A8
Fulbar Ave PA4 94 C4
Fulbar Cres PA2 112 F2
Fulbar Ct PA4 94 D4
Fulbar La PA4 94 D4
Fulbar Rd
Glasgow G51 115 C7
Paisley PA2 112 F3
Fulbar St PA4 94 D4

FULLARTON
Glasgow 119 A3
Irvine 219 B1
Fullarton Ave
Dundonald KA2 225 F2
Glasgow G32 119 A2
Fullarton Cres KA10 229 F1
Fullarton Ct KA1 222 E1
Fullarton Ctyd KA10 230 B1
Fullarton Dr
Glasgow G32 119 A1
Troon KA10 229 F1
Fullarton La G32 119 A2
Fullarton Pl
Coatbridge ML5 121 E3
Stevenston KA20 217 D8
Troon KA10 230 A4
Fullarton Rd
Cambuslang G72 138 F8
Cumbernauld G68 61 E5
Glasgow G32 118 F1
Prestwick KA9 236 C6
Fullarton Rdbt KA12 219 B2
Fullarton St
Ayr KA7 238 F8
Coatbridge ML5 121 E3
Irvine KA12 219 B2
Kilmarnock KA1 222 E1
Fullers Gate G81 74 C7
Fullerton Dr KA23 190 B4
Fullerton La PA15 46 F3
Fullerton Sq KA22 205 C2
Fullerton St PA3 113 D7
Fullerton Terr PA3 113 E7
Fulmar Cres FK5 23 C5
Fulmar Ct 4 G64 97 F8
Fulmar Pk G74 159 D3
Fulmar Pl PA5 131 C6
Fulshaw Cres KA8 236 F2
Fulshaw Ct KA9 236 D5
Fulshaw Pl KA8 236 E3
Fulton Cres PA10 111 B3
Fulton Dr PA6 111 E8
Fulton Gdns PA6 111 E8
Fulton Rd
Milngavie G62 55 B1
Milngavie G62 55 B1
Fulton's La 10 KA3 222 F1
Fulton St G13 95 E7
Fulwood Ave
Glasgow G13 94 F7
Linwood PA3 112 B6
Fulwood Park Ind Est
ML3 162 B4
Fulwood Pl G13 94 F7
Furlongs The ML3 162 E5
Furnace Ct KA1 228 E6
Furnace Rd ML3 183 F3
Fyfe Park Terr PA14 47 F1
FYFE SHORE 47 E2
Fyfe Shore Rd PA14 47 F1
Fyffe Park Rd PA14 47 E1
Fyneart St ML2 165 E4
Fyne Ave ML4 141 E6
Fyne Cres ML9 184 F5
Fyne Ct ML3 162 A1
Fyne La ML7 146 E6
Fyne Way ML1 143 A5
Fynloch Pl G81 73 E7
Fyvie Ave G43 136 B5
Fyvie Cres ML6 123 F7

G

Gaaf Cl KA24 191 A6
Gaberston Ave FK10 10 C7
Gabriel St PA15 46 B2
Gadburn Sch G21 98 C5
Gadie Ave PA4 94 E2
Gadie St G33 118 D8
Gadloch Ave G66 79 D2
Gadloch Gdns G66 79 D3
Gadloch St G22 97 C6
Gadloch View G66 79 D2
Gadsburn Ct G21 98 C6
Gadshill St G21 97 F1
Gael St PA16 45 C4
Gagarin Terr KA13 207 E2
GAILES 224 F3
Gailes Pk G71 140 F2
Gailes Pl KA1 227 E4
Gailes Rd
Cumbernauld G68 61 F5
Irvine KA11 224 E5
Troon KA10 229 E7
Gailes St G40 118 B4
Gainburn Cres G67 81 F6
Gainburn Ct G67 81 F6
Gainburn Gdns G67 81 F5
Gainburn Pl G67 81 F6
Gainburn View G67 82 A6
Gainford Pl KA3 222 F4
Gain Rd
Annathill ML5 81 F1
Cumbernauld G67, ML5 82 A1
Gain & Shankburn Rd
G67 82 C2
Gainside Rd ML5 101 C6
Gairbraid Ave G20 96 D6
Gairbraid Ct G20 96 C6
Gairbraid Pl G20 96 D6
Gairbraid Terr G69 121 A5
Gair Cres
Carluke ML8 188 A3
Wishaw ML2 165 B1
Gairdoch Dr FK2 24 C3
Gairdoch St FK2 42 B8
Gairloch Gdns G66 59 B1
Gair Rd ML8 188 B6
Gair Wynd ML7 147 B3
Gaitskell Ave G83 27 D7
Gala Ave PA4 94 E2
Gala Cres ML2 165 A5
Gala St G33 98 E2
Galbraith Cres
Law ML8 187 A6
Stenhousemuir FK5 23 C4
Galbraith Dr
Glasgow G51 115 E8
Milngavie G62 75 F8
Galdenoch St G33 99 B2
Gallacher Ave PA2 113 A1
Gallacher Cres G83 19 F1
Gallacher Ct
Motherwell ML1 164 B3
Paisley PA1 113 C5
Gallacher Way G82 27 D2
Gallahill Ave PA14 69 A7
Gallamuir Dr FK7 12 D3
Gallamuir Rd FK7 12 D5
Gallan Ave 3 G23 76 E1
Gallery Gr ML5 122 A6
Gallery of Modern Art*
G1 241 A2
Gallion Wlk 14 KA1 227 F8
Galloway Ave
Ayr KA8 236 C2
Hamilton ML3 183 C7
Paisley PA3 113 E7
Wishaw ML2 165 C4
Galloway Ct
Falkirk FK1, FK2 42 B6
Irvine KA11 220 B6
Galloway Dr G73 138 B3
Galloway Pl KA21 216 E8
Galloway Rd
Airdrie ML6 122 F4
East Kilbride G74 160 C3
Galloway St
Falkirk FK1 42 B6
Glasgow G21 97 F6
Galloway Terr PA3 113 E7
GALLOWFLAT 138 C7
Gallowflat St G73 138 B8
GALLOWGATE 118 A5
Gallowgate G1, G40, G31 117 F6
GALLOWHILL 114 A7
GALLOW HILL 215 B5
Gallowhill ML9 185 A2
Gallowhill Ave G66 79 C6
Gallowhill Gr G66 79 C7
Gallowhill Prim Sch PA3 114 B7
Gallowhill Rd
Carmunnock G76 158 E8
Kirkintilloch G66 79 C6
Lanark ML11 215 A4
Paisley PA3 114 A6
Galrigside Rd KA1 227 D7
Galston Ave G77 157 A5
Galston Ct ML3 183 E7
Galston Pl KA3 223 B6
Galston Rd KA1 228 F6
Galston St G53 134 F6
Galt Ave KA12 219 D3
Galt Pl G75 180 D7
Galt St PA15 46 C3
Gambeson Cres FK7 7 D3
Gameshill View KA3 211 E8
Gamrie Dr G53 135 A7
Gamrie Gdns G53 135 A7
Gamrie Rd G53 135 A8
Gannel Hill View FK10 5 E4
Gannochy Dr G64 78 C1
Gantock Cres G33 119 B7
Ganton Ct KA13 207 B3
Gara Rd ML6 123 D5
Garden Ct 2 KA8 235 F1
Gardenhall G75 179 E8
Gardenhall Ct G75 179 E8
Garden Ho G66 58 B6
Garden Pl KA10 229 B3
GARDENSIDE 140 E5
Gardenside ML4 142 A4
Gardenside Ave
Glasgow G32 139 B8
Uddingston G71 140 F6
Gardenside Cres G32 139 B8
Gardenside Gr G32 139 B8
Gardenside Pl G32 139 B8
Gardenside Rd ML3 162 D2
Gardenside St G71 140 E6
Garden Square La KA13 207 E3
Garden Square Wlk ML6 122 D8
Garden St
Ayr KA8 235 F1
Falkirk FK1 42 C5
Kilmarnock KA3 222 F1
Gardens The KA11 220 C6
Garden Terr FK1 42 C5
Garden Veteran's Cotts
PA7 72 F5
Gardiner St KA9 236 C8
Gardner Gr G71 141 A8
Gardner St G11 96 B2
Gardrum Gdns FK1 66 D7
Gardrum Pl KA3 222 F4
Gardyne St G34 100 A1
Garelet Pl KA11 220 B2
Gareloch Ave
Airdrie ML6 102 F2
Paisley PA2 113 A2
Gareloch Cl PA15 46 A2
Gareloch La PA14 68 D8
Gareloch Rd
Greenock PA15 46 A3
Gareloch Rd *continued*
Port Glasgow PA14 68 E8
Rhu G84 15 E4
Gare Rd G84 15 B3
Garfield Ave ML4 142 C5
Garfield Dr ML4 142 C4
Garfield Pl G33 99 E6
Garfield St G31 118 A6
Garforth Rd G69 119 F4
Gargieston Prim Sch
KA2 227 C6
Gargrave Ave G69 119 F4
Garion Dr G13 95 B5
Garlieston Rd G33 119 F6
Garmouth Ct 3 G51 116 A8
Garmouth Gdns 4 G51 116 A8
Garmouth St G51 115 F8
Garnetbank Prim Sch
G3 240 B4
GARNETHILL 240 B4
Garnethill St G3 240 B4
Garnet St G3 240 B4
Garngaber Ave G66 79 D5
Garngaber Ct G66 79 E5
Garngrew Rd FK4 38 F3
Garnhall Ditch* G68 38 E1
Garnhall Farm Rd G68 62 E8
Garnie Ave PA8 93 D8
Garnie Cres PA8 73 D1
Garnie La PA8 93 D8
Garnieland Rd PA8 73 D1
Garnie Oval PA8 73 D1
Garnie Pl PA8 73 D1
GARNKIRK 100 B6
Garnkirk La G33 99 E5
Garnock Acad KA25 149 A2
Garnock Ct
Irvine KA12 219 C2
4 Kilbirnie KA25 149 A1
Garnock Pk G74 160 B1
Garnock Rd
Kilmarnock KA1 228 A5
Stevenston KA20 217 D8
Stevenston, Stevenston Site
KA20 218 C6
Garnockside KA14 170 B6
Garnock St
Dalry KA24 191 C7
Glasgow G21 97 F2
Kilbirnie KA25 149 B2
Garnock Swimming Pool
KA25 149 A1
Garnock View
Glengarnock KA14 170 B7
Kilwinning KA13 207 E4
GARNQUEEN 101 E5
Garnqueen Cres ML5 101 D6
Garpel Way PA12 129 B2
Garrallan KA13 207 C2
Garraway Pl G84 16 F1
Garrawy Rd G84 16 F2
Garrell Ave G65 36 D1
Garrell Gr G65 36 D2
Garrell Pl G65 60 C8
Garrell Rd G65 60 C8
Garrell Way
Cumbernauld G67 61 E2
Kilsyth G65 60 C8
Garret Pl G68 61 D5
Garrick Ave G77 156 D2
Garrick Ct G77 156 D2
Garrier Ct KA11 220 F2
Garrier Pl KA1 222 D2
Garrier Rd KA11 220 F2
Garrioch Cres 1 G20 96 D5
Garrioch Dr G20 96 D5
Garrioch Gate 8 G20 96 D5
Garriochmill Rd
Glasgow G20 96 E3
Glasgow G20 96 F3
Garriochmill Way 3 G20 96 F3
Garrioch Quadrant 2
G20 96 D5
Garrioch Rd G20 96 D5
Garrion Bsns Pk ML2 186 A8
Garrion Pl ML9 185 F1
Garrion St ML2 186 C6
Garrison Pl FK1 42 B5
GARROWHILL 120 A5
Garrowhill Dr G69 119 F5
Garrowhill Prim Sch
G69 120 A5
Garrowhill Sta G69 119 F6
Garry Ave G61 76 B2
Garry Dr PA2 113 A2
Garryhorn KA9 236 D6
Garry Pl
Falkirk FK1 42 D2
Kilmarnock KA1 228 A5
Troon KA10 229 G5
Garry St G44 137 A7
Garry Way ML7 146 E6
Garscadden Prim Sch
G13 94 F7
Garscadden Rd G15 75 A2
Garscadden Road S G13 95 A8
Garscadden Sta G14 95 A6
Garscadden View 5 G81 74 D3
Garscube Mill G61 76 A2
Garscube Rd G4, G20 97 B2
Garshake Ave G82 50 C5
Garshake Rd G82 50 C5
Garshake Terr G82 50 C5
Gartartan Rd PA1 114 F5
Gartcarron Hill G68 61 C3
Gartcloss Rd ML5 101 C2
Gartclush Gdns FK7 11 E8
Gartconnell Dr G61 75 E6
Gartconnell Gdns G61 75 E6
Gartconnell Rd G61 75 E6
Gartconner Ave G66 80 B8
Gartconner Prim Sch G66 80 B8
GARTCOSH 100 F5
Gartcosh Business
Interchange G69 101 B4
Gartcosh Prim Sch G69 100 F4
Gartcosh Rd ML5 101 A1
Gartcosh Sta G69 101 A4
Gartcosh Wlk ML4 141 F5
Gartcows Ave FK1 42 A4
Gartcows Cres FK1 42 A3
Gartcows Dr FK1 42 A4
Gartcows Gdns FK1 41 F4
Gartcows Pl FK1 42 A3
Gartcows Rd FK1 42 A3
Gartcraig Pl
Glasgow G33 98 F1
Glasgow G33 99 A1
Gartcraig Rd G33 118 F8
Garten Dr ML7 147 B3
Gartferry Ave G69 80 F2
Gartferry Rd G68, G69 81 B4
Gartferry St G21 98 A4
Gartfield St ML6 123 B6
Gartgill Rd ML5 101 E2
GARTHAMLOCK 99 E2
Garthamlock Rd G33 99 E1
Garth Dr G81 94 B7
Garthill Gdns FK1 42 A4
Garthill La FK1 42 A4
Garthland Dr
Ardrossan KA22 205 C4
Glasgow G31 118 A7
Garthland La PA1 113 F5
Garth St G1 241 A2
GARTLEA 123 B6
Gartlea Ave ML6 123 B7
Gartlea Gdns 1 ML6 123 B7
Gartleahill ML6 123 B6
Gartlea Rd ML6 123 A7
Gartliston Rd ML5 101 F3
Gartliston Terr G69 121 A5
Gartloch Ct G69 100 C3
Gartloch Rd
Glasgow, Gartcosh G69 100 C3
Glasgow, Ruchazie G33 99 A1
Gartloch Way G69 100 C3
Gartly St G44 136 F4
Gartmore Gdns G71 140 E8
Gartmore La G69 81 A2
Gartmore Rd PA1 114 C4
Gartmore Terr G72 138 F3
Gartmorn Rd FK10 5 D1
Gartnavel General Hospl
G12 96 A4
Gartnavel Royal Hospl
G12 96 A4
Gartnavel Royal Hospl Sch
G12 96 A4
GARTNESS 123 E5
Gartness Dr ML6 123 E5
Gartness Rd ML6 124 A3
GARTOCHARN 20 F8
Gartocher Dr G32 119 C5
Gartocher Rd G32 119 C5
Gartocher Terr G32 119 C5
Gartons Rd G21 98 C4
GARTSHERRIE 101 E1
Gartsherrie Ave ML5 101 F5
Gartsherrie Ind Est ML5 101 F1
Gartsherrie Prim Sch
ML5 121 E8
Gartsherrie Rd ML5 121 F8
Gartshore Cres G65 59 F2
Gartshore Gdns G68 60 F1
Garturk St
Coatbridge ML5 122 B4
Glasgow G42 117 B2
Garvald Ct G40 118 B3
Garvald La FK6 21 C1
Garvald Rd FK6 39 D7
Garvald St
Glasgow G40 118 B3
Greenock PA15 46 C3
Garvally Cres FK10 10 A8
Garve Ave G44 137 A5
Garvel Cres G33 119 E6
Garvel Dr PA15 45 D3
Garvel Pl G62 54 D2
Garvel Rd
Glasgow G33 119 E6
Milngavie G62 54 E2
Garvel Specl Sch PA16 44 E5
Garven Ct KA1 228 B7
Garven Rd KA20 217 E6
Garvie Ave PA19 44 F6
Garvin Lea ML4 142 A8
Garvock Dr
Glasgow G43 136 B6
Greenock PA15 45 E3
Garwhitter Dr G62 55 B2
Gascoigne Ct 8 FK2 42 A8
Gascoyne G75 180 C7
Gaskin Path G33 99 E5
Gask Pl G13 94 F8
Gas St PA5 112 A3
Gasworks Rd ML8 187 D3
GATEHEAD 226 E5
Gatehead Cvn Pk KA2 226 E5
Gatehead Rd KA2 221 E1
Gatehouse St G32 119 C4
GATESIDE
Barrhead 133 F1
Beith 171 E7
Greenock 45 B4
Gateside KA11 219 F6
Gateside Ave
Bonnybridge FK4 40 C6
Cambuslang G72 139 D5
Greenock PA16 45 B4
Kilsyth G65 60 B8
Gateside Cres
Airdrie ML6 123 A8
Barrhead G78 134 A1
Gateside Gdns
Barrhead G78 133 F2
Greenock PA16 45 B4
Gateside Gr PA16 45 B4
Gateside Pk G65 60 B8
Gateside Pl
Kilbarchan PA10 111 A3
Kilmarnock KA1 227 F4
Gateside Prim Sch KA15 171 E8
Gateside Rd
Barrhead G78 134 A3
Stirling FK7 7 A3
Wishaw ML2 164 E4
Gateside St
Glasgow G31 118 B6
Hamilton ML3 162 E3
West Kilbride KA23 190 D6
Gates Rd PA12 129 D3
Gateway The G74 160 A4
Gaughan Quadrant ML1 163 D5
Gauldry Ave G52 115 C3
Gauze St PA1 113 F5
Gavel Gr 6 ML11 215 C3
Gavel La 4 ML11 215 C3
Gavell Rd
Kilsyth G65 60 A7
Queenzieburn G65 59 F7
Gavinburn Gdns G60 73 A7
Gavinburn Pl G60 73 A7
Gavinburn Prim Sch G60 72 F7
Gavinburn St G60 73 A7
Gavin Hamilton Ct KA7 239 C6
Gavin's Mill Rd G62 55 A1
Gavins Rd
Alloa FK10 4 F1
Clydebank G81 74 B5
Gavin St ML1 163 F5
Gavinton St G44 136 F5
Gayne Dr ML5 101 C6
Gean Ct G67 62 F4
Gean Rd FK10 9 F8
Gearholm Rd KA7 238 D3
Gear Terr G40 118 B2
Geary St 3 G23 76 D1
Geddes Hill G74 160 B4
Geddes Rd G21 98 C7
Geelong Gdns G66 33 D1
Geils Ave G82 50 C2
Geilsland Rd KA15 171 D7
Geilsland Sch KA15 171 C8
Geils Quadrant G82 50 C2
GEILSTON 48 B8
Geilston Ct G82 48 A8
Geilston House & Gdns*
G82 25 H1
Geilston Pk G82 48 A7
Geirston Rd KA25 148 F2
Gelston St G32 119 B4
Gemini Gr ML1 143 B5
Gemmell Cres KA8 236 C1
Gemmell Ct KA8 236 C1
Gemmell Way ML9 198 E2
Gemmel Pl G77 156 C4
General Roy Way ML8 202 C8
Generals Gate G71 140 E6
Gentle Row G81 73 F6
George Aitken Ct KA22 205 D3
George Ave G81 74 C3
George Cres G81 74 C3
George Ct
5 Hamilton ML3 162 A5
Irvine KA12 219 C3
Paisley PA1 113 D4
George Laing Ct FK5 23 E2
George Mann Terr G73 138 A4
George Pl
Doonfoot KA7 238 B2
Paisley PA1 113 E4
George Rd PA19 44 E6
George Reith Ave G12 95 F5
George's Ave KA8 236 B3
Georges Cl 7 ML3 162 A5
George Sq
Ayr KA8 236 A1
Glasgow G1 241 A2
Greenock PA15 45 E6
George St
Airdrie ML6 122 F7
Alexandria G83 27 F3
Alva FK12 5 A6
3 Ayr KA8 235 F1
Barrhead G78 134 B3
Chapelhall ML6 123 D3
Falkirk FK2 42 B5
Glasgow, Baillieston G69 120 B4
Glasgow G1 241 B2
Hamilton ML3 162 A5
Helensburgh G84 16 E1
Howwood PA9 130 F5
Johnstone PA5 111 F3
Laurieston FK2 42 F3
Motherwell ML1 163 F4
Motherwell, New Stevenston
ML1 143 B4
Paisley PA1 113 D4
Stenhousemuir FK5 23 C3
Stevenston KA20 217 D7

George Stewart Gdns [3]
ML3 162 A5
George Street La G83 27 F3
George Terr KA12 219 C3
George View ML2 164 F2
George Way [10] ML9 185 B4
Georgian Ct PA16 45 E6
Gerald Terr FK5 23 E3
Gerardine Ct G83 28 A8
Gerard Pl ML4 142 B7
GERMISTON 98 B2
Germiston Cres G75 180 A4
Germiston Ct G75 180 A4
Gertrude Pl G78 134 A2
Ghillies La ML1 142 C1
Gibb Ct ML9 198 E2
Gibbdun Pl FK6 39 E7
Gibbon Cres G74 160 C3
Gibbshill Pl ML7 127 D5
Gibb St
Chapelhall ML6 123 D2
Cleland ML1 144 B1
GIBSHILL 46 E2
Gibshill Rd PA15 46 E2
Gibson Ave G82 50 B4
Gibson Cres PA5 111 F2
Gibsongray St FK2 42 A7
Gibson Hts G4 241 C2
Gibson La PA13 69 D1
Gibson Quadrant ML1 142 C1
Gibson Rd PA4 94 B1
Gibson St
Denny FK6 21 E1
Dumbarton G82 50 B4
Glasgow G4 241 C1
Glasgow, Kelvingrove G12 96 E2
Greenock PA15 46 E2
Kilmarnock KA1 222 D1
Salsburgh ML7 125 B2
Giffen Rd KA21 217 A8
GIFFNOCK 136 C2
Giffnock Park Ave G46 136 C4
Giffnock Prim Sch G46 136 C2
Giffnock Sta G46 136 C3
Gifford Dr G52 115 A5
Gifford Pl ML5 121 E3
Gifford Wynd PA2 112 F2
Gigha Cres KA11 220 B2
Gigha Gdns ML8 202 A8
Gigha La KA11 220 B2
Gigha Pl KA11 220 B2
Gigha Quadrant [4] ML2 164 E1
Gigha Terr KA11 220 B2
Gigha Wynd KA11 220 B2
Gilbertfield Path G33 99 B2
Gilbertfield Pl
Glasgow G33 99 B2
Irvine KA12 219 D2
Gilbertfield Rd G72 139 E3
Gilbertfield St G33 99 B2
Gilbert Sheddon Ct KA3 195 E1
Gilbert St G3 116 C8
Gilburn Pl ML7 146 F4
Gilchrist Dr FK1 41 E4
Gilchrist St ML5 122 B8
Gilchrist Way ML2 165 B1
Gilderdale G74 159 C2
Gilfillan Ave KA21 206 A2
Gilfillan Pl
Falkirk FK2 24 C2
Overtown ML2 186 C7
Gilfillan Way PA2 132 E8
Gilhill St G20 96 D7
Gillbank Ave ML8 187 D2
Gillbank La [6] ML9 185 C2
Gillburn Gate PA13 89 D8
Gillburn Rd PA13 89 D8
Gillburn St ML2 186 C6
Gillespie Dr G84 16 D4
Gillespie Pl FK7 7 B1
Gillespie Terr FK7 12 D2
Gillie-burn Gdns ML7 146 F4
Gillies Cres G74 160 D5
Gillies Dr FK7 7 C4
Gillies Hill FK7 6 D5
Gillies La G69 120 C4
Gillies St KA10 229 E3
Gill Pk FK6 21 E2
Gill Rd ML2 186 C7
Gillsburn Gdns KA3 223 A2
Gilmartin Rd PA3 111 E6
Gilmerton St G32 119 A4
Gilmour Ave
Clydebank G81 74 B5
Thorntonhall G74 158 B2
Gilmour Cres
Eaglesham G76 178 E5
Rutherglen G73 137 F8
Gilmour Dr ML3 161 F2
Gilmour Pl
Bellshill ML4 141 F5
Coatbridge ML5 121 F8
[7] Glasgow G5 117 C4
Gilmour St
Alexandria G83 27 D5
Clydebank G81 74 C4
Eaglesham G76 178 E5
Greenock PA15 46 D2
Kilmarnock KA1 228 A7
Paisley PA1 113 E5
Stewarton KA3 195 E1
Gilmourton Cres G77 156 D3
Gilmour Wynd KA20 206 E1
Gilroy Cl ML11 215 C5
Gilsay Ct FK1 42 C2
GILSHOCHILL 96 E8
Gilshochill Sta G23 96 E7
Gimmerscroft Cres [1]
ML6 123 F6
Girdle Gate KA11 219 F5
GIRDLE TOLL 220 A6
Girdle Toll KA11 220 A5
Girdons Way G71 140 E6
Girthon St G32 119 C4
Girvan Cres ML6 123 D1
Girvan St G33 118 D8
Glade The ML9 185 B2
Gladney Ave G13 94 E8
Gladsmuir Rd G52 115 A6
Gladstone Ave
Barrhead G78 134 B2
Johnstone PA5 131 D7
Gladstone Ct [1] ML3 162 A5
Gladstone Dr G74 179 D8
Gladstone Pl FK8 7 A6
Gladstone Rd
Saltcoats KA21 217 A8
Stenhousemuir FK5 23 D3
Gladstone St
Bellshill ML4 142 B5
Clydebank G81 73 F2
[11] Glasgow G4 97 A2
Glaive Ave FK7 7 D3
Glaive Rd G13 75 D1
Glamis Ave
Carluke ML8 187 F2
Elderslie PA5 112 B1
Newton Mearns G77 156 F5
Glamis Cres [3] G72 161 D3
Glamis Ct ML1 143 C2
Glamis Dr
East Kilbride G74 159 F3
Greenock PA16 45 A5
Glamis Gait [2] G72 161 E3
Glamis Gdns G64 78 B4
Glamis La [4] G72 161 D3
Glamis Pl PA16 45 A5
Glamis Rd G31 118 D4
Glanderston Ave
Barrhead G78 134 E2
Newton Mearns G77 156 B6
Glanderston Ct G13 95 A7
Glanderston Dr G13 95 A7
Glanderston Gate G77 156 C6
Glanderston Rd G77 155 D5
GLASGOW 241 C2
Glasgow Acad The [4] G12 96 F3
Glasgow Acad The (Atholl)
G62 55 A3
Glasgow Botanic Gdns*
G12 96 D4
Glasgow Caledonian Univ
G4 241 A4
Glasgow Cath (St Mungo)*
G4 241 C3
Glasgow Central Sta G2 240 C2
Glasgow Coll of Nautical
Studies G5 117 C5
Glasgow Dental Hospl
G2 240 B3
Glasgow Dental Sch G3 240 B4
Glasgow & Edinburgh Rd
Calderbank ML1 123 A1
Coatbridge ML5 121 D3
Glasgow G69 120 D5
Motherwell, Newhouse
ML1 143 C8
Motherwell, Newhouse
ML1 143 E7
Glasgow Fort Sh Ctr G34 99 E1
Glasgow Gaelic Sch G3 116 E8
Glasgow Harbour Terr
G11 96 A1
Glasgow Homeopathic Hospl
G12 96 A4
Glasgow La KA22 205 C2
Glasgow Metropolitan Coll
(Cathedral St Campus)
G1 241 B3
Glasgow Metropolitan Coll
(Dornoch St Campus)
G40 117 F5
Glasgow Metropolitan Coll
(Florence St Campus)
G5 117 C5
Glasgow Metropolitan Coll
(North Hanover St Campus)
G1 241 A3
Glasgow Metropolitan Coll
(Rogart St Campus)
G40 117 F5
Glasgow Museum Resource
Ctr & Open Mus* G53 134 F5
Glasgow Necropolis (cemy)*
G4 241 C2
Glasgow Prestwick Int
Airport KA9 233 E2
Glasgow Rd
Barrhead G78 134 D4
Cambuslang, Silverbank
G72 138 F6
Cambuslang, Whitlawburn G72,
G73 138 F1
Clydebank G81 94 C7
Clydebank, Hardgate G81 74 C6
Coatbridge ML5 121 D5
Cumbernauld G67 82 D8
Cumbernauld, Kildrum G67 62 B4
Denny FK6 21 E1
Dumbarton, Dennystown
G82 49 E4
Dumbarton, Dumbuck G82 50 C2
Eaglesham G76 178 E7
Glasgow Rd *continued*
Falkirk FK1 41 C6
Glasgow G71 120 A4
Hamilton G72 161 E7
Kilmarnock KA3 223 B5
Kilsyth G65 60 B8
Kirkintilloch G66 79 A8
Lanark ML11 214 E4
Longcroft FK4 39 C4
Milngavie G62 55 B1
Nerston G72 160 A8
Nerston G74 160 A7
Paisley PA1 114 C4
Port Glasgow PA14 47 E1
Renfrew PA4 94 F2
Rutherglen G73 117 F1
Stirling FK7 7 B2
Strathblane G63 31 B4
Uddingston G71 140 E7
Wishaw ML2 164 E3
Glasgow Royal Concert
Hall* G1 241 A3
Glasgow Sch of Art The
Glasgow G3 240 B4
Glasgow G3 240 C4
Glasgow Science Ctr*
G3 116 D7
Glasgow St
Ardrossan KA22 205 C2
Glasgow G12 96 E2
Helensburgh G84 16 C2
Kilbirnie KA25 149 A2
Glasgow Steiner Sch G3 96 D1
Glasgow Vennel KA12 219 C2
Glassel Rd G34 100 D1
Glasserton Pl G43 136 F5
Glasserton Rd G43 136 F5
GLASSFORD 198 A4
Glassford Rd ML3, ML9 198 D5
Glassford St
Glasgow G1 241 A2
Milngavie G62 55 B2
Motherwell ML1 164 A4
Glassford Twr ML1 164 B3
Glasshouse Loan FK10 10 A6
Glassock Rd KA3 222 F5
Glaudhall Ave G69 100 E7
Glazertbank G66 57 C8
Glazert Mdw G66 57 E7
Glazert Park Dr G66 57 E7
Glazert Pl G66 58 B5
Glazert Rd KA3 195 C7
Glebe Ave
Bothwell G71 141 B2
Carmunnock G76 158 D7
Coatbridge ML5 121 D4
Irvine KA11 225 C8
Kilmarnock KA1 228 A8
Stirling FK8 7 A7
Glebe Cres
Airdrie ML6 123 D8
Alva FK12 5 B7
Ayr KA8 235 F2
East Kilbride G74 159 F1
Hamilton ML3 162 C2
Stirling FK8 7 A7
Glebe Ct
Beith KA15 171 B8
East Kilbride G74 160 D5
Glasgow G4 241 B3
Kilmacolm PA13 89 D8
[2] Kilmarnock KA1 228 A8
[23] Lanark ML11 215 A4
Glebe Dr [1] ML11 215 A4
Glebefield Rd G84 15 E5
Glebe Gdns
Alexandria G83 27 E4
Houston PA6 91 B2
Glebe Hollow G71 141 B2
Glebe La G77 156 D4
Glebelands Way KA15 171 B7
Glebe Pk G82 50 B5
Glebe Pl
Cambuslang G72 139 B5
Rutherglen G73 137 F8
Saltcoats KA21 216 F8
Glebe Prim Sch KA12 219 C2
Glebe Rd
Ayr KA8 235 F2
Beith KA15 171 B8
Glengarnock KA25 170 B7
Kilmacolm PA13 89 D8
Kilmarnock KA1 228 A8
Newton Mearns G77 156 D4
Glebe St
Bellshill ML4 141 F5
Denny FK6 21 E2
East Kilbride G74 159 F1
Falkirk FK1 42 B5
Glasgow G1 241 C3
Hamilton ML3 162 D2
Kilwinning KA13 207 E4
Renfrew PA4 94 D3
Saltcoats KA21 216 F8
Stevenston KA20 206 C1
Glebe Terr
Alloa FK10 10 A6
Fenwick KA3 213 A3
Glebe The
Alva FK12 5 B7
Bothwell G71 141 B2
Irvine KA11 225 C8
Lanark ML11 214 F4
Symington KA1 231 C3
Glebe Wynd G71 141 B2
GLED CRAIG 70 B3
Gleddoch Cl G52 114 E6
Gleddoch Ct G52 114 E6
Gleddoch Gate [4] G52 114 F6
Gleddoch Rd G52 114 F6
Gleddoch View G82 49 D2
Gleddoch Wynd PA14 70 D5
Gledstane Rd PA7 72 B2
Glenacre Cres G71 140 E8
Glenacre Dr
Airdrie ML6 123 D6
Glasgow G45 137 D3
Glenacre Gr G45 137 E4
Glenacre Rd G67 82 F8
Glenacre St G45 137 D3
Glenacre Terr G45 137 D3
Glenafeoch Rd ML8 188 A1
Glen Affric G74 160 B1
Glen Affric Ave G53 135 D4
Glen Affric Pl KA1 227 C6
Glen Affric Way ML6 123 D1
Glen Afton Ct KA1 227 C6
Glenafton Gr ML5 121 F5
Glenafton View ML3 183 B8
Glen Alby Pl G53 135 C4
Glenalla Cres KA7 238 D1
Glenallan Terr ML1 142 D1
Glenallan Way PA2 132 E7
Glen Almond G74 160 D2
Glenalmond Rd [3] G73 138 D3
Glenalmond St G32 119 A4
Glenalva Ct G65 36 D1
Glenan Gdns G84 16 C2
Glenapp Ave PA2 114 B1
Glenapp Ct KA13 207 C2
Glenapp Pl
Kilwinning KA13 207 C2
Moodiesburn G69 80 F3
Glenapp Quadrant KA1 228 B7
Glenapp Rd PA2 114 B1
Glenapp St G41 116 F3
Glenarklet Cres PA2 134 A8
Glenarklet Dr PA2 114 A1
Glenarn Rd G84 15 E4
Glen Arroch G74 160 B1
Glenartney PA6 91 A2
Glenartney Rd G69 80 C1
Glenashdale Way PA2 114 A1
Glen Ave
Balloch G83 28 A8
Glasgow G32 119 B6
Gourock PA19 44 F6
Larkhall ML9 184 F1
Moodiesburn G69 80 F2
Neilston G78 154 E7
Port Glasgow PA14 47 B2
Glenavon Ct
Hamilton ML3 162 B1
Larkhall ML9 199 B7
Glen Avon Dr ML6 123 D1
Glenavon Rd G20 96 D7
Glenbank FK1 42 B1
Glenbank Ave G66 79 D4
Glenbank Ct G46 135 F2
Glenbank Dr G46 135 F2
Glenbank Rd G66 79 D4
Glenbarr St G21 97 F1
Glenbervie FK5 23 A4
Glen Bervie G74 160 B2
Glenbervie Ave FK5 23 A3
Glenbervie Bsns Pk FK5 23 A4
Glenbervie Cres
Cumbernauld G68 61 F5
Larbert FK5 23 B3
Glenbervie Dr
Kilwinning KA13 207 B3
Larbert FK5 23 A3
Glenbervie Pl
[15] Glasgow G23 76 D1
Gourock PA19 44 B6
Newton Mearns G77 156 A5
Glenbervie Wynd KA11 224 F8
Glenbo Dr FK6 39 E7
GLENBOIG 101 F6
Glenboig Farm Rd ML5 101 E6
Glenboig New Rd ML5 101 F6
Glenboig Prim Sch ML5 101 F5
Glenboig Rd
Glenboig G69 101 B7
Glenboig ML5 101 C6
Glen Brae
Bridge of Weir PA11 110 D8
Falkirk FK1 42 A3
Glenbrae Ct FK1 42 B3
Glenbrae Rd
Greenock PA15 46 B2
Port Glasgow PA14 68 D7
Glenbride Rd KA23 190 C3
Glenbrittle Dr PA2 114 A1
Glenbrittle Way PA2 114 A1
Glenbuck Ave G33 98 F6
Glenbuck Dr G33 98 F6
GLENBURN 133 C8
Glenburn Ave
Cambuslang G72 138 E5
Glasgow G69 120 C5
Moodiesburn G69 80 F2
Motherwell ML1 143 C4
Glenburn Cl
Greengairs ML6 103 C8
Kilwinning KA13 207 C6
Glenburn Cres
Milton of Campsie G66 58 C5
Paisley PA2 133 D7
Uddingston G71 141 C8
Glenburn Ct
East Kilbride G74 159 A3
[3] Kirkintilloch G66 79 D8
Glenburn Dr PA13 69 D1
Glenburn Gdns
Bishopbriggs G64 77 F2
Glenburn Gdns *continued*
Glenboig ML5 101 C6
Glenburnie Pl G34 119 F7
Glenburn Ind Est KA9 236 E8
Glenburn La
Glasgow G20 96 E7
Kilmacolm PA13 69 D1
Glenburn Pl PA13 69 D1
Glenburn Prim Sch KA9 236 E8
Glenburn Rd
Bearsden G61 75 E5
East Kilbride G74 159 A3
Falkirk FK1 42 D1
Glasgow G46 136 B1
Hamilton ML3 162 B3
Kilmacolm PA13 69 D1
Paisley PA2 133 D7
Prestwick KA9 236 E8
Glenburn Sch PA16 44 E3
Glenburn St
Glasgow G20 96 E7
Port Glasgow PA14 47 A2
Glenburn Terr
Carluke ML8 201 E8
Motherwell ML1 143 C1
Glenburn Way G74 158 F3
Glenburn Wlk G69 120 C5
Glenburn Wynd [3] ML9 185 B4
Glencairn Ave ML2 164 D4
Glencairn Dr
Coatbridge ML5 121 E5
Glasgow G41 116 E2
Moodiesburn G69 80 E2
Rutherglen G73 137 F8
Glencairn Gdns
Cambuslang G72 139 D5
Glasgow G41 116 E2
Stevenston KA20 206 D1
Glencairn Ind Est KA1 227 F6
Glencairn La G41 116 F2
Glencairn Prim Sch
Motherwell ML1 163 F5
Stevenston KA20 217 D8
Glencairn Rd
Ayr KA7 239 C6
Cumbernauld G67 62 C2
Dumbarton G82 49 C4
Greenock PA16 44 E3
Kilmacolm PA13 89 E8
Langbank PA14 70 C7
Paisley PA3 114 A7
Glencairn Ret Pk KA1 227 F6
Glencairn Sq KA1 227 F7
Glencairn St
Falkirk FK1 41 B5
Kirkintilloch G66 79 D7
Motherwell ML1 163 F5
Saltcoats KA21 216 F7
Stevenston KA20 206 D1
Stirling FK7 7 B3
Glencairn Terr
Kilmaurs KA3 222 B7
Stevenston KA20 206 D1
Glencairn Twr [1] ML1 163 F5
Glencalder Cres ML4 142 C3
Glen Cally G74 160 B2
Glencally Ave PA2 114 B1
Glen Cannich G74 160 B1
Glen Carron G74 160 B1
Glencart Gr PA10 111 C1
Glencleland Rd ML2 164 D4
Glenclora Dr PA2 114 A1
Glen Clova G74 160 B2
Glen Clova Dr G68 61 C4
Glenclova Gdns KA2 227 C6
Glencloy St G20 96 C7
Glenclune PA14 47 E1
Glenclune Ct PA13 89 C7
Glen Clunie G74 160 D2
Glen Clunie Dr G53 135 C4
Glen Clunie Pl G53 135 C4
Glencoates Prim Sch
PA3 113 A6
Glencoats Bsns Ctr PA3 113 B5
Glencoats Dr PA3 113 A4
Glencoe Ct PA16 45 B5
Glencoe Dr ML1 143 A5
Glencoe Pl
Glasgow G13 95 F7
Hamilton ML3 183 B8
Glencoe Rd
Carluke ML8 202 A8
Rutherglen G73 138 D3
Stirling FK8 2 A1
Glencoe St G13 95 F7
Glen Cona Dr G53 135 C5
Glenconner Pl KA7 239 B6
Glenconner Rd KA7 239 B6
Glenconner Way G66 59 A1
Glencorse Rd PA2 113 C2
Glencorse St G32 118 E7
Glencraigs Dr KA3 222 F5
Glencraig St ML6 122 E7
Glencraig Terr KA3 213 B3
Glen Creran Cres G78 154 C6
Glen Cres
Falkirk FK1 42 B1
Glasgow G13 94 E7
Stevenston KA20 206 C1
Glencroft Ave G71 140 E8
Glencroft Rd G44 137 D5
Glencryan Rd G67 62 B1
Glencryan Sch G67 82 E7
Glen Ct
Coatbridge ML5 121 D5
Dalry KA24 191 A6
Motherwell ML1 164 B4
Glendale Ave ML6 123 D6

Glendale Cres
Ayr KA7 239 C4
Bishopbriggs G64 98 C8
Glendale Dr G64 98 C8
Glendale Gr ML5 121 E3
Glendale Pl
Ayr KA7 239 B4
Bishopbriggs G64 98 C7
Glasgow G31 118 B6
Glendale Prim Sch G41 116 F4
Glendale St G31 118 B6
Glendaruel Ave G61 76 B4
Glendaruel Rd G73 138 E2
Glendarvel Gdns G22 97 D4
Glendee Gdns PA4 94 D2
Glendee Rd PA4 94 D2
Glen Dene Way G53 135 C4
Glendentan Rd PA11 110 C6
Glendermott Ct ML8 187 F3
Glen Derry G74 160 D3
Glen Dessary G74 181 B8
Glendeveron Way ML1 143 B2
Glen Devon G74 160 D1
Glendevon Dr FK8 1 F2
Glendevon Pl
Clydebank G81 73 F3
Hamilton ML3 183 B8
Glendevon Sq G33 99 B2
Glen Dewar Pl G53 135 C4
Glendinning Pl G76 178 D4
Glendinning Rd G13 75 E1
Glen Dochart Dr G68 61 C5
Glendoick Pl G77 156 A5
Glen Doll G74 160 B2
Glen Doll Rd G78 154 B6
Glendorch Ave ML2 165 C7
Glendore St G14 95 E2
Glen Douglas Dr G68 61 C4
Glen Douglas Pl PA16 45 C3
Glen Douglas Rd PA16 45 C3
Glen Douglas Way PA16 45 D3
Glendoune KA3 228 D7
Glendoune Rd G76 157 E5
Glendower Way PA2 132 E8
Glen Dr
Helensburgh G84 16 D4
Motherwell ML1 143 B5
Glenduffhill Rd G69 119 F5
Glen Dye G74 160 B2
Glen Eagles G74 160 C1
Gleneagles Ave
Cumbernauld G68 62 A5
Kilwinning KA13 207 C4
Gleneagles Dr
Bishopbriggs G64 78 A3
Gourock PA19 44 A6
Newton Mearns G77 157 B4
Gleneagles Gate G77 157 B4
Gleneagles Gdns G64 78 A3
Gleneagles Lane N G14 95 C4
Gleneagles Lane S G14 95 C3
Gleneagles Pk G71 140 F2
Glenelg Cres G66 59 A1
Glenelg Path ML5 101 C6
Glenelg Quadrant G34 100 D1
Glenelm Pl ML4 142 A6
Glen Esk G74 160 C2
Glenesk Cres G53 135 C4
Glen Esk Dr G53 135 C4
Glenesk Pl G53 135 C4
Glen Etive Pl G73 138 E2
Glen Falloch G74 160 C1
Glen Falloch Cres G78 154 D5
Glen Falloch Way G68 61 C5
Glen Farg G74 160 D1
Glenfarg Cres G61 76 B4
Glenfarg Ct ML3 183 B8
Glenfarg Rd G73 138 B4
Glenfarg St 12 G20 97 A2
Glenfarm Rd ML1 143 E4
Glen Farrar G74 160 B1
Glen Farrar Way KA2 227 C6
Glen Feshie G74 181 B8
Glenfield Ave PA2 133 E7
Glenfield Cres PA2 133 E6
Glenfield Gdns
Kilmarnock KA1 227 F6
Paisley PA2 133 D6
Glenfield Gr PA2 133 D6
Glenfield Grange PA2 133 E6
Glenfield Pl KA1 227 F6
Glenfield Rd
East Kilbride G75 181 A6
Paisley PA2 133 D6
Glenfinlas St G84 16 E1
Glen Finlet Cres G78 154 C5
Glenfinnan Dr
Bearsden G61 76 C3
Glasgow G20 96 D6
Glenfinnan Gr ML4 142 D4
Glenfinnan Pl 4 G20 96 D6
Glenfinnan Rd G20 96 D6
Glenfoot Gdns KA2 225 F1
Glenfruin Cres PA2 114 B1
Glen Fruin Dr 9 ML9 185 C1
Glen Fruin Pl ML6 123 D1
Glenfruin Rd G72 161 C8
Glen Fruin Rd PA16 45 D3
Glenfuir Ct FK1 41 D4
Glenfuir Rd FK1 41 E5
Glenfuir St FK1 41 C5
Glen Fyne Rd G68 61 B4
Glen Gairn G74 160 D2
Glen Gairn Cres G78 154 C6
GLENGARNOCK 170 C6
Glengarnock Prim Sch
KA14 170 B7
Glengarnock Sta KA14 170 C6
Glengarnock Tech Ctr
KA14 170 C7
Glengarnock Workshops
KA14 170 C7
Glen Garrell Pl G65 36 C1
Glengarriff Rd ML4 142 B8
Glen Garry G74 181 B8
Glengarry Cres FK1 41 F2
Glengarry Dr G52 115 C5
Glengavel Cres G33 98 F6
Glengavel Gdns ML2 165 C7
Glen Gavin Way PA2 114 B1
Glen Gdns
Elderslie PA5 112 C3
Falkirk FK1 42 A3
Glengonnar St ML9 199 A8
Glengowan Ct ML9 185 A3
Glengowan Prim Sch
Caldercruix ML6 105 A4
Larkhall ML9 185 A3
Glengowan Rd
Bridge of Weir PA11 110 C8
Caldercruix ML6 105 A4
Glengoyne Dr 3 ML1 143 A2
Glen Gr
East Kilbride G75 180 D7
Kilsyth G65 36 D2
Glengyre St G34 100 C1
Glenhead Cres
Clydebank G81 74 A7
Glasgow G22 97 C6
Glenhead Dr ML1 163 E4
Glenhead Rd
Clydebank G81 74 A5
Kirkintilloch G66 79 D4
Glenhead St G22 97 D6
Glenheath Dr ML5 101 C6
Glenholme Ave PA2 113 B1
Glenhove Rd G67 62 B2
Glenhuntly Rd PA14 47 C1
Glenhuntly Terr PA14 47 C1
Gleniffer Ave G13 95 A6
Gleniffer Braes Ctry Pk*
PA2 132 E6
Gleniffer Cres PA5 112 C2
Gleniffer Ct PA2 133 B7
Gleniffer Dr G78 134 B5
Gleniffer High Sch PA2 133 A8
Gleniffer Rd
Paisley G78, PA2 132 D3
Paisley, Gallowhill PA4 114 B8
Renfrew PA4 94 B1
Uplawmoor G78 152 D4
Gleniffer View
4 Clydebank G81 74 D3
Neilston G78 154 E8
Gleninver Rd PA16 45 A4
Glen Isla G74 160 C2
Glenisla Ave G69 81 A4
Glen Isla Ave G78 154 C5
Glen Isla Pl ML8 202 B7
Glen Isla Quadrant ML1 165 B8
Glenisla St G31 118 D3
Glen Kinchie FK10 4 A2
Glenkinchie Rd KA3 222 E3
Glen Kinglas Ave PA16 45 D2
Glen Kinglas Rd PA16 45 D2
Glenkirk Dr G15 75 B2
Glen Kyle Dr G53 135 C4
Glen La
Paisley PA3 113 E5
Uplawmoor G78 153 A3
Glen Lednock Dr G68 61 B4
Glen Lee G74 160 C2
Glenlee Prim Sch 8
ML3 162 A5
Glenlee St ML3 161 F5
Glenleith Pl KA11 220 C2
Glen Lethnot G74 160 C2
Glenlivet Pl KA3 223 B3
Glen Livet Pl G53 135 C4
Glenlivet Rd G78 154 C6
Glen Lochay Gdns G68 61 B4
Glenlora Dr G53 135 A7
Glenlora Terr G53 135 B7
Glen Loy Pl G53 135 C4
Glenluce Dr G32 119 D4
Glenluce Gdns 4 G69 81 A3
Glenluce Terr G74 159 C2
Glenluggie Rd G66 80 A7
Glenlui Ave G73 138 B5
Glen Luss Gdns G68 61 B4
Glen Luss Pl
Coatbridge ML5 122 D5
Glasgow G53 135 C4
Glen Luss Rd PA16 45 C2
Glen Luss Way PA16 45 D2
Glen Lyon G74 160 C1
Glen Lyon Cres KA2 227 C6
Glenlyon Ct ML3 183 B8
Glen Lyon Ct G68 61 B4
Glenlyon Gr KA11 219 F5
Glenlyon Pl G73 138 C3
Glen Lyon Rd G78 154 C6
Glen Lyon Wlk ML1 164 C3
Glen Mallie G74 160 C1
Glenmalloch Pl PA5 112 C3
Glenmanor Ave G69 80 E2
Glenmanor Prim Sch G69 80 E2
Glenmanor Rd G69 80 E2
Glenmare Ave G66 80 A7
Glen Mark G74 160 C2
Glen Mark Rd G78 154 C6
GLENMAVIS 102 E3
Glenmavis Cres ML8 188 A1
Glenmavis Ct ML8 188 A1
Glenmavis Rd ML6 102 E2
Glenmavis St G4 240 C4
Glen Mews 4 ML8 202 B8
Glen More
Carluke ML8 202 C8
East Kilbride G74 160 A1
Glenmore Ave
Alexandria G83 27 D6
Bellshill ML4 142 B3
Glasgow G42 137 E8
Glenmore Dr FK4 39 F6
Glenmore Rd ML1 143 C3
Glen Moriston G74 160 B1
Glen Moriston Rd
Cumbernauld G68 61 B4
Glasgow G53 135 C4
Glenmoss Ave PA8 72 F1
Glenmosston Rd PA13 89 E8
Glenmount Pl KA7 238 B1
Glen Moy G74 160 C1
Glenmuir Ave G53 135 C5
Glenmuir Cres G53 135 C5
Glenmuir Ct
Ayr KA8 236 D2
Glasgow G53 135 D5
Glenmuir Dr G53 135 B5
Glenmuir Pl KA8 236 D2
Glenmuir Rd KA8 236 D2
Glen Muir Rd G78 154 C6
Glenmuir Sq KA8 236 C2
Glen Nevis G74 181 B8
Glen Nevis Pl KA2 227 C6
Glen Noble ML1 165 B8
Glenochil Pk FK10 4 E4
Glenochil Rd FK1 42 A3
Glen Ochil Rd ML6 123 D1
Glenochil Terr FK10 4 E4
Glen Ogilvie G74 160 C2
Glen Ogle St G32 119 D4
Glenoran La 1 ML9 185 B4
Glenoran Rd G84 16 A4
Glenorchard Rd G64 56 D1
Glen Orchy Ct G68 61 B5
Glen Orchy Dr
Cumbernauld G68 61 B4
Glasgow G53 135 D4
Glen Orchy Gr G53 135 D4
Glen Orchy Pl
Chapelhall ML6 123 D1
Cumbernauld G68 61 B4
Glasgow G53 135 D4
Kilmarnock KA2 227 C6
Glen Orchy Rd ML1 165 A7
Glen Ord Rd ML1 143 B2
Glen Orrin Ave KA2 227 C6
Glenorrin Way G78 154 C6
Glenpark ML6 123 E6
Glenpark Ave
Glasgow G46 136 A2
Prestwick KA9 236 C6
Glenpark Dr PA14 47 A1
Glenpark Gdns G72 138 E7
Glenpark Ind Est G31 118 B6
Glenpark Pl KA7 239 B3
Glenpark Rd PA12 129 C3
Glenpark St
Glasgow G31 118 B6
Wishaw ML2 165 A4
Glenpark Terr G72 138 E7
Glenpath G82 50 C3
Glenpatrick Bldgs PA5 112 C1
Glenpatrick Rd PA5 112 D2
Glen Pl G76 157 D7
Glen Prosen G74 160 C2
Glen Quoich G74 160 D3
Glenraith Path G33 99 B3
Glenraith Rd G33 99 B2
Glenraith Sq G33 99 B3
Glenraith Wlk G33 99 B3
Glen Rannoch Dr ML6 123 D1
Glen Rd
Airdrie ML6 123 E6
Bishopton PA7 72 A4
Caldercruix ML6 104 F4
East Kilbride G74 158 F5
Glasgow G32 119 B7
Lennoxtown G66 33 B2
Motherwell ML1 143 D7
Old Kilpatrick G60 73 B6
Plean FK5 22 D8
Shotts ML7 146 F4
Torwood FK5 22 D7
West Kilbride KA23 190 D5
Wishaw ML2 165 A4
Glenriddel Rd KA7 239 B6
Glenriddet Ave KA25 170 B8
Glenrigg Ct ML6 122 F5
Glen Rinnes Dr G78 154 D6
Glen Rosa Gdns G68 61 B4
Glen Roy Dr G78 154 C6
Glen Sannox Dr G68 61 C4
Glen Sannox Gr G68 61 C4
Glen Sannox Loan G68 61 C4
Glen Sannox View G68 61 B4
Glen Sannox Way G68 61 C4
Glen Sannox Wynd G68 61 C4
Glen Sax Dr PA4 94 E1
Glen Shee G74 160 C2
Glen Shee Ave G78 154 C6
Glen Shee Cres ML6 123 D1
Glenshee Ct G31 118 D3
Glen Shee Ct ML8 202 B8
Glenshee Gdns G31 118 E4
Glen Shee Gdns ML8 202 B8
Glen Shee La ML8 202 C8
Glenshee St G31 118 D4
Glenshee Terr ML3 183 B8
Glenshiel Ave PA2 114 A1
Glen Shiel Cres KA2 227 C6
Glenshira Ave PA2 114 A1
Glen Shirva Rd G65 59 F4
Glenside Ave G53 115 B2
Glenside Cres KA23 190 D5
Glenside Dr G73 138 E6
Glenside Gr KA23 190 D5
Glenside Rd
Dumbarton G82 50 C6
Port Glasgow PA14 68 D7
Glenspean Pl ML5 122 D5
Glenspean St G43 136 D6
Glen St
Barrhead G78 134 C3
Cambuslang G72 139 D4
Greenock PA16 45 D7
Motherwell ML1 142 E1
Motherwell, Whittagreen
ML1 143 D4
Paisley PA3 113 E5
Glentanar Ct PA1 114 A4
Glentanar Dr G69 81 A2
Glentanar Pl G22 97 B8
Glentanar Rd G22 97 B7
Glen Tanner G74 160 D2
Glen Tarbert Dr G78 154 C6
Glentarbert Rd G73 138 D3
Glen Tennet G74 160 C2
Glen Terr
Caldercruix ML6 104 F4
Denny FK6 21 D1
Glen The FK10 4 C3
Glentore Quadrant ML6 103 A2
Glentrool Gdns
Glasgow G22 97 D4
Moodiesburn G69 81 A3
Glen Trool Wlk KA2 227 C7
Glen Truim View KA2 227 C6
Glen Turret G74 160 D2
Glenturret St G32 119 A4
Glen Twr ML1 164 B3
Glentyan Ave PA10 111 A4
Glentyan Dr G53 135 A6
Glentye Dr FK10 4 D4
Glentye Gdns FK1 41 E2
Glen Tye Rd FK7 7 D5
Glentynan Pl G53 135 A7
Glen Urquhart G74 160 B1
Glenview
Airdrie ML6 123 D6
Frankerton FK6 21 A3
1 Kirkintilloch G66 79 D8
Larkhall ML9 184 F4
Menstrie FK11 4 A6
West Kilbride KA23 190 D4
Glen View
Bonnybridge FK4 39 D5
Cumbernauld G67 62 C3
Hamilton ML3 183 D7
Renton G82 27 D2
Glenview Ave
Banknock FK4 38 F3
Caldercruix ML6 105 A4
Glenview Cres G69 81 A4
Glenview Ct ML9 184 F4
Glenview Dr FK1 41 F2
Glenview Pl G72 140 D1
Glenview St ML6 102 E4
Glenview Terr PA15 45 E4
GLEN VILLAGE 42 B1
Glenville Ave G46 136 B3
Glenville Gate G76 158 A5
Glenville Terr G76 158 A5
Glenward Ave G66 57 E8
Glenwell St ML6 102 E3
Glenwinnel Rd FK12 4 E7
Glenwood Ave ML6 123 C4
Glenwood Bsns Ctr G45 137 F3
Glenwood Ct G66 79 A5
Glenwood Dr G46 135 F2
Glenwood Gdns G66 79 A5
Glenwood Path G45 137 E3
Glenwood Pl
Glasgow G45 137 E3
Kirkintilloch G66 79 A5
Glenwood Rd G66 79 A5
Glenyards Rd FK4 39 F2
Glidden Ct ML2 186 C7
Glorat Ave G66 57 E8
Gloucester Ave
Clarkston G76 157 D7
Rutherglen G73 138 D5
Gloucester St G5 117 A5
Glowrorum Dr FK6 39 E7
Glynwed Ct FK2 42 C7
Goatfell View KA10 229 F7
GOCKSTON 113 D8
Gockston Rd PA3 113 D7
Goddard Pl ML2 166 B5
Godfrey Ave FK6 21 D1
Godfrey Cres FK5 23 C1
Goethe-Institute G3 240 A4
Gogar Loan FK9 3 D5
Gogar Pl
Glasgow G33 118 E8
Stirling FK7 7 C2
Gogar St G33 118 E8
Goil Ave ML4 141 D6
Goil Way ML1 143 A5
Goldberry Ave G14 95 B5
Goldcraig Ct KA11 220 A5
Goldcrest Ct ML1 164 F1
Goldenacre Pl ML6 103 F3
Goldenberry Ave KA23 190 C4
Goldenhill Ct G81 74 B6
Goldenhill Prim Sch G81 74 B6
Golden Jubilee National
Hospl G81 73 E2
Goldenlee View PA6 111 A8
Goldie Pl KA20 206 C1
Goldie Rd G71 141 A4
Golf Ave
Bellshill ML4 142 A3
Stevenston KA20 217 F6
Golf Course Rd
Balmore G64 77 E8
Bridge of Weir PA11 110 C7
Fluchter G64 56 C1
Golf Cres KA10 229 E2
Golf Ct G44 136 E2
Golf Dr
Clydebank G15 74 F1
Clydebank G15 75 A1
Paisley PA1 114 C4
Port Glasgow PA14 68 D8
Golffields Rd KA12 219 D1
Golf Gdns ML9 185 C2
Golfhill Dr
Alexandria G83 27 F5
Glasgow G31 118 A8
Helensburgh G84 16 F2
Golfhill Nursing Home
G31 117 F8
Golfhill Prim Sch
Airdrie ML6 102 E2
Glasgow G31 118 B7
Golfhill Quadrant ML6 103 A2
Golfhill Rd ML2 164 E4
Golfloan KA3 211 F8
Golf Pl
Bellshill ML4 142 B3
Greenock PA16 45 C7
Helensburgh G84 17 A2
Irvine KA12 219 B5
Troon KA10 229 E2
Golf Rd
Bishopton PA7 72 B4
Clarkston G76 157 D8
Gourock PA19 44 C6
Rutherglen G73 138 B4
Golfview G61 75 C5
Golf View G81 73 F4
Golfview Dr ML5 121 D7
Golfview Pl ML5 121 D6
Golspie Ave ML6 122 E4
Golspie St G51 116 A8
Golspie Way G72 161 C3
Goodview Gdns ML9 185 C2
Goosecroft Rd FK8 7 B8
Goosedubbs G1 241 A1
Goosedubs Pl 5 FK2 41 F8
Gooseholm Cres G82 50 A5
Gooseholm Rd G82 50 A5
Gopher Ave G71 141 B8
GORBALS 117 C4
Gorbals Cross
Glasgow G5 117 C5
Larkhall ML9 185 A3
Gorbals L Ctr G52 117 C5
Gorbals St G5 117 C5
Gordon Ave
Bishopton PA7 72 B4
Glasgow, Garrowhill G69 119 F5
Glasgow, Netherlee G44 136 E2
Hillington G52 114 E7
Gordon Cres
Bridge of Allan FK9 2 A8
Newton Mearns G77 156 E6
Stirling FK8 1 F2
Gordon Ct ML6 123 E8
Gordon Dr
Alloa FK10 10 C7
East Kilbride G74 160 B3
Glasgow G44 136 E3
Gordon La G1 240 C2
Gordon McMaster Gdns
PA5 112 A3
Gordon Pl
Bellshill ML4 141 F2
Falkirk FK1 41 E5
Gordon Rd
Glasgow G44 136 E2
Hamilton ML3 161 F4
Gordon Sq PA5 111 F2
Gordon St
Ayr KA8 236 A3
Glasgow G1 240 C2
Greenock PA15 45 E4
Paisley PA1 113 E4
Gordon Terr
Ayr KA8 239 A8
Blantyre G72 140 C1
Hamilton ML3 161 F3
Gorebridge St G32 118 E7
Goremire Rd ML8 202 B8
Gorget Ave G13 75 C1
Gorget Pl G13 75 C1
Gorget Quadrant G13 75 B1
Gorrie St FK6 21 D2
Gorse Cres PA11 110 E7
Gorse Dr G78 134 B4
Gorsehall St ML1 144 B2
Gorse Pk KA7 239 C3
Gorse Pl G71 141 B8
Gorsewood G64 77 E1
Gorstan Pl G20 96 C5
Gorstan St G23 96 D8
Goschen Terr KA8 236 B2
Gosford La G14 95 A4
Goshen Pl FK5 23 E2
Gotterbank PA11 89 E2
Gottries Rd KA12 219 A1
Goudie St PA3 113 D7
Gough St G33 118 D8
Goukscroft Ct KA7 238 D3

Goukscroft Pk KA7 . . . . . . 238 D3
Gould St KA8 . . . . 236 C2
Gourlay G74 . . . . 160 D5
Gourlay Dr ML2 . . . . 186 C6
Gourlay St 1 G21 . . . . 97 E4
GOUROCK 44 D7
Gourock High Sch PA19 . . . 44 D7
Gourock Prim Sch PA19 . . . 44 E7
Gourock St G5 . . . . 117 A4
Gourock Sta PA19 . . . . 44 E8
GOVAN 116 A7
Govan Cross Sh Ctr G51. 116 A8
Govan Dr G83 . . . . 27 D6
Govan High Sch G51 . . . . . 115 E7
GOVANHILL 117 B2
Govanhill St
Glasgow G42 . . . . 117 B2
Glasgow G42 . . . . 117 C2
Govan Rd
Glasgow G51 . . . . 115 E8
Glasgow, Plantation G51 . . 116 C6
Govan Underground Sta
G51 . . . . 116 A8
Gowan Ave FK2 . . . . 42 B6
Gowanbank Gdns PA5 . . . . 111 E2
Gowanbank Prim Sch
G53 . . . . 135 A5
Gowanbank Rd KA7 . . . . . . 239 B2
Gowanbrae G66 . . . . 79 C6
Gowan Brae ML6 . . . . 105 B5
Gowanhill Gdns FK8 . . . . 1 F1
Gowan La FK2 . . . . 42 B6
Gowanlea Ave G15 . . . . 75 A1
Gowanlea Dr
Glasgow G46 . . . . 136 D4
Slamannan FK1 . . . . 86 B6
Gowanlea Terr G71 . . . . . . 141 B7
Gowanside Pl ML8 . . . . . . 187 D2
Gower Pl KA7 . . . . 239 B3
Gower St G51 . . . . 116 C4
Gower Terr G41 . . . . 116 C5
Gowkhall Ave ML1 . . . . . . 143 F3
Gowkhouse Rd PA13 . . . . . . 89 E8
GOWKTHRAPPLE 186 A8
Goyle Ave G15 . . . . 75 C3
Grace Ave G69 . . . . 120 F5
Grace St G3 . . . . 240 A2
Grace Wynd ML3 . . . . 162 E3
Gracie Cres FK7 . . . . 8 D4
Gradlon Pl FK1 . . . . 42 B3
Graeme Ct ML1 . . . . 142 D2
Graeme High Sch FK1 . . . . 42 E4
Graeme Pl FK1 . . . . 41 E1
Graffham Ave G46 . . . . 136 E3
Grafton Pl G1 . . . . 241 A3
Graham Ave
Cambuslang G72 . . . . 139 D5
Clydebank G81 . . . . 74 B3
East Kilbride G74 . . . . 159 E2
Hamilton ML3 . . . . 183 D8
Larbert FK5 . . . . 23 B3
Stevenston KA20 . . . . 206 B1
Stirling FK9 . . . . 2 C4
Graham Cres G82 . . . . 48 B7
Graham Ct KA1 . . . . 228 E6
Graham Dr
East Kilbride G75 . . . . 180 F5
Milngavie G62 . . . . 54 F2
Grahamfield Pl KA15 . . . . 171 A7
Graham Ho G67 . . . . 61 E2
Graham Pl
Ashgill ML9 . . . . 185 F1
Helensburgh G84 . . . . 17 A2
Kilmarnock KA3 . . . . 223 D2
Kilsyth G65 . . . . 36 C2
Graham Rd
Crossford ML8 . . . . 201 B1
Dumbarton G82 . . . . 49 D4
Grahams Ave PA12 . . . . . . 129 D3
Grahamsdyke Cres FK4 . . . 40 A3
Grahamsdyke Rd
Bonnybridge FK4 . . . . 40 A4
Kirkintilloch G66 . . . . 58 E1
Grahamsdyke St FK2 . . . . . . 42 F4
Grahamshill Ave ML6 . . . 123 D8
Grahamshill St ML6 . . . . . 123 C8
Graham Sq G31 . . . . 117 F6
Grahams Rd FK1 . . . . 42 B6
Grahams Road Rdbt FK1 . . 42 B5
Graham St
Airdrie ML6 . . . . 123 A7
Barrhead G78 . . . . 134 B3
Bridge of Allan FK9 . . . . 2 B7
Greenock PA16 . . . . 45 C5
Hamilton ML3 . . . . 162 E3
Johnstone PA5 . . . . 111 E2
Motherwell ML1 . . . . 143 A5
Wishaw ML2 . . . . 165 B2
GRAHAMSTON 42 A6
Grahamston Ave KA14 . . . 170 B7
Grahamston Cres PA2 . . . 134 C8
Grahamston Ct PA2 . . . . . 134 C8
Grahamston Pk G78 . . . . . 134 B5
Grahamston Pl PA2 . . . . . 134 C8
Grahamston Rd G78 . . . . . 134 C6
Graham Terr
Airth FK2 . . . . 14 D4
Bishopbriggs G64 . . . . 98 B7
Stewarton KA3 . . . . 195 D1
Graham Wlk KA3 . . . . 223 C2
Graham Wynd G75 . . . . . . 180 F5
Graignestock Pl 2 G40 . . 117 E5
Graigside Pl G68 . . . . 81 F7
Grainger Rd G64 . . . . 78 D1
Grammar Prim Sch KA7 . . 238 F7
Grammar School Sq
ML3 . . . . 162 E4
Grampian Ave PA2 . . . . . . 133 D8
Grampian Cres
Chapelhall ML6 . . . . 123 F1
Glasgow G32 . . . . 119 B4
Grampian Ct
Bearsden G61 . . . . 75 C8
Greenock PA16 . . . . 45 B5
Irvine KA11 . . . . 220 A8
Grampian Dr G75 . . . . 180 B4
Grampian Pl G32 . . . . 119 B4
Grampian Rd
Kilmarnock KA1 . . . . 228 B3
Port Glasgow PA14 . . . . 69 A6
Stirling FK7 . . . . 6 E6
Wishaw ML2 . . . . 164 F4
Grampian St G32 . . . . 119 B4
Grampian Way
Barrhead G78 . . . . 134 C1
Bearsden G61 . . . . 75 C7
Cumbernauld G68 . . . . 61 A2
Granary Rd FK2 . . . . 42 A8
Granary Sq FK2 . . . . 42 B7
Granby Ho 8 G12 . . . . 96 E3
Granby La G12 . . . . 96 D3
Grandtuly Dr G12 . . . . 96 C6
GRANGE 227 D8
Grange Acad KA1 . . . . 227 D8
Grange Ave
Ayr KA7 . . . . 239 B2
Falkirk FK2 . . . . 42 D6
Milngavie G62 . . . . 55 B2
Wishaw ML2 . . . . 164 E1
Grange Ct
Lanark ML11 . . . . 214 F5
Stevenston KA20 . . . . 206 C1
Grange Dr FK2 . . . . 42 D6
Grange Gdns
Bothwell G71 . . . . 141 B1
Bridge of Allan FK9 . . . . 2 C7
Grangemouth Rd FK2 . . . . 42 E5
Grangemuir Ct KA9 . . . . . 236 B7
Grangemuir Rd KA9 . . . . . 236 B7
Grangeneuk Gdns G68 . . . . 61 C1
Grange Pl
Alexandria G83 . . . . 27 E5
Kilmarnock KA1 . . . . 227 F8
Grange Rd
Alloa FK10 . . . . 9 F6
Bearsden G61 . . . . 75 F5
Bridge of Allan FK9 . . . . 2 C6
Glasgow G42 . . . . 137 A8
Stevenston KA20 . . . . 206 D1
Granger Rd
Balloch G83 . . . . 27 F8
Kilmarnock KA1 . . . . 227 E5
Grange St
Kilmarnock KA1 . . . . 227 F8
Motherwell ML1 . . . . 164 A4
Grange Terr KA1 . . . . 227 D8
Grange The KA11 . . . . 220 C6
Grange Twr ML1 . . . . 164 B2
Grange View FK5 . . . . 23 E1
Grannoch Pl ML5 . . . . 122 D2
Gran St G81 . . . . 94 E8
Grant Cres G82 . . . . 27 D1
Grant Ct
Airdrie ML6 . . . . 123 E8
Hamilton ML3 . . . . 183 C7
Grant Gr ML4 . . . . 142 A4
Grantholm Ave ML1 . . . . . 143 B6
Grantlea Gr G32 . . . . 119 D4
Grantlea Terr G32 . . . . . . 119 D4
Grantley Gdns G41 . . . . . . 136 D8
Grantley St G41 . . . . 136 D8
Grantoften Path G75 . . . . 180 E6
Granton St G5 . . . . 117 E2
Grantown Ave ML6 . . . . . . 123 E6
Grantown Gdns
Airdrie ML6 . . . . 103 A5
Glenmavis ML6 . . . . 102 F5
Grant Pl
Kilmarnock KA3 . . . . 223 C2
Stirling FK9 . . . . 2 B4
Grants Ave PA2 . . . . 113 D1
Grants Cres PA2 . . . . 133 D8
Grants Pl PA2 . . . . 133 C8
Grant St
Alloa FK10 . . . . 9 F6
Glasgow G3 . . . . 240 A4
Greenock PA15 . . . . 46 C3
Helensburgh G84 . . . . 16 D1
Helensburgh G84 . . . . 16 D2
Grants Way PA2 . . . . 113 D1
Granville St
Clydebank G81 . . . . 74 B3
Glasgow G3 . . . . 240 A3
Helensburgh G84 . . . . 16 F1
Grasmere G75 . . . . 179 F5
Grasmere Ct ML3 . . . . 183 D6
Grassyards Intc KA3 . . . . 223 D3
Grassyards Rd KA3 . . . . . . 223 C2
Grathellen Ct ML1 . . . . . . 164 A8
Grawhall Pl FK5 . . . . 23 B2
Gray Cres KA12 . . . . 224 E8
Gray Dr G61 . . . . 75 F3
Gray's Cl ML11 . . . . 214 C4
Grayshill Rd G68 . . . . 81 E6
Gray's Rd G71 . . . . 141 B5
Gray St
Alexandria G83 . . . . 27 E5
Cleland ML1 . . . . 144 B1
Glasgow G3 . . . . 96 E1
Greenock PA15 . . . . 46 B3
Kirkintilloch G66 . . . . 80 B7
Larkhall ML9 . . . . 185 A4
Prestwick KA9 . . . . 236 C8
Gray St *continued*
Shotts ML7 . . . . 147 A4
Graystale Rd FK7 . . . . 7 A3
Graystonelee Rd ML7 . . . 146 D6
Graystones KA13 . . . . 207 E5
Grayston Manor G69 . . . . . . 80 E1
Great Dovehill G1, G4 . . . 241 B1
Great George La 6 G12 . . 96 D3
Great George St
Glasgow G12 . . . . 96 D3
Glasgow G12 . . . . 96 E2
Great Hamilton St PA2 . . . 113 E2
Great Kelvin La G12 . . . . . . 96 E2
Great Western Rd
Bowling G60 . . . . 72 D8
Clydebank G81 . . . . 74 C4
Glasgow, Dowanhill G4,
G12 . . . . 96 D3
Glasgow, Knightswood G15 . . 95 D7
Great Western Terr 13
G12 . . . . 96 C4
Great Western Terrace La 12
G12 . . . . 96 C4
Greenacre Ct FK7 . . . . 7 E1
Greenacre Dr FK4 . . . . 40 A3
Greenacre Pl
Bannockburn FK7 . . . . 7 E1
Bonnybridge FK4 . . . . 40 A3
Greenacre Rd FK4 . . . . 40 A3
Greenacres
Ardrossan KA22 . . . . 205 E3
Motherwell ML1 . . . . 163 C5
Greenacres Ct G53 . . . . . . 135 C4
Greenacres Cvn Pk KA20 206 F1
Greenacres Dr G53 . . . . . 135 C4
Greenacres Rdbt 4 G64 . . 98 D8
Greenacres View ML1 . . . 163 C5
Greenacres Way G53 . . . . 135 C4
Greenan Ave G42 . . . . 137 E7
Greenan Gr KA7 . . . . 238 B3
Greenan Pk KA7 . . . . 238 B3
Greenan Pl KA7 . . . . 238 C3
Greenan Rd
Doonfoot KA7 . . . . 238 C3
Kilmarnock KA3 . . . . 228 B8
Greenan Terr KA9 . . . . 236 D7
Greenan Way KA7 . . . . 238 B3
Green Ave KA12 . . . . 219 C4
GREENBANK 41 C3
Greenbank 6 G72 . . . . 161 D7
Green Bank KA24 . . . . 191 C7
Greenbank Ave G46 . . . . . 157 A7
Greenbank Ct
Falkirk FK1 . . . . 41 D4
Irvine KA12 . . . . 219 C1
Greenbank Dr PA2 . . . . . . 133 D7
Greenbank Gdn* G76 . . . 157 C6
Greenbank Mews PA16 . . . . 45 D5
Greenbank Pl FK1 . . . . 41 D4
Greenbank Rd
Falkirk FK1 . . . . 41 D3
Falkirk FK1 . . . . 41 D4
Irvine KA12 . . . . 219 C1
Wishaw ML2 . . . . 165 C3
Green Bank Rd G68 . . . . 61 C2
Greenbank St 3 G73 . . . . 138 A8
Greenbank Terr 4 ML8 . . 187 F2
Greenburn Specl Sch
G74 . . . . 160 A2
Greencornhills Rdbt FK7 . . 11 F8
Greencraig Ave FK1 . . . . . . 66 C6
Green Dale ML2 . . . . 165 D5
Greendyke St G1 . . . . 241 B1
GREENEND 122 D5
Greenend Ave PA5 . . . . . . 111 D1
Greenend Pl G32 . . . . 119 C7
Greenend View ML4 . . . . . 141 F5
Greenfarm Rd
Linwood PA3 . . . . 112 B6
Newton Mearns G77 . . . . . 156 B6
GREENFAULDS 82 E7
Greenfaulds Cres G67 . . . . 83 A8
Greenfaulds High Sch
G67 . . . . 82 D7
Greenfaulds Rd G67 . . . . . . 82 E7
Greenfaulds Sta G67 . . . . . . 82 F7
GREENFIELD 119 B6
Greenfield Ave
Alloway KA7 . . . . 238 E2
Glasgow G32 . . . . 119 B7
Greenfield Cres ML2 . . . . 165 D4
Greenfield Dr
Irvine KA12 . . . . 219 D2
Wishaw ML2 . . . . 165 D4
Greenfield Pl G32 . . . . 119 B6
Greenfield Prim Sch
G51 . . . . 115 F7
Greenfield Quadrant
ML1 . . . . 143 F4
Greenfield Rd
Carluke ML8 . . . . 187 F3
Clarkston G76 . . . . 157 E6
Glasgow G32 . . . . 119 C6
Hamilton ML3 . . . . 162 A5
Greenfield St
Alloa FK10 . . . . 10 B7
Bonnybridge FK4 . . . . 40 B6
Glasgow G51 . . . . 115 F7
Wishaw ML2 . . . . 165 D4
Greenfinch Ave G68 . . . . . . 81 F8
GREENFOOT 102 A7
Greenfoot KA13 . . . . 207 E3
GREENGAIRS 83 F1
Greengairs Ave G51 . . . . . 115 D8
Greengairs Prim Sch ML6 83 E2
Greengairs Rd ML6 . . . . 83 E1
Green Gdns ML1 . . . . 144 C2
Greenhall Pl G72 . . . . 161 C6
GREENHEAD 165 D2
Greenhead FK12 . . . . 5 B6
Greenhead Ave
Dumbarton G82 . . . . 50 B3
Stevenston KA20 . . . . 206 E2
Greenhead Gdns G82 . . . . . 50 B3
Greenhead Holdings
KA20 . . . . 206 D3
Greenhead Moss Com Nature
Pk* ML2 . . . . 165 E2
Greenhead Rd
Bearsden G61 . . . . 75 F4
Dumbarton G82 . . . . 50 C3
Inchinnan PA4 . . . . 93 C6
Lennoxtown G66 . . . . 57 E8
Wishaw ML2 . . . . 165 D2
Greenhead St G40 . . . . . . 117 E4
GREENHILL 102 B1
GREEN HILL 40 A2
Greenhill G64 . . . . 98 C8
Greenhill Ave
Glasgow G46 . . . . 136 C1
Mount Ellen G69 . . . . 100 E7
Greenhill Bsns Ctr ML5 . . 102 A1
Greenhill Bsns Pk PA3 . . 113 C6
Greenhill Cres
Elderslie PA5 . . . . 112 D2
Linwood PA3 . . . . 112 C6
Greenhill Ct
Irvine KA11 . . . . 220 B6
Rutherglen G73 . . . . 138 A8
Greenhill Dr PA3 . . . . 112 C6
Greenhill Ind Est ML5 . . . 102 A1
Greenhill Prim Sch ML5. 122 A8
Greenhill Rd
Blackridge EH48 . . . . 107 E3
Bonnybridge FK4 . . . . 40 A3
Cleland ML1 . . . . 144 F3
Paisley PA3 . . . . 113 C6
Rutherglen G73 . . . . 138 A8
GREENHILLS 180 C6
Greenhills KA15 . . . . 172 A2
Greenhills Cres G75 . . . . . 180 B5
Greenhill Smallholdings
KA2 . . . . 222 A2
Greenhills Prim Sch
G75 . . . . 180 C5
Greenhill Sq FK4 . . . . 40 A3
Greenhills Rd G75 . . . . . . 180 C5
Greenhills Sq G75 . . . . 180 B5
Greenhill St G73 . . . . 138 A7
Greenhill Terr KA2 . . . . . . 221 F3
Greenholm Ave
Clarkston G76 . . . . 157 E7
Uddingston G71 . . . . 140 E7
Greenholme Ct G44 . . . . . 137 B7
Greenholme St G44 . . . . . 137 B6
Greenholm St KA1 . . . . . . 227 F6
Greenhorn's Well Ave FK1 41 F3
Greenhorn's Well Cres
FK1 . . . . 41 F3
Greenhorn's Well Dr FK1 . . 41 F3
Greenknowe Dr ML8 . . . . . 186 F6
Greenknowe Pk KA9 . . . . 233 D4
Greenknowe Rd G43 . . . . . 136 B6
Greenknowe St ML2 . . . . . 186 B6
Greenlady Wlk ML11 . . . . 215 C4
Greenlaw Ave
Paisley PA1 . . . . 114 A5
Wishaw ML2 . . . . 165 C5
Greenlaw Cres PA1 . . . . . 114 A6
Greenlaw Ct G14 . . . . 94 D6
Greenlaw Dr
Newton Mearns G77 . . . . . 156 D5
Paisley PA1 . . . . 114 A5
Greenlaw Gdns PA1 . . . . . 114 A6
Greenlaw Ho PA1 . . . . 114 A5
Greenlaw Ind Est PA3 . . . 113 F6
Greenlaw Rd
Glasgow G14 . . . . 94 E6
Newton Mearns G77 . . . . . 156 D5
Greenlea Rd G69 . . . . 100 B8
Greenlea St G13 . . . . 95 E6
GREENLEES 139 A3
Greenlees Ct KA24 . . . . . . 191 B8
Greenlees Gdns G72 . . . . . 138 F3
Greenlees Gr ML5 . . . . . . 122 D5
Greenlees Pk G72 . . . . 139 A4
Greenlees Rd G72 . . . . 139 A4
Green Loan ML1 . . . . 143 A3
Greenloan Ave G51 . . . . . 115 D8
Greenloan View ML9 . . . . 185 B1
Greenmoss Pl ML4 . . . . . . 142 C5
Greenmount G22 . . . . 97 A7
Greenmount Dr FK1 . . . . . . 66 C6
Greenoakhill Cres G71 . . 120 A2
Greenoakhill Gate G71 . . 120 B2
Greenoakhill Pl G71 . . . . 120 A2
Greenoakhill Rd G69,
G71 . . . . 120 A2
GREENOCK 45 C6
Greenock Acad PA16 . . . . . 45 D7
Greenock Ave G44 . . . . . . 137 B5
Greenock Central Sta
PA15 . . . . 46 A4
Greenock Rd
Bishopton PA7 . . . . 71 D5
Greenock PA15 . . . . 46 F2
Inchinnan PA4 . . . . 93 C6
Langbank PA14 . . . . 70 C7
Paisley PA3 . . . . 113 D7
Port Glasgow PA14 . . . . 47 D1
Renfrew PA4 . . . . 94 A5
Greenock Sp Ctr PA16 . . . . 45 E5
GREENOCK WEST 45 C6
Greenock West Sta PA15 . . 45 E5
Green Pl
Bothwell G71 . . . . 141 B2
Green Pl *continued*
Calderbank ML6 . . . . 123 B2
Green Rd
Paisley PA2 . . . . 113 B3
Rutherglen G73 . . . . 138 A8
Greenrig G71 . . . . 140 F6
Greenrigg Cotts ML7 . . . . 127 F5
Greenrigg Prim Sch ML7 127 F6
Greenrigg Rd G67 . . . . 62 B1
Greenrigg St G71 . . . . 140 F6
Greenrig Rd ML11 . . . . 214 B1
Greenrig St G33 . . . . 98 D3
Greens Ave G66 . . . . 79 C7
Greens Cres G66 . . . . 79 C7
Greenshields Rd G69 . . . . 120 B5
Greenside
Carmunnock G76 . . . . 158 E8
Irvine KA11 . . . . 220 A4
Greenside Ave
Kilbirnie KA25 . . . . 170 A7
Prestwick KA9 . . . . 236 D7
Springside KA11 . . . . 221 A1
Greenside Cl 6 ML11 . . . 215 A4
Greenside Cres G33 . . . . . . 98 E3
Greenside La 7 ML11 . . . 215 A4
Greenside Pl G61 . . . . 75 C8
Greenside Rd
Clydebank G81 . . . . 74 B7
Motherwell ML1 . . . . 143 C8
Wishaw ML2 . . . . 165 C2
Greenside St
Alloa FK10 . . . . 10 B6
Coatbridge ML5 . . . . 122 B8
Glasgow G33 . . . . 98 E3
Motherwell ML1 . . . . 143 F4
Greenside Terr KA11 . . . . 221 A2
Greenside Way KA11 . . . . 220 A4
Greens Rd G67 . . . . 82 F6
Green St
Ayr KA8 . . . . 235 F2
Bothwell G71 . . . . 141 B2
Clydebank G81 . . . . 74 A3
Glasgow G40 . . . . 117 E5
6 Kilmarnock KA1 . . . . . . 227 F8
Saltcoats KA21 . . . . 216 F7
Stonehouse ML9 . . . . 198 F2
Green Street La
Ayr KA8 . . . . 235 F1
Ayr KA8 . . . . 235 F2
Green Street Lane Bsns Pk
4 KA8 . . . . 235 F2
Green The
Alva FK12 . . . . 5 A7
Glasgow G40 . . . . 117 E4
Greentowers Rd ML11 . . . 214 E8
Greentree Dr G69 . . . . 119 F3
Greentree Pk KA7 . . . . 239 C4
Greenview Sch G22 . . . . 97 D6
Greenview St G43 . . . . 136 C8
Greenway La G72 . . . . 161 C5
Greenways Ave PA2 . . . . . 113 B2
Greenways Ct PA2 . . . . . . 113 A2
Greenwood Acad KA11 . . 220 A1
Greenwood Ave
Cambuslang G72 . . . . 139 E6
Moodiesburn G69 . . . . 80 F2
Stirling FK8 . . . . 7 A8
Greenwood Cres ML5 . . . 122 D5
Greenwood Ct G76 . . . . . . 157 E6
Greenwood Dr
Bearsden G61 . . . . 76 A4
Johnstone PA5 . . . . 131 E8
Greenwood Gate KA11 . . 220 A1
Greenwood Intc KA11 . . . 225 A8
Greenwood Quadrant
G81 . . . . 74 D1
Greenwood Rd
Clarkston G76 . . . . 157 D7
Irvine KA11 . . . . 220 C1
Greenwood St ML7 . . . . . . 146 E5
Greenyards Intc G67 . . . . . 62 C1
Greer Quadrant G81 . . . . . . 74 B4
Grenada Pl G75 . . . . 159 B1
Grenadier Gdns ML1 . . . . 163 D4
Grenadier Pk G72 . . . . 139 A4
Grendon Ct FK8 . . . . 7 A6
Grendon Gdns FK8 . . . . 7 A6
Grenville Ct FK1 . . . . 41 F4
Grenville Dr G72 . . . . 138 F4
Grenville Rd PA19 . . . . 44 F6
Gresham View ML1 . . . . . . 164 B2
Greta Meek La G66 . . . . 58 C6
Gretna St G40 . . . . 118 B4
Greyfriars Ct ML11 . . . . . . 214 F4
Greyfriars Rd G71 . . . . 140 C8
Greyfriars St G32 . . . . 118 F7
Greygoran FK10 . . . . 5 C2
Grey Pl PA15 . . . . 45 F6
Greystone Ave G73 . . . . . . 138 C6
Greystone Bauks ML11 . . . 214 F4
Greystone Baulks ML11 . 214 A4
Greystone Gdns G73 . . . . 138 C6
Greywood St G13 . . . . 95 E7
Grier Path G31 . . . . 118 D5
Grier Pl ML9 . . . . 184 F2
Grierson Cres FK7 . . . . 6 D6
Grierson La G33 . . . . 118 D8
Grierson St G33 . . . . 118 D8
Griers Wlk KA11 . . . . 225 D6
Grieve Croft G71 . . . . 140 F1
Grieve Rd
Cumbernauld G67 . . . . 62 A3
Greenock PA16 . . . . 45 B5
Griffen Ave PA1 . . . . 112 E5
Griffin Dock Rd KA8 . . . . . 235 E2
Griffin Pl ML4 . . . . 142 A8
Griffiths St FK1 . . . . 42 B4
Griffiths Way ML8 . . . . 186 F4

Griqua Terr G71 141 B2
Grodwell Dr FK12 4 E7
Grogarry Rd G15 75 A4
Grossart St ML7 125 A2
Grosvenor Cres 9 G12 96 D3
Grosvenor La
Glasgow G12 96 D3
Greenock PA15 46 D3
Grosvenor Rd PA15 46 D3
Grosvenor Terr 12 G12 96 D3
Grougar Dr KA3 223 B4
Grougar Gdns KA3 223 B4
Grougar Rd KA3 228 D8
Groveburn Ave G46 136 A4
Grove Cres
Falkirk FK2 24 A2
Larkhall ML9 185 C2
Grovepark Ct G20 97 A2
Grovepark Gdns G20 97 A2
Grovepark St G20 97 A3
Grove Pk G66 79 D4
Grove St FK6 21 C2
Groves The G64 98 C7
Grove The
Bishopton PA7 72 A3
Bridge of Weir PA11 110 E6
Kilbarchan PA10 111 A3
Neilston G78 154 C6
Rutherglen G46 157 B8
Grove Way ML4 141 F4
Grove Wood G71 121 D1
Grovewood Bsns Ctr
ML4 141 E8
Grove Wynd ML1 143 A3
Grudie St G34 120 A8
Gryfebank Ave PA6 91 E1
Gryfebank Cl PA6 91 E1
Gryfebank Cres PA6 91 E1
Gryfebank Way PA6 91 E1
Gryfe Rd
Bridge of Weir PA11 110 D7
Port Glasgow PA14 68 E7
Gryfe St PA15 46 B2
Gryfewood Cres PA6 91 E1
Gryfewood Way PA6 91 E1
Gryffe Ave PA11 90 C1
Gryffe Castle PA11 90 C1
Gryffe Cres PA2 112 F1
Gryffe Gr PA11 110 D8
Gryffe High Sch PA6 91 A1
Gryffe Rd PA13 89 D7
Gryffe St G44 137 A7
Guildford St G33 99 C1
Guiltreehill KA7 239 A1
Gullane Cres G68 61 F6
Gullane Ct
Hamilton ML3 183 B7
Irvine KA11 224 F8
Gullane Dr ML5 121 F2
Gullane Pl KA13 207 B3
Gullane St G11 96 B1
Gulliland Ave KA2 225 F2
Gulliland Pl KA12 219 D1
Gullin Dr KA9 236 E5
Gullion Pk G74 160 A4
Gunn Mews ML2 164 F2
Gunn Quadrant ML4 141 E3
Gushet Ho ML6 122 E7
Gushet Pl ML11 214 A3
Guthrie Cres FK5 23 B2
Guthrie Ct ML1 163 C6
Guthrie Dr G71 121 A1
Guthrie Pl
East Kilbride G74 159 F2
Rhu G84 15 D4
Torrance G64 57 C1
Guthrie Rd KA21 217 A8
Guthrie St
Glasgow G20 96 D6
Hamilton ML3 162 D4
Guthrie Terr KA1 227 B7
Guy Mannering Rd G84 25 C8
Gyle Pl ML2 165 E3

H

Habbieauld Rd KA3 222 B8
Haberlea Ave G53 135 C3
Haberlea Gdns G53 135 C2
Haddington Gdns KA11 220 B6
Haddington Way ML5 121 E3
Haddow Gr 6 G71 141 A8
Haddow St ML3 162 E3
Hadrian Terr ML1 163 C8
Hagart Rd PA6 91 B2
Hagen Dr ML1 143 E1
Hagg Cres PA5 111 E3
Hagg Pl PA5 111 E3
Hagg Rd PA5 111 E2
HAGGS 39 A3
Haggs La G41 116 C2
Haggs Rd G41 116 C1
Haggswood Ave G41 116 C2
Haghill Park Prim Sch
G31 118 B7
Haghill Pk Sp Ctr G45 118 C8
Haghill Rd G31 118 C7
Hagholm Rd ML11 215 F7
Hagmill Cres ML5 122 C2
Hagmill Rd ML5 122 B2
Hagthorn Ave KA25 170 A8
Haig Ave FK8 2 A2
Haig Dr G69 119 F4
Haig St
Glasgow G21 98 A4
Greenock PA15 45 F6
Hailes Ave G32 119 D5
Haining Ave KA1 228 B5
Haining Rd PA4 94 D3
Haining The PA4 94 D2
HAIRMYRES 179 F8
Hairmyres G75 158 F1
Hairmyres Dr G75 179 F8
Hairmyres Hospl G75 179 F8
Hairmyres Hospl Sch
G75 158 F1
Hairmyres La G75 158 E1
Hairmyres Pk G75 179 F8
Hairmyres Rdbt G75 158 F1
Hairmyres St G42 117 C2
Hairmyres Sta G75 158 F1
Hairst St PA4 94 D4
Halbeath Ave G15 74 F3
Halberts Cres FK7 7 B2
Halbert St G41 116 E1
Haldane Ave FK9 2 A6
Haldane Ct G83 27 F8
Haldane La 9 G14 95 D3
Haldane Pl G75 180 F7
Haldane Prim Sch G83 27 F8
Haldane St G14 95 D3
Haldane Terr G83 19 F1
Haldon Gr ML5 101 F7
Halfmerke Prim Sch
G74 160 A3
Halfmerk N G74 160 A2
Halfmerk S G74 160 A2
HALFWAY 139 D4
Halfway St KA23 190 C5
Halgreen Ave G15 74 E3
Halidon Ave G67 82 F7
Halifax Way 7 PA4 94 C1
Halket Cres FK2 24 C2
Halkett Cres G83 27 E7
Halkett Pl KA21 217 A8
Halkirk Gate G72 161 C4
Hallam Rd FK5 23 D2
Hall Bar Gdns ML8 201 E4
Hallbrae St G33 98 E2
Hallcraig St ML6 123 A8
Halley Ct G13 94 E7
Halley Dr G13 94 E7
Halley Pl G13 94 E7
Halley Sq G13 94 F7
Halley St G13 94 E7
Hallforest St G33 99 B2
HALLGLEN 42 D1
Hallglen Prim Sch FK1 42 B1
Hallglen Rd FK1 42 B1
Hallglen Sh Ctr FK1 42 B1
Hallglen Terr FK1 42 B1
Hallgraig Pl ML8 187 D2
Hallhill Cres G33 119 E6
Hallhill Rd
Glasgow, Barlanark G32, G33 119 E6
Glasgow, Garrowhill G69 120 A6
Glasgow, Greenfield G32 119 B5
Johnstone PA5 131 C7
Halliburton Cres G33 119 F7
Halliburton Terr G34 120 A7
Hallidale Cres PA4 94 F2
Hallinan Gdns ML2 164 F1
Hall La KA10 230 B4
Hallpark
Alloa FK10 10 C8
Sauchie FK10 5 C1
Hall Pl
Lanark ML11 215 A4
Stepps G33 99 F5
Hall Rd
Nemphlar ML11 214 B6
Rhu G84 15 D5
Hallrule Dr G52 115 C5
HALLSIDE 139 F5
Hallside Ave G72 139 E5
Hallside Bvd G72 139 F4
Hallside Cres G72 139 E5
Hallside Dr G72 139 E5
Hallside Gdns ML2 165 E4
Hallside Pl G5 117 C4
Hallside Prim Sch G72 139 E4
Hallside Rd G72 139 E4
Hallside St PA9 130 F5
Hall St
Alexandria G83 27 F4
Clydebank G81 74 B1
Hamilton ML3 162 D1
Motherwell ML1 143 A4
Renton G82 49 D8
Halls Vennal 3 KA8 235 F2
Hallydown Dr G13 95 C5
Halpin Cl ML4 141 D5
Halton Gdns G69 119 F4
Haltons Path G71 141 A6
Hamersley Pl G75 180 B7
Hamilcomb Rd ML4 142 A3
Hamill Dr G65 60 F8
HAMILTON 162 C3
Hamilton Ave
Glasgow G41 116 C3
Stenhousemuir FK5 23 E4
Hamilton Bsns Pk ML3 162 D5
Hamilton Central Sta
ML3 162 E3
Hamilton Coll ML3 162 D5
Hamilton Cres
Ayr KA7 239 A7
Bearsden G61 75 E7
Bishopton PA7 71 F3
Cambuslang G72 139 C4
Coatbridge ML5 122 A5
Renfrew PA4 94 D5
Stevenston KA20 206 F2
Hamilton Ct KA3 222 B7
Hamilton Dr
Airdrie ML6 103 B1
Bothwell G71 141 B1
Cambuslang G72 139 A5
Erskine PA8 72 F3
Falkirk FK1 42 A4
Glasgow G12 96 E3
Glasgow, Giffnock G46 136 D2
Hamilton G72 161 B5
Motherwell ML1 163 F4
Stirling FK9 2 C4
Hamilton Drive La G12 /
G20 96 E3
Hamilton Gate 6 PA15 45 F5
Hamilton Gdns KA3 195 E1
Hamilton Gram Sch ML3 162 D3
HAMILTONHILL 97 B4
Hamiltonhill Cres G22 97 B4
Hamiltonhill Gdns G22 97 B3
Hamiltonhill Rd G22 97 B3
Hamilton Int Tech Pk
G72 161 C5
Hamilton Mausoleum*
ML3 162 F5
Hamilton Park Ave G12 96 E3
Hamilton Park N ML3 162 D6
Hamilton Park S ML3 162 D6
Hamilton Pl
East Kilbride G75 180 E7
Hamilton ML3 183 D6
Motherwell ML1 143 B4
Motherwell, Whittagreen
ML1 143 C4
Hamilton Rd
Bellshill ML4 141 F4
Bothwell G71 141 B1
Cambuslang G72 139 C4
East Kilbride G74 160 C5
Glasgow G32 119 D2
Hamilton G72 161 B6
Larkhall ML9 184 F5
Motherwell ML1 163 D6
Rutherglen G72, G73 138 D7
Rutherglen G73 138 C7
Stenhousemuir FK5 23 D6
Hamilton Sch for the Deaf 9
ML3 162 A5
Hamilton St
Carluke ML8 187 F1
Clydebank G81 94 D7
Dumbarton G82 50 A4
Falkirk FK1 41 D6
Glasgow G42 117 C1
Kilwinning KA13 207 E4
Larkhall ML9 185 A4
Paisley PA3 113 F5
Saltcoats KA21 216 E7
Hamilton Terr G81 94 D7
Hamilton Twr G71 140 D4
Hamilton View G71 141 A7
Hamilton Water Pal ML3 162 D4
Hamilton Way
8 Greenock PA15 45 F5
Prestwick KA9 233 C2
Stonehouse ML9 198 E2
Hamilton West Sta ML3 162 C4
Hamlet G74 160 B5
Hampden Dr G42 137 B7
Hampden La G42 137 B8
Hampden Pk-Scotland's Nat
Stadium (Queen's Park FC)
G42 137 B7
Hampden Specl Sch G42 137 E7
Hampden Terr G42 137 B8
Hampden Way 4 PA4 94 D1
Handel Pl 3 G5 117 C4
HANGINGSHAW 137 C8
Hangingshaw Pl G42 137 C8
Hannah Dr KA2 221 F3
Hannah Pl G82 27 E2
Hannah Research Pk The
KA6 237 A4
Hanover Cl G42 137 A8
Hanover Ct
Glasgow G1 241 A3
Johnstone PA5 111 F3
Paisley PA1 114 A5
Stirling FK9 2 D4
Hanover Gdns
Bishopbriggs G64 78 A1
Paisley PA1 113 C4
Hanover St
Glasgow G1 241 A2
Helensburgh G84 25 A8
HANSEL VILLAGE 231 C1
Hanson Pk G31 117 F8
Hanson St G31 117 F8
Hapland Ave G53 115 C2
Hapland Rd G53 115 C2
Happyhills KA23 190 C5
Haran Rd G83 19 F1
Harbour Ind Est KA22 205 C2
Harbour Pl
Ardrossan KA22 205 B1
Glasgow G11 96 A1
Harbour Point KA21 216 F7
Harbour Rd
Ardrossan KA22 216 B8
Irvine KA12 219 B1
Paisley PA3 113 E6
Troon KA10 229 B3
Harbour St
Irvine KA12 219 A1
Saltcoats KA21 216 F7
Harburn Pl G23 76 E1
Harbury Pl G14 94 F6
Harcourt Dr G31 118 B8
Hardacres ML11 215 A5
HARDGATE 74 C5
Hardgate Dr G51 115 C8
Hardgate Gdns G51 115 C7
Hardgate Pl G51 115 C8
Hardgate Rd G51 115 C8
Hardie Ave G73 138 C8
Hardie Cres FK7 8 C4
Hardie Ct FK7 7 C3
Hardie St
Alexandria G83 27 D7
Hamilton, Blantyre G72 161 D7
Hamilton, Laighstonehall
ML3 162 B2
Motherwell ML1 163 E8
Hardmuir Gdns 1 G66 58 E1
Hardmuir Rd G66 58 E1
Hardridge Ave G52 115 E2
Hardridge Pl G52 115 E2
Hardridge Rd G52 115 E2
Hardwood Ct PA16 45 E7
Hardy Hill G84 17 A2
Harebell Pl KA7 239 B3
Harefield Dr G14 95 B5
Harelaw Ave
Barrhead G78 134 D1
Glasgow G44 136 E4
Neilston G78 154 D6
Port Glasgow PA14 68 D8
Harelaw Cres PA2 133 C7
HARELEESHILL 185 C1
Hareleeshill Prim Sch 23
ML9 185 C1
Hareleeshill Rd ML9 185 C2
Hareleeshill Sp Barn
ML9 185 C1
HARESHAW 144 E6
Hareshaw Dr KA3 223 A5
Hareshaw Gdns KA3 223 A5
Hareshaw Rd ML1 144 D5
HARESTANES 59 A2
Harestanes Gdns G66 59 A1
Harestanes Ind Est ML8 201 F5
Harestanes Prim Sch G66 59 A1
Harestanes Rd ML8 201 E4
Harestone Cres ML2 165 C2
Harestone Rd ML2 165 C2
Harfield Dr G33 119 E6
Harfield Gdns G33 119 E6
Harhill St G51 116 A8
Harkins Ave G72 161 C7
Harkness Ave G66 58 B5
Harland Cotts G14 95 C3
Harland St G14 95 C3
Harlands The FK10 9 E7
Harlaw Gdns G64 78 D2
Harlequin Ct ML3 182 F7
Harley Ct FK2 42 B8
Harley Gdns FK4 40 B5
Harley Pl KA21 205 E1
Harley St G51 116 C6
Harling Dr KA10 229 E2
Harmetray St G22 97 D6
Harmony Pl G51 116 A7
Harmony Row 1 G51 116 A8
Harmony Sq G51 116 A7
Harmsworth St G11 95 F2
Harper Cres ML2 165 E4
Harperland Dr KA1 227 D7
Harperland Holdings
KA2 226 A4
Harport St G46 135 E4
Harrier Way PA16 45 B4
Harriet Pl G43 136 B6
Harriet Rd KA3 223 A2
Harriet St G73 138 A7
Harrington Rd G74 159 E1
Harris Cl G77 156 B6
Harris Cres G60 73 B5
Harris Ct
Alloa FK10 10 B5
Irvine KA11 225 C8
Harris Dr G60 73 B5
Harris Gdns G60 73 C5
Harrison Dr G51 116 B6
Harrison Pl
Falkirk FK1 41 F5
Renton G82 27 D2
Harris Pl
Airdrie ML6 123 C5
Kilmarnock KA3 223 B5
Harris Quadrant ML2 165 E5
Harris Rd
Glasgow G23 76 E1
Old Kilpatrick G60 73 C5
Port Glasgow PA14 69 B7
Harris Terr KA11 225 C8
Harrow Ct G15 74 F3
Harrow Pl G15 74 F3
Hartfield Cres G78 154 E7
Hartfield Ct G82 50 A4
Hartfield Gdns G82 50 A4
Hartfield Rd KA7 238 F5
Hartfield Terr
Paisley PA2 113 F2
Shotts ML7 167 B8
Harthall KA8 236 E2
HARTHILL 127 F5
Harthill Ind Est ML7 127 D5
Harthill Rd EH48 107 D2
Hartlaw Cres G52 115 A6
Hartree Ave G13 94 E8
Hart St
Clydebank G81 74 D7
Glasgow G31 118 E5
Linwood PA3 112 C5
Hartstone Pl G53 135 B7
Hartstone Rd G53 135 B7
Hartstone Terr G53 135 B7
HARTWOOD 146 A3
Hartwood Gdns
Hartwood ML7 146 A2
Newton Mearns G77 156 D2
Hartwoodhill Hospl ML7 146 C4
Hartwood Rd
Hartwood ML7 145 F2
Shotts ML7 146 A3
Hart Wynd FK7 7 F1
Harvest Dr ML1 163 D4
Harvest St FK9 2 A4
Harvey Cotts PA12 129 D2
Harvey Ct PA12 129 C2
Harvey Gdns KA22 205 C3
Harvey Sq PA12 129 C2
Harvey St
Ardrossan KA22 205 C3
Glasgow G4 97 C2
Harvey Terr PA12 129 C2
Harvey Way ML4 142 C7
Harvey Wynd FK8 2 A1
Harvie Ave G77 156 D6
Harvie St G51 116 D6
Harwood Gdns 1 G69 81 A3
Harwood St G32 118 E7
Hastie St G3 96 D1
Hastings G75 180 B7
Hatfield Ct PA13 89 C7
Hatfield Dr G12 96 A5
Hathaway Dr G46 136 B2
Hathaway La G20 96 E5
Hathaway St G20 96 E5
Hathersage Ave G69 120 B5
Hathersage Dr G69 120 B5
Hathersage Gdns 2 G69 120 B5
Hatton Gdns G52 115 A4
Hattonhill ML1 143 C2
Hatton Path G52 115 A4
Hatton Pl ML1 143 C2
HATTONRIG 142 B6
Hattonrigg Rd ML4 142 B6
Hatton Terr ML1 143 C2
Haughburn Pl G53 135 B7
Haughburn Rd G53 135 B7
Haughburn Terr G53 135 C7
Haugh Gdns FK2 24 B1
HAUGHHEAD 32 F3
Haugh Pl ML3 162 E1
Haugh Rd
Glasgow G3 116 D8
Kilsyth G65 60 C8
Stirling FK9 2 B2
Haugh St FK2 24 B1
Haughs Way FK6 21 E2
Haughton Ave G65 60 E8
Haughview Rd ML1 163 B6
Haupland Rd KA22 205 B5
Hauplands Way KA23 190 E5
Havelock La G11 96 C2
Havelock Pk 9 G75 159 A1
Havelock Pl G84 16 F2
Havelock St
Glasgow G11 96 C2
Helensburgh G84 16 E2
Haven Pk G75 179 F6
Haven The FK7 9 F3
Havoc Rd G82 49 C4
Hawbank Rd G74 159 B3
Hawbank Rdbt G74 159 B2
Hawick Ave PA2 113 B1
Hawick Cres ML9 185 A2
Hawick Ct 10 PA15 46 B3
Hawick Dr ML5 122 D3
Hawick St
Glasgow G13 94 E7
Wishaw ML2 165 C5
Hawkhead Ave PA2 114 B2
Hawkhead Rd PA2 114 B3
Hawkhead Sta PA1 114 B4
Hawkhill Ave KA8 236 B2
Hawkhill Avenue La KA8 236 B2
Hawkhill Dr KA20 206 F1
Hawkhill Pl KA20 206 F2
Hawkhill Rd FK10 10 C6
Hawkhill Ret Pk KA20 206 F2
Hawksland Wlk ML3 162 E1
Hawkwood G75 180 D5
Hawkwood Rd ML6 102 F4
Hawley Rd FK1 42 D4
Hawthorn Ave
Bearsden G61 76 A7
Bishopbriggs G64 98 B8
Dumbarton G82 49 B5
Erskine PA8 93 E8
Johnstone PA5 112 A1
Kirkintilloch G66 79 C5
Prestwick KA9 236 C7
Rutherglen G72 138 E5
Wishaw ML2 166 C6
Hawthorn Cres
Beith KA15 171 A8
Erskine PA8 93 E8
Fallin FK7 8 D4
Stirling FK8 1 F2
Hawthorn Ct
Clarkston G76 157 E6
Kilwinning KA13 207 E2
Hawthornden Gdns G23 76 E1
Hawthorn Dr
Airdrie ML6 123 D6
Ayr KA7 239 C4
Banknock FK4 38 E2
Barrhead G78 155 D8
Coatbridge ML5 122 D5
Denny FK6 21 D3

Hawthorn Dr *continued*
Falkirk FK1 41 E4
Fallin FK7 8 C4
Harthill ML7 127 E6
Motherwell ML1 143 B3
Shotts ML7 147 C4
Stevenston KA20 206 E3
Wishaw ML2 165 C3
Hawthorne Pl
Gourock PA19 44 B6
Stenhousemuir FK5 23 D1
Hawthorn Gdns
Bellshill ML4 142 C4
Cambuslang G72 139 E4
Clarkston G76 157 E6
11 Larkhall ML9 185 C2
Prestwick KA9 236 C7
Hawthorn Gr ML8 186 F6
Hawthorn Hill ML3 162 E1
Hawthornhill Rd G82 49 C5
Hawthorn Pl
Kilwinning KA13 207 E2
Shotts ML7 167 A8
Troon KA10 229 E4
Hawthorn Quadrant G22 97 C5
Hawthorn Rd
Clarkston G76 157 E6
Cumbernauld G67 62 F4
Erskine PA8 93 E8
Hawthorn Sq KA1 227 D8
Hawthorn St
Clydebank G81 74 A4
Glasgow G22 97 D5
Torrance G64 57 C1
Hawthorn Terr
East Kilbride G75 180 B6
Uddingston G71 141 B7
Hawthorn Way
Dumbarton G82 49 B4
Erskine PA8 93 E8
Milton of Campsie G66 58 C5
Quarter ML3 183 F4
Rutherglen G72 138 E5
Hawthorn Wlk G72 138 D5
Hay Ave PA7 72 C3
Hayburn Cres G11 96 A3
Hayburn Ct G11 96 A1
Hayburn Gate G11 96 B2
Hayburn La
Glasgow G11 96 A3
Glasgow G11 96 A4
Hayburn St G11 96 B2
Hayes Gr G83 27 E6
Hayfield FK2 42 C7
Hayfield Ct G5 117 D4
Hayfield Rd FK2 42 C7
Hayfield St G5 117 D4
Hayfield Terr FK6 39 E7
Hayford Mills FK7 6 D6
Hayford Pl FK7 6 D6
Hayhill KA8 239 D8
Hayhill Rd G74 179 C7
Hayle Gdns G69 80 F3
Haylynn St G14 95 E2
Haymarket St G32 118 F7
Hayocks Prim Sch KA20 206 E2
Hayocks Rd KA20 206 E2
Hayocks Rdbt KA20 206 E1
Haypark Rd FK6 39 D6
Haysholm Sch KA12 219 E4
Hay St PA15 45 F4
Haystack Pl G66 79 E4
HAYSTON 79 A8
Hayston Cres G22 97 B5
Hayston Rd
Cumbernauld G68 61 E4
Kirkintilloch G66 79 A8
Hayston St G22 97 B5
Hayward Ave ML8 202 C8
Hayward Ct ML8 202 C8
Haywood St G22 97 C6
Hazel Ave
Ardrossan KA22 205 C4
Bearsden G61 76 A7
Dumbarton G82 49 B5
Glasgow G44 136 F4
Johnstone PA5 112 A1
Kilmarnock KA1 227 D7
Kirkintilloch G66 79 D6
Menstrie FK11 3 F6
Hazelbank
Motherwell ML1 143 B5
Plains ML6 103 F3
Hazel Bank G66 58 B4
Hazelbank Gdns FK8 2 A2
Hazelbank Wlk ML6 122 D8
Hazel Cres FK6 21 D3
Hazeldean Cres ML2 165 C5
Hazel Dene G64 98 B8
Hazeldene La 3 ML9 185 C1
Hazeldene Pk KA13 207 F4
Hazelden Gdns G44 136 E4
Hazelden Pk G44 136 E4
Hazelden Rd G77 177 C7
Hazelfield Gr ML6 123 E1
Hazel Gdns ML1 163 E3
Hazel Gr
Falkirk FK2 42 D7
Kirkintilloch G66 79 D6
Law ML8 186 F6
Shotts ML7 147 B4
Hazelgrove KA13 208 A4
Hazelhead G74 160 B2
Hazellea Dr G46 136 E4
Hazelmere Rd PA13 89 B8
Hazel Path ML1 144 B1
Hazel Pk ML3 162 E2
Hazel Rd
Banknock FK4 38 E2
Cumbernauld G67 62 D3
Hazel Terr
Gourock PA19 44 C6
Uddingston G71 141 B7
Hazelton ML1 163 D5
Hazel Wood ML2 165 D5
Hazelwood Ave
Bridge of Weir PA11 110 E7
Newton Mearns G77 156 E4
Paisley PA2 132 E7
Hazelwood Dr G72 161 C8
Hazelwood Gdns G73 138 C4
Hazelwood Gr G69 121 A6
Hazelwood La PA11 110 D7
Hazelwood Rd
Ayr KA7 238 F6
Bridge of Weir PA11 110 D6
Glasgow G41 116 C4
Hazelwood Sch G41 116 A3
Hazlitt Gdns G20 97 A6
Hazlitt Pl G20 97 B6
Hazlitt St G20 97 B6
Headhouse Ct G75 180 D8
Headhouse Gn G75 180 E8
Headlands Gr KA15 171 C8
Headlesscross Rd EH47 147 F2
HEAD OF MUIR 39 E6
Head of Muir Prim Sch FK6 39 D6
Headrigg Gdns KA23 190 C5
Headrigg Rd KA23 190 C5
Headsmuir Ave ML8 187 D2
Head St KA15 171 C8
Heath Ave
Bishopbriggs G64 98 B8
Kirkintilloch G66 79 C4
Heathcliffe Ave G72 140 C1
Heathcot Ave G15 74 E2
Heathcot Pl G15 74 E2
Heather Ave
Alexandria G83 27 E6
Barrhead G78 134 A5
Bearsden G61 75 E7
Clydebank G81 74 A7
Motherwell ML1 143 A5
Shieldhill FK1 66 C6
Heatherbank Ave G69 100 C3
Heatherbank Dr G69 100 C3
Heatherbank Gr G69 100 C3
Heatherbank Wlk ML6 122 D7
Heatherbell Ct ML7 127 D5
Heatherbrae G64 77 E1
Heatherdale Gdns FK6 39 E7
Heather Dr G66 79 A4
Heather Gdns
Kirkintilloch G66 79 A4
Uddingston G71 141 C7
Heather Gr 3 G75 180 E7
Heatherhouse Ind Est KA12 224 D8
Heatherhouse Rd KA12 224 D8
Heather Pk KA7 239 C3
Heather Pl
Johnstone PA5 112 A2
Kilmarnock KA1 227 D7
Kirkintilloch G66 79 A4
Heather Rd ML11 214 B6
Heather Row ML8 187 E4
Heather St ML6 105 A5
Heatherstane Bank KA11 220 C2
Heatherstane Way KA11 220 C2
Heatherstane Wlk KA11 220 C2
Heather View G66 33 E1
Heather Way ML1 143 A4
Heatheryford Gdns ML6 104 A3
Heathery Knowe G75 180 E7
Heathery Knowe Prim Sch G75 180 E7
Heatheryknowe Rd
Coatbridge G69 120 F7
Glasgow G69 120 F7
Heathery Lea Ave ML5 122 D3
Heathery Rd ML2 164 F3
HEATHFIELD 236 C4
Heathfield ML2 186 A7
Heathfield Ave G69 81 A2
Heathfield Dr G62 55 B3
Heathfield Ho KA12 219 B3
Heathfield Ind Est KA8 236 D4
Heathfield Prim Sch KA8 236 B5
Heathfield Rd KA8 236 D4
Heathpark KA8 236 C5
Heath Rd ML9 185 B3
Heathside Rd G46 136 D3
Heathwood Dr G46 136 A3
Hecla Ave G15 74 F3
Hecla Pl G15 74 F3
Hecla Sq G15 74 F3
Hector Rd G41 136 D8
Hedges Loan FK7 7 E1
Hedges The FK1 41 E5
Heggies Ave PA14 69 A8
Heights Rd EH48 107 D4
Helena Pl G76 157 E8
Helen Gdns 4 PA14 47 A2
HELENSBURGH 16 A1
Helensburgh Central Sta G84 16 D1
Helensburgh Dr G13 95 E6
Helensburgh Upper Sta G84 16 D3
Helenslea G72 139 E4
Helenslea Pl ML4 141 F4
Helenslee Cres G82 49 D3
Helenslee Ct G82 49 D3
Helenslee Rd
Dumbarton G82 49 D3
Langbank PA14 70 C7
Helen St
Glasgow, Drumoyne G51, G52 115 F5
Glasgow, Govan G51 116 A7
Helen's Terr KA13 207 E2
Helenvale Ct G31 118 D5
Helenvale St G31 118 D4
Helen Way G83 27 F2
Helen Wynd ML9 185 A2
Helmsdale Ave G72 140 C3
Helmsdale Cl G72 161 D4
Helmsdale Ct G72 139 D5
Helmsdale Dr PA2 112 F2
Hemlock St G13 95 F7
Hemmingen Ct ML8 187 E3
Hemphill View KA2 221 F3
Henderland Dr G61 75 E2
Henderland Rd G61 75 E1
Henderson Ave
Alloa FK10 10 A8
Cambuslang G72 139 E6
Henderson Ct ML1 163 D7
Henderson Pl
Alva FK12 5 A7
Plean FK7 12 C4
Henderson Rd KA10 229 E2
Henderson St
Airdrie ML6 123 B8
Bridge of Allan FK9 2 B7
Clydebank G81 94 E8
Coatbridge ML5 121 F6
Glasgow G20 96 F3
Paisley PA1 113 D5
Henderson Terr PA19 44 E6
Hendry St FK2 42 B7
Hennings The FK10 5 C1
Henrietta St G14 95 C3
Henry Bell Gn 5 G75 180 F8
Henry Bell St G84 16 F1
Henry Quadrant ML1 144 A5
Henryson Cres FK5 23 B2
Henry St
Alva FK12 5 A6
Barrhead G78 134 B3
Hepburn Hill ML3 183 C8
Hepburn Rd G52 115 B7
Hepburn Way KA11 220 C7
Herald Ave G13 75 D1
Herald Gr ML1 163 D4
Herald Way 2 PA4 94 C1
Herbertshire St FK6 21 E2
Herbertson Cres KA12 219 D4
Herbertson Gr G72 140 C1
Herbertson St
4 Glasgow G5 117 B5
2 Hamilton G72 161 E7
Herbert St G20 96 F3
Herbison Ct ML9 185 B4
Hercules Way PA4 94 D1
Herdshill Ave FK1 66 C6
Heriot Ave PA2 132 F8
Heriot Cres G64 78 A3
Heriot Ct PA2 132 F8
Heriot Prim Sch PA2 132 F8
Heriot Rd G66 79 C3
Heriot Way PA2 132 F8
Heritage Ct
Greenock PA16 45 E7
Newton Mearns G77 156 E5
Heritage Dr FK2 24 A3
Heritage Pk KA23 190 D6
Heritage View ML5 121 F8
Heritage Way ML5 121 F7
Herma St G23 96 F7
Hermes Way ML4 142 F5
Hermiston Ave G32 119 C6
Hermiston Gdns G69 80 C1
Hermiston Pl
Glasgow G32 119 C6
Motherwell ML1 143 A5
Hermiston Rd G32 119 B6
Hermitage Acad G84 25 C8
Hermitage Ave G13 95 C6
Hermitage Cres ML5 122 B3
Hermitage Prim Sch G84 16 D2
Hermitage Rd FK9 2 E6
Herndon Ct G77 157 A6
Heron Ct G81 74 B5
Heron Pl PA5 131 D7
Heron Rd PA16 45 A4
Heronswood KA13 207 E5
Heron Way PA4 94 C1
Herries Rd G41 116 C1
Herriet St G41 116 F3
Herriot Ave KA25 149 A4
Herriot St ML5 121 E8
Herschell St G13 95 F6
Hertford Ave G12 96 B6
Hervey St FK10 10 A8
Hestan Pl KA3 223 B5
Heugh St FK1 42 A3
Hewett Cres PA6 91 C1
Hexham Gdns G41 116 D1
Heys St G78 134 C2
Hibernia St PA16 45 D4
Hickman St G42 117 C2
Hickman Terr G42 117 C2
Hickory Cres G71 141 C8
Hickory St G22 97 E5
High Avon St ML9 184 F4
HIGH BALMALLOCH 36 C1
High Banton Rd G65 37 D4
High Barholm PA10 111 B3
High Barrwood Rd G65 60 F8
High Beeches G76 158 E8
HIGH BLANTYRE 161 C5
High Blantyre Prim Sch G72 161 B7
High Blantyre Rd ML3 161 F5
HIGH BONNYBRIDGE 40 C3
Highburgh Ave ML11 215 B4
Highburgh Ct ML11 215 B4
Highburgh Dr G73 138 C5
Highburgh Rd G12 96 C2
HIGH BURNSIDE 138 D4
High Burnside Ave ML5 121 E5
High Calside PA2 113 E3
High Carnegie Rd PA14 68 F8
High Church La 2 KA3 222 F1
High Coats ML5 122 B7
High Common Rd G74 181 B7
High Cotts G64 78 B5
Highcraig Ave PA5 111 D1
High Craigends G65 60 E8
High Craighall Rd G4 97 B2
Highcroft Ave G44 137 D5
Highcross Ave ML5 121 D4
HIGH CROSSHILL 138 B6
Highdykes Prim Sch G83 28 B2
Higherness Way ML5 121 E3
Highet Gdns KA12 219 B4
HIGHFIELD 169 F1
Highfield Ave
Kilmarnock KA3 223 A3
Kirkintilloch G66 58 E1
Paisley PA2 133 D7
Prestwick KA9 236 D7
Highfield Bsns Pk KA6 237 A6
Highfield Cres
3 Kirkintilloch G66 58 E1
Motherwell ML1 164 A8
Paisley PA2 133 D7
Highfield Ct G66 58 F1
Highfield Dr
Ayr KA8 236 E3
Clarkston G76 157 D7
Glasgow G12 96 B6
Rutherglen G73 138 C4
Stevenston KA20 206 E1
Highfield Gr
Kilmarnock KA3 223 A3
2 Kirkintilloch G66 58 E1
Highfield Pl
East Kilbride G74 159 F3
Glasgow G12 96 B6
Irvine KA11 219 F6
Highfield Rd
Ayr KA7 239 B4
Kirkintilloch G66 58 E1
Larkhall ML9 185 B3
Highfield St KA13 207 F4
High Flender Rd G76 157 D5
HIGH GALLOWHILL 79 A6
High Glencairn St KA1 227 F7
Highgrove Rd PA4 94 E3
Highholm Ave PA14 47 B1
Highholm Prim Sch PA14 47 C1
Highholm St PA14 47 B2
High Kirk View PA5 111 F2
Highland Ave G72 161 C8
Highland Dr FK5 23 C3
Highland Dykes Cres FK4 40 A6
Highland Dykes Dr FK4 40 B6
Highlanders Acad Prim Sch PA15 45 E4
Highlander Way FK10 4 D2
Highlandman's Rd G84 15 F5
Highland Mary Pl 5 PA15 45 F5
HIGHLAND PARK 36 D2
Highland Pk G65 36 D1
Highland Pl G65 36 C2
Highland Rd G62 55 A2
High Mains Ave G82 50 C3
High Mair PA4 94 C2
High Mdw ML8 188 C1
High Mill Prim Sch 5 ML8 187 F2
High Mill Rd ML8 188 A2
High Overton St ML9 200 D4
High Parksail PA8 93 C8
High Parks Cres ML3 183 D6
High Patrick St ML3 162 E3
High Pleasance ML9 185 A3
High Rd
Ayr KA8 236 E3
Motherwell ML1 163 E7
Paisley PA2 113 C3
Saltcoats KA21 205 F1
Stevenston KA20 206 C1
High Sch of Glasgow The (Jun Sch) G61 75 D4
High Sch of Glasgow The (Senior Sch) G13 95 F5
High St
Airdrie ML6 122 F8
Airth FK2 14 D3
Alloa FK10 10 B6
Ayr KA7 238 F8
Bonnybridge FK4 40 A5
Carluke ML8 187 F2
Clackmannan FK10 10 F4
Dumbarton G82 49 E3
Falkirk FK1 42 B4
Glasgow G1 241 B2
Greenock PA15 45 F5
Irvine KA12 219 C2
Johnstone PA5 111 F3
Kilbirnie KA25 149 B3
Kilmacolm PA13 69 D1
Kilmarnock KA3 223 A1
High St *continued*
Kirkintilloch G66 58 C1
Lanark ML11 215 A4
Lochwinnoch PA12 129 C2
Motherwell ML1 143 F4
Neilston G78 154 E7
Paisley PA1 113 E4
Renfrew PA4 94 E3
Rutherglen G73 138 A8
Shotts ML7 146 F4
Slamannan FK1 86 B7
Stewarton KA3 195 E1
High Station Ct FK1 42 A3
High Station Rd FK1 42 A3
Highstonehall Rd ML3 162 A1
High Street Ind Est G66 58 C1
High Street Sta G1 241 B2
Highthorne Cres KA23 190 E5
High Thorneyflat Wynd KA8 236 F3
High View Gr FK1 66 D6
High Whitehills Rd G75 180 E5
High Wood Gdns ML4 141 E5
Hilary Cres KA7 239 A6
Hilary Dr G69 119 F5
Hilda Cres G33 98 E4
Hillary Ave G73 138 D6
Hillary Rd FK5 23 E1
Hill Ave G77 156 C4
Hillbank Rd KA3 222 E3
Hillbank St G83 27 F4
Hillbrae St 4 G51 115 D6
Hill Cres G76 157 F6
Hillcrest
Carmunnock G76 158 D8
Chryston G69 100 D8
Stewarton KA3 211 E8
Hillcrest Ave
Clydebank G81 74 A7
Coatbridge ML5 122 C6
Cumbernauld G67 82 F8
Glasgow, Carmyle G32 139 B8
Glasgow, Muirend G44 136 E4
Paisley PA2 133 C6
Wishaw ML2 164 E3
Hillcrest Ct G67 61 F1
Hillcrest Dr
Alloa FK10 10 C6
Newton Mearns G77 157 A5
Stevenston KA20 206 E1
Hillcrest Pl
Denny FK6 39 D7
Kilwinning KA13 207 F3
Hillcrest Rd
Bearsden G61 75 F4
Falkirk FK1 41 F2
Glasgow G72 139 C8
Queenzieburn G65 59 E8
Uddingston G71 141 A7
Hillcrest Sq FK2 66 F7
Hillcrest St G62 55 B2
Hillcrest Terr G71 141 B3
Hillcrest View ML9 185 B3
Hillcroft Terr 6 G64 97 F8
Hill Dr G76 178 E4
HILLEND 105 B3
Hillend Cres
Clarkston G76 157 C6
Duntocher G81 73 F7
Hillend Dr PA15 46 C3
Hillend Pl PA15 46 C3
Hillend Rd
Clarkston G76 157 D6
Glasgow G22 97 A7
Rutherglen G73 138 B5
Hillfoot
Houston PA6 111 E8
Renton G82 27 D2
Hillfoot Ave
Bearsden G61 75 F5
Dumbarton G82 50 C4
Rutherglen G73 138 A7
Wishaw ML2 165 D7
Hillfoot Cres
Ayr KA7 239 B5
Wishaw ML2 165 D7
Hillfoot Dr
Bearsden G61 75 F5
Coatbridge ML5 121 D6
Howwood PA9 130 F5
Wishaw ML2 165 D7
Hillfoot Gdns
Uddingston G71 140 E7
Wishaw ML2 165 D7
Hillfoot Rd
Airdrie ML6 123 B6
Ayr KA7 239 C6
Hillfoots Rd
Menstrie FK9 3 C6
Stirling FK9 2 E4
Hillfoot St G31 118 A7
Hillfoot Sta G61 76 A5
Hillfoot Terr ML8 188 A1
HILLHEAD
Kilmarnock 222 F2
Kirkintilloch 79 E8
Hillhead Ave
Banknock FK4 38 E3
Carluke ML8 188 A2
Moodiesburn G69 80 F2
Motherwell ML1 143 A2
Rutherglen G73 138 B4
Hillhead Cres
Hamilton ML3 161 F3
Motherwell ML1 143 A2
Hillhead Dr
Airdrie ML6 123 B6
Falkirk FK1 41 F2

Hillhead Dr *continued*
Motherwell ML1 143 A1
Hillhead High Sch 1 G12 96 E2
Hillhead Pl G73 138 B4
Hillhead Prim Sch
8 Glasgow G12 96 D3
Kilmarnock KA3 222 E3
Kirkintilloch G66 79 E8
Hillhead Rd
Glasgow G21 98 D7
Kirkintilloch G66 58 E1
Stevenston KA20 206 E3
Hillhead Rdbt 2 G66 58 D1
Hillhead Sq KA3 222 F3
Hillhead St
Glasgow G12 96 D2
Milngavie G62 55 A2
Hillhead Terr ML3 161 E3
Hillhead Underground Sta
G12 96 D3
HILLHOUSE 161 E4
Hill House* G84 16 E4
Hillhouse Bsns Ctr ML3 162 A4
Hillhouse Cres ML3 161 F3
Hillhouse Farm Gate
ML11 214 E5
Hillhouse Farm Rd ML11 214 E4
Hillhouse Gate ML8 202 C8
Hillhouse Gdns KA10 229 E6
Hillhouse Park Ind Est
ML3 161 F3
Hillhouse Pl KA3 195 D1
Hillhouse Rd
Denny FK6 39 E7
Hamilton, High Blantyre
G72 161 B5
Hamilton, Hillhouse ML3 161 E4
Troon KA10 229 E6
Hillhouseridge Rd ML7 146 D5
Hillhouse St G21 98 A5
Hillhouse Terr ML3 161 F3
HILLINGTON 115 A5
Hillington East Sta G52 115 B6
Hillington Gdns G52 115 C4
Hillington Ind Est
Glasgow G52 114 E8
Glasgow, North Cardonald
G52 115 A7
Hillington Park Cir G52 115 C5
Hillington Park Ret &
Amenities Ctr G52 114 F8
Hillington Pk* G52 114 F8
Hillington Prim Sch G52 115 A6
Hillington Quadrant G52 115 A5
Hillington Rd
Glasgow G52 115 A7
Hillington Industrial Estate
G52 115 A8
Renfrew G52 94 F1
Hillington Road S G52 115 A5
Hillington Sh Ctr G52 114 F8
Hillington Terr G52 115 A5
Hillington West Sta G52 114 F7
Hill Intc KA11 219 E6
Hillkirk Pl G21 97 F4
Hillkirk St G21 97 F4
Hillkirk Street La 3 G21 97 F4
Hill La KA22 205 C1
Hillmoss KA3 222 B7
Hillneuk Ave G61 76 A5
Hillneuk Dr G61 76 A5
Hillocks Pl KA10 229 F7
Hill of Kinnaird FK2 23 E7
HILLPARK 136 C5
Hillpark KA6 237 F6
Hillpark Ave PA2 113 D1
Hillpark Cres FK7 7 C2
Hillpark Dr
Bannockburn FK7 7 D2
Glasgow G43 136 C6
2 Kilmarnock KA3 222 F2
Hillpark Rise KA13 207 B3
Hillpark Sec Sch G43 136 C5
Hill Pk FK10 10 B7
Hill Pl
Alloa FK10 10 A8
Ardrossan KA22 205 C1
Bellshill ML4 141 F3
Motherwell ML1 143 C2
Shotts ML7 146 E5
Hill Rd
Cumbernauld G67 61 E2
Harthill ML7 127 D5
Howwood PA9 130 F5
Kilsyth G65 36 D2
Netherburn ML9 199 F5
Stonehouse ML9 198 E2
Hillrigg ML6 83 D1
Hillrigg Ave ML6 123 C8
Hillsborough Rd G69 119 F5
Hillshaw Foot KA11 220 C2
Hillshaw Gn KA11 220 C2
Hillside
Alloa FK10 5 C2
Croy G65 60 F4
Gourock PA19 43 D4
Houston PA6 111 E8
West Kilbride KA23 190 C4
Hillside Ave
Alexandria G83 27 D3
Bearsden G61 75 F5
Clarkston G76 157 D7
Kilmacolm PA13 69 D1
Hillside Cotts
Dalry KA24 191 E7
Glenboig ML5 101 E6
Hillside Cres
Coatbridge ML5 121 F4
Hillside Cres *continued*
Hamilton ML3 162 D2
Motherwell ML1 143 D4
Neilston G78 154 D7
Prestwick KA9 236 D8
Hillside Ct
Glasgow G46 135 F3
Stevenston KA20 217 C8
Hillside Dr
Barrhead G78 134 A3
Bearsden G61 76 A5
Bishopbriggs G64 78 A2
Blackridge EH48 107 D3
Port Glasgow PA14 47 B1
Hillside Gardens La 3
G11 96 B3
Hillside Gr G78 134 A2
Hillside La ML3 162 C2
Hillside Pk G81 74 B6
Hillside Pl
Blackridge EH48 107 D3
Motherwell ML1 143 D3
Hillside Quadrant G43 136 B5
Hillside Rd
Barrhead G78 134 A3
Cardross G82 26 B1
Glasgow G43 136 B5
Gourock PA19 44 D7
Greenock PA15 46 B2
Neilston G78 154 D7
Paisley PA2 114 A1
Hillside St KA20 217 C8
Hillside Terr
Alloa FK10 10 B7
Hamilton ML3 162 C2
Milton of Campsie G66 58 B5
Old Kilpatrick G60 73 B5
Hill St
Alexandria G83 27 D5
Alloa FK10 10 B7
Ardrossan KA22 205 C1
Caldercruix ML6 104 F5
Chapelhall ML6 123 D2
Dumbarton G82 49 D3
Glasgow G3 240 B4
Greenock PA15 46 A4
Hamilton ML3 161 F3
Irvine KA12 219 C2
Kilmarnock, Hillhead KA3 222 F2
Kilmarnock KA3 222 F1
Larkhall ML9 185 B2
Saltcoats KA21 216 F7
Stirling FK7 7 B3
Wishaw ML2 165 A3
Hill Street Ind Est KA22 205 C1
Hills Trust Prim Sch
G51 116 A8
Hillswick Cres G22 97 B8
Hill Terr ML1 143 C2
Hilltop Ave ML4 142 A7
Hilltop Cres PA19 44 F6
Hilltop Pl KA7 239 D5
Hilltop Rd
Gourock PA19 44 F5
Moodiesburn G69 80 F2
Hillview
Banton G65 37 D3
Greengairs ML6 83 F2
Hill View
East Kilbride G75 180 E8
Milton G82 50 F1
Hillview Ave
Kilsyth G65 60 E7
Lennoxtown G66 57 E8
Hillview Cotts G65 59 F4
Hillview Cres
Bellshill ML4 142 A8
Larkhall ML9 185 B2
Uddingston G71 140 E8
Hillview Ct G81 73 F3
Hillview Dr
Blantyre G72 140 D1
Bridge of Allan FK9 2 A6
Clarkston G76 157 E7
Helensburgh G84 16 D4
Hillview Gdns
Bishopbriggs G64 98 D7
Clydebank G81 73 F3
Hillview Pl
Alexandria G83 27 D6
Clarkston G76 157 E7
Fallin FK7 8 C4
Newton Mearns G77 156 D4
Hillview Rd
Bonnybridge FK4 40 C3
Bridge of Weir PA11 110 E7
Elderslie PA5 112 C2
Kirkfieldbank ML11 214 A3
Stenhousemuir FK5 23 C3
Hillview St G32 118 F5
Hillview Terr
Alloa FK10 10 C6
Old Kilpatrick G60 73 B6
Hilton FK7 12 E8
Hiltonbank St ML3 162 B4
Hilton Cres FK10 10 D7
Hilton Ct
Bishopbriggs G64 78 A3
7 Hamilton ML3 162 E2
Saltcoats KA21 205 E3
Hilton Gdns G13 95 F7
Hilton Pk G64 77 F4
Hilton Rd
Alloa FK10 10 D7
Bishopbriggs G64 78 A3
Milngavie G62 54 E2
Hilton Terr
Bishopbriggs G64 77 F3
Hilton Terr *continued*
Cambuslang G72 138 E3
Fallin FK7 8 C4
Glasgow G13 95 E7
Hilton View ML4 142 A8
Hindog Pl KA24 191 A8
Hindsland Rd ML9 185 B1
Hinshaw St G20 97 A3
Hinshelwood Dr G51 116 A5
Hinshelwood Pl G51 116 B5
Hirsel Pl G71 141 B2
Hirst Cres FK7 8 D4
Hirst Ct FK7 8 D4
Hirst Gdns ML7 146 C5
Hirst Rd ML7 126 D3
Hobart Cres G81 73 D5
Hobart Quadrant ML2 165 E3
Hobart Rd G75 180 C7
Hobart St G22 97 B4
Hobden St G21 98 A3
Hoddam Ave G45 138 A3
Hoddam Terr G45 138 A3
Hodge St FK1 42 B4
Hoey Dr ML2 186 C7
Hogan Ct G81 73 F6
Hogan Way ML1 143 E1
Hogarth Ave
Glasgow G32 118 D7
Saltcoats KA21 205 E2
Hogarth Cres G32 118 D7
Hogarth Ct G83 27 E6
Hogarth Dr G32 118 D7
Hogarth Gdns G32 118 D7
HOGGANFIELD 98 F2
Hogganfield Ct G33 98 D2
Hogganfield St G33 98 D2
Hoggan Way FK12 4 F6
Hogg Ave PA5 111 E1
Hogg Rd ML6 123 D4
Hogg St ML6 123 A7
Holbourne Pl FK11 4 A7
Holeburn Rd G43 136 C6
Hole Farm Rd PA15, PA16 45 D3
HOLEHILLS 103 B2
Holehills Dr ML6 103 B2
Holehills Pl ML6 103 B2
HOLEHOUSE 154 C7
Holehouse Brae G78 154 C7
Holehouse Dr
Glasgow G13 95 A6
Kilbirnie KA25 149 B3
Holehouse Rd
Eaglesham G76 178 F6
Kilmarnock KA3 228 B8
Holehouse Terr G78 154 C7
Hollandbush Ave FK4 38 E3
Hollandbush Cres FK4 38 F3
Hollandbush Gr ML3 183 D8
HOLLANDHURST 101 F2
Hollandhurst Rd ML5 101 F1
Holland St G2 240 B3
Hollinwell Rd G23 76 D1
Hollowglen Rd G32 119 B6
Hollow Park Ct KA7 239 B2
Hollow Pk KA7 239 B2
Hollows Ave PA2 132 F7
Hollows Cres PA2 132 F7
Hollows The G46 136 B1
Holly Ave
Milton of Campsie G66 58 B5
Stenhousemuir FK5 23 F3
Holly Bank KA7 239 D5
Hollybank Pl G72 139 B4
Hollybank St G21 98 A1
Hollybrook Pl 2 G42 117 B2
Hollybrook Specl Sch
G42 117 B2
Hollybrook St G42 117 B2
Hollybush Ave PA2 133 B7
Hollybush La PA14 69 B8
Hollybush Pl KA3 223 B6
Hollybush Rd G52 114 F5
Holly Dr
Dumbarton G82 49 B5
Glasgow G21 98 A3
Holly Gr
Banknock FK4 38 F2
Bellshill ML4 142 F5
Menstrie FK11 3 F6
Hollyhill Gr G69 121 A6
Hollymount G61 75 F2
Holly Pl
Johnstone PA5 132 A8
Kilmarnock KA1 222 D1
Holly St
Airdrie ML6 123 C6
Clydebank G81 74 B4
Hollytree Gdns G66 57 C7
Holm Ave
Paisley PA2 113 F2
Uddingston G71 140 E7
Holmbank Ave G41 136 D7
Holmbrae Ave G71 140 F7
Holmbrae Rd G71 140 F8
Holmbyre Ct G45 137 B1
Holmbyre Rd G45 137 B1
Holmbyre Terr G45 137 C2
Holm Cres KA3 213 B3
Holm Crest ML8 201 B2
Holm Ct ML8 201 B2
Holmes Ave PA4 94 C1
Holmes Cres KA1 227 D6
Holmes Farm Rd KA1 227 D6
Holmes Park Ave KA1 227 D6
Holmes Park Cres KA1 227 D6
Holmes Park Gdns KA1 227 D6
Holmes Park View KA1 227 D6
Holmes Park Wynd KA1 227 D6
Holmes Quadrant ML4 142 B4
Holmes Rd KA1 227 D6
Holmes Village KA1 227 D6
Holmfauldhead Dr G51 115 E8
Holmfauldhead Pl 3
G51 115 E8
Holmfauld Rd G51 95 E1
Holmfield G66 79 E7
Holm Gdns ML4 142 C4
Holmhead KA25 170 A8
Holmhead Cres G44 137 A6
Holmhead Dr KA3 195 F2
Holmhead Pl G44 137 A6
Holmhead Rd G44 137 A5
Holmhill Ave G72 139 A4
Holmhills Dr G72 138 F3
Holmhills Gdns G72 138 F4
Holmhills Gr G72 138 F4
Holmhills Pl G72 138 F4
Holmhills Rd G72 138 F4
Holmhills Terr G72 138 F4
Holm La G74 159 E1
Holmlands Pl KA1 227 D6
Holmlea Dr KA1 227 E6
Holmlea Pl KA1 227 E6
Holmlea Rd G44 137 A7
Holmpark PA7 72 B3
Holm Pk (Clydebank & Yorker Athletic FC's)
G81 94 C7
Holm Pl
Larkhall ML9 184 E2
Linwood PA3 112 B7
Holmquarry Rd KA1 227 F6
Holm Rd ML8 201 B2
Holms Ave KA11 220 D1
Holms Cres PA8 72 F2
Holmscroft Ave PA15 45 E4
Holmscroft St PA15 45 E5
Holmscroft Way PA15 45 E4
Holms Pl G69 100 E7
Holms Rd KA14 170 B6
Holm St
Carluke ML8 187 E2
Glasgow G2 240 C2
Motherwell ML1 143 A3
Stewarton KA3 211 E8
HOLMSTON 239 D7
Holmston Cres KA7 239 C7
Holmston Dr KA7 239 C6
Holmston Gdns KA7 239 A7
Holmston Prim Sch KA7 239 A7
Holmston Rd KA7 239 C7
Holmston Rdbt KA7 239 E7
Holmswood Ave G72 140 D1
Holmwood Ave G71 140 F7
Holmwood Gdns G71 140 F6
Holmwood Gn ML8 201 A3
Holmwood House* G44 137 B4
Holmwood Pk ML8 201 A3
Holton Cotts FK10 5 C1
Holton Cres FK10 5 C1
Holton Ct FK10 5 C1
Holton Sq FK10 5 C1
Holy Cross High Sch
ML3 162 C5
Holy Cross Prim Sch
Croy G65 60 F4
Glasgow G42 117 B2
Holy Family Prim Sch
Bellshill ML4 142 C5
Kirkintilloch G66 79 B6
Holyknowe Cres G66 57 E8
Holyknowe Rd G66 57 F7
Holyoake Ct KA1 228 F7
Holyrood Cres G20 96 F2
Holyrood Pl FK5 23 E4
Holyrood Quadrant 2
G20 96 F2
Holyrood Sec Sch G42 117 C1
Holyrood Sp Ctr G42 117 C1
Holyrood St ML3 162 A5
HOLYTOWN 143 A6
Holytown Prim Sch ML1 143 B5
Holytown Rd ML1 142 E5
Holytown Sta ML1 143 A3
Holywell St G31 118 B5
Homeblair Ho G46 136 C5
Homebriar Ho KA7 238 F8
Homeburn Ho G46 136 C3
Home Farm Cotts FK6 39 F6
Home Farm Rd
Ayr KA7 239 A2
Hartwood ML7 145 F3
Homeglen Ho G46 136 C2
Homer Pl ML4 142 E5
Homeshaw Ho G77 156 F4
Home St ML11 215 C3
Homesteads The FK8 6 D7
Homeston Ave G71 141 A3
Honeybank Cres ML8 188 A3
Honeybog Rd G52 114 E6
Honeycomb Pl ML9 200 D4
Honeyman Cres ML11 215 C4
Honeysuckle Dr G67 82 D6
Honeysuckle La G83 27 F7
Honeysuckle Pk KA7 239 B2
Honeywell Ave G33 100 A4
Honeywell Cres ML6 123 E1
Honeywell Ct
2 Glasgow G34 120 C8
Stepps G33 100 A4
Honeywell Dr G33 100 A4
Honeywell Gr G33 100 A4
Honeywell Pl G33 100 A4
Hood Ct G84 16 A2
Hood St
Clydebank G81 74 D2
Hood St *continued*
Greenock PA15 45 F6
Hookney Terr FK6 21 C2
Hooper Pl ML4 142 B5
Hope Ave PA11 89 E2
Hope Cres ML9 185 B3
Hopefield Ave G12 96 C5
Hopehill Gdns G20 97 A3
Hopehill Rd G20 97 A3
Hopeman PA8 73 A3
Hopeman Ave G46 135 E4
Hopeman Dr G46 135 E4
Hopeman Path G46 135 E5
Hopeman Rd G46 135 E4
Hopeman St G46 135 E4
Hopepark Dr G65 / G68 60 E2
Hopepark Terr FK4 39 F6
Hope St
Ayr KA7 238 F8
Bellshill ML4 142 C5
Carluke ML8 188 A2
Falkirk FK1 42 B5
Glasgow G2 240 C3
Greenock PA15 45 F4
Hamilton ML3 162 E3
Helensburgh G84 25 B8
Lanark ML11 215 A4
Motherwell ML1 163 E7
Stirling FK8 1 F1
Wishaw ML2 166 A4
Hopeton St PA19 44 E8
Hopetoun Bank KA11 220 C2
Hopetoun Dr FK9 2 A8
Hopetoun Pl G23 76 E1
Hopetoun Terr G21 98 A3
Hopkin's Brae 3 G66 58 D1
Horatius St ML1 142 B1
Hornal Rd G71 141 A4
Hornbeam Dr G81 74 A4
Hornbeam Rd
Cumbernauld G67 62 E5
Uddingston G71 141 B8
Horndean Ct G64 78 A4
Horne St G22 97 E5
Hornock Cotts ML5 121 F8
Hornock Rd ML5 101 F1
Hornshill Dr ML1 144 B2
Hornshill Farm Rd G33 99 E6
Hornshill St G21 98 A4
Horsburgh Ave G65 36 D1
Horsburgh St G33 99 D2
Horse Isle View KA22 205 A4
Horse Shoe KA23 190 C5
Horse Shoe La G61 75 F4
Horse Shoe Rd G61 75 E4
Horsewood Rd PA11 110 C8
Horslethill Rd G12 96 C3
Horslet St ML5 121 C4
Horsley Brae ML2 186 B4
Horton Pl G84 17 A3
Hosiery Ct KA10 229 E3
Hospital Rd ML2 165 C1
Hospital St
Coatbridge ML5 122 A4
Glasgow G5 117 B4
Hospitland Dr ML11 215 C4
Hotspur St G20 96 E4
Houldsworth Cres ML7 167 A8
Houldsworth Ct ML2 165 C2
Houldsworth La 7 G3 116 E8
Houldsworth St G3 240 A3
Househillmuir Cres G53 135 C7
Househillmuir La G53 135 C7
Househillmuir Pl G53 135 C7
Househillmuir Rd G53 135 B6
HOUSEHILLWOOD 135 A7
Househillwood Cres G53 135 B7
Househillwood Rd G53 135 B6
Housel Ave G13 95 B7
House O' Muir Rd ML7 126 B3
HOUSTON 91 B2
Houston Cres KA24 191 B7
Houston Ct
Kilbirnie KA25 149 A2
Renfrew PA4 94 D4
Houstonfield Quadrant
PA6 91 A2
Houstonfield Rd PA6 91 A2
Houston Pl
Elderslie PA5 112 C2
Glasgow G5 240 A1
Houston Prim Sch PA6 91 B1
Houston Rd
Bridge of Weir PA11 90 E1
Houston PA6 91 B1
Houston PA6 91 B2
Houston PA6 91 D2
Inchinnan PA3, PA4, PA6 92 D3
Kilmacolm PA11 89 E7
Linwood PA3 91 C1
Houston St
Glasgow G5 116 F5
Greenock PA16 45 E6
Hamilton ML3 162 D1
Renfrew PA4 94 D4
Wishaw ML2 165 D2
Houston Terr G74 159 D2
Houstoun Ct PA5 111 F3
Houstoun Sq PA5 111 F3
Howacre ML11 214 F5
Howard Ave G74 160 A5
Howard Ct
East Kilbride G74 160 A5
Kilmarnock KA1 227 F8
Howard Park Dr KA1 227 E7

Howard St
Falkirk FK1 41 F4
Glasgow G1 241 A1
Kilmarnock KA1 227 F8
Larkhall ML9 185 C1
Paisley PA1 114 A4
Howat Cres KA12 219 E3
Howatshaws Rd G82 50 B6
Howat St G51 116 A8
Howburn Cres ML7 127 E6
Howburn Rd ML7 127 D6
Howden Ave
Kilwinning KA13 207 E4
Motherwell ML1 143 D8
Howden Dr PA3 112 A5
Howden Pl ML1 143 A5
Howe Gdns G71 141 A7
Howe Rd G65 60 D7
Howes St ML5 122 B4
Howe St PA1 112 F4
Howetown FK10 5 D4
Howford Rd G52 115 B4
Howford Specl Sch G53 115 A2
Howgate KA13 207 D3
Howgate Ave G15 74 F3
Howgate Rd ML3 183 C8
Howgate Sh Ctr 6 FK1 42 B4
Howie Bldgs G76 157 E8
Howie Cres G84 15 A3
Howieshill Ave G72 139 B5
Howieshill Rd G72 139 B5
Howie's Pl FK1 41 B4
Howie St ML9 185 B1
Howlands Rd FK7 7 A3
Howletnest Rd ML6 123 D6
Howlet Pl ML3 162 E1
Howson Lea ML1 164 B4
Howson View ML1 163 B7
Howth Dr G13 95 F8
Howth Terr G13 95 F8
HOWWOOD 130 E6
Howwood Prim Sch PA9 131 A5
Howwood Sta PA9 130 F5
Hoylake Pk G71 140 F2
Hoylake Pl G23 76 E1
Hoylake Sq KA13 207 C4
Hozier Cres G71 140 F8
Hozier Loan 8 ML9 185 B4
Hozier Pl 9 G71 141 B3
Hozier St
Carluke ML8 187 F2
Coatbridge ML5 122 A4
Hudson Pl KA9 233 C2
Hudson Terr G75 180 C8
Hudson Way G75 180 C8
Hudspeth Ct G83 27 D7
Hughenden Ct G12 96 B4
Hughenden Dr G12 96 B4
Hughenden Gdns G12 96 B4
Hughenden La G12 96 B4
Hughenden Rd G12 96 B4
Hughenden Terr G12 96 B4
Hugh Murray Gr G72 139 C5
Hugh Watt Pl KA3 222 A7
Hugo St G20 96 F5
Hulks Rd
Greengairs ML6 83 D4
Greengairs ML6 84 B4
Humbie Ct G77 156 F2
Humbie Gate G77 156 E2
Humbie Gr G77 156 E3
Humbie Lawns G77 156 E2
Humbie Rd
Eaglesham G76 178 C7
Newton Mearns G77 156 F2
Hume Cres FK9 2 A6
Hume Ct FK9 2 A6
Hume Dr
Bothwell G71 141 A3
Uddingston G71 140 E7
Hume Pl G75 180 D8
Hume Rd G67 62 A3
Hume St G81 74 B1
Hunter Ave KA22 205 D2
Hunter Cres KA10 230 A2
Hunter Dr
Irvine KA12 219 B6
Newton Mearns G77 156 B3
Hunterfield Dr G72 138 E5
Hunter Gdns
Bonnybridge FK4 40 A5
Denny FK6 21 D2
HUNTERHILL 114 A2
Hunterhill Ave PA2 113 F3
Hunterhill Rd PA2 113 F3
Hunter House Mus★
G74 160 C4
Hunterian Art Gall★ G12 96 D2
Hunterian Mus★ G12 96 D2
Hunterlees Rd ML10 198 B3
Hunter Pl
Kilbarchan PA10 111 A2
Kilwinning KA13 208 A3
Milngavie G62 54 E1
Shotts ML7 146 E5
Stenhousemuir FK2 24 A4
Hunter Prim Sch G74 160 C2
Hunter Rd
Crosshouse KA2 221 F1
Hamilton ML3 162 B6
Milngavie G62 54 E2
Rutherglen G73 118 C1
Hunter's Ave
Ayr KA8 236 B4
Dumbarton G82 50 D3
Hunter's Cl 14 ML11 215 A4
Hunters Cres G74 160 C3
Huntersfield Rd PA5 111 D1
Hunters Gr G74 160 C3
Hunters Hill Ct G21 97 F6
Huntershill Rd G64 98 A8
Huntershill St G21 97 E6
Huntershill Village G64 97 F8
Huntershill Way G64 97 F7
Hunters Pl
East Kilbride G74 160 C3
Greenock PA15 45 F5
Hunter St
Airdrie ML6 103 A1
Bellshill ML4 142 A5
East Kilbride G74 159 F2
Glasgow G4 241 C2
Paisley PA1 113 E5
Prestwick KA9 236 C8
Shotts ML7 146 D5
Hunterston Rd KA23 190 D5
Hunters Way PA12 129 C2
Hunt Hill G68 60 C1
Hunthill La G72 161 B6
Hunthill Pl G76 158 A5
Hunthill Rd G72 161 B7
Hunt Hill Rdbt G68 60 C1
Huntingdon Rd G21 97 E2
Huntingdon Sq G21 97 E2
Hunting Lodge Gdns
ML3 163 A2
Huntingtower Rd
Baillieston G69 119 F4
Glasgow G69 120 A3
Huntly Ave
Bellshill ML4 142 A6
Glasgow G46 136 D2
Huntly Cres FK8 1 F2
Huntly Ct
Bishopbriggs G64 98 A8
Kilmarnock KA3 223 C3
Huntly Dr
Bearsden G61 75 E7
Cambuslang G72 139 B4
Coatbridge ML5 121 D4
Greenock PA16 44 F3
Huntly Gdns
Glasgow G12 96 D3
Hamilton G72 161 D3
Huntly Path G69 81 A2
Huntly Pl
Kilmarnock KA3 223 C2
Port Glasgow PA14 47 B2
Huntly Quadrant ML2 165 B5
Huntly Rd
Glasgow, Dowanhill G12 96 C3
Glasgow, Hillington G52 114 F8
Glasgow (Hillington Ind Est)
G52 94 F1
Huntly Terr
Paisley PA2 114 A1
Port Glasgow PA14 47 B2
Shotts ML7 147 B3
Hurlawcrook Rd G75 180 F2
HURLET 134 E7
Hurlet Cotts G53 134 F6
Hurlethill Ct G53 134 F7
Hurlet Rd PA2, G53 134 D7
HURLFORD 228 F6
Hurlford Ave G13 94 F7
Hurlford Prim Sch KA1 228 E6
Hurlford Rd KA1 228 A5
Hurly Hawkin G64 98 D8
Hurworth St FK1 41 F3
Hutcheson Rd G46 136 A2
Hutchesons Gram Sch
Glasgow, Crossmyloof
G41 116 E2
Glasgow G42 117 A2
Hutcheson St G1 241 A2
HUTCHESONTOWN 117 D3
Hutchinson Pl G72 139 E3
Hutchinson St ML2 186 D7
Hutchinson Town Ct 8
G5 117 C4
Hutchison Ct G46 136 B1
Hutchison Dr G61 76 A2
Hutchison Pl ML5 121 F6
Hutchison St ML3 162 D1
Hutton G12 96 A6
Hutton Ave PA6 111 C8
Hutton Dr
East Kilbride G74 159 F4
Glasgow G51 115 E8
Hutton Pk FK10 10 C7
Huxley Pl G20 96 F6
Hyacinth Way ML8 201 F8
Hydepark Bsns Ctr G21 97 E3
Hydepark St G3 240 A2
Hyndal Ave G53 115 C1
Hyndford Pl 19 ML11 215 A4
Hyndford Rd ML11 215 D2
HYNDLAND 96 A3
Hyndland Ave G11 96 B2
Hyndland Ct 11 G12 96 C3
Hyndland Prim Sch G11 96 B2
Hyndland Rd G12 96 B3
Hyndland Sec Sch G12 96 B3
Hyndland St G11 96 C2
Hyndland Sta G12 96 A4
Hyndlee Dr G52 115 C5
Hyndman Rd KA23 190 C3
Hyndshaw Rd ML8 187 C8
Hyndshaw View ML8 187 A4
Hyslop Pl G81 74 A3
Hyslop Rd KA20 206 F2
Hyslop St ML6 122 E8

I

Iain Dr G61 75 C6
Iain Rd G61 75 C6
Ian Smith Ct G81 94 D8
IBM Sta PA16 44 D1
IBROX 116 B6
Ibroxholm Ave G51 116 B5
Ibroxholm Oval G51 116 B5
Ibroxholm Pl G51 116 B5
Ibrox Ind Est G51 116 C6
Ibrox Prim Sch G51 116 B5
Ibrox St G51 116 C6
Ibrox Stadium (Rangers FC)
G51 116 B6
Ibrox Terr G51 116 B6
Ibrox Underground Sta
G51 116 B6
Ida Quadrant ML4 141 F5
Iddesleigh Ave G62 55 A2
Ilay Ave
Bearsden G61 95 F8
Glasgow G61 96 A8
Ilay Ct G61 96 A8
Ilay Rd G61 96 A8
Imex Bsns Ctr ML5 122 C6
Imlach Pl ML1 163 D5
Imperial Dr ML6 122 F6
Imperial Pl G71 141 A2
Imperial Way G71 141 A2
Inchbrae Rd G52 115 C4
Inch Colm Ave FK5 23 C4
Inchcolm Gdns G69 81 A3
Inchcolm Pl G74 159 C2
Inchconnachan Ave G83 19 E2
Inchcruin G83 27 D8
Inchcruin Pl G15 74 E4
Inches Rd KA22 216 B8
Inches Rdbt FK5 23 C4
Inchfad Cres G15 74 E3
Inchfad Dr G15 74 E3
Inchfad Pl G15 74 E3
Inchfad Rd G83 19 E2
Inch Garve G74 160 D1
Inch Garvie Terr FK5 23 C4
Inchgotrick Rd KA1 227 E4
Inchgower Gr G84 15 D5
Inchgower Pl 2 ML1 143 A2
Inchgower Rd G33 99 E6
Inchgreen St PA14 46 F2
Inchholm La G11 95 E2
Inchholm St G11 95 E2
INCHINNAN 93 D6
Inchinnan Bsns Pk PA4 93 B4
Inchinnan Dr PA4 93 C4
Inchinnan Ind Est PA4 93 B5
Inchinnan Prim Sch PA4 93 D7
Inchinnan Rd
Bellshill ML4 141 F7
Paisley PA3 113 E7
Renfrew PA4 94 C4
Inch Keith G74 160 D1
Inchkeith Pl
Falkirk FK1 42 B2
Glasgow G32 119 B7
Inchlaggan Pl G15 74 E4
Inchlee St G14 95 E3
Inchlonaig Dr G83 19 E1
Inch Marnock G74 160 D1
Inchmoan Pl G15 74 E4
Inch Murrin G74 160 D1
Inchmurrin Ave G66 80 B8
Inchmurrin Cres G83 19 E2
Inchmurrin Dr
Kilmarnock KA3 223 A5
Rutherglen G73 138 D2
Inchmurrin Gdns G73 138 D2
Inchmurrin Pl G73 138 D2
Inchna FK11 4 A6
Incheuk Path ML5 101 D6
Incheuk Rd ML5 101 E6
Inchnock Ave G69 101 A6
Inchoch Gr G33 99 E2
Inchoch St G33 99 E2
Inchrory Pl G15 74 E4
Inchtavannach G83 27 D8
Inchwood Ct G68 82 A7
Inchwood Pl G68 81 F7
Inchwood Rd G68 81 F7
Incle St PA1 113 F5
Indale Ave KA9 236 E7
India Cotts G83 27 E5
India Dr PA4 93 C5
India St
Alexandria G83 27 E5
Glasgow G2 240 B3
Industry St G66 79 D7
Inga St G20 96 E7
Ingerbreck Ave G73 138 D4
Ingleby Ct PA11 110 D8
Ingleby Dr
Glasgow G31 118 B7
Rutherglen G31 118 A7
Ingleby Pl G78 154 E7
Inglefield Ct ML6 123 A7
Inglefield St G42 117 B2
Ingleneuk Ave G33 99 B5
Ingleside G66 79 C6
Ingleston Ave FK6 21 D4
Inglestone Ave G46 136 A2
Ingleston Pk PA15 46 A3
Ingleston St PA15 46 A3
Inglewood Cres
East Kilbride G75 180 A8
Paisley PA2 112 F2
Inglewood Gdns FK10 10 A8
Inglewood Ho FK10 4 F1
Inglewood Rd FK10 9 F8
Inglis Ct ML9 198 F3
Inglis Dr FK2 24 C2
Inglis Pl G75 180 F7
Inglis St
Glasgow G31 118 A6
Wishaw ML2 164 D2
Ingliston Dr PA7 71 F3
Ingram Pl KA3 223 A3
Ingram St G1 241 A2
Inishail Rd G33 99 C1
Inkerman Ct 8 KA7 235 E1
Inkerman Pl KA1 222 E1
Inkerman Rd G52 114 F5
Inkwood Way ML1 143 B2
Innellan Cres ML7 146 E6
Innellan Dr KA3 222 F3
Innellan Gdns G20 96 B7
Innellan Pl G20 96 B7
Inner City Trad Est G4 241 B4
Inner Clyde Nature Reserve★
PA7 71 E7
Innerleithen Dr ML2 165 D6
Innermanse Quadrant
ML1 143 F5
Innerpeffray Dr FK2 24 A3
Innerwick Dr G52 115 B5
Innerwood Rd KA13 207 E5
Innes Ct
Airdrie ML6 123 E8
East Kilbride G74 159 E4
International Ave G72 161 D4
Inverallan Ct FK9 1 F8
Inverallan Dr FK9 1 F7
Inverallan Rd FK9 1 F7
Inveraray Gdns ML1 143 C2
Inverarish PA8 93 C7
Inverary Dr
Bishopbriggs G64 78 B4
Gartcosh G69 100 E4
Stenhousemuir FK5 23 F5
Inveravon Dr ML1 163 C5
Inverbervie PA8 73 A2
Invercanny Dr G15 75 A4
Invercanny Pl G15 75 A4
Invercargill G75 180 A7
Invercloy Ct G75 180 B4
Invercloy Pl KA3 222 E4
Inverclyde Acad PA16 44 F3
Inverclyde Gdns G73 138 E3
Inverclyde Royal Hospl
PA16 44 F4
Invercree Wlk ML5 101 C6
Inveresk Pl ML5 122 A8
Inveresk Quadrant G32 119 A6
Inveresk St G32 119 A6
Inverewe Ave G46 135 D2
Inverewe Dr G46 135 D2
Inverewe Gdns G46 135 D2
Inverewe Pl G46 135 D3
Inverewe Way G77 156 B5
Invergarry Ave G46 135 D1
Invergarry Ct G46 135 E1
Invergarry Dr G46 135 E2
Invergarry Gdns G46 135 D1
Invergarry Gr G46 135 D2
Invergarry Pl G46 135 E2
Invergarry Quad G46 135 E2
Invergarry View G46 135 E2
Inverglas Ave PA4 94 F1
Invergordon Ave G43 136 F7
Invergordon Pl ML6 123 A6
Invergyle Dr G52 115 C5
Invergyle La G52 115 B5
Inverkar Dr PA2 113 A2
Inverkar Rd KA7 239 A6
Inverkip Dr ML7 146 E5
Inverkip Rd
Greenock, Cowdenknowes
PA16 45 C4
Greenock, Spango Valley
PA16 44 D2
Inverkip St PA15 45 E5
Inverlair Ave G44 136 F6
Inverleith St G32 118 E7
Inverleven Pl KA11 219 F7
Inverlochy Rd ML6 122 E6
Inverlochy St G33 99 D1
Inverness St G51 115 D6
Inveroran Dr G61 76 B4
Inver Rd G33 119 E7
Invershiel Rd G23 76 E1
Invershin Dr 6 G20 96 D5
Inverurie St G21 97 D3
Invervale Ave 3 ML6 123 F6
Inzievar Terr G32 119 B1
Iona ML6 123 D6
Iona Ave G74 160 A4
Iona Cres
Gourock PA19 44 D6
Old Kilpatrick G60 73 C5
Iona Ct KA11 225 C8
Iona Dr PA2 133 D7
Iona Gdns G60 73 C5
Iona La G69 81 A2
Iona Path G72 161 C7
Iona Pl
Coatbridge ML5 101 D1
Falkirk FK1 42 B2
Irvine KA11 225 C8
Kilmarnock KA3 223 A5
Old Kilpatrick G60 73 C5
Iona Quadrant ML2 165 E5
Iona Rd
Port Glasgow PA14 69 A7
Renfrew PA4 94 C1
Rutherglen G73 138 E3
Wishaw ML2 165 F6
Iona Ridge ML3 161 F1
Iona St
Glasgow G51 116 B7
Greenock PA16 45 C4
Motherwell ML1 142 D1
Iona Way
Kirkintilloch G66 80 B8
Stepps G33 99 E4
Iona Wlk
Coatbridge ML5 121 E4
Gourock PA19 44 C6
Iona Wynd G83 27 F1
Iris Ave G45 138 A3
Iris Ct KA7 239 C3
Irongray St G31 118 C7
IRVINE 219 B4
Irvine Burns Mus & Club★
KA12 219 C3
Irvine Cres ML5 122 C7
Irvine Ct G40 118 B3
Irvine Dr PA3 111 F7
Irvine Gdns G66 58 B5
Irvine Ind Est KA12 224 D7
Irvine Mains Cres KA12 219 C4
Irvine Pl
Kilsyth G65 36 B1
Stirling FK8 7 A8
Irvine Rd
Crosshouse KA2 221 E1
Kilmarnock KA1 222 C1
Kilmaurs KA3 222 B7
Kilwinning KA13 208 A1
Irvine Royal Acad KA12 219 B5
Irvine St
Glasgow G40 118 B3
Glenmavis ML6 102 F4
Irvine Sta KA12 219 B1
Irvine Terr ML3 183 D8
Irving Ave G81 74 B6
Irving Ct
Clydebank G81 74 B6
Falkirk FK1 41 E5
Irving Quadrant G81 74 B5
Irwin St PA15 46 E2
Isabella Gdns ML3 163 C1
Iser La G41 136 F8
Isla Ave ML2 165 F6
Island Rd G67 82 D8
Islands Cres FK1 42 B2
Island View KA22 205 B4
Islay ML6 123 E6
Islay Ave
Port Glasgow PA14 69 B7
Rutherglen G73 138 E3
Islay Cres
Old Kilpatrick G60 73 C5
Paisley PA2 133 D7
Saltcoats KA21 205 F2
Islay Ct
Hamilton ML3 161 F2
Irvine KA11 225 C8
Islay Dr
Newton Mearns G77 156 B5
Old Kilpatrick G60 73 C5
Islay Gdns
Carluke ML8 202 A8
Larkhall ML9 185 B3
Islay Pl KA3 223 B5
Islay Quadrant 2 ML2 164 E1
Islay Rd G66 80 A8
Islay Way ML5 121 D4
Isle of Pin Rd KA10 230 A1
Isobel Mair Sch G76 136 D1
Ivanhoe G74 160 D4
Ivanhoe Cres ML2 165 B3
Ivanhoe Ct ML8 187 D1
Ivanhoe Dr
Kirkintilloch G66 79 E8
Saltcoats KA21 206 A1
Ivanhoe Pl
Motherwell ML1 143 B5
Stirling FK8 2 A2
Ivanhoe Rd
Cumbernauld G67 82 F8
Glasgow G13 95 D8
Paisley PA2 112 F1
Ivanhoe Way PA2 112 F1
Ivybank Ave G72 139 C4
Ivybank Cres PA14 47 A1
Ivybank Rd PA14 47 B2
Ivy Cres PA19 44 E6
Ivy Gr ML5 122 B6
Ivy Pl
Ayr KA7 239 D5
Hamilton G72 161 C8
Motherwell ML1 143 A3
Ivy Rd G71 141 C8
Ivy Terr ML1 143 A5
Ivy Way ML6 123 E3
Izatt St FK10 10 B7

J

Jackson Ct ML5 122 B6
Jackson Dr G33 100 A5
Jackson Pl
Bearsden G61 75 E3
Carluke ML8 187 E3
Renton G82 27 D2
Jackson St ML5 122 B7
Jack's Rd
Bothwell G71 141 A5
Saltcoats KA21 205 F1
Jack St
Hamilton ML3 183 D8
Motherwell ML1 164 B4
Jacks View KA23 190 C5

JACKTON 179 C7
Jackton Bsns Ctr G75 179 C7
Jackton Rd G75 179 D5
Jacobite Pl ML4 142 D4
Jacob Pl FK1 42 B3
Jacobs Dr PA19 44 D6
Jacob's Ladder Way
ML2 186 C6
Jade Terr ML4 142 A4
Jagger Gdns G69 119 F4
Jamaica Dr G75 159 B1
Jamaica La PA15 45 E6
Jamaica St
Glasgow G1 240 C1
Greenock PA15 45 F6
James Aiton Prim Sch
G72 139 A6
James Boyle Sq G66 58 B6
James Brown Ave KA8 236 E3
James Campbell Rd KA8 239 C8
James Clements Cl
KA13 207 D4
James Cres KA12 219 C4
James Croft Dr FK1 41 F1
James Dempsey Ct ML5 121 F6
James Dempsey Gdns
ML5 121 F6
James Dunlop Gdns G64 98 B7
James Gray St G41 136 E8
James Hamilton Acad
KA3 223 C1
James Hamilton Dr ML4 142 B5
James Hamilton Heritage
Pk* G74 159 D4
James Healy Dr ML3 183 C7
James Hemphill Ct G66 57 E8
James Johnston Pl KA3 223 A3
James Leeson Ct G66 58 C6
James Little St KA1 227 F7
James MacFarlane Sch
KA22 205 C3
James Miller Cres KA21 217 A7
James Morrison St G1 241 B1
James Murdie Gdns 3
ML3 162 A6
James Nisbet St G21 97 F1
James Reid Sch KA21 206 B2
James Shaw La 5 KA1 222 F1
James Short Pk FK1 42 B3
James St
3 Alexandria G83 27 E5
Alva FK12 5 A6
Ayr KA8 236 A1
Bannockburn FK7 7 C1
Bellshill ML4 141 E7
Carluke ML8 187 F1
Dalry KA24 191 B8
Falkirk FK2 42 B6
Glasgow G40 117 E4
Haggs FK4 39 A3
Helensburgh G84 16 D2
Laurieston FK2 42 F3
Motherwell ML1 163 D7
Prestwick KA9 236 B5
Stenhousemuir FK5 23 D2
Stirling FK8 2 B1
James Sym Cres KA1 227 E6
JAMESTOWN 27 F7
Jamestown Ind Est G83 27 F7
Jamestown Prim Sch G83 27 F7
James View ML1 142 F3
James Watt Ave G75 181 A8
James Watt Coll (Finnart
Campus) PA15 45 E5
James Watt Coll (North
Ayrshire Campus)
KA13 207 E4
James Watt Coll (Waterfront
Campus) PA15 46 A5
James Watt Pl G74 159 B3
James Watt Rd G62 54 F3
James Watt St G2 240 B2
James Watt Way PA15 46 C4
James Wilson Pl ML8 201 B2
Jamieson Ave FK5 23 E3
Jamieson Ct
Clydebank G81 74 B7
1 Glasgow G42 117 B2
Jamieson Dr G74 160 A2
Jamieson Gdns
Shotts ML7 146 E5
Uddingston G71 140 E6
Jamieson Pl KA3 195 D1
Jamieson St
Glasgow G42 117 B2
Glasgow G42 117 C2
Jamieson Way KA15 171 A7
Janebank Ave G72 139 C4
Jane Ct ML9 185 A2
Janefield Ave PA5 111 E2
Janefield Pl
Beith KA15 150 B1
Hamilton G72 161 C6
Lennoxtown G66 33 D1
Janefield St
Glasgow G31 118 B5
Glasgow G31 118 C4
Jane Pl G5 117 C4
Jane Rae Gdns G81 94 D8
Jane's Brae G67 82 F8
Jane's Brae Intc G67 82 F7
Janesmith St ML2 164 C4
Janetta St G81 74 A4
Jardine St G20 96 F3
Jardine Terr
Gartcosh G69 100 F5
Greenock PA16 45 E7
Jarvie Ave ML6 104 B2
Jarvie Cres G65 60 D7
Jarvie Pl 6 FK2 42 A8
Jarvie Way PA2 132 E8
Jasmine Pl G67 82 B6
Jasmine Rd KA1 227 C7
Jasmine Way ML8 201 E8
Java St ML1 142 C1
Jean Armour Dr
Clydebank G81 74 C3
Kilmarnock KA1 227 B7
Jean Armour La PA16 44 E3
Jean Armour Pl KA21 206 A2
Jean Armour Terr PA16 44 E3
Jeanette Ave ML3 183 D7
Jeanie Deans Dr G84 25 C8
Jean MacLean Pl G64 78 B4
Jean St PA14 47 B2
Jedburgh Ave G73 138 B7
Jedburgh Ct 4 PA15 46 B3
Jedburgh Dr PA2 113 A1
Jedburgh Gdns 1 G20 96 F3
Jedburgh Pl
Coatbridge ML5 121 F3
East Kilbride G74 159 F2
Jedburgh St
Hamilton G72 161 D7
Wishaw ML2 165 C5
Jedworth Ave G15 75 B3
Jedworth Ct 3 G61 75 E5
Jedworth Rd G15 75 C3
Jeffrey Pl G65 36 C1
Jeffrey St KA1 227 F5
Jellicoe Pl G84 17 A2
Jellicoe St G81 73 E3
Jellyholm Rd FK10 10 E8
Jennie Lee Dr ML2 186 B7
JENNY LIND 135 D2
Jenny Lind Ct G46 135 E2
Jennys Well Ct PA2 114 B2
Jennys Well Rd PA2 114 C2
Jermond Dr KA12 219 D5
Jervis Pl G84 17 A2
Jervis Terr G75 180 B7
Jerviston Ct ML1 143 A1
Jerviston Rd
Glasgow G33 99 C2
Motherwell ML1 143 A1
Jerviston St
Motherwell ML1 163 F8
Motherwell, New Stevenston
ML1 143 A3
New Stevenston ML1 143 A4
Jerviswood ML1 143 A1
Jerviswood Dr ML11 215 F7
Jerviswood Rd ML11 215 A4
Jessie St G42 117 D1
Jessiman Sq PA4 94 B1
Jimmy Sneddon Way
ML1 142 D2
Joanna Terr G72 161 D8
Jocelyn Sq G1 241 A1
Jock Stein Ctr ML3 161 E4
Jockshorn Terr KA3 222 C6
John Bassy Dr FK4 38 D3
John Bowman Gdns ML4 142 B6
John Brannan Way ML4 141 D6
John Brogan Pl KA20 217 B8
John Brown Pl G69 100 C8
John Burnside Dr G81 74 D7
John Burtt Pl KA3 223 A3
John Campbell Ct PA19 44 F7
John Campbell St PA19 44 F7
John Cowane Row FK9 2 A4
John Davidson Dr FK6 21 C4
John Dickie St 9 KA1 222 F1
John Ewing Gdns ML9 185 A4
John Finnie St KA1 227 F8
John Galt Prim Sch
KA12 219 D4
John Gregor Pl PA12 129 C2
John Hendry Rd G71 141 A4
John Hillhouse Ind Est
G72 138 D8
John Jarvis Sq G65 36 D1
John Kennedy Pl KA3 223 A3
John Knox La ML3 161 D4
John Knox St
Clydebank G81 94 C7
Glasgow G4 241 C2
John Lang St PA5 112 A3
John Logie Baird Prim Sch
G84 17 A2
John McEwan Way G64 78 B8
John Marshall Dr G64 97 E8
John Murray Ct ML1 163 E3
John Murray Dr FK9 2 A8
John Neilson Ave PA1 113 A4
John Ogilvie High Sch
ML3 161 F4
John O'Hara Ct FK1 41 D5
John Paul Acad G23 76 D1
John Paul II Prim Sch
Glasgow G45 137 D1
Uddingston G71 141 C7
John Paul Sp Ctr G23 76 D1
John Pl ML9 199 B7
John Rushforth Pl FK8 1 F3
Johnsburn Dr G53 135 B6
Johnsburn Rd G53 135 B6
Johnshaven PA8 73 A2
Johnshaven St 1 G43 136 C7
Johnshill PA12 129 D3
John Smith Ct ML6 122 F8
John Smith Gate G78 134 C4
John Smith Gdns ML5 122 D5
John Smith Way ML7 146 D5
Johnson Ct G84 16 F1
Johnson Dr G72 139 B5
John St
Ayr KA8 236 A1
Barrhead G78 134 B3
Bellshill ML4 142 A5
Carluke ML8 187 F1
Falkirk FK2 42 B7
Glasgow G1 241 A2
Gourock PA19 44 E8
Greenock PA15 46 B3
Haggs FK4 39 A3
Hamilton, Blantyre G72 161 E8
Hamilton ML3 162 E3
Helensburgh G84 16 C2
Helensburgh G84 16 C3
Kirkintilloch G66 58 D1
Larkhall ML9 185 B2
Renton G82 49 D8
Wishaw ML2 164 C4
Johnston Ave
Clydebank G81 94 D8
Kilsyth G65 60 D7
Stenhousemuir FK5 23 F3
Stirling FK9 2 B3
Johnston Ct 7 FK2 42 A8
Johnston Dr KA10 229 E6
JOHNSTONE 112 A4
Johnstone Ave G52 115 B7
Johnstone Ct FK12 5 A6
Johnstone Dr
Lochwinnoch PA12 129 C2
Rutherglen G73 138 A7
Johnstone High Sch
PA5 131 C7
Johnstone Hospl PA5 111 F4
Johnstone La ML8 188 B1
Johnstone Rd ML3 162 E2
Johnstone St
Alva FK12 5 A6
Bellshill ML4 142 C5
Menstrie FK11 3 F6
Johnstone Sta PA5 112 A2
Johnstone Terr G65 59 F2
Johnston Pl FK6 21 C1
Johnston Rd G69 101 B6
Johnston St
Airdrie ML6 123 B8
Bannockburn FK7 7 C1
Greenock PA16 45 D7
1 Paisley PA1 113 E4
Johnston Terr PA16 45 D7
John Street La G84 16 C2
John Walker Dr KA3 222 D3
John Wheatley Coll
(Easterhouse Campus)
G34 120 B8
John Wheatley Coll (The
East End Campus) G31 118 C6
John Wilson Dr G65 36 B1
John Wilson St PA15 46 D2
John Wood St PA14 47 C1
John Wright Sports Ctr
G74 160 A2
Joiners La KA3 195 B7
Jones Ave FK5 41 C8
Jones Wynd ML1 143 E1
Jonquil Way ML8 201 F8
Joppa St G33 118 E8
JORDANHILL 95 E5
Jordanhill Cres G13 95 D5
Jordanhill Dr G13 95 D6
Jordanhill La G13 95 E5
Jordanhill Sch G13 95 E5
Jordanhill Sta G11 95 F4
Jordan Pl ML1 144 C3
Jordan St G14 95 D2
Jordanvale Ave G14 95 D2
Jowitt Ave G81 74 D1
Jubilee Bank G66 79 C3
Jubilee Ct
Glasgow G52 114 F7
Larkhall ML9 185 A4
Jubilee Dr KA3 195 F1
Jubilee Gdns G61 75 F4
Jubilee Pl KA3 195 F1
Jubilee Rd
Denny FK6 21 E3
Troon KA10 229 D3
Jubilee Terr PA5 111 D2
Jubilee Way FK4 39 F5
Julian Ave G12 96 C4
Julian La G12 96 C4
Junction Pl 12 FK10 10 B6
Juniper Ave
East Kilbride G75 180 D6
Quarriers Village PA11 89 F1
Juniper Ct G66 79 B5
Juniper Dr
Hamilton ML3 182 F7
Milton of Campsie G66 58 B4
Juniper Gn KA7 239 D6
Juniper Gr ML3 162 F2
Juniper Pl
Glasgow G32 119 F4
Johnstone PA5 132 A8
Uddingston G71 141 D8
Juniper Rd G71 141 D8
Juniper Terr G32 119 E4
Juniper Wynd ML1 143 B5
Juno La PA16 44 D3
Juno St ML1 142 D2
Juno Terr PA16 44 D3
Jupiter La PA16 44 D3
Jupiter Pl G84 15 D6
Jupiter St ML1 142 D1
Jupiter Terr PA16 44 D3
Jura G74 181 B7
Jura Ave PA4 94 D1
Jura Ct
Glasgow G52 115 E5
Irvine KA11 225 C8
Jura Dr
Blantyre G72 140 C3
Kirkintilloch G66 80 A8
Newton Mearns G77 156 B6
Old Kilpatrick G60 73 C5
Jura Gdns
Carluke ML8 202 A8
Hamilton ML3 162 A2
Kilmarnock KA3 222 D3
Larkhall ML9 185 C3
Old Kilpatrick G60 73 C5
Jura Pl
Old Kilpatrick G60 73 C5
Troon KA10 229 F7
Jura Quadrant 3 ML2 164 E1
Jura Rd
Old Kilpatrick G60 73 C5
Paisley PA2 133 D7
Jura St
Glasgow G52 115 F5
Greenock PA16 45 C4
Jura Wynd ML5 101 C6
Jutland Ct G84 16 A3

K

Kaim Dr G53 135 C6
Kairnhill Ct ML11 214 E4
Kames Ct KA11 220 B6
Kames Rd ML7 146 E6
Kane Pl ML9 198 D1
Kane St G82 27 D2
Karadale Gdns ML9 185 A2
Karries Ct FK6 39 B8
Kateswell Dr ML7 125 B1
Katewell Ave G15 74 E4
Katewell Pl G15 74 E4
Katherine St ML6 123 E8
Kathleen Pk G84 16 A3
Katrine Ave
Bishopbriggs G64 78 B1
Uddingston ML4 141 D6
Katrine Cres ML6 102 F1
Katrine Ct
Alloa FK10 10 C5
Kilmarnock KA1 228 A5
Katrine Dr
Newton Mearns G77 157 B4
Paisley PA2 113 A2
Katrine Pl
Cambuslang G72 139 A6
Coatbridge ML5 101 D1
Denny FK6 39 D6
Irvine KA12 219 D6
Katrine Rd
Greenock PA15 46 A3
Shotts ML7 146 E6
Katrine Way 5 G71 141 A3
Katrine Wynd ML1 143 A5
Katriona Path 12 ML9 185 C1
Kay Gdns ML1 163 B6
Kay Park Cres KA3 223 B1
Kay Park Gr KA3 223 A1
Kay Park Terr KA3 223 B1
Kay St G21 97 F4
Kaystone Rd G15 75 A1
Keal Ave G15 95 B8
Keal Cres G15 95 A8
Keal Dr G15 95 A8
Keal Pl G15 95 A8
Keane Path ML1 164 B3
Kearn Ave G15 75 B1
Kearn Pl G15 75 B1
Keats Pk G71 141 B3
KEILARSBRAE 10 D8
Keilarsbrae
Alloa FK10 5 C1
Sauchie FK10 10 C8
Keil Cres G82 49 D3
Keil Ct G84 25 B8
Keir Ave FK8 2 A2
Keir Cres ML2 165 B4
Keir Ct FK9 2 A7
Keir Dr G64 77 F2
Keirfold Ave FK10 4 D3
Keir Gdns FK9 2 A7
Keir Hardie Ave
Laurieston FK2 42 F3
Motherwell ML1 143 B5
Keir Hardie Cres KA13 208 A3
Keir Hardie Ct G64 78 A1
Keir Hardie Dr
Ardrossan KA22 205 B4
Bellshill ML4 141 F4
Kilbirnie KA25 149 A1
13 Kilsyth G65 60 D8
Keir Hardie Meml Prim Sch
ML1 143 D3
Keir Hardie Pl
Bellshill ML4 141 F4
Saltcoats KA21 206 A2
Keir Hardie Rd
Alva FK12 5 C7
Larkhall ML9 185 C1
Stevenston KA20 206 E1
Keir Hardie St PA15 46 E2
Keir St
Bridge of Allan FK9 2 A7
Glasgow G41 116 F3
Keir's Wlk G72 139 A6
Keith Ave
Glasgow G46 136 D3
Stirling FK7 7 C4
Keith Ct G11 96 C1
Keith Pl KA3 223 C2
Keith Quadrant ML2 165 B5
Keith St
Bellshill ML4 142 A6
Glasgow G11 96 C2
Hamilton ML3 162 F4
Kelbourne Cres ML4 141 F5
Kelbourne Sch G20 96 E4
Kelbourne St G20 96 E4
KELBURN 47 F1
Kelburn Bsns Pk PA14 48 B1
Kelburn Cres KA1 227 E4
Kelburne KA13 207 C2
Kelburne Dr PA1 114 B5
Kelburne Gdns
Glasgow G69 120 A3
Paisley PA1 114 A5
Kelburne Oval PA1 114 A5
Kelburn St G78 134 B2
Kelburn Terr PA14 48 A1
Kelhead Ave G52 114 F4
Kelhead Dr G52 114 F5
Kelhead Path G52 114 F5
Kelhead Pl G52 114 F5
Kelliebank FK10 9 E6
Kellie Gr G74 159 D3
Kellie Pl FK10 10 A7
Kells Pl G15 74 E4
Kelly Ct FK8 7 A8
Kelly Dr FK6 21 E3
Kelly's La ML8 188 B1
Kelly St
Greenock PA16 45 D5
Greenock PA16 45 E6
Kelso Ave
Bridge of Weir PA11 110 D7
Paisley PA2 113 A1
Rutherglen G73 138 B7
Kelso Cres ML2 165 B6
Kelso Ct 5 PA15 46 B3
Kelso Dr
Carluke ML8 188 C1
East Kilbride G74 160 A3
Kelso Gdns G69 80 F3
Kelso Pl
Glasgow G14 94 E6
Renton G82 27 E2
Kelso Quadrant ML5 121 F8
Kelso St G13 94 F7
Kelton St G32 119 B4
Kelt Rd FK4 38 E4
KELVIN 181 B6
Kelvin Ave
Glasgow G52 114 F8
Glasgow (Hillington Ind Est)
G52 94 F1
Kilwinning KA13 207 F1
Kelvinbridge Rdbt G64 78 B8
Kelvinbridge Underground
Sta G4 96 E2
Kelvin Cres
Bearsden G61 75 F2
East Kilbride G75 181 A7
Kelvin Ct
East Kilbride G75 181 A7
Glasgow G12 96 A5
1 Kirkintilloch G66 58 C1
4 Troon KA10 229 E5
KELVINDALE 96 A7
Kelvindale G64 57 C1
Kelvindale Gdns G20 96 D6
Kelvindale Pl 3 G20 96 D6
Kelvindale Prim Sch G12 96 A5
Kelvindale Rd G12, G20 96 C5
Kelvindale Sta G20 96 B7
Kelvin Dr
Airdrie ML6 103 B1
Barrhead G78 134 D1
Bishopbriggs G64 78 A2
East Kilbride G75 180 F7
Glasgow G20 96 D4
Kirkintilloch G66 79 A8
Moodiesburn G69 80 E2
Shotts ML7 147 B4
Kelvin Gdns
Hamilton ML3 161 E4
Kilsyth G65 60 D7
KELVINGROVE 96 D2
Kelvingrove Mus & Art Gall*
G3 96 D1
Kelvingrove St G3 116 E8
Kelvin Hall International
Sports Arena G3 96 C1
Kelvinhall Underground Sta
G11 96 C2
KELVINHAUGH 96 C1
Kelvinhaugh Gate G3 116 D8
Kelvinhaugh Pl G3 116 D8
Kelvinhaugh Prim Sch
G3 116 C8
Kelvinhaugh St G3 116 D8
Kelvinhead G65 37 F2
Kelvinhead Rd G65 37 E2
Kelvin Ind Est G75 181 A6
Kelvin Park S G75 181 A4
Kelvin Pl G75 181 A7
Kelvin Rd
Bellshill ML4 142 B7
Cumbernauld G67 83 A8
East Kilbride G75 181 A7
Milngavie G62 54 E3
Uddingston G71 140 E7
Kelvin Road N G67 83 A8
KELVINSIDE 96 A5
Kelvinside Acad G12 96 D4

Kelvinside Ave
Glasgow G20 ... 96 E4
Glasgow G20 ... 96 F4
Kelvinside Cres G65 ... 37 E3
Kelvinside Dr G20 ... 96 F4
Kelvinside Gardens La 4
G20 ... 96 E4
Kelvinside Gdns G20 ... 96 E4
Kelvinside Gdns E G20 ... 96 F4
Kelvinside Terrace S 3
G20 ... 96 E3
Kelvinside Terrace W 2
G20 ... 96 E3
Kelvin South Bsns Pk
G75 ... 180 F3
Kelvin St ML5 ... 122 C5
Kelvin Terr G65 ... 59 F3
Kelvinvale G66 ... 58 D1
Kelvin View
Torrance G64 ... 78 C8
Twechar G65 ... 59 F3
Kelvinview Ave FK4 ... 38 E2
Kelvin Way
1 Bothwell G71 ... 141 A3
Glasgow G3, G12 ... 96 E1
Kilsyth G65 ... 36 C1
Kirkintilloch G66 ... 79 A8
Kemp Ave PA3 ... 94 A1
Kemp Ct
Hamilton ML3 ... 162 E3
Saltcoats KA21 ... 205 E3
Kemper Ave FK1 ... 42 C3
Kempock Pl PA19 ... 44 E8
Kempock St PA19 ... 44 E8
Kemp St
7 Glasgow G21 ... 97 E4
Hamilton ML3 ... 162 E3
Kempsthorn Cres G53 ... 115 B1
Kempsthorn Pl G53 ... 115 B1
Kempsthorn Rd G53 ... 115 A1
Kenbank Cres PA11 ... 110 D8
Kenbank Rd PA11 ... 110 D8
Kendal Ave
Glasgow G12 ... 96 A6
Glasgow, Giffnock G46 ... 136 C3
Kendal Dr G12 ... 96 A6
Kendal Rd G75 ... 179 F6
Kendoon Ave G15 ... 74 E3
Kenilburn Ave ML6 ... 103 B2
Kenilburn Cres ML6 ... 103 B2
Kenilworth G74 ... 160 E4
Kenilworth Ave
Glasgow G41 ... 136 D8
Helensburgh G84 ... 25 C7
Paisley PA2 ... 132 F8
Wishaw ML2 ... 165 B3
Kenilworth Cres
Bearsden G61 ... 75 C6
Bellshill ML4 ... 142 A6
Greenock PA16 ... 45 D3
Hamilton ML3 ... 161 F4
Kenilworth Ct
Bridge of Allan FK9 ... 2 B7
Carluke ML8 ... 187 E1
Cumbernauld G67 ... 82 E8
Motherwell ML1 ... 143 A5
Kenilworth Dr
Airdrie ML6 ... 123 D8
Laurieston FK2 ... 42 F4
Saltcoats KA21 ... 206 A2
Kenilworth Rd
Bridge of Allan FK9 ... 2 B7
Kirkintilloch G66 ... 79 E8
Lanark ML11 ... 215 B4
Kenilworth Way PA2 ... 112 F1
Kenley Rd PA4 ... 94
Kenmar Gdns G71 ... 140 E8
Kenmar Rd ML3 ... 162 B5
Kenmar Terr ML3 ... 162 B5
Kenmore KA10 ... 229 E4
Kenmore Ave KA9 ... 236 C6
Kenmore Dr PA16 ... 45 A4
Kenmore Gdns G61 ... 76 B5
Kenmore Pl
Greenock PA16 ... 45 A4
Troon KA10 ... 229 E4
Kenmore Rd
Cumbernauld G67 ... 62 B2
Kilmacolm PA13 ... 89 C7
Kenmore St G32 ... 119 A5
Kenmore Way
Carluke ML8 ... 187 F3
Coatbridge ML5 ... 122 C3
Kenmuiraid Pl ML4 ... 141 F3
Kenmuir Ave G32 ... 119 E3
Kenmuirhill Gate G32 ... 119 D2
Kenmuirhill Gdns G32 ... 119 D2
Kenmuirhill Rd G32 ... 119 D2
Kenmuir Rd
Glasgow, Carmyle G32 ... 139 D8
Glasgow, Mount Vernon
G32 ... 119 E2
Kenmuir St
Coatbridge ML5 ... 121 C4
Falkirk FK1 ... 41 A5
Kenmure Ave G64 ... 77 F1
Kenmure Cres G64 ... 77 F1
Kenmure Dr G64 ... 77 F1
Kenmure Gdns G64 ... 77 E1
Kenmure La G64 ... 77 F1
Kenmure Pl FK5 ... 23 F4
Kenmure Rd G46 ... 157 B6
Kenmure St G41 ... 116 F3
Kenmure View PA9 ... 130 E5
Kenmure Way G73 ... 138 B3
Kennard St FK2 ... 42 C6
Kennedar Dr G51 ... 115 E8
Kennedy Ave G65 ... 60 A3
Kennedy Ct
Alexandria G83 ... 27 C7
Glasgow G46 ... 136 C4
Kilmarnock KA3 ... 223 C3
Kennedy Dr
Airdrie ML6 ... 122 E7
Helensburgh G84 ... 16 D4
Kilmarnock KA3 ... 223 C4
Kennedy Gdns ML2 ... 186 B7
Kennedy Path G4 ... 241 B3
Kennedy Pk KA11 ... 220 B1
Kennedy Rd
Saltcoats KA21 ... 205 F1
Troon KA10 ... 229 B2
Kennedy's La PA15 ... 46 B3
Kennedy St
Glasgow G4 ... 241 B3
Kilmarnock KA1 ... 227 F6
Wishaw ML2 ... 165 C3
Kennedy Way FK2 ... 14 E3
Kennelburn Rd ML6 ... 123 D2
Kenneth Rd ML1 ... 163 C5
Kennihill ML6 ... 103 A1
Kennihill Quadrant ML6 ... 103 A1
Kenningknowes Rd FK7 ... 6 E5
KENNISHEAD ... 135 F5
Kennishead Ave G46 ... 135 F5
Kennishead Path G46 ... 135 E5
Kennishead Pl G46 ... 135 E5
Kennishead Rd
Glasgow G43, G46 ... 136 A6
Glasgow G53, G46, G43 ... 135 D5
Kennishead Sta G46 ... 135 E5
Kennisholm Ave G46 ... 135 E5
Kennisholm Path G46 ... 135 E5
Kennisholm Pl G46 ... 135 E5
Kennoway Cres ML3 ... 163 C1
Kennoway Dr G11 ... 95 F2
Kennyhill Sq G31 ... 118 B8
Ken Rd KA1 ... 228 A5
Kenshaw Ave ML9 ... 199 A8
Kenshaw Pl ML9 ... 199 A8
Kensington Dr G46 ... 136 D1
Kensington Gate 1 G12 ... 96 C4
Kensington Gate La 2
G12 ... 96 C4
Kensington Rd G12 ... 96 C4
Kentallen Rd G33 ... 119 E6
Kent Ct G84 ... 17 A3
Kent Dr
Helensburgh G84 ... 17 A3
Rutherglen G73 ... 138 D5
Kentigern Terr G64 ... 98 B8
Kentmere Cl G75 ... 180 A6
Kentmere Dr G75 ... 180 A6
Kentmere Pl G75 ... 180 A6
Kent Pl G75 ... 179 F6
Kent Rd
Alloa FK10 ... 9 F8
Bellshill ML4 ... 141 D6
Glasgow G3 ... 116 E8
Glasgow G3 ... 240 A3
Stirling FK7 ... 7 B5
Kent St G40 ... 241 C1
Keppel Dr G44 ... 137 E6
Keppochhill Dr G21 ... 97 D3
Keppochhill Rd G22 ... 97 D3
Keppoch St G21 ... 97 D3
Keppock Pl FK1 ... 41 F1
Kerelaw Ave KA20 ... 206 E2
Kerelaw Rd KA20 ... 206 D2
Kerfield La G15 ... 74 E4
Kerfield Pl G15 ... 74 E4
Kerr Ave KA21 ... 217 A8
Kerr Cres
Haggs FK4 ... 39 A3
Hamilton ML3 ... 162 C1
Ker Rd G62 ... 54 E3
Kerr Dr
Glasgow G40 ... 117 F5
Irvine KA12 ... 219 D2
Motherwell ML1 ... 163 C6
Kerrera Pl G33 ... 119 D6
Kerrera Rd G33 ... 119 D6
Kerr Gdns G71 ... 141 A8
Kerr Grieve Ct 5 ML1 ... 163 E5
Kerrix Rd
Monkton KA9 ... 233 D7
Symington KA9, KA1 ... 230 F1
Kerrmuir Ave KA1 ... 228 F5
Kerr Pl
Denny FK6 ... 21 D2
Glasgow G40 ... 117 F5
Irvine KA12 ... 219 D2
Kerr Rd KA3 ... 223 D2
Kerrs La KA21 ... 216 E8
Kerr St
Barrhead G78 ... 134 B2
Glasgow G40 ... 117 F5
Hamilton G72 ... 161 E8
Kirkintilloch G66 ... 79 C8
Paisley PA3 ... 113 D5
Kerrycroy Ave G42 ... 137 D8
Kerrycroy Pl G42 ... 137 D8
Kerrycroy St G42 ... 137 D8
Kerrydale St G40 ... 118 B4
Kerrylamont Ave G42 ... 137 E7
Kerry Pl G15 ... 74 E3
Kerse Ave KA24 ... 191 E7
Kersebonny Rd FK7 ... 6 C7
Kerse Gdns FK2 ... 42 E5
Kersegreen Rd FK10 ... 10 F5
Kersehill Circ FK2 ... 42 C7
Kersehill Cres FK2 ... 42 C7
Kerse La FK1 ... 42 C4
Kerse Pk KA7 ... 239 B1
Kerse Pl FK1 ... 42 C5
Kerse Rd
Stirling FK7 ... 7 C6
Stirling, Loanhead FK7 ... 7 E5
Kershaw St ML2 ... 186 C7
Kersie Rd FK7 ... 9 A3
Kersie Terr FK7 ... 9 E3
Kersland Cres KA1 ... 228 E6
Kersland Dr G62 ... 55 B2
Kersland Foot KA11 ... 219 F5
Kersland Gait KA3 ... 211 E8
Kersland La
1 Glasgow G12 ... 96 D3
Milngavie G62 ... 55 B2
Kersland Rd KA14 ... 170 C6
Kersland Specl Sch PA2 ... 114 C1
Kersland St G12 ... 96 D3
Ker St PA15 ... 45 F6
Kerswinning Ave KA25 ... 170 A7
Kessington Dr G61 ... 76 A4
Kessington Rd G61 ... 76 B3
Kessington Sq G61 ... 76 B3
Kessock Dr G22 ... 97 B3
Kessock Pl G22 ... 97 B3
Kessog Gdns G83 ... 27 F7
Kestrel Cres PA16 ... 45 A5
Kestrel Ct
Clydebank G81 ... 74 A5
Coatbridge ML5 ... 122 E3
Kestrel Pl
Greenock PA16 ... 45 A5
Johnstone PA5 ... 131 D7
Kestrel Rd G13 ... 95 C6
Kestrel View
Bellshill ML4 ... 141 E8
Motherwell ML4 ... 121 E1
Keswick Dr ML3 ... 183 C6
Keswick Rd G75 ... 179 F6
Kethers La ML1 ... 163 C7
Kethers St ML1 ... 163 C6
Keverkae FK10 ... 9 F6
Kevoc Cotts KA6 ... 237 A5
Kew Gdns G71 ... 141 B7
Kew Terr G12 ... 96 D3
Keynes Sq ML4 ... 142 D4
Keystone Ave G62 ... 76 B8
Keystone Quadrant G62 ... 76 A8
Keystone Rd G62 ... 76 B8
Kibble Education & Care Ctr
PA3 ... 113 C8
Kibbleston Rd PA10 ... 130 F7
Kidlaw Cres FK10 ... 4 D3
Kidsneuk KA12 ... 219 A6
Kidsneuk Gdns KA12 ... 219 A6
Kidston Dr G84 ... 16 A2
Kidston Pl 5 G5 ... 117 C4
Kidston Terr 4 G5 ... 117 C4
Kier Ct FK9 ... 2 B7
Kier Hardie Ct KA15 ... 171 A8
Kierhill Rd G68 ... 61 C2
Kilallan Ave PA11 ... 90 D1
Kilallan Rd PA6 ... 90 C6
KILBARCHAN ... 111 A3
Kilbarchan Intc PA10 ... 111 C2
Kilbarchan Prim Sch
PA10 ... 111 A4
Kilbarchan Rd
Bridge of Weir PA11 ... 110 F6
Johnstone PA5 ... 111 D2
Johnstone PA10 ... 111 C2
Kilbarchan St 2 G5 ... 117 B5
Kilbean Dr FK1 ... 41 E2
Kilbeg Terr G46 ... 135 D3
Kilberry St G21 ... 98 A1
KILBIRNIE ... 149 B1
Kilbirnie Pl G5 ... 117 A4
Kilbirnie St G5 ... 117 A4
Kilbirnie Terr FK6 ... 21 D3
Kilblain Ct 12 PA15 ... 45 F5
Kilblain St 11 PA15 ... 45 F5
KILBOWIE ... 74 C3
Kilbowie Pl ML6 ... 123 D6
Kilbowie Prim Sch G81 ... 74 B3
Kilbowie Rd
Clydebank G81 ... 74 B3
Clydebank, Hardgate G81 ... 74 B5
Cumbernauld G67 ... 62 A1
Kilbowie Ret Pk G81 ... 74 C2
Kilbrandon Cres KA7 ... 238 B2
Kilbrandon Way KA7 ... 238 B2
Kilbrannan Ave KA21 ... 205 F2
Kilbrannan Dr PA16 ... 45 B3
Kilbreck Gdns G61 ... 75 C8
Kilbreck La ML1 ... 143 C3
Kilbrennan Dr
Falkirk FK1 ... 41 B4
Motherwell ML1 ... 163 B7
Kilbrennan Rd PA3 ... 112 B6
Kilbride Dr G84 ... 16 E3
Kilbride Rd KA3 ... 195 D1
Kilbride St G5 ... 117 D2
Kilbride Terr G5 ... 117 D3
Kilbride View G71 ... 141 A7
Kilburn Gr G72 ... 140 D1
Kilburn Pl G13 ... 95 B6
Kilchattan Dr G44 ... 137 C7
Kilchoan Rd G33 ... 99 C2
Kilcloy Ave G15 ... 75 A4
Kilcreggan View PA15 ... 46 C2
Kildale Rd PA12 ... 129 B2
Kildale Way G73 ... 137 F8
Kildare Dr ML11 ... 215 B4
Kildare Pl
Lanark ML11 ... 215 B4
Wishaw ML2 ... 166 A5
Kildare Rd ML11 ... 215 B4
Kildary Ave G44 ... 137 A5
Kildary Rd G44 ... 137 A5
Kildean Hospl FK8 ... 1 F2
Kildermorie Path G34 ... 120 A8
Kildermorie Rd G34 ... 120 A8
Kildonan Ct ML2 ... 165 F7
Kildonan Dr
Glasgow G11 ... 96 A2
Helensburgh G84 ... 16 F2
Kildonan Ho KA9 ... 236 B5
Kildonan Pl
Motherwell ML1 ... 163 C7
Saltcoats KA21 ... 205 F2
Kildonan St ML5 ... 122 B7
Kildrostan St G41 ... 116 F2
KILDRUM ... 62 B4
Kildrummy Ave FK5 ... 23 F4
Kildrummy Dr G69 ... 100 F4
Kildrummy Pl G74 ... 159 D3
Kildrum Prim Sch G67 ... 62 B2
Kildrum Rd G67 ... 62 C3
Kildrum South Rdbt G67 ... 62 B1
Kilearn Rd PA3 ... 114 B7
Kilearn Sq PA3 ... 114 B7
Kilearn Way PA3 ... 114 B7
Kilfinan Rd ML7 ... 146 D6
Kilfinan St G22 ... 97 B7
Kilgarth St ML5 ... 121 C4
Kilgraston Rd PA11 ... 110 D6
Kilkerran KA13 ... 207 C3
Kilkerran Ct G77 ... 156 B4
Kilkerran Dr
Glasgow G33 ... 98 F6
Troon KA10 ... 229 E7
Kilkerran Pk G77 ... 156 B4
Kilkerran Way G77 ... 156 B4
Killearn Cres ML6 ... 104 B3
Killearn Dr PA1 ... 114 F4
Killearn Rd PA15 ... 46 B2
Killearn St
Glasgow G21, G22 ... 97 D4
Glasgow G22 ... 97 C4
Killellan Pl PA19 ... 43 F4
Killermont Ave G61 ... 76 A2
Killermont Ct G61 ... 76 B3
Killermont Mdws G71 ... 140 E2
Killermont Pl KA13 ... 207 B3
Killermont Prim Sch G61 ... 76 A4
Killermont Rd
Bearsden G61 ... 76 A2
Milngavie G62 ... 55 B1
Killermont St G2 ... 241 A3
Killermont View G20 ... 76 B2
Killiegrew Rd G41 ... 116 D2
Killin Ct ML5 ... 122 B3
Killin Dr PA3 ... 111 F5
Killin Pl
Greenock PA16 ... 45 A4
Troon KA10 ... 229 F4
Killin St G32 ... 119 B4
Killoch Ave PA3 ... 113 A5
Killoch Dr
Barrhead G78 ... 134 D1
Glasgow G13 ... 95 A6
Killochend Dr PA15 ... 45 E3
Killoch La PA3 ... 113 A5
Killoch Pl
Ayr KA7 ... 238 F7
Irvine KA11 ... 219 F4
Killoch Rd PA3 ... 113 A5
Killoch Way
Irvine KA11 ... 219 F4
Paisley PA3 ... 113 A5
KILMACOLM ... 89 C7
Kilmacolm Pl PA15 ... 46 C2
Kilmacolm Prim Sch
PA13 ... 89 C7
Kilmacolm Rd
Bridge of Weir PA11 ... 90 B2
Greenock PA15 ... 46 B2
Houston PA6 ... 91 B3
Port Glasgow PA14 ... 69 A6
Kilmahew Ave G82 ... 26 B1
Kilmahew Ct
Ardrossan KA22 ... 205 C1
Cardross G82 ... 26 A1
Kilmahew Dr G82 ... 26 A1
Kilmahew Gr G82 ... 26 B1
Kilmahew St KA22 ... 205 C2
Kilmailing Rd G44 ... 137 B6
Kilmair Pl G20 ... 96 D5
Kilmaluag Terr G46 ... 135 D3
Kilmannan Gdns G62 ... 54 E3
Kilmany Dr G32 ... 118 F5
Kilmany Gdns G32 ... 118 F5
Kilmardinny Ave G61 ... 75 F6
Kilmardinny Cres G61 ... 76 A6
Kilmardinny Dr G61 ... 75 F5
Kilmardinny Gate G61 ... 75 F5
Kilmardinny Gr G61 ... 75 F6
Kilmari Gdns G15 ... 74 E4
KILMARNOCK ... 227 C8
Kilmarnock Acad KA1 ... 228 A8
Kilmarnock Coll KA3 ... 228 A8
Kilmarnock Coll of Sporting
Excellence KA3 ... 223 A2
Kilmarnock Rd
Crosshouse KA2 ... 221 F1
Dundonald KA2 ... 225 F2
Glasgow G43 ... 136 D7
Kilmaurs KA3 ... 222 C6
Monkton KA9 ... 233 E6
Prestwick KA1, KA9 ... 234 A8
Springside KA11 ... 221 A2
Symington KA1 ... 231 D3
Troon KA10 ... 229 F6
Kilmarnock Sta KA1 ... 222 F1
Kilmartin La ML8 ... 187 F3
Kilmartin Pl
Airdrie ML6 ... 123 D6
Glasgow G46 ... 135 E4
Motherwell G71 ... 121 A1
KILMAURS ... 222 D7
Kilmaurs Dr G46 ... 136 E3
Kilmaurs Prim Sch KA3 ... 222 B7
Kilmaurs Rd
Crosshouse KA2 ... 221 E2
Fenwick KA3 ... 212 F2
Fenwick KA3 ... 213 A2
Kilmarnock KA3 ... 222 E4
Knockentiber KA2 ... 221 F3
Kilmaurs St G51 ... 115 F6
Kilmaurs Sta KA3 ... 222 B7
Kilmeny Cres ML2 ... 165 C5
Kilmeny Ct KA22 ... 205 D1
Kilmeny Terr KA22 ... 205 D1
Kilmichael Ave ML2 ... 166 A6
Kilmore Cres G15 ... 74 E4
Kilmore Gr ML5 ... 121 F4
Kilmorie Dr G73 ... 137 F7
Kilmory Ave G71 ... 141 A7
Kilmory Ct
East Kilbride G75 ... 180 C4
Falkirk FK1 ... 41 C4
Kilmory Dr G77 ... 156 E6
Kilmory Gdns ML8 ... 188 A3
Kilmory Pl
Kilmarnock KA3 ... 222 E4
Troon KA10 ... 229 G5
Kilmory Rd
Carluke ML8 ... 202 B8
Saltcoats KA21 ... 205 F2
Kilmory Wlk KA3 ... 195 D1
Kilmuir Cres G46 ... 135 D4
Kilmuir Dr G46 ... 135 E3
Kilmuir Rd
Glasgow G46 ... 135 E3
Uddingston G71 ... 120 F1
Kilmun Rd PA15 ... 46 A3
Kilmun St G20 ... 96 D7
Kilnbank Cres KA7 ... 239 D7
Kilnburn Rd ML1 ... 163 C7
KILNCADZOW ... 203 B5
Kilncadzow Rd ML8 ... 202 E8
Kilncraigs Ct FK10 ... 10 C5
Kilncraigs Rd FK10 ... 10 C6
Kilncroft La PA2 ... 113 E2
Kiln Ct KA12 ... 219 C2
Kilnford Cres KA2 ... 225 D2
Kilnford Dr KA2 ... 225 E2
Kilnknowe Cotts PA9 ... 131 A6
Kilnside Rd PA1 ... 114 A4
Kilns Pl FK2 ... 41 F6
Kilns Rd FK1 ... 42 A5
Kilnwell Quadrant ML1 ... 163 D7
Kiln Wlk KA12 ... 219 C2
Kiloran Gr G77 ... 156 A4
Kiloran Pl G77 ... 156 A4
Kiloran St G46 ... 135 F4
Kilpatrick Ave PA2 ... 113 B2
Kilpatrick Cres PA2 ... 133 D8
Kilpatrick Ct
Irvine KA11 ... 220 A3
Old Kilpatrick G60 ... 73 A6
Stepps G33 ... 99 F5
Kilpatrick Dr
Bearsden G61 ... 75 C8
East Kilbride G75 ... 180 B3
Erskine PA8 ... 73 B2
Paisley PA4 ... 114 B8
Stepps G33 ... 99 F5
Kilpatrick Gdns G76 ... 157 C8
Kilpatrick Pl KA11 ... 220 A2
Kilpatrick Sch G81 ... 73 E6
Kilpatrick Sta G60 ... 73 B6
Kilpatrick View G82 ... 50 B4
Kilpatrick Way 9 G71 ... 141 A8
Kilrig Ave KA13 ... 207 E4
Kilruskin Dr KA23 ... 190 D4
KILSYTH ... 60 C7
Kilsyth Acad G65 ... 36 C1
Kilsyth Cres KA11 ... 220 A3
Kilsyth Gdns G75 ... 180 A3
Kilsyth Prim Sch G65 ... 60 D8
Kilsyth Rd
Banknock FK4 ... 38 D3
Kirkintilloch G66 ... 58 E1
Queenzieburn G65, G66 ... 59 E7
Kilsyth Wlk KA11 ... 220 A3
Kiltarie Cres ML6 ... 123 F6
Kiltearn Rd G33 ... 119 F7
Kiltongue Cotts ML6 ... 122 D8
Kilvaxter Dr G46 ... 135 E3
KILWINNING ... 207 F2
Kilwinning Abbey*
KA13 ... 207 E3
Kilwinning Acad KA13 ... 207 E4
Kilwinning Cres
Airdrie ML6 ... 103 E1
Hamilton ML3 ... 161 E1
Kilwinning Rd
Dalry KA24 ... 191 B6
Irvine KA12 ... 219 B5
Stevenston KA20 ... 206 F1
Stewarton KA3 ... 211 C8
Kilwinning Sta KA13 ... 207 D4
Kilwynet Way PA3 ... 114 A7
Kimberley Gdns G75 ... 180 C8
Kimberley St
Clydebank G81 ... 73 E5
Wishaw ML2 ... 164 D3
Kinalty Rd G44 ... 137 A5
Kinarvie Cres G53 ... 134 F7
Kinarvie Gdns G53 ... 134 F7
Kinarvie Pl G53 ... 134 F7
Kinarvie Rd G53 ... 134 F7

Kirk Wynd *continued*
2 Falkirk FK1 ... 42 B4
Stirling FK7 ... 7 B4
Kirn Dr PA19 ... 44 D6
Kirn Rd KA3 ... 222 F2
Kirn St G20 ... 96 C8
Kirriemuir G74 ... 160 D5
Kirriemuir Ave G52 ... 115 C4
Kirriemuir Gdns G64 ... 78 C2
Kirriemuir Pl G52 ... 115 C4
Kirriemuir Rd G64 ... 78 C1
Kirstie Pl G83 ... 27 F2
Kirtle Dr PA4 ... 94 E2
Kirtle Pl G75 ... 179 E7
Kirtonholme Cres G74 ... 159 D2
Kishorn Pl G33 ... 99 C1
Kitchener St ML2 ... 165 A3
Kittoch Pl 5 G74 ... 159 F2
Kittoch Sch G75 ... 180 D8
Kittochside Rd G76 ... 158 F6
Kittoch St G74 ... 159 F2
Kittyshaw Pl KA24 ... 191 A7
Kittyshaw Rd KA24 ... 191 A7
Klondike Ct ML1 ... 143 B3
Knapdale St G22 ... 97 A7
Knightsbridge St G13 ... 95 D7
Knightscliffe Ave G13 ... 95 E7
Knights Gate G71 ... 140 E5
Knights Way FK6 ... 21 C2
KNIGHTSWOOD ... 95 C7
Knightswood Ct G13 ... 95 D6
Knightswood Prim Sch G13 ... 95 E7
Knightswood Rd
Glasgow G13 ... 95 D7
Glasgow G13 ... 95 D8
Knightswood Sec Sch G13 ... 95 D6
Knightswood Terr G72 ... 140 E1
Knivysbridge Pl ML4 ... 141 F3
KNOCKBUCKLE ... 89 B8
Knockbuckle Ave PA13 ... 69 B1
Knockbuckle Rd PA13 ... 89 C8
Knockburnie Rd G71 ... 141 A4
Knockdhu Pl PA19 ... 43 F5
Knock Dr ML6 ... 122 E6
KNOCKENTIBER ... 221 F3
Knockentiber Rd KA11, KA2 ... 221 A2
Knockhall St G33 ... 99 D1
Knockhill Dr G44 ... 137 B7
Knockhill Rd PA4 ... 94 B1
KNOCKINLAW ... 222 F4
Knockinlaw Mount KA3 ... 222 F4
Knockinlaw Rd KA3 ... 222 F4
Knock Jargon Ct KA21 ... 205 E3
Knockland Hill KA3 ... 222 A7
Knockmarloch Dr KA1 ... 227 F3
Knockmilly Pl 7 G69 ... 81 A3
Knocknair St PA14 ... 68 E8
Knockrivoch Gdns KA22 ... 205 E4
Knockrivoch Pl KA22 ... 205 E4
Knockrivoch Wynd KA22 ... 205 E4
Knockside Ave PA2 ... 133 D7
Knock Way PA3 ... 114 A7
Knoll Croft Rd ML7 ... 147 A3
Knollpark Dr G76 ... 157 D6
Knoll Pk KA7 ... 238 F3
Knowe Cres ML1 ... 143 D4
Knowehead Dr G71 ... 140 E6
Knowehead Gdns
2 Glasgow G41 ... 116 E3
Uddingston G71 ... 140 E6
Knowehead Rd
Clachan of Campsie G66 ... 32 F4
Hurlford KA1 ... 228 F5
Kilmarnock KA1 ... 227 F4
Wishaw ML2 ... 165 C2
Knowehead Terr 1 G41 ... 116 E3
Knoweholm KA7 ... 238 C2
Knowenoble St ML1 ... 144 B2
Knowe Rd
Chryston G69 ... 100 C8
Greenock PA15 ... 46 B4
Paisley PA3 ... 114 B7
Knowes Ave G77 ... 156 E5
Knowes Rd G77 ... 156 F5
Knowe St G62 ... 54 F2
Knowes View G81 ... 74 C7
Knowetap St G20 ... 96 E7
Knowe The
Alloa FK10 ... 5 C2
Troon KA10 ... 229 G7
Knowetop Ave ML1 ... 163 F4
Knowetop Cres G82 ... 49 C5
Knowetop Prim Sch ML1 ... 163 F4
Knowfaulds Rd FK10 ... 4 B3
Knox Ave PA11 ... 110 C7
Knoxland Prim Sch G82 ... 50 A3
Knoxland Sq G82 ... 50 A2
Knoxland St G82 ... 50 A2
Knox Pl
Newton Mearns G77 ... 156 B4
Saltcoats KA21 ... 206 A2
Knox St
Airdrie ML6 ... 123 B8
Paisley PA1 ... 113 C4
Knoxville Rd KA25 ... 149 B1
Kronborg Way G75 ... 180 E5
Kyle Acad KA7 ... 239 D7
Kyleaken Dr G72 ... 140 B2
Kyleakin Rd G46 ... 135 D3
Kyleakin Terr G46 ... 135 D3
Kyle Ave
Cowie FK7 ... 12 E7
Kyle Ave *continued*
Springside KA11 ... 220 F2
Kyle Cres KA10 ... 230 A4
Kyle Ct
Ayr KA7 ... 239 A7
Cambuslang G72 ... 139 A6
Kyle Ctr KA7 ... 238 F8
Kyle Dr
Glasgow G46 ... 136 E3
Troon KA10 ... 229 E5
Kyle Gr ML1 ... 143 A3
Kylemore Cres ML1 ... 142 D2
Kylemore La PA16 ... 44 E3
Kylemore Terr PA16 ... 44 E3
KYLEPARK ... 140 D7
Kylepark Ave G71 ... 140 D6
Kylepark Cres G71 ... 140 D7
Kylepark Dr G71 ... 140 D7
Kyle Pl ML5 ... 121 F5
Kyle Quadrant
Motherwell ML1 ... 143 C3
Wishaw ML2 ... 164 E1
Kyle Rd
Cumbernauld G67 ... 62 B3
Irvine KA12 ... 224 D7
Kylerhea Rd G46 ... 135 D3
Kyleshill KA21 ... 216 F7
Kyle Sq G73 ... 137 F5
Kyle St
Ayr KA7 ... 238 F8
Glasgow G4 ... 241 A4
Motherwell ML1 ... 163 B7
Prestwick KA9 ... 236 C8
Kyleswell St KA13 ... 207 E3
Kyle Terr G82 ... 49 B5

L

La Belle Allee 3 G3 ... 96 E1
La Belle Pl 2 G3 ... 96 E1
Laberge Gdns
Flemington ML1 ... 164 B5
New Stevenston ML1 ... 143 B3
Laburnum Ave
Beith KA15 ... 171 A8
Cambuslang G72 ... 139 F3
East Kilbride G75 ... 180 C6
Laburnum Cres ML2 ... 165 B5
Laburnum Ct G75 ... 180 C6
Laburnum Dr G66 ... 58 B5
Laburnum Gdns G66 ... 79 B5
Laburnum Gr
Coatbridge ML5 ... 122 B6
Kirkintilloch G66 ... 79 B5
Stirling FK8 ... 6 F5
Troon KA10 ... 229 E4
Laburnum Lea ML3 ... 162 E2
Laburnum Pl PA5 ... 132 A8
Laburnum Rd
Ayr KA7 ... 239 C6
Banknock FK4 ... 38 E2
Cumbernauld G67 ... 62 D2
Glasgow G41 ... 116 C4
Kilmarnock KA1 ... 227 C7
Uddingston G71 ... 141 D8
Laburnum St PA15 ... 46 F2
Lachlan Cres PA8 ... 72 E1
La Crosse Terr G12 ... 96 E3
Lacy St PA1 ... 114 A4
Ladder Ct G75 ... 180 B4
Lade Ct PA12 ... 129 C2
Lade Dr FK5 ... 41 C8
Lade Mill FK7 ... 7 C1
Lade Rd FK4 ... 40 A5
Ladeside KA3 ... 222 C8
Ladeside Cl G77 ... 156 C6
Ladeside Cres FK5 ... 23 E1
Ladeside Ct KA25 ... 170 A8
Ladeside Dr
Johnstone PA5 ... 111 D2
Kilsyth G65 ... 36 E1
Ladeside Gdns KA3 ... 222 C7
Ladeside Prim Sch FK5 ... 41 C8
Ladeside Rd KA3 ... 222 C7
Lade Terr G52 ... 115 A4
Lade The G83 ... 27 F6
Ladhope Pl G13 ... 94 E8
Ladyacre KA13 ... 207 E4
Ladyacre Rd ML11 ... 215 B3
Ladyacres PA4 ... 93 D6
Ladyacres Way PA4 ... 93 D6
Lady Alice Prim Sch PA16 ... 45 C4
Lady Ann Cres ML6 ... 123 C6
Lady Anne St G14 ... 94 F6
Ladybank G68 ... 61 F6
Ladybank Ct G74 ... 159 E2
Ladybank Dr G52 ... 115 E4
Ladybank Gdns G74 ... 159 F2
Ladybank Pl 2 G74 ... 159 F2
LADYBURN ... 46 E3
Ladyburn Ct KA11 ... 219 F6
Ladyburn St
Greenock PA15 ... 46 D3
Greenock PA15 ... 46 E3
Paisley PA1 ... 114 A4
Ladyford Ave KA13 ... 207 E3
Ladyha Ct KA11 ... 220 B5
Ladyhill Dr G69 ... 120 A4
Lady Isle Cres G71 ... 140 E6
Lady Jane Gate G71 ... 140 E4
Ladykirk Cres
Glasgow G52 ... 115 B6
Paisley PA2 ... 113 F3
Ladykirk Dr G52 ... 115 C6
Ladykirk Rd KA9 ... 236 C8
Ladykirk Way G74 ... 159 F4
Lady La PA1 ... 113 D4
Ladyland Dr KA25 ... 149 B3
Ladyloan Ave G15 ... 74 F4
Ladyloan Ct G15 ... 74 E4
Ladyloan Gdns G15 ... 74 F4
Ladyloan Gr G15 ... 74 F4
Ladyloan Pl G15 ... 74 E4
Lady Margaret Dr KA10 ... 230 A2
Lady Mary Wlk ML3 ... 162 E1
Ladymuir Circ PA8 ... 72 F1
Ladymuir Cres G53 ... 115 C2
Lady Octavia Recn Ctr PA15 ... 46 C2
Lady's Gate G83 ... 27 F1
Ladysgate Ct FK2 ... 24 B3
Ladysmill FK2 ... 42 D5
Ladysmill Ind Est FK1 ... 42 C5
Ladysmith Ave PA10 ... 111 C2
Ladysmith Dr G75 ... 180 A4
Ladysmith Rd KA25 ... 149 A1
Ladysmith St ML2 ... 164 D4
Ladysneuk Rd FK9 ... 2 D2
Ladyton G83 ... 27 F3
Ladyton Prim Sch G83 ... 28 A3
Ladyton Sh Ctr G83 ... 28 A3
Lady Watson Gdns ML3 ... 162 A2
Lady Well ML11 ... 214 B6
Ladywell Ct FK5 ... 23 A3
Ladywell Dr FK10 ... 4 B3
Ladywell Pl FK10 ... 4 B3
Ladywell Prim Sch ML1 ... 163 D7
Ladywell Rd ML1 ... 163 C7
Ladywell St G4 ... 241 C2
Lady Wilson St ML6 ... 123 B7
Ladywood G62 ... 55 B2
Lafferty Pl FK6 ... 21 F1
Lagan Rd ML8 ... 188 A1
Laggan Ave ML7 ... 147 B3
Laggan Ho KA9 ... 236 B5
Laggan Path ML7 ... 146 E6
Laggan Quadrant ML6 ... 102 F1
Laggan Rd
Airdrie ML6 ... 102 F1
Bishopbriggs G64 ... 78 B1
Glasgow G43 ... 136 E5
Newton Mearns G77 ... 156 D7
Laggan Terr PA4 ... 94 B4
Laggan Way ML2 ... 165 F7
Laggary Pk G84 ... 15 E5
Laggary Rd G84 ... 15 E5
Lagoon L Ctr PA1 ... 113 F4
Lagos La G73 ... 138 C2
Laidlaw Ave ML1 ... 142 F3
Laidlaw Gdns G71 ... 120 F1
Laidlaw St G5 ... 240 B1
Laidon Rd ML6 ... 102 F1
Laidon Wlk 3 ML2 ... 165 F6
Laighcartside St PA5 ... 112 A3
Laigh Ct KA15 ... 150 B1
Laighdykes Rd KA21 ... 205 E1
LAIGH FENWICK ... 213 A2
LAIGH GLENGALL ... 239 B2
Laighland KA9 ... 236 C5
Laighlands Rd G71 ... 141 B2
Laigh Milton Viaduct* KA2 ... 226 C6
Laigh Mount KA7 ... 238 F1
Laighmuir St G71 ... 140 F5
LAIGH PARK ... 113 F7
Laighpark Ave PA7 ... 72 B3
Laighpark View PA3 ... 113 E7
Laigh Rd
Beith KA15 ... 150 B1
Newton Mearns G77 ... 157 C5
LAIGHSTONEHALL ... 162 C2
Laighstonehall Rd ML3 ... 162 B2
Laightoun Ct G67 ... 82 A6
Laightoun Dr G67 ... 82 A6
Laightoun Gdns G67 ... 82 A6
Lainshaw KA13 ... 207 C2
Lainshaw Ave KA1 ... 227 E4
Lainshaw Dr G45 ... 137 B2
Lainshaw Prim Sch KA3 ... 211 D8
Lainshaw St KA3 ... 211 D8
Laird Gr G71 ... 141 A8
Laird Pl G40 ... 117 F4
Lairds Gate G71 ... 140 D5
Lairds Hill G67 ... 61 E2
Laird's Hill Ct G65 ... 60 B8
Laird's Hill Pl G65 ... 60 A8
Lairdsland Prim Sch 5 G66 ... 79 C8
Laird St
Coatbridge ML5 ... 122 B7
Greenock PA15 ... 45 F6
Laird Weir KA22 ... 205 D3
Lairg Dr G72 ... 140 C2
Lairhills Rd G75 ... 180 F7
Lairox Terr FK6 ... 21 D3
Lake Ave ML11 ... 215 D2
Lamberton Ave FK7 ... 7 C3
Lamberton Dr G52 ... 115 C5
Lamberton Gdns KA11 ... 220 C5
Lamberton Rd KA3 ... 195 D1
Lambert Terr FK10 ... 10 C7
LAMBHILL ... 97 A7
Lambhill Quadrant 2 G41 ... 116 E5
Lambhill St G41 ... 116 D5
Lambie Cres G77 ... 156 C5
Lambie Ct KA21 ... 216 E8
Lamb St
Glasgow G22 ... 97 B6
Hamilton ML3 ... 162 E3
Lamerton Rd G67 ... 62 C2
Lamford Dr KA7 ... 238 C1
Lamington Rd G52 ... 115 B5
Lamlash Cres G33 ... 119 B8
Lamlash Pl
East Kilbride G75 ... 180 B4
Glasgow G33 ... 119 B8
Helensburgh G84 ... 16 F2
Motherwell ML1 ... 163 C7
Lamlash Sq G33 ... 119 C8
Lammerknowes Rd G65 ... 37 E3
Lammermoor G74 ... 160 E4
Lammermoor Ave G52 ... 115 C4
Lammermoor Cres G66 ... 79 F8
Lammermoor Dr G67 ... 82 E7
Lammermoor Gdns G66 ... 79 F8
Lammermoor Prim Sch ML2 ... 165 B5
Lammermoor Rd G66 ... 79 F8
Lammermoor Terr ML2 ... 165 B3
Lammermuir Ct
Irvine KA11 ... 220 A3
Paisley PA2 ... 133 E8
Lammermuir Dr PA2 ... 133 E8
Lammermuir Gdns G61 ... 75 C7
Lammermuir Pl ML1 ... 143 A5
Lammermuir Rd KA1 ... 228 A3
Lammermuir Way ML6 ... 123 F1
Lammermuir Wynd ML9 ... 184 F5
Lammer Wynd 7 ML9 ... 185 C1
Lamond View FK5 ... 23 D1
Lamont Ave PA7 ... 72 C3
Lamont Cres
Fallin FK7 ... 8 D5
Renton G82 ... 27 D2
Lamont Dr KA12 ... 224 E8
Lamont Pl KA12 ... 224 E8
Lamont Rd G21 ... 98 B6
LANARK ... 215 C3
Lanark Ave ML6 ... 123 A4
Lanark Gram Sch ML11 ... 215 B3
Lanark Ind Est ML11 ... 215 E5
Lanark Mus* ML11 ... 214 F4
Lanark Prim Sch ML11 ... 215 B5
Lanark Rd
Ashgill ML9 ... 186 A3
Braidwood ML8, ML11 ... 202 B3
Carluke ML8 ... 187 F1
Crossford ML8 ... 201 A2
Kirkfieldbank ML11 ... 214 A4
Lanark ML11 ... 214 D6
Larkhall ML2, ML9 ... 185 D6
Netherburn ML8 ... 200 D7
Lanark St G1 ... 241 B1
Lanark Sta ML11 ... 215 B4
Lancaster Ave
Beith KA15 ... 171 B7
Chapelhall ML1 ... 143 E8
Lancaster Cres G12 ... 96 C4
Lancaster Crescent La G12 ... 96 C4
Lancaster Rd G64 ... 78 B4
Lancaster Terr 11 G12 ... 96 C4
Lancaster Terrace La 10 G12 ... 96 C4
Lancaster Way 4 PA4 ... 94 C1
Lancefield Quay G3 ... 116 E7
Lancefield St G3 ... 240 A2
Landemer Dr G73 ... 138 A6
Landemer Gait G73 ... 138 A6
Landressy Pl G40 ... 117 F4
Landressy St G40 ... 117 F4
Landsborough Ct KA21 ... 205 E2
Landsborough Dr KA3 ... 223 A3
Landsborough Pl KA20 ... 206 F2
Landsdowne Gdns ML3 ... 162 F3
Landsdowne Rd ML9 ... 185 C2
Lane The G68 ... 61 D6
Lanfine Rd PA1 ... 114 C4
Lanfine Row KA11 ... 220 A6
Lanfine Terr KA11 ... 219 F6
Lanfine Way KA11 ... 220 A6
Langa St G20 ... 96 F7
Lang Ave
Bishopton PA7 ... 72 C3
Renfrew PA4 ... 94 D1
LANGBANK ... 70 B7
Langbank Dr PA13 ... 69 E1
Langbank Holdings G62 ... 76 E8
Langbank Prim Sch PA14 ... 70 B7
Langbank Rise PA13 ... 69 E1
Langbank St 1 G5 ... 117 B5
Langbank Sta PA14 ... 70 D7
Langbar Cres G33 ... 119 E7
Langbar Gdns G33 ... 119 F7
Langbyres Rd ML1 ... 144 D1
Langcraig Rd KA1 ... 227 F2
Langcraigs Ct PA2 ... 133 C8
Langcraigs Dr PA2 ... 133 D6
Langcraigs Prim Sch PA2 ... 133 C7
Langcraigs Terr PA2 ... 133 C6
Langcroft Ave KA9 ... 233 E1
Langcroft Dr G72 ... 139 C4
Langcroft Pl G51 ... 115 C7
Langcroft Rd G51 ... 115 D7
Langcroft Terr G51 ... 115 D7
Langdale
East Kilbride G74 ... 159 C3
Newton Mearns G77 ... 157 B5
Langdale Ave G33 ... 98 E3
Langdale Rd G69 ... 80 F2
Langdales Ave G68 ... 61 D2
Langdale St G33 ... 98 E3
Langfaulds Cres G81 ... 74 D6
Langfaulds Prim Sch G15 ... 74 F4
Langford Dr G53 ... 135 B3
Langford Pl G53 ... 135 B3
Langhaul Ave G53 ... 114 F1
Langhaul Ct G53 ... 114 F1
Langhaul Pl G53 ... 114 F1
Langhaul Rd G53 ... 114 F1
Langhill Dr G68 ... 61 D3
Langhill Pl FK6 ... 21 C1
Langholm G75 ... 179 F6
Langholm Cres ML2 ... 165 B6
Langholm Ct
6 Greenock PA15 ... 46 B3
Moodiesburn G69 ... 81 A2
Langholm Dr PA3 ... 112 C5
Langholm Path 1 G72 ... 161 C7
Langlands Ave
East Kilbride G75 ... 180 F4
Glasgow G51 ... 115 D7
Langlands Brae 8 KA1 ... 222 F1
Langlands Ct
East Kilbride G75 ... 180 F4
Glasgow G51 ... 115 F8
Langlands Dr
East Kilbride G75 ... 180 F4
Glasgow G51 ... 115 C8
Langlands Gate G75 ... 180 F3
Langlands Moss Nature Reserve* G75 ... 181 C5
Langlands Pl G75 ... 180 F4
Langlands Rd
East Kilbride G75 ... 180 E3
Glasgow G51 ... 115 E8
Glasgow G51 ... 116 A8
Langlands-Seafar Intc G67 ... 82 E8
Langlands Sq G75 ... 180 F3
Langlands St KA1 ... 222 F1
Langlands Terr G82 ... 50 B6
Langlea Ave G72 ... 138 D4
Langlea Ct G72 ... 138 E4
Langlea Dr G72 ... 138 E5
Langlea Gdns G72 ... 138 E5
Langlea Gr G72 ... 138 E4
Langlea Rd G72, G73 ... 138 E4
Langlea Way G72 ... 138 E5
LANGLEES ... 24 D1
Langlees Ave G77 ... 157 B5
Langlees Prim Sch FK2 ... 42 B8
Langlees St FK2 ... 24 C1
Langley Ave G13 ... 95 B8
LANGLOAN ... 121 E5
Langloan Cres ML5 ... 121 E6
Langloan Pl ML5 ... 121 E6
Langloan Prim Sch ML5 ... 121 E6
Langloan St ML5 ... 121 E6
Langlook Pl G53 ... 134 F8
Langlook Rd G53 ... 114 F1
LANGMUIR ... 59 B1
Langmuir Ave
Kirkintilloch G66 ... 58 E1
Perceton KA11 ... 220 C5
Langmuir Ct KA11 ... 220 C5
Langmuirhead Rd G66 ... 79 D1
Langmuir Rd
Coatbridge G69 ... 121 A5
Kirkintilloch G66 ... 59 B1
Langmuir Way G69 ... 121 A5
Langness Rd G33 ... 119 B8
Langoreth Ave ML3 ... 161 F2
Lang Pl PA5 ... 111 F3
Lang Rd KA10 ... 229 F7
Langrig Rd
Glasgow G21 ... 98 A4
Newton Mearns G77 ... 156 D3
Langs Gr G20 ... 96 E7
Langshaw Cres ML8 ... 187 F2
Langshaw Ct KA3 ... 195 C1
Langshot St 2 G51 ... 116 D5
LANGSIDE ... 136 E8
Langside G81 ... 74 E6
Langside Ave
Glasgow G41 ... 136 F8
Kilmarnock KA1 ... 227 F3
Uddingston G71 ... 141 C6
Langside Coll (Glenwood Campus) G45 ... 137 F3
Langside Coll (Govanhill Campus) G42 ... 117 B3
Langside Coll (Langside Campus) G42 ... 137 A8
Langside Coll (Rutherglen Campus) G73 ... 138 B6
Langside Coll (Toryglen Campus) G42 ... 137 D8
Langside Ct G71 ... 141 B1
Langside Dr
Blackridge EH48 ... 107 B3
Glasgow G43 ... 136 E5
Kilbarchan PA10 ... 111 A2
Langside Gdns G42 ... 137 A7
Langside La G42 ... 117 A1
Langside Pk PA10 ... 111 A2
Langside Pl
Glasgow G41 ... 136 F8
Kilbirnie KA25 ... 149 A1
Langside Prim Sch G41 ... 136 E8
Langside Rd
Bothwell G71 ... 141 B1
Glasgow, Govanhill G42 ... 117 A2
Glasgow, Langside G42 ... 137 A8
Langside Sta G43 ... 136 E6
Langside Terr PA14 ... 68 D8
Lang St PA1 ... 114 A4
Langstile Pl G52 ... 114 F5
Langstile Rd G52 ... 114 F5
Langton Cres
Barrhead G78 ... 134 D1
Glasgow G53 ... 115 C1
Langton Gate G77 ... 156 C5
Langton Gdns G69 ... 119 F4
Langton Pl G77 ... 156 C5
Langton Rd G53 ... 115 C1
Langtree Ave G46 ... 136 A1
Lanrig Pl G69 ... 100 C8

Lanrig Rd G69 100 C8
Lansbury Gdns PA3 113 D7
Lansbury St
  Alexandria G83 27 E7
  Greenock PA15 46 F2
Lansbury Terr ML9 185 C1
Lansdowne Cres
  Glasgow G20 96 F2
  Shotts ML7 147 B3
Lansdowne Crescent La
  G20 96 F2
Lansdowne Dr G68 61 F4
Lansdowne Rd KA8 236 A3
Lantana Gr [1] ML1 163 D8
Lanton Dr G52 115 B5
Lanton Path ML6 123 E1
Lanton Rd G43 136 E5
Lappin St G81 94 D8
Lapsley Ave PA2 113 E1
Laputa Pl KA1 227 E3
Lapwing Rd PA4 94 E4
LARBERT 23 B2
Larbert High Sch FK5 23 E1
Larbert Rd FK4 40 B6
Larbert St G4 240 C4
Larbert Sta FK5 23 C2
Larbert Village Prim Sch
  FK5 23 B1
Larch Ave
  Bishopbriggs G64 98 B8
  Kirkintilloch G66 79 C6
Larch Cl [1] G72 139 E3
Larch Cres G66 79 C6
Larch Ct
  Cambuslang G72 139 F3
  Cumbernauld G67 62 E4
  East Kilbride G75 180 B5
  Hamilton G72 161 C8
Larch Dr
  Banknock FK4 38 E2
  East Kilbride G75 180 B5
Larches The G69 81 A4
Larchfield G84 16 D2
Larchfield Ave
  Glasgow G14 95 B4
  Newton Mearns G77 156 E5
  Wishaw ML2 165 D6
Larchfield Cres ML2 165 C6
Larchfield Ct G77 156 D4
Larchfield Dr G73 138 C4
Larchfield Gdns ML2 165 D6
Larchfield Gr ML2 165 D7
Larchfield Path ML7 147 B2
Larchfield Pl
  Glasgow G14 95 B4
  Wishaw ML2 165 D6
Larchfield Rd G61 75 F1
Larch Gait G72 139 F3
Larch Gr
  Cumbernauld G67 62 E4
  Hamilton ML3 162 F2
  Milton of Campsie G66 58 B5
  Motherwell ML1 143 A5
  Stenhousemuir FK5 23 F3
Larchgrove Ave G32 119 C6
Larchgrove Pl G32 119 C7
Larchgrove Rd G32 119 C7
Larch Ho KA9 236 C6
Larch Pl
  [2] Cambuslang G72 139 E3
  Cumbernauld G67 62 D4
  East Kilbride G75 180 B5
  Johnstone PA5 132 A8
  Kilmarnock KA1 227 D8
  Uddingston G71 141 D8
Larch Rd
  Cumbernauld G67 62 E4
  Glasgow G41 116 B4
Larch Sq [3] G72 139 E3
Larch Terr KA15 171 C8
Larch Way ML3 183 F4
Larchwood Rd KA7 239 C4
Larchwood Terr G78 155 D8
Larghill La KA7 239 B5
Largie Rd G43 136 F5
Largo La G72 161 D3
Largo Pl G51 115 E7
Largs Ave KA3 223 B3
Largs Rd KA25 148 D1
LARKFIELD 44 D4
Larkfield Ct G72 161 C6
Larkfield Dr G72 161 D6
Larkfield Gr PA16 44 F4
Larkfield Ind Est PA16 44 C5
Larkfield Rd
  Gourock PA19 44 E6
  Greenock PA16, PA19 44 F4
  Kirkintilloch G66 79 E6
Larkfield St [2] G42 117 B3
LARKHALL 185 B3
Larkhall Acad ML9 184 F1
Larkhall L Ctr ML9 185 A2
Larkhall Sta
  Larkhall ML9 185 A3
  Maryhill G20 96 E5
Larkhill Ind Est ML9 199 B8
Larkin Gdns PA3 113 D7
Larkin Way ML4 141 F7
Larksfield Dr ML8 202 A8
Larkspur Dr G74 159 C4
Larkspur Way ML8 201 F8
Lark Way ML4 141 F8
Lashley Gr ML2 186 C7
Lasswade St G14 94 E6
Latherton Dr [5] G20 96 D5
Latimer Gdns G52 115 A4
Latimer Path [8] G52 115 A4
Latta Ct KA9 236 D6
Latta St G82 50 A4
Lauchlan Way KA13 207 E3
Lauchlin Pl G66 80 B7
Lauchope Rd ML6 143 D7
Lauchope St ML6 123 E2
Lauder Cres ML2 165 B6
Lauder Ct KA3 223 C3
Lauderdale Dr G77 156 C3
Lauderdale Gdns G12 96 B3
Lauderdale La G12 96 B3
Lauder Dr
  Linwood PA3 112 B5
  Rutherglen G73 138 D6
Lauder Gdns
  Blantyre G72 140 C2
  Coatbridge ML5 122 D3
Lauder Gn G74 160 B4
Lauder La ML3 161 E3
Lauder St [4] G5 117 A4
Laudervale Gdns G83 27 D8
Laughland Dr ML1 143 D3
Laughlanglen Rd KA7 239 A3
Laundry La G33 99 C5
Lauranne Pl ML4 141 E5
Laurel Ave
  Clydebank G81 73 D4
  Kirkintilloch G66 79 D6
Laurelbank ML5 122 A8
Laurel Bank
  Ayr KA7 239 C4
  Hamilton ML3 183 C8
Laurelbank Ave FK4 40 A3
Laurelbank Rd
  Glasgow G32 139 C8
  Muirhead G69 100 B7
Laurel Ct
  Cambuslang G72 139 E4
  Denny FK6 21 D3
  East Kilbride G75 180 D5
  Falkirk FK1 41 C6
Laurel Dr
  East Kilbride G75 180 D5
  Larkhall ML9 185 D2
  Wishaw ML2 164 E3
Laurel Gait G72 139 E3
Laurel Gdns
  Chapelhall ML6 123 E2
  Uddingston G71 140 F8
Laurel Gr
  Bonnybridge FK4 39 F3
  Greengairs ML6 83 F2
Laurelhill Bsns Pk FK7 6 F6
Laurelhill Bsns Pk FK8 7 A6
Laurelhill Gdns FK8 6 F5
Laurelhill Pl FK8 7 A5
Laurel La
  Cambuslang G72 139 E3
  [5] Larkhall ML9 185 C1
Laurel Park Cl G13 95 C5
Laurel Park Gdns G13 95 C5
Laurel Pl
  Bonnybridge FK4 39 F3
  East Kilbride G75 180 D5
  Glasgow G11 96 A2
  Kilmarnock KA1 227 D7
Laurel Sq FK4 38 E2
Laurel St G11 96 A2
Laurels The
  [6] Motherwell ML1 143 B2
  Newton Mearns G77 156 D5
  Tullibody FK10 4 B1
Laurel Way
  Barrhead G78 134 B3
  Quarriers Village PA11 89 F1
Laurel Wlk G73 138 C3
Laurel Wynd G72 139 F3
Laurencecroft Rd FK8 2 B2
Laurence Ct G15 74 E3
Laurence Dr
  Bearsden G61 75 D6
  Clydebank G15 74 E3
Laurence Gdns G15 74 E3
Laurenstone Terr G74 160 B3
Lauren View ML6 122 F7
Lauren Way PA2 113 A1
Laurie Ct G71 141 A7
Laurieland Ave KA2 221 E1
LAURIESTON
  Falkirk 42 F4
  Glasgow 117 B5
Laurieston Cres ML6 123 D1
Laurieston Ct KA2 225 F1
Lauriestone Pl ML5 122 D3
Laurieston Ind Est FK2 42 F3
Laurieston Rd G5 117 C5
Laurieston Way G73 138 A4
Lauriston Ct KA22 205 D1
Lauriston Gr G77 156 B5
Lauriston Way KA3 223 B6
Lavelle Dr ML5 122 C7
Lavender Ct G71 141 C7
Lavender Dr G75 180 D5
Lavender La ML8 201 E8
Laverock Ave
  Greenock PA15 45 D3
  Hamilton ML3 163 A2
Laverockhall ML11 215 B5
Laverockhall St G21 97 F3
Laverock Rd ML6 103 B3
Laverock Terr G69 80 F1
Lavery Ave FK5 23 B1
LAW 186 F5
Law Brae KA23 190 D5
Law Dr ML1 143 C4
Lawers Cres KA1 228 A4
Lawers Dr G61 75 C7
Lawers La ML1 143 C3
Lawers Pl
  Greenock PA16 45 A4
  Irvine KA11 220 A4
Lawers Rd
  Glasgow G43 136 B5
  Kilmarnock KA1 228 A4
  Renfrew PA4 94 C1
Lawfield Ave
  Newton Mearns G77 157 B5
  West Kilbride KA23 190 E4
LAW HILL 187 A4
Lawhill Ave G45 137 D4
Lawhill Rd ML8 187 B3
Lawhope Mill Rd ML6 123 F3
Lawmarnock Cres PA11 110 C7
Lawmarnock Ho PA11 110 C7
Lawmarnock Rd PA11 110 C7
Lawmoor Rd G5 117 C3
Lawmoor St G5 117 C3
Lawmuir Cres G81 74 E7
Lawmuir Pl ML4 142 A2
Lawmuir Prim Sch ML4 142 A3
Lawmuir Rd
  Bellshill ML4 142 A3
  Law ML8 186 F6
Lawn Pk G62 55 C1
Lawn St PA1 113 F5
Law Pl
  Denny FK6 21 E1
  East Kilbride G74 159 F5
Law Prim Sch ML8 187 A5
Law Rdbt G74 159 E4
Lawrence Ave
  Glasgow G46 136 D1
  Helensburgh G84 25 C7
Lawrence Ct FK5 23 B5
Lawrence Dr G83 19 F1
Lawrence St G11 96 C2
Lawrie Pl ML1 143 E1
Lawrie St
  Glasgow G11 96 B2
  Stonehouse ML9 198 E3
  Wishaw ML2 165 F5
Lawrie Way [11] ML9 185 C1
Lawson Ave ML1 163 E3
Lawson Dr KA22 205 D4
Lawson St
  Ayr KA8 236 B2
  Kilmarnock KA1 228 A7
Law St G40 118 B5
Lawswell FK10 5 E3
LAWTHORN 220 C6
Lawthorn Prim Sch
  KA11 220 A6
Lawthorn Rd KA11 220 B6
Lawthorn Rdbt KA11 220 B6
Law View ML2 186 C6
Laxdale Dr FK6 39 D7
Laxford Ave G44 137 A4
Laxford Pl ML5 122 D5
Laxford Rd PA8 72 E1
Laxford Way ML1 143 C4
Laxton Dr G66 79 E4
Laymoor Ave PA4 94 F3
Lea Ave G78 154 D7
Leabank Ave PA2 133 E8
Leadburn Rd G21 98 C4
Leadburn St G32, G33 118 E7
Leader St G33 98 D1
Leadhills Rd KA1 228 A3
Leaend Rd ML6 102 E1
Leander Cres
  Bellshill ML4 142 E5
  Renfrew PA4 94 E2
Leapark Dr FK4 39 F3
Learigg Rd ML6 104 B3
Learmonth St FK1 42 B4
Learmont Pl G62 54 F2
Leathem Pl ML2 164 C1
Leathen Pl PA8 72 E1
Lec Ct FK2 42 F4
Leckethill Ave G68 81 F7
Leckethill Ct G68 81 F7
Leckethill Pl G68 81 F7
Leckethill View G68 81 F7
Leckie Ct ML3 162 C4
Leckie Dr ML3 162 C4
Leckie Pl G83 27 E6
Leckie St G41 136 C8
Lecropt Sch (Barnardo's)
  FK1 41 C6
Ledaig Pl G31 118 C7
Ledaig St G31 118 C7
Ledard Rd G42 137 A7
Ledcameroch Cres G61 75 E4
Ledcameroch Pk G61 75 D4
Ledcameroch Rd G61 75 E4
Ledgate G66 58 D1
Ledgowan Pl G20 96 D8
Ledi Ave FK10 4 B2
Ledi Dr G61 75 B7
Ledi Path ML1 143 C3
Ledi Pl FK1 66 E7
Ledi Rd G43 136 C5
Ledi View FK9 2 B3
Ledmore Dr G15 74 F4
Ledmore Pl FK1 42 E1
Lednock Rd
  Glasgow G52 115 A5
  Stepps G33 99 C5
Ledrish Ave G83 19 F2
Ledvinka Cres ML3 162 A6
Lee Ave G33 98 E1
Leebank Dr G44 136 F2
Leeburn Ave PA6 91 C1
Leeburn Gdns PA6 91 C1
Leechford ML11 215 B5
Leechlee Rd ML3 162 E3
Lee Cres G64 98 A8
Leefield Dr G44 136 F2
Leehill Rd G21 97 E7
Lee Meadow Rd ML8 202 A4
Leemuir View ML8 202 B8
Lee Pl ML4 142 D4
Lees Burn Ct G74 160 A5
Leesburn Pl G74 159 F4
Lee's Ct ML5 122 A5
Leeside Rd G21 97 E7
Leesland G71 141 A8
Leeward Circ G75 159 A1
Leeward Pk KA7 239 A1
Leewood Dr G44 137 A2
Le Froy Gdns G75 180 C8
Le Froy La G75 180 C8
Lefroy St ML5 121 E7
Legbrannock Ave ML1 143 D7
Legbrannock Cres ML1 143 D4
Legbrannock Rd ML1 143 E5
Leggate Way ML4 142 A8
Leggatson Dr G53 135 C3
Legion Pl ML9 185 A3
Leglen Wood Cres G33 98 D6
Leglen Wood Dr G21 98 D5
Leglen Wood Gdns G21 98 D6
Leglen Wood Pl G21 98 E6
Leglen Wood Rd G21 98 D6
Leicester Ave G12 96 B5
Leighton St
  Glasgow G20 96 F6
  Wishaw ML2 165 B2
Leishman Ct EH48 107 D2
Leishman Pl ML6 103 D1
Leishman Twr FK1 42 C4
Leisuredrome G64 77 E3
Leisure Way ML9 185 A2
Leitchland Rd PA2 132 D8
Leitch St PA15 46 E3
Leith Ave ML9 198 F2
Leithland Ave [2] G53 115 B1
Leithland Rd G53 115 B1
Leith Pl FK6 39 D7
Leith St G33 118 D8
Leman Dr PA6 111 D8
Leman Gr PA6 111 D8
Lembert Dr G76 157 D8
Lemmon St PA15 45 D4
Lendale La G64 78 A4
Lendalfoot Gdns ML3 161 D2
Lendal Pl G75 179 E6
Lendel Pl G51 116 D5
Lendrick Ave FK1 41 F2
Lenihall Dr G45 137 E2
Lenihall Terr G45 137 E2
Lennox Ave
  Bishopton PA7 72 B3
  Coatbridge ML5 121 E7
  Glasgow G14 95 D3
  Milngavie G62 55 A1
  Stirling FK7 7 A4
Lennoxbank Ho [7] G83 27 E8
Lennox Cres
  Bishopbriggs G64 97 F8
  Kilmarnock KA1 222 D1
Lennox Ct [16] G65 60 D8
Lennox Dr
  Bearsden G61 75 F6
  Clydebank G81 74 C7
  Newton Mearns G77 156 E2
  Prestwick KA9 236 C5
Lennox Gdns
  Dumbarton G82 49 A4
  Glasgow G14 95 D4
Lennox Lane E G14 95 D3
Lennox Lane W
  Glasgow G14 95 C3
  Glasgow G14 95 D4
Lennoxmill La G66 57 C8
Lennox Pl G81 73 E3
Lennox Rd
  Cumbernauld G67 61 F2
  Dumbarton G82 50 B3
  Lennoxtown G66 33 C1
  Milton G82 50 F1
Lennox St
  Alexandria G83 27 E5
  Dumbarton G82 50 A3
  Glasgow G20 96 C7
  Renton G82 49 D8
  Wishaw ML2 165 E4
Lennox Terr PA3 114 A8
LENNOXTOWN 57 E8
Lennoxtown Prim Sch
  G66 57 D8
Lennox Wynd KA21 205 F2
Lentran St G34 120 D7
Lenwood Gdns G83 27 F3
Leny Cres FK1 42 A1
Leny St G20 96 F4
LENZIE 79 D5
Lenzie Acad G66 79 C6
LENZIEMILL 83 B8
Lenziemill Rd
  Cumbernauld, Greenfaulds
  G67 82 F7
  Cumbernauld, Lenziemill
  G67 83 B8
Lenzie Moss Nature
  Reserve* G66 79 B4
Lenzie Moss Prim Sch
  G66 79 B5
Lenzie Pl G21 97 F6
Lenzie Prim Sch G66 79 C5
Lenzie Rd
  Kirkintilloch G66 79 D7
  Stepps G33 99 D6
Lenzie St G21 97 F5
Lenzie Sta G66 79 C4
Lenzie Terr G21 97 F5
Lenzie Way G21 97 E6
Leonard Gr ML1 143 E1
Leperstone Ave
  Kilmacolm PA13 69 D2
  Port Glasgow PA14 68 E7
Leperstone Rd PA13 69 D2
Lerwick Pl KA3 223 A6
Lesley Pl KA20 206 E1
Lesley Quadrant ML4 141 F2
Leslie Ave
  Bishopton PA7 72 B3
  Newton Mearns G77 156 E7
Leslie Cres KA7 239 A6
Leslie Pl KA3 223 B2
Leslie Rd
  Glasgow G41 116 E3
  Kilmarnock KA3 223 B2
Leslie St
  Glasgow G41 116 F3
  Motherwell ML1 163 F7
Leslie Terr KA9 236 C8
Lesmahagow Rd ML11 214 A4
Lesmuir Dr G14 95 A5
Lesmuir Pl G14 94 F5
Lestrange Ave FK12 5 B7
LETHAM 24 C8
Letham Cotts FK2 24 D8
Letham Ct G43 136 E5
Letham Dr
  Bishopbriggs G64 98 D8
  Glasgow G43 136 E5
Letham Grange G68 61 F4
Lethamhill Cres G33 98 F1
Lethamhill Pl G33 98 E1
Lethamhill Rd G33 98 F1
Letham Oval G64 98 D8
Letham Terrs FK2 14 C1
Lethbridge Pl [4] G75 180 C8
Lethen View FK10 4 C3
Letherby Dr G44 137 B7
Letheron Dr ML2 165 B5
Lethington Ave G41 136 E8
Lethington Pl G41 136 F8
Lethington Rd G46 157 A7
Letterfearn Rd G23 76 E1
Letterickhills Cres G72 139 E3
LEVAN 43 E5
Levanne Gdns PA19 43 F6
Levanne Pl PA19 43 F6
Levan Point PA19 43 F5
Leven Ave
  Bishopbriggs G64 78 B1
  Helensburgh G84 25 C8
  Kilmarnock KA3 223 A3
Levenbank Gdns G83 27 F7
Levenbank Rd G83 27 F7
Levenbank Terr G83 27 F7
Levencroft Mews G83 27 F3
Leven Ct
  Alloa FK10 10 C5
  Barrhead G78 134 B5
  Dumbarton G82 49 E3
  Hurlford KA1 228 F6
Leven Dr
  Bearsden G61 75 F3
  Hamilton ML3 183 B8
  Hurlford KA1 228 F6
Levenford Terr G82 49 E3
Levengrove Ct G82 49 E3
Levengrove Terr G82 49 E3
Levenhowe Pl G83 27 E7
Levenhowe Rd G83 27 E7
Leven Path ML1 143 A5
Leven Pl
  Erskine PA8 72 E1
  Greenock PA15 46 C1
  Irvine KA12 219 D6
  Shotts ML7 146 E6
Leven Quadrant ML6 102 F2
Leven Rd
  Coatbridge ML5 101 D1
  Greenock PA15 46 C1
  Langbank PA14 70 C7
  Troon KA10 229 G5
Leven Sq PA4 94 B4
Leven St
  Alexandria G83 27 E4
  Dumbarton G82 50 A3
  Falkirk FK2 42 B8
  Glasgow G41 116 F3
  Motherwell ML1 163 E4
  Renton G82 49 D8
Leven Terr ML1 143 C2
LEVENVALE 27 D7
Levenvale Prim Sch G83 27 D7
Leven Valley Ent Ctr G82 49 D4
Leven View G81 74 B3
Leven Way
  [6] Cumbernauld G67 61 F1
  East Kilbride G75 179 F6
  Paisley PA2 112 E1
Leveret Lea KA3 228 D8
Levern Bridge Ct G53 134 F7
Levern Bridge Gr G53 134 F6
Levern Bridge Pl G53 134 F6
Levern Bridge Rd G53 134 F6
Levern Bridge Way G53 134 F6
Levern Cres G78 134 B1
Leverndale Ct G53 114 F1
Leverndale Hospl G53 114 F2
Leverndale Rd G53 114 F1
Levern Gdns G78 134 B3
Levern Grove Ct G53 134 F6

Levern Rd G53 134 E6
LEVERNSIDE 134 A4
Levernside Ave
Barrhead G78 134 A2
Glasgow G53 135 C8
Levernside Cres G53 135 C8
Levernside Rd G53 135 C8
Lever Rd G84 16 F3
Lewis Ave
Renfrew PA4 94 D1
Wishaw ML2 165 E5
Lewis Cres
Irvine KA11 220 A2
Johnstone PA10 111 C2
Old Kilpatrick G60 73 C5
Lewis Ct
Alloa FK10 10 B5
Falkirk FK1 42 B2
Irvine KA11 220 A2
Lewis Dr
Kilmarnock KA3 223 B5
Old Kilpatrick G60 73 B5
Lewis Gdns
Bearsden G61 75 B6
Old Kilpatrick G60 73 C5
Lewis Gr G60 73 C5
Lewis Pl
Airdrie ML6 123 D6
Newton Mearns G77 156 B6
Old Kilpatrick G60 73 C5
Lewis Rd
Greenock PA16 45 C4
Port Glasgow PA14 69 B7
Lewis Rise KA11 220 A2
Lewis Terr KA11 220 A2
Lewiston Dr 5 G23 76 D1
Lewiston Pl 6 G23 76 D1
Lewiston Rd G23 76 D1
Lewis Wynd KA11 220 A2
Lexwell Ave PA5 112 D3
Leyden Ct G20 96 E5
Leyden Gdns G20 96 F5
Leyden St G20 96 E5
Leyland Ave ML3 183 A8
Leyland Wynd ML3 183 A7
Leys Pk ML3 162 A4
Leys The G64 78 A1
Liath Ave ML1 164 C3
Libberton Way ML3 162 A3
Liberator Dr KA8 236 E4
Liberton St G33 118 E8
Liberty Ave G69 121 A5
Liberty Path 7 G72 161 D7
Liberty Rd
Bellshill ML4 142 A3
Caldercruix ML6 105 A5
Libo Ave
Glasgow G53 115 D1
Uplawmoor G78 153 B3
Libo Pl PA8 72 E1
Library Gdns 2 G72 138 F6
Library La G46 135 F3
Library Rd ML2 165 B3
Lichtenfels Gdns KA9 236 E8
Lickprivick Rd G75 180 B6
Liddell Gr G75 180 D7
Liddells Ct G64 98 A7
Liddell St G32 119 C1
Liddel Rd G67 61 E1
Liddesdale Pass G22 97 C7
Liddesdale Pl G22 97 E7
Liddesdale Rd G22 97 C7
Liddesdale Sq G22 97 E7
Liddesdale Terr G22 97 E7
Liddoch Way G73 137 F8
Liff Gdns G64 98 D8
Liff Pl G34 100 C1
Lifnock Ave KA1 228 F6
LIGHTBURN 119 A7
Lightburn Hospl G32 119 B7
Lightburn Pl G32 119 B7
Lightburn Rd G72 139 E3
Lighthouse The★ G1 240 C2
Lilac Ave
Clydebank G81 73 D4
Cumbernauld G67 62 F5
Lilac Cres G71 141 C8
Lilac Ct G67 62 F5
Lilac Gdns G64 98 B8
Lilac Gr ML2 164 F1
Lilac Hill
Cumbernauld G67 62 F5
Hamilton ML3 162 F2
Lilac Pl
Cumbernauld G67 62 F5
Kilmarnock KA1 227 E8
Lilac Way ML1 143 B5
Lilac Wynd G72 139 F4
Lillie Art Gall★ G62 55 B2
Lillyburn Pl G15 74 E5
Lillyloch Gdns ML6 104 F4
LILYBANK 47 A2
Lilybank Ave
Airdrie ML6 103 B2
Cambuslang G72 139 C4
Muirhead G69 100 C7
Lilybank Ct FK10 5 D1
Lilybank Gardens La G12 96 D2
Lilybank Gdns G12 96 D2
Lilybank La G12 96 D2
Lilybank Rd
Greenock PA15 46 F2
Port Glasgow PA14 47 A2
Prestwick KA9 236 B5
Lilybank Sch PA14 47 A2
Lilybank St ML3 162 C4
Lilybank Terr G12 96 D2
Lilybank Terrace La G12 96 D2
Lily St G40 118 B3
Limecraigs Ave PA2 133 C7
Limecraigs Cres PA2 133 C7
Limecraigs Rd PA2 133 C7
Lime Cres
Airdrie ML6 123 C7
Cumbernauld G67 62 E3
Lime Gr
Blantyre G72 140 D1
Kirkintilloch G66 79 D5
Motherwell ML1 163 E4
Stenhousemuir FK5 23 D1
Limegrove St ML4 142 A7
LIMEKILNBURN 183 B2
Limekilnburn Rd ML3 183 D3
Limekiln Rd
Ayr KA8 235 F3
Stevenston KA20 217 E7
Limekilns Rd G67 82 F5
Limekilns St G81 74 D7
Lime La 4 G14 95 D3
Limelands Quadrant
ML6 104 F4
Lime Loan ML1 143 B4
Lime Pl KA1 227 D8
Lime Rd
Dumbarton G82 49 F4
Falkirk FK1 41 B4
LIMERIGG 86 B2
Limerigg Prim Sch FK1 86 C1
Limeside Ave G73 138 C7
Limeside Gdns G73 138 C7
Lime St
Glasgow G14 95 D3
Greenock PA15 45 E4
Limes The G44 137 B4
Limetree Ave G71 141 C8
Limetree Cres G77 156 D4
Limetree Ct 2 ML3 162 A5
Limetree Dr G81 74 A4
Limetree Quadrant G71 141 C7
Limetree Wlk G66 58 B4
Limeview Ave PA2 133 B7
Limeview Cres PA2 133 B7
Limeview Rd PA2 133 B7
Limeview Way PA2 133 B7
Limewood Pl G69 121 A6
Limonds Ct KA8 236 A1
Limonds Wynd KA8 236 A1
Limpetlaw ML11 215 B5
Linacre Dr G32 119 C5
Linacre Gdns G32 119 D5
LINBURN 72 E1
Linburn Pl G52 115 A6
Linburn Rd
Erskine PA8 72 E1
Glasgow G52 114 F7
Linburn Specl Sch G52 114 F6
Linclive Intc PA3 112 D5
Linclive Terr PA3 112 D5
Lincluden Path 2 G41 116 F4
Lincoln Ave
Glasgow G13 95 C6
Uddingston G71 120 F1
Lincoln Ct 4 ML5 122 A8
Lincoln Rd PA16 44 D4
Lincuan Ave G46 157 C8
Lindams G71 140 F5
Linden Ave
Denny FK6 21 C3
Stirling FK7 7 C6
Wishaw ML2 165 C6
Linden Ct G81 74 A6
Linden Dr
Banknock FK4 38 E2
Clydebank G81 74 A6
Linden Lea
Hamilton ML3 162 B4
Milton of Campsie G66 58 B5
Linden Pl G13 95 F7
Linden St G13 95 F7
Lindens The G71 141 A1
Linden Way G13 95 F7
Lindores Ave G73 138 C7
Lindores Dr G74 159 C1
Lindores Pl G74 159 C1
Lindores St G42 137 B8
Lind Pl FK4 39 C4
Lindrick Dr 4 G23 76 E1
Lindsay Ave
Kilbirnie KA25 149 B3
Saltcoats KA21 205 F1
Lindsaybeg Ct G69 100 C8
Lindsaybeg Rd
Chryston G66 80 B2
Lenzie G66 79 E4
Lindsay Dr
Glasgow G12 96 B6
Kilmarnock KA3 223 D3
Stirling FK9 2 B4
LINDSAYFIELD 180 A4
Lindsayfield Ave G75 180 C4
Lindsayfield Rd G75 180 B4
Lindsay Gdns
Alexandria G83 27 E6
Kilmarnock KA3 223 D3
Lindsay Gr G74 159 F2
Lindsay Loan ML11 215 C5
Lindsay Pl
East Kilbride G74 160 A1
Glasgow G12 96 B6
Johnstone PA5 112 A3
Kirkintilloch G66 79 D3
Lindsay Quadrant G83 28 A8
Lindsay Rd G74 159 F1
Lindsay St
Ayr KA8 236 C2
Kilmarnock KA1 227 E8
Lindsay Terr G66 57 E8
Lindston Pl KA7 239 A2
Lindum Cres ML1 163 B8
Lindum St ML1 163 B8
Lineside Wlk G84 15 E5
Linfern Ave KA1 228 C8
Linfern Avenue E KA1 228 C7
Linfern Avenue W KA1 228 C7
Linfern Pl KA7 239 B3
Linfern Rd G12 96 C3
Linghope Pl ML2 185 E7
Lingley Ave ML6 123 A6
Linhead Dr G53 135 C6
Linhope Pl G75 179 E7
Linister Cres PA9 130 E5
Links Cres KA10 229 F6
Links Rd
Glasgow G44 137 C4
Glasgow, Mount Vernon
G32 119 D3
Prestwick KA9 233 B1
Saltcoats KA21 205 F2
Links The G68 62 B6
Links View ML9 185 C2
Linksview Rd ML1 143 B1
Linkwood Ave G15 74 F3
Linkwood Cres G15 75 A3
Linkwood Ct KA11 220 A6
Linkwood Dr G15 75 A3
Linkwood Gdns G15 75 B3
Linkwood Gr 4 G15 75 B3
Linkwood Pl
Clydebank G15 74 F3
Irvine KA11 220 A6
Linkwood Rd ML6 103 B3
Linlithgow Gdns G32 119 D5
Linlithgow Pl
Gartcosh G69 100 E4
Stenhousemuir FK5 23 E4
Linnbank ML11 214 A4
Linnburn Terr KA22 205 B4
Linn Cres
Kirkfieldbank ML11 214 A4
Paisley PA2 133 C8
Linndale Oval G45 137 C2
Linndale Way G45 137 C2
Linn Dr G44 136 F3
Linnet Ave PA5 131 C7
Linnet Pl G13 94 F7
Linnet Rd
Bellshill ML4 142 B4
Greenock PA16 45 B4
Linnet Way ML4 141 F8
Linn Gate G68 61 A2
Linn Gdns G68 61 A2
Linn Glen G66 57 F8
Linnhead Dr G53 135 C5
Linnhead Pl G14 95 B4
Linnhe Ave
Bishopbriggs G64 78 B1
Glasgow G44 137 A4
Hamilton ML3 162 A1
Linnhe Cres ML2 165 B1
Linnhe Ct ML9 184 F5
Linnhe Dr G78 134 B5
Linnhe Pl
Blantyre G72 140 C2
Erskine PA8 72 E1
Linn Park★ G44 137 A3
Linnpark Ave G44 136 F2
Linnpark Ct
Glasgow G44 136 D2
2 Netherlee G44 136 F2
Linn Park Gdns PA5 112 A2
Linn Park Ind Est G45 137 B2
Linn Pl FK2 14 E3
Linn Rd KA22 205 C4
LINNVALE 74 D1
Linnvale Prim Sch G81 74 D1
Linnvale Way G68 61 C6
Linn Valley View G45 137 D3
LINNVILLE 214 A3
Linnwell Cres PA2 133 D7
Linrigg Rd ML1 144 D7
Linside Ave PA1 114 B4
Lint Brae KA3 195 E1
Lint Butts 8 G72 161 C7
Lintfield Loan G71 141 A5
Linthaugh Gdns ML9 198 E1
Linthaugh Rd G53 115 A3
Linthaugh Terr G53 115 D1
Linthill ML11 215 B6
LINTHOUSE 95 E1
Linthouse Bldgs 1 G51 115 E8
Linthouse Rd G51 95 E1
Linthouse Vennel KA12 219 A1
Lintie Rd ML1 143 C4
Lintlaw G72 140 D2
Lintlaw Dr G52 115 B6
Lintmill Terr G78 154 C6
Lint Mill Way G68 61 A2
Linton Pl ML5 121 E3
Linton St G33 118 E8
Lint Riggs FK1 42 B5
Lintview FK1 86 B5
Lintwhite Cres PA11 110 E7
Lintwhite Ct PA11 110 E8
LINWOOD 112 B6
Linwood Ave
Clarkston G76 157 F7
East Kilbride G74 159 A2
Linwood Ct G44 137 A5
Linwood High Sch PA3 111 F6
Linwood Ind Est PA3 112 B4
Linwood Rd PA1 112 E4
Linwood Sp Ctr PA3 112 B7
Linwood Terr ML3 162 B4
Lion Bank G66 58 D1
Lionthorn Rd FK1 41 F1
Lipney FK11 4 A6
Lipton Gdns G5 117 D3
Lisburn Rd KA8 236 A4
Lismore G74 181 C8
Lismore Ave
Motherwell ML1 163 B8
Port Glasgow PA14 69 B7
Renfrew PA4 94 D1
Lismore Ct FK1 42 B2
Lismore Dr
Coatbridge ML5 121 E4
Irvine KA11 225 B8
Linwood PA3 111 F5
Paisley PA2 133 D7
Lismore Gdns PA10 111 C2
Lismore Hill ML3 161 D3
Lismore Ho KA9 236 B5
Lismore Pl
Airdrie ML6 123 C5
11 Moodiesburn G69 81 A3
Newton Mearns G77 156 B6
Lismore Rd G12 96 B5
Lismore Way KA11 225 C8
Lissens Wlk KA13 207 C5
Lister Ct FK9 2 A6
Lister Gdns G76 158 A5
Lister Hts G4 241 C2
Lister Pl G52 115 A7
Lister Rd G52 115 A7
Lister St
Crosshouse KA2 222 A1
Glasgow G4 241 B4
Lister Twr G75 180 F8
Lister Way G72 161 C5
Lister Wlk ML4 142 C7
Lithgow Ave
Kirkintilloch G66 79 E7
Langbank PA14 70 B7
Lithgow Cres PA2 114 A2
Lithgow Dr ML1 144 B1
Lithgow Pl
Denny FK6 39 C8
East Kilbride G74 159 B2
Lithgow Way
Greenock PA15 46 F3
Port Glasgow PA14 47 A3
Little Bellsland Rd KA1 227 F6
Little Corseford Farm
PA10 131 C7
Little Denny Rd FK6 21 D1
Little Dovehill G1 241 B1
LITTLE EARNOCK 162 A2
Littlehill St G21 98 A4
Littleholm Pl G81 73 E4
Little John Gdns ML2 165 F4
Littlemill Ave G68 60 E1
Littlemill Cres G53 135 A8
Littlemill Ct G60 72 B8
Littlemill Dr G53 135 A8
Littlemill Gdns 10 G53 135 A8
Littlemill La G60 72 C8
Littlemill Way ML1 143 B1
Littlesdale Ave PA2 132 D7
Little St G3 240 A2
Littlestane Ct KA11 220 A6
Littlestane Rd KA11 220 A6
Littlestane Rdbt KA11 220 A6
Littlestane Rise KA11 220 A6
Littlestane Row KA11 220 A6
Littleston Gdns PA8 72 F1
Littleton Dr 8 G23 76 D1
Littleton St G23 76 D1
Live Language G3 240 A3
Lively Pl 4 G72 161 C7
Livery Wlk PA11 110 D8
Livilands Ct FK8 7 B5
Livilands Gate FK8 7 B5
Livilands La FK8 7 B5
Livingston Dr ML6 104 A3
Livingstone Ave G52 115 A8
Livingstone Bvd G72 161 D4
Livingstone Cres
Blantyre G72 140 D1
East Kilbride G75 180 D7
Falkirk FK2 42 E5
Livingstone Ct KA3 223 C3
Livingstone Dr
East Kilbride G75 180 E7
Laurieston FK2 42 F2
Livingstone Gdns ML9 185 B3
Livingstone La
3 Bothwell G71 141 A3
Cambuslang G72 139 A3
Livingstone Pk G65 36 C2
Livingstone Pl ML6 123 B7
Livingstone Quadrant
ML7 127 D4
Livingstone St
Clydebank G81 74 D1
Hamilton ML3 161 F4
Livingstone Terr KA12 219 C5
Livingstone Terr KA3 195 B7
Lloyd Ave G32 119 A2
Lloyd Dr ML1 143 A1
Lloyds St ML5 122 A4
Lloyd St
Glasgow G31 118 A8
Motherwell ML1 143 A1
Rutherglen G73 118 B1
Lloyd Wlk KA3 211 C8
Llynallan Rd ML7 126 F4
Loach Ave KA12 219 D1
Loadingbank KA25 170 A7
Loadingbank Ct KA25 170 A7
Loanbank Pl G51 116 A7
Loanbank Quadrant G51 116 A7
Loancroft Ave G69 120 C4
Loancroft Gate G71 140 E5
Loancroft Gdns G71 140 F5
Loancroft Pl G69 120 B3
Loanend Cotts G72 139 F1
Loanfoot Ave
Glasgow G13 95 B7
Kilmarnock KA1 222 D1
Neilston G78 154 D6
Loanfoot Gdns
Braidwood ML8 201 F4
Plean FK7 12 C4
Loanfoot Rd G72 161 D5
LOANHEAD
Renfrew 94 C3
Stirling 7 E6
Loanhead Ave
Denny FK4 39 D6
Linwood PA3 112 A6
Motherwell ML1 143 D3
Renfrew PA4 94 D3
Loanhead Cres ML1 143 D3
Loanhead La PA3 112 A6
Loanhead Prim Sch 4
KA1 228 A8
Loanhead Rd
Ardrossan KA22 205 D2
Linwood PA3 112 A6
Motherwell ML1 143 C3
Loanhead St
Coatbridge ML5 121 E3
Glasgow G32 118 F7
Kilmarnock KA1 228 A8
Loaning 1 ML9 185 C2
Loaninghead Dr G82 50 B6
Loaning The
Alloway KA7 238 F1
4 Bearsden G61 75 E5
Kirkintilloch G66 79 C7
Motherwell ML1 163 C7
Rutherglen G46 157 A7
Loan Lea Cres ML9 185 B1
Loan Pl ML7 127 E6
LOANS 230 A4
Loan The G62 54 C4
Lobnitz Ave PA4 94 D3
Loccard Rd KA20 206 C1
Lochaber Cres ML7 147 B3
Lochaber Dr
Rutherglen G73 138 D4
Stenhousemuir FK5 23 F3
Lochaber Path 8 G72 161 D7
Lochaber Pl G74 159 F3
Lochaber Rd G61 76 B2
Lochaber Wlk G66 58 C7
Loch Achray Gdns G32 119 C4
Loch Achray St G32 119 C4
Lochaline Ave PA2 113 A2
Lochaline Dr G44 137 A4
Lochalsh Cres G66 58 C7
Lochalsh Dr PA2 113 A2
Lochalsh Pl
Airdrie ML6 123 C5
Blantyre G72 140 B2
Lochans The G84 15 B3
Lochar Cres G53 115 D2
Lochard Dr PA2 113 A2
Loch Ardinning Nature
Reserve★ G63 55 D8
Loch Ardinning Nature
Trail★ G63 55 C8
Lochar Pl G75 179 E7
Loch Assynt G74 181 B8
Loch Ave ML8 201 F4
Loch Awe G74 181 A8
Loch Awe Pl ML5 121 F6
Lochay Pl KA10 229 G5
Lochay St G32 119 C4
Lochbrae FK10 5 D2
Lochbrae Dr G73 138 D4
Lochbridge Rd G34 120 A7
Lochbroom Ct G77 156 F6
Lochbroom Dr
Newton Mearns G77 156 F6
Paisley PA2 113 A2
Loch Brora Cres ML5 121 E6
Lochbuie La ML6 102 E4
Lochburn Cres G20 96 E7
Lochburn Gate G20 96 E7
Lochburn Gdns G20 96 F7
Lochburn Gr G20 96 E7
Lochburn Pas G20 96 E7
Lochburn Rd G20 96 E7
Lochcraig Ct KA11 220 A3
Lochdochart Path G34 120 D7
Lochdochart Rd G34 120 D8
Loch Dr G84 16 A2
Lochearn Cres
Airdrie ML6 102 F2
Paisley PA2 113 A2
Lochearnhead Rd G33 99 C5
Lochend Ave G69 100 E7
Lochend Com High Sch
G34 120 C8
Lochend Cotts G83 20 E3
Lochend Cres G61 75 D3
Lochend Dr G61 75 E3
Lochend Pl KA10 229 F1
Lochend Rd
Bearsden G61 75 E3
Gartcosh G69 100 F5
Glasgow G69 100 D1
Glengarnock KA14 170 C7
Troon KA10 229 E1
Lochend St ML1 163 F6
Locher Ave PA6 91 E1

Locherburn Ave PA6 111 D8
Locherburn Gr PA6 111 D8
Locherburn Pl PA6 111 D8
Locher Cres PA6 111 E8
Locher Gait PA6 111 E8
Locher Gdns PA6 111 E8
Locher Pl ML5 122 D3
Locher Rd PA10, PA11 110 F4
Locher Way PA6 111 E8
Locher Wlk ML5 122 C3
Lochfauld Rd G23 77 B2
LOCHFIELD 113 F1
Lochfield Cres PA2 113 F1
Lochfield Dr PA2 114 A1
Lochfield Gdns G34 100 D1
Lochfield Prim Sch PA2 113 F1
Lochfield Rd PA2 113 F1
Lochgarry Way ML5 121 E4
Lochgilp St G20 96 C7
Loch Goil G74 160 A1
Lochgoin Ave G15 74 F4
Lochgoin Gdns G15 74 E4
Lochgreen Ave KA10 229 G7
Lochgreen Pl
Coatbridge ML5 101 C2
Hamilton ML3 183 B8
Kilmarnock KA1 227 E4
Lochgreen Rd FK1 41 E2
Lochgreen Rdbt FK1 41 F2
Lochgreen St G33 98 D3
Lochhead Ave
Denny FK6 21 E1
Linwood PA3 112 B5
Lochhead Ct KA3 211 E8
Lochiel Ct ML6 122 D7
Lochiel Dr G66 58 C6
Lochiel La G73 138 D4
Lochiel Rd G46 135 F4
Lochies Sch FK10 5 F1
Lochinch Pl G77 156 A5
Lochinvar Pl FK4 40 C3
Lochinvar Rd G67 82 E7
Lochinver Cres
Hamilton G72 161 C3
Paisley PA2 113 A2
Lochinver Dr G44 137 A5
Lochinver Gr G72 139 B5
Lochknowe St ML8 201 F5
Loch Laidon St G32 119 D4
Lochlands Ave FK1 41 B8
Lochlands Bsns Pk FK5 41 B8
Lochlands Ind Est FK5 41 A8
Lochlands Loan FK1 41 B7
Loch Laxford G74 181 B8
Lochlea
East Kilbride G74 160 D4
Kilmarnock KA1 227 B7
Loch Lea G66 58 F2
Lochlea Ave
Clydebank G81 74 C3
Troon KA10 229 G4
Lochlea Dr KA7 239 B6
Lochlea Rd
Clarkston G76 157 E5
Cumbernauld G67 62 C3
Glasgow G43 136 D6
Rutherglen G73 137 F5
Saltcoats KA21 206 A3
Lochlea Way ML1 143 E4
Lochlee Loan 4 ML9 185 C2
Lochleven La G42 137 A7
Lochleven Rd G42 137 A7
LOCHLIBO 134 A1
Lochlibo Ave G13 94 F7
Lochlibo Cres G78 134 A1
Lochlibo Ct KA11 220 A6
Lochlibo Rd
Barrhead G78 134 A1
Burnhouse, Auchentiber KA13 193 E3
Burnhouse KA15 172 E3
Irvine KA11 220 A6
Lugton KA15, KA3 173 C7
Neilston G78 154 C7
Torranyard KA11, KA13 209 D4
Uplawmoor G78 153 C5
Lochlibo Terr G78 134 A1
Lochlie Pl 2 KA20 206 E1
Lochlip Rd PA12 129 D2
Loch Lomond Shores★ G83 19 C1
Loch Lomond & The Trossachs National Pk★ G83 19 D5
Loch Lomond YH★ G83 18 F4
Loch Long G74 181 A8
Loch Loyal G74 181 B8
Lochmaben Dr FK5 23 F4
Lochmaben Rd
Gartcosh G69 100 F4
5 Glasgow G52 115 A4
Lochmaben Wynd KA3 223 B6
Lochmaddy Ave G44 137 A4
Loch Maree G74 181 B8
Loch Meadie G74 181 B8
Lochmill Holdings G66 59 A5
Lochnagar Dr G61 75 B7
Lochnagar Rd
Kilmarnock KA1 228 A4
Motherwell ML1 164 C3
Lochnagar Way 20 ML9 185 C1
Loch Naver G74 181 B8
Lochore Ave PA3 114 A7
Lochpark KA7 238 C3
Loch Park Ave ML8 201 F8
Loch Park Ind Est ML9 198 F3
Lochpark Pl
Denny FK6 21 E2
Lochpark Pl *continued*
Larkhall ML9 185 A1
Loch Pk ML2 165 C3
Loch Pl PA11 110 D8
Loch Prim Sch G73 138 D4
Lochranza Ct
Kilmarnock KA3 223 B6
2 Motherwell ML1 143 B2
Lochranza Dr
East Kilbride G75 180 B4
Helensburgh G84 16 F2
Lochranza La G75 180 C4
Lochranza Pl KA21 206 A2
Loch Rd
Bridge of Weir PA11 110 D8
Chapelhall ML6 123 D2
Kirkintilloch G66 79 E7
Milngavie G62 55 B3
Stepps G33 99 D5
Lochridge Pl FK6 21 D1
Lochrig Ct KA3 195 C1
Loch Shin G74 181 B8
Lochshore East Ind Est KA14 170 D7
Lochshore Ind Est KA25 170 B7
LOCHSIDE 236 A2
Lochside
Bearsden G61 75 F3
Gartcosh G69 100 F6
Lochside Cres 6 ML6 103 A3
Lochside Ct
Ayr KA8 236 A1
Dundonald KA2 225 F1
Lochside Rd
Ayr KA8 236 B2
Ayr KA8 236 C3
Slamannan FK1 86 C1
Lochside St 2 G41 116 E1
Lochsloy Ct G22 97 D4
Loch St ML6 123 B2
Loch Striven G74 160 A1
Loch Torridon G74 181 B8
Loch View
Calderbank ML6 123 B2
Caldercruix ML6 105 A5
Kilmarnock KA3 223 C2
Lochview Ave PA19 45 A7
Lochview Cres G33 98 F3
Lochview Dr G33 98 F4
Lochview Gate G33 98 F3
Lochview Gdns G33 98 F3
Lochview Pl G33 98 F3
Lochview Quadrant ML4 141 F3
Lochview Rd
Bearsden G61 75 E3
Beith KA15 170 F7
Coatbridge ML5 101 C1
Port Glasgow PA14 47 B1
Lochview Terr G69 100 F5
Loch Voil St G32 119 D4
LOCHWINNOCH 129 B3
Lochwinnoch Community Mus★ PA12 129 C2
Lochwinnoch Prim Sch PA12 129 C3
Lochwinnoch Rd PA13 89 C7
Lochwinnoch RSPB Nature Reserve★ PA12 129 E1
Lochwinnoch Sta PA12 150 E8
Lochwood Cl KA13 207 C5
Lochwood Loan G69 81 A3
Lochwood Pl KA11 219 F6
Lochwood St G33 98 E2
Lochy Ave PA4 94 F1
Lochy Gdns G64 78 B1
Lochy Pl PA8 72 F1
Lochy St ML2 165 A1
Locke Gr ML1 143 F1
Lockerbie Ave G43 136 F6
Locket Yett View ML4 141 E5
Lockhart Ave G72 139 D6
Lockhart Ct G77 156 D2
Lockhart Dr
Cambuslang G72 139 D6
Lanark ML11 214 E5
Newton Mearns G77 156 D2
Lockhart Hospl ML11 215 C3
Lockhart Pl
Stonehouse ML9 198 F3
Wishaw ML2 165 E4
Lockhart St
Carluke ML8 187 F2
Glasgow G21 98 B2
Hamilton ML3 183 C6
Stonehouse ML9 199 A3
Lockhart Terr G74 160 B2
Lock Sixteen FK1 41 D5
Locksley Ave
Cumbernauld G67 82 E7
Glasgow G13 95 C8
Locksley Cres G67 82 E6
Locksley Ct G67 82 E6
Locksley Pl G67 82 E6
Locksley Rd
Cumbernauld G67 82 E6
Paisley PA2 112 F1
Locksley Way PA2 112 F1
Locks St ML5 122 D6
Lodge Cres PA13 89 E8
Lodge Dr FK5 23 F2
Lodge Gdns PA13 69 E1
Lodge Gr PA13 69 E1
Lodge Pk PA13 69 E1
Lodge Twr ML1 164 B3
Logan Ave G77 156 C6
Logan Ct KA10 229 E3
Logandale Ave ML2 165 F6
Logan Dr
Cumbernauld G68 61 D3
Troon KA10 229 E4
Logan Gdns ML1 165 B8
Loganlea Dr ML1 143 A1
Logans Prim Sch ML1 163 B7
Logans Rd ML1 163 C8
Logan St
Glasgow G5 117 D3
Hamilton G72 161 E7
Loganswell Dr G46 135 E2
Loganswell Gdns G46 135 E2
Loganswell Pl G46 135 E2
Loganswell Rd G46 135 E2
Logan Tower G72 139 E4
Logie Dr FK5 23 A3
Logie La
Bridge of Allan FK9 2 C7
Stirling FK9 2 D4
Logie Pk G74 160 A3
Logie Pl G84 17 A1
Logie Rd FK9 2 D4
Logie Sq G74 160 A3
Lomax St G33 118 D8
Lomond G75 180 E5
Lomond Ave
Hurlford KA1 228 F6
Port Glasgow PA14 68 E8
Renfrew PA4 94 B1
Lomond Castle G83 18 F5
Lomond Cres
Alexandria G83 27 D7
Beith KA15 150 C2
Bridge of Weir PA11 110 C8
Cumbernauld G67 82 C7
Paisley PA2 133 D8
Stenhousemuir FK5 23 F3
Stirling FK9 2 B4
Lomond Ct
Alloa FK10 10 C5
Barrhead G78 134 C2
Coatbridge ML5 122 D7
Cumbernauld G67 82 C7
Dumbarton G82 49 E4
Helensburgh G84 16 E1
Lomond Dr
Airdrie ML6 102 F2
Alexandria G83 27 D7
Bannockburn FK7 7 E1
Barrhead G78 134 B4
Bishopbriggs G64 78 A3
Bothwell G71 141 B3
Cumbernauld G67 82 B7
Dumbarton G82 50 B6
Falkirk FK2 24 C1
Newton Mearns G77 156 D7
Wishaw ML2 165 B1
Lomond Galleries Sh Ctr G83 27 D6
LOMONDGATE 50 A6
Lomond Gate G83 28 A8
Lomond Gdns PA5 112 C2
Lomond Gr
Cumbernauld G67 82 C7
Helensburgh G84 25 C8
Lomond Ind Est G83 27 E6
Lomond Pl
Coatbridge ML5 101 E1
Cumbernauld G67 82 B7
Erskine PA8 72 E1
Irvine KA12 219 D6
Stepps G33 99 E4
Lomond Rd
Alexandria G83 27 D8
Balloch G83 27 E8
Bearsden G61 75 F2
Coatbridge ML5 101 D2
Greenock PA15 46 B3
Kilmarnock KA1 228 A4
Kirkintilloch G66 79 D5
Shotts ML7 146 E6
Uddingston G71 120 F1
Lomond Sch G84 16 C3
Lomondside Ave G76 157 C7
Lomond St
Alloa FK10 4 E1
Glasgow G22 97 B5
Helensburgh G84 16 E1
Lomond Trad Ctr G83 27 E6
Lomond View
Cambuslang G72 139 A1
Cumbernauld G67 82 C7
Hamilton ML3 161 F2
Symington KA1 231 D4
Lomondview Ind Est PA5 111 F3
Lomond Way
Denny FK6 39 D6
Irvine KA11 220 A4
Motherwell ML1 143 A5
Lomond Wlk
7 Larkhall ML9 185 B4
Motherwell ML1 143 C4
London Dr G32 119 E2
London La G1 241 B1
London Rd
Glasgow G31 118 D4
Kilmarnock KA3 228 B8
London St
Larkhall ML9 185 A4
Renfrew PA4 94 D5
London Way G1 241 B1
Lonend PA1 113 F3
Loney Cres FK6 39 E8
Longay Pl G22 97 C8
Longay St G22 97 C8
Longbank Dr KA7 239 A4
Longbank Rd KA7 239 A4
LONGBAR 170 D6
Longbar Ave KA14 170 D6
Long Calderwood Prim Sch G74 160 C4
Long Crags View G82 50 C6
Longcraigs Ave KA22 205 C5
LONGCROFT 39 B3
Longcroft Dr PA4 94 C4
Longcroft Holdings FK4 39 B3
Longdales Ave FK2 42 A8
Longdales Ct FK2 42 A8
Longdales Pl FK2 42 A8
Longdales Rd FK2 42 A8
Longden St G81 94 D8
Long Dr
Irvine KA11, KA12 219 F5
Irvine, Shewalton KA11 225 A7
Longdyke Pl FK2 24 C4
Longfield Ave KA21 205 E2
Longfield Pl KA21 205 E2
Longford Ave KA13 207 E1
Longford St G33 118 D8
Longhill Ave KA7 238 C1
Longlands Pk KA7 238 F4
Longlee G69 120 B4
Longmeadow PA5 111 D1
Longmorn Pl 1 ML1 143 B2
LONGPARK 222 F3
Longpark Ave KA3 222 F2
LONGRIGGEND 85 B1
Longriggend Rd ML6 85 C2
Long Row
Glasgow G69 120 C6
Kirkintilloch G66 80 B7
Lanark ML11 214 F2
Menstrie FK11 4 A7
Longrow Gdns KA11 219 F7
Longstone Rd G33 119 B8
Longwill Terr G67 62 B4
Lonmay Dr G33 119 D8
Lonmay Pl G33 119 D8
Lonsdale Ave G46 136 D3
Loom Wlk PA10 111 A3
Lora Dr G52 115 E4
Lord Way G69 120 F5
Loreny Dr KA1 227 E2
Loreny Ind Est KA1 227 E3
Loretto Pl G33 118 F8
Loretto St G33 118 F8
Lorien Ct KA8 236 C4
Lorimar Pl FK2 24 B2
Lorimer Cres G75 180 D7
Lorn Ave G69 100 D8
Lorn Dr G83 19 F1
Lorne Arc KA7 238 F8
Lorne Cres G64 78 D2
Lorne Dr
Linwood PA3 112 A5
Motherwell ML1 142 D2
Lorne Gdns
Laurieston FK2 42 F3
Salsburgh ML7 125 A2
Lorne Pl ML5 122 D5
Lorne Rd
Glasgow G52 114 F8
Stenhousemuir FK5 23 C2
Lorne St
Glasgow G51 116 D6
Hamilton ML3 162 C4
Helensburgh G84 16 D2
Lorne Street Prim Sch G51 116 D6
Lorne Terr G72 138 F3
Lorn Pl G66 59 C1
Lornshill Acad FK10 4 E2
Lornshill Cres FK10 9 F8
Lorraine Gardens La 5 G12 96 C4
Lorraine Gdns 4 G12 96 C4
Lorraine Rd 3 G12 96 C4
Lorraine Way G83 27 F1
Loskin Dr G22 97 B7
Losshill FK11 4 A6
Lossie Cres PA4 94 F2
Lossie St G33 98 D1
Lothian Cres
Paisley PA2 113 D1
Stirling FK9 2 C3
Lothian Dr G76 157 D8
Lothian Gdns 1 G20 96 E3
Lothian Rd
Ayr KA7 239 A7
Greenock PA16 44 D4
Stewarton KA3 211 C8
Lothian St
Glasgow G52 114 E8
Glasgow G52 114 F8
Lothian Way G74 160 D3
Louburn EH48 107 D3
Louden Hill Dr G33 98 E6
Louden Hill Pl G33 98 E6
Louden Hill Rd G33 98 E6
Louden Hill Way G33 98 E6
Loudens Wlk FK6 21 D5
Loudon G75 180 E5
Loudon Gdns PA5 112 A3
Loudonhill Ave ML3 183 E8
Loudon Rd G33 99 B4
Loudon St ML2 165 B6
Loudon Terr
Bearsden G61 75 D7
Glasgow G12 96 D3
Loudoun Ave KA1 228 A4
Loudoun Cres KA13 207 B4
Loudoun-Montgomery Prim Sch KA12 219 C1
Loudoun Pl
Crosshouse KA2 226 F8
Symington KA1 231 D4
Loudoun Rigg KA12 219 C1
Loudoun St KA3 211 E7
Loudoun Terr KA9 236 D7
Louise Gdns ML1 142 F5
Louisville Ave ML2 165 D5
LOUNSDALE 113 A2
Lounsdale Ave PA2 113 B3
Lounsdale Cres PA2 113 B2
Lounsdale Dr PA2 113 B2
Lounsdale Gr PA2 113 B3
Lounsdale House PA2 113 A1
Lounsdale Pl G14 95 B4
Lounsdale Rd PA2 113 B2
Lounsdale Way PA2 113 B3
Lourdes Ave G52 115 D4
Lourdes Ct G52 115 D4
Lourdes Prim Sch G52 115 C5
Lourdes Sec Sch G52 115 D4
Lovat Ave G61 75 F7
Lovat Dr G66 79 B8
Lovat Path 2 ML9 185 C2
Lovat Pl
Glasgow G52 114 E7
Rutherglen G73 138 D4
Love Ave PA11 89 E2
Love Dr ML4 142 B6
Love La KA24 191 C8
Lovers Loan FK12 5 B7
Lovers Wlk FK8 2 B1
Love St
Kilwinning KA13 208 A3
Paisley PA3 113 E6
Low Barholm PA10 111 B2
Low Broadlie Rd G78 154 D7
Low Church La 3 KA1 227 F8
Low Craigends G65 60 E8
Low Cres G81 94 E8
Lower Auchingramont Rd ML3 162 E4
Lower Bourtree Dr G73 138 C4
Lower Bouverie St PA14 47 D1
Lower Bridge St FK8 2 A1
Lower Castlehill FK8 2 A1
Lower Millgate G71 140 F6
Lower Mill Rd G76 157 F6
Lower Nethan Gorge★ ML8 200 F2
Lower Stoneymollan Rd G83 27 C8
Lower Sutherland Cres G84 16 B3
Lower Vennel KA11 220 A3
Low Flender Rd G76 157 D5
Low Glencairn St KA1 227 F6
Low Green Rd KA12 219 B2
Lowland Ct G33 99 E6
Low Moss Ind Est G64 78 B4
Lowmoss Rdbt G64 78 C5
Lowndes St G78 134 C2
Low Parksail PA8 93 C7
Low Parks Mus★ ML3 162 E4
Low Patrick St ML3 162 F3
Low Pleasance ML9 185 B3
Low Quarry Gdns ML3 162 D2
Low Rd
Ayr KA8 236 E3
Paisley PA2 113 C3
Lowther Ave G61 75 C7
Lowther Bank KA11 220 C2
Lowther Pl KA1 228 A4
Lowther Terr 15 G12 96 C4
LOW WATERS 162 E1
Low Waters Rd ML3 162 D1
Loyal Ave PA8 72 F1
Loyal Gdns G61 75 B8
Loyal Pl PA8 72 F1
Loyne Dr PA4 94 F2
Luath St G51 116 A8
Lubas Ave G42 137 D7
Lubas Pl G42 137 D7
Lubnaig Dr PA8 72 E1
Lubnaig Gdns G61 75 C7
Lubnaig Pl ML6 102 E2
Lubnaig Rd G43 136 E6
Lubnaig Wlk ML1 143 A5
Luce Ave KA1 228 A5
Luckenhill Dr ML6 84 D3
Luckiesfauld G78 154 D7
Luckingsford Ave PA4 93 D7
Luckingsford Dr PA4 93 D7
Luckingsford Rd PA4 93 C7
Lucy Brae G71 140 E8
Ludgate FK10 10 A6
Ludovic Sq PA5 111 F3
Luffness Gdns G32 119 B2
Lugar Ave KA11 220 A6
Lugar Cres KA9 236 B5
Lugar Dr G52 115 E4
Lugar Pl
Glasgow G44 137 F5
Troon KA10 229 G5
Lugar St ML5 122 B8
Lugar Wynd KA3 223 B6
Luggiebank Pl G69 121 A4
Luggiebank Rd
Kirkintilloch, Eastside G66 58 D1
Kirkintilloch, Townhead G66 79 D8
Luggieburn Wlk ML5 121 F5
Luggie Gr G66 80 A7
Luggie Rd ML8 187 E3
Luggie View G67 82 A6
LUGTON 173 C6
Lugton Ct KA12 219 C1
Lugton Rd KA3 195 B8
Luing ML6 123 E6

Luing Rd 1 G52 115 E5
Luma Gdns G51 115 C7
Lumloch St G21 98 A4
Lumsden La G3 96 D1
Lumsden Pl KA20 206 E1
Lumsden St G3 96 D1
Lunan Dr G64 98 C8
Lunan Pl G51 115 E7
Lunar Path ML6 123 D1
Luncarty Pl G32 119 A3
Luncarty St G32 119 A3
Lunderston Cl G53 135 B6
Lunderston Dr G53 135 A7
Lunderston Gdns G53 135 B6
Lundholm Rd KA20 217 E7
Lundie Gdns G64 98 D8
Lundie St G32 118 E3
Lurg St PA14 68 D8
Luss Ave PA15 46 B1
Luss Brae ML3 161 F2
Lusset Glen G60 73 B6
Lusset Rd G60 73 B6
Lusshill Terr G71 120 B2
Luss Pl PA15 46 B1
Luss Rd
Alexandria G83 27 D7
Glasgow G51 115 F7
Helensburgh G84 17 B5
Lybster Cres 2 G73 138 D3
Lybster Way G72 161 C3
Lychgate Rd FK10 4 B2
Lye Brae G67 62 B2
Lyell Gr G74 159 E3
Lyell Pl G74 159 E3
Lyle Cres PA7 72 A4
Lylefoot Cres PA16 45 B8
Lylefoot Pl PA16 45 B7
Lyle Gdns KA12 219 D1
Lyle Gr PA16 45 B7
Lyle Pl
Greenock PA16 45 A7
Paisley PA2 113 F2
Lyle Rd
Airdrie ML6 123 F8
Greenock PA16 45 B7
Kilmacolm PA13 89 D8
Lyle's Land PA6 91 B3
Lylesland Ct PA2 113 E2
Lyle Sq G62 54 E2
Lyle St
Greenock, Central PA15 45 F4
Greenock PA15 46 A4
Lylestone Terr KA13 208 D7
Lyman Dr ML2 165 C7
Lymburn Pl KA8 239 B8
Lymburn St G3 116 D8
Lymekilns Rd G74 159 D3
Lyndale Pl G20 96 D8
Lyndale Rd G20 96 D8
Lyndhurst Gardens La G20 96 F3
Lyndhurst Gdns G20 96 F3
Lynebank Gr G77 156 D2
Lynebank Pl G77 156 D2
Lyne Croft G64 78 A4
Lynedoch Cres G3 240 A4
Lynedoch Ct 4 PA15 46 A4
Lynedoch Ind Est PA15 46 A4
Lynedoch Pl G3 240 A4
Lynedoch St
Glasgow G3 240 A4
Greenock PA15 45 F4
Lynedoch Terr G3 240 A4
Lyne St ML2 165 A5
Lynmouth Pl PA19 44 E5
Lynn Ave KA24 191 C7
Lynnburn Ave ML4 142 A6
Lynn Ct ML9 185 A2
Lynn Dr
Eaglesham G76 178 E6
Kilbirnie KA25 149 B3
Milngavie G62 55 C2
Lynne Dr G23 76 E1
Lynnhurst G71 140 F7
Lynn Wlk
3 Balloch G83 27 E8
Bothwell G71 141 A5
Lynnwood Rd ML2 166 C6
Lynton Ave G46 136 A1
Lyon Cres FK9 2 A6
Lyoncross FK4 39 D4
Lyoncross Ave G78 134 D3
Lyoncross Cres G78 134 D3
Lyoncross Rd G53 115 B2
Lyon Rd
Erskine PA8 72 E1
Linwood PA3 112 B4
Paisley PA2 112 F1
Lyons Quadrant ML2 164 D4
Lysander Way 2 PA4 94 D1
Lysa Vale Pl ML4 141 E5
Lytham Dr G23 76 E1
Lytham Mdws G71 140 E2
Lythgow Way ML11 215 C5
Lyttleton G75 180 B7

M

Mabel St ML1 163 E5
Maberry Cl KA3 195 D1
Maberry Pl KA10 229 F6
McAdam Ct
Prestwick KA9 236 D5
Troon KA10 229 G4
MacAdam Gdns ML4 142 A6
MacAdam Pl
Ayr KA8 236 A1
East Kilbride G75 180 E8
Falkirk FK1 41 D6
Irvine KA11 219 F1
Kilmarnock KA3 223 C1
McAdam Sq KA8 236 A1
McAlister Rd G83 27 E5
McAllan Mews ML1 143 B2
McAllan Pl KA11 219 F7
McAllister Ave ML6 123 D8
McAllister Ct FK7 7 D1
MacAllister Pl KA3 223 C1
MacAlpine Ct FK10 4 D3
McAlpine Pl KA3 223 C2
McAlpine St
Glasgow G3 240 B2
Wishaw ML2 165 B2
MacAndrew Pl KA3 223 C1
Macara Dr KA12 219 E3
McArdle Ave ML1 163 B7
MacArthur Ave ML6 102 D3
MacArthur Cres G74 159 C4
MacArthur Ct G74 159 C3
MacArthur Dr G74 159 C3
MacArthur Gdns G74 159 C3
McArthur Pk G66 79 C7
McArthur St G43 136 C7
McArthur Wynd G72 139 C5
McAslin Ct G4 241 B3
McAslin St G4 241 C3
McAulay Brae FK7 12 C3
McAulay Pl G84 16 A2
McAuley Pl KA3 223 C1
McAuslan Pl G84 16 F2
Macbeth G74 160 B5
Macbeth Dr KA3 223 C1
Macbeth Gdns KA3 223 C1
Macbeth Pl G31 118 D4
Macbeth Rd
Greenock PA16 45 A5
Stewarton KA3 195 D1
Macbeth St G31 118 D4
Macbeth Wlk KA3 223 C1
McBride Ave G66 79 C7
McBride Path G33 99 E5
MacCabe Gdns G66 57 F7
McCall's Ave KA8 236 A2
McCallum Ave G73 138 B8
McCallum Cres PA19 44 E7
McCallum Ct G74 159 B4
MacCallum Dr G72 139 C5
McCallum Gdns ML4 141 F2
McCallum Gr G74 159 B4
McCallum Pl G74 159 B4
MacCallum Pl KA3 223 C1
McCallum Rd ML9 185 B1
McCambridge Pl FK5 23 C5
McCann Ct FK7 12 B4
McCardel Way KA3 211 E8
McCardle Way ML2 166 A6
McCarrison Rd ML2 166 A6
McCartney Rd FK5 23 C4
McCash Pl G66 79 C7
McCaull Pl KA10 229 F6
McCloy Gdns G53 134 F5
McClue Ave PA4 94 B3
McClue Rd PA4 94 C4
McClure Gdns KA12 219 C3
McClurg Ct 3 ML1 163 E5
McColgan Pl KA8 236 C3
McColl Ave G83 27 C7
McColl Pl G83 27 C6
McConnell Rd PA12 129 B2
McCormack Gdns ML1 143 E4
McCormack Pl FK5 23 D4
McCourt Gdns ML4 142 C5
McCracken Ave PA4 94 B2
McCracken Dr G71 141 C8
McCraken Ct FK1 66 F5
McCreery St G81 94 D8
MacCrimmon Pk G74 159 B4
McCrorie Pl PA10 111 A3
McCulloch Ave G71 141 D6
McCulloch La G83 27 D7
McCulloch St G41 116 F4
McCulloch Way
Neilston G78 154 D7
Stepps G33 99 F5
MacDairmid Dr ML3 183 B7
McDonald Ave PA5 111 E1
MacDonald Ave G74 159 A4
McDonald Cres G81 94 D8
MacDonald Cres G65 60 A3
MacDonald Ct
Beith KA15 171 A7
Larbert FK5 23 B5
McDonald Dr KA12 219 D4
MacDonald Dr
Kilmarnock KA3 223 C1
Stirling FK7 7 A4
MacDonald Gdns KA3 223 C1
MacDonald Gr ML4 141 F2
McDonald Pl
Motherwell ML1 143 A5
Neilston G78 154 E7
MacDonald Pl KA3 223 C1
MacDonald St
3 Motherwell ML1 163 F5
1 Rutherglen G73 138 A7
MacDonald Wlk 5 G83 27 E8
McDougal Dr G72 139 C5
MacDougall Dr KA3 223 C1
MacDougall Pl KA3 223 C1
MacDougall St
Glasgow G43 136 C7
Greenock PA15 46 D4
MacDougal Quadrant ML4 141 F2
McDowall Ave KA22 205 D2
McDowall Pl KA22 205 D2
MacDowall St
Johnstone PA5 111 F3
Paisley PA3 113 D6
Macduff PA8 73 A2
Macduff Pl G31 118 D4
Macduff St G31 118 D4
Mace Ct FK7 7 D3
Macedonian Gr ML1 143 C4
Mace Rd G13 75 C1
McEwan Dr G84 16 F3
McEwan Gdns G74 159 A4
MacEwan Pl KA3 228 C8
McEwans Way ML9 198 D1
McEwan Wlk G83 27 E6
MacFarland Rd 5 G61 75 F3
Macfarlane Cres
Cambuslang G72 139 C5
Falkirk FK1 42 B5
Macfarlane Dr KA3 223 C1
McFarlane Rd G83 28 A8
Macfarlane Rd G61 76 A3
McFarlane St
Glasgow G4 241 C1
Paisley PA3 113 C7
Macfie Pl G74 159 B4
McGavin Ave KA13 208 A3
McGavin Way KA13 207 D4
McGhee Pl FK1 41 F2
McGhee St G81 74 B4
McGibney Dr KA12 219 D1
McGillivray Ave KA21 205 F2
MacGillvary Ave PA15 46 E3
McGoldrick Pl G33 99 F5
McGowan Pl ML3 162 A5
MacGowan Way PA15 46 E3
McGown St PA3 113 D6
McGregor Ave
Airdrie ML6 123 D8
Balloch G83 28 A8
Renfrew PA4 94 B2
Stevenston KA20 206 D1
MacGregor Ct G72 139 C5
McGregor Dr G82 50 C4
MacGregor Dr KA3 228 C8
McGregor La G82 27 D2
McGregor Path ML5 101 C6
McGregor Rd G67 61 E1
MacGregor Rd PA15 46 E3
McGregor St
Clydebank G81 94 D8
Glasgow G51 115 F6
Wishaw ML2 164 D4
McGregor Wlk G83 27 C7
McGrigor Rd
Milngavie G62 54 F3
Stirling FK7 7 A4
McGurk Way ML4 141 D6
MACHAN 185 A2
Machan Ave ML9 185 A3
Machanhill ML9 185 B2
Machanhill Prim Sch ML9 185 B3
Machanhill View ML9 185 B2
Machan Rd ML9 185 B1
McHardy Cres KA15 171 F3
Machrie Ct FK1 41 C4
Machrie Dr
Glasgow G45 137 F4
Helensburgh G84 16 F3
Newton Mearns G77 156 E6
Machrie Gn G75 180 B4
Machrie Pl KA13 207 C3
Machrie Rd
Glasgow G45 137 F4
Kilmarnock KA3 222 E4
Machrie St
Glasgow G45 137 F3
Motherwell ML1 163 B7
Mcilvanney Cres KA3 222 F2
Mcilvanney Dr KA3 223 A2
McInally Cres 1 FK2 41 F7
McInnes Ct ML2 165 B2
MacInnes Dr ML1 144 A5
McInnes Gr ML9 198 E1
MacInnes Mews ML1 143 E4
McInnes Pl ML2 186 B7
MacInnes Pl KA3 223 C1
McInnes St G83 28 A8
McIntosh Ct 1 G31 117 F7
Macintosh Pl
East Kilbride G75 180 C7
Falkirk FK1 42 A1
Kilmarnock KA3 223 C1
McIntosh Quadrant ML4 141 F2
McIntosh St G31 117 F7
McIntosh Way
Bellshill ML4 141 F3
Cumbernauld G67 61 F1
Motherwell ML1 163 C5
McIntyre Ave KA9 233 D2
McIntyre Pl PA2 113 E2
MacIntyre Pl KA3 223 C1
MacIntyre Rd KA9 233 C2
McIntyre St G3 240 A2
McIntyre Terr
6 Balloch G83 27 E8
Cambuslang G72 139 A6
McIsaac Rd KA21 217 A7
McIver St G72 139 E6
MacIvor Cres G74 159 A4
MacIvor Pl KA3 223 C1
McKay Cres PA5 112 B2
McKay Ct G77 156 C3
McKay Gr ML4 141 F5
McKay Pl
East Kilbride G74 159 A4
Newton Mearns G77 156 C4
MacKean St PA3 113 D6
McKechnie St G51 116 A8
MacKeith St G40 117 F4
McKellar Ave KA22 205 D2
MacKellar Pl KA3 223 C2
McKell Ct FK1 42 A3
MacKendrick Pl KA3 228 C8
McKenna Dr ML6 122 E7
McKenzie Ave G81 74 B4
McKenzie Dr G83 19 F1
Mackenzie Dr
Johnstone PA10 111 B1
Kilmarnock KA3 223 B1
McKenzie Gate G72 139 E6
Mackenzie Gdns G74 159 A4
McKenzie Pl FK1 42 A2
Mackenzie Pl FK1 41 F2
McKenzie's Cl 16 ML11 215 A4
McKenzie St PA3 113 C5
Mackenzie St PA15 46 D4
Mackenzie Terr ML4 142 A7
McKeown Gdns ML4 142 D4
McKerrell St PA1 114 A5
Mackie Ave
Greenock PA14 46 F1
Port Glasgow PA14 47 A1
Stewarton KA3 195 D2
Mackie Pl KA3 223 C1
Mackie's Mill Rd PA5 132 D8
Mackie St KA8 236 C2
McKillop Pl KA21 205 F2
McKim Wlk G82 49 D8
McKinlay Ave G83 20 A1
McKinlay Cres
Alloa FK10 10 C7
Irvine KA12 219 B1
Mackinlay Pl KA1 228 B8
Mackinley Pl G77 156 D4
MacKinnon Dr KA3 228 C8
McKinnon Pl KA21 206 A2
MacKinnon Terr KA12 219 E4
Mackintosh Ct G72 139 A3
Mackintosh Pl KA11 219 F1
McKnight Ave KA3 213 E4
Mack St ML6 123 A8
McLachlan Ave FK7 7 B2
MacLachlan Ave FK6 21 C1
MacLachlan Pl G84 16 E3
MacLachlan Rd G84 16 E3
McLachlan St FK5 23 C2
McLaren Ave PA4 94 C1
McLaren Cres G20 96 E7
McLaren Ct
Glasgow G46 136 B1
Stenhousemuir FK5 23 D2
Troon KA10 229 G4
McLaren Ct KA10 229 G4
McLaren Dr ML4 142 D4
McLaren Gdns G20 96 E7
McLaren Gr G74 159 A4
McLaren Pl G82 27 E2
MacLaren Pl
Kilmarnock KA3 228 C8
3 Netherlee G44 136 F2
McLaren Terr FK7 7 B3
MacLaren Terr FK2 24 A2
McLauchlan View ML7 127 F6
McLaurin Cres PA5 111 D1
Maclay Ave PA10 111 A2
McLean Cres G83 19 F1
Maclean Cres FK12 5 C7
Maclean Ct
East Kilbride G74 159 B4
Stirling FK7 7 C3
McLean Dr
Bellshill ML4 141 F2
Irvine KA11 225 D8
Maclean Dr KA3 223 B1
McLean Gdns ML9 198 E2
Maclean Gr G74 159 B4
McLean Mus & Art Gall* PA16 45 E6
McLean Pl PA3 113 D7
Maclean Pl G74 159 B4
Maclean Sq G51 116 E6
McLean St KA8 236 C2
Maclean St
Clydebank G81 94 E8
Glasgow G51 116 D6
Maclean Terr EH48 107 C3
McLees La ML1 163 B7
MacLehose Ct PA16 45 E7
MacLehose Rd G67 62 C3
McLelland Dr
Kilmarnock KA1 227 E7
Plains ML6 104 B2
McLellan Galleries* G3 240 C3
MacLellan Rd G78 154 E6
MacLellan St G41 116 D5
McLennan St G42 137 B8
MacLeod Cres G84 16 B4
MacLeod Dr
Helensburgh G84 16 C4
Kilmarnock KA3 228 C8
MacLeod Pl
East Kilbride G74 160 B3
Kilmarnock KA3 228 C8
McLeod Rd G82 50 C4
McLeod St PA15 46 D3
McLeod Way G72 139 C5
McLuckie Dr KA13 207 C4
McLuckie Pk KA13 207 C4
McMahon Dr ML2 166 A6
McMahon Gr ML4 142 B6
McMillan Cres KA15 171 A7
McMillan Ct KA10 229 F4
McMillan Dr KA22 205 A4
Macmillan Dr
Gourock PA19 44 D6
Kilmarnock KA3 223 C1
Macmillan Gdns G71 121 A1
McMillan Pl KA11 224 H6
Macmillan Pl KA3 223 C1
McMillan Rd ML2 164 D2
Macmillan Sch of Music & Drama PA1 113 C4
Macmillan St ML9 184 F2
McMillan Way ML8 186 F5
McNab Gdns FK1 41 F2
MacNab Pl KA3 223 B1
McNair St G32 119 A5
MacNaughton Dr KA3 223 C1
MacNaughton Wlk KA3 223 C1
McNaught Pl
Kilmaurs KA3 222 A7
Renton G82 27 D1
McNay Cres KA21 206 A1
McNee Rd KA9 233 C3
McNeil Ave G81 74 E1
McNeil Dr ML1 143 A8
McNeil Gdns G5 117 D4
McNeill Ave KA9 233 D1
MacNeill Dr G74 159 B4
MacNeill Gdns G74 159 B4
McNeil Pl ML2 186 C7
MacNeil Pl KA3 223 B1
McNeil St G5 117 D4
MacNeil St ML9 184 F3
McNeish Way G74 159 C4
MacNichol Gdns KA3 223 C1
MacNichol Pl KA3 223 C1
MacNicol Ct G74 159 A4
MacNicol Pk G74 159 A4
MacNicol Pl G74 159 A4
McNiven Ct ML9 198 E1
McPhail Ave ML1 143 F5
MacPhail Dr KA3 223 C1
McPhail St
Glasgow G40 117 E4
Greenock PA15 46 D3
McPhater St G4 240 C4
McPherson Cres ML6 123 E1
McPherson Dr
Bothwell G71 141 B3
Gourock PA19 44 D7
Macpherson Dr FK8 2 A2
Macpherson Gdns KA3 223 C1
McPherson La G83 27 D7
Macpherson Pk G74 159 C3
Macpherson Pl
Falkirk FK1 41 F2
Kilmarnock KA3 223 C1
McPherson St
Bellshill ML4 142 D5
Glasgow G1 241 B1
Macpherson Wlk KA3 223 C1
Macphie Rd G82 50 C4
Macrae Dr KA9 233 C2
Macrae Gdns G74 159 C3
Macredie Pl KA11 220 D6
Macrimmon Pl G75 180 E8
MacRobert Ave KA11 220 B1
McShane Ct ML2 166 B5
McShannon Gr ML4 142 A3
McSparran Rd G65 60 F4
McTaggart Ave FK6 21 E2
MacTaggart Rd G67 82 E8
McVean Pl FK4 39 B4
Madeira La PA16 45 D7
Madeira St PA16 45 D7
Madill Pl FK5 23 F3
Madison Ave G44 137 B5
Madison Path 9 G72 161 D7
Madras Pl
Glasgow G40 117 F3
Neilston G78 154 E7
Madras St G40 117 F3
Mafeking St
Glasgow G51 116 B6
Wishaw ML2 164 D4
Mafeking Terr G78 154 C7
Magdalen Way PA2 132 E7
Maggie Wood's Loan
Falkirk FK1 41 F4
Falkirk FK1 41 F5
Magna St ML1 163 B8
Magnolia Dr G72 139 F3
Magnolia Gdns
Ashgill ML9 185 E1
Motherwell ML1 143 C3
Magnolia Pl G71 141 C8
Magnolia St ML2 165 B5
Magnolia Terr G72 139 F3
Magnum L Ctr KA12 218 F1
Magnus Cres G44 137 B4
Magnus Rd PA6 111 D8
Mahon Ct G69 80 F1
Maidens G74 159 D3
Maidens Ave G77 157 A5
Maidland Rd G53 135 C8
Maid Morville Ave KA11 225 C8
Mailerbeg Gdns G69 80 F3
Mailie Wlk ML1 143 C3
Mailing Ave G64 78 C2
Mailings Ct G65 37 E3
Mailings Rd G65 37 E3
Mailings The G65 37 E4
Maimhor Rd KA23 190 B4
Mainhead Terr G67 62 B5
Mainhill Ave G69 120 D5
Mainhill Dr G69 120 C5
Mainhill Pl G69 120 D6
Mainhill Rd G69 120 F5

Mainholm Cres KA8 236 D1
Mainholm Ct KA8 236 E1
Mainholm Rd
Ayr, Braehead KA8 236 D1
Ayr KA6, KA8 239 E8
Main Rd
Ayr KA8 236 E2
Cardross G82 48 A8
Crookedholm KA3 228 E7
Cumbernauld, Condorrat G67 82 A7
Cumbernauld, Mollinsburn G67 81 E5
Elderslie PA5 112 D3
Fenwick KA3 213 A3
Gatehead KA2 226 E5
Gateside KA15 171 E8
Langbank PA14 70 D7
Paisley PA2 113 D3
Rosneath G84 15 A3
Springside KA11 220 F2
Waterside KA3 213 F3
Mains Ave
Beith KA15 150 A1
Glasgow G46 136 B1
Helensburgh G84 16 A3
Mainscroft PA8 73 C1
Mains Ct ML11 215 C5
Mains Dr PA8 73 C1
Mains Hill PA8 73 B1
Mainshill Ave PA8 73 B1
Mainshill Gdns PA8 73 B1
Mains Pl ML4 142 A3
Mains Rd
Beith KA15 150 A1
East Kilbride G74 159 F5
Harthill ML7 127 E5
Mains River PA8 73 C1
Main St
Airth FK2 14 D4
Alexandria, Dalmonach G83 27 E5
Alexandria G83 27 E4
Alloa FK10 5 D1
Ayr KA8 235 F1
Balloch G83 19 F1
Bannockburn FK7 7 D1
Banton G65 37 D3
Barrhead G78 134 C2
Beith KA15 150 B1
Bellshill ML4 141 F5
Bellshill ML4 142 B5
Blackridge EH48 107 C3
Bonhill, Dalmonach G83 27 F6
Bonhill G83 27 F3
Bonnybridge FK4 40 B5
Bothwell G71 141 A2
Bridge of Weir PA11 110 D8
Calderbank ML6 123 C2
Caldercruix ML6 105 A4
California FK1 66 F5
Cambusbarron FK7 6 D5
Cambus FK10 9 B8
Cambuslang G72 139 A6
Chapelhall ML6 123 E3
Chryston G69 80 D1
Clarkston G76 157 F6
Cleland ML1 144 C1
Coatbridge, Cliftonville ML5 122 C6
Coatbridge ML5 122 A7
Cowie FK7 12 D7
Cumbernauld G67 62 B5
Dalry KA24 191 C7
Drybridge KA11 225 E6
Dundonald KA2 225 F2
Dunlop KA3 195 B7
East Kilbride G74 159 F2
Falkirk, Bainsford FK2 42 B7
Falkirk, Camelon FK1 41 E5
Falkirk, Carronshore FK2 24 C3
Fallin FK7 8 E3
Gateside KA15 171 E8
Glasgow G40 117 F4
Glasgow, Muirhead G69 120 C4
Glasgow, Thornliebank G46 135 F3
Glenboig ML5 101 E6
Glengarnock KA14 170 B6
Greenock PA15 46 C4
Hamilton G72 161 D6
Hamilton G72 161 E5
Houston PA6 91 B2
Howwood PA9 130 F5
Irvine KA11 220 D1
Irvine KA11 220 D1
Kilbirnie KA25 149 B1
Kilmaurs KA3 222 C7
Kilsyth G65 36 D1
Kilsyth G65 60 D8
Kilwinning KA13 207 E3
Lennoxtown G66 57 D8
Lochwinnoch PA12 129 C2
Longriggend ML6 85 A1
Milngavie G62 76 A8
Monkton KA9 233 D4
Monkton KA9 233 D5
Motherwell ML1 143 B6
Neilston G78 154 D7
Overtown ML2 186 C6
Plains ML6 104 B2
Plean FK7 12 D3
Prestwick KA9 236 C8
Renton G82 27 D2
Rutherglen G73 138 B8
Salsburgh ML7 125 B2
Shieldhill FK1 66 D6
Shotts ML7 147 A3
Slamannan FK1 86 B7
Main St *continued*
Stenhousemuir FK5 23 C2
Stenhousemuir FK5 23 E2
Stevenston KA20 206 D1
Stewarton KA3 211 D8
Stirling FK7 7 B4
Symington KA1 231 C4
Thornliebank G46 136 A4
Torrance G64 78 B8
Troon KA10 230 A4
Tullibody FK10 4 B2
Twechar G65 59 F4
Uddingston G71 140 F5
West Kilbride KA23 190 D5
Wishaw ML2 164 F4
Wishaw, Newmains ML2 166 A3
Main Street E FK11 4 A6
Main Street W FK11 3 F6
Mains Wood PA8 73 D1
Mair Ave KA24 191 E7
Mair St G51 116 E6
Maitland Ave FK7 7 D1
Maitland Bank ML9 185 C3
Maitland Cres FK7 7 B3
Maitland Ct G84 16 D1
Maitland Dr G64 57 B1
Maitland Pl PA4 94 B2
Maitland St
Glasgow G4 240 C4
Helensburgh G84 16 D1
Majors Loan FK1 42 A4
Majors Pl FK1 42 A3
Malcolm Ct KA3 195 F1
Malcolm Dr FK5 23 E4
Malcolm Gdns
East Kilbride G74 159 C2
Irvine KA12 219 D2
Malcolm Pl G84 17 A2
Malcolm's Ct KA3 222 C6
Malcolm St ML1 163 C6
Mal Fleming's Brae G65 60 F7
Malin Pl G33 118 F8
Mallaig Pl G51 115 D7
Mallaig Rd
Glasgow G51 115 E7
Port Glasgow PA14 68 F7
Mallaig Terr PA16 44 E4
Mallard Cres
East Kilbride G75 180 A5
Greenock PA16 45 A6
Mallard La
7 Bothwell G71 141 B3
Greenock PA16 45 A6
Mallard Pl G75 180 A5
Mallard Rd G81 74 B5
Mallard Terr G75 180 A5
Mallard Way ML4 141 F8
Malleable Gdns ML1 142 C2
Malleny Gr G77 156 B3
Malletsheugh Rd G77 156 B3
Malletsheugh Rdbt G77 156 B3
Malloch Cres PA5 112 B2
Malloch Pl G74 160 B2
Malloch St G20 96 E5
Mallot's View G77 156 B4
Malov Ct G75 180 E6
Malplaquet Ct ML8 188 B1
Malta Terr G5 117 B4
Maltbarns St G20 97 A3
Maltings The FK1 41 F5
Malvaig La 3 G72 161 C6
Malvern Ct G31 118 A6
Malvern Way 4 PA3 113 D8
Mambeg Dr G51 115 E8
Mamore Pl G43 136 C6
Mamore St G43 136 C6
Mamre Dr FK1 66 F5
Manchester Dr G12 96 B6
Mandela Ave FK2 42 C7
Manderston Ct G77 156 B4
Manderston Mdw G77 156 B4
Mandora Ct ML8 188 B1
Manitoba Cres G75 159 B1
Mannering G74 160 D4
Mannering Ct G41 136 C8
Mannering Rd
Glasgow G41 136 C8
Paisley PA2 132 E8
Mannering Way PA2 112 E1
Mannfield Ave FK4 39 F4
Mannoch Pl ML5 122 D3
Mannofield G61 75 D4
Manor Ave KA3 223 A4
Manor Cres
Gourock PA19 44 F7
Tullibody FK10 4 B2
Manor Dr
Airdrie ML6 122 E8
Coatbridge ML5 121 D7
Manor Gate
Bothwell G71 141 B1
Newton Mearns G77 156 F4
Manor Loan FK9 3 B5
Manor Park Ave PA2 113 B1
Manor Pk ML3 162 D2
MANOR POWIS 3 B3
Manor Powis Cotts FK9 3 B3
Manor Rd
Clydebank G15 74 F1
Gartcosh G69 100 F5
Glasgow G14 95 E4
Paisley PA2 112 F1
Manor St FK1 42 B4
Manor Steps FK9 3 C3
Manor View
Calderbank ML6 123 B2
Larkhall ML9 185 C2
Manor Way G73 138 C4
Manrahead Rdbt KA15 171 A7
Manresa Pl 1 G4 97 B2
Manse Ave
Bearsden G61 75 F5
Bothwell G71 141 A2
Coatbridge ML5 121 D4
Manse Brae
Ashgill ML9 200 B8
Cambuslang G72 139 F2
Dalserf ML9 186 B1
Glasgow G44 137 B6
Rhu G84 15 D5
Manse Bridge ML8 187 F1
Manse Cres
Houston PA6 91 B2
Stirling FK7 7 B4
Manse Ct
Barrhead G78 134 D3
Kilsyth G65 60 D7
Kilwinning KA13 207 E3
Law ML8 187 A4
Manse Dr G83 27 F8
Mansefield Ave G72 139 A4
Mansefield Cres
Clarkston G76 157 D6
Old Kilpatrick G60 73 A6
Mansefield Rd
Clarkston G76 157 E6
Quarter ML3 183 E6
Mansefield Terr KA3 195 B7
Manse Garden's G83 27 F8
Manse Gdns
Balloch G83 27 E7
Glasgow G32 119 D4
Manse La G74 159 F3
Mansel St G21 98 A5
Manse Mews ML2 166 A4
Manse Pl
Airdrie ML6 123 A7
Bannockburn FK7 7 E1
Falkirk FK1 42 B4
Rhu G84 15 D5
Slamannan FK1 86 B7
Manse Rd
Bearsden G61 75 F5
Bowling G60 72 D8
Carmunnock G76 158 D7
Glasgow, Barrachnie G32 119 D4
Glasgow, Easterhouse G69 120 E6
Kilsyth G65 60 E7
Lanark ML11 214 F4
Motherwell ML1 163 F4
Neilston G78 154 E8
Salsburgh ML7 125 D1
Shotts ML7 147 A3
Stonehouse ML9 198 C2
West Kilbride KA23 190 D5
Wishaw ML2 166 A4
Manse Road Gdns G61 75 F5
Manse St
Coatbridge ML5 121 F6
Kilmacolm PA13 89 D8
Kilmarnock KA1 228 A8
Renfrew PA4 94 D4
Saltcoats KA21 216 F7
Manseview ML9 185 B2
Manse View
Hamilton G72 161 C6
Motherwell ML1 143 F5
Manseview Terr G76 178 E5
Mansewell Rd KA9 233 C1
MANSEWOOD 136 B5
Mansewood Dr G82 50 B5
Mansewood Rd G43 136 B5
Mansfield Ave FK10 5 D1
Mansfield Dr G71 141 A6
Mansfield Rd
Bellshill ML4 141 F4
Glasgow G52 114 F8
Lochwinnoch PA12 129 C3
Prestwick KA9 236 B6
Mansfield St G11 96 C2
Mansfield Way KA11 220 A5
Mansion Ave PA14 69 A8
Mansion Ct G72 139 A6
Mansionhouse Ave G32 139 C8
Mansionhouse Dr G32 119 C6
Mansionhouse Gdns G41 136 E7
Mansionhouse Gr G32 119 E3
Mansionhouse Rd
Falkirk FK1 41 D5
Glasgow G32 119 E3
Glasgow, Langside G41 136 E7
Paisley PA1 114 A5
Mansion St
Cambuslang G72 139 A6
Glasgow G22 97 B5
Glasgow G22 97 C5
Manson Ave KA9 233 D1
Manson Pl G75 181 B5
Manson Rd KA12 219 E4
Manuel Ave KA15 171 A7
Manuel Ct
Irvine KA11 225 C8
Kilbirnie KA25 170 A8
Manuel Terr KA11 225 C8
Manus Duddy Ct
Blantyre G72 140 D1
Hamilton G72 161 D8
Maple Ave
Dumbarton G82 49 B5
Milton of Campsie G66 58 B5
Newton Mearns G77 156 D4
Stenhousemuir FK5 23 F3
Maple Bank ML3 162 F2
Maple Cres G72 139 F3
Maple Ct
10 Alloa FK10 10 B6
Cumbernauld G67 62 F5
Maple Dr
Ayr KA7 239 D5
Barrhead G78 155 D8
Beith KA15 150 B2
Clydebank G81 74 A5
Johnstone PA5 132 A8
Kirkintilloch G66 79 A5
Larkhall ML9 185 A5
Maple Gr
Coatbridge G69 121 A6
East Kilbride G75 180 B6
Troon KA10 229 E4
Maple Pl
Banknock FK4 38 E2
Denny FK6 21 C3
East Kilbride G75 180 B6
Kilmarnock KA1 227 D7
Uddingston G71 141 D8
Maple Quadrant ML6 123 D6
Maple Rd
Cumbernauld G67 62 F5
Glasgow G41 116 B4
Greenock PA16 45 B3
Motherwell ML1 143 B5
Maple Terr
East Kilbride G75 180 B6
Irvine KA12 219 D4
Maple Way 7 G72 161 C7
Maple Wlk G66 58 B5
Maplewood ML2 164 D1
Mar Ave PA7 72 B3
Marble Ave KA11 220 D1
Marchbank Gdns PA1 114 D4
Marchburn Ave KA9 236 E8
Marchdyke Cres KA1 227 E3
Marches The
Lanark ML11 215 B5
8 Stirling FK8 7 B7
Marchfield G64 77 E3
Marchfield Ave PA3 113 E8
Marchfield Quadrant KA8 236 B5
Marchfield Rd KA8 236 B5
Marchglen FK13 5 F5
Marchglen Pl 1 G51 115 D7
Marchmont Ct KA1 228 F7
Marchmont Gdns G64 77 F2
Marchmont Rd KA7 238 F6
Marchmont Road La KA7 238 F7
Marchmont Terr 2 G12 96 C3
Marchside Ct FK10 5 C1
March St G41 116 F2
Marcus Way 3 ML1 163 C8
Mardale G74 159 C3
Mar Dr G61 75 F7
Maree Ct FK10 10 C6
Maree Dr
Cumbernauld G67 82 B7
Glasgow G52 115 E4
Maree Gdns G64 78 B1
Maree Pl KA12 219 D7
Maree Rd PA2 113 A2
Maree Way G72 161 D8
Maree Wlk 7 ML2 165 F6
Marfield St G32 118 F6
Margaret Ave
Haggs FK4 39 A3
Salsburgh ML7 125 B2
Margaret Ct
Denny FK6 21 E1
Lennoxtown G66 57 D8
Margaret Dr
Alexandria G83 27 D5
Bonnybridge FK4 40 A6
Motherwell ML1 164 B3
Margaret Gdns ML3 162 B6
Margaret Pl ML4 141 E5
Margaret Rd
Bannockburn FK7 7 C2
Hamilton ML3 162 B6
Margaret's Pl ML9 185 A3
Margaret St
Coatbridge ML5 122 A4
Gourock PA19 44 F7
Greenock PA16 45 D7
Margaretta Bldgs G44 137 A6
Margaret Terr FK5 23 E4
Margaretvale Dr ML9 185 A2
Mar Gdns G73 138 D4
Marguerite Ave G66 79 C6
Marguerite Dr G66 79 C6
Marguerite Gdns
Bothwell G71 141 B2
Kirkintilloch G66 79 C6
Marguerite Gr G66 79 C6
Marguerite Pl
Ayr KA7 239 C3
Milton of Campsie G66 58 B6
Marian Dr ML1 143 C2
Maric La ML6 104 A2
Marigold Ave ML1 163 E8
Marigold Sq KA7 239 B3
Marigold Way ML8 201 F8
Marina Ct ML4 141 F3
Marina Rd KA9 236 B8
Marine Cres G51 116 E6
Marine Dr KA11, KA12 224 D6
Marine Gdns G51 240 A1
Mariner Ave FK1 41 B5
Mariner Ct G81 74 A2
Mariner Dr FK1 41 B5
Mariner Gdns FK1 41 C6
Mariner Rd FK1 41 C5
Mariner St FK1 41 B5
Mariners View KA22 205 B1
Marine View Ct KA10 229 D2
Marion St ML4 142 D5
Mariscat Rd G41 116 E2
Marius Cres ML1 142 C1
Marjory Dr PA3 114 B7
Marjory Rd PA4 94 A1
Markdow Ave G53 115 A1
Market Cl 7 G65 60 D8
Market Ct
15 Kilsyth G65 60 D8
18 Lanark ML11 215 A4
Market End 17 ML11 215 A4
Markethill Rd
East Kilbride, East Mains G74 159 E3
East Kilbride G74 159 E5
Markethill Rdbt G74 159 E3
Market Pl
Carluke ML8 187 F2
Kilmacolm PA13 89 D8
5 Kilsyth G65 60 D8
Uddingston G71 141 C7
Market Rd
2 Carluke ML8 187 F2
Kirkintilloch G66 80 A7
Uddingston G71 141 C7
Market Sq 6 G65 60 D8
Market St
Airdrie ML6 123 A7
Kilsyth G65 60 D8
Uddingston G71 141 C7
Markinch Rd PA14 68 F6
Marlach Pl 13 G53 135 A8
Marlborough Ave G11 95 F3
Marlborough Ct 3 KA7 235 E1
Marlborough Dr FK9 2 C3
Marlborough Lane N 1 G11 95 F3
Marlborough Lane S G11 95 F3
Marlborough Pk G75 180 A7
Marldon La G11 95 F3
Marle Pk KA7 239 A3
Marley Way G66 58 B6
Marlfield Gdns ML4 142 A8
Marloch Ave PA14 69 A6
Marlow St G41 116 E5
Marlow Terr G41 116 E4
Marmion Ave G84 25 C7
Marmion Cres ML1 142 D1
Marmion Ct PA2 132 F8
Marmion Dr G66 79 F8
Marmion Pl G67 82 E7
Marmion Rd
Cumbernauld G67 82 E7
Paisley PA2 132 E8
Marmion St FK2 42 B8
Marne St G31 118 B8
Marnoch Dr ML5 101 D6
Marnoch Way G69 80 F2
MARNOCK 101 D6
Marnock Terr PA2 114 A2
Mar Pl
Alloa FK10 10 A7
Alloa, Sauchie FK10 5 C1
Stirling FK8 7 A8
Marquis Ave ML3 162 B6
Marquis Gate G71 140 E5
Marr Coll KA10 229 F4
Marr Dr KA10 229 E4
Marress Rd KA12 219 B3
Marress Rdbt KA12 219 B2
Marrswood Gr ML3 162 A4
Marrs Wynd ML11 215 C5
Marr's Wynd ML11 215 C5
Marrwood Ave G66 80 B6
Marschal Ct FK7 7 D3
Marsden Ct FK9 2 D4
Marshall Dr FK1 66 F5
Marshall Gdns KA3 222 A7
Marshall Gr ML3 162 B3
Marshall La ML2 165 A3
Marshall Rd ML1 143 D7
Marshall's La PA1 113 E4
Marshall St
Larkhall ML9 185 A2
Wishaw ML2 164 F2
Marshall Twr FK1 42 D4
Marshall Way FK10 4 C4
Marshill FK10 10 A6
Marsmount Rd KA9 233 F1
Mars Rd PA16 44 C2
Mar St FK10 10 B6
Martha Pl ML9 185 B2
Martha St G1 241 A3
Martin Ave
Balloch G83 28 A8
Irvine KA12 219 D5
Martin Cres G69 120 C5
Martin Ct ML3 162 C3
Martin Gannon Ct G82 49 D8
Martin Pl ML1 143 C3
Martinside G75 180 E5
Martin Sq KA21 206 A2
Martin St
Coatbridge ML5 122 D7
Glasgow G40 117 F3
Martlet Dr PA5 131 C7
Mart St G1 241 A1
Martyn St ML6 122 E6
Martyrs Pl G64 98 A8
Marwick St G31 118 B7
Maryborough Ave KA9 236 B6
Maryborough Rd KA9 236 A6
Mary Dr ML4 141 E3

Maryfield Pl
Ayr KA8 236 B4
Falkirk FK1 41 B4
Maryfield Rd KA8 236 B4
Mary Fisher Cres G82 50 C2
Mary Glen ML2 165 D5
MARYHILL 96 C7
Maryhill Rd
Bearsden G61, G20 76 A1
Glasgow G20 97 A2
Glasgow, Maryhill G20 96 D6
Maryhill Sta G20 96 C8
Maryknowe Rd ML1 143 C2
Maryland Dr G52 115 E5
Maryland Gdns G52 115 E5
Maryland Rd G82 50 C6
Mary Love Pl KA20 206 B1
Marypark Rd PA14 70 B7
Mary Rae Rd ML4 141 E3
Mary Russell Sch The PA2 114 C2
Mary Slessor Wynd G73 138 C2
Mary Sq G69 120 F5
Mary St
Greenock PA16 45 C4
Hamilton ML3 162 D2
Johnstone PA5 112 A3
Laurieston FK2 42 F4
Paisley PA2 113 E2
Port Glasgow PA14 47 A2
Mary Stevenson Dr FK10 10 A8
Maryston St G33 98 D2
Mary Street Rdbt FK2 42 F3
MARYVILLE 140 C8
Maryville Ave G46 136 C2
Maryville Gdns G46 136 C2
Maryville La G71 140 E8
Maryville View G71 120 D1
Marywell Path G68 60 F2
Marywood Sq G41 116 F2
Mary Young Pl G76 157 F6
Mashock Path ML8 201 B1
Mason Ct ML1 163 E6
Masonfield Ave G68 61 D2
MASONHILL 239 D6
Masonhill Pl KA7 239 C5
Masonhill Rd KA7 239 D6
Mason La ML1 163 E6
Mason St
Larkhall ML9 185 C2
Motherwell ML1 163 E6
Masterton St G21 97 C3
Masterton Way G71 121 B1
Mather Terr FK2 42 F4
Matherton Ave G77 157 B5
Matheson Wlk G83 27 E7
Mathew Smith Ave KA1 227 E6
Mathie Cres PA19 44 E6
Mathieson Cres G33 99 F5
Mathieson Rd G73 118 C1
Mathieson St PA1 114 B5
Mathieson Terr 6 G5 117 D4
Mathieson Wlk G83 27 F8
Matilda Rd G41 116 E4
Matthew McWhirter Pl ML9 185 B4
Matthew Pl KA13 207 E5
Matyr's Sch* G4 241 C3
Mauchline G74 160 E3
Mauchline Ave G66 59 A2
Mauchline Ct
Hamilton ML3 161 D2
Kilmarnock KA3 223 B6
Kirkintilloch G66 59 A2
Mauchline La PA16 44 E3
Mauchline Rd KA1 228 F6
Mauchline St G5 117 A4
Mauchline Terr PA16 44 E3
Maukinfauld Ct G32 118 D3
Maukinfauld Gdns G31 118 E4
Maukinfauld Rd G32 118 E3
Mauldslie Dr ML8 187 A6
Mauldslie Pl ML9 199 F8
Mauldslie Rd ML8 187 B2
Mauldslie St
Bellshill ML4 142 A4
Coatbridge ML5 122 A5
Glasgow G40 118 B4
Maule Dr G11 96 A2
Maunsheugh Rd KA3 213 A3
Maurice Ave FK7 7 D4
Mausoleum Dr ML3 162 F5
Mavis Bank
Bishopbriggs G64 97 F8
6 Hamilton G72 161 C7
Mavisbank Ave FK1 66 C6
Mavisbank Gdns
Bellshill ML4 142 A6
Glasgow G5 240 A1
Glasgow G51 116 E6
Mavisbank Rd G51 116 D6
Mavisbank Specl Sch ML6 122 F8
Mavisbank St
Airdrie ML6 122 E8
Wishaw ML2 166 C5
Mavisbank Terr
Johnstone PA5 111 F2
Paisley PA1 113 F3
Mavis Rd PA16 45 B4
Mavor Ave G74 160 A4
Mavor Rdbt G74 159 F4
Maxholm Rd KA1 227 E5
Maxton Ave G78 134 A3
Maxton Cres
Alva FK12 5 C7
Wishaw ML2 165 C6
Maxton Gr G78 134 A3
Maxton Terr G72 138 F3
Maxwell Ave
Bearsden G61 75 E1
Glasgow G69 120 A5
Glasgow, Pollokshields G41 116 F4
Maxwell Cres G72 161 D6
Maxwell Ct
Beith KA15 171 A7
Coatbridge ML5 122 A7
Kilmarnock KA3 223 D3
Maxwell Dr
East Kilbride G74 160 A2
Erskine PA8 72 F3
Glasgow, Garrowhill G69 120 A5
Glasgow, Pollokshields G41 116 C4
Glasgow, Pollokshields G41 116 E4
Maxwell Gdns
Glasgow G41 116 D4
Hurlford KA1 228 E6
Maxwell Gn KA11 220 A4
Maxwell Gr G41 116 D4
Maxwell La G41 116 E4
Maxwell Oval 1 G41 116 F4
Maxwell Park Sta G41 116 D2
Maxwell Path 10 ML9 185 C2
Maxwell Pl
Bridge of Weir PA11 110 D8
Coatbridge ML5 121 F5
Glasgow G41 117 A3
Kilsyth G65 36 D1
Stevenston KA20 206 E2
6 Stirling FK8 7 B8
Uddingston G71 141 A6
Maxwell Rd
Bishopton PA7 72 B3
Glasgow G41 116 F4
Maxwell St
Clydebank G81 73 F4
Glasgow G2 241 A1
Glasgow, Muirhead G69 120 B4
4 Paisley PA3 113 E5
Port Glasgow PA14 47 E1
Maxwell Terr G41 116 F4
Maxwellton Ave G74 160 B3
Maxwellton Ct PA2 113 C4
Maxwellton Pl G74 160 B3
Maxwellton Prim Sch G74 160 B3
Maxwellton Rd
East Kilbride G74 160 C4
Paisley PA1 113 B3
Port Glasgow PA14 68 F6
Maxwellton St PA1, PA2 113 C3
Maxwell Twr FK1 42 D3
Maxwelton Rd G33 98 D2
Maxwood Pl KA11 220 A5
Maybank La G42 117 A1
Maybank St G42 117 A1
Mayberry Cres G32 119 D5
Mayberry Gdns G32 119 D5
Mayberry Gr G32 119 D5
Mayberry Pl G72 161 D8
Maybole Cres G77 157 A4
Maybole Dr ML6 123 A4
Maybole Gdns ML3 161 D2
Maybole Gr G77 157 A4
Maybole Pl ML5 122 D3
Maybole Rd
Ayr KA7 239 B3
Port Glasgow PA14 68 F6
Maybole St G53 134 F6
Mayfield Ave G76 157 E7
Mayfield Cres
Howwood PA9 130 F6
Stevenston KA20 206 C1
Mayfield Ct
Howwood PA9 130 F6
Stirling FK7 7 B3
Mayfield Dr
Howwood PA9 130 F6
Longcroft FK4 39 B3
Mayfield Gdns ML8 202 A7
Mayfield Gr KA20 206 C1
Mayfield Mews FK1 41 F4
Mayfield Pl
Carluke ML8 202 A7
Coatbridge ML5 122 A3
Saltcoats KA21 217 A8
Mayfield Prim Sch KA21 206 A2
Mayfield Rd
Hamilton ML3 161 F4
Saltcoats KA21 217 A8
Stevenston KA20 206 C1
Mayfield St
Glasgow G20 96 F5
Stirling FK7 7 B4
May Gdns
Hamilton ML3 162 C5
Wishaw ML2 165 A4
Mayne Ave FK9 2 B6
May Rd PA2 133 E7
May St ML3 162 D5
May Terr
Glasgow G46 137 B8
Glasgow, Merrylee G46 136 C3
Mayville St KA20 206 C1
May Wynd ML3 162 C5
M&D's Scotland's Theme Pk* ML1 141 E1
Meadow Ave
Hamilton G72 161 D6
Meadow Ave *continued*
Irvine KA12 219 C4
Meadowbank La
Prestwick KA9 236 B7
Uddingston G71 140 E6
Meadowbank Pl G77 156 D5
Meadowbank St G82 49 E4
Meadowburn
Bishopbriggs G64 78 A3
Bishopbriggs G64 78 A4
Meadowburn Ave
Kirkintilloch G66 79 E5
Newton Mearns G77 156 D5
Meadowburn Prim Sch G64 78 A3
Meadowburn Rd ML2 165 C3
Meadow Cl G75 180 A4
Meadow Ct
Carluke ML8 188 C1
Denny FK6 21 D4
Dumbarton G82 49 F5
Meadowfield Pl ML2 166 C6
MEADOWFOOT 190 E5
Meadowfoot Rd KA23 190 D4
Meadowforth Rd FK7 7 C7
Meadow Gn FK10 5 B1
Meadowhead Ave
Irvine KA11 224 G4
Moodiesburn G69 80 F2
Meadowhead Ind Est KA11 224 G4
Meadowhead Rd
Irvine KA11 224 H3
Plains ML6 103 F2
Wishaw ML2 164 C4
Meadowhead Rdbt KA11 224 H2
MEADOWHILL 185 B4
Meadowhill G77 156 D5
Meadowhill St ML9 185 B4
Meadow La
Bothwell G71 141 B2
Renfrew PA4 94 D5
Meadowland Rd FK9 2 A6
Meadowpark KA7 239 A5
Meadowpark Dr KA7 239 B5
Meadow Park Rd KA13 207 C5
Meadowpark St G31 118 B7
Meadow Path ML6 123 D1
Meadow Pk FK12 5 A6
Meadow Pl FK8 2 C1
Meadow Rd
Dumbarton G82 50 A4
Glasgow G11 96 A2
Motherwell ML1 163 F5
Meadow Rise G77 156 C5
Meadows Ave
Erskine PA8 73 C1
Larkhall ML9 185 B3
Meadows Dr PA8 73 C1
Meadowside
Beith KA15 171 A8
Crookedholm KA3 228 E8
Hamilton ML3 183 D6
West Kilbride KA23 190 D5
Meadowside Ave PA5 112 D2
Meadowside Gdns ML6 123 D7
Meadowside Ind Est PA4 94 D6
Meadowside Pl ML6 123 D7
Meadowside Rd G65 59 F8
Meadowside St PA4 94 D5
Meadow St
Coatbridge ML5 122 B4
Falkirk FK1 42 C4
Meadows The
Falkirk, Carronshore FK2 24 B2
Falkirk FK1 42 C4
Helensburgh G84 16 F4
Houston PA6 91 E1
Kilwinning KA13 207 D4
Stirling FK9 2 B3
Meadow View
Cumbernauld G67 62 C4
Kilwinning KA13 207 C5
Plains ML6 104 A3
Meadow Way
Kilwinning KA13 207 D5
Newton Mearns G77 156 D6
Meadowwell St G32 119 B5
Meadow Wlk ML5 122 C6
Meadside Ave PA10 111 A4
Meadside Rd PA10 111 A4
Mealkirk St G81 74 C7
Mealybrae Rd G64 56 D3
MEARNS 156 E3
Mearns Castle High Sch G77 157 A3
Mearnscroft Gdns G77 156 F3
Mearnscroft Rd G77 156 F3
Mearns Ct ML3 183 E7
Mearnskirk Rd G77 156 D2
Mearns Prim Sch G77 156 B3
Mearns Rd
Motherwell ML1 163 C8
Newton Mearns, Mearns G77 156 D1
Newton Mearns, Whitecraigs G77 157 B7
Mearns St
Greenock PA15 45 F4
Greenock PA15 45 F5
Mearns Terr PA15 45 F4
Mearns Way G64 78 D2
Medine Ave KA15 150 B1
Medine Ct KA15 150 B1
Medlar Ct G72 139 F3
Medlar Rd G67 62 D2
Medrox Gdns G67 81 F5
Medwin Ct G75 179 E7
Medwin Gdns G75 179 E7
Medwin St G72 139 E5
Medwyn Pl FK10 9 F6
Medwyn St
Glasgow G14 95 D3
Glasgow G14 95 E2
Meek Pl G72 139 B5
Meeks Rd FK2 42 B5
Meetinghouse La 5 PA1 113 E5
Megan Gate G40 117 F4
Megan St G40 117 F4
Meigle Rd ML6 122 F5
Meikelaught Pl KA21 205 F3
Meikle Ave PA4 94 C2
Meikle Bin Brae G66 57 F7
Meikle Cres
Greengairs ML6 103 D8
Hamilton ML3 183 C7
Meikle Ct KA3 195 E1
Meikle Cutstraw Farm KA3 211 F8
Meikle Drumgray Rd ML6 103 E8
MEIKLE EARNOCK 183 A7
Meikle Earnock Rd ML3 183 B7
Meiklehill Ave 4 G66 58 E1
Meiklehill Rd G66 58 E1
Meikle Pl KA11 220 B6
Meikle Rd G53 135 C8
Meiklerig Cres G53 115 C2
MEIKLERIGGS 113 B2
Meikleriggs Dr PA2 113 A1
Meiklewood Ave KA9 233 D1
Meiklewood Bsns Ctr KA3 223 D8
Meiklewood Rd
Glasgow G51 115 D6
Kilmarnock KA3 222 F5
Melbourne Ave
Clydebank G81 73 D5
East Kilbride G75 180 C8
Melbourne Ct G46 136 D3
Melbourne Gn 5 G75 180 C8
Melbourne Rd KA21 216 E7
Melbourne St G31 117 F6
Melbourne Terr KA21 216 E7
Meldon Pl G51 115 D7
Meldrum Gdns G41 116 D2
Meldrum Mains ML6 102 E4
Meldrum St G81 94 D8
Melford Ave
Glasgow G46 136 D2
Kirkintilloch G66 79 B8
Shotts ML7 147 B3
Melford Rd ML4 141 E7
Melford Way PA3 114 B7
Melfort Ave
Clydebank G81 74 C3
Glasgow G41 116 B4
Melfort Ct G81 74 C2
Melfort Dr FK7 7 C4
Melfort Est PA10 111 C1
Melfort Gdns
Clydebank G81 74 C2
Johnstone PA10 111 C1
Melfort Path ML2 165 F7
Melfort Quadrant ML1 143 D3
Melfort Rd ML3 161 E2
Mellerstain Dr G14 94 F6
Mellerstain Gr G14 94 F6
Mellock Gdns FK1 41 E2
Melness Pl 2 G51 115 D7
Melrose Ave
Chapelhall ML6 123 D2
Coatbridge G69 120 F6
Linwood PA3 112 B5
Motherwell ML1 143 B6
Paisley PA2 113 A1
Rutherglen G73 138 B7
Melrose Cres ML2 165 A5
Melrose Ct
7 Greenock PA15 46 B3
Rutherglen G73 138 B7
Melrose Gdns
Glasgow G20 96 F3
Twechar G65 59 F4
Uddingston G71 120 F1
Melrose Pl
Blantyre G72 140 C1
Coatbridge ML5 121 F7
9 Falkirk FK1 42 B4
Larkhall ML9 185 A1
Melrose Rd
Cumbernauld G67 82 E7
Port Glasgow PA14 68 F7
Melrose St
6 Glasgow G4 97 A2
Hamilton ML3 162 B5
Melrose Terr
East Kilbride G74 159 F3
Hamilton ML3 162 B6
Melvaig Pl G20 96 D5
Melvick Pl 3 G51 115 D7
Melville Cres ML1 163 F6
Melville Ct G1 241 A1
Melville Dr ML1 163 E6
Melville Gdns G64 78 A2
Melville La FK1 42 B5
Melville Pk G74 160 B3
Melville Pl
Bridge of Allan FK9 2 A7
Carluke ML8 187 E2
Melville St
Falkirk FK1 42 B5
Glasgow G41 116 F3
Kilmarnock KA3 228 B8
Melville Terr FK8 7 B6
Melvinhall Rd ML11 215 A5
Memel St G21 97 E5
Memorial Way ML1 143 C6
Memus Ave G52 115 C4
Mendip La G75 180 A4
Mennock Ct ML3 161 E2
Mennock Dr G64 78 A4
Mennock La KA10 229 G5
Mennock St ML1 144 C2
Menock Rd G44 137 D6
MENSTRIE 3 E6
Menstrie Bsns Ctr FK11 3 F6
Menstrie Castle* FK11 3 F6
Menstrie Pl FK10 4 A6
Menstrie Prim Sch FK11 4 A6
Menstrie Rd FK10 4 C3
Menteith Ave G64 78 B1
Menteith Ct
Alloa FK10 10 C6
Motherwell ML1 163 F6
Menteith Dr G73 138 D2
Menteith Gdns G61 75 C8
Menteith Loan ML1 143 A5
Menteith Pl G73 138 D2
Menteith Rd
Motherwell ML1 163 E7
Stirling FK9 2 A3
Menzies Dr
Glasgow G21 98 B5
Stirling FK8 2 A2
Menzies Pl G21 98 B5
Menzies Rd G21 98 A5
Mercat Wynd 2 FK10 10 B6
Merchant La G1 241 A1
Merchants Cl PA10 111 A3
Merchiston Ave
Falkirk FK2 42 A7
Linwood PA3 111 F5
Merchiston Dr PA5 111 D5
Merchiston Gdns FK2 42 A6
Merchiston Ind Est FK2 42 C8
Merchiston Rd
Falkirk, Grahamston FK2 42 A6
Falkirk, Mungal FK2 42 A7
Merchiston Rdbt FK2 42 A6
Merchiston St G32 118 F7
Merchiston Terr FK2 42 A7
Mercury La PA16 44 D3
Mere Ct G68 61 D6
Meredith Dr FK5 23 F3
Merino Rd PA15 45 E3
Merkins Ave G82 50 B6
MERKLAND 58 F1
Merkland Ct
Glasgow G11 96 B1
Kirkintilloch G66 59 A1
Merkland Dr
Falkirk FK1 42 E1
Kirkintilloch G66 80 A8
Merkland Pk KA2 225 F1
Merkland Pl
Dundonald KA2 225 F1
Kirkintilloch G66 59 A1
Merkland Rd
Ayr KA7 239 A2
Coatbridge ML5 101 C2
Merkland Sch G66 58 F1
Merkland St G11 96 B2
Merkland Way G75 180 C4
Merksworth Ave KA24 191 C7
Merksworth Way PA3 113 E7
Merlewood Ave G71 141 B4
Merlewood Rd KA23 190 B4
Merlin Ave
Bellshill ML4 142 A8
Greenock PA16 45 B6
Merlinford Ave PA4 94 E3
Merlinford Cres PA4 94 E3
Merlinford Dr PA4 94 E3
Merlinford Way PA4 94 E3
Merlin La PA16 45 A6
Merlin Way PA3 114 B7
Merrick Ave
Prestwick KA9 233 D1
Troon KA10 229 G4
Merrick Ct ML6 103 A2
Merrick Gdns
Bearsden G61 75 C7
Glasgow G51 116 B5
Quarter ML3 183 E3
Merrick Path G51 116 B5
Merrick Pl
Irvine KA11 220 B2
Symington KA1 231 D4
Merrick Rd KA1 228 B4
Merrick Terr G71 141 B7
Merrick View KA3 195 E1
Merrick Way G73 138 B3
Merryburn Ave G46 136 D4
Merrycrest Ave G46 136 D4
Merrycroft Ave G46 136 D4
Merry Ct G72 161 E6
Merryflats G65 59 F4
Merrygreen Pl KA3 195 E1
Merryland Pl G51 116 C7
Merryland St
Glasgow G51 116 B7
Glasgow G51 116 C7
MERRYLEE 136 D4
Merrylee Ave PA14 68 E7
Merrylee Cres G46 136 C5
Merrylee Park Ave G46 136 D4
Merrylee Park Mews G46 136 C5
Merrylee Prim Sch G44 136 F6
Merrylee Rd G44 136 E5
Merrylees Rd G72 161 C7
Merry St ML1 163 F7
Merryston Ct ML5 121 E6

Merrystone St ML5 121 F7
Merryton Ave
Clydebank G15 75 B3
Glasgow, Merrylee G46 136 D4
Merryton Gdns 3 G15 75 B3
Merryton Rd
Larkhall ML9 184 F6
Motherwell ML1 164 C2
Merryton St ML9 184 F5
Merryton Sta ML9 184 F5
Merryton Twr ML1 164 B2
Merryvale Ave G46 136 D4
Merryvale Pl G46 136 D5
Merryvale Rd KA12 219 C1
Merryvale Rdbt KA12 219 C1
Merton Dr G52 115 A5
Merville Cres FK1 66 F5
Merville Terr FK1 66 F5
Meryon Gdns G32 119 D2
Meryon Rd G32 119 D3
Metcalfe Pl KA11 224 H6
Methil Rd PA14 68 F6
Methil St G14 95 C3
Methil Way G72 161 D2
Methlan Park Gdns G82 49 D2
Methlan Pk G82 49 E2
Methlick Ave ML6 122 E4
Methuen Rd
Paisley PA3 113 F8
Renfrew PA3 93 F1
Methven Ave
Bearsden G61 76 B5
Kilmarnock KA1 227 F4
Methven Pl
East Kilbride G74 159 C2
Kilmarnock KA1 227 F4
Methven Rd G46 157 A7
Methven St
Clydebank G81 73 F4
Glasgow G31 118 D4
Methven Terr ML5 102 B1
Metropole La G1 241 A1
Mews Ho KA7 238 E8
Mews La
Ayr KA7 238 E8
Greenock PA16 45 C8
Kilmarnock KA1 227 F7
Paisley PA3 113 F7
Mey Ct G77 156 A4
Mey Pl G77 156 A4
Mharie Pl G83 27 F2
Michael McParland Dr
G64 78 B8
Michael Terr ML6 123 D1
Micklehouse Oval 2
G69 120 B6
Micklehouse Pl 1 G69 120 B6
Micklehouse Rd G69 120 B6
Micklehouse Wynd 3
G69 120 B6
Midas Pl ML4 142 E5
MID AUCHINLECK 68 E7
Mid Ave PA14 68 F8
Mid Barrwood Rd G65 60 F8
Mid Carbarns ML2 164 D1
Midcroft G64 77 E3
Midcroft Ave G44 137 E5
MIDDLEFIELD 42 D6
Middlefield G75 180 E5
Middlefield Ind Est FK2 42 D7
Middlefield Rd FK2 42 D6
Middlefield Residential Sch
G11 96 B2
Middlehouse Ct ML8 187 D2
Middlemass Ct FK2 42 B6
Middlemass Dr KA1 228 B8
Middlemuir Ave G66 79 D5
Middlemuir Rd
Kirkintilloch G66 79 D6
Stirling FK7 7 C6
Middlepart KA20 206 C2
Middlepart Cres KA21 206 A1
Middlepenny Pl PA14 70 B7
Middlepenny Rd PA14 70 B7
Middlerigg Rd G68 61 D2
Middlesex Gdns 3 G41 116 E6
Middlesex St G41 116 E5
Middleton FK11 4 A5
Middleton Ave ML9 199 B8
Middleton Dr
Helensburgh G84 25 B8
Milngavie G62 55 C2
Middleton La G84 25 B8
Middleton Pk KA11 220 A4
Middleton Pl G68 60 F2
Middleton Rd
Irvine KA11 220 A4
Linwood PA3 112 D7
Paisley PA3 113 B6
Middleton St
Alexandria G83 27 D5
Glasgow G51 116 C6
Middle Ward St G81 74 D7
Mid Dykes Rd KA21 205 E2
Midfaulds Ave PA4 94 E2
Midland Craft Ctr KA3 213 C2
Midland St G1 240 C2
Midlem Dr G52 115 C5
Midlem Oval G52 115 C5
Mid-Loan St ML8 201 E4
Midlock St G51 116 C6
Midlothian Dr G41 116 D1
Mid Pk G75 180 E8
Mid Rd
Beith KA15 150 B1
Cumbernauld G67 82 F6
Eaglesham G76 178 E4
Mid Rig KA11 220 A4
Midthorn Cres FK2 42 E5
MIDTON 44 D6
Midton Ave KA9 236 B8
Midton Cres 10 G69 81 A3
Midton Rd
Ayr KA7 238 F6
Howwood PA9 131 B6
Kilmarnock KA1 227 F2
Prestwick KA9 236 C8
Midton St G21 97 F3
Midtown FK11 3 F7
Mid-Wharf St G4 97 C2
Migvie Pl G20 96 D5
Milford G75 180 B7
Milford Ct G33 119 A8
Milford St G33 119 A8
Milgarholm Ave KA12 219 D1
Milgarholm Rdbt KA12 219 D1
Millands Ave G72 140 C2
Millarbank St G21 97 E4
Millard Ave ML1 143 B2
Millar Gr ML3 162 B3
Millar Pl
5 Bishopbriggs G64 98 D8
Bonnybridge FK4 40 B3
Stenhousemuir FK2 24 A5
Stirling FK8 2 C1
Millar Rd KA21 217 A8
Millars Pl G66 79 D4
Millar St
Greenock PA15 46 B2
Paisley PA1 113 F5
Stonehouse ML9 198 F2
MILLARSTON 113 A3
Millarston Ave PA1 113 A4
Millarston Dr PA1 113 A4
Millarston Ind Est PA1 113 A3
Millars Wynd FK10 5 C2
Millar Terr G73 118 B1
Mill Ave KA3 222 C7
Millbank Ave ML4 142 C3
Millbank Ct ML5 121 F3
Millbank Rd
Port Glasgow PA14 68 C8
Wishaw ML2 164 F1
Millbank Row KA11 220 D1
Millbarr Gr KA15 171 F4
Millbeg Cres G33 119 F5
Millbeg Pl G33 119 F5
Mill Brae
Ayr KA7 239 A7
Bridge of Weir PA11 110 D8
Millbrae Ave G69 100 D8
Millbrae Cres
Clydebank G81 94 D7
Glasgow G42 136 F7
Millbrae Ct
Ayr KA7 239 A7
Glasgow G42 136 F7
Mill Brae Ct ML5 121 D5
Millbrae Gdns G42 136 F7
Millbrae Rd G42 136 F7
Millbrix Ave G14 95 A5
Millbrook G74 159 B1
Millbrook Pl FK11 3 F6
Millburn Ave
Clydebank G81 94 E8
Renfrew PA4 94 E3
Rutherglen G73 138 A6
Millburn Cres G82 50 B3
Millburn Ct G75 179 E7
Millburn Dr
Kilmacolm PA13 89 B8
Renfrew PA4 94 E3
Millburn Gate ML9 185 F1
Millburn Gdns G75 179 E7
Millburn La ML9 185 C2
Millburn Pl ML9 199 B8
Millburn Rd
Alexandria G83 27 D3
Ashgill ML9 186 A1
Dumbarton G82 50 B3
Port Glasgow PA14 68 C8
Renfrew PA4 94 D3
Millburn St
Falkirk FK2 42 D5
Glasgow G21 98 A1
Lennoxtown G66 57 E8
Motherwell ML1 163 E7
Millburn Terr KA11 220 A6
Millburn Way
East Kilbride G75 179 E7
Renfrew PA4 94 E3
Mill Cres
Glasgow G40 117 F4
Irvine KA12 219 E3
Torrance G64 57 C1
Millcroft Rd
Cumbernauld, Carbrain
G67 62 B1
Cumbernauld G67 82 E4
Rutherglen G73 117 F2
Mill Ct
Falkirk FK2 24 B3
Hamilton ML3 162 C2
Kilbirnie KA25 149 B1
Kilmarnock KA1 228 A7
Rutherglen G73 138 A8
Milldam Rd G81 74 C7
Milldown Pl KA11 220 C2
Milledge ML8 188 A2
Millennium Ct G34 120 C8
Millennium Gdns G34 120 C7
Millennium Gr 1 G34 120 C8
Millennium Wheel Dr FK1 41 A5
Miller Cl G64 98 D8
Miller Ct G82 50 B4
Miller Dr G64 98 D8
Millerfield Pl
Glasgow G40 118 B3
Hamilton ML3 162 F3
Millerfield Rd G40 118 B3
Miller Gdns
Bishopbriggs G64 98 D8
Hamilton ML3 162 F3
Miller La G81 74 B1
Miller Pl
Airth FK2 14 E4
Ardrossan KA22 205 B4
Harthill ML7 127 F6
Miller Prim Sch G45 137 F2
Miller Rd
Ayr KA7 238 F7
Balloch G83 27 F8
Millerslea G82 50 F1
Millerslea Gdns G84 16 F1
MILLERSNEUK 79 F5
Millersneuk Ave G66 79 D3
Millersneuk Cres G33 99 B5
Millersneuk Ct G66 79 D4
Millersneuk Dr G66 79 D4
Millersneuk Prim Sch
G66 79 E4
Millersneuk Rd G66 79 D4
Miller's Pl ML6 123 B7
Miller Sq KA9 233 C2
Miller St
Carluke ML8 188 A2
Clydebank G81 74 B1
Coatbridge ML5 122 B5
Dumbarton G82 50 B4
Glasgow G1 241 A2
Glasgow, Muirhead G69 120 B4
Hamilton ML3 162 F3
Harthill ML7 127 E6
Johnstone PA5 112 B3
Larkhall ML9 185 B3
Wishaw ML2 165 A3
MILLERSTON
Busby 157 E4
Stepps 99 A4
Millerston St G31 118 B6
Miller Wlk G64 98 D8
Mill Farm KA22 205 D5
Millfield Ave
Erskine PA8 72 F1
Motherwell ML1 163 F8
Millfield Cres PA8 73 A1
Millfield Dr PA8 73 A1
Millfield Gdns PA8 73 A1
Millfield Hill PA8 72 F1
Millfield La PA8 72 F1
Millfield Mdws PA8 72 F1
Millfield Pl PA8 72 F1
Millfield View PA8 72 F1
Millfield Wlk PA8 73 A1
Millfield Wynd PA8 72 F1
Millflats St FK2 24 A1
Millford Dr PA3 112 B5
Millfore Ct KA11 220 A3
Millgate G71 140 F8
Millgate Ave G71 140 F8
Millgate Cres ML6 105 A4
Millgate Ct G71 140 F7
Millgate Rd ML3 162 C1
Millgate Terr ML3 162 C1
Millglen Cvn Pk KA22 205 C6
Millglen Pl KA22 205 D4
Millglen Rd KA22 205 D4
Mill Gr
Cambuslang G72 139 D5
Hamilton ML3 162 C2
Millhall Ct ML6 104 B3
Millhall Rd
Eaglesham G76 179 C3
Stirling FK7 7 D5
MILLHEUGH 184 F2
Millheugh ML9 184 E2
Millheugh Brae ML9 184 E2
Millheugh Pl G72 161 C6
Millheugh Rd ML3 198 E5
Mill Hill FK7 6 D6
Millhill Ave KA3 222 C7
Millhill Rd KA20 206 D1
Millhill Terr KA3 222 E4
Millholm Rd G44 137 B4
Millhouse Cres G20 96 C7
Millhouse Dr G20 96 C7
Millichen Rd G23 76 E5
Millig St G84 16 C3
Milliken Dr PA10 111 C2
MILLIKENPARK 111 C1
Milliken Park Rd PA10 111 C1
Milliken Park Sta PA5 131 C8
Milliken Rd PA10 111 C2
Mill La G84 16 A3
Mill Loan ML6 123 A8
Mill of Airthrey Ct FK9 1 F8
Mill of Gryffe Rd PA11 110 D8
MILL OF HALDANE 28 A8
Mill Pk
Dalry KA24 191 D8
Hamilton ML3 162 C2
Mill Pl
Linwood PA3 112 A6
Uddingston G71 140 F6
Millport Ave G44 137 C7
Millport Rd PA14 68 F6
Mill Rd
Airdrie ML6 103 A1
Alloa FK10 10 B6
Banton G65 37 D3
Bothwell G71 141 A1
Cambusbarron FK7 6 D6
Cambuslang G72 139 D5
Cardross G82 26 A1
Mill Rd *continued*
Carluke ML8 187 E1
Clydebank G81 94 D7
Falkirk FK2 24 B3
Hamilton ML3 162 C1
Harthill ML7 127 F5
Hartwood ML7 145 F1
Irvine KA12 219 E2
Kilbirnie KA25 149 B1
Motherwell ML1 163 F8
Queenzieburn G65 59 E7
Shotts ML7 166 F8
Wattston ML6 83 B1
Wishaw ML2 166 E5
Mill Rig G75 180 D5
Mill Rise G66 79 D4
Millroad Dr G40 241 C1
Millroad Gdns 2 G40 117 F6
Millroad St G40 117 F6
Millrock Ct KA10 229 D3
Millside Gdns KA13 207 F4
Mill St
Alloa FK10 10 B6
Ayr KA7 239 A8
Caldercruix ML6 104 F5
Glasgow G40 117 F3
Greenock PA15 45 E4
Kilmarnock KA1 227 F7
Paisley PA1 113 F4
Rutherglen G73 138 A6
Millstream Cres ML6 105 A4
Millstream Ct PA1 113 F4
Mill Street Ind Est ML6 123 A8
Mill Trail Visitor Ctr* FK12 4 F7
Mill Vennel PA4 94 D3
Millview G78 134 D3
Millview Mdws G78 154 C7
Millview Pl G53 135 B4
Millview Terr G78 154 C7
Mill Waulk KA3 211 E8
Mill Way G66 80 A7
Mill Wlk G72 139 D5
Millwood St G41 136 E8
Mill Wynd
Ayr KA7 238 F8
Waterside KA3 213 F3
Milnbank St G31 118 A8
Milncroft Pl G33 99 A1
Milncroft Rd G33 99 A1
Milndavie Cres G63 31 C3
Milndavie Rd G63 31 C2
Milne Ct ML2 165 E4
Milne Park Rd FK7 11 E8
Milner Rd G13 95 E5
Milne Way G71 141 A6
MILNGAVIE 55 C3
Milngavie Ent Ctr G62 55 A2
Milngavie Prim Sch G62 55 A2
Milngavie Rd
Bearsden G61 76 A6
Strathblane G63 31 C2
Milngavie Sta G62 55 B1
Milnpark Gdns 1 G41 116 E5
Milnpark St G41 116 E5
Milnquarter Rd FK4 40 A3
MILNWOOD 142 D4
Milnwood Dr
Bellshill ML4 142 D4
Motherwell ML1 142 C2
Milovaig Ave G23 76 D1
Milovaig St G23 76 D1
Milrig Rd G73 137 F7
Milroy Gdns ML4 142 A8
MILTON
Dumbarton 50 F2
Glasgow 97 C7
Milton Ave
Cambuslang G72 138 E5
Kilmarnock KA3 223 C1
Miltonbank Prim Sch G22 97 C8
Milton Brae
Milton G82 50 F2
Stirling FK7 7 B2
Milton Cl FK6 21 D3
Milton Cres
Bannockburn FK7 7 C1
Carluke ML8 187 F1
Irvine KA11 220 C1
Troon KA10 229 F6
Milton Ct
Airdrie ML6 123 A8
Irvine KA11 220 D1
Milton G82 50 F2
Milton Douglas Rd G81 74 B5
Milton Dr
1 Bishopbriggs G64 97 F7
Kilmarnock KA3 223 C1
Milton Est G83 27 F6
Milton Gdns
Stirling FK7 7 B1
Uddingston G71 140 E8
Milton Gr FK7 7 C1
Milton Hill G82 50 F1
Milton Mains Rd G81 74 A5
MILTON OF CAMPSIE 58 D6
Milton Pk
Ayr KA7 239 B3
Kilbirnie KA25 149 B2
Milton Pl FK6 21 D3
Milton Quadrant KA25 149 A3
Milton Rd
Bannockburn FK7 7 C1
Carluke ML8 201 D7
East Kilbride G74 159 A2
Irvine KA11 220 C1
Kilbirnie KA25 149 A3
Kilmarnock KA3 228 C8
Kilmarnock KA3 228 D8
Milton Rd *continued*
Kirkintilloch G66 58 C1
Lennoxtown G66 57 E7
Port Glasgow PA14 68 E6
Milton Row FK6 21 E3
Milton Sch G22 97 E7
Milton St
Airdrie ML6 123 A8
Carluke ML8 187 E2
Glasgow G4 241 A4
Hamilton ML3 162 A4
Motherwell ML1 163 E8
Milton Terr
Hamilton ML3 162 A5
Stirling FK7 7 B1
Milton View KA2 226 E5
Milverton Ave G61 75 D6
Milverton Rd
Glasgow G46 136 B1
Rutherglen G46 157 A8
Mimosa Rd PA11 110 D8
Minard Rd
Glasgow G41 116 E1
Port Glasgow PA14 68 E7
Shotts ML7 146 D6
Minard Way G71 141 A7
Mincher Cres ML1 163 E4
Minch Way ML6 123 D5
Minella Gdns ML4 142 A8
Mine Rd FK9 2 A8
Minerva Ct 10 G3 116 E8
Minerva La PA16 44 D3
Minerva St G3 116 E8
Minerva Terr PA16 44 D3
Minerva Way G3 116 E8
Mingarry St G20 96 E4
Mingulay Cres G22 97 D8
Mingulay Pl G22 97 E8
Mingulay St G22 97 D8
Ministers Pk G74 158 F4
Minmoir Rd G53 134 F7
Minster Wlk G69 120 F5
Minstrel Rd G13 75 D1
Minthill Pl ML7 127 D5
Mintlaw Way G69 80 C1
Minto Ave G73 138 D4
Minto Cres G52 115 F5
Minto Ct FK12 5 B6
Minto Gdns FK12 5 B6
Minto Pk ML2 165 C6
Minto St
Glasgow G52 115 F5
Greenock PA16 45 D4
Mireton St G22 97 B5
Mirin Dr PA3 113 E7
Mirren Dr G81 73 F7
Mirren's Shore PA14 47 C2
Mirrin Wynd PA3 113 E7
Mirrlees Dr G12 96 C4
Mirrlees La G12 96 C4
Misk Knowes KA20 217 E6
Misk Rd KA20 218 C6
Mission Gdns ML2 165 C5
Mission La 8 FK1 42 B4
Mission Pl ML1 163 E8
Mitchell Arc G73 138 B8
Mitchell Ave
Cambuslang G72 139 E6
Renfrew PA4 94 B2
Mitchell Cres FK10 9 F7
Mitchell Ct
East Kilbride G74 159 C2
3 Kilmarnock KA1 228 A8
Mitchell Dr
Cardross G82 48 B6
Milngavie G62 55 C1
Rutherglen G73 138 B6
Mitchell Gr G74 159 C2
Mitchell Hill Rd G45 137 F2
Mitchell La G1 240 C2
Mitchell Liby* G3 240 C3
Mitchell Pl
Falkirk FK1 41 E1
Saltcoats KA21 205 E1
Mitchell Rd G67 62 A3
Mitchell St
Airdrie ML6 122 F8
Beith KA15 150 B1
Coatbridge ML5 121 C5
Glasgow G1 240 C2
Greenock PA15 46 F2
Mitchell Way G83 27 E5
Mitchison Rd G67 62 A3
Mitre Ct 2 G11 95 F4
Mitre Gate 1 G11 95 F4
Mitre La G14 95 E4
Mitre Lane W G14 95 D4
Mitre Rd
Glasgow G11 95 F4
Glasgow G14 95 E4
Moat Ave G13 95 C7
Mochray Ct FK4 39 E5
Mochrum Ct KA9 236 D6
Mochrum Rd G43 136 E6
Modan Rd FK7 7 A3
Moffat Ave FK2 24 C3
Moffat Ct G75 179 E7
Moffat Gdns G75 179 E7
Moffathill ML6 123 E5
MOFFAT MILLS 123 F6
Moffat Pl
Airdrie ML6 123 F8
Blantyre G72 140 D1
Bonnybridge FK4 40 A4
Coatbridge ML5 122 E4

Moffat Pl *continued*
East Kilbride G75 179 E7
Moffat Rd
Airdrie ML6 123 F7
Prestwick KA9 233 C3
Moffat St
Glasgow G5 117 D4
Greenock PA15 46 C3
Moffat View ML6 104 A3
Moffat Wynd KA21 205 F3
Mogarth Ave PA2 132 F8
Moidart Ave PA4 94 B4
Moidart Cres G52 115 F5
Moidart Ct G78 134 B4
Moidart Gdns
Kirkintilloch G66 59 B1
Newton Mearns G77 156 E6
Moidart Pl G52 115 F5
Moidart Rd
Glasgow G52 115 E5
Port Glasgow PA14 68 E7
Moir St
Alloa FK10 10 A8
Glasgow G1 241 B1
Molendinar St G1 241 B1
Molendinar Terr G78 154 C6
Mollanbowie Rd G83 19 F2
MOLLINSBURN 81 D4
Mollinsburn Rd
Annathill G67, ML5 81 F2
Glenboig ML5, ML6 101 F8
Glenmavis ML6 102 C6
Mollinsburn St G21 97 E3
Mollins Ct G68 81 D5
Mollins Rd G68 81 C7
Mollison Ave ML7 127 E6
Monach Gdns KA11 225 B8
Monach Rd
Glasgow G33 119 C8
Port Glasgow PA14 69 A7
Monaebrook Pl G84 25 B8
Monar Dr G22 97 B3
Monar Pl G22 97 B3
Monar St G22 97 B3
Monart Pl G20 96 F4
Monar Way [5] ML2 165 F6
Moncks Rd FK1 42 D4
Moncreiff Gdns G66 79 D5
Moncrieff Ave G66 79 D5
Moncrieffe Rd ML6 123 D4
Moncrieff St [1] PA3 113 E5
Moncur Ct KA13 207 C5
Moncur Rd KA13 208 A3
Moncur St G40 241 C1
Moness Dr G52 115 E4
Money Gr ML1 164 B4
Monieburgh Cres G65 36 E1
Monieburgh Rd G65 36 E1
Monifieth Ave G52 115 D3
Monikie Gdns G64 78 D1
Monkcastle Dr G72 139 A6
Monkland Ave G66 79 D6
Monklands KA10 229 G7
Monklands Hospl ML6 122 D7
Monklands Ind Est ML5 121 F2
Monkland St ML6 123 B7
Monkland Terr ML5 101 D6
Monkland View
Calderbank ML6 123 B2
Uddingston G71 121 A1
Monkland View Cres
G69 121 A5
Monkreddan Cres KA13 207 C5
Monksbridge Ave G13 75 D1
Monkscourt Ave ML6 122 E7
Monkscroft Ave [1] G11 96 A3
Monkscroft Ct G11 96 A2
Monkscroft Gdns G11 96 A2
Monks La ML8 201 E4
Monks Rd ML6 123 C4
MONKTON 233 D4
Monkton Brae G69 80 C1
Monkton Cres ML5 121 E4
Monkton Ct KA9 233 D2
Monkton Dr G15 75 C2
Monkton Gdns G77 157 A4
Monktonhill Rd
Monkton KA9 233 B7
Troon KA10 232 F8
Monktonhill Rdbt KA9 233 D6
Monkton Pl PA14 68 F7
Monkton Prim Sch KA9 233 D4
Monkton Rd KA9 233 C1
Monkwood Pl KA7 239 B2
Monmouth Ave G12 96 A5
Monreith Ave G61 75 D2
Monreith Rd G43 136 E6
Monreith Road E G44 137 A5
Monroe Dr G71 120 F1
Monroe Pl G71 120 F1
Montague La G12 96 B4
Montague St G4 96 F2
Montalto Ave ML1 143 B1
Montclair Pl PA3 112 B6
Montego Gn [2] G75 159 A1
Monteith Dr G76 158 A8
Monteith Gdns G76 157 F8
Monteith Pl
[3] Glasgow G40 117 E5
Hamilton G72 161 E8
Monteith Row
Glasgow G1 241 B1
Glasgow G40 117 E5
Monteith Wlk ML7 146 E6
Montfode Ct KA22 205 B4
Montfode Dr KA22 205 B4
Montford Ave G44 137 E7
Montfort Pl FK1 42 B3
Montgarrie St [3] G51 115 D6
Montgomerie Cres KA21 216 E8
Montgomerie Ct KA22 205 C1
Montgomerie Dr KA3 211 B7
Montgomerie Pier Rd
KA22 205 B1
Montgomerie Rd
Prestwick KA9 233 B1
Saltcoats KA21 216 E8
Montgomerie St
Ardrossan KA22 205 C1
Port Glasgow PA14 47 D1
Montgomerieston Pl [8]
KA25 149 A1
Montgomerieston St [9]
KA25 149 A1
Montgomerie Terr
Ayr KA7 235 E1
Kilwinning KA13 208 A3
Montgomery Ave
Beith KA15 171 C8
Coatbridge ML5 121 F7
Paisley PA3 114 B7
Montgomery Cres
Falkirk FK2 24 B2
Wishaw ML2 185 E8
Montgomery Ct
Eaglesham G76 178 E3
Kilbirnie KA25 149 B2
Paisley PA3 114 B7
Montgomery Dr
Falkirk FK2 24 B2
Glasgow G46 136 C1
Kilbarchan PA10 111 A4
Montgomeryfield KA11 225 B8
Montgomery Pl
[3] East Kilbride G74 159 F2
Falkirk FK2 24 B2
Irvine KA12 219 A1
[1] Kilmarnock KA3 222 F2
Larkhall ML9 185 B2
Montgomery Rd PA3 114 B8
Montgomery Sq G76 178 E4
Montgomery St
Cambuslang G72 139 E5
Eaglesham G76 178 E4
[4] East Kilbride G74 159 F2
Falkirk FK2 42 E5
Glasgow G40 118 A4
Irvine KA12 219 A1
Kilmarnock KA3 222 F2
Larkhall ML9 185 A4
Montgomery Terr G66 58 C5
Montgomery Way FK9 2 B3
Montgomery Well FK2 24 B2
Montgreenan View KA13 207 F3
Montport Gate G78 134 E3
Montraive St G73 118 C1
Montrave St G52 115 D4
Montreal Ho G81 73 D6
Montreal Pk G75 159 C1
Montrose Ave
Glasgow, Carmyle G32 119 C1
Glasgow G52 114 E8
Glasgow G52 114 F8
Glasgow (Hillington Ind Est)
G52 94 E1
Port Glasgow PA14 68 E6
Montrose Cres ML3 162 D4
Montrose Ct
[7] Motherwell ML1 143 B2
Paisley PA2 132 F8
Montrose Dr G61 75 E7
Montrose Gdns
Blantyre G72 140 C2
Kilsyth G65 36 C1
Milngavie G62 55 A3
Montrose La ML3 162 C4
Montrose Pl PA3 112 A6
Montrose Rd
Paisley PA2 132 F8
Stirling FK9 2 C4
Montrose St
Clydebank G81 74 C2
Glasgow G1 241 B2
Motherwell ML1 142 D1
Montrose Terr
Bishopbriggs G64 98 C7
Bridge of Weir PA11 110 D7
Montrose Way
Bonnybridge FK4 39 D5
Paisley PA2 132 F8
Monument Cres KA9 233 F1
Monument Rd KA7 238 F4
Monument View FK8 2 B2
Monymusk Gdns G64 78 D2
Monymusk Pl G15 74 E5
Moodie Ct KA1 227 F5
MOODIESBURN 80 E2
Moodiesburn St G33 98 E2
Moonlight Pl KA22 205 B2
Moorburn Ave G46 136 B3
Moorburn Pl PA3 111 F6
Moorcroft Dr ML6 123 E7
Moorcroft Rd G77 156 C3
Moore Dr
Bearsden G61 75 F3
Helensburgh G84 25 C7
Moore Gdns ML3 183 E7
Moorend Workshops
KA11 224 G7
Moore Pl KA20 217 D8
Moore St
Glasgow G31, G40 117 F6
Motherwell ML1 143 A3
MOORFIELD 227 B8
Moorfield Ave
Kilmarnock KA1 227 D6
Port Glasgow PA14 68 D7
Moorfield Cres ML6 123 F7
Moorfield Ind Est KA2 227 A7
Moorfield La PA19 44 C6
Moorfield Pl KA2 226 D5
Moorfield Rd
Gourock PA19 44 C7
Hamilton G72 161 C6
Prestwick KA9 236 C7
Moorfield Rdbt KA1 227 A7
Moorfoot G64 78 C2
Moorfoot Ave
Glasgow G46 136 A3
Paisley PA2 113 D1
Moorfoot Dr
Gourock PA19 44 C6
Wishaw ML2 164 F3
Moorfoot Gdns G75 180 B3
Moorfoot Path PA2 133 D8
Moorfoot Pl KA11 220 A3
Moorfoot Prim Sch PA19 44 C6
Moorfoot St G32 118 E6
Moorfoot Way
Bearsden G61 75 C8
Irvine KA11 220 A3
Moorhill Cres G77 156 C4
Moorhill Rd G77 156 C3
Moorhouse Ave
Glasgow G13 94 F6
Paisley PA2 113 B2
Moorhouse St G78 134 C2
Moorings The PA2 113 C3
Moorland Dr ML6 123 E7
Moorlands Wlk G71 141 A5
MOORPARK 94 B2
Moorpark Ave
[3] Airdrie ML6 123 E7
Glasgow G52 114 F6
Muirhead G69 100 C7
Moor Park Cres KA9 236 C5
Moorpark Ct G51 116 A7
Moorpark Dr G52 115 A6
Moorpark Ind Est KA20 217 D7
Moorpark Pl
[1] Glasgow G52 114 F6
Kilbirnie KA25 149 A3
Stevenston KA20 217 D7
Moor Park Pl KA9 236 C5
Moorpark Prim Sch
Kilbirnie KA25 149 A3
Renfrew PA4 94 B2
Moorpark Road E KA20 217 D8
Moorpark Road W KA20 217 D7
Moorpark Sq PA4 94 B2
Moor Pk KA9 236 C5
Moor Pl KA8 236 C4
Moor Rd
Ayr KA8 236 C4
Cartland ML8, ML11 202 E2
Eaglesham G76 178 D4
Milngavie G62 55 B2
Strathblane G63 31 C1
Moorside St ML8 188 A2
Morag Ave G72 140 C1
Moraine Ave G15 75 B1
Moraine Cir G15 75 B1
Moraine Dr
Clarkston G76 157 D8
Clydebank G15 75 B1
Moraine Pl G15 75 B1
Morar Ave G81 74 B4
Morar Cres
Airdrie ML6 102 E2
Bishopbriggs G64 77 F2
Bishopton PA7 72 C2
Clydebank G81 74 B4
Coatbridge ML5 101 D1
Morar Ct
Clydebank G81 74 B4
Cumbernauld G67 82 B8
Hamilton ML3 162 A1
Larkhall ML9 184 F5
Morar Dr
Bearsden G61 76 B3
Clydebank G81 74 B4
Cumbernauld G67 82 B8
Falkirk FK2 24 C1
Linwood PA3 112 A5
Paisley PA2 113 A2
Rutherglen G73 138 B3
Morar Pl
Clydebank G81 74 B4
East Kilbride G74 159 F3
Irvine KA12 219 C6
Newton Mearns G77 156 D7
Renfrew PA4 94 B4
Morar Rd
Clydebank G81 74 B4
Glasgow G52 115 E5
Port Glasgow PA14 68 E7
Morar St ML2 165 A1
Morar Terr
Rutherglen G73 138 D4
Uddingston G71 141 B7
Morar Way
Motherwell ML1 143 C3
Shotts ML7 147 B3
Moravia Ave G71 141 A3
Moray Ave ML6 123 A5
Moray Ct G73 138 A8
Moray Dr
Clarkston G76 157 F7
Torrance G64 57 B1
Moray Gate G71 140 F4
Moray Gdns
Clarkston G76 157 F8
Cumbernauld G68 61 F5
Uddingston G71 140 F8
Moray Pl
Bishopbriggs G64 78 C1
Chryston G69 100 D8
Glasgow G41 116 F2
Hamilton G72 161 C6
Kirkintilloch G66 59 B1
Linwood PA3 112 A6
Moray Quadrant ML4 142 A5
Moray Rd PA14 47 C1
Moray Way ML1 143 A5
Mordaunt St G40 118 A3
Moredun Cres G32 119 C7
Moredun Dr PA2 113 B1
Moredun Rd PA2 113 B1
Moredun St G32 119 C7
Morefield Rd [10] G51 115 D7
Morgan Ct FK7 7 C3
Morgan Mews [4] G42 117 B3
Morgan St
Hamilton ML3 162 D2
Larkhall ML9 184 F3
Morina Gdns G53 135 C3
Morion Rd G13 95 D8
Moriston Ct ML2 165 F6
Morland G74 160 D4
Morley Cres FK7 7 A3
Morley St G42 137 A7
Morna La G14 95 E2
Mornay Way ML7 146 D5
MORNINGSIDE 166 C3
Morningside Prim Sch
ML2 166 B4
Morningside Rd ML2 166 C3
Morningside St G33 118 E8
Morrin Path G21 97 E3
Morrin St G21 97 E4
Morris Cres
Hamilton G72 161 D7
Hurlford KA1 228 E6
Motherwell ML1 143 E1
Morris Ct KA24 191 B8
Morrishall Rd G74 160 C3
Morrishill Dr KA15 171 A7
Morris La KA3 223 A1
Morris Moodie Ave KA20 217 E7
Morrison Ave
Bonnybridge FK4 39 F6
Stevenston KA20 206 E1
Morrison Ct KA20 206 E1
Morrison Dr
Bannockburn FK7 7 C2
Lennoxtown G66 57 F7
Morrison Gdns
Ayr KA8 239 B8
Torrance G64 78 C8
Morrison Ho G67 62 A2
Morrison Pl KA3 223 D2
Morrison Quadrant G81 74 E1
Morrison Rd KA9 233 C3
Morrison St
Duntocher G81 73 F6
Glasgow G5 240 B1
Morris Rd KA9 233 D1
Morris St
Greenock PA15 46 C3
Hamilton ML3 162 D1
Larkhall ML9 185 C1
Morris Terr FK8 7 A8
Morriston Cres PA4 94 F1
Morriston Park Dr G72 139 A6
Morriston St G72 139 A6
Morton Ave KA7 239 A5
Morton Gdns G41 116 C1
Morton Pl KA1 222 F1
Morton Rd
Ayr KA7 239 A5
Stewarton KA3 211 C8
Morton St ML1 163 E8
Morven Ave
Bishopbriggs G64 78 C1
Blantyre G72 140 C1
Kilmarnock KA3 222 F3
Paisley PA2 133 D8
Morven Cres KA10 229 E2
Morven Ct FK1 42 C2
Morven Dr
Clarkston G76 157 D8
Linwood PA3 112 A5
Motherwell ML1 164 C4
Troon KA10 229 E3
Morven Gait PA8 93 E8
Morven Gate ML1 164 C4
Morven Gdns G71 140 F8
Morven La G72 140 C1
Morven Rd
Bearsden G61 75 E6
Cambuslang G72 138 F3
Morven St
Coatbridge ML5 122 A8
Glasgow G52 115 E5
Morven Way
[1] Bothwell G71 141 B3
Kirkintilloch G66 80 B8
Morville Cres KA13 207 E5
Mosesfield St G21 97 F5
Mosque Ave G5 117 C5
Mossacre Rd ML2 165 C4
Moss Ave
Caldercruix ML6 105 A5
Linwood PA3 112 B6
Mossband La ML7 146 E6
Mossbank
East Kilbride G75 179 F8
Hamilton G72 161 D6
Mossbank *continued*
Prestwick KA9 236 E7
Mossbank Ave G33 98 F4
Mossbank Cres ML1 143 F4
Mossbank Dr G33 98 F4
Mossbank Rd ML2 165 C4
Mossbell Rd ML4 141 E6
MOSSBLOWN 237 F7
Mossblown St ML9 184 F3
Mossburn Ave
Balloch G83 19 F1
Harthill ML7 127 D5
Mossburn Ind Est ML7 127 D5
Mossburn Rd ML2 165 D3
Mossburn St ML2 165 D1
Mosscastle Rd
Glasgow G33 99 C2
Slamannan FK1 86 A7
Moss Ct KA1 228 F5
Mossdale G74 159 C3
Mossdale Ct ML4 142 D5
Mossdale Gdns ML3 161 E2
Moss Dr
Barrhead G78 134 A5
Erskine PA8 93 B7
Irvine KA11 224 H5
Mossedge Ind Est PA3 112 C6
MOSSEND 142 D5
Mossend Ave
Helensburgh G84 16 F1
Kilbirnie KA25 170 A8
Mossend La G33 119 D8
Mossend Pl G84 16 F1
Mossend Prim Sch ML4 142 C4
Mossend St G33 119 D8
Mossgiel G75 180 B7
Mossgiel Ave
Cowie FK7 12 D7
Kilmarnock KA3 228 C8
Rutherglen G73 138 A5
Stirling FK8 2 A2
Troon KA10 229 G4
Mossgiel Cres G76 157 F5
Mossgiel Dr
Clydebank G81 74 C3
Irvine KA12 219 D3
Mossgiel Gdns
Kirkintilloch G66 58 F1
Uddingston G71 140 E8
Mossgiel La [1] ML9 185 C1
Mossgiel Pl
Ayr KA7 239 A6
Rutherglen G73 138 A5
[1] Stevenston KA20 206 E1
Mossgiel Rd
Ardrossan KA22 205 D4
Ayr KA7 239 A6
Cumbernauld G67 62 B2
Glasgow G43 136 D6
Saltcoats KA21 206 A3
Mossgiel St FK1 41 B5
Mossgiel Terr G72 140 C2
Mossgiel Way ML1 143 C4
Mosshall Gr ML1 143 F4
Mosshall Rd ML1 143 D7
Mosshall St ML1 143 F3
Mosshead Prim Sch G61 75 E7
Mosshead Rd
Bearsden G61 76 A7
Kilmarnock KA1 228 A3
Moss Heights Ave G52 115 D5
Mosshill Rd ML4 142 B7
Mosshouse FK7 6 F4
Mosside Pl KA3 222 F4
Mosside Rd KA8 236 C4
Mossknowe G67 62 C2
Mossland Dr ML2 165 C4
Mossland Rd
Glasgow G52 114 E8
Glasgow (Hillington Ind Est)
G52 94 E1
Mosslands Rd PA3 113 E7
Mosslingal G75 180 E5
Mossmulloch G75 180 E5
MOSSNEUK 179 F7
Mossneuk Ave G75 179 E8
Mossneuk Cres ML2 165 D4
Mossneuk Dr
East Kilbride G75 179 F7
Paisley PA2 133 C8
Wishaw ML2 165 C4
Mossneuk Pk ML2 165 D4
Mossneuk Prim Sch G75 179 F7
Mossneuk Rd G75 180 A8
Mossneuk St ML5 121 F3
MOSSPARK 115 E3
Mosspark Ave
Glasgow G52 115 F3
Milngavie G62 55 A3
Mosspark Bvd G52 115 E4
Mosspark Dr G52 115 E3
Mosspark La G52 115 E3
Mosspark Oval G52 115 E3
Mosspark Prim Sch G52 115 E3
Mosspark Rd
Coatbridge ML5 121 D8
Milngavie G62 55 A3
Mosspark Sq G52 115 E3
Mosspark Sta G52 115 C3
Moss Path G69 119 F3
Moss Rd
Airdrie ML6 123 A6
Airth FK2 13 E5
Bridge of Weir PA11 110 E7
Cumbernauld G67 62 F4
East Kilbride G75 180 C4
Fallin FK7 8 C4
Glasgow G51 115 D8

Moss Rd *continued*
Helensburgh G82 25 E4
Kilmacolm PA13 89 D8
Kirkintilloch G66 80 B7
Kirkintilloch, High Gallowhill G66 79 B6
Linwood PA3 112 C7
Muirhead G69 100 C7
Port Glasgow PA14 68 F7
Wishaw ML2 165 E3
Moss Side Ave ML6 122 E8
Moss-Side Ave ML8 187 D2
Moss-Side Rd G41 116 E1
Moss St PA1 113 E5
Mossvale Cres G33 99 C2
Mossvale La PA3 113 D6
Mossvale Path G33 99 C3
Mossvale Prim Sch PA3 113 D7
Mossvale Rd G33 99 C2
Mossvale Sq
Glasgow G33 99 B2
Paisley PA3 113 D7
Mossvale St PA3 113 D7
Mossvale/St James Prim Sch PA3 113 D7
Mossvale Terr 13 G69 81 A3
Mossvale Way G33 99 C2
Mossvale Wlk G33 99 C2
Mossview Cres ML6 123 A5
Mossview La G52 115 C5
Mossview Quadrant G52 115 D5
Mossview Rd G33 99 E5
Mosswater Wynd G68 60 F2
Mosswell Rd G62 55 B3
Mossyde Ave PA14 69 A7
Mossywood Ct
Airdrie ML6 123 D8
Cumbernauld G68 81 F7
Mossywood Pl G68 81 F7
Mossywood Rd G68 81 F7
Mote Hill ML3 162 E5
Mote Hill Ct ML3 162 E5
Mote Hill Gr ML3 162 E5
Motehill Rd PA3 114 A7
Mote View KA2 221 D1
MOTHERWELL 163 D8
Motherwell Bsns Ctr ML1 163 F7
Motherwell Coll ML1 164 B5
Motherwell Heritage Ctr* ML1 163 D7
Motherwell Rd
Bellshill ML4 142 B4
Hamilton ML3 163 A4
Motherwell, Carfin ML1 143 C1
Motherwell ML1 142 B1
Motherwell ML1 144 A6
Motherwell St ML6 123 C8
Motherwell Sta ML1 163 D7
Motoring Heritage Ctr* G83 27 D6
Motte Gdns KA22 205 B4
Moubray Gdns FK10 4 B1
Moubrey Row FK7 12 D8
Moulin Cir G52 115 A4
Moulin Pl G52 115 A4
Moulin Rd G52 115 A4
Moulin Terr G52 115 A4
Mountainblue St G31 118 B5
Mount Annan Dr G44 137 B7
Mount Ave
Kilmarnock KA1 227 D6
Symington KA1 231 D4
Mount Bartholomew FK4 40 A5
MOUNTBLOW 73 D5
Mountblow House G81 73 D5
Mountblow Rd G81 73 E5
Mount Cameron Drive N 3 G74 181 A8
Mount Cameron Drive S G74 181 B8
Mount Cameron Prim Sch G74 181 B7
Mount Carmel Prim Sch KA3 222 F5
Mountcastle Wynd KA13 207 D6
Mountcharles KA7 238 D2
Mount Charles Cres KA7 238 D2
MOUNT ELLEN 100 E6
MOUNT FLORIDA 137 C8
Mount Florida Prim Sch G42 137 B7
Mount Florida Sta G42 137 A8
Mountgarrie Path 8 G51 115 D7
Mountgarrie Rd 9 G51 115 D7
Mount Harriet Ave G33 99 E6
Mount Harriet Dr G33 99 E6
Mountherrick G75 180 E5
Mount Ho KA2 227 B7
Mount Hope FK9 2 B7
Mount Lockhart G71 120 B2
Mount Lockhart Gdns G71 120 B2
Mount Lockhart Pl G71 120 B2
Mount Oliphant FK7 12 D7
Mount Oliphant Cres KA7 239 B6
Mount Oliphant Pl KA7 239 B6
Mount Pl KA1 227 D6
Mount Pleasant KA20 206 D1
Mount Pleasant Cres G66 58 B6
Mount Pleasant Dr G60 73 B6
Mount Pleasant Pl G60 73 B6
Mount Pleasant St PA15 45 E4
Mount Pleasant Way KA3 222 F1
Mount St G20 96 F3
Mount Stewart St ML8 187 E2
Mount Stuart St G41 136 E8
Mount The
Ayr KA7 239 B4
Motherwell ML1 163 D6
MOUNT VERNON 119 D2
Mount Vernon Ave
Coatbridge ML5 121 E7
Glasgow G32, G69 119 E3
Mount Vernon Prim Sch G32 119 D3
Mount Vernon Sta G32 119 F2
Mount View KA11 220 C1
Mount Village KA1 227 C7
Mount William FK10 5 E1
Mournian Way ML3 162 D1
Mousa Pk G72 138 F3
Mousebank La ML11 214 F4
Mousebank Rd ML11 214 F5
Mousemill Rd ML11 214 D5
Mowbray G74 160 C4
Mowbray Ave G69 100 F5
Mowbrey Ct FK7 7 D4
Moyne Rd G53 115 A2
Moy Path 4 ML2 165 F6
Moy St G11 96 C2
Muckcroft Rd G69 80 C4
Mudale Ct FK1 42 D1
MUGDOCK 55 C6
Mugdock Ctry Pk* G62 55 A6
Mugdock Rd
Milngavie G62 55 A2
Milngavie G62 55 B4
Muiralehouse Rd FK7 11 E8
Muirbank Ave G73 137 F8
Muirbank Gdns G73 137 F7
Muirbrae Rd G73 138 B4
Muirbrae Way G73 138 B4
Muirburn Ave G44 136 E4
Muirburn Rd
Beith KA15 150 A3
Stonehouse ML10 198 A2
Muir Cl KA3 195 C1
Muir Cres G83 27 D7
Muircroft Dr ML1 144 B2
Muir Ct G44 136 F2
Muir Dr
Irvine KA12 219 D3
Stevenston KA20 217 C8
Troon KA10 229 E6
Muir Drive Cotts KA20 217 C8
Muirdrum Ave G52 115 D3
Muirdyke Ave FK2 24 C3
Muirdyke Rd
Coatbridge, Brackenhirst ML5, ML6 102 A5
Coatbridge, Drumpellier ML5 121 D8
Glenboig ML5 101 F4
Muirdykes Ave
2 Glasgow G52 115 A5
Port Glasgow PA14 68 D7
Muirdykes Rd
Glasgow G52 115 A5
Paisley PA3 113 B6
Muiredge Ct G71 140 F6
Muiredge & Jersy Rd
Cleland ML1, ML7 145 B6
Shotts ML7 146 A8
Muiredge Prim Sch G71 141 A6
Muiredge Terr G69 120 B4
MUIREND 136 E4
Muirend Ave G44 136 F5
Muirend Rd
Cardross G82 48 A8
Glasgow G44 136 E4
Kilmarnock KA3 222 F5
Stirling FK7 7 B5
Muirend St KA25 149 B2
Muirend Sta G44 136 F4
Muirfield Cres 6 G23 76 E1
Muirfield Ct
Glasgow G44 136 F4
Irvine KA11 224 G7
Muirfield Mdws G71 140 E2
Muirfield Pl KA13 207 C4
Muirfield Rd
Cumbernauld G68 62 A5
Stenhousemuir FK5 23 E2
Muir Glen 5 ML11 215 C3
Muirhall Pl
Irvine KA11 220 C1
Stenhousemuir FK5 23 C3
Muirhall Rd FK5 23 C3
Muirhall Terr ML7 125 B2
MUIRHEAD
Glasgow 120 C4
Stepps 100 D7
Troon 229 G4
Muirhead Ave FK2 42 A8
Muirhead Cotts G66 80 B7
Muirhead Ct G69 120 C4
Muirhead Dr
Law ML8 187 A6
Linwood PA3 112 A5
Motherwell ML1 143 F4
Muirhead Gate 4 G71 141 A8
Muirhead Gdns
Glasgow G69 120 C4
Salsburgh ML7 125 B2
Muirhead Gr G69 120 C4
Muirhead Pl ML7 127 D4
Muirhead Prim Sch KA10 229 F4
Muirhead Rd
Glasgow G69 120 B3
Stenhousemuir FK5 23 E4
Muirhead Rdbt G67 62 B3
Muirhead St
Kirkintilloch G66 79 D7
Lochwinnoch PA12 129 D2
Muirhead Terr ML1 163 E4
Muirhead Way G64 78 D1
Muirhill Ave G44 136 E5
Muirhill Cres G13 95 A7
Muirhill Ct ML3 162 D4
MUIRHOUSE 164 B2
Muirhouse Ave
Motherwell ML1 164 B3
Wishaw ML2 166 B6
Muirhouse Dr ML1 164 C2
Muirhouse La 4 G75 180 F8
Muirhouse Pk G61 75 D8
Muirhouse Prim Sch ML1 164 B2
Muirhouse Rd
Motherwell ML1 164 B2
Symington KA1 231 F5
Muirhouse St 1 G41 117 A3
Muirhouse Twr ML1 164 B3
Muirkirk Dr
Glasgow G13 95 F7
Hamilton ML3 161 D2
Muirlee Rd ML8 188 B1
Muirlees Cres G62 54 E2
Muirmadkin Rd ML4 142 B5
Muirmaillen Ave ML1 144 C1
Muirpark Ave PA4 94 C2
Muirpark Dr
Bishopbriggs G64 98 A8
Shieldhill FK1 66 D6
Muirpark Gdns FK10 4 E4
Muirpark Rd KA15 150 B1
Muirpark St G11 96 B2
Muirpark Terr G64 98 A8
Muir Rd G82 50 C6
Muirshiel Ave G53 135 C6
Muirshiel Cres G53 135 D6
Muirshiel Ct G53 135 C5
Muirshiel Ctry Pk* PA12 108 A3
Muirshiel La PA14 68 D8
Muirshiel Rd PA14 68 D8
Muirshot Rd ML9 185 B4
Muirside Ave
Glasgow G32 119 E3
Kirkintilloch G66 80 A8
Tullibody FK10 4 C3
Muirside Ct KA13 207 C2
Muirside Pl
Kilwinning KA13 207 C2
21 Wishaw ML2 165 F6
Muirside Rd
Glasgow G69 120 B4
Kilwinning KA13 207 C2
Tullibody FK10 4 C3
Muirside St G69 120 B4
Muirskeith Cres G44 137 A6
Muirskeith Pl G43 136 F6
Muirskeith Rd G43 136 F6
Muir St
Alexandria G83 27 D8
Bishopbriggs G64 78 A1
Coatbridge ML5 121 E7
Hamilton, High Blantyre G72 161 D6
Hamilton ML3 162 E4
Larkhall ML9 185 A3
Law ML8 186 F6
Motherwell ML1 163 D7
Renfrew PA4 94 D4
Stenhousemuir FK5 23 D2
Muirs The FK10 4 C4
Muir Street Prim Sch 5 ML1 163 D8
Muir Terr PA3 114 A7
MUIRTON 7 E6
Muirton Dr G64 77 F3
Muirton Rd FK7 7 E6
Muirton Rdbt FK7 7 F7
Muiryfauld Dr G31 118 E5
Muiryhall St
Coatbridge, Cliftonville ML5 122 B7
Coatbridge ML5 122 A7
Muiryhall Street E ML5 122 C7
Mulben Cres G53 134 F7
Mulben Pl G53 134 F7
Mulben Terr G53 134 F8
Mulberry Cres ML6 123 E3
Mulberry Dr G75 180 C5
Mulberry Rd
Glasgow G43 136 D5
Motherwell G71 121 C1
Mulberry Way G75 180 C5
Mulberry Wynd G72 139 F3
Muldron Terr ML7 147 B2
Mulgrew Ave KA21 206 A2
Mull
Airdrie ML6 123 D5
East Kilbride G74 181 C8
Mullardoch St 12 G23 76 D1
Mull Ave
Paisley PA2 133 E7
Port Glasgow PA14 69 A7
Renfrew PA4 94 C1
Mull Cres KA11 220 A2
Mull Ct
Alloa FK10 10 B5
Hamilton ML3 161 F1
Irvine KA11 220 A2
Mullen Ct G33 99 F5
Mulloch Ave 1 FK2 42 A8
Mull Pl KA11 220 A2
Mull Quadrant ML2 165 E5
Mull St G21 98 B2
Mull Terr KA11 220 A2
Mulvey Cres ML6 122 E7
MUNGAL 42 A8
Mungalend FK2 42 B7
Mungalend Rdbt FK2 42 B8
Mungalhead Rd FK2 42 A7
Mungal Mill Ct 4 FK2 41 F8
Mungal Pl FK2 42 B8
Mungo Pk G75 180 D8
Mungo Pl G71 121 A1
Munlochy Rd G51 115 D7
Munnoch Cres KA22 205 B5
Munnoch Way FK7 12 C4
Munro Ave
Kilmarnock KA1 222 D1
Stirling FK9 2 B4
Munro Ct G81 73 F6
Munro Dr
Kilbirnie KA25 170 B8
Milton of Campsie G66 58 B5
Munro Drive E G84 16 E3
Munro Drive W G84 16 D3
Munro Gate FK9 2 A5
Munro Gdns FK2 42 F3
Munro Pl
Alloa FK10 9 F6
East Kilbride G74 160 B3
Glasgow G13 95 E6
Kilmarnock KA1 222 E2
Saltcoats KA21 206 A2
Munro Rd
Glasgow G13 95 E5
Stirling FK7 7 E6
Munro St
4 Alexandria G83 27 E5
Greenock PA16 45 A4
Stenhousemuir FK5 23 E3
Munro Wlk KA21 206 A2
Murano Pl G20 96 F4
Murano St G20 96 F4
Murchie Dr KA9 236 D5
Murchison G12 96 A6
Murchison Dr G75 180 B7
Murchison Rd PA6 91 C1
Murchland Ave KA3 213 A3
Murchland Way KA12 219 C3
Murdieston St PA15 45 D4
Murdoch Cres KA20 217 D7
Murdoch Ct
Saltcoats KA21 205 E3
1 Troon KA10 229 E5
Murdoch Dr G62 76 D8
Murdoch Pl
Irvine KA11 224 H6
Motherwell ML1 142 F3
Murdoch Rd G75 180 E8
Murdoch's Lone KA7 238 E1
Murdoch Sq ML4 142 C7
Murdock Ct KA10 229 E5
Murdostoun Cres ML7 127 F6
Murdostoun Gdns ML2 165 B5
Murdostoun Terr ML1 144 E1
Murdostoun View ML2 165 F6
Mure Ave KA3 223 B5
Mure Pl G78 153 B3
Muriel Blue Ct PA19 44 F7
Muriel La G78 134 C3
Muriel St G78 134 C3
Muriel Street Ind Est G78 134 C4
Murnin Ct FK7 7 C3
Murnin Rd FK4 40 A4
Murnin Road Ind Est FK4 40 A4
Murray Ave
Kilsyth G65 60 D8
Saltcoats KA21 205 E2
Murray Bsns Area PA3 113 D6
Murray Cres
Hamilton G72 161 E6
Wishaw ML2 166 A7
Murray Ct ML3 162 A3
Murray Dr ML9 198 F2
Murrayfield G64 78 A3
Murrayfield Dr G61 75 E1
Murrayfield Pl FK7 7 D1
Murrayfield St G32 118 E7
Murrayfield Terr FK7 7 D1
Murray Gdns G66 58 C5
Murray Gr G61 75 B8
Murrayhill G75 180 D8
Murray Path G71 140 E6
Murray Pl
Ayr KA8 236 C3
Barrhead G78 134 D4
Bellshill ML4 141 E7
Cambusbarron FK7 6 D5
Dumbarton G82 50 C4
Gourock PA19 44 E6
Kilmarnock KA3 223 D2
Stirling FK8 7 B7
Murray Prim Sch G75 180 E8
Murray Rd
Bothwell G71 141 A3
Law ML8 186 F4
Murray Rdbt The G75 180 F8
Murray Rd The G75 180 E7
Murray Row FK7 12 E8
Murrayshall Rd FK7 7 B3
Murrayside ML9 198 D1
Murray Sq The 2 G75 180 E7
Murray St
Ayr KA8 236 C2
Greenock PA16 45 C5
Paisley PA3 113 D6
Renfrew PA4 94 C3
Murray Terr ML1 163 B7
MURRAY THE 180 E7
Murray Wlk G72 161 E6
Murrin Ave G64 78 D1
Murroch Ave G82 50 C6
Murroch Cres G83 28 B1
Murroes Rd G51 115 D7
Museum Bsns Pk G53 134 F5
Museum of Transport* G3 96 C1
Musgrove Pl G75 180 C8
Muslin St G40 117 F4
Muttonhole Rd ML3 182 E7
Mybster Pl G51 115 D7
Myers Cres G71 141 A5
Myers Ct ML4 141 D6
Myles Ho FK8 7 A8
Mylne Pl FK2 24 B2
Myothill Rd FK6 39 D7
Myot View FK6 21 A3
Myreside Pl G32 118 D6
Myreside St G32 118 E6
Myres Rd G53 135 D8
Myreton FK11 4 A6
Myreton Ave PA13 89 C7
Myreton Dr FK7 11 E8
Myreton Way FK1 41 F3
Myretoungate FK12 4 E6
Myrie Gdns G64 78 B2
Myroch Pl G34 100 C1
Myrtle Ave G66 79 C5
Myrtle Bank KA15 171 A8
Myrtle Dr
Motherwell ML1 143 B5
Wishaw ML2 164 D4
Myrtle Hill La G42 137 C8
Myrtle La ML9 185 C1
Myrtle Pk G42 117 C1
Myrtle Pl G42 137 C8
Myrtle Rd
Clydebank G81 73 D4
Uddingston G71 141 B8
Myrtle Sq G64 98 A8
Myrtle St G72 140 D1
Myrtle View Rd G42 137 C8
Myrtle Wlk G72 138 F6
Myvot Ave G67 82 B6
Myvot Rd
Cumbernauld, Dalshannon G67 82 B6
Cumbernauld, Mollinsburn G67 81 F4

N

Naburn Gate 6 G5 117 C4
Nagle Gdns ML1 164 F8
Nailer Rd
Falkirk FK1 41 E6
Stirling FK7 7 B2
Nairn Ave
Bellshill ML4 142 A6
Blantyre G72 140 C2
Nairn Cl KA3 195 C1
Nairn Cres ML6 123 A5
Nairn Ct
Falkirk FK1 42 D1
Kilwinning KA13 207 B3
Nairn Dr PA16 44 D5
Nairn Pl
Clydebank G81 73 F3
East Kilbride G74 160 C3
Nairn Quadrant ML2 165 B5
Nairn Rd PA16 44 D4
Nairnside Rd G21 98 C7
Nairn St
Clydebank G81 73 F3
Glasgow G3 96 D1
Hamilton G72 161 C6
Larkhall ML9 184 F2
Nairn Way G68 62 A5
Naismith Ct ML9 198 E1
Naismith St G32 139 C8
Naismith Wlk ML4 142 C7
Nansen St G20 97 A3
Napier Ave G82 48 B8
Napier Cres
Dumbarton G82 49 D3
Falkirk FK2 42 A7
Napier Ct
Cardross G82 48 B8
Cumbernauld G68 62 D8
Old Kilpatrick G60 73 C5
Napier Dr G51 116 B8
Napier Gdns PA3 112 C6
Napier Hill G75 180 E8
Napier La G75 180 E8
Napier Pk G68 62 C7
Napier Pl
Cumbernauld G68 62 D8
Falkirk FK2 42 A7
Glasgow G51 116 B8
Old Kilpatrick G60 73 C5
Napier Rd
Cumbernauld G68 62 C7
Glasgow, Govan G51 116 B8
Glasgow (Hillington Ind Est) G52 94 F1
Glasgow, North Cardonald G52 114 F8
Napiershall La G4 96 F2
Napiershall Pl 3 G20 96 F2
Napiershall St G20 96 F2
Napier Sq ML4 142 C7
Napier St
Clydebank G81 94 D7
Glasgow G51 116 B8

Napier St *continued*
Johnstone PA5 111 E3
Linwood PA3 112 C6
Napierston Rd G83 27 F5
Napier Terr G51 116 B8
Napier Way G68 62 C7
Naproch Pl G77 157 C5
Naseby Ave G11 95 F3
Naseby La G11 95 F4
Nasmyth Ave
Bearsden G61 75 B8
East Kilbride G75 181 A7
Nasmyth Pl G75 180 F7
Nasmyth Rd G52 115 A7
Nasmyth Road N G52 115 A7
Nasmyth Road S G52 115 A7
Nassau Pl 1 G75 159 A1
National Bank La G1 240 C2
National Mus of Rural Life The* G76 158 F4
National Piping Ctr The G4 240 C4
National Wallace Monument The* FK9 2 E4
Navar Ct ML7 147 A3
Navar Pl PA2 114 A2
Naver St G33 98 E1
Navy Way G84 15 B3
Naylor La ML6 123 B8
Naysmyth Bank G75 180 F8
Nebit The FK12 4 E6
Needle Gn ML8 187 F2
Neidpath G69 120 A3
Neidpath Ave ML5 122 B3
Neidpath Dr FK5 24 A4
Neidpath E G74 159 D2
Neidpath Pl ML5 122 A3
Neidpath Rd ML8 187 E3
Neidpath Road E G46 157 A6
Neidpath Road W G46 157 A7
Neidpath W G74 159 D1
Neil Ave KA12 219 D5
Neilsland Dr
Hamilton ML3 183 C7
Motherwell ML1 163 B6
Neilsland Oval G53 115 D1
Neilsland Prim Sch ML3 162 A1
Neilsland Rd ML3 162 B1
Neilsland Sq
Glasgow G53 115 D1
Hamilton ML3 162 C1
Neilsland St ML3 162 C1
Neilson Ct ML3 162 E2
Neilson St
Bellshill ML4 142 A5
Falkirk FK1 42 B4
Neil St
Greenock PA16 45 A4
Renfrew PA4 94 D5
NEILSTON 154 E6
Neilston Ave G53 135 C5
Neilston Ct G53 135 C5
Neilston L Ctr G78 154 E7
Neilston Pl G65 36 B1
Neilston Prim Sch G78 154 E7
Neilston Rd
Barrhead G78 134 A1
Neilston G78 154 E8
Paisley PA2 113 E2
Uplawmoor G78 153 B3
Neilston Sta G78 154 D7
Neilston Wlk G65 36 D1
Neilvaig Dr G73 138 C3
Neistpoint Dr G33 119 A7
Nellfield Ct ML8 202 A4
Nellfield Gdns ML8 202 A4
Nellfield La ML8 202 A4
Nelson Ave ML5 121 E4
Nelson Cres ML1 164 B4
Nelson Mandela Pl G1 241 A3
Nelson Pl
Ayr KA8 236 A2
Glasgow G69 120 B4
Helensburgh G84 17 A2
Stirling FK7 7 C6
Nelson Rd
Gourock PA19 44 F6
Saltcoats KA21 217 B8
Nelson St
Glasgow G5 240 B1
Glasgow, Muirhead G69 120 B4
Greenock PA15 45 E5
Kilmarnock KA1 227 F8
Nelson Terr G74 181 A8
NEMPHLAR 214 A6
Nemphlar Moor Rd
Crossford ML8 201 D1
Nemphlar ML11 214 A7
Nemphlar Rd ML11 214 A6
Nemphlat Hill ML11 214 F5
Neptune St G51 116 B7
Neptune Way ML4 142 E5
NERSTON 159 F4
Nerston Rd G74 159 E6
Nerston Residential Sch G74 160 A7
Ness Ave PA5 131 C8
Ness Dr
Blantyre G72 140 E1
East Kilbride G74 160 B1
Ness Gdns
Bishopbriggs G64 78 B1
Hulford KA1 228 F6
Larkhall ML9 199 A8
Ness Pl KA10 229 G5
Ness Rd
Greenock PA16 45 C5
Renfrew PA4 94 B4
Ness St
Glasgow G33 98 E1
Wishaw ML2 186 B8
Ness Terr ML3 162 A1
Ness Way ML1 143 A5
Nethan Ave ML2 164 C1
NETHANFOOT 201 A3
Nethanfoot Brig Rd ML8 201 B2
Nethan Gate ML3 162 C3
Nethan Glen ML8 201 A2
Nethan Path ML9 199 A8
Nethan Pl ML3 183 D6
Nethan St
Glasgow G51 116 A8
Motherwell ML1 142 C2
Nethan View ML8 201 A2
Nether Auldhouse Rd G43 136 C6
Netherbank Rd ML2 164 D2
Netherblane G63 31 A4
Netherbog Ave G82 50 B4
Netherbog Rd G82 50 B4
NETHERBURN 200 C4
Netherburn Ave
Glasgow G44 136 F2
Houston PA6 111 E8
Netherburn Gdns PA6 111 E8
Netherburn Prim Sch ML9 200 B3
Netherburn Rd ML9 200 A7
Netherby Dr G41 116 D4
Netherby Rd FK2 14 D4
Nethercairn Pl G77 157 C5
Nethercairn Rd G43 136 C4
Nethercliffe Ave G44 136 F2
Nethercommon Ind Est PA3 113 E7
Nethercraigs Dr PA2 133 C8
Nethercraigs Rd PA2 133 B7
Nethercraigs Sports Complex G52 115 D2
Nethercroy Rd G65 60 E5
Netherdale G77 157 B5
Netherdale Cres ML2 164 C2
Netherdale Dr PA1 114 F4
Netherdale Rd ML2 164 E2
Netherfaulds Dr FK6 21 D1
Netherfield St G31 118 C6
Nethergate The FK12 4 E6
Nethergreen Cres PA4 94 B3
Nethergreen Wynd PA4 94 B3
Netherhall Rd ML2 164 D2
Netherhill Ave G44 136 F1
Netherhill Cotts PA3 114 B7
Netherhill Cres PA3 114 A6
Netherhill Rd
Moodiesburn G69 80 F2
Paisley PA3 113 F6
Netherhill Way PA3 114 B7
Netherhouse Ave
Coatbridge ML5 121 F3
Kirkintilloch G66 79 E4
Netherhouse Pl G34 120 E8
Netherhouse Rd G34, G69 120 E7
NETHER KIRKTON 154 F8
Nether Kirkton Ave G78 154 E8
Nether Kirkton View G78 154 E8
Nether Kirkton Way G78 154 F8
Nether Kirkton Wynd G78 154 E8
Netherland Rd KA3 211 E8
NETHERLEE 136 F2
Netherlee Cres KA24 169 B1
Netherlee Ct G44 136 F2
Netherlee Pl G44 137 A4
Netherlee Prim Sch G44 136 F2
Netherlee Rd G44 137 A4
Nethermains Prim Sch FK6 21 D1
Nethermains Rd
Denny FK6 21 C2
Kilwinning KA13 207 E2
Milngavie G62 76 A8
Nethermiln Rd KA23 190 D4
Netherpark Ave G44 136 F1
Netherplace Cres
Glasgow G53 135 B8
Newton Mearns G77 156 C3
Netherplace Rd
Glasgow G53 135 B8
Newton Mearns G77 156 A3
Newton Mearns G77 156 C4
Nether Robertland Prim Sch KA3 195 F1
NETHERTON
Glasgow 95 E8
Strathblane 31 B4
Wishaw 164 D1
Netherton Ave
Glasgow G13 95 E8
Port Glasgow PA14 69 A7
Netherton Ct
Glasgow G45 137 F2
Newton Mearns G77 157 A7
Netherton Dr G78 134 E1
Netherton Farm La 1 G61 95 F8
Netherton Hill G66 57 B8
Netherton Ind Est ML2 164 E2
Netherton Oval G66 33 B1
Netherton Prim Sch ML2 164 E1
Netherton Rd
East Kilbride G75 180 A4
Netherton Rd *continued*
East Kilbride, The Murray G75 180 C7
Glasgow G13 95 F7
Glasgow G13 95 F8
Newton Mearns G77 156 F6
Wishaw ML2 164 E1
Netherton St
Harthill ML7 127 D5
Wishaw ML2 164 F2
Nethervale Ave G44 136 F1
Netherview Rd G44 137 A1
Netherway G44 136 F1
Netherwood Ave G68 81 F8
Netherwood Ct
Cumbernauld G68 82 A8
Motherwell ML1 164 B2
Netherwood Gr G68 82 A8
Netherwood Pl G68 81 F8
Netherwood Rd
Cumbernauld G68 81 F8
Motherwell ML1 164 B3
Netherwood Twr ML1 164 B2
Netherwood Way G68 82 A8
Nethy Way PA4 94 F1
NETTLEHIRST 171 F1
Neuk Ave
Houston PA6 91 C1
Muirhead G69 100 C7
Neuk Cres PA6 91 C2
Neukfoot La G78 153 A3
Neuk The ML2 164 E3
Neuk Way G72 139 C8
Nevan Rd KA10 229 G6
Neville G74 160 C4
Nevis Ave ML3 162 A1
Nevis Cres FK10 10 B8
Nevis Ct
Barrhead G78 134 C1
Coatbridge ML5 122 C3
Greenock PA16 45 B5
Motherwell ML1 163 E4
Nevis Dr
Motherwell ML1 164 C3
Torrance G64 57 B1
Nevison St ML9 185 B2
Nevis Pl
Falkirk FK1 42 C2
Kilmarnock KA1 228 A4
Shotts ML7 147 B3
Nevis Rd
Bearsden G61 75 B7
Glasgow G43 136 B5
Renfrew PA4 94 B1
Nevis Way
Irvine KA11 220 A4
Renfrew PA3 93 E1
New Abbey Rd G69 100 F4
New Albion Ind Est G13 94 E7
Neward Cres KA9 236 D6
Newark KA13 207 C2
Newark Ave PA16 45 C7
Newark Castle* PA14 47 D2
Newark Cres KA7 238 B1
Newark Dr
Glasgow G41 116 E3
Paisley PA2 133 C8
Wishaw ML2 165 C6
Newark Gate ML7 166 F8
Newark Ho PA2 113 B1
Newark Pl
Port Glasgow PA14 47 D1
Wishaw ML2 165 D6
Newark Prim Sch 2 PA14 68 F8
Newark St
Greenock PA16 45 C8
Port Glasgow PA14 47 D1
Newark Terr KA9 236 D7
NEWARTHILL 143 E3
Newarthill Prim Sch ML1 143 E3
Newarthill Rd ML1 143 C2
New Ashtree St ML2 164 E3
New Ave PA9 130 F6
Newbank Ct G31 118 E4
Newbank Gdns G31 118 D4
Newbank Rd G31 118 E4
Newbarns St ML8 187 F3
Newbattle Ave ML6 123 B2
Newbattle Ct G32 119 B2
Newbattle Gdns G32 119 B2
Newbattle Pl G32 119 B2
Newbattle Rd G32 119 B2
Newbiggin Cres FK10 4 C2
New Bldgs ML11 215 A2
Newbold Ave 2 G21 97 F7
New Branziet Cotts G22 77 B8
Newbridge G66 33 A2
New Bridge St KA7 235 F1
Newburgh PA8 73 A3
Newburgh St G43 136 D7
Newcarron Ct 3 FK2 42 A8
New Carron Rd FK2, FK5 24 A3
Newcastleton Dr 9 G23 76 E1
New Century Dr ML7 146 E4
New City Rd
Glasgow G4 240 B4
Glasgow G4 240 C4
New City Row G63 31 B4
New Cordale Rd G82 27 D2
Newcraigs Dr G76 158 D7
Newcroft Dr G44 137 D5
New Cross ML3 162 E3
New Dock La PA15 46 A5
New Douglas Pk (Hamilton Academicals FC) ML3 162 C5
Newdyke Ave G66 79 E8
Newdyke Rd G66 79 E8
Newdykes Rd KA9 233 D1
New Edinburgh Rd G71, ML4 141 B6
New England Rd KA21 206 A2
NEW FARM LOCH 223 C2
New Farm Prim Sch KA3 223 C1
Newfield Cres ML3 162 B4
Newfield Dr KA2 225 F2
Newfield La 8 G71 141 B3
Newfield Pl
Dundonald KA2 225 F2
Glasgow G46 135 F2
Irvine KA11 220 B5
Rutherglen G73 137 F8
Newfield Rd ML9 198 E1
Newfield Sq G53 135 A6
Newford Gr G76 157 E5
Newgrove Gdns G72 139 A6
New Hallglen Rd FK1 42 D2
Newhall St G40 117 F3
Newhaven Rd G33 119 B8
Newhaven St G32 119 A7
New Hill Rd KA20 218 C4
Newhills Rd G33 119 E7
NEWHOUSE 144 A7
Newhouse FK8 7 A5
Newhouse Dr
Falkirk FK1 41 E2
Kilbirnie KA25 169 F8
Newhouse Ind Est ML1 143 D7
Newhouse Intc KA11 224 G5
Newhousemill Cotts G74 181 C7
Newhousemill Rd
East Kilbride G74 181 D7
Hamilton G72, ML3 161 C1
Newhouse Way KA11 220 A5
Newhut Rd ML1 142 D1
New Inchinnan Rd PA3 113 E7
Newington La FK5 22 D6
Newington St G32 118 F6
New Kirk Rd G61 75 E5
New La ML6 123 B3
New Lairdsland Rd G66 79 D8
NEW LANARK 215 A2
New Lanark Prim Sch ML11 215 A2
New Lanark Rd ML11 214 F2
New Lanark World Heritage Village* ML11 215 A2
Newlandcraigs Ave PA5 112 D1
Newlandcraigs Dr PA5 112 D2
NEWLANDS 136 D6
Newlands Ct FK7 12 D2
Newlands Dr
Hamilton ML3 183 D8
Kilmarnock KA3 222 E5
Newlandsfield Rd G43 136 D7
Newlands Gdns PA5 112 C1
NEWLANDSMUIR 180 A6
Newlandsmuir Rd G75 180 A6
Newlands Pl
East Kilbride G74 159 E1
Kilmarnock KA3 222 E4
Tullibody FK10 4 C3
Newlands Rd
Bannockburn FK7 11 D8
East Kilbride G75 179 E5
East Kilbride, Newlandsmuir G75 180 A7
Glasgow G44 136 E6
Uddingston G71 140 F8
Newlands St
Coatbridge ML5 122 A4
Lanark ML11 215 C3
Newlands Terr
Carluke ML8 187 F2
Milton of Campsie G66 58 C6
New Line Rd FK7 11 A7
Newliston Dr G5 117 D3
New Luce Dr G32 119 D3
NEWMAINS 166 B5
Newmains Ave PA4 93 B5
Newmains Prim Sch
Renfrew PA4 94 C1
Wishaw ML2 166 A4
Newmains Rd PA4 94 C1
Newmarket FK7 7 E1
Newmarket Ctr FK1 42 B5
Newmarket St
Ayr KA7 238 F8
Falkirk FK1 42 B5
Newmill & Canthill Rd ML7 146 B6
Newmill Gdns ML7 145 F3
Newmill Rd
Dunlop KA3 195 C8
Glasgow G21 98 C5
New Mill Rd KA1 228 B7
Newmills FK10 4 B3
Newmilns Gdn KA3 223 B6
Newmilns Gdns G72 161 D2
Newmilns St G53 134 F6
NEW MONKLAND 102 E5
New Monkland Prim Sch ML6 102 E4
Newmoor Intc KA11 219 F1
Newnham Rd PA1 114 E4
Newpark Cres
Cambuslang G72 139 A7
Stirling FK7 7 A2
Newpark Rd FK7 7 B2
New Park St ML3 162 C5
New Plymouth G75 180 A7
New Rd
Ayr KA8 235 F2
Bannockburn FK7 7 D2
Cambuslang G72 139 E4
Newrose Ave ML4 142 C7
Newshot Dr PA8 73 C1
New Sneddon St PA3 113 E6
New St
Beith KA15 171 B8
Bridge of Allan FK9 1 F8
Clydebank G81 74 A6
Dalry KA24 191 C7
Hamilton G72 161 C7
Irvine KA12 219 B2
Kilbarchan PA10 111 A3
Kilmarnock KA1 227 F5
Lochwinnoch PA12 129 C2
Paisley PA1 113 E4
Slamannan FK1 86 B7
Stevenston KA20 217 D8
Stewarton KA3 195 D1
Stonehouse ML9 198 F2
Newstead Gdns G23 76 E1
NEW STEVENSTON 143 B4
New Stevenston Prim Sch ML1 142 F4
New Stevenston Rd
Motherwell ML1 143 B2
Motherwell ML1 143 C2
New Struan Sch FK10 9 F6
NEWTON 140 A6
Newton Ave
Cambuslang G72 139 D7
Elderslie PA5 112 E3
Skinflats FK2 24 F3
Newton Brae G72 139 F6
Newton Ct
Cambuslang G72 139 D6
Newton Mearns G77 156 D3
Newton Dr
Elderslie PA5 112 E3
Uddingston G71 141 A7
Wishaw ML2 166 A5
Newton Farm Rd G72 140 A6
Newton Gr G77 156 D3
Newtongrange Ave G32 119 B2
Newtongrange Gdns G32 119 B3
Newtonhead KA11 220 B5
Newtonlea Ave G77 156 F4
NEWTON MEARNS 156 B4
Newton of Barr PA12 129 B2
NEWTON ON AYR 236 B3
Newton-on-Ayr Sta KA8 236 A3
Newton Park Ct KA8 236 B2
Newton Pl
Glasgow G3 240 A4
Newton Mearns G77 156 E3
Newton Prim Sch KA8 236 A1
Newton Rd
Bishopton PA7 72 A3
Kirkintilloch G66 79 E4
Newtonshaw FK10 5 C1
Newton St
Glasgow G2, G3 240 B3
Greenock PA16 45 D6
Kilbirnie KA25 149 B1
Paisley PA1 113 C4
Newton Sta G72 139 E5
Newton Station Rd G72 139 E5
Newton Terr
Glasgow G3 240 A3
Greenock PA16 45 D6
Paisley PA1 112 F3
Newton Terrace La G3 240 A3
Newton Trad Est KA8 236 A2
Newton Way PA3 114 B7
Newton Wlk KA1 228 A7
Newtown St G65 60 D8
Newtyle Dr G53 114 F1
Newtyle Pl
Bishopbriggs G64 78 D1
Glasgow G53 114 F1
Newtyle Rd PA1 114 C4
New View Cres ML4 142 A3
New View Dr ML4 142 A3
New View Pl ML4 142 A3
New Wynd G1 241 A1
Niamh Ct PA4 93 C7
Nicholas St G1 241 B2
Nicholson Pl FK1 41 F2
Nicklaus Way ML1 143 E7
Nicol Dr PA16 45 B5
Nicolson Ct G33 99 E5
Nicolson St
Greenock PA15 45 E5
Greenock PA15 45 F5
Nicol St
Airdrie ML6 103 C1
Greenock PA16 45 B4
Niddrie Rd G42 117 A2
Niddrie Sq 1 G42 116 F2
Niddry St PA3 113 F5
Nigel Gdns G41 116 D1
Nigel St ML1 163 D6
Nigg Pl G34 120 A8
Nightingale Pl PA5 131 D6
Nikitas Ave ML9 199 B7
Nile Ct KA7 238 F8
Nile St PA15 45 F4
Nimmo Dr G51 115 F7
Nimmo Pl
Carluke ML8 187 E3
Wishaw ML2 165 C3
Nimmo Rd PA16 45 C4
Nimmo St PA16 45 C4
Nineyard St KA21 216 F7
Ninian Ave PA6 111 C8
Ninian Rd ML6 123 C5
Ninian's Rise G66 79 F7
Ninian's Terr KA13 207 F2

Nisbet Dr
Denny FK6 21 D2
Prestwick KA9 236 D5
Nisbet St G31 118 D5
Nisbett Pl ML6 123 E2
Nisbett St ML6 123 E2
Nissen Pl G53 114 F1
Nith Dr
Hamilton ML3 183 A8
Renfrew PA4 94 E2
Nith La 24 ML2 165 F6
Nith Path ML1 144 C2
Nith Pl KA1 228 B5
Nith Quadrant ML1 143 C3
Nithsdale G74 160 D3
Nithsdale Cres G61 75 C6
Nithsdale Cross G41 116 D3
Nithsdale Dr G41 116 F2
Nithsdale Pl G41 116 F3
Nithsdale Rd
Ardrossan KA22 205 D4
Glasgow G41 116 D3
Nithsdale St G41 116 F2
Nith St G33 98 D1
NITSHILL 134 F5
Nitshill Rd G53 135 C3
Nitshill Sta G53 135 A5
Niven Ct KA3 223 D4
Niven St G20 96 C6
Noble Prim Sch ML4 142 A7
Noble Rd ML4 142 B5
Nobles Pl ML4 141 F4
Nobleston G83 28 A2
Nobles View ML4 141 F4
Noldrum Ave G32 139 C8
Noldrum Gdns G32 139 C8
Noltmire Rd KA8 236 C4
Noran Cres KA10 229 G5
Norbreck Dr G46 136 C4
Norby Rd G11 95 F3
Nordic Cres G72 161 E7
Nordic Gdns 3 G72 161 E7
Nordic Gr 6 G72 161 E7
Noremac Way ML4 141 F7
Norfield Dr G44 137 B7
Norfolk Cres G64 77 E3
Norfolk Ct G5 117 B5
Norfolk Rd PA16 44 E4
Norfolk St G5 117 B5
Norham St G41 116 E1
Norman Cres KA12 219 B5
Norman St G40 117 F3
Norse Lane N G14 95 C4
Norse Lane S 14 G14 95 C4
Norse Pl G14 95 C4
Norse Rd G14 95 C4
Northacre KA13 207 E5
Northacre Gr KA13 207 D5
Northall Quadrant ML1 143 B1
Northampton Dr G12 96 B6
Northampton La G12 96 B6
North Ave
Cambuslang G72 138 F6
Carluke ML8 187 D2
Clydebank G81 74 A2
North Ayrshire Mus*
KA21 216 F7
Northbank Ave
Cambuslang G72 139 D6
Kirkintilloch G66 79 C8
North Bank Pl G81 94 C7
Northbank Rd G66 79 C8
Northbank St 1 G72 139 D6
North Bank St G81 94 C8
NORTH BARR 73 A2
North Barr PA8 73 B3
North Barr Ave PA8 73 A3
NORTH BARRWOOD 36 F1
North Berwick Ave G68 61 F5
North Berwick Cres G75 180 A6
North Berwick Gdns G68 61 F5
North Biggar Rd ML6 123 B8
North Birbiston Rd G66 57 E8
Northbrae Pl G13 95 B6
North Bridge St 1 ML6 122 F8
North British Rd G71 140 F6
NORTH BROOMAGE 23 A4
North Broomage Rdbt
FK5 23 A3
Northburn Ave ML6 103 B1
Northburn Pl ML6 103 B2
Northburn Rd ML5 102 C1
Northburn St ML6 104 B2
North Bute St ML5 122 B4
North Caldeen Rd ML5 122 C5
North Calder Dr ML6 123 D6
North Calder Gr G71 120 B2
North Calder Pl G71 120 B2
North Calder Rd G71 121 C1
North Campbell Ave G62 54 F1
North Canal Bank G4 97 D2
North Canal Bank St G4 97 C2
North Carbrain Rd G67 61 F1
NORTH CARDONALD 115 B7
North Castle St FK10 10 A5
North Claremont La G62 55 A2
North Claremont St 4
G3 96 E1
North Corsebar Rd PA2 113 C2
North Court La G1 241 A2
Northcraig Rd KA3 223 A3
North Crescent Ave
KA22 205 C3
North Crescent Rd KA22 205 B3
Northcroft Rd G69 80 F2
North Croft St PA3 113 F5
North Ct G1 241 A2
North Dean Park Ave
G71 141 A2
Northdoon Pl KA7 238 D3
North Douglas St G81 94 C8
North Dr
Glasgow G1 240 C2
Kilbirnie KA25 170 A8
Linwood PA3 112 B6
Troon KA10 229 G4
North Dryburgh Rd ML2 165 B6
North Dumgoyne Ave G62 54 F3
North Elgin Pl G81 94 C7
North Elgin St G81 94 D8
North End FK7 6 D6
North Erskine Pk G61 75 D5
North Faulds Rd ML11 215 E5
NORTHFIELD 36 B1
Northfield G75 179 F7
Northfield Ave
Ayr KA8 236 B3
Port Glasgow PA14 68 F8
Shotts ML7 147 B2
Northfield Dr G83 27 F5
Northfield Pl KA8 236 A3
Northfield Rd
Alexandria G83 28 A5
Denny FK6 21 C4
Kilsyth G65 36 B1
Northfield St ML1 163 E8
Northflat Pl ML8 202 C8
North Frederick St G1 241 A3
North Gardner St 6 G11 96 B3
North Gargieston Rd
KA1 227 C6
Northgate Quadrant G21 98 C6
Northgate Rd G21 98 C7
North Glasgow Coll G21 97 F3
North Gower St 1 G51 116 C5
North Grange Rd G61 75 E6
North Green Dr FK2 14 D4
North Hamilton Pl KA1 222 E1
North Hamilton St KA1 222 E1
North Hanover St G1, G4 241 A3
North Harbour Ind Est 10
KA8 235 F1
North Harbour St KA8 235 F1
Northinch Ct G14 95 D2
Northinch St G14 95 D2
North Iverton Park Rd
PA5 112 B3
NORTH KELVIN 96 F4
North Kilmeny Cres ML2 165 C6
North La PA3 112 C6
Northland Ave G14 95 C5
Northland Dr G14 95 C5
Northland Gdns G14 95 C5
Northland La G14 95 C4
North Lodge Ave ML1 163 E4
North Lodge Rd PA4 94 C4
North Main St
Alexandria G83 27 D6
Falkirk FK2 24 C3
North Moraine La G15 75 C2
NORTH MOTHERWELL 163 C8
NORTH MOUNT
VERNON 119 F3
Northmuir Dr ML2 165 D4
Northmuir Rd G15 75 B4
North Neuk KA10 229 F7
North Newmoor Ind Est
KA11 219 F2
North Orchard St ML1 163 D7
Northpark Ave KA8 236 B3
North Park Ave
Barrhead G78 134 B3
Glasgow G46 135 F4
Northpark St G20 96 F4
North Portland St G1, G4 241 B2
North Porton Rd PA7 72 C4
North Rd
Bellshill ML4 142 A7
Coatbridge ML5 122 A2
Cumbernauld G68 82 A8
Johnstone PA5 111 F2
Port Glasgow PA14 68 E8
West Kilbride KA23 190 C5
North Ring Rd KA20 218 B5
North Shore Rd
Troon KA10 229 D4
Troon KA10 229 E5
North & South Rd ML2 165 E8
North Sq ML5 121 E8
North St
Alexandria G83 27 E5
Alloa FK10 10 A7
Dalry KA24 191 C8
Falkirk FK2 42 B8
Glasgow G3 240 A3
Greenock PA16 45 C8
Houston PA6 91 B3
Larkhall ML9 185 A4
Motherwell ML1 163 F8
Paisley PA3 113 E6
Stirling FK9 2 D1
North Street Ind Est G83 27 E5
Northumberland St G20 96 E4
North Vennel
Irvine KA11 220 A3
Lanark ML11 215 A4
North View G61 75 D2
North View Rd PA11 110 F6
North Wallace St G4 241 B4
Northway G72 140 C1
Northwood Dr ML2 166 A6
Northwood Rd FK10 4 D2
North Woodside L Ctr G4 97 A2
North Woodside Rd G20 96 F3
Norton St FK12 5 B7
Norval St G11 96 A2
Norwich Dr G12 96 B5
Norwood Ave
Alloa FK10 9 F7
Bonnybridge FK4 40 B7
Kirkintilloch G66 79 B8
Norwood Cres FK10 9 F7
Norwood Ct FK4 40 B7
Norwood Dr G46 136 A1
Norwood Gr FK10 9 F7
Norwood Pk G61 75 F3
Norwood Pl FK4 40 B7
Norwood Terr G71 141 A7
Notre Dame High Sch
Glasgow G12 96 C3
Greenock PA16 45 D3
Notre Dame Prim Sch
G12 96 C3
Nottingham Ave G12 96 B6
Nottingham La G12 96 B6
Novar Dr G12 96 B4
Novar Gdns G64 77 E2
Novar St ML3 162 D2
Nuneaton St G40 118 A4
Nuneaton Street Ind Est
G40 118 A4
Nurseries Rd G69 119 F6
Nursery Ave
Erskine PA7 72 E4
Kilmarnock KA1 228 A8
Prestwick KA9 236 B6
Nursery Bldgs ML11 215 A2
Nursery Ct
Carluke ML8 187 E3
Lanark ML11 214 E4
Nursery Dr
Ashgill ML9 200 A8
Kilwinning KA13 207 C5
Nursery Gdns
Kilmarnock KA1 228 B7
Springside KA11 221 A2
Nursery Gr
Ayr KA7 239 B5
Kilmacolm PA13 69 C1
Nursery Hall KA8 236 D2
Nursery La
Glasgow G41 116 F2
Kilmacolm PA13 69 C1
Kilmarnock KA1 228 B8
Nursery Pk ML8 187 E2
Nursery Pl
Ardrossan KA22 205 D2
Hamilton G72 161 D6
Nursery Rd
Ayr KA7 239 B5
Falkirk FK1 41 E4
Nursery St
Glasgow G41 117 A3
Helensburgh G84 25 B8
Kilmarnock KA1 227 F7
Nursery Wynd
Ayr KA7 239 B5
Kilmarnock KA1 228 A7
Kilwinning KA13 207 C5
Nutberry Ct G42 117 B1

O

Oak Ave
Bearsden G61 75 F7
East Kilbride G75 180 B6
Oakbank Ave ML2 164 E1
Oakbank Dr G78 155 E8
Oakbank Ind Est G20 97 B3
Oakbank Rd PA14 68 F8
Oakbank St ML6 123 D7
Oakburn Ave G62 54 F1
Oakburn Cres G62 54 F2
Oakburn Gdns G83 27 F5
Oakburn Wlk G83 27 F6
Oak Cres
Glasgow G69 120 A4
Plean FK7 12 C3
Oakdene Ave
Bellshill ML4 142 A7
Uddingston G71 141 B7
Oakdene Cres ML1 143 C3
Oak Dr
Cambuslang G72 139 C4
Fallin FK7 8 D4
Kirkintilloch G66 79 B5
Stenhousemuir FK5 23 D1
Oak Fern Dr G74 159 D4
Oak Fern Gr G74 159 D4
Oakfield Ave 7 G12 96 E3
Oakfield Dr
Alexandria G83 27 F5
2 Motherwell ML1 163 E6
Oakfield La 2 G12 96 E2
Oakfield Rd ML1 163 E6
Oakfield Terr PA15 46 C4
Oakfield Twr 1 ML1 163 E5
Oak Gr ML6 123 E3
Oakgrove Prim Sch 14 G4 97 A2
Oakhill Ave G69 119 F3
Oakland Dr KA20 206 E2
Oaklands Ave KA12 219 C4
Oak Lea ML3 162 F2
Oaklea Cres G72 161 C8
Oakleigh Dr PA16 45 D8
Oakley Dr G44 136 F3
Oakley Terr 4 G31 117 F7
Oak Mall Sh Ctr 3 PA15 45 F5
Oak Mall The 7 PA15 45 F5
Oak Path ML1 143 B5
Oak Pk
Bishopbriggs G64 78 B1
Oak Pk *continued*
Motherwell ML1 163 D4
Oak Pl
Coatbridge ML5 122 C5
East Kilbride G75 180 B6
Kilmarnock KA1 227 D8
Uddingston G71 141 C7
Oak Rd
Ardrossan KA22 205 C4
Clydebank G81 73 F5
Cumbernauld G67 62 E4
Paisley PA2 114 A1
Oakridge Cres PA3 113 B5
Oakridge Rd G69 121 B6
Oakshaw Brae PA1 113 D5
Oakshawhead PA1 113 D5
Oakshaw Street E PA1 113 E5
Oakshaw Street W PA1 113 D5
Oakside Pl ML3 183 D7
Oak St
Glasgow G2 240 B2
Stirling FK8 1 F1
Oaks The
Glasgow G44 137 B4
Johnstone PA5 111 E2
Oaktree Gdns
Dumbarton G82 50 C2
Glasgow G45 137 F4
Oakwood Ave
Ayr KA8 236 E2
Paisley PA2 113 B1
Oakwood Cres G34 100 D1
Oakwood Dr
Beith KA15 171 A8
Coatbridge ML5 121 D5
Glasgow G34 100 D1
Newton Mearns G77 156 F4
Oakwood Prim Sch G34 120 D8
Oakwood Sch FK2 42 F4
Oak Wynd G72 139 F3
Oates Gdns ML1 164 B4
Oatfield St G21 98 B3
OATLANDS 117 E2
Oban Ct 2 G20 96 E4
Oban Dr G20 96 E4
Oban La G20 96 E4
Oban Pl ML6 123 D6
Oban Terr PA16 44 E4
Oban Way ML1 143 B2
Oberon FK10 9 F8
Obiston Gdns G32 119 A5
Obree Ave KA9 236 E5
Observatory La 10 G12 96 D3
Observatory Rd G12 96 C3
Ocean Field G81 73 F6
Ocein Dr G74 179 C8
Ochel Path ML6 123 F1
Ochil Cres FK8 2 B2
Ochil Ct
East Kilbride G75 180 B4
Irvine KA11 220 A4
Tullibody FK10 4 C3
Ochil Dr
Barrhead G78 134 C1
Paisley PA2 133 E8
Stenhousemuir FK5 23 E3
Ochil Gdns FK4 39 F2
Ochil Hills Woodland Pk*
FK12 5 D7
Ochilmount FK7 7 F1
Ochil Pl
Glasgow G32 119 A4
Kilmarnock KA1 228 B3
Ochil Rd
Alva FK12 5 B7
Bearsden G61 75 B7
Bishopbriggs G64 78 C1
Menstrie FK11 4 A7
Renfrew PA4 94 B1
Stirling FK9 2 C4
Ochil St
Alloa FK10 10 A7
Fallin FK7 8 C4
Glasgow G32 119 A4
Tullibody FK10 4 B3
Wishaw ML2 164 F4
Ochil Terr FK2 24 B2
Ochiltree Ave G13 95 F7
Ochiltree Cres ML5 121 E5
Ochiltree Dr ML3 161 E1
Ochiltree Pl KA3 223 B6
Ochiltree Terr FK1 41 B5
Ochilvale Terr FK10 5 D3
Ochilview
Alva FK12 5 A7
Cowie FK7 12 E6
Ochil View
Denny FK6 39 D8
Shieldhill FK1 66 D7
8 Uddingston G71 141 A8
Ochil View Ct FK5 23 C5
Ochilview Pk
(Stenhousemuir FC & East
Stirlingshire FC) FK5 23 D3
Ochre Cres FK7 12 C8
O'Connor Ct KA21 216 E8
Octavia Ct PA15 46 D2
Octavia Terr PA16 45 C8
Octavia Wlk 2 PA14 47 A2
Odense Ct G75 180 E6
Ogilface Cres EH48 107 C2
Ogilvie Pl
Bridge of Allan FK9 2 A6
Glasgow G31 118 D4
Kilmarnock KA3 223 C2
Ogilvie Rd FK8 7 A5
Ogilvie St G31 118 D4
O'Hanlon Way FK8 1 F2
O'Hare G83 28 A3
Oki Way G68 62 C7
Old Aisle Rd G66 79 F7
Old Auchans View KA2 225 E2
Old Avon Rd ML3 163 A2
Old Balmore Rd G64 77 E7
OLD BALORNOCK 98 B5
Oldbarhills TP Site PA2 134 D8
Old Bars Dr 6 G69 81 A3
Old Bellsdyke Rd FK5 23 A3
Old Biggar Rd ML6 83 B1
Old Bore Rd ML6 123 E8
Old Bothwell Rd
Bothwell G71 141 B1
Hamilton G71 162 B8
Old Brewery La FK10 10 B7
Old Bridgend ML8 187 F1
Old Bridge of Weir Rd
PA6 91 A2
Old Bridge Rd KA8 236 E3
Old Bridge St
11 Alloa FK10 10 B6
Ayr KA7 235 F1
Old Bridge Wynd FK9 2 A4
Old Caley Rd KA12 219 C4
Old Castle Gdns G44 137 B6
Old Castle Rd G44 137 B5
Old Church Gdns G69 121 A5
Old Coach Rd G74 159 F3
Old Cross
4 Airdrie ML6 123 A8
Hamilton ML3 162 F4
Old Dalmarnock Rd G40 117 F4
Old Dalnottar Rd G60 73 C5
Old Denny Rd FK5 23 A3
Old Drove Rd FK7 6 C5
OLD DRUMCHAPEL 75 A1
Old Dullatur Rd G68 61 D6
Old Dumbarton Rd
Glasgow G3 96 C1
Glasgow G3 96 D1
Old Eastfield St ML7 127 D5
Old Edinburgh Rd
Uddingston, Calderbraes
G71 140 D8
Uddingston, Calderbraes
G71 140 F8
Uddingston G71 141 C7
Old Farm Rd
Ayr KA8 236 D3
2 Bearsden G61 95 F8
Old Gartloch Rd G69 100 F5
Old Glasgow Rd
Cumbernauld G67 62 A4
Kilwinning KA13 207 F4
Stewarton KA3 195 F2
Uddingston G71 140 E5
Uddingston, Kylepark G71 140 D7
Old Govan Rd PA4 94 F3
Old Greenock Rd
Bishopton, Kingston PA7,
PA8 72 D2
Bishopton PA7 71 D5
Erskine, Inchinnan PA4 93 D7
Erskine, West Craigend PA4 93 A8
Langbank PA14 70 C6
Port Glasgow PA14 69 D7
OLDHALL 114 D5
Oldhall Dr PA13 69 D1
Oldhall Rd PA1 114 D5
Oldhall Rdbt KA11 224 H5
Oldhall West Ind Est
KA11 224 H6
Old Hillfoot Rd KA7 239 B5
Old Humbie Rd G77 156 E2
Old Inns Intc G67 62 C5
Old Inns Rdbt G68 62 B6
Old Inverkip Rd PA16 45 C4
Old Irvine Rd KA1 227 E8
OLD KILPATRICK 73 A6
Old Lanark Rd
Braidwood ML8, ML11 202 B4
Carluke ML8 201 F8
Cartland ML11 202 E1
Old Largs Rd PA15, PA16 45 E2
Old Luss Rd
Balloch G83 19 B1
Helensburgh G84 16 F1
Old Manse Gdns ML5 122 A7
Old Manse Rd
Glasgow G32 119 D5
Wishaw ML2 164 E1
Old Market Rd ML11 215 B3
Old Military Rd G83 20 E8
Old Mill Ct G81 74 A5
Old Mill Gate G73 138 A6
Old Mill La G71 140 F7
Old Mill Park Ind Est G66 58 C1
Old Mill Rd
Bothwell G71 141 B1
Cambuslang G72 139 D5
Clydebank G81 74 A6
East Kilbride G74 159 F2
Hartwood ML7 146 B1
Kilmarnock KA1 228 A7
Paisley PA1, PA2 113 B3
Uddingston G71 140 F7
Old Mill View G65 60 F3
Old Mill Way FK6 21 B2
Old Mill Wlk 4 G83 27 E8
OLD MONKLAND 121 E4
Old Monkland Prim Sch
ML5 121 C4
Old Monkland Rd ML5 121 E4
Old Mugdock Rd G63 31 C2

Old Perceton KA11 220 B6
Old Playfield Rd G76 158 D8
Old Quarry Rd
Cumbernauld G68 81 D5
Stevenston KA20 217 D8
Old Raise Rd KA21 206 A1
Old Rd PA5 112 C3
Old Redding Rd FK2 42 F3
Old Rome Dr KA1 227 B7
Old Rome Way KA2 226 E5
Old Rutherglen Rd G5 117 D4
Old School Ct
Coatbridge ML5 122 A4
Tullibody FK10 4 B2
Old School Flats PA11 110 D8
Old Schoolhouse La PA6 91 B3
Old School Sq PA10 111 A3
Old Sch Pl ML8 187 A4
Old Sheriffmuir Rd FK9 2 C6
Old Shettleston Rd G32 119 A5
Old Sneddon St PA3 113 E5
Old St
Duntocher G81 73 F6
Kilmarnock KA1 227 F5
Old Stable Row ML5 122 B7
Old Station Brae KA10 229 F3
Old Station Ct G71 141 A2
Old Station Wynd KA10 229 F3
OLD TOLL 239 F6
Old Town FK7 7 D1
Old Town Jail★ KF8 7 A8
Old Twr Rd G68 60 F2
Old Union St ML6 123 B7
Old Vic Ct G74 160 C4
Old Willowyard Rd KA15 171 A7
Old Wood Rd G69 120 A4
Old Woodwynd Rd KA13 207 E4
Old Wynd G1 241 A1
Olifard Ave G71 141 B3
Oliphant Cres
Clarkston G76 157 E5
Paisley PA2 132 E8
Oliphant Ct
Paisley PA2 132 F8
Stirling FK8 2 B1
Oliphant Dr KA3 228 C8
Oliphant Oval PA2 132 E8
Olive Bank G71 121 C1
Olive Ct ML1 143 B5
Olive Rd KA1 227 D8
Oliver Rd FK1 42 D4
Olive St G33 98 D4
Ollach PA8 93 C7
Olympia Ct G75 180 F8
Olympia St [3] G40 117 F5
Olympia Way G74 159 F1
Olympic Bsns Pk KA2 225 D4
OMOA 144 A4
Omoa Rd ML1 144 B1
O'Neill Ave G64 98 B8
O'Neil Terr G83 27 E4
Onich Pl ML7 147 B3
Onslow G75 180 C7
Onslow Dr G31 118 A7
Onslow Rd G81 74 D2
Onslow Sq G31 118 A7
Ontario Pk G75 159 B1
Ontario Pl G75 159 B1
ONTHANK 222 E5
Onthank Dr KA3 222 F4
Onthank Prim Sch KA3 222 F5
Onyx St ML4 142 A4
Open Shore PA15 46 A5
Oran Gate G20 96 E5
Oran Gdns G20 96 E5
Orangefield PA15 45 E5
Orangefield Dr KA9 233 D1
Orangefield Ind Est KA9 233 D2
Orangefield La PA15 45 E5
Oran Pl G20 96 E4
Oran St G20 96 E4
ORBISTON 141 F4
Orbiston Ct ML1 164 A5
Orbiston Dr
Bellshill ML4 142 C4
Clydebank G81 74 D7
Orbiston Pl G81 74 D7
Orbiston Rd ML4 141 F4
Orbiston Sq ML4 141 F3
Orbiston St ML1 163 F5
Orbital Ct [12] G74 179 E8
Orcades Dr G44 137 C4
Orchard Ave
Ayr KA7 239 B6
Bothwell G71 141 B1
Orchard Brae
Hamilton ML3 162 D4
Kirkintilloch G66 79 E4
Orchard Cres PA14 47 A2
Orchardcroft [5] FK8 7 B7
Orchard Ct
Glasgow G32 139 B8
Glasgow, Orchard Pk G46 136 A3
Renfrew PA4 94 D4
Orchard Dr
Glasgow G46 136 B3
Hamilton G72 161 D8
Rutherglen G73 137 F7
Orchard Field G66 79 E4
Orchard Gate ML9 185 A2
Orchard Gn G74 160 B4
Orchard Gr
Coatbridge ML5 122 B6
Glasgow G46 136 B4
Kilmacolm PA13 89 C8
Orchard Gr *continued*
Kilwinning KA13 207 E4
Orchard House Day Unit
FK8 2 A1
ORCHARD PARK 136 B3
Orchard Park Ave G46 136 B3
Orchard Pk G46 136 C3
Orchard Pl
Ayr KA7 239 B6
Bellshill ML4 141 F3
Hamilton ML3 162 D3
Kilwinning KA13 207 E4
Kirkintilloch G66 80 A7
Orchard Rd FK9 2 A6
Orchardson Rd FK5 23 B2
Orchard St
Carluke ML8 187 F1
Falkirk FK1 42 B5
Glasgow G69 119 F3
Greenock PA15 46 B3
Hamilton ML3 162 E3
[3] Kilmarnock KA3 222 F2
Motherwell ML1 163 D7
Overtown ML2 186 B6
Paisley PA1 113 E4
Renfrew PA4 94 D4
West Kilbride KA23 190 C5
Orchard The FK10 4 B2
Orchardton Rd G68 81 D7
Orchardton Woods Ind Pk
G68 81 C8
Orchard View Dr ML11 214 A4
Orchid Pl G66 57 C8
Orchill Dr ML6 104 A3
Orchy Ave
Clarkston G76 157 F8
Glasgow G76 136 F1
Orchy Cres
Airdrie ML6 123 C4
Bearsden G61 75 D1
Paisley PA2 112 F1
Orchy Ct G81 74 C5
Orchy Dr G76 136 F1
Orchy Gdns G76 136 F1
Orchy St G44 137 A6
Orchy Terr G74 160 A1
Orefield Pl G74 159 E3
Oregon Pl G5 117 C4
Orion Pl ML4 142 E5
Orion Way
Cambuslang G72 139 A6
Carluke ML8 187 D2
Orkney Ct FK10 10 B5
Orkney Dr KA3 223 A5
Orkney Pl
Falkirk FK1 42 B2
Glasgow G51 116 B7
Orkney Quadrant ML2 165 D4
Orkney St G51 116 B7
Orlando G74 160 C5
Orleans Ave G14 95 E4
Orleans La G14 95 E3
Orlington Ct ML5 121 F8
Ormiston Ave G14 95 C4
Ormiston Dr
Alloa FK10 4 E2
Hamilton ML3 183 C8
Ormiston La [10] G14 95 C4
Ormiston Lane N [6] G14 95 C4
Ormiston Lane S [12] G14 95 C4
Ormiston Pl KA11 220 C7
Ormond Ct FK5 23 A3
Ormonde Ave G44 136 F3
Ormonde Cres G44 136 F3
Ormonde Ct G44 136 F3
Ormonde Dr G44 136 F3
Ornsay St G22 97 D7
Oronsay Ave PA14 69 B6
Oronsay Cres
Bearsden G61 76 B3
Old Kilpatrick G60 73 C6
Oronsay Ct G60 73 C6
Oronsay Gdns G60 73 C6
Oronsay Pl
Old Kilpatrick G60 73 C6
Wishaw ML2 165 B1
Oronsay Rd ML6 123 D5
Oronsay Sq G60 73 C6
Orr Sq PA1 113 E5
Orr Square Church PA1 113 D5
Orr St
Glasgow G40 117 F5
Glasgow G40 117 F6
Paisley, Castlehead PA1 113 E5
Paisley PA2 113 E3
Orr Terr
Harthill ML7 127 C4
Neilston G78 154 C6
Orton Pl G51 116 A6
Osborne Cres G74 158 B3
Osborne Gdns FK1 41 F3
Osborne St
Clydebank G81 74 A3
Falkirk FK1 41 F3
Glasgow G1 241 A1
Oskaig PA8 93 C7
Oslie View KA3 195 F1
Osprey Cres
Paisley PA3 113 D8
Wishaw ML2 165 B4
Osprey Dr
Kilmarnock KA1 228 C7
Uddingston G71 141 A7
Osprey Rd
Greenock PA16 45 B4
Paisley PA3 113 D8
Osprey View PA3 113 D8
Ossian Ave PA1 114 F5
Ossian Rd G43 136 E6
Oster Pl KA3 195 F2
Oswald Ct KA8 236 A3
Oswald Dr KA9 233 C1
Oswald Gdns ML8 201 E4
Oswald La KA8 235 E2
Oswald Pl KA8 236 A5
Oswald Rd KA8 236 A4
Oswald St
Falkirk FK1 42 B4
Glasgow G1 240 C2
Oswald Wlk G62 76 C8
Otago La G12 96 E2
Otago Lane N G12 96 E2
Otago Pk G75 159 A1
Otago Pl G82 50 C2
Otago St G12 96 E2
Othello G74 160 B5
Ottawa Cres G81 73 D4
Otterburn Ave KA3 223 B3
Otterburn Dr G46 136 C1
Otterswick Pl G33 99 C2
Ottoline Dr KA10 229 G2
Oudenarde Ct ML8 188 B1
Our Holy Redeemer's RC
Prim Sch G81 94 D7
Our Lady of Loretto Prim Sch
G81 73 E3
Our Lady of Lourdes Prim
Sch G75 180 D8
Our Lady of Peace Prim Sch
Glasgow G33 119 F6
Linwood PA3 112 A5
Our Lady of the Annunciation
Prim Sch G43 136 E5
Our Lady of the Assumption
Prim Sch G20 97 A6
Our Lady of the Missions
Prim Sch G46 136 A2
Our Lady of the Rosary Prim
Sch G52 115 D4
Our Lady & St Francis RC
Prim Sch ML1 143 C2
Our Lady & St Patricks High
Sch G82 49 C4
Our Ladys High Sch
Cumbernauld G67 61 D1
Motherwell ML1 164 A3
Our Lady's Prim Sch FK8 1 E2
Outdale Ave KA9 236 E8
Oval The
Glasgow G76 136 F1
Glenboig ML5 101 C6
Overbrae Gdns G15 74 F5
Overbrae Pl G15 74 F5
Overburn Ave G82 49 F4
Overburn Cres G82 49 F5
Overburn Terr G82 50 A5
Overcroy Rd G65 60 F4
Overdale Ave G42 136 F8
Overdale Cres KA9 236 C6
Overdale Gdns G42 136 F8
Overdale Pl ML2 186 C6
Overdale St G42 136 F8
Overjohnstone Dr ML2 164 D4
Overlea Ave G73 138 D6
Overlee Ho G76 157 F7
Overlee Rd G76 157 F7
Overmills Cres KA7 239 D8
Overmills Rd KA7 239 E7
Overnewton Pl G3 116 D8
Overnewton Sq G3 96 D1
Overnewton St G3 96 D1
Overton Cres
Denny FK6 21 D1
Greenock PA15 45 D3
Johnstone PA5 112 B3
West Kilbride KA23 190 C5
Overton Ct KA23 190 C5
Overton Dr KA23 190 C5
Overton Gdns PA13 69 E1
Overton Gr PA13 69 E1
Overton Pl
Glasgow G31 118 A5
Irvine KA11 220 B5
Overton Prim Sch PA15,
PA16 45 D3
Overton Rd
Alexandria G83 27 D4
Cambuslang G72 139 D4
Johnstone PA5 112 A2
Netherburn ML9 200 C5
Overton St
Alexandria G83 27 E5
Cambuslang G72 139 D4
Overton Terr FK6 21 C2
Overtoun Ave G82 50 B3
Overtoun Ct KA11 221 A2
Overtoun Dr
Clydebank G81 73 F4
Rutherglen G73 138 A7
Overtoun Estate★ G82 50 F5
Overtoun Rd
Clydebank G81 73 F4
Springside KA11 220 F3
OVERTOWN 186 C6
Overtown Ave G53 135 B6
Overtown Prim Sch ML2 186 C7
Overtown Rd ML2 165 F2
Overtown St G31 118 A5
Overwood Dr
Dumbarton G82 50 B4
Glasgow G44 137 C6
Overwood Gr G82 50 B4
Owen Ave G75 180 C7
Owendale Ave ML4 142 B7
Owen Kelly Pl KA21 205 E1
Owen Pk G75 180 D7
Owen St ML1 163 E8
O'wood Ave ML1 143 B6
Oxenward Rd KA13 207 E3
Oxford Ave PA19 45 A6
Oxford Dr PA3 112 B6
Oxford La
Glasgow G5 117 B5
Renfrew PA4 94 C3
Oxford Rd
Greenock PA16 44 D4
Renfrew PA4 94 C3
Oxford St
Coatbridge ML5 121 F6
Glasgow G5 240 C1
Kirkintilloch G66 79 C8
OXGANG 79 F7
Oxgang Holdings G66 79 F7
Oxgang Pl G66 79 E7
Oxgang Prim Sch G66 79 F8
Oxgang Rdbt G66 79 F7
Oxhill Pl G82 49 D3
Oxhill Rd G82 49 D4
Oxton Dr G52 115 B5

P

Pacemuir La PA13 89 B8
Pacemuir Rd PA13 89 B8
Paddock Ct ML8 202 B8
Paddock Dr ML8 202 B8
Paddockholm North Ind Est
KA25 149 B2
Paddockholm Rd KA25 149 B1
Paddockholm South Ind Est
KA25 149 B1
Paddock St ML5 122 D4
Paddock The
Clarkston G76 158 A5
Hamilton ML3 162 D6
Lanark ML11 214 D7
Perceton KA11 220 C5
Paddock View KA2 221 C1
Paduff Pl KA25 149 A2
Paidmyre Cres G77 156 D3
Paidmyre Gdns G77 156 D3
Paidmyre Rd G77 156 D3
PAISLEY 113 C2
Paisley Abbey★ PA1 113 F4
Paisley Arts Ctr PA1 113 E4
Paisley Canal Sta PA1 113 E3
Paisley Gilmour Street Sta
PA3 113 E5
Paisley Gram Sch [2]
PA1 114 A5
Paisley Mus & Art Gallery★
PA1 113 D4
Paisley Rd
Barrhead G78 134 B4
Glasgow G5 240 B1
Renfrew PA4 94 C2
Paisley Rd W
Glasgow G51, G52 115 D4
Glasgow, Ibrox G52 116 A5
Paisley St James Sta
PA3 113 C6
Paisley Sh Ctr The PA1 113 E4
Paisley St KA22 205 C2
Palacecraig St ML5 122 A3
Palace Grounds Rd ML3 162 F4
Palace of Art★ G41 115 F5
Palacerigg Country Pk★
G67 83 F7
Paladin Ave G13 95 B8
Palermo St [2] G21 97 E4
Palladium Pl G14 95 D3
Palmer Ave G13 75 D1
Palmerston G75 180 A7
Palmerston Pl
Glasgow G3 116 D8
Johnstone PA5 131 C8
Palm Pl G71 121 C1
Pandora Way G71 141 A7
Pankhurst Pl G74 159 F2
Panmure Path G68 60 F2
Panmure Pl G22 97 B5
Panmure St G20 97 A5
Panrock Ct KA10 229 D3
Pantonville Rd KA23 190 C3
Papermill Rd PA15, PA16 45 D2
Papingo Cl KA13 207 C6
Pappert
Bonhill G83 28 B3
Dumbarton G82 50 F4
Parcville Way G53 134 F3
Pardovan Pl FK1 41 F6
Paris Ave FK6 21 E1
Parkandarroch Cres
ML8 188 A1
Park Ave
Balloch G83 19 F1
Barrhead G78 134 B1
Beith KA15 150 B1
Bishopbriggs G64 78 B3
Carluke ML8 187 F3
Denny FK4 39 E6
Dumbarton G82 50 B3
Elderslie PA5 112 C2
Glasgow G3 96 F2
Greenock PA16 45 A7
Kilwinning KA13 207 E3
Kirkintilloch G66 79 C8
Laurieston FK2 42 F4
Milngavie G62 55 A1
Motherwell ML1 143 A5
Paisley PA2 113 D1
Prestwick KA9 236 B8
Stenhousemuir FK5 23 D1
Park Ave *continued*
Stirling FK8 7 A6
Twechar G65 59 F4
Park Bank PA8 73 B1
Park Brae PA8 93 C8
Parkbrae Ave G20 97 A6
Parkbrae Dr G20 97 A6
Parkbrae Gate G20 97 A6
Parkbrae Gdns G20 97 A6
Parkbrae La G20 97 A6
Parkbrae Pl G20 97 A6
Parkburn Ave G66 79 C7
Park Burn Ct ML3 162 A6
Park Burn Ind Est ML3 162 A6
Parkburn Rd G65 36 D1
Park Cir
Ayr KA7 238 F7
Carluke ML8 187 F3
Glasgow G3 240 A4
Park Circus La
Ayr KA7 238 F7
Glasgow G3 240 A4
Park Circus Pl G3 240 A4
Park Cres
Airdrie ML6 122 E8
Alloa FK10 5 C1
Bannockburn FK7 7 D2
Bearsden G61 75 C5
Bishopbriggs G64 78 A2
Dumbarton G82 49 F5
Eaglesham G76 178 E5
Falkirk FK2 24 A2
Hamilton G72 161 C6
Inchinnan PA4 93 D7
Stewarton KA3 211 D8
Torrance G64 57 C1
Park Ct
Beith KA15 171 C8
Bishopbriggs G64 78 B3
Clydebank G81 73 E4
Glasgow G46 136 B3
Shotts ML7 146 F4
Symington KA1 231 D3
Parkdale Gr G53 135 A3
Parkdale Way G53 135 A3
Park Dr
Bannockburn FK7 7 D2
Bellshill ML4 142 A4
Erskine PA8 93 B8
Glasgow G3 240 A4
Hamilton ML3 163 C1
Lanark ML11 214 F4
Rutherglen G73 138 A7
Stenhousemuir FK5 23 D2
Thorntonhall G74 158 C3
Wishaw ML2 166 A5
Parkdyke FK7 6 E6
Parkend Ave KA21 217 A7
Parkend Cres FK1 66 C6
Parkend Gdns KA21 217 A7
Parkend Rd KA21 217 A7
Parkend Terr KA21 217 A7
Parker Pl
[12] Kilsyth G65 60 D8
Larkhall ML9 185 B4
PARK FARM 69 B7
Parkfield G75 180 E5
PARKFOOT
Banknock 39 C4
Falkirk 42 C3
Parkfoot Ct FK1 42 B3
Parkfoot St G65 36 D1
Park Gardens La G3 96 E1
Parkgate FK12 4 F6
Park Gate
Erskine PA8 93 B8
Glasgow G3 96 E1
Park Gate Pl ML4 141 F5
Park Gdns
Bannockburn FK7 7 D2
Glasgow G3 96 E1
Kilbarchan PA10 111 B4
Park Glade PA8 93 B8
Park Gn PA8 93 B8
Park Gr
Cardross G82 48 B8
Erskine PA8 93 C8
Parkgrove Ave G46 136 D4
Parkgrove Terr G3 96 E1
Parkgrove Terrace La [6]
G3 96 E1
PARKHALL 74 A5
Parkhall Rd G81 73 F4
Parkhall St G74 159 F2
Parkhall Terr G81 73 F5
PARKHEAD 118 C3
Parkhead Ave KA13 207 F3
Parkhead Cross G31 118 D5
Parkhead Ct FK10 10 C8
Parkhead Hospl G31 118 D5
Parkhead La [3] ML6 123 A8
Parkhead Rd
Alloa FK10 10 C8
Falkirk FK1 42 B1
Parkhead St
Airdrie ML6 123 A8
Motherwell ML1 163 F5
Park Hill PA8 73 B1
Parkhill Ave
Crosshouse KA2 226 E8
Port Glasgow PA14 69 A8
Parkhill Dr
Dalry KA24 191 D7
Lochwinnoch PA12 129 D3
Rutherglen G73 138 A7
Parkhill Rd G43 136 D8
Parkhill Sch G31 118 C8
Parkholm Ave G53 134 F3

Parkholm Dr G53 . . . . 135 A3
Parkholm Gdns G53 . . . . 135 A3
Parkholm La G5 . . . . 240 A1
Parkholm Quadrant G53 135 A3
Parkhouse Dr 6 KA25 . . 149 A1
Parkhouse Gdns KA22. . . 205 D1
Parkhouse Rd
Ardrossan KA22. . . . . 205 D2
Glasgow G53 . . . . 135 A4
Parkhouse St KA7 . . . . . . .238 F7
Parkinch PA8 . . . . .93 C8
Park La
Ardrossan KA22. . . . . 205 C3
Carluke ML8. . . . . .187 E1
Glasgow G40 . . . . .117 F5
Hamilton G72. . . . . 161 D8
Kilsyth G65 . . . . .60 D8
Kilwinning KA13. . . . . 207 D5
Stirling FK8 . . . . .7 B8
Parklands Oval G53. . . . . .114 F2
Parklands Rd G44 . . . . . . .136 F3
Parklands Sch G84 . . . . . . .16 E2
Parklands View G53. . . . . .114 F2
Parklea G64 . . . . .77 E3
Park Lea ML6. . . . . 105 A4
Parklee Dr G76 . . . . .158 E7
PARK MAINS. 93 C8
Park Mains High Sch PA8 .73 B1
Parkmanor Ave G53. . . . . 135 A3
Parkmanor Gn G53 . . . . . 135 A3
Parkmeadow Ave G53. . . . 135 A3
Parkmeadow Way G53 . . 135 A3
Park Moor PA8 . . . . .93 B8
PARKNEUK. 161 B2
Parkneuk Rd
Glasgow G43 . . . . 136 C4
Hamilton G72. . . . . .161 B1
Parkneuk St ML1 . . . . .163 E8
Parknook Way 6 ML9 . . . .185 B4
Park Pl
Alloa FK10 . . . . .10 C7
Bellshill ML4 . . . . .141 E3
Coatbridge ML5. . . . . 122 D4
Denny FK6 . . . . .21 D2
Irvine KA12 . . . . .219 B5
Johnstone PA5. . . . . .111 F2
Lanark ML11 . . . . .214 F4
Stirling FK7 . . . . 6 F6
Strathblane G63 . . . . .31 B3
Thorntonhall G74. . . . . 158 C3
Park Prim Sch FK10. . . . . . .10 B5
Park Quadrant
Glasgow G3. . . . . 240 A4
6 Wishaw ML2. . . . . .164 E1
Park Rd
Ardrossan KA22. . . . . 205 C2
Bellshill ML4 . . . . 142 A4
Bishopbriggs G64 . . . . .78 B2
Blackridge EH48 . . . . .107 E3
Bridge of Weir PA11 . . . . . . .90 D1
Calderbank ML6. . . . . .123 B3
Chryston G69. . . . . 100 C8
Clydebank G81. . . . . .73 F3
Coatbridge G69 . . . . 121 A5
Falkirk FK2. . . . . .24 A1
Glasgow, Carmyle G32. . . . 139 C8
Glasgow G4 . . . . .96 E2
Glasgow, Giffnock G46. . . . 136 C2
Hamilton ML3 . . . . 162 D3
Inchinnan PA4 . . . . .93 D7
Johnstone PA5. . . . . .111 F2
Kilmacolm PA13. . . . . .89 C8
Menstrie FK11. . . . . .4 A6
Milngavie G62 . . . . .55 A1
Motherwell ML1. . . . . .143 B2
Paisley PA2 . . . . 113 D1
Saltcoats KA21 . . . . .216 E7
Shotts ML7. . . . . 146 D5
Park Ridge PA8. . . . . .93 C7
Parksail PA8. . . . . .93 C7
Parksail Dr PA8 . . . . .93 C8
Park Sch KA1. . . . . 227 D8
PARKSIDE. 144 C2
Parkside KA11 . . . . .220 B3
Parkside Ct FK7 . . . . .12 C3
Parkside Gdns G20 . . . . . . .97 A6
Parkside Pl G20 . . . . .97 A6
Parkside Rd
Motherwell ML1. . . . . .163 B6
Shotts ML7. . . . . 146 D4
Park St
Airdrie ML6 . . . . .122 E8
Alexandria G83 . . . . .27 D5
Alva FK12. . . . . .5 A7
Bonnybridge FK4 . . . . .40 C4
Carluke ML8. . . . . .187 F1
Cleland ML1. . . . . .144 B3
Coatbridge ML5. . . . . .122 B8
Cowie FK7 . . . . .12 E8
Dumbarton G82 . . . . .50 A3
Falkirk FK1. . . . . .42 B5
Kilmarnock KA1. . . . . .222 E1
Kirkintilloch G66 . . . . .80 B7
Motherwell ML1. . . . . .163 F6
Motherwell, New Stevenston
ML1. . . . . 143 A3
Park Street S G3 . . . . .96 E1
Parks View ML3. . . . . 183 D6
Park Terr
Ayr KA7 . . . . .238 E8
Cardross G82. . . . . .48 A8
East Kilbride G74. . . . . .159 E1
Glasgow G3. . . . . .96 E1
Gourock PA19 . . . . .44 E7
Stirling FK8 . . . . .7 A6
Tullibody FK10. . . . . .4 B1
Park Terrace East La G3 240 A4
Park Terrace La 1 G3 . . . .96 E1
Parkthorn View KA2. . . . . .225 E2
Park Top PA8 . . . . .73 C1
Parkvale Ave PA8 . . . . .93 D8
Parkvale Cres PA8 . . . . .93 D8
Parkvale Dr PA8 . . . . .93 D8
Parkvale Gdns PA8. . . . . . . .93 D8
Parkvale Pl PA8 . . . . .93 D8
Parkvale Way PA8 . . . . .93 D8
Parkview KA7 . . . . .238 F2
Park View
Ardrossan KA22. . . . . 205 D3
Caldercruix ML6. . . . . 105 A5
Kilbarchan PA10. . . . . 111 A4
Kilbirnie KA25 . . . . 149 A1
Larkhall ML9 . . . . .185 B2
Paisley PA2 . . . . 113 D2
Parkview Ave
Falkirk FK1. . . . . .41 F2
Kirkintilloch G66 . . . . .79 D6
Parkview Cres ML2 . . . . . 166 A4
Parkview Ct G66. . . . . .79 D7
Park View Ct FK1 . . . . .41 E5
Parkview Dr
Coatbridge ML5. . . . . .121 E7
Stepps G33 . . . . .99 E6
Parkview Prim Sch G23. . .96 D8
Parkville Ct EH48 . . . . .107 E3
Parkville Dr
Hamilton G72. . . . . .161 E6
Hamilton G72. . . . . .161 F6
Parkville Rd ML4 . . . . 142 C7
Parkway
Alloa FK10 . . . . .10 B7
Erskine PA8 . . . . .93 B8
Parkway G72 . . . . 139 C8
Park Way G67 . . . . .62 B4
Parkway Ct
Alloa FK10 . . . . .10 A7
Coatbridge ML5. . . . . .121 E6
Glasgow G69 . . . . .120 B7
Parkway Pl ML5 . . . . .121 E5
Park Winding PA8 . . . . .93 C8
Park Wood PA8. . . . . .73 C1
Parkwood Lea 1 ML3. . . 162 A6
Parkwood Terr 2 ML3 . . 162 A6
Parliament Rd G66 . . . . . . .79 D7
Parnell St ML6. . . . . .122 F5
Parnie St G1 . . . . 241 A1
Parry Terr G75. . . . . .159 B1
Parsonage Row G1 . . . . . .241 B2
Parsonage Sq G4 . . . . .241 B2
Parson St G4. . . . . 241 C3
Parterre KA12 . . . . 219 C2
PARTICK. 96 B2
Partick Bridge St G11. . . . . .96 C1
PARTICKHILL. 96 B3
Partickhill Ave G11 . . . . . . .96 B3
Partickhill Ct G11. . . . . .96 B3
Partickhill Rd G11 . . . . .96 B2
Partick St ML5. . . . . 122 C5
Partick Sta (Underground)
G11 . . . . .96 B1
Partridge Rd PA16 . . . . .45 A6
Patchy Pk ML9 . . . . 199 A8
Paterson Ave KA12. . . . . . .219 E5
Paterson Cres KA12. . . . . . 219 D5
Paterson Dr
Helensburgh G84. . . . . .16 B4
Shieldhill FK1. . . . . .66 C6
Paterson Pl
Bearsden G61 . . . . .75 C8
Bonnybridge FK4 . . . . .40 C5
Bridge of Allan FK9 . . . . .2 A6
Paterson's Laun G64. . . . . .77 E7
Paterson St
Ayr KA8 . . . . .236 B4
Glasgow G5. . . . . .240 B1
Motherwell ML1. . . . . .163 E8
Paterson Terr G75 . . . . . . 180 D7
Paterson Twr FK1 . . . . .42 D4
PATHER. 165 A1
Pather St ML2 . . . . .165 B2
Pathfoot KA13 . . . . .207 F3
Pathfoot Ave FK9 . . . . .2 C7
Pathfoot Dr FK9 . . . . .2 C7
Pathfoot Rd FK9 . . . . .2 C6
Pathfoot View KA13 . . . . . .207 F3
Pathhead Gdns G33. . . . . . .98 F6
Pathhead Rd G76 . . . . 158 D7
Path The
Airth FK2 . . . . .14 D4
Bannockburn FK7. . . . . .7 D2
Pat Kelly Ave FK7. . . . . .6 F4
Patna Ct ML3. . . . . .161 E1
Patna St G40 . . . . .118 B3
Paton Ct ML2. . . . . 164 D1
Paton St
Alloa FK10 . . . . .10 A7
Glasgow G31. . . . . .118 B7
Greenock PA16 . . . . .45 C5
Patrick Ave KA20 . . . . 206 C1
Patrickbank Cres PA5. . . . 112 D1
Patrickbank Gdns PA5 . . . 112 C1
Patrickbank View PA5. . . . 112 C1
Patrickbank Wynd PA5. . . 112 D1
Patrick Dr FK1. . . . . .66 E7
Patrickholm Ave ML9 . . . .198 E1
Patrick St
Greenock PA16 . . . . .45 E6
Paisley PA2 . . . . .113 F3
Patterson Dr ML8. . . . . 187 A6
Patterton Dr G78 . . . . 134 D1
Patterton Sta G77 . . . . 156 D8
Pattison St G81. . . . . .73 E3
Pattle Pl KA7. . . . . .238 F1
Paul Dr FK2 . . . . .14 E4
Pavilion Pl KA22 . . . . 205 C1
Pavilion Rd KA7 . . . . .238 E8
Pavilions Bsns Pk FK10 . . . . 9 E7
Pavilions The FK10. . . . . .9 E7
Pavilion View FK10. . . . . .9 F8
Paxstone Cres ML7 . . . . . .127 E5
Paxstone Dr ML7 . . . . .127 E5
Paxton Cres G74. . . . . .159 F4
Paxton Ct G74 . . . . .159 F4
Paxton Pl KA1 . . . . 228 A7
Payne St G4 . . . . 241 A4
Peace Ave
Kilmarnock KA1. . . . . 222 D1
Quarriers Village PA11 . . . . .89 F2
Peach Ct ML1 . . . . 143 D1
Peacock Ave PA2 . . . . .112 F2
Peacock Cross ML3. . . . . . 162 C4
Peacock Cross Ind Est
ML3 . . . . 162 C4
Peacock Ct ML8 . . . . .202 B8
Peacock Dr
Hamilton ML3 . . . . 162 C4
Paisley PA2 . . . . .112 F2
Peacock Loan ML8. . . . . . . .187 F3
Pearce La G51. . . . . 116 A8
Pearce St G51. . . . . 116 A8
Pear Gr ML1. . . . . 143 D1
Pearl St ML4 . . . . .142 B3
Pearson Ave FK4 . . . . .39 D5
Pearson Dr PA4. . . . . .94 D3
Pearson Pl
Bonnybridge FK4 . . . . .39 D5
Linwood PA3 . . . . .112 B5
Pearson View FK10. . . . . . . .10 C8
Peathill Ave G69. . . . . .80 B1
Peathill Rd FK4. . . . . .40 A6
Peathill St G21 . . . . .97 C3
Peathill Terr FK4. . . . . .40 A5
Peatland Quadrant KA1 . 228 A3
Peatland Rd KA1. . . . . 228 A3
Peat Pl G53 . . . . 135 A5
Peat Rd
Bridge of Weir PA11 . . . . . .110 E7
Glasgow G53. . . . . .135 B6
Greenock PA15 . . . . .45 D3
Pebble Dr ML9 . . . . 198 D1
Peden Ave KA24 . . . . .191 B7
Peden Pl KA12. . . . . 219 C2
Peden St ML7 . . . . 127 C5
Pedmyre La G76. . . . . 158 D7
Peebles Ct 8 PA15 . . . . . . .46 B3
Peebles Dr G73. . . . . 138 D7
Peebles Path ML5 . . . . 122 D3
Peebles St KA8 . . . . .235 F2
Peel Ave ML1. . . . . .163 E4
Peel Brae G66. . . . . .58 C1
Peel Ct G72 . . . . 139 A6
Peel Glen Gdns G15 . . . . . . .75 A5
Peel Glen Rd G15, G61. . . . .75 A5
Peel La G11 . . . . .96 B2
Peel Park Pl G74 . . . . .158 F2
Peel Pl
Bothwell G71. . . . . 141 A3
Coatbridge ML5. . . . . 121 D5
Peel Rd G74. . . . . .158 B2
Peel St
Cardross G82. . . . . .48 B7
Glasgow G11. . . . . .96 B2
Peel View 2 G81 . . . . .74 D3
Pegasus Ave
Carluke ML8. . . . . .187 E2
Paisley PA1 . . . . 112 D5
Pegasus Rd ML4. . . . . .142 E5
Peggieshill Pl KA7. . . . . . . .239 B5
Peggieshill Rd KA7 . . . . . .239 B5
Peile La PA16. . . . . .45 D6
Peile St PA16. . . . . .45 C6
Peiter Pl 5 G72. . . . . 161 C7
Pelham Ct 2 G74 . . . . 179 D8
Pelstream Ave FK7. . . . . .7 B4
Pemberton Valley KA7. . . 239 A2
Pembroke G74. . . . . 160 D4
Pembroke Rd PA16. . . . . . . .44 D4
Pembroke St
Glasgow G3 . . . . 240 A3
Stenhousemuir FK5. . . . . . . .23 C3
Pembury Cres ML3. . . . . . . .182 F7
Penbreck Ct KA11 . . . . . . .220 B6
Penbury Cres ML3 . . . . .182 F7
Pencaitland Dr G32. . . . . . 119 A3
Pencaitland Gr G32. . . . . . 119 A3
Pencaitland Pl G23 . . . . . . .76 E1
Pendale Rise G45. . . . . 137 D3
Pendeen Cres G33. . . . . . . .119 E5
Pendeen Pl G33 . . . . .119 F6
Pendeen Rd G33. . . . . .119 F5
Penders La FK1. . . . . .42 A5
Pendicle Cres G61. . . . . .75 D3
Pendicle Rd G61. . . . . .75 E3
Pendle Ct G69. . . . . .100 F6
Pendreich Way FK9 . . . . .2 D6
Penfold Cres G75. . . . . 180 D8
Penicuik St G32 . . . . 118 D6
PENILEE. 114 E6
Penilee Rd G52. . . . . .114 E6
Penilee Terr G52. . . . . .114 E6
Peninver Dr G51. . . . . .115 E8
Penman Ave G73 . . . . .137 F8
Pennan PA8 . . . . .73 A3
Pennan Pl G14 . . . . .95 A5
Penneld Rd G52 . . . . .114 F5
Penniecroft Ave G82. . . . . .50 C5
Pennine Gr ML6 . . . . .123 F1
Pennyburn Local Ctr
KA13. . . . . 207 C2
Pennyburn Prim Sch
KA13. . . . . 207 D2
Pennyburn Rd KA13. . . . . 207 D2
Pennyburn Rdbt KA20. . . 207 A2
PENNY FERN. 45 B3
Pennyfern Dr PA16. . . . . . . .45 B3
Pennyfern Rd PA16 . . . . . . .45 B3
Pennyroyal Ct G74 . . . . . . 159 D4
Pennyvenie Way KA11. . . 220 A5
Penrioch Dr G75. . . . . 180 C4
Penrith Ave G46 . . . . 136 C2
Penrith Dr G12 . . . . .96 A6
Penrith Pl G75. . . . . .179 F6
Penryn Gdns G32 . . . . 119 D3
Penston Rd G33 . . . . 119 D8
Pentland Ave
Linwood PA3 . . . . 112 A5
Port Glasgow PA14 . . . . .68 F6
Pentland Cres
Larkhall ML9 . . . . .184 E5
Paisley PA2 . . . . 133 D8
Pentland Ct
Airdrie ML6 . . . . .103 B2
Barrhead G78 . . . . 134 C1
Coatbridge ML5. . . . . 122 C3
Greenock PA16 . . . . .45 B5
Pentland Dr
Barrhead G78 . . . . 134 C1
Bishopbriggs G64 . . . . .78 D2
Paisley PA4 . . . . .114 B8
Prestwick KA9. . . . . 236 D5
Pentland Gdns ML9. . . . . .184 F5
Pentland Pl
Bearsden G61 . . . . .75 B7
Irvine KA11. . . . . 220 A3
Pentland Rd
Chryston G69. . . . . 100 D8
East Kilbride G75. . . . . 180 A3
Glasgow G43. . . . . 136 C5
Kilmarnock KA1 . . . . 228 A3
Wishaw ML2 . . . . .164 E4
Pentland Sch ML5 . . . . 101 C1
Pentland Way ML3. . . . . . 183 A7
Penzance Way G69 . . . . . . .80 F2
Peockland Gdns PA5. . . . . 112 A3
Peockland Pl PA5. . . . . . . 112 A3
People's Palace (Mus) &
Winter Gdns* G40 . . . . .117 E5
Peploe Ave FK5. . . . . .23 B2
Peploe Dr G74. . . . . 160 D5
PERCETON. 220 C5
Perceton Gate KA11 . . . . .220 E7
Perceton Mains KA11 . . . 220 D6
Perceton Rdbt KA11 . . . . .220 B6
Perceton Row KA11. . . . . .220 D3
Perchy View ML2 . . . . 165 C1
Percy Dr G46. . . . . 136 C1
Percy Rd PA4. . . . . .94 A1
Percy St
Glasgow G51. . . . . 116 D5
Larkhall ML9 . . . . 185 A4
Perran Gdns G69 . . . . .80 E2
Perray Ave G82. . . . . .49 B5
Perrays Cres G82 . . . . .49 A5
Perrays Ct G82 . . . . .49 A5
Perrays Dr G82 . . . . .49 A5
Perrays Gr G82 . . . . .49 A5
Perrays Way G82 . . . . .49 A5
Perth Ave ML6. . . . . 123 A4
Perth Cres G81 . . . . .73 D5
Perth St G3 . . . . 240 A2
Peter Coats Bldg PA2. . . . .113 E3
Peter D Stirling Rd 1
G66 .58 D1
Peter McEachran Ho
G31 . . . . 118 C8
Peters Ave G83 . . . . .28 A8
PETERSBURN 123 D5
Petersburn Pl ML6. . . . . . . 123 D6
Petersburn Prim Sch
ML6 . . . . 123 C6
Petersburn Rd ML6 . . . . . 123 D6
PETERSHILL 98 B3
Petershill Ct G21 . . . . .98 C3
Petershill Dr G21 . . . . .98 C3
Petershill Pl G21 . . . . .98 B4
Petershill Rd G21. . . . . .98 A3
Peterson Dr G13. . . . . .94 E8
Peterson Gdns G13 . . . . . . .94 E8
Peter St KA12 . . . . 219 A1
Peterswell Brae FK7 . . . . .7 E1
Petition Pl G71 . . . . 141 A5
Pettigrew St G32 . . . . 119 A5
Peveril Ave
Glasgow G41. . . . . 116 D1
Rutherglen G73 . . . . 138 C5
Peveril Ct G73. . . . . 138 C5
Pharonhill St G31. . . . . . . 118 D5
Pheasantry The FK10. . . . . .10 E5
Philip Ct ML4. . . . . 142 A4
Philip Dr FK5 . . . . .23 D2
Philip Murray Rd ML4. . . 141 D6
PHILIPSHILL 158 E4
Philipshill Gate G74. . . . . .158 E3
Philipshill Ind Est G74 . . . .158 E3
Philipshill Rd G76 . . . . . . .158 E4
Philip Sq KA8. . . . . 236 A1
Philip St FK2 . . . . .42 B7
Philips Wlk ML3 . . . . .162 B2
Philips Wynd ML3. . . . . . . .162 B2
Phoenix Bsns Pk PA1 . . . . .112 E5
Phoenix Cres ML4 . . . . . . .141 F8
Phoenix Ct G74. . . . . 160 D5
Phoenix Ho G81 . . . . .74 A2
Phoenix Ind Est
Paisley PA3 . . . . .113 E8
Stirling FK7 . . . . .7 C7
Phoenix Leisure Pk The
PA1. . . . . .112 E5
Phoenix Pl
Elderslie PA5 . . . . 112 D3
Motherwell ML1. . . . . 143 A3
Phoenix Rd ML4 . . . . .142 E5
Phoenix Ret Pk PA1. . . . . .112 F5
Piazza Sh Ctr PA1. . . . . . . .113 E5
Piccadilly St G3 . . . . 240 A2
Picken St KA1 . . . . .227 F5
PICKERSTONHILL. 144 A5
Pickerstonhill ML1. . . . . . . .143 E4
Picketlaw Dr G76 . . . . 158 D7
Picketlaw Farm Rd G76 . 158 C7
Pienchorran PA4. . . . . .93 C7
Pier Rd
Balloch G83 . . . . .19 D1
Rhu G84. . . . . .15 E4
Piershill St G32. . . . . .118 F7
Piersland Pl KA11. . . . . . . 220 A5
Pikeman Rd G13. . . . . .95 C7
Pike Rd FK7 . . . . .7 D4
Pillans Ave ML8. . . . . 187 D2
Pillans Ct ML3 . . . . 162 A6
Pilmuir Ave G44 . . . . .136 F4
Pilmuir Holdings G77 . . . .155 F2
Pilrig St G32 . . . . .118 E7
Pilton Rd G15 . . . . .75 A4
Pineapple The* FK2 . . . . . .14 B6
Pine Ave G72 . . . . .139 F3
Pine Brae KA7. . . . . 239 C5
Pine Cl G67 . . . . .62 E4
Pine Cres
Cumbernauld G67 . . . . .62 E4
East Kilbride G75. . . . . .180 B5
Hamilton ML3 . . . . 183 A7
Johnstone PA5. . . . . 112 A1
Menstrie FK11. . . . . 3 F6
Pine Ct
Cumbernauld G67 . . . . .62 E4
East Kilbride G75. . . . . 180 C5
Pine Gr
Alloa FK10 . . . . .10 C6
Calderbank ML6. . . . . .123 B2
Coatbridge G69 . . . . 121 A6
Cumbernauld G67 . . . . .62 E4
Motherwell ML1. . . . . .143 B5
Uddingston G71. . . . . .141 B8
Pine Ho
East Kilbride G75. . . . . .180 B5
Prestwick KA9. . . . . 236 C5
Pinelands G64. . . . . .78 A4
Pine Lawn ML2 . . . . 165 D5
Pine Mews ML1. . . . . 143 D2
Pine Pk ML3. . . . . .162 E1
Pine Pl
Cumbernauld G67 . . . . .62 E4
Glasgow G5 . . . . 117 C4
Pine Quadrant ML6 . . . . . .123 E3
Pine Rd
Clydebank G81. . . . . .73 D4
Cumbernauld G67 . . . . .62 E4
Dumbarton G82. . . . . .49 F4
Kilmarnock KA1. . . . . 227 D7
Pine St
Airdrie ML6 . . . . 123 D7
Greenock PA15 . . . . .45 E4
Lennoxtown G66 . . . . .57 E8
Paisley PA2 . . . . 114 A2
Pines The G44 . . . . .137 B4
Pineview Ct G15 . . . . .75 B3
Pine Wlk FK5. . . . . .23 D1
Pinewood 1 G61. . . . . .75 F3
Pinewood Ave G66. . . . . . . .79 A5
Pinewood Ct
Dumbarton G82. . . . . .50 C5
Kirkintilloch G66 . . . . .79 A5
Pinewood Pl G66 . . . . .79 A5
Pinewood Sq G15. . . . . .75 B3
Pinkerton Ave G73. . . . . . .137 F8
Pinkerton La PA4 . . . . .94 D1
Pinkston Dr G21 . . . . .97 E2
Pinkston Rd G4, G21 . . . . .97 D2
Pinmore KA13 . . . . 207 C2
Pinmore Pl G53. . . . . .134 F5
Pinmore St G53 . . . . .134 F5
Pinwherry Dr G33 . . . . .98 F6
Pinwherry Pl G71. . . . . 141 A3
Pioneer Pk G82. . . . . .50 A2
Piper Ave PA6 . . . . 111 C8
Piperhill KA7 . . . . 239 A2
Piper Rd
Airdrie ML6 . . . . 123 C5
Houston PA6 . . . . 111 C8
Pirleyhill Dr FK1. . . . . .66 D6
Pirleyhill Gdns FK1 . . . . . . .42 A2
Pirnhall Rd
Bannockburn, Chartershall
FK7. . . . . .11 A8
Bannockburn FK7. . . . . .11 D7
Bannockburn FK7. . . . . .11 E8
Pirnie Pl G65 . . . . .60 D8
Pirnmill Ave
East Kilbride G75. . . . . .180 B4
Motherwell ML1. . . . . .163 B7
Pirnmill Pl G84 . . . . .16 F2
Pirnmill Rd KA21 . . . . .205 F2
Pitcairn Cres G75. . . . . . . .179 F8
Pitcairn Gr G75. . . . . 180 A8
Pitcairn Pl G75 . . . . .179 F8
Pitcairn St G31 . . . . .118 E4
Pitcairn Terr ML3 . . . . 162 A4
Pitcaple Dr G43 . . . . .136 B6
Pitfairn Rd FK10 . . . . .5 E3
Pitlochry Dr
Glasgow G52 . . . . 115 C4
Larkhall ML9 . . . . 185 C1
Pitlochry Pl G72. . . . . .161 E2
Pitmedden Rd G64. . . . . . . .78 D2
Pitmilly Rd G15. . . . . .75 C4

Pit Rd
Bellshill ML4 .... 141 F6
Kirkintilloch G66 .... 80 C7
Pitreavie Ct ML3 .... 183 B8
Pitreavie Pl G33 .... 99 C1
Pittenweem Path G72 .... 161 D3
Pitt St G2 .... 240 B3
Pitt Terr FK8 .... 7 B6
Place of Bonhill G82 .... 27 D3
Place View KA25 .... 149 A1
Pladda Ave
Irvine KA11 .... 220 B2
Port Glasgow PA14 .... 69 B7
Pladda Cres KA11 .... 220 A2
Pladda Ct KA11 .... 220 B2
Pladda Dr KA9 .... 236 C6
Pladda Rd
Renfrew PA4 .... 94 D1
Saltcoats KA21 .... 205 F2
Pladda St ML1 .... 163 B7
Pladda Terr KA11 .... 220 B2
Pladda Way G84 .... 16 F2
Pladda Wynd KA11 .... 220 B2
PLAINS 104 A3
Plains Prim Sch ML6 .... 104 A2
Plaintrees Ct PA2 .... 113 E1
Plane Pl G71 .... 121 C1
Planetree Pl PA5 .... 112 A1
Planetree Rd G81 .... 74 A5
Plann Cotts KA2 .... 221 F3
Plann Ho KA2 .... 221 F3
Plann Rd KA2 .... 221 F4
PLANTATION 116 D6
Plantation Ave ML1 .... 143 B6
Plantation Park Gdns [3]
G51 .... 116 D5
Plantation Sq G51 .... 116 E6
Plant St G31 .... 118 C6
Plan View KA25 .... 149 B3
Plateau Dr KA10 .... 229 G7
Platthorn Dr G74 .... 159 F1
Platthorn Rd G74 .... 159 F1
Players Rd FK7 .... 7 C7
Playfair St G40 .... 118 A3
Playingfield Cres KA2 .... 221 E1
Playingfield Rd KA2 .... 221 E1
Pleaknowe Cres G69 .... 80 F2
Pleamuir Pl G68 .... 61 C2
PLEAN 12 C3
Pleanbank Cotts FK7 .... 12 B3
Plean Ctry Pk* FK7 .... 12 B2
Plean Ind Est FK7 .... 12 D1
Plean St G14 .... 95 A5
Pleasance FK1 .... 42 B4
Pleasance Ct [12] FK2 .... 42 B4
Pleasance Gdns FK1 .... 42 B4
Pleasance Rd FK1 .... 42 B3
Pleasance Sq [11] FK1 .... 42 B4
Pleasance St G43 .... 136 D7
Pleasance Way G43 .... 136 D7
Pleasantfield Rd KA9 .... 236 B5
Pleasantside Ave PA14 .... 69 A8
Pleasures The FK10 .... 9 E7
Plotcock Rd ML3 .... 198 D7
Ploughland Holdings
KA2 .... 225 F3
Plover Dr G75 .... 180 A5
Plover Pl PA5 .... 131 C7
Plusgarten Loan ML2 .... 165 F7
Plymouth Ave PA19 .... 44 E5
Pochard Way ML4 .... 141 F8
Poet's View G66 .... 79 F7
Poindfauld Terr G82 .... 50 A4
Pointhouse Rd G3 .... 116 D8
Pokelly Pl KA3 .... 195 F1
Polbae Cres G76 .... 178 E5
Polden Ave G75 .... 180 A3
Polden Ct G75 .... 180 A3
Poles Rd KA3 .... 213 A3
Polkemmet Dr ML7 .... 127 F6
Polkemmet La ML7 .... 127 F5
Polkemmet Rd ML7 .... 127 F6
Pollick Ave G78 .... 153 B3
Pollick Farm La G78 .... 153 A2
Pollock Ave
Eaglesham G76 .... 178 E5
Hamilton ML3 .... 162 A4
Pollock Cres KA13 .... 207 E2
Pollock Morris Dr KA2 .... 226 B7
Pollock Rd
Bearsden G61 .... 76 A3
Newton Mearns G77 .... 156 C4
Pollock St
Bellshill ML4 .... 142 C5
Motherwell ML1 .... 163 E7
POLLOK 115 B1
Pollok Ave G43 .... 136 B8
Pollok Ctry Pk* G43 .... 116 B1
Pollok Dr G64 .... 77 E1
Pollok House* G43 .... 135 F8
Pollok La G74 .... 160 B3
Pollok L Ctr G53 .... 135 C7
Pollok Pl [2] G74 .... 160 B3
POLLOKSHAWS 136 C7
Pollokshaws East Sta
G43 .... 136 D7
Pollokshaws Rd
Glasgow, Gorbals G41 .... 117 B4
Glasgow, Pollokshaws
G43 .... 136 C8
Glasgow, Strathbungo G41 .... 116 F1
Pollokshaws West Sta
G43 .... 136 B7
POLLOKSHIELDS 116 E3
Pollokshields East Sta
G41 .... 117 A3
Pollokshields Prim Sch
G41 .... 116 F3
Pollokshields Prim Sch
Annexe (Infs) [1] G41 .... 116 F3
Pollokshield Sq G41 .... 116 E2
Pollokshields Sq G41 .... 116 E2
Pollokshields West Sta
G41 .... 116 F2
POLMADIE 117 C2
Polmadie Ave G5 .... 117 D2
Polmadie Ind Est G5,
G73 .... 117 E2
Polmadie Rd G5 .... 117 D2
Polmadie St G42 .... 117 C1
Polmaise Ave FK7 .... 7 B3
Polmaise Cres FK7 .... 8 C5
Polmaise Ct FK7 .... 7 B3
Polmaise Rd
Cambusbarron FK7 .... 6 E3
Stirling FK7 .... 6 F5
Polnoon Ave G13 .... 95 A6
Polnoon Dr G76 .... 178 E5
Polnoon Mews G76 .... 178 E5
Polnoon St G76 .... 178 D4
Polo Ave KA10 .... 229 F2
Polo Gdns KA10 .... 229 F2
Polquhap Ct [4] G53 .... 135 A8
Polquhap Gdns [6] G53 .... 135 A8
Polquhap Pl [5] G53 .... 135 A8
Polquhap Rd G53 .... 135 A8
Polson Dr PA5 .... 111 E2
Polsons Cres PA2 .... 113 D2
Polwarth La
Glasgow G12 .... 96 B3
Glasgow G12 .... 96 B4
Polwarth St G12 .... 96 B3
Pomona Pl ML3 .... 161 F2
Pompee Rd FK10 .... 5 B1
Poplar Ave
Bishopton PA7 .... 72 B2
Glasgow G11 .... 95 F4
Johnstone PA5 .... 112 A1
Newton Mearns G77 .... 156 E4
Poplar Cres
Bishopton PA7 .... 72 B2
Quarter ML3 .... 183 F4
Poplar Dr
Clydebank G81 .... 73 F5
Kirkintilloch G66 .... 79 A5
Milton of Campsie G66 .... 58 C5
Poplar Gdns G75 .... 180 C5
Poplar Pl
Blantyre G72 .... 140 C1
Gourock PA19 .... 44 C6
Hamilton G72 .... 161 C8
Motherwell ML1 .... 143 B4
Uddingston G71 .... 141 D8
Poplar Rd G82 .... 49 F4
Poplar St
Airdrie ML6 .... 123 D7
Greenock PA15 .... 46 F2
Poplars The
Bearsden G61 .... 75 D8
Tullibody FK10 .... 4 B1
Poplar Way
Ayr KA7 .... 239 D5
Cambuslang G72 .... 139 F3
Motherwell ML1 .... 143 D2
Poplin St G40 .... 118 A3
Porchester St G33 .... 99 D2
Portal Rd G13 .... 95 C8
Portdownie FK1 .... 41 D5
PORT DUNDAS 97 C2
Port Dundas Pl G2 .... 241 A3
Port Dundas Rd G4 .... 241 A4
PORT EGLINTON 117 A4
Portencross Rd KA23 .... 190 C5
Porter Ave [3] FK9 .... 2 B3
Porter Dr KA2 .... 227 B6
Porterfield Rd
Kilmacolm PA13 .... 89 E7
Renfrew PA4 .... 94 B3
Porters La ML6 .... 123 D2
Porter St G51 .... 116 C5
Porters Well G71 .... 140 E5
Portessie PA8 .... 73 A2
PORT GLASGOW 47 F1
Port Glasgow High Sch
PA14 .... 69 A6
Port Glasgow Ind Est
PA14 .... 68 E7
Port Glasgow Rd
Greenock PA15 .... 46 E3
Greenock PA15 .... 46 F2
Kilmacolm PA13 .... 69 B2
Port Glasgow Sta PA14 .... 47 C1
Portia Pl ML1 .... 163 E7
Porting Cross Pl KA3 .... 223 B6
Portland Ave KA12 .... 224 D8
Portland Brae KA1 .... 228 E6
Portland Ct KA1 .... 228 E6
Portland High Sch ML5 .... 122 B7
Portland Pk ML3 .... 162 E2
Portland Pl
Hamilton ML3 .... 162 E2
Irvine KA11 .... 219 E6
Irvine KA12 .... 224 D8
Kilmarnock KA1 .... 227 E8
Lanark ML11 .... 215 B4
Stevenston KA20 .... 217 D7
Portland Place Ind Est
KA20 .... 217 D7
Portland Rd
Cumbernauld G68 .... 61 F5
Irvine KA12 .... 224 C8
Kilmarnock KA1 .... 227 E8
Portland Rd *continued*
Paisley PA2 .... 114 B3
Portland Rdbt KA12 .... 219 A1
Portland Sq ML3 .... 162 E2
Portland St
Coatbridge ML5 .... 122 B7
Kilmarnock KA1 .... 222 F1
Troon KA10 .... 229 D3
Portland Terr KA10 .... 229 C2
Portland Wynd [4] ML9 .... 185 B4
Portlethen PA8 .... 73 A2
Portman St G41 .... 116 E5
Portmark Ave KA7 .... 238 C1
Portmarnock Dr G23 .... 96 E8
Porton Pl PA7 .... 72 A3
Portpatrick Rd G60 .... 72 F7
Port Ranald Dr KA10 .... 229 C3
Portreath Rd G69 .... 80 F3
Portree Ave
Coatbridge ML5 .... 121 E4
Kilmarnock KA3 .... 223 A6
Portree Pl G15 .... 74 E4
Portree Terr PA16 .... 44 E4
Portsmouth Dr PA19 .... 44 F5
Portsoy PA8 .... 73 A2
Portsoy Ave G13 .... 94 F8
Portsoy Pl G13 .... 94 F8
Port St
Glasgow G3 .... 240 A2
Stirling FK8 .... 7 B7
Portugal St G5 .... 117 B5
Portwell ML3 .... 162 E4
Possil Cross G22 .... 97 C3
POSSIL PARK 97 D5
Possilpark & Parkhouse Sta
G22 .... 97 B6
Possil Rd G4 .... 97 B3
Postgate ML3 .... 162 E4
Posthill FK10 .... 5 D1
Potassels Rd G69 .... 100 C7
Potrail Pl ML3 .... 162 A3
Potter Cl G32 .... 118 E3
POTTERFIELD 94 B2
Potter Gr G32 .... 118 E3
POTTERHILL 113 E1
Potterhill Ave PA2 .... 133 E8
Potterhill Rd G53 .... 115 B2
Potter Pl
Glasgow G32 .... 118 E3
Skinflats FK2 .... 24 F3
Potter St G32 .... 118 E3
Potters Wynd ML11 .... 215 C5
Pottery Pl KA3 .... 222 F2
Pottery St PA15 .... 46 E3
Pottis Rd FK7 .... 7 D3
Potts Way ML1 .... 142 C1
Powbrone G75 .... 180 E5
Powburn Cres G71 .... 140 D7
Power Plant Rd KA20 .... 218 B6
Powfoot St G31 .... 118 D5
Powforth Cl ML9 .... 184 E3
Powgree Cres KA15 .... 171 C5
Powmill Gdns KA9 .... 233 D2
Powmill Rd KA9 .... 233 D2
Powrie St G33 .... 99 C3
Poynter Ct G71 .... 140 E5
Prentice La [5] G71 .... 141 A8
Prentice Rd ML1 .... 163 B5
President Kennedy Dr
FK7 .... 12 C3
Prestonfield G62 .... 54 E1
Prestonfield Ave KA13 .... 207 B4
Preston Pl
Glasgow G42 .... 117 B2
Gourock PA19 .... 44 D7
Preston St G42 .... 117 B2
Preston Terr FK10 .... 5 D1
PRESTWICK 236 A7
Prestwick Acad KA9 .... 233 D1
Prestwick Ct G68 .... 61 F4
Prestwick Int Airport Sta
KA9 .... 233 B3
Prestwick Pl G77 .... 157 A4
Prestwick Pool KA9 .... 236 C7
Prestwick Rd KA8 .... 236 A4
Prestwick St G53 .... 135 A6
Prestwick Town Sta KA9 .... 233 B1
Pretoria Ct G75 .... 180 B4
Pretoria Rd FK5 .... 23 B1
Priestfield Ind Est G72 .... 161 D5
Priestfield St G72 .... 161 C6
PRIESTHILL 135 A6
Priesthill Ave G53 .... 135 C6
Priesthill Cres G53 .... 135 C6
Priesthill & Darnley Sta
G53 .... 135 C5
Priesthill Gdns G53 .... 135 C6
Priesthill Rd G53 .... 135 C6
Priestknowe Rdbt G74 .... 159 F1
Priestland Cl KA3 .... 223 B6
Priestley Way G72 .... 138 E8
Prieston Rd PA11 .... 110 D7
Primrose Ave
Bellshill ML4 .... 142 A7
Larkhall ML9 .... 199 A8
Primrose Cres ML1 .... 163 E5
Primrose Ct
Alloa FK10 .... 10 B6
[1] Glasgow G14 .... 95 D3
Primrose Pk KA7 .... 239 C3
Primrose Pl
Alloa FK10 .... 10 B6
Cumbernauld G67 .... 82 B6
Kilmarnock KA1 .... 222 D1
Saltcoats KA21 .... 206 A2
Uddingston G71 .... 141 C8
Primrose St
Alloa FK10 .... 10 B7
Primrose St *continued*
Bonnybridge FK4 .... 40 B6
Glasgow G14 .... 95 D3
Primrose Way
Carluke ML8 .... 201 E8
Lennoxtown G66 .... 57 E7
Prince Albert Rd G12 .... 96 B3
Prince Albert Terr G84 .... 16 D2
Prince Edward St [2]
G42 .... 117 A2
Prince of Wales Gdns
G20 .... 96 C8
Prince Pl ML2 .... 166 A6
Princes Ct KA8 .... 236 A2
Princes Gardens La [5]
G12 .... 96 B3
Princes Gate
Hamilton ML3 .... 162 F4
Rutherglen G73 .... 138 A8
Uddingston G71 .... 140 E4
Prince's Gdns G12 .... 96 B3
Princes Pk PA7 .... 72 E4
Princes Pl KA22 .... 205 B1
Prince's Pl [8] G12 .... 96 C3
Princess Anne Quadrant
ML1 .... 142 F5
Princess Cres PA1 .... 114 B6
Princess Ct
Helensburgh G84 .... 16 C1
Kilmarnock KA1 .... 228 B4
Princess Dr G69 .... 121 A5
Princes Sq
Barrhead G78 .... 134 D3
Troon KA10 .... 229 D3
Princes Square Shop Ctr
G1 .... 241 A2
Princess Rd ML1 .... 142 F4
Princess Sq ML2 .... 165 F5
Princess St FK4 .... 40 B5
Princes St
Ardrossan KA22 .... 205 B1
Caldercruix ML6 .... 105 A5
California FK1 .... 66 F5
Falkirk FK1 .... 42 B5
Greenock PA15 .... 45 E5
Kilmarnock KA1 .... 227 F8
Motherwell ML1 .... 163 E8
Port Glasgow PA14 .... 47 C2
Rutherglen G73 .... 138 A8
Stirling FK8 .... 7 B8
Princes Street E G84 .... 16 E1
Princess Way G84 .... 15 B3
Prince's Terr G12 .... 96 C3
Printers Land G76 .... 158 A6
Printers Lea G66 .... 57 C8
Priorwood Ct [7] G13 .... 95 D6
Priorwood Gate G77 .... 156 B4
Priorwood Gdns [8] G13 .... 95 D6
Priorwood Pl G13 .... 95 D6
Priorwood Rd G77 .... 156 A4
Priorwood Way G77 .... 156 A4
Priory Ave PA3 .... 114 A7
Priory Dr G71 .... 140 D7
Priory Gate ML2 .... 186 B7
Priory Pl
Cumbernauld G68 .... 60 E1
Glasgow G13 .... 95 D7
Priory Rd G13 .... 95 D7
Priory St G72 .... 161 D8
Priory Terr ML2 .... 164 C2
Priory Wynd KA13 .... 207 C5
Procession Rd PA2 .... 133 D6
Professors' Sq G12 .... 96 D2
Progress Dr ML6 .... 105 A5
Promenade KA8 .... 236 A4
Propulsives Rd KA20 .... 218 B4
Prosen St G32 .... 118 F3
Prospect Ave
Cambuslang G72 .... 138 F5
Uddingston G71 .... 140 F7
Prospect Ct G72 .... 161 D5
Prospect Dr ML9 .... 199 F8
Prospecthill Cir G42 .... 137 D8
Prospecthill Cres G42 .... 137 E8
Prospecthill Ct PA15 .... 45 E4
Prospecthill Dr G42 .... 137 C8
Prospecthill Gr G42 .... 137 A8
Prospecthill Pl
Glasgow G42 .... 137 E8
Greenock PA15 .... 45 E4
Prospecthill Rd
Falkirk FK1 .... 42 A2
Glasgow G42 .... 137 D8
Saltcoats KA21 .... 206 A1
Prospecthill Sq G42 .... 137 D8
Prospecthill St PA15 .... 45 E4
Prospecthill Way G42 .... 137 A8
Prospect Rd
Dullatur G68 .... 61 D6
Glasgow G43 .... 136 D8
Prospect St FK1 .... 41 F5
Provand Hall Cres G69 .... 120 B3
Provand's Lordship* G4 .... 241 C3
Provan Hall* G34 .... 99 F1
Provanhill St G21 .... 97 F1
PROVANMILL 98 C2
Provanmill Rd G33 .... 98 E2
Provan Rd G33 .... 118 D8
Provan Wlk G34 .... 99 E1
Provost Cl PA5 .... 111 F3
Provost Driver Ct PA4 .... 94 E2
Provost Gate ML9 .... 185 A3
Provost Hunter Ave FK12 .... 5 C7
Pular Ave ML1 .... 164 B4
Pullar Ave FK9 .... 2 A6
Pullar Ct FK9 .... 2 A6
Pundeavon Ave KA25 .... 149 B2
Purdie G74 .... 160 D5
Purdie St ML3 .... 162 A5
Purdon St G11 .... 96 B2
Putyan Ave KA24 .... 191 B7
Pyatshaw Rd ML9 .... 185 B1

Q

Quadrangle The G20 .... 96 E5
Quadrant Rd G43 .... 136 E5
Quadrant Sh Ctr ML5 .... 122 A7
Quadrant The G76 .... 157 F8
Quail Rd KA8 .... 236 A4
Quakerfield FK7 .... 7 E1
Quantock Dr G75 .... 180 A4
QUARRELTON 111 F1
Quarrelton Gr PA5 .... 111 F1
Quarrelton Rd PA5 .... 111 E2
Quarrier St PA15 .... 46 D3
QUARRIERS VILLAGE 89 F2
Quarrolhall Cres FK2 .... 24 B3
Quarry Ave G72 .... 139 E3
Quarrybank PA10 .... 111 C2
Quarrybrae Ave G76 .... 157 D7
Quarrybrae Gdns G71 .... 141 C6
Quarry Brae Prim Sch
G31 .... 118 D5
Quarrybrae St G31 .... 118 E5
Quarry Cotts EH48 .... 107 C3
Quarry Ct ML3 .... 162 E3
Quarry Dr
Kilmacolm PA13 .... 69 D2
Kirkintilloch G66 .... 79 F8
Quarryknowe
Lanark ML11 .... 215 A4
Rutherglen G73 .... 137 F7
Quarry Knowe
Bannockburn FK7 .... 11 E8
Dumbarton G82 .... 49 D5
Rhu G84 .... 15 E5
Quarryknowe Pl ML4 .... 141 F3
Quarryknowe St
Clydebank G81 .... 74 E7
Glasgow G31 .... 118 E5
Quarry La
Dumbarton G82 .... 49 E3
Eaglesham G76 .... 178 D4
Lennoxtown G66 .... 33 D1
Quarry Pk G75 .... 180 E8
Quarry Pl
Alloa FK10 .... 10 C8
Cambuslang G72 .... 138 E6
Dumbarton G82 .... 49 D5
Hamilton ML3 .... 162 E3
Shotts ML7 .... 146 D5
Quarry Rd
Airdrie ML6 .... 103 A1
Barrhead G78 .... 134 B4
Cambusbarron FK7 .... 6 C5
East Kilbride G75 .... 180 D5
Irvine KA12 .... 219 C3
Larkhall ML9 .... 185 A2
Law ML8 .... 187 A3
Paisley PA2 .... 113 F1
Port Glasgow PA14 .... 68 F7
Shotts ML7 .... 146 D5
Quarryside St ML6 .... 102 E4
Quarry St
Coatbridge ML5 .... 122 D7
Hamilton ML3 .... 162 E3
Johnstone PA5 .... 111 F2
Larkhall ML9 .... 185 B1
Motherwell ML1 .... 143 A4
Shotts ML7 .... 146 D5
Wishaw ML2 .... 165 A3
Quarrywood Ave G21 .... 98 C4
Quarrywood Rd G21 .... 98 D4
QUARTER 183 F3
Quarter Prim Sch ML3 .... 183 F3
Quay Pend G82 .... 49 E3
Quay Rd
Glasgow G73 .... 118 A1
Rutherglen G73 .... 137 F8
Quay Road N G73 .... 118 A1
Quay St
Dumbarton G82 .... 49 F3
Saltcoats KA21 .... 216 F7
Quebec Dr G75 .... 159 C1
Quebec Gn G75 .... 159 C1
Quebec Ho G81 .... 73 D6
Quebec Wynd G32 .... 139 C8
Queen Elizabeth Ave
G52 .... 114 F7
Queen Elizabeth Ct
Clydebank G81 .... 74 A3
Motherwell ML1 .... 163 D7
Queen Elizabeth Gdns
Clydebank G81 .... 74 A3
[11] Glasgow G5 .... 117 C4
Queen Elizabeth Sq [12]
G5 .... 117 C4
Queen Margaret Acad
KA7 .... 239 C4
Queen Margaret Ct [3]
G20 .... 96 E4
Queen Margaret Dr G20 .... 96 E4
Queen Margaret Rd G20 .... 96 E4
Queen Mary Ave
Clydebank G81 .... 74 D2
Glasgow G42 .... 117 B1
Queen Mary Gdns G81 .... 74 A3
Queen Mary St G40 .... 118 A4
Queen Rd KA12 .... 219 C5
Queen's Ave
Bridge of Allan FK9 .... 2 B6
Cambuslang G72 .... 139 B5
Queensbank Ave G69 .... 100 E7

Queensberry Ave
Bearsden G61 75 E7
Clarkston G76 157 E7
Glasgow G52 114 F7
Queensborough Gdns 4
G12 96 B3
Queensby Ave 6 G69 120 B6
Queensby Dr G69 120 A6
Queensby Pl G69 120 C6
Queensby Rd G69 120 C6
Queens Cres
Bellshill ML4 141 F4
Motherwell ML1 142 F4
Queen's Cres
Carluke ML8 188 A2
Chapelhall ML6 123 D3
Cleland ML1 144 B2
Coatbridge G69 120 F5
Falkirk FK1 41 F5
7 Glasgow G4 97 A2
Glasgow G4 240 B4
Queens Ct
Ayr KA7 238 F8
Irvine KA12 219 D2
Stenhousemuir FK5 23 D3
Queen's Ct
Bridge of Allan FK9 1 F7
Helensburgh G84 25 A8
Milngavie G62 76 B8
Queensdale Ave ML9 199 B8
Queensdale Rd ML9 199 B8
Queens Dr
Bishopton PA7 72 C3
Denny FK6 21 E3
Falkirk FK1 41 F5
Hamilton ML3 183 D6
Stenhousemuir FK5 23 C3
Queen's Dr
Alexandria G83 27 D4
Ardrossan KA22 205 D3
California FK1 66 F5
Cumbernauld G68 61 F6
Glasgow G42 117 A1
Kilmarnock KA1 228 B6
Monkton KA9 233 D5
Stenhousemuir FK5 23 C2
Troon KA10 229 E6
Queen's Drive La G42 117 A1
Queens Drive Ret Pk
KA1 228 A6
Queensferry St G5 117 E2
Queen's Gate G76 157 E8
Queens Gate La 9 G12 96 C3
Queens Gdns FK9 1 F7
Queen's Gdns G12 96 C3
Queens Gr G66 79 C4
Queenshaugh Dr FK8 2 C1
Queenside Cres PA8 72 F1
Queen's La FK9 2 A7
Queensland Ct G52 115 C6
Queensland Dr G52 115 C6
Queensland Gdns G51 115 D6
Queensland Lane E G52 115 C6
Queensland Lane W G52 115 C6
QUEENSLIE 119 E8
Queenslie Ind Est G33 119 D8
Queenslie St G33 98 D2
Queen's Park Ave G42 117 B1
Queen's Park Sta G42 117 A2
Queen's Pl
Glasgow G12 96 C3
Kilwinning KA13 208 A3
Queens Point G84 15 B8
Queen Sq G41 116 F2
Queen's Quadrant KA8 236 A1
Queen's Rd
Elderslie PA5 112 C2
Stirling FK8 6 F7
Queen's St FK1 66 F5
Queen St
Alexandria G83 27 D4
Alloa FK10 10 B7
Alva FK12 5 A7
Ayr KA8 236 A1
Bannockburn FK7 7 C2
Falkirk FK2 42 C5
Fallin FK7 8 C4
Glasgow G1 241 A2
Hamilton ML3 162 A5
Helensburgh G84 16 C3
11 Kilmarnock KA1 227 F8
Kilwinning KA13 208 A3
Kirkintilloch G66 79 C8
Motherwell ML1 163 E7
Paisley PA1 113 C4
Port Glasgow PA14 47 C2
Renfrew PA4 94 D3
Rutherglen G73 138 A8
Stirling FK8 7 A8
Stonehouse ML9 198 E2
Wishaw ML2 165 F6
Queens Terr KA9 233 B1
Queen's Terr
Ayr KA7 238 E8
Bridge of Allan FK9 2 A7
Queen's Terrace La KA7 238 E8
Queen Street Sta G1 241 A3
Queens View G64 78 B8
Queensway
East Kilbride G75 180 E8
Gourock PA19 44 C6
Queens Way G83 27 D4
Queen Victoria Ct G14 95 C4
Queen Victoria Dr G14 95 C4
Queen Victoria Gate G13 95 C5
Queen Victoria St ML6 122 F7
QUEENZIEBURN 59 F7
Queenzieburn Ind Est
G65 59 F7
Quendale Dr G32 118 F3
Quentin St G41 116 E1
Quinton Gdns G69 120 A5

R

Raasay Cres ML6 123 E6
Raasay Dr PA2 133 D7
Raasay Gdns G77 156 B5
Raasay Pl
Glasgow G22 97 C8
Kilmarnock KA3 223 A6
Raasay St G22 97 C8
Racecourse Pl KA12 219 A5
Racecourse Rd KA7 238 E6
Racecourse View
Ayr KA7 238 E5
Hamilton ML3 162 E5
RADNOR PARK 74 A4
Radnor St
Clydebank G81 74 A3
Clydebank, Kilbowie G81 74 B3
Glasgow G3 96 D1
Raeberry St G20 96 F3
Raebog Cres ML6 102 F2
Raebog Rd ML6 102 F4
Raeburn Ave
East Kilbride G74 160 B4
Paisley PA1 114 A4
Raeburn Cres ML3 161 E3
Raeburn Pl G74 160 B4
Raeburn Rd FK5 23 B2
Raeburn Wlk ML4 142 A7
Rae Ct FK2 24 C3
Raeside Ave G77 156 D3
Raes Rd ML8 201 B8
Rae St FK5 23 D3
Raeswood Dr G53 134 F8
Raeswood Gdns G53 134 F8
Raeswood Pl 3 G53 135 A8
Raeswood Rd G53 134 F8
Raewell Cres ML4 141 F3
Raggithill Ave KA6 237 F6
Raglan St
Alexandria G83 27 F3
Glasgow G4 97 A2
Raglan Street La G83 27 F3
Railway Ct G66 57 D8
Railway Rd ML6 122 D7
Raise St KA21 216 F8
Raith Ave
Glasgow G45 137 D4
Prestwick KA9 236 E7
Raithburn Ave
Glasgow G45 137 C3
Kilmarnock KA3 222 F4
Raithburn Rd G45 137 C3
Raith Dr
Bellshill ML4 142 B4
Cumbernauld G68 60 D1
Raithhill KA7 239 B1
Raith Rd KA3 213 B3
Raith Terr KA9 236 E7
Raleigh Ct FK1 41 E5
RALSTON 114 D4
Ralston Ave
Glasgow G52 114 F4
Glasgow PA1 114 F3
Ralston Ct G52 114 F4
Ralston Dr
Crookedholm KA3 228 D8
Glasgow G52 114 F4
Ralston Path G52 114 F4
Ralston Pl G52 114 F4
Ralston Prim Sch PA1 114 E5
Ralston Rd
Barrhead G78 134 C2
Bearsden G61 75 E5
Ralston St
Airdrie ML6 122 E7
5 Paisley PA1 114 A4
Ralstonyards Rd KA3 228 E7
Ramage Rd ML8 188 B1
Ramillies Ct
Carluke ML8 188 A1
Clydebank G81 74 C2
Ramoth ML11 214 D4
Rampart Ave G13 95 B8
Ramsay Ave
Johnstone PA5 111 E1
Laurieston FK2 42 F3
Ramsay Cres PA10 111 B2
Ramsay Ct
Newton Mearns G77 156 E3
Troon KA10 229 G4
Ramsay Hill 3 G74 160 A3
Ramsay Pl
Coatbridge ML5 121 C5
Johnstone PA5 111 E1
Stirling FK8 2 A2
Ramsay St G81 73 F3
Ramsey Ind Est G66 58 B1
Ramsey Tullis Dr FK10 4 C1
Ramsey Wynd ML4 142 B7
Ram St G32 118 F5
Ramstane Pl KA11 220 C5
Ranald Gdns G73 138 D3
Randolph Ave G76 137 A1
Randolph Cres FK7 7 C1
Randolph Ct FK8 7 A5
Randolph Dr
Clarkston G76 137 A1
Glasgow G76 136 F1
Randolphfield FK8 7 A5
Randolph Gate G11 95 F4
Randolph Gdns
Denny FK6 21 D1
Glasgow G76 136 F1
Randolph La G11 95 F3
Randolph Pl FK7 7 C2
Randolph Rd
Glasgow G11 95 F4
Stirling FK8 7 B4
Randolph Terr FK7 7 A4
Randyford Rd FK2 42 D5
Randyford St FK2 42 E5
RANFURLY 110 E6
Ranfurly Ct PA11 110 D7
Ranfurly Dr G68 61 E4
Ranfurly Pl PA11 110 D7
Ranfurly Rd
Bridge of Weir PA11 110 E6
Glasgow G52 114 F5
Range Pl ML3 162 E1
Range Rd ML1 164 B4
Rangerhouse Rd G75 180 F5
Range Road Ind Est ML2 164 C3
Range St ML1 164 B4
Ranken Cres KA12 219 D3
Ranken Dr KA12 219 D4
Rankin Cres
Bonnybridge FK4 39 D5
Greengairs ML6 83 F2
Rankin Ct
Greenock PA16 45 C4
Kilmarnock KA3 223 C3
Muirhead G69 100 C7
Rankin Dr G77 156 C6
Rankine Ave G75 181 A7
Rankine Ho G4 97 C2
Rankine Pl
East Kilbride G75 181 A7
Johnstone PA5 111 F3
Rankine St PA5 111 F3
Rankine Wynd FK10 4 C2
Rankin Gate Ctr 3 ML8 187 F2
Rankin Rd ML2 165 E4
Rankin St
Carluke ML8 187 F2
Greenock PA16 45 C4
Rankin Way G78 134 E3
Rannoch Ave
Bishopbriggs G64 78 B1
Coatbridge ML5 101 D1
Hamilton ML3 162 A1
Newton Mearns G77 156 D7
Rannoch Cl KA3 195 D1
Rannoch Ct
Alloa FK10 10 C5
Cumbernauld G67 82 B6
Hamilton G72 161 F5
Rannoch Dr
Bearsden G61 76 B3
Cumbernauld G67 82 B6
Kirkintilloch G66 59 B1
Renfrew PA4 94 C4
Wishaw ML2 165 B1
Rannoch Gdns G64 78 C2
Rannoch Gn G74 159 F3
Rannoch La G69 81 A2
Rannoch Pl
Irvine KA12 219 C6
Paisley PA2 114 A3
Shieldhill FK1 66 E7
Shotts ML7 146 E6
Stenhousemuir FK5 23 F4
Rannoch Rd
Airdrie ML6 102 F1
Johnstone PA5 131 F8
Kilmacolm PA13 89 C7
Uddingston G71 120 E1
Rannoch St G44 137 A6
Rannoch Terr ML9 185 C1
Rannoch Way 6 G71 141 A3
Rannoch Wynd G73 138 D2
RAPLOCH
Larkhall 184 F3
Stirling 1 F2
Raploch Ave G14 95 B4
Raploch Com Campus FK8 1 E2
Raploch La G14 95 B4
Raploch Prim Sch FK8 1 E2
Raploch Rd
Larkhall ML9 184 F3
Stirling FK8 1 F1
Raploch St ML9 184 F3
Rashieburn PA8 73 B2
Rashieglen PA8 73 A2
Rashiehill PA8 73 A2
Rashiehill Rd FK1 86 A6
RASHIELEE 73 A2
Rashielee PA8 73 B2
Rashielee Ave PA8 73 B2
Rashielee Prim Sch PA8 73 B2
Rashielee Rd PA8 73 A2
Rashiewood PA8 73 B2
Rashley Sq KA22 205 D4
Rathlin Ave KA1 227 F4
Rathlin Ho KA9 236 B5
Rathlin St G51 116 A8
Rathlin Terr G82 49 C5
Ratho Dr
Cumbernauld G68 61 E5
Glasgow G21 97 E4
Ratho Pk ML3 183 B7
Ratho St PA15 46 C4
Rattray PA8 73 A3
Rattray St G32 118 E3
Ravel Row G31 118 D5
Ravelston Rd G61 75 E2
Ravelston St G32 118 E6
Ravel Wynd G71 141 B8
Raven Rd PA16 45 A5
Ravenscliffe Dr G46 136 B3
Ravenscourt G74 158 C2
RAVENSCRAIG 45 A3
Ravenscraig Ave PA2 113 C2
Ravenscraig Ct
Bellshill ML4 142 B5
Greenock PA16 45 A4
Ravenscraig Dr G53 135 C6
Ravenscraig Hospl PA16 45 A3
Ravenscraig Prim Sch
PA16 44 E3
Ravenscraig Rd KA3 211 D8
Ravenscraig Stadium & Recn
Ctr PA16 44 E3
Ravenscraig Terr G53 135 C5
Ravenscroft KA12 219 B5
Ravens Ct 5 G64 97 F8
Ravenshall ML1 165 B8
Ravenshall Rd G41 136 C8
Ravenshill Dr ML1 144 C1
Ravenstone Dr G46 136 C4
Ravenswood Ave PA2 132 E7
Ravenswood Dr G41 116 D1
Ravenswood Prim Sch
G67 82 E8
Ravenswood Rd G69 120 C5
Raven Wynd ML2 165 B3
RAWYARDS 103 C1
Rawyards Ave ML6 103 B2
Raylight Pl KA22 205 B1
Raymond Pl G75 159 C1
Rayne Pl G15 75 B4
Ream Ave 2 ML6 123 F6
Reay Ave
Cardross G82 48 A8
East Kilbride G74 159 B2
Reay Gdns G74 159 B2
Recawr Pk KA7 239 B3
Recreation Pk (Alloa Athletic
FC) FK10 10 C6
Redan St 2 G40 117 F5
Redbrae Pl 7 G66 58 D1
Redbrae Rd
Falkirk FK1 41 D6
Kirkintilloch G66 79 E8
Red Bridge Ct 3 ML5 122 A8
Redburn G83 28 A2
Redburn Ave G46 157 B8
Redburn Ct G67 62 F6
Redburn Cvn Pk KA12 219 A7
Redburn Gate KA12 219 A7
Redburn Ind Est KA12 219 C7
Redburn Pl
Cumbernauld G67 62 F6
Irvine KA12 219 B6
Redburn Rd
Blackridge EH48 107 B2
Cumbernauld G67 62 F6
Redburn Rdbt KA12 219 A8
Redburn Sch G67 62 C2
Redcastle Sq G33 99 D1
Redcliffe Dr G75 180 B8
Redclyffe Gdns G84 16 D4
Reddance Terr KA24 191 A8
Reddans Pk KA3 195 D1
Red Deer Rd G75 180 C8
Redding Ave KA3 222 F4
REDDING MUIR 66 F6
Redding Rd FK2 42 F2
Redding Road Rdbt FK2 42 F2
Rederech Cres ML3 161 F2
Redford St G33 118 D8
Red Fox Dr G83 27 E8
Red Fox Terr G83 27 E8
Red Gables Sq KA22 205 B3
Redgate Pl G14 95 B4
Redgauntlet Rd G84 25 C8
Redgrave G74 160 D5
Redhall FK7 8 A4
Redhaws Rd ML7 147 A3
Redheugh Ave KA25 149 B3
Redheugh Ct KA25 149 B4
Redheugh Ho KA25 149 B4
Redhill Rd G68 61 D3
Redhills View G66 57 F7
Redholme ML9 185 B1
Redhouse La ML8 187 F3
Redhurst Cres PA2 133 C7
Redhurst La PA2 133 C7
Redhurst Way PA2 133 C7
Redlands La G12 96 C4
Redlands Rd FK10 4 A3
Redlands Terr 14 G12 96 C4
Redlawood Pl G72 140 A6
Redlawood Rd G72 140 A6
Redmire Cres ML7 167 B8
Redmoss Rd
Duntocher G81 73 F7
Milton of Campsie G66 58 B5
Redmoss St G22 97 B5
Rednock St G22 97 C4
Redpath Dr
Cambuslang G72 139 D6
Glasgow G52 115 C5
Stenhousemuir FK2 24 A4
Red Rd
Glasgow G21 98 B4
Helensburgh G82 25 G4
Red Road Ct G21 98 B3
Red Row G82 27 D2
Redshank Ave PA4 94 E4
Redstone Ave KA13 208 A4
Redwell Pl FK10 9 F7
Redwing Cres ML5 122 E2
Redwing Gdns ML2 165 A1
Redwood Ave G74 158 E1
Redwood Cl ML3 183 A7
Redwood Cres
Bishopton PA7 72 C3
Cambuslang G72 139 F3
East Kilbride G74 158 E2
Hamilton ML3 183 A7
Uddingston G71 141 C8
Redwood Ct
East Kilbride G75 179 E8
Greenock PA16 45 E7
Redwood Dr
East Kilbride G74 158 E3
Glasgow G21 98 A3
Redwood Gr ML5 122 B6
Redwood La ML3 183 A7
Redwood Pl
East Kilbride G74 158 E2
Kirkintilloch G66 79 B5
Uddingston G71 141 C8
Redwood Rd
Cumbernauld G67 62 D2
Motherwell ML1 143 B5
Redwood Way G72 139 F3
Reedlands Dr FK6 39 D7
Reedloch Dr KA10 229 G7
Reek St KA15 171 E7
Reelick Ave G13 94 E8
Reelick Quadrant G13 94 E8
Reema Rd ML4 142 B6
Reen Pl G71 141 B4
Reform St KA15 150 B1
Regal Ct KA24 191 C8
Regal Gr ML7 146 E4
Regalia View KA12 219 E6
Regency Ct ML3 163 A2
Regency Way ML1 142 F4
Regent Ct
Glasgow G12 96 B4
1 Greenock PA15 45 F4
Regent Dr G73 138 A8
Regent Moray St G3 96 D1
Regent Park Sq G41 116 F2
Regent Pk KA9 233 C1
Regent Pl G81 73 E4
Regents Gate G71 140 E4
Regent Sh Ctr 2 G66 79 C8
Regent Sq G66 79 C4
Regent St
Clydebank G81 73 E4
Greenock PA15 45 F4
Kirkintilloch G66 79 C8
Paisley PA1 114 B5
Regent Way ML3 162 F3
Register Ave ML4 142 A3
Register Rd G65 60 E8
Regwood St G41 136 D8
Reid Ave
Bearsden G61 76 A6
Dalry KA24 191 B6
Linwood PA3 112 B5
Reid Ct
Hurlford KA3 228 E7
Rutherglen G73 138 B8
Reid Gr
Motherwell ML1 164 B4
Stonehouse ML9 198 F2
Reidhouse St G21 97 F4
Reid Kerr Coll PA3 113 F6
Reid Pl
Glasgow G40 117 F4
Larbert FK5 23 B2
Reid's Ave KA20 206 D2
Reid St
Airdrie ML6 103 B1
Coatbridge ML5 122 B8
Glasgow G40 117 F3
Hamilton ML3 161 F5
Rutherglen G73 138 B8
Salsburgh ML7 125 B2
Reid Terr KA21 217 A7
Reidvale St G31 118 A6
Reilly Gdns FK4 40 B3
Reilly Rd
Bonnybridge FK4 40 B3
Houston PA6 91 C8
Reith Dr G75 180 D7
Remus Pl ML4 142 E5
Renfield La G2 240 C2
Renfield St
Glasgow G2 240 C3
Renfrew PA4 94 D4
RENFREW 94 E4
Renfrew Ct G2 241 A3
Renfrew High Sch PA4 94 D2
Renfrew La G2 240 C3
Renfrew L Ctr PA4 94 B2
Renfrew Mus* PA4 94 D4
Renfrew Pl ML5 121 C4
Renfrew Rd
Glasgow G51 95 A1
Glasgow G51 95 C1
Paisley PA3 114 A8
Renfrew St
Coatbridge ML5 121 C4
Glasgow G2 240 C3
Rennie Bsns Units KA21 216 F7
Rennie Pl
East Kilbride G74 159 A3
Saltcoats KA21 216 F8
Rennie Rd G65 36 B1
Rennie St
Falkirk FK1 42 A3
Kilmarnock KA1 228 A8
Renshaw Dr G52 115 B6
Renshaw Pl ML4 142 F8

Renshaw Rd
Bishopton PA7 .... 72 B3
Elderslie PA5 .... 112 C2
RENTON 27 C1
Renton Pk KA11 .... 220 C7
Renton Prim Sch G82 .... 27 D1
Renton Rd
Dumbarton G82 .... 49 D6
Greenock PA15 .... 46 C1
Renton G82 .... 49 D8
Renton St G4 .... 241 A4
Renton Sta G82 .... 27 D1
Renwick Pl ML11 .... 215 C5
Renwick Way KA9 .... 236 D5
Reservoir Rd PA19 .... 44 F6
Resipol Rd G33 .... 99 E5
Reston Dr G52 .... 115 B6
Reuther Ave G73 .... 138 B7
Revoch Dr G13 .... 95 A7
Reynolds Ave G75 .... 181 A7
Reynolds Dr G33 .... 99 F5
Reynolds Path ML2 .... 165 D1
Rhannan Rd G44 .... 137 A5
Rhannan Terr G44 .... 137 A5
Rhindhouse Pl G69 .... 120 D5
Rhindhouse Rd G69 .... 120 D5
Rhindmuir Ave G69 .... 120 C5
Rhindmuir Cres G69 .... 120 D6
Rhindmuir Ct G69 .... 120 C6
Rhindmuir Dr G69 .... 120 C6
Rhindmuir Gate G69 .... 120 D6
Rhindmuir Gdns G69 .... 120 C6
Rhindmuir Gr G69 .... 120 D6
Rhindmuir Path G69 .... 120 D6
Rhindmuir Pl G69 .... 120 D6
Rhindmuir Rd G69 .... 120 C6
Rhindmuir View G69 .... 120 D6
Rhindmuir Wynd G69 .... 120 D6
Rhindsdale Cres G69 .... 120 C5
Rhinds St ML5 .... 121 C4
Rhodders Gr FK12 .... 5 B7
RHU 15 D5
Rhu-Ellen Ct G84 .... 15 D4
Rhumhor Gdns PA10 .... 111 C2
Rhu Prim Sch G84 .... 15 D5
Rhu Quadrant ML2 .... 186 C6
Rhu Rd Lower G84 .... 16 A2
Rhu Road Higher G84 .... 16 A3
Rhyber Ave ML11 .... 215 B5
Rhymebank ML9 .... 198 C1
Rhymer St G21 .... 97 F1
Rhymie Rd G32 .... 119 D3
Rhynie Dr G51 .... 116 B5
Riach Gdns ML1 .... 142 C1
Ribblesdale G74 .... 159 C3
RICCARTON 227 E5
Riccarton G75 .... 180 B7
Riccarton Path ML3 .... 163 B1
Riccarton Rd KA1 .... 228 D6
Riccarton St G42 .... 117 C2
Riccartsbar Ave PA2 .... 113 C3
Rice Way ML1 .... 164 B4
Richardland Pl KA1 .... 228 A7
Richardland Rd 3 KA1 .... 227 F7
Richard Pl KA10 .... 229 E4
Richard Quinn St FK7 .... 12 D8
Richardson Ave KA1 .... 228 F5
Richard St G2 .... 240 B2
Richie Ave G82 .... 48 A8
Richmond Ave G76 .... 157 E7
Richmond Ct G73 .... 138 C8
Richmond Dr
Bishopbriggs G64 .... 78 B4
Cambuslang G72 .... 138 E5
Linwood PA3 .... 112 A7
Rutherglen G73 .... 138 D7
Richmond Gdns G69 .... 100 B8
Richmond Gr G73 .... 138 C7
Richmond Park Sch G5 .... 117 D3
Richmond Pl G73 .... 138 C8
Richmond Rd G73 .... 138 D7
Richmond St
Clydebank G81 .... 74 C1
Glasgow G1 .... 241 B2
Richmond Terr KA2 .... 225 F1
Riddell St
Clydebank G81 .... 74 C3
Coatbridge ML5 .... 122 D7
Riddon Ave G13 .... 94 E8
Riddon Pl G13 .... 94 E8
RIDDRIE 98 D1
Riddrie Cres G33 .... 118 E8
RIDDRIE KNOWES 98 E1
Riddrie Knowes G33 .... 118 E8
Riddrievale Ct G33 .... 98 E1
Riddrievale St G33 .... 98 E1
Ridgepark Dr ML11 .... 214 F5
Ridgepark Sch ML11 .... 214 F6
Rigby St G32 .... 118 E6
Rigfoot KA11 .... 220 B5
Rigghead KA3 .... 211 C8
Rigghead Ave G67 .... 62 B5
Rigg Pl G33 .... 119 E7
Riggs Cotts KA20 .... 217 C8
Riggside Rd G33 .... 99 C2
Rigg St KA3 .... 211 D8
Riggs The
Milngavie G62 .... 55 A3
Prestwick KA9 .... 233 C1
Righead Ind Est ML4 .... 141 D7
Righead Rdbt G74 .... 159 D1
Riglands Gate PA4 .... 94 C4
Riglands Way PA4 .... 94 C3
Riglaw Pl G13 .... 95 A7
Rigmuir Rd G51 .... 115 C7
Rigwoodie Pl KA7 .... 238 E1
Rimmon Cres ML7 .... 146 E6
Rimsdale St G40 .... 118 A5
Ringans La FK7 .... 6 F3
Ringford St G21 .... 97 F3
Ring Rd FK10 .... 10 B7
Ringsdale Ave ML9 .... 199 A8
Ringsdale Ct ML9 .... 199 A8
Ripon Dr G12 .... 96 A6
Risk St
Clydebank G81 .... 73 F4
Dumbarton G82 .... 49 F3
Ristol Rd G13 .... 95 B5
Ritchie Cres PA5 .... 112 C3
Ritchie Ct KA3 .... 223 C2
Ritchie Pk PA5 .... 112 B3
Ritchie Pl G77 .... 156 C4
Ritchie's Cl 13 ML11 .... 215 A4
Ritchie St
3 Glasgow G5 .... 117 A4
West Kilbride KA23 .... 190 C5
Wishaw ML2 .... 164 D3
Ritchie Terr G83 .... 27 D5
Ritz Pl G5 .... 117 D3
Riverbahk View FK8 .... 2 C1
Riverbank Dr ML4 .... 142 D3
Riverbank Pl KA1 .... 228 A7
Riverbank St G43 .... 136 C7
Riverbank View FK8 .... 7 C8
River Ct G76 .... 157 F6
Riverdale Gdns ML3 .... 162 E1
River Dr PA4 .... 93 D5
Riverford Rd
Glasgow G43 .... 136 D7
Rutherglen G73 .... 118 C1
Rivergate Sh Ctr KA12 .... 219 B2
River Pl KA25 .... 149 B1
River Rd G32 .... 139 B8
Riversdale La G14 .... 95 A4
RIVERSIDE 2 B1
Riverside
Balloch G83 .... 27 E8
Houston PA6 .... 91 D1
Milngavie G62 .... 55 A2
Riverside Bsns Pk KA11 .... 224 H7
Riverside Ct
Eaglesham G76 .... 157 E1
Glasgow G44 .... 137 A2
1 Netherlee G44 .... 136 F2
Riverside Dr FK8 .... 2 C1
Riverside Gdns
8 Balloch G83 .... 27 E8
Clarkston G76 .... 157 F5
Gourock PA19 .... 44 F7
Larkhall ML9 .... 199 A8
Riverside La G82 .... 49 E3
Riverside Pk G44 .... 137 A1
Riverside Pl
Ayr KA8 .... 239 A8
Cambuslang G72 .... 139 E6
Kilbirnie KA25 .... 149 B1
Riverside Prim Sch FK8 .... 2 B1
Riverside Rd
Glasgow G43 .... 136 E7
Greenock PA15 .... 46 B3
Irvine KA11 .... 220 D1
Kilbirnie KA25 .... 149 B1
Kirkfieldbank ML11 .... 214 C4
Larkhall ML9 .... 199 A8
Stewarton KA3 .... 211 E8
Waterfoot G76 .... 178 E8
Riverside Rdbt KA11 .... 225 A7
Riverside Terr G76 .... 157 F6
Riverside View FK10 .... 10 B4
Riverside Way KA11 .... 224 H8
Riverside Wlk ML1 .... 163 F8
River St
Ayr KA8 .... 235 F1
Falkirk FK2 .... 24 A1
River Terr KA8 .... 235 F1
Riverton Dr G75 .... 180 B8
Riverview FK10 .... 10 A7
River View KA7 .... 238 F8
River View Cres G82 .... 48 B8
Riverview Dr G5 .... 240 B1
Riverview Gdns G5 .... 240 B1
Riverview Pl G5 .... 240 B1
Riverway KA12 .... 219 B1
Riverway Ret Pk KA12 .... 219 B1
River Wlk KA13 .... 207 F5
River Wynd FK9 .... 2 A4
Roaden Ave PA2 .... 132 F7
Roaden Rd PA2 .... 132 F7
Roadhead PA12 .... 150 F8
ROADMEETINGS 202 D8
Roadmeetings Hospl
ML8 .... 202 C7
Roadside G67 .... 62 B5
Roadside Pl ML6 .... 103 D8
Robb Terr G66 .... 80 A6
Robert Bruce Ct FK5 .... 23 A2
Robert Burns Ave
Clydebank G81 .... 74 C3
Motherwell ML1 .... 143 E4
Robert Burns Ct KA15 .... 150 B1
Robert Burns Quadrant
ML4 .... 141 F5
Robert Creighton Pl KA3 .... 222 F1
Robert Dick Ct FK10 .... 4 C2
Robert Dr G51 .... 116 A7
Robert Gilson Gdns ML5 .... 122 B5
Robert Hardie Ct FK5 .... 23 C2
Robert Kay Pl FK5 .... 23 C5
Robert Kinmond Ave FK10 .... 4 C2
Robert Knox Ave FK10 .... 4 C2
Robertland Rigg KA3 .... 195 E1
Robertland Sq KA3 .... 211 E8
Robert Noble Pl KA1 .... 222 D2
Roberton Ave G41 .... 116 C2
Roberton St ML6 .... 123 E3
Robert Owen Meml Prim Sch
ML11 .... 215 C4
Robert Smillie Cres ML9 .... 185 A1
Robert Smillie Memorial
Prim Sch 1 ML9 .... 185 A1
Robertson Ave
Bonnybridge FK4 .... 40 B6
Renfrew PA4 .... 94 B3
Robertson Cl PA4 .... 94 C3
Robertson Cres
Ayr KA8 .... 236 D1
Neilston G78 .... 154 D7
Saltcoats KA21 .... 217 A7
Robertson Ct FK5 .... 23 D2
Robertson Dr
Bellshill ML4 .... 142 A4
East Kilbride G74 .... 160 B2
Renfrew PA4 .... 94 B3
Robertson Gait PA2 .... 113 E3
Robertson La G2 .... 240 C2
Robertson Pk* PA2 .... 132 F6
Robertson Pl
Kilmarnock KA1 .... 228 A8
Stirling FK7 .... 7 B3
Robertson Rd KA9 .... 233 C3
Robertson St
Airdrie ML6 .... 122 E8
Alva FK12 .... 5 B7
Barrhead G78 .... 134 B2
Glasgow G2 .... 240 C2
Greenock PA16 .... 45 E6
Hamilton ML3 .... 161 F5
Robertson Terr G69 .... 120 C5
Roberts Quadrant ML4 .... 142 B3
Roberts St
Clydebank G81 .... 73 E3
Wishaw ML2 .... 165 A3
Robert St
Glasgow G51 .... 116 A8
Port Glasgow PA14 .... 47 E1
Shotts ML7 .... 146 E4
Robert Stewart Pl KA1 .... 222 E1
Robert Templeton Dr
G72 .... 139 B5
Robert West Service Ct
KA13 .... 207 E2
Robert Wilson Gate ML9 .... 199 A8
Robert Wynd ML2 .... 166 A6
Robin Pl ML2 .... 165 B3
Robin Rd PA16 .... 45 B5
Robinsfield G22 .... 77 A7
Robin Way G72 .... 139 C8
ROBROYSTON 98 F6
Robroyston Ave G33 .... 98 E3
Robroyston Oval G33 .... 98 E5
Robroyston Rd
Bishopbriggs G64, G66 .... 78 F1
Glasgow, Barmulloch G33 .... 98 D4
Glasgow, Blackhill G33 .... 98 E3
Glasgow G33 .... 98 E6
Robroyston Way G33 .... 98 E5
Robshill Ct G77 .... 156 D4
Robsland Ave KA7 .... 238 F5
Robslee Cres G46 .... 136 B3
Robslee Dr G46 .... 136 B4
Robslee Prim Sch G46 .... 136 A2
Robslee Rd G46 .... 136 A3
Robson Gr 3 G42 .... 117 B3
Rocep Dr G51 .... 94 F2
Rochdale Pl 4 G66 .... 79 C8
Roche Way KA24 .... 191 C7
Rochsoles Cres ML6 .... 103 A2
Rochsoles Dr ML6 .... 103 A2
Rochsolloch Farm Cotts
ML6 .... 122 E7
Rochsolloch Prim Sch
ML6 .... 122 E6
Rochsolloch Rd ML6 .... 122 D6
Rockall Dr G44 .... 137 C4
Rockbank Cres ML5 .... 101 E6
Rockbank Pl
Clydebank G81 .... 74 C6
Glasgow G40 .... 118 A5
Rockbank St G40 .... 118 A5
Rockburn Cres ML4 .... 142 A7
Rockburn Dr G76 .... 157 D8
Rockcliffe Path ML6 .... 123 F1
Rockcliffe St G40 .... 117 F3
Rock Dr PA10 .... 111 B2
Rockfield Pl G21 .... 98 C5
Rockfield Rd G21 .... 98 C5
Rock Gdns ML9 .... 198 D1
Rockhampton Ave G75 .... 180 B7
Rockliffe Path ML6 .... 123 E1
Rockmount Ave
Barrhead G78 .... 134 D1
Glasgow G46 .... 136 A3
Rockrose Pk KA7 .... 239 B3
Rockshill Pl ML6 .... 123 B2
Rock St G4 .... 97 B3
Rockwell Ave PA2 .... 133 C8
Rockwood Pl ML6 .... 104 D4
Rocop Bsns Pk PA4 .... 94 F2
Roddinghead Rd G46 .... 157 A6
Rodding The ML11 .... 215 B5
Rodger Ave G77 .... 156 C5
Rodger Dr G73 .... 138 B6
Rodger Pl G73 .... 138 A6
Rodgers St FK6 .... 21 E1
Rodger Way ML1 .... 144 C3
Rodil Ave G44 .... 137 C4
Rodney Pl G84 .... 17 A2
Rodney Rd PA19 .... 44 F6
Rodney St G4 .... 97 B2
Roebank Dr G78 .... 134 C1
Roebank Rd KA15 .... 150 C2
Roebank St G31 .... 118 B8
Roffey Park Rd PA1 .... 114 D5
Rogart St G40 .... 117 F5
Rogerfield Rd G34, G69 .... 120 C7
Rogers Ct ML9 .... 198 D2
ROGERTON 159 D6
Rokeby La G12 .... 96 E3
Roland Cres G77 .... 156 F3
Roman Ave
Bearsden G61 .... 75 F5
Clydebank G15 .... 75 A1
Roman Cres G60 .... 72 F7
Roman Ct
Bearsden G61 .... 75 F5
Cleghorn ML11 .... 215 F7
Clydebank G81 .... 74 A6
Roman Dr
Bearsden G61 .... 75 F5
Bellshill ML4 .... 142 B4
Falkirk FK1 .... 41 D5
Roman Gdns G61 .... 75 F5
Roman Hill Rd G81 .... 74 B7
Roman Pl ML4 .... 141 E3
Roman Rd
Ayr KA7 .... 239 C5
Bearsden G61 .... 75 F5
Bonnybridge FK4 .... 40 A4
Clydebank G81 .... 74 A6
Kirkintilloch G66 .... 79 B8
Motherwell ML1 .... 163 E7
Roman Way G71 .... 141 C6
Romney Ave G44 .... 137 C5
Romulus Ct ML1 .... 142 C1
Rona Ave PA14 .... 69 B7
Ronades Rd FK2 .... 42 A8
Ronald Cres FK5 .... 23 B1
Ronald Pl FK8 .... 7 B8
Ronaldsay Ct KA11 .... 225 B8
Ronaldsay Dr G64 .... 78 D2
Ronaldsay Pass G22 .... 97 D7
Ronaldsay Pl G67 .... 82 D8
Ronaldsay St G22 .... 97 D7
Ronaldshaw Pk KA7 .... 238 E6
Ronald St 2 ML5 .... 122 A8
Rona Pl KA3 .... 223 B5
Rona St G21 .... 98 B2
Rona Terr G72 .... 138 F3
Ronay St
Glasgow G22 .... 97 D8
Wishaw ML2 .... 165 E5
Rook Rd PA16 .... 45 A5
Rooksdell Ave PA2 .... 113 C1
Ropework La G1 .... 241 A1
Rorison Pl ML9 .... 185 F1
Rosa Burn Ave G75 .... 180 B4
Rosaburn Cres G75 .... 180 B5
Rosa Pl KA21 .... 206 A2
ROSEBANK
Carluke 200 C8
Denny 21 D4
Kirkintilloch 80 A8
Rosebank FK10 .... 5 D1
Rosebank Ave
Blantyre G72 .... 140 E1
Falkirk FK1 .... 41 F5
Kirkintilloch G66 .... 79 E8
Rosebank Cres KA7 .... 238 F5
Rosebank Ct G72 .... 161 E8
Rosebank Dr
Cambuslang G72 .... 139 C4
Uddingston G71 .... 141 C7
Rosebank Gdns
Alloa FK10 .... 10 C8
Glasgow G71 .... 120 B2
Irvine KA11 .... 219 F7
Johnstone PA5 .... 112 A2
Rosebank La 3 G71 .... 141 B3
Rosebank Pl
Dullatur G68 .... 61 C6
Falkirk FK1 .... 41 F5
Glasgow G71 .... 120 B2
Hamilton ML3 .... 162 A3
Kilmarnock KA3 .... 222 F2
Rosebank Rd
Bellshill ML4 .... 142 B8
Overtown ML2 .... 186 C6
Rosebank Rdbt FK1 .... 41 F5
Rosebank St ML6 .... 123 E8
Rosebank Terr
Coatbridge G69 .... 121 A4
Kilmacolm PA13 .... 89 D8
Rosebank Twr G72 .... 139 A6
Rosebay Pk KA7 .... 239 B2
Roseberry Ct 13 G12 .... 96 C3
Roseberry La ML6 .... 123 E3
Roseberry Pl ML3 .... 162 A4
Roseberry Rd ML6 .... 123 E4
Roseberry St G5 .... 117 E2
Rosebery Ct KA25 .... 149 A2
Rosebery Pl FK8 .... 2 B1
Roseburn Ct G67 .... 62 F6
Roseburn Pl ML5 .... 122 A6
Rose Cres
Gourock PA19 .... 44 D6
Hamilton ML3 .... 161 F4
Rosedale G74 .... 159 C3
Rose Dale G64 .... 98 B8
Rosedale Ave PA2 .... 132 D7
Rosedale Dr G69 .... 120 A4
Rosedale Gdns
Glasgow G20 .... 96 C8
Helensburgh G84 .... 16 F1
Rosedale St ML11 .... 214 F2
Rosedene Terr ML4 .... 142 A6
Rosefield Gdns G71 .... 140 E7
Rose Gdns ML5 .... 121 F3
Rosegreen Cres ML4 .... 142 A8
ROSEHALL 122 B4
Rosehall Ave ML5 .... 122 B4
Rosehall Ind Est ML5 .... 122 A3
Rosehall Rd
Bellshill ML4 .... 141 F6
Shotts ML7 .... 146 C3
Rosehall Terr
Falkirk FK1 .... 42 B4
8 Wishaw ML2 .... 164 E1
Rosehill Cres G53 .... 135 A6
Rosehill Dr
Cumbernauld G67 .... 82 A6
Glasgow G53 .... 135 A6
Rosehill Rd G64 .... 78 C8
Roseholm Ave KA12 .... 219 E2
Rose Knowe Rd G42 .... 137 D8
Roselea ML6 .... 104 F4
Roselea Dr G62 .... 55 B3
Roselea Gdns G13 .... 95 F7
Roselea Pl G72 .... 140 D1
Roselea Rd G71 .... 140 E8
Roselea St ML9 .... 185 B4
Rosemary Cres G74 .... 159 D4
Rosemary Ct FK6 .... 21 D2
Rosemary Pl G74 .... 159 D4
Rosemead Terr FK1 .... 66 F5
Rosemount
Cumbernauld G68 .... 61 F5
Kilwinning KA13 .... 207 C2
Rosemount Ave G77 .... 156 D2
Rosemount Ct
Carluke ML8 .... 188 A2
Newton Mearns G77 .... 156 D1
Rose Mount Ct ML6 .... 123 C8
Rosemount Dr KA10 .... 229 E8
Rosemount Gdns
Prestwick KA9 .... 236 C6
Shieldhill FK1 .... 66 D6
Rosemount La
Bridge of Weir PA11 .... 110 B6
4 Larkhall ML9 .... 185 C1
Rosemount Mdws G71 .... 140 F2
Rosemount Pl PA19 .... 44 A6
Rosemount St G21 .... 97 F1
Rosendale Way G72 .... 161 E7
Roseneath Prim Sch G84 .... 15 A3
Roseneath St PA16 .... 45 C8
Roseness Pl G33 .... 119 A8
Rosenheath Gate G74 .... 159 C2
Rosepark Ave G71 .... 141 C6
Rosepark Cotts ML5 .... 121 E3
Rose St
Alloa FK10 .... 4 E1
Bonnybridge FK4 .... 40 B6
Cumbernauld G67 .... 82 B6
Glasgow G3 .... 240 C4
Greenock PA16 .... 45 C4
Kirkintilloch G66 .... 79 D8
Motherwell ML1 .... 164 A5
Tullibody FK10 .... 4 D4
Rose Terr
Denny FK6 .... 21 D1
Stenhousemuir FK5 .... 23 F3
Rosevale Cres
Bellshill ML4 .... 142 C4
Hamilton ML3 .... 162 B2
Rosevale Rd G61 .... 75 E4
Rosevale Sch G22 .... 97 D7
Rosevale St G11 .... 96 A2
Rosewood ML2 .... 164 D1
Rosewood Ave
Bellshill ML4 .... 142 B7
Paisley PA2 .... 113 B2
Rosewood Path ML4 .... 141 E5
Rosewood Pl G69 .... 121 A6
Rosewood St G13 .... 95 E7
Roseyard Pl PA14 .... 47 C1
Roslea Dr G31 .... 118 A7
Roslin Ct PA13 .... 89 C7
Roslin Pl ML6 .... 123 E2
Roslin St PA15 .... 45 F6
Roslin Twr G72 .... 138 E3
Roslyn Dr G69 .... 120 F6
ROSNEATH 15 A3
Rosneath Castle Cvn Pk
G84 .... 15 E1
Rosneath Dr G84 .... 16 B2
Rosneath Rd
Port Glasgow PA14 .... 68 D8
Rosneath G84 .... 15 B2
Rosneath St G51 .... 116 A8
Ross Ave
Kirkintilloch G66 .... 79 F8
Renfrew PA4 .... 94 A1
Rossbank Rd PA14 .... 47 A2
Ross Cres
Falkirk FK1 .... 41 C5
Motherwell ML1 .... 163 C5
Ross Ct FK7 .... 7 B3
Ross Dr
Airdrie ML6 .... 122 E5
Motherwell, Braedale ML1 .... 163 C5
Motherwell, Tannochside
G71 .... 121 C1
Rossendale Ct G43 .... 136 C8
Rossendale Rd G43 .... 136 C8
Ross Gdns ML1 .... 163 C5
ROSSHALL 114 F3
Rosshall Acad G52 .... 115 A4
Rosshall Ave PA1 .... 114 C4
Ross Hall Hospl (Private)
G52 .... 115 A3
Rosshall Pl PA4 .... 94 D3
Rosshill Ave G52 .... 114 F5
Rosshill Rd G52 .... 114 F5
Rossie Cres G64 .... 98 C8
Rossie Gr G77 .... 156 B5
ROSSLAND 72 B1
Rossland Cres PA7 .... 72 A3

Rossland Gdns PA7 ... 72 A3
Rossland View PA7 ... 72 A3
Rosslea Dr G46 ... 136 C2
Rosslyn Ave
East Kilbride G74 ... 160 A3
Rutherglen G73 ... 138 C7
Rosslyn Ct ML3 ... 162 A4
Rosslyn Ho 12 G12 ... 96 C3
Rosslyn Pl KA8 ... 236 B3
Rosslyn Rd
Ashgill ML9 ... 199 F8
Bearsden G61 ... 75 B6
Rosslyn Terr 18 G12 ... 96 C4
Ross Pl
East Kilbride G74 ... 160 C3
Rutherglen G73 ... 138 D4
Ross Rd KA21 ... 205 F2
Ross St
Ayr KA8 ... 236 C2
Coatbridge ML5 ... 122 A7
Glasgow G40 ... 241 B1
Paisley PA1 ... 114 A3
Ross Terr ML3 ... 163 C1
Ross Wlk
Kilmarnock KA3 ... 223 B2
Renton G82 ... 27 D2
Rostan Rd G43 ... 136 C5
Rosyth Rd G5 ... 117 E2
Rosyth St G5 ... 117 E2
Rotherwick Dr PA1 ... 114 E4
Rotherwood Ave
Glasgow G13 ... 75 E1
Paisley PA2 ... 132 F8
Rotherwood La G13 ... 75 C2
Rotherwood Pl 1 G13 ... 95 D8
Rotherwood Way PA2 ... 132 F8
Rothesay Cres ML5 ... 122 B4
Rothesay Pl
Coatbridge ML5 ... 122 B4
Kilmarnock KA3 ... 222 F3
Rothesay Rd PA16 ... 44 F3
Rothesay St G75 ... 180 E8
Rothes Dr G23 ... 96 D8
Rothes Pl G23 ... 76 C1
Rottenrow
Glasgow G4 ... 241 B3
Glasgow G4 ... 241 C2
Rottenrow E G4 ... 241 B2
Roughburn Rd FK9 ... 2 A6
Roughcraig St ML6 ... 103 A2
Roughlands Cres FK2 ... 24 B3
Roughlands Dr FK2 ... 24 A3
Roughlea Pl KA10 ... 229 G6
ROUGHMUSSEL ... 134 F8
ROUGHRIGG ... 85 B2
Roughrigg Rd ML6 ... 124 C6
Roukenburn St G46 ... 135 F4
Rouken Glen Pk* G46 ... 135 F1
Rouken Glen Rd G46 ... 136 A1
Roundel The
Falkirk FK2 ... 42 D7
Wishaw ML2 ... 165 C2
Roundelwood FK10 ... 5 B1
Roundhill Dr PA5 ... 112 E3
Roundhouse FK7 ... 12 D8
Roundknowe Rd G71 ... 120 C1
Round Riding Rd G82 ... 50 B4
Rousay Wynd KA3 ... 223 A6
Rowallan KA13 ... 207 C2
Rowallan Cres KA9 ... 236 D7
Rowallan Ct 6 KA7 ... 235 E1
Rowallan Dr
Bannockburn FK7 ... 11 F8
Kilmarnock KA3 ... 223 A4
Rowallan Gdns G11 ... 96 A3
Rowallan La
Clarkston G76 ... 157 E7
Glasgow G11 ... 96 A3
Rowallan Rd G46 ... 135 F2
Rowallan St G84 ... 16 B3
Rowallan Terr G33 ... 99 B4
Rowan Ave
Beith KA15 ... 171 C8
Milton of Campsie G66 ... 58 C5
Renfrew PA4 ... 94 C4
Rowanbank Pl ML6 ... 122 D8
Rowanbank Rd KA9 ... 236 E7
Rowan Cres
Ayr KA7 ... 239 C5
Chapelhall ML6 ... 123 E3
Falkirk FK1 ... 41 A4
Kirkintilloch G66 ... 79 C5
Menstrie FK11 ... 3 F6
Shotts ML7 ... 147 B4
Rowan Ct
Bannockburn FK7 ... 7 E1
Cambuslang G72 ... 139 F3
Wishaw ML2 ... 164 D2
Rowandale Ave G69 ... 120 A4
Rowand Ave G46 ... 136 C3
Rowanden Ave ML4 ... 142 A6
Rowan Dr
Banknock FK4 ... 38 E2
Bearsden G61 ... 76 A7
Clydebank G81 ... 73 F4
Dumbarton G82 ... 49 A4
Rowan Gdns
Glasgow G41 ... 116 B4
Larkhall ML9 ... 185 B2
Rowan Gr ML3 ... 183 F3
Rowanhill Pl KA1 ... 227 D7
Rowan Ho KA9 ... 236 C6
Rowan La ML1 ... 143 A2
Rowanlea ML6 ... 103 F3
Rowanlea Ave PA2 ... 132 E7
Rowanlea Dr G46 ... 136 D4
Rowanpark Dr G78 ... 134 A5
Rowan Pl
Beith KA15 ... 171 C8
Cambuslang G72 ... 139 C6
Coatbridge ML5 ... 121 E4
Hamilton G72 ... 161 D8
Kilmarnock KA1 ... 227 D7
Troon KA10 ... 229 E4
Rowan Rd
Cumbernauld G67 ... 62 D3
Glasgow G41 ... 116 B4
Linwood PA3 ... 111 F7
Rowan Rise ML3 ... 162 E2
Rowans Gate PA2 ... 113 F2
Rowans Gdns G71 ... 141 B4
Rowanside Terr KA22 ... 205 C4
Rowan St
Greenock PA16 ... 45 C5
Paisley PA2 ... 113 F2
Wishaw ML2 ... 165 B5
Rowans The
Alloa FK10 ... 5 C2
Bishopbriggs G64 ... 77 F2
Rowan Terr KA12 ... 219 D4
Rowantree Ave
Motherwell ML1 ... 143 D7
Rutherglen G73 ... 138 B5
Uddingston G71 ... 141 C7
Rowantree Gdns
Irvine KA11 ... 220 A5
Rutherglen G73 ... 138 B5
Rowantree Gr G83 ... 27 E4
Rowantreehill Rd PA13 ... 89 E8
Rowantree Pl
Johnstone PA5 ... 111 F1
Larkhall ML9 ... 185 D2
Lennoxtown G66 ... 57 E7
Rowantree Rd PA5 ... 112 A1
Rowantree Terr
Lennoxtown G66 ... 57 E7
Motherwell ML1 ... 143 B5
Rowantree Wlk FK5 ... 23 B4
Rowan View ML11 ... 215 B2
Rowanwood Cres ML5 ... 121 D5
Rowchester St G40 ... 118 A5
Rowena Ave G13 ... 75 D1
Rowmore Quays G84 ... 15 E4
Roxburgh Ave PA15 ... 45 E4
Roxburgh Dr
Bearsden G61 ... 75 E7
Coatbridge ML5 ... 122 D4
Roxburgh Pk G74 ... 159 F1
Roxburgh Pl
5 Hamilton G72 ... 161 D7
Stenhousemuir FK5 ... 23 F4
Roxburgh Rd
Hurlford KA1 ... 228 E6
Paisley PA2 ... 132 D7
Roxburgh Row FK7 ... 12 E8
Roxburgh St
Glasgow G12 ... 96 D3
Greenock PA15 ... 45 E5
Roxburgh Way PA15 ... 45 E4
Royal Alexandra Hospl
PA2 ... 113 D2
Royal Bank Pl G1 ... 241 A2
Royal Cres G3 ... 116 E8
Royal Ct PA15 ... 45 E5
Royal Dr ML3 ... 163 A2
Royal Exchange Ct G1 ... 241 A2
Royal Exchange Sq G1 ... 241 A2
Royal Gdns
Bothwell G71 ... 140 E2
Stirling FK8 ... 7 A8
Royal Highland Fusiliers
Regimental Mus* G2 ... 240 B4
Royal Hospl for Sick Children
(Yorkhill) G3 ... 96 C1
Royal Inch Cres PA4 ... 94 D5
Royal Infmy Hospl G4 ... 241 C3
Royal Scottish Acad of Music
& Drama G2 ... 240 C3
Royal St PA19 ... 44 E8
Royal Stuart Way FK7 ... 7 E8
Royal Terr
Glasgow G3 ... 96 E1
Wishaw ML2 ... 165 C7
Royal Terrace La G3 ... 96 E1
Royal Troon Golf Club*
KA10 ... 232 D8
Royellen Ave ML3 ... 161 F2
Roy St G21 ... 97 D3
Roystonhill G21 ... 97 F1
Roystonhill Pl G21 ... 97 F1
Royston Prim Sch G21 ... 97 F1
Royston Rd G21, G33 ... 98 C3
Royston Sq G21 ... 241 C4
Roy Young Ave G83 ... 28 A8
ROZELLE ... 239 A2
Rozelle Ave
Clydebank G15 ... 75 B3
Newton Mearns G77 ... 156 B4
Rozelle Dr G77 ... 156 B4
Rozelle House & MacLaurin
Galleries* KA7 ... 238 F2
Rozelle Pl G77 ... 156 B4
Rozelle Terr KA7 ... 239 B1
Rubie Cres KA12 ... 219 C1
Rubislaw Dr G61 ... 75 E3
Ruby St G40 ... 118 A4
Ruby Terr ML4 ... 142 A4
RUCHAZIE ... 99 B1
Ruchazie Pl G32, G33 ... 118 F8
Ruchazie Rd G33 ... 118 F7
RUCHILL ... 97 A5
Ruchill Pl G20 ... 96 F5
Ruchill Prim Sch G20 ... 96 F6
Ruchill St G20 ... 96 F5
Rue End St PA15 ... 46 A4
Ruel St G44 ... 137 A7
Rufflees Ave G78 ... 134 D4
Rugby Ave G13 ... 95 B8
Rugby Cres KA1 ... 227 D7
Rugby Pk (Kilmarnock FC)
KA1 ... 227 E7
Rugby Rd KA1 ... 227 D7
Rulley View FK6 ... 21 C4
Rullion Pl G33 ... 118 F8
Rumford Pl KA3 ... 223 C6
Rumford St G40 ... 117 F3
Rumlie The FK1 ... 86 A6
Runciman Pl G74 ... 160 B4
Rundell Dr G66 ... 58 C5
Rupert St G4 ... 96 F2
Rush Hill KA7 ... 239 C2
Rushyhill St G21 ... 98 A4
Ruskie Rd FK9 ... 2 B3
Ruskin La G12 ... 96 E3
Ruskin Pl
Glasgow G12 ... 96 E3
Kilsyth G65 ... 60 D8
Ruskin Sq G64 ... 78 A1
Ruskin Terr
Glasgow G12 ... 96 E3
Rutherglen G73 ... 118 B1
Russell Colt St ML5 ... 122 A8
Russell Ct KA3 ... 223 C3
Russell Dr
Alexandria G83 ... 27 C7
Ayr KA8 ... 236 A2
Bearsden G61 ... 75 F6
Dalry KA24 ... 191 D8
Russell Gdns
Newton Mearns G77 ... 156 C4
10 Uddingston G71 ... 141 A8
Russell Hill Ct FK5 ... 23 B1
Russell La ML2 ... 165 A2
Russell Pl
Bonnybridge FK4 ... 39 D5
Clarkston G76 ... 158 A5
East Kilbride G75 ... 180 C7
Linwood PA3 ... 111 F6
Russell Rd
Duntocher G81 ... 73 E7
Lanark ML11 ... 215 B5
Russell St
Ayr KA8 ... 236 A1
Bellshill ML4 ... 142 D5
Chapelhall ML6 ... 123 E2
Hamilton ML3 ... 161 F5
Johnstone PA5 ... 112 A3
Paisley PA3 ... 113 D7
6 Port Glasgow PA14 ... 47 A2
Wishaw ML2 ... 165 B2
Russel St FK2 ... 42 B6
Rutherford Ave
Bearsden G61 ... 75 B8
Kirkintilloch G66 ... 80 B6
Rutherford Ct
Bridge of Allan FK9 ... 2 A8
Clydebank G81 ... 74 A2
Rutherford Grange G66 ... 79 C6
Rutherford La G75 ... 180 F8
Rutherford Sq G75 ... 180 F8
RUTHERGLEN ... 138 D8
Rutherglen High Sch
G73 ... 138 C8
Rutherglen Ind Est G73 ... 118 A1
Rutherglen Rd G5, G73 ... 117 E2
Rutherglen Sh Ctr G73 ... 138 B8
Rutherglen Sta G73 ... 138 B8
Ruthven Ave G46 ... 136 D1
Ruthven La
7 Glasgow G12 ... 96 D3
Glenboig ML5 ... 101 C6
Ruthven Pl
Bishopbriggs G64 ... 98 C8
Troon KA10 ... 229 F4
Ruthven St G12 ... 96 D3
Rutland Cres G51 ... 116 E6
Rutland Ct G51 ... 116 E6
Rutland Pl G51 ... 116 E6
Ryan Rd G64 ... 78 B1
Ryan Way G73 ... 138 C3
Ryat Dr G77 ... 156 C6
Ryat Gn G77 ... 156 C5
Ryatt Linn PA8 ... 72 F1
Rydal Gr G75 ... 179 F6
Rydal Pl G75 ... 179 F6
Ryden Mains Rd ML6 ... 102 D4
Ryde Rd ML2 ... 165 C4
Ryebank Rd G21 ... 98 C5
Rye Cres G21 ... 98 B5
Ryecroft Dr G69 ... 120 B5
Ryedale Pl G15 ... 75 B4
Ryefield Ave
Coatbridge ML5 ... 121 D7
Johnstone PA5 ... 111 D1
Ryefield Ho KA24 ... 169 B1
Ryefield Pl PA5 ... 111 D1
Ryefield Rd G21 ... 98 B5
Ryehill Pl G21 ... 98 C5
Ryehill Rd G21 ... 98 C4
Ryemount Rd G21 ... 98 C5
Rye Rd G21 ... 98 C5
Ryeside Pl KA24 ... 169 C1
Ryeside Rd G21 ... 98 B4
Rye Way PA2 ... 112 E1
Ryewraes Rd PA3 ... 112 B5
Rylands KA9 ... 236 C6
Rylands Dr G32 ... 119 D4
Rylands Gdns G32 ... 119 E4
Rylees Cres G52 ... 114 E6
Rylees Pl G52 ... 114 E6
Rylees Rd G52 ... 114 E6
Rysland Ave G77 ... 156 E5
Rysland Cres G77 ... 156 E5
Rysland Dr KA3 ... 213 A4
Ryvra Rd G13 ... 95 D6

S

Sachelcourt Ave PA7 ... 72 B2
Sackville Ave G13 ... 95 F5
Sackville La G13 ... 95 F5
Sacred Heart Prim Sch
Bellshill ML4 ... 142 A3
Glasgow G40 ... 117 F4
Greenock PA16 ... 44 E4
Saddell Rd G15 ... 75 B4
Sadler's Wells Ct G74 ... 160 B4
Saffron Cres ML2 ... 164 E1
Saffronhall Cres ML3 ... 162 D4
Saffronhall Gdns ML3 ... 162 D4
Saffronhall La ML3 ... 162 D4
Sainford Cres FK2 ... 24 A1
St Abb's Dr PA2 ... 113 A1
St Agathas Prim Sch G66 ... 80 B8
St Agnes Prim Sch G23 ... 96 E8
St Aidans High Sch ML2 ... 165 B4
St Aidan's Path ML2 ... 165 C6
St Aidans RC Prim Sch
ML2 ... 165 C5
St Aidans Sch G32 ... 118 D6
St Alberts Prim Sch G41 ... 116 E4
St Aloysius Coll G3 ... 240 B4
St Aloysius Prim Sch G22 ... 97 E5
St Aloysius RC Prim Sch
ML6 ... 123 E2
St Ambrose High Sch
ML5 ... 121 E8
St Andrews Acad PA2 ... 114 C1
St Andrews Ave G71 ... 141 A1
St Andrew's Ave
Bishopbriggs G64 ... 77 E2
Prestwick KA9 ... 236 C6
St Andrew's Brae G82 ... 50 B5
St Andrews Cl 3 G41 ... 116 F4
St Andrews Cres G41 ... 116 E4
St Andrew's Cres
Dumbarton G82 ... 50 B5
Paisley PA3 ... 113 C8
St Andrew's Cross G41 ... 117 A3
St Andrews Ct
Bellshill ML4 ... 142 B5
East Kilbride G75 ... 180 C6
Kirkintilloch G66 ... 79 D7
Motherwell ML1 ... 143 A6
Saltcoats KA21 ... 205 F3
St Andrew's Ct
Carluke ML8 ... 187 E1
Larbert FK5 ... 23 B3
St Andrews Dr
Bearsden G61 ... 75 D7
Bridge of Weir PA11 ... 110 C6
Coatbridge ML5 ... 121 E6
Cumbernauld G68 ... 62 B6
Gourock PA19 ... 44 A6
Law ML8 ... 187 A6
St Andrew's Dr
Airth FK2 ... 14 B7
Glasgow G41 ... 116 D3
Hamilton ML3 ... 161 D4
Paisley PA3 ... 113 D8
Renfrew PA3 ... 93 E1
St Andrew's Drive W
Paisley PA3 ... 113 D8
Renfrew PA3 ... 93 C1
St Andrews Gate ML4 ... 141 F5
St Andrew's Gdns
Airdrie ML6 ... 123 B8
Dalry KA24 ... 191 B6
St Andrews High Sch
ML5 ... 121 F3
St Andrew's High Sch
G81 ... 94 C8
St Andrews La
Alexandria G83 ... 27 E4
Gourock PA19 ... 44 A6
St Andrew's La G1 ... 241 B1
St Andrews Path 10 ML9 ... 185 C1
St Andrews Pl
Beith KA15 ... 171 A7
10 Falkirk FK1 ... 42 B4
Kilsyth G65 ... 36 C1
St Andrew's Pl KA20 ... 206 F2
St Andrews Prim Sch
Airdrie ML6 ... 102 E1
Bearsden G61 ... 75 C6
Cumbernauld G68 ... 61 D5
Kilmarnock KA3 ... 223 B2
St Andrew Sq PA15 ... 46 B4
St Andrew's RC Cath*
G1 ... 241 A1
St Andrews RC Prim Sch
FK1 ... 42 E4
St Andrews RC Sec Sch
G32 ... 119 A7
St Andrew's Rd
Ardrossan KA22 ... 205 D4
Glasgow G41 ... 116 F4
Renfrew PA4 ... 94 C2
St Andrews & St Brides High
Sch G74 ... 160 A1
St Andrew's Sq G1 ... 241 B1
St Andrews St ML1 ... 143 A5
St Andrew's St
Ayr KA7 ... 239 A7
Glasgow G1 ... 241 B1
St Andrew St
Greenock PA15 ... 46 B4
Kilmarnock KA1 ... 227 F8
St Andrews Way KA12 ... 224 F8
St Andrew's Way ML2 ... 165 C6
St Andrew's Wlk 2 KA1 ... 227 F7
St Andrews Wynd G84 ... 16 E3
St Angelas Prim Sch
G53 ... 135 C3
St Annes Ave PA8 ... 93 D8
St Anne's Cres FK7 ... 7 E1
St Anne's Ct ML3 ... 183 D8
St Annes Prim Sch
Erskine PA8 ... 93 C8
Glasgow G40 ... 118 A5
St Annes RC Prim Sch
ML3 ... 183 D8
St Annes Wynd PA8 ... 93 D8
St Ann's Dr G46 ... 136 C2
St Anthonys Prim Sch
Johnstone PA5 ... 131 C7
Rutherglen G73 ... 138 D4
Saltcoats KA21 ... 205 E2
St Athanasius' Prim Sch
ML8 ... 187 F1
St Augustine's Prim Sch
ML5 ... 121 F6
St Barbaras Prim Sch
G69 ... 100 D7
St Barchan's Rd PA10 ... 111 B2
St Bartholomews Prim Sch
ML5 ... 101 D1
St Bartholomew's Prim Sch
G45 ... 137 F4
St Benedicts High Sch
PA3 ... 111 F5
St Benedict's Prim Sch
G34 ... 100 C1
St Bernadette's Prim Sch
ML1 ... 163 B8
St Bernadette's RC Prim Sch
FK10 ... 4 A2
St Bernards Prim Sch
G53 ... 135 A5
St Bernards RC Prim Sch
ML5 ... 122 B3
St Blane's Dr G73 ... 137 F6
St Blanes Prim Sch
Glasgow G23 ... 76 D1
Hamilton G72 ... 161 C8
St Boswell's Cres PA2 ... 113 A1
St Boswells Dr ML5 ... 122 D4
St Brendans Prim Sch
G13 ... 94 F7
St Brendans RC Prim Sch
ML1 ... 164 B2
St Brennans Ct KA25 ... 170 A7
St Bride's Ave G71 ... 141 C7
St Bride's Dr KA23 ... 190 D5
St Bride's Pl KA12 ... 219 C5
St Bride's Prim Sch G72 ... 139 A5
St Brides Prim Sch
G71 ... 141 A4
St Bride's Rd
Glasgow G43 ... 136 D6
West Kilbride KA23 ... 190 D6
St Brides Way G71 ... 141 A4
St Bridgets Prim Sch
Glasgow G69 ... 120 B5
Kilbirnie KA25 ... 170 A8
St Brigid's Prim Sch
Glasgow G42 ... 137 E8
Wishaw ML2 ... 166 A5
St Bryde La G74 ... 159 F2
St Bryde St 8 G74 ... 159 F2
St Cadocs Prim Sch G77 ... 156 C5
St Cadoc's Prim Sch
G72 ... 139 C4
St Catherines Cres ML7 ... 146 E6
St Catherine's Prim Sch
PA3 ... 113 F6
St Catherines RC Prim Sch
G21 ... 98 C5
St Catherines Rd KA8 ... 236 F2
St Catherine's Rd G46 ... 136 C2
St Charles Prim Sch
Cambuslang G72 ... 139 F6
Glasgow G20 ... 96 F4
Paisley PA2 ... 113 F2
St Clair PA9 ... 130 F5
St Clair Ave G46 ... 136 C3
St Clair St G20 ... 96 F2
St Clares Prim RC Sch
G15 ... 75 A4
St Columba Dr G66 ... 79 E7
St Columba Mews G84 ... 16 D2
St Columba Pl KA20 ... 206 F2
St Columbas High Sch
PA16 ... 45 A6
St Columba's High Sch
G81 ... 74 C4
St Columba's Sch (Junior)
PA13 ... 89 C8
St Columba's Sch (Senior)
PA13 ... 89 D8
St Columbkilles Prim Sch 1
G73 ... 138 B7
St Constantine's Prim Sch
G51 ... 115 E7
St Convals Prim Sch
G43 ... 136 D8
St Crispin's Pl FK1 ... 42 B4
St Cuthbert's Cres KA9 ... 236 D6
St Cuthberts Ct KA21 ... 216 E8
St Cuthberts Prim Sch
Glasgow G22 ... 97 B4
10 Hamilton ML3 ... 162 A5
St Cuthbert's Rd KA9 ... 236 C6
St Cuthbert Way ML3 ... 161 F5
St Cyrus Gdns G64 ... 78 C1

St Cyrus Rd G64 .... 78 C1
St David's Ct FK5 .... 23 B1
St Davids Dr ML6 .... 123 C4
St David's Pl ML9 .... 185 A3
St David's Prim Sch PA5 111 D1
St Davids RC Prim Sch
ML6 .... 104 A2
St Denis Prim Sch G31 ... 118 B7
St Denis Way ML5 .... 121 F8
St Dominics RC Prim Sch
ML6 .... 123 D6
St Edmunds Gr G62 .... 55 A3
St Edwards Prim Sch
ML6 .... 123 C7
St Elizabeths Prim Sch
ML3 .... 183 D7
St Enoch Ave G71 .... 141 C8
St Enoch Pl G1 .... 240 C2
St Enoch Sh Ctr G1 .... 241 A1
St Enoch Sq G1 .... 240 C2
St Enoch Underground Sta
G1 .... 240 C1
St Eunan's Prim Sch G81 .. 74 C2
St Fergus' Prim Sch PA3 . 113 B5
St Fillans Dr PA6 .... 91 A2
St Fillans Prim Sch G44 .. 137 B5
St Fillan's Prim Sch PA6 .. 91 B1
St Fillans Rd G33 .... 99 C5
St Flanan Rd G65, G66 .... 59 D2
St Flannans Prim Sch
G66 .... 58 F1
St Francis of Assisi Prim Sch
Cumbernauld G68 .... 82 A7
Glasgow G69 .... 119 F3
St Francis Prim Sch
Glasgow G5 .... 117 D4
Port Glasgow PA14 .... 68 F7
St Francis RC Prim Sch
FK2 .... 42 A6
St Francis Rigg 4 G5 ... 117 D4
St Francis Xavier Coll
ML5 .... 122 C4
St Gabriels Prim Sch
PA16 .... 44 D3
St George's Cross 10 G3 .. 97 A2
St George's Ct FK5 .... 23 B1
St George's Gate 2 PA1 . 113 E4
St George's Pl
8 Glasgow G3 .... 97 A2
Glasgow G4 .... 240 B4
St Georges Prim Sch
G52 .... 114 F5
St George's Rd
Ayr KA8 .... 236 B3
Glasgow G3 .... 97 A2
St George's Underground Sta
G20 .... 97 A2
St Gerards Prim Sch
ML4 .... 142 B7
St Gerards Sec Sch G51 .. 116 B7
St Germains G61 .... 75 E4
St Gilberts RC Prim Sch
G21 .... 98 C3
St Giles Pk ML3 .... 162 B2
St Giles Sq FK1 .... 41 B6
St Giles Way
Falkirk FK1 .... 41 B6
Hamilton ML3 .... 162 B2
St Gregory's Prim Sch
G20 .... 96 D6
St Helena Cres G81 .... 74 C6
St Helens Gdns G42 .... 136 F8
St Helens Prim Sch
Bishopbriggs G64 .... 78 C2
Cumbernauld G67 .... 82 B7
St Hilarys Prim Sch G74 . 181 B8
St Ignatius' RC Prim Sch 1
ML2 .... 165 C3
St Inan Ave KA12 .... 219 E3
St Inan's Dr KA15 .... 150 C1
St Ives Rd G69 .... 80 F3
St James Ave PA3 .... 113 C7
St James Bsns Ctr PA1 ... 112 E4
St James Ct
Coatbridge ML5 .... 121 E3
East Kilbride G75 .... 158 E1
St James' Orch FK9 .... 2 D1
St James' Pl KA20 .... 206 F2
St James Prim Sch G40 .. 117 E5
St James' Prim Sch PA4 ... 94 C3
St James Rd G4 .... 241 B3
St James' St PA1 .... 113 E5
St James Way ML5 .... 121 E3
St Joachims Cath Prim Sch
G32 .... 119 C1
St Joan of Arc Sec Sch
G22 .... 97 B7
St Joan's Cres KA13 .... 207 E2
St John Bosco Prim Sch
PA8 .... 72 F2
St John Ogilvie Prim Sch
Irvine KA11 .... 220 B3
Paisley PA1 .... 114 B4
St John's Ave FK2 .... 42 C6
St Johns Bvd G71 .... 141 A6
St John's Ct
Falkirk FK2 .... 42 C6
Glasgow G41 .... 116 E4
St John's Gate FK6 .... 21 C2
St John's Gdns FK6 .... 21 C2
St John's Gr FK6 .... 21 C2
St John's Manor PA19 .... 44 E8
St John's Pl
Ardrossan KA22 .... 205 C2
Stevenston KA20 .... 206 F2
St Johns Prim Sch
Ayr KA8 .... 236 A1
Barrhead G78 .... 134 C4
Hamilton ML3 .... 162 D3
7 Port Glasgow PA14 .... 47 A2
Stevenston KA20 .... 206 F1
St John's Prim Sch FK10 ... 9 F6
St John's Quadrant G41 .. 116 E4
St John's Rd
Glasgow G41 .... 116 E4
Gourock PA19 .... 44 E8
St John St
6 Ayr KA7 .... 235 F1
Coatbridge ML5 .... 122 A7
Prestwick KA9 .... 236 C8
Stirling FK8 .... 7 A8
St Johns Way G65 .... 59 F3
St John The Baptist Prim Sch
G71 .... 141 A6
St Josephs Acad (Kilmarnock
Campus) KA3 .... 223 B2
St Joseph's Ct G21 .... 97 F1
St Joseph's Pl G21 .... 97 F1
St Josephs Prim Sch
Clarkston G76 .... 157 E5
Glasgow G4 .... 97 B2
Hamilton G72 .... 161 D8
Helensburgh G84 .... 16 F2
Milngavie G62 .... 54 F1
Stepps G33 .... 99 E5
St Joseph's Prim Sch
Clydebank G81 .... 74 D7
Greenock PA16 .... 45 A4
St Josephs RC Prim Sch
FK4 .... 40 B4
St Joseph's View G21 .... 97 F1
St Kenneth Dr G51 .... 115 E8
St Kenneths Prim Sch
G74 .... 159 E2
St Kenneth's Prim Sch
PA15 .... 46 D2
St Kentigerns Rd ML11 ... 215 B5
St Kessog's Prim Sch 1
G83 .... 27 F8
St Kevins Prim Sch G69 . 121 A5
St Kevins Sch G21 .... 97 E2
St Kilda Bank KA11 .... 220 A2
St Kilda Ct KA11 .... 220 A2
St Kilda Dr G14 .... 95 E4
St Kilda Pl KA11 .... 220 A2
St Kilda Way ML2 .... 165 E5
St Laurence Cres FK1 .... 86 B6
St Laurence's Prim Sch
PA15 .... 46 A3
St Lawrence Pk G75 .... 159 C1
St Lawrence Pl KA21 .... 206 A1
St Lawrence St PA15 .... 46 B4
ST LEONARDS 160 D1
St Leonard's Ct KA7 .... 239 A5
St Leonard's Dr G46 .... 136 C3
St Leonard's Prim Sch
G74 .... 160 D3
St Leonards Rd G74 .... 160 D2
St Leonard's Rd
Ayr KA7 .... 239 A5
Lanark ML11 .... 215 B4
St Leonard's Sq G74 .... 160 C1
St Leonard St ML11 .... 215 B5
St Leonards Wlk ML5 .... 122 C3
St Leonard's Wynd KA7 . 239 A6
St Louise Prim Sch G75 .. 180 E6
St Louises Prim Sch
G46 .... 135 D4
St Lucy's Prim Sch G67 ... 62 E4
St Luke's Ave ML8 .... 201 E8
St Lukes High Sch G78 .. 155 C8
St Lukes Pl G5 .... 117 C5
St Lukes Prim Sch KA13 . 207 B2
St Lukes Terr G5 .... 117 C5
St Machan's Prim Sch
G66 .... 33 D1
St Machan's Way G66 .... 33 D1
St Machars Rd PA11 .... 110 E7
St Margaret Ave KA24 .... 191 B7
St Margaret Mary's Sec Sch
G45 .... 137 D2
St Margaret of Scotland Prim
Sch 1 G67 .... 82 F8
St Margarets Ave PA3 ... 114 A7
St Margaret's Ave G65 .... 37 E3
St Margaret's Cath*
KA8 .... 236 A1
St Margarets Ct ML4 .... 142 B5
St Margaret's Ct
Greenock PA16 .... 45 B5
Paisley PA3 .... 113 F7
St Margaret's Dr ML2 .... 164 E1
St Margarets High Sch
ML6 .... 123 B8
St Margaret's Pl G1 .... 241 A1
St Margarets Prim Sch
PA5 .... 111 E2
St Margarets RC Prim Sch
FK7 .... 12 D7
St Margaret's Rd KA22 .. 205 D4
St Maria Groetti Prim Sch
G33 .... 119 B8
St Mark Gdns G32 .... 118 F5
St Mark's Ct ML2 .... 165 C6
St Marks Prim Sch
Barrhead G78 .... 134 C1
Glasgow G31 .... 118 E5
Hamilton ML3 .... 161 F1
Irvine KA12 .... 219 E4
Rutherglen G73 .... 138 B5
St Mark St G32 .... 118 E5
St Marnock Pl 10 KA1 .... 227 F8
St Marnocks Prim Sch
G53 .... 115 C1
St Marnock St
Glasgow G40 .... 118 A5
Kilmarnock KA1 .... 227 F8
St Marthas RC Prim Sch
G21 .... 98 B5
St Martins Gate ML5 .... 122 A4
St Martins Prim Sch G83 .. 27 E3
St Mary's Cres G78 .... 134 D2
St Marys Ct ML11 .... 215 C4
St Mary's Ct ML2 .... 165 B2
St Marys Gdns G78 .... 134 D2
St Marys (Maryhill) Sch
G20 .... 96 C7
St Mary's Pl KA21 .... 205 F1
St Marys Prim Sch
Caldercruix ML6 .... 104 F5
Cumbernauld G67 .... 61 E1
Greenock PA16 .... 45 E6
Hamilton ML3 .... 162 D4
Lanark ML11 .... 215 C3
Paisley PA1 .... 113 C3
St Mary's Prim Sch
1 Clydebank G81 .... 74 A6
Larkhall ML9 .... 184 F2
St Marys RC Prim Sch
Bannockburn FK7 .... 7 D2
Cleland ML1 .... 144 B1
Coatbridge ML5 .... 122 A5
St Mary's RC Prim Sch
G83 .... 27 E5
St Mary's Rd
Bellshill ML4 .... 141 E5
Bishopbriggs G64 .... 77 E1
St Marys Sch Kenmure
G64 .... 77 D1
St Mary's Way G82 .... 49 F3
St Mary's Wynd 5 FK8 .... 7 A8
St Matthew's Acad KA21 . 205 F1
St Matthews Prim Sch
G64 .... 78 B2
St Matthew's Prim Sch
ML2 .... 164 E4
St Maurices High Sch
G68 .... 82 A8
St Maurice's Rdbt G68 .... 61 A1
St Maur's Cres KA3 .... 222 E3
St Maurs Gdns KA3 .... 222 C7
St Maur's Pl KA3 .... 222 E3
St Medan's Pl KA21 .... 205 F1
St Meddans Cres KA10 .... 229 E3
St Meddans Ct KA10 .... 229 D2
St Meddans Cvn Site
KA10 .... 229 E3
St Meddans St KA10 .... 229 D2
St Michael Dr G84 .... 16 E2
St Michael Rd ML2 .... 164 C1
St Michael's Ct G31 .... 118 C5
St Michael's La G31 .... 118 C5
St Michael's Mount KA1 . 227 B7
St Michaels Prim Sch
Glasgow G31 .... 118 C5
Moodiesburn G69 .... 81 A2
1 Port Glasgow PA14 .... 68 F8
St Michael's RC Prim Sch
G82 .... 49 D4
St Mirin's Cath PA1 .... 113 F5
St Mirins Prim Sch G44 . 137 C5
St Mirren Park (St Mirren
FC) PA3 .... 113 D6
St Mirren's Rd G65 .... 60 E8
St Mirren St PA1 .... 113 E4
St Modans Ct 13 FK1 .... 42 B4
St Modans High Sch FK7 ... 7 A3
St Modan's Way G84 .... 15 B3
St Monach's Pl KA20 .... 206 F2
St Monance St G21 .... 97 F5
St Monicas-Milton Prim Sch
G22 .... 97 C7
St Monicas Prim Sch
Coatbridge ML5 .... 121 D4
Glasgow G53 .... 115 B1
St Monicas Way ML5 .... 121 D4
St Mungo Ave G4 .... 241 B3
St Mungo Ct PA11 .... 110 E8
St Mungo Museum of
Religious Life & Art*
G4 .... 241 C3
St Mungo Pl
Glasgow G4 .... 241 B3
Hamilton ML3 .... 161 D4
St Mungo's ML11 .... 215 A3
St Mungo's Acad G40 .... 118 A5
St Mungos Cres 5 ML1 .. 143 B2
St Mungos High Sch FK2 .. 42 A6
St Mungos Prim Sch G4 241 C3
St Mungo's RC Prim Sch
FK10 .... 10 C5
St Mungo's Rd G67 .... 61 F1
St Mungo St G64 .... 97 F8
St Mungo's Wlk G67 .... 61 F2
St Mungo's Wynd FK10 .... 10 A6
St Nicholas Rd
Lanark ML11 .... 215 B5
Prestwick KA9 .... 236 B7
ST NINIANS 7 B4
St Ninian's ML11 .... 215 B5
St Ninian's Cres PA2 .... 113 F2
St Ninian's Dr KA22 .... 205 D4
St Ninians Gr ML2 .... 165 D6
St Ninians High Sch G64 .. 78 D2
St Ninian's High Sch
G46 .... 136 B2
St Ninians Pl ML9 .... 198 E1
St Ninian's Pl ML3 .... 161 F3
St Ninians Prim Sch
Hamilton ML3 .... 161 F3
St Ninians Prim Sch *continued*
Prestwick KA9 .... 236 E8
Stirling FK7 .... 7 A4
St Ninian's Prim Sch
Glasgow G13 .... 75 C1
Gourock PA19 .... 44 D6
St Ninians Rd
Cambusbarron FK7 .... 6 E5
Paisley PA2 .... 113 F2
Stirling FK8 .... 7 B6
St Ninian's Rd
Hamilton ML3 .... 161 E3
Prestwick KA9 .... 236 B7
St Ninian Terr G5 .... 117 C5
St Oswold's Sch G44 .... 137 A5
St Palladius Prim Sch
KA24 .... 191 C7
St Palladius Terr KA24 .. 191 D8
St Patrick's Ct ML11 .... 214 F4
St Patricks Prim Sch
Coatbridge ML5 .... 122 B7
Glasgow G3 .... 240 A2
Greenock PA15 .... 45 E4
Kilsyth G65 .... 60 D8
Troon KA10 .... 229 D2
St Patrick's Prim Sch
ML1 .... 142 F3
St Patricks RC Prim Sch
Denny FK6 .... 21 E3
Shotts ML7 .... 146 E3
St Patrick's RC Prim Sch
G82 .... 50 A3
St Patrick's Rd ML11 .... 214 F4
St Pauls High Sch G53 .. 135 D8
St Pauls Prim Sch
Glasgow, Shettleston
G32 .... 119 A3
Hamilton ML3 .... 162 B6
Paisley PA2 .... 112 F1
St Paul's Prim Sch G14 .... 95 D3
St Peter's La G2 .... 240 B2
St Peter's Path 13 G4 .... 97 A2
St Peters Prim Sch
Ardrossan KA22 .... 205 C4
Hamilton ML3 .... 162 B1
Paisley PA2 .... 133 D8
St Peter's Prim Sch G11 .. 96 C2
St Peter's RC Prim Sch
G82 .... 50 B6
St Peter's St G4 .... 97 A2
St Philips Sch ML6 .... 103 F1
St Phillans Ave KA7 .... 239 B6
St Philomena's RC Prim Sch
G33 .... 98 D3
ST QUIVOX 237 B5
St Quivox Rd KA9 .... 236 D8
St Raymond's Specl Sch
G45 .... 137 B2
St Rhonans La G83 .... 27 E4
St Roberts Gdns G53 .... 135 C5
St Rochs RC Prim Sch
G21 .... 98 A1
St Roch's Sec Sch G21 .. 241 C4
St Ronans Dr G73 .... 138 C6
St Ronan's Dr
Glasgow G41 .... 136 D8
Hamilton ML3 .... 183 C8
St Ronan's RC Prim Sch
G83 .... 28 A3
St Rose of Lima Prim Sch
G33 .... 99 C2
St Saviours Prim Sch
G51 .... 116 B7
St Serf's Pl FK10 .... 4 B3
St Serfs Prim Sch ML6 ... 103 B2
St Serf's Prim Sch FK10 .... 4 B3
St Serf's Rd FK10 .... 4 B3
St Serf's Wlk FK12 .... 4 E6
St Stephens Ave G73 .... 138 D3
St Stephen's Ave G73 .... 138 D3
St Stephen's Cres G73 ... 138 E3
St Stephens Ct G81 .... 73 F3
St Stephen's High Sch
PA14 .... 69 A7
St Stephen's Pl KA20 .... 206 F2
St Stephen's Prim Sch
Clydebank G81 .... 73 F3
Glasgow G21 .... 97 E2
St Stephens RC Prim Sch
ML5 .... 122 D5
St Teiling ML11 .... 215 B6
St Teresa's Prim Sch
(Keppoch Campus) G21 .97 C3
St Teresas RC Prim Sch
ML1 .... 143 D3
St Thomas Aquinas Sec Sch
G14 .... 95 E4
St Thomas Prim Sch
Glasgow G33 .... 118 D8
Neilston G78 .... 154 D7
St Thomas' Prim Sch
ML2 .... 165 A2
St Thomas's Pl FK7 .... 6 E6
St Thomas's Well FK7 .... 6 D7
St Timothys Prim Sch
G32 .... 119 A6
St Timothy's Prim Sch
ML5 .... 121 F4
St Valentine Terr 5 G5 .. 117 D4
St Valery Ct FK7 .... 7 A4
St Valery Dr FK7 .... 7 A4
St Vigeans Ave G77 .... 156 C3
St Vigeans Pl G77 .... 156 C3
St Vincent Cres
Ayr KA7 .... 239 A2
Glasgow G3 .... 116 E8
St Vincent Crescent La
G3 .... 116 E8
St Vincent La G2 .... 240 C2
St Vincent Pl
East Kilbride G75 .... 180 A8
Glasgow G1 .... 241 A2
Lanark ML11 .... 215 B4
Motherwell ML1 .... 163 E7
St Vincent's Prim Sch
East Kilbride G75 .... 180 B5
Glasgow G46 .... 135 E4
St Vincents Sch Tollcross
G32 .... 119 A2
St Vincent St G2 .... 240 B3
St Vincent Terr G3 .... 240 A3
St Winifred's Way ML2 .. 165 A4
St Winning's La KA13 .... 207 E3
St Winnings Prim Sch
KA13 .... 207 D3
St Winning's Rd
Kilwinning KA13 .... 207 D3
Kilwinning KA13 .... 207 E3
St Winning's Well KA13 . 207 D3
St Winnoc Rd PA12 .... 129 D3
Salamanca St G31 .... 118 D5
Salasaig Ct G33 .... 119 A7
Salen Loan ML7 .... 147 B3
Salen St G52 .... 115 F5
Salford Pl 2 G66 .... 58 C1
Saline St ML6 .... 122 D6
Salisbury G74 .... 160 D4
Salisbury Ave KA1 .... 228 F6
Salisbury Cres ML1 .... 163 B8
Salisbury Pl
Clydebank G81 .... 73 D5
Prestwick KA9 .... 236 C8
Salisbury St 2 G5 .... 117 B4
Salkeld St G5 .... 117 B5
Salmona St G22 .... 97 B4
Salmon Dr FK1 .... 41 E1
Salmon St PA15 .... 45 E5
SALSBURGH 125 C2
Saltaire Ave G71 .... 141 A5
SALTCOATS 216 D8
Saltcoats KA20 .... 206 E1
SALTCOATS CAMPBELL . 217 C7
Saltcoats Rd KA20 .... 217 B8
Saltcoats Sta KA21 .... 216 F7
Salterland Rd G78 .... 134 E4
Salters Way KA21 .... 205 F3
Saltfield La 2 KA8 .... 235 F2
Saltire Cres ML9 .... 185 C2
Saltmarket G1 .... 241 B1
Saltmarket Pl G1 .... 241 A1
Saltoun St G12 .... 96 D3
Saltpans Rd KA8 .... 235 F3
Salvador Ave ML9 .... 200 C3
Salvia St G72 .... 138 F6
Samson Ave KA1 .... 228 B7
Samson Cres ML8 .... 202 C8
Sandaig Prim Sch G33 ... 119 F6
Sandaig Rd G33 .... 119 E6
Sandale Path 2 G72 .... 161 C6
Sandalwood ML2 .... 164 D1
Sandalwood Ave G74 .... 159 D4
Sandalwood Ct G74 .... 159 D4
Sanda Pl
Kilmarnock KA3 .... 223 B5
Saltcoats KA21 .... 205 F2
Sanda St G20 .... 96 E4
Sanda Way PA2 .... 133 D7
Sandbank Ave G20 .... 96 D6
Sandbank Cres
Alexandria G83 .... 27 F5
Glasgow G20 .... 96 D6
Sandbank Dr G20 .... 96 D7
Sandbank St G20 .... 96 D7
Sandbank Terr G20 .... 96 D7
Sandbed La 7 KA1 .... 227 F8
Sandbed St KA1 .... 227 F8
Sandend PA8 .... 73 A3
Sandend Rd G53 .... 135 A7
Sanderling Pl
East Kilbride G75 .... 180 A5
Johnstone PA5 .... 131 D6
Sanderling Rd PA3 .... 113 E8
Sanderson Ave
Irvine KA12 .... 219 B1
Uddingston G71 .... 141 D6
Sanderson High Sch
G74 .... 181 C8
Sandfield Ave G62 .... 55 A3
Sandfield Rd KA9 .... 236 C8
Sandfield St G20 .... 96 E5
Sandford Gdns G69 .... 120 B5
Sandgate KA7 .... 238 F8
Sandgate Ave G32 .... 119 D3
Sandhaven Pl G53 .... 135 A7
Sandhaven Rd G53 .... 135 A7
Sandhead Cres ML6 .... 123 E1
Sandhead Terr G72 .... 161 D2
Sandhill Gdns KA10 .... 229 G3
Sandholes Rd PA5 .... 111 C6
Sandholes St PA1 .... 113 C4
Sandholm Pl G14 .... 94 F5
Sandholm Terr G14 .... 94 F5
Sandiefield Rd 1 G5 .... 117 C4
Sandielands Ave PA8 .... 93 D8
Sandilands KA10 .... 229 E1
Sandilands Cres ML1 .... 163 C5
Sandilands St G32 .... 119 C5
Sandmill St G21 .... 98 A1
Sandpiper Cres ML5 .... 122 D3
Sandpiper Dr G75 .... 180 A5
Sandpiper Mdw FK10 .... 10 D5
Sandpiper Pl G75 .... 180 A5
Sandpiper Rd PA12 .... 129 D2
Sandpiper Way ML4 .... 141 E8
Sandra Rd G64 .... 78 C2
Sandray Ave PA14 .... 69 B7

Sandringham Ave G77 .. 157 A6
Sandringham Ct G77 .... 157 A5
Sandringham Dr PA5 ..... 112 B1
Sandringham La 2 G12 ... 96 D3
Sandringham Terr PA16 ... 45 E7
Sandvale Pl ML7 .... 147 A3
Sandwood Cres 4 G52 . 115 A5
Sandwood Path 1 G52 . 115 A5
Sandwood Prim Sch 6
G52 .... 115 A5
Sandwood Rd G52 ...... 115 A5
Sandy Ct KA23 .... 190 C3
Sandyfaulds St 1 G5 ... 117 D4
Sandyford Ave ML1 ..... 143 D7
Sandyford Pl
Glasgow G3 .... 240 A3
Motherwell ML1 .... 143 D7
Sandyford Place La G3 .. 240 A3
Sandyford Rd
Mossblown KA6 .... 237 F6
Motherwell ML1 .... 143 D7
Paisley PA3 .... 114 A8
Prestwick KA9 .... 234 B1
Sandyford St G3 .... 116 C8
Sandyford Toll Rdbt
KA9 .... 237 C8
Sandyhill Ave ML7 ...... 147 A3
SANDYHILLS 119 C5
Sandyhills Cres G32 ..... 119 B3
Sandyhills Dr G32 .... 119 B3
Sandyhills Gr G32 .... 119 B2
Sandyhills Pl G32 .... 119 B3
Sandyhills Rd G32 ...... 119 C3
Sandyhill Terr KA6 ...... 239 E6
Sandyknowes Rd G67 ..... 83 A8
Sandy La G11 .... 96 A2
Sandylands Prom KA21 .. 217 A7
Sandy Rd
Carluke ML8 .... 187 F2
Glasgow G11 .... 96 A2
Irvine KA12 .... 219 B5
Renfrew PA4 .... 94 C2
West Kilbride KA23 ...... 190 C3
Sandyvale ML9 .... 198 D1
Sanford Pl 11 G3 .... 116 E8
Sannox Dr
Motherwell ML1 .... 163 B7
Saltcoats KA21 .... 206 A2
Sannox Gdns G31 .... 118 B8
Sannox Pl
Ayr KA8 .... 236 D2
East Kilbride G75 .... 180 B4
Helensburgh G84 .... 16 F3
Sannox Rd KA1 .... 222 C2
Sannox View KA8 .... 236 E2
Sanquhar Ave KA9 ...... 236 D7
Sanquhar Dr G53 .... 135 A8
Sanquhar Farm Rd KA8 . 236 D3
Sanquhar Gdns
Blantyre G72 .... 140 B2
1 Glasgow G53 .... 135 A8
Sanquhar Pl 2 G53 ..... 135 A8
Sanquhar Rd G53 .... 115 A1
Sanson La ML8 .... 202 C8
Sapphire Rd ML4 .... 142 B4
Saracen Head Rd G1 ..... 241 C1
Saracen Prim Sch (Keppoch
Campus) G22 .... 97 C4
Saracen St
Glasgow G22 .... 97 C4
Glasgow G22 .... 97 C5
Sarazen Ct ML1 .... 164 E8
Sarazen Dr KA10 .... 232 E8
Sardinia La G12 .... 96 D3
Sark Dr KA10 .... 229 G5
Saskatoon Pl G75 .... 159 B1
Saturn Ave PA1 .... 112 E5
Saucel Cres PA1 .... 113 E4
Saucelhill Terr PA2 ...... 113 F3
Saucel Pl PA1 .... 113 E3
Saucel St PA1 .... 113 F4
Sauchenford Smallholdings
FK7 .... 12 A5
Sauchenhall Path 8 G69 .. 81 A3
SAUCHIE 5 E1
Sauchie Ct FK7 .... 7 F1
Sauchiehall La
Glasgow G2 .... 240 B3
Glasgow G2 .... 240 C3
Sauchiehall St
Glasgow, Cranston Hill
G3 .... 116 E8
Glasgow G2 .... 240 B3
Sauchiesmoor Rd ML8 .. 202 A8
Sauchie St FK7 .... 7 A2
Saugh Ave G78 .... 173 D8
Saughs Ave G33 .... 98 F6
Saughs Dr G33 .... 98 F6
Saughs Gate G33 .... 98 F6
Saughs Pl G33 .... 98 F6
Saughs Rd G33 .... 98 F6
Saughton St G32 .... 118 E7
Saughtree Ave KA21 ..... 205 F2
Saunders Ct G78 .... 134 B3
Saunterne Rd KA9 ...... 233 C1
Savoy Ct KA7 .... 238 E7
Savoy Pk KA7 .... 238 E7
Savoy Sh Ctr G2 .... 240 C3
Savoy St G40 .... 117 F4
Sawers Ave FK6 .... 21 D1
Sawmillfield St G4 .... 97 B2
Sawmill Rd G11 .... 95 F2
Saxon Rd G13 .... 95 D7
Scadlock Rd PA3 .... 113 B5
Scalloway La G72 .... 138 F3
Scalloway Rd
Cambuslang G72 .... 138 E3
Gartcosh G69 .... 100 E4
Scalpay G74 .... 160 C1
Scalpay Pass G22 .... 97 D7
Scalpay Pl
Glasgow G22 .... 97 D7
Kilmarnock KA3 .... 223 A5
Scalpay St G22 .... 97 D7
Scamadale Rd ML6 .... 84 D3
Scapa St G23 .... 96 F8
Scapa Way G33 .... 99 E6
Scapesland Terr G82 ...... 50 A4
Scaraway Dr G22 .... 97 D8
Scaraway Pl G22 .... 97 D8
Scaraway St G22 .... 97 D8
Scaraway Terr G22 .... 97 D8
Scarba Dr G43 .... 136 B6
Scarba Quadrant 5 ML2 164 E1
Scarffe Ave PA3 .... 111 F5
Scargie Rd KA1 .... 227 E4
Scarhill Ave ML6 .... 122 F5
Scarhill La ML6 .... 123 A5
Scarhill St
Cleland ML1 .... 144 B2
Coatbridge ML5 .... 121 F3
Scarletmuir ML11 .... 214 F5
Scarlow St PA14 .... 47 C2
Scarrel Dr G45 .... 138 A4
Scarrel Gdns G45 .... 138 A3
Scarrel Rd G45 .... 138 A3
Scarrel Terr G45 .... 138 A4
Scaur O' Doon Rd KA7 .. 238 C3
Scavaig Cres G15 .... 74 E4
Schaw Ct
Alloa FK10 .... 5 D1
Bearsden G61 .... 75 E6
Schaw Dr
Bearsden G61 .... 75 E6
Clydebank G81 .... 74 E7
Schawpark Ave FK10 ...... 5 D1
Schaw Rd PA3 .... 114 A6
Schiltron Way FK7 .... 7 D3
Scholar's Gate G75 ...... 180 D6
School Ave G72 .... 139 B5
School Ho PA11 .... 89 E3
Schoolhouse La G72 .... 161 C6
School La
Bothwell G71 .... 141 B1
Cambuslang G72 .... 139 E4
Carluke ML8 .... 187 E2
Dumbarton G82 .... 49 D4
Irvine KA12 .... 219 C1
Lennoxtown G66 .... 57 D8
Menstrie FK11 .... 4 A7
Milton of Campsie G66 .... 58 C6
Shotts ML7 .... 167 B8
School Mews FK11 .... 4 A7
School Pl KA22 .... 205 C2
School Quadrant ML6 .... 102 F2
School Rd
Gartocharn G83 .... 20 F7
Kilbirnie KA25 .... 149 A2
Newton Mearns G77 ..... 156 D4
Paisley PA1 .... 114 E5
Rhu G84 .... 15 D5
Salsburgh ML7 .... 125 D3
Stepps G33 .... 99 E6
Torrance G64 .... 57 C1
Tullibody FK10 .... 4 B2
Wishaw ML2 .... 166 A4
Wishaw, Morningside ML2 . 166 B4
School St
Chapelhall ML6 .... 123 D2
Coatbridge ML5 .... 122 A4
Hamilton ML3 .... 162 D1
Shotts ML7 .... 146 F4
School View ML1 .... 163 E5
Schoolwell St KA20 ...... 206 D1
School Wlk FK5 .... 23 D3
School Wynd
Dundonald KA2 .... 225 F2
Kilbirnie KA25 .... 149 A2
Paisley PA1 .... 113 E5
Quarriers Village PA11 .... 89 E3
Scioncroft Ave G73 ..... 138 C7
Sclandersburn Rd FK6 .... 39 C8
Scone Pl
East Kilbride G74 .... 159 D3
Newton Mearns G77 ..... 157 B4
Scone St G21 .... 97 C3
Scone Wlk 3 G69 .... 120 A3
Sconser PA4 .... 93 C7
Sconser St G23 .... 76 E1
Scorton Gdns G69 .... 119 F4
Scotia Cres ML9 .... 185 A1
Scotia Gdns ML3 .... 183 C7
Scotia Pl FK2 .... 42 C5
Scotia St ML1 .... 163 C7
Scotland St G5 .... 116 F5
Scotland Street School
Mus* G5 .... 116 F5
Scotland Street W G41 .. 116 D5
Scotsblair Ave G66 .... 79 C7
Scotsburn Rd G21 .... 98 C4
SCOTSTOUN 95 B4
SCOTSTOUNHILL 95 B6
Scotstounhill Sta G13 ...... 95 B5
Scotstoun L Ctr G14 ...... 95 D4
Scotstoun Prim Sch G14 .. 95 C4
Scotstoun Rd FK7 .... 12 E7
Scotstoun St G14 .... 95 C3
Scotstoun Way ML5 ..... 122 C5
Scott Ave
Bowling G60 .... 72 D8
Johnstone PA5 .... 131 E8
Milton of Campsie G66 .... 58 C6
Scott Cres
Alloa FK10 .... 10 B5
Cumbernauld G67 .... 82 D7
Kilmarnock KA1 .... 227 E7
Scott Cres *continued*
Troon KA10 .... 229 G4
Scott Ct
Alexandria G83 .... 27 E4
Alva FK12 .... 5 B6
Helensburgh G84 .... 16 C1
Scott Dr
Bearsden G61 .... 75 C6
Cumbernauld G67 .... 82 D7
Law ML8 .... 187 A6
Scott Gdns G82 .... 48 A8
Scott Gr ML3 .... 162 D2
Scott Hill 1 G74 .... 160 A3
Scott Ho G67 .... 62 A3
Scottish Agricultural Coll
KA6 .... 237 C3
Scottish Exhibition &
Conference Ctr G3 .... 116 D7
Scottish Maritime Mus*
KA12 .... 219 A1
Scottish Sch of Herbal
Medicine G51 .... 95 E1
Scott Pl
Bellshill ML4 .... 142 B7
Johnstone PA5 .... 131 E8
Saltcoats KA21 .... 205 E1
Troon KA10 .... 229 E5
Scott Rd
Glasgow G52 .... 114 F8
Irvine KA12 .... 219 C1
Kilmarnock KA1 .... 227 E7
Scott's Pl ML6 .... 123 B8
Scott's Rd PA2 .... 114 D3
Scott St
Alexandria G83 .... 27 F4
Clydebank G81 .... 73 E4
Glasgow G69 .... 120 B4
Glasgow, Garnethill G3 .. 240 B4
Greenock PA15 .... 46 A4
Hamilton ML3 .... 162 D1
Larkhall ML9 .... 185 B2
Motherwell ML9 .... 163 E7
Stirling FK8 .... 2 A2
Scott Way PA14 .... 47 A3
Scotus Coll G61 .... 75 D4
Seabank Rd
Ayr KA7 .... 235 E1
Prestwick KA9 .... 233 B1
Seabank St KA21 .... 217 A7
Seabegs Cres FK4 .... 40 A4
Seabegs Pl FK4 .... 39 F4
Seabegs Rd FK4 .... 39 F4
Seabegs Wood Antonine
Wall* FK4 .... 39 E3
SEAFAR 61 E1
Seafar Rd G67 .... 61 F2
Seafar Rdbt G67 .... 82 E8
SEAFIELD 238 D5
Seafield Ave G61 .... 75 F7
Seafield Cottage La PA16 . 45 D8
Seafield Cres
Ayr KA7 .... 238 E5
Cumbernauld G68 .... 60 E1
Seafield Ct
Ardrossan KA22 .... 205 B3
Falkirk FK1 .... 41 F2
Seafield Dr
Ardrossan KA22 .... 205 C3
Ayr KA7 .... 238 D5
Rutherglen G73 .... 138 D3
Seafield Ho PA16 .... 45 E7
Seafield Rd KA7 .... 238 E6
Seafield Sch KA22 .... 205 B3
Seaford St KA1 .... 227 E8
Seaforth Cres
Ayr KA8 .... 236 B4
Barrhead G78 .... 134 B4
Seaforth La G69 .... 81 A2
Seaforth Pl
Bellshill ML4 .... 141 F3
Stirling FK8 .... 7 B8
5 Stirling FK8 .... 7 B8
Seaforth Rd
Ayr KA8 .... 236 B4
Clydebank G81 .... 74 B2
Falkirk FK2 .... 24 C1
Glasgow G52 .... 115 A7
Seaforth Road N G52 .... 115 A7
Seaforth Road S G52 .... 115 A7
Seagate
Irvine KA12 .... 219 B3
Prestwick KA9 .... 233 C2
Seagrove St G32 .... 118 D6
Sea Life Loch Lomond*
G83 .... 19 D1
SEAMILL 190 C2
Seamill Gdns G74 .... 159 D2
Seamill Path G53 .... 134 F5
Seamill St G53 .... 134 F5
Seamill Way ML5 .... 121 F5
Seamore St 4 G20 .... 96 F2
Seath Ave
Airdrie ML6 .... 122 E7
Langbank PA14 .... 70 D6
Seath Rd G73 .... 118 A1
Seath St G42 .... 117 C2
Seaton Pl FK1 .... 42 D4
Seaton Terr
Hamilton ML3 .... 162 A4
Irvine KA12 .... 219 C5
Sea Tower Ct KA7 .... 238 E6
Seaview Rd KA21 .... 216 F7
Seaview Terr KA10 ...... 230 A4
Seaward La
Glasgow G5 .... 240 A1
Glasgow G41, G5 .... 116 E6
Seaward Pl G41 .... 116 F5
Seaward St
Glasgow G5, G41 .... 116 F5
3 Glasgow G41 .... 116 E5
Second Ave
Alexandria G83 .... 27 F5
Auchinloch G66 .... 79 D1
Bearsden G61 .... 76 A3
Clydebank G81 .... 74 A3
Dumbarton G82 .... 50 C2
Glasgow G44 .... 137 B6
Irvine KA12 .... 224 E8
Millerston G33 .... 99 B4
Renfrew PA4 .... 94 C2
Uddingston G71 .... 120 E1
Second Avenue La G44 .. 137 B7
Second Gdns G41 .... 116 A4
Second Rd G72 .... 161 E5
Second St G71 .... 140 F8
SEEDHILL 114 A3
Seedhill PA1 .... 113 F4
Seedhill Rd PA1 .... 114 A4
Seggielea La G13 .... 95 D6
Seggielea Rd G13 .... 95 D6
Segton Ave KA13 .... 207 C3
Seil Dr G44 .... 137 C4
Selborne Pl 1 G13 .... 95 E5
Selborne Rd G13 .... 95 E5
Selby Gdns G32 .... 119 D5
Selby Pl ML5 .... 101 D2
Selby St ML5 .... 101 D2
Selkirk Ave
Glasgow G52 .... 115 C4
Paisley PA2 .... 133 A8
Selkirk Ct 9 PA15 .... 46 B3
Selkirk Dr G73 .... 138 C7
Selkirk Pl
East Kilbride G74 .... 160 D3
Hamilton ML3 .... 162 E2
Selkirk Rd PA14 .... 68 D8
Selkirk St
Hamilton, Blantyre G72 .. 161 D7
Hamilton, Silvertonhill ML3 162 E2
Wishaw ML2 .... 165 C5
Selkirk Way
Bellshill ML4 .... 142 B7
Coatbridge ML5 .... 122 E3
Sella Rd G64 .... 78 D2
Selvieland Farm Cotts
PA3 .... 92 D3
Selvieland Rd G52 ...... 114 F5
Semphill Gdns G74 ..... 160 B2
Sempie St ML3 .... 161 F4
Semple Ave PA8 .... 72 F2
Semple Ave
Bishopton PA7 .... 72 B3
Lochwinnoch PA12 .... 129 C3
Semple Pl PA3 .... 112 B7
Semple Rd KA9 .... 236 D5
Semple View PA9 .... 130 F5
Senate Pl ML1 .... 142 C1
Senga Cres ML4 .... 142 A7
Seres Rd G76 .... 157 D8
Sergeant Law Rd
Paisley G78, PA2 .... 132 E3
Uplawmoor G78 .... 153 B7
Seright Cres KA3 .... 228 D7
Seright Sq KA3 .... 228 D8
Serpentine Wlk PA15 ..... 46 C3
Sersley Dr KA25 .... 148 F1
Service St G66 .... 33 C1
Seton Dr FK7 .... 7 C4
Seton La KA22 .... 205 C2
Seton St KA22 .... 205 C2
Seton Terr 3 G31 .... 117 F7
Settle Gdns G69 .... 119 F4
Seven Sisters G66 .... 79 E5
Seventh Ave G71 .... 140 F8
Seventh Rd G72 .... 161 E5
Severn Rd G75 .... 179 F7
Seymour Ave KA13 ...... 207 F2
Seymour Gn G75 .... 180 B7
Seyton Ave G46 .... 136 C1
Seyton Ct G46 .... 136 C1
Seyton La G74 .... 159 E3
Shaftesbury Ct G74 ..... 160 C5
Shaftesbury St
Alloa FK10 .... 10 A7
Clydebank G81 .... 73 F2
Glasgow G3 .... 240 A3
Shafton Pl G13 .... 95 E8
Shafton Rd G13 .... 95 E8
Shaftsbury Ave G81 ...... 73 F2
Shaftsbury Cres ML1 ... 143 D3
Shakespeare Ave G81 .... 73 F4
Shakespeare St G20 ...... 96 E5
Shalloch Pk KA7 .... 238 C2
Shalloch Pl KA11 .... 220 B2
Shamrock St
Glasgow G4 .... 240 B4
Kirkintilloch G66 .... 79 D8
Shand La ML8 .... 187 F3
Shandon Brae G83 .... 27 F8
Shandon Cres
Balloch G83 .... 27 F8
Bellshill ML4 .... 142 A8
Shandon Pl PA15 .... 46 C2
Shandon Terr ML3 .... 161 F3
Shand St ML2 .... 165 B3
Shandwick Square Sh Ctr
G34 .... 120 A8
Shandwick St G34 .... 120 A8
Shankland Gr PA15 .... 46 F2
Shankland Rd PA15 .... 46 F2
Shankly Dr ML2 .... 166 C3
Shanks Ave
Barrhead G78 .... 134 C2
Denny FK6 .... 39 E8
Shanks Cres PA5 .... 111 E2
Shanks Ct KA3 .... 222 F2
Shanks Ind Pk G78 ...... 134 C4
Shanks St
Airdrie ML6 .... 103 A1
Glasgow G20 .... 96 E5
Shanks Way G78 .... 134 C5
Shannon Dr FK1 .... 41 F4
Shannon St G20 .... 96 F5
Shanter Pl
Alloway KA7 .... 238 E1
Kilmarnock KA3 .... 228 C8
Shanter Way KA7 .... 238 E1
Shanter Wynd KA7 ...... 238 E1
Shantron Rd G83 .... 27 E6
Shapinsay St G22 .... 97 D8
Sharlee Wynd KA23 ..... 190 D6
**Sharnothshield Small
Holdings** ML2 .... 166 E6
Sharon St KA24 .... 191 B8
Sharp Ave ML5 .... 121 C4
Sharpe Ave KA11 .... 220 D1
Sharphill Ind Est KA21 .. 206 A3
Sharphill Rd KA21 ...... 216 F8
Sharp St
Gourock PA19 .... 44 F7
Motherwell ML1 .... 163 B7
Shavian Terr KA13 ...... 207 E2
Shavin Brae KA7 .... 239 D6
Shaw Ave PA7 .... 72 C3
Shawbank Pl KA1 .... 228 A7
Shawbridge Arc G43 .... 136 C8
Shawbridge Ind Est G43 . 136 B7
Shawbridge St G43 ..... 136 C7
Shawburn Cres ML3 ..... 162 B4
Shawburn St ML3 .... 162 B4
Shaw Cres ML2 .... 164 D1
Shaw Ct
Erskine PA8 .... 72 F3
Newton Mearns G77 ..... 156 F4
Shawfarm Ct KA9 .... 233 D1
Shawfarm Gdns KA9 .... 233 D2
Shaw Farm Ind Est KA9 .. 233 F1
Shawfarm Pl KA9 .... 233 D1
Shawfarm Rd KA9 .... 233 E1
SHAWFIELD 117 F2
Shawfield Ave KA7 ..... 239 A4
Shawfield Cres ML8 ..... 186 F6
Shawfield Dr G73 .... 117 F2
Shawfield Ind Est G73 ... 117 F2
Shawfield Rd G73 .... 117 F2
Shawfoot Rd ML1 .... 122 F1
Shawgill Ct ML8 .... 186 F4
SHAWHEAD 122 A3
Shawhead Ave ML5 ..... 122 B4
Shawhead Cotts ML5 .... 122 B3
Shawhead Prim Sch
ML5 .... 122 B3
Shawhill Cres G77 ...... 156 E3
Shawhill Rd G43 .... 136 D8
Shawholm Cres G43 ..... 136 C7
Shawholm Gdns KA12 ... 219 C3
SHAWLANDS 136 E8
Shawlands Acad G41 ..... 116 E1
Shawlands Arcade Sh Ctr
G41 .... 136 D8
Shawlands Cres ML9 .... 199 D6
Shawlands Cross 5 G41 . 116 E1
Shawlands Prim Sch
G41 .... 136 D8
Shawlands Sta G41 ...... 136 D8
Shawmoss Rd G41 ...... 116 D1
Shawpark St G20 .... 96 E6
Shaw Pl
Dalry KA24 .... 191 B7
Greenock PA15 .... 45 F5
Linwood PA3 .... 112 B5
Saltcoats KA21 .... 206 A2
Shaw Rd
Milngavie G62 .... 76 A8
Newton Mearns G77 ..... 156 E4
Prestwick KA9 .... 233 D1
Prestwick KA9 .... 233 E1
Shawrigg Rd ML9 .... 185 C2
SHAWSBURN 185 E2
Shawsgate ML9 .... 185 E1
Shaws Rd ML9 .... 199 C8
Shaw St
Glasgow G51 .... 116 A8
Larkhall ML9 .... 199 B8
SHAWSTONEFOOT 144 F1
Shawstonfoot Rd ML1 ... 145 A1
Shawwood Cres G77 .... 156 E3
Shearer Dr ML3 .... 183 C7
Shearer Quadrant G83 .... 28 A8
SHEDDENS 157 F7
Sheena Dr G83 .... 27 F2
Sheepburn Rd G71 ...... 140 E7
Sheila St G33 .... 98 E4
Sheildhill 3 G75 .... 180 F7
Sheiling Hill ML3 .... 162 E4
Sheilings The FK10 .... 4 B1
Sheldrake Pl PA5 .... 131 D6
Shellbridge Way KA22 .. 205 C2
Shelley Ct G12 .... 96 A5
Shelley Dr
Bothwell G71 .... 141 B2
Clydebank G81 .... 74 A4
Shelley Rd G12 .... 96 A5
Shells Rd G66 .... 58 E1
Shepford Pl ML5 .... 121 D7
Sherbrooke Ave G41 .... 116 C3
Sherbrooke Dr G41 ..... 116 C4
Sherbrooke Gdns G41 ... 116 C3
Sherbrooke Pl G75 ...... 159 C1
Sherburn Gdns G69 ..... 119 F3

Sherdale Ave ML6 . . . . . . 123 D2
Sheriffmuirlands FK9 . . . . . . 2 C3
Sheriffmuir Rd FK9 . . . . 2 D7
Sheriff Park Ave G73. . . . 138 A7
Sherriff La FK5 . . . . 23 F3
Sherry Ave ML1. . . . . 143 A5
Sherry Dr ML3. . . . . 162 A1
Sherry Hts G72 . . . . 139 A6
Sherwood Ave
Paisley PA1 . . . . 114 A5
Uddingston G71. . . . . 141 A5
Sherwood Dr G46. . . . . . . 136 A3
Sherwood Pl G15 . . . . 75 B4
Sherwood Rd
Glenboig ML5. . . . . 101 F6
Hurlford KA1 . . . . 228 F6
Prestwick KA9 . . . . 236 E8
Shetland Ct FK10 . . . . 10 B5
Shetland Dr
Glasgow G44 . . . . 137 C4
Kilmarnock KA3 . . . . 223 A6
Shettleston Rd G32 . . . . . . 119 B5
Shettleston Sheddings
G32 . . . . 118 E5
Shettleston Sta G32. . . . . . 119 B5
SHEWALTON 224 H6
Shewalton Dr KA11 . . . . . 225 D6
Shewalton Moss KA11. . . 225 D6
Shewalton Rd
Drybridge KA11 . . . . 225 B6
Irvine KA11 . . . . 224 F6
Shewalton Rdbt KA11 . . . 225 A6
Shewalton Sandpits Nature
Reserve* KA11. . . . . 224 F7
Shewalton Sand Quarry
KA11. . . . . 224 G7
Shiel Ave G74 . . . . 159 F3
Shielbridge Gdns G23. . . . . 76 E1
Shiel Ct G78. . . . . 134 B5
Shieldaig Dr G73 . . . . 138 B4
Shieldaig Rd G22 . . . . 97 B8
Shieldburn Rd G51. . . . . . . 115 D7
SHIELDHALL 115 D8
Shieldhall Gdns G51 . . . . 115 C7
Shieldhall Rd
Glasgow, Shieldhall G51 . . 115 C7
Glasgow, West Drumoyne
G51. . . . . 115 E6
SHIELDHILL. 66 D6
Shieldhill Prim Sch FK1. . . 66 D6
Shieldhill Rd
Carluke ML8. . . . . 201 E8
Shieldhill FK2. . . . . 66 F7
Shieldmuir St ML2. . . . . . 164 C4
Shieldmuir Sta ML2. . . . . . 164 C3
Shiel Dr ML9 . . . . 184 F5
Shields Ct ML1 . . . . 164 B3
Shields Dr ML1 . . . . 164 B3
Shields Holdings PA12 . . . 130 B6
Shields Loan ML11. . . . . . . 214 F5
Shields Rd
East Kilbride G75. . . . . 180 B3
Glasgow G41 . . . . 116 E2
Glasgow G41 . . . . 116 F3
Glasgow G41 . . . . 116 F4
Motherwell ML1. . . . . 164 B3
Shields Road Underground
Sta G5. . . . . 116 F5
Shields Twr ML1 . . . . 164 B3
Shiel Gdns
Falkirk FK2. . . . . 24 C1
Shotts ML7. . . . . 147 A3
Shiel Hill KA7 . . . . 239 B2
Shielhope Ct KA11 . . . . . . 220 A4
Shieling Pk KA7 . . . . 238 E7
Shiel Pl
Coatbridge ML5 . . . . 122 D5
East Kilbride G74. . . . . 159 F3
Irvine KA12 . . . . 219 C6
Shiel Rd G64 . . . . 78 B1
Shiel Terr ML2 . . . . 165 F6
Shierlaw Gdns FK2. . . . . 14 D4
Shilford Ave G13. . . . . 95 A7
Shilford Rd G78 . . . . 132 C1
Shillay St G22 . . . . 97 E8
SHILLFORD 153 D5
Shilliaw Dr KA9. . . . . 236 D5
Shilliaw Pl KA9 . . . . 236 D5
Shillinghill FK10 . . . . 10 B6
Shillingworth Pl PA11 . . . 110 D6
Shilton Dr G53 . . . . 135 C5
Shilton La PA7. . . . . 72 E4
Shinwell Ave G81. . . . . 74 D1
Shipbank La G1 . . . . 241 A1
Shiphaugh Pl FK8. . . . . 2 C1
Shira Terr G74 . . . . 160 B1
Shire Way FK10. . . . . 9 F6
Shirley Quadrant ML1. . . . 163 D4
Shirley's Cl 10 ML11 . . . . 215 A4
Shirra's Brae Rd FK7. . . . . . . 7 B4
SHIRREL. 142 B7
Shirrel Ave ML4. . . . . 142 A7
Shirrel Rd ML1 . . . . 143 B4
Shirva Lea G65 . . . . 59 F4
Shiskine Dr
Glasgow G20. . . . . 96 C8
Kilmarnock KA3. . . . . 222 E4
Shiskine Pl
Glasgow G20. . . . . 96 C8
Helensburgh G84. . . . . 16 F2
Shiskine St G20 . . . . 96 C7
Sholto Cres ML4. . . . . 141 D7
SHORE 7 C8
Shore Rd
Airth FK2 . . . . 14 D4
Shore Rd *continued*
Ayr KA8 . . . . 235 F3
Stevenston KA20. . . . . 217 D7
Stirling FK8 . . . . 7 C8
Troon KA10 . . . . 229 C2
Shore St
Glasgow G40. . . . . 118 A2
Gourock PA19 . . . . 44 E8
Port Glasgow PA14 . . . . 47 B2
Shore The FK10. . . . . 10 A5
SHORTLEES. 227 E3
Shortlees Cres KA1 . . . . . . 227 F3
Shortlees Prim Sch KA1. . 227 F3
Shortlees Rd KA1 . . . . 227 F2
Shortridge St G20 . . . . 96 E5
SHORTROODS. 113 D7
Shortroods Ave PA3. . . . . 113 E7
Shortroods Cres PA3. . . . 113 D7
Shortroods Rd PA3. . . . . . 113 D7
SHOTTS 146 F5
Shottsburn Rd ML7 . . . . . 126 A3
Shottskirk Rd ML7 . . . . . . 146 C6
Shotts L Ctr ML7. . . . . 146 F4
Shotts Rd ML7. . . . . 126 E2
Shotts St G33. . . . . 119 D8
Shotts Sta ML7 . . . . 146 E4
Shuna Cres G20 . . . . 96 F5
Shuna Gdns G20. . . . . 96 F5
Shuna Pl
Glasgow G20. . . . . 96 E5
Newton Mearns G77 . . . . . 156 B6
Shuna St G20. . . . . 96 E5
Shuttle St
Glasgow G1. . . . . 241 B2
Kilbarchan PA10. . . . . 111 A3
Kilsyth G65 . . . . 60 D8
Paisley PA1 . . . . 113 E4
Sidehead Rd
Harthill ML7. . . . . 127 E5
Stonehouse ML9 . . . . 198 E1
Sidland Rd G21. . . . . 98 C5
Sidlaw Ave
Barrhead G78 . . . . 134 C1
Hamilton ML3 . . . . 161 F2
Port Glasgow PA14 . . . . 68 F6
Sidlaw Ct ML5. . . . . 122 C3
Sidlaw Dr ML2. . . . . 164 F3
Sidlaw Foot KA11. . . . . . . 220 C2
Sidlaw Pl KA1 . . . . 228 A3
Sidlaw Rd G61. . . . . 75 B7
Sidlaw Way
Chapelhall ML6 . . . . 123 F1
Larkhall ML9 . . . . 184 F5
Sidney St KA21 . . . . 216 E7
Sielga Pl G34. . . . . 120 A8
Siemens Pl G21. . . . . 98 B1
Siemens St G21 . . . . 98 B1
Sievewright St G73 . . . . . 118 C1
SIGHTHILL 97 D2
Sighthill Loan 5 ML9. . . . 185 B4
Sighthill Prim Sch G21. . . . 97 D3
Sighthill Terr ML7. . . . . . . 125 B2
SIKESIDE 122 E5
Sikeside Pl ML5 . . . . 122 D5
Sikeside Prim Sch ML5. . 122 D5
Sikeside St ML5 . . . . 122 D5
Silk Ho FK1. . . . . 42 B5
Silkin Ave G81. . . . . 74 D1
Silk St PA1 . . . . 113 F5
Sillars Mdw KA12. . . . . . . 219 E2
Silvan Pl G76. . . . . 158 A5
SILVERBANK 138 E6
Silverbanks Ct 3 G72. . . . 138 E6
Silverbanks Gait 2 G72. . 138 E6
Silverbanks Rd 1 G72. . . 138 E6
Silver Birch Dr 4 G51 . . 115 D7
Silverbirch Gdns ML3 . . . . 183 F3
Silver Birch Gdns 5
G51 . . . . 115 D7
Silverbirch Gr ML3. . . . . . . 183 F3
Silverburn Cres ML1 . . . . 143 D3
Silverburn Gdns FK12 . . . . . . 5 C7
Silverburn Sh Ctr G53. . . 135 C7
Silverburn St G33. . . . . . . 118 E8
Silverdale G74. . . . . 159 C3
Silverdale Cres ML11. . . . . 214 F4
Silverdale Ct ML11. . . . . . . 214 F4
Silverdale St G31. . . . . . . 118 C4
Silverdale Terr ML6 . . . . . 103 F3
Silver Firs ML1 . . . . 143 C3
Silverfir St G5. . . . . 117 D3
Silver Glade G52. . . . . 115 B4
Silvergrove St G40. . . . . . . 117 E5
Silvermuir Ave ML11 . . . . . 215 F7
SILVERTON. 50 A4
Silverton Ave G82. . . . . 50 B3
SILVERTONHILL 162 E2
Silvertonhill Ave ML3 . . . . 162 E1
Silvertonhill La G82. . . . . . . 50 B3
Silvertonhill Pl ML3. . . . . . 183 D7
Silverwells G71. . . . . 141 B1
Silverwells Cres G71. . . . . 141 A1
Silverwood Ct G71. . . . . . . 141 B1
Silverwood Prim Sch
KA3 . . . . 223 C3
Silverwood Rd KA3 . . . . . 228 D8
Simonsburn Rd KA1 . . . . . 227 E3
Simons Cres
Kilmarnock KA1. . . . . 227 E4
Renfrew PA4 . . . . 94 D5
Simpson Ct
Clydebank G81. . . . . 74 A2
Troon KA10 . . . . 229 G3
Uddingston G71. . . . . 140 F6
Simpson Dr
East Kilbride G75. . . . . 180 D7
Saltcoats KA21 . . . . 205 F3
Simpson Gdns G78. . . . . . . 134 B2
Simpson Hts G4 . . . . 241 C2
Simpson Pl
East Kilbride G75. . . . . 180 D7
Kilwinning KA13. . . . . 207 F1
Simpson Quadrant G83 . . . 28 A8
Simpson St
Crosshouse KA2 . . . . 222 A1
Falkirk FK1. . . . . 41 E6
Glasgow G20 . . . . 96 F3
Simpson Way ML4 . . . . . . 142 C7
Simshill Rd G44 . . . . 137 C4
Simson Ave KA23 . . . . 190 E4
Sim St KA3 . . . . 211 C8
Sinclair Ave G61. . . . . 75 E6
Sinclair Cres FK6 . . . . 21 D1
Sinclair Ct
Bannockburn FK7. . . . . 7 E1
Kilmarnock KA3. . . . . 223 C3
Sinclair Dr
Coatbridge ML5. . . . . 121 D7
Fallin FK7. . . . . 8 D4
Glasgow G42 . . . . 136 F7
Helensburgh G84. . . . . 16 E3
Sinclair Gdns G64 . . . . 98 B8
Sinclair Gr ML4. . . . . 141 F2
Sinclair La G84 . . . . 16 E4
Sinclair Pk 3 G75 . . . . . . 180 F8
Sinclair Pl
East Kilbride G75. . . . . 180 F8
Falkirk FK2. . . . . 24 A1
Sinclair St
Clydebank G81. . . . . 94 D8
Greenock PA15 . . . . 46 D3
Helensburgh G84. . . . . 16 D2
Milngavie G62 . . . . 55 A2
Stevenston KA20. . . . . 206 C1
Singer Rd
Clydebank G81. . . . . 73 F3
East Kilbride G75. . . . . 180 F6
Singers Pl FK4. . . . . 39 E5
Singer St G81 . . . . 74 B3
Singer Sta G81 . . . . 74 B2
Sir James Clark Bldg
PA1. . . . . 113 F4
Sir John Graham Ct FK5 . . 23 B1
Sir John Maxwell Prim Sch
G43 . . . . 136 C7
Sir Matt Busby Sports
Complex ML4 . . . . 141 F5
Sir Michael Ct 13 PA15. . . . 45 F5
Sir Michael Pl
Greenock PA15 . . . . 45 F5
Paisley PA1 . . . . 113 D4
Sir Michael St PA15. . . . . . . 45 F5
Sir Thomas Lipton Way 5
G72 . . . . 138 F6
Sir William Wallace Ct
FK5. 23 B3
Siskin Way
Coatbridge ML5. . . . . 122 D3
Cumbernauld G68 . . . . 81 F8
Sixth Ave PA4. . . . . 94 C1
Sixth St G71. . . . . 120 E1
Skaethorn Rd G20 . . . . 96 B7
Skaithmuir Ave FK2. . . . . . . 24 B3
Skaithmuir Cres FK2. . . . . . 24 B3
Skara Wlk ML2 . . . . 165 F7
Skaterigg Dr G13 . . . . 95 F5
Skaterigg Gdns G13 . . . . . . 95 F5
Skaterigg La G13 . . . . 95 E5
Skelbo Path G34. . . . . 100 D1
Skelbo Pl G34 . . . . 100 D1
Skellyton Cres ML9 . . . . . 185 B2
Skelmorlie Pl
Kilwinning KA13. . . . . 207 D3
Stenhousemuir FK5 . . . . 23 F4
Skene Rd
Glasgow G51. . . . . 116 B5
Kilmarnock KA3. . . . . 223 C3
Skene St FK4 . . . . 40 A6
Skerne Gr G75. . . . . 179 F6
Skernieland Rd KA3. . . . . 213 A4
Skerray Quadrant G22 . . . . 97 C8
Skerray St G22 . . . . 97 C8
Skerryvore Pl G33 . . . . . . 119 B8
Skerryvore Rd G33. . . . . . 119 B8
Skibo La G46. . . . . 135 E3
Skibo Pl G69 . . . . 100 E4
Skimmers Hill G66. . . . . 58 B4
SKINFLATS. 24 F3
Skipness Ave ML8. . . . . . . 202 A8
Skipness Dr G51. . . . . 115 E8
Skirsa Ct G23. . . . . 97 A8
Skirsa Pl G23. . . . . 96 F7
Skirsa Sq G23 . . . . 97 A7
Skirsa St G23. . . . . 96 F8
Skirving St G41. . . . . 136 E8
Skovlunde Way G75. . . . . 180 E6
Skye G74. . . . . 160 C1
Skye Ave PA4. . . . . 94 C1
Skye Cres
Gourock PA19 . . . . 44 D6
Old Kilpatrick G60 . . . . 73 C5
Paisley PA2 . . . . 133 D8
Skye Ct
Cumbernauld G67 . . . . 82 D8
Irvine KA11 . . . . 225 C8
Skye Dr
Cumbernauld G67 . . . . 82 D8
Old Kilpatrick G60 . . . . 73 C5
Skye Gdns
Bearsden G61 . . . . 75 B6
Kilmarnock KA3. . . . . 223 A6
Skye Pl
Airdrie ML6 . . . . 123 D6
Cumbernauld G67 . . . . 82 D8
Stevenston KA20. . . . . 206 F2
Skye Quadrant ML2. . . . . . 165 E5
Skye Rd
Cumbernauld G67 . . . . 82 D8
Port Glasgow PA14 . . . . 69 B6
Prestwick KA9 . . . . 233 E1
Rutherglen G73 . . . . 138 D3
Skye St PA16 . . . . 45 C4
Skye Wynd ML3. . . . . 161 F1
Skylands Gr ML3. . . . . 183 A8
Skylands Pl ML3. . . . . 183 A7
Skylands Rise ML3. . . . . . 183 A8
Skythorn Way FK1 . . . . 41 E2
SLAEMUIR 69 A6
Slaemuir Ave PA14. . . . . 68 F6
Slaemuir Gdns PA14 . . . . . . 68 F6
Slakiewood Ave G69 . . . . . 100 E7
SLAMANNAN. 86 A6
Slamannan Prim Sch FK1 . 86 A7
Slamannan Rd
Avonbridge FK1 . . . . 87 F6
Falkirk FK1. . . . . 42 A2
Slamannan FK1 . . . . 86 B2
Slatefield G66 . . . . 57 D8
Slatefield Ct G31 . . . . 118 A6
Slatefield St G31 . . . . 118 A6
Slate Mill Gdns KA12. . . . . 219 E2
Sleaford Ave ML1 . . . . 163 D4
Slenavon Ave G73 . . . . . . 138 D3
Slessor Dr G75 . . . . 180 F7
Slioch Sq ML1. . . . . 143 C4
Sloan Ave KA12. . . . . 219 D2
Sloan Pl
Ayr KA8 . . . . 236 D2
Irvine KA12 . . . . 219 D2
Sloan St KA8 . . . . 236 D2
Sloy St
Glasgow G22. . . . . 97 D4
Wishaw ML2 . . . . 165 A1
Small Cres G72. . . . . 161 D7
Smart Village Bsns Campus
FK10. 9 E7
Smeaton Ave G64. . . . . 78 B8
Smeaton Ct KA10 . . . . 229 G4
Smeaton Dr G64. . . . . 78 A4
Smeaton Gr G20. . . . . 96 F6
Smeaton St G20 . . . . 96 F6
Smiddy Ct
Kilmarnock KA1. . . . . 227 F6
Kilwinning KA13. . . . . 207 E3
Lanark ML11 . . . . 215 A4
Smiddy View FK7 . . . . 6 D6
Smiddy Wynd FK12 . . . . 5 A6
Smillie Pl KA2. . . . . 227 C6
Smillie St PA15 . . . . 46 E2
Smillie Terr 2 FK9. . . . . 2 B3
Smith Art Gallery & Mus*
FK8. . . . . 7 A8
Smith Ave
Glengarnock KA14. . . . . . . 170 D6
Irvine KA12 . . . . 219 D4
Wishaw ML2 . . . . 186 A8
Smith Cl G64 . . . . 98 D8
Smith Cres
Balloch G83 . . . . 27 F8
Clydebank G81. . . . . 74 B5
Kilwinning KA13. . . . . 207 F2
Smith Dr KA21. . . . . 217 A8
Smithfield Loan FK10 . . . . . 9 E6
Smithfield Mdws FK10 . . . . . 9 E6
Smith Gdns G64 . . . . 98 D8
Smith Gr G64. . . . . 98 D8
Smithhills St PA1 . . . . 113 E5
Smith Pl FK6 . . . . 21 D1
Smith Quadrant ML5. . . . . 122 C7
Smith's La PA3 . . . . 113 E6
Smith St
Ayr KA7 . . . . 239 A8
Dalry KA24. . . . . 191 C7
Falkirk FK2. . . . . 42 B7
Glasgow G14. . . . . 95 E2
Greenock PA15 . . . . 45 F5
Prestwick KA9 . . . . 236 C8
SMITHSTON. 45 A4
Smithston Cotts PA16 . . . . . 45 B3
Smithstone Cres G65 . . . . . 60 F5
Smithstone Ct KA11. . . . . . 219 F5
Smithstone Rd G68 . . . . 60 F2
Smithstone Terr KA13 . . . . 207 B8
Smithstone Way KA11. . . . 219 F6
Smith Terr G73 . . . . 118 B1
Smithview ML2 . . . . 186 C7
Smith Way G64 . . . . 98 D8
Smithy Brae PA13. . . . . 89 D8
Smithycroft ML3. . . . . 163 A3
Smithycroft Rd G33 . . . . . . 98 E1
Smithycroft Sec Sch G33. . 98 E1
Smithy Ct G82. . . . . 48 A8
Smithyends G67 . . . . 62 B5
Smithy Rd G82 . . . . 48 A8
Smollett Rd G82 . . . . 50 B3
Smollett St G83. . . . . 27 D5
Smugglers Brig Rd ML8. . 201 B2
Smuggler's Way G84. . . . . . 15 D6
Smyllum Ho ML11 . . . . . . 215 C4
Smyllum Pk ML11. . . . . . . 215 C4
Smyllum Rd ML11. . . . . . . 215 C4
Snaefell Ave G73 . . . . 138 C4
Snaefell Cres G73. . . . . . . 138 C5
Snead View ML1 . . . . 143 E1
Sneddon Ave ML2. . . . . . . 165 C1
Sneddon Pl FK2 . . . . 14 D3
Sneddon St ML3. . . . . 162 A6
Sneddon Terr ML3 . . . . . . 161 F6
Snowden Sch FK8 . . . . 7 A7
Snowdon Pl
2 Glasgow G5 . . . . 117 D4
Stirling FK8 . . . . 7 A6
Snowdon Place La FK7. . . . . 7 A6
Snowdon St 3 G5. . . . . . 117 D4
Snowdon Terr KA23 . . . . . 190 B5
Snowdrop Sq KA7 . . . . 239 B3
Snuff Mill Rd G44. . . . . . . 137 A5
Society St G31. . . . . 118 B5
Solar Ct ML9 . . . . 199 B8
Sollas Pl G13 . . . . 94 E8
Solomon's View KA3 . . . . 195 C7
Solsgirth Gdns G66 . . . . 59 B1
Solvents Rd KA20. . . . . 218 B5
Solway Ct ML3. . . . . 183 B8
Solway Dr FK6. . . . . 39 D7
Solway Pl
Chryston G69. . . . . 80 D1
Kilmarnock KA1. . . . . 228 B4
Troon KA10 . . . . 229 F5
Solway Rd G64 . . . . 78 D2
Solway St G73. . . . . 117 F2
Somerford Rd G61. . . . . 75 F1
Somerled Ave PA3 . . . . 94 A1
Somerset Ave ML3 . . . . 162 B4
Somerset Pl G3 . . . . 240 A4
Somerset Place Meuse
G3 . . . . 240 A4
Somerset Rd KA8. . . . . 236 B2
Somervell St G72. . . . . 138 F6
Somerville Ct KA15 . . . . . . 150 B1
Somerville Dr
East Kilbride G75. . . . . 180 F7
Glasgow G42. . . . . 137 B8
Somerville La 2 G75 . . . . 180 F7
Somerville Pk KA11. . . . . . . 220 B7
Somerville Pl G84 . . . . 25 B8
Somerville Terr 1 G75. . . 180 F7
Somerville Way KA11 . . . . . 220 B7
Sommerville Dr KA20 . . . . 217 E6
Sophia Cres KA12. . . . . 219 B6
Sorbie Dr ML9. . . . . 198 E1
Sorbie Rd
Ardrossan KA21, KA22 . . . . 205 E3
Ardrossan, South Beach
KA22. . . . . 205 D1
Sorby St G31 . . . . 118 D5
Sorley St G11. . . . . 95 F2
Sorn St G40 . . . . 118 B3
Sorrel Dr KA7 . . . . 239 C3
Souillac Dr FK6. . . . . 21 C1
Soulis St KA3. . . . . 223 A1
Sourlie Rdbt KA11 . . . . . . 220 A7
Sourlie Terr KA11 . . . . 219 F5
Souter Dr KA3 . . . . 228 C8
Souterhouse Path ML5. . . 121 F5
Souterhouse Rd ML5. . . . . 121 F5
Souter Pl KA7 . . . . 239 B5
Souter Way FK5 . . . . 23 C4
SOUTH ALLOA. 9 F3
Southampton Dr G12 . . . . . 96 B6
South Annandale St G42 . 117 B2
South Approach Rd FK2. . . 24 F8
South Ave
Carluke ML8. . . . . 187 E2
Clydebank G81. . . . . 74 A2
Hamilton G72. . . . . 161 E5
Paisley PA2 . . . . 133 F8
Renfrew PA4 . . . . 94 D3
Southbank Bsns Pk G66. . . 79 C7
Southbank Dr G66. . . . . 79 C7
Southbank Rd G66. . . . . 79 C8
Southbank St G31 . . . . . . 118 D5
South Bank St G81. . . . . 94 C7
South Bantaskine Dr FK1. . 42 A3
South Bantaskine Rd FK1 . 42 A3
Southbar Ave G13 . . . . 95 A7
Southbar Rd PA8 . . . . 93 A7
SOUTH BARRWOOD 60 F7
South Barrwood Rd G65 . . 60 E7
South Beach KA10 . . . . . . 229 D2
South Beach Espl KA10 . 229 D2
South Beach La KA10 . . . . 229 E1
South Beach Rd
Ardrossan KA22. . . . . 205 D1
Ayr KA7 . . . . 235 E1
South Beach Way KA22 . 205 D1
South Biggar Rd ML6 . . . . 123 B7
South Brae G66. . . . . 57 C7
Southbrae Ave PA11 . . . . . 110 B7
Southbrae Dr G13 . . . . 95 D4
Southbrae La 3 G13. . . . . . 95 E5
South Bridge St ML6. . . . 123 A8
SOUTH BROOMAGE. 23 D1
South Broomage Ave FK5 . 23 C1
Southburn Rd G63 . . . . 31 C3
South Burn Rd ML6 . . . . . 122 D7
South Caldeen Rd ML5. . . 122 B5
South Calder ML1. . . . . 163 F8
South Campbell St PA2 . . 113 E3
South Carbrain Rd G67 . . . 62 B1
SOUTH CARDONALD. . . . 115 C4
South Cathkin Cotts
G73 . . . . 159 C8
South Chester St G32. . . 119 A5
South Church Pl G83 . . . . . 27 F3
South Circular Rd ML5. . 122 A6
South Claremont La G62 . . 55 A1
South Commonhead Ave
ML6 . . . . 103 A1
Southcraig Ave KA3. . . . . . 223 C7
Southcraig Dr KA3. . . . . . . 223 B6
Southcraig Holdings
KA3 . . . . 223 C5
South Crescent Rd KA22 205 D1
Southcroft FK12 . . . . 4 F6
Southcroft Rd G73. . . . . 117 F1
Southcroft St G51 . . . . 116 B7
South Crosshill Rd G64 . . . 78 A1
South Dean Park Ave
G71 . . . . 141 A2
South Dean Rd KA3. . . . . . 223 B2
Southdeen Ave G15. . . . . . . 75 B3

Southdeen Gr [5] G15 75 B3
Southdeen Rd G15 75 A3
South Douglas St G81 94 C8
South Dr
- Kilbirnie KA25 169 F8
- Linwood PA3 112 B6
- Troon KA10 229 G3
South Dumbreck Rd G65 60 B8
South Elgin Pl G81 94 C7
South Elgin St G81 94 C7
Southend Pl ML4 141 F4
Southend Rd G81 74 B5
Southern Ave G73 138 B5
Southerness Dr G68 62 A5
Southern General Hospl G51 115 D8
South Erskine Pk G61 75 D5
Southesk Ave G64 77 F2
Southesk Gdns G64 77 F3
South Exchange Ct G1 241 A2
Southfield Ave
- Paisley PA2 133 E8
- Port Glasgow PA14 68 F8
- Shotts ML7 147 B4
Southfield Cres
- Coatbridge ML5 122 D5
- Glasgow G53 135 C8
- Shotts ML7 147 B4
- Stirling FK8 7 A6
Southfield Dr FK1 86 A6
Southfield Pk KA7 239 A5
Southfield Rd
- Cumbernauld G68 61 C1
- Shotts ML7 147 B4
South Frederick St G1 241 A2
South Gargieston Dr KA1 227 C6
Southgate G62 55 A1
South Glassford St G62 55 B1
South Green Dr FK2 14 E3
South Hamilton Ct [1] KA1 227 E8
South Hamilton Pl KA1 227 E7
South Hamilton St KA1 227 E8
South Harbour St KA7 235 E1
Southhill Ave G73 138 C5
South Hirst Rd ML7 126 D3
Southhook Rd
- Kilmarnock KA1 222 D2
- Knockentiber KA2 221 F3
Southinch Ave G14 94 E6
Southinch La G14 94 E6
South Isle Rd KA22 205 C5
South Kersebonny Steading FK8 6 C7
South King St G84 16 F1
South Lanarkshire Coll G75 181 B7
Southlea Ave G46 136 A3
South Line View ML2 164 E2
South Loan G69 100 D8
Southloch Gdns [1] G21 97 F3
Southloch St G21 97 F3
South Lodge Ct KA7 238 E6
South Mains FK7 9 B1
South Mains Rd G62 54 F1
South Medrox St ML5 101 C7
South Melville La FK1 42 B5
South Moraine La G15 75 C2
South Mound PA6 91 A2
South Muirhead Ct G67 62 A2
South Muirhead Rd G67 62 A2
Southmuir Pl G20 96 D5
South Neuk KA25 170 A7
South Newmoor Ave KA11 219 F1
South Newmoor Ind Est KA11 219 F2
South Nimmo St [2] ML6 123 B7
SOUTH NITSHILL 135 A4
Southook Row KA11 220 B5
Southpark Ave
- Glasgow G12 96 E2
- Prestwick KA9 236 B7
South Park Ave G78 134 C3
South Park Dr PA2 113 E2
South Park Gr ML3 162 D3
South Park Prim Sch G75 180 C6
Southpark Rd KA7 238 E6
South Park Rd ML3 162 D2
South Park Sch KA7 239 A5
Southpark Terr G12 96 E2
South Pl ML4 141 F4
South Pleasance Ave FK1 42 B4
South Portland St [5] G5 117 B5
South Prim Sch PA2 113 E2
South Rd
- Clarkston G76 158 A5
- Port Glasgow PA14 68 E8
- West Kilbride KA23 190 C4
South Ring Rd KA20 218 B5
South Ring Round KA20 218 A5
South Robertson Pl ML6 122 E7
South Scott St G69 120 B4
Southside Cres [2] G5 117 C4
South St
- Cambus FK10 9 B8
- Glasgow G14 95 C3
- Greenock PA16 45 D6
- Houston PA6 91 A2
- Inchinnan PA4 93 B4
- Stirling FK9 2 D1
South Vennel
- Irvine KA11 220 A3
- Lanark ML11 215 A4
South Vesalius St G32 119 A5
Southview G61 75 C5
South View
- Bellshill ML4 141 E4
- Blantyre G72 140 C1
- Clydebank G81 73 F3
- Stenhousemuir FK5 23 D1
Southview Ave G76 157 F5
Southview Cres PA11 90 D1
Southview Ct [3] G64 97 F7
Southview Dr G63 31 B3
Southview Gr G61 75 C5
Southview Pl G69 100 E6
Southview Rd G63 31 C3
Southview Terr G64 97 F7
Southward Way KA10 229 G7
South William St PA5 111 F2
Southwold Rd PA1 114 E5
Southwood Ct G77 156 D1
Southwood Dr G44 137 C6
Southwood Pl G77 156 D2
Southwood Rd KA10 232 F8
South Woodside Rd
- Glasgow G4 96 E2
- Glasgow G4 96 F3
Soutra Pl G33 119 B8
Spairdrum Rd ML6 82 F4
Spalehall Dr ML1 143 F3
Spallander Rd KA10 229 G6
SPANGO VALLEY 44 D2
Sparrow Gdns KA1 228 C7
Spateston Rd PA5 131 C7
Spean Ave G74 160 B1
Spean St G44 137 A6
Spectrum Ho G81 74 B2
Speedwell Sq KA7 239 B3
Speirsfield Gdns PA2 113 E3
Speirshall Cl G14 94 F5
Speirshall Terr G14 94 F6
Speirs Rd G61 76 B3
Speirs Wharf G4 97 B2
Spencer Dr PA2 132 E8
Spencerfield Gdns ML3 162 F3
Spencer St
- Clydebank G81 74 A3
- Glasgow G13 95 F7
Spence St
- Bonnybridge FK4 40 A6
- Glasgow G20 96 C8
Spey Ave
- Kilmarnock KA1 228 A5
- Paisley PA2 112 E1
Speyburn Pl
- [8] Airdrie ML6 103 A3
- Irvine KA11 219 F6
- Stepps G33 99 E6
Spey Ct
- Airdrie ML6 123 C5
- Stirling FK7 7 C5
- [22] Wishaw ML2 165 F6
Spey Dr
- Coatbridge ML5 121 E4
- Renfrew PA4 94 E2
Spey Gdns ML3 183 B8
Spey Gr G75 179 F7
Spey Pl PA5 131 C8
Spey Rd
- Bearsden G61 75 C2
- Troon KA10 229 G4
Spey St G33 118 F8
Spey Terr G75 179 F7
Spey Wlk
- [8] Cumbernauld G67 61 F1
- Motherwell ML1 143 B5
Spey Wynd ML9 199 A8
Spiers Ave KA15 171 A7
Spiersbridge Ave G46 135 E2
Spiersbridge Bsns Pk G46 135 E3
Spiersbridge La G46 135 E3
Spiersbridge Rd G46 135 F3
Spiersbridge Rdbt G46 135 F2
Spiersbridge Terr G46 135 E3
Spiers Gate ML8 187 A5
Spiers Gr G46 135 F3
Spiersland Way KA15 171 C7
Spiers Pl PA3 112 C7
Spiers Rd
- Houston PA6 91 B2
- Johnstone PA5 112 B3
- Lochwinnoch PA12 129 B3
Spindlehowe Rd
- Uddingston G71 140 F5
- Uddingston, Tannochside G71 141 A7
SPINDLESIDE 144 D1
Spindleside Rd ML1 144 D1
Spindrift Wynd KA21 205 F3
Spinkhill FK2 42 F2
Spinners Ct G81 74 B7
Spinners Gdns PA2 113 B3
Spinners La G81 74 B7
Spinningdale ML9 198 D1
Spital Rd ML9 198 F1
SPITTAL 137 F5
Spittal Hill FK9 2 C4
Spittal Prim Sch G73 137 F5
Spittal Rd G73 137 F5
Spittal St FK8 7 A8
Spoolers Rd PA1 113 C3
Spoutmouth G1 241 B1
Sprig Way ML7 127 E5
Springbank Cres
- Glasgow G31 118 C4
- Hamilton ML3 183 A7
- Motherwell ML1 143 A2
Springbank Gdns
- Falkirk FK2 42 C5
- Irvine KA11 220 A7
Springbank Ind Est KA12 224 E8
Springbank Rd
- Ayr KA8 236 B4
- Paisley PA3 113 D7
- Shotts ML7 146 D6
- Stirling FK7 7 C6
Springbank St G20 97 A4
Springbank Terr
- Paisley PA3 113 D7
- Plains ML6 103 F3
Springbank View ML6 103 F3
SPRINGBOIG 119 D6
Springboig Ave G32 119 C6
Springboig Rd G32 119 C6
Springboig St Johns Sch G33 119 D7
SPRINGBURN 97 F3
Springburn Acad G21 97 F5
Springburn L Ctr G21 97 F4
Springburn Pl G74 159 A3
Springburn Rd G21 97 E4
Springburn Sh Ctr [4] G21 97 F4
Springburn Sports Pk G21 98 B4
Springburn Sta G21 97 F4
Springburn Way
- [3] Glasgow G21 97 E4
- Glasgow G21 97 F4
Springcroft Ave G69 120 B6
Springcroft Cres G69 120 B6
Springcroft Dr G69 120 A6
Springcroft Gdns G69 120 C6
Springcroft Gr
- Bonhill G83 27 F3
- Glasgow G69 120 B6
Springcroft Rd G69 120 C6
Springcroft Wynd G69 120 B6
Springfield Ave
- Bishopbriggs G64 98 A7
- Paisley PA1 114 B4
- Prestwick KA9 236 D7
- Uddingston G71 140 F5
Springfield Cres
- Bishopbriggs G64 98 A8
- Carluke ML8 201 F8
- Hamilton G72 161 C7
- Uddingston G71 140 F5
Springfield Ct
- Bishopbriggs G64 78 B1
- Glasgow G1 241 A2
Springfield Dr
- Barrhead G78 134 E1
- Falkirk FK1 41 F5
Springfield Gdns
- Irvine KA11 220 A7
- Lanark ML11 214 F5
- Uddingston G71 140 F5
Springfield Gr G78 155 D8
Springfield Park Rd G73 138 C6
Springfield Pk PA5 112 A2
Springfield Quay G5 240 A1
Springfield Quay Leisure Pk G5 240 A1
Springfield Rd
- Airdrie ML6 123 E8
- Alloa FK10 10 C7
- Barrhead G78 155 C8
- Bishopbriggs G64 78 A1
- Crosshouse KA2 221 F2
- Cumbernauld G67 62 A4
- Denny FK6 21 F2
- Glasgow G40 118 B4
- Salsburgh ML7 125 A1
- Stirling FK7 7 C5
Springfield Sq G64 98 A8
Springfield Woods PA5 112 A2
Springfield Works G64 78 A1
SPRINGHALL 138 E4
Springhall Ct G73 138 D3
Springhead Rd ML7 167 A8
SPRINGHILL
- Barrhead 134 C1
- Shotts 147 B2
Springhill Ave
- Airdrie ML6 123 B8
- Coatbridge ML5 121 C4
- Crosshouse KA2 226 F8
Springhill Drive S G69 120 A6
Springhill Farm Gr [3] G69 120 A6
Springhill Farm Pl [1] G69 120 A6
Springhill Farm Rd G69 120 A6
Springhill Farm Way [2] G69 120 A6
Springhill Gdns
- Glasgow G41 116 E1
- Kilmarnock KA1 227 E8
Springhill & Leadloch Rd ML7, EH47 147 E2
Springhill Parkway G69 120 A7
Springhill Pl
- Coatbridge ML5 121 C4
- Kilmarnock KA1 227 E8
Springhill Prim Sch G78 134 B1
Springhill Rd
- Barrhead G78 134 B1
- Clarkston G76 157 F7
- Glasgow G69 120 A5
- Port Glasgow PA14 47 C1
- Shotts ML7 147 B3
Springhill Terr KA11 220 F2
Springhill View ML7 147 B3
Springholm Dr ML6 102 F2
Springkell Ave G41 116 C2
Springkell Dr G41 116 B2
Springkell Gate G41 116 D2
Springkell Gdns G41 116 D2
Springkell St PA15 46 B4
Springkerse Bsns Pk FK7 7 E7
Springkerse Ind Est FK7 7 D6
Springkerse Rd FK7 7 D6
Springkerse Rdbt FK7 7 E7
Springkerse Ret Pk FK7 7 E6
Spring La ML6 104 F4
SPRINGSIDE 220 F2
Springside KA23 190 E7
Springside Gdns G15 75 A5
Springside Pl G15 75 A4
Springside Prim Sch KA11 220 F2
Springside Terr KA11 220 F2
Springvale Ct KA21 216 F7
Springvale Dr PA2 112 F2
Springvale Pk KA7 238 F6
Springvale Pl KA21 216 F8
Springvale Rd KA7 238 F6
Springvale St KA21 216 F8
Springvale Terr [8] G21 97 E4
Springwell Cres G72 161 F7
Springwell Pl KA3 195 E1
Springwells Ave ML6 123 C8
Springwells Cres ML6 123 C8
Springwood FK7 6 F5
Springwood Ave FK8 6 F5
Springwood Dr PA13 69 D2
Spring Wynd G5 117 C4
Sprotwell Terr FK10 5 D1
Spruce Ave
- Hamilton, Silvertonhill ML3 162 F2
- Hamilton, Wheatlands G72 161 C8
- Johnstone PA5 112 A1
Sprucebank Ave PA14 70 C7
Spruce Ct ML3 162 E1
Spruce Dr
- Cambuslang G72 139 F4
- Kirkintilloch G66 79 A5
Spruce Ho KA9 236 B5
Spruce Pk KA7 239 D5
Spruce Rd
- Cumbernauld G67 62 D4
- Motherwell G71 121 C1
Spruce St G22 97 D5
Spruce Way
- Cambuslang G72 139 F4
- Motherwell ML1 143 B4
Spur Rd KA8 235 E2
Spynie Pl G64 78 D2
Spynie Way [1] ML2 165 F6
Spy's La G84 15 E4
Square of Ales [3] KA1 222 F1
Square The FK7 8 D4
Squire St G14 95 E2
Sraehouse Wynd ML8 188 B1
Stable Gr PA1 113 B4
Stable Houses KA1 231 F6
Stable Pl G62 54 F3
Stable Rd
- Milngavie G62 54 F3
- Shotts ML7 147 A4
Stables The
- Glasgow G52 115 A3
- Mugdock G62 55 B6
- Paisley PA1 113 B4
Stable Wynd KA10 230 B4
Staffa G74 181 C8
Staffa Ave
- Port Glasgow PA14 69 A7
- Renfrew PA4 94 C1
Staffa Ct KA11 225 B8
Staffa Dr
- Airdrie ML6 123 F7
- Kirkintilloch G66 80 B8
- Paisley PA2 133 E7
Staffa Pl FK1 42 B2
Staffa Rd G72 138 F3
Staffa St
- Glasgow G31 118 B8
- Gourock PA19 44 E6
Staffin Dr G23 76 D1
Staffin Path [10] G23 76 E1
Staffin Rd KA10 229 G5
Staffin St G23 76 E1
Stafflar Dr KA1 227 E4
Stafford Cres PA16 44 F4
Stafford Rd PA16 44 F4
Stafford St
- Bellshill ML4 141 F4
- Glasgow G4 241 B4
- Helensburgh G84 16 D2
- Kilmarnock KA3 222 F2
Stafford Street W G84 16 C3
Staffordway S PA16 44 F4
Stag Ct G71 141 C6
Stag St G51 116 B7
Staig Wynd ML1 164 A4
Staikhill ML11 214 F5
Staineybraes Pl ML6 102 F2
Stairlie Cres KA23 190 D5
Stalker St ML2 164 C4
Stamford Gate G31 118 B5
Stamford Pl G31 118 B5
Stamford Rd G31 118 B5
Stamford St G31 118 B5
STAMPERLAND 157 F8
Stamperland Ave G76 157 F8
Stamperland Cres G76 157 E8
Stamperland Dr G76 157 F8
Stamperland Gdns G76 157 F8
Stamperland Hill G76 136 F1
Stanalane St G46 135 F4
STAND 103 B6
Standa La KA3 222 C8
Standalane KA3 211 D8
Standburn Rd
- Glasgow G21 98 D6
Standburn Rd *continued*
- Glasgow G21 98 D7
Standford Hall G72 139 A6
STANE 147 A3
Staneacre Pk ML3 162 F3
Stane Brae KA3 211 E7
STANECASTLE 219 E5
Stanecastle Dr KA11 219 E5
Stanecastle Gate KA11 219 F5
Stanecastle Intc KA12 219 F4
Stanecastle Rd KA11 219 F4
Stanecastle Sch [2] KA11 220 A5
Stanecraigs Pl [20] ML2 165 F6
Stanefield Dr ML1 143 E4
Stane Gr ML7 147 A3
Stanely Ave PA2 113 B1
Stanely Cres PA2 133 B8
Stanely Dr PA2 113 D1
Stanely Gr PA2 133 B8
Stanely Grange PA2 133 B7
Stanely Rd PA2 113 C1
Stane Prim Sch ML7 147 A4
Stane Rd
- Port Glasgow PA14 68 E8
- Shotts ML7 147 A2
Stanford St G81 74 C1
Stanhope Dr G73 138 D5
Stanhope Pl ML2 186 A7
Stanistone Rd ML8 188 A2
Stanley Ave KA22 205 C3
Stanley Bvd G72 161 D4
Stanley Dr
- Ardrossan KA22 205 C3
- Bellshill ML4 142 A6
- Bishopbriggs G64 78 B2
- Bridge of Allan FK9 2 B7
- Brookfield PA5 111 C5
Stanley La PA5 111 C5
Stanley Pk ML6 123 B8
Stanley Pl
- Blantyre G72 140 D1
- Saltcoats KA21 205 E1
Stanley Prim Sch KA22 205 C3
Stanley Rd
- Ardrossan KA22 205 D3
- Saltcoats KA21 216 E8
Stanley St
- Glasgow G41 116 E5
- Hamilton ML3 161 F4
Stanley Street La G41 116 E5
Stanley Terr FK12 5 A6
Stanmore Ave ML11 215 B5
Stanmore Cres ML11 215 C5
Stanmore Gdns ML11 215 D6
Stanmore House Sch ML11 215 D6
Stanmore Rd
- Glasgow G42 137 B8
- Lanark ML11 215 D6
Stanners La PA15 46 B4
Stanrigg St ML6 104 A2
Stanton Ave FK10 9 F6
Stark Ave
- Clydebank G81 73 E6
- Falkirk FK1 41 D5
Starling Way ML4 141 E8
Starryshaw Rd ML7 146 E6
Startpoint St G33 119 A8
Station Ave
- [2] Greenock PA15 46 A4
- Greenock PA15 46 A5
- Howwood PA9 130 F5
Station Brae
- Irvine KA11 220 C1
- Neilston G78 154 C8
Station Brae Gdns KA11 220 C1
Station Bridge KA7 239 A7
Station Cres PA4 94 D4
Station Ct
- Bellshill ML4 141 F5
- Kilbirnie KA14 170 C6
- Netherburn ML9 200 C4
Station Dr
- Hurlford KA1 228 D6
- Prestwick KA9 233 C1
- Springside KA11 220 F3
Station Gate
- Hamilton G72 161 E8
- Netherburn ML9 200 C4
Station Pk G69 120 C4
Station Pl ML8 187 A6
Station Plaza KA13 207 D3
Station Rd
- Airdrie ML6 123 E8
- Ayr KA7, KA8 239 A8
- Bannockburn FK7 7 E1
- Bardowie G62 77 B7
- Bearsden G61 75 D4
- Bishopton PA7 72 B2
- Blackridge EH48 107 D2
- Blanefield G63 30 F4
- Blantyre G72 140 E1
- Bothwell G71 141 A2
- Bridge of Allan FK9 1 F8
- Caldercruix ML6 105 A4
- Cambus FK10 4 B1
- Cardross G82 48 A7
- Carluke ML8 187 E1
- Clarkston G46 158 A5
- Cleland ML1 144 B1
- Cowie FK7 12 D6
- Dumbarton G82 49 F4
- Dunlop KA3 195 B7
- Glasgow G69 120 C4
- Glasgow, Giffnock G46 136 C3

Station Rd *continued*
Glasgow, Maryhill G20 96 C8
Gourock PA19 44 E8
Hamilton ML3 162 E3
Helensburgh G84 25 B8
Howwood PA10 130 F6
Kilbarchan PA10 111 B2
Kilsyth G65 36 D1
Kirkintilloch G66 79 C4
Langbank PA14 70 C6
Larkhall ML9 185 B4
Law ML8 187 A6
Lennoxtown G66 57 D8
Longcroft FK4 39 B4
Millerston G33 99 A5
Milngavie G62 55 A1
Milngavie G62 55 B1
Monkton KA9 233 C4
Motherwell ML1 143 B3
Muirhead G69 100 C6
Neilston G78 154 D7
Netherburn ML9 200 C4
Old Kilpatrick G60 73 B6
Paisley PA1, PA2 113 A3
Plains ML6 104 B2
Port Glasgow PA14 47 C1
Prestwick KA9 233 C1
Renfrew PA4 94 E4
Rhu G84 15 E5
Shotts ML7 146 E4
Slamannan FK1 86 B6
Springside KA11 220 F2
Stepps G33 99 D5
Stevenston KA20 217 D7
7 Stirling FK8 7 B8
Strathblane G63 31 A4
Uddingston G71 140 E6
Wishaw ML2 165 A2
Station Rise PA12 129 C2
Station Row
Drybridge KA11 225 E6
Law ML8 187 A6
Slamannan FK1 86 B5
Station St G82 27 D1
Station Way G71 140 E5
Station Wynd PA10 111 B2
Staybrae Dr G53 114 F1
Staybrae Gr G53 114 F1
Steadings Dr G83 28 A6
Steadings The
Airth FK2 13 E5
Fallin FK7 8 A4
Steading The ML2 165 B5
Steadman Pl KA11 225 A8
Steel Cres FK6 21 F1
Steele Cres G83 28 A8
Steele Wlk G83 28 A8
Steel Pl ML2 164 F2
Steel St
Glasgow G1 241 B1
Gourock PA19 44 F7
Wishaw ML2 165 B2
Steeple Sq PA10 111 A3
Steeple St PA10 111 A3
Steeples View KA10 229 F7
Stein Pl ML2 166 C3
Stein Sq FK7 7 F1
Stemac La ML6 104 A2
Stenhouse Ave G69 100 C7
STENHOUSEMUIR 23 D3
Stenhousemuir Prim Sch
FK5 23 D3
Stenhouse Rd FK2 23 F2
Stenton Cres ML2 164 D1
Stenton Pl ML2 164 D1
Stenton St G32 118 E7
Stenzel Pl G33 99 F5
Stepends Rd
Airdrie ML6 124 C8
Plains ML6 104 D2
Stepford Pl G33 119 F7
Stepford Rd G33 120 A7
Stephen Cres G69 119 F5
Stephens Ave ML6 104 F4
Stephens Croft 6 FK2 41 F8
Stephenson Pl 3 G75 180 D8
Stephenson Sq 4 G75 180 D8
Stephenson St G52 114 E8
Stephenson Terr G75 180 D8
STEPPS 99 C6
Stepps Prim Sch G33 99 E6
Stepps Rd
Glasgow G33 119 C8
Kirkintilloch G66 79 E2
Stepps Sta G33 99 E5
Steps Rd KA12 219 C5
Steps St FK5 23 E3
Steuart Rd FK9 1 F7
Steven Pl KA25 149 B2
Stevens La ML1 143 A3
Stevenson Ct
Bridge of Allan FK9 2 A5
Falkirk FK2 24 B1
Stevenson Pl ML4 142 B7
Stevenson St
Carluke ML8 187 E2
Clydebank G81 73 F3
Glasgow G40 117 E5
Glasgow G40 241 C1
Kilmarnock KA1 222 D1
Paisley PA2 113 E3
Stevens Pl PA19 44 E6
Steven St G83 27 E5
STEVENSTON 217 E8
Stevenston Ct ML1 143 A4
Stevenston Ind Est KA20 217 F7
Stevenston Rd KA13, KA20 207 C3
STEVENSTON SITE 218 B5
Stevenston St ML1 143 A4
Stevenston Sta KA20 217 D7
Stewart Ave
Falkirk FK2 24 A2
Hamilton, Blantyre G72 161 C7
Hamilton, Meikle Earnock
ML3 183 A7
Newton Mearns G77 156 E6
Renfrew PA4 94 B1
Stewart Cres
Barrhead G78 134 D4
Wishaw ML2 166 A5
Stewart Ct
Barrhead G78 134 C4
Coatbridge ML5 122 C6
Rutherglen G73 138 C7
Stewart Ctr PA15 45 F5
Stewart Dr
Clarkston G76 157 E8
Clydebank G81 74 B6
Coatbridge G69 121 B6
Irvine KA12 219 D4
STEWARTFIELD 159 D4
Stewartfield Cres G74 159 D3
Stewartfield Dr G74 159 D4
Stewartfield Gdns G74 159 C4
Stewartfield Rd G74 159 C3
Stewartfield Way
East Kilbride, Philipshill
G74 158 F4
East Kilbride, Stewartfield
G74 159 D4
Stewartgill Pl ML9 185 F1
Stewart Gr ML7 127 F5
Stewart Ho PA15 45 E6
STEWARTON 211 B8
Stewarton Acad KA3 195 F1
Stewarton Cres KA3 223 B6
Stewarton Dr G72 138 F5
Stewarton Rd
Dunlop KA3 195 B7
Fenwick KA3 213 A4
Glasgow G46 135 E1
Newton Mearns G77 156 C7
Stewarton St ML2 165 C2
Stewarton Sta KA3 195 D1
Stewarton Terr ML2 165 C2
Stewart Pl
Barrhead G78 134 D4
1 Carluke ML8 187 F2
Stewart Quadrant ML1 143 B6
Stewart Rd
Ayr KA8 236 C4
Falkirk FK2 42 C5
Paisley PA2 133 F8
Stewarts La ML2 165 C3
Stewart Sq FK8 2 A2
Stewart St
Barrhead G78 134 D4
Bellshill ML4 142 D5
Bonnybridge FK4 39 F5
Cambusbarron FK7 6 D6
Carluke ML8 187 E2
Clydebank G81 73 E3
Coatbridge ML5 122 A8
Glasgow G4 240 C4
Hamilton ML3 162 A5
Milngavie G62 55 A1
Stewartville St G11 96 B2
STIRLING 7 C8
Stirling Ave
Bearsden G61 75 E2
Kilmarnock KA1 222 C1
Stirling Br* FK8 2 B2
Stirling Bsns Ctr FK8 7 B6
Stirling Castle* FK8 7 A8
Stirling Cres KA1 222 C1
Stirling Dr
Bearsden G61 75 D6
Bishopbriggs G64 77 E3
East Kilbride G74 160 A3
Gourock PA19 43 F5
Hamilton ML3 161 E4
Johnstone PA5 111 D2
Linwood PA3 111 F5
Rutherglen G73 138 B5
Stirling Ent Pk FK7 7 C7
Stirlingfauld Pl 7 G5 117 B5
Stirling Gate PA3 112 A6
Stirling Gdns G64 77 E3
Stirling High Sch FK8 7 A5
Stirling Ind Est ML6 103 B3
Stirling Pl
Lennoxtown G66 57 E8
Plean FK7 12 C3
Stirling Rd
Airdrie ML6 103 B5
Alexandria G83 27 F1
Alloa FK10 9 E8
Alva FK12 4 F7
Balloch G83 20 A2
Carluke ML8 187 E4
Chapelhall ML6 123 D3
Cumbernauld G67 83 A6
Dumbarton, Bellsmyre G82 50 A7
Dumbarton, Crosslet G82 50 C3
Fallin FK7 8 C4
Glasgow G4 241 B3
Kilsyth G65 36 F1
Larbert, North Broomage
FK5 23 A3
Larbert, South Broomage FK2,
FK5 41 C7
Torwood FK5 22 E5
Stirling Rd *continued*
Tullibody FK10 4 B3
Wattston G67 83 A3
Stirling Royal Infmy FK8 7 B5
Stirling Sports Village FK7 7 E8
Stirling St
Airdrie ML6 123 A7
Alva FK12 5 A7
Coatbridge ML5 121 D4
Cumbernauld G67 62 B4
Denny, Dunipace FK6 21 D4
Denny FK6 21 E2
Motherwell ML1 164 B4
Renton G82 27 D2
Stirling Sta FK8 7 B8
Stirling Way
Glasgow G69 120 A4
1 Renfrew PA4 94 D1
Stirrat St
Glasgow G20 96 C6
Paisley PA3 113 C7
Stobbs Cres KA13 207 E2
Stobbs Terr
Irvine KA13 218 E7
Kilwinning KA13 207 E2
Stobcross Bsns Pk 6
G3 116 E8
Stobcross Rd G3 116 D8
Stobcross St
Coatbridge ML5 122 A6
Glasgow G3 116 E7
Stobcross Wynd G3 116 D8
Stobhill Cotts G21 98 A7
Stobhill Cres KA7 239 B5
Stobhill Hospl G21 98 A6
Stobhill Rd G21 97 F7
Stobo G74 160 C4
Stobo Ct G74 160 C4
Stobo St ML2 165 C5
Stobs Dr G78 134 B4
Stobs Pl G34 100 C1
Stock Ave PA2 113 E3
Stockbridge Cres KA25 149 B4
Stockholm Cres PA2 113 F3
Stockiemuir Ave G61 75 E7
Stockiemuir Ct G61 75 E7
Stockiemuir Rd
Bearsden G61 75 D7
Milngavie G61, G62 54 C1
Stocks Rd
Cleland ML1 144 F1
Wishaw ML2 166 A8
Stock St PA2 113 E2
Stockwell Pl G1 241 A1
Stockwell St G1 241 A1
Stoddard Sq PA5 112 D3
Stonebank Gr G45 137 D3
Stonebyres Ct ML3 162 A3
Stonecraig Rd ML2 165 C2
Stonecrop Pl KA7 239 C4
Stonedyke Cres ML8 188 A3
Stonedyke Gr G15 75 B2
Stonedyke Prim Sch G15 75 B2
Stonedyke Rd ML8 188 B3
Stonefield Ave
Glasgow G12 96 C6
Paisley PA2 113 F1
Stonefield Cres
Clarkston G76 157 C8
Hamilton G72 161 C7
Paisley PA2 113 F1
Stonefield Dr PA2 113 F1
Stonefield Gdns
Carluke ML8 187 F3
Paisley PA2 113 F1
Stonefield Gn PA2 113 E1
Stonefield Gr PA2 113 F1
Stonefield Park Gdns
G72 161 E8
Stonefield Pk
Doonfoot KA7 238 C2
Paisley PA2 133 E8
Stonefield Pl G72 161 C6
Stonefield Rd G72 161 C7
Stonefield St ML6 103 B1
Stonehall Ave ML3 162 B2
Stonehaven Cres ML6 122 E5
Stonehaven Rd PA16 44 F3
STONEHOUSE 198 F2
Stonehouse Hospl ML9 198 D1
Stonehouse Prim Sch
ML9 198 E1
Stonelaw Ct G73 138 B7
Stonelaw Dr G73 138 B6
Stonelaw High Sch 2
G73 138 B7
Stonelaw Rd G73 138 B6
Stonelaw Twrs G73 138 C6
Stoneleigh G12 96 B5
Stoneleigh Pl PA16 45 C7
Stoneleigh Rd PA16 45 C7
Stoneside Dr G43 136 B6
Stoneside Sq G43 136 A6
Stoney Brae
2 Paisley, Laigh Pk PA3 113 E5
Paisley PA2 133 E8
Stoneyetts Rd G69 80 F2
Stoneyflatt Ave G82 50 B5
Stoneyflatt Ct G82 50 B5
Stoneyflatt Gdns G82 50 B5
Stoneyflatt Rd G82 50 B5
Stoneyholm Rd KA25 149 B2
Stoneymeadow Rd G74 160 D5
Stoneymollan Rd
Cardross G82 26 A6
Helensburgh G82 25 H5
STONEYWOOD 21 C2
Stoneywood Pk FK6 21 B2
Stonyhill Ave KA1 227 E5
Stonyhurst St
Glasgow, Firhill G22 97 B4
Glasgow G22 97 C4
Stonylee Rd G67 62 A1
Stoopshill Cres KA24 191 E7
Store Row ML3 183 F3
Storie St PA1 113 E4
Stormlight Rd KA22 205 B1
Stormyland Way G78 134 C2
Stornoway Cres ML2 165 E5
Stornoway Dr KA3 223 A6
Stornoway St G22 97 C8
Stow Brae PA1 113 E3
Stow Coll (City Campus)
G3 240 B4
Stow Coll (West Campus)
G20 96 E4
Stow St PA1 113 E4
Strachan Pl G72 161 D3
Strachan St
Bellshill ML4 142 A4
Falkirk FK1 41 E4
Strachur Cres G22 97 A7
Strachur Gdns 2 G22 97 A7
Strachur Gr 5 G22 97 A7
Strachur Pl 4 G22 97 A7
Strain Cres ML6 123 B6
Straiton Dr ML3 161 D2
Straiton Pl G72 161 D8
Straiton St G32, G33 118 E7
Strand KA15 171 B8
Strandhead KA3 211 C8
Strand St KA1 222 F1
Strang Pl KA9 236 D5
Strang's Pl FK1 66 F5
Stranka Ave PA2 113 C3
Stranraer Dr G15 75 C2
Stratford G74 160 D5
Stratford St G20 96 E5
Strathallan Ave G75 180 A8
Strathallan Cres 2 ML6 103 A3
Strathallan Ct FK9 2 A6
Strathallan Gate 11 G75 159 A1
Strathallan Gdns 4 G66 79 D8
Strathallan Rd FK9 2 A6
Strathallan Wynd G75 158 F1
Strathallon Pl G73 138 D3
Strathaven Acad G75 180 B4
Strathaven Rd
Eaglesham G76 178 F4
East Kilbride G74, G75 181 B7
Hamilton ML3 183 C5
Stonehouse ML9 198 D1
Strathavon Cres ML6 103 A2
Strathayr Pl KA8 239 A8
STRATHBLANE 31 D3
Strathblane Cres ML6 103 A3
Strathblane Dr G75 179 E8
Strathblane Gdns
Glasgow G13 95 D5
Glasgow G13 95 F8
Strathblane Prim Sch
G63 31 C3
Strathblane Rd
Clachan of Campsie G66 32 F3
Greenock PA15 46 C2
Milngavie G62 55 C3
Strathblane G63 31 E3
Strathbran St G31 118 D4
STRATHBUNGO 116 F1
Strathcairn Cres ML6 103 A3
Strath Carron ML8 187 A5
Strathcarron Cres PA2 134 B8
Strathcarron Dr PA2 114 B1
Strathcarron Pl
7 Glasgow G20 96 D6
Paisley PA2 134 B8
Strathcarron Rd PA2 134 B8
Strathcarron Way PA2 114 B1
Strathclyde Ave KA22 205 D3
Strathclyde Bsns Ctr
Cambuslang G72 139 E3
Greenock PA15 46 E3
Motherwell ML1 142 F4
Strathclyde Bsns Pk
ML4 141 E8
Strathclyde CP Visitor Ctr*
ML1 141 D1
Strathclyde Ct G84 16 B3
Strathclyde Ctry Pk* ML1,
ML3 162 E8
Strathclyde Ctry Pk ML1 141 F1
Strathclyde Dr G73 138 A6
Strathclyde Gdns G72 139 E3
Strathclyde Homes Stadium
(Dumbarton FC) G82 50 A2
Strathclyde Hospl ML1 163 D5
Strathclyde Path G71 140 E6
Strathclyde Pl G84 16 A2
Strathclyde Rd
Dumbarton G82 50 A5
Motherwell ML1 163 B6
Strathclyde St G40 118 A2
Strathclyde View G71 141 B1
Strathclyde Way ML4 142 C7
Strathcona Dr G13 96 A7
Strathcona Gdns G13 96 A7
Strathcona Ho G75 180 E7
Strathcona La 4 G75 180 E7
Strathcona Pl
East Kilbride G75 180 E7
5 Rutherglen G73 138 D4
Strathcona St G13 95 F6
Strathconon Gdns 1
G75 179 E8
Strath Dearn ML8 187 A5
Strathdearn Gr G75 179 E8
Strathdee Ave G81 74 B5
Strathdee Rd G44 136 E2
Strathdon Ave
Glasgow G44 136 F2
Paisley PA2 113 C2
Strathdon Dr G44 136 F2
Strathdon Pl 3 G75 179 E8
Strathdoon Pl KA7 238 D2
Strathearn Gr G66 59 B1
Strathearn Rd G76 157 E6
Strath Elgin ML8 187 A5
Strathendrick Dr G44 136 E4
Strathfillan Rd G74 159 D2
Strathgoil Cres ML6 103 A3
Strathgryffe Cres PA11 90 C1
Strath Halladale ML8 187 A5
Strathhalladale Ct 9
G75 179 E8
Strathisla Way 3 ML1 143 B2
Strathkelvin Ave 4 G64 97 F7
Strathkelvin La 8 G75 179 E8
Strathkelvin Ret Pk G64 78 C5
Strathlachlan Ave ML8 188 A1
Strathleven Dr G83 27 F1
Strathleven Pl G82 49 F3
Strathmiglo Ct 7 G75 179 E8
Strathmiglo Pl FK5 23 F4
Strathmore Ave
Blantyre G72 140 C1
Paisley PA1 114 D4
Strathmore Cres
1 Airdrie ML6 103 A2
Stirling FK9 2 A3
Strathmore Ct G14 95 F4
Strathmore Dr FK9 2 A3
Strathmore Gdns 2
G73 138 D4
Strathmore Gr G75 179 E8
Strathmore Pk KA11 220 B6
Strathmore Pl ML5 122 D5
Strathmore Rd
Glasgow G22 97 B7
Hamilton ML3 162 E3
Strathmore Wlk ML5 122 D5
Strathmungo Cres ML6 102 F2
Strath Nairn ML8 187 A5
Strathnairn Ave G75 179 E8
Strathnairn Ct 4 G75 179 E8
Strathnairn Dr G75 179 E8
Strathnairn Way 5 G75 179 E8
Strath Naver ML8 187 A5
Strathnaver Cres ML6 103 A3
Strathnaver Gdns 6
G75 179 E8
Strathord Pl G69 81 A4
Strathord St G32 119 A3
Strath Peffer ML8 186 F5
Strathpeffer Cres 5
ML6 103 A2
Strathpeffer Dr 2 G75 179 E8
Strathrannoch Way G75 179 E8
Strathspey Ave G75 179 E8
Strathspey Cres 1 ML6 103 A3
Strathtay Ave
East Kilbride G75 158 F1
Glasgow G44 136 E2
Strathtummel Cres 3
ML6 103 A3
Strathview Gr G44 136 E2
Strathview Pk G44 136 E2
Strathview Rd ML4 141 F3
Strathvithie Gr 10 G75 179 E8
Strathwhillan Ct G75 179 F8
Strathwhillan Dr G75 179 F8
Strathy Pl
5 Glasgow G20 96 D6
Kilmarnock KA1 228 B5
Strathyre Ct 11 G75 179 E8
Strathyre Gdns
Bearsden G61 76 B5
East Kilbride G75 179 E8
Glenmavis ML6 102 F5
12 Moodiesburn G69 81 A3
Strathyre Pl FK1 42 A1
Strathyre Rd G72 161 F6
Strathyre St G41 136 E8
Stratton Dr G46 136 B2
Strauss Ave G81 74 E1
Stravaig Path PA2 133 A7
Stravaig Wlk PA2 133 B7
Stravanan Ct G45 137 E2
Stravanan Gdns G45 137 C1
Stravanan Pl G45 137 D2
Stravanan Rd G45 137 D2
Stravanan St G45 137 D2
Stravanan Terr G45 137 D2
Stravenhouse Rd ML8 186 F4
Strawberrybank Rd KA3 223 A2
Strawberry Field Rd PA6 91 B1
Strawhill Ct G76 157 F7
Strawhill Rd G76 157 F7
Streamfield Gate G33 98 D7
Streamfield Gdns G33 98 E7
Streamfield Lea G33 98 E8
Streamfield Pl G33 98 E7
Strenabey Ave G73 138 D4
Stripehead 3 FK10 10 B6
Striven Cres ML2 165 A1
Striven Ct ML5 122 B3
Striven Dr FK2 24 C1
Striven Gdns G20 96 F3
Striven Terr ML3 162 A1
Stroma Ave PA14 69 B6
Stroma Ct KA11 225 C8
Stroma St G21 98 B2
Stromness St G5 117 A4
STRONE 46 D2
Strone Cres PA15 46 B3

Strone Gdns G65 60 B8
Stronend St G22 97 B5
Strone Path ML5 101 C6
Strone Pl ML6 123 C5
Strone Rd
Alexandria G83 27 F6
Glasgow G33 119 B7
Stronsay Ct KA11 220 A2
Stronsay Pl
Bishopbriggs G64 78 D2
Kilmarnock KA3 223 A5
Stronsay St G21 98 B2
Stronsay Way KA11 220 A2
Stronvar Dr G14 95 B4
Stroud Rd G75 180 D6
Strowan Cres G32 119 B4
Strowan's Rd G82 50 C3
Strowan St G32 119 C4
Strowan's Well Rd G82 50 C3
Struan Ave G46 136 C3
Struan Gdns G44 137 A5
Struan Rd G44 137 A5
Strude Howe FK12 5 B7
Strude Mill FK12 5 B7
Strude St FK12 5 B7
Struie St G34 120 A8
Struma Dr G76 157 C8
STRUTHERHILL 199 B8
Strutherhill ML9 199 B8
Strutherhill Ind Est ML9 199 C8
Struthers Ave KA3 228 D8
Struthers Cres G74 160 B4
Struthers Pl KA10 229 G8
Struthers Prim Sch KA10 229 G5
Struther St ML9 199 B8
Struther & Swinhill Rd ML9 199 D6
Stuart Ave
Old Kilpatrick G60 73 B5
Rutherglen G73 138 B5
Stuart Dr
Bishopbriggs G64 97 E8
Lanark ML11 215 B5
Larkhall ML9 185 C1
Stuart Ho G67 62 B3
Stuarton Pk G74 159 E2
Stuart Pl KA2 225 F2
Stuart Quadrant 7 ML2 164 E1
Stuart Rd
Bishopton PA7 72 B3
Carmunnock G76 158 D8
Dumbarton G82 50 C4
Stuart St
East Kilbride G74 159 F2
Old Kilpatrick G60 73 B5
Stuckleckie Rd G84 17 A1
Sturrock St KA1 227 F8
Styles Pl FK1 41 F2
Succoth St G13 95 F7
Sudbury Cres G75 159 B1
Suffolk Rd PA16 44 E4
Suffolk St
Glasgow G40 241 B1
Helensburgh G84 16 C2
Sugworth Ave G69 120 B5
Suisnish PA4 93 C7
Sumburgh St G33 119 A7
Summerfield Cotts G14 95 E2
Summerfield Rd G67 82 A6
Summerfield St G40 118 B3
SUMMERFORD 41 D4
Summerford FK1 41 D4
Summerford Gdns FK1 41 D4
Summerford Rd FK1 41 D4
Summerhill Ave ML9 185 A2
Summerhill Dr G15 75 B4
Summerhill & Garngibbock Rd G67 82 D4
Summerhill Gdns G15 75 B4
Summerhill Pl
Clydebank G15 75 B4
Shotts ML7 166 F8
Summerhill Rd
Clarkston G76 157 F7
Clydebank G15 75 B4
Summerhill Way ML4 141 F4
Summerlea Rd
Glasgow G46 135 F4
West Kilbride KA23 190 B4
SUMMERLEE 121 F7
Summerlee Cotts ML5 121 F7
Summerlee-Mus of Scottish Ind Life* ML5 121 F8
Summerlee Rd
Larkhall ML9 184 F5
Wishaw ML2 164 C4
Summerlee St
Coatbridge ML5 121 F7
Glasgow G33 119 C7
Summer St G40 117 F5
SUMMERSTON 76 D1
Summerston Sta G20 96 D8
Summertown Rd G51 116 B7
Suna Path ML7 147 B3
Sunart Ave PA4 94 B4
Sunart Ct ML3 162 A1
Sunart Gdns G64 78 C1
Sunart Rd
Bishopbriggs G64 78 C1
Glasgow G52 115 F5
Sunart St ML2 165 A1
Sunbury Ave G76 157 C7
Sundale Ave G76 157 D6
Sunderland Ave G82 49 C4
Sunderland Ct KA25 170 A7
Sundrum Pl KA13 207 D2
Sunflower Gdns ML1 163 D8
Sunningdale Ave
Ayr KA7 239 A3
Newton Mearns G77 156 F6
Sunningdale Dr PA11 110 C6
Sunningdale Pl G84 25 B8
Sunningdale Rd G23 96 E8
Sunningdale Sq KA13 207 C4
Sunningdale Wynd G71 140 E3
Sunnybank ML7 146 F5
Sunnybank Dr G76 157 D7
Sunnybank Gr G76 157 D6
Sunnybank Rd FK7 7 B3
Sunnybank St G40 118 B3
Sunnydale Dr EH48 107 E3
Sunnydale Rd EH48 107 E3
Sunnyhill G65 59 F3
Sunnylaw Dr PA2 113 B2
Sunnylaw Pl
Falkirk FK1 41 F3
Glasgow G22 97 B5
Sunnylaw Rd FK9 2 A8
Sunnylaw St G22 97 B4
SUNNYSIDE 122 A8
Sunnyside
Kilmaurs KA3 222 B7
Stirling FK7 7 A4
Sunnyside Ave
Motherwell ML1 143 B5
Port Glasgow PA14 69 A8
Uddingston G71 140 F5
Sunnyside Cres ML1 143 A5
Sunnyside Ct FK10 10 B7
Sunnyside Dr
Clarkston G76 157 D8
Clydebank G15 75 A1
Coatbridge G69 121 A5
Sunnyside Gate ML1 143 A5
Sunnyside Oval PA2 113 E1
Sunnyside Pl
Barrhead G78 134 B2
Clydebank G15 75 A1
Motherwell ML1 143 A5
Stirling FK9 2 A4
Sunnyside Prim Sch
1 Alloa FK10 10 B7
Glasgow G33 99 C3
Sunnyside Rd
Alloa FK10 10 B7
Cleland ML1 165 B8
Coatbridge ML5 122 A8
Falkirk FK1 41 F5
Kilmarnock KA1 227 F2
Kirkfieldbank ML11 214 D5
Larkhall ML3, ML9 184 C3
Paisley PA2 113 D1
Sunnyside Square E KA1 227 F2
Sunnyside Square W KA1 227 F2
Sunnyside St
Falkirk FK1 41 E6
Larkhall ML9 184 F4
Sunnyside Terr ML1 143 B5
Surcoat Loan FK7 7 E3
Surrey La 1 G5 117 B4
Surrey St 3 G5 117 B4
Susannah St 2 G83 27 E5
Sussex St G41 116 E5
Sutcliffe Ct G13 95 E7
Sutcliffe Rd G13 95 F7
Sutherland Ave
Alloa FK10 10 C7
Bearsden G61 75 E7
Glasgow G41 116 C3
Stirling FK8 2 C1
Sutherland Cres ML3 162 A4
Sutherland Ct G41 116 E4
Sutherland Dr
Airdrie ML6 122 F5
Denny FK6 39 D8
Dumbarton G82 50 C3
Glasgow G46 136 D1
Kilmarnock KA3 223 D2
Sutherland La G12 96 D2
Sutherland Pl
Bellshill ML4 141 F2
Helensburgh G84 16 B2
Sutherland Rd
Clydebank G81 74 B2
Greenock PA16 45 A4
Sutherland St
Hamilton G72 161 C5
Helensburgh G84 16 B2
Paisley PA1 113 D5
Sutherland Way G74 160 C3
Sutherness Dr G33 119 A8
Suttie Way FK9 1 F8
Sutton Ct KA13 207 B3
Sutton Park Cres FK5 23 E3
Sutton Pl FK2 42 D5
Swaledale G74 159 C3
Swallow Dr PA5 131 C7
Swallow Gdns G13 94 F7
Swallow Pl KA3 228 C7
Swallow Rd
Clydebank G81 74 D7
Wishaw ML2 165 B3
Swan Pl PA5 131 C7
Swanson Rd G83 27 D7
Swan St
Clydebank G81 73 F3
Glasgow G4 241 A4
Swanston St G40 118 A2
Swan Way ML8 186 F4
Sween Ave G44 137 A4
Sween Dr ML3 162 A1
Sween Path ML4 142 C3
Sweethill Terr ML5 122 D3
Sweethill Wlk ML4 142 C7
Sweethope Gdns G71 141 B2
Sweethope Pl G71 141 A3
Swift Bank ML3 161 E1
Swift Cl ML2 165 B3
Swift Cres G13 94 F8
Swift Pl
East Kilbride G75 179 F6
Johnstone PA5 131 D7
Swinburne Ave G72 161 B7
Swinburne Dr FK10 5 B1
Swindon St G81 73 E3
SWINHILL 199 C6
Swinhill Ave ML9 199 C6
Swinhill Rd ML9 199 C6
Swinstie Rd ML1 165 D8
Swinstie View ML1 144 C1
SWINTON 120 C6
Swinton Ave G69 120 D5
Swinton Cres
Coatbridge ML5 121 B4
Glasgow G69 120 D5
Swinton Dr G52 115 B5
Swinton Gdns G69 120 D5
Swinton Path G69 120 D5
Swinton Pl
Coatbridge ML5 121 B4
Glasgow G52 115 B5
Irvine KA11 220 B7
Swinton Prim Sch G69 120 C6
Swinton Rd G69 120 C5
Swinton View G69 120 C5
Swisscot Ave ML3 183 B8
Swisscot Wlk ML3 183 B8
Switchback Rd G61 75 F1
Swordale Pl G34 120 A8
Sword St
Airdrie ML6 122 F7
Glasgow G31 117 F6
Sword's Way FK2 24 A1
Sycamore Ave
Beith KA15 150 B2
Johnstone PA5 112 A1
Kirkintilloch G66 79 D5
Uddingston G71 141 C8
Sycamore Cres
Airdrie ML6 123 D6
Ayr KA7 239 D6
East Kilbride G75 180 D6
Sycamore Ct
Beith KA15 150 B1
East Kilbride G75 180 D6
Sycamore Dr
Airdrie ML6 123 D6
Clydebank G81 74 A4
Hamilton ML3 162 F2
Sycamore Gr G72 161 C8
Sycamore Pl
East Kilbride G75 180 D6
Gourock PA19 44 C6
Motherwell ML1 143 C3
Stirling FK8 6 F5
Sycamores The FK10 4 B1
Sycamore Way
Cambuslang G72 139 F4
Carmunnock G76 158 D7
Milton of Campsie G66 58 C5
Sydenham Ct G12 96 B4
Sydenham La G12 96 C3
Sydenham Rd G12 96 C3
Sydes Brae G72 161 B4
Sydney Dr G75 180 C8
Sydney Pl 6 G75 180 C8
Sydney St
Clydebank G81 73 D4
Glasgow G31 241 C1
Sykehead Ave ML4 142 B5
Sykeside Rd ML6 122 F4
Sykes Terr G78 154 F7
Sylvania Way G81 74 B2
Sylvania Way S G81 74 B1
SYMINGTON 231 C3
Symington Ct 6 KA10 229 E5
Symington Dr G81 74 B2
Symington Pl
Falkirk FK2 24 B3
Irvine KA11 224 H7
Symington Prim Sch KA1 231 D4
Symington Road N KA1 231 D3
Symington Road S KA1 231 C3
Symington Sq 8 G75 180 F8
Symon Twr FK1 42 D4
Syms La KA8 236 A1
Syriam Pl 1 G21 97 F4
Syriam St G21 97 F5

T

Tabard Pl G13 95 C8
Tabard Rd G13 95 C8
Tabernacle La G72 139 A5
Tabernacle St G72 139 A5
Taggart Rd G65 60 F3
Taig Rd G66 80 B7
Tain Terr G72 161 C3
Tait Ave G78 134 D3
Tait Dr FK5 41 C8
Tait Wlk ML8 201 B1
Takmadoon Rd G65, FK6 37 A7
Tak-Ma-Doon Rd G65 36 F3
Talbot G74 160 C4
Talbot Cres ML5 121 E4
Talbot Ct G13 95 B5
Talbot Dr G13 95 B5
Talbot Pl G13 95 B5
Talbot Rd G83 28 A8
Talbot Terr
Glasgow G13 95 B5
Uddingston G71 140 E8
Talisker FK10 4 B2
Talisker Ave KA3 222 E4
Talisker Cres ML6 103 B3
Talisman G81 74 D2
Talisman Ave G82 49 C4
Talisman Cres
Helensburgh G84 25 B8
Motherwell ML1 142 D2
Talisman Rd
Glasgow G13 95 C6
Paisley PA2 132 E7
Talisman Wlk KA21 206 A2
Tallant Rd G15 75 B3
Tallant Terr G15 75 C3
Talla Rd G52 115 B5
Tall Ship The* G3 116 C8
Tamarack Cres G71 141 C8
Tamar Dr G75 179 F6
Tambowie Ave G62 54 F2
Tambowie Cres G62 54 F2
Tambowie St G13 95 E8
TAMFOURHILL 41 C4
Tamfourhill Ave FK1 41 C4
Tamfourhill Ind Est FK1 41 C4
Tamfourhill Rd FK1 41 C4
Tammy Dale's Rd KA13 207 F3
Tam O'Shanter Dr FK7 12 D7
Tam O'Shanter Experience* KA7 238 E1
Tam's Brig KA8 236 A3
Tamshill St G20 96 F5
Tanar Ave PA4 94 F1
Tanar Way PA4 94 E1
TANDLEHILL 111 B1
Tandlehill Rd PA10 111 B1
Tanera Ave G44 137 C4
Tanera Ct FK1 42 B2
Tanfield Pl G32 119 C7
Tanfield St G32 119 C7
Tankerland Rd G44 137 A6
Tannadice Ave G52 115 C4
Tannadice Path G52 115 C4
Tanna Dr G52 115 F3
Tannahill Cres
Johnstone PA5 111 E1
Johnstone PA5 111 F1
Tannahill Ctr The PA3 113 B6
Tannahill Dr G74 160 C3
Tannahill Rd
Glasgow G43 136 F6
Paisley PA3 113 B6
Tannahill Terr PA3 113 B6
Tanners Rd FK1 42 A4
Tannery La FK8 2 A1
Tannoch Dr
Cumbernauld G67 82 F7
Milngavie G62 55 B3
Tannoch Pl G67 82 F7
Tannoch Rd G78 153 B3
TANNOCHSIDE 141 B8
Tannochside Dr G71 121 B1
Tannochside Pk
Motherwell G71 121 B1
Uddingston G71 141 B8
Tannochside Prim Sch G71 141 B8
Tannock St
Glasgow G22 97 B4
Kilmarnock KA1 227 F6
Tantallon Ave PA19 43 F5
Tantallon Ct ML8 187 E3
Tantallon Dr
Coatbridge ML5 101 C2
Falkirk FK2 24 A3
Paisley PA2 113 A1
Tantallon Pk G74 159 D2
Tantallon Rd
2 Bothwell G71 141 B3
Glasgow, Baillieston G69 120 A3
Glasgow, Langside G41 136 E8
Tanzieknowe Ave G72 139 B3
Tanzieknowe Dr G72 139 B3
Tanzieknowe Pl G72 139 A3
Tanzieknowe Rd G72 139 B3
Tappoch Pl FK5 23 A3
Taransay Ct G22 97 E7
Taransay St G51 116 A8
Tarbert Ave
Blantyre G72 140 C2
West Kilbride KA23 190 E5
Wishaw ML2 165 A1
Tarbert Ct ML3 162 A1
Tarbert Pl ML8 188 A1
Tarbert Way ML5 121 E4
Tarbet St PA19 44 F7
Tarbolton G74 160 D3
Tarbolton Cres ML6 123 D1
Tarbolton Dr G81 74 C3
Tarbolton Path ML9 184 F3
Tarbolton Pl KA3 223 C6
Tarbolton Rd
Cumbernauld G67 62 B2
Dundonald KA2 225 F1
Glasgow G43 136 D6
Monkton KA9 233 E4
Symington KA1 231 F5
Tarbolton Sq G81 74 C3
Tarbrax Path ML7 147 A3
Tarbrax Way ML3 162 A3
Tarduff Pl FK6 21 B2
Tarff Ave G76 178 E5
Tarfside Ave G52 115 C4
Tarfside Gdns G52 115 D4
Tarfside Oval G52 115 D4
Target Rd ML6 123 B6
Targe Wynd FK7 7 E3
Tarland St G51 115 F6
Tarn Gr G33 98 E8
Tarquin Pl 4 ML1 163 C8
Tarras Dr PA4 94 E1
Tarras Pl G72 139 D5
TARRYHOLME 224 F8
Tarryholme Dr KA12 219 D2
Tasker St PA16 45 C5
Tasman Dr G75 180 B8
Tasmania Quadrant ML2 165 E3
Tassie Pl G74 160 A2
Tassie St G41 136 D8
Tattershall Rd G33 99 C1
Tavistock Dr G43 136 D5
Tay Ave PA4 94 E3
Taybank Dr KA7 239 A3
Tay Cres
Bishopbriggs G64 78 B1
Glasgow G33 98 E1
Tay Ct
Alloa FK10 10 C6
East Kilbride G75 179 E7
Tay Gdns ML3 183 B8
Tay Gr G75 179 E7
Tayinloan Dr ML8 202 B8
Tay La ML2 166 A5
Tay Loan ML1 143 A5
Taylor Ave
Kilbarchan PA10 110 F3
Motherwell ML1 143 D2
Taylor Brown Cl KA3 211 E8
Taylor Ct
1 Ayr KA8 235 F2
Falkirk FK2 42 C7
Taylor High Sch ML1 143 A3
Taylor Pl
Glasgow G4 241 B3
Saltcoats KA21 216 F8
Taylor's Rd FK5 23 C1
Taylor St
Alexandria G83 27 C7
Ayr KA8 235 F2
Clydebank G81 94 C8
Glasgow G4 241 B3
Taymouth Dr PA19 43 F5
Taymouth St G32 119 B3
Taynish Dr G44 137 B5
Tay Pl
Dumbarton G82 50 B7
East Kilbride G75 179 E7
Johnstone PA5 131 C8
Kilmarnock KA1 228 A5
Larkhall ML9 199 A8
Shotts ML7 146 E6
Tay Rd
Bearsden G61 75 D2
Bishopbriggs G64 78 B1
Troon KA10 229 G4
Tayside ML6 102 F1
Tay St
Coatbridge ML5 101 C1
Falkirk FK2 24 C1
Greenock PA16 45 B5
Tay Terr G75 179 E7
Tay Wlk 10 G67 61 F1
Teak Pl G71 121 D1
Teal Cres G75 179 F5
Teal Ct ML4 141 E8
Teal Dr G13 95 A7
Tealing Ave G52 115 C4
Tealing Cres G52 115 C4
Teasel Ave G53 135 B3
Teawell Rd G77 156 D5
Technology Ave G72 161 C4
Teesdale G74 159 C3
Teign Gr G75 179 F6
Teith Ave PA4 94 F2
Teith Dr G61 75 D3
Teith Pl
Cambuslang G72 139 D5
Kilmarnock KA1 228 B5
Teith St G33 98 E1
Telegraph Rd ML6 105 B7
Telephone La G12 96 C2
Telford Ave ML9 199 C8
Telford Ct
Bannockburn FK7 7 D1
Clydebank G81 74 A2
3 Troon KA10 229 E5
Telford Pl
Cumbernauld G67 83 A8
Irvine KA11 219 F1
Telford Rd
Cumbernauld G67 83 A8
East Kilbride G75 180 E8
Telford Sq FK1 41 E6
Telford St ML4 142 A6
Telford Terr 7 G75 180 F8
Teme Pl G75 179 F7
Templand Cres KA24 191 C8
Templand Rd KA24 191 C8
Templar Ave G13 75 D1
TEMPLE 95 E7
Temple Cotts G67 82 B7
Temple Ct ML8 187 A6
Temple Denny Rd FK6 21 D2
Temple Gdns G13 95 F7
Templehill KA10 229 C3
Templeland Rd G53 115 C2
Temple Locks Ct 1 G13 95 F7
Temple Locks Pl 2 G13 95 F7
Temple Rd G13 96 A7
Templerigg Ct KA9 233 C1
Templerigg St KA9 233 C1

Templeton Bsns Ctr G40 .117 E5
Templeton Cres KA9 . . . . 236 D8
Templeton Ct G40 . . . . . . .117 E5
Templeton St G40 . . . . . . .117 E5
Ten Acres FK10 . . . . .5 B1
Tennant Ave G74. . . . . 159 A1
Tennant Complex The
G74 . . . . 159 A1
Tennant St PA4 . . . . .94 D4
Tennant Wynd ML4 . . . . . 142 A8
Tennent St ML5. . . . . .122 B5
Tennyson Dr G31 . . . . .118 E4
Tennyson Gdns G72. . . . . 161 D7
Tenters Way PA2. . . . . .113 B3
Tern Pl PA5. . . . . 131 D7
Tern Way ML5 . . . . .122 E3
Terrace Rd PA15 . . . . .46 A4
Terregles Ave G41 . . . . . . 116 D2
Terregles Cres G41 . . . . . 116 C2
Terregles Dr G41 . . . . 116 C2
Teviot Ave
Bishopbriggs G64 . . . . .78 A4
Paisley PA2 . . . . .132 E8
Teviot Cres G61. . . . . .75 D2
Teviotdale
East Kilbride G74. . . . . 159 D2
Newton Mearns G77 . . . . . .157 B5
Teviot Dr PA7. . . . . .72 C2
Teviot Pl
Cambuslang G72 . . . . .139 E5
Troon KA10 . . . . .229 F4
Teviot Rd PA14 . . . . .68 F6
Teviot Sq G67 . . . . .61 F2
Teviot St
Ayr KA8 . . . . .236 B3
Coatbridge ML5. . . . . 101 D2
Falkirk FK1. . . . . .41 F4
Glasgow G3. . . . . 116 C8
Teviot Terr PA5 . . . . 131 C8
Teviot Way 2 G72. . . . . . . 161 C7
Teviot Wlk G67 . . . . .61 F2
Tewkesbury Rd G74. . . . . 160 D4
Thane Rd G13 . . . . .95 C6
Thanes Gate G71 . . . . .140 E5
Thankerton Ave ML1 . . . . .142 F5
Thankerton Rd ML9. . . . . .185 B1
Tharsis St G21. . . . . .97 F1
Theatre Royal* G2 . . . . . 240 C3
THE GREENS. 79 B6
Thetford Gr ML5. . . . . .101 F6
Thimble St G82. . . . . .27 D2
Third Ave
Alexandria G83 . . . . .27 F5
Auchinloch G66 . . . . .79 D1
Dumbarton G82. . . . . .50 C2
Glasgow G44. . . . . .137 B7
Irvine KA12 . . . . 224 D8
Millerston G33. . . . . .99 C5
Renfrew PA4 . . . . .94 C2
Third Ave La G44 . . . . .137 B7
Third Gdns G41. . . . . 116 A4
Thirdpart Cres G13 . . . . .94 E7
Thirdpart Holdings KA23 190 A8
Thirdpart Pl KA1. . . . . 227 D7
Third Rd G72 . . . . .161 E5
Third St G71. . . . . .140 F8
Thirlmere G75. . . . . .179 F5
Thistle Ave FK6. . . . . .21 D3
Thistlebank PA11 . . . . .90 C1
Thistle Bank G66 . . . . .79 D4
Thistlebank Gdns ML5 . . .121 E3
Thistle Chambers 4 FK8. . . 7 B7
Thistle Cres ML9. . . . . .185 B1
Thistle Ctr The FK8 . . . . 7 B7
Thistledown Gr ML5 . . . . 122 C6
Thistle Gdns ML1 . . . . 143 A5
Thistle Ind Est FK7. . . . . 7 C6
Thistle Mews KA20. . . . . . .217 E7
Thistle Neuk G60 . . . . .73 A7
Thistle Pl
East Kilbride G74. . . . . 159 D3
Stirling FK8 . . . . .2 A2
Thistle Quadrant ML6. . . .103 B1
Thistle Rd ML1 . . . . 143 A3
Thistles Sh Ctr The FK8 . . . . 7 B7
Thistle St
Airdrie ML6 . . . . .103 B1
Alloa FK10. . . . . .10 C6
Cleland ML1. . . . . 144 C1
Falkirk FK2. . . . . .42 C6
Glasgow G5. . . . . 117 C5
Kirkintilloch G66 . . . . .79 D7
Paisley PA2 . . . . 113 C2
Thistle Terr
Glasgow G5. . . . . 117 C4
Stevenston KA20. . . . . .206 E2
Thistle Wlk KA7 . . . . 239 C3
Thomas Baird Gdns KA3 223 A3
Thomas Campbell St
KA21. . . . . 217 A8
Thomas Muir Ave G64 . . . .98 A8
Thomas Muir La PA15. . . . .46 F2
Thomas Muir St PA15 . . . . .46 F2
Thomas St
Alexandria G83 . . . . .27 E4
Paisley PA1 . . . . .113 B4
Thomas Taylor Ave
ML11 . . . . .215 B4
Thompson Brae PA1 . . . . . .113 E3
Thompson Pl G81. . . . . .74 C6
Thomson Ave
Johnstone PA5. . . . . .111 E3
Kirkintilloch G66 . . . . .79 E8
Wishaw ML2 . . . . 164 D1
Thomson Cres FK1. . . . . . . .41 E3
Thomson Ct ML9. . . . . .198 F3
Thomson Dr
Airdrie ML6 . . . . .122 F6
Bearsden G61 . . . . .75 F6
Bellshill ML4 . . . . 141 D5
Motherwell ML1. . . . . 163 D5
Thomson Gr G72 . . . . 139 A7
Thomson Pl
Cambusbarron FK7 . . . . .6 D5
Slamannan FK1 . . . . .86 B3
Thomson's Cl 22 ML11 . . 215 A4
Thomson St
Ayr KA8 . . . . 236 C2
Carluke ML8. . . . . .187 F2
Glasgow G31 . . . . 118 A6
Johnstone PA5. . . . . .111 E2
Kilmarnock KA3 . . . . .222 F2
Renfrew PA4 . . . . .94 C2
Thomson Terr
Shotts ML7. . . . . 146 D6
Stewarton KA3. . . . . 211 C8
Thom St PA16 . . . . .45 D4
Thorn Ave
2 Hamilton G72. . . . . 161 D3
Thorntonhall G74. . . . . 158 C3
Thornbank St G3 . . . . 116 C8
Thorn Brae PA5. . . . . 112 A3
Thornbridge Ave
1 Glasgow G12 . . . . .96 C5
1 Glasgow, Garrowhill
G69. . . . . .120 B5
Thornbridge Gdns
Falkirk FK2. . . . . .42 E4
3 Glasgow G69 . . . . 120 A5
Thornbridge Rd
Falkirk FK2. . . . . .42 E5
Glasgow G69. . . . . 120 A5
Thornbridge Sq FK2 . . . . . .42 E5
Thorncliffe Gdns G41 . . . .116 E2
Thorncroft Dr G44 . . . . . . 137 D4
Thorn Ct PA5 . . . . .112 B2
Thorndale Gdns FK4 . . . . . .39 B2
Thorndean Ave ML4. . . . . .142 B4
Thorndean Cres ML4. . . . .142 B4
Thorndene PA5 . . . . .112 B3
Thorndene Ave ML1. . . . . 143 C2
Thorndene Ct FK1 . . . . .41 F2
Thorndene Terr FK1. . . . . . .86 B7
Thorndene La G14 . . . . .95 A4
Thorn Dr
Bearsden G61 . . . . .75 D5
Rutherglen G73. . . . . 138 C4
Thorndyke G74 . . . . 160 C5
Thorne Rd FK10 . . . . .4 E1
Thornhill PA5. . . . . .112 B2
Thornhill Ave
Blantyre G72 . . . . 140 D1
Elderslie PA5 . . . . .112 B2
Hamilton G72. . . . . 161 D8
Thornhill Ct
Falkirk FK2. . . . . .42 C6
Kilwinning KA13. . . . . .207 B3
Thornhill Dr PA5. . . . . .112 B2
Thornhill Gdns G77 . . . . . 156 D2
Thornhill La 4 G71. . . . . . .141 B3
Thornhill Path G31 . . . . . . 118 D5
Thornhill Pl KA1. . . . . .227 E3
Thornhill Rd
Falkirk FK2. . . . . .42 C6
Hamilton ML3 . . . . .161 E4
Thornhill Way ML5. . . . . . 122 D3
Thornhouse Ave KA12. . . 219 D3
Thornhouse Ct KA12 . . . 219 D3
Thorniecroft Dr G67 . . . . . . .82 C6
Thorniecroft Pl G67. . . . . . .82 C6
Thornielee G74. . . . . .160 B2
Thorniewood Gdns G71. . 141 A7
Thorniewood Rd G71 . . . .140 F8
Thornkip Pl ML5. . . . . 122 D5
Thornlea Dr G46. . . . . 136 D4
Thornlea Gdns 2 ML6 . . .103 B1
Thornlea Pl ML11. . . . . . . .215 F7
Thornlea St ML8. . . . . 202 A8
Thornley Ave G13. . . . . .95 B6
THORNLIEBANK. 135 F3
Thornliebank Ind Est
G46 . . . . .135 E3
Thornliebank Prim Sch
G46 . . . . 136 A4
Thornliebank Rd G46 . . . .136 B5
Thornliebank Sta G46. . . 136 A4
Thornlie Gill ML2 . . . . .165 B2
Thornlie Prim Sch ML2 . 165 A1
Thornly Park Ave PA2. . . 134 A8
Thornly Park Dr PA2 . . . . .133 F8
Thornly Park Gdns PA2 . .113 E1
Thornly Park Rd PA2. . . . .133 F8
Thornly Park Residence
PA2. . . . . .133 F7
Thorn Prim Sch PA5 . . . . 112 A2
Thorn Rd
Bearsden G61 . . . . .75 D5
Bellshill ML4 . . . . .142 B5
Thornside Rd PA5. . . . . . . 112 A3
Thorn Terr KA3 . . . . 223 A4
Thornton Ave
Bonnybridge FK4 . . . . .40 B6
Crosshouse KA2 . . . . .221 E1
Thornton Gdns FK4 . . . . . . .40 B6
THORNTONHALL 158 C3
Thorntonhall Sta G74. . . . .158 B3
Thornton La G20. . . . . .96 E7
Thornton Pl ML3. . . . . 183 D6
Thornton Rd G74 . . . . 158 C2
Thornton St
Coatbridge ML5. . . . . 101 D2
Glasgow G20. . . . . .96 E7
Thorntree Ave
Beith KA15. . . . . 150 C2
Hamilton ML3 . . . . .161 F5
Thorntree Dr ML5. . . . . . . .121 F5
Thorntree Prim Sch G32 119 A6
Thorntree Way G71 . . . . . .141 B3
Thornwood Ave
Ayr KA8 . . . . .236 E2
Glasgow G11 . . . . .96 A2
Kirkintilloch G66 . . . . .79 B5
Thornwood Cres G11 . . . . .95 F3
Thornwood Dr
Bridge of Weir PA11 . . . . . .110 B7
Glasgow G11 . . . . .95 F2
4 Glasgow G11 . . . . .96 A3
Irvine KA12 . . . . 219 C2
Paisley PA2 . . . . .113 B1
Thornwood Gdns G11. . . . .96 A2
Thornwood Pl G11. . . . . . . .96 A3
Thornwood Prim Sch G11 95 F2
Thornwood Quadrant G11 95 F3
Thornwood Rd G11 . . . . . . .95 F2
Thornwood Terr G11 . . . . . .95 F2
Thornyburn Dr G69 . . . . . 120 D4
Thornyburn Pl G69 . . . . . 120 C4
Thornycroft Terr FK7. . . . . .12 C3
Thornyflat Cres KA8 . . . . .236 F2
Thornyflat Dr KA8 . . . . . . .236 E2
Thornyflat Pl KA8. . . . . . . .236 F2
Thornyflat Rd KA8 . . . . . . .236 E2
Thornyflat St KA8. . . . . . . .236 E2
THRASHBUSH. 103 A2
Thrashbush Ave ML2. . . . . 165 D4
Thrashbush Cres ML2. . . 165 D4
Thrashbush La ML6 . . . . . .103 B2
Thrashbush Quadrant
ML6 . . . . 103 A2
Thrashbush Rd
Airdrie ML6 . . . . .103 B2
Wishaw ML2 . . . . 165 D4
Thread St PA1 . . . . .113 F3
Threave Ct ML8. . . . . .187 E3
Threave Pl
Gartcosh G69. . . . . .100 E4
Newton Mearns G77 . . . . . .156 B5
Three Bridges Rdbt FK1. . .41 A6
Threepwood Rd KA15 . . . .150 E2
Three Rivers Wlk G75. . . .180 B8
Three Sisters Ct KA21. . . .205 E2
Three Stanes Rdbt KA11 .224 F6
Threestonehill Ave G32 . 119 C6
Threshold G74. . . . . 160 A2
Threshold Pk G74. . . . . . . 160 A2
Thriplee Rd PA11 . . . . 110 C8
THROSK 9 A3
Thrums G74 . . . . 160 D5
Thrums Ave G64. . . . . .78 C1
Thrums Gdns G64. . . . . .78 C1
Thrushcraig Cres PA2. . . . .113 F2
Thrush Pl PA5 . . . . 131 D7
Thurso St G11 . . . . .96 C1
Thurston Rd G52 . . . . .115 B5
Thyme Sq ML1. . . . . .163 E8
Tianavaig PA4 . . . . .93 C7
Tibbermore Rd 6 G11. . . . .96 A3
Tibbies Loan FK7 . . . . .12 D8
Tiber Ave ML1 . . . . 142 C1
Tighnasheen Way G72 . . 140 D1
Tig Rd KA8 . . . . 236 A3
Tillanburn Rd ML1 . . . . . . .143 F3
Tillet Oval PA3. . . . . .113 D7
Tillie St G20. . . . . .96 F3
Till St ML2 . . . . .165 B6
Tillycairn Ave G33 . . . . .99 D2
Tillycairn Dr G33 . . . . .99 D2
Tillycairn Pl G33. . . . . .99 E2
Tillycairn Rd G33 . . . . .99 E2
Tillycairn St G33. . . . . .99 E2
Tilt Rd ML2. . . . . .165 F6
Tilt St G33 . . . . .98 E2
Time Capsule* ML5 . . . . .121 F6
Timmons Gr ML4 . . . . 142 D5
Timmons Pl FK6 . . . . .21 D1
Timmons Terr ML6. . . . . . 123 D1
Tinker's La ML1. . . . . 163 C5
Tintagel Gdns G69. . . . . . . .80 F3
Tinto Ave KA1 . . . . 228 A4
TINTOCK. 59 C2
Tintock Dr G66 . . . . .58 F1
Tintock Pl G68 . . . . .61 D6
Tintock Rd G66. . . . . .59 B2
Tinto Cres ML2 . . . . 165 D2
Tinto Ct ML5 . . . . 122 C3
Tinto Dr
Barrhead G78 . . . . 134 C1
Cumbernauld G68 . . . . .61 D2
Tinto Gr G69 . . . . .121 B6
Tinto Prim Sch G43. . . . . 136 C6
Tinto Rd
Airdrie ML6 . . . . .123 B6
Bearsden G61 . . . . .75 C6
Bishopbriggs G64 . . . . .78 D1
Glasgow G43. . . . . 136 C5
Tinto St ML2 . . . . 165 C2
Tinto View ML3 . . . . .183 E8
Tinto Way
Cleland ML1. . . . . 144 C2
East Kilbride G75. . . . . .180 B5
Tinwald Path G52. . . . . . . 115 A5
Tipperary Pl FK5. . . . . .23 E2
Tiree G74 . . . . 181 C7
Tiree Ave
Paisley PA2 . . . . 133 D7
Port Glasgow PA14 . . . . .69 A7
Renfrew PA4 . . . . .94 C1
Tiree Cres ML2 . . . . .165 F6
Tiree Ct
Cumbernauld G67 . . . . .82 D8
Tiree Ct *continued*
Irvine KA11 . . . . .225 B8
Tiree Dr G67 . . . . .82 D8
Tiree Gdns
Bearsden G61 . . . . .75 B6
Glenmavis ML6 . . . . .102 F5
Old Kilpatrick G60 . . . . .73 C6
Tiree Grange ML3 . . . . . . .161 F1
Tiree Pl
Coatbridge ML5. . . . . 121 D4
Falkirk FK1. . . . . .42 B1
Newton Mearns G77 . . . . . .156 B5
Old Kilpatrick G60 . . . . .73 C6
Stevenston KA20. . . . . .206 F1
Tiree Rd G67 . . . . .82 D8
Tiree St G21. . . . . .98 C2
Tirry Ave PA4. . . . . .94 F2
Tirry Way PA4 . . . . .94 F2
Titania FK10. . . . . .10 A8
Titchfield Rd KA10 . . . . . . .229 B2
Titchfield St KA1 . . . . .227 F8
Titchfield Way KA11 . . . . . 220 A5
Titwood Dr KA3. . . . . .222 F4
Titwood Rd
Glasgow G41. . . . . 116 D1
Glasgow G41. . . . . .116 E1
Newton Mearns G77 . . . . . 156 D1
Tiverton Ave G32 . . . . 119 D3
Tivoli Ct G75 . . . . .180 E6
Tobago Pl
East Kilbride G75. . . . . 159 A1
Glasgow G40 . . . . .117 F5
Tobago St
Glasgow G40. . . . . .117 E5
Greenock PA15 . . . . .45 F5
Tobermory Dr KA3. . . . . . 222 D3
Tobermory Gdns 7 ML6 103 A3
Tobermory Rd G73. . . . . . 138 D2
Todburn Dr PA2. . . . . .133 F7
Todd Pl G31 . . . . 118 C7
Todd St G31 . . . . 118 C7
Todhill Ave KA3. . . . . .222 F4
Todhills 9 G75 . . . . .180 F8
Todhills N G75. . . . . .180 F8
Todhills S G75. . . . . .180 F8
Todholm Cres PA2 . . . . . . .114 B2
Todholm Prim Sch PA2. . .114 B2
Todholm Rd PA2 . . . . .114 B2
Todholm Terr PA2. . . . . . . .114 B2
Todrig Dr KA1 . . . . .227 E3
Toftcombs Ave ML9. . . . . 198 D1
Toftcombs Cres ML9 . . . . 198 D1
Tofthill Ave G64 . . . . .77 F2
Tofthill Gdns G64 . . . . .77 F2
Tofts KA24. . . . . 191 D7
Tofts Cres KA24. . . . . 191 D7
Togo Pl PA15 . . . . .45 E4
Tolbooth St 3 FK1. . . . . . . .42 B4
Tollbrae Ave ML6 . . . . .123 B7
Tollbrae Prim Sch ML6. . .123 B7
Tollcross Park Gdns G32 .118 E3
Tollcross Park Gr G32. . . .118 F3
Tollcross Park L Ctr G32 .118 F4
Tollcross Park View G32. .118 F3
Tollcross Rd G31, G32 . . . .118 E4
Tollerton Dr KA12. . . . . . . 219 D4
Tollhouse Gdns ML4 . . . . 142 C3
Tollhouse Way KA11 . . . . 220 A5
Toll La G51. . . . . .116 E6
Tollpark Cres ML2 . . . . . . 166 A5
Tollpark Pl G68 . . . . .62 E8
Tollpark Rd G68 . . . . .62 E8
Toll St ML1 . . . . .163 F5
Toll The G76. . . . . .157 E8
Toll Wynd ML3. . . . . 183 C7
Tolmount Cres ML1 . . . . . 164 D3
Tolsta St 2 G23 . . . . .76 E1
Tom-a-Mhoid G84. . . . . .15 A3
Tomtain Brae G68 . . . . .81 F7
Tomtain Ct G68. . . . . .81 F7
Toner Gdns ML2 . . . . .186 B7
Tontine Cres G82 . . . . .49 D8
Tontine La G1 . . . . .241 B1
Tontine Pk G82 . . . . .49 C7
Tontine Pl G73 . . . . .138 E4
Topaz Terr ML4 . . . . 142 A3
Tophill Entry FK1 . . . . .41 F5
Toponthank La KA3 . . . . . 223 A6
Toppersfield PA10. . . . . . . 111 C2
Torbeg Gdns G75 . . . . .180 B4
Torbeg Ho KA9 . . . . 236 C5
TORBOTHIE 147 B4
Torbothie Rd ML7. . . . . . . .147 B4
Torbracken PA9. . . . . 131 A6
Torbreck St G52 . . . . .115 F5
TORBREX 6 F5
Torbrex Farm Rd FK7 . . . . . .7 A4
Torbrex La FK7, FK8 . . . . . . .7 A5
Torbrex Rd
Cumbernauld G67 . . . . .62 A1
Stirling FK7 . . . . .6 F4
Torburn Ave
Glasgow G46 . . . . .136 B4
Plean FK7 . . . . .12 D3
TORBUSH. 166 C3
Tordene Path G68 . . . . .61 D3
Torgyle St G23. . . . . .76 D1
Torlea Pl FK5. . . . . .23 B3
Tormeadow Rd G77 . . . . . 156 D5
Tormore Ct G33 . . . . .99 E6
Tormore St 1 G51. . . . . . . 115 D6
Tormusk Dr G45 . . . . 138 A4
Tormusk Gdns G45. . . . . . 138 A4
Tormusk Gr G45 . . . . 138 A4
Tormusk Rd G45. . . . . 138 A4
Torness St G11 . . . . .96 C2
Torogay Pl G22 . . . . .97 E8
Torogay St G22 . . . . .97 D7
Torogay Terr G22 . . . . .97 C8
Toronto Wlk G72. . . . . 139 C8
Torphin Cres G32 . . . . 119 A7
Torphin Wlk G32. . . . . .119 B7
TORRANCE. 57 C1
Torrance Ave
Airdrie ML6 . . . . 123 D7
East Kilbride G75. . . . . .181 B5
Torrance Ct G75 . . . . .181 B4
Torrance Gait G75 . . . . . . .181 B4
Torrance La G75. . . . . .181 B4
Torrance Prim Sch G64 . . .57 B1
Torrance Rd
East Kilbride G74. . . . . .159 E2
Greenock PA15 . . . . .46 B2
Torrance G64. . . . . .78 C7
Torrance Rdbt
Bishopbriggs G64 . . . . .78 C6
East Kilbride G75. . . . . .181 B5
Torrance Wynd G75. . . . . .181 B4
Torran Dr PA8 . . . . .93 E8
Torran Rd G33. . . . . .119 F7
TORRANYARD 209 D5
Torranyard Cvn Pk KA11,
KA13. . . . . 209 D4
Torranyard Terr ML3 . . . . .161 E1
Torr Ave PA11 . . . . .89 E2
Torr Cres G84 . . . . .15 E5
Torr Gdns G22. . . . . .97 D4
Torriden Ct ML5 . . . . .121 E5
Torriden Pl ML5 . . . . .121 E5
Torriden St ML5 . . . . .121 E5
Torridon Ave
Falkirk FK2. . . . . .24 C1
Glasgow G41. . . . . .116 B4
Motherwell ML1. . . . . 143 D3
Torridon Ct FK10. . . . . .10 C5
Torridon Dr PA4 . . . . .94 E2
Torridon Gdns
Bearsden G61 . . . . .75 C7
Newton Mearns G77 . . . . . .157 B4
Torrinch Dr G83 . . . . .19 E2
Torrington Ave
Giffnock G46 . . . . 136 A1
Rutherglen G46 . . . . 157 A8
Torrington Cres G32 . . . . 119 D3
Torrin Loan ML7 . . . . .147 B3
Torrin Rd G23 . . . . .76 D1
Torrisdale Pl ML5 . . . . .121 E7
Torrisdale St
Coatbridge ML5. . . . . .121 E7
1 Glasgow G42 . . . . 117 A2
Torr La PA11. . . . . .89 E2
Torr Pl G22. . . . . .97 D4
Torr Rd
Bishopbriggs G64 . . . . .78 D1
Bridge of Weir PA11 . . . . . 110 C8
Torr St G22. . . . . .97 D4
Torryburn Rd G21. . . . . .98 C4
Torry Dr FK12. . . . . .4 E7
TORWOOD 22 E6
Torwood Ave FK5 . . . . .23 B2
Torwood Brae ML3. . . . . . .161 F2
Torwoodhill G84. . . . . .15 F4
Torwoodhill Pl G84 . . . . . . .15 F4
Torwoodhill Rd G84. . . . . . .15 F4
Torwood La G69 . . . . .81 A2
Torwood Sch FK5. . . . . .22 E6
TORYGLEN. 137 D8
Toryglen Prim Sch G42 . .137 E8
Toryglen Rd G73. . . . . .137 F8
Toryglen St G5 . . . . .117 E2
Touchhill Cres FK7. . . . . . . .12 C3
Touch Rd FK7, FK8 . . . . .6 B6
Toul Gdns ML1. . . . . 164 C3
Tourhill Ind Est KA3. . . . . .222 B6
Tourhill Rd KA3. . . . . .222 F4
Tourmaline Terr ML4. . . . .142 B3
Tournai Path 10 G72 . . . . 161 D7
Towans Ct KA9 . . . . 233 D2
Toward Ct
Blantyre G72 . . . . .140 E1
Hamilton G72. . . . . .161 E8
Toward Rd G33 . . . . 119 C8
Toward Way PA2. . . . . 133 D7
Tower Ave G78 . . . . 134 D4
Tower Cres PA4. . . . . .94 B2
Tower Dr
Gourock PA19 . . . . .44 D6
Renfrew PA4 . . . . .94 B2
Tower Gdns PA19 . . . . .44 E8
Towerhill Ave KA3 . . . . . . 222 C6
Towerhill Rd
Glasgow G13 . . . . .75 C1
Kilmaurs KA3. . . . . 222 C6
Towerlands Farm Ctr
KA11. . . . . .220 B3
Towerlands Farm Rd
KA11. . . . . .220 B3
Towerlands Gate KA11 . . .220 B2
Towerlands Intc KA11 . . . .219 F3
Towerlands Prim Sch
KA11. . . . . 220 C2
Towerlands Rd KA11 . . . . 220 C2
Tower Pl
Clackmannan FK10 . . . . .10 F5
Helensburgh G84. . . . . .16 D1
Johnstone PA5. . . . . 112 A1
Kilmarnock KA1 . . . . 227 D3
Milngavie G62 . . . . .55 B2
Tower Rd
Cumbernauld G67 . . . . .83 A6
Fluchter G64 . . . . .56 E3
Johnstone PA5. . . . . .111 F1
Towers Ct FK2 . . . . .42 B6
Towerside Cres G53. . . . . 115 A2
Towerside Rd G53 . . . . . . 115 A2

Towers Pl
Airdrie ML6 123 F7
Stirling FK9 2 D4
Tower Sq FK10 10 B5
Towers Rd ML6 123 F7
Tower St
Alloa FK10 10 A7
Glasgow G41 116 E5
Tower Terr PA1 113 D4
Tower View FK10 5 E1
Towie Pl
2 Glasgow G20 96 D6
Uddingston G71 140 F6
Town Burn FK7 6 F4
TOWN CENTRE 61 F2
TOWNEND 50 A4
Townend KA3 222 C7
Townend Brae KA1 231 B3
Townend La KA24 191 C7
Townend Pl KA1 231 B3
Townend Rd
Dumbarton G82 50 A5
Kilmarnock KA1 227 E3
Symington KA1 231 C4
Townend St KA24 191 C7
Townend Terr KA1 231 C4
Townfoot KA11 220 C1
TOWNHEAD
Coatbridge 101 C2
Glasgow 241 B3
Kirkintilloch 79 C8
Townhead
Beith KA15 171 B8
Irvine KA12 219 D2
Kilbirnie KA25 149 B2
Kilmaurs KA3 222 C8
Kilwinning KA13 207 D3
Kirkintilloch G66 79 D7
Kirkintilloch G66 79 D8
Townhead Apartments 9 FK10 10 B6
Townhead Ave ML1 142 E8
Townhead Dr ML1 143 F3
Townhead Gdns KA3 223 A2
Townhead Pl G71 141 A8
Townhead Prim Sch ML5 101 D2
Townhead Rd
Coatbridge ML5 101 C1
Helensburgh G84 17 A2
Newton Mearns G77 156 D4
Saltcoats KA21 217 A8
Townhead Rdbt G66 79 D8
Townhead St
Hamilton ML3 162 F3
Kilsyth G65 60 D8
Stevenston KA20 206 D1
Stonehouse ML10 198 E2
Townhead Terr PA1 113 D4
Townhill Prim Sch ML3 161 E2
Townhill Rd ML3 161 E3
Townhill Terr 1 ML3 161 E3
TOWNHOLM 223 A2
Townholm KA3 223 A2
Town House St FK6 21 E2
Townmill Rd G31 118 A8
Townsend St G4 97 C2
Traction Bsns Ctr ML1 163 C6
TRADESTON 117 A5
Tradeston Ind Est G5 117 A4
Tradeston St G5 117 A5
Trafalgar Ct G68 61 D6
Trafalgar St
Clydebank G81 73 F2
Glasgow G40 117 F3
Greenock PA15 45 F4
Greenock PA15 45 F5
Trainard Ave G32 118 F4
Tramore Cres KA9 236 C8
Tramway & the Hidden Gdns* G41 117 A3
Tranchard Ct 5 KA7 235 E1
Tranent Pl
Cleland ML1 144 C2
Glasgow G33 118 E8
Traquair Ave
Paisley PA2 132 E8
Wishaw ML2 165 C5
Traquair Dr G52 115 B5
Traquair Wynd 10 G72 161 C7
Treebank Cres KA7 239 C5
Treeburn Ave G46 136 B3
Treemain Rd G46 157 A8
Treesbank KA13 207 C2
Treesbank Rd KA1 227 F4
Treespark Ave G78 134 B4
Treespark Gdns G78 134 B4
Treeswoodhead Rd KA1 228 A2
Trefoil Ave G41 136 D8
Trefoil Pl KA7 239 C3
Trelawney Terr KA20 217 E6
Trent Pl G75 179 E6
Trent St ML5 101 D2
Tresta Rd G23 96 F8
Treviot Pl 1 PA15 46 B3
Triangle Sh Ctr The G64 78 A1
Tribboch St ML9 184 F3
Trident Way PA4 94 C1
Trinidad Gn 3 G75 159 A1
Trinidad Way G75 159 A1
Trinity Ave G52 115 C4
Trinity Cres KA15 150 C1
Trinity Dr
Cambuslang G72 139 C3
Dalry KA24 191 B6
Trinity High Sch
Hamilton ML3 162 E4
Renfrew PA4 94 D3
Trinity Pl G82 27 D1
Trinity Way 14 ML9 185 C1
Trinley Rd G13 75 D1
Triton Pl ML4 142 F5
Tron Ct FK10 4 B2
Trondra Gdns KA3 223 A6
Trondra Path G34 119 F8
Trondra Pl G34 119 F7
Trongate
Glasgow G1 241 A1
Stonehouse ML9 198 F2
TROON 229 C2
Troon Ave G75 180 A6
Troon Ct G75 180 B6
Troon Dr PA11 110 C7
Troon Gdns G68 61 F6
Troon Pl G77 157 A4
Troon Prim Sch KA10 229 D3
Troon Rd KA10 230 B3
Troon St G40 118 B3
Troon Sta KA10 229 E2
Trossachs Ave ML1 143 A5
Trossachs Ct G20 97 A3
Trossachs Rd G73 138 D2
Trossachs St G20 97 A3
Troubridge Ave PA10 111 B1
Troubridge Cres PA10 111 B2
Trovaig PA8 93 C7
Trows Rd ML2 186 B6
Truce Rd G13 95 B8
Truro Ave G69 80 F3
Tryfield Pl KA8 236 A2
Tryst Pk FK5 23 C5
Tryst Rd
Cumbernauld, Carbrain G67 62 A2
Cumbernauld G67 61 F1
Stenhousemuir FK5 23 D2
Stenhousemuir FK5 23 D3
Tryst Sp Ctr G67 62 A1
Tryst Wlk G67 61 F1
Tudhope Cres G83 27 D7
Tudor Lane S G14 95 E3
Tudor Rd G14 95 E3
Tudor St G69 119 F3
Tulley Wynd ML1 142 D2
Tulliallan Pl
East Kilbride G74 181 A8
Stenhousemuir FK5 24 A4
TULLIBODY 4 C3
Tullibody Rd FK10 9 F8
TULLICHEWAN 27 C7
Tullichewan Cres G83 27 D7
Tullichewan Dr G83 27 D7
Tullichewan Rd G83 27 D8
Tulligarth Pk FK10 10 A7
Tullis Ct G40 117 E4
Tullis Gdns G40 117 F4
Tullis St G40 117 F4
Tullochard Pl 1 G73 138 D3
Tulloch Gdns ML1 164 B4
Tulloch Rd ML7 147 B3
Tulloch St G44 137 A6
Tullymet Rd ML3 183 D8
Tummel Dr ML6 102 F2
Tummel Gn G74 159 E3
Tummell Way PA2 112 F1
Tummel Pl FK5 23 E3
Tummel St G33 98 E2
Tunnel St G3 116 E7
Tuphall Rd ML3 162 D2
Turnberry Ave
2 Glasgow G11 96 B3
Gourock PA19 44 B6
Turnberry Cres
Chapelhall ML6 123 E1
Coatbridge ML5 121 E4
Turnberry Ct KA13 207 B3
Turnberry Dr
Bridge of Weir PA11 110 C6
Hamilton ML3 161 D2
Kilmarnock KA1 227 F4
Newton Mearns G77 157 A5
Rutherglen G73 137 F5
Turnberry Gdns G68 61 F5
Turnberry Pl
Dumbarton G82 49 C8
East Kilbride G75 180 B6
Rutherglen G73 137 F4
Turnberry Rd
Glasgow G11 96 A3
Glasgow G11 96 B3
Turnberry Wynd
Bothwell G71 140 E2
Irvine KA11 224 F8
Turnbull Ave G83 27 D3
Turnbull Cres G83 27 D3
Turnbull High Sch G64 77 E2
Turnbull St G1 241 B1
Turner Pl KA3 223 A3
Turner Rd PA3 113 F8
Turners Ave PA1 113 B3
Turner St ML5 121 F6
Turnhill Ave PA8 93 B7
Turnhill Cres PA8 93 B7
Turnhill Dr PA8 93 B7
Turnhill Gdns PA8 93 B7
Turningshaw Rd PA6 91 E5
Turnlaw G75 180 D5
Turnlaw Rd G72 139 A2
Turnlaw St G5 117 D4
Turnyland Mdws PA8 93 B7
Turnyland Way PA8 93 B7
Turpie Dr FK5 23 B2
Turquoise Terr ML4 142 B3
Turret Cres G13 95 D8
Turret Ct FK10 10 C6
Turret Rd G13 95 C8
Turriff St G5 117 B4
TV ML2 186 A8
Twain Ave FK5 24 A3
TWECHAR 59 F3
Twechar Prim Sch G65 60 A3
Tweed Ave PA2 112 F2
Tweed Cres
Glasgow G33 98 E1
Kilmarnock KA1 228 A5
Renfrew PA4 94 E2
Wishaw ML2 165 C5
Tweed Ct ML6 123 C5
Tweed Dr G61 75 D3
Tweed La ML1 143 B5
Tweedmuir Pl ML5 122 D3
Tweed Pl PA5 131 C8
Tweedsmuir G64 78 C2
Tweedsmuir Cres G61 75 E7
Tweedsmuir Pk ML3 183 C8
Tweedsmuir Rd G52 115 B5
Tweed St
Ayr KA8 236 B3
Coatbridge ML5 122 A3
East Kilbride G75 179 F7
Greenock PA16 45 B5
Larkhall ML9 185 A1
Tweedvale Ave G14 94 E6
Tweedvale Pl G14 94 E6
Tweed Wlk G67 61 F2
Twinlaw St G34 100 D1
Tygetshaugh Ct FK6 21 D4
Tylney Rd PA1 114 D5
Tyndrum Rd G61 76 B5
Tyndrum St G4 241 A4
Tynecastle Cres G32 119 B7
Tynecastle Path G32 119 B7
Tynecastle Pl G32 119 B7
Tynecastle St G32 119 B7
Tyne Pl G75 179 E6
Tynron Ct ML3 161 E1
Tynwald Ave G73 138 D4

U

UDDINGSTON 140 E5
Uddingston Gram Sch G71 140 E6
Uddingston Rd G71 141 A3
Uddingston Sta G71 140 E6
UDSTON 161 F4
Udston Hospl ML3 161 F4
Udston Prim Sch ML3 161 E4
Udston Rd ML3 161 F5
Udston Terr ML3 161 F5
Uig Pl G33 119 E5
Uig Way ML7 147 A3
Uist Ave PA14 69 A7
Uist Cres G33 99 E4
Uist Dr G66 80 A8
Uist La KA3 222 F6
Uist Pl ML6 123 D6
Uist St G51 115 F7
Uist Way ML2 165 E5
Ullswater G75 179 F5
Ulundi Rd PA5 111 E2
Ulva St G52 115 F5
Ulverston Terr ML3 183 D6
Umachan PA4 93 C7
Umberly Rd KA1 227 E3
Underwood KA13 207 D5
Underwood Cotts FK7 6 D5
Underwood Ct PA3 113 D5
Underwood Dr ML2 166 A7
Underwood La PA1 113 D5
Underwood Pl KA1 227 F3
Underwood Rd
Cambusbarron FK7 6 D5
Paisley PA3 113 D5
Prestwick KA9 236 D7
Rutherglen G73 138 C6
Underwood St G41 136 E8
Union Arc KA7 238 F7
Union Ave KA8 236 A3
Union Gdns FK1 41 D5
Union Pl
Glasgow G1 240 C2
Larbert FK5 23 B1
Union Rd FK1 41 D5
Union St
Alexandria G83 27 F4
4 Alloa FK10 10 B6
Bridge of Allan FK9 2 A7
Carluke ML8 187 F1
Falkirk FK2 42 B7
Glasgow G1 240 C2
Greenock PA16 45 E6
Hamilton ML3 162 D3
Hurlford KA1 228 E6
1 Kilmarnock KA3 222 F1
Kirkintilloch G66 79 C8
Larkhall ML9 185 A3
Motherwell ML1 143 A4
Paisley PA2 113 E2
Saltcoats KA21 216 F7
Shotts ML7 146 D5
Stenhousemuir FK5 23 E3
Stirling FK8 2 B1
Stonehouse ML9 198 F2
Troon KA10 229 C3
Union Street La G83 27 F4
Unitas Cres ML8 187 E1
Unitas Rd ML4 142 C5
Unity Pk ML7 146 D4
Unity Pl G4 97 A2
Universal Rd FK2 42 E7
University Ave G12 96 D2
University Gdns G12 96 D2
University Pl G12 96 D2
University Road W FK9 2 C6
Univ of Glasgow (Main Campus) G11, G12 96 D2
Univ of Glasgow (St Andrew's Building) G3 96 E2
Univ of Glasgow (Veterinary Medicine) G61 96 A8
Univ of Stirling FK9 2 D6
Univ of Strathclyde (John Anderson Campus) G1, G4 241 B3
Univ of Strathclyde (Jordanhill Campus) G13 95 D5
Univ of the West of Scotland (Ayr Campus) KA8 239 C7
Univ of the West of Scotland (Hamilton Campus) ML3 162 D4
Univ of the West of Scotland (Paisley Campus) PA1 113 D4
Unsted Pl 4 PA1 114 A4
Unst La G72 138 E2
Unthank Rd ML4 142 C5
Uphall Pl G33 118 E7
UP La G65 60 D8
Upland La 2 G14 95 C4
Upland Rd G14 95 C4
UPLAWMOOR 153 B3
Uplawmoor Prim Sch G78 153 B3
Uplawmoor Rd
Neilston G78 154 B6
Uplawmoor G78 153 E4
Upper Adelaide St G84 16 F1
Upper Arthur St G83 27 D4
Upper Bourtree Ct G73 138 C4
Upper Bourtree Dr G73 138 C4
Upper Bridge St
Alexandria G83 27 D4
Stirling FK8 2 A1
Upper Carman Rd G82 27 D1
Upper Cartsburn St PA15 46 A3
Upper Castlehill 2 FK8 7 A8
Upper Colquhoun St G84 16 D4
Upper Craigs FK8 7 B7
Upper Crofts KA7 238 F1
Upper Glenburn Rd G61 75 D5
Upper Glenfinlas St G84 16 E2
Upper Hall Rd G84 15 D5
Upper Loaning KA7 238 F1
Upper Mill St ML6 123 A8
Upper Mill Street Ind Est ML6 123 A8
Upper Newmarket St FK1 42 B5
Upper Smollett St G83 27 D4
Upper Stoneymollan Rd G83 27 B8
Upper Sutherland Cres G84 16 B3
Upper Sutherland St G84 16 B3
Upper Torwoodhill Rd G84 15 F4
UP Rd G65 60 D8
Ure Cres FK4 40 A6
Urquhart Cres PA4 94 C2
Urquhart Dr
East Kilbride G74 160 A3
Gourock PA19 43 F5
Urquhart Pl
Gartcosh G69 100 F4
Helensburgh G84 16 D4
Urquhart Rd KA3 223 D2
Urrdale Rd G41 116 B5
Usmore Pl G33 119 E5

V

Vaila La G72 138 F3
Vaila Pl G23 97 A7
Vaila St G23 96 F7
Vale Gr FK9 1 F5
Valence Twr G71 140 D4
Vale of Bonny View FK4 39 F5
VALE OF LEVEN 27 E4
Vale of Leven Acad G83 27 D3
Vale of Leven Hospl G83 27 C6
Vale of Leven Ind Est G82 27 E1
Vale of Leven Swim Pool G83 27 D6
Vale Pl FK6 21 E3
Valerio Ct G72 161 D8
Valetta Pl G81 73 D3
Valeview FK5 23 D2
Valeview Terr
Dumbarton G82 50 A6
Glasgow G42 137 A8
Vale Wlk G64 98 C8
Vallantine Cres G71 141 A8
Vallay St G22 97 D8
Valleybank G65 37 D3
Valley Ct ML3 162 C2
Valleyfield
East Kilbride G75 159 D1
Milton of Campsie G66 58 B6
Valleyfield Dr G68 60 E1
Valleyfield Pl FK7 7 C6
Valleyfield St 1 G21 97 E3
Valley International Pk* ML8 201 C2
Valley View ML1 164 B3
Valleyview Dr FK2 42 A8
Valleyview Pl FK2 42 A7
Vancouver Ct G75 159 B1
Vancouver Dr G75 159 B1
Vancouver La
15 Glasgow G14 95 C4
Glasgow G14 95 D4
Vancouver Pl G81 73 D4
Vancouver Rd G14 95 D4
Vanguard St G81 74 D2
Vanguard Way PA4 94 C1
Vardar Ave G76 157 C8
Vardon Lea ML1 143 E1
Varna La G14 95 E3
Varna Rd G14 95 E4
Varnsdorf Way ML6 123 E6
Vasart Pl G20 96 F4
Vatersay Pl KA3 223 A6
Vaults La KA13 207 E3
Veir Terr G82 49 E3
Veitches Ct G81 74 A6
Veitch Pl G66 57 D8
Venachar Rd FK1 42 A1
Vennachar St ML7 146 E6
Vennacher Rd PA4 94 B4
Vennard Gdns G41 116 F2
Vennel La KA3 211 E8
Vennel (Mus) The* KA12 219 C2
Vennel St
Dalry KA24 191 B7
Stewarton KA3 211 E8
Vennel The FK6 21 E2
Vermont Ave G73 138 A7
Vermont St G41 116 E5
Vernon Bank G74 159 E3
Vernon Dr PA3 112 A6
Vernon Pl KA2 225 E2
Vernon St KA21 216 F7
Verona Ave G14 95 C4
Verona Gdns 4 G14 95 C4
Verona La G14 95 C4
Verona Pl KA22 205 D1
Vesalius St G32 119 A5
Vesuvius Dr ML1 164 B4
Viaduct Circ KA13 207 E5
Viaduct Rd G76 157 F7
Vicarfield Pl G51 116 B7
Vicarfield St G51 116 B7
Vicarland Pl G72 139 A4
Vicarland Rd G72 139 A5
Vicars Rd ML9 198 E2
Vicar St FK1 42 B5
Vicars Wlk G72 139 B5
Vickers St ML1 163 B8
Victoria Ave
Barrhead G78 134 B4
Carluke ML8 187 E1
Victoria Buildings Bsns Ctr PA1 114 A4
Victoria Cir G12 96 C3
Victoria Cottage Hospl G65 60 B8
Victoria Cres
Airdrie ML6 122 F6
Barrhead G78 134 B4
Clarkston G76 157 F7
Irvine KA12 219 B1
Kilsyth G65 60 B8
Wishaw ML2 164 D4
Victoria Crescent La G12 96 C3
Victoria Crescent Pl 4 G12 96 C3
Victoria Crescent Rd G12 96 C3
Victoria Cross G42 117 A2
Victoria Ct
Larkhall ML9 185 A4
Newton Mearns G77 156 D2
Victoria Dr
Barrhead G78 134 B4
Troon KA10 229 E2
Victoria Drive E PA4 94 C2
Victoria Drive W PA4 94 B3
Victoria East Rd KA1 228 A7
VICTORIA GARDENS 94 C1
Victoria Gdns
Airdrie ML6 122 F7
Barrhead G78 134 B4
Kilmacolm PA13 69 C1
Paisley PA2 113 C2
Victoria Glade G68 61 D6
Victoria Gr G78 134 B4
Victoria Infmy
Glasgow G42 137 A8
Helensburgh G84 16 F1
Victoria La G77 156 D2
Victoria Mans KA7 238 E6
Victoria Park* G14 95 E3
Victoria Park Cnr G14 95 D3
Victoria Park Drive N G14 95 E3
Victoria Park Drive S G14 95 D3
Victoria Park Gardens N G11 95 F3
Victoria Park Gardens S G11 95 F3
Victoria Park Lane N G14 95 D3
Victoria Park Lane S G14 95 D3
Victoria Park Sch 6 ML8 187 F2
Victoria Park St 7 G14 95 D3
Victoria Pk
Ayr KA7 238 E6
Kilsyth G65 60 B8
Victoria Pl
Airdrie ML6 122 E6
Barrhead G78 134 C4
Bellshill ML4 141 F4
Kilsyth G65 60 C8
Milngavie G62 55 B1

Victoria Pl *continued*
4 Rutherglen G73 138 A8
Stirling FK8 7 A7
Victoria Prim Sch
Airdrie ML6 122 F7
Falkirk FK2 42 D6
3 Glasgow G42 117 B2
Victoria Quadrant ML1 142 F5
Victoria Rd
Barrhead G78 134 B4
Brookfield PA5 111 D5
Dullatur G68 61 D6
Falkirk FK2 42 C6
Glasgow G42 117 A3
Gourock PA19 44 C7
Harthill ML7 127 E5
Helensburgh G84 16 E2
Kirkintilloch G66 79 C3
Larbert FK5 23 B1
Paisley PA2 113 C2
Rutherglen G73 138 B6
Saltcoats KA21 217 A8
Stepps G33 99 D5
Stirling FK8 7 A8
Victoria Rdbt KA12 219 B2
Victoria Sq
Newton Mearns G77 156 D2
Stirling FK8 7 A7
Victoria St
Alexandria G83 27 E4
Alloa FK10 10 A7
Ayr KA8 236 A1
Dumbarton G82 50 A3
Hamilton, Blantyre G72 161 D7
Hamilton, Whitehill ML3 162 B6
Harthill ML7 127 E5
Kirkintilloch G66 79 C8
Larkhall ML9 185 A4
Rutherglen G73 138 B8
Wishaw ML2 166 A4
Victoria Terr
Dullatur G68 61 D6
Kilmarnock KA1 228 A7
Menstrie FK11 4 B7
Victoria Way KA3 195 F1
Victor St ML6 104 A2
Victory Dr PA10 111 A4
Victory Way G69 120 B4
Viewbank G46 136 A3
Viewbank Ave ML6 123 B2
Viewbank St ML5 101 F5
Viewfield
Airdrie ML6 122 E7
Moodiesburn G69 80 E4
Viewfield Ave
Bishopbriggs G64 97 E8
Blantyre G72 140 E1
Glasgow G69 119 F5
Kirkintilloch G66 79 C5
Lochwinnoch PA12 129 B2
Milton of Campsie G66 58 B5
Viewfield Bsns Ctr KA8 236 A2
Viewfield Dr
Alva FK12 4 F6
Bishopbriggs G64 97 E8
Glasgow G69 119 F5
Viewfield La G12 96 E2
Viewfield Pl
Harthill ML7 127 F6
3 Stirling FK8 7 B8
Viewfield Rd
Ayr KA8 236 A2
Banknock FK4 38 D3
Bellshill ML4 141 F3
Bishopbriggs G64 97 E8
Coatbridge ML5 121 C4
Viewfield St
Harthill ML7 127 F6
4 Stirling FK8 7 B8
Viewforth FK8 7 B6
Viewglen Ct G45 137 D1
Viewmount Dr G20 96 D7
VIEWPARK 141 C7
Viewpark
Beith KA15 150 B1
Milngavie G62 55 B1
Viewpark Ave G31 118 B8
Viewpark Ct G73 138 C6
Viewpark Dr G73 138 B6
Viewpark Gdns PA4 94 B2
Viewpark Pl ML1 163 C6
Viewpark Rd ML1 163 C6
Viewpark Sh Ctr G71, ML4 141 D6
Viewpoint Gate G21 97 F6
Viewpoint Pl G21 97 F6
Viewpoint Rd G21 97 F6
Viking Cres PA6 111 D8
Viking Rd ML6 123 B5
Viking Terr G75 180 E6
Viking Way
Glasgow G46 135 F5
Renfrew PA4 94 C1
Villabank FK6 21 E2
Villafield Ave G64 78 A3
Villafield Dr G64 78 A3
Villafield Loan G64 78 A3
Village Gdns G72 140 E1
Village Rd G72 139 F5
VILLAGE THE 159 F2
Vincent Ct ML4 142 A4
Vineburgh Ave KA12 219 C4
Vineburgh Ct KA12 219 B4
Vine Park Ave KA3 222 B7
Vine Park Dr KA3 222 B7
Vine St G11 96 B2
Vines The KA12 219 C4
Vinicombe La 3 G12 96 D3
Vinicombe St G12 96 D3
Vintner St G4 97 C2
Viola Pl G64 78 C8
Violet Gdns ML8 201 E8
Violet Pl ML1 143 B6
Violet St PA1 114 A4
Virginia Ct G1 241 A2
Virginia Gdns
Ayr KA8 236 A2
Milngavie G62 76 C8
Virginia Gr ML3 182 F8
Virginia Pl G1 241 A2
Virginia St
Glasgow G1 241 A2
1 Greenock PA15 46 A4
Virtue Well View ML6 102 E3
Viscount Ave PA4 94 C1
Viscount Gate G71 140 E5
Vivian Ave G62 54 F1
Voil Dr G44 137 A4
Voil Rd FK9 2 A3
Vorlich Ct G78 134 C1
Vorlich Dr FK1 66 E7
Vorlich Gdns G61 75 C7
Vorlich Pl
Kilmarnock KA1 228 A4
Stirling FK9 2 A3
Vorlich Wynd ML1 143 C4
Vrackie Pl KA1 228 A4
Vryburg Cl G75 180 A4
Vryburg Cres G75 180 A4
Vulcan St
4 Glasgow G21 97 E4
Motherwell ML1 163 E8

W

Waddell Ave ML6 102 D4
Waddell Ct
Glasgow G5 117 D5
Kilmarnock KA3 222 F4
Waddell St
Airdrie ML6 103 A1
Falkirk FK2 24 C2
Glasgow G5 117 D4
Waggon Rd
Ayr KA8 235 F2
Falkirk FK2 42 B7
Waid Ave G77 156 C6
Waldemar Rd G13 95 C7
Walden Rd KA1 228 E6
Waldo St 3 G13 95 F7
Walker Ave
Kilmarnock KA3 228 B8
Troon KA10 229 E5
Walkerburn Dr ML2 165 C6
Walkerburn Rd G52 115 B4
Walker Ct
Glasgow G11 96 B1
Hurlford KA1 228 F6
Walker Dr
Bonnybridge FK4 39 D5
Elderslie PA5 112 C2
Walker Path 2 G71 141 A8
Walker Rd KA8 236 B2
Walkers Ct ML2 166 A4
Walker St
Glasgow G11 96 B1
Greenock PA16 45 C5
5 Kilbirnie KA25 149 A1
Paisley PA1 113 D4
Walkinshaw Rd PA4 93 C3
Walkinshaw St
Glasgow G40 118 A4
Johnstone PA5 112 A3
Walkinshaw Way PA3 113 E7
Walkmill La G81 74 B6
Walk The FK10 10 A5
Wallace Ave
Bishopton PA7 72 B3
Dundonald KA2 225 F2
Elderslie PA5 112 C2
Stevenston KA20 206 D1
Troon KA10 229 E6
Wallace Bldgs FK2 42 B6
Wallace Cres
Denny FK6 21 C2
Plean FK7 12 D3
Wallace Ct
Kilmarnock KA1 228 E6
2 Lanark ML11 215 A4
Prestwick KA9 236 D7
Stirling FK8 2 B1
Wallace Dr
3 Bishopbriggs G64 98 D8
Larkhall ML9 185 C2
Wallacefield Rd KA10 229 E3
Wallace Gate 2 G64 98 D8
Wallace Gdns
Stirling FK9 2 D3
Torrance G64 57 B1
Wallace High Sch FK9 2 C4
Wallacehill Rd KA1 227 F4
Wallace Ho G67 61 E2
Wallace Pl
1 Bishopbriggs G64 98 D8
Blantyre G72 140 E1
Cambusbarron FK7 6 D5
Falkirk FK2 42 C6
Fallin FK7 8 C4
Greenock PA15 45 F5
Hamilton ML3 163 A2
Wallace Prim Sch PA5 112 D2
Wallace Rd
Irvine KA12 219 C4
Motherwell ML1 143 B2
Renfrew PA4 94 A1
Wallace St
Alloa FK10 10 C7
Bannockburn FK7 7 E1
Clydebank G81 74 B1
Coatbridge ML5 122 A5
Dumbarton G82 50 A3
Falkirk FK2 42 C6
Glasgow G5 117 A5
Greenock PA16 45 D4
Kilmarnock KA1 227 E7
Motherwell ML1 163 D7
Paisley PA3 113 E6
Plains ML6 104 A2
Port Glasgow PA14 47 E1
Rutherglen G73 138 A7
Stirling FK8 2 B1
WALLACETOWN 236 B1
Wallacetown Ave KA3 223 C6
Wallace View
Kilmarnock KA1 227 F5
Shieldhill FK1 66 D7
Tullibody FK10 4 D3
Wallace Way ML11 215 C4
Wallacewell Cres G21 98 B5
Wallacewell Pl G21 98 B5
Wallacewell Prim Sch G21 98 D6
Wallacewell Quadrant G21 98 C6
Wallacewell Rd G21 98 C6
Wallace Wynd
Cambuslang G72 139 A3
Law ML8 187 A6
Wallbrae Rd G67 82 F8
Wall Gdns FK1 41 C5
Wallneuk 2 PA1 113 F5
Wallneuk Rd PA3 113 F5
Walls St G1 241 B2
Wall St FK1 41 C5
Wallstale Rd FK7 7 A3
Walmer Cres G51 116 C5
Walnut Cl G75 180 C6
Walnut Cres
Glasgow G22 97 D5
Johnstone PA5 112 B1
Walnut Ct G66 58 B5
Walnut Dr G66 79 B6
Walnut Gate G72 139 F4
Walnut Gr G75 180 C6
Walnut Pl
Glasgow G22 97 D5
Motherwell G71 121 C1
Walnut Rd
Glasgow G22 97 D5
Kilmarnock KA1 227 C7
Walpole Pl PA5 131 C7
Walter St
Glasgow G31 118 C7
Wishaw ML2 165 D3
Walton Ave G77 156 C6
Walton Ct G46 136 C2
Walton St
Barrhead G78 134 C3
Glasgow G41 136 E8
Wamba Ave G13 95 E8
Wamphray Pl G75 179 D7
Wandilla Ave G81 74 D2
Wanlock St G51 116 A8
Ward Ct KA8 236 B4
Wardend Rd G64 57 B1
Warden Rd G13 95 D7
Wardhill Rd G21 98 B5
Wardhouse Rd PA2 133 C7
Wardie Pl G33 119 F7
Wardie Rd G34 120 A7
Wardlaw Ave G73 138 B7
Wardlaw Cres
East Kilbride G75 181 A7
Troon KA10 230 A4
Wardlaw Dr G73 138 B8
Wardlaw Gdns KA11 220 B7
Wardlaw Pl FK2 24 C2
Wardlaw Rd
Bearsden G61 75 F1
Kilmarnock KA3 223 E5
Wardneuk KA9 236 C6
Wardneuk Ct KA11 220 A6
Wardneuk Dr KA3 223 A4
WARDPARK 62 C7
Wardpark Ct G67 62 D6
Wardpark East Ind Est G68 62 E8
Wardpark North Ind Est G68 62 D7
Wardpark Pl G67 62 D6
Wardpark Rd G67 62 D6
Wardpark Rdbt G68 62 D7
Wardpark South Ind Est G67 62 D6
Ward Rd KA8 236 B4
Wardrop Pl G74 159 F3
Wardrop St
Beith KA15 171 C8
2 Glasgow G51 116 A8
Paisley PA1 113 E4
Wardrop Terr KA15 171 C8
Wards Cres ML5 121 E5
Wards Pl KA1 227 F7
Ward St FK10 10 A5
Ware Rd G34 120 A7
Warilda Ave G81 74 C2
Warlock Dr PA11 90 D1
Warlock Rd PA11 90 D3
Warly Dr KA2 225 F1
Warly Pl KA2 225 F1
Warner St KA20 217 D7
Warnock Cres ML4 142 B4
Warnock Rd G77 156 C7
Warnock St G31 241 C3
Warren Rd ML3 183 D8
Warren St G42 117 B1
Warren Wlk G66 57 E7
Warriston Cres G33 118 D8
Warriston Ct G33 118 F8
Warriston Pl G32 119 B7
Warriston St G33 118 E8
Warriston Way 1 G73 138 D4
WARRIX 224 G7
Warrix Ave KA12 219 D2
Warrix Gdns KA10 232 E8
Warrix Intc KA11 219 E1
Warroch St G3 240 A2
Warwick G74 160 C4
Warwick Gr ML3 161 E5
Warwickhill KA11 220 B5
Warwickhill Pl KA1 222 E2
Warwickhill Rd KA1 222 D1
Warwick Rd PA16 44 E4
Warwick Villas G81 94 E7
Washington Rd
Kirkintilloch G66 79 B8
Paisley PA3 113 F8
Washington St G3 240 B2
Watchmeal Cres G81 74 C7
Waterbank Rd G76 158 D5
Watercut Rd KA13 218 F8
WATERFOOT 157 D2
Waterfoot Ave G53 135 C8
Waterfoot Rd
Newton Mearns, Kirkhill G77 157 B3
Newton Mearns, Mearns G77 156 F3
Waterfoot Row G76 157 D3
Waterfoot Terr G53 135 C8
Waterford Ct G46 136 B2
Waterford Rd G46 136 B3
Waterfront L Complex PA15 46 A6
Waterfront Way FK9 2 A3
Waterfurs Dr FK2 42 A8
Waterhaughs Gdns G33 98 D7
Waterhaughs Gr G33 98 D7
Water La 8 KA1 227 F8
Waterlands Gdns ML8 188 A3
Waterlands Pl ML8 187 A4
Waterlands Rd ML8 187 B6
WATERLOO 165 D1
Waterloo Cl G66 58 D1
Waterloo Dr ML11 215 A5
Waterloo Gdns 6 G66 58 D1
Waterloo La G2 240 C2
Waterloo Rd
Lanark ML11 215 A5
Prestwick KA9 236 B5
Waterloo St G2 240 C2
Watermill Ave G66 79 D4
Water Rd G78 134 C3
Water Row G51 116 A8
Watersaugh Dr ML1 144 B2
Watersedge Ct G84 15 D4
Waters End FK2 24 B2
WATERSIDE
Fenwick 213 F4
Glasgow 134 E5
Kirkintilloch 80 B7
Waterside
Clarkston G76 157 F5
Irvine KA12 219 B3
Waterside Ave G77 156 C4
Waterside Ct
Carmunnock G76 158 D7
Kilmarnock KA1 227 F8
Waterside Dr G77 156 C4
Waterside Gdns
Cambuslang G72 139 E3
Carmunnock G76 158 D7
Hamilton ML3 162 E1
Waterside La PA10 111 C2
Waterside Pl G5 117 D4
Waterside Rd
Carmunnock G76 158 D6
Carmunnock G76 158 D8
Kilwinning KA13 207 F4
Kirkintilloch G66 79 E7
Waterside St
Glasgow G5 117 D4
Kilmarnock KA1 227 F8
Waterside Terr PA10 111 C2
Waterside Way PA10 111 C2
Waterslap KA3 213 A2
Water St PA14 47 C2
Waterston Way PA12 129 C3
Wateryetts Dr PA13 69 D1
Watling Ave FK1 41 C5
Watling Dr FK1 41 D5
Watling Gdns FK1 41 D6
Watling Pl 7 G75 159 A1
Watling St
Falkirk FK1 41 C5
Motherwell ML1 142 C1
Uddingston G71 140 E8
Watson Ave
Linwood PA3 112 B5
Rutherglen G73 137 F7
Stonehouse ML9 199 A3
Watson Cres G65 60 E8
Watson Pl
Hamilton G72 161 B7
Longcroft FK4 39 C4
Watson St
Falkirk FK2 42 B5
Watson St *continued*
Glasgow G1 241 B1
Hamilton G72 161 C7
Kilmarnock KA3 228 B8
Larkhall ML9 184 F3
Motherwell ML1 163 E5
4 Motherwell ML1 163 E6
Uddingston G71 140 F6
Watson Terr KA12 219 D2
Watsonville Pk 3 ML1 163 E6
Watstone Rd ML9 199 A2
Watt Ave G33 99 F5
Watt Cres ML4 142 B7
Watt Ct
Dalry KA24 191 C7
Stonehouse ML9 198 E1
Wattfield Rd KA7 238 F6
Watt Gdns FK1 41 E6
Watt La PA11 110 E7
Watt Liby & McLean Mus & Art Gall* PA16 45 E6
Watt Low Ave G73 137 F6
Watt Pl
Greenock PA15 46 A5
Hamilton G72 161 C4
Milngavie G62 54 F3
Watt Rd
Bridge of Weir PA11 110 D7
Glasgow G52 115 A7
Watt St
Airdrie ML6 103 C1
Glasgow G5 240 A1
Greenock PA16 45 E6
WATTSTON 103 C8
Waukglen Ave G53 135 B2
Waukglen Cres G53 135 C3
Waukglen Dr G53 135 B3
Waukglen Gdns G53 135 B2
Waukglen Path G53 135 B3
Waukglen Pl G53 135 B3
Waukglen Rd G53 135 B3
Waulker St FK8 1 F2
Waulking Mill Rd G81 74 C7
Waulkmill Ave G78 134 D4
Waulkmill Pl KA1 228 A7
Waulkmill St G46 135 E4
Waulkmill Way G78 134 D4
Waverley
Clydebank G81 74 C2
East Kilbride G74 160 D4
Waverley Ave
Helensburgh G84 25 C7
Kilmarnock KA1 222 C1
Waverley Cres
Bonnybridge FK4 40 B3
Cumbernauld G67 82 D7
Hamilton ML3 161 F4
Kirkintilloch G66 79 D8
Lanark ML11 215 C4
Stirling FK8 2 C1
Waverley Ct
Bothwell G71 141 A2
Helensburgh G84 16 D2
Waverley Dr
Airdrie ML6 103 B1
Rutherglen G73 138 C7
Wishaw ML2 165 B4
Waverley Gdns
Elderslie PA5 112 D2
Glasgow G41 116 E1
WAVERLEY PARK 116 D1
Waverley Park Rdbt G66 79 E8
Waverley Pk G66 79 D8
Waverley Pl KA21 205 E1
Waverley Rd
Paisley PA2 132 F8
Stenhousemuir FK5 23 C2
Waverley St
Coatbridge ML5 102 B1
Falkirk FK2 42 B8
Glasgow G41 116 E1
Greenock PA16 45 C3
Hamilton ML3 161 F4
Larkhall ML9 199 A8
Waverley Terr
Dumbarton G82 49 B4
Hamilton G72 161 D5
Stenhousemuir FK5 23 C2
Waverley Way PA2 132 F7
Weardale La G33 119 C8
Weardale St G33 119 C8
Weaver Ave G77 156 C7
Weaver Cres ML6 123 A5
Weaver La PA10 111 A4
Weaver Pl G75 179 F7
Weaver Row FK7 7 A4
Weavers Ave PA2 113 B3
Weaver's Cott* PA10 111 A3
Weavers Ct
1 East Kilbride G74 159 F2
3 Hamilton ML3 162 E2
Kilbarchan PA10 111 A3
Weavers Gate PA1 113 B3
Weavers Rd PA2 113 B3
Weaver St
Ayr KA8 235 F2
Glasgow G4 241 B2
Weavers Way
Saltcoats KA21 205 F3
Stonehouse ML9 198 E1
Weavers Wlk ML11 215 A3
Weaver Terr PA2 114 A3
Webster Ave FK2 24 B4
Webster Groves ML2 165 D5
Webster St
Clydebank G81 94 E8
Glasgow G40 118 A3
Wedderlea Dr G52 115 B5

Wee Cl KA15 .... 171 B8
Weensmoor Rd G53 .... 134 F4
Weeple Dr PA3 .... 112 A6
Wee Row FK2 .... 42 B6
Wee Sunnyside Rd ML9 .. 184 B2
Weighhouse Cl PA1 .... 113 E4
Weighhouse Rd ML8 .... 187 E3
Weir Ave
Barrhead G78 .... 134 C2
Prestwick KA9 .... 233 D1
Weir Dr FK7 .... 8 D4
Weir Pl
Greenock PA15 .... 46 D3
Kilbirnie KA25 .... 149 B1
Law ML8 .... 186 F4
Weir Rd
Ardrossan KA22 .... 205 D4
Ayr KA8 .... 235 F3
Weir St
Coatbridge ML5 .... 122 A7
Falkirk FK1 .... 42 C5
Greenock PA15 .... 46 D2
Paisley PA1, PA3 .... 113 F5
Stirling FK8 .... 1 F2
Weirston Rd KA13 .... 208 A3
Weirwood Ave G69 .... 120 A5
Weirwood Gdns G69 .... 119 F4
Welbeck Cres KA10 .... 229 C2
Welbeck Ct KA10 .... 229 C2
Welbeck Rd G53 .... 135 B4
Welbeck St
Greenock PA16 .... 45 C8
Kilmarnock KA1 .... 228 A7
Weldon Pl G65 .... 60 F3
Welfare Ave G72 .... 139 D4
Welland Pl G75 .... 179 E7
Wellbank Gdns KA23 .... 190 C5
Wellbank Pl G71 .... 140 F5
Wellbeck Ho 7 G74 .... 159 F2
Wellbeck Mews KA10 .... 229 C2
Wellbrae
Larkhall ML9 .... 185 A2
Stonehouse ML9 .... 198 E2
Wellbrae Rd ML3 .... 162 B1
Wellbrae Terr G69 .... 80 F2
Wellbuttslea Dr ML11 .... 214 E3
Wellcroft Pl G5 .... 117 B4
Wellcroft Rd ML3 .... 161 E3
Wellcroft Terr ML3 .... 161 E3
Welldale La ML11 .... 214 B5
Well Dr ML11 .... 214 E3
Wellesley Cres
Cumbernauld G68 .... 81 E8
East Kilbride G75 .... 179 F7
Wellesley Dr
Cumbernauld G68 .... 60 D1
East Kilbride G75 .... 179 F8
Wellesley Pl G68 .... 60 D1
Wellfield Ave G46 .... 136 B3
Wellfield St G21 .... 97 F4
Wellgate ML11 .... 215 A4
Wellgate Ct ML9 .... 185 A4
Wellgate Dr FK9 .... 2 C7
Wellgatehead ML11 .... 215 A3
Wellgate St ML9 .... 185 A4
Well Gn G43 .... 136 C8
Well Green Ct G43 .... 136 C8
Wellgreen Pl FK8 .... 7 B6
Wellgreen Rd FK8 .... 7 B7
Wellhall Ct ML3 .... 162 B4
Wellhall Rd ML3 .... 162 B3
Wellhead Ct ML11 .... 215 B4
Wellhouse Cres G33 .... 119 F7
Wellhouse Gdns G33 .... 119 F7
Wellhouse Gr G33 .... 119 F7
Wellhouse Rd G33 .... 119 F7
Wellington G75 .... 180 B7
Wellington Ave KA3 .... 228 D8
Wellington Gdns KA3 .... 228 E8
Wellington La
Ayr KA7 .... 238 E8
Glasgow G2 .... 240 C2
Wellington Path G69 .... 120 B4
Wellington Pl
Clydebank G81 .... 73 D3
Coatbridge ML5 .... 121 C5
4 Kilmarnock KA3 .... 222 F2
Wishaw ML2 .... 186 D8
Wellington Rd G64 .... 78 B4
Wellington Sch KA7 .... 238 E7
Wellington Sq KA7 .... 238 E8
Wellington St
Airdrie ML6 .... 103 A1
Glasgow G2 .... 240 C2
Greenock PA15 .... 45 E4
Kilmarnock KA3 .... 222 F1
Paisley PA3 .... 113 D5
Prestwick KA9 .... 236 B5
Wishaw ML2 .... 164 C5
Wellington Terr ML11 .... 214 F5
Wellington Way
Greenock PA15 .... 45 E4
5 Renfrew PA4 .... 94 C1
Wellknowe Ave G74 .... 158 C2
Wellknowe Pl G74 .... 158 C3
Wellknowe Rd G74 .... 158 C3
Well La G66 .... 57 D8
Wellmeadow Cl G77 .... 156 D5
Wellmeadow Gn G77 .... 156 D5
Wellmeadow Rd G43 .... 136 B6
Wellmeadows Ct ML3 .... 162 A2
Wellmeadows La ML3 .... 162 A2
Wellmeadow St PA1 .... 113 D4
Wellmeadow Way G77 .. 156 D6
Wellpark KA7 .... 238 F2
Wellpark Ave KA3 .... 228 C8
Wellpark Bldgs 3 PA15 .. 46 A4
Wellpark Cres FK7 .... 6 F4
Wellpark Ct
Greenock PA15 .... 45 F4
Kilmarnock KA3 .... 228 C8
Wellpark Gr KA3 .... 228 C8
Wellpark La
Neilston G78 .... 154 D6
Saltcoats KA21 .... 216 F8
Wellpark Pl KA3 .... 228 C8
Wellpark Rd
Banknock FK4 .... 38 D2
Motherwell ML1 .... 163 C6
Saltcoats KA21 .... 216 F8
Wellpark St G31 .... 241 C2
Wellpark Terr
Bonnybridge FK4 .... 40 A5
Neilston G78 .... 154 D6
Well Rd
Bridge of Allan FK9 .... 2 A8
Falkirk FK1 .... 41 F3
Kilbarchan PA10 .... 111 A3
Lanark ML11 .... 215 B3
Wellsbourne Ho KA7 .... 238 E7
Wellshot Dr G72 .... 138 F5
Wellshot Prim Sch G32 .. 118 F4
Wellshot Rd G32 .... 118 F4
WELLSIDE 139 D4
Wellside Ave ML6 .... 103 A1
Wellside Ct FK1 .... 42 A5
Wellside Dr G72 .... 139 C4
Wellside La ML6 .... 103 B1
Wellside Pl FK1 .... 42 A5
Wellside Quadrant ML6 . 103 A1
Wells Quarry Rd G76,
G74 .... 159 C5
Wells St G81 .... 73 F3
Well St
Paisley PA1, PA3 .... 113 C5
West Kilbride KA23 .... 190 C5
Wellstood Ct FK4 .... 40 C6
Wellview Dr ML1 .... 163 D6
Wellwood KA13 .... 207 C2
Wellwood Ave ML11 .... 215 B5
Wellwynd ML6 .... 122 F8
Wellwynd Gdns 2 ML6 .. 122 F8
Wellyard La PA16 .... 44 C3
Wellyard Way PA16 .... 44 C2
Wellyard Wynd PA16 .... 44 C2
Welsh Ct FK6 .... 21 F1
Welsh Dr
Hamilton, Blantyre G72 .. 161 D6
Hamilton, Eddlewood ML3. 183 C7
Welsh Gdns FK9 .... 2 A8
Welsh Pl KA21 .... 205 E1
Welsh Rd KA9 .... 233 D2
Welsh Row ML6 .... 123 C3
Wemyss Ave G77 .... 156 C7
Wemyss Bay St PA15 .... 45 E3
Wemyss Cres KA10 .... 229 F1
Wemyss Dr G68 .... 60 E1
Wemyss Gdns G69 .... 120 A3
Wendur Way 5 PA3 .... 113 D8
Wenlock Rd PA2 .... 113 F2
Wensleydale G74 .... 159 C3
Wentworth Dr 5 G23 .... 76 E1
Wentworth Sq KA13 .... 207 C4
Wesley St ML6 .... 122 F7
West Abercromby St G84 .. 16 D3
West Academy St ML2 .. 164 E3
West Acad St ML2 .... 164 E3
Westacres Rd G77 .... 156 B4
WEST ARTHURLIE 134 A2
West Ave
Carluke ML8 .... 187 E1
Hamilton G72 .... 161 E5
Paisley PA1 .... 112 D4
Plains ML6 .... 104 A3
Renfrew PA4 .... 94 D3
Stepps G33 .... 99 D5
Uddingston G71 .... 141 C6
WEST BALGROCHAN 57 A1
West Balgrochan Rd G64 .. 57 B1
Westbank Ct 7 G12 .... 96 E2
Westbank La G12 .... 96 E2
Westbank Quadrant G12 .. 96 E2
West Barmoss Ave PA14 .. 68 F7
WEST BENHAR 127 B4
West Benhar Rd ML7 .... 127 B3
West Blackhall St
1 Greenock PA15 .... 45 F5
Greenock PA15 .... 45 F6
West Boreland Rd FK6 .... 21 D2
Westbourne Gdns G84 .... 16 C2
Westbourne Ave KA9 .... 236 D8
Westbourne Cres G61 .... 75 C5
Westbourne Ctr G78 .... 134 B2
Westbourne Dr G61 .... 75 D5
Westbourne Gardens La 6
G12 .... 96 C4
Westbourne Gardens N 7
G12 .... 96 C4
Westbourne Gardens S
G12 .... 96 C4
Westbourne Gardens W 8
G12 .... 96 C4
Westbourne Gdns KA9 .. 236 D8
Westbourne Rd G12 .... 96 B4
Westbourne Terrace Lane N
9 G12 .... 96 C4
Westbourne Terrace Lane S
3 G12 .... 96 B4
West Bowhouse Gdns
KA11 .... 220 A5
West Bowhouse Head
KA11 .... 220 A5
West Bowhouse Way
KA11 .... 220 A5
West Bowhouse Workshops
KA11 .... 220 A5
West Brae PA1 .... 113 D4
Westbrae Dr G13, G14 .... 95 E4
Westbrae Rd G77 .... 156 F6
West Bridgend G82 .... 49 E4
West Bridge St FK1 .... 42 A5
West Buchanan Pl PA1 .. 113 D4
WESTBURN 139 E6
Westburn Ave
Cambuslang G72 .... 139 D6
Falkirk FK1 .... 41 F4
Paisley PA3 .... 113 B5
Westburn Bldgs 2 PA15 .. 45 F5
Westburn Cres
Clydebank G81 .... 74 B7
Rutherglen G73 .... 137 F7
Westburn Dr G72 .... 139 B6
Westburn Farm Rd G72 .. 139 B6
Westburn Rd
Cambuslang, Newton
G72 .... 140 B5
Cambuslang, Westburn
G72 .... 139 D6
Stewarton KA3 .... 195 E1
West Burnside St G65 .... 60 D8
West Burn St PA15 .... 45 F5
West Byrehill Ind Est
KA13 .... 207 B2
West Campbell St
Glasgow G2 .... 240 C3
Paisley PA1 .... 113 B4
West Canal St ML5 .... 121 F7
West Carmuirs Loan FK5 .. 40 F6
Westcastle Cres G45 .... 137 D3
Westcastle Ct G45 .... 137 D3
Westcastle Gdns G45 .... 137 D3
Westcastle Gr G45 .... 137 D3
West Chapelton Ave G61 .. 75 F4
West Chapelton Cres G61 . 75 F4
West Chapelton Dr G61 .... 75 F4
West Chapelton La G61 .... 75 F4
Westcliff G82 .... 49 B4
West Clyde St
Helensburgh G84 .... 16 C1
Larkhall ML9 .... 185 B2
Westclyffe St 3 G41 .... 116 E1
West Coats Prim Sch
G72 .... 138 F5
West Coats Rd G72 .... 138 F5
Westcott Pl ML11 .... 215 C5
WEST CRAIGEND 72 F1
Westcraigs Pk EH48 .... 107 C3
Westcraigs Rd
Blackridge EH48 .... 107 D2
Harthill ML7 .... 127 F6
West Cres KA10 .... 229 G4
West Cross ML2 .... 165 A3
Westcross Rdbt G77 .... 156 A5
West Ct
Clydebank G81 .... 73 E4
Irvine KA12 .... 219 B2
West Dhuhill Dr G84 .... 16 D4
West Doura Ave KA21 .... 205 F1
West Doura Ct KA13 .... 207 B3
West Doura Way KA13 .. 207 C3
West Dr
Airdrie ML6 .... 123 E6
Stenhousemuir FK5 .... 23 C1
WEST DRUMOYNE 115 E7
Westend G61 .... 76 A2
West End KA24 .... 191 B7
Westend Ct ML8 .... 186 F4
West End Dr ML4 .... 141 F4
West End Gdns FK10 .... 10 A6
Westend Park St G3 .... 96 F2
West End Pl ML4 .... 141 F4
Westend Ret Pk G11 .... 96 A2
WESTER AUCHINLOCH 79 C2
Wester Boghead G66 .... 78 F4
Westerburn St G32 .... 118 F6
Wester Carriagehill PA2 .. 113 E2
Wester Cleddens Prim Sch
G64 .... 78 A2
Wester Cleddens Rd G64 .. 78 C2
Wester Cochno Holdings
G81 .... 74 A8
Wester Common Dr G22 .. 97 A4
Westercommon Prim Sch
G22 .... 97 A4
Wester Common Rd G22 .. 97 A4
Westercraigs G31 .... 117 F7
Westercraigs Ct 7 G31 .. 117 F7
Westerdale G74 .... 159 C3
Westerfield Rd G76 .... 158 D4
Westergate Sh Ctr G2 .. 240 C2
Westergill Ave ML6 .... 123 E6
Westerglen Rd FK1 .... 42 A2
Westergreens Ave G66 .... 79 C6
Westerhill Rd G64 .... 78 D3
WESTER HOLYTOWN 142 E6
Westerhouse Ct ML8 .... 187 D2
Westerhouse Rd G34 .... 119 F8
Westerkirk Dr G23 .... 76 E1
Westerlands G12 .... 96 A6
Westerlands Dr
Newton Mearns G77 .... 156 B4
Stirling FK8 .... 7 B5
Westerlands Gdns G77 .... 156 B4
Westerlands Gr G77 .... 156 B4
Westerlands Pl G77 .... 156 B5
Westerlea Ct FK9 .... 2 A5
Westerlea Dr FK9 .... 2 A5
Wester Leddriegreen Rd
G63 .... 31 B4
WESTERMAINS 79 B8
Westermains Ave G66 .... 79 B7
Wester Mavisbank Ave
ML6 .... 122 F8
Wester Moffat Ave ML6 .. 123 E7
Wester Moffat Cres 2
ML6 .... 123 E7
Wester Moffat Hospl
ML6 .... 123 F8
Wester Myvot Rd G67 .... 82 A4
Western Ave
Falkirk FK2 .... 42 B6
Rutherglen G73 .... 137 F8
Western Cres KA25 .... 170 A7
Western Ind Est KA3 .... 222 E2
Western Infmy G11 .... 96 C2
Western Isles Rd G60 .... 73 C5
Western Pl KA3 .... 223 A4
Western Rd
Cambuslang G72 .... 138 F3
Kilmarnock KA1, KA3 .... 222 E2
Westerpark Ave G72 .... 161 C3
Wester Rd G32 .... 119 D3
Westerton
Cowie FK7 .... 12 D8
Lennoxtown G66 .... 57 F8
Westerton Ave
Clarkston G76 .... 158 A5
Glasgow G61 .... 95 F8
Larkhall ML9 .... 185 A1
Westerton Ct G76 .... 158 A5
Westerton Dr FK9 .... 2 A7
Westerton La G76 .... 158 A5
Westerton of Mugdock
G62 .... 55 B6
Westerton Prim Sch G61 .. 75 E2
Westerton Rd G68 .... 61 D6
Westerton Sta G61 .... 75 E1
Westerton Terr FK2 .... 24 C3
West Fairholm St ML9 .... 184 F5
Westfarm Ave G72 .... 139 D6
Westfarm Cres G72 .... 139 D6
Westfarm Ct G72 .... 139 D7
Westfarm Dr G72 .... 139 D7
Westfarm Gr G72 .... 139 D7
Westfarm La G72 .... 139 D7
Westfarm Wynd G72 .... 139 D6
West Faulds Rd ML11 .... 215 E5
WESTFIELD
Cumbernauld 81 F7
Kilsyth 36 A1
Westfield
Dumbarton G82 .... 49 C4
Kilbirnie KA25 .... 170 B8
Westfield Ave G73 .... 137 F7
Westfield Cres G61 .... 75 E2
Westfield Ct KA21 .... 216 E7
Westfield Dr
Bearsden G61 .... 75 E2
Cumbernauld G68 .... 81 F7
Glasgow G52 .... 115 A5
Greenock PA16 .... 45 C8
Kilmacolm PA13 .... 89 B8
Westfield Ind Area G68 .. 81 D6
Westfield Pl
Cumbernauld G68 .... 81 D6
Denny FK6 .... 21 E1
Westfield Prim Sch G68 .. 81 F7
Westfield Rd
Ayr KA7 .... 238 E6
Cumbernauld G68 .... 61 A1
Cumbernauld G68 .... 81 E7
Glasgow G46 .... 136 A3
Kilmarnock KA3 .... 223 C6
Kilsyth G65 .... 36 B1
Motherwell ML1 .... 143 C7
Port Glasgow PA14 .... 68 F8
Westfield Rdbt FK2 .... 42 F6
Westfields G64 .... 77 E3
Westfield St FK2 .... 42 E5
Westfield Trad Est FK6 .... 21 E1
West Fullarton St KA1 .. 222 E1
Westgarth Pl G74 .... 159 A3
West Gate ML2 .... 165 D3
Westgate Way ML4 .... 141 F5
West George La G2 .... 240 C3
West George St
Coatbridge ML5 .... 122 A8
Glasgow G2 .... 240 C3
7 Kilmarnock KA1 .... 222 F1
West Glebe G76 .... 178 F5
West Glebe Terr ML3 .... 162 C2
West Glen Gdns PA13 .... 69 E1
West Glen Rd PA13, PA14 .. 69 E1
West Gr KA10 .... 229 G4
West Graham St G3 .... 240 B4
West Greenhill Pl G3 .... 116 E8
West Hamilton St ML1 .... 163 E6
Westhaugh Cvn Site FK10 .. 5 A4
Westhaugh Rd FK9 .... 1 F4
West High St G66 .... 58 C1
Westhorn Dr G32 .... 119 A1
Westhouse Ave G73 .... 137 E7
Westhouse Gdns G73 .... 137 E7
West James St FK12 .... 5 A6
West Johnstone St FK12 .... 5 A6
WEST KILBRIDE 190 D3
West Kilbride Mus*
KA23 .... 190 C5
West Kilbride Prim Sch
KA23 .... 190 C5
West Kilbride Rd KA24 .. 191 A7
West Kilbride Sta KA23 .. 190 D5
West King St G84 .... 16 B2
West Kirklands Pl KA24 .. 191 B7
West Kirk St ML6 .... 122 F8
Westknowe Gdns G73 .... 138 B5
West La PA1 .... 113 B4
Westland PA13 .... 89 C8
Westland Dr G14 .... 95 D4
Westland Drive La 8 G14 95 D3
Westlands Gdns PA2 .... 113 D2
West Langlands St KA1 .. 222 E1
Westlea Pl ML6 .... 123 B6
West Lennox Dr G84 .... 16 D3
West Link Rd FK9 .... 2 D5
West Lodge Gdns FK10 .... 9 F8
West Lodge Rd PA4 .... 94 B4
WEST MAINS 159 D1
West Mains Ind Est FK3 .. 42 F7
West Mains Rd
East Kilbride G74 .... 159 D2
Falkirk FK3 .... 42 F7
West Mains Sch G74 .... 160 A3
West Main St ML7 .... 127 E5
Westminster Pl FK5 .... 23 E4
Westminster Terr 3 G3 .. 116 E8
West Montrose St G84 .... 16 C2
Westmoor Cres KA1 .... 227 D7
Westmoreland St G42 .... 117 A2
Westmorland Rd PA16 .... 44 E4
Westmuir Pl G73 .... 137 F8
Westmuir St G31 .... 118 D5
West Murrayfield FK7 .... 7 D1
West Nemphlar Rd ML11 214 C6
West Netherton St KA1 .. 227 F7
West Nile St G1 .... 241 A3
West of Scotland Science Pk
(Kelvin Campus) G20 .... 76 B1
West of Scotland Science Pk
(Todd Campus) G20 .... 76 B1
Westonbirt Gr ML5 .... 101 F6
Weston Pl KA9 .... 236 D6
Weston Terr KA23 .... 190 C5
Westpark Cres 3 FK2 .... 41 F8
West Park Cres KA3 .... 222 B8
Westpark Ct
8 Falkirk FK2 .... 41 F8
Stevenston KA20 .... 217 C7
Westpark Dr PA3 .... 113 B5
West Park Dr KA3 .... 222 B8
Westpark Wynd KA24 .... 191 B8
West Pl ML2 .... 166 A5
Westport
East Kilbride G75 .... 159 A1
Lanark ML11 .... 214 E3
West Port ML11 .... 214 F4
West Portland St KA10 .. 229 C2
WEST PORTON 72 A4
West Porton Pl PA7 .... 71 F4
Westport St 10 G65 .... 60 D8
West Prim Sch PA1 .... 113 C4
West Princes St G84 .... 16 C2
West Prince's St
6 Glasgow G4 .... 96 E2
Glasgow G4 .... 96 F2
West Quay PA14 .... 47 C2
Westray Ave
Newton Mearns G77 .... 156 C7
Port Glasgow PA14 .... 69 B6
Westray Cir G22 .... 97 D6
Westray Ct G67 .... 82 E8
Westray Dr KA3 .... 223 A6
Westray Pl
Bishopbriggs G64 .... 78 D2
Glasgow G22 .... 97 D7
Westray Rd G67 .... 82 E8
Westray Sq G22 .... 97 D7
Westray St G22 .... 97 C7
Westray Terr FK1 .... 42 C2
Westray Wynd 2 ML2 .... 165 F6
West Rd
Irvine KA12 .... 219 B3
Irvine KA12 .... 219 B7
Kilbarchan PA10 .... 111 A4
Port Glasgow PA14 .... 68 E8
Stevenston KA20 .... 218 A6
Torrance G64 .... 57 B1
West Regent St G2 .... 240 C3
Westreron Ho
Bridge of Allan FK9 .... 2 A8
Stirling FK9 .... 2 A1
WESTRIGG 107 F3
West Rossdhu Dr G84 .... 16 D3
West Row G63 .... 31 A4
West Sanquhar Ave KA8 .. 236 B2
West Sanquhar Pl KA8 .. 236 B2
West Sanquhar Rd KA8 .. 236 B3
West Scott Terr ML3 .... 162 D1
West Shaw St
Greenock PA15 .... 45 E5
Kilmarnock KA1 .... 227 F6
Westside Gdns G11 .... 96 C2
West St
Clydebank G81 .... 94 E8
Glasgow G5 .... 117 A5
Paisley PA1 .... 113 C4
West Stewart St
Greenock PA15 .... 45 F5
Hamilton ML3 .... 162 C4
West Stirling St FK12 .... 4 F7
West Street Underground
Sta G5 .... 117 A5
West Thomson St G81 .... 74 B3
West Thornlie St ML2 .... 165 A2
West Vennel 6 FK10 .... 10 B6
West View KA3 .... 213 E4
Westview Cres FK10 .... 4 C2
West View Terr KA3 .... 195 B8
Westward Way KA10 .... 229 F7
West Wellbrae Cres ML3 .. 183 B8
West Whitby St G31 .... 118 C4
WESTWOOD 180 A8
Westwood Ave
Ayr KA8 .... 236 E2
Glasgow G46 .... 136 B3
Westwood Cres
Ayr KA8 .... 236 E2

Westwood Cres *continued*
Hamilton ML3 .... 162 C2
1 Stirling FK9 .... 2 B3
Westwood Dr ML1 .... 144 E1
Westwood Gdns PA3 ..... 113 B5
Westwood Hill G75 ...... 180 B7
Westwood Quadrant G81 .. 74 D1
Westwood Rd
East Kilbride G75 .... 180 B8
Glasgow G43 .... 136 B6
Wishaw ML2 .... 165 F7
Wishaw ML2 .... 166 A5
West Woodside Ave PA14 .. 68 F6
Westwood Sq G75 .... 180 B8
West Woodstock Ct 3
KA1 .... 227 E8
West Woodstock St KA1 . 227 E8
Weymouth Cres PA19 ..... 44 E5
Weymouth Ct G12 .... 96 B6
Weymouth Dr G12 .... 96 A6
Whamflet Ave G69 ...... 120 C7
Whamond Twr ML1 ...... 163 E5
Whangie The* G63 .... 29 A5
Wharf Rd KA12 .... 218 D3
Wharry Rd FK12 .... 4 E7
Whatriggs Rd KA1 ...... 228 A4
Wheatear Gr ML5 .... 122 E3
Wheatfield Rd
Ayr KA7 .... 238 E7
Bearsden G61 .... 75 D2
Wheatholm Cres ML6 .... 103 B1
Wheatholm St ML6 ...... 103 B1
Wheatland Ave G72 ..... 161 C8
Wheatland Dr ML11 ..... 214 F5
Wheatlandhead Ct G72 . 161 C8
WHEATLANDS 161 C8
Wheatlands Ave FK4 ...... 40 A6
Wheatlands Dr PA10 .... 111 A4
Wheatlands Farm Rd
PA10 .... 111 A4
Wheatlandside ML11 ..... 214 F5
Wheatley Cres G65 .... 60 D7
Wheatley Ct G32 .... 119 A5
Wheatley Dr G32 .... 119 A5
Wheatley Loan G64 .... 98 C8
Wheatley Pl G32 .... 119 A5
Wheatley Rd
Saltcoats KA21 .... 206 A2
Stevenston KA20 .... 206 E1
Wheatpark Pl KA8 ...... 236 F3
Wheatpark Rd
Ayr KA8 .... 236 E3
Lanark ML11 .... 214 F4
WHIFFLET 122 B5
Whifflet Ct ML5 .... 122 B5
Whifflet St ML5 .... 122 B4
Whifflet Sta ML5 .... 122 B5
Whimbrel Wynd PA4 ...... 94 E5
Whin Ave G78 .... 134 B4
Whinfell Dr G75 .... 180 A6
Whinfell Gdns G75 ...... 180 A6
Whinfield Ave
Cambuslang G72 .... 138 E7
Prestwick KA9 .... 236 C6
Whinfield Gdns KA9 ..... 236 C6
Whinfield Rd
Glasgow G53 .... 135 A4
Prestwick KA9 .... 236 B6
WHINHALL 122 E8
Whinhall Ave ML6 .... 102 F1
Whinhall Rd ML6 .... 102 E1
Whin Hill G74 .... 160 B4
Whinhill Cres PA15 .... 46 B2
Whinhill Ct 2 PA15 .... 45 F4
Whinhill Gdns G53 ...... 115 A3
Whinhill Pl G53 .... 115 A3
Whinhill Rd
Glasgow G53 .... 115 A3
Greenock PA15 .... 46 A3
Paisley PA2 .... 114 B2
Whin Hill Rd KA7 .... 239 B2
Whinhill Sta PA15 .... 46 B3
Whinknowe ML9 .... 199 F8
Whin Loan G65, G66 ...... 59 D8
Whinney Gr ML2 .... 165 E4
Whinnie Knowe ML9 ..... 184 F1
Whinpark Ave ML4 ...... 141 F3
Whin Pl G74 .... 160 B5
Whinriggs ML9 .... 198 D1
WHINS OF MILTON 7 B2
Whins Rd
Alloa FK10 .... 10 C7
Glasgow G41 .... 116 C1
Stirling FK7 .... 7 B2
Troon KA10 .... 229 F7
Whin St G81 .... 74 B4
Whinwell Rd FK8 .... 2 A1
Whirlie Dr PA6 .... 111 B8
Whirlie Rd PA6 .... 91 B1
Whirlies Rdbt The G74 .. 160 A3
Whirlow Gdns G69 ...... 120 A5
Whirlow Rd G69 .... 120 B5
Whistleberry Cres ML3 ... 162 B7
Whistleberry Dr ML3 .... 162 B7
Whistleberry Ind Est
ML3 .... 162 A7
Whistleberry Ind Pk
ML3 .... 162 A6
Whistleberry La ML3 .... 162 B6
Whistleberry Pk ML3 .... 162 A7
Whistleberry Rd ML3 .... 162 A7
Whistleberry Ret Pk G72 161 F7
Whistleberry Wynd ML3 . 162 A6
Whistlefield Ct G61 .... 75 F3
Whitacres Path G53 ..... 135 A4
Whitacres Rd G53 ...... 135 A4
Whitburn St G32 .... 118 F7
Whiteadder Pl G75 ...... 179 D7
White Ave G82 .... 50 B4
White Cart Ct G43 ...... 136 D7
White Cart Rd PA3 ...... 113 E8
White-Cart Twr G74 ..... 181 B7
White Craig Rd KA22 .... 205 D4
WHITECRAIGS 157 B7
Whitecraigs Ct G46 ..... 157 A8
Whitecraigs Pl G23 .... 96 E8
Whitecraigs Sta G46 ..... 157 A8
WHITECROFT 47 B1
WHITECROOK 94 C8
Whitecrook Bsns Ctr G81 . 74 C1
Whitecrook Prim Sch
G81 .... 74 C1
Whitecrook St G81 .... 74 C1
Whitefield Ave G72 ..... 139 A4
Whitefield Rd G51 ...... 116 C6
Whitefield Terr G66 .... 33 C1
Whiteford Ave G82 .... 50 C5
Whiteford Cres G82 .... 50 C5
Whiteford Ct ML3 .... 183 C6
Whiteford Gdns G82 .... 50 B5
Whiteford Pl G82 .... 50 C5
Whiteford Rd
Paisley PA2 .... 114 A2
Stepps G33 .... 100 A5
Whiteford View KA7 ..... 239 D7
Whitegates G66 .... 79 C7
Whitegates Pl FK1 .... 41 C4
Whitehall Ave KA9 ...... 236 D8
Whitehall St G3 .... 240 A2
WHITEHAUGH 114 A5
Whitehaugh Ave PA1 ..... 114 B6
Whitehaugh Dr PA1 ...... 114 B5
Whitehaugh Pl G53 ...... 135 B4
Whitehaugh Rd G53 ..... 135 A4
WHITEHILL 162 A6
Whitehill Ave
Airdrie ML6 .... 103 A1
Cumbernauld G68 .... 61 D2
Kirkintilloch G66 .... 58 F1
Stepps G33 .... 99 D6
Whitehill Cres
Carluke ML8 .... 187 F3
Clydebank G81 .... 74 E7
Kirkintilloch G66 .... 58 F1
Lanark ML11 .... 214 F4
Whitehill Ct
Glasgow G31 .... 118 A7
Kirkintilloch G66 .... 58 F1
Whitehill Farm Rd G33 .... 99 D6
Whitehill Gdns G31 ..... 118 A7
Whitehill Gr G77 .... 156 F2
Whitehill La G61 .... 75 D4
Whitehill Pl FK8 .... 7 A5
Whitehill Pool G31 .... 118 B7
Whitehill Rd
Bearsden G61 .... 75 D4
Hamilton ML3 .... 162 B5
WHITEHILLS 180 E5
Whitehills PA8 .... 73 B3
Whitehills Dr G75 .... 180 E7
Whitehill Sec Sch G31 ... 118 B7
Whitehills Pl G75 .... 180 E7
Whitehill St G31 .... 118 A7
Whitehills Terr G75 ..... 180 E7
Whitehill Street La G31 . 118 A7
Whitehill Terr ML11 ..... 214 F4
Whitehirst Farm Ctyd
KA13 .... 207 B5
WHITEHIRST PARK 207 A3
Whitehirst Park Prim Sch
KA13 .... 207 C3
Whitehirst Park Rd KA13 207 B3
Whitehope Gn KA11 ..... 220 A4
Whitehorse Wlk G75 ..... 180 B8
Whitehouse Rd FK7 .... 7 D7
Whitehurst G61 .... 75 C6
Whitehurst Pk G61 .... 75 C6
WHITEINCH 95 D2
Whiteinch Bsns Pk G14 .. 95 D2
Whiteinch Prim Sch G14 .. 95 E2
Whitekirk Pl G15 .... 75 A2
Whitelaw Ave ML5 .... 101 F5
Whitelaw Cres ML4 ...... 142 D4
Whitelaw Gdns G64 .... 78 A3
Whitelaw St
Blackridge EH48 .... 107 D1
Glasgow G20 .... 96 C7
Whitelaw Terr G65 .... 59 F4
Whitelea Ave PA13 .... 89 D8
Whitelea Cres PA13 .... 89 D8
Whitelea Ct PA13 .... 89 D8
Whitelea Rd PA13 .... 89 C8
Whitelee G75 .... 180 D5
Whitelee Cres G77 ...... 156 B6
Whitelee Gate G77 ...... 156 B6
WHITELEES 231 F4
Whitelees Prim Sch G67 .. 62 F5
Whitelees Rd
Cumbernauld G67 .... 62 F6
Greenock PA15 .... 46 F2
Lanark, Cleghorn ML11 ... 203 F2
Lanark ML11 .... 215 C3
Whitelees Rdbt G67 .... 62 F5
Whiteloans G71 .... 141 B3
Whitemoss Ave
East Kilbride G74 .... 159 F1
Glasgow G44 .... 136 F4
Whitemoss Gr G74 ...... 160 A2
Whitemoss Rd G74 ...... 160 A1
Whitemoss Rdbt G74 .... 160 A1
Whitepond Ave ML4 ..... 141 F3
Whiterigg Ct ML6 .... 122 D8
Whites Bridge Ave PA3 ... 112 F4
Whites Bridge Cl PA3 .... 113 A5
Whiteshaw Ave ML8 ..... 187 D1
Whiteshaw Dr ML8 ...... 187 D2
Whiteshaw Rd ML8 ...... 187 B3
Whiteside Dr KA9 .... 233 E4
Whiteside Gdns KA9 ..... 233 E4
Whiteside Pk KA9 .... 233 E4
Whiteside Pl KA9 .... 233 E4
Whiteside Rd KA9 ...... 236 D7
Whiteside Terr KA9 ..... 236 D7
White's Neuk ML11 ..... 215 C5
White St
Ayr KA8 .... 236 B4
Clydebank G81 .... 94 D7
Glasgow G11 .... 96 C2
Whitestone Ave G68 ...... 61 B2
Whitevale St G31 .... 118 A6
Whitewisp Ct KA11 ...... 220 A4
Whiteyetts Cres FK10 .... 5 D2
Whiteyetts Dr FK10 .... 5 D2
Whiteyetts Pl FK10 .... 5 D2
Whitfield Dr KA8 .... 236 D3
Whithope Rd G53 .... 134 F4
Whithope Terr G53 ...... 134 F4
Whithorn Cres G69 .... 80 F3
WHITLAWBURN 138 F3
Whitlawburn Ave G72 .... 138 E4
Whitlawburn Rd G72 ..... 138 E4
Whitlawburn Terr G72 ... 138 E4
Whitlees Cres KA22 ..... 205 D3
Whitlees Ct KA22 .... 205 E3
WHITLETTS 236 D3
Whitletts Ct KA8 .... 236 E2
Whitletts Prim Sch KA8 .. 236 E3
Whitletts Rd KA8 .... 236 C2
Whitletts Rdbt KA6 ...... 236 F3
Whitriggs Rd G53 .... 134 F4
Whitslade St G34 .... 100 A1
Whitsun Dale G74 ...... 159 C3
WHITTAGREEN 143 C3
Whittagreen Ave ML1 ... 143 D3
Whittagreen Cres ML1 .. 143 D2
Whittagreen Ct ML1 .... 143 D3
Whittingehame Dr G12 .... 96 A5
Whittingehame Gdns G12 96 A5
Whittingehame La G13 .... 95 F5
Whittingehame Pk G12 ... 95 F5
Whittington Pl G69 ..... 101 A6
Whittington St ML5 ..... 122 A6
Whittlemuir Ave G44 .... 136 F4
Whittle Pl KA11 .... 219 F2
Whittle Rd KA8 .... 236 C3
Whitton Dr G46 .... 136 E3
Whitton St G20 .... 96 C8
Whitworth Dr
Clydebank G81 .... 74 A2
Glasgow G20 .... 97 A6
Whitworth Gate G20 ...... 97 A5
Whitworth Gdns G20 ...... 97 A6
Whyte Ave
Cambuslang G72 .... 138 E6
Irvine KA12 .... 219 D1
Whyte Cnr G82 .... 50 F1
Whyte St ML7 .... 127 F6
Wick Ave ML6 .... 122 E4
Wickets The PA1 .... 114 A3
Wickham Ave G77 ...... 156 D6
Wide Cl ML11 .... 215 A4
Wigton Ave G77 .... 156 C7
Wigtoun Pl G67 .... 62 B4
Wildcat Rd KA23 .... 190 B4
Wilderness The FK2 .... 14 D4
WILDMANBRIDGE 187 C7
Wildman Rd ML8 .... 187 B7
Wilfred Ave G13 .... 95 D7
Wilkie Cres ML9 .... 185 B2
Wilkie Loan ML4 .... 142 B7
Wilkie Pl FK5 .... 23 B2
Wilkie Rd G71 .... 141 A5
William Booth Pl FK7 .... 7 A3
William Burns Pl KA11 .. 220 C1
William Dr ML3 .... 183 D7
Williamfield Ave FK7 .... 7 A4
Williamfield Gr KA12 .... 219 B4
Williamfield Pk KA12 .... 219 B4
William Mann Dr G77 ... 156 C4
WILLIAMSBURGH 114 B5
Williamsburgh Prim Sch 1
PA1 .... 114 A5
Williamsburgh Terr PA1 . 114 A5
Williamson Ave
Dumbarton G82 .... 50 A4
Falkirk FK2 .... 24 A1
Williamson Dr G84 .... 17 A1
Williamson Pl
Falkirk FK2 .... 42 C7
Johnstone PA5 .... 112 B2
Williamson St
Clydebank G81 .... 74 B4
Falkirk FK1 .... 42 B4
Glasgow G31 .... 118 C4
William Spiers Pl ML9 ... 185 B1
William St
Clydebank G81 .... 74 A6
Coatbridge ML5 .... 122 B4
Glasgow G3 .... 240 A3
Greenock PA15 .... 46 A5
Hamilton ML3 .... 162 B5
Helensburgh G84 .... 16 C2
Johnstone PA5 .... 111 F3
Kilmarnock KA3 .... 222 F2
11 Kilsyth G65 .... 60 D8
Paisley PA1 .... 113 C4
Port Glasgow PA14 .... 47 B2
William Tricker Cres
KA15 .... 171 C8
William Ure Pl G64 .... 78 B5
William Wilson Ct G65 .... 36 D1
WILLIAMWOOD 157 D8
Williamwood Dr G44 ..... 136 F2
Williamwood High Sch
G76 .... 157 E5
Williamwood Park W
G44 .... 136 F2
Williamwood Pk G44 ..... 136 F2
Williamwood Sta G46 ... 136 D1
Willie Mair's Brae KA3 .. 223 A2
Willie Ross La G73 ...... 118 B1
Willie Ross Pl KA3 ...... 223 D4
Willison's La PA14 .... 47 C1
Willock Pl G20 .... 96 E7
Willock St KA1 .... 227 F5
Willockston Rd KA10 .... 229 F2
Willoughby Dr G13 .... 95 F6
Willoughby La G13 .... 95 F6
Willow Ave
Bishopbriggs G64 .... 98 A8
Elderslie PA5 .... 112 C2
Kirkintilloch G66 .... 79 C5
Motherwell ML1 .... 143 A2
Willowbank ML9 .... 185 A5
Willowbank Cres 1 G3 ... 96 F2
Willowbank Gdns G66 ..... 79 D8
Willowbank Pl G83 .... 27 F4
Willowbank Prim Sch G3 .. 96 F2
Willowbank Specl Sch 1
ML5 .... 121 E6
Willowbank St G3 ...... 240 A4
Willow Brae FK7 .... 12 C3
Willowburn Rd KA15 ..... 170 F7
Willow Cres ML5 .... 122 A4
Willow Ct
Clydebank G81 .... 73 F4
East Kilbride G75 .... 180 B6
Willowdale Cres G69 ..... 120 B4
Willowdale Gdns G69 ... 120 A4
Willow Dr
Airdrie ML6 .... 123 D7
Banknock FK4 .... 38 E2
Hamilton G72 .... 161 C8
Johnstone PA5 .... 112 A1
Kilmacolm PA13 .... 89 D8
Milton of Campsie G66 ..... 58 C5
Willowford Rd G53 ...... 135 A4
Willow Gdns KA11 ...... 219 E5
Willow Gr
Menstrie FK11 .... 3 E6
Motherwell ML1 .... 143 B5
Willow La
Glasgow G32 .... 119 B2
Troon KA10 .... 229 E4
Willowpark Ct 3 ML6 .... 122 F8
Willow Pk KA7 .... 239 D4
Willow Pl
Johnstone PA5 .... 112 A2
Lanark ML11 .... 215 B3
Uddingston G71 .... 141 D8
Willow Rd KA1 .... 227 D8
Willow St G13 .... 95 F7
Willows The
Carmunnock G76 .... 158 E8
Tullibody FK10 .... 4 B1
Willow Way ML3 .... 162 E2
Willowyard Ind Est KA15 . 170 F7
Willowyard Rd KA15 ..... 170 F7
Wills Rd KA8 .... 236 C2
Willwood Dr ML2 .... 165 C7
Willwood Rd ML2 .... 165 C7
Wilmot Rd G13 .... 95 D6
Wilsgait St ML1 .... 144 C2
Wilson Ave
Denny FK6 .... 21 D2
Falkirk FK1 .... 41 C5
Irvine KA12 .... 219 C4
Kilmarnock KA3 .... 228 B8
Linwood PA3 .... 112 A5
Troon KA10 .... 230 A2
Wilson Ct
Bellshill ML4 .... 141 F5
4 Hamilton ML3 .... 162 A5
Wilson Dr
Bannockburn FK7 .... 7 C2
Falkirk FK1 .... 41 C5
Wilson Gdns FK1 .... 41 C6
Wilson Pl
Bonnybridge FK4 .... 40 C4
Dundonald KA2 .... 225 E2
East Kilbride G74 .... 160 A4
Newton Mearns G77 ...... 156 C4
Saltcoats KA21 .... 205 F3
Wilson Rd
Falkirk FK1 .... 41 C6
Shotts ML7 .... 167 A8
Wilsons Rd
Hareshaw ML1 .... 144 E6
Motherwell ML1 .... 144 E7
Wilson St
Airdrie ML6 .... 122 F8
Alexandria G83 .... 27 E5
Ayr KA8 .... 236 B2
Beith KA15 .... 150 C1
Coatbridge ML5 .... 122 C7
Glasgow G1 .... 241 A2
Hamilton ML3 .... 162 A5
Larkhall ML9 .... 185 B2
Motherwell ML1 .... 163 F7
Paisley PA1 .... 113 C4
Port Glasgow PA14 .... 47 D1
Renfrew PA4 .... 94 D4
Wilson Wynd KA24 ...... 191 A7
Wiltonburn Rd G53 ...... 135 A4
Wilton Crescent La G20 ... 96 F3
Wilton Dr G20 .... 96 F3
Wilton Rd ML8 .... 202 A8
Wilton St
Coatbridge ML5 .... 101 D2
Wilton St *continued*
Glasgow G20 .... 96 F3
Wilverton Rd G13 .... 95 E8
Winburne Cres ML3 ...... 162 B4
Winchester Ave FK6 ...... 21 E3
Winchester Avenue Ind Est
FK6 .... 21 F3
Winchester Ct FK6 .... 21 F3
Winchester Dr
Denny FK6 .... 21 F2
Glasgow G12 .... 96 B6
Windelstraw Ct KA11 .... 220 A3
Winderemere St ML4 .... 141 F4
Windermere G75 .... 179 F5
Windermere Gdns ML3 .. 183 C6
Windhill Cres G43 ...... 136 B5
Windhill Pk G76 .... 157 E2
Windhill Pl G43 .... 136 C5
Windhill Rd G43 .... 136 C5
Windlaw Ct G45 .... 137 D2
Windlaw Gdns G44 ...... 136 F4
Windlaw Park Gdns G44 . 136 F4
Windlaw Rd
Carmunnock G76 .... 158 D8
Glasgow G76 .... 137 D1
Windmill Ct
Hamilton ML3 .... 162 D4
Motherwell ML1 .... 163 F6
Windmill Gdns ML8 ...... 187 F2
Windmillhill St ML1 ..... 163 F5
Windmill Rd ML3 .... 162 D4
Windmill St KA21 .... 216 E7
Windmill View FK10 .... 5 D2
Windrow Terr ML2 ...... 165 C7
Windsor Ave
Falkirk FK1 .... 41 E4
Newton Mearns G77 ...... 156 F5
Windsor Cres
Clydebank G81 .... 74 A3
Elderslie PA5 .... 112 B1
Falkirk FK1 .... 41 E4
Paisley PA1 .... 114 A6
Windsor Crescent La G81 . 74 B3
Windsor Ct ML8 .... 187 F2
Windsor Dr
Denny FK6 .... 21 D3
Falkirk FK1 .... 41 F4
Glenmavis ML6 .... 102 F4
Windsor Gdns
Alloa FK10 .... 9 F8
Falkirk FK1 .... 41 E4
Hamilton ML3 .... 162 A5
Windsor Park Sch FK1 .... 41 E4
Windsor Path 8 ML9 ... 185 C2
Windsor Pl
Shotts ML7 .... 146 E5
Stirling FK8 .... 7 A7
Windsor Quadrant ML8 .. 187 F2
Windsor Rd
Falkirk FK1 .... 41 E4
Motherwell ML1 .... 143 A5
Renfrew PA4 .... 94 C2
Windsor St
Coatbridge ML5 .... 121 E3
4 Glasgow G20 .... 97 A2
Glasgow, Springboig G32 .. 119 C6
Menstrie FK11 .... 3 F6
Shotts ML7 .... 146 E5
Windsor Terr G20 .... 97 A2
Windsor Wlk G71 .... 141 B7
Windward Pk KA7 ...... 239 A1
Windward Rd G75 ...... 159 A1
Windyedge Cres G13 ...... 95 C5
Windyedge Pl G13 .... 95 C5
Windyedge Rd ML1 ...... 144 C3
Windyridge ML3 .... 162 E1
Windyridge Pl 11 G72 ... 161 C7
Windy Yetts G65 .... 59 F3
Winehouse Yett KA2 ..... 225 E2
Wingate Ave KA24 ...... 191 B7
Wingate Cres G74 ...... 160 C4
Wingate Dr G74 .... 160 C4
Wingate Pk G74 .... 160 C4
Wingate St ML2 .... 164 E4
Wingfaulds Ave KA24 .... 191 A8
Wingfield Gdns G71 ..... 141 B1
Winifred St G33 .... 98 D4
Winning Ct G72 .... 140 E1
Winning Quadrant ML2 . 164 D3
Winning Row G31 .... 118 D5
Winnipeg Dr G75 .... 180 B8
Winstanley Wynd KA13 .. 207 C5
Winston Ave KA9 .... 236 D7
Winston Cres G66 .... 57 D8
Winston Rd G84 .... 17 A2
Wintergreen Ct G74 ..... 159 D4
Wintergreen Dr G74 .... 159 D4
Winton Ave
Eaglesham G76 .... 178 F4
Glasgow G46 .... 136 C2
Kilwinning KA13 .... 207 C3
Winton Bldgs KA22 ..... 205 B1
Winton Cir KA21 .... 216 E7
Winton Cres G72 .... 161 D7
Winton Ct KA22 .... 205 C1
Winton Dr G12 .... 96 C5
Winton Gdns G71 ...... 140 F7
Winton La
Ardrossan KA22 .... 205 C2
Glasgow G12 .... 96 C5
Winton Pk G75 .... 159 A1
Winton Pl
Ardrossan KA22 .... 205 C2
Irvine KA12 .... 219 C4
Winton Prim Sch KA22 .. 205 C2
Winton St
Ardrossan KA22 .... 205 D2
Saltcoats KA21 .... 216 E8

Wirran Pl G13 94 E8
Wishart Dr FK7 7 D3
Wishart La ML8 187 A5
Wishart St G4, G31 241 C3
WISHAW 165 B4
Wishaw Acad Prim Sch 2 ML2 165 C3
Wishaw Bsns Ctr 1 ML2 165 B2
Wishaw General Hospl ML2 164 E3
Wishaw High Rd ML1 165 C8
Wishawhill St ML2 164 F4
Wishaw Low Rd ML1 165 A7
Wishaw Rd ML2 186 E8
Wishaw Sp Ctr ML2 164 F2
Wishaw Sta ML2 165 A2
Wisner Ct G46 135 F4
Wisteria La ML8 201 F8
Wiston St G72 139 E5
Witches Linn KA22 205 B4
Witchhill Pl KA3 222 F2
Witchhill Sch KA3 222 F2
Witchknowe Ave KA1 227 F5
Witchknowe Ct
Kilmarnock KA1 227 F4
2 Kilmarnock KA1 228 A4
Witchknowe Rd KA1 227 F4
Witch Rd KA3 222 F2
Witchwood Ct ML5 101 D2
Witcutt Way ML2 164 E1
Witherspoon St PA1 113 E4
Woddrop St G40 118 B2
Wolcott Dr G72 161 D8
Wolfe Ave G77 156 C7
Wolfe Rd FK1 42 D4
Wolseley St G5 117 D3
Wood Aven Dr G74 159 D4
Wood Avens FK10 4 B1
Woodbank Cres
Clarkston G76 157 E6
Johnstone PA5 111 F2
Woodbank Ct G83 27 C7
Woodbank Gdns G83 27 C7
Woodbank Rd KA2 221 F1
Woodburn Ave
Airdrie ML6 122 F6
Balloch G83 27 F7
Clarkston G76 157 E6
Hamilton G72 161 E8
Kilwinning KA13 207 E4
Woodburn Cres FK4 39 F3
Woodburn Ct
Lanark ML11 215 C2
Rutherglen G73 138 B6
Woodburn Dr FK10 4 F1
Woodburn Gait ML11 215 B3
Woodburn Gdns FK2 42 E5
Woodburn Gr ML3 162 E3
Woodburn Pk ML3 162 E3
Woodburn Pl PA6 111 E7
Woodburn Rd
Beith KA15 171 C8
Falkirk FK2 42 D5
Glasgow G43 136 D5
Motherwell ML1 143 D7
Woodburn St
Falkirk FK2 42 E5
Motherwell ML1 163 E8
Woodburn Terr 9 ML9 185 C2
Woodburn Way
Alva FK12 5 A6
Cumbernauld G68 61 C2
Milngavie G62 55 A1
Wood Cres
Kilwinning KA13 207 E4
Motherwell ML1 142 E1
Woodcroft Ave G11 95 F4
Wood Ct KA10 229 B2
Wooddale ML1 163 D4
Woodend G72 161 D6
Woodend Cotts KA6 239 E2
Woodend Ct G32 119 E2
Wood End Cvn Site ML7 166 F8
Woodend Dr
Airdrie ML6 103 C1
Glasgow G13 95 E5
Paisley PA1 114 D4
Woodend Gdns G32 119 D2
Woodend La 2 G13 95 E5
Woodend Oval KA6 239 E2
Woodend Pl PA5 112 B2
Woodend Rd
Alloway KA7 238 F1
Ayr KA7 239 A1
Carluke ML8 188 A2
Glasgow G32 119 E2
Rutherglen G73 138 B4
Woodend St G84 16 B2
Woodfarm Cl KA13 207 D6
Woodfarm High Sch G46 136 A3
Wood Farm Rd G46 136 A2
WOODFIELD 236 A5
Woodfield G71 141 C6
Woodfield Ave
Ayr KA8 236 A5
Bishopbriggs G64 98 B8
Woodfield Cres KA8 236 A4
Woodfield Rd KA8 236 A4
Woodfoot Rd ML3 162 A2
Woodford Pl PA3 112 A6
Woodford St G41 136 E7
Wood Gr KA11 220 C1
Woodgreen Ave G44 137 C6
Woodgreen Ct ML2 186 A8
Woodgreen Wynd KA13 207 C5
WOODHALL 69 A8
Woodhall ML1 143 A8
Woodhall Ave
Calderbank ML6 123 B2
Coatbridge ML5 121 F3
Hamilton ML3 162 B4
Motherwell ML1 142 F5
Woodhall Cottage Rd
ML6 123 C1
Woodhall Mill Rd ML6 123 B1
Woodhall Pl ML5 121 F3
Woodhall Rd
Braidwood ML8 201 E3
Calderbank ML6 123 B2
Wishaw ML2 165 F3
Woodhall St
Chapelhall ML6 123 D2
Glasgow G40 118 B2
Woodhall Sta PA14 48 A1
Woodhall Terr PA14 69 B8
Woodhead Ave
Bothwell G71 141 B1
Cumbernauld G68 81 F7
Kirkintilloch G66 79 D7
Woodhead Cres
Glenmavis ML6 102 E3
Hamilton ML3 183 A8
Uddingston G71 140 F7
Woodhead Ct G68 81 F7
Woodhead Gdns G71 162 B8
Woodhead Gn ML3 183 B8
Woodhead Gr G68 81 F7
WOODHEAD GREEN 183 B8
Woodhead Pl G68 81 F7
Woodhead Prim Sch
ML3 183 A8
Woodhead Rd
Cumbernauld G68 81 F7
Garnkirk G69 100 B6
Glasgow G53 135 A5
Woodhead Terr G69 100 B7
Woodhead View G68 81 F7
Woodhill Cres KA11 220 B5
Woodhill Pl KA3 222 B6
Woodhill Prim Sch G64 78 C2
Woodhill Rd
Blackridge EH48 107 B3
Glasgow G21 98 B6
Kilmarnock KA3 222 E3
Woodholm Ave G44 137 C6
Woodhouse Ct G76 158 A5
Woodhouse St G13 95 E7
Woodilee Cotts G66 79 E6
Woodilee Ind Est G66 79 E6
Woodilee Rd
Kirkintilloch G66 79 E6
Motherwell ML1 143 E4
Wood La G64 98 C8
Woodland Ave
Airdrie ML6 123 C4
Kirkintilloch G66 79 B8
Paisley PA2 133 E8
Woodland Cres
Cambuslang G72 139 C4
Eaglesham G76 178 D5
Woodland Gdns
Carmunnock G76 158 D7
Hamilton ML3 162 F2
Woodland Pl KA22 205 C3
WOODLANDS 42 B4
Woodlands
Glasgow G46 135 F3
Sauchie FK10 5 E1
Woodlands Ave
Bothwell G71 141 A3
Irvine KA12 219 D4
Lanark ML11 215 B3
Law ML8 187 A6
Mount Ellen G69 100 E6
Woodlands Cres
Ayr KA7 239 B4
Bothwell G71 141 A3
Falkirk FK1 42 A4
Glasgow G46 135 F3
Johnstone PA5 131 E8
Woodlands Ct
Alexandria G83 27 C7
8 Glasgow, Kelvingrove G3 96 E1
Glasgow, Thornliebank
G46 135 F2
Old Kilpatrick G60 73 B5
Woodlands Dr
Coatbridge ML5 121 D7
Glasgow G4 96 F2
Lanark ML11 215 B2
Motherwell ML1 142 F5
Woodlands Gate
Glasgow G3 240 A4
Glasgow, Thornliebank
G46 135 F3
Woodlands Gdns G71 141 A4
Woodlands Gr
Kilmarnock KA3 223 B4
Milngavie G62 55 A3
Woodlands Pk G46 135 F3
Woodlands Pl
Coatbridge ML5 121 D7
Kilmarnock KA3 223 B4
Woodlands Prim Sch
Cumbernauld G67 82 E7
Irvine KA12 219 D3
Linwood PA3 112 A5
Woodlands Rd
Glasgow G3 240 A4
Glasgow, Thornliebank
G46 135 F2
Motherwell, Holytown
ML1 143 D7
Motherwell ML1 163 F4
Thornliebank G46 136 A2
Woodlands St
Milngavie G62 55 A2
Motherwell ML1 163 F4
Prestwick KA9 236 B8
Woodlands Terr G3 240 A4
Woodlands The ML4 142 D3
Woodlands View ML9 199 A3
Woodland Terr ML9 185 C1
Woodland Way
Cumbernauld G67 62 B3
Denny FK6 39 D7
Woodlea Ave ML6 123 C4
Woodlea Cres KA2 221 F2
Woodlea Ct KA2 221 F2
Woodlea Dr
Glasgow G46 136 D4
Hamilton ML3 183 D8
Woodlea Gdns
Alloa FK10 5 A1
Bonnybridge FK4 39 F5
Woodlea La PA19 45 A7
Woodlea Pk
Alloa FK10 10 B8
Sauchie FK10 5 A1
Woodlea Pl
Airdrie ML6 103 C1
Ayr KA7 239 B2
Woodlinn Ave G44 137 B5
Woodmill KA13 207 F1
Woodmill Dr G64 57 C1
Woodmill Gdns G67 81 F6
Woodneuk La G69 100 F5
Woodneuk Rd
Gartcosh G69 100 F5
Glasgow G53 135 B5
Woodneuk St ML6 123 D1
Woodneuk Terr G69 100 F5
Woodpark KA9 236 B5
Wood Pk KA7 239 B4
Wood Pl
Strathblane G63 31 A5
Troon KA10 229 B2
Wood Quadrant G81 94 E8
Wood Rd KA10 229 B2
Woodrow ML1 143 B8
Woodrow Ave
Kilmacolm PA13 69 D1
Motherwell ML1 143 B2
Woodrow Cir G41 116 D4
Woodrow Pl G41 116 C4
Woodrow Rd G41 116 D4
WOODSIDE 97 B3
Woodside
Houston PA6 91 D1
Motherwell ML1 142 E8
West Kilbride KA23 190 D3
Woodside Ave
Bridge of Weir PA11 90 D1
Glasgow G46 136 A3
5 Hamilton ML3 162 E2
Kilmarnock KA1 227 D6
Kilsyth G65 60 F8
Kirkintilloch G66 79 D5
Rutherglen G73 138 C7
Woodside Cres
Alexandria G83 28 A6
Barrhead G78 134 D2
Glasgow G3 240 A4
Paisley PA1 113 C4
Wishaw ML2 166 B6
Woodside Ct
Cambusbarron FK7 6 D5
Coatbridge ML5 121 D5
Falkirk FK1 42 B3
4 Hamilton ML3 162 E2
Woodside Dr
Calderbank ML6 123 B2
Eaglesham G76 157 D2
Woodside Gdns
Carmunnock G76 158 D7
Clarkston G76 157 D7
Coatbridge ML5 121 D4
Woodside Gr
Larbert FK5 41 D8
Rutherglen G73 138 C7
Woodside La
Brookfield PA5 111 D6
Lanark ML11 215 C2
Woodside Pl
Dunlop KA3 195 C7
Fallin FK7 8 C4
Glasgow G3 240 A4
Uddingston G71 141 C8
Woodside Place La G3 240 A4
Woodside Prim Sch ML3 162 E2
Woodside Rd
Alloa FK10 4 F1
Beith KA15 150 B1
Brookfield PA5 111 D6
Carmunnock G76 158 D7
Forrestfield ML6 106 A3
Kilwinning KA13 207 C4
Stirling FK8 2 A3
Tullibody FK10 4 A1
Woodside St
Chapelhall ML6 123 D2
Coatbridge ML5 121 D4
Motherwell ML1 164 B4
Motherwell, New Stevenston
ML1 143 A3
Woodside Terr
Clackmannan FK10 10 F4
Falkirk FK1 42 B3
Glasgow G3 240 A4
Woodside Terrace La
G3 240 A4
Woodside Twr ML1 164 B3
Woodside Wlk ML3 162 E2
Wood St
Airdrie ML6 103 C1
Coatbridge ML5 121 E7
Glasgow G31 118 B8
Greenock PA16 45 C8
Kilwinning KA13 207 E4
Motherwell ML1 163 F8
Paisley PA2 114 B3
Woodstock Ave
Glasgow G41 116 D1
Kirkintilloch G66 79 F8
Lanark ML11 215 C4
Paisley PA2 132 F8
Woodstock Dr
Lanark ML11 215 B4
Wishaw ML2 165 C4
Woodstock Pl KA1 222 E1
Woodstock Rd
Greenock PA16 45 C3
Lanark ML11 215 B4
Woodstock Specl Sch
KA1 227 E8
Woodstock St KA1 227 E8
Woodstock Way PA2 132 E8
Woodstone Ct G84 15 E4
Woodvale Ave
Airdrie ML6 123 D4
Bearsden G61 76 B2
Rutherglen G46 157 B8
Woodvale Dr PA3 113 A5
Woodview G71 141 D8
Wood View
Motherwell ML1 143 B5
Shotts ML7 166 F8
Woodview Dr
Airdrie ML6 123 A5
Bellshill ML4 142 C7
Woodview La ML6 123 A5
Woodview Rd ML9 199 A8
Woodview Terr ML3 162 B4
Woodville Park Ind Est
G51 116 B6
Woodville Pk G51 116 B6
Woodville St G51 116 B6
Woodwynd KA13 207 E4
Woodyard Rd G82 49 E3
Woodyett Pk G76 157 F5
Woodyett Rd G76 157 F5
Wooer St 4 FK1 42 B4
Woolcarders Ct FK7 6 D6
Wordle Rd FK7 6 F4
Wordsworth Way G71 141 B3
Workshop Rd KA20 218 B5
Worsley Cres G77 156 C7
Wotherspoon Dr KA15 150 B2
Wraes Ave G78 134 D4
Wraes View G78 133 F1
Wraisland Cres PA7 71 F4
Wrangholm Cres ML1 143 B3
Wrangholm Dr ML1 143 B3
Wren Ct ML4 141 E8
Wren Pl
Johnstone PA5 131 D7
Wishaw ML2 165 B3
Wren Rd PA16 45 A4
Wright Ave G78 134 A2
Wrightfield Pl KA7 238 E2
Wrightlands Cres PA8 93 E8
Wright St
Falkirk FK2 42 B6
Renfrew PA4 94 A1
Wright Way ML1 143 A3
Wyburn Pl KA8 236 A3
Wye Cres ML5 101 D1
Wykeham Pl G13 95 C6
Wykeham Rd G13 95 C6
Wyler Twr ML3 162 E3
Wylie G74 160 D5
Wylie Ave
Alexandria G83 27 D4
Newton Mearns G77 156 D7
Wylie Pl
Renton G82 27 E2
Stewarton KA3 195 E1
Wylie St ML3 162 D2
Wyllie Rd KA21 217 A8
Wyndford Dr G20 96 D5
Wyndford Pl 3 G20 96 D5
Wyndford Prim Sch G20 96 D5
Wyndford Rd
Cumbernauld G68 62 D8
Glasgow G20 96 D5
Wyndford Terr G71 141 B7
Wyndham Ct G12 96 D4
Wyndham St G12 96 D4
Wynd The
Alva FK12 5 A7
Cumbernauld G67 62 B5
Wynyard Gn G75 180 B8
Wyper Pl G31 118 A6
Wyvil Ave G13 75 E1
Wyvis Ave
Bearsden G61 75 C7
Glasgow G13 94 F8
Wyvis Ct G77 156 D2
Wyvis Gdns KA1 228 A3
Wyvis Pl
Glasgow G13 94 F8
Irvine KA11 220 A4
Newton Mearns G77 156 C2
Shotts ML7 147 B3
Wyvis Quadrant G13 94 F8
Wyvis Rd KA1 228 A3
Wyvis Way ML1 164 D3

X

Xscape* PA4 94 F4

Y

Yair Dr G52 115 A6
Yardley Pl FK2 24 A1
Yardside Rd KA3 222 B7
Yarrow Cres
Bishopton PA7 72 C2
Wishaw ML2 165 B4
Yarrow Ct G72 139 E5
Yarrow Gardens La 2
G20 96 F3
Yarrow Gdns G20 96 F3
Yarrow Pk G74 160 A1
Yarrow Rd G64 78 A4
Yarrow Way G72 161 E8
Yate Gr G31 118 B5
Yate Rd G31 118 B5
Yate St G31 118 B5
Yementry Ct G72 138 F3
Yerton Brae KA23 190 C4
Yetholm Gdns G74 159 F4
Yetholm St G14 94 E6
Yetholm Terr ML3 161 E3
Yett Rd ML1 143 D3
Yetts Ave PA13 69 D1
Yetts Cres G66 79 F8
Yetts Hole Rd ML6 102 B5
Yetts The FK7 6 C5
Yew Dr G21 98 A3
Yew Pl PA5 111 F1
Yews Cres ML3 162 B5
YIELDSHIELDS 188 E2
Yieldshields Rd ML8 189 D3
YOKER 94 E7
Yokerburn Pl G13 94 E7
Yokerburn Terr G81 94 D7
Yoker Ferry Rd G14 94 E6
Yoker Mill Gdns G13 94 E7
Yoker Mill Rd G13 94 F8
Yoker Prim Sch G14 94 F6
Yoker Sp Ctr G14 94 F6
Yoker Sta G81 94 D7
Yonderton Pl KA23 190 D4
York Ct KA10 229 E3
York Dr
Falkirk FK2 42 D6
Rutherglen G73 138 D5
Yorke Ct KA10 229 E2
Yorke Pl KA1 222 D1
Yorke Rd KA10 229 E2
Yorkhill Par G3 96 C1
Yorkhill St G3 96 D1
York Pl
Ayr KA8 235 F2
Bellshill ML4 142 A5
1 Kirkintilloch G66 79 C8
York Rd
Greenock PA16 44 E5
Motherwell ML6 143 D8
York St
Ayr KA8 235 F2
Clydebank G81 74 D2
Falkirk FK2 42 D6
Glasgow G2 240 B2
Wishaw ML2 165 B2
York Street La KA8 235 F2
York Way PA4 94 C1
Young Ave KA10 229 E6
Younger Dr KA9 233 C3
Younger Quadrant G64 78 A1
Young Pl
East Kilbride G75 181 A5
1 Uddingston G71 141 A8
Wishaw ML2 166 B5
Young Rd ML11 215 E5
Young St
Ardrossan KA22 205 C2
Clydebank G81 74 B4
Prestwick KA8 236 B5
Wishaw ML2 165 B3
Young Terr G21 98 A4
Young Wynd ML4 142 A8
Yukon Terr G75 180 B8
Yule Way G67 62 A2
Yvetot Ave ML11 215 B4
Yvetot Ct ML8 187 E3

Z

Zambesi Dr G72 140 C1
Zena Cres G33 98 D4
Zena Pl G33 98 D4
Zena St G33 98 D4
Zetland Pl FK2 24 F3
Zetland Rd G52 114 F8

Notes

Notes

Notes